THE K&W GUIDE TO
COLLEGES

FOR STUDENTS WITH
LEARNING DISABILITIES OR
ATTENTION DEFICIT DISORDER

6TH EDITION

"Filling a glaring need for reliable information about programs for students with learning differences, *The K&W Guide to Colleges for Students with Learning Disabilities or Attention Deficit Disorder* is a comprehensive, accurate, and valuable addition to any college counselor's professional library."

Andrew Roth, Dean of Enrollment Services,
Mercyhurst College

"*The K&W Guide* has been most helpful and is very thorough. . . . Until now, I've not found so much useful material available in such concentrated format. So happy to have discovered your book!"

A parent of three sons with learning disabilities,
Cardiff by the Sea, California

"I knew something had to exist. My tenth-grade son will thrive in a correct college setting. . . . I saw [*The K&W Guide*] mentioned in *USA Today*."

Parent of a student with learning disabilities,
Santa Fe, New Mexico

"*The K&W Guide* is distinctive in its design. The Landmark students who have used it have found that it sets the standard for clear presentation of pertinent material."

Director of Admissions,
Landmark College

"Many colleges have programs and services for students with learning disabilities. A very informative guidebook you might want to consult is *The K&W Guide to Colleges for Students with Learning Disabilities or Attention Deficit Disorder*."

Jeffrey Zaslow,
Chicago Sun Times

"[*The K&W Guide*] is outstanding in content, scope, coverage, and authority. . . . [T]he authors have developed a major new reference source in a field that is crying for reference material."

Jack Hicks, Administrative Librarian at the Deerfield Public Library,
Deerfield, Illinois

THE PRINCETON REVIEW

THE K&W GUIDE TO COLLEGES

FOR STUDENTS WITH LEARNING DISABILITIES OR ATTENTION DEFICIT DISORDER

6TH EDITION

MARYBETH KRAVETS

AND IMY F. WAX

RANDOM HOUSE, INC.

NEW YORK

www.review.com

Princeton Review Publishing, L.L.C.
2315 Broadway
New York, NY 10024
E-mail: comments@review.com

ISBN: 0-375-76220-5
ISSN: 1094-9356

Manufactured in the United States of America on partially recycled paper.

9 8 7 6 5 4 3 2 1

6th Edition

DEDICATION

This book is a labor of love written to help individuals throughout the world who have been identified as having learning disabilities or attention deficit disorder. Just as important, it is for those students who have never been officially identified as learning disabled. And of course, it is an educational tool for all of the families, professionals, and friends who know someone who has a learning disability.

ACKNOWLEDGMENTS

To the families of Marybeth Kravets and Imy F. Wax for their patience and support in this endeavor: Alan, Wendy, Steve, Allison, Connor, Mark, Sara, David, Robert, Cathy, Cliff, Dan, Andrea, Howard, Lisa, Bill, Gary, Debrah, and Greg.

To Deerfield High School and High School District 113 for their ongoing support of learning disability programs and services and their belief in promoting the development of independence for all students and guiding them toward making good decisions about life after high school.

To all of the colleges who provide services and programs to promote the educational endeavors and dreams of students with learning disabilities or attention deficit disorder.

To Michael Barron, Lydia Block, Loring Brinkerhoff, Joan Fisher, Jeanne Kincaid Esq., Dr. Dennis Ray Kinder, Dr. Diane Perriera, and Dr. Julie Steck, for sharing their thoughts and experiences with learning disabilities and attention deficit/hyperactivity disorder.

To Stephanie Gordon, learning disability specialist, Deerfield High School, Deerfield, Illinois, for her professional assistance.

To Karen Rodgers Photography for the authors' pictures.

CONTENTS

Contents

FOREWORD

It is my pleasure to introduce the sixth edition of *The K&W Guide to Colleges for Students with Learning Disabilities or Attention Deficit Disorder*. As Chairman of the National Center for Learning Disabilities (NCLD), I congratulate The Princeton Review on this excellent resource. There is an enormous need for the sharing of information about learning disabilities. So many organizations, programs, schools, and materials that benefit individuals with learning disabilities exist; people just need to have access to them. This book achieves that goal in a very effective way.

My heart goes out to all children and adults with learning disabilities, as well as to their families. Given my experiences with my daughter, I can certainly empathize with the constant struggles so many young people face throughout their school years and after their transition to the work world. Accurate diagnosis, proper interventions, and the informed and caring support of parents, teachers, and professionals can make a difference in assuring that these children and adults enjoy productive and satisfying lives. An important first step is to have access to accurate and useful information.

When I first found out my daughter had learning disabilities, my instinct was to do everything humanly possible to help her. Much to my shock and dismay, I learned that there was little help available. I felt alone and helpless. At that time, I wondered if other families and professionals were going through the same frustration and disappointment. I now realize they were, and still are. If only this type of resource had been around twenty years ago!

As one of the nation's leading not-for-profit organizations committed to helping individuals with learning disabilities, the National Center for Learning Disabilities considers the sharing of accurate information and referrals to services among our highest priorities. In fact, our efforts in this area began in the early 1980s, when we published the *Guide for Parents of Children with Learning Disabilities*. This effort later evolved into NCLD's National Information and Referral Service, which today provides free information and referrals to local, state, and national resources, including diagnostic clinics, camps, and specialized schools.

We applaud The Princeton Review's *K&W Guide to Colleges for Students with Learning Disabilities or Attention Deficit Disorder*. This book captures so many types of helpful resources for parents, teachers, counselors, physicians, and advocates, it is sure to be a valuable addition to your library.

Anne Ford, Chairman
National Center for Learning Disabilities
New York, New York

INTRODUCTION

The K&W Guide was conceived independently by the authors over twenty years ago, but it took until 1987 for the paths of the authors to cross.

Imy Wax is a licensed psychotherapist and educational consultant. She is also the mother of two children—one with a learning disability and the other with a mild learning disability and attention deficit/hyperactivity disorder (ADHD). The truth is that this book is a dedication to Imy's daughter, who at the age of two was identified as having multiple learning disabilities, a large delay in her language skills, and a dismal prognosis for her future. Several professionals indicated that a traditional public elementary and high school experience would not be possible, and college was never even mentioned.

Imy was always optimistic, however, and she absolutely refused to accept such a diagnosis. She set goals, became a visionary, and exerted significant influence to allow her daughter to compensate for her limitations. She became an advocate for her daughter. She researched, read every book and every article she could find, and gave herself hope to believe in her child and in herself. Imy made it her goal to understand the learning disability and the strategies that would best contribute to her daughter's well-being.

Imy's daughter ultimately attended both public school and a special private school for students with learning disabilities. When her daughter was in the eighth grade in a private school, Imy volunteered in the College Resource Center at Deerfield High School so that she could get a better grasp of what might be in store for her daughter if she were to enroll in the local public high school. This was in 1987, and the paths of the two authors crossed for the first time.

Marybeth Kravets is the college consultant at Deerfield High School where Imy volunteered. Deerfield High School is a public high school that has comprehensive programs and services for students with learning disabilities (LD) and attention deficit/hyperactivity disorder (ADHD). Deerfield High School is also a school from which 98 percent of students matriculate to college, including those students identified as having LD or ADHD. Imy discovered that her daughter could be accommodated in the high school, and that the professionals there had hopes of mainstreaming her into regular college preparatory courses with appropriate accommodations and modifications.

Hidden under Imy's "commitment to the dream," however, lived the growing concern that she experienced when she listened to a college representative visiting with students at the high school. It seemed to her that all colleges were after the same student, one with at least a 3.0 GPA, an ACT score of 24 or an SAT score of 1000, a ranking in the top 50 percent of their class, and a four-year curriculum consisting of every subject at Deerfield High School. Imy's daughter had begun the ninth grade with only special education courses, which were individualized to meet her special needs. By junior year, she had mainstreamed into college preparatory courses in English, science, fine arts, and social studies, but was still enrolled in special education classes in math. She was not even close to learning about algebra (the typical freshman curriculum), and she had never taken a foreign language.

One day, Imy asked to meet with Marybeth to talk about her concern that there was not enough information about colleges that were prepared to accommodate students with learning disabilities. As the two began to explore the available resources for information, they realized most guidebooks only offered computer-generated information that said almost the same thing about every college regarding special services and special admissions. Thus began their search for more pertinent information to help Imy in her quest for a possible match for her daughter and those that she saw in her office, and to help Marybeth provide better college counseling for the students at her high school.

The first edition of the resulting book included extensive information about 150 colleges. The next four editions grew. This sixth edition of *The K&W Guide* has expanded to include more college profiles with detailed information about what these schools do and do not provide. It also gives specific information about documentation guidelines for students with learning disabilities and attention deficit/hyperactivity disorder (ADHD), and important information highlighting how services and accommodations are individually tailored for each student at the college level.

Through the information provided in this book and the tips and strategies provided to help students identify their priorities and explore their options, students can determine if the services or programs offered at a particular school match their individual needs. In this edition, you'll find:

- Special programs and services for students with multiple learning disabilities and/or ADHD, or for those needing limited accommodations

- Information professionals need to know in order to help advise and counsel students and parents in their college search process

- Detailed information about general and special admission procedures, the application process, services, programs, accommodations, remedial or developmental courses, and opportunities for basic skills classes

- Policies and procedures regarding course waivers or substitutions

- General profiles of colleges and universities

The main focus of *The K&W Guide* is to provide comprehensive information about the services or programs available at colleges and universities for students with learning disabilities or attention deficit disorder. Many colleges and universities will include students with LD or ADHD in their structured programs or special services. In most high schools, students identified as having only ADHD are categorized under "other health-related disabilities" and protected by Section 504 of the Rehabilitation Act of 1973. These students can request and receive accommodations in high school and college, as long as they present current and appropriate documentation from a certified professional.

Colleges that provide descriptions of the level of support and accommodations available on their campuses, whether they are basic services complying with the mandates of Section 504 or enhanced services that go beyond the mandates, provide this population of students with the best opportunity for good decision-making. The end result is that students will choose colleges where the services match their needs.

It is extremely important that readers understand that the fact that a college offers a service or accommodation does not necessarily mean that every student with LD/ADHD can access it. Each student requesting accommodations must submit current and appropriate documentation, and the disability support personnel will determine what accommodations are "reasonable." Too often, students assume that because they received specific services or accommodations in high school, they will receive the same level of services once they enroll in college. This is not the case for all students, and colleges have the right to reexamine the documentation and identify the services they feel are reasonable and appropriate.

Students and their parents are encouraged to read the college catalogs, talk to the admissions staff and the directors of the special support services, and visit the campuses. This is a good time to provide a copy of the student's documentation and get an idea of what services and/or accommodations may be offered to the students. Before planning a trip, however, begin with a thorough reading of this guide. Students need to have well-ordered priorities to determine the criteria they will use for selecting an appropriate college.

Students with unique learning needs should approach the college search with the goal of identifying colleges that will fill all of their needs—educationally, culturally, and socially. There is more than one "right" college for any student, learning disabled or not. Although no single source can provide all of the information needed to help students make educated decisions about appropriate college choices, the availability of other resource books with extensive information is very limited. The ultimate goal of *The K&W Guide* is to give descriptive and honest information so that all students have equal access to this knowledge. This guide is the first place to look to find colleges providing:

- **Structured Programs:** Schools that have specific programs for students with LD/ADHD with much more than the mandated services. These services might include special admissions procedures, specialized and trained professionals, compensatory strategies, one-on-one tutoring, additional fees, compulsory participation, and monitoring.

- **Coordinated Services:** Schools that have some involvement with admissions decisions, voluntary participation, more than just mandated services, small or no fees, and less structure.

- **Basic Services:** Schools that comply with Section 504 mandates that rarely have specialized LD staff, do not have monitoring, and are totally dependent on student advocacy.

The authors gratefully acknowledge the time and effort of all the service providers at the colleges and universities who responded to our request for current information about their services and programs. It is these colleges and others like them that are willing to work closely with students who have learning disabilities, believe in empowering students to articulate their needs, and help students to become independent and successful learners as they pursue a college education.

It is essential that college services and accommodations for individuals with learning disabilities and ADHD be visible, honored, funded, maintained, and expanded to meet the needs of identified students. Because learning disabilities are being identified earlier, diagnosed students are being provided with individualized educational plans to meet their needs, becoming self-advocates, learning compensatory skills, and making the transition in greater numbers from high school to college.

This must be a joint effort. The colleges and universities need to support the efforts and the ongoing learning process of these individuals. Those who believe in the merit of helping these individuals should reach out to those who do not understand. Those who do not understand should open their minds to the fact that learning disabilities are neurological and are life-long; they do not go away. The authors of this guide applaud these students. No children choose to be born with a learning disability or ADHD. However, if they hold fast to their dreams and aspirations and look beyond the imperfections and hidden handicaps, they can make things happen for themselves.

Marybeth Kravets and Imy Wax

THOUGHTS FROM . . .

Michael Barron, Director of Admissions, University of Iowa: More than thirty years ago, when I first became an admission officer at a medium-size public university in Texas, my mentors and colleagues suggested that I would encounter applicants who had not performed very well in high school. I was told to expect that some of those students would "claim" to have a reading problem and others would actually use the term dyslexia. It seems that many of my admission colleagues were somewhat dubious about the true extent of such a disability (although the term dyslexia was not in widespread use at the time). It is with horror that I look back on those times when many of us simply discounted such students as just being lazy, dumb, or under-prepared.

We are blessed today with greater knowledge about learning disabilities, and more important, with compassionate understanding of those individuals who cope with one or more of the growing list of what we now call learning disabilities. Often these students exhibit superior intellectual capacity, but lack the ability to mark the appropriate bubble or write an answer on paper in the prescribed time period. They are a resource that cannot be overlooked or swept aside by our application of some of the more odious and inappropriate labels used in the past.

We must take risks along with these students in order to help them develop their potential. We have learned that there are many disorders that impact an individual's ability to learn, but do not impair their intellectual capacity. I am pleased to say that now there are many more of my colleagues who understand these needs and, working carefully with disabilities specialists and faculty, are developing ways to provide these students with the opportunity for higher education.

At Iowa, the Office of Admissions has a special relationship with the Office of Services for Disabled Students, and has operated a very successful program of alternative admission consideration for such students. We seek students with learning disabilities who have used the resources available to them to their fullest potential.

A diverse student body with a variety of talents, interests, and backgrounds is necessary in a university. Iowa welcomes applications from students with documented learning disabilities and/or attention deficit disorder. The staff in the Office of Services for Disabled Students, as well as that in the Office of Admissions, carefully evaluates the overall academic performance of these students for evidence that they will be able to successfully pursue a demanding and rigorous collegiate program. We keep in mind that we are looking for students with the ability to do college work that is reflected in the strength of the courses they have taken, as well as the compensatory strategies that they have employed during their high school years.

Some students fulfill all of our regular admission requirements despite documented learning disabilities. This does not mean that they no longer need compensatory strategies or a special office to assist them in advising faculty of their special needs. They do. We have also had excellent success at Iowa with our special admission process for students with learning disabilities who do not meet our regular admission requirements, and recent data suggest that with proper attention, as many as eight out of ten such students succeed at the University. Faculty members are recruited to be partners in this process.

We recognize that the decision for students to self-identify themselves as learning disabled is a personal choice. A student's decision not to self-identify is respected. However, it has been our experience that students with learning disabilities who acknowledge the existence of a disability and seek assistance early are more likely to achieve academic success than those who wait for problems to develop. It was not too long ago that such students probably would never graduate from high school. Even if they did, they could not look forward to a future with very many options for employment.

Thankfully, we are making breakthroughs for many of these students and are now providing them with access to and opportunities for higher education. While there are programs like Iowa's that are beginning to achieve success, we have by no means provided a paradigm that is consistently accepted and used throughout the country. That will only come through public discussion of the successes and failures of those of us who have met the challenge and taken the risk. This book, *The K&W Guide to Colleges for Students with Learning Disabilities or Attention Deficit Disorder*, is certainly one of the resources I hope will be widely used in that effort.

While we are working to educate our colleagues, to modify our systems to accommodate these students, and to provide them with the opportunity to obtain the education that they desire, we also must begin to work as partners with industry. It will not be enough to provide an environment where an individual can complete a university degree and yet fail miserably in the world of work because of its lack of understanding and inappropriate job placement procedures. Our experience at Iowa is that these students desperately want to succeed, and they want to stand on the merits of their own achievements. To deny them the opportunity to be an asset at the highest level of their ability is to squander a valuable human resource, creating an unnecessary and unwanted liability for society. I urge students with learning disabilities and their families to demand the services they need and to be patient with those of us in the education establishment, as we seek to understand. I also encourage educators at all levels to be sensitive to and aware of these individuals as a resource not to be wasted, and to work diligently to provide educational opportunity to all.

◆ ◆ ◆

Joan Fisher, Past Director of Support Services, Office of Equal Opportunity, Cornell University: Yes, students with learning disabilities do succeed in highly selective colleges! For the past twelve years I have worked with students with disabilities at Cornell University, where approximately 20,000 students apply and 5,000 are offered admission to fill approximately 3,000 places in each freshman class. In 1987, nineteen students on campus self-identified as having learning disabilities. In 1998 that number had risen to 225. Similar increases have taken place in other selective colleges.

During this time I have met with or spoken to hundreds of prospective students and their parents and shared with them some thoughts about preparation for an Ivy League education. I have explained the admissions process and provided tips on preparation strategies for students, parents, and high school guidance counselors and teachers. I'd like to share some of these tips and strategies with you.

Think about college long before senior year

Freshman year of high school or even middle school is not too soon to think about college. Many students who are capable of attending a highly selective college find themselves ineligible because they have not met the necessary course requirements. Students are often encouraged to bypass the more difficult math, science, or English courses and often do not attempt foreign language courses. Although many highly selective colleges may offer a waiver or substitution policy for foreign languages to students with specific types of learning disabilities, don't assume that this is an automatic process. If you are an intellectually gifted student with a learning disability and are thinking of applying to a highly selective college, insist that your secondary school provide you with the reasonable accommodations you need to succeed in these classes, rather than discourage you from participating. If you can't handle these classes in a secondary setting, perhaps a highly selective college is not your best choice.

Good self-advocacy is vital to success

When students move from the jurisdiction of IDEA to that of Section 504 of the Rehabilitation Act of 1073 and the Americans with Disabilities Act (ADA), a major shift in responsibility takes place. IDEA places direct responsibility on the schools to identify students with disabilities and provide services to them. Section 504 and the ADA place the burden on self-identification and request for reasonable accommodations directly on the student. Many colleges also require the student to provide updated (usually within three years) documentation of learning disabilities and attention deficit disorder. Check with the schools you are applying to for specific documentation requirements. Failure of students to self-identify and request the accommodations for which they are legally eligible is a primary reason for lack of success in college. Students who finally come for help in November (I call it my "crying season") say "I didn't want special treatment," or "I thought I could do it on my own." My recommendation to all eligible students is "start with all of the accommodations for which you are eligible. If you don't need them, you don't have to use them."

The role of parents, teachers, and guidance counselors in preparation

One of the most difficult parts of the transition process is the changing of roles by parents and others. Parents who have been used to advocating for their sons or daughters (a necessary role in many cases) may have difficulty turning this process over to their children as they enter post-secondary education. However, Mom and Dad have to begin making this transition well before the student begins college. Schools also must play a role in the transition by including students in all discussions regarding accommodations, class selection, and other decisions regarding their education. When I ask a student who is sitting in my office with his parents during a campus visit to describe his disability and the student looks at Mom and says "What do I have?" I know that student is going to have a difficult time in college. Below are some ideas for beginning the transition process.

- Include the student in discussion of disability issues. Students who can describe and understand how they learn can best explain what accommodations they will need to succeed in college and later in life.

- Role-play examples of conversations between the student and professors. Practice approaching a teacher and discussing learning and accommodations needs. One high school calls it training in "teacher-pleasing behaviors." I have found that faculty members are most impressed by a student who can really explain his or her learning needs and can explain how they can be met. I have seen many students who assume that it is necessary to fight for every accommodation and approach faculty with negative expectations. It has been my experience that most faculty members are fully aware of applicable laws and want to see students succeed. If you come to them expecting support, you will find most professors are caring and helpful.

- Assist the student in the use of adaptive technology. Many students benefit greatly from equipment originally designed for persons with visual or other disabilities as well as the many software programs specifically designed to aid those with learning disabilities. Programs are available which read books and articles out loud to students, correct spelling and grammar, and even finish sentences. Many students also do well with voice-activated programs such as Dragon Dictate. In my experience, the ability to utilize adaptive programs is a great equalizer and allows the student greater independence.

- Encourage students to make their own contacts with colleges and respond themselves to questions in interviews, whether with a person in the disability service office or with an admissions director. College personnel see this ability as a sign of the maturity necessary for success in a highly competitive environment. Because most of my contacts are with parents, I am especially impressed by the student who makes his own contacts.

The admissions process

The questions most often asked by applicants is, "Should I even bother to apply if I'm not in the top 10 percent of my class and have 1200 on my SAT?" The second is, "Should I self-identify as having a disability during the application process?"

Although most students applying to highly selective colleges have excelled in school and on SAT or ACT exams (often with extended time), many others are admitted who do not meet all of the criteria. Remember, an average SAT score means many applicants are above the score and others are below it. The same goes for class rank, GPA, and all the other variables. Highly selective colleges look at the whole application (not just GPA and test scores). They look at leadership skills, talents, and the attributes that make you unique. The essay portion of the application gives you the opportunity to share this information with admission personnel. The quality of your essays may well make the difference between acceptance and denial.

Whether or not to self-identify is your choice. By law, the college cannot ask an applicant if he has disability. You do not have to self-identify in the application process to receive accommodations. You also do not need to send documentation with the application unless you are applying specifically to a formal learning disability program that requires it.

On the flip side, there are reasons you might want to self-identify. You may do so through one of your required essays or through a letter from your guidance counselor. These reasons may include, but are not limited to such criteria as

- You didn't meet all of the curriculum requirements, such as taking a foreign language.

- Grades in a class such as math or English were consistently lower than in your other classes. For example, if you do less well in math than in your other classes because of a math learning disability, you might want to let the college know that.

- You were first identified in secondary school and your grades improved dramatically once you began receiving accommodations. It's not uncommon to see "C's" become "B's," or even "A's." Explain this on the application.

- Your disability has contributed to your career choice or some of your activities grew out of your disability experience. For example, were you active in the Learning Disability Association? Did you present at a conference or make presentations to other students? Has your disability contributed to your desire to become a special education teacher? This information can be a plus on your application.

Succeeding on the college campus

Students who are the most successful have learned to distinguish between "reasonable accommodation" as defined by law and "special privilege" as defined by wishful thinking. I frequently told students and faculty that a reasonable accommodation levels the playing field and gives everyone an even chance to succeed.

It does not mean

- being given an "A" because you have a disability, or being immune from failing a class.

- not doing required assignments, having test grades changed, or demonstrating unacceptable classroom behaviors.

- being given easier assignments or getting morning "wake-up" calls.

It does mean

- making early contact with the campus disability services office, preferably in the first week you are on campus.

- meeting with professors well before the first exam to discuss specific accommodation requirements. Most colleges will either send a letter in advance to your professors or provide you with a letter to deliver to them.

- taking advantage of peer support groups, tutoring programs, writing assistance, adaptive technology, faculty office hours, and any other help which is available. Support services are like a smorgasbord. All kinds of help are available, but the choice to use them is yours.

Many students told me that they have to work much harder than their peers, and sometimes it took longer to graduate. However, as I hear from former students who are now lawyers, doctors, teachers, or successful business professionals, I can assure you that the results are worth the extra effort. If you have a dream, having a learning disability does not have to stop your pursuit of it.

◆ ◆ ◆

Lydia S. Block, PhD, Educational Consultant, Block Educational Consulting: For many students the idea of attending a large university is very intriguing. These schools offer large sports programs, many majors, different types of living situations, and a multitude of cultural and social activities. Successfully negotiating the large university setting also requires a considerable amount of initiative on the student's part. How do students and their parents know when a large school is a good match? How does a student know that he or she will be able to get what is necessary in terms of academic support and accommodations from a large university? These are important things to find out before applying. *The K&W Guide* is the best resource available to provide families with information gleaned first-hand both from school visitations and directly from the schools' Disability Service Providers.

With few exceptions most large universities have disability service programs to serve students with all disabilities. Some campuses have limited staff to work with students, and students will find that it is up to them to seek the help that they need. By the nature of their size, there is far less personal attention at a large university then at a small school and students must learn to advocate for themselves. Students at large schools must be very independent. The classes are generally large the first year or two, some are taught by graduate students, and it is less likely that a faculty member will be able to get to know a student well. Students must know what they need in terms of academic support and accommodations and be prepared to ask for it. Generally, students are responsible for filing paperwork with the appropriate office to receive accommodation, and for meeting with faculty members to explain their disability.

In addition to knowing what they need in terms of accommodations, students at large universities must also be able to identify when they do not understand material or an assignment. This is true at any school, but a large university offers fewer opportunities for class discussion and often less access to faculty members than a small school. So it is up to the students to seek help when they need it.

Students with attention deficit/hyperactivity disorder sometimes find it difficult to structure their academic and social lives at a large university. Students must rely on motivation and their ability to independently make decisions and follow them through. This is a challenge for all college freshmen, but it is particularly difficult for some students with LD and ADHD.

For students who have been successfully involved in activities in high school, and shown the ability to structure their lives and advocate for themselves, a large institution can be full of wonderful opportunities. For certain majors, large schools offer the best programs, noted faculty, and research and internship opportunities. It is important for students to consider what being a student at a large campus environment will be like. When the student visits a large university, it is essential that she sit in on large lecture classes and meet with the disability service provider. These are important steps in realistically evaluating what life would be like in a setting where everything will not always be clearly defined.

◆ ◆ ◆

Julie T. Steck, PhD, HSPP; and Dennis Ray Kinder, PhD, HSPP; Children's Resource Group:

Dear Parents:

As soon as our adolescents enter high school, most of us begin to worry about what they will do after high school. Increasingly, a parent's dream for their child includes a college education. As parents strive to assist their adolescent in traversing the rocky path through high school, college begins to seem more like a nightmare than a dream. It somehow seems like an insurmountable task. How can a student who loses homework in their backpack be expected to organize, complete, and turn in a term paper? How can a student who misses the bus on a regular basis ever make it to an 8 A.M. class without a parent to awaken him? How can a student who forgets the combination to her locker keep track of a dorm key?

These are the scenarios that haunt families of students with attention deficit/hyperactivity disorder (ADHD). So, is a college education a realistic expectation? Yes, but it takes a great deal of planning, thought, commitment, and (most importantly) patience. All too often the goal of families with students with ADHD is to get the student into college. But if a college education is the goal, the goal must also include staying on path to complete a college education, finding some enjoyment in the process, and becoming a successful adult. Leaving home and going to college does not mean that the characteristics of ADHD are left behind. It only means that the parents no longer see evidence of the disability on a daily basis. The young adult must still deal with the disorder, and he or she will be doing it in an environment with much less internal structure and with many more distractions.

What can parents do to prepare their student to be successful in college? The first step toward achieving the dream is to confront the problem. If you suspect that your student has ADHD or if he or she has been diagnosed but not adequately addressed, you and your child need to recognize the disorder and develop an appreciation for how it impacts his or her progress. The impact of ADHD is far-reaching and often has social, educational, emotional, and organizational implications. Just as with any other medical disorder, a young adult must become increasingly responsible for managing his or her own care. For example, students with asthma must know how much they should exercise, what type of weather and climate is best for them, and when and how much medication to take. Similarly, students with ADHD need to know how to structure their day, what type of classes and social situations are best for them, and how to appropriately use their medications. All too often, parents have willingly provided these supports for their student with ADHD without the student realizing why they needed to be done. As students approach young adulthood, parents need to assist in educating their student about ADHD and the potential impact of the disorder on the young person's life.

The second step toward the dream of college is to ensure that the disorder is appropriately diagnosed. The evaluation should be conducted by a qualified medical provider or psychologist who has been trained in ADHD. In order to meet the criteria required by most colleges and universities for special programs, accommodations, or adaptations, the evaluation must include the use of standardized measures which document the disability and its impact on educational performance.

In addition, the report should contain specific recommendations for accommodations and programming. This evaluation should not be considered just another hurdle to cross, but should be viewed by the parent and student as an opportunity to obtain information regarding the student's performance and levels of functioning. The evaluation should also serve as a forum to gain insight into the student's strengths and needs, providing helpful information for both the parent and the student.

The third step toward the dream is to review the student's elementary, junior high, and high school career objectively. How has the student performed overall? In what types of classes did the student do well? What types of classes were difficult for the student? If medication has been used, how did it impact grades and performance? What types of learning environments did the student prefer? Did he or she do well in the environments they preferred? It is likely that these factors will impact college performance just as they have previously. The best predictor of the future is often a realistic assessment of the past.

The fourth step in achieving the dream of college is to choose a college or university in which the student can be successful. Most students with ADHD have experienced a great deal of frustration in high school largely because there were so few choices available to them regarding their school environment. Selecting an appropriate college provides an opportunity to choose an environment more tailored to the student's needs. In general, students with ADHD do best when they chose colleges with the following:

- Smaller classroom environments

- Opportunities to interact directly with instructors and professors

- Structured support services for students with disabilities

- Academic expectations that will not be a "reach" for the student

- An adult mentor within the university or living nearby

- On-campus living environments

- Tutoring services in areas of weakness

- Academic counselors knowledgeable about ADHD

The most important step in achieving the dream of a college education is for parents to work jointly with their young adult to build a plan for success. Most students with ADHD do not complete a four-year college program in four years. Generally, this is due to the student dropping out of college (or being asked to leave) due to frustration or failure. It is far better to anticipate college taking longer and build in a five-year (or longer) plan. Many students benefit from taking a class in the summer at a local college prior to starting their freshman year. This provides an opportunity for the student to experience a college-level class before leaving home. Most students will do better with a slightly lighter class load than normal. Instead of starting with five classes and dropping one, start with four classes that will require a realistic amount of time and study. If the student will be working to support themselves, the course load may need to be even lighter.

In working with high school and college students with ADHD, we have typically observed that these students seldom consistently achieve grades at a level at which they, or others, expect they are capable. Thus, it's usually preferable to set goals that are attainable and to focus on completion. If completion of a degree is viewed as success, students with ADHD and their families can achieve success. If success is viewed as a consistent level of high performance there is a likelihood of failure that may result in a decision to abort the dream. In our experience, it is far better to set realistic expectations and succeed than it is to reach for the stars and fail.

◆ ◆ ◆

INFORMATION FROM AN ATTORNEY ON DISABILITY LAW

Jeanne M. Kincaid, Esq.; Due Process Special Education Hearing Officer, New Hampshire; Adjunct Faculty Member of the University of New Hampshire's Graduate School of Education and the Franklin Pierce Law Center; co-author of Section 504, the ADA and the Schools; contributing author to the publication Disability Compliance for Higher Education: *The K&W Guide* offers potential students and their families the opportunity to make an educated decision when selecting the proper college or university to meet the student's needs, in light of his or her learning disability. Although nearly every college in the country is subject to Section 504 of the Rehabilitation Act and many also fall within the coverage of the Americans with Disabilities Act (ADA) (both of which prohibit discrimination on the basis of disability), the range of accommodations and services offered by each institution varies considerably.

The following information is designed to assist the student and family in helping to understand what the law minimally requires, determining if the student requires more, and learning what other services might be available. I begin with a brief outline of how the laws for students from kindergarten through twelfth grade differ from those for individuals in a higher-education institution. This will provide a framework for my further comments.

K–12	Higher Education
Guaranteed an education	Have no right to an education
Districts must screen and identify	Students responsible for identification
Free evaluation	Students pay for evaluations
District must develop a plan	Students responsible for plan
IEP	No IEP
District ensures plan implemented	Students responsible for plan
Right to fundamental service	No fundamental rights
Right to due process hearing	No right to due process
Parents are legal advocates	Students act as own advocates

Admissions

Generally, institutions of higher education may not inquire about one's disability prior to acceptance, unless the inquiry is made for affirmative action purposes. However, students and families should consider contacting the college's Section 504/ADA Coordinator, or the Disabled Student Services (DSS) Office, to determine what services the student is likely to receive if accepted by the college. The DSS office may also be helpful in advising the student whether to disclose her disability in the application. Additionally, should the student choose to enroll at the college, the DSS office can advise the student as to what documentation he may need, in order to ensure that he receives timely and effective services.

Documentation

Documentation serves two important purposes: 1) It establishes that the student has a disability as defined by Section 504 and the ADA; and 2) guides the college in providing appropriate accommodations for the adult learner. Many colleges require that documentation be conducted within the past three years. Moreover, as federal law does not obligate a college to conduct assessments, a student should consider requesting that his/her high school update the assessment, consistent with any requirements of the college in which the student seeks enrollment. For example, some colleges have established guidelines for the type of documentation they require. Checking with the DSS office in advance, however, may yield information about what assessments the college may provide the student free of charge.

Accommodations

At a minimum, a student with a learning disability should be able to expect the following accommodations if the nature of the disability requires such adjustments and is supported by the documentation: a reduced courseload, extended time to complete tests and assignments, extended time to complete degree requirements, a note-taker, course substitution of nonessential courses, a quiet testing room, books on tape, the right to tape-record classes, and in some cases, an alternate format for taking tests.

The law does not obligate an institution of higher education to provide all recommended accommodations, but rather effective accommodations. A student should therefore not presume that what he/she received in high school will necessarily be honored at the post-secondary level.

With respect to courseload, often students with disabilities benefit greatly from taking less than the average number of courses, particularly during the first year, as the student makes the transition to the rigors of higher education. Nonetheless, as many students with learning disabilities may take five or more years to complete an undergraduate degree, it is important to consider the impact a reduced courseload may have upon financial aid. Although most loans and scholarships should be pre-rated, rather than lost entirely, colleges handle this issue in a variety of ways. Again, the DSS office should be able to apprise the student of the college's policy.

A critical consideration for college selection is determining the college's general education requirement imposed on all students in order to obtain a degree as well as requirements for graduating with a particular major. Many colleges/universities require one or more courses in foreign language and mathematics. For some students with learning disabilities, no amount of accommodation will result in their successful completion of such requirements. It cannot be emphasized enough how vital it is to review such requirements before selecting your college, as such requirements typically need not be waived based upon disability.

Services

Beyond the accommodations mentioned above, colleges often provide a vast array of additional services. Although a college may not charge for legally mandated accommodations, it may impose a fee for services that go beyond the minimal legal requirements. For example, as discussed throughout this guide, some colleges provide tutoring by personnel specifically trained in working with students with learning disabilities. As tutoring is considered a personal service and not an accommodation, a college may generally charge for such services, to the extent they go beyond the minimum legal standard. Other such services may include assessments, study-skills training, priority registration, counseling, and case management services.

Securing Accommodations

Each campus has its own unique system for providing students with disability-related accommodations. Many give the student a letter detailing recommended accommodations, with instructions to the student to approach the professors in each course so that classroom accommodations are provided in a timely fashion. Some DSS offices send the letter directly to the student's professors. However, the former approach is the trend, as it promotes self-advocacy, a necessary skill for the student's long-term success, both as a student and, in the future, as an employee. Although many professors have received training on the ADA and Section 504, many have not. Therefore, should a professor fail to agree to the recommendations or neglect to carry them out, it is imperative that the student promptly notifies the DSS office, which should intervene on the student's behalf. Unlike public high school, civil rights laws in institutions of higher education do not require that the institution monitor the student's progress or shadow the student to ensure that the accommodations are provided and effective. Again, it is up to the student to take affirmative steps when problems arise. Remember, no one is likely to ever know if a note-taker fails to consistently show for a class unless the student notifies the DSS office.

As a Final Cautionary Note

Students with hidden disabilities, such as learning disabilities, often wish to attempt college without accommodation. Many students have been "labeled" their entire educational lives and are committed to attempting college on their own terms, without special assistance. Although some succeed without accommodation, court and agency rulings have consistently ruled that a student who fails to take advantage of available disability-related accommodations does so at his peril. Although the ADA is based on promoting success, it also gives individuals with disabilities the right to fail. Before making a decision to forego accommodations, I strongly encourage the student to consult with the DSS office.

◆ ◆ ◆

GUIDELINES FOR DOCUMENTATION OF LEARNING DISABILITIES

One of the more confusing things about applying to college as a student with a learning disability is answering the questions "What documentation should I send?" and "How will the college use that documentation?" It is important to keep in mind that documentation of your disability cannot be considered during the admission process unless you are requesting special consideration of your application. In cases of special consideration, your disability documentation may help the review committee understand the nature of your learning disability and how it impacted your high school studies. It may also help to explain why you did not complete some high school classes commonly required for admission to your favorite college or university.

Though documentation may be important during the admission process, for most students current, comprehensive documentation becomes critical for receiving appropriate accommodations guaranteed under either the ADA or Section 504. Guidelines for documenting learning disabilities in post-secondary-age individuals have been developed by the Association on Higher Education and Disability (AHEAD). These guidelines provide a standard by which many colleges and universities may verify the existence of a student's learning disability and may determine what accommodations are appropriate to support each student's enrollment.

IDEA no longer requires that a disability be re-evaluated every three years. It is true that learning disabilities do not go away with age, but the nature of the disability may change and functional limitations may result in difficulties not experienced until college. For this reason, many colleges and universities are requiring that documentation of disability be "current," in many cases within the last three years.

Comprehensive documentation, including measures of aptitude, achievement, and information processing are essential for any college or university to implement the best possible academic accommodation plan. Accommodations are to be provided based on the individual student's functional limitations and each evaluation should point to a link between the test scores and the recommendations the evaluator is making regarding the student's needs. Students sometimes believe that because an evaluator made recommendations in his or her documentation report that those recommendations will be followed. This may not be true. The post-secondary service provider must be able to identify how the functional limitations of the disability necessitate a particular accommodation.

Documentation of learning disabilities should include results of a clinical interview with a medical, family, school and psychosocial history. This information not only helps to add to the credibility of a diagnosis of learning disability, it frequently helps the service provider to understand the full scope of a student's needs.

Providing comprehensive, current documentation of your learning disability in the form of a report compiled by a well-trained professional will help to assure you the most appropriate support services in college. Make sure you do everything you can to set the stage for your success!

Diane C. Perreira, Ed. Director,

The S.A.L.T. Center

The University of Arizona

GUIDELINES FOR DOCUMENTATION OF A LEARNING DISABILITY IN ADOLESCENTS AND ADULTS

July 1997

The Board of Directors established an Ad Hoc Committee to study issues surrounding the documentation of a learning disability. The board wishes to thank the members of the AHEAD Ad Hoc Committee on LD Guidelines for their efforts in laying the foundation of these Guidelines for use by the Association's members.

Loring Brinckerhoff, Ad Hoc Committee Chairperson, Educational Testing Service, Recording for the Blind and Dyslexic

Joan McGuire, Ad Hoc Committee Liaison to the Board, University of Connecticut—Storrs

Kim Dempsey, Law School Admission Council

Cyndi Jordan, University of Tennessee—Memphis

Shelby Keiser, National Board of Medical Examiners

Catherine Nelson, Educational Testing Service

Nancy Pompian, Dartmouth College

Louise Russell, Harvard University

Additional copies of this publication are available for purchase for $10.00 U.S. each. This publication is available in alternate formats upon request.

TABLE OF CONTENTS

INTRODUCTION

In response to the expressed need for guidance related to the documentation of a learning disability in adolescents and adults, the Association on Higher Education And Disability (AHEAD) has developed the following guidelines. The primary intent of these guidelines is to provide students, professional diagnosticians and service providers with a common understanding and knowledge base of those components of documentation which are necessary to validate a learning disability and the need for accommodation. The information and documentation that establishes a learning disability should be comprehensive in order to make it possible for a student to be served in a post-secondary setting.

The document presents guidelines in four important areas: 1) qualifications of the evaluator, 2) recency of documentation, 3) appropriate clinical documentation to substantiate the learning disability, and 4) evidence to establish a rationale supporting the need for accommodations. Under the Americans with Disabilities Act (ADA) and Section 504 of the Rehabilitation Act of 1973, individuals with learning disabilities are guaranteed certain protections and rights of equal access to programs and services; thus the documentation should indicate that the disability substantially limits some major life activity. The following guidelines are provided in the interest of assuring that LD documentation is appropriate to verify eligibility and to support requests for accommodations, academic adjustments and/or auxiliary aids. It is recommended that post-secondary institutions using these guidelines consult with their legal counsel before establishing a policy on documentation relating to individuals with disabilities. In countries not regulated by this legislation further modification may be appropriate.

These guidelines are designed to be a framework for institutions to work from in establishing criteria for eligibility. It is acknowledged that different educational settings with different student populations will need to modify and adapt these guidelines to meet the needs and backgrounds of their student populations. Recommendations for consumers are presented in Appendix A to assist them in finding and working with a qualified professional in regard to documentation.

DOCUMENTATION GUIDELINES

I. Qualifications of the Evaluator

Professionals conducting assessments, rendering diagnoses of learning disabilities, and making recommendations for appropriate accommodations must be qualified to do so. Comprehensive training and direct experience with an adolescent and adult LD population is essential. The name, title and professional credentials of the evaluator, including information about license or certification (e.g., licensed psychologist) as well as the area of specialization, employment and state/province in which the individual practices should be clearly stated in the documentation. For example, the following professionals would generally be considered qualified to evaluate specific learning disabilities provided that they have additional training and experience in the assessment of learning problems in adolescents and adults: clinical or educational psychologists, school psychologists, neuropsychologists, learning disabilities specialists, medical doctors, and other professionals. Use of diagnostic terminology indicating a learning disability by someone whose training and experience are not in these fields is not acceptable. It is of utmost importance that evaluators are sensitive and respectful of cultural and linguistic differences in adolescents and adults during the assessment process. It is not considered appropriate for professionals to evaluate members of their families. All reports should be on letterhead, typed, dated, signed and otherwise legible.

II. Documentation

The provision of all reasonable accommodations and services is based upon assessment of the impact of the student's disabilities on his or her academic performance at a given time in the student's life. Therefore, it is in the student's best interest to provide recent and appropriate documentation relevant to the student's learning environment. Flexibility in accepting documentation is important, especially in settings with significant numbers of nontraditional students. In some instances, documentation may be outdated or inadequate in scope or content. It may not address the student's current level of functioning or need for accommodations because observed changes may have occurred in the student's performance since the previous assessment was conducted. In such cases, it may be appropriate to update the evaluation report. Since the purpose of the update is to determine the student's current need for accommodations, the update, conducted by a qualified professional, should include a rationale for ongoing services and accommodations.

III. Substantiation of the Learning Disability

Documentation should validate the need for services based on the individual's current level of functioning in the educational setting. A school plan such as an individualized education program (IEP) or a 504 plan is insufficient documentation, but it can be included as part of a more comprehensive assessment battery. A comprehensive assessment battery and the resulting diagnostic report should include a diagnostic interview, assessment of aptitude, academic achievement, information processing and a diagnosis.

A. Diagnostic Interview

An evaluation report should include the summary of a comprehensive diagnostic interview. Learning disabilities are commonly manifested during childhood, but not always formally diagnosed. Relevant information regarding the student's academic history and learning processes in elementary, secondary and post-secondary education should be investigated. The diagnostician, using professional judgment as to which areas are relevant, should conduct a diagnostic interview which may include: a description of the presenting problem(s); developmental, medical, psycho social and employment histories; family history (including primary language of the home and the student's current level of English fluency); and a discussion of dual diagnosis where indicated.

B. Assessment

The neuropsychological or psycho-educational evaluation for the diagnosis of a specific learning disability must provide clear and specific evidence that a learning disability does or does not exist. Assessment, and any resulting diagnosis, should consist of and be based on a comprehensive assessment battery which does not rely on any one test or subtest.

Evidence of a substantial limitation to learning or other major life activity must be provided. A list of commonly used tests is included in Appendix B. Minimally, the domains to be addressed must include the following:

1. Aptitude

   A complete intellectual assessment with all subtests and standard scores reported.

2. Academic Achievement

   A comprehensive academic achievement battery is essential with all subtests and standard scores reported for those subtests administered. The battery should include current levels of academic functioning in relevant areas such as reading (decoding and comprehension), mathematics, and oral and written language.

3. Information Processing

   Specific areas of information processing (e.g., short- and long-term memory, sequential memory, auditory and visual perception/processing, processing speed, executive functioning and motor ability) should be assessed.

   Other assessment measures such as nonstandard measures and informal assessment procedures or observations may be helpful in determining performance across a variety of domains. Other formal assessment measures may be integrated with the above instruments to help determine a learning disability and differentiate it from co-existing neurological and/or psychiatric disorders (i.e., to establish a differential diagnosis). In addition to standardized tests, it is also very useful to include informal observations of the student during the test administration.

C. Specific Diagnosis

   Individual "learning styles," "learning differences," "academic problems," and "test difficulty or anxiety," in and of themselves do not constitute a learning disability. It is important to rule out alternative explanations for problems in learning such as emotional, attentional or motivational problems that may be interfering with learning but do not constitute a learning disability. The diagnostician is encouraged to use direct language in the diagnosis and documentation of a learning disability, avoiding the use of terms such as "suggests" or "is indicative of." If the data indicate that a learning disability is not present, the evaluator should state that conclusion in the report.

D. Test Scores

   Standard scores and/or percentiles should be provided for all normed measures. Grade equivalents are not useful unless standard scores and/or percentiles are also included. The data should logically reflect a substantial limitation to learning for which the student is requesting the accommodation. The particular profile of the student's strengths and weaknesses must be shown to relate to functional limitations that may necessitate accommodations. The tests used should be reliable, valid and standardized for use with an adolescent/adult population. The test findings should document both the nature and severity of the learning disability. Informal inventories, surveys and direct observation by a qualified professional may be used in tandem with formal tests in order to further develop a clinical hypothesis.

E. Clinical Summary

A well-written diagnostic summary based on a comprehensive evaluation process is a necessary component of the report. Assessment instruments and the data they provide do not diagnose; rather, they provide important elements that must be integrated by the evaluator with background information, observations of the client during the testing situation, and the current context. It is essential, therefore, that professional judgment be utilized in the development of a clinical summary. The clinical summary should include:

1. demonstration of the evaluator's having ruled out alternative explanations for academic problems as a result of poor education, poor motivation and/or study skills, emotional problems, attentional problems and cultural/language differences;

2. indication of how patterns in the student's cognitive ability, achievement and information processing reflect the presence of a learning disability;

3. indication of the substantial limitation to learning or other major life activity presented by the learning disability and the degree to which it impacts the individual in the learning context for which accommodations are being requested; and

4. indication as to why specific accommodations are needed and how the effects of the specific disability are accommodated.

The summary should also include any record of prior accommodation or auxiliary aids, including any information about specific conditions under which the accommodations were used (e.g., standardized testing, final exams, licensing or certification examinations).

IV. Recommendations for Accommodations

It is important to recognize that accommodation needs can change over time and are not always identified through the initial diagnostic process. Conversely, a prior history of accommodation does not, in and of itself, warrant the provision of a similar accommodation. The diagnostic report should include specific recommendations for accommodations as well as an explanation as to why each accommodation is recommended. The evaluators should describe the impact the diagnosed learning disability has on a specific major life activity as well as the degree of significance of this impact on the individual. The evaluator should support recommendations with specific test results or clinical observations.

If accommodations are not clearly identified in a diagnostic report, the disability service provider should seek clarification and, if necessary, more information. The final determination for providing appropriate and reasonable accommodations rests with the institution.

In instances where a request for accommodations is denied in a post-secondary institution, a written grievance or appeal procedure should be in place.

V. Confidentiality

The receiving institution has a responsibility to maintain confidentiality of the evaluation and may not release any part of the documentation without the student's informed and written consent.

Recommendations for Consumers

1. For assistance in finding a qualified professional

   - Contact the disability services coordinator at the institution you attend or plan to attend to discuss documentation needs, and discuss your future plans with the disability services coordinator.

   - If additional documentation is required, seek assistance in identifying a qualified professional.

2. In selecting a qualified professional

   - Ask what his or her credentials are.

   - Ask what experience he or she has had working with adults with learning disabilities.

   - Ask if he or she has ever worked with the service provider at your institution or with the agency to which you are sending material.

3. In working with the professional

   - Take a copy of these guidelines to the professional.

   - Encourage him or her to clarify questions with the person who provided you with these guidelines.

   - Be prepared to be forthcoming, thorough and honest with requested information.

   - Know that professionals must maintain confidentiality with respect to your records and testing information.

4. As follow-up to the assessment by the professional

   - Request a written copy of the assessment report.

   - Request the opportunity to discuss the results and recommendations.

   - Request additional resources if you need them.

   - Maintain a personal file of your records and reports.

APPENDIX B

Tests for Assessing Adolescents and Adults

When selecting a battery of tests, it is critical to consider the technical adequacy of instruments including their reliability, validity and standardization on an appropriate norm group. The professional judgment of an evaluator in choosing tests is important.

The following list is provided as a helpful resource, but it is not intended to be definitive or exhaustive.

Aptitude

- Wechsler Adult Intelligence Scale-Revised (WAIS-R)
- Woodcock-Johnson Psychoeducational Battery-Revised: Tests of Cognitive Ability
- Kaufman Adolescent and Adult Intelligence Test
- Stanford-Binet Intelligence Scale (4th ed.)

The Slosson Intelligence Test-Revised and the Kaufman Brief Intelligence Tests are primarily screening devices that are not comprehensive enough to provide the kinds of information necessary to make accommodation decisions.

Academic Achievement

- Scholastic Abilities Test for Adults (SATA)
- Stanford Test of Academic Skills
- Woodcock-Johnson Psychoeducational Battery-Revised: Tests of Achievement
- Wechsler Individual Achievement Test (WIAT)

Or specific achievement tests such as

- Nelson-Denny Reading Skills Test
- Stanford Diagnostic Mathematics Test
- Test of Written Language-3 (TOWL-3)
- Woodcock Reading Mastery Tests-Revised

Specific achievement tests are useful instruments when administered under standardized conditions and interpreted within the context of other diagnostic information. The Wide Range Achievement Test-3 (WRAT-3) is not a comprehensive measure of achievement and therefore is not useful if used as the sole measure of achievement.

Information Processing

Acceptable instruments include the Detroit Tests of Learning Aptitude-3 (DTLA-3), the Detroit Tests of Learning Aptitude-Adult (DTLA-A), information from subtests on WAIS-R, Woodcock-Johnson Psychoeducational Battery-Revised: Tests of Cognitive Ability, as well as other relevant instruments.

Reprinted with permission from the Association On Higher Education And Disability.

GUIDELINES FOR DOCUMENTATION OF ADHD

In the fall of 1997, seven members of the Association on Higher Education and Disability (AHEAD) met at Dartmouth College to develop a set of guidelines for documenting ADHD. The primary purpose of these guidelines is to educate our colleagues and consumers as to how to determine whether ADHD documentation is sufficient to support the disability claim and the accommodations being requested. The final draft of these guidelines was sent out for further review to some of the leading physicians, neuropsychologists, post-secondary service providers, and university scholars in the field.

Criteria that are addressed in the consortium's guidelines include: qualifications of the evaluator; recency of the documentation; comprehensive documentation components including evidence of early and current impairment; relevant testing; identification criteria from the Diagnostic and Statistical Manual of Mental Disorders-Fourth Edition (DSM-IV) (American Psychiatric Association, 1994), a specific diagnosis and interpretive summary; and a rationale for the recommendation(s).

These guidelines were developed in reaction to the number of post-secondary disability service providers who felt they should no longer be placed in a position of having to accept "incredibly insufficient little notes on a prescription pad" as documentation for an attention deficit disorder. Although the consortium guidelines may best be viewed as a "work in progress," it is hoped that they will provide our field with additional guidance and an acceptable standard so that misconceptions regarding the documentation of ADHD in adolescents and adults can be minimized and opportunities for a productive dialogue can be facilitated. An additional intent of the guidelines is to provide "a springboard" for unique needs of a given setting, state, or region. The guidelines are the development of policies that could be tailored; they are not designed to be a "boilerplate." Practitioners are encouraged to tailor these guidelines to suit the needs of their respective settings.

At the secondary level, it is hoped that guidance counselors, school psychologists, special education personnel, and parents will also find the consortium guidelines helpful as they prepare for IEP meetings, the submission of ADHD documentation to licensing and testing agencies, and the mapping-out of individual transition plans (ITPs) for students. Given that the number of ADHD students has almost doubled during the last decade (Gordon & Murphy, 1998) secondary school personnel need to be aware that testing agencies and post-secondary disability service providers are reviewing ADHD documentation with greater scrutiny. Evaluators, high school personnel, and parents may need to be reminded that the assessment of an adolescent with a suspected ADHD must not only establish a diagnosis of ADHD, but also demonstrate the current impact of the ADHD on an individual's ability in academically related settings. At high school level, a complete psycho-educational evaluation in addition to the ADHD diagnosis may be necessary in order to clearly establish the degree the ADHD impacts the individual in school. ADHD documentation that does not include an early history of ADHD symptoms, or ADHD documentation that states the student has only "problems" with attention, or ADHD documentation that is based solely on the self-reported symptoms of the student are hard to establish as credible (Gordon & Murphy, 1998).

Adherence to these guidelines should help high school professionals and parents so they can plan ahead by requesting comprehensive documentation of ADHD that demonstrates that the attention problems are so significant as to impact the student's ability to perform within a specific educational, vocational or testing situation. The documentation should validate the need for the accommodations being requested and if there is a history of accommodations these should be stated. The bottom line is that all requests for accommodations should be supported by the evaluator's clinical observations, backed-up with diagnostic data, and further collaborated by parents, teachers, and the students themselves.

Loring C. Brinckerhoff, PhD

Educational Testing Service/Recording for the Blind & Dyslexic

References:

Gordon, M. & Murphy, K. "Attention-Deficit/Hyperactivity Disorder" in M. Gordon & S. Keiser, *Accommodations in Higher Education Under the Americans with Disabilities Act (ADA)*. New York: Guilford Press, 1998.

GUIDELINES FOR DOCUMENTATION OF ATTENTION DEFICIT/HYPERACTIVITY DISORDER IN ADOLESCENTS AND ADULTS

CONSORTIUM ON ADHD DOCUMENTATION

Loring C. Brinckerhoff, Chairperson Educational Testing Service

Kim M. Dempsey, Law School Admission Council

Cyndi Jordan, University of Tennessee—Memphis

Shelby R. Keiser, National Board of Medical Examiners

Joan M. McGuire, University of Connecticut—Storrs

Nancy W. Pompian, Dartmouth College

Louise H. Russell, Harvard University

ACKNOWLEDGMENTS

The consortium wishes to acknowledge the contributions of the following individuals and expresses its appreciation and gratitude for their time invested in reviewing these guidelines and for their insightful comments:

Russell Barkley, PhD, Director of Psychology, University of Massachusetts Medical Center

Michael Gordon, PhD, Professor, Department of Psychiatry; Director, ADHD Program, State University of New York Health Science Center

Mark S. Greenberg, PhD, Neuropsychologist, Department of Psychiatry, Harvard Medical School

Leighton Y. Huey, MD, Department of Psychiatry, Dartmouth Hitchcock Medical Center

Peter S. Jensen, MD, Chief, Developmental Psychopathology Research Branch, National Institute of Mental Health

Lynda Katz, PhD, President, Landmark College

Kevin R. Murphy, PhD, Assistant Professor of Psychiatry; Chief, Adult Attention Deficit/Hyperactivity Disorder Clinic, Department of Psychiatry, University of Massachusetts Medical Center

Laura F. Rothstein, JD, Law Foundation Professor of Law, Law Center, University of Houston

Larry B. Silver, MD, Diplomat: General Psychiatry; Child/Adolescent Psychiatry

Marc Wilchesky, PhD, C. Psych. Coordinator, Learning Disabilities Program, Counseling and Development Center, York University

Joan Wolforth, MA, Coordinator, Office for Students with Disabilities, McGill University

OUTLINE

Introduction

Documentation Guidelines

   I. A Qualified Professional Must Conduct the Evaluation

   II. Documentation Should be Current

   III. Documentation Should be Comprehensive

      A. Evidence of Early Impairment

      B. Evidence of Current Impairment

         1. Statement of Presenting Problem

         2. Diagnostic Interview

      C. Rule Out of Alternative Diagnoses or Explanations

      D. Relevant Testing

      E. Identification of DSM-IV Criteria

      F Documentation Must Include a Specific Diagnosis

      G. An Interpretative Summary Should be Provided

   IV. Each Accommodation Recommended by the Evaluator Should include a Rationale

APPENDIX A: DSM IV Diagnostic Criteria for ADHD (American Psychiatric Association, 1994)

APPENDIX B: Recommendations for Consumers

INTRODUCTION

The Consortium's mission is to develop standard criteria for documenting attention deficit disorder, with or without hyperactivity (ADHD). These guidelines can be used by post-secondary personnel, examining, certifying, and licensing agencies, and consumers who require documentation to determine reasonable and appropriate accommodation(s) for individuals with ADHD. Although the more generic term, Attention Deficit Disorder (ADD), is frequently used, the official nomenclature in the Diagnostic and Statistical Manual of Mental Disorders (4th ed.) (DSM-IV) (American Psychiatric Association, 1994) is Attention-Deficit/Hyperactivity Disorder (ADHD) which is used in these guidelines. The guidelines provide consumers, professional diagnosticians, and service providers with a common understanding and knowledge base of the components of documentation which are necessary to validate the existence of ADHD, its impact on the individual's educational performance, and the need for accommodation(s). The information and documentation to be submitted should be comprehensive in order to avoid or reduce unnecessary time delays in decision-making related to the provision of services.

In the main section of the document, the Consortium presents guidelines in four important areas:

1) qualifications of the evaluator; 2) recency of documentation; 3) comprehensiveness of the documentation to substantiate the ADHD; and 4) evidence to establish a rationale to support the need for accommodation(s). Attached to these guidelines are appendices giving diagnostic criteria for ADHD from the Diagnostic and Statistical Manual of Mental Disorders (4th ed.) (DSM-IV) (American Psychiatric Association, 1994), and Recommendations for Consumers.

Under the Americans with Disabilities Act (ADA) and Section 504 of the Rehabilitation Act of 1973, individuals with disabilities are protected from discrimination and assured services. In order to establish that an individual is covered under the ADA, the documentation must indicate that the disability substantially limits some major life activity, including learning. The following documentation guidelines are provided in the interest of assuring that documentation of ADHD demonstrates an impact on a major life activity and supports the request for accommodations, academic adjustments, and/or auxiliary aids.

DOCUMENTATION GUIDELINES

I. A Qualified Professional Must Conduct the Evaluation

Professionals conducting assessments and rendering diagnoses of ADHD must have training in differential diagnosis and the full range of psychiatric disorders. The name, title, and professional credentials of the evaluator, including information about license or certification as well as the area of specialization, employment, and state or province in which the individual practices should be clearly stated in the documentation. The following professionals would generally be considered qualified to evaluate and diagnose ADHD provided they have comprehensive training in the differential diagnosis of ADHD and direct experience with an adolescent or adult ADHD population: clinical psychologists, neuropsychologists, psychiatrists, and other relevantly trained medical doctors. It may be appropriate to use a clinical team approach consisting of a variety of educational, medical, and counseling professionals with training in the evaluation of ADHD in adolescents and adults.

Use of diagnostic terminology indicating an ADHD by someone whose training and experience are not in these fields is not acceptable. It is also not appropriate for professionals to evaluate members of their own families. All reports should be on letterhead, typed, dated, signed, and otherwise legible. The receiving institution or agency has the responsibility to maintain the confidentiality of the individual's records.

II. Documentation Should be Current

Because the provision of all reasonable accommodations and services is based upon assessment of the current impact of the disability on academic performance, it is in an individual's best interest to provide recent and appropriate documentation. In most cases, this means that a diagnostic evaluation has been completed within the past three years. Flexibility in accepting documentation which exceeds a three-year period may be important under certain conditions if the previous assessment is applicable to the current or anticipated setting.

If documentation is inadequate in scope or content, or does not address the individual's current level of functioning and need for accommodation(s), reevaluation may be warranted. Furthermore, observed changes may have occurred in the individual's performance since previous assessment, or new medication(s) may have been prescribed or discontinued since the previous assessment was conducted. In such cases, it may be necessary to update the evaluation report. The update should include a detailed assessment of the current impact of the ADHD and interpretive summary of relevant information (see Section III, G) and the previous diagnostic report.

III. Documentation Should be Comprehensive

A. Evidence of Early Impairment

Because ADHD is, by definition, first exhibited in childhood (although it may not have been formally diagnosed) and manifests itself in more than one setting, relevant historical information is essential. The following should be included in a comprehensive assessment: clinical summary of objective, historical information establishing symptomology indicative of ADHD throughout childhood, adolescence, and adulthood as garnered from transcripts, report cards, teacher comments, tutoring evaluations, past psychoeducational testing, and third party interviews when available.

B. Evidence of Current Impairment

In addition to providing evidence of a childhood history of an impairment, the following areas must be investigated:

1. Statement of Presenting Problem

A history of the individual's presenting attentional symptoms should be provided, including evidence of ongoing impulsive/hyperactive or inattentive behaviors that significantly impair functioning in two or more settings.

2. Diagnostic Interview

The information collected for the summary of the diagnostic interview should consist of more than self-report, as information from third party sources is critical in the diagnosis of ADHD. The diagnostic interview with information from a variety of sources should include, but not necessarily be limited to, the following:

- history of presenting attentional symptoms, including evidence of ongoing impulsive/hyperactive or inattentive behavior that has significantly impaired functioning over time;

- developmental history;

- family history for presence of ADHD and other educational, learning, physical, or psychological difficulties deemed relevant by the examiner;

- relevant medical and medication history, including the absence of a medical basis for the symptoms being evaluated;

- relevant psychosocial history and any relevant interventions;

- a thorough academic history of elementary, secondary, and post-secondary education;

- review of prior psychoeducational test reports to determine whether a pattern of strengths or weaknesses is supportive of attention or learning problems;

- relevant employment history;

- description of current functional limitations pertaining to an educational setting that are presumably a direct result of problems with attention;

- relevant history of prior therapy.

C. Rule Out of Alternative Diagnoses or Explanations

The evaluator must investigate and discuss the possibility of dual diagnoses, and alternative or co-existing mood, behavioral, neurological, and/or personality disorders that may confound the diagnosis of ADHD. This process should include exploration of possible, alternative diagnoses, and medical and psychiatric disorders as well as educational and cultural factors impacting the individual which may result in behaviors mimicking an attention-deficit/hyperactivity disorder.

D. Relevant Testing

Neuropsychological or psychoeducational assessment is important in determining the current impact of the disorder on the individual's ability to function in academically related settings. The evaluator should objectively review and include with the evaluation report relevant background information to support the diagnosis. If grade equivalents are reported, they must be accompanied by standard scores and/or percentiles. Test scores or subtest scores alone should not be used as a sole measure for the diagnostic decision regarding ADHD. Selected subtest scores from measures of intellectual ability, memory functions tests, attention or tracking tests, or continuous performance tests do not in and of themselves establish the presence or absence of ADHD. Checklists and/or surveys can serve to supplement the diagnostic profile but in and of themselves are not adequate for the diagnosis of ADHD and do not substitute for clinical observations and sound diagnostic judgment. All data must logically reflect a substantial limitation to learning for which the individual is requesting the accommodation.

E. Identification of DSM-IV Criteria

According to the DSM-IV, "the essential feature of ADHD is a persistent pattern of inattention and/or hyperactivity-impulsivity that is more frequent and severe than is typically observed in individuals at a comparable level of development" (p. 78). A diagnostic report should include a review and discussion of the DSM-IV criteria for ADHD both currently and retrospectively and specify which symptoms are present (see Appendix A for DSM-IV criteria).

In diagnosing ADHD, it is particularly important to address the following criteria:

- symptoms of hyperactivity/impulsivity or inattention that cause impairment which must have been present in childhood;

- current symptoms that have been present for at least the past six months;

- impairment from the symptoms present in two or more settings (for example, school, work, and home);

- clear evidence of significant impairment in social, academic, or occupational functioning; and

- symptoms which do not occur exclusively during the course of a Pervasive Developmental Disorder, Schizophrenia, or other Psychotic Disorder and are not better accounted for by another mental disorder (e.g., Mood Disorder, Anxiety Disorder, Dissociative Disorder, or a Personality Disorder).

F. Documentation Must Include a Specific Diagnosis

The report must include a specific diagnosis of ADHD based on the DSM-IV diagnostic criteria. The diagnostician should use direct language in the diagnosis of ADHD, avoiding the use of terms such as "suggests," "is indicative of," or "attention problems." Individuals who report only problems with organization, test anxiety, memory and concentration in selective situations do not fit the proscribed diagnostic criteria for ADHD. Given that many individuals benefit from prescribed medications and therapies, a positive response to medication by itself does not confirm a diagnosis, nor does the use of medication in and of itself either support or negate the need for accommodation(s).

G. An Interpretative Summary Should be Provided

A well-written interpretative summary based on a comprehensive evaluative process is a necessary component of the documentation. Because ADHD is in many ways a diagnosis that is based upon the interpretation of historical data and observation, as well as other diagnostic information, it is essential that professional judgment be utilized in the development of a summary, which should include:

1. demonstration of the evaluator's having ruled out alternative explanations for inattentiveness, impulsivity, and/or hyperactivity as a result of psychological or medical disorders or noncognitive factors;

2. indication of how patterns of inattentiveness, impulsivity, and/or hyperactivity across the life span and across settings are used to determine the presence of ADHD;

3. indication of whether or not the student was evaluated while on medication, and whether or not there is a positive response to the prescribed treatment;

4. indication and discussion of the substantial limitation to learning presented by the ADHD and the degree to which it impacts the individual in the learning context for which accommodations are being requested; and

5. indication as to why specific accommodations are needed and how the effects of ADHD symptoms, as designated by the DSM-IV, are mediated by the accommodation(s).

IV. Each Accommodation Recommended by the Evaluator Should Include a Rationale

The evaluator(s) should describe the impact, if any, of the diagnosed ADHD on a specific major life activity as well as the degree of impact on the individual. The diagnostic report should include specific recommendations for accommodations that are realistic and that post-secondary institutions, examining, certifying, and licensing agencies can reasonably provide. A detailed explanation should be provided as to why each accommodation is recommended and should be correlated with specific functional limitations determined through interview, observation, and/or testing. Although prior documentation may have been useful in determining appropriate services in the past, current documentation should validate the need for services based on the individual's present level of functioning in the educational setting. A school plan such as an Individualized Education Program (IEP) or a 504 plan is insufficient documentation in and of itself but can be included as part of a more comprehensive evaluative report. The documentation should include any record of prior accommodations or auxiliary aids, including information about specific conditions under which the accommodations were used (e.g., standardized testing, final exams, licensing or certification examinations) and whether or not they benefited the individual. However, a prior history of accommodations, without demonstration of a current need, does not in itself warrant the provision of a like accommodation. If no prior accommodations were provided, the qualified professional and/or the individual should include a detailed explanation as to why no accommodations were used in the past and why accommodations are needed at this time.

Because of the challenge of distinguishing normal behaviors and developmental patterns of adolescents and adults (e.g., procrastination, disorganization, distractibility, restlessness, boredom, academic underachievement or failure, low self-esteem, and chronic tardiness or inattendance) from clinically significant impairment, a multifaceted evaluation should address the intensity and frequency of the symptoms and whether these behaviors constitute an impairment in a major life activity.

Reasonable accommodation(s) may help to ameliorate the disability and to minimize its impact on the student's attention, impulsivity, and distractibility. The determination for reasonable accommodation(s) rests with the designated disability contact person working in collaboration with the individual with the disability and when appropriate, college faculty. The receiving institution or agency has a responsibility to maintain confidentiality of the evaluation and may not release any part of the documentation without the individual's informed consent.

DSM-IV Diagnostic Criteria for ADHD*

The following diagnostic criteria for ADHD are specified in the DSM-IV (American Psychiatric Association, 1994):

A. Either (1) or (2):

1. six (or more) of the following symptoms of inattention have persisted for at least 6 months to a degree that is maladaptive and inconsistent with developmental level:

Inattention:

   a. often fails to give close attention to details or makes careless mistakes in schoolwork, work, or other activities

   b. often has difficulty sustaining attention in tasks or play activities

   c. often does not seem to listen when spoken to directly

   d. often does not follow through on instructions and fails to finish schoolwork, chores, or duties in the workplace (not due to oppositional behavior or failure to understand instructions)

   e. often has difficulty organizing tasks and activities

   f. often avoids, dislikes, or is reluctant to engage in tasks that require sustained mental effort (such as schoolwork or homework)

   g. often loses things necessary for tasks or activities (e.g., toys, school assignments, pencils, books, or tools)

   h. is often easily distracted by extraneous stimuli

   i. is often forgetful in daily activities

2. six (or more) of the following symptoms of hyperactivity-impulsivity have persisted for at least 6 months to a degree that is maladaptive and inconsistent with developmental level:

Hyperactivity:

   a. often fidgets with hands or feet or squirms in seat

   b. often leaves seat in classroom or in other situations in which remaining seated is expected

   c. often runs about or climbs excessively in situations in which it is inappropriate (in adolescents or adults, may be limited to subjective feelings of restlessness)

   d. often has difficulty playing or engaging in leisure activities quietly

   e. is often "on the go" or often acts as if "driven by a motor"

   f. often talks excessively

Impulsivity:

   g. often blurts out answers before questions have been completed

   h. often has difficulty awaiting turn

   i. often interrupts or intrudes on others (e.g., butts into conversations or games)

B. Some hyperactive-impulsive or inattentive symptoms that caused impairment were present before age 7 years.

C. Some impairment from the symptoms is present in two or more settings (e.g., at school [or work] and at home).

D. There must be clear evidence of clinically significant impairment in social, academic, or occupational functioning.

E. The symptoms do not occur exclusively during the course of a Pervasive Developmental Disorder, Schizophrenia, or other Psychotic Disorder and are not better accounted for by another mental disorder (e.g., Mood Disorder, Anxiety Disorder, Dissociative Disorder, or a Personality Disorder).

The DSM-IV specifies a code designation based on type:

314.01 Attention-Deficit/Hyperactivity Disorder, Combined Type: if both Criteria A1 and A2 are met for the past 6 months

314.00 Attention-Deficit/Hyperactivity Disorder, Predominantly Inattentive Type: if Criterion A1 is met but Criterion A2 is not met for the past 6 months

314.01 Attention-Deficit/Hyperactivity Disorder, Predominantly Hyperactive-Impulsive Type: if Criterion A1 is met but Criterion A2 is not met for the past 6 months.

Coding note: For individuals (especially adolescents and adults) who currently have symptoms that no longer meet full criteria, "In Partial Remission" should be specified.

314.9 Attention-Deficit/Hyperactivity Disorder Not Otherwise Specified: This category is for disorders with prominent symptoms of inattention or hyperactivity-impulsivity that do not meet criteria for Attention-Deficit/Hyperactivity Disorder.

* Note. From Diagnostic and Statistical Manual of Mental Disorders (4th ed.) (pp. 83–85), by the American Psychiatric Association, 1994, Washington, D.C. Copyright 1994 by the American Psychiatric Association. Reprinted with permission.

Appendix B

Recommendations for Consumers

1. For assistance in finding a qualified professional:

   a. contact the disability services coordinator at a college or university for possible referral sources; and/or

   b. contact a physician who may be able to refer you to a qualified professional with demonstrated expertise in ADHD.

2. In selecting a qualified professional:

   a. ask what experience and training he or she has had diagnosing adolescents and adults;

   b. ask whether he or she has training in differential diagnosis and the full range of psychiatric disorders.

      Clinicians typically qualified to diagnose ADHD may include clinical psychologists, physicians, including psychiatrists, and neuropsychologists;

   c. ask whether he or she has ever worked with a post-secondary disability service provider or with the agency to whom you are providing documentation; and

   d. ask whether you will receive a comprehensive written report.

3. In working with the professional:

   a. take a copy of these guidelines to the professional; and

   b. be prepared to be forthcoming, thorough, and honest with requested information.

4. As follow-up to the assessment by the professional:

   a. schedule a meeting to discuss the results, recommendations, and possible treatment;

   b. request additional resources, support group information, and publications if you need them;

   c. maintain a personal file of your records and reports; and

   d. be aware that any receiving institution or agency has a responsibility to maintain confidentiality.

GETTING READY

The purpose of *The K&W Guide* is to help students with learning disabilities acquire the basic knowledge necessary to begin the college exploration process and get ready to make appropriate college selections.

STUDENT PREPARATION CHECKLIST

- Understand their strengths and weaknesses.
- Be able to articulate the nature of their learning disabilities.
- Understand the compensatory skills developed to accommodate the learning differences.
- Be able to describe the services they received in high school.
- Identify short-term and long-term goals.
- Select appropriate college choices to match individual needs.

GUIDELINES FOR THE SEARCH AND SELECTION PROCESS

SELF ASSESSMENT

- What is the student's learning disability?
- When was the disability diagnosed?
- What is the student's level of performance in high school?
- Is the student enrolled in college-prep courses, modified courses, or individualized, special-education courses?
- What are the student's individual strengths and weaknesses?
- Is it easier for the student to learn from a lecture, reading the material, or having the material read to her?
- Does the student perform better on written assignments or oral presentations?
- Which subjects are easier, and which are more difficult?
- What are the student's favorite and least favorite courses and why?
- What are the student's short-term and long-term goals?
- Are these goals realistic?
- Is the student striving to improve in academic areas?
- What accommodations are being provided?
- Is the student actively utilizing resource assistance and learning compensatory strategies?
- What does the student plan to study in college?
- What skills and competencies are required for the career goals being pursued?
- When were the last diagnostic tests given?
- What level of services/accommodations are needed in college? Structured programs, comprehensive services, or basic services?

ARTICULATION

- Does the student understand the disability?
- Can the student describe the learning disability?
- Does the student comprehend how the disability impacts learning?
- Can the student explain the nature of the disability?
- Can the student explain the accommodations being utilized as well as any curriculum modifications received?
- Can the student explain necessary accommodations to teachers?

ACADEMIC ASSESSMENT

Does the student have difficulty with written language?

- Using appropriate words
- Organizing thoughts
- Writing lengthy compositions
- Using correct punctuation and sentence structure
- Expressing thoughts clearly

Does the student have trouble with verbal expression?

- Retrieving appropriate words
- Understanding what others are saying
- Using words in the correct context
- Carrying on conversations

Does the student have a problem with hand-eye coordination?

- Fnding certain information on a page
- Performing tasks that require fine motor coordination

Does the student get frustrated reading?

- Decoding unfamiliar words
- Understanding reading assignments
- Completing reading assignments within a time frame

Does the student often misspell words?

- Mix up the sequence of letters
- Become confused when spelling irregular words

Does the student experience difficulty performing mathematics?

- Multiplication table and fractions
- Sequencing of steps of various mathematical questions

What are the student's study habits?

- Attentive in class for an extended period of time
- Easily distracted
- Needs extra time to respond to questions
- Note-taking skills
- Memory
- Time management
- Time orientation
- Organization

How is the student's handwriting ability?

- Assignments are difficult to read
- Appropriate capitalization used
- Stays within the lines when writing
- Leaves enough space between words

EXPLORATION AND TIMELINES

SOPHOMORE YEAR

- Explore options.
- Consider taking the PLAN (if available)—request appropriate testing accomodations.
- Meet with counselor and case manager.
- Review testing and documentation.
- Review course registration for junior year. Students considering four-year colleges should be enrolled in as many college prepatory courses as possible.
- Write to colleges or use college websites to explore schools.
- Contact the service providers on the college campus.

JUNIOR YEAR

- Consider taking the PSAT—request appropriate testing accomodations.
- Review achievement level.
- Review course registration for senior year. Students considering four-year colleges should be enrolled in as many college prepatory courses as possible.
- Review the level of services in high school.
- Identify the level of services needed in college.
- Visit colleges.
- Register for the ACT/SAT, standardized or nonstandardized.
- Request necessary updated psychoeducational testing (including the WAIS-R)

- Submit general applications.
- Submit special applications (if required).
- Schedule interviews (if appropriate).
- Write essays (if required).
- Disclose learning disability to college.
- Release current psycho-educational testing.*
- Release documentation of other health-related disabilities.*

  * Students under the age of eighteen must have their parents' signature to release information to each of the colleges.

CAMPUS VISITS

- The student should call to make an arrangement for a visit.
- Visit while classes are in session.
- Meet with admissions and special support service providers.
- Take a guided tour.
- Attend a class.
- Eat a meal on campus.
- Drive around the boundaries of the campus.
- Take pictures, take notes, and talk to students on campus.
- Take parents or family members along (but not in the interview).
- Pick up college catalogue, view book, video, and support service brochures.
- Write thank-you notes.

INTERVIEWS

To prepare for interviews, students should know the following:

- Strengths and weaknesses
- The accommodations needed
- How to describe learning disability

If an interview is required prior to an admission decision:

- View the interview as an opportunity.
- Prepare a list of questions.
- Know that interviews, if required, are either required of all applicants or required for a special program or special admission practice.

Questions the Director of Support Services may ask

- When was the learning disability first diagnosed?
- What type of assistance has the student been receiving in high school?
- What kind of accommodations will the student need in college?
- Can the student describe the learning difficulties?
- Can the student articulate strengths and weaknesses?
- How has the disability affected the student's learning?
- What high school courses were easy (or more difficult)?
- Is the student comfortable with the learning disability?
- Can the student self-advocate?
- What does the student plan to choose as a major?
- Is the student motivated?

Questions students and/or parents may ask

- What are the admission requirements?
- Is there any flexibility in admission policy? Course substitutions? GPA?
- What is the application procedure?
- Is a special application required?
- What auxiliary testing is required?
- Are there extra charges or fees for the special programs or services?
- Are there remedial or developmental courses?
- What is the procedure for requesting waivers or substitutions?
- Who is the contact person for learning disabilities?
- What are the academic qualifications of the individual who provides services to students with learning disabilities?
- What services and accommodations are available: Testing accommodations? Note takers? Books on tape? Skills classes? Support groups? Priority registration? Professional tutors? Peer tutors? Advising? Computer-aided technology? Scribes? Proctors? Oral tests? Use of computers and spell-checker in class? Use of calculators in class? Distraction-free environment for tests? Learning disability specialists? Advocacy with professors? Faculty in-services?
- How long has the program been in existence?
- How many students are receiving services?
- How long can students access services?
- What is the success rate of students receiving services?

For a successful interview

- Develop a list of questions.
- Know the accommodations needed.
- Provide new information.
- Practice interviewing.
- Be able to describe strengths and weaknesses.
- Talk about extracurricular activities.
- Take notes.
- Get the business card of the interviewer.
- Try to relax.
- Have fun!

LETTERS OF RECOMMENDATION

- Obtain descriptive letters from counselors, teachers, and case managers.
- Have recommenders address learning style, degree of motivation, level of achievement, abilities, attitudes, self-discipline, determination, creativity, mastery of subject matter, academic risks, and growth.
- Have a teacher describe the challenge in a difficult course.
- Advise recommenders when letters are due.

We have just highlighted some of the areas of importance. Now it is time to begin to use the information in this guide that describes the various programs and services at various colleges and universities in the United States.

HOW TO USE THIS GUIDE

The K&W Guide to Colleges for Students with Learning Disabilities or Attention Deficit Disorder includes information on colleges and universities that offer services to students with learning disabilities. No two colleges are identical in the programs or services they provide, but there are some similarities. For the purpose of this guide, the services and programs at the various colleges have been grouped into three categories.

Structured Programs (SP)

Colleges with Structured Programs offer the most comprehensive services for students with learning disabilities. The director and/or staff are certified in learning disabilities or related areas. The director is actively involved in the admission decision and, often, the criteria for admission may be more flexible than general admission requirements. Services are highly structured and students are involved in developing plans to meet their particular learning styles and needs. Often students in Structured Programs sign a contract agreeing to actively participate in the program. There is usually an additional fee for the enhanced services. Students who have participated in a Structured Program or Structured Services in high school such as Learning Disabilities Resource Program, individualized or modified coursework, tutorial assistance, academic monitoring, note-takers, test accommodations, or skill classes might benefit from exploring colleges with Structured Programs or Coordinated Services.

Coordinated Services (CS)

Coordinated Services differ from Structured Programs in that the services are not as comprehensive. These services are provided by at least one certified learning disability specialist. The staff is knowledgeable and trained to provide assistance to students to develop strategies for their individual needs. The director of the program or services may be involved in the admission decision, or be in a position to offer recommendations to the admissions office on the potential success of the applicant, or to assist the students with an appeal if denied admission to the college. Receiving these services generally requires specific documentation of the learning disability—students are encouraged to self-identify prior to entry. Students voluntarily request accommodations or services in the Coordinated Services category, and there may be specific skills courses or remedial classes available or required for students with learning disabilities who are admitted probationally or conditionally. High school students who may have enrolled in some modified or remedial courses, utilized test accommodations, required tutorial assistance, but who typically requested services only as needed, might benefit from exploring colleges with Coordinated Services.

Services (S)

Services is the least comprehensive of the three categories. Colleges offering Services generally are complying with the federal mandate requiring reasonable accommodations to all students with appropriate and current documentation. These colleges routinely require documentation of the disability in order for the students with LD/ADHD to receive accommodations. Staff and faculty actively support the students by providing basic services to meet the needs of the students. Services are requested on a voluntarily basis, and there may be some limitations as to what is reasonable and the degree of services available. Sometimes, just the small size of the student body allows for the necessary personal attention to help students with learning disabilities succeed in college. High school students who require minimum accommodations, but who would find comfort in knowing that services are available, knowing who the contact person is, and knowing that this person is sensitive to students with learning disabilities, might benefit from exploring colleges providing Services or Coordinated Services.

CATEGORIES USED TO DESCRIBE THE PROGRAMS AND SERVICES AT COLLEGES AND UNIVERSITIES

The categories on the following pages describe the topics of information used in this guide. Each college in the book is covered on two pages, beginning with pertinent information describing the learning disability program or services. This is followed by special admission procedures, then specific information about services offered, and concludes with general college information. Please note the statement preceding the section on services and accommodations which states "Services and Accommodations are determined individually for each student based on current and appropriate documentation." Some categories are answered with: N/A (not applicable) because not all colleges were able to fit into every category included in this guide; NR (not reported) because some colleges were unable to provide the information we requested; and Y/N (Yes/No) because the answer is dependent on individual situations.

The authors have made a conscientious effort to provide the most current information possible. However, names, costs, dates, policies, and other information are always subject to change, and colleges of particular interest or importance to the reader should be contacted directly for verification of the data.

DEFINITIONS OF TESTING INSTRUMENTS AND ASSESSMENTS

INTELLIGENCE TESTS

Stanford-Binet: Stanford-Binet Intelligence Scale, Fourth Edition

The Stanford-Binet Intelligence Scale is administered to individuals aged two through adult. Verbal responses are emphasized more than nonverbal responses. Thus children tested at age two might score quite differently when tested on another IQ test several years later.

WISC-III: Wechsler Intelligence Scale for Children III

The WISC-III is a revision of the Wechsler Intelligence Scale for Children-Revised (WISC-R). The WISC-III is given to children aged six through sixteen as a measure of general intelligence. This scale provides three IQ scores: verbal, performance, and full-scale. It yields information about strengths and weaknesses in language and performance areas.

WAIS-III: Wechsler Adult Intelligence Scale, Third Edition

The Wechsler Adult Intelligence Scale assesses the intellectual ability of adults aged sixteen through eighty-nine. The WAIS-III yields the three composite IQ scores: verbal, performance, and full-scale, as well as four index scores, in verbal comprehension, perceptual organization, working memory, and processing speed. Adolescents between the ages of sixteen to eighteen who are in high school must have this test conducted. This test is used to identify areas of learning strengths and weaknesses or disabilities.

ACHIEVEMENT TESTS

PIAT-R

The PIAT-R is an updated, revised, and re-standardized battery of the old PIAT, and includes a new written expression sub-test. This test is used to measure general academic achievement in reading mechanics and comprehension, spelling, math, and general knowledge. The PIAT-R is administered to individuals from grades K through 12, and aged 5 through 18.

SDAT: Stanford Diagnostic Achievement Tests

The SDAT measures performance in academic subjects such as spelling, grammar, arithmetic, and reading. This test also provides instructional objectives and suggestions for teaching.

TOWL: Test of Written Language

The TOWL identifies strengths and weaknesses in various writing abilities. It can be used to compare students to their peers, and determine performance levels in written expression.

WRAT-R: Wide Range Achievement Test-Revised

The WRAT-R evaluates oral reading, spelling, and arithmetic computation. This test is used from kindergarten through college, and scores are by grade level for each skill.

WJ-R: Woodcock-Johnson Psychoeducational Battery-Revised

The WJ-R is a battery of tests used from pre-school through adult level to measure achievement in reading, math, written language, and general knowledge. These tests also assess the level of academic versus nonacademic accomplishments.

SAT/ACT CONVERSION CHART

SAT I to ACT		ACT to SAT I	
SAT I Verbal + Math Score	ACT Composite Score	ACT Composite Score	SAT I Verbal + Math Score
		36	1600
1570-1600	35	35	1580
1510-1560	34	34	1530
1450-1500	33	33	1460
1390-1440	32	32	1410
1350-1380	31	31	1360
1310-1340	30	30	1320
1270-1300	29	29	1280
1230-1260	28	28	1240
1200-1220	27	27	1210
1160-1190	26	26	1170
1120-1150	25	25	1140
1090-1110	24	24	1100
1050-1080	23	23	1060
1010-1040	22	22	1030
970-1000	21	21	990
930-960	20	20	950
890-920	19	19	910
840-880	18	18	860
800-830	17	17	820
750-790	16	16	770
700-740	15	15	720
630-690	14	14	670
570-620	13	13	600
510-560	12	12	540
450-500	11	11	480
410-440	10	10	430
400	9	1-9	400

SCHOOL PROFILES

JACKSONVILLE STATE UNIVERSITY

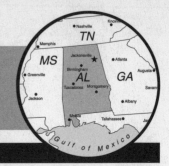

700 Pelham Road North, Jacksonville, AL 36265
Phone: 256-782-5400 • Fax: 256-782-5121
E-mail: lbedford@jsucc.jsu.edu • Web: www.jsu.edu
Support level: CS • Institution type: 4-year public

LEARNING DISABILITY PROGRAM AND SERVICES

Under the Disability Support Services the Academic Center for Excellence offers support for students with learning disabilities and ADHD. It is an inclusive service community promoting academic excellence and empowering students for success. Once a student has been admitted, DSS assists the qualified student with a documented disability in receiving academic support services. Accommodations are based solely on the supporting documentation. Required documents for a student with LD are current intelligence tests, current achievement tests, certified professional validation of the LD, or high school records documenting prior identification and/or services as a student with LD. Students with IQs below 85 do not qualify for services. Each student with appropriate documentation identifying a learning disability will develop an Individualized Postsecondary Plan. The IPP is prepared from the documentation received, input from the student (and parents, if appropriate) and the staff in support services. Copies of the IPP are given to the student, who is responsible for identifying him/herself and giving a copy to each instructor.

LD/ADHD ADMISSIONS INFORMATION

College entrance tests required: Yes
Nonstandardized tests accepted: Yes
Interview required: No
Essay required: No
Documentation required for LD: Psychoeducational evaluation
Documentation required for ADHD: Yes
Documentation submitted to: Disability Support Services
Special Ed. HS course work accepted: Yes

Specific course requirements for all applicants: Yes
Separate application required for services: No
# of LD applications submitted yearly: 25
# of LD applications accepted yearly: 25
Total # of students receiving LD/ADHD services: 25
Acceptance into program means acceptance into college: Student must be admitted and enrolled in the University first and then request services.

ADMISSIONS

All applicants must meet the general entrance requirements. The middle 50 percent of the applicants have an ACT of 18–22. All students must have at least 3 years of English and no more than 4 of the 15 required courses in high school may be in vocational courses. Interviews are recommended but not required. Students with an ACT below 16 may enter through successful completion of a summer bridge program. The program, Experiencing Success in Education and Life, offers skill-building classes. Students with an ACT between 16 and 19 are conditionally admitted.

ADDITIONAL INFORMATION

DSS is funded to provide programming only for sensory impaired (blind/low vision and deaf/hard of hearing). However, DSS does, of course, provide services for all disabilities. Disability Support Services will provide services to any student with LD/ADHD with appropriate documentation, and accommodations are based solely on the supporting documentation. DSS requires formal documentation (current within the last three years) and the academic accommodations needed are determined from this documentation. Services available may include note-takers, readers, scribes, priority registration, assistive technology, testing modifications, distraction-free environment for tests, and an Individualized Postsecondary Plan. Academic Success Skills offers skills classes in time management, test strategies, organizational skills, and other areas. These courses are offered for college credit. All students have access to tutoring, supplemental instruction, structured study sessions, and online tutorials. Disabilities is a support group for students with disabilities whose purpose is to spread disability awareness on campus and in the community.

SUPPORT SERVICES CONTACT INFORMATION

Learning Disability Program/Services: Academic Center for Excellence: Disability Support Services
Director: Dan Miller
  E-mail: dmiller@jsucc.jsu.edu
  Telephone: 256-782-5093
  Fax: 256-782-5025
Contact: Same

LEARNING DISABILITY SERVICES

Requests for the following services/accommodations will be evaluated individually based on appropriate and current documentation.

Allowed in Exams
  Calculator: Yes
  Dictionary: Yes
  Computer: Yes
  Spellchecker: Yes
Extended test time: Yes
Scribes: Yes
Proctors: Yes
Oral exams: Yes
Notetakers: Yes

Distraction-reduced environment: Yes
Tape recording in class: Yes
Books on tape from RFBD: Yes
Taping of books not from RFBD: Yes
Accommodations for students with
  ADHD: Yes
Reading machine: Yes
Other assistive technology: Yes
Priority registration: Yes

Added costs for services: No
LD specialists: Yes (4)
Professional tutors: No
Peer tutors: 40
Max. hours/wk. for services:
  Unlimited
How professors are notified of
  LD/ADHD: By both student and
  director

GENERAL ADMISSIONS INFORMATION

Director of Admissions: Martha Mitchell
Telephone: 256-782-5363

ENTRANCE REQUIREMENTS
15 total are required; 15 total are recommended; 3 English required, 4 elective required. 19 ACT or 900 SAT for unconditional admission. Conditional admission with 16–18 ACT or 750–890 SAT. High school diploma or GED required. Minimum TOEFL is 500. TOEFL required of all international applicants.

Application deadline: September 3
Notification: Rolling
Average GPA: 3.1

Average SAT I Math: NR
Average SAT I Verbal: NR
Average ACT: 20

Graduated top 10% of class: NR
Graduated top 25% of class: NR
Graduated top 50% of class: NR

COLLEGE GRADUATION REQUIREMENTS

Course waivers allowed: No
Course substitutions allowed: Yes
In what subjects: Determined on a case-by-case basis

ADDITIONAL INFORMATION

Environment: Located in a small town about 75 miles from Birmingham.

Student Body
  Undergrad enrollment: 6,640
  Female: 57%
  Male: 43%
  Out-of-state: 10%

Cost Information
  In-state tuition: $2,440
  Out-of-state tuition: $4,880
  Room & board: $3,100
Housing Information
  University housing: Yes
  Percent living on campus: 60%

Greek System
  Fraternity: Yes
  Sorority: Yes
Athletics: NCAA Division I

UNIVERSITY OF ALABAMA

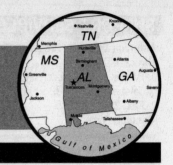

Box 870132, Tuscaloosa, AL 35487-0132
Phone: 205-348-5666 • Fax: 205-348-9046
E-mail: admissions@ua.edu • Web: www.ua.edu
Support level: CS • Institution type: 4-year public

LEARNING DISABILITY PROGRAM AND SERVICES

Any student enrolled with a documented LD is eligible for services and accommodations. Students must provide documentation, including a written report of an LD evaluation; a summary of areas of testing; actual test scores; overall summary and diagnosis; and recommendations and suggested strategies for student, professors, and academic advisors. The Office of Disability Services may request further testing.

LD/ADHD ADMISSIONS INFORMATION

College entrance tests required: Yes
Nonstandardized tests accepted: Yes
Interview required: No
Essay required: No
Documentation required for LD: Psychological and academic achievement
Documentation required for ADHD: Yes
Documentation submitted to: ODS
Special Ed. HS course work accepted: Yes, if teacher is certified in area

Specific course requirements for all applicants: Yes
Separate application required for services: No
# of LD applications submitted yearly: 150–175
# of LD applications accepted yearly: All who are admissible
Total # of students receiving LD/ADHD services: 450
Acceptance into program means acceptance into college: Students must be admitted and enrolled in the University prior to requesting services.

ADMISSIONS

All students must meet regular entrance requirements. An interview with the Office of Disabilities is recommended. Students with an acceptable GPA but not test scores, or vice versa, may be considered for Summer Trial Admissions. Students who fall within this category are encouraged to submit teacher/counselor recommendations that could substantiate the student's potential for success. Students admitted through Summer Trial Admissions will be required to attend the summer session and enroll in an appropriate math class and human development class. Additionally, students will take a study skills lab, which will provide strategies and monitoring of the student's notes taken during the classes. The strategies are practical rather than theoretical. Students need a 2.0 GPA in the summer courses to be admitted for the fall.

ADDITIONAL INFORMATION

Accommodations are tailored to individual needs according to diagnostic testing. Accommodations may include early registration; testing modifications; academic aids such as taping lectures, use of calculators, dictionaries, spellcheckers, notetakers, and taped materials; and reading assistance.

SUPPORT SERVICES CONTACT INFORMATION

Learning Disability Program/Services: Office of Disability Services
Director: Dr. Jim Saski
  E-mail: jsaski2@sa.ua.edu
  Telephone: 205-348-7966
  Fax: 205-348-5291
Contact: Same

LEARNING DISABILITY SERVICES

Requests for the following services/accommodations will be evaluated individually based on appropriate and current documentation.

Allowed in Exams
  Calculator: Yes
  Dictionary: Yes
  Computer: Yes
  Spellchecker: Yes
Extended test time: Yes
Scribes: Yes
Proctors: Yes
Oral exams: Yes
Notetakers: Yes

Distraction-reduced environment: Yes
Tape recording in class: Yes
Books on tape from RFBD: Yes
Taping of books not from RFBD: No
Accommodations for students with
  ADHD: Yes
Reading machine: Yes
Other assistive technology: Yes
Priority registration: No

Added costs for services: No
LD specialists: Yes (1)
Professional tutors: No
Peer tutors: 20
Max. hours/wk. for services:
  Unlimited
How professors are notified of
  LD/ADHD: By student with verification
  from Disability Services

GENERAL ADMISSIONS INFORMATION

Director of Admissions: Tom Davis
Telephone: 205-348-5666

ENTRANCE REQUIREMENTS
15 total are required; 4 English required, 4 English recommended, 3 math required, 4 math recommended, 3 science required, 4 science recommended, 2 science lab required, 1 foreign language required, 2 foreign language recommended, 3 social studies required, 4 social studies recommended, 1 history required, 1 history recommended, 5 elective required, 5 elective recommended. High school diploma or GED required. Minimum TOEFL is 500. TOEFL required of all international applicants.

Application deadline: July 1
Notification: Rolling beginning 9/1
Average GPA: 3.4

Average SAT I Math: NR
Average SAT I Verbal: NR
Average ACT: 24

Graduated top 10% of class: 28%
Graduated top 25% of class: 55%
Graduated top 50% of class: 81%

COLLEGE GRADUATION REQUIREMENTS

Course waivers allowed: No
Course substitutions allowed: Yes
In what subjects: Core curriculum has built-in substitutions: computer language for foreign language, logic for math.

ADDITIONAL INFORMATION

Environment: The University is located 55 miles from Birmingham.

Student Body
  Undergrad enrollment: 15,318
  Female: 52%
  Male: 48%
  Out-of-state: 21%

Cost Information
  In-state tuition: $3,014
  Out-of-state tuition: $8,162
  Room & board: $3,800
Housing Information
  University housing: Yes
  Percent living on campus: 28%

Greek System
  Fraternity: Yes
  Sorority: Yes
Athletics: NCAA Division I

UNIV. OF ALABAMA—HUNTSVILLE

301 Sparkman Drive, Huntsville, AL 35899
Phone: 256-824-6070 • Fax: 256-824-6073
E-mail: admitme@email.uah.edu • Web: www.uah.edu
Support level: S • Institution type: 4-year public

LEARNING DISABILITY PROGRAM AND SERVICES

The Office of Student Development Services offers a variety of services and accommodations to assist students with disabilities in eliminating barriers they encounter in pursuing higher education. The main objective is to provide access to academic, social, cultural, recreational, and housing opportunities at the University. The services offered encourage students to achieve and maintain autonomy.

LD/ADHD ADMISSIONS INFORMATION

College entrance tests required: Yes
Nonstandardized tests accepted: Yes
Interview required: No
Essay required: No
Documentation required for LD: Psychoeducational evaluation
Documentation required for ADHD: Yes
Documentation submitted to: Services for Students with Disabilities
Special Ed. HS course work accepted: Yes

Specific course requirements for all applicants: Yes
Separate application required for services: Yes
# of LD applications submitted yearly: N/A
# of LD applications accepted yearly: N/A
Total # of students receiving LD/ADHD services: 145
Acceptance into program means acceptance into college: Students must be admitted and enrolled at the University first and then may request services.

ADMISSIONS

Admission is based on grades and test scores. Additionally, applicants should have 4 years English, 3 years social studies, 3 years math, 2 years science, and a total of 20 Carnegie units.

ACT	SAT	GPA
17 or below	700 or below	3.25
18	740	3.00
19	790	2.75
20-21	860	2.50
22	920	2.25
23	970	2.00
24 or above	1010 or above	1.15

There is no special LD admission process. If a student becomes subject to academic suspension, the suspension is for a minimum of one term, and the student must petition the Admissions Committee for approval to re-enroll.

ADDITIONAL INFORMATION

Students should forward their documentation to Services for Students with Disabilities. Student Development Services provides the mandated services, including testing accommodations, distraction-free environments for tests, readers, proctors, scribes, note-takers, peer tutoring on an unlimited basis, specialized adaptive computers, and study skills classes that can be taken for credit. Math labs, chemistry labs, writing centers, and tutorial services are available for all students on campus. Additionally, all students have access to skills classes in time management, test-taking strategies, and study skills. Services and accommodations are available for undergraduate and graduate students.

SUPPORT SERVICES CONTACT INFORMATION

Learning Disability Program/Services: Services for Students with Disabilities
Director: Delois H. Smith
  E-mail: smithdh@email.uah.edu
  Telephone: 256-890-6203
  Fax: 256-890-6672
Contact: Rosemary Robinson
  E-mail: robins@mail.uah.edu
  Telephone: 256-890-6203
  Fax: 256-824-6672

LEARNING DISABILITY SERVICES

Requests for the following services/accommodations will be evaluated individually based on appropriate and current documentation.

Allowed in Exams
  Calculator: Yes
  Dictionary: Yes
  Computer: Yes
  Spellchecker: Yes
Extended test time: Yes
Scribes: Yes
Proctors: Yes
Oral exams: Yes
Notetakers: Yes

Distraction-reduced environment: Yes
Tape recording in class: Yes
Books on tape from RFBD: Yes
Taping of books not from RFBD: Yes
Accommodations for students with ADHD: Yes
Reading machine: Yes
Other assistive technology: Yes
Priority registration: Yes

Added costs for services: No
LD specialists: No
Professional tutors: 3
Peer tutors: 10
Max. hours/wk. for services: Unlimited
How professors are notified of LD/ADHD: By both student and director

GENERAL ADMISSIONS INFORMATION

Director of Admissions: Scott Verzyl
Telephone: 256-824-6070

ENTRANCE REQUIREMENTS
20 total are required; 4 English required, 3 math required, 2 science required, 3 social studies required, 8 elective required. Minimum ACT of 917 and minimum GPA of 3.25 or minimum ACT of 24 and minimum GPA of 1.75 required. High school diploma or GED required. Minimum TOEFL is 500. TOEFL required of all international applicants.

Application deadline: August 15
Notification: Rolling beginning 9/1
Average GPA: 3.4
Average SAT I Math: 560
Average SAT I Verbal: 549
Average ACT: 25
Graduated top 10% of class: 36%
Graduated top 25% of class: 63%
Graduated top 50% of class: 94%

COLLEGE GRADUATION REQUIREMENTS

Course waivers allowed: No
Course substitutions allowed: Yes
In what subjects: Substitutions determined on a case-by-case basis

ADDITIONAL INFORMATION

Environment: The University is located on 337 acres 100 miles north of Birmingham and 100 miles south of Nashville.

Student Body
  Undergrad enrollment: 5,220
  Female: 51%
  Male: 49%
  Out-of-state: 10%

Cost Information
  In-state tuition: $3,284
  Out-of-state tuition: $6,890
  Room & board: $4,300
Housing Information
  University housing: Yes
  Percent living on campus: 13%

Greek System
  Fraternity: Yes
  Sorority: Yes
Athletics: NCAA Division II

SHELDON JACKSON COLLEGE

801 Lincoln Street, Sitka, AK 99835
Phone: 800-478-4556 • Fax: 907-747-6366
E-mail: yukonjohn@sj-alaska.edu • Web: www.sj-alaska.edu
Support level: CS • Institution type: 4-year private

AK
Anchorage
Sitka
Gulf of Alaska

LEARNING DISABILITY PROGRAM AND SERVICES

The Learning Assistance Program is available to aid students who are "differently abled." The College seeks to help students find their forté, best learning modes, and best modes of expression; and seeks to help students prepare to find the greatest possible joy in vocation and service to others. The College seeks guidance from the students in its effort to guide them toward the aids and resources that will be the most helpful and meaningful. The Sheldon Jackson College Learning Assistance Program provides individualized attention, a structured academic program, and special support services during the students' first semester. This program is designed to provide a structured support system that will allow students to succeed in college. Students sign a Participation Agreement. This program also addresses the out-of-classroom experiences. Additional attention and support services are provided by the Office of Residence Life, including giving appropriate information to trained Residence Advisors. Residence Advisors provide encouragement on the peer level.

LD/ADHD ADMISSIONS INFORMATION

College entrance tests required: No
Nonstandardized tests accepted: Yes
Interview required: No
Essay required: No
Documentation required for LD: Psychoeducational evaluation
Documentation required for ADHD: Yes
Documentation submitted to: Learning Assistance Center
Special Ed. HS course work accepted: Individually evaluated

Specific course requirements for all applicants: Yes
Separate application required for services: Yes
# of LD applications submitted yearly: 10
# of LD applications accepted yearly: 8
Total # of students receiving LD/ADHD services: 4
Acceptance into program means acceptance into college: Students must request services after admission.

ADMISSIONS
Students with a GPA above 2.0 are admitted without restriction other than to provide learning disability documentation if they plan to seek special services. Students with a GPA below 2.0 are contacted to participate in the Achievement Program. This program requires the students to take a two-credit course in Academic Success Skills, and to spend five or more hours a week in monitored study at the Learning Center.

ADDITIONAL INFORMATION
The Academic Programs Committee coordinates the Learning Assistance Program. The committee evaluates each participant based on semester GPA, a recommendation of the assigned advisor, etc. The Learning Resource Center provides the academic resources for the program. The LRC Coordinator serves as an advisor. Additional faculty and administrative advisors are assigned when needed. Advisors instruct the Academic Success Skills classes; determine orientation activities; advise during registration; monitor academic progress; liaison with faculty; and instruct students to write narratives describing their classes and to demonstrate responsibility for behavior relating to academic progress. Participants agree to enroll in Academic Success Skills Class; participate in New Student Orientation; attend all classes regularly; attend all scheduled meetings with advisor; review all course syllabi with advisor; attend study hall, tutoring sessions, and resource labs; and communicate academic difficulties.

SUPPORT SERVICES CONTACT INFORMATION

Learning Disability Program/Services: Learning Assistance Program
Director: Alice Smith
 E-mail: asmith@sj-alaska.edu
 Telephone: 907-747-5235
 Fax: 907-747-5237
Contact: Admissions
 E-mail: yukonjohn@sj-alaska.edu

LEARNING DISABILITY SERVICES

Requests for the following services/accommodations will be evaluated individually based on appropriate and current documentation.

Allowed in Exams
 Calculator: Y/N
 Dictionary: Y/N
 Computer: Y/N
 Spellchecker: Y/N
Extended test time: Yes
Scribes: Yes
Proctors: Yes
Oral exams: Y/N
Notetakers: Yes

Distraction-reduced environment: Yes
Tape recording in class: Yes
Books on tape from RFBD: Yes
Taping of books not from RFBD: Yes
**Accommodations for students with
 ADHD:** Yes
Reading machine: Yes
Other assistive technology: Yes
Priority registration: No

Added costs for services: No
LD specialists: Yes
Professional tutors: Yes
Peer tutors: Yes
Max. hours/wk. for services:
 Individually evaluated
**How professors are notified of
 LD/ADHD:** Student and program
 director

GENERAL ADMISSIONS INFORMATION

Director of Admissions: Elizabeth Lower
Telephone: 800-478-4556

ENTRANCE REQUIREMENTS

4 English recommended, 4 math recommended, 4 science recommended, 2 science lab recommended, 4 social studies recommended. High school diploma or GED required. No ACT/SAT scores required. Minimum TOEFL is 550. TOEFL required of all international applicants.

Application deadline: Rolling
Notification: Rolling beginning 12/1
Average GPA: 2.9

Average SAT I Math: NR
Average SAT I Verbal: NR
Average ACT: NR

Graduated top 10% of class: 20%
Graduated top 25% of class: 40%
Graduated top 50% of class: 75%

COLLEGE GRADUATION REQUIREMENTS

Course waivers allowed: Yes
Course substitutions allowed: Yes
In what subjects: Varies; students petition the Academic Programs Committee

ADDITIONAL INFORMATION

Environment: The College is located on 345 acres in a small town 800 miles north of Seattle.

Student Body
 Undergrad enrollment: 235
 Female: 56%
 Male: 44%
 Out-of-state: 70%

Cost Information
 Tuition: $7,250
 Room & board: $5,150
Housing Information
 University housing: Yes
 Percent living on campus: 60%

Greek System
 Fraternity: Yes
 Sorority: Yes
Athletics: NAIA

UNIVERSITY OF ALASKA—ANCHORAGE

3211 Providence Drive, Room 158, Anchorage, AK 99508-8046
Phone: 907-786-1480 • Fax: 907-786-4888
E-mail: ayenrol@alaska.edu • Web: www.uaa.alaska.edu
Support level: S • Institution type: 4-year public

LEARNING DISABILITY PROGRAM AND SERVICES

The University of Alaska—Anchorage provides equal opportunities for students who experience disabilities. Academic support services are available to students with learning disabilities. Staff trained to work with students with disabilities coordinate these services. To allow time for service coordination, students are encouraged to contact the Disability Support Services office several weeks before the beginning of each semester. Ongoing communication with the staff throughout the semester is encouraged.

LD/ADHD ADMISSIONS INFORMATION

College entrance tests required: Yes
Nonstandardized tests accepted: Yes
Interview required: No
Essay required: No
Documentation required for LD: Psychoeducational evaluation including WAIS-III, WJ, and WRAT
Documentation required for ADHD: Yes
Documentation submitted to: DSS
Special Ed. HS course work accepted: Yes, if regular-level classes

Specific course requirements for all applicants: Yes
Separate application required for services: No
# of LD applications submitted yearly: N/A
# of LD applications accepted yearly: N/A
Total # of students receiving LD/ADHD services: 90
Acceptance into program means acceptance into college: UAA has open enrollment; students are accepted to the University and then may request services.

ADMISSIONS

All students must meet the same admission requirements. The University has an open enrollment policy. However, admission to specific programs of study may have specific coursework or testing criteria that all students will have to meet. While formal admission is encouraged, the University has an open enrollment policy that allows students to register for courses in which they have the adequate background. Open enrollment does not guarantee subsequent formal admission to certificate or degree programs. Individuals with learning disabilities are admitted via the standard admissions procedures that apply to all students submitting applications for formal admission. Students with documentation of a learning disability are eligible to receive support services once they are enrolled in the University. LD students who self-disclose during the admission process are referred to DSS for information about services and accommodations.

ADDITIONAL INFORMATION

Slingerland Language Arts classes are available for all students in the areas of vocabulary building and study skills. There is no separate tutoring for students with learning disabilities. Tutorial help is available in the Reading and Writing Labs and the Learning Resource Center for all students. With appropriate documentation students with LD or ADHD may have access to accommodations such as: testing modifications; distraction-free environment for tests; scribes; proctors; note-takers; caculators, dictionary and computers in exams; and assistive technology. Services and accommodations are available for undergraduate and graduate students.

SUPPORT SERVICES CONTACT INFORMATION

Learning Disability Program/Services: Disability Support Services
Director: Lyn Stoller
  E-mail: anlms1@uaa.alaska.edu
  Telephone: 907-786-4530
  Fax: 907-786-4531
Contact: Same

LEARNING DISABILITY SERVICES

Requests for the following services/accommodations will be evaluated individually based on appropriate and current documentation.

Allowed in Exams
  Calculator: Yes
  Dictionary: Yes
  Computer: Yes
  Spellchecker: Yes
Extended test time: Yes
Scribes: Yes
Proctors: Yes
Oral exams: Yes
Notetakers: Yes

Distraction-reduced environment: Yes
Tape recording in class: Yes
Books on tape from RFBD: Yes
Taping of books not from RFBD: Yes
Accommodations for students with
  ADHD: Yes
Reading machine: Yes
Other assistive technology: Yes
Priority registration: Yes

Added costs for services: No
LD specialists: No
Professional tutors: No
Peer tutors: Yes
Max. hours/wk. for services:
  Unlimited
How professors are notified of
  LD/ADHD: By both student and
  director

GENERAL ADMISSIONS INFORMATION

Director of Admissions: Cecile Mitchell
Telephone: 907-786-1480

ENTRANCE REQUIREMENTS

4 English recommended, 2 math recommended, 3 science recommended, 1 foreign language recommended, 3 social studies recommended, 1 history recommended. High school diploma or GED required. Minimum TOEFL is 450. TOEFL required of all international applicants.

Application deadline: September 10
Notification: Rolling
Average GPA: 2.5

Average SAT I Math: 459
Average SAT I Verbal: 422
Average ACT: 20

Graduated top 10% of class: 11%
Graduated top 25% of class: 30%
Graduated top 50% of class: 60%

COLLEGE GRADUATION REQUIREMENTS

Course waivers allowed: Yes
Course substitutions allowed: Yes
In what subjects: Determined by petition on a case-by-case basis

ADDITIONAL INFORMATION

Environment: The University of Alaska is an urban campus on 350 acres 7 miles from downtown Anchorage.

Student Body
  Undergrad enrollment: 14,167
  Female: 61%
  Male: 39%
  Out-of-state: 4%

Cost Information
  In-state tuition: $2,559
  Out-of-state tuition: $7,329
  Room & board: $5,200
Housing Information
  University housing: Yes
  Percent living on campus: 7%

Greek System
  Fraternity: Yes
  Sorority: Yes
Athletics: NCAA Division II

UNIVERSITY OF ALASKA—FAIRBANKS

PO Box 757480, Fairbanks, AK 99775-7480
Phone: 907-474-7500 • Fax: 907-474-5379
E-mail: fyapply@uaf.edu • Web: www.uaf.edu
Support level: S • Institution type: 4-year public

LEARNING DISABILITY PROGRAM AND SERVICES

The University of Alaska is committed to providing equal opportunity to students with disabilities. Disability Services at UAF provides assistance to students with permanent or temporary disabilities. The purpose of the program is to enable students who have disabilities to be successful in college. Campus services include the Academic Advising Center, which is responsible for advising incoming freshmen and students with undeclared majors. It provides explanations of programs and requirements and assists students with choosing a major, selecting electives, and choosing classes consistent with their academic and career goals. Student Support Services provides academic and personal support including developmental classes and tutoring for students who are economically disadvantaged, do not have a parent who graduated from college, or have a documented disability. Disabled Students of UAF provides peer support groups for UAF students experiencing disabilities. The Student Development and Learning Center provides tutoring, individual instruction in basic skills, counseling, career planning services, and assessment testing. Disability Services welcomes inquiries and seeks to make the College experience a success for students with disabilities.

LD/ADHD ADMISSIONS INFORMATION

College entrance tests required: Yes
Nonstandardized tests accepted: Yes
Interview required: No
Essay required: No
Documentation required for LD: WAIS-III
Documentation required for ADHD: Yes
Documentation submitted to: Disability Services
Special Ed. HS course work accepted: Yes

Specific course requirements for all applicants: Yes
Separate application required for services: No
# of LD applications submitted yearly: N/A
# of LD applications accepted yearly: N/A
Total # of students receiving LD/ADHD services: 60–70
Acceptance into program means acceptance into college: Students must be admitted and enrolled at the University and then request services.

ADMISSIONS
There is no special admissions process for students with learning disabilities. The University has a liberal admissions policy. To qualify for admission freshman students must meet one of the following: associate's degree program requires a high school diploma or GED, and students must maintain a "C" average with 14 credits to enter a baccalaureate degree program; baccalaureate degree requires a high school diploma with a 2.0 GPA, and admission to specific programs requires different combinations of GPA and high school courses. Students must also complete, with a minimum GPA of 2.5, a core curriculum including 4 years English, 3 years math, 3 years social sciences, and 3 years natural or physical sciences. Foreign language is recommended. Students can be provisionally accepted if they make up course deficiencies with a C or better in each of the developmental or university courses, and complete 9 credits of general degree requirements with a C or better. Being accepted to the University does not depend on minimum test scores; however, these test scores are used to determine placement in English, math, and other freshman-level courses.

ADDITIONAL INFORMATION
Services include individual counseling to determine necessary accommodations; arrangements for special services such as readers, scribes, and note-takers; advocacy with faculty and staff; assistance to faculty and staff in determining appropriate accommodations; help in determining specific needs for students with learning disabilities; and referral to campus and community agencies for additional services. Basic study-skills classes are offered for all students and may be taken for credit. Services and accommodations are provided for undergraduate and graduate students.

SUPPORT SERVICES CONTACT INFORMATION

Learning Disability Program/Services: Disability Services
Director: Cindy Slats, Administrative Assistant
  E-mail: fyheaco@aurora.alaska.edu
  Telephone: 907-474-5655
  Fax: 907-474-6777
Contact: Same

LEARNING DISABILITY SERVICES

Requests for the following services/accommodations will be evaluated individually based on appropriate and current documentation.

Allowed in Exams
  Calculator: No
  Dictionary: Yes
  Computer: Yes
  Spellchecker: Yes
Extended test time: Yes
Scribes: Yes
Proctors: Yes
Oral exams: Yes
Notetakers: Yes

Distraction-reduced environment: Yes
Tape recording in class: Yes
Books on tape from RFBD: Yes
Taping of books not from RFBD: Yes
Accommodations for students with ADHD: Yes
Reading machine: Yes
Other assistive technology: Yes
Priority registration: No

Added costs for services: None if in tutoring lab; private tutoring varies
LD specialists: No
Professional tutors: No
Peer tutors: No
Max. hours/wk. for services: No; referred to same tutors as all other students
How professors are notified of LD/ADHD: By student

GENERAL ADMISSIONS INFORMATION

Director of Admissions: Nancy Dicks
Telephone: 907-474-7500

ENTRANCE REQUIREMENTS

16 total are required; 4 English required, 3 math required, 3 science required, 1 science lab required, 2 foreign language recommended, 3 social studies required, 3 elective required. High school diploma or GED required. Must have a minimum 2.0 GPA. Specific programs require a 2.5 GPA. Applicants may be admitted with deficiencies. Minimum TOEFL is 550. TOEFL required of all international applicants.

Application deadline: August 1
Notification: Rolling beginning 9/1
Average GPA: 3.0

Average SAT I Math: NR
Average SAT I Verbal: NR
Average ACT: 20

Graduated top 10% of class: 13%
Graduated top 25% of class: 28%
Graduated top 50% of class: 58%

COLLEGE GRADUATION REQUIREMENTS

Course waivers allowed: No
Course substitutions allowed: Yes
In what subjects: Requests are considered on an individual case-by-case basis.

ADDITIONAL INFORMATION

Environment: The University is in a small town close to Fairbanks.

Student Body
  Undergrad enrollment: 6,358
  Female: 60%
  Male: 40%
  Out-of-state: 15%

Cost Information
  In-state tuition: $2,550
  Out-of-state tuition: $7,620
  Room & board: $4,610
Housing Information
  University housing: Yes
  Percent living on campus: 30%

Greek System
  Fraternity: Yes
  Sorority: Yes
Athletics: NCAA Division II

ARIZONA STATE UNIVERSITY

PO Box 870112, Tempe, AZ 85287-0112
Phone: 480-965-7788 • Fax: 480-965-3610
E-mail: ugradinq@asuvm.inre.asu.edu • Web: www.asu.edu
Support level: CS • Institution type: 4-year public

LEARNING DISABILITY PROGRAM AND SERVICES

ASU's Disablility Resources for Students strives to facilitate resources, services, and auxiliary aids to allow each qualified student with disabilities to equitably access educational, social, and career opportunities. Students utilizing the services through the DRS program are mainstreamed in all courses. Support is available but students need to be assertive and have a desire to succeed. The services are geared to the needs of the particular student and are individually based. Each student is encouraged to seek out methods for attaining the highest possible goals. All services and accommodations are provided upon request on an individual basis as appropriate for qualified/eligible individuals with learning disabilities.The goal of DRS is to assist the student in becoming academically and socially independent. The DRS staff includes professionals who facilitate a wide range of academic support services and accommodations. The center also provides consultation on disability issues to the surrounding community.

LD/ADHD ADMISSIONS INFORMATION

College entrance tests required: Yes
Nonstandardized tests accepted: Yes
Interview required: No
Essay required: No
Documentation required for LD: WAIS-III; WJ
Documentation required for ADHD: Yes
Documentation submitted to: DRS
Special Ed. HS course work accepted: Yes, but must be approved

Specific course requirements for all applicants: Yes
Separate application required for services: No
# of LD applications submitted yearly: 150
# of LD applications accepted yearly: 150+
Total # of students receiving LD/ADHD services: 350
Acceptance into program means acceptance into college: Students must be admitted and enrolled at the University first and then may request services.

ADMISSIONS
Students with LD submit the regular ASU application. Students should self-disclose their LD and submit documentation. Courses required: 4 years English, 4 years math, 3 years science, 2 years social science, and 1 year fine arts. Arizona residents should rank in the top quarter or have a 22 ACT/930 SAT or a 3.0 GPA in core courses. Nonresidents should rank in the top quarter or have a 24 ACT/1010 SAT or a 3.0 GPA in core courses. Nonresidents who have a strong high school background and who rank in the top 50 percent or have a GPA of 2.5–2.9 will be considered individually. To appeal a denial an applicant should: Write a letter stating reasons for wanting to attend ASU and describing ability for success; send three recommendations showing motivation and perseverance; and send a transcript showing gradual upward trend in courses and grades. Appeals are reviewed by admissions and disability support personnel. If applicant is ultimately denied after an appeal or if six hours of credit or less is desired per semester, a non-degree-seeking application is available. Transcripts are not required. Students can earn up to 15 nondegree hours to be applied toward a degree program. Non-degree candidates may live in residential housing at ASU and attend ASU and the local community college. After 24 credits and a GPA of 2.0 the student may apply for regular admission at ASU.

ADDITIONAL INFORMATION
Academic support accommodations include consultation; individualized program recommendations; registration information and advisement referrals; academic tutoring; Computer Technology Center; learning strategies instruction; library research assistance; supplemental readers in coordination with RFBD; mastery of Alternative Learning Techniques Lab; in-class note-taking; testing accommodations; and diagnostic testing referrals. DSR provides in-service training for faculty/staff. Services and accommodations are available for undergraduate and graduate students. DSR will accept current diagnosis of ADHD that is based on appropriate diagnostic information given by a licensed/certified professional. The diagnosis must be written on professional letterhead and include a clinical history, instruments used for the diagnosis, narrative, DSM-IV diagnosis, and recommendations for accommodations. All students have access to skills classes in time management, note-taking strategies, test-taking, and career awareness.

SUPPORT SERVICES CONTACT INFORMATION

Learning Disability Program/Services: Disability Resources for Students (DRS)
Director: Tedde Scharf
  E-mail: tedde@asu.edu
  Telephone: 602-965-1234
  Fax: 602-965-0441
Contact: Phyllis Jones
  E-mail: Phyllis.jones@asu.edu
  Telephone: 602-965-1234
  Fax: 602-965-0441

LEARNING DISABILITY SERVICES

Requests for the following services/accommodations will be evaluated individually based on appropriate and current documentation.

Allowed in Exams
  Calculator: Yes
  Dictionary: Yes
  Computer: Yes
  Spellchecker: Yes
Extended test time: Yes
Scribes: Yes
Proctors: Yes
Oral exams: Yes
Notetakers: Yes

Distraction-reduced environment: Yes
Tape recording in class: Yes
Books on tape from RFBD: Yes
Taping of books not from RFBD: Yes
Accommodations for students with ADHD: Yes
Reading machine: Yes
Other assistive technology: Yes
Priority registration: Yes

Added costs for services: No
LD specialists: Yes (4)
Professional tutors: No
Peer tutors: No
Max. hours/wk. for services: 3 hours
How professors are notified of LD/ADHD: By the student

GENERAL ADMISSIONS INFORMATION

Director of Admissions: Timothy Desch
Telephone: 480-965-2604

ENTRANCE REQUIREMENTS

16 total are required; 4 English required, 4 math required, 3 science required, 3 science lab required, 2 foreign language required, 2 social studies required. In-state: top 25 percent or 22 ACT or 930 SAT or 3.0 GPA. Out of state: top 25 percent or 24 ACT or 1010 SAT or 3.0 GPA. Nonresidents with 2.5–2.9 GPA and top 50 percent may be considered individually. High school diploma or GED required. Minimum TOEFL is 500. TOEFL required of all international applicants.

Application deadline: Rolling
Notification: Rolling beginning 1/15
Average GPA: 3.3

Average SAT I Math: 552
Average SAT I Verbal: 538
Average ACT: 23

Graduated top 10% of class: 26%
Graduated top 25% of class: 52%
Graduated top 50% of class: 82%

COLLEGE GRADUATION REQUIREMENTS

Course waivers allowed: No
Course substitutions allowed: Yes
In what subjects: Substitutions granted by the College Standards Committee as appropriate to documentation and history attempts.

ADDITIONAL INFORMATION

Environment: Arizona State University is a city school about 5 miles from Phoenix.

Student Body
  Undergrad enrollment: 33,985
  Female: 52%
  Male: 48%
  Out-of-state: 23%

Cost Information
  In-state tuition: $2,272
  Out-of-state tuition: $9,728
  Room & board: $5,240
Housing Information
  University housing: Yes
  Percent living on campus: 16%

Greek System
  Fraternity: Yes
  Sorority: Yes
Athletics: NCAA Division I

NORTHERN ARIZONA UNIVERSITY

PO Box 4084, Flagstaff, AZ 86011-4084
Phone: 520-523-5511 • Fax: 520-523-6023
E-mail: undergraduate.admissions@nau.edu • Web: www.nau.edu
Support level: CS • Institution type: 4-year public

LEARNING DISABILITY PROGRAM AND SERVICES

Disability Support Services promotes educational opportunities for students with disabilities at Northern Arizona University. DSS assists students in their persistence to graduate and to realize their life goals by providing resources, services, and auxiliary aids.The goal is to assist students in achieving their academic goals while at the same time creating an environment conducive to learning and building self-esteem. The belief is that in providing supportive assistance the student will become an independent learner and self-advocate.

LD/ADHD ADMISSIONS INFORMATION

College entrance tests required: Yes
Nonstandardized tests accepted: Yes
Interview required: No, but recommended
Essay required: No
Documentation required for LD: Psychoeducational evaluation
Documentation submitted to: Disability Support Services
Special Ed. HS course work accepted: Yes with approval from admissions

Specific course requirements for all applicants: Yes
Separate application required for services: No
# of LD applications submitted yearly: N/A
# of LD applications accepted yearly: N/A
Total # of students receiving LD/ADHD services: 117
Acceptance into program means acceptance into college: Students must be admitted and enrolled at the University first and then may request services.

ADMISSIONS

There are no special admissions criteria for students with learning disabilities. General admission requirements for unconditional admission include 4 years English, 4 years math, 2 years social science with 1 year being American history, 2–3 years lab science with additional requirements, and 1 year fine arts, 2 years foreign language; (students may be admitted conditionally with course deficiencies, but not in both math and science). GPA of 2.5 or top 50 percent for in-state residents (3.0 GPA or the upper 25 percent of the graduating class for nonresidents) or SAT of 930 (1010 for nonresidents) or an ACT of 22 (24 for nonresidents). Conditional admission is possible with a 2.5–2.99 GPA or top 50 percent of graduating class and ACT/SAT scores. Exceptional admission may be offered to 10 percent of the new freshmen applicants or transfer applicants.

ADDITIONAL INFORMATION

Skills classes are available in note-taking, study techniques, reading, memory and learning, overcoming math anxiety, speed reading, time management, test-taking strategies, "How to Make Math Easy," "How to Get Started Writing," "How to Edit Writing," and "How to Prepare for Final Exams." All services and accommodations are available for undergraduate and graduate students.

SUPPORT SERVICES CONTACT INFORMATION

Learning Disability Program/Services: Disability Support Services
Director: Marsha Fields, EdD
  E-mail: Marsha.Fields@nau.edu
  Telephone: 520-523-8773
  Fax: 520-523-8747
Contact: Kim Dobson
  E-mail: Kim.Dobson@nau.edu
  Telephone: 520-523-8773
  Fax: 520-523-8747

LEARNING DISABILITY SERVICES

Requests for the following services/accommodations will be evaluated individually based on appropriate and current documentation.

Allowed in Exams
  Calculator: Yes
  Dictionary: Yes
  Computer: Yes
  Spellchecker: Yes
Extended test time: Yes
Scribes: Yes
Proctors: Yes
Oral exams: Yes
Notetakers: Yes

Distraction-reduced environment: Yes
Tape recording in class: Yes
Books on tape from RFBD: Yes
Taping of books not from RFBD: Yes
Accommodations for students with
  ADHD: Yes
Reading machine: Yes
Other assistive technology: Yes
Priority registration: Yes

Added costs for services: No
LD specialists: Yes (1)
Professional tutors: No
Peer tutors: 100+
Max. hours/wk. for services:
  Unlimited
How professors are notified of
  LD/ADHD: By the student

GENERAL ADMISSIONS INFORMATION

Director of Admissions: Molly Munger
Telephone: 520-523-6002

ENTRANCE REQUIREMENTS
4 English required, 4 math required, 3 science required, 3 science lab required, 2 foreign language required, 1 social studies required, 1 history required. High school diploma or GED required. Minimum TOEFL is 500. TOEFL required of all international applicants.

Application deadline: Rolling
Notification: Rolling
Average GPA: 3.4

Average SAT I Math: 530
Average SAT I Verbal: 520
Average ACT: 22

Graduated top 10% of class: 24%
Graduated top 25% of class: 49%
Graduated top 50% of class: 83%

COLLEGE GRADUATION REQUIREMENTS

Course waivers allowed: Yes
Course substitutions allowed: Yes
In what subjects: Math; a substitution program is available for individuals with a math learning disability; it applies only to lower-level, liberal arts math

ADDITIONAL INFORMATION

Environment: The University is located on 320 acres in an urban area.

Student Body
  Undergrad enrollment: 13,947
  Female: 58%
  Male: 42%
  Out-of-state: 19%

Cost Information
  In-state tuition: $2,188
  Out-of-state tuition: $8,304
  Room & board: $3,802
Housing Information
  University housing: Yes
  Percent living on campus: 47%

Greek System
  Fraternity: Yes
  Sorority: Yes
  Athletics: NCAA Division I

UNIVERSITY OF ARIZONA

PO Box 210040, Tucson, AZ 85721-0040
Phone: 520-621-3237 • Fax: 520-621-9799
E-mail: appinfo@arizona.edu • Web: www.arizona.edu
Support level: SP • Institution type: 4-year public

LEARNING DISABILITY PROGRAM AND SERVICES

Student Alternative Learning Techniques (SALT) challenges students with LD to succeed in their pursuit of higher education. Supporting the ideal of education for life, SALT encourages and provides experiences and opportunities to build confidence beyond the classroom. SALT encourages growth and independence, training individuals to improve learning, expression, and decision-making. A major philosophy is to provide intensive service for the first year with the goal of increasing independence as the student learns the coping strategies to succeed in college. The following guidelines clarify the process of documenting LD at UA: Assessment and testing must be comprehensive and include a diagnostic interview and results of a neuropsychological or psychoeducational evaluation, a specific diagnosis and actual test scores, and evaluation by a qualified professional. All documentation must be current. Recommended accommodations should include a rationale that correlates the accommodations to specific test results and clinical observations. Students providing documentation express a desire to qualify for consideration as an individual with a disability. Being identified as LD/ADD does not afford any individual automatic access to university accommodations or for privileges as an individual with disabilities. The University has established guidelines to meet diverse needs while maintaining the integrity of academic and nonacademic programming.

LD/ADHD ADMISSIONS INFORMATION

College entrance tests required: Yes
Nonstandardized tests accepted: Yes
Interview required: No, but recommended
Essay required: Yes
Documentation required for LD: WAIS-III; or WISC; WJ
Documentation required for ADHD: Yes
Documentation submitted to: SALT Coordinator
Special Ed. HS course work accepted: No

Specific course requirements for all applicants: Yes
Separate application required for services: Yes
# of LD applications submitted yearly: 500+
# of LD applications accepted yearly: 130
Total # of students receiving LD/ADHD services: 500
Acceptance into program means acceptance into college: Students are admitted to the University and then to SALT.

ADMISSIONS

The majority of students with disabilities seeking admission to UA meet the general admission requirements, which include either an ACT of 25 (22 in-state) or SAT of 1010 (930 in-state); top 25 percent of class (top 50 percent in-state) or 3.0 GPA (2.5 in-state); and 4 years English, 4 years math, 3 years science, 2 years social studies, and 2 years foreign language. Candidates with disabilities who desire special consideration are expected to provide all documentation they feel necessary to represent the specific circumstances. If the candidate has a learning disability or attention deficit disorder and is requesting special consideration through admission to the SALT program, the student should submit all documentation of disability directly to UA admissions. Students may apply to SALT at any time beginning in August preceding their senior year of high school. A student may submit documentation with the SALT application as well, but one copy *must* accompany the UA application for admission in order to receive special consideration. Whenever possible, the SALT Center will announce its decision regarding a student's application for admission to SALT concurrently with the University's notification of acceptance. Incomplete records at SALT could delay a decision. Students denied admission to UA will not be considered for SALT.

ADDITIONAL INFORMATION

Basic services include advocacy, auxiliary aids for classroom accommodations, and special testing; there is no charge for these services. Enhanced services provide a full-service program with academic monitoring, registration assistance, staff contact and trained learning specialists, tutoring, a writing enhancement program, a specially equipped computer learning laboratory, and personalized tutorial services. Each student works with a trained specialist to identify learning preferences, learning strategies, and appropriate compensatory, productive learning techniques. There is a fee for enhanced services. Support services include both academic programs and counseling components. Students receive assistance with academic planning and registration followed by regularly scheduled staff contact to monitor progress. A Drop-In Center is available for study, tutoring, and student/staff interaction. The SALT program is staffed by persons trained and experienced in working with students with LD.

SUPPORT SERVICES CONTACT INFORMATION

Learning Disability Program/Services: Strategic Alternative Learning Techniques (SALT)
Director: Dr. Sue Kroeger
　E-mail: suek@u.arizona.edu
　Telephone: 520-626-7674
　Fax: 520-621-5500
Contact: Pat Cooper
　E-mail: pcooper@u.arizona.edu
　Telephone: 520-621-3884
　Fax: 520-626-5500

LEARNING DISABILITY SERVICES

Requests for the following services/accommodations will be evaluated individually based on appropriate and current documentation.

Allowed in Exams
　Calculator: Yes
　Dictionary: Yes
　Computer: Yes
　Spellchecker: Yes
Extended test time: Yes
Scribes: Yes
Proctors: Yes
Oral exams: Yes
Notetakers: Yes

Distraction-reduced environment: Yes
Tape recording in class: Yes
Books on tape from RFBD: No
Taping of books not from RFBD: No
Accommodations for students with ADHD: Yes
Reading machine: Yes
Other assistive technology: Yes
Priority registration: Yes

Added costs for services: $1,800 per semester
LD specialists: Yes (10)
Professional tutors: NR
Peer tutors: 110
Max. hours/wk. for services: Unlimited
How professors are notified of LD/ADHD: By student

GENERAL ADMISSIONS INFORMATION

Director of Admissions: Lori Goldman
Telephone: 520-621-3237

ENTRANCE REQUIREMENTS

16 total are required; 16 total are recommended; 4 English required, 4 English recommended, 4 math required, 4 math recommended, 3 science required, 3 science recommended, 3 science lab required, 3 science lab recommended, 2 foreign language required, 2 foreign language recommended, 1 social studies required, 1 social studies recommended, 1 history required, 1 history recommended. High school diploma or GED required.

Application deadline: April 1
Notification: Rolling beginning 11/1
Average GPA: 3.4

Average SAT I Math: 556
Average SAT I Verbal: 545
Average ACT: 24

Graduated top 10% of class: 33%
Graduated top 25% of class: 61%
Graduated top 50% of class: 88%

COLLEGE GRADUATION REQUIREMENTS

Course waivers allowed: Yes
Course substitutions allowed: Yes
In what subjects: Math and foreign language

ADDITIONAL INFORMATION

Environment: Situated in downtown Tucson on 325 acres, the University is surrounded by the Santa Catalina Mountain range in the Sonora Desert.

Student Body
　Undergrad enrollment: 26,404
　Female: 53%
　Male: 47%
　Out-of-state: 27%

Cost Information
　In-state tuition: $2,272
　Out-of-state tuition: $9,728
　Room & board: $5,888
Housing Information
　University housing: Yes
　Percent living on campus: 20%

Greek System
　Fraternity: Yes
　Sorority: Yes
Athletics: NCAA Division I

HARDING UNIVERSITY

900 East Center, PO Box 12255, Searcy, AR 72149
Phone: 501-279-4407 • Fax: 501-279-4865
E-mail: admissions@harding.edu • Web: www.harding.edu
Support level: CS • Institution type: 4-year private

LEARNING DISABILITY PROGRAM AND SERVICES

The philosophy and goals of Student Support Services are to foster an institutional climate supportive of the success of high-risk (first-generation, low-income, or disabled) students at Harding University. SSS strives to deliver a program of services that will result in increasing the College retention and graduation rates of these students. Each student in the program receives a high level of personal attention and support for his/her needs throughout the school year. Students meet with an academic counselor concerning their specific needs. Students are given the opportunity to discuss their needs and goals with someone to help them better understand what those needs and goals are. There are many workshops offered to provide students with hands-on learning. There is also a ropes course, which consists of three levels of activities on a special outdoor obstacle course. The readiness-level activities consist of games and problem-solving activities. Low elements use various apparatus to pose problems for the group to overcome. In the high elements mountain-climbing techniques and safety procedures are used to allow the individual to reach goals with the support of the group. The ropes course teaches a variety of skills ranging from communication to trust and faith to working as a team. The course demonstrates that people can learn to overcome many fears by overcoming just one.

LD/ADHD ADMISSIONS INFORMATION

College entrance tests required: Yes
Nonstandardized tests accepted: Yes
Interview required: No
Essay required: Yes
Documentation required for LD: Current psychological evaluation (preferred senior year in high school) by licensed professional
Documentation required for ADHD: Evaluation by medical doctor
Documentation submitted to: Admissions and SSS
Special Ed. HS course work accepted: No

Specific course requirements for all applicants: Yes
Separate application required for services: No
# of LD applications submitted yearly: 48
# of LD applications accepted yearly: 48
Total # of students receiving LD/ADHD services: 36
Acceptance into program means acceptance into college: Students must be admitted and enrolled at the University first and then may request services.

ADMISSIONS

Admission criteria for students with learning disabilities are the same as for students in general, except that scores made on special administrations of college entrance exams (ACT/SAT) are accepted. These scores, however, must meet the accepted admissions criteria. Students who score 18 or below on the ACT (or equivalent SAT) are admitted into the Developmental Studies Program called Advance. Transfer students with low GPAs are accepted on probation. Course requirements include 4 years English, 3 years math, 3 years social studies, and 2 years science; 2 years of foreign language are recommended. The minimum GPA is a 2.0. The director of SSS makes admission decisions for the program and the director of admissions determines admissibility into the University. Students may self-disclose in the admission process and this information could be used as one component in making an admission decision.

ADDITIONAL INFORMATION

Testing accommodations are provided with documented evidence of a disability. These accommodations include extended time on exams, readers, taking the test in parts with breaks, use of computer with spellcheck, and providing a distraction-free environment. Classroom accommodations may include computer with spellcheck; extra time for proofreading and editing of written assignments; note-taker; books on tape; and taping outside reading assignments. Professors do not receive documentation or explanation unless the student signs a release form that would permit the release of such sensitive information. Each semester the student is asked to sign a permission form designating which professors should receive letters. Skills classes for college credit are offered in Beginning Algebra, Basic English, College Reading, and Study Skills. The CAPS (coaches and players) mentoring program targets primarily students with ADHD/ADHD.

SUPPORT SERVICES CONTACT INFORMATION

Learning Disability Program/Services: Student Support Services (SSS)
Director: Linda Thompson, EdD
  E-mail: lthompson@harding.edu
  Telephone: 501-279-4416
  Fax: 501-279-4217
Contact: Teresa McLeod, M.Ed
  E-mail: tmcleod@harding.edu
  Telephone: 501-279-4019
  Fax: 501-279-4217

LEARNING DISABILITY SERVICES

Requests for the following services/accommodations will be evaluated individually based on appropriate and current documentation.

Allowed in Exams
  Calculator: Yes
  Dictionary: Yes
  Computer: Yes
  Spellchecker: Yes
Extended test time: Yes
Scribes: Yes
Proctors: Yes
Oral exams: Yes
Notetakers: Yes

Distraction-reduced environment: Yes
Tape recording in class: Yes
Books on tape from RFBD: Yes
Taping of books not from RFBD: Yes
Accommodations for students with ADHD: Yes
Reading machine: Yes
Other assistive technology: Yes
Priority registration: Yes

Added costs for services: No
LD specialists: Yes (1)
Professional tutors: 1
Peer tutors: 6
Max. hours/wk. for services: Unlimited
How professors are notified of LD/ADHD: By both student and director

GENERAL ADMISSIONS INFORMATION

Director of Admissions: Mike Williams
Telephone: 501-279-4407

ENTRANCE REQUIREMENTS
15 total are required; 20 total are recommended; 4 English required, 3 math required, 4 math recommended, 2 science required, 3 science recommended, 2 foreign language recommended, 3 social studies required, 4 social studies recommended, 3 elective required. High school diploma is required and GED is not accepted. Minimum TOEFL is 500. TOEFL required of all international applicants.

Application deadline: June 1
Notification: Rolling beginning 5/1
Average GPA: 3.3

Average SAT I Math: 560
Average SAT I Verbal: 570
Average ACT: 24

Graduated top 10% of class: 35%
Graduated top 25% of class: 62%
Graduated top 50% of class: 90%

COLLEGE GRADUATION REQUIREMENTS

Course waivers allowed: No
Course substitutions allowed: N/A
In what subjects: N/A

ADDITIONAL INFORMATION

Environment: The University is located on 200 acres in a small town 50 miles northeast of Little Rock.

Student Body
  Undergrad enrollment: 3,982
  Female: 55%
  Male: 45%
  Out-of-state: 63%

Cost Information
  Tuition: $8,175
  Room & board: $4,336
Housing Information
  University housing: Yes
  Percent living on campus: 71%

Greek System
  Fraternity: Yes
  Sorority: Yes
Athletics: NCAA Division II

UNIVERSITY OF THE OZARKS

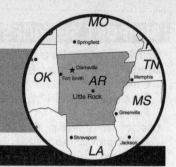

415 College Avenue, Clarksville, AR 72830
Phone: 501-979-1227 • Fax: 501-979-1355
E-mail: jdecker@ozarks.edu • Web: www.ozarks.edu
Support level: SP • Institution type: 4-year private

LEARNING DISABILITY PROGRAM AND SERVICES

The Jones Learning Center believes that students with specific learning disabilities are entitled to services that allow them to compete with other students. The Learning Center program emphasizes a total learning environment. Instruction is individualized and personalized. Enhanced services include individualized programming; a technology unit; centralized accessibility; and a supportive atmosphere with low student-to-staff ratio, which provides students even greater opportunity to realize their true academic potential. Ideas, instructional materials, and activities are presented on a variety of different levels commensurate with the educational needs of the individual student. This program is very comprehensive in every area. At the beginning of each semester the course load and needs of the student are assessed to determine what services will be needed.

LD/ADHD ADMISSIONS INFORMATION

College entrance tests required: No
Nonstandardized tests accepted: Yes
Interview required: Yes
Essay required: Yes
Documentation required for LD: Psychoeducational evaluation
Documentation required for ADHD: Yes
Documentation submitted to: Jones Learning Center
Special Ed. HS course work accepted: Yes

Specific course requirements for all applicants: Yes
Separate application required for services: Yes
# of LD applications submitted yearly: 50–60
# of LD applications accepted yearly: 20–30
Total # of students receiving LD/ADHD services: 68
Acceptance into program means acceptance into college: Students admitted to the Learning Center are automatically accepted to the University.

ADMISSIONS

Students complete a special application. Applicants must be 18 or older; complete high school or obtain a GED; demonstrate average or above-average IQ; have a learning disability or attention deficit disorder as a primary disability; provide diagnostic information from previous evaluations; complete the admissions packet; visit campus; and participate in a two-day psychoeducational evaluation that includes interviews. Applicants with some areas of concern for the admissions committee may be admitted on a one-year trial basis. This conditional admission is only available to students applying to the Jones Learning Center. There are no specific high school courses and no minimum ACT/SAT scores required for admission. Admission decisions are made by the Admissions Committee. Motivation is a key factor in the admission decision. Students are encouraged to begin the application to the Jones Learning Center during the spring semester of their junior year or early in the senior year. The JLC has a rolling admission policy. Once students are admitted into the JLC they are automatically admitted to the University.

ADDITIONAL INFORMATION

Students are assigned to a program coordinator who is responsible for the individualized planning of each student's program of study, acts as an advocate, and monitors the student's progress. Students receive help understanding learning styles, utilizing strengths, circumventing deficits, building skills, and becoming independent learners and self-advocates. Skills classes are offered in study skills (for credit), writing (for credit), reading, and math. Enhanced services include testing accommodations; one-to-one administration of a test with a reader and staff to take dictation if needed; assistive technology including Dragon Dictate and a Kurzweil Scanner/Reader; peer tutoring; and note-takers. Developmental services include opportunities to improve basic skills in reading, writing, and math. Students with ADHD and/or LD may receive services from the Learning Center.

SUPPORT SERVICES CONTACT INFORMATION

Learning Disability Program/Services: Jones Learning Center
Director: Julia Frost
  E-mail: jfrost@ozarks.edu
  Telephone: 501-979-1403
  Fax: 501-979-1429
Contact: Shannon Rutledge
  E-mail: srutledg@ozarks.edu
  Telephone: 501-979-1403
  Fax: 501-979-1429

LEARNING DISABILITY SERVICES

Requests for the following services/accommodations will be evaluated individually based on appropriate and current documentation.

Allowed in Exams
  Calculator: Yes
  Dictionary: Yes
  Computer: Yes
  Spellchecker: Yes
Extended test time: Yes
Scribes: Yes
Proctors: Yes
Oral exams: Yes
Notetakers: Yes

Distraction-reduced environment: Yes
Tape recording in class: Yes
Books on tape from RFBD: Yes
Taping of books not from RFBD: Yes
Accommodations for students with ADHD: Yes
Reading machine: Yes
Other assistive technology: Yes
Priority registration: No

Added costs for services: $6,265 per semester
LD specialists: Yes (16)
Professional tutors: 16
Peer tutors: 100
Max. hours/wk. for services: Unlimited
How professors are notified of LD/ADHD: By both student and director

GENERAL ADMISSIONS INFORMATION

Director of Admissions: Jim Decker
Telephone: 501-979-1227

ENTRANCE REQUIREMENTS
15 total are required; 4 English required, 2 math required, 2 science required, 2 foreign language required, 2 social studies required, 2 history required. High school diploma or GED required. Minimum TOEFL is 500. TOEFL required of all international applicants.

Application deadline: Rolling
Notification: Rolling
Average GPA: 3.3

Average SAT I Math: 505
Average SAT I Verbal: 509
Average ACT: 22

Graduated top 10% of class: 21%
Graduated top 25% of class: 44%
Graduated top 50% of class: 87%

COLLEGE GRADUATION REQUIREMENTS

Course waivers allowed: No
Course substitutions allowed: Yes
In what subjects: College algebra and foreign language

ADDITIONAL INFORMATION

Environment: The University is located on 56 acres 100 miles northwest of Little Rock. Clarksville is a town of 5,000 residents in the Arkansas River Valley.

Student Body
  Undergrad enrollment: 573
  Female: 55%
  Male: 45%
  Out-of-state: 33%

Cost Information
  Tuition: $9,200
  Room & board: $4,080
Housing Information
  University housing: Yes
  Percent living on campus: 60%

Greek System
  Fraternity: Yes
  Sorority: Yes
  Athletics: NAIA

BAKERSFIELD COLLEGE

1801 Panorama Drive, Bakersfield, CA 93305
Phone: 805-395-4301
Web: www.bc.cc.ca.us
Support: CS • Institution: 2-year public

LEARNING DISABILITY PROGRAM AND SERVICES

The goals of the Bakersfield College Learning Disabilities program are to foster academic success, encourage lifelong learning, and ensure that students with disabilities have an equitable opportunity for success in an educational setting. The LD program at BC provides services for students with learning disabilities and assists with transferring to four-year colleges, gaining AA degrees, completing certificates in specialized fields, and developing as an individual. There are no special classes; students attend regular classes and are expected to compete on that level. The purpose of Supportive Services is to ensure that students with disabilities can participate in the mainstream programs and activities. The counselors in Supportive Services understand how having a disability may affect a student's success in college and on the job. Supportive Services provides academic, vocational, and personal counseling to address academic and disability-related needs. Counselors also work with students to identify appropriate individualized accommodations and services. Once the disability has been verified, the counselors develop an individualized list of appropriate accommodations for each student. Many of these services are coordinated through the Accommodations Desk in the Learning Center.

LD/ADHD ADMISSIONS INFORMATION

College entrance tests required: Yes
Nonstandardized tests accepted: Yes
Interview required: No
Essay required: No
Documentation required for LD: WAIS-III or WJ-I; and WJ-II, WRAT
Documentation required for ADHD: Yes
Submitted to: Supportive Services
Special Ed. HS course work accepted: Yes

Specific course requirements for all applicants: Yes
Separate application required for services: No
# of LD applications submitted yearly: 100
# of LD applications accepted yearly: All who apply
Total # of students receiving LD/ADHD services: 300
Acceptance into program means acceptance into college: Student must be admitted and enrolled at the College first and then may request services.

ADMISSIONS

There is no special application for admission. The College has an "open-door" policy. Students must meet the California Community College LD Eligibility Model, which includes an IQ of 85+, a processing deficit, and a discrepancy between aptitude and achievement. Students with recent testing may submit this evaluation. The LD program will give students the Woodcock-Johnson assessment to determine the existence of a learning disability if they enter college without a diagnosis of a learning disability. All students take a college-designed test called Asset that is similar to an ACT and helps the College obtain curricular information used in placement. This test is given timed and with extended time.

ADDITIONAL INFORMATION

All courses have reading-level requirements, and some have prerequisites that must be met before entrance. It is recommended that students be able to read at least at a sixth-grade level in order to be successful in the College courses. Often students reading below sixth-grade level are unable to find courses that are appropriate. Services include counseling, tutoring, test accommodations, study skills classes, and individualized instructional accommodations materials. Bakersfield College offers a variety of services designed to maximize success for students in their college courses. Skills courses are offered in reading, math, writing, and study strategies. Students with attention deficit disorder will receive Section 504 accommodations from Disabled Student Services.

SUPPORT SERVICES CONTACT INFORMATION

Learning Disability Program/Services: Supportive Services
Director: Tim Bohan
E-mail: tbohan@bc.cc.ca.us
Telephone: 661-395-4334
Fax: 661-395-4025
Contact: Same

LEARNING DISABILITY SERVICES

Requests for the following services/accommodations will be evaluated individually based on appropriate and current documentation.

Allowed in Exams
  Calculator: Yes
  Dictionary: Yes
  Computer: Yes
  Spellchecker: Yes
Extended test time: Yes
Scribes: Yes
Proctors: Yes
Notetakers: Yes

Distraction-reduced environment: Yes
Tape recording in class: Yes
Books on tape from RFBD: Yes
Taping of books not from RFBD: Yes
Accommodations for students with
  ADHD: Yes
Reading machine: Yes
Other assistive technology: Yes
Priority registration: Yes

Added costs for services: No
LD specialists: Yes (2)
Professional tutors: No
Peer tutors: 50–75
Max. hours/wk. for services: 2 hours
How professors are notified of
  LD/ADHD: By student

GENERAL ADMISSIONS INFORMATION

Director of Admissions: Sue Vaughn
Telephone: 661-395-4301

ENTRANCE REQUIREMENTS
High school diploma or GED required. ACT/SAT not required for admission.

Application deadline: Rolling
Notification: Rolling beginning 9/1
Average GPA: NR

Average SAT I Math: NR
Average SAT I Verbal: NR
Average ACT: NR

Graduated top 10% of class: NR
Graduated top 25% of class: NR
Graduated top 50% of class: NR

COLLEGE GRADUATION REQUIREMENTS

Course waivers allowed: No
Course substitutions allowed: Yes
In what subjects: Determined on a case-by-case basis; course substitutions vary.

ADDITIONAL INFORMATION

Environment: The College is located on a 175-acre campus 100 miles north of Los Angeles.

Student Body
  Undergrad enrollment: 12,267
  Female: 56%
  Male: 44%
  Out-of-state: 1%

Cost Information
  In-state tuition: $140
  Out-of-state tuition: $3,500
  Room & board: N/A
Housing Information
  University housing: Yes
  Percent living on campus: 1%

Greek System
  Fraternity: Yes
  Sorority: Yes
Athletics: Intercollegiate sports

CAL POLYTECHNIC STATE U.—SAN LUIS OBISPO

Admissions Office, Cal Poly, San Luis Obispo, CA 93407
Phone: 805-756-2311 • Fax: 805-756-5400
E-mail: admissions@calpoly.edu • Web: www.calpoly.edu
Support level: CS • Institution type: 4-year public

LEARNING DISABILITY PROGRAM AND SERVICES

The goal of the program is to assist students with learning disabilities in using their learning strengths. Disability Resources Center (DRC) assists students with disabilities in achieving access to higher education, promotes personal and educational success, and increases the awareness and responsiveness of the campus community. DRC is actively involved with students and faculty and provides a newsletter and open house to keep the College population aware of what it is and what it does. Incoming students are encouraged to meet with DRC staff to receive assistance in the planning of class schedules. This allows for the selection of appropriate classes to fit particular needs and personal goals. It is the responsibility of each student seeking accommodations and services to provide a written, comprehensive psychological and/or medical evaluation verifying the diagnosis. The Cal Poly Student Learning Outcomes model promotes student personal growth and the development of self-advocacy for full inclusion of qualified students with verified disabilities. The promotion of student self-reliance and responsibility are necessary adjuncts to educational development. For learning disabilities the assessments must be done by a licensed educational psychologist, psychologist, neurologist, or LD specialist. The diagnosis of ADHD must be made by a licensed therapist, educational psychologist, psychologist, psychiatrist, neurologist, or physician.

LD/ADHD ADMISSIONS INFORMATION

College entrance tests required: Yes
Nonstandardized tests accepted: Yes
Interview required: No
Essay required: No
Documentation required for LD: Psychoeducational evaluation
Documentation required for ADHD: Yes
Documentation submitted to: DRC
Special Ed. HS course work accepted: Yes

Specific course requirements for all applicants: Yes
Separate application required for services: No
# of LD applications submitted yearly: 100–150
# of LD applications accepted yearly: NR
Total # of students receiving LD/ADHD services: 450–510
Acceptance into program means acceptance into college: Students must be admitted and enrolled at the University first and then may request services.

ADMISSIONS
Students with LD must meet the same admission criteria as all applicants, and should submit a general admission application to the Admissions Office. General requirements include 4 years English, 3 years math, 1 year U.S. history or government, 1 year lab science, 2 years foreign language, 1 year fine arts, and 3 years electives. On a case-by-case basis, foreign language substitutions may be allowed. Some courses taken in the Special Education Department may be accepted. All documentation should be sent directly to the Support Program, and students who self-disclose will receive information. Admission decisions are made by the admissions office.

ADDITIONAL INFORMATION
Incoming students are strongly urged to schedule an appointment with DRC to receive assistance in the planning of classes. Academic accommodations are designed to meet a student's disability-related needs without fundamentally altering the nature of the instructional program, and are not intended to provide remediation. Supportive services may include academic advising, alternative format materials, assistive listening devices, note-taking, taped textbooks, test accommodations, tutorial services, and writing assistance. DRC may recommend the services of the Academic Skills Center of Student Academic Services and enrollment in English and math classes offering additional support. There is also a peer mentoring program and Partners for Success and a career mentoring program available to all students. Students requesting accommodations, which include using a computer, dictionary, or spellcheck during an exam, will need the professor's permission. The University can provide some free psychoeducational assessment services, but there is a lengthy waiting period for these limited services. Services and accommodations are available to undergraduate and graduate students.

SUPPORT SERVICES CONTACT INFORMATION

Learning Disability Program/Services: Disability Resource Center (DRC)
Director: William Bailey
   E-mail: wbailey@calpoly.edu
   Telephone: 805-756-1395
   Fax: 805-756-5451
Contact: Dr. Steven Kane
   E-mail: skane@calpoly.edu
   Telephone: 805-756-1395
   Fax: 805-756-5451

LEARNING DISABILITY SERVICES

Requests for the following services/accommodations will be evaluated individually based on appropriate and current documentation.

Allowed in Exams
  Calculator: Yes
  Dictionary: Yes
  Computer: Yes
  Spellchecker: Yes
Extended test time: Yes
Scribes: Yes
Proctors: Yes
Oral exams: Yes
Notetakers: Yes

Distraction-reduced environment: Yes
Tape recording in class: Yes
Books on tape from RFBD: Yes
Taping of books not from RFBD: Yes
Accommodations for students with ADHD: Yes
Reading machine: Yes
Other assistive technology: Yes
Priority registration: Limited

Added costs for services: No
LD specialists: Yes (2)
Professional tutors: No
Peer tutors: 25
Max. hours/wk. for services: Depends on the service
How professors are notified of LD/ADHD: By student

GENERAL ADMISSIONS INFORMATION

Director of Admissions: James Maraviglia
Telephone: 805-756-2913

ENTRANCE REQUIREMENTS
15 total are required; 4 English required, 3 math required, 3 science required, 1 science lab required, 2 foreign language required. High school diploma or GED required. Minimum TOEFL is 550. TOEFL required of all international applicants.

Application deadline: November 30
Notification: Rolling beginning 3/1
Average GPA: 3.6

Average SAT I Math: 569
Average SAT I Verbal: 532
Average ACT: 23

Graduated top 10% of class: 38%
Graduated top 25% of class: 73%
Graduated top 50% of class: 94%

COLLEGE GRADUATION REQUIREMENTS

Course waivers allowed: No
Course substitutions allowed: Yes
In what subjects: On a case-by-case basis, individuals may be granted course substitutions in quantitative reasoning (in very limited non-math-related majors) by the VP of academic affairs and foreign language substitutions with departmental approval.

ADDITIONAL INFORMATION

Environment: The campus is located 100 miles north of Santa Barbara.

Student Body
  Undergrad enrollment: 15,867
  Female: 44%
  Male: 56%
  Out-of-state: 4%

Cost Information
  In-state tuition: $2,100
  Out-of-state tuition: $4,560
  Room & board: $6,246
Housing Information
  University housing: Yes
  Percent living on campus: 18%

Greek System
  Fraternity: Yes
  Sorority: Yes
Athletics: NCAA Division I

Cal State Polytechnic U.—Pomona

3801 West Temple Avenue, Pomona, CA 91768
Phone: 909-468-5020 • Fax: 909-869-4529
E-mail: cppadmit@csupomona.edu • Web: www.csupomona.edu
Support level: CS • Institution type: 4-year public

LEARNING DISABILITY PROGRAM AND SERVICES

The mission of the Office of Disabled Student Services is to help students with disabilities compete on an equal basis with their nondisabled peers by providing reasonable accommodations. This will allow them access to any academic program or to facilitate participation in any university activity that is offered to fellow students. The major purposes of DSS are to determine reasonable accommodations based on disability as assessed by knowledgeable professionals; to emphasize self-advocacy; to maximize learning experience and continuously assess students' needs; to actively recruit and increase retention and graduation rates of students with disabilities and provide greater educational equity; to facilitate the University in meeting requirements of the Americans with Disabilities Act; and to prepare students with disabilities for life, leadership, and careers in a changing world.

LD/ADHD ADMISSIONS INFORMATION

College entrance tests required: Yes
Nonstandardized tests accepted: Yes
Interview required: No
Essay required: No
Documentation required for LD: Psychoeducational evaluation
Documentation required for ADHD: Yes
Documentation submitted to: Disabled Student Services
Special Ed. HS course work accepted: Yes

Specific course requirements for all applicants: Yes
Separate application required for services: No
# of LD applications submitted yearly: N/A
# of LD applications accepted yearly: N/A
Total # of students receiving LD/ADHD services: 400+
Acceptance into program means acceptance into college: Students must be admitted and enrolled at the University prior to requesting services.

ADMISSIONS

Students must meet the University's regular entrance requirements, including C or better in the subject requirements of 4 years English, 3 years math, 1 year U.S. history, 1 year lab science, 2 years foreign language, 1 year visual or performing arts, and 3 years electives, and a qualifiable eligibility index based on high school GPA and scores on either ACT or SAT. Special admits are very limited. Applicants with LD are encouraged to complete college-prep courses. However, if students are unable to fulfill a specific course requirement because of a learning disability, alternative college-prep courses may be substituted. Substitutions may be granted in foreign language, lab science, and math. Substitutions may be authorized on an individual basis after review and recommendation by applicant's guidance counselor in consultation with the director of DSS. Course substitutions could limit access to some majors. Students who self-disclose are reviewed by DSS, which provides a recommendation to admissions.

ADDITIONAL INFORMATION

Support services include counseling, advocacy services, registration, note-takers, readers, tutors, testing accommodations, and specialized equipment. Skills classes are not offered through DSS but are available in other departments in the areas of reading skills, test preparation, test-taking strategies, and study skills. Services and accommodations are available to undergraduate and graduate students. Cal Poly offers a summer program for any high school student.

SUPPORT SERVICES CONTACT INFORMATION

Learning Disability Program/Services: Disabled Student Services (DSS)
Director: Fred Henderson
   E-mail: fdhenderson@csupomona.edu
   Telephone: 909-869-3005
   Fax: 909-869-3271
Contact: Same

LEARNING DISABILITY SERVICES

Requests for the following services/accommodations will be evaluated individually based on appropriate and current documentation.

Allowed in Exams
   Calculator: Yes
   Dictionary: Yes
   Computer: Yes
   Spellchecker: Yes
Extended test time: Yes
Scribes: Yes
Proctors: Yes
Oral exams: Yes
Notetakers: Yes

Distraction-reduced environment: Yes
Tape recording in class: Yes
Books on tape from RFBD: Yes
Taping of books not from RFBD: Yes
Accommodations for students with
   ADHD: Yes
Reading machine: Yes
Other assistive technology: Yes
Priority registration: Yes

Added costs for services: No
LD specialists: Yes
Professional tutors: No
Peer tutors: Yes
Max. hours/wk. for services: 2
How professors are notified of
   LD/ADHD: By student

GENERAL ADMISSIONS INFORMATION

Director of Admissions: George Gaines (interim director)
Telephone: 909-869-7659

ENTRANCE REQUIREMENTS

15 total are required; 15 total are recommended; 4 English required, 4 English recommended, 3 math required, 3 math recommended, 1 science required, 1 science recommended, 1 science lab required, 1 science lab recommended, 2 foreign language required, 3 foreign language recommended, 1 history required, 1 history recommended, 3 elective required, 3 elective recommended. High school diploma or GED required. Minimum TOEFL is 525. TOEFL required of all international applicants.

Application deadline: April 1
Notification: Rolling beginning 11/1
Average GPA: 3.3

Average SAT I Math: 534
Average SAT I Verbal: 480
Average ACT: 20

Graduated top 10% of class: NR
Graduated top 25% of class: NR
Graduated top 50% of class: NR

COLLEGE GRADUATION REQUIREMENTS

Course waivers allowed: No
Course substitutions allowed: Yes
In what subjects: It depends on the nature of the disability. Foreign language and math are the most common. Testing verification and documentation is required.

ADDITIONAL INFORMATION

Environment: The University is located on 1,437 acres in a suburban area 30 miles east of Los Angeles.

Student Body
   Undergrad enrollment: 16,450
   Female: 44%
   Male: 56%
   Out-of-state: 3%

Cost Information
   In-state tuition: $1,800
   Out-of-state tuition: $9,100
   Room & board: $6,113
Housing Information
   University housing: Yes
   Percent living on campus: 13%

Greek System
   Fraternity: Yes
   Sorority: Yes
   Athletics: NCAA Division II

CALIFORNIA STATE UNIV.—CHICO

400 West First Street, Chico, CA 95929-0720
Phone: 530-898-4428 • Fax: 530-898-6456
E-mail: info@csuchico.edu • Web: www.csuchico.edu
Support level: CS • Institution type: 4-year pubic

LEARNING DISABILITY PROGRAM AND SERVICES

The goal of Disability Support Services is to facilitate accommodation requests and provide the support services necessary to ensure equal access to university programs for students with disabilities. This goal is consistent with university policy and with federal and state laws. DSS provides a variety of services to university students at no charge. DSS advisors who specialize in various disabilities are available to assist students with individual accommodations. It is the student's responsibility to initiate accommodation requests early to ensure proper coordination of services. Students must provide current and appropriate documentation to support their requests for services/accommodations.

LD/ADHD ADMISSIONS INFORMATION

College entrance tests required: Yes
Nonstandardized tests accepted: Yes
Interview required: No
Essay required: No
Documentation required for LD: Psychoeducational evaluation
Documentation required for ADHD: Yes
Documentation submitted to: DSS
Special Ed. HS course work accepted: Yes, if approved

Specific course requirements for all applicants: Yes
Separate application required for services: No
# of LD applications submitted yearly: N/A
# of LD applications accepted yearly: N/A
Total # of students receiving LD/ADHD services: 300+
Acceptance into program means acceptance into college: Students must be admitted and enrolled at the University and then may request services.

ADMISSIONS

There are no special admission procedures for students with learning disabilities. Applicants must meet the general admission requirements that are based on GPA, test scores, and subject requirements. Course requirements include 4 years English, 3 years math, 1 year U.S. history, 1 year science, 2 years foreign language, and 1 year visual and performing arts. Applicants with disabilities are encouraged to complete college-prep courses. If the applicant is judged unable to fulfill a specific course requirement because of a verified disability, alternate college-prep courses may be substituted for specific subject requirements. Substitutions may be authorized on an individual basis after review and recommendation by the high school counselor or academic advisor in consultation with the director of a CSU Disability Support Services program.

ADDITIONAL INFORMATION

General accommodations may include priority registration, note-takers, readers, scribes, test accommodations, computer access assistance, LD assessment, liaison with faculty and administration. Students are also eligible for certain student services, including tutoring and supplemental instruction at the Student Learning Center. Advisors are available to discuss all accommodation requests. There is a math lab, a writing center, a tutoring center, and a Student Learning Center available to all students. The University is committed to making electronic information available to all students. Designated computer stations throughout campus have adaptive hardware and software installed. Software, hardware, and equipment include: Open Book Unbound Reading System, Kurzweil Reading System, DeckTalk PC, Double Talk LT, Vocal/Window Eyes, Jaws for Windows, Ducksberry Software, and ZoomText Plus, and most computers are networked for library and Internet access.

SUPPORT SERVICES CONTACT INFORMATION

Learning Disability Program/Services: Disability Support Services
Director: Billie Jackson
 E-mail: bfjackson@csu.chico.edu
 Telephone: 530-898-5959
 Fax: 530-898-4411
Contact: Van Alexander
 E-mail: vanalexander@csu.chico.edu
 Telephone: 530-898-5989
 Fax: 530-898-4411

LEARNING DISABILITY SERVICES

Requests for the following services/accommodations will be evaluated individually based on appropriate and current documentation.

Allowed in Exams	**Distraction-reduced environment:** Yes	**Added costs for services:** No
Calculator: Yes	**Tape recording in class:** Yes	**LD specialists:** Yes (2)
Dictionary: Yes	**Books on tape from RFBD:** Yes	**Professional tutors:** 25
Computer: Yes	**Taping of books not from RFBD:** Yes	**Peer tutors:** 25
Spellchecker: Yes	**Accommodations for students with**	**Max. hours/wk. for services:** 280
Extended test time: Yes	**ADHD:** Yes	**How professors are notified of**
Scribes: Yes	**Reading machine:** Yes	**LD/ADHD:** Student contact with letter
Proctors: Yes	**Other assistive technology:** Yes	
Oral exams: Yes	**Priority registration:** Yes	
Notetakers: Yes		

GENERAL ADMISSIONS INFORMATION

Director of Admissions: John Swiney
Telephone: 800-542-4426

ENTRANCE REQUIREMENTS

15 total are required; 4 English required, 3 math required, 1 science required, 1 science lab required, 2 foreign language required, 1 history required, 3 elective required. High school diploma or GED required. Minimum TOEFL is 500. TOEFL required of all international applicants.

Application deadline: November 30	**Average SAT I Math:** 487	**Graduated top 10% of class:** 35%
Notification: Rolling beginning 3/1	**Average SAT I Verbal:** 486	**Graduated top 25% of class:** 76%
Average GPA: 3.1	**Average ACT:** 20	**Graduated top 50% of class:** 100%

COLLEGE GRADUATION REQUIREMENTS

Course waivers allowed: No
Course substitutions allowed: Yes
In what subjects: Case-by-case basis

ADDITIONAL INFORMATION

Environment: The University is located in a small town 100 miles from Sacramento.

Student Body	**Cost Information**	**Greek System**
Undergrad enrollment: 13,397	**In-state tuition:** $1,990	**Fraternity:** Yes
Female: 54%	**Out-of-state tuition:** $9,380	**Sorority:** Yes
Male: 46%	**Room & board:** $5,860	**Athletics:** NCAA Division II
Out-of-state: 1%	**Housing Information**	
	University housing: Yes	
	Percent living on campus: 13%	

CALIF. STATE UNIV.—NORTHRIDGE

PO Box 1286, Northridge, CA 91328-1286
Phone: 818-677-3773 • Fax: 818-677-4665
E-mail: lorraine.newlon@csun.edu • Web: www.csun.edu
Support level: CS • Institution type: 4-year public

LEARNING DISABILITY PROGRAM AND SERVICES

The Office of Disabled Student Services recognizes that students with learning disabilities can be quite successful in a university setting if appropriate educational support services are offered to them. In an effort to assist students with learning disabilities in reaching their full potential, the program offers a comprehensive and well-coordinated system of educational support services that allow students to be judged on the basis of their ability rather than disability. The professional staff includes LD specialists trained in the diagnosis of learning disabilities and the provision of educational support services. Additionally, the program employs graduate students (Educational Support Specialists) who work under the direction of the professional staff and assist students with study skills, time-management procedures, test-taking techniques, and other individualized programs.

LD/ADHD ADMISSIONS INFORMATION

College entrance tests required: Yes
Nonstandardized tests accepted: Yes
Interview required: Yes
Essay required: No
Documentation required for LD: Psychoeducational evaluation
Documentation required for ADHD: Yes
Documentation submitted to: Students with Disability Resources
Special Ed. HS course work accepted: Yes

Specific course requirements for all applicants: Yes
Separate application required for services: No
# of LD applications submitted yearly: N/A
# of LD applications accepted yearly: N/A
Total # of students receiving LD/ADHD services: 500
Acceptance into program means acceptance into college: Students must be accepted and enrolled at the University first and then may request services.

ADMISSIONS

There is no special admission process. However, the Special Admission Committee of Students with Disabilities Resources makes recommendations to the Admissions Office. Students must get a C or better in: 4 years English, 3 years math, 1 year U.S. history, 1 year science, 2 years foreign language, 1 year visual/performing arts, and 3 years electives. Students with LD may request course substitutions. An eligibility index combining GPA and ACT or SAT is used, and grades used are from 10th through 12th grade (bonus points for honor courses). Index is calculated by multiplying GPA by 800 and adding SAT, or multiplying GPA by 200 and adding 10 times the ACT. California residents need an index of 2900 using SAT or 694 using ACT. Nonresidents must have a minimum index of 3502 (SAT) or 842 (ACT). No test scores needed if GPA is a 3.0+ for residents or 3.61 for nonresidents.

ADDITIONAL INFORMATION

The following services and accommodations are available for students presenting appropriate documentation: the use of calculators, dictionary, computer, and spellchecker for tests; extended testing time; scribes; proctors; oral exams; note-takers; distraction-free testing environments; tape recorder in class; books on tape; and priority registration. Testing accommodations may be arranged through the program without the "integrity" of the test being sacrificed. The Computer Access Lab provides computers along with professional assistance. The program and the CSUN Career Center work cooperatively to assist students with LD in planning and attaining their career goals. Diagnostic testing is available for students who suspect they may have a learning disability. Counselors are available to assist students in meeting their social/emotional needs as well as their academic requirements. Assistance in developing appropriate learning strategies is provided on an individual basis. Additionally, a support group for students with learning disabilities meets regularly. There are also workshops, a reader service, and note-takers. Services and accommodations are available for undergraduate and graduate students.

SUPPORT SERVICES CONTACT INFORMATION

Learning Disability Program/Services: Students with Disabilities Resources
Director: Lee Axelrod
  E-mail: lee.axelrod@csun.edu
  Telephone: 818-677-2684
  Fax: 818-677-4932
Contact: Same

LEARNING DISABILITY SERVICES

Requests for the following services/accommodations will be evaluated individually based on appropriate and current documentation.

Allowed in Exams
  Calculator: Yes
  Dictionary: Yes
  Computer: Yes
  Spellchecker: Yes
Extended test time: Yes
Scribes: Yes
Proctors: Yes
Oral exams: Yes
Notetakers: Yes

Distraction-reduced environment: Yes
Tape recording in class: Yes
Books on tape from RFBD: Yes
Taping of books not from RFBD: Yes
Accommodations for students with ADHD: Yes
Reading machine: Yes
Other assistive technology: Yes
Priority registration: Yes

Added costs for services: No
LD specialists: Yes (2)
Professional tutors: No
Peer tutors: 3
Max. hours/wk. for services: 2
How professors are notified of LD/ADHD: By student

GENERAL ADMISSIONS INFORMATION

Director of Admissions: Lorraine Newlon
Telephone: 818-667-3773

ENTRANCE REQUIREMENTS

4 English required, 3 math required, 1 science required, 1 science lab required, 2 foreign language required, 3 elective required. High school diploma or GED required. Minimum TOEFL is 500. TOEFL required of all international applicants.

Application deadline: November 30
Notification: Rolling beginning 11/30
Average GPA: 3.1

Average SAT I Math: NR
Average SAT I Verbal: NR
Average ACT: NR

Graduated top 10% of class: NR
Graduated top 25% of class: 33%
Graduated top 50% of class: NR

COLLEGE GRADUATION REQUIREMENTS

Course waivers allowed: No
Course substitutions allowed: Yes
In what subjects: Determined on a case-by-case basis

ADDITIONAL INFORMATION

Environment: The University has a large suburban campus in the San Fernando Valley northwest of Los Angeles.

Student Body
  Undergrad enrollment: 20,955
  Female: 57%
  Male: 43%
  Out-of-state: 1%

Cost Information
  In-state tuition: $1,800
  Out-of-state tuition: $9,200
  Room & board: $6,600
Housing Information
  University housing: Yes
  Percent living on campus: 8%

Greek System
  Fraternity: Yes
  Sorority: Yes
Athletics: NCAA Division II

California State University—Northridge

CALIF. STATE U.—SAN BERNARDINO

5500 University Parkway, San Bernardino, CA 92407-2397
Phone: 909-880-5000 • Fax: 909-880-5200
E-mail: cppadmit@csupomona.edu • Web: www.csusb.edu
Support level: CS • Institution type: 4-year public

LEARNING DISABILITY PROGRAM AND SERVICES

The Learning Disability Program is dedicated to assuring each student an opportunity to experience equity in education. Each student must complete an assessment and then the staff helps to develop compensatory methods for handling assignments and classroom projects. Careful attention is paid to helping the student acquire learning skills and formulating and implementing specific strategies for note-taking and management of written materials. Recommendations are designed for each student as a result of the psychometric assessment, personal interview, and academic requirements. The emphasis of the plan is to assist the students with a learning disability in finding techniques to deal with the disabilities in college and in the job market.

LD/ADHD ADMISSIONS INFORMATION

College entrance tests required: No
Nonstandardized tests accepted: Yes
Interview required: No
Essay required: No
Documentation required for LD: Psychoeducational evaluation
Documentation required for ADHD: Yes
Documentation submitted to: Services to Students with Disabilities
Special Ed. HS course work accepted: Y/N

Specific course requirements for all applicants: Yes
Separate application required for services: Yes
# of LD applications submitted yearly: 75–101
# of LD applications accepted yearly: 45–66
Total # of students receiving LD/ADHD services: 140–156
Acceptance into program means acceptance into college: Students must be admitted and enrolled at the University first and then may request services.

ADMISSIONS

Applicants with learning disabilities must follow the same application procedure as all students. Entrance requirements include a minimum GPA of 2.0; 4 years English, 3 years math, 1 year U.S. history, 1 year science, 2 years foreign language, 1 year visual or performing arts, and 3 years electives from any of the previous areas including agriculture. The middle 50 percent have an ACT of 15–19 and SAT of 800–1020. Special admission may be requested through the Learning Disability Program if the student has a deficiency in course entrance requirements. The director of the LD Program provides recommendations on the admissibility of those students who do not meet regular admissions requirements. Occasionally the special admit will consider students who are below the required GPA or test scores. These requirements can be substituted and the student can make up the deficiency on campus once enrolled.

ADDITIONAL INFORMATION

Services and accommodations for students with appropriate documentation could include the following: the use of calculators, dictionary, computer or spellchecker in exams; extended time on tests; distraction-free testing environment; oral exams; note-taker; proctors; scribes; tape recorder in class; books on tape; assistive technology; and priority registration. Specific services include assessment counseling and testing accommodations. Students on academic probation have two quarters to raise their GPA to a 2.0. The LD Program provides continual academic support.

SUPPORT SERVICES CONTACT INFORMATION

Learning Disability Program/Services: Services to Students with Disabilities
Director: Nicholas Erickson
  E-mail: nerickson@csusb.edu
  Telephone: 909-880-5238
  Fax: 909-880-7090
Contact: Melissa Scarfone
  E-mail: scarfone@csusb.edu
  Telephone: 909-880-5238
  Fax: 909-880-7090

LEARNING DISABILITY SERVICES

Requests for the following services/accommodations will be evaluated individually based on appropriate and current documentation.

Allowed in Exams
  Calculator: Yes
  Dictionary: Yes
  Computer: Yes
  Spellchecker: Yes
Extended test time: Yes
Scribes: Yes
Proctors: Yes
Oral exams: Yes
Notetakers: Yes

Distraction-reduced environment: Yes
Tape recording in class: Yes
Books on tape from RFBD: Yes
Taping of books not from RFBD: Yes
Accommodations for students with ADHD: Yes
Reading machine: Yes
Other assistive technology: Yes
Priority registration: Yes

Added costs for services: No
LD specialists: Yes (1)
Professional tutors: No
Peer tutors: No
Max. hours/wk. for services: N/A
How professors are notified of LD/ADHD: By student

GENERAL ADMISSIONS INFORMATION

Director of Admissions: Alan Liebrecht
Telephone: 909-880-5188

ENTRANCE REQUIREMENTS

13 total are required; 3 English required, 2 math required, 1 science required, 2 foreign language required, 1 social studies required, 1 history required, 3 elective required. High school diploma or GED required. Minimum TOEFL is 500. TOEFL required of all international applicants.

Application deadline: September 15
Notification: Rolling
Average GPA: 3.22

Average SAT I Math: 524
Average SAT I Verbal: 470
Average ACT: 20

Graduated top 10% of class: NR
Graduated top 25% of class: NR
Graduated top 50% of class: NR

COLLEGE GRADUATION REQUIREMENTS

Course waivers allowed:
Course substitutions allowed: Yes
In what subjects: Evaluated individually based on appropriate and current documentation

ADDITIONAL INFORMATION

Environment: The University is located in a suburban area in the foothills of the San Bernadino Mountains.

Student Body
  Undergrad enrollment: 11,007
  Female: 62%
  Male: 38%
  Out-of-state: 3%

Cost Information
  In-state tuition: $1,800
  Out-of-state tuition: $9,200
  Room & board: $6,800
Housing Information
  University housing: Yes
  Percent living on campus: 4%

Greek System
  Fraternity: Yes
  Sorority: Yes
Athletics: NCAA Division III

COLLEGE OF THE SISKIYOUS

800 College Avenue, Weed, CA 96094
Phone: 530-938-4461 • Fax: 530-938-5367
E-mail: ar@siskiyous.edu • Web: www.siskiyous.edu
Support level: CS • Institution type: 2-year private

LEARNING DISABILITY PROGRAM AND SERVICES

The Disabled Student Services Programs and Services Office is dedicated to meeting the needs of students with disabilities. The goal of DSP&S is to assist students to overcome barriers to allow access to the College's regular programs and activities. Support services are provided for students with a wide variety of disabilities. Any student who has a documented disability and demonstrates a need for a service that is directly related to the educational limitation is eligible for support services.

LD/ADHD ADMISSIONS INFORMATION

College entrance tests required: Yes
Nonstandardized tests accepted: Yes
Interview required: No
Essay required: No
Documentation required for LD: Psychoeducational evaluation
Documentation required for ADHD: Yes
Submitted to: Disabled Student Services
Special Ed. HS course work accepted: Yes

Specific course requirements for all applicants: No
Separate application required for services: No
# of LD applications submitted yearly: N/A
# of LD applications accepted yearly: N/A
Total # of students receiving LD/ADHD services: 100
Acceptance into program means acceptance into college: Students must be admitted and enrolled and then request services.

ADMISSIONS

Students with LD/ADHD who self-disclose during the admission process may receive advice from DSP&S during the admission process. Basically this advice would provide descriptions of appropriate courses the students may take and the services and accommodations they may be eligible to receive. There are not any minimum admission requirements for a specific class rank, GPA or ACT/SAT score. Applicants must have a high school diploma or equivalent certification.

ADDITIONAL INFORMATION

There is an LD specialist available in the Disability Support Services Office. There are support services available for students who have a documented disability and demonstrate a need for a service that is directly related to their educational limitations. They may include academic advising, registration assistance, the development of an individualized educational plan, LD assessment, tutoring, readers, note-takers, testing accommodations, and adaptive educational equipment. The COS High-Tech Center is designed to provide computer access and technology to students with disabilities to educate and prepare them for academic success and today's workforce. In addition, all students have access to skills classes in areas such as time management, organization, study strategies, and test-taking strategies.

SUPPORT SERVICES CONTACT INFORMATION

Learning Disability Program/Services: Disabled Student Services
Director: Karen Zeigler
  Telephone: 530-938-5297
  Fax: 530-938-5379
Contact: Donna Prather
  Telephone: 530-938-5814

LEARNING DISABILITY SERVICES

Requests for the following services/accommodations will be evaluated individually based on appropriate and current documentation.

Allowed in Exams
  Calculator: Yes
  Dictionary: Yes
  Computer: Yes
  Spellchecker: Yes
Extended test time: Yes
Scribes: Yes
Proctors: Yes
Oral exams: Yes
Notetakers: Yes

Distraction-reduced environment: Yes
Tape recording in class: Yes
Books on tape from RFBD: Yes
Taping of books not from RFBD: Yes
Accommodations for students with
  ADHD: Yes
Reading machine: No
Other assistive technology: Yes
Priority registration: No

Added costs for services: No
LD specialists: Yes
Professional tutors: 2
Peer tutors: 30
Max. hours/wk. for services:
  Unlimited
How professors are notified of
  LD/ADHD: By student

GENERAL ADMISSIONS INFORMATION

Director of Admissions: Teresa Winkleman
Telephone: 530-938-5217

ENTRANCE REQUIREMENTS
Open admissions. High school diploma or GED required.

Application deadline: Rolling
Notification: Rolling
Average GPA: NR

Average SAT I Math: NR
Average SAT I Verbal: NR
Average ACT: NR

Graduated top 10% of class: NR
Graduated top 25% of class: NR
Graduated top 50% of class: NR

COLLEGE GRADUATION REQUIREMENTS

Course waivers allowed: No
Course substitutions allowed: Yes
In what subjects: Case-by-case

ADDITIONAL INFORMATION

Environment: The College is located at the base of Mount Shasta.

Student Body
  Undergrad enrollment: 944
  Female: 54%
  Male: 46%
  Out-of-state: 5%

Cost Information
  In-state tuition: $350
  Out-of-state tuition: $4,460
  Room & board: $4,112
Housing Information
  University housing: Yes
  Percent living on campus: NR

Greek System
  Fraternity: No
  Sorority: No
Athletics: Intercollegiate

LOYOLA MARYMOUNT UNIVERSITY

7900 Loyola Boulevard, Los Angeles, CA 90045
Phone: 310-338-2750 • Fax: 310-338-2797
E-mail: admissns@lmumail.lmu.edu • Web: www.lmu.edu
Support level: S • Institution type: 4-year private

LEARNING DISABILITY PROGRAM AND SERVICES

The Office of Disability Support Services (DSS) provides specialized assistance and resources that enable students with physical, perceptual, emotional, and learning disabilities to achieve maximum independence while they pursue their educational goals. Assisted by staff specialists from all areas of the University, the DSS Office works to eliminate physical and attitudinal barriers. To be eligible for services, students must provide documentation of the disability from a licensed professional. At the Learning Resource Center students can receive tutoring in over 250 LMU classes, attend workshops, and access assistance in writing, reading, and math with LRC specialists.

LD/ADHD ADMISSIONS INFORMATION

College entrance tests required: Yes
Nonstandardized tests accepted: Yes
Interview required: N/A
Essay required: Yes
Documentation required for LD: Psychoeducational evaluation
Documentation required for ADHD: Yes
Documentation submitted to: DSS
Special Ed. HS course work accepted: No

Specific course requirements for all applicants: Yes
Separate application required for services: No
# of LD applications submitted yearly: N/A
# of LD applications accepted yearly: N/A
Total # of students receiving LD/ADHD services: 200
Acceptance into program means acceptance into college: Students must be admitted by the University first and then may request services.

ADMISSIONS

There is no special admissions process for students with Learning Disabilities or Attention Deficit Hyperactive Disorder. The admission decision will be based upon the student's grade point average, SAT/ACT scores, strength of curriculum, the application essay, letters of recommendation, and extracurricular activities. Enrolled students have an average GPA of 3.3, 25 ACT, and 1130 SAT I. Students are encouraged to have completed 4 years English, 3 years social sciences, 3 years foreign language, 3 years math (4 years for engineering and science), and 1 year elective.

ADDITIONAL INFORMATION

There is a Learning Resource Center where all students can find specialists and tutors. There is course-specific tutoring, study-skills programs (which include learning time management, overcoming test anxiety, conquering math word problems, mastering the textbook, preparing for exams, and studying efficiently), and other academic support programs with full-time professional staff members prepared to assist with writing, reading, math, ESL, and Disability Support Services. Assistive technology includes equipment that enlarges print, Windows Bridge 21000, screen-reading program, Kurzweil Reader, and Dragon Dictate. Specific accommodations for LD students with appropriate documentation could include: priority registration, note-takers, readers, transcribers, alternate testing conditions, taped books, and advocacy.

SUPPORT SERVICES CONTACT INFORMATION

Learning Disability Program/Services: Office of Disability Support Services (DSS)
Director: Patricia Robbins
   E-mail: probbins@lmu.edu
   Telephone: 310-338-4535
   Fax: 310-338-7657
Contact: Same

LEARNING DISABILITY SERVICES

Requests for the following services/accommodations will be evaluated individually based on appropriate and current documentation.

Allowed in Exams
   Calculator: Yes
   Dictionary: Yes
   Computer: Yes
   Spellchecker: Yes
Extended test time: Yes
Scribes: Yes
Proctors: Yes
Oral exams: Yes
Notetakers: Yes

Distraction-reduced environment: Yes
Tape recording in class: Yes
Books on tape from RFBD: Yes
Taping of books not from RFBD: No
Accommodations for students with ADHD: Yes
Reading machine: Yes
Other assistive technology: Yes
Priority registration: Yes

Added costs for services: No
LD specialists: No
Professional tutors: No
Peer tutors: 60–80
Max. hours/wk. for services: 5
How professors are notified of LD/ADHD: By student

GENERAL ADMISSIONS INFORMATION

Director of Admissions: Dale Marini
Telephone: 310-338-2750

ENTRANCE REQUIREMENTS

16 total are recommended; 4 English recommended, 3 math recommended, 2 science recommended, 2 science lab recommended, 3 foreign language recommended, 3 social studies recommended, 1 elective recommended. High school diploma or GED required. Minimum TOEFL is 550. TOEFL required of all international applicants.

Application deadline: Rolling
Notification: Rolling beginning 1/1
Average GPA: 3.3

Average SAT I Math: 571
Average SAT I Verbal: 567
Average ACT: 24

Graduated top 10% of class: 27%
Graduated top 25% of class: 58%
Graduated top 50% of class: 89%

COLLEGE GRADUATION REQUIREMENTS

Course waivers allowed: No
Course substitutions allowed: No
In what subjects: N/A

ADDITIONAL INFORMATION

Environment: The University is located on 125 acres in a suburban setting.

Student Body
   Undergrad enrollment: 4,727
   Female: 57%
   Male: 43%
   Out-of-state: 22%

Cost Information
   Tuition: $19,600
   Room & board: $7,608
Housing Information
   University housing: Yes
   Percent living on campus: 51%

Greek System
   Fraternity: Yes
   Sorority: Yes
Athletics: NCAA Division I

REEDLEY COLLEGE

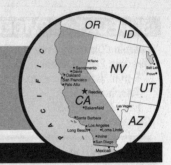

995 N. Reed Ave., Reedley, CA 93654
Phone: 559-638-3641, ext. 3624 • Fax: 559-638-5040
E-mail: letty.alvarez@scccd.com • Web: www.rc.cc.ca.us
Support level: CS • Institution type: 2-year private

LEARNING DISABILITY PROGRAM AND SERVICES

The Disabled Student Program & Services (DSP&S) focuses on abilities, not disabilities. DSP&S offers services to students with learning disabilities beyond those provided by conventional programs at the College and enables students to successfully pursue their individual educational, vocational, and personal goals. The Learning Disabilities Program assesses the needs and skill levels of each student, tailoring a specific educational course of study designed to bring out the best in an individual at a college level. The instructional program in reading, writing, math, and other academics prepares students to function in the classroom, in their chosen vocation, and throughout life. The LD Program provides special instruction and attention for students with specific educational needs available in mainstream classes.

LD/ADHD ADMISSIONS INFORMATION

College entrance tests required: No
Nonstandardized tests accepted: Yes
Interview required: No
Essay required: No
Documentation required for LD: Psychoeducational evaluation
Documentation required for ADHD: Yes
Submitted to: DSP&S
Special Ed. HS course work accepted: Yes

Specific course requirements for all applicants: No
Separate application required for services: No
# of LD applications submitted yearly: N/A
# of LD applications accepted yearly: N/A
Total # of students receiving LD/ADHD services: 200
Acceptance into program means acceptance into college: Students must be admitted and enrolled in the College and then request services.

ADMISSIONS
Reedley is an open-door admission college. Students must present a high school diploma or equivalent. There is no minimum GPA or required courses required for admission. ACT/SAT tests are not required for admission. There is a separate application to access services for students with learning disabilities. This application, however, is submitted after admission.

ADDITIONAL INFORMATION
The LD Program offers the following services: LD assessments; small class sessions; adaptive instruction; matriculation and integration with mainstream classes; individualized student contact; and specialized educational counseling. In addition students can access the following accommodations if they provide appropriate documentation: the use of calculators, dictionary, computer or spellcheck in exams; extended time on tests; scribes; proctors; oral exams; notetakers; tape recorder in class; books on tape; assistive technology; three LD specialists; and priority registration. American Sign Language may be substituted for foreign language and students are responsible for providing information about their disability to their professors.

SUPPORT SERVICES CONTACT INFORMATION

Learning Disability Program/Services: Disabled Students Program & Services (DSP&S)
Director: Dr. Janice Emerzian
  E-mail: emerzian@lightspeed.net
  Telephone: 559-442-8237
  Fax: 539-485-7304
Contact: Same

LEARNING DISABILITY SERVICES

Requests for the following services/accommodations will be evaluated individually based on appropriate and current documentation.

Allowed in Exams
  Calculator: Yes
  Dictionary: Yes
  Computer: Yes
  Spellchecker: Yes
Extended test time: Yes
Scribes: Yes
Proctors: Yes
Oral exams: Yes
Notetakers: Yes

Distraction-reduced environment: Yes
Tape recording in class: Yes
Books on tape from RFBD: Yes
Taping of books not from RFBD: Yes
Accommodations for students with ADHD: Yes
Reading machine: Yes
Other assistive technology: Yes
Priority registration: Yes

Added costs for services: No
LD specialists: Yes
Professional tutors: 2
Peer tutors: 30
Max. hours/wk. for services: Unlimited
How professors are notified of LD/ADHD: By student

GENERAL ADMISSIONS INFORMATION

Director of Admissions: Letty Alvarez
Telephone: 559-638-0323

ENTRANCE REQUIREMENTS
Open door admissions. High school diploma or GED required. No SAT/ ACT required.

Application deadline: August 18
Notification: Rolling
Average GPA: NR

Average SAT I Math: NR
Average SAT I Verbal: NR
Average ACT: NR

Graduated top 10% of class: NR
Graduated top 25% of class: NR
Graduated top 50% of class: NR

COLLEGE GRADUATION REQUIREMENTS

Course waivers allowed: N/A
Course substitutions allowed: N/A
In what subjects: N/A

ADDITIONAL INFORMATION

Environment: The College is located 30 miles southeast of Fresno.

Student Body
  Undergrad enrollment: 10,078
  Female: 61%
  Male: 39%
  Out-of-state: 3%

Cost Information
  In-state tuition: $352
  Out-of-state tuition: $4,252
  Room & board: $3,820
Housing Information
  University housing: Yes
  Percent living on campus: NR

Greek System
  Fraternity: No
  Sorority: No
Athletics: NJCAA

SAN DIEGO STATE UNIVERSITY

5500 Campanile Drive, San Diego, CA 92182-7455
Phone: 619-594-7800 • Fax: 619-594-4802
E-mail: admissions@sdsu.edu • Web: www.sdsu.edu
Support level: CS • Institution type: 4-year public

LEARNING DISABILITY PROGRAM AND SERVICES

The Learning Disability Program at San Diego State is under the umbrella of Disabled Student Services. The LD Program is designed to provide assessment, accommodations, and advocacy. Students must provide documentation prior to receiving services. Students with learning disabilities may be assessed using nationally standardized batteries. The University believes that students with learning disabilities can be successful at San Diego State and will try to provide the appropriate services to foster their success.

LD/ADHD ADMISSIONS INFORMATION

College entrance tests required: Yes
Nonstandardized tests accepted: Yes
Interview required: No
Essay required: No
Documentation required for LD: WAIS-III; WJ
Documentation required for ADHD: Yes
Documentation submitted to: DSS
Special Ed. HS course work accepted: No

Specific course requirements for all applicants: Yes
Separate application required for services: No
# of LD applications submitted yearly: N/A
# of LD applications accepted yearly: N/A
Total # of students receiving LD/ADHD services: 520
Acceptance into program means acceptance into college: Students must be admitted to the University first and then may request services.

ADMISSIONS

Students with learning disabilities who are not admissible by the general admission criteria or who are denied admission may request a review through special admission. Students need to write a letter to the director of the LD Program explaining why they feel they should be admitted. Three recommendations are required for special admit. No student will be admitted with a GPA below 2.0. Students must provide documentation verifying the disability and meeting the California State definition of a learning disability. The director of Disabled Student Services reviews documentation and makes a recommendation to the Admissions Office.

ADDITIONAL INFORMATION

Students are encouraged to get volunteer note-takers from among other students enrolled in the class. Students with learning disabilities may request permission to tape a lecture. Students will also need permission from the professor to use a calculator, dictionary, computer, or spellchecker in exams. Tutoring services are provided at no charge. High-Tech Center is a learning center available for all students with disabilities. Services and accommodations are available for undergraduates and graduate students.

SUPPORT SERVICES CONTACT INFORMATION

Learning Disability Program/Services: Disabled Student Services
Director: Margo Behr
  E-mail: mbehr@mail.sdsu.edu
  Telephone: 619-594-6473
  Fax: 619-594-4315
Contact: Same

LEARNING DISABILITY SERVICES

Requests for the following services/accommodations will be evaluated individually based on appropriate and current documentation.

Allowed in Exams
  Calculator: Y/N
  Dictionary: Y/N
  Computer: Y/N
  Spellchecker: Y/N
Extended test time: Yes
Scribes: No
Proctors: Yes
Oral exams: No
Notetakers: Yes

Distraction-reduced environment: Yes
Tape recording in class: Yes
Books on tape from RFBD: Yes
Taping of books not from RFBD: Yes
Accommodations for students with ADHD: Yes
Reading machine: Yes
Priority registration: Yes

Added costs for services: No
LD specialists: Yes (2.5)
Professional tutors: No
Peer tutors: Yes
Max. hours/wk. for services: Depends on need
How professors are notified of LD/ADHD: By the student

GENERAL ADMISSIONS INFORMATION

Director of Admissions: Sandra Cook
Telephone: 619-594-5200

ENTRANCE REQUIREMENTS

15 total are required; 4 English required, 3 math required, 1 science required, 1 science lab required, 2 science lab recommended, 2 foreign language required, 1 social studies recommended, 1 history required, 3 elective required. High school diploma or GED required. Minimum TOEFL is 550. TOEFL required of all international applicants.

Application deadline: November 30
Notification: Rolling beginning 3/1
Average GPA: 3.4

Average SAT I Math: 532
Average SAT I Verbal: 512
Average ACT: 21

Graduated top 10% of class: NR
Graduated top 25% of class: NR
Graduated top 50% of class: NR

COLLEGE GRADUATION REQUIREMENTS

Course waivers allowed: Yes
Course substitutions allowed: Yes
In what subjects: Substitutions allowed based on attempts and disability-related services

ADDITIONAL INFORMATION

Environment: San Diego State is located on 300 acres 12 miles from the ocean.

Student Body
  Undergrad enrollment: 25,658
  Female: 57%
  Male: 43%
  Out-of-state: 3%

Cost Information
  In-state tuition: $1,776
  Out-of-state tuition: $9,156
  Room & board: $7,586
Housing Information
  University housing: Yes
  Percent living on campus: 11%

Greek System
  Fraternity: Yes
  Sorority: Yes
Athletics: NCAA Division I

SAN FRANCISCO STATE UNIVERSITY

1600 Holloway Avenue, Adm. 154, San Francisco, CA 94132
Phone: 415-338-1113 • Fax: 415-338-3880
E-mail: ugadmit@sfsu.edu • Web: www.sfsu.edu
Support level: CS • Institution type: 4-year public

LEARNING DISABILITY PROGRAM AND SERVICES

The Disability Resource Center (DRC) is available to promote and provide equal access to the classroom and to campus-related activities. A full range of support services is provided in order that students may define and achieve personal autonomy at SFSU. The staff is sensitive to the diversity of disabilities, including those only recently recognized as disabilities requiring reasonable accommodations. Confidential support services are available for all students with a verified temporary or permanent disability who are enrolled at the University. All students registered with DRC are eligible for disability management advising. This consists of helping students access services from DRC; manage DRC services and school in general; problem solve conflicts/concerns that are disability-related with individuals, programs, and services on campus; and understand "reasonable accommodation" under the law. The DRC seizes every opportunity to educate the campus community about reasonable accommodations for students with disabilities. Generally the campus community is sensitive, but if an oversight occurs, students do have protection under Section 504 and ADA. Students are encouraged to contact DRC for guidance in pursuing a grievance. Resolution of a violation can often be achieved informally without completing the formal grievance procedure.

LD/ADHD ADMISSIONS INFORMATION

College entrance tests required: Yes
Nonstandardized tests accepted: Yes
Interview required: Yes
Essay required: No
Documentation required for LD: Psychoeducational evaluation
Documentation required for ADHD: Yes
Documentation submitted to: DRC
Special Ed. HS course work accepted: Yes, case-by-case

Specific course requirements for all applicants: Yes
Separate application required for services: Yes
# of LD applications submitted yearly: N/A
# of LD applications accepted yearly: N/A
Total # of students receiving LD/ADHD services: 300–400
Acceptance into program means acceptance into college: Students must be admitted and enrolled at the University first and then may request services.

ADMISSIONS

All students should apply through the regular admission process. General admission requirements include 4 years English, 3 years math, 2 year science, 2 years foreign language, 1 year history, 3 years electives. Students must also meet the in-state or out-of-state eligibility index based on test scores and GPA. Students not admissible because of a disability may request special admissions assistance from DRC. To obtain DRC assistance, students must register with DRC, provide documentation, and notify Admissions that DRC has appropriate verification. Admissions will consult with DRC before making a decision. Students with LD who are judged unable to fulfill specific requirements may take course substitutions in math, foreign language, or science. Substitutions are authorized on an individual basis after review and recommendation by the high school or community college counselor. Students taking substitutions must have 15 units of college-prep study. High school case managers may write summaries and provide a clinical judgment. DRC wants information about achievement deficits and may require the student to attend an admissions interview.

ADDITIONAL INFORMATION

The Disability Resource Center can arrange for test accommodations and note-takers and will advocate for the student. The staff is very involved and offers comprehensive services through a team approach. There are no developmental courses offered at the University. However, there are skills classes. Students with documented learning disabilities may request assistance in locating tutors. Other services may include registration assistance, campus orientation, note-takers, readers, test-taking assistance, tutoring, disability-related counseling, and referral information.

SUPPORT SERVICES CONTACT INFORMATION

Learning Disability Program/Services: Disability Resource Center
Director: Deidre Defreese
  E-mail: defreese@sfs.edu
  Telephone: 415-338-6356
  Fax: 415-338-1041
Contact: Same

LEARNING DISABILITY SERVICES

Requests for the following services/accommodations will be evaluated individually based on appropriate and current documentation.

Allowed in Exams
  Calculator: Yes
  Dictionary: Yes
  Computer: Yes
  Spellchecker: Yes
Extended test time: Yes
Scribes: Yes
Proctors: Yes
Oral exams: Yes
Notetakers: Yes

Distraction-reduced environment: Yes
Tape recording in class: Yes
Books on tape from RFBD: Yes
Taping of books not from RFBD: No
Accommodations for students with ADHD: Yes
Reading machine: Yes
Other assistive technology: Yes
Priority registration: Yes

Added costs for services: No
LD specialists: Yes (2)
Professional tutors: No
Peer tutors: Yes
Max. hours/wk. for services: Limited
How professors are notified of LD/ADHD: By student

GENERAL ADMISSIONS INFORMATION

Director of Admissions: Patricia Schofield
Telephone: 415-338-2037

ENTRANCE REQUIREMENTS

3 English required, 3 math required, 1 science required, 1 science lab required, 2 foreign language required, 1 history required, 3 elective required. High school diploma or GED required. Minimum TOEFL is 550. TOEFL required of all international applicants.

Application deadline: August 1
Notification: Rolling beginning 12/15
Average GPA: 3.1

Average SAT I Math: 485
Average SAT I Verbal: 466
Average ACT: 19

Graduated top 10% of class: NR
Graduated top 25% of class: NR
Graduated top 50% of class: NR

COLLEGE GRADUATION REQUIREMENTS

Course waivers allowed: Yes
Course substitutions allowed: Yes
In what subjects: Determined on a case-by-case basis

ADDITIONAL INFORMATION

Environment: The school is located in downtown San Francisco on a 130-acre campus.

Student Body
  Undergrad enrollment: 21,044
  Female: 59%
  Male: 41%
  Out-of-state: 1%

Cost Information
  In-state tuition: $1,904
  Out-of-state tuition: $7,802
  Room & board: $6,720
Housing Information
  University housing: Yes
  Percent living on campus: 5%

Greek System
  Fraternity: Yes
  Sorority: Yes
Athletics: NCAA Division II

SAN JOSE STATE UNIVERSITY

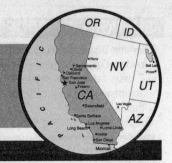

1 Washington Square, San Jose, CA 95112-0009
Phone: 408-283-7500 • Fax: 408-924-2050
E-mail: contact@.sjsu.edu • Web: www.sjsu.edu
Support level: CS • Institution type: 4-year public

LEARNING DISABILITY PROGRAM AND SERVICES

The goal of the Disability Resource Center is to provide appropriate academic adjustments and support services to students with disabilities while training them to become self-advocates and to develop maximum independence. The Disability Resource Center provides services to students and consultation to faculty to educate every department so that they best serve students with disabilities.

LD/ADHD ADMISSIONS INFORMATION

College entrance tests required: Yes
Nonstandardized tests accepted: Yes
Interview required: No
Essay required: No
Documentation required for LD: WAIS-III; WJ
Documentation required for ADHD: Yes
Documentation submitted to: DRC
Special Ed. HS course work accepted: No

Specific course requirements for all applicants: Yes
Separate application required for services: No
# of LD applications submitted yearly: N/A
# of LD applications accepted yearly: N/A
Total # of students receiving LD/ADHD services: 600
Acceptance into program means acceptance into college: Students must be admitted and enrolled at the University first and then may request services.

ADMISSIONS

Students with learning disabilities apply directly to the Admissions Office; there is no special handling of the student's applications through the DRC. All assessments and disability verifications go directly to DRC for establishment of a confidential file. (The assessment should include the WJ-R Parts 1 & 2 or the WAIS and WJ-R Part 2, and other skills tests.) Students must have at least a 2.0 GPA, and a sliding scale is used combining GPA and test scores. Only courses from grades 10–12 are used to compute GPA. High school courses required are: 4 years English, 3 years math, 1 year lab science, 1 year U.S. history, 2 years foreign language, 1 year visual and performing arts, and 3 years electives. Foreign language admission requirements can be waived for students with learning disabilities if their high school sends a letter stating that other college-prep courses have been substituted for the foreign language. Those students not meeting general entrance criteria can petition the Exceptional Admissions Committee of the Admissions Office. These students must submit a personal statement and two letters of recommendation, plus disclosure of their learning disability, to be eligible for special consideration. The Admissions Committee has a representative from Disabled Student Services.

ADDITIONAL INFORMATION

No skills courses are offered by DRC, nor is tutoring offered by DRC. Referral for skills courses and tutoring is made to regular university services. Recent changes in CSU policy require that any remediation needed in math and English be cleared during the student's first year if he or she enters as a freshman. Transfer students must have completed Oral Communication, English 1A equivalent, critical thinking, and math past intermediate algebra. Books on tape are provided through RFB. Students who request the use of a calculator in an exam will need to secure permission from the professor, as well as have appropriate documentation identifying that this is a necessary accommodation to compensate for the disability. Students who are transferring to San Jose State University from another campus in California do not need to provide new documentation of the learning disability.

SUPPORT SERVICES CONTACT INFORMATION

Learning Disability Program/Services: Disability Resource Center (DRC)
Director: Martin Schulter
  E-mail: marty@drc.sjsu.edu
  Telephone: 408-924-6000
  Fax: 408-924-5999
Contact: Donna Ellis
  E-mail: donna@drc.sjsu.edu
  Telephone: 408-924-6000

LEARNING DISABILITY SERVICES

Requests for the following services/accommodations will be evaluated individually based on appropriate and current documentation.

Allowed in Exams
  Calculator: Y/N
  Dictionary: Y/N
  Computer: Yes
  Spellchecker: Yes
Extended test time: Yes
Scribes: Yes
Proctors: Yes
Oral exams: Yes
Notetakers: Yes

Distraction-reduced environment: Yes
Tape recording in class: Yes
Books on tape from RFBD: Yes
Taping of books not from RFBD: Yes
Accommodations for students with ADHD: Yes
Reading machine: Yes
Other assistive technology: Yes
Priority registration: Yes

Added costs for services: No
LD specialists: Yes (1)
Professional tutors: No
Peer tutors: No
Max. hours/wk. for services: Case-by-case
How professors are notified of LD/ADHD: By the student

GENERAL ADMISSIONS INFORMATION

Director of Admissions: John Bradbury
Telephone: 408-924-1000

ENTRANCE REQUIREMENTS

4 English required, 3 math required, 1 science required, 1 science lab required, 2 foreign language required, 1 history required, 3 elective required. High school diploma or GED required. Minimum TOEFL is 550. TOEFL required of all international applicants.

Application deadline: Rolling
Notification: Rolling
Average GPA: 2.0–2.9

Average SAT I Math: 510
Average SAT I Verbal: 472
Average ACT: 20

Graduated top 10% of class: NR
Graduated top 25% of class: NR
Graduated top 50% of class: NR

COLLEGE GRADUATION REQUIREMENTS

Course waivers allowed: No
Course substitutions allowed: Yes
In what subjects: General education quantitative reasoning substitutions made on a case-by-case basis

ADDITIONAL INFORMATION

Environment: The University is located on 117 acres in an urban area in the center of San Jose.

Student Body
  Undergrad enrollment: 20,679
  Female: 51%
  Male: 49%
  Out-of-state: 2%

Cost Information
  In-state tuition: $1,900
  Out-of-state tuition: $9,800
  Room & board: $6,534
Housing Information
  University housing: Yes
  Percent living on campus: 10%

Greek System
  Fraternity: Yes
  Sorority: Yes
Athletics: NCAA Division I

SANTA CLARA UNIVERSITY

500 El Camino Real, Santa Clara, CA 95053
Phone: 406-554-4700 • Fax: 408-554-5255
E-mail: ugadmissions@scu.edu • Web: www.scu.edu
Support level: CS • Institution type: 4-year private

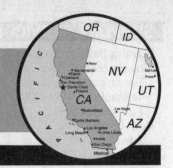

LEARNING DISABILITY PROGRAM AND SERVICES

The primary mission of Disabilities Resources is to enhance academic progress, promote social involvement, and build bridges connecting the various services of the University for all students. This goal is met by providing academic intervention programs; opportunities to increase students' personal understanding of their disability; role models; and community outreach. Disabilities Resources is a resource area within the Drahmann Center that helps to ensure equal access to all academic and programmatic activities for students with disabilities. This goal is met through the provision of Academic Support Services, contact with other university offices, educational programming on disability issues for the University, and, most importantly, assistance in teaching students effective self-advocacy skills under the student development model. Students with disabilities must have documentation of their disability from a qualified professional.

LD/ADHD ADMISSIONS INFORMATION

College entrance tests required: Yes
Nonstandardized tests accepted: Yes
Interview required: No
Essay required: Yes
Documentation required for LD: Psychoeducational evaluation
Documentation required for ADHD: Yes
Documentation submitted to: Disability Resources
Special Ed. HS course work accepted: No

Specific course requirements for all applicants: Yes
Separate application required for services: No
# of LD applications submitted yearly: N/A
# of LD applications accepted yearly: N/A
Total # of students receiving LD/ADHD services: 125
Acceptance into program means acceptance into college: Students must be accepted and enrolled at the University first and then may request services.

ADMISSIONS

All students submit the same general application. Santa Clara takes pride in the personal nature of its admission process. All applicants are carefully reviewed. Freshman applicants are offered admission based upon (1) high school record; (2) ACT/SAT; (3) recommendations; and (4) personal factors. Applicants submitting a nonstandardized ACT/SAT are encouraged to write a personal statement to assist the admission committee in evaluating the application.

ADDITIONAL INFORMATION

The Disabilities Resources staff meets individually with students. Some of the academic accommodations provided by DSR include note-taking, library assistance, proofreading, and test accommodations. Other support services include priority registration; tutoring or academic counseling; and workshops on legal issues and self-advocacy. The DR is in the process of purchasing computer-aided technology to assist the students. Graduate students with learning disabilities are offered the same services and accommodations as those provided for undergraduate students. Students can be better served if the professional documentation they submit specifically identifies the accommodations needed for the student to be successful in college. This should include the student's strengths and weaknesses and any required modifications. All students have access to peer tutoring, drop-in-math lab, and a drop-in-writing center.

SUPPORT SERVICES CONTACT INFORMATION

Learning Disability Program/Services: Disability Resources (DR)
Director: Ann Ravenscroft, Coordinator
   E-mail: eravenscroft@scu.edu
   Telephone: 408-554-4111
   Fax: 408-554-2709
Contact: Same

LEARNING DISABILITY SERVICES

Requests for the following services/accommodations will be evaluated individually based on appropriate and current documentation.

Allowed in Exams
   Calculator: Yes
   Dictionary: Yes
   Computer: Yes
   Spellchecker: Yes
Extended test time: Yes
Scribes: Yes
Proctors: Yes
Oral exams: Yes
Notetakers: Yes

Distraction-reduced environment: Yes
Tape recording in class: Yes
Books on tape from RFBD: Yes
Taping of books not from RFBD: Yes
**Accommodations for students with
   ADHD:** Yes
Reading machine: No
Other assistive technology: Yes
Priority registration: Yes

Added costs for services: No
LD specialists: Yes (1)
Professional tutors: No
Peer tutors: Yes
Max. hours/wk. for services: 1 hour
   per course or more if necessary
**How professors are notified of
   LD/ADHD:** By both student and
   director

GENERAL ADMISSIONS INFORMATION

Director of Admissions: Sandra Hayes
Telephone: 406-554-4000

ENTRANCE REQUIREMENTS

17 total are required; 26 total are recommended; 4 English required, 4 English recommended, 4 math required, 4 math recommended, 3 science required, 4 science recommended, 1 science lab required, 2 science lab recommended, 4 foreign language required, 4 foreign language recommended, 1 social studies required, 2 social studies recommended, 1 history required, 2 history recommended, 2 elective required, 4 elective recommended. High school diploma is required and GED is not accepted. TOEFL required of all international applicants.

Application deadline: January 15
Notification: Rolling beginning 12/1
Average GPA: 3.6

Average SAT I Math: 618
Average SAT I Verbal: 601
Average ACT: NR

Graduated top 10% of class: 43%
Graduated top 25% of class: 80%
Graduated top 50% of class: 97%

COLLEGE GRADUATION REQUIREMENTS

Course waivers allowed: No
Course substitutions allowed: Yes
In what subjects: Foreign language and math, all decided on an individual basis

ADDITIONAL INFORMATION

Environment: The University is located 1 hour south of San Francisco in "Silicon Valley," 3 miles from San Jose airport and 4 hours from Lake Tahoe.

Student Body
   Undergrad enrollment: 4,308
   Female: 54%
   Male: 46%
   Out-of-state: 31%

Cost Information
   Tuition: $19,776
   Room & board: $8,034
Housing Information
   University housing: Yes
   Percent living on campus: 58%

Greek System
   Fraternity: Yes
   Sorority: Yes
Athletics: NCAA Division I

SANTA ROSA JUNIOR COLLEGE

1501 Mendocino Avenue, Santa Rosa, CA 95401
Phone: 707-527-4685 • Fax: 707-524-1768
E-mail: admininfo@santarose.edu • Web: www.santarosa.edu
Support: CS • Institution: 2-year public

LEARNING DISABILITY PROGRAM AND SERVICES

The Disability Resources Department provides students with disabilities equal access to a community college education through specialized instruction, disability-related support services, and advocacy activities. Santa Rosa Junior College is a state-supported school that accepts all students with learning disabilities who apply and meet the mandatory state eligibility requirements that verify their learning disability. If a student is eligible for the program, an Individualized Educational Plan is developed and implemented. Students may participate in a combination of special and mainstream college classes with appropriate support services as needed. The College encourages and fosters autonomy, independence, and responsibility in students with disabilities and challenges them to become self-advocates. The College also creates a campus climate in which diverse learning styles are respected and equal access for students with disabilities can be realized.

LD/ADHD ADMISSIONS INFORMATION

College entrance tests required: No
Nonstandardized tests accepted: Yes
Interview required: No
Essay required: No
Documentation required for LD: WAIS-III, Woodcock-Johnson
Documentation required for ADHD: Yes
Submitted to: Disability Resources Department
Special Ed. HS course work accepted: Yes

Specific course requirements for all applicants: No
Separate application required for services: No
# of LD applications submitted yearly: 50–100
# of LD applications accepted yearly: 100–300
Total # of students receiving LD/ADHD services: 30–40
Acceptance into program means acceptance into college: Students must be admitted and enrolled at the College first and then may request services.

ADMISSIONS

Admission to Santa Rosa is open to students with a high school diploma or a GED. There are no specific requirements for admission. Students with learning disabilities must meet state eligibility requirements verifying a learning disability to qualify to receive services. Students must demonstrate: average to above-average intellectual ability, adequate measured achievement in at least one academic area or employment setting, a severe processing deficit in one or more areas, a severe discrepancy between aptitude and achievement in one or more academic areas, and adaptive behavior appropriate to a college setting. Students may also qualify on the basis of a communicative disorder and head injuries. All students must demonstrate appropriate behavior and an ability to benefit from the instructional program.

ADDITIONAL INFORMATION

The Learning Skills Program offers small specialized classes in the following areas for nontransferable credit: basic academic skills, guidance/independent living, sensory-motor integration, and speech and language. Support services include assessment for learning disabilities, counseling, tutoring, speech/language skills development, and liaison. Skills classes are offered in spelling, writing, math, study strategies, computers, and art process. All of these courses may be taken for college credit.

SUPPORT SERVICES CONTACT INFORMATION

Learning Disability Program/Services: Disability Resources Dept.
Director: Kari Vigeland
  E-mail: kvigeland@santarosa.edu
  Telephone: 707-527-4278
  Fax: 707-524-1768
Contact: Marcie Baer
  E-mail: mbaer@santarosa.edu
  Telephone: 707-527-4278
  Fax: 707-527-4685

LEARNING DISABILITY SERVICES

Requests for the following services/accommodations will be evaluated individually based on appropriate and current documentation.

Allowed in Exams
  Calculator: Yes
  Dictionary: Yes
  Computer: Yes
  Spellchecker: Yes
Extended test time: Yes
Scribes: Yes
Proctors: Yes
Oral exams: Yes
Notetakers: Yes

Distraction-reduced environment: Yes
Tape recording in class: Yes
Books on tape from RFBD: Yes
Taping of books not from RFBD: Yes
Accommodations for students with ADHD: Yes
Reading machine: Yes
Other assistive technology: Yes
Priority registration: Yes

Added costs for services: No
LD specialists: Yes
Professional tutors: 10
Peer tutors: No
Max. hours/wk. for services: Decided on an individual basis
How professors are notified of LD/ADHD: By student and LD specialist

GENERAL ADMISSIONS INFORMATION

Director of Admissions: Ricardo Navarrette
Telephone: 707-527-4685

ENTRANCE REQUIREMENTS
High school diploma or GED is accepted. ACT/SAT not required.

Application deadline: Rolling
Notification: Rolling
Average GPA: NR

Average SAT I Math: NR
Average SAT I Verbal: NR
Average ACT: NR

Graduated top 10% of class: NR
Graduated top 25% of class: NR
Graduated top 50% of class: NR

COLLEGE GRADUATION REQUIREMENTS

Course waivers allowed: Yes
Course substitutions allowed: Yes
In what subjects: Math; after student attempts regular math courses

ADDITIONAL INFORMATION

Environment: The College is located on 93 acres with easy access to San Francisco.

Student Body
  Undergrad enrollment: 28,223
  Female: 59%
  Male: 41%
  Out-of-state: 2%

Cost Information
  In-state tuition: $315
  Out-of-state tuition: $3,630
  Room & board: $2,035
Housing Information
  University housing: Yes
  Percent living on campus: 22%

Greek System
  Fraternity: Yes
  Sorority: Yes
Athletics: Intercollegiate

SIERRA COLLEGE

5000 Rocklin Road, Rocklin, CA 95677
Phone: 916-624-3333 • Fax: 916-781-0403
Web: www.sierra.cc.ca.us
Support: CS • Institution: 2-year public

LEARNING DISABILITY PROGRAM AND SERVICES

The goals of the program are to assist students with learning disabilities in reaching their academic/vocational goals, and to help the students strengthen and develop their perceptual skills; and to provide the support needed to maximize student success. Sierra College subscribes to the psychometric-evaluation model established by the California Community College System. This six-step process includes: (1) intake screening; (2) measured achievement; (3) ability level; (4) processing deficit; (5) aptitude-achievement discrepancy; and (6) eligibility recommendation. Students are evaluated individually through the Learning Disabilities Orientation course. This is a mainstreamed program with no special classes, but it does provide support and accommodations for students with learning disabilities.

LD/ADHD ADMISSIONS INFORMATION

College entrance tests required: No
Nonstandardized tests accepted: Yes
Interview required: No
Essay required: No
Documentation required for LD: WAIS-III; WJ
Documentation required for ADHD: Yes
Submitted to: Learning Opportunities Center
Special Ed. HS course work accepted: Yes

Specific course requirements for all applicants: No
Separate application required for services: No
# of LD applications submitted yearly: N/A
# of LD applications accepted yearly: N/A
Total # of students receiving LD/ADHD services: 400+
Acceptance into program means acceptance into college: Students must be admitted and enrolled at the College first and then may request services.

ADMISSIONS

Sierra College has an open admissions policy for those students who meet the regular entrance requirements and who have completed testing and evaluation by a learning disabilities specialist. ACT/SAT are not required, and there are no cutoffs for GPA, class rank, or test scores. Additionally, no specific courses are required for admission. Any student who holds a high school diploma or GED is admitted. Services are provided to all enrolled students with appropriate documentation.

ADDITIONAL INFORMATION

In order to receive services and accommodations, students must meet the eligibility requirements set forth by the state of California for students with learning disabilities. Skills courses are available in reading, math, writing, study strategies, English as a Second Language, and spelling. These skills classes are offered for college credit. In addition, students can get assistance in test-taking techniques, priority registration, and peer tutoring. Other services include assessment and evaluation of learning disabilities; individual education plans; identification of students' learning styles and modalities; perceptual training programs; test-taking facilitation; compensatory learning strategies/techniques; computer-assisted instruction; and classroom accommodations.

SUPPORT SERVICES CONTACT INFORMATION

Learning Disability Program/Services: Learning Opportunites Center
Director: Dr. Jim Hirschinger
  E-mail: jhirschinger@scmail.sierra.cc.ca.us
  Telephone: 916-781-0599
  Fax: 916-789-2967
Contact: Denise Stone
  E-mail: dstone@scmail.sierra.cc.ca.us
  Telephone: 916-789-2697
  Fax: 916-789-2967

LEARNING DISABILITY SERVICES

Requests for the following services/accommodations will be evaluated individually based on appropriate and current documentation.

Allowed in Exams
  Calculator: Yes
  Dictionary: Yes
  Computer: Yes
  Spellchecker: Yes
Extended test time: Yes
Scribes: No
Proctors: Yes
Oral exams: Yes
Notetakers: Yes

Distraction-reduced environment: Yes
Tape recording in class: Yes
Books on tape from RFBD: Yes
Taping of books not from RFBD: Yes
Accommodations for students with ADHD: Yes
Reading machine: No
Other assistive technology: Yes
Priority registration: Yes

Added costs for services: No
LD specialists: 3
Professional tutors: No
Peer tutors: 100
Max. hours/wk. for services: Unlimited
How professors are notified of LD/ADHD: By student and program director

GENERAL ADMISSIONS INFORMATION

Director of Admissions: Mandy Davis
Telephone: 916-781-0525

ENTRANCE REQUIREMENTS
High school diploma or GED is accepted. ACT/SAT not required for admission.

Application deadline: Rolling
Notification: Rolling
Average GPA: NR

Average SAT I Math: NR
Average SAT I Verbal: NR
Average ACT: NR

Graduated top 10% of class: NR
Graduated top 25% of class: NR
Graduated top 50% of class: NR

COLLEGE GRADUATION REQUIREMENTS

Course waivers allowed: Yes
Course substitutions allowed: Yes
In what subjects: Waivers or substitutions are provided on an individual basis.

ADDITIONAL INFORMATION

Environment: The school is located on a 327-acre campus in a rural setting with easy access to Sacramento.

Student Body
  Undergrad enrollment: 17,000
  Female: 56%
  Male: 44%
  Out-of-state: 1%

Cost Information
  In-state tuition: $410
  Out-of-state tuition: $3,120
  Room & board: $4,892
Housing Information
  University housing: Yes
  Percent living on campus: 1%

Greek System
  Fraternity: Yes
  Sorority: Yes
  Athletics: Intercollegiate

SONOMA STATE UNIVERSITY

1801 East Cotati Avenue, Rohnert Park, CA 94928
Phone: 707-664-2778 • Fax: 707-664-2060
E-mail: admitme.@sonoma.edu • Web: www.sonoma.edu
Support level: S • Institution type: 4-year public

LEARNING DISABILITY PROGRAM AND SERVICES

The goal of the Disabled Student Services is to provide reasonable accommodations and equal access to the educational process while helping students with disabilities become self-advocates. Services at Sonoma State University are provided primarily through two offices on campus. DSS offers support services and advocacy, and Learning Skills Services provides academic support and skill development. One-to-one sessions and workshops are given by specialists in various subject areas. In addition, a campus Tutorial Program offers individual peer tutoring. Appropriate documentation for LD/ADHD student is required and must be completed by a qualified professional. The documentation should be submitted to DSS.

LD/ADHD ADMISSIONS INFORMATION

College entrance tests required: Yes
Nonstandardized tests accepted: Yes
Interview required: No
Essay required: No
Documentation required for LD: Psychoeducational evaluation, WAIS-III
Documentation required for ADHD: Yes
Documentation submitted to: Disabled Student Services
Special Ed. HS course work accepted: No

Specific course requirements for all applicants: Yes
Separate application required for services: Yes
# of LD applications submitted yearly: 40–50
# of LD applications accepted yearly: 20–25
Total # of students receiving LD/ADHD services: 170–230
Acceptance into program means acceptance into college: Students must be admitted and enrolled at the University first and then may register for services.

ADMISSIONS

Admission is based on a combination of high school GPA, test scores, and college-preparatory classes. Required courses include 4 years English, 3 years math, 1 year social studies, 1 year science, 2 years foreign language, 1 year visual or performing arts, and 3 electives. SAT/ACT score requirements depend on the GPA. However, a 2.0 GPA is the absolute minimum. Students with learning disabilities submit a general application. If a limited number of required courses are missing, students can be granted a conditional admission and these courses must be made up in college. Students not meeting either regular or conditional admission may initiate a request for special admission by writing a letter to the DSS director providing information about strengths, weaknesses, and why special admission is needed. LD diagnostic evaluation and 2 letters of recommendation are also required for conditional admission. All special admission applicants are interviewed in person or by phone. Special admission is only available to designated groups of students. Special admission applicants need to submit a letter to Linda Lipps describing what subject areas are missing or if the GPA or SAT/ACT are low. The staff of DSS makes recommendations, but the final decision is made by the Office of Admission.

ADDITIONAL INFORMATION

DSS does not offer skills classes or tutoring. Reading, writing, and math are offered through the Learning Skills Services. Tutorial assistance is available in the Tutorial Center. There are no LD specialists in the DSS; however, there are disability management advisors who authorize accommodations. With appropriate documentation some of the services or accommodations offered include: the use of calculators, dictionary, computer or spellchecker in exams; extended time on tests; scribes; proctors; oral exams; note-takers; distraction-free testing environments; tape recorder in class; taped text; and priority registration.

SUPPORT SERVICES CONTACT INFORMATION

Learning Disability Program/Services: Disabled Student Services (DSS)
Director: Linda Lipps
  Telephone: 707-664-2677
  Fax: 707-644-2505
Contact: Aurelia Melgar
  Telephone: 707-664-2677
  Fax: 707-644-2505

LEARNING DISABILITY SERVICES

Requests for the following services/accommodations will be evaluated individually based on appropriate and current documentation.

Allowed in Exams
  Calculator: Yes
  Dictionary: Yes
  Computer: Yes
  Spellchecker: Yes
Extended test time: Yes
Scribes: Yes
Proctors: Yes
Oral exams: Yes
Notetakers: Yes

Distraction-reduced environment: Yes
Tape recording in class: Yes
Books on tape from RFBD: Yes
Taping of books not from RFBD: Yes
Accommodations for students with
  ADHD: Yes
Reading machine: Yes
Other assistive technology: Yes
Priority registration: Yes

Added costs for services: No
LD specialists: No
Professional tutors: No
Peer tutors: 30–45
Max. hours/wk. for services: 4
How professors are notified of
  LD/ADHD: By student with verification from DSS

GENERAL ADMISSIONS INFORMATION

Director of Admissions: Dr. Katharyn Crabbe
Telephone: 707-664-2778

ENTRANCE REQUIREMENTS
16 total are required; 4 English required, 3 math required, 2 science required, 1 science lab required, 2 foreign language required, 1 history required, 3 elective required. High school diploma or GED required. Minimum TOEFL is 500. TOEFL required of all international applicants.

Application deadline: January 31
Notification: Rolling beginning 11/1
Average GPA: 3.2

Average SAT I Math: 514
Average SAT I Verbal: 513
Average ACT: NR

Graduated top 10% of class: 10%
Graduated top 25% of class: 40%
Graduated top 50% of class: 78%

COLLEGE GRADUATION REQUIREMENTS

Course waivers allowed: No
Course substitutions allowed: Yes, limited
In what subjects: Allowed in math by petition. The University offers an alternative math class to fulfill the general education requirement. May substitute foreign language only.

ADDITIONAL INFORMATION

Environment: The school is located on 220 acres with easy access to San Francisco.

Student Body
  Undergrad enrollment: 6,211
  Female: 65%
  Male: 35%
  Out-of-state: 3%

Cost Information
  In-state tuition: $2,130
  Out-of-state tuition: $9,400
  Room & board: $6,471
Housing Information
  University housing: Yes
  Percent living on campus: 31%

Greek System
  Fraternity: Yes
  Sorority: Yes
Athletics: NCAA Division II

UNIV. OF CALIFORNIA—BERKELEY

Office of Undergraduate Admission and Relations,
110 Sproul Hall #5800, Berkeley, CA 94720-5800
Phone: 510-642-3175 • Fax: 510-642-7333
E-mail: ouars@uclink.berkeley.edu • Web: www.berkeley.edu
Support level: CS • Institution type: 4-year public

LEARNING DISABILITY PROGRAM AND SERVICES

DSP seeks to ensure that students with disabilities have equal access to educational opportunities and student life at UC Berkeley. DSP works to sustain a supportive environment that provides appropriate and necessary disability-related accommodations, enables students to demonstrate their knowledge and skills, facilitates students' success in academic pursuits, and promotes independence. DSP's services assist students as they develop their skills and the qualities needed to meet their educational, personal, and professional goals. DSP also works to support the efforts of the campus community to ensure full participation of students with disabilities in every aspect of university life. DSP is a recipient of a TRIO Student Support Services Grant. Funds are used to provide a variety of services for students, helping them to complete graduation requirements and plan successful post-graduation educations or careers. For services, DSP must have verification of the disability on file. Students with LD must submit a psychoeducational evaluation done by a qualified professional. Students with ADHD must submit a certification form from a qualified professional who has an expertise in diagnosing ADHD in adults. Additional testing may be requested if it is deemed necessary for the planning and provision of appropriate accommodations and services.

LD/ADHD ADMISSIONS INFORMATION

College entrance tests required: Yes
Nonstandardized tests accepted: Yes
Interview required: No
Essay required: Yes
Documentation required for LD: WAIS-III; WJ; current
Documentation required for ADHD: Yes
Documentation submitted to: DSP
Special Ed. HS course work accepted: No

Specific course requirements for all applicants: Yes
Separate application required for services: No
# of LD applications submitted yearly: N/A
# of LD applications accepted yearly: N/A
Total # of students receiving LD/ADHD services: 242
Acceptance into program means acceptance into college: Students must be admitted and enrolled at the University first and then may request services.

ADMISSIONS

All applicants must submit the general application for admission, and are expected to meet the same standards as other students. The deadline for freshman applications is November 30. The University requires the SAT I or ACT and three SAT II tests (writing, math, and one other). Students with learning disabilities should submit a copy of their application for admission and verification of the disability to the DSP. The student will be asked to fill out a questionnaire explaining how the student's academic experience has been affected by the disability.

ADDITIONAL INFORMATION

DSP staff provide the following services: recommending and ensuring the provision of academic accommodations; consulting with instructors about accommodations; authorizing auxiliary services; teaching academic strategies and study skills; promoting on-campus awareness; academic advising; adaptive technology; support groups; a special section of the course "Facilitating Success" for students with LD and ADHD that centers on understanding learning differences, maximizing strengths, academic planning, research, writing, exam preparation, and using university resources; priority registration; specialist to help in developing problem-solving strategies and solutions to difficult problems; and a series of informational workshops on topics like understanding disabilities and individual learning styles, improving reading, writing, and research efficiency, memory strategies, self-advocacy, computer applications that facilitate learning, and career or graduate school planning. There are 242 students with LD and 100 students with ADD receiving services. Specialists may recommend a reduced course load.

SUPPORT SERVICES CONTACT INFORMATION

Learning Disability Program/Services: Disabled Student's Program (DSP)
Director: Ed Rogers
   E-mail: edrogers@uclink4.berkeley.edu
   Telephone: 510-642-0518
Contact: Connie Chiba
   E-mail: cchiba@uclink4.berkeley.edu
   Telephone: 510-642-0518
   Fax: 510-643-9686

LEARNING DISABILITY SERVICES

Requests for the following services/accommodations will be evaluated individually based on appropriate and current documentation.

Allowed in Exams
   Calculator: Yes
   Dictionary: Y/N
   Computer: Y/N
   Spellchecker: Yes
Extended test time: Yes
Scribes: Yes
Proctors: Y/N
Oral exams: Y/N
Notetakers: Yes

Distraction-reduced environment: Yes
Tape recording in class: Yes
Books on tape from RFBD: Yes
Taping of books not from RFBD: Yes
Accommodations for students with ADHD: Yes
Reading machine: Yes
Other assistive technology: Yes
Priority registration: Yes

Added costs for services: No
LD specialists: Yes (4)
Professional tutors: No
Peer tutors: Student Learning Center
Max. hours/wk. for services: Student Learning Center
How professors are notified of LD/ADHD: By student

GENERAL ADMISSIONS INFORMATION

Director of Admissions: Pamela Hicks
Telephone: 510-642-6442

ENTRANCE REQUIREMENTS

15 total are required; 19 total are recommended; 4 English required, 3 math required, 4 math recommended, 2 science required, 3 science recommended, 2 science lab required, 3 science lab recommended, 2 foreign language required, 3 foreign language recommended, 2 history required, 2 elective required. SAT I and SAT II required. High school diploma or GED required. Minimum TOEFL is 550. TOEFL required of all international applicants.

Application deadline: November 30
Notification: March 31
Average GPA: 3.9

Average SAT I Math: 685
Average SAT I Verbal: 655
Average ACT: NR

Graduated top 10% of class: 95%
Graduated top 25% of class: 100%
Graduated top 50% of class: NR

COLLEGE GRADUATION REQUIREMENTS

Course waivers allowed: No
Course substitutions allowed: Yes
In what subjects: Foreign language requirement can be substituted with cultural courses on a case-by-case basis; math waivers are considered on a case-by-case basis.

ADDITIONAL INFORMATION

Environment: The 1,232-acre campus is in an urban area, 10 miles east of San Francisco.

Student Body
   Undergrad enrollment: 22,261
   Female: 50%
   Male: 50%
   Out-of-state: 11%

Cost Information
   In-state tuition: $4,050
   Out-of-state tuition: $14,221
   Room & board: $8,122
Housing Information
   University housing: Yes
   Percent living on campus: 23%

Greek System
   Fraternity: Yes
   Sorority: Yes
   Athletics: NCAA Division I

UNIV. OF CALIFORNIA—LOS ANGELES

405 Hilgard Avenue, Los Angeles, CA 90095
Phone: 310-825-3101 • Fax: 310-206-1206
E-mail: ugadm@saonet.ucla.edu • Web: www.ucla.edu
Support level: CS • Institution type: 4-year public

LEARNING DISABILITY PROGRAM AND SERVICES

UCLA complies with state, federal, and university guidelines that mandate full access for students with disabilities, including learning disabilities. UCLA complies with the requirement to provide reasonable accommodations for documented students to allow them to participate in their academic program to the greatest extent possible. Students with other documented types of learning disabilities, including Attention Deficit (Hyperactive) Disorder and Traumatic Brain Injury, are also served by the Learning Disabilities Program. The UCLA Learning Disabilities Program is coordinated by a full-time learning disabilities specialist, and offers a full range of accommodations and services. Services are individually designed, and include counseling, special test arrangements, note-taker services, readers, priority enrollment, adaptive technology, and individual tutoring. An active support group provides opportunities for students to discuss mutual concerns and enhance learning strategies. Workshops and speakers address skill development and topics of interest. In the Peer-Mentor program, continuing students with learning disabilities serve as resources to entering students.

LD/ADHD ADMISSIONS INFORMATION

College entrance tests required: Yes
Nonstandardized tests accepted: Yes
Interview required: No
Essay required: Yes
Documentation required for LD: Psychoeducational evaluation
Documentation required for ADHD: Yes
Documentation submitted to: Office for Students with Disabilities
Special Ed. HS course work accepted: No

Specific course requirements for all applicants: Yes
Separate application required for services: No
# of LD applications submitted yearly: N/A
# of LD applications accepted yearly: N/A
Total # of students receiving LD/ADHD services: 225–300
Acceptance into program means acceptance into college: Students must be admitted and enrolled at the University first and then may request services.

ADMISSIONS

There are no special admissions criteria for students with learning disabilities. In an academic review the University will assess and balance a variety of academic factors to determine the overall scholastic strength of each applicant. UCLA does not use a formula. The comprehensive review includes the remainder of the freshman applicants after the academic review. While commitment to intellectual development and academic progress continues to be of primary importance, the personal statement also forms an integral part of this review. All applicants are required to submit the SAT I or ACT and SAT II (including the Writing Test, Mathematics Level 1 or 2, and either English Literature, Foreign Language, Science, or Social Studies). To be competitive, students usually score in the high 20s on the ACT or high 1100s on the SAT I, and between 500–600 on each of the SAT II: Subject Tests. High school courses required are: 4 years English, 2 years history/social science, 3 years math, 2 years foreign language (3 years recommended), 2 years lab science (3 years recommended), and 2 years electives. Additional criteria are based on an eligibility index using test scores and class rank. Selected students are admitted for winter. Admissions readers pay attention to significant obstacles and challenges related in personal statements. The LD specialists provide disability-related information to admissions staff.

ADDITIONAL INFORMATION

LD Program includes tutors for individual classes; peer mentors; support group meetings; learning skills workshops; advocacy; referrals to campus resources; priority enrollment; orientation program; LD screening; and disability management counseling by four LD specialists, including disability awareness, learning and time-management strategies, self-advocacy skills, and interpretation of evaluation reports. Compensations could include alternatives in (1) printed materials: taped textbooks, computerized voice synthesizer, RFBD; (2) test-taking procedures: extended time, proctor to assist with reading and writing, distraction-free test area, computer for essay exams, alternative test formats including essay-type rather than multiple choice-type or taped exams rather than written exams, use of calculator or spellchecker; (3) note-taking: note-takers, taped lecture; (4) writing essays and papers: word processors with voice synthesizers, composition tutors; (5) reduced course load; (6) extended time to complete a program; and (7) tutors for individual classes.

SUPPORT SERVICES CONTACT INFORMATION

Learning Disability Program/Services: Office for Students with Disabilities
Director: Kathy Molini
  E-mail: kmolini@saonet.ucla.edu
  Telephone: 310-825-1501
  Fax: 310-825-9656
Contact: Same

LEARNING DISABILITY SERVICES

Requests for the following services/accommodations will be evaluated individually based on appropriate and current documentation.

Allowed in Exams
  Calculator: Yes
  Dictionary: Yes
  Computer: Yes
  Spellchecker: Yes
Extended test time: Yes
Scribes: Yes
Proctors: Yes
Oral exams: Yes
Notetakers: Yes

Distraction-reduced environment: Yes
Tape recording in class: Yes
Books on tape from RFBD: Yes
Taping of books not from RFBD: Yes
Accommodations for students with
  ADHD: Yes
Reading machine: Yes
Other assistive technology: Yes
Priority registration: Yes

Added costs for services: No
LD specialists: Yes (4)
Professional tutors: No
Peer tutors: Yes
Max. hours/wk. for services:
  Unlimited
How professors are notified of
  LD/ADHD: By student

GENERAL ADMISSIONS INFORMATION

Director of Admissions: Joanne Woosley
Telephone: 323-343-3901

ENTRANCE REQUIREMENTS
4 English required, 3 math required, 4 math recommended, 2 science lab required, 3 science lab recommended, 2 foreign language required, 3 foreign language recommended, 2 history required, 2 elective required. High school diploma or GED required. Minimum TOEFL is 550. TOEFL required of all international applicants.

Application deadline: November 30
Notification: Rolling beginning 3/1
Average GPA: NR

Average SAT I Math: 660
Average SAT I Verbal: 617
Average ACT: 26

Graduated top 10% of class: 97%
Graduated top 25% of class: NR
Graduated top 50% of class: NR

COLLEGE GRADUATION REQUIREMENTS

Course waivers allowed: No
Course substitutions allowed: Yes
In what subjects: Foreign language and math as appropriate based on documentation, history, and recommendation

ADDITIONAL INFORMATION

Environment: The University is located on 419 acres in an urban area of Los Angeles.

Student Body
  Undergrad enrollment: 24,668
  Female: 55%
  Male: 45%
  Out-of-state: 3%

Cost Information
  In-state tuition: $3,701
  Out-of-state tuition: $14,315
  Room & board: $8,565
Housing Information
  University housing: Yes
  Percent living on campus: 25%

Greek System
  Fraternity: Yes
  Sorority: Yes
  Athletics: NCAA Division I

University of California—Los Angeles

UNIVERSITY OF CALIF.—SAN DIEGO

9500 Gilman Drive, 0021, La Jolla, CA 92093-0021
Phone: 858-534-4831 • Fax: 858-543-5723
E-mail: admissionsinfo@ucsd.edu • Web: www.ucsd.edu
Support level: CS • Institution type: 4-year public

LEARNING DISABILITY PROGRAM AND SERVICES

The primary objective of the Office for Students with Disabilities (OSD) is to integrate mainstream students with learning disabilities into campus programs, services, and activities. Academic accommodations are designed to meet disability-related needs without fundamentally altering the program; are not remedial; and may include part-time enrollment, exception to minimum academic progress requirements, substitution of course work required for graduation, and alternative test formats. This program is not intended to provide remediation. Students seeking accommodations must provide a comprehensive written evaluation that meets the following requirements: Assessment must be comprehensive and include: Aptitude (WAIS-R with subtest scores and/or WJ-R); Achievement (WJ-R); Information Processing (WAIS-R subtests or WJ-R-cognitive portions) within three years; diagnostic report with written summary of educational, medical, and family histories and behavioral observation; test scores, testing procedures followed, interpretation, dates, evaluator; specified intracognitive and/or cognitive-achievement discrepancies; statement of how the LD substantially interferes with the student's educational progress; and recommendations for academic accommodations. OSD's peer mentoring program is designed to match new students who have disabilities (mentees) with continuing students (Mentors) who have the same major, interests, and/or disabilities. Mentors and mentees meet as a group once a week throughout the academic year. The group provides for informal meetings and serves as a place to receive emotional support from several students who understand and have something in common. The group also gives students a place where they can feel comfortable discussing issues. Topics covered in the past include: problem-solving techniques, study strategies, test-taking problems, and social issues.

LD/ADHD ADMISSIONS INFORMATION

College entrance tests required: Yes
Nonstandardized tests accepted: Yes
Interview required: No
Essay required: Yes
Documentation required for LD: Psychoeducational evaluation
Documentation required for ADHD: Yes
Documentation submitted to: Office for Students with Disabilities
Special Ed. HS course work accepted: Y/N

Specific course requirements for all applicants: Yes
Separate application required for services: No
# of LD applications submitted yearly: 40–50
# of LD applications accepted yearly: 50
Total # of students receiving LD/ADHD services: 150
Acceptance into program means acceptance into college: Students are admitted and enrolled at the University and then reviewed for LD services.

ADMISSIONS

There is no special admissions process for students with learning disabilities. All applicants must meet the same admission criteria. Course requirements include 2 years social science (including U.S. history and 1/2 year government), 4 years English, 3 years math, 2 years lab science, 2 years foreign language (courses taken in 7th or 8th grade may be used to fulfill part of this requirement), 2 years electives. There is an Eligibility Index based on ACT/SAT and GPA such as 2.82 GPA and 36 ACT/1590–1600 SAT up to 3.29 GPA and 12 ACT/490–570 SAT. Meeting the Eligibility Index requirements does not guarantee admission. The minimum GPA for a California resident is 2.8 and for a nonresident a 3.4. Students must submit 3 SAT II Tests. There is a Summer Bridge Program for conditional admits that is available to a specific group of students.

ADDITIONAL INFORMATION

Depending upon the nature of the disability and level of functional limitation, LD coordination may include the following: note-takers; readers; peer mentoring; priority registration; typists; problem-resolution assistance; peer mentoring; extended time for tests; distraction-free testing environment; calculators, dictionary, computer or spellchecker in exams; scribes; proctors; tape recorders in class; peer tutoring; and priority registration. Course substitutions are dependent on the College and major requirements. Skills classes are offered for all students in study and time management, and skill building.

SUPPORT SERVICES CONTACT INFORMATION

Learning Disability Program/Services: Office for Students with Disabilities (OSD)
Director: Roberta J. Gimblett
  E-mail: rgimblett@ucsd.edu
  Telephone: 858-534-4382
  Fax: 858-534-4650
Contact: Same

LEARNING DISABILITY SERVICES

Requests for the following services/accommodations will be evaluated individually based on appropriate and current documentation.

Allowed in Exams
  Calculator: Yes
  Dictionary: Yes
  Computer: Yes
  Spellchecker: Yes
Extended test time: Yes
Scribes: Yes
Proctors: Yes
Oral exams: Yes
Notetakers: Yes

Distraction-reduced environment: Yes
Tape recording in class: Yes
Books on tape from RFBD: Yes
Taping of books not from RFBD: Yes
Accommodations for students with ADHD: Yes
Reading machine: Yes
Other assistive technology: Yes
Priority registration: Yes

Added costs for services: No
LD specialists: Yes
Professional tutors: 5
Peer tutors: 200–300
Max. hours/wk. for services: Unlimited
How professors are notified of LD/ADHD: By student

GENERAL ADMISSIONS INFORMATION

Director of Admissions: Mae Brown
Telephone: 858-534-3156

ENTRANCE REQUIREMENTS
15 total are required; 4 English required, 3 math required, 4 math recommended, 2 science required, 3 science recommended, 2 science lab required, 3 science lab recommended, 2 foreign language required, 3 foreign language recommended, 2 history required, 2 elective required. High school diploma or GED required. Minimum TOEFL is 550. TOEFL required of all international applicants.

Application deadline: November 30
Notification: March 15
Average GPA: 3.9

Average SAT I Math: 647
Average SAT I Verbal: 609
Average ACT: 25

Graduated top 10% of class: 95%
Graduated top 25% of class: 100%
Graduated top 50% of class: 100%

COLLEGE GRADUATION REQUIREMENTS

Course waivers allowed: Yes
Course substitutions allowed: Yes
In what subjects: Dependent on college and major requirements

ADDITIONAL INFORMATION

Environment: The University has a suburban campus north of downtown San Diego.

Student Body
  Undergrad enrollment: 15,840
  Female: 51%
  Male: 49%
  Out-of-state: 2%

Cost Information
  In-state tuition: $3,848
  Out-of-state tuition: $14,250
  Room & board: $7,290
Housing Information
  University housing: Yes
  Percent living on campus: 33%

Greek System
  Fraternity: Yes
  Sorority: Yes
Athletics: NCAA Division II

UNIV. OF CALIF.—SANTA BARBARA

Office of Admissions, 1210 Cheadle Hall, Santa Barbara, CA 93106
Phone: 805-893-2881 • Fax: 805-893-2676
E-mail: appinfo@sa.ucsb.edu • Web: www.ucsb.edu
Support level: CS • Institution type: 4-year public

LEARNING DISABILITY PROGRAM AND SERVICES

The Disabled Student Program (DSP) is a department within the NCAA Division of Student Affairs that works to increase the retention and graduation ratio of students with temporary and permanent disabilities, assure equal access to all educational and academic programs, and foster student independence. The University is strongly committed to maintaining an environment that guarantees students with disabilities full access to educational programs and activities. The DSP office serves as campus liaison regarding issues and regulations related to students with disabilities. DSP provides reasonable accommodations to students with learning disabilities; specific accommodations are determined on an individual basis. Admitted students should send LD documentation to DSP and schedule an appointment with the LD specialist. Accommodations and academically related services are not designed to provide remediation, but to accommodate a disorder that impairs the student's ability to acquire, process, or communicate information. Each accommodation will be made available to the extent that it does not compromise the academic integrity of the student's program. In all cases, it is the student's responsibility to communicate special needs to the professor and/or DSP.

LD/ADHD ADMISSIONS INFORMATION

College entrance tests required: Yes
Nonstandardized tests accepted: Yes
Interview required: NR
Essay required: Yes
Documentation required for LD: WAIS-III; WJ; Achievement
Documentation required for ADHD: Yes
Documentation submitted to: DSP
Special Ed. HS course work accepted: No

Specific course requirements for all applicants: Yes
Separate application required for services: No
# of LD applications submitted yearly: N/A
# of LD applications accepted yearly: N/A
Total # of students receiving LD/ADHD services: 220+
Acceptance into program means acceptance into college: Students must be accepted and enrolled at the University first and then may request services.

ADMISSIONS

There is no special application for students with learning disabilities. All students must meet the same admission criteria. However, students may self-disclose the existence of a learning disability. Students should use their autobiographical statement to address their disability and how they have coped with it in high school. All documentation is submitted to the Office of Admissions, including tests and letters that could be helpful in determining the student's ability to succeed in college. General admission requirements include 4 years English, 3 years math, 1 year world history, 1 year U.S. history, 2 years lab science, 2 years foreign language, 2 years electives. The ACT or SAT is required and 3 SAT II in English Composition, Math, and one other additional subject. DSP does not admit students but may consult with Admissions.

ADDITIONAL INFORMATION

Academic accommodations may include substitution of courses required for graduation, nonremedial individualized tutoring, and instruction in reading and writing strategies and in compensatory study skills. Academic support services include priority registration; assistance with reading, writing, test-taking, and note-taking; and liaison with faculty. Skills classes and tutoring are provided through CLASS, the Campus Learning Assistance Program. These classes are available for all students on campus. DSP Office does not have the space to provide areas for testing accommodations, but individual professors assist by securing space. Students are not required to attend a special orientation prior to the fall quarter. Services and accommodations are available for undergraduate and graduate students.

SUPPORT SERVICES CONTACT INFORMATION

Learning Disability Program/Services: Disabled Student Program (DSP)
Director: Diane Glenn
  E-mail: Glenn-d@ucsb.edu
  Telephone: 805-893-2182
  Fax: 805-893-7127
Contact: Claudia Batty
  E-mail: batty-c@sa.ussb.edu
  Telephone: 805-893-8897
  Fax: 805-890-7127

LEARNING DISABILITY SERVICES

Requests for the following services/accommodations will be evaluated individually based on appropriate and current documentation.

Allowed in Exams
  Calculator: Yes
  Dictionary: No
  Computer: Yes
  Spellchecker: Yes
Extended test time: Yes
Scribes: Yes
Proctors: Yes
Oral exams: No
Notetakers: Yes

Distraction-reduced environment: Yes
Tape recording in class: Yes
Books on tape from RFBD: Yes
Taping of books not from RFBD: Yes
Accommodations for students with ADHD: Yes
Reading machine: Yes
Other assistive technology: Yes
Priority registration: Yes

Added costs for services: No
LD specialists: Yes (1)
Professional tutors: No
Peer tutors: Yes, at tutoring center 1 hour per week individually, or 3 hours per week in group
Max. hours/wk. for services: 1
How professors are notified of LD/ADHD: Students self-identify with letter from DSP

GENERAL ADMISSIONS INFORMATION

Director of Admissions: Diane Glenn
Telephone: 805-893-2881

ENTRANCE REQUIREMENTS
15 total are required; 4 English required, 3 math required, 4 math recommended, 2 science required, 2 foreign language required, 3 foreign language recommended, 1 social studies required, 2 history required, 2 elective required. High school diploma or GED required. Minimum TOEFL is 500. TOEFL required of all international applicants.

Application deadline: November 30
Notification: March 15
Average GPA: 3.7

Average SAT I Math: 609
Average SAT I Verbal: 580
Average ACT: 24.5

Graduated top 10% of class: NR
Graduated top 25% of class: NR
Graduated top 50% of class: NR

COLLEGE GRADUATION REQUIREMENTS

Course waivers allowed: No
Course substitutions allowed: Yes
In what subjects: Requires petition process and is determined on a case-by-case basis

ADDITIONAL INFORMATION

Environment: The University is located on 813 acres in a small city 10 miles west of Santa Barbara.

Student Body
  Undergrad enrollment: 17,538
  Female: 53%
  Male: 47%
  Out-of-state: 5%

Cost Information
  In-state tuition: $3,836
  Out-of-state tuition: $14,450
  Room & board: $7,706
Housing Information
  University housing: Yes
  Percent living on campus: 20%

Greek System
  Fraternity: Yes
  Sorority: Yes
Athletics: NCAA Division I

UNIVERSITY OF REDLANDS

PO Box 3080, Redlands, CA 92373-0999
Phone: 909-335-4074 • Fax: 909-335-4089
E-mail: admissions@uor.edu • Web: www.redlands.edu
Support level: S • Institution type: 4-year private

LEARNING DISABILITY PROGRAM AND SERVICES

Students identified as learning disabled are eligible for tutoring and individual assistance from Academic Support Services. While the University does not have a formal program for students with learning disabilities, the goal is to help students succeed in college once they are enrolled. Although the services and accommodations offered are minimal, they do comply with the mandates of Section 504 of the Rehabilitation Act of 1973. Academic Support Services is sensitive to the needs of students with disabilities, and strives to provide the services and accommodations that are identified in the professional documentation.

LD/ADHD ADMISSIONS INFORMATION

College entrance tests required: Yes
Nonstandardized tests accepted: Yes
Interview required: No
Essay required: Yes
Documentation required for LD: Psychoeducational evaluation
Documentation required for ADHD: Yes
Documentation submitted to: Academic Support Services
Special Ed. HS course work accepted: No

Specific course requirements for all applicants: Yes
Separate application required for services: No
# of LD applications submitted yearly: Unknown
# of LD applications accepted yearly: 35–50
Total # of students receiving LD/ADHD services: 90–110
Acceptance into program means acceptance into college: Students must be admitted and enrolled at the University first and then may request services.

ADMISSIONS
Students with learning disabilities are required to submit the general application form and meet the same admission standards as all applicants. "Faculty admits" are for those students whose GPAs or SAT/ACT scores do not meet admissions standards, but who show promise of success in college. Students are encouraged to self-disclose during the admission process. The director of Academic Support Services is involved in the admission decision for students with learning disabilities; however, the final decision is made by the office of admissions.

ADDITIONAL INFORMATION
Each service provided by Academic Support Services encourages students to take personal responsibility for their academic success. Study skills courses are available as well as basic skills classes in math, writing, and learning strategies. Students have access to tutoring on a one-to-one basis. The peer tutoring program provides friendly, supportive assistance for most academic subjects. Peer tutors must have faculty recommendations in the subjects they wish to tutor and at least a 3.0 GPA in the area they tutor. The director of Academic Support Services will work with students to assist them in identifying their needs and securing appropriate accommodations. Additionally, students may make individual appointments for assistance with time management and study skills. However, it is the student's responsibility to seek out help and request assistance. There are currently 70–80 students with LD and 20–30 with ADHD receiving services.

SUPPORT SERVICES CONTACT INFORMATION

Learning Disability Program/Services: Academic Support Services/Disabled Student Services
Director: Judy Bowman
  E-mail: jbowman@uor.edu
  Telephone: 909-335-4079
  Fax: 909-335-5297
Contact: Same

LEARNING DISABILITY SERVICES

Requests for the following services/accommodations will be evaluated individually based on appropriate and current documentation.

Allowed in Exams
  Calculator: Yes
  Dictionary: Yes
  Computer: Yes
  Spellchecker: Yes
Extended test time: Yes
Scribes: Yes
Proctors: Yes
Oral exams: Yes
Notetakers: Yes

Distraction-reduced environment: Yes
Tape recording in class: Yes
Books on tape from RFBD: Yes
Taping of books not from RFBD: No
Accommodations for students with ADHD: Yes
Reading machine: No
Other assistive technology: No
Priority registration: N/A

Added costs for services: No
LD specialists: No
Professional tutors: No
Peer tutors: 50
Max. hours/wk. for services: 2 hours per week for LD/ADHD
How professors are notified of LD/ADHD: By student and coordinator

GENERAL ADMISSIONS INFORMATION

Director of Admissions: Paul Driscoll
Telephone: 909-335-4074

ENTRANCE REQUIREMENTS

13 total are required; 16 total are recommended; 4 English required, 4 English recommended, 3 math required, 3 math recommended, 2 science required, 3 science recommended, 2 science lab required, 3 science lab recommended, 2 foreign language required, 3 foreign language recommended, 2 social studies required, 3 social studies recommended, 2 history recommended. High school diploma or GED required. Minimum TOEFL is 550. TOEFL required of all international applicants.

Application deadline: July 1
Notification: Rolling beginning 12/1
Average GPA: 3.4

Average SAT I Math: 566
Average SAT I Verbal: 562
Average ACT: 23

Graduated top 10% of class: NR
Graduated top 25% of class: NR
Graduated top 50% of class: NR

COLLEGE GRADUATION REQUIREMENTS

Course waivers allowed: No
Course substitutions allowed: Yes
In what subjects: Substitutions in math and foreign language

ADDITIONAL INFORMATION

Environment: The University is located on 130 acres in a small town 60 miles east of Los Angeles.

Student Body
  Undergrad enrollment: 1,734
  Female: 56%
  Male: 44%
  Out-of-state: 29%

Cost Information
  Tuition: $21,180
  Room & board: $7,840
Housing Information
  University housing: Yes
  Percent living on campus: 74%

Greek System
  Fraternity: Yes
  Sorority: Yes
Athletics: NCAA Division III

UNIVERSITY OF SAN FRANCISCO

2130 Fulton Street, San Francisco, CA 94117
Phone: 415-422-6563 • Fax: 415-422-2217
E-mail: admission@usfca.edu • Web: www.usfca.edu
Support level: CS • Institution type: 4-year private

LEARNING DISABILITY PROGRAM AND SERVICES

The University of San Francisco believes that students with learning disabilities are capable of succeeding and becoming contributing members of the University community and society. To this end, USF provides educational support and assistance to those students whose goals are successful completion of college and who take an active participatory role in their own education. Services provided enable students to achieve grades that accurately reflect their ability, promote healthy self-images, remediate deficit areas, and promote USF's LD program by conducting in-services for faculty, admissions, and other staff; providing brochures; advertising services; and working closely with faculty to provide accommodations to students with learning disabilities.

LD/ADHD ADMISSIONS INFORMATION

College entrance tests required: Yes
Nonstandardized tests accepted: Yes
Interview required: No
Essay required: No
Documentation required for LD: Psychoeducational evaluation
Documentation required for ADHD: Yes
Documentation submitted to: Admissions and LD Services
Special Ed. HS course work accepted: Yes

Specific course requirements for all applicants: Yes
Separate application required for services: No
# of LD applications submitted yearly: 40
# of LD applications accepted yearly: 20
Total # of students receiving LD/ADHD services: 190
Acceptance into program means acceptance into college: Students must be admitted and enrolled at the University first and then may request services.

ADMISSIONS

If a student who is a borderline admit self-discloses on the regular application form, the director of USF Services reviews the documentation and gives an evaluation before an admission decision is made. The final decision is made jointly between the director of the program and the Office of Admissions. Students who are accepted to the University under "conditional" status are encouraged to participate in the Summer Forward program. This voluntary program focuses on the academic needs of the students and prepares them for the demands of college life.

ADDITIONAL INFORMATION

Services include trained tutors, instruction in study skills and coping strategies, academic advising, maintaining regular contact with the LD coordinator, diagnostic testing, individual or small group instruction for educational skills building, and helping students improve their understanding of their learning disability. Assistive technology includes Dragon Naturally Speaking. Services and accommodations are available for undergraduate and graduate students. Students with Attention Deficit Disorder request services through Disability Related Services.

SUPPORT SERVICES CONTACT INFORMATION

Learning Disability Program/Services: Learning Disability Services
Director: Tom Merrell
  Telephone: 415-422-6876
  Fax: 415-422-5906
Contact: Teresa Ong
  E-mail: ongt@usfca.edu
  Telephone: 415-422-6876
  Fax: 415-422-5906

LEARNING DISABILITY SERVICES

Requests for the following services/accommodations will be evaluated individually based on appropriate and current documentation.

Allowed in Exams
  Calculator: Yes
  Dictionary: Yes
  Computer: Yes
  Spellchecker: Yes
Extended test time: Yes
Scribes: Yes
Proctors: Yes
Oral exams: Yes
Notetakers: Yes

Distraction-reduced environment: Yes
Tape recording in class: Yes
Books on tape from RFBD: Yes
Taping of books not from RFBD: No
Accommodations for students with ADHD: Yes
Reading machine: Yes
Other assistive technology: Yes
Priority registration: Yes

Added costs for services: No
LD specialists: Yes (2)
Professional tutors: 20
Peer tutors: 100
Max. hours/wk. for services: 3
How professors are notified of LD/ADHD: By student

GENERAL ADMISSIONS INFORMATION

Director of Admissions: William Henley
Telephone: 415-422-6563

ENTRANCE REQUIREMENTS
20 total are recommended; 4 English recommended, 3 math recommended, 2 science recommended, 2 foreign language recommended, 3 social studies recommended, 6 elective recommended. High school diploma or GED required. Minimum TOEFL is 550. TOEFL required of all international applicants.

Application deadline: February 15
Notification: Rolling
Average GPA: 3.3

Average SAT I Math: 540
Average SAT I Verbal: 540
Average ACT: 22.5

Graduated top 10% of class: 23%
Graduated top 25% of class: 52%
Graduated top 50% of class: 82%

COLLEGE GRADUATION REQUIREMENTS

Course waivers allowed: NR
Course substitutions allowed: Yes
In what subjects: Determined on a case-by-case basis based on the diagnosis

ADDITIONAL INFORMATION

Environment: The University of San Francisco is located on 52 acres in the heart of the city.

Student Body
  Undergrad enrollment: 4,572
  Female: 62%
  Male: 38%
  Out-of-state: 16%

Cost Information
  Tuition: $18,860
  Room & board: $8,242
Housing Information
  University housing: Yes
  Percent living on campus: 36%

Greek System
  Fraternity: Yes
  Sorority: Yes
Athletics: NCAA Division I

UNIVERSITY OF SOUTHERN CALIFORNIA

University Park, Los Angeles, CA 90089-0911
Phone: 213-740-1111 • Fax: 213-740-6364
E-mail: admap@usc.edu • Web: www.usc.edu
Support level: CS • Institution type: 4-year private

LEARNING DISABILITY PROGRAM AND SERVICES

Disability Services and Programs is responsible for delivery of services to students with learning disabilities. It offers a comprehensive support program in the areas of educational therapy, content area tutoring, study skills instruction, special exam administration, liaison with textbook taping services, advocacy, and network referral system. The learning specialists, graduate assistants, and learning assistants are available to students for academic therapy. A computer lab is available for computer-assisted learning and for word processing when working with a staff person. After admission, students with LD are counseled by advisors who dialogue with the learning specialist, and who are sensitive to special needs. Educational counseling is done by the learning specialist. Off-campus referrals are made to students desiring comprehensive diagnostic testing. The support structure for students with documented learning disabilities is one that is totally individualized. There is no "special program" per se. Support is given at the request of the student. The Learning Disabilities Specialist and/or grad assistants at USC are prepared to act as advocates when appropriate for any student experiencing academic problems that are related to the learning disability. USC aims to assure close, personal attention to its students even though it is a large campus.

LD/ADHD ADMISSIONS INFORMATION

College entrance tests required: Yes
Nonstandardized tests accepted: Yes
Interview required: No, recommended
Essay required: Yes
Documentation required for LD: WAIS-III; WJ; Achievement
Documentation required for ADHD: Yes
Documentation submitted to: Disability Services and Programs
Special Ed. HS course work accepted: Yes

Specific course requirements for all applicants: Yes
Separate application required for services: No
# of LD applications submitted yearly: N/A
# of LD applications accepted yearly: N/A
Total # of students receiving LD/ADHD services: 350
Acceptance into program means acceptance into college: Students must be accepted and enrolled at the University first and then may request services.

ADMISSIONS

There are no special admissions for students with learning disabilities. Students may self-disclose during the admission process and provide documentation. Disability Services may be asked for consultation and interpretation. However, all admission decisions are made by the Office of Admission. Course requirements include 4 years English, 3 years math, 2 years natural science, 2 years social studies, 2 years foreign language, and 4 year-long electives. (The foreign language requirement is not waived in the admission process). Transfer students are admitted on the basis of their college course work as well as the high school record. It is the student's responsibility to provide recent educational evaluations for documentation as part of the admissions application process. Testing must be current within 3 years, or 5 years for transfer or returning students.

ADDITIONAL INFORMATION

The services provided are modifications that are determined to be appropriate for students with LD. During the first 3 weeks of each semester, students are seen on a walk-in basis by the staff in the LD Support Services. Students requesting assistance must have a planning appointment with an LD specialist or grad assistant; provide a copy of the current class schedule; and be sure that eligibility has been determined by documentation of specific learning disabilities. Learning assistance most often involves one-to-one attention for academic planning, scheduling, organization, and methods of compensation. Students may have standing appointments with learning assistants and subject tutors. After 1 "no-show" or 3 canceled appointments, standing appointments will be canceled. Course accommodations could include taping of lectures; note-taking; extended time for tests; use of word processor; proofreader; limiting scheduling of consecutive exams; and advocacy. Other services include support groups, counseling, and coaching.

SUPPORT SERVICES CONTACT INFORMATION

Learning Disability Program/Services: Disability Services and Programs
Director: Janet Eddy, PhD
  E-mail: jeddy@usc.edu
  Telephone: 213-740-0776
  Fax: 213-740-8216
Contact: Dr. Patricia Tobey
  E-mail: tobey@usc.edu
  Telephone: 213-740-0776
  Fax: 213-740-8216

LEARNING DISABILITY SERVICES

Requests for the following services/accommodations will be evaluated individually based on appropriate and current documentation.

Allowed in Exams
  Calculator: Y/N
  Dictionary: Y/N
  Computer: Yes
  Spellchecker: Yes
Extended test time: Yes
Scribes: Yes
Proctors: Yes
Oral exams: No
Notetakers: Yes

Distraction-reduced environment: Yes
Tape recording in class: Yes
Books on tape from RFBD: Yes
Taping of books not from RFBD: Yes
Accommodations for students with ADHD: Yes
Reading machine: Yes
Other assistive technology: Yes
Priority registration: No

Added costs for services: No
LD specialists: Yes (1)
Professional tutors: Yes
Peer tutors: 15
Max. hours/wk. for services: 2 hours per class per week—may be extended
How professors are notified of LD/ADHD: By student and program director

GENERAL ADMISSIONS INFORMATION

Director of Admissions: Laurel Tews (interim)
Telephone: 213-740-1111

ENTRANCE REQUIREMENTS
16 total are required; 4 English required, 3 math required, 4 math recommended, 2 science required, 3 science recommended, 2 science lab required, 3 science lab recommended, 2 foreign language required, 3 foreign language recommended, 2 social studies required, 3 social studies recommended, 3 elective required. High school diploma is required and GED is not accepted.

Application deadline: January 10
Notification: April 1
Average GPA: 3.9
Average SAT I Math: 670
Average SAT I Verbal: 640
Average ACT: 29
Graduated top 10% of class: 75%
Graduated top 25% of class: 90%
Graduated top 50% of class: 99%

COLLEGE GRADUATION REQUIREMENTS

Course waivers allowed: No
Course substitutions allowed: Yes
In what subjects: Foreign language, literature in translation, linguistics, classics, logic, and computer languages

ADDITIONAL INFORMATION

Environment: The University is located on 150 acres in an urban area, 2 miles south of downtown Los Angeles.

Student Body
  Undergrad enrollment: 15,705
  Female: 50%
  Male: 50%
  Out-of-state: 30%

Cost Information
  Tuition: $24,230
  Room & board: $7,610
Housing Information
  University housing: Yes
  Percent living on campus: 35%

Greek System
  Fraternity: Yes
  Sorority: Yes
Athletics: NCAA Division I

University of the Pacific

3601 Pacific Avenue, Stockton, CA 95211
Phone: 209-946-2211 • Fax: 209-946-2413
E-mail: admissions@uop.edu • Web: www.uop.edu
Support level: CS • Institution type: 4-year private

LEARNING DISABILITY PROGRAM AND SERVICES

There is no special program for students with learning disabilities, but the University does have a Learning Disabilities Support program. This program offers assistance through tutoring, study skills classes, support groups, and testing accommodations. Documentation for LD must include psychoeducational evaluations from a professional. The documentation for ADHD must be from a medical doctor. Documentation should be sent to the Director of the Educational Resource Center. Students register for services after admission by contacting the Educational Resource Center. Student confidentiality is protected. The ultimate goal is for the student to earn a degree that is "unmodified and unflagged." Faculty and staff are dedicated to providing students with learning disabilities all reasonable accommodations so that they may enjoy academic success. The LD Support program helps keep UOP in compliance with the Americans with Disabilities Act and Section 504 of the Rehabilitation Act. Compliance is accomplished without compromising UOP standards, placing undue financial or administrative burden on the University, fundamentally altering the nature of programs, or extending unreasonable accommodations.

LD/ADHD ADMISSIONS INFORMATION

College entrance tests required: Yes
Nonstandardized tests accepted: Yes
Interview required: No
Essay required: Yes
Documentation required for LD: Psychoeducational evaluation
Documentation required for ADHD: Yes
Documentation submitted to: Learning Disability Support
Special Ed. HS course work accepted: Yes

Specific course requirements for all applicants: Yes
Separate application required for services: No
# of LD applications submitted yearly: N/A
# of LD applications accepted yearly: N/A
Total # of students receiving LD/ADHD services: 140–160
Acceptance into program means acceptance into college: Students must be accepted and enrolled at the University first and then may request services.

ADMISSIONS

UOP welcomes students with learning disabilities. Although there is no special admission procedure, students are given special consideration. There is no minimum ACT/SAT requirement. There are two alternative methods for admissions: (1) Probationary Admissions for the marginal student: "C/D" average with no special requirements, but the University advisor is notified of status, no required test score, and no quota regarding the number of students admitted; and (2) Special Admissions: students who begin college courses in the summer prior to freshman year and receive at least a "C" average in 2 courses and 1 study skills class (can take those courses at any local community college).

ADDITIONAL INFORMATION

All admitted students are eligible for LD services with the appropriate assessment documentation. Academic Support Services offers services to improve learning opportunities for students with LD and are provided within reasonable limits. These services could include: diagnostic assessment, accommodations for academic needs, taped texts, readers, tutorials for academic courses, and referrals to appropriate resources. Other related services include: career development and guidance, counseling, and LD support groups. The Educational Resource Center is open to all students on campus. Skills courses for credit are available in reading, study skills, writing, and math. Services and accommodations are available for undergraduate and graduate students. The University offers a special summer program for pre-college freshmen students with learning disabilities.

SUPPORT SERVICES CONTACT INFORMATION

Learning Disability Program/Services: Learning Disabilities Support
Director: Howard Houck
  E-mail: hhouck@uop.edu
  Telephone: 209-946-2458
  Fax: 209-946-2278
Contact: Same

LEARNING DISABILITY SERVICES

Requests for the following services/accommodations will be evaluated individually based on appropriate and current documentation.

Allowed in Exams
  Calculator: Yes
  Dictionary: Yes
  Computer: Yes
  Spellchecker: Yes
Extended test time: Yes
Scribes: Yes
Proctors: Yes
Oral exams: Yes
Notetakers: Yes

Distraction-reduced environment: Yes
Tape recording in class: Yes
Books on tape from RFBD: Yes
Taping of books not from RFBD: Yes
**Accommodations for students with
  ADHD:** Yes
Reading machine: Yes
Other assistive technology: Yes
Priority registration: Yes

Added costs for services: No
LD specialists: Yes
Professional tutors: 3
Peer tutors: 80
Max. hours/wk. for services: 10
**How professors are notified of
  LD/ADHD:** By director

GENERAL ADMISSIONS INFORMATION

Director of Admissions: Thomas Rajala
Telephone: 209-946-2211

ENTRANCE REQUIREMENTS
16 total are required; 4 English recommended, 3 math recommended, 2 science recommended, 2 science lab recommended, 2 foreign language recommended, 1 history recommended, 4 elective recommended. High school diploma or GED required. Minimum TOEFL is 475. TOEFL required of all international applicants.

Application deadline: March 1
Notification: Rolling beginning 12/15
Average GPA: 3.5

Average SAT I Math: 576
Average SAT I Verbal: 545
Average ACT: 24

Graduated top 10% of class: 42%
Graduated top 25% of class: 71%
Graduated top 50% of class: 91%

COLLEGE GRADUATION REQUIREMENTS

Course waivers allowed: Yes
Course substitutions allowed: Yes
In what subjects: NR

ADDITIONAL INFORMATION

Environment: The University is located on 150 acres 90 miles east of San Francisco.

Student Body
  Undergrad enrollment: 3,093
  Female: 58%
  Male: 42%
  Out-of-state: 16%

Cost Information
  Tuition: $20,350
  Room & board: $6,378
Housing Information
  University housing: Yes
  Percent living on campus: 58%

Greek System
  Fraternity: Yes
  Sorority: Yes
Athletics: NCAA Division I

WHITTIER COLLEGE

13406 Philadelphia Street, PO Box 634, Whittier, CA 90608
Phone: 562-907-4238 • Fax: 562-907-4870
E-mail: admission@whittier.edu • Web: www.whittier.edu
Support level: S • Institution type: 4-year private

LEARNING DISABILITY PROGRAM AND SERVICES

Learning Support Services is designed to assist at-risk students, including students with learning disabilities. The director of Learning Support Services provides assistance to students with documented disabilities. Accommodation requests are made through the director's office. Students with disabilities must make their needs known to the director of LSS in order to receive accommodations. To arrange for services students must self-disclose the learning disability, and make an individual appointment to discuss their accommodation requests with the director. The Learning Support Services offers peer tutoring, workshops on study skills, and basic English and math skills assistance. These services are provided at no cost.

LD/ADHD ADMISSIONS INFORMATION

College entrance tests required: Yes
Nonstandardized tests accepted: Yes
Interview required: No
Essay required: Yes
Documentation required for LD: Psychoeducational evaluation
Documentation required for ADHD: Yes
Documentation submitted to: Learning Support Services after admission
Special Ed. HS course work accepted: N/A

Specific course requirements for all applicants: Yes
Separate application required for services: No
# of LD applications submitted yearly: 10–15
# of LD applications accepted yearly: N/A
Total # of students receiving LD/ADHD services: 30
Acceptance into program means acceptance into college: Students must be admitted to the College and then reviewed for LD services.

ADMISSIONS

There is no special admissions process for students with learning disabilities. All applicants are expected to meet the same admission criteria. Students must submit the ACT or SAT I and have a minimum of a 2.0 GPA; the recommended courses include 4 years English, 3–4 years math, 2–3 years foreign language, 2–3 years social studies, and 2–3 years lab science.

ADDITIONAL INFORMATION

Skills courses are offered for credit in time management, test-taking strategies, text reading, and note-taking. The use of calculators, dictionary, computer, or spellchecker in exams would be considered on a case-by-case basis depending on appropriate documentation and student needs. Students with appropriate documentation will have access to note-takers, readers, extended exam time, alternative exam locations, proctors, scribes, oral exams, books on tape, and priority registration. All students have access to math lab, writing center, learning lab, and academic counseling.

SUPPORT SERVICES CONTACT INFORMATION

Learning Disability Program/Services: Learning Support Services
Director: Jamie Shepherd, MA
  E-mail: tthomsen@whittier.edu
  Telephone: 562-907-4233
  Fax: 562-907-4980
Contact: Same

LEARNING DISABILITY SERVICES

Requests for the following services/accommodations will be evaluated individually based on appropriate and current documentation.

Allowed in Exams
  Calculator: Yes
  Dictionary: Yes
  Computer: Yes
  Spellchecker: Yes
Extended test time: Yes
Scribes: Yes
Proctors: Yes
Oral exams: Yes
Notetakers: Yes

Distraction-reduced environment: Yes
Tape recording in class: Yes
Books on tape from RFBD: Yes
Taping of books not from RFBD: Yes
Accommodations for students with
  ADHD: Yes
Reading machine: Yes
Other assistive technology: Yes
Priority registration: Y/N

Added costs for services: No
LD specialists: No
Professional tutors: No
Peer tutors: 15
Max. hours/wk. for services:
  Unlimited
How professors are notified of
  LD/ADHD: By director

GENERAL ADMISSIONS INFORMATION

Director of Admissions: Urmi Kas
Telephone: 562-907-4870

ENTRANCE REQUIREMENTS
11 total are required; 16 total are recommended; 4 English required, 3 math required, 1 science required, 3 science recommended, 2 science lab recommended, 2 foreign language required, 3 foreign language recommended, 1 social studies required, 2 social studies recommended, 3 history recommended. High school diploma is required and GED is not accepted. Minimum TOEFL is 550. TOEFL required of all international applicants.

Application deadline: Rolling
Notification: Rolling beginning 3/1
Average GPA: 3.1

Average SAT I Math: 528
Average SAT I Verbal: 536
Average ACT: 22

Graduated top 10% of class: 14%
Graduated top 25% of class: 30%
Graduated top 50% of class: 52%

COLLEGE GRADUATION REQUIREMENTS

Course waivers allowed: No
Course substitutions allowed: Yes
In what subjects: Case-by-case basis with appropriate documentation

ADDITIONAL INFORMATION

Environment: The College is on a suburban campus 20 miles southeast of Los Angeles.

Student Body
  Undergrad enrollment: 1,297
  Female: 55%
  Male: 45%
  Out-of-state: 40%

Cost Information
  Tuition: $20,300
  Room & board: $6,736
Housing Information
  University housing: Yes
  Percent living on campus: 62%

Greek System
  Fraternity: Yes
  Sorority: Yes
Athletics: NCAA Division III

REGIS UNIVERSITY

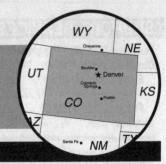

3333 Regis Boulevard, Denver, CO 80221-1099
Phone: 303-458-4900 • Fax: 303-964-5534
E-mail: regisadm@regis.edu • Web: www.regis.edu
Support level: SP • Institution type: 4-year private

LEARNING DISABILITY PROGRAM AND SERVICES

Regis University does not have a specific structured program for students with LD/ADHD. Disability Services provides services to all students with documented disabilities on an individualized basis. The philosophy is a commitment to ensure equal opportunity for students to succeed by providing equal access to programs and services. The Freshman Commitment Program is not specifically for students with LD/ADHD, although students with disabilities may be in the program. This program is not connected with disability services. Freshman Commitment offers a specialized program for approximately 40 students who show sufficient evidence of motivation and ability to succeed in college, even though they may not have the required GPA or test scores. Recommendations from high school teachers and evidence of extracurricular activities, as well as all other information a student provides, are considered for selection of these students. The goals of the Commitment Program are to provide a means for underachieving students to enter college; to provide the support needed to be a successful learner; and to help students develop the analytical processes that lead to high achievement. Students remain in the program for two semesters. To be successful, students must attend and pass all required Commitment courses with a "C" or better; cannot fall below a 2.0 GPA in nonCommitment courses; may not participate in varsity sports, forensics, or other activities that could interfere with class attendance; and must limit outside work, events, or other extracurricular activities that could impact their scholastic success.

LD/ADHD ADMISSIONS INFORMATION

College entrance tests required: Yes
Nonstandardized tests accepted: Yes
Interview required: N/A
Essay required: Yes
Documentation required for LD: Psychoeducational evaluation
Documentation required for ADHD: Yes
Documentation submitted to: Disability Services
Special Ed. HS course work accepted: N/A

Specific course requirements for all applicants: Yes
Separate application required for services: N/A
# of LD applications submitted yearly: N/A
# of LD applications accepted yearly: N/A
Total # of students receiving LD/ADHD services: 110
Acceptance into program means acceptance into college: Students are reviewed by Freshman Commitment and a recommendation is provided to the Admissions Committee for a final decision.

ADMISSIONS
There is no special admission procedure for students with learning disabilities. Although an interview is not required, the College would prefer that the student visit the school and have a minimum GPA of 2.56, an SAT of 930 or ACT of 20, and 15 academic units. Students may be considered with 17 ACT or 810 SAT and 2.3 GPA. Students need to show sufficient evidence of motivation and ability to succeed in college, even though they may not have the required GPA or test scores. Recommendations from counselors and evidence of extracurricular activities will be used in their decision-making process. Students admitted on probation are typically students with stronger test scores and lower GPA. These students are admitted into the College's degree program on a one-semester probation. They must have a 2.0 GPA to return the second semester. Other students may be admitted into the Freshman Commitment Program. These students usually have lower test scores and a C+ average. The probationary admission is for two semesters.

ADDITIONAL INFORMATION
Disability Services provides the following services for students with appropriate documentation: self-advocacy training, test-taking and learning strategies assistance, mentoring program; note-takers; readers; scribes; extended testing time; course substitutions; and priority registration. Students in the Commitment Program remain for one year and, with successful completion, are officially admitted to the College. They must pass all required Commitment courses with a C or better, not fall below a 2.0 GPA in non-Commitment course work, and agree not to participate in varsity sports or other activities that may interfere with class attendance while involved in the program. There are Learning Support Courses, study groups, and tutorials as needed. Three study rooms are staffed by tutors during the daytime and in the evening. All students must pass 3 hours of math, but there is a math learning support course or a remedial math class available for students to take prior to taking the regular college algebra class. The program offers learning support classes in reading skills, writing skills, and study skills, which apply toward elective credit. Special advising, tutoring, diagnostic academic testing, and study and testing assistance are other services offered.

SUPPORT SERVICES CONTACT INFORMATION

Learning Disability Program/Services: Disability Services
Director: Dr. KoKo Oyler
  E-mail: koyler@regis.edu
  Telephone: 303-458-4941
  Fax: 303-964-3647
Contact: Same

LEARNING DISABILITY SERVICES

Requests for the following services/accommodations will be evaluated individually based on appropriate and current documentation.

Allowed in Exams
  Calculator: Yes
  Dictionary: Yes
  Computer: Yes
  Spellchecker: Yes
Extended test time: Yes
Scribes: Yes
Proctors: Yes
Oral exams: Yes
Notetakers: Yes

Distraction-reduced environment: Yes
Tape recording in class: Yes
Books on tape from RFBD: Yes
Taping of books not from RFBD: Yes
Accommodations for students with ADHD: Yes
Reading machine: Yes
Other assistive technology: Yes
Priority registration: Yes

Added costs for services: $1,350
LD specialists: No
Professional tutors: No
Peer tutors: 22
Max. hours/wk. for services: Unlimited
How professors are notified of LD/ADHD: By student

GENERAL ADMISSIONS INFORMATION

Director of Admissions: Vic Davolt
Telephone: 800-388-2366, ext. 4900

ENTRANCE REQUIREMENTS
16 total are recommended; 4 English recommended, 2 math recommended, 2 science recommended, 2 foreign language recommended, 2 social studies recommended, 1 history recommended. High school diploma or GED required. Minimum TOEFL is 550. TOEFL required of all international applicants.

Application deadline: Rolling
Notification: Rolling
Average GPA: 3.1

Average SAT I Math: 543
Average SAT I Verbal: 546
Average ACT: 23

Graduated top 10% of class: 21%
Graduated top 25% of class: 47%
Graduated top 50% of class: 70%

COLLEGE GRADUATION REQUIREMENTS

Course waivers allowed: No
Course substitutions allowed: Yes
In what subjects: Foreign language; foreign culture courses are substituted if the documentation verifies a disability. All students must take 3 hours of math.

ADDITIONAL INFORMATION

Environment: The University is on a 90-acre campus in a suburban area of Denver.

Student Body
  Undergrad enrollment: 1,022
  Female: 54%
  Male: 46%
  Out-of-state: 39%

Cost Information
  Tuition: $17,570
  Room & board: $6,800
Housing Information
  University housing: Yes
  Percent living on campus: 48%

Greek System
  Fraternity: Yes
  Sorority: Yes
Athletics: NCAA Division II

UNIVERSITY OF COLORADO—BOULDER

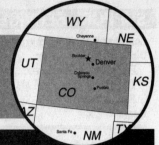

Campus Box 30, Boulder, CO 80309-0030
Phone: 303-492-6301 • Fax: 303-492-7115
E-mail: apply@colorado.edu • Web: www.colorado.edu
Support level: CS • Institution type: 4-year public

LEARNING DISABILITY PROGRAM AND SERVICES

The Academic Access and Resource Program (AAR) is a component of Disability Services. The Academic Access and Resource Program provides services to students with nonvisible disabilities such as learning disabilities, attention deficit disorder, head injuries, and psychiatric disabilities. The philosophy is that a student with a disability can be successful in a competitive post-secondary environment given self-acknowledgment of the disability and appropriate support services. Inherent in this philosophy is the importance of the student understanding his/her diagnostic profile so that relevant learning strategies can be learned and applied. The goal is for the student 'to become an independent learner who takes ownership and responsibility for the learning process. This process begins with the student understanding his/her areas of strengths and weaknesses and then building both awareness of needs and the development of appropriate compensatory strategies. In this process it is imperative that students take ownership for their own learning process and self-acknowledge the disability. The student develops compensatory strategies and builds a network of resources. A profile of individual strengths and weaknesses is developed between the student and the diagnostician. This information enables the student to understand how learning occurs and how strategies may be developed. Students need to be aware that there are no waivers or substitutions provided at the University. The goal of the program is to help students be successful within this academic community and provide them with skills and tools to be productive members of society. Disability Services has established documentation guidelines for LD and ADHD. Students should request information from Disability Services or can access it directly off the website.

LD/ADHD ADMISSIONS INFORMATION

College entrance tests required: Yes
Nonstandardized tests accepted: Yes
Interview required: No
Essay required: No
Documentation required for LD: Psychoeducational evaluation
Documentation required for ADHD: Yes
Documentation submitted to: Disability Services
Special Ed. HS course work accepted: No

Specific course requirements for all applicants: Yes
Separate application required for services: No
# of LD applications submitted yearly: N/A
# of LD applications accepted yearly: N/A
Total # of students receiving LD/ADHD services: 486
Acceptance into program means acceptance into college: Students must be admitted and enrolled at the University first and then may request services.

ADMISSIONS
There is not a special admission process for students with LD. All students are considered under the same competitive admissions criteria. All application information should be submitted to admissions by February 15, but documentation should be submitted directly to Disability Services. For the College of Arts and Sciences minimum academic requirements include 4 years English, 3 years math, 3 years natural science (must include chemistry or physics, and include 2 years of lab science), 3 years social science (including geography) and 3 years foreign language. UC Boulder is a competitive institution and admitted students must meet the same requirements as all other students. Graduation requirements are never waived. Students with documented LD/ADHD who struggle with foreign language learning may qualify for enrollment in the Modified Foreign Language. Students who struggle with math need to speak with a disability specialist about options for satisfying this requirement.

ADDITIONAL INFORMATION
Services are provided through Disability Services, of which AAR is a component. The Academic Access and Resources Program provides an opportunity to meet with a disability specialist to work on academic strategies. If tutoring is needed, the disability specialist can refer the student to the appropriate resources, but the student pays for the service. Other services include advocacy and support; evening writing lab; assistive technology lab; and a career program for students with disabilities. Lectures may be taped with the professor's permission. Priority registration is provided only if it directly responds to the disability. Support services and accommodations are available to undergraduate and graduate students who provide documentation of a disability. Students may seek an assessment to determine the possibility of the existence of a learning disability. The AAR will respond to all students with appropriate documentation who request services.

SUPPORT SERVICES CONTACT INFORMATION

Learning Disability Program/Services: Disability Services
Director: Cindy Donahue
  E-mail: dsinfo@spot.colorado.edu
  Telephone: 303-492-8671
  Fax: 303-492-5601
Contact: Jayne MacArthur, Coordinator of Academic Access and Resources Program
  E-mail: Jayne.MacArthur@colorado.edu
  Telephone: 303-492-8671
  Fax: 303-492-5601

LEARNING DISABILITY SERVICES

Requests for the following services/accommodations will be evaluated individually based on appropriate and current documentation.

Allowed in Exams
  Calculator: Yes
  Dictionary: No
  Computer: No
  Spellchecker: Yes
Extended test time: Yes
Scribes: Yes
Proctors: No
Oral exams: No
Notetakers: Yes

Distraction-reduced environment: Yes
Tape recording in class: Yes
Books on tape from RFBD: Yes
Taping of books not from RFBD: Yes
Accommodations for students with ADHD: Yes
Reading machine: No
Other assistive technology: Yes
Priority registration: Yes

Added costs for services: No
LD specialists: Yes (4)
Professional tutors: No
Peer tutors: No
Max. hours/wk. for services: Varies
How professors are notified of LD/ADHD: By student

GENERAL ADMISSIONS INFORMATION

Director of Admissions: Barbara Schneider
Telephone: 303-492-6301

ENTRANCE REQUIREMENTS

16 total are recommended; 4 English recommended, 3 math recommended, 3 science recommended, 2 science lab recommended, 3 foreign language recommended, 1 social studies recommended, 1 history recommended. High school diploma or GED required. Minimum TOEFL is 500. TOEFL required of all international applicants.

Application deadline: February 15
Notification: Rolling beginning 11/1
Average GPA: 3.4

Average SAT I Math: 584
Average SAT I Verbal: 569
Average ACT: 25

Graduated top 10% of class: 21%
Graduated top 25% of class: 53%
Graduated top 50% of class: 88%

COLLEGE GRADUATION REQUIREMENTS

Course waivers allowed: No
Course substitutions allowed: No
In what subjects: Decisions on academic requirements are within the domain of the academic deans. Decisions are made on an individual basis. There are no waivers/substitutions for entrance to College of Liberal Arts.

ADDITIONAL INFORMATION

Environment: The school is located at the base of the Rocky Mountains, 45 minutes from Denver.

Student Body
  Undergrad enrollment: 23,342
  Female: 48%
  Male: 52%
  Out-of-state: 32%

Cost Information
  In-state tuition: $3,155
  Out-of-state tuition: $15,940
  Room & board: $5,538
Housing Information
  University housing: Yes
  Percent living on campus: 26%

Greek System
  Fraternity: Yes
  Sorority: Yes
Athletics: NCAA Division I

University of Colorado—Boulder

U. of Colorado—Colorado Sprgs.

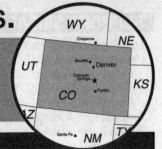

Admissions Office, PO Box 7150, Colorado Springs, CO 80933-7150
Phone: 719-262-3383 • Fax: 719-262-3116
E-mail: admrec@mail.eccs.edu • Web: www.uccs.edu
Support level: CS • Institution type: 4-year public

LEARNING DISABILITY PROGRAM AND SERVICES

University of Colorado—Colorado Springs is committed to providing equal educational opportunity for all students who meet the academic admission requirements. The purpose of Disability Services is to provide comprehensive support to meet the individual needs of students with disabilities.

LD/ADHD ADMISSIONS INFORMATION

College entrance tests required: Yes
Nonstandardized tests accepted: Yes
Interview required: No
Essay required: No
Documentation required for LD: WAIS-III; WJ
Documentation required for ADHD: Yes
Documentation submitted to: Disability Services—after admission
Special Ed. HS course work accepted: No

Specific course requirements for all applicants: Yes
Separate application required for services: No
# of LD applications submitted yearly: N/A
# of LD applications accepted yearly: N/A
Total # of students receiving LD/ADHD services: 150–200
Acceptance into program means acceptance into college: Students must be accepted and enrolled in the University prior to requesting services.

ADMISSIONS

An applicant's learning disability is not considered in an admission decision. All applicants are required to meet the Minimum Academic Preparation Standards (MAPS), including 4 years English, 3 years math (4 years for engineering and business), 3 years natural science, 2 years social science, 2 years foreign language, and 1 year elective; fine and performing arts are encouraged. Courses taken before 9th grade are accepted as long as the documentation provided shows that the courses were completed. Successfully completing 2 years of foreign language will satisfy the foreign language requirement regardless of whether the courses were taken before the 9th grade. Students with deficiencies may be admitted to the University provided they meet the other admission standards of test scores, rank in class, and GPA (minimum of 2.8), and provided they make up any deficiencies in the MAPS prior to graduation.

ADDITIONAL INFORMATION

Students with learning disabilities receive information in their acceptance letter about contacting Disability Services if they wish to request accommodations or services. Strategy development is offered in study skills, reading, test performance, stress reduction, time management, and writing skills. Disability Services offers the use of volunteers who use carbonless paper provided by the support services. Services and accommodations are available for undergraduate and graduate students with learning disabilities. Tutors are available for all university students in labs; tutors are also provided for students with disabilities.

SUPPORT SERVICES CONTACT INFORMATION

Learning Disability Program/Services: Disability Services
Director: Kaye Simonton
  E-mail: ksimonto@mail.uccs.edu
  Telephone: 719-262-3065
  Fax: 719-262-3354
Contact: Same

LEARNING DISABILITY SERVICES

Requests for the following services/accommodations will be evaluated individually based on appropriate and current documentation.

Allowed in Exams
  Calculator: Varies
  Dictionary: Yes
  Computer: Yes
  Spellchecker: Yes
Extended test time: Yes
Scribes: Yes
Proctors: Yes
Oral exams: Y/N
Notetakers: No

Distraction-reduced environment: Yes
Tape recording in class: Yes
Books on tape from RFBD: Yes
Taping of books not from RFBD: Yes
Accommodations for students with ADHD: Yes
Reading machine: Yes
Other assistive technology: Yes
Priority registration: No

Added costs for services: No
LD specialists: Yes (1)
Professional tutors: No
Peer tutors: 9–12
Max. hours/wk. for services: 3
How professors are notified of LD/ADHD: Student with letter from Disability Services

GENERAL ADMISSIONS INFORMATION

Director of Admissions: Randy Kouba
Telephone: 719-262-3383

ENTRANCE REQUIREMENTS

15 total are required; 4 English required, 3 math required, 4 math recommended, 3 science required, 2 science lab required, 2 foreign language required, 2 social studies required, 1 elective required. High school diploma or GED required. Minimum TOEFL is 550. TOEFL required of all international applicants.

Application deadline: July 1
Notification: Rolling beginning 10/1
Average GPA: 3.4

Average SAT I Math: 534
Average SAT I Verbal: 526
Average ACT: 23

Graduated top 10% of class: 14%
Graduated top 25% of class: 46%
Graduated top 50% of class: 75%

COLLEGE GRADUATION REQUIREMENTS

Course waivers allowed: No
Course substitutions allowed: Yes
In what subjects: Depends on documentation

ADDITIONAL INFORMATION

Environment: The University has an urban campus 70 miles south of Denver.

Student Body
  Undergrad enrollment: 5,054
  Female: 61%
  Male: 39%
  Out-of-state: 13%

Cost Information
  In-state tuition: $3,362
  Out-of-state tuition: $11,732
  Room & board: $5,893
Housing Information
  University housing: Yes
  Percent living on campus: 9%

Greek System
  Fraternity: Yes
  Sorority: Yes
Athletics: NCAA Division II

UNIVERSITY OF DENVER

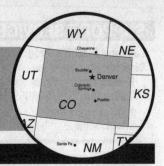

University Hall, Room 155, 2199 S. University Blvd., Denver, CO 80208
Phone: 303-871-2036 • Fax: 303-871-3301
E-mail: admission@du.edu • Web: www.du.edu
Support level: CS • Institution type: 4-year private

LEARNING DISABILITY PROGRAM AND SERVICES

Learning Effectiveness Program (LEP) is a comprehensive program structured to provide students with individualized support. LEP counselors work one-on-one with students to determine their learning strengths and to develop skills that will make them successful university students. Three crucial areas of skill development are encouraged: self-advocacy, articulation of strengths and weaknesses, and independent learning strategies. Cognitive strategy development is a basic part of individual sessions with a learning specialist. Students participate in regular course work and do not take special classes. One major focus of the LEP is reducing anxiety about learning in a college environment. Students learn how to focus on higher-level thought processes in order to compensate for lower-level processing deficits. They are also taught nontraditional study skills designed to increase reading, writing, and memory. Students are treated as responsible adults and are expected to participate in the program willingly.

LD/ADHD ADMISSIONS INFORMATION

College entrance tests required: Yes
Nonstandardized tests accepted: Yes
Interview required: Yes
Essay required: No
Documentation required for LD: Psychoeducational evaluation
Documentation required for ADHD: Yes
Documentation submitted to: LEP
Special Ed. HS course work accepted: No

Specific course requirements for all applicants: Yes
Separate application required for services: Yes
# of LD applications submitted yearly: 450
# of LD applications accepted yearly: 80
Total # of students receiving LD/ADHD services: 230–250
Acceptance into program means acceptance into college: Student must be admitted first to the University to enroll in the LEP.

ADMISSIONS

Admission to the University and LEP are two distinct processes. All potential candidates with LD/ADHD must submit a general admissions application, essay, recommendations, activity sheet, high school transcript, and ACT/SAT scores. Students applying to LEP must also provide: documentation of LD/ADHD; recent diagnostic tests; the completed LEP Intake Form provided upon disclosure of an LD; and a letter from a counselor, teacher, or LD specialist. The verification form from an appropriate specialist is critical and should describe the student's learning deficit and the support services necessary for success. Strengths, weaknesses, maturity level, ability to handle frustration, and feelings about limitations should also be included in documentation sent to the LEP. A successful background in college-prep classes is desirable. The minimum GPA is 3.1. A campus visit and interview are recommended after submission of all documentation and testing. Interviews should be scheduled as far in advance as possible. Interviews are required for all students who apply Early Action.

ADDITIONAL INFORMATION

LEP services are only available to students who are enrolled in the program. The LEP is a fee-for-service program that provides services beyond the mandated services provided under Section 504. There is a $2,550 fee per year for this program. The director and associate director are LD specialists, and the staff is composed of professionals in a variety of academic disciplines. Professional tutoring is also available to students enrolled in this program. Students who feel that they need only basic accommodations and do not wish to participate in the comprehensive program should contact Disability Services Program at 303-871-2455 to make those arrangements. The use of a calculator, dictionary, computer, and/or spellchecker require the professor's permission. Services and accommodations are available for undergraduate and graduate students. Learning disability assessments are available on campus.

SUPPORT SERVICES CONTACT INFORMATION

Learning Disability Program/Services: Learning Effectiveness Program (LEP)
Director: Ted F. May, Director, University Disability Services
  E-mail: tmay@du.edu
Telephone: 303-871-2372
  Fax: 303-871-3938
Contact: David Luker, Associate Director, LEP
  E-mail: dluker@du.edu
  Telephone: 303-871-2372
  Fax: 303-871-3939

LEARNING DISABILITY SERVICES

Requests for the following services/accommodations will be evaluated individually based on appropriate and current documentation.

Allowed in Exams
  Calculator: Y/N
  Dictionary: Y/N
  Computer: Y/N
  Spellchecker: No
Extended test time: Yes
Scribes: Yes
Proctors: Yes
Oral exams: Yes
Notetakers: Yes

Distraction-reduced environment: Yes
Tape recording in class: Yes
Books on tape from RFBD: N/A
Taping of books not from RFBD: N/A
**Accommodations for students with
  ADHD:** Yes
Reading machine: Yes
Other assistive technology: Yes
Priority registration: Yes

Added costs for services: $5,100 per
  semester
LD specialists: Yes (2)
Professional tutors: 50
Peer tutors: 20
Max. hours/wk. for services:
  Unlimited
**How professors are notified of
  LD/ADHD:** By student

GENERAL ADMISSIONS INFORMATION

Director of Admissions: John Dolan
Telephone: 303-871-3383

ENTRANCE REQUIREMENTS

4 English required, 4 math required, 3 science required, 2 science lab required, 2 foreign language required. High school diploma or GED required. Minimum TOEFL is 500. TOEFL required of all international applicants. Interviews required for all Early Action applicants.

Application deadline: Rolling
Notification: After 1/1
Average GPA: 3.4

Average SAT I Math: 569
Average SAT I Verbal: 555
Average ACT: 24

Graduated top 10% of class: 32%
Graduated top 25% of class: 57%
Graduated top 50% of class: 85%

COLLEGE GRADUATION REQUIREMENTS

Course waivers allowed: Yes
Course substitutions allowed: Yes
In what subjects: Foreign language

ADDITIONAL INFORMATION

Environment: The University has a 230-acre campus 7 miles southeast of Denver.

Student Body
  Undergrad enrollment: 3,809
  Female: 58%
  Male: 42%
  Out-of-state: 56%

Cost Information
  Tuition: $20,560
  Room & board: $6,400
Housing Information
  University housing: Yes
  Percent living on campus: 41%

Greek System
  Fraternity: Yes
  Sorority: Yes
Athletics: NCAA Division I

UNIVERSITY OF NORTHERN COLORADO

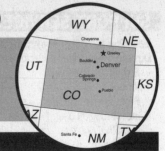

UNC Admissions Office, Greeley, CO 80639
Phone: 970-351-2881 • Fax: 970-351-2984
E-mail: unc@mail.unco.edu • Web: www.unco.edu
Support level: S • Institution type: 4-year public

LEARNING DISABILITY PROGRAM AND SERVICES

Although the University does not offer a formal LD program, individual assistance is provided whenever possible. The Disability Access Center (DAC) provides access, accommodations, and advocacy for UNC students who have documented disabilities. Academic needs are determined by the documentation and a student interview. Students with disabilities have an equal opportunity to pursue their educational goals. DAC provides test accommodations, adaptive hardware and software, learning strategies, organizational skills, and a reader program. Students requesting accommodations at UNC must provide test instruments from a certified professional that measure general intellect, aptitude, and more specific information processing tests; academic and vocational measures of achievement; and a clinical interview, which is the primary measure of previous educational and psychological functioning. Suggestions of reasonable accommodations which might be appropriate at the post-secondary level are encouraged. These recommendations should be supported by the diagnosis. Students with ADHD must provide a medical or clinical diagnosis from a developmental pediatrician, neurologist, psychiatrist, licensed clinical or educational psychologist, family physician, or a combination of such professionals.

LD/ADHD ADMISSIONS INFORMATION

College entrance tests required: Yes
Nonstandardized tests accepted: Yes
Interview required: Yes
Essay required: No
Documentation required for LD: Current psychological evaluation, including aptitude and achievement
Documentation required for ADHD: Yes
Documentation submitted to: Disability Access Center
Special Ed. HS course work accepted: Yes

Specific course requirements for all applicants: Yes
Separate application required for services: No
# of LD applications submitted yearly: 80–100
# of LD applications accepted yearly: N/A
Total # of students receiving LD/ADHD services: N/A
Acceptance into program means acceptance into college: Students must be admitted and enrolled at the University first and then may request services.

ADMISSIONS

There is no special admission process for students with learning disabilities. All students with disabilities are admitted to UNC under the standard admission requirements of the University. The UNC has a special "window" for admitting students who do not meet UNC's freshman admission requirements but want to earn full admission into a degree program. Students wishing to participate in this program need to call the Admissions Office. Each applicant is judged on an individual basis. Students do not need to be LD to apply for this DAC program, but must have a documented disability. To assist in determining eligibility for the program, current medical/clinical information is necessary. In order to receive services students must request accommodations upon arrival at UNC. Students enrolled in the Challenge Program must take 12 hours of college credit and earn a GPA of 2.0 after one or two semesters in order to remain at UNC.

ADDITIONAL INFORMATION

Services for individuals with LD/ADHD include learning strategies/organizational skills/advocacy skills; reader program; test accommodations; assistance in arranging for note-takers; assistive technology, including voice synthesizers, screen readers, screen enlargers, scanners, voice-recognition computer systems, large monitors, and word processing with spellcheck. Workshops are offered in student skills, organizational skills, study strategies, and time management. These workshops are electives and are not for credit. There is a support group for students with LD/ADHD, facilitated by DAC staff, which assists students in developing a support network. Services and accommodations are available for undergraduate and graduate students.

SUPPORT SERVICES CONTACT INFORMATION

Learning Disability Program/Services: Disability Access Center (DAC)
Director: Nancy Kauffman
　E-mail: nlkauff@unco.edu
　Telephone: 970-351-2289
　Fax: 970-351-4166
Contact: Same

LEARNING DISABILITY SERVICES

Requests for the following services/accommodations will be evaluated individually based on appropriate and current documentation.

Allowed in Exams
　Calculator: Yes
　Dictionary: Yes
　Computer: Yes
　Spellchecker: Yes
Extended test time: Yes
Scribes: Yes
Proctors: Yes
Oral exams: Yes
Notetakers: Yes

Distraction-reduced environment: Yes
Tape recording in class: Yes
Books on tape from RFBD: Yes
Taping of books not from RFBD: Yes
Accommodations for students with
　ADHD: Yes
Reading machine: Yes
Other assistive technology: Yes
Priority registration: Yes

Added costs for services: No
LD specialists: No
Professional tutors: No
Peer tutors: 20
Max. hours/wk. for services: Varies
How professors are notified of
　LD/ADHD: By student

GENERAL ADMISSIONS INFORMATION

Director of Admissions: Gary Gullickson
Telephone: 970-351-2891

ENTRANCE REQUIREMENTS
15 total are required; 4 English recommended, 3 math required, 2 science recommended, 1 science lab recommended, 2 social studies recommended. High school diploma or GED required. Minimum TOEFL is 520. TOEFL required of all international applicants.

Application deadline: August 1
Notification: Rolling
Average GPA: 3.2

Average SAT I Math: 511
Average SAT I Verbal: 513
Average ACT: 22

Graduated top 10% of class: 12%
Graduated top 25% of class: 33%
Graduated top 50% of class: 69%

COLLEGE GRADUATION REQUIREMENTS

Course waivers allowed: No
Course substitutions allowed: No
In what subjects: N/A

ADDITIONAL INFORMATION

Environment: The University is located on 240 acres in a small town 50 miles north of Denver.

Student Body
　Undergrad enrollment: 10,134
　Female: 60%
　Male: 40%
　Out-of-state: 12%

Cost Information
　In-state tuition: $2,754
　Out-of-state tuition: $9,737
　Room & board: $4,996
Housing Information
　University housing: Yes
　Percent living on campus: 28%

Greek System
　Fraternity: Yes
　Sorority: Yes
Athletics: NCAA Division II

UNIVERSITY OF SOUTHERN COLORADO

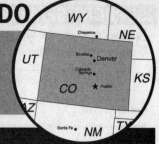

Admissions, 2200 Bonforte Blvd., Pueblo, CO 81001
Phone: 719-546-2461 • Fax: 719-549-2419
E-mail: info@uscolo.edu • Web: www.uscolo.edu
Support level: S • Institution type: 4-year public

LEARNING DISABILITY PROGRAM AND SERVICES

The Disabilities Services Office, an affiliate of the Learning Assistance Center, strives to provide optimal services to students who have disabilities to enhance learning and increase retention. Students with learning disabilities or Attention Deficit Disorder are encouraged to submit additional documentation, as well as letters of recommendation from counselors, teachers, or special education specialists. Documentation must include a comprehensive psychological evaluation with diagnostic and description of manifestations of the disability to the learning environment with recommendations for specific accommodations.

LD/ADHD ADMISSIONS INFORMATION

College entrance tests required: Yes
Nonstandardized tests accepted: Yes
Interview required: No
Essay required: No
Documentation required for LD: Psychoeducational evaluation
Documentation required for ADHD: Yes
Documentation submitted to: Disability Resources
Special Ed. HS course work accepted: Yes

Specific course requirements for all applicants: Yes
Separate application required for services: No
# of LD applications submitted yearly: N/A
# of LD applications accepted yearly: N/A
Total # of students receiving LD/ADHD services: 14
Acceptance into program means acceptance into college: Students must be admitted and enrolled and then may request services.

ADMISSIONS

All first-time freshmen must submit their high school transcripts with GPA and ACT/SAT scores along with the general application. There is no special admission procedure for students with disabilities, but all information submitted will be considered in making an admission decision. Twenty percent of the freshmen applicants are eligible for admission based on criteria in addition to GPA and test scores. Students who do not meet the general admission criteria should submit letters of recommendation with information describing their ability to be successful in the University curriculum. Since there are no course requirements for admission, only recommendations, waivers are not necessary.

ADDITIONAL INFORMATION

Skills classes are offered in note-taking strategies, study skills, and textbook-reading strategies. The request for the use of a dictionary, computer, or spellchecker during exams will depend on the student's documented needs and permission from the professor. Students with specific needs are encouraged to provide documentation that specifically identifies the specific disability and the accommodations identified to compensate for the deficit. Services and accommodations are available for undergraduate and graduate students.

SUPPORT SERVICES CONTACT INFORMATION

Learning Disability Program/Services: Disabilities Resources Office
Director: Pam Chambers
 E-mail: chambersp@uscolo.edu
 Telephone: 719-549-2581
 Fax: 719-549-2195
Contact: Same

LEARNING DISABILITY SERVICES

Requests for the following services/accommodations will be evaluated individually based on appropriate and current documentation.

Allowed in Exams
 Calculator: Yes
 Dictionary: Yes
 Computer: Yes
 Spellchecker: Yes
Extended test time: Yes
Scribes: Yes
Proctors: Yes
Oral exams: Yes
Notetakers: Yes

Distraction-reduced environment: Yes
Tape recording in class: Yes
Books on tape from RFBD: Yes
Taping of books not from RFBD: Yes
Accommodations for students with
 ADHD: Yes
Reading machine: Yes
Other assistive technology: Yes
Priority registration: No

Added costs for services: No
LD specialists: No
Professional tutors: 1
Peer tutors: 5
Max. hours/wk. for services:
 Unlimited
How professors are notified of
 LD/ADHD: By student

GENERAL ADMISSIONS INFORMATION

Director of Admissions: Pam Anastioussa
Telephone: 719-549-2461

ENTRANCE REQUIREMENTS

4 English recommended, 3 math recommended, 2 science recommended, 1 science lab recommended, 2 foreign language recommended, 2 social studies recommended. High school diploma or GED required. Minimum TOEFL is 500. TOEFL required of all international applicants.

Application deadline: July 21
Notification: Rolling beginning 8/1
Average GPA: 3.1

Average SAT I Math: 476
Average SAT I Verbal: 460
Average ACT: 20

Graduated top 10% of class: 13%
Graduated top 25% of class: 34%
Graduated top 50% of class: 68%

COLLEGE GRADUATION REQUIREMENTS

Course waivers allowed: No
Course substitutions allowed: Yes
In what subjects: Substitutions determined on a case-by-case basis

ADDITIONAL INFORMATION

Environment: The University is located 100 miles south of Denver in an urban area.

Student Body
 Undergrad enrollment: 5,082
 Female: 57%
 Male: 43%
 Out-of-state: 7%

Cost Information
 In-state tuition: $1,808
 Out-of-state tuition: $8,448
 Room & board: $4,768
Housing Information
 University housing: Yes
 Percent living on campus: 18%

Greek System
 Fraternity: Yes
 Sorority: Yes
Athletics: NCAA Division II

CONNECTICUT COLLEGE

270 Mohegan Avenue, New London, CT 06320
Phone: 860-439-2200 • Fax: 860-439-4301
E-mail: admit@conncoll.edu • Web: www.conncoll.edu
Support level: CS • Institution type: 4-year private

LEARNING DISABILITY PROGRAM AND SERVICES

The College has established the Office of Disability Services to ensure equal access to educational activities for all students with disabilities. The direct services to students include: learning strategies, self-advocacy training sessions, learning disability evaluations, and review of petitions to the Committee on Academic Standing for modifications to the College curriculum. Reasonable and appropriate accommodations are available to students who have identified themselves to the Office, provided appropriate documentation of a disability, and made a timely request for the accommodations. Evidence to support a claim of a disability should include information regarding the nature of the disability and the accommodations or modifications considered appropriate. The Office of Disability Services must receive written permission from a student prior to exchanging information about the student's disability with anyone on campus. With permission the Director of Disability Services can advocate for a student with a faculty member who questions a course modification or can support a petition to the Committee on Academic Standing.

LD/ADHD ADMISSIONS INFORMATION

College entrance tests required: Yes
Nonstandardized tests accepted: Yes
Interview required: N/A
Essay required: Yes
Documentation required for LD: Psychoeducational evaluation
Documentation required for ADHD: Yes
Documentation submitted to: ODS—after admission
Special Ed. HS course work accepted: N/A

Specific course requirements for all applicants: Yes
Separate application required for services: N/A
# of LD applications submitted yearly: N/A
# of LD applications accepted yearly: N/A
Total # of students receiving LD/ADHD services: 100
Acceptance into program means acceptance into college: NR

ADMISSIONS

Students may self-disclose their disability through a personal statement during the admission process. However, students with learning disabilities and attention deficits must meet the regular admissions criteria for Connecticut College.

ADDITIONAL INFORMATION

The Office of Disability Services will provide general information about disabilities, make referrals to appropriate campus resources, assist with registration, and coordinate requests for accommodations. Academic accommodations depend on the individual needs as supported by documentation. These accommodations may include a reduced course load, course substitutions, use of a tape recorder or computer, and testing modifications such as extended time. Direct services may include learning strategy and self-advocacy training sessions, LD evaluations, review of petitions to the Committee on Academic Standing for modifications to the College curriculum, and certification of eligibility for special accommodations on graduate entry and professional licensure exams.

SUPPORT SERVICES CONTACT INFORMATION

Learning Disability Program/Services: Office of Disability Services (ODS)
Director: Susan L. Duques, PhD
  E-mail: slduq@conncoll.edu
  Telephone: 860-439-5428
  Fax: 860-439-5430
Contact: Barbara L. McLlarky
  E-mail: blmcl@conncoll.edu
  Telephone: 860-439-5240
  Fax: 860-439-5430

LEARNING DISABILITY SERVICES

Requests for the following services/accommodations will be evaluated individually based on appropriate and current documentation.

Allowed in Exams
  Calculator: Yes
  Dictionary: Yes
  Computer: Yes
  Spellchecker: Yes
Extended test time: Yes
Scribes: Yes
Proctors: Yes
Oral exams: Yes
Notetakers: Yes

Distraction-reduced environment: Yes
Tape recording in class: Yes
Books on tape from RFBD: Yes
Taping of books not from RFBD: Yes
Accommodations for students with
  ADHD: Yes
Reading machine: Yes
Other assistive technology: Yes
Priority registration: Y/N

Added costs for services: No
LD specialists: Yes (1)
Professional tutors: No
Peer tutors: Yes
Max. hours/wk. for services: Unlimited
How professors are notified of
  LD/ADHD: By both student and
  director

GENERAL ADMISSIONS INFORMATION

Director of Admissions: Lee Coffin
Telephone: 860-439-2202

ENTRANCE REQUIREMENTS
22 total are recommended; 4 English recommended, 3 math recommended, 3 science recommended, 3 foreign language recommended, 3 social studies recommended, 3 history recommended, 3 elective recommended. High school diploma or GED required. Minimum TOEFL is 600. TOEFL required of all international applicants.

Application deadline: January 1
Notification: April 1
Average GPA: N/A

Average SAT I Math: 650
Average SAT I Verbal: 660
Average ACT: 27

Graduated top 10% of class: 49%
Graduated top 25% of class: 85%
Graduated top 50% of class: 100%

COLLEGE GRADUATION REQUIREMENTS

Course waivers allowed: Yes
Course substitutions allowed: Yes
In what subjects: Foreign language

ADDITIONAL INFORMATION

Environment: Located 60 miles from Boston and 100 miles from New York City.

Student Body
  Undergrad enrollment: 1,814
  Female: 57%
  Male: 43%
  Out-of-state: 79%

Cost Information
  Comprehensive Tuition: $35,588
Housing Information
  University housing: Yes
  Percent living on campus: 96%

Greek System
  Fraternity: No
  Sorority: No
Athletics: NCAA Division III

FAIRFIELD UNIVERSITY

1073 North Benson Road, Fairfield, CT 06430-5195
Phone: 203-254-4100 • Fax: 203-254-4199
E-mail: admis@fair1.fairfield.edu • Web: www.fairfield.edu
Support level: CS • Institution type: 4-year private

LEARNING DISABILITY PROGRAM AND SERVICES

The University provides services for students with disabilities through Student Support Services. There is no LD program, only services that are available for all students with disabilities These services are designed to provide equal access to the learning environment. Students are supported while being encouraged to be self-advocates. Students with learning disabilities must provide documentation from an appropriate testing agent. For students with learning disabilities, cognitive and academic achievement tests and information processing must be administered. Students with ADHD must have documentation from appropriate professionals who can provide behavior rating scales, ruling out other disabilities and showing the onset of the ADHD between age 7–12. All documentation should be submitted to Student Support Services.

LD/ADHD ADMISSIONS INFORMATION

College entrance tests required: Yes
Nonstandardized tests accepted: Yes
Interview required: No
Essay required: No
Documentation required for LD: Psychoeducational evaluation
Documentation required for ADHD: Yes
Documentation submitted to: Office of Student Support Services—after admission
Special Ed. HS course work accepted: Yes

Specific course requirements for all applicants: Yes
Separate application required for services: No
# of LD applications submitted yearly: N/A
# of LD applications accepted yearly: N/A
Total # of students receiving LD/ADHD services: 300
Acceptance into program means acceptance into college: Students must be accepted and enrolled at the University first and then may request services.

ADMISSIONS

There is no special admissions process for students with learning disabilities. Admission criteria include: top 40% of graduating class or better; B average; 25 ACT; counselor recommendations; and college-prep courses including 4 years English, 3–4 years math, 2–4 years foreign language, 1–3 years lab science, and 2–3 years history. Courses taken in the Special Educstion deptarpemnt may be acceptable. The middle 50 percent SAT I scores are 1120–1270. Once students have been admitted and have enrolled they may initiate a contact for services.

ADDITIONAL INFORMATION

Skills courses are offered in study skills, note-taking strategies, time management skills, and strategies for success. These skills courses are not for credit. Students are offered meetings with a professional who has a background in teaching students with disabilities. Letters are sent to professors upon student's request. All students have access to content tutoring and a writing center. Services and accommodations are available for undergraduate and graduate students.

SUPPORT SERVICES CONTACT INFORMATION

Learning Disability Program/Services: Office of Student Support Services
Director: Rev. W. Laurence O'Neil, S.J.
  E-mail: wloneil@mail.fairfield.edu
  Telephone: 203-254-4000
  Fax: 203-254-4014
Contact: David Ryan-Soderlund
  E-mail: drsoderlund@mail.fairfield.edu
  Telephone: 203-254-2445
  Fax: 203-254-4014

LEARNING DISABILITY SERVICES

Requests for the following services/accommodations will be evaluated individually based on appropriate and current documentation.

Allowed in Exams
  Calculator: Yes
  Dictionary: Yes
  Computer: Yes
  Spellchecker: Yes
Extended test time: Yes
Scribes: Yes
Proctors: Yes
Oral exams: Yes
Notetakers: Yes

Distraction-reduced environment: Yes
Tape recording in class: Yes
Books on tape from RFBD: Yes
Taping of books not from RFBD: Yes
Accommodations for students with ADHD: Yes
Reading machine: Yes
Other assistive technology: Yes
Priority registration: No

Added costs for services: No
LD specialists: Yes (1)
Professional tutors: No
Peer tutors: 90
Max. hours/wk. for services: Unlimited
How professors are notified of LD/ADHD: By student

GENERAL ADMISSIONS INFORMATION

Director of Admissions: Judith Dobai (acting director)
Telephone: 203-254-4100

ENTRANCE REQUIREMENTS

15 total are required; 18 total are recommended; 4 English required, 4 English recommended, 3 math required, 4 math recommended, 3 science required, 4 science recommended, 2 science lab required, 2 science lab recommended, 2 foreign language required, 4 foreign language recommended, 3 history required, 4 history recommended, 1 elective required. High school diploma is required and GED is not accepted. Minimum TOEFL is 550. TOEFL required of all international applicants.

Application deadline: February 1
Notification: April 1
Average GPA: 3.6

Average SAT I Math: 591
Average SAT I Verbal: 580
Average ACT: 26

Graduated top 10% of class: 30%
Graduated top 25% of class: 75%
Graduated top 50% of class: 96%

COLLEGE GRADUATION REQUIREMENTS

Course waivers allowed: No
Course substitutions allowed: Yes
In what subjects: Math and foreign language; must have severe impairment

ADDITIONAL INFORMATION

Environment: The University is located on 200 acres in a suburban area 60 miles northeast of New York City.

Student Body
  Undergrad enrollment: 4,173
  Female: 55%
  Male: 45%
  Out-of-state: 75%

Cost Information
  Tuition: $21,000
  Room & board: $7,630
Housing Information
  University housing: Yes
  Percent living on campus: 75%

Greek System
  Fraternity: No
  Sorority: No
  Athletics: NCAA Division I

MITCHELL COLLEGE

437 Pequot Avenue, New London, CT 06320
Phone: 800-443-2811 • Fax: 860-444-1209
E-mail: admissions@mitchell.edu • Web: www.mitchell.edu
Support level: SP • Institution type: 2-year and 4-year private

LEARNING DISABILITY PROGRAM AND SERVICES

Mitchell College is dedicated to providing a student-centered supportive learning environment that addresses the educational needs of all students, including those with LD, through 2- and 4-year programs. The Academic Support Center offers the Learning Resource Center, which provides a spectrum of academic support services to students with disabilities at three levels of support; a Tutoring Center that provides tutoring across the content areas to all students enrolled at the College by appointment and walk-in accommodations; and a Testing Center to monitor, proctor, and administer tests and exams. The LRC's three levels of support include a Level I fee-based program that is the most comprehensive (a team of specialists); the non-fee-based Level II standard support services, including weekly consultation and review sessions, accommodations and modifications; and Level III accommodations and modifications. The fundamental components that characterize the Level I Enhanced Support are individual appointments or small group; guided reading and structured study sessions; regularly scheduled skills mini workshops; collaboration with academic advisor to assist in planning a program of study; collaboration with other C.A.R.E.S. staff as necessary; reviews and modifications of course selections or credit loads if necessary; assurance of documented modifications and/or accommodations. The staff is comprised of specialists trained in working with students who have difficulties with reading, mathematics, writing, and organization. Generally, successful students have a college-prep curriculum in high school; solid level of skills in reading, writing, and math; plus determination, persistence, and motivation to achieve personal goals.

LD/ADHD ADMISSIONS INFORMATION

College entrance tests required: Yes
Nonstandardized tests accepted: Yes
Interview required: No
Essay required: Yes
Documentation required for LD: Psychoeducational evaluation
Documentation required for ADHD: Yes
Documentation submitted to: Admissions and LRC
Special Ed. HS course work accepted: N/A

Specific course requirements for all applicants: Yes
Separate application required for services: No
# of LD applications submitted yearly: 100–120
# of LD applications accepted yearly: 90
Total # of students receiving LD/ADHD services: 225–275
Acceptance into program means acceptance into college: Students are reviewed by both the program and Admissions, but the final decision is with Admissions. Once admitted students may request services.

ADMISSIONS

Students with LD may apply through the LRC program. Students complete an application process that includes the high school transcript; documentation of the LD and/or ADHD; current assessment information; and aptitude and achievement test scores reflecting all subtest and summative scores in the form of standard scores and/or percentile ranks, ACT/SAT, and recommendations from LD teacher(s) and counselors. In addition, each applicant is required to submit a writing sample that is part of the formal application itself. Often, an interview with the LRC staff is requested following a review of the completed application. The applicant's academic program should be within a mainstream and/or inclusion framework, with a consistent C or better performance reflected in the core academic subjects. Evidence of commitment, motivation, and preparedness for college-level study is desired. While they require the SAT/ACT, admission is dependent more on potential and the student's desire to be successful than what he/she has necessarily done in the past. The director and learning specialists review LRC applicant information and make recommendations to admissions. Students are notified of a decision as soon as all of the credentials are received and reviewed.

ADDITIONAL INFORMATION

During the first year, students accepted into the LRC program are expected to work with their assigned learning specialists at least four hours per week, divided between individual and small-group sessions. These training sessions focus on developing and/or strengthening skills in a variety of learning-study strategies, as well as other ancillary skills and strategies that are designed to promote academic success. The LRC students are expected to fulfill all degree requirements for their chosen major program of study, and to follow all college requirements and procedures in the Student Catalog.

SUPPORT SERVICES CONTACT INFORMATION

Learning Disability Program/Services: Learning Resource Center (LRC)
Director: Patricia A. Pezzullo, PhD
  E-mail: pezzullo_p@mitchell.edu
  Telephone: 860-701-5141
  Fax: 860-701-5090
Contact: Same

LEARNING DISABILITY SERVICES

Requests for the following services/accommodations will be evaluated individually based on appropriate and current documentation.

Allowed in Exams
  Calculator: Yes
  Dictionary: Yes
  Computer: Yes
  Spellchecker: Yes
Extended test time: Yes
Scribes: Yes
Proctors: Y/N
Oral exams: Yes
Notetakers: Yes

Distraction-reduced environment: Yes
Tape recording in class: Yes
Books on tape from RFBD: Yes
Taping of books not from RFBD: Yes
**Accommodations for students with
  ADHD:** Yes
Reading machine: Yes
Other assistive technology: Yes
Priority registration: N/A

Added costs for services: Yes
LD specialists: Yes (16)
Professional tutors: 8
Peer tutors: No
Max. hours/wk. for services:
  Unlimited
**How professors are notified of
  LD/ADHD:** By both student and
  director

GENERAL ADMISSIONS INFORMATION

Director of Admissions: Kevin Mayne
Telephone: 860-701-5036

ENTRANCE REQUIREMENTS
High school diploma or GED required. Minimum TOEFL is 500. TOEFL required of all international applicants.

Application deadline: March 31
Notification: Rolling beginning 10/1
Average GPA: 2.4

Average SAT I Math: 401
Average SAT I Verbal: 415
Average ACT: 23

Graduated top 10% of class: 2%
Graduated top 25% of class: 4%
Graduated top 50% of class: 36%

COLLEGE GRADUATION REQUIREMENTS

Course waivers allowed: NR
Course substitutions allowed: Yes
In what subjects: Varies based on the student's history with the subject area and the school policies and procedures

ADDITIONAL INFORMATION

Environment: The 65-acre campus sits on a former estate, located in a safe and quiet residential area of historic New London. The campus includes 26 wooded acres, ponds, hiking trails, and two private beaches with a dock and fleet of sailboats.

Student Body
  Undergrad enrollment: 621
  Female: 52%
  Male: 48%
  Out-of-state: 50%

Cost Information
  Tuition: $14,800
  Room & board: $7,100
Housing Information
  University housing: Yes
  Percent living on campus: 90%

Greek System
  Fraternity: Yes
  Sorority: Yes
Athletics: NJCAA

SOUTHERN CONNECTICUT STATE UNIV.

SCSU-Admissions House, 131 Farnham Avenue, New Haven, CT 06515
Phone: 203-392-5656 • Fax: 203-392-5727
E-mail: adminfo@scsu.ctstateu.edu • Web: www.southernct.edu
Support level: CS • Institution type: 4-year public

LEARNING DISABILITY PROGRAM AND SERVICES

The purpose of the Disability Resource Office (DRO) is to ensure educational equity for students with disabilities. The DRO works to provide access to full participation in all aspects of campus life. The DRO assists students in arranging for individualized accommodations and support services. The DRO is a resource to students, faculty, and the University at large. Use of DRO services is voluntary and confidential. The DRO provides academic, career, and personal support for all university students with disabilities, including students with specific learning disabilities and attention deficit disorders. The DRO is a component of Student Supportive Services.

LD/ADHD ADMISSIONS INFORMATION

College entrance tests required: Yes
Nonstandardized tests accepted: Yes
Interview required: No
Essay required: Yes
Documentation required for LD: Psychoeducational evaluation
Documentation required for ADHD: Yes
Documentation submitted to: DRO
Special Ed. HS course work accepted: Yes, with appropriate documentation

Specific course requirements for all applicants: Yes
Separate application required for services: No
# of LD applications submitted yearly: N/A
# of LD applications accepted yearly: N/A
Total # of students receiving LD/ADHD services: 400
Acceptance into program means acceptance into college: Students must be admitted and enrolled at the University first and then may request services.

ADMISSIONS

There is no special admissions process for students with learning disabilities. All applicants must meet the same criteria. Conditional admission is considered and based on the following: WAIS scores and subscores, achievement tests, SAT/ACT scores, and transcript. Applicants who wish DRO to be involved in the admission decision should note "disability" on the application, which goes to Admissions. They should also submit current psychoeducational testing information to DRO.

ADDITIONAL INFORMATION

The DRO assists students in arranging for individualized accommodations and support services. Services are available to both prospective and current students as follows: prospective students should attend one of the several workshops offered each fall for prospective students and their parents seeking information regarding the program and should obtain an application to the University. Current students should make an appointment with the office and bring educational documentation including achievement testing and psychoeducational evaluation or medical documentation. Services include course selection and registration; course and testing accommodations; support from learning specialists in developing time management and study skills, in identifying strengths and weaknesses, and in acquiring compensatory strategies; liaison with faculty and university departments; and advocacy and self-advocacy information and training. Services and accommodations are available for undergraduate and graduate students.

SUPPORT SERVICES CONTACT INFORMATION

Learning Disability Program/Services: Disability Resource Office (DRO)
Director: Suzanne Tucker
 E-mail: tucker@southernct.edu
 Telephone: 203-392-6828
 Fax: 203-392-6829
Contact: Debbie Fairchild

LEARNING DISABILITY SERVICES

Requests for the following services/accommodations will be evaluated individually based on appropriate and current documentation.

Allowed in Exams
 Calculator: Yes
 Dictionary: Yes
 Computer: Yes
 Spellchecker: Yes
Extended test time: Yes
Scribes: Yes
Proctors: Yes
Oral exams: Yes
Notetakers: Yes

Distraction-reduced environment: Yes
Tape recording in class: Yes
Books on tape from RFBD: Yes
Taping of books not from RFBD: Yes
Accommodations for students with ADHD: Yes
Reading machine: Yes
Other assistive technology: Yes
Priority registration: Y/N

Added costs for services: No
LD specialists: Yes (3)
Professional tutors: No
Peer tutors: Yes
Max. hours/wk. for services: Usually a half-hour per week
How professors are notified of LD/ADHD: By student

GENERAL ADMISSIONS INFORMATION

Director of Admissions: Sharon Brennan
Telephone: 203-392-5656

ENTRANCE REQUIREMENTS
15 total are required; 4 English required, 3 math required, 2 science required, 2 foreign language required, 2 social studies required, 2 history required. High school diploma or GED required. Minimum TOEFL is 525. TOEFL required of all international applicants.

Application deadline: May 1
Notification: Rolling beginning 12/1
Average GPA: NR

Average SAT I Math: 451
Average SAT I Verbal: 466
Average ACT: NR

Graduated top 10% of class: 5%
Graduated top 25% of class: 22%
Graduated top 50% of class: 57%

COLLEGE GRADUATION REQUIREMENTS

Course waivers allowed: Yes
Course substitutions allowed: Yes
In what subjects: Foreign language

ADDITIONAL INFORMATION

Environment: The University is located on 168 acres in an urban area 35 miles south of Hartford and 90 miles from New York City.

Student Body
 Undergrad enrollment: 7,624
 Female: 59%
 Male: 41%
 Out-of-state: 5%

Cost Information
 In-state tuition: $3,709
 Out-of-state tuition: $8,321
 Room & board: $5,934
Housing Information
 University housing: Yes
 Percent living on campus: 24%

Greek System
 Fraternity: Yes
 Sorority: Yes
Athletics: NCAA Division II

UNIVERSITY OF CONNECTICUT

2131 Hillside Road, U-88, Storrs, CT 06268-3088
Phone: 860-486-3137 • Fax: 860-486-1476
E-mail: beahusky@uconn.edu • Web: www.uconn.edu
Support level: CS • Institution type: 4-year public

LEARNING DISABILITY PROGRAM AND SERVICES

The major goal of the University Program for College Students with LD (UPLD) is to assist qualified students with LD to become independent and successful learners. The program is designed to complement and support, but not to duplicate, the University's existing campus services and programs. Three types of program services are offered along a continuum leading to independence: (1) Direct Instruction, in which students meet with learning specialists weekly to learn compensatory skills to strengthen learning strategies; (2) Monitoring for students who need periodic contact; and (3) Consultation with UPLD staff on a student-initiated basis. Most students find that it is beneficial to access services at the Direct Instruction Level, and to progress at an individual rate through the UPLD continuum as they experience increasing confidence and competence. Staff of UPLD are not qualified to serve as academic advisors. In cases where the disability does not include a specific LD, such as ADHD/ADHD, students can receive support services from the Center for Students with Disabilities (CSD). Students diagnosed with LD and ADHD have services coordinated through UPLD and CSD.

LD/ADHD ADMISSIONS INFORMATION

College entrance tests required: Yes
Nonstandardized tests accepted: Yes
Interview required: No
Essay required: No
Documentation required for LD: Psychoeducational evaluation
Documentation required for ADHD: Yes
Documentation submitted to: UPLD
Special Ed. HS course work accepted: No

Specific course requirements for all applicants: Yes
Separate application required for services: No
# of LD applications submitted yearly: 350+
# of LD applications accepted yearly: 40–50
Total # of students receiving LD/ADHD services: 150
Acceptance into program means acceptance into college: Student must be admitted and enrolled at the University first and then may request services.

ADMISSIONS

There is no separate application process for students with LD, and they must meet regular admissions criteria. The typical academic profile is: rank in top third of graduating class; academic GPA of 3.2 in college-prep courses; and SAT I of 1100 and above. Transfer students need a cumulative GPA of at least a 2.5 and must be in good standing at their current institution. To access services, students must refer themselves to UPLD and submit documentation that meets the criteria of the University's Guidelines for Documentation of a Specific LD. Documentation must verify eligibility and support requests for reasonable accommodations, academic adjustments, and/or auxiliary aids. Testing must be comprehensive. Minimally, domains to be addressed include: Aptitude; Achievement (current levels of functioning in reading, math, and written language); and Information Processing. Testing must be current, usually within three years, with clear and specific evidence of an LD. Individual "learning styles" and "learning differences" in and of themselves do not constitute an LD. Actual test scores must be provided including interpretation of the results. A written summary about relevant educational, medical, and family histories that relate to LD must be included. Recommendations for accommodations should be based on objective evidence of a current substantial limitation to learning, and descriptions of any accommodation and/or auxiliary aid used in high school or college should be discussed. IEPs and Section 504 plans alone are useful but are not sufficient to establish the rationale for services.

ADDITIONAL INFORMATION

Trained staff work with students on developing learning strategies and offer individual structured sessions. Students are encouraged to plan their course work to ensure success, including a reduced course load and extending their time for graduation. Learning specialists help students in self-advocacy, identify and monitor needs, and develop individualized goals. Reasonable accommodations are determined on a case-by-case basis. The CSD coordinates requests for proctors or scribes and provides services to students with ADHD without a diagnosed LD. The University has a formal course substitution policy for students with LD which requires current, valid diagnostic evidence that the nature and severity of the LD precludes completion of courses in foreign language or math despite the provision of accommodations. A "waiver" of a subject in high school does not guarantee a substitution at the University.

SUPPORT SERVICES CONTACT INFORMATION

Learning Disability Program/Services: University Program for College Students with LD (UPLD)
Director: Joseph W. Madaus, PhD
  Telephone: 860-486-0178
Contact: Same

LEARNING DISABILITY SERVICES

Requests for the following services/accommodations will be evaluated individually based on appropriate and current documentation.

Allowed in Exams
  Calculator: Yes
  Dictionary: Yes
  Computer: Yes
  Spellchecker: Yes
Extended test time: Yes
Scribes: Yes
Proctors: Yes
Oral exams: Yes
Notetakers: Yes

Distraction-reduced environment: Yes
Tape recording in class: Yes
Books on tape from RFBD: Yes
Taping of books not from RFBD: Yes
Accommodations for students with ADHD: No
Reading machine: No
Other assistive technology: No
Priority registration: No

Added costs for services: No
LD specialists: Yes (5)
Professional tutors: No
Peer tutors: No
Max. hours/wk. for services: 2
How professors are notified of LD/ADHD: By student

GENERAL ADMISSIONS INFORMATION

Director of Admissions: Wayne Locust
Telephone: 860-486-3137

ENTRANCE REQUIREMENTS

16 total are required; 4 English required, 3 math required, 2 science required, 2 science lab required, 2 foreign language required, 3 foreign language recommended, 2 social studies required, 3 elective required. High school diploma or GED required. Minimum TOEFL is 550. TOEFL required of all international applicants. Combined SAT I of 1100 and rank in top third of class recommended.

Application deadline: March 1
Notification: Rolling beginning 12/15
Average GPA: NR

Average SAT I Math: 563
Average SAT I Verbal: 577
Average ACT: NR

Graduated top 10% of class: 23%
Graduated top 25% of class: 62%
Graduated top 50% of class: 95%

COLLEGE GRADUATION REQUIREMENTS

Course waivers allowed: No
Course substitutions allowed: Yes
In what subjects: Math and foreign language

ADDITIONAL INFORMATION

Environment: University of Connecticut is located 30 miles northeast of Hartford.

Student Body
  Undergrad enrollment: 13,208
  Female: 52%
  Male: 48%
  Out-of-state: 21%

Cost Information
  In-state tuition: $5,596
  Out-of-state tuition: $14,370
  Room & board: $6,062
Housing Information
  University housing: Yes
  Percent living on campus: 67%

Greek System
  Fraternity: Yes
  Sorority: Yes
Athletics: NCAA Division I

UNIVERSITY OF HARTFORD

200 Bloomfield Avenue, West Hartford, CT 06117
Phone: 860-768-4296 • Fax: 860-768-4961
E-mail: admissions@mail.hartford.edu • Web: www.hartford.edu
Support level: CS • Institution type: 2-year private

LEARNING DISABILITY PROGRAM AND SERVICES

The Learning Plus program facilitates equal opportunity for academic achievement and is available to any student diagnosed with LD. Program objectives include help to: understand strengths and weaknesses; provide learning strategies; develop self-advocacy skills; connect with campus resources; develop decision-making skills; facilitate appropriate testing modifications; provide information to faculty and students regarding LD, classroom accommodations and testing modifications, and legal rights and responsibilities; and protect the confidentiality of student records. Learning Plus services include: Direct Strategies, in which students are assigned to an LP tutor and meet weekly for instruction in metacognitive skills such as information processing or organizational strategies; Check In, where students meet every other week with tutor for monitoring and organizational strategies; and Drop-In, for "as needed" assistance. Service determination depends on semester standing, GPA, and course curricula. Freshmen are assigned to Direct Strategies Instruction. Students with documentation are advised to contact the director of LP during the first week of classes. The director will discuss the disability, appropriate services, and classroom accommodations. Students are encouraged to discuss effective accommodations with professors. To receive services and accommodations from Learning Plus students should submit comprehensive documentation to the director of Learning Plus, not Admissions, after being accepted to the University.

LD/ADHD ADMISSIONS INFORMATION

College entrance tests required: Yes
Nonstandardized tests accepted: Yes
Interview required: No
Essay required: No
Documentation required for LD: WAIS-III and achievement testing
Documentation required for ADHD: Yes
Documentation submitted to: Disabled Student Services
Special Ed. HS course work accepted: Sometimes

Specific course requirements for all applicants: Yes
Separate application required for services: No
# of LD applications submitted yearly: N/A
# of LD applications accepted yearly: N/A
Total # of students receiving LD/ADHD services: 150-425
Acceptance into program means acceptance into college: Students must be accepted and enrolled at the University first and then may request services.

ADMISSIONS

Students with learning disabilities do not apply to the Learning Plus Program, but do apply directly to one of the nine schools and colleges within the University. If admitted, students with learning disabilities may then elect to receive the support services offered. The Admissions Committee pays particular attention to the student's individual talents and aspirations, especially as they relate to programs available at the University. Some borderline applicants may be admitted as a summer admission. Course requirements include 4 years English, 3–3.5 years math, 2 years science, 2 years social studies, plus electives. Substitutions are allowed on rare occasions and depend on disability and major. Students may also apply to Hillyer College, which is a two-year program with more flexible admission criteria. This is a developmental program, with flexible admission standards, offering many services. Hillyer provides students with the opportunity to be in a college atmosphere and, if successful, transfer into the four-year program. Hillyer is not necessarily for students with LD, although some students with LD are enrolled.

ADDITIONAL INFORMATION

Learning Plus is voluntary and students are required to seek assistance and to maintain contact. All modifications are determined on a case-by-case, course-by-course basis. The learning specialists are not content tutors. It is their goal to help students develop learning strategies and understand specific course material. Students are responsible for disclosing their LD to their professors. Skills classes are offered in study skills and math. Students can also receive one individual appointment weekly consisting of learning strategies from master's-level professionals. Instruction focuses on time management, organization strategies, reading, writing, mathematics, and course-specific study techniques. Some students with learning disabilities choose not to avail themselves of Learning Plus services. That is their privilege. The director of Learning Plus maintains confidential files of all documentation, should students request services at any time during their college career.

SUPPORT SERVICES CONTACT INFORMATION

Learning Disability Program/Services: Disabled Students Services
Director: Susan Fitzgerald
  E-mail: fitzgeral@mail.hartford.edu
  Telephone: 860-768-5129
Contact: Same

LEARNING DISABILITY SERVICES

Requests for the following services/accommodations will be evaluated individually based on appropriate and current documentation.

Allowed in Exams	**Distraction-reduced environment:** Yes	**Added costs for services:** No
Calculator: Yes	**Tape recording in class:** Yes	**LD specialists:** Yes (4)
Dictionary: No	**Books on tape from RFBD:** Yes	**Professional tutors:** No
Computer: Yes	**Taping of books not from RFBD:** No	**Peer tutors:** No
Spellchecker: Yes	**Accommodations for students with**	**Max. hours/wk. for services:** 1 time
Extended test time: Yes	**ADHD:** Yes	per week
Scribes: No	**Reading machine:** No	**How professors are notified of**
Proctors: Yes	**Other assistive technology:** No	**LD/ADHD:** By student
Oral exams: No	**Priority registration:** No	
Notetakers: Yes		

GENERAL ADMISSIONS INFORMATION

Director of Admissions: Rick Zeiser
Telephone: 860-768-4296

ENTRANCE REQUIREMENTS

16 total are required; 11 total are recommended; 4 English required, 2 math required, 3 math recommended, 2 science required, 3 science recommended, 2 foreign language recommended, 2 social studies required, 3 social studies recommended, 2 history required, 4 elective required. High school diploma or GED required. Minimum TOEFL is 550. TOEFL required of all international applicants.

Application deadline: Rolling	**Average SAT I Math:** 527	**Graduated top 10% of class:** 9%
Notification: Rolling beginning 10/1	**Average SAT I Verbal:** 522	**Graduated top 25% of class:** 28%
Average GPA: NR	**Average ACT:** 23	**Graduated top 50% of class:** 64%

COLLEGE GRADUATION REQUIREMENTS

Course waivers allowed: No
Course substitutions allowed: Yes
In what subjects: On rare occasions. Depends on disability and major.

ADDITIONAL INFORMATION

Environment: The University is located on a 320-acre campus in a residential section of West Hartford, 90 minutes from Boston.

Student Body	**Cost Information**	**Greek System**
Undergrad enrollment: 5,367	**Tuition:** $19,700	**Fraternity:** Yes
Female: 52%	**Room & board:** $8,074	**Sorority:** Yes
Male: 48%	**Housing Information**	**Athletics:** NCAA Division I
Out-of-state: 61%	**University housing:** Yes	
	Percent living on campus: 65%	

University of Hartford

UNIVERSITY OF NEW HAVEN

300 Orange Avenue, West Haven, CT 06516
Phone: 203-932-7139 • Fax: 203-931-6093
E-mail: adminfo@charger.newhaven.edu • Web: www.newhaven.edu
Support level: S • Institution type: 4-year

LEARNING DISABILITY PROGRAM AND SERVICES

The primary responsibility of the Disability Services and Resource Office is to provide services and support that promote educational equity for students with disabilities. Students must self-identify and submit documentation of a disability and the need for accommodations. Documentation should be submitted upon acceptance. Students must complete a DSR Student Intake Form with their signature requesting accommodations and following the established procedures for making arrangements for accommodations each semester. Staff members act as advocates, liaisons, planners, and troubleshooters. Staff is responsible for assuring access, but at the same time, they avoid creating an artificial atmosphere of dependence on services that cannot reasonably be expected after graduation. The Center for Learning Resources offers academic help and free tutoring for all students. The Office of Academic Skills focuses on assisting all students to be academically successful. Counselors work one-on-one with students to strengthen abilities and develop individualized study strategies, which focus on reading, note-taking, time management, learning/memory and test taking skills.

LD/ADHD ADMISSIONS INFORMATION

College entrance tests required: Yes
Nonstandardized tests accepted: Yes
Interview required: No
Essay required: No
Documentation required for LD: Intelligence
  test/achievement test information processing
Documentation required for ADHD: Yes
Documentation submitted to: Disability Services and
  Resources
Special Ed. HS course work accepted: Yes

Specific course requirements for all applicants: Yes
Separate application required for services: No
# of LD applications submitted yearly: N/A
# of LD applications accepted yearly: N/A
Total # of students receiving LD/ADHD services: N/A
Acceptance into program means acceptance into
  college: Students must be admitted and enrolled and then
  request services.

ADMISSIONS

All applicants must meet the same admission requirements. Foreign language is not required for admission. The College will accept courses taken in the special education department. Students with LD may self-disclose if they feel that it may make a difference in whether or not they are accepted.

ADDITIONAL INFORMATION

DSR provides services that include the coordination of classroom accommodations such as extended time for exams; use of a tape recorder, calculator, note-takers etc.; readers, scribes or books on tape; assistance during course registration process; proctoring of tests when accommodations cannot be arranged for in the classroom; proctoring of English course post-tests and the Writing Proficiency Exam; and provides training in time management, organizational skills and test-anxiety management. The office includes testing rooms and a mini computer lab. The Center for Learning Resources has a math lab, writing lab, and computer lab. The CLR presents free workshops in improving study skills, preparing resumes, and preparing for the Writing Proficiency Exam.

SUPPORT SERVICES CONTACT INFORMATION

Learning Disability Program/Services: Disability Services and Resources
Director: Linda Cupney-Okeke
  E-mail: lcokeke@charger.newhaven.edu
  Telephone: 203-932-7331
  Fax: 203-931-6082
Contact: Same

LEARNING DISABILITY SERVICES

Requests for the following services/accommodations will be evaluated individually based on appropriate and current documentation.

Allowed in Exams	**Distraction-reduced environment:** Yes	**Added costs for services:** N/A
Calculator: Yes	**Tape recording in class:** Yes	**LD specialists:** No
Dictionary: Yes	**Books on tape from RFBD:** Yes	**Professional tutors:** N/A
Computer: Yes	**Taping of books not from RFBD:** Yes	**Peer tutors:** N/A
Spellchecker: Yes	**Accommodations for students with**	**Max. hours/wk. for services:** N/A
Extended test time: Yes	**ADHD:** Yes	**How professors are notified of**
Scribes: Yes	**Reading machine:** Yes	**LD/ADHD:** By both student and
Proctors: Yes	**Other assistive technology:** Yes	director
Oral exams: Yes	**Priority registration:** No	
Notetakers: Yes		

GENERAL ADMISSIONS INFORMATION

Director of Admissions: Jane C. Sangeloty
Telephone: 203-932-7312

ENTRANCE REQUIREMENTS

16 total are required; 4 English required, 3 math required, 2 science required, 2 foreign language recommended, 2 social studies recommended, 2 history required, 3 elective required. High school diploma or GED required. Minimum TOEFL is 500. TOEFL required of all international applicants.

Application deadline: NR	**Average SAT I Math:** 470	**Graduated top 10% of class:** 8%
Notification: Rolling beginning 9/15	**Average SAT I Verbal:** 464	**Graduated top 25% of class:** 24%
Average GPA: 2.9	**Average ACT:** N/A	**Graduated top 50% of class:** 54%

COLLEGE GRADUATION REQUIREMENTS

Course waivers allowed: No
Course substitutions allowed: No
In what subjects: N/A

ADDITIONAL INFORMATION

Environment: Located close to New Haven and 75 miles from New York City.

Student Body	**Cost Information**	**Greek System**
Undergrad enrollment: 2,537	Tuition: $15,600	Fraternity: Yes
Female: 40%	Room & board: $6,960	Sorority: Yes
Male: 60%	**Housing Information**	Athletics: NCAA Division II
Out-of-state: 28%	University housing: Yes	
	Percent living on campus: 36%	

WESTERN CONNECTICUT STATE UNIV.

Undergrad. Admiss. Office, 181 White Street, Danbury, CT 06810-6860
Phone: 203-837-9000 • Fax: 203-837-8338
E-mail: weasil@wcsu.cstateu.edu • Web: www.wcsu.edu
Support level: CS • Institution type: 4-year public

LEARNING DISABILITY PROGRAM AND SERVICES

Two primary purposes of Students with Disabilities Services are to provide the educational development of disabled students and to improve understanding and support in the campus environment. Students with learning disabilities will be assisted in receiving the services necessary to achieve their goals.

LD/ADHD ADMISSIONS INFORMATION

College entrance tests required: Yes
Nonstandardized tests accepted: Yes
Interview required: Yes
Essay required: No
Documentation required for LD: Psychoeducational evaluation
Documentation required for ADHD: Yes
Documentation submitted to: Students with Disability Services
Special Ed. HS course work accepted: Yes

Specific course requirements for all applicants: Yes
Separate application required for services: No
# of LD applications submitted yearly: N/A
# of LD applications accepted yearly: N/A
Total # of students receiving LD/ADHD services: 70
Acceptance into program means acceptance into college: Students must be admitted and enrolled at the University first and then may request services.

ADMISSIONS

Students with learning disabilities submit the general application form. No alternative admission policies are offered. Students should have a 2.5 GPA (C+ or better) and the average SAT is 894 (ACT may be substituted). Students are encouraged to self-disclose their disability on the application, and submit documentation to be used after admission to determine services and accommodations.

ADDITIONAL INFORMATION

Services include priority registration, tutoring, testing accommodations, and advocacy and counseling. The University does not offer any skills classes. The University offers a special summer program for pre-college freshmen with learning disabilities. Services and accommodations are available for undergraduate and graduate students.

SUPPORT SERVICES CONTACT INFORMATION

Learning Disability Program/Services: Students with Disabilities Services
Director: Helen Kreuger
 Telephone: 203-837-9252
Contact: Same

LEARNING DISABILITY SERVICES

Requests for the following services/accommodations will be evaluated individually based on appropriate and current documentation.

Allowed in Exams
 Calculator: Yes
 Dictionary: No
 Computer: Y/N
 Spellchecker: Y/N
Extended test time: Yes
Scribes: Yes
Proctors: Yes
Oral exams: Yes
Notetakers: Yes

Distraction-reduced environment: Yes
Tape recording in class: Yes
Books on tape from RFBD: Yes
Taping of books not from RFBD: Yes
Accommodations for students with ADHD: Yes
Reading machine: No
Other assistive technology: No
Priority registration: Yes

Added costs for services: $2 per hour for tutor
LD specialists: Yes (1)
Professional tutors: Yes
Peer tutors: Yes
Max. hours/wk. for services: As needed
How professors are notified of LD/ADHD: Student and Disability Specialist

GENERAL ADMISSIONS INFORMATION

Director of Admissions: William Hawkins
Telephone: 203-877-9000

ENTRANCE REQUIREMENTS

16 total are required; 4 English required, 3 math required, 2 science required, 2 science lab required, 2 foreign language required, 3 foreign language recommended, 1 social studies required, 1 history required, 3 elective required. High school diploma or GED required. Minimum TOEFL is 550. TOEFL required of all international applicants.

Application deadline: May 1
Notification: Rolling beginning 12/1
Average GPA: NR

Average SAT I Math: 482
Average SAT I Verbal: 483
Average ACT: 18

Graduated top 10% of class: 2%
Graduated top 25% of class: 14%
Graduated top 50% of class: 47%

COLLEGE GRADUATION REQUIREMENTS

Course waivers allowed: Yes
Course substitutions allowed: Yes
In what subjects: Those required by the student's disability

ADDITIONAL INFORMATION

Environment: The University is located on 315 acres 60 miles from New York City.

Student Body
 Undergrad enrollment: 4,881
 Female: 55%
 Male: 45%
 Out-of-state: 11%

Cost Information
 In-state tuition: $3,758
 Out-of-state tuition: $8,370
 Room & board: $5,668
Housing Information
 University housing: Yes
 Percent living on campus: 28%

Greek System
 Fraternity: Yes
 Sorority: Yes
Athletics: NCAA Division III

UNIVERSITY OF DELAWARE

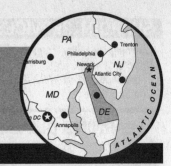

116 Hullihen Hall, Newark, DE 19716
Phone: 302-831-8123 • Fax: 302-831-6905
E-mail: admissions@udel.edu • Web: www.udel.edu
Support level: CS • Institution type: 4-year public

LEARNING DISABILITY PROGRAM AND SERVICES

The University of Delaware is committed to providing reasonable and timely academic accommodations for students with disabilities. The Academic Services Center focuses primarily on serving students with learning disabilities and ADHD. ASC is not a program but rather a center that provides services and accommodations to help students. ASC works jointly with other units. The staff has been trained to understand learning disabilities and ADHD and is available to assist faculty in providing accommodations for students whose documentation is complete. Independent, highly motivated students will do well at the University.

LD/ADHD ADMISSIONS INFORMATION

College entrance tests required: Yes
Nonstandardized tests accepted: Yes
Interview required: Yes
Essay required: Yes
Documentation required for LD: WAIS-III; WRAT-3; WJ-R: within 3–5 years
Documentation required for ADHD: Yes
Documentation submitted to: Academic Services Center
Special Ed. HS course work accepted: Y/N

Specific course requirements for all applicants: Yes
Separate application required for services: No
# of LD applications submitted yearly: N/A
# of LD applications accepted yearly: N/A
Total # of students receiving LD/ADHD services: 500
Acceptance into program means acceptance into college: Students must be admitted and enrolled at the University first and then may request LD services.

ADMISSIONS

Students must be "otherwise qualified" for university admissions, which means they must meet university and college admissions criteria. In other words, students are admitted on the basis of their abilities. Once admitted, students are encouraged to self-disclose their individual disability by returning a form they receive during orientation, or by making an appointment to discuss their needs with an ASC staff member. Documentation sent as part of the admissions application does not constitute the official notification to the University that the student is seeking services. We request documentation sent directly from the psychologist or medical doctor.

ADDITIONAL INFORMATION

With appropriate documentation students with learning disabilities could be eligible for some of the following services: the use of calculators, computer and spellchecker in exams; extended time on tests; proctors; oral exams; note-takers; distraction-free environment for tests; tape recorders in class; books on tape; and priority registration. There are one-credit courses offered through the School of Education that assist students in their study skills, critical thinking, and problem solving. In addition the ASC offers College Intensive Literacy for students who need additional assistance. Students with ADHD are provided assistance jointly by the ASC and the Center for Counseling and Student Development. All students have access to a writing center, math center, and tutoring and study-skills workshops in the academic services center.

SUPPORT SERVICES CONTACT INFORMATION

Learning Disability Program/Services: Academic Services Center
Director: David Johns
  E-mail: djohns@udel.edu
  Telephone: 302-831-1639
  Fax: 302-831-4128
Contact: Ruth Smith
  E-mail: rasmith@udel.edu
  Telephone: 302-831-1639

LEARNING DISABILITY SERVICES

Requests for the following services/accommodations will be evaluated individually based on appropriate and current documentation.

Allowed in Exams
  Calculator: Yes
  Dictionary: No
  Computer: Yes
  Spellchecker: Yes
Extended test time: Yes
Scribes: No
Proctors: Yes
Oral exams: Yes
Notetakers: Yes

Distraction-reduced environment: Yes
Tape recording in class: Yes
Books on tape from RFBD: Yes
Taping of books not from RFBD: Yes
**Accommodations for students with
  ADHD:** Yes
Reading machine: Yes
Other assistive technology: Yes
Priority registration: Yes

Added costs for services: No
LD specialists: Yes (2)
Professional tutors: No
Peer tutors: 40
Max. hours/wk. for services: Varies;
  students make appointments
**How professors are notified of
  LD/ADHD:** By both student and director

GENERAL ADMISSIONS INFORMATION

Director of Admissions: Larry Griffin
Telephone: 302-831-8123

ENTRANCE REQUIREMENTS

16 total are required; 19 total are recommended; 4 English required, 4 English recommended, 2 math required, 4 math recommended, 2 science required, 3 science recommended, 1 science lab required, 2 foreign language required, 4 foreign language recommended, 1 social studies required, 2 social studies recommended, 2 history required, 2 history recommended, 3 elective required. High school diploma or GED required. Minimum TOEFL is 550. TOEFL required of all international applicants.

Application deadline: February 15
Notification: Rolling
Average GPA: 3.5

Average SAT I Math: 580
Average SAT I Verbal: 570
Average ACT: N/A

Graduated top 10% of class: 30%
Graduated top 25% of class: 69%
Graduated top 50% of class: 95%

COLLEGE GRADUATION REQUIREMENTS

Course waivers allowed: No
Course substitutions allowed: Yes
In what subjects: Foreign language; The Educational Affairs Committee of the College of Arts and Sciences makes decisions on a case-by-case basis. Students are asked to attempt the class and work closely with a tutor before submitting a petition for a substitute.

ADDITIONAL INFORMATION

Environment: The 1,100-acre campus is in a small town 12 miles southwest of Wilmington and midway between Philadelphia and Baltimore.

Student Body
  Undergrad enrollment: 17,314
  Female: 59%
  Male: 41%
  Out-of-state: 59%

Cost Information
  In-state tuition: $5,100
  Out-of-state tuition: $13,800
  Room & board: $5,312
Housing Information
  University housing: Yes
  Percent living on campus: 53%

Greek System
  Fraternity: Yes
  Sorority: Yes
Athletics: NCAA Division I

AMERICAN UNIVERSITY

4400 Massachusetts Avenue, NW, Washington, DC 20016-8001
Phone: 202-885-6000 • Fax: 202-885-1025
E-mail: afa@american.edu • Web: www.american.edu
Support level: CS • Institution type: 4-year private

LEARNING DISABILITY PROGRAM AND SERVICES

The focus of the Learning Services Program is to assist students with their transition from high school to college during their freshman year. The Learning Services Program is a mainstream program offering additional support in college writing and finite math. Support continues to be available until graduation.

LD/ADHD ADMISSIONS INFORMATION

College entrance tests required: Yes
Nonstandardized tests accepted: Yes
Interview required: Yes
Essay required: Yes
Documentation required for LD: Psychoeducational
evaluation; WAIS-III; WISC-III: within 3 years
Documentation required for ADHD: Yes
Documentation submitted to: Learning Services Program
Special Ed. HS course work accepted: Yes, if it meets
college-prep standards

Specific course requirements for all applicants: Yes
Separate application required for services: Yes
# of LD applications submitted yearly: 200
# of LD applications accepted yearly: NR
Total # of students receiving LD/ADHD services: 220
**Acceptance into program means acceptance into
college:** Students must be admitted and enrolled at the
University first and then may request services.

ADMISSIONS

Students with LD must be admitted to the University and then to the Learning Services Program. Students who wish to have program staff consult with Admissions about their LD during the admissions process must submit a Supplemental Application to the Learning Services Program that requires documentation of the LD. Students using a Common Application should indicate interest in the program on their application. Special education courses taken in high school may be accepted if they meet the criteria for the Carnegie Units. The academic credentials of successful applicants with LD fall within the range of regular admissions criteria; the mean GPA is 2.9 for LD admits and 3.2 for regularly admitted students; ACT ranges from 24–29 for regular admits and 24–28 for LD admits or SAT 1110–1270 for regular admits and 1131 for LD admits. American Sign Language is an acceptable substitution for foreign language. The admission decision is made by a special admissions committee and is based on the high school record, recommendations, and all pertinent diagnostic reports. For selected students, admission to the University will be contingent upon enrollment in the program; for others, the Learning Services Program will be optional though strongly recommended. Conditional admission is offered to some students through the Excell Program.

ADDITIONAL INFORMATION

Students have an academic advisor experienced in advising students with LD. All entering freshmen have the same requirements, including College Writing (a section is reserved for students in the program) and College Reading. Students meet weekly with a learning specialist for individual tutorial sessions that help them further develop college-level reading, writing, and study strategies. Peer tutors assist with course content tutoring. Individual and group counseling is offered through Psychological Services. The staff of the program will consult professors with students' written permission. All modifications are based upon diagnostic testing and educational recommendations, and students are held to the same academic standards but may meet these standards through nontraditional means. As sophomores, basic skills tutorial sessions are offered on an as-needed basis.

SUPPORT SERVICES CONTACT INFORMATION

Learning Disability Program/Services: Learning Services Program
Director: Helen Steinberg
   Telephone: 202-885-3360
   Fax: 202-885-1042
Contact: Same

LEARNING DISABILITY SERVICES

Requests for the following services/accommodations will be evaluated individually based on appropriate and current documentation.

Allowed in Exams
   Calculator: Yes
   Dictionary: Y/N
   Computer: Y/N
   Spellchecker: Y/N
Extended test time: Yes
Scribes: Yes
Proctors: Yes
Oral exams: Y/N
Notetakers: No

Distraction-reduced environment: Yes
Tape recording in class: Yes
Books on tape from RFBD: No
Taping of books not from RFBD: Yes
Accommodations for students with ADHD: Yes
Reading machine: Yes
Other assistive technology: Yes
Priority registration: Yes

Added costs for services: $1,000
LD specialists: Yes (5)
Professional tutors: No
Peer tutors: Yes
Max. hours/wk. for services: Unlimited
How professors are notified of LD/ADHD: By the student and the program director

GENERAL ADMISSIONS INFORMATION

Director of Admissions: Dr. Sharon Alston
Telephone: 202-885-6066

ENTRANCE REQUIREMENTS
16 total are required; 18 total are recommended; 4 English required, 3 math required, 4 math recommended, 2 science recommended, 2 science lab recommended, 2 foreign language required, 3 social studies recommended, 4 elective recommended. High school diploma or GED required.

Application deadline: February 1
Notification: Mid-March
Average GPA: 3.2

Average SAT I Math: 592
Average SAT I Verbal: 599
Average ACT: 26

Graduated top 10% of class: 28%
Graduated top 25% of class: 70%
Graduated top 50% of class: 92%

COLLEGE GRADUATION REQUIREMENTS

Course waivers allowed: No
Course substitutions allowed: No
In what subjects: Math department does not offer waivers/course substitutions, however, a special section of finite math is offered for students with learning disabilities. This section meets 3 rather than 2 days a week and has a professor and a math tutor who are familiar with LD.

ADDITIONAL INFORMATION

Environment: The University is located on 77 acres close to the Capitol in a residential area.

Student Body
   Undergrad enrollment: 5,705
   Female: 61%
   Male: 39%
   Out-of-state: 92%

Cost Information
   Tuition: $21,144
   Room & board: $8,392
Housing Information
   University housing: Yes
   Percent living on campus: 59%

Greek System
   Fraternity: Yes
   Sorority: Yes
Athletics: NCAA Division I

CATHOLIC UNIVERSITY OF AMERICA

102 McMahon Hall, Washington, DC 20064
Phone: 202-319-5305 • Fax: 202-319-6533
E-mail: cua-admissions@cua.edu • Web: www.cua.edu
Support level: CS • Institution type: 4-year private

LEARNING DISABILITY PROGRAM AND SERVICES

The University does not have a specially designated "program" for students with LD, but offers comprehensive support services and accommodations. The University has an Advisory Committee on Students with LD that is composed of faculty members and administrators with expertise in a variety of specialized areas. The committee assists students with an LD that might preclude their full participation in university academic activities. The goals of the services are to facilitate academic success, support personal growth, and encourage self-advocacy. Students with LD are required to meet the same academic standards as other students at the University. Students must submit current diagnostic verification of the LD. To initiate services and accommodations students make an appointment with an advisor to Students with LD as soon as possible after arrival on campus. A disabilities advisor will consult with students to determine appropriate accommodations and coordinate services. Students with LD/ADHD that impairs their ability to acquire a foreign language may apply to substitute for the requirement. The decision to grant a substitution is based on an individual's learning history, documentation of a disability that impairs foreign language acquisition, and future educational goals.

LD/ADHD ADMISSIONS INFORMATION

College entrance tests required: Yes
Nonstandardized tests accepted: Yes
Interview required: No
Essay required: Yes
Documentation required for LD: Psychoeducational evaluation
Documentation required for ADHD: Yes
Documentation submitted to: Admissions
Special Ed. HS course work accepted: Yes

Specific course requirements for all applicants: Yes
Separate application required for services: Yes
# of LD applications submitted yearly: 60–90
# of LD applications accepted yearly: N/A
Total # of students receiving LD/ADHD services: 188
Acceptance into program means acceptance into college: Students must be admitted and enrolled at the University first and then may request services.

ADMISSIONS

Students with LD may apply for admission through the regular admission procedures or may request a special admissions review. If an otherwise intellectually qualified applicant feels that there are weaknesses in admissions material due to a pre-existing learning disability and voluntarily informs the Office of Admissions, the application will be referred to a Special Admissions Committee for review. The review process will be used to provide a fuller assessment of the total student than regular admissions material might provide. Applicants wishing to be considered under the special admissions policy for students with LD/ADHD should submit the following along with regular admissions requirements: diagnostic reports certifying the LD and the ability to do college work; three teacher evaluations from the most recent teachers of math, English, and one other subject; a supervised handwritten writing sample, on a topic of the applicant's choice; and an optional interview. These optional procedures are intended to enhance each applicant's opportunity for admission to the University and will not be used to discriminate against the individual.

ADDITIONAL INFORMATION

Services include advocacy; advising and referral to tutoring or study skills; faculty consultation and support; assistance in arranging note-takers and recorded texts; support and positive feedback; tape recording; extended time on tests; priority registration; and reasonable extension of deadlines on written papers. The Academic Tutoring and Learning Assistance Services offers individual and group tutoring, "study strategies," writing skills assistance, counseling, and an ADHD/LD support group. Students with LD that impairs the ability to learn a foreign language (two semesters required for graduation) may apply for a substitution by: providing LD documentation; completing basic language testing; writing a letter formally requesting the substitution; and meeting with LD advisor. If granted a foreign language substitution, students meet with Associate Dean of Arts and Sciences to determine alternate courses.

SUPPORT SERVICES CONTACT INFORMATION

Learning Disability Program/Services: Disability Support Services
Director: Bonnie McClellan
  E-mail: mcclellan@cua.edu
  Telephone: 202-319-5618
  Fax: 202-319-5126
Contact: Same

LEARNING DISABILITY SERVICES

Requests for the following services/accommodations will be evaluated individually based on appropriate and current documentation.

Allowed in Exams
  Calculator: Yes
  Dictionary: Yes
  Computer: Yes
  Spellchecker: Yes
Extended test time: Yes
Scribes: Yes
Proctors: Yes
Oral exams: Yes
Notetakers: Yes

Distraction-reduced environment: Yes
Tape recording in class: Yes
Books on tape from RFBD: Yes
Taping of books not from RFBD: Yes
Accommodations for students with
  ADHD: Yes
Reading machine: Yes
Other assistive technology: Yes
Priority registration: Yes

Added costs for services: No
LD specialists: Yes (1)
Professional tutors: 2
Peer tutors: As needed
Max. hours/wk. for services: 3
How professors are notified of
  LD/ADHD: By both student and director

GENERAL ADMISSIONS INFORMATION

Director of Admissions: Dale Herald
Telephone: 202-319-5305

ENTRANCE REQUIREMENTS

17 total are recommended; 4 English recommended, 3 math recommended, 3 science recommended, 1 science lab recommended, 2 foreign language recommended, 4 social studies recommended, 1 history recommended. High school diploma or GED required. Minimum TOEFL is 550. TOEFL required of all international applicants.

Application deadline: February 15
Notification: March 20
Average GPA: 3.4

Average SAT I Math: 575
Average SAT I Verbal: 590
Average ACT: 25

Graduated top 10% of class: 24%
Graduated top 25% of class: 54%
Graduated top 50% of class: 86%

COLLEGE GRADUATION REQUIREMENTS

Course waivers allowed: No
Course substitutions allowed: Yes
In what subjects: Foreign language

ADDITIONAL INFORMATION

Environment: The University is situated in northeast Washington, D.C., within minutes of the Capitol.

Student Body
  Undergrad enrollment: 2,609
  Female: 54%
  Male: 46%
  Out-of-state: 92%

Cost Information
  Tuition: $20,050
  Room & board: $8,382
Housing Information
  University housing: Yes
  Percent living on campus: 58%

Greek System
  Fraternity: Yes
  Sorority: Yes
  Athletics: NCAA Division III

Catholic University of America

GEORGE WASHINGTON UNIVERSITY

2121 I Street NW, Suite 201, Washington, DC 20052
Phone: 202-994-6040 • Fax: 202-994-0325
E-mail: gwadm@gwu.edu • Web: www.gwu.edu
Support level: CS • Institution type: 4-year private

LEARNING DISABILITY PROGRAM AND SERVICES

Disability Support Services (DSS) was established to provide support to disabled students so that they might participate fully in university life, derive the greatest benefit from their educational experiences, and achieve maximum personal success. There is no LD program at GW with a fee for service. Students with LD/ADHD are served through DSS. Services are designed to eliminate competitive disadvantages in an academic environment while preserving academic integrity. The staff is committed to providing student-centered services that meet the individual needs of each student. The ultimate goal of DSS is to assist students with disabilities as they gain knowledge to recognize strengths, accommodate differences, and become strong self-advocates. Staff are available to discuss issues such as course load, learning strategies, academic accommodations, and petitions for course waivers or substitutions. DSS offers individual assistance in addressing needs not provided through routine services. Students with LD must provide documentation, including a comprehensive diagnostic interview, psychoeducational evaluation, and a treatment plan; include test scores and an interpretation of overall intelligence, information processing, executive functioning, spatial ability, memory, motor ability, achievement skills, reading, writing, and math, and a specific diagnosis and description of the student's functional limitations in an educational setting.

LD/ADHD ADMISSIONS INFORMATION

College entrance tests required: Yes
Nonstandardized tests accepted: Yes
Interview required: No
Essay required: Yes
Documentation required for LD: WAIS-III;
  neuropsychological or psychoeducational evaluation:
  within 3 years
Documentation required for ADHD: Yes
Documentation submitted to: DSS—after admission
Special Ed. HS course work accepted: No

Specific course requirements for all applicants: Yes
Separate application required for services: No
# of LD applications submitted yearly: N/A
# of LD applications accepted yearly: N/A
Total # of students receiving LD/ADHD services: 260
**Acceptance into program means acceptance into
  college:** Students must be admitted and enrolled at the
  University first and then reviewed for services with
  Disability Support Services.

ADMISSIONS
GWU does not discriminate on the basis of handicap in the recruitment and admission of students. There are no separate admissions procedures or criteria for disabled students. The minimal course requirements include 2 years math (prefer 4), 4 years English, 2 years foreign language (prefer 4), 2–3 years social sciences (prefer 4), and 2–3 years science (prefer 4). The score range for the ACT is 25–30 or SAT 1160–1320. The SAT II is optional. Since there is no automatic referral from Admissions or other campus offices, students are encouraged to contact DSS directly prior to or upon admission.

ADDITIONAL INFORMATION
Students need to make a specific request for services or accommodations. Based upon the documentation, the director of DSS authorizes the needed academic adjustments. DSS provides services without charge, including advocacy, readers, scribes, test proctors, LD advising, and assistance with registration and note-taking. Students may be referred for additional services, including diagnostic testing, tutors, and specialized noncredit courses that are available on a fee basis. There is a learning disabilities support group that meets twice throughout the academic year. This group focuses on issues important to students with LD and/or ADHD. In addition to providing an opportunity for peer support, the group discusses topics ranging from study strategies, note-taking, and the planning of papers, to social issues facing the GW student with LD/ADHD. Also, there is a Disability Resource Association, which is a student organization that has a Speakers Bureau and offers support groups.

SUPPORT SERVICES CONTACT INFORMATION

Learning Disability Program/Services: Disability Support Services (DSS)
Director: Christy Willis
  E-mail: cwillis@gwu.edu
  Telephone: 202-994-8250
  Fax: 202-994-7610
Contact: Becky McCloskey
  E-mail: beckymc@gwu.edu
  Telephone: 202-994-8250
  Fax: 202-994-7610

LEARNING DISABILITY SERVICES

Requests for the following services/accommodations will be evaluated individually based on appropriate and current documentation.

Allowed in Exams		
Calculator: Yes	**Distraction-reduced environment:** Yes	**Added costs for services:** No
Dictionary: Yes	**Tape recording in class:** Yes	**LD specialists:** Yes (2)
Computer: Yes	**Books on tape from RFBD:** Yes	**Professional tutors:** 2
Spellchecker: Yes	**Taping of books not from RFBD:** Yes	**Peer tutors:** Yes
Extended test time: Yes	**Accommodations for students with ADHD:** Yes	**Max. hours/wk. for services:** Unlimited
Scribes: Yes	**Reading machine:** Yes	**How professors are notified of LD/ADHD:** By both student and director
Proctors: Yes	**Other assistive technology:** Yes	
Oral exams: No	**Priority registration:** Yes	
Notetakers: Yes		

GENERAL ADMISSIONS INFORMATION

Director of Admissions: Kathryn Napper
Telephone: 202-994-6040

ENTRANCE REQUIREMENTS

4 English required, 4 English recommended, 2 math required, 4 math recommended, 2 science required, 4 science recommended, 1 science lab required, 2 foreign language required, 4 foreign language recommended, 2 social studies required, 4 social studies recommended. High school diploma is required and GED is not accepted. Minimum TOEFL is 550. TOEFL required of all international applicants.

Application deadline: January 15	**Average SAT I Math:** 620	**Graduated top 10% of class:** 45%
Notification: March 15	**Average SAT I Verbal:** 620	**Graduated top 25% of class:** 85%
Average GPA: NR	**Average ACT:** 26	**Graduated top 50% of class:** 99%

COLLEGE GRADUATION REQUIREMENTS

Course waivers allowed: No
Course substitutions allowed: Yes
In what subjects: Primarily math; determined on a case-by-case basis

ADDITIONAL INFORMATION

Environment: The University has an urban campus 3 blocks from the White House.

Student Body	Cost Information	Greek System
Undergrad enrollment: 8,837	**Tuition:** $25,000	**Fraternity:** Yes
Female: 57%	**Room & board:** $8,538	**Sorority:** Yes
Male: 43%	**Housing Information**	**Athletics:** NCAA Division I
Out-of-state: 94%	**University housing:** Yes	
	Percent living on campus: 58%	

GEORGETOWN UNIVERSITY

37th and P Streets, NW, Washington, DC 20057
Phone: 202-687-3600 • Fax: 202-687-5084
E-mail: gwr@georgetown.edu • Web: www.georgetown.edu
Support level: CS • Institution type: 4-year private

LEARNING DISABILITY PROGRAM AND SERVICES

Georgetown University will not discriminate against or deny access to any otherwise qualified student with a disability. Learning Services requires that all students with learning disabilities provide documentation. Once the disability is on record the University will provide reasonable accommodations. Learning Services will advise students about their college course work and provide study-skills assistance on an as-available basis.

LD/ADHD ADMISSIONS INFORMATION

College entrance tests required: Yes
Nonstandardized tests accepted: Yes
Interview required: No
Essay required: Yes
Documentation required for LD: Psychoeducational evaluation
Documentation required for ADHD: Yes
Documentation submitted to: Disability Support Services
Special Ed. HS course work accepted: No

Specific course requirements for all applicants: Yes
Separate application required for services: No
# of LD applications submitted yearly: N/A
# of LD applications accepted yearly: N/A
Total # of students receiving LD/ADHD services: NR
Acceptance into program means acceptance into college: Students must be admitted and enrolled at the University first and then may request services.

ADMISSIONS
Students with learning disabilities are admitted under the same competitive standards used for all students. Services are offered to enrolled students.

ADDITIONAL INFORMATION
Georgetown uses AHEAD (Association for Higher Education and Disability) guidelines for documentation of LD/ADHD. Testing must be comprehensive and address the following areas: Aptitude; Achievement, including current levels of functioning in reading, math, and written language; and Information Processing. Testing must be current within the last three years. There must be clear and specific evidence and identification of an LD. Actual test scores must be provided including interpretation of results. Professionals conducting assessment and rendering diagnoses of LD must be qualified. Test used to document eligibility must be technically sound and standardized for use with an adult population. A written summary of the student's relevant educational, medical, and family histories that relate to the LD must be included. Recommendations for accommodations should be based on objective evidence of a substantial limitation to learning and should establish rationale for any accommodation recommended.

SUPPORT SERVICES CONTACT INFORMATION

Learning Disability Program/Services: Disability Support Services/Learning Services
Director: Marcia Fulk
  Telephone: 202-687-6985
  Fax: 202-687-6158
Contact: Same

LEARNING DISABILITY SERVICES

Requests for the following services/accommodations will be evaluated individually based on appropriate and current documentation.

Allowed in Exams
  Calculator: Yes
  Dictionary: Y/N
  Computer: Yes
  Spellchecker: Yes
Extended test time: Yes
Scribes: No
Proctors: No
Oral exams: Yes
Notetakers: Yes

Distraction-reduced environment: Yes
Tape recording in class: Yes
Books on tape from RFBD: Yes
Taping of books not from RFBD: Yes
Accommodations for students with ADHD: Yes
Reading machine: Yes
Other assistive technology: Yes
Priority registration: Yes

Added costs for services: No
LD specialists: Yes (1)
Professional tutors: 2
Peer tutors: Yes
Max. hours/wk. for services: Tutorial referrals
How professors are notified of LD/ADHD: By the student and the program director

GENERAL ADMISSIONS INFORMATION

Director of Admissions: Dean Charles Deacon
Telephone: 202-687-3600

ENTRANCE REQUIREMENTS

4 English required, 4 English recommended, 2 math required, 4 math recommended, 2 science required, 4 science recommended, 1 science lab recommended, 2 foreign language required, 4 foreign language recommended, 2 social studies required, 4 social studies recommended. High school diploma or GED required. Minimum TOEFL is 550. TOEFL required of all international applicants.

Application deadline: January 10
Notification: April 1
Average GPA: NR

Average SAT I Math: 675
Average SAT I Verbal: 675
Average ACT: 29

Graduated top 10% of class: 78%
Graduated top 25% of class: 94%
Graduated top 50% of class: 98%

COLLEGE GRADUATION REQUIREMENTS

Course waivers allowed: No
Course substitutions allowed: Yes
In what subjects: Foreign language can be substituted if not required for major.

ADDITIONAL INFORMATION

Environment: The University is located on 110 acres, 1.5 miles north of downtown Washington, D.C.

Student Body
  Undergrad enrollment: 6,418
  Female: 54%
  Male: 46%
  Out-of-state: 99%

Cost Information
  Tuition: $24,200
  Room & board: $9,103
Housing Information
  University housing: Yes
  Percent living on campus: 67%

Greek System
  Fraternity: Yes
  Sorority: Yes
Athletics: NCAA Division I

BARRY UNIVERSITY

11300 North East Second Avenue, Miami Shores, FL 33161-6695
Phone: 305-899-3100 • Fax: 305-899-2971
E-mail: admissions@mail.barry.edu • Web: www.barry.edu
Support level: SP • Institution type: 4-year private

LEARNING DISABILITY PROGRAM AND SERVICES

Barry offers a special program for students with LD. The Center for Advanced Learning Program (CAL) is a comprehensive, intensive, highly structured, and individualized approach to assisting students with LD throughout their college careers. It is designed to move students gradually toward increasing self-direction in academic, personal, and career activities. This program affirms Barry University's commitment to expand college opportunities to students with LD and to provide the specialized services which can enhance college success. To apply to the CAL Program students must: complete and return to CAL, the general Barry application for admission and the CAL Application; write a one- to-two-page personal statement on how the student would benefit from the CAL Program; have a personal interview with the CAL; sign the Informed Consent Form and present this form to their high school in order for documentation to be released; forward Psychoeducational Evaluation Report including the WAIS-R, Achievement Tests, and Information Processing Testing; and provide a copy of the most recent IEP, high school transcript, and a letter of recommendation from a school counselor or LD specialist. It is important for students with LD to understand the need for a commitment to working with the CAL Program to achieve success at college.

LD/ADHD ADMISSIONS INFORMATION

College entrance tests required: Yes
Nonstandardized tests accepted: Yes
Interview required: NR
Essay required: Yes
Documentation required for LD: Psychoeducational evaluation
Documentation required for ADHD: Yes
Documentation submitted to: Center for Advanced Learning
Special Ed. HS course work accepted: Yes

Specific course requirements for all applicants: Yes
Separate application required for services: Yes
# of LD applications submitted yearly: 75
# of LD applications accepted yearly: 25
Total # of students receiving LD/ADHD services: 45
Acceptance into program means acceptance into college: Students must be admitted and enrolled at the University first and then may receive services from CAL.

ADMISSIONS

Students with learning disabilities must meet the regular admission criteria for the University, which include 2.0 GPA; ACT of 17 or above or SAT I of 800 or above; and 4 years English, 3–4 years math, 3 years natural science, and 3–4 years social science. However, there is a process of individual review by learning disability professionals for those students who have a diagnosed disability and who do not meet the general admission criteria. These students must have an interview and provide appropriate and current LD documentation. An essay is required for admission into the LD Program. Students admitted to the CAL Program will be expected to meet all requirements established for them and those of the specific university program in which they enroll.

ADDITIONAL INFORMATION

The Center for Advanced Learning (CAL) Program includes a full range of professionally managed and intensive support services that includes the following: individual diagnostic evaluation allowing for development of a personalized educational plan; intensive scheduled classes to improve math, reading, and written and oral communication skills; individual and small-group, subject-area tutoring; instruction in learning and study strategies based on individual needs; academic advising; assistance in developing interpersonal skills; individual and small-group personal, academic, and career counseling; assistance in obtaining study aids; computer access; special test administration services; advocacy with faculty; and optional summer college transition program. Additionally, all students have access to math labs, writing centers, reading clinics, and educational seminars. All instructional staff hold advanced degrees in their area of specialization. Services are available for both undergraduate and graduate students.

SUPPORT SERVICES CONTACT INFORMATION

Learning Disability Program/Services: Center for Advanced Learning
Director: Professor Jill M. Reed
 E-mail: jreed@mail.barry.edu
 Telephone: 305-899-3485
 Fax: 305-899-3778
Contact: Vivian Castro
 E-mail: vcastro@mail.barry.edu
 Telephone: 305-899-3485
 Fax: 305-899-3778

LEARNING DISABILITY SERVICES

Requests for the following services/accommodations will be evaluated individually based on appropriate and current documentation.

Allowed in Exams
 Calculator: Yes
 Dictionary: Yes
 Computer: Yes
 Spellchecker: Yes
Extended test time: Yes
Scribes: Yes
Proctors: Yes
Oral exams: Yes
Notetakers: Yes

Distraction-reduced environment: Yes
Tape recording in class: Yes
Books on tape from RFBD: Yes
Taping of books not from RFBD: Yes
Accommodations for students with ADHD: Yes
Reading machine: Yes
Other assistive technology: Yes
Priority registration: No

Added costs for services: $1,850 per semester
LD specialists: Yes (2)
Professional tutors: 14
Peer tutors: No
Max. hours/wk. for services: Unlimited
How professors are notified of LD/ADHD: By the student and program director

GENERAL ADMISSIONS INFORMATION

Director of Admissions: Tracey Fontaine
Telephone: 305-899-3100

ENTRANCE REQUIREMENTS
4 English recommended, 3 math recommended, 3 science recommended, 3 social studies recommended. High school diploma or GED required. Minimum TOEFL is 500. TOEFL required of all international applicants.

Application deadline: Rolling
Notification: Rolling
Average GPA: 2.9

Average SAT I Math: 430
Average SAT I Verbal: 430
Average ACT: 21

Graduated top 10% of class: 15%
Graduated top 25% of class: 40%
Graduated top 50% of class: 50%

COLLEGE GRADUATION REQUIREMENTS

Course waivers allowed: No
Course substitutions allowed: Yes
In what subjects: With appropriate documentation, and if the course is not deemed to be an "essential requirement."

ADDITIONAL INFORMATION

Environment: Located 7 miles from Miami.

Student Body
 Undergrad enrollment: 5,777
 Female: 65%
 Male: 35%
 Out-of-state: 10%

Cost Information
 Tuition: $15,530
 Room & board: $6,220
Housing Information
 University housing: Yes
 Percent living on campus: 31%

Greek System
 Fraternity: Yes
 Sorority: Yes
 Athletics: NCAA Division II

BEACON COLLEGE

105 E. Main Street, Leesburg, FL 34748
Phone: 352-395-4302
Web: www.sundial.net/beacon
Support: SP • Institution: 4-year private

LEARNING DISABILITY PROGRAM AND SERVICES

The philosophy of Beacon College is to offer our students academic programs supplemented by appropriate accommodations and support services that will help them prepare for meaningful participation in society. The purpose of Beacon College is to create a campus community that facilitates academic and personal success. The mission of Beacon College is to offer academic degree programs to students with learning disabilities. To accomplish this, the College provides Associate of Arts and Bachelor of Arts programs in human services and liberal studies. The human services programs provide a practical experience in the professional fields associated with public and community services. The liberal studies program provides a broad-based liberal arts education for students seeking intellectual growth and personal change. Liberal studies exposes students to a variety of subjects designed to establish a basis for effective lifelong learning and attainment of personal goals.

LD/ADHD ADMISSIONS INFORMATION

College entrance tests required: Yes
Nonstandardized tests accepted: Yes
Interview required: Yes
Essay required: Yes
Documentation required for LD: Psychoeducational evaluation, WAIS-III
Documentation required for ADHD: Yes
Submitted to: Admissions
Special Ed. HS course work accepted: Yes

Specific course requirements for all applicants: Yes
Separate application required for services: No
# of LD applications submitted yearly: 40–60
# of LD applications accepted yearly: 18–25
Total # of students receiving LD/ADHD services: 66
Acceptance into program means acceptance into college: Students are admitted directly into the College and the program simultaneously.

ADMISSIONS

Applicants must submit current (within two years) academic reports and test scores, recent psychoeducational evaluations documenting a learning disability, and records that may help clarify presenting learning problems. Students must also submit a high school transcript, personal statements, and three recommendation forms. All applicants must have a high school diploma or the GED. Each applicant must have an interview prior to an admission decision being made. There are no specific high school courses required for admission, and courses taken in a special education curriculum are accepted. The College does not require either the ACT or SAT. The admission decision is made by the Admissions Committee. Beacon may admit students on a provisional basis.

ADDITIONAL INFORMATION

Beacon College is a growing program that serves college students with documented learning disabilities who each have the ability, desire, and perseverence to earn either an AA or BA degree. Some students are recent high school graduates while others are older students who transfer from other colleges or who enter after being in the workforce. Beacon serves a culturally diverse group of men and women from 22 different states. Small class size, average of 10, helps to meet the needs of the individual students. Beacon's Academic Mentoring Program guides students with a focus on self-awareness, time management/organization skills, and strategies for academic success. The Field Placement Program assists students with goal setting, career exploration, and work experience. Students gain life skills through living within the Leesburg community in apartments leased by the College. Beacon students graduate with a college academic degree and the life skills to live independently. In addition to the ability to set personal goals, graduates are also prepared to seek gainful employment or explore additional academic or vocational training.

SUPPORT SERVICES CONTACT INFORMATION

Learning Disability Program/Services: Beacon College
Director: Deborah Brodbeck, President
  E-mail: admissions@beaconcollege.edu
  Telephone: 352-787-7660
  Fax: 352-787-0721
Contact: Betsy Stout Morrill
  E-mail: beaconl@sundail.net
  Telephone: 352-787-7249
  Fax: 352-787-0721

LEARNING DISABILITY SERVICES

Requests for the following services/accommodations will be evaluated individually based on appropriate and current documentation.

Allowed in Exams
  Calculator: Yes
  Dictionary: Yes
  Computer: Yes
  Spellchecker: Yes
Extended test time: Yes
Scribes: Yes
Proctors: Yes
Oral exams: Yes
Notetakers: Yes

Distraction-reduced environment: Yes
Tape recording in class: Yes
Books on tape from RFBD: Yes
Taping of books not from RFBD: Yes
Accommodations for students with ADHD: Yes
Reading machine: Yes
Other assistive technology: Yes
Priority registration: Yes

Added costs for services: Part of total tuition
LD specialists: Yes
Professional tutors: Yes
Peer tutors: N/A
Max. hours/wk. for services: Unlimited
How professors are notified of LD/ADHD: By both student and director

GENERAL ADMISSIONS INFORMATION

Director of Admissions: Betsy Stout Morrill
Telephone: 352-787-7660

ENTRANCE REQUIREMENTS
Students must write a personal statement and a submit current psychoeducational evaluation. Three letters of recommendation must be provided. ACT/SAT not required.

Application deadline: Open
Notification: Rolling beginning 9/1
Average GPA: NR

Average SAT I Math: NR
Average SAT I Verbal: NR
Average ACT: NR

Graduated top 10% of class: NR
Graduated top 25% of class: NR
Graduated top 50% of class: NR

COLLEGE GRADUATION REQUIREMENTS

Course waivers allowed: Yes
Course substitutions allowed: Yes
In what subjects: The College meets the individual needs of all students

ADDITIONAL INFORMATION

Environment: The College is located in the city of Leesburg, 1 hour from Orlando.

Student Body
  Undergrad enrollment: 66
  Female: 40%
  Male: 60%
  Out-of-state: 83%

Cost Information
  Tuition: $18,300
  Room & board: $5,700
Housing Information
  University housing: Yes
  Percent living on campus: 100%

Greek System
  Fraternity: No
  Sorority: No
Athletics: Individual sports

FLORIDA A&M UNIVERSITY

Suite G-9, Foote-Hilyer Administration Center, Tallahassee, FL 32307
Phone: 850-599-3796 • Fax: 850-599-3069
E-mail: bcox2@famu.edu • Web: www.famu.edu
Support level: CS • Institution type: 4-year public

LEARNING DISABILITY PROGRAM AND SERVICES

Florida A&M offers an education for students with LD and meets the challenge consistent with the objective indicated by the Learning Development and Evaluation Center (LDEC) club name, "Excellence Through Caring." The goals of the LDEC are threefold: first, students with specific learning disabilities can successfully pursue college-level studies with a reasonable level of expectation for degree success; second, preparation for college-level studies for students with specific learning disabilities should begin early; and third, postsecondary students should actively engage in developmental learning. The need for life-long learning is evident in the ever-changing society and for the learning disabled person is mandatory for continued success. Tutoring for developmental learning is a major component. The program does not offer "blanket" accommodations, but services offered are very comprehensive, such as preparation classes for tests, adapted courses, opportunities for test retakes, alternative courses, and academic activities structured according to students' diagnostic evaluation. A reduced course load is considered a viable option to maintaining an acceptable GPA. The LDEC is a multifaceted program providing psychoeducational evaluation, personalized prescription, and comprehensive support services.

LD/ADHD ADMISSIONS INFORMATION

College entrance tests required: Yes
Nonstandardized tests accepted: Yes
Interview required: NR
Essay required: No
Documentation required for LD: Psychoeducational evaluation
Documentation required for ADHD: Yes
Documentation submitted to: Learning Development and Evaluation Center
Special Ed. HS course work accepted: Y/N

Specific course requirements for all applicants: Yes
Separate application required for services: Yes
# of LD applications submitted yearly: 40–60
# of LD applications accepted yearly: 20–25
Total # of students receiving LD/ADHD services: 275
Acceptance into program means acceptance into college: Students are admitted directly into LDEC and attend the summer LD program as part of special admissions to the University.

ADMISSIONS
Acceptance into the LDEC does not ensure admission to the University. If students with learning disabilities apply and are rejected, they may ask for "special admission" consideration and send verifying information of a learning disability. The Office of Admissions gives all information to the LDEC director for a recommendation for admission to the University based upon acceptance into the LDEC program. Applicants must have a regular high school diploma, take the ACT/SAT, have a recent psychoeducational evaluation, and attend a summer program. Most students who have learning disabilities and who seek admission through the LDEC enter Florida A&M through the special admission process. ACT scores should be 12 or higher. The required GPA is 1.7 or above.

ADDITIONAL INFORMATION
Specific course offerings in reading, study skills, English, and math with additional class meetings and assignments to meet the individual needs of the students are available. Students must register for reading and student life-skills courses each semester until the student and program staff feel that optimal learning development skills have been reached. When appropriate, students may have a peer tutor attend classes and take notes (student and tutor will exchange notes in the LDEC) or the peer tutor may only need to help the student organize notes from a taped lecture. LDEC offers a two-week Summer Transition Program (required for incoming students with LD) to students entering 11th or 12th grade or recent graduates from high school. This program provides students a chance to focus on certain skills such as memory, technology, or a particular academic area. Mastery of the College Study Skills Institute provides a firm foundation for students with learning disabilities to enhance success in college and their future employment.

SUPPORT SERVICES CONTACT INFORMATION

Learning Disability Program/Services: Learning Development and Evaluation Center (LDEC)
Director: Dr. Sharon M. Wooten
  Telephone: 850-599-8474
  Fax: 850-561-2513
Contact: Dr. William Hudson/Mrs. Gwen McGee
  Telephone: 850-599-3180

LEARNING DISABILITY SERVICES

Requests for the following services/accommodations will be evaluated individually based on appropriate and current documentation.

Allowed in Exams
  Calculator: Yes
  Dictionary: Yes
  Computer: Yes
  Spellchecker: Yes
Extended test time: Yes
Scribes: Yes
Proctors: Yes
Oral exams: Yes
Notetakers: Yes

Distraction-reduced environment: No
Tape recording in class: Yes
Books on tape from RFBD: Yes
Taping of books not from RFBD: Yes
Accommodations for students with ADHD: Yes
Reading machine: Yes
Other assistive technology: Yes
Priority registration: No

Added costs for services: $1,000
LD specialists: Yes (3)
Professional tutors: Yes
Peer tutors: Yes
Max. hours/wk. for services: Varies
How professors are notified of LD/ADHD: By student and program director

GENERAL ADMISSIONS INFORMATION

Director of Admissions: Barbara Cox
Telephone: 850-599-3796

ENTRANCE REQUIREMENTS

19 total are required; 4 English required, 3 math required, 3 science required, 1 science lab required, 2 foreign language required, 3 social studies required, 4 elective required. High school diploma or GED required. Minimum TOEFL is 500. TOEFL required of all international applicants.

Application deadline: May 13
Notification: Rolling
Average GPA: 3.2

Average SAT I Math: NR
Average SAT I Verbal: NR
Average ACT: 20

Graduated top 10% of class: NR
Graduated top 25% of class: NR
Graduated top 50% of class: NR

COLLEGE GRADUATION REQUIREMENTS

Course waivers No
Course substitutions allowed: Yes
In what subjects: Varies based on the major elective requirements and the student's disability

ADDITIONAL INFORMATION

Environment: The University is located on 419 acres 169 miles west of Jackson.

Student Body
  Undergrad enrollment: 10,691
  Female: 58%
  Male: 42%
  Out-of-state: 21%

Cost Information
  In-state tuition: $2,300
  Out-of-state tuition: $9,000
  Room & board: $3,896
Housing Information
  University housing: Yes
  Percent living on campus: 77%

Greek System
  Fraternity: Yes
  Sorority: Yes
Athletics: NCAA Division I

FLORIDA ATLANTIC UNIVERSITY

PO Box 3091, Boca Raton, FL 33431
Phone: 561-297-3040 • Fax: 561-297-2758
E-mail: admisweb@acc.fau.edu • Web: www.fau.edu
Support level: CS • Institution type: 4-year public

LEARNING DISABILITY PROGRAM AND SERVICES

The Office for Students with Disabilities (OSD) offers equal access to a quality education by providing reasonable accommodations to qualified students. Students who have a documented LD may receive strategy tutoring from the LD Specialist by appointment. Students are expected to be self-sufficient and strong self-advocates. There is a Counseling Center with professionally trained staff to help students with interpersonal conflicts and concerns, test anxiety, poor concentration, and guidance services.

LD/ADHD ADMISSIONS INFORMATION

College entrance tests required: Yes
Nonstandardized tests accepted: Yes
Interview required: No
Essay required: No
Documentation required for LD: Test of aptitude (WAIS-III preferred), achievement battery, tests of information processing
Documentation required for ADHD: Yes
Documentation submitted to: OSD
Special Ed. HS course work accepted: Yes

Specific course requirements for all applicants: Yes
Separate application required for services: No
# of LD applications submitted yearly: N/A
# of LD applications accepted yearly: N/A
Total # of students receiving LD/ADHD services: 250
Acceptance into program means acceptance into college: Students must be accepted and enrolled at the University first (they can appeal a denial) and then may request services.

ADMISSIONS

There is no special application process for students with LD. However, students with LD may be eligible to substitute for certain admission requirements. Students not meeting admission criteria may be admitted by a faculty admission committee, if they possess the potential to succeed in university studies or will enhance the University. Supporting documentation explaining circumstances that adversely affected the student's past academic performances will be required. An admissions counselor will assess each applicant in developing supporting materials to be presented to the committee by the Director of Admissions. Students are expected to have a minimum ACT of 20 or SAT of 860. A sliding scale is used with GPA and test scores. Students who self-disclose and are admitted are then reviewed for services. In some cases, these students are reviewed by the OSD, which provides a recommendation to admissions.

ADDITIONAL INFORMATION

Students must provide documentation including aptitude (WAIS preferred) and achievement battery. The diagnostician's report must indicate standardized assessment measures on attention, reported history, and corroboration of current symptoms using two rating scales. With appropriate documentation students may receive the following accommodations or services: the use of calculators, dictionary, computer or spellcheck in exams; extended time on tests; distraction-free environment for tests; oral exams; proctors; scribes; tape recorders in class; textbooks on tape; note-takers; and course substitutions. Skills classes are offered in study-skills techniques and organizational strategies.

SUPPORT SERVICES CONTACT INFORMATION

Learning Disability Program/Services: Office for Students with Disabilities (OSD)
Director: Nicole Robes, MEd
  Telephone: 561-297-3880
  Fax: 561-297-2184
Contact: Same

LEARNING DISABILITY SERVICES

Requests for the following services/accommodations will be evaluated individually based on appropriate and current documentation.

Allowed in Exams
  Calculator: Yes
  Dictionary: No
  Computer: Yes
  Spellchecker: Yes
  Extended test time: Yes
  Scribes: Yes
  Proctors: Yes
  Oral exams: Yes
  Notetakers: Yes

Distraction-reduced environment: Yes
Tape recording in class: Yes
Books on tape from RFBD: Yes
Taping of books not from RFBD: Yes
Accommodations for students with ADHD: Yes
Reading machine: Yes
Other assistive technology: Yes
Priority registration: No

Added costs for services: No
LD specialists: Yes (2)
Professional tutors: No
Peer tutors: No
Max. hours/wk. for services: Unlimited
How professors are notified of LD/ADHD: By both student and director

GENERAL ADMISSIONS INFORMATION

Director of Admissions: Albert Colom
Telephone: 561-297-3040

ENTRANCE REQUIREMENTS

19 total are required; 4 English required, 3 math required, 3 science required, 2 science lab required, 2 foreign language required, 3 social studies required, 4 elective required. High school diploma or GED required. Minimum TOEFL is 550. TOEFL required of all international applicants.

Application deadline: June 1
Notification: Rolling beginning 9/1
Average GPA: 3.3

Average SAT I Math: 530
Average SAT I Verbal: 520
Average ACT: 21

Graduated top 10% of class: NR
Graduated top 25% of class: NR
Graduated top 50% of class: NR

COLLEGE GRADUATION REQUIREMENTS

Course waivers allowed: No
Course substitutions allowed: Yes
In what subjects: Determined on a case-by-case basis

ADDITIONAL INFORMATION

Environment: The University is located on 1,000 acres 1.5 miles from the ocean and in proximity to Miami and Ft. Lauderdale.

Student Body
  Undergrad enrollment: 17,016
  Female: 61%
  Male: 39%
  Out-of-state: 8%

Cost Information
  In-state tuition: $2,396
  Out-of-state tuition: $9,734
  Room & board: $4,993
Housing Information
  University housing: Yes
  Percent living on campus: 5%

Greek System
  Fraternity: Yes
  Sorority: Yes
Athletics: NCAA Division I

FLORIDA STATE UNIVERSITY

2249 University Center, Tallahassee, FL 32306-2400
Phone: 850-644-6200 • Fax: 850-644-0197
E-mail: admissions@admin.fsu.edu • Web: www.fsu.edu
Support level: CS • Institution type: 4-year public

LEARNING DISABILITY PROGRAM AND SERVICES

The Student Disability Resource Center at FSU is the primary advocate on campus for students with disabilities. The center works with faculty and staff to provide accommodations for the unique needs of students both in and out of the classroom. Learning specialists can meet individually, on a regular or occasional basis, with students who have LD, attention deficit disorder or other impairments. FSU is noted for its sensitivity to students with disabilities. By providing support services at no cost to students with disabilities, the Student Disability Resource Center offers an opportunity for students with disabilities to achieve their academic and personal goals. Students who self-disclose their disability must complete a "Request for Services" form in order to receive accommodations. LD documentation must be no more than three years old and submitted from a licensed psychologist.

LD/ADHD ADMISSIONS INFORMATION

College entrance tests required: Yes
Nonstandardized tests accepted: Yes
Interview required: N/A
Essay required: No
Documentation required for LD: Psychoeducational evaluation
Documentation required for ADHD: Yes
Documentation submitted to: Admissions and Disability Resource Center
Special Ed. HS course work accepted: Yes

Specific course requirements for all applicants: Yes
Separate application required for services: Yes
# of LD applications submitted yearly: NR
# of LD applications accepted yearly: NR
Total # of students receiving LD/ADHD services: 500
Acceptance into program means acceptance into college: Students must be admitted and enrolled and then request services.

ADMISSIONS

Students with LD or ADHD who are borderline candidates for admission are encouraged to self-disclose in the admission process. These students can choose to apply for special consideration based on a disability. Special consideration is specifically designed for students who do not meet general admissions requirements. A disability subcommittee reviews the documentation, personal statement, recommendations, transcripts, and standardized test scores to determine eligibility for admissions. Under certain circumstances students may be offered summer admission.

ADDITIONAL INFORMATION

Students who choose to disclose their disability to receive accommodations must complete a "Request for Services" form available from the Student Disability Resource Center. For an LD, documentation less than three years old is required from a licensed psychologist. Staff members assist students in exploring their needs and determining the necessary services and accommodations. Academic accommodations include alternative testing/extended time, editing, note-takers, registration assistance, test writing, tutors, and study partners. Learning Specialists meet individually with students with LD/ADHD. Services include teaching study skills, memory enhancement techniques, organizational skills, test-taking strategies, stress management techniques, ways to structure tutoring for best results, skills for negotiating accommodations with instructors, and supportive counseling. Advocates for Disability Awareness act as a support group for students with disabilities. Through their participation, students and others in the University community involved develop skills in leadership, self-advocacy, and career development.

SUPPORT SERVICES CONTACT INFORMATION

Learning Disability Program/Services: Student Disability Resource Center
Director: Lauren Kennedy
  E-mail: sdrc@admin.fsu.edu
  Telephone: 850-644-9566
  Fax: 850-644-7164
Contact: Same

LEARNING DISABILITY SERVICES

Requests for the following services/accommodations will be evaluated individually based on appropriate and current documentation.

Allowed in Exams
  Calculator: Yes
  Dictionary: Yes
  Computer: Yes
  Spellchecker: Yes
Extended test time: Yes
Scribes: Yes
Proctors: Yes
Oral exams: Yes
Notetakers: Yes

Distraction-reduced environment: Yes
Tape recording in class: Yes
Books on tape from RFBD: Yes
Taping of books not from RFBD: Yes
Accommodations for students with
  ADHD: Yes
Reading machine: Yes
Other assistive technology: Yes
Priority registration: Yes

Added costs for services: N/A
LD specialists: Yes (1)
Professional tutors: N/A
Peer tutors: N/A
Max. hours/wk. for services: N/A
How professors are notified of
  LD/ADHD: By student

GENERAL ADMISSIONS INFORMATION

Director of Admissions: John Burnhill
Telephone: 850-644-6200

ENTRANCE REQUIREMENTS
19 total are required; 4 English required, 3 math required, 3 science required, 2 science lab required, 2 foreign language required, 4 elective required. High school diploma or GED required. Minimum TOEFL is 550. TOEFL required of all international applicants.

Application deadline: March 1
Notification: Rolling beginning 9/20
Average GPA: 3.6

Average SAT I Math: 595
Average SAT I Verbal: 592
Average ACT: 26

Graduated top 10% of class: 57%
Graduated top 25% of class: 75%
Graduated top 50% of class: 98%

COLLEGE GRADUATION REQUIREMENTS

Course waivers allowed: Yes
Course substitutions allowed: Yes
In what subjects: Math and foreign language

ADDITIONAL INFORMATION

Environment: Located 160 miles from Jacksonville.

Student Body
  Undergrad enrollment: 27,014
  Female: 56%
  Male: 44%
  Out-of-state: 14%

Cost Information
  In-state tuition: $2,200
  Out-of-state tuition: $8,900
  Room & board: $5,610
Housing Information
  University housing: Yes
  Percent living on campus: 16%

Greek System
  Fraternity: Yes
  Sorority: Yes
Athletics: NCAA Division I

LYNN UNIVERSITY

3601 North Military Trail, Boca Raton, FL 33431-5598
Phone: 561-237-7900 • Fax: 561-237-7100
E-mail: admission@lynn.edu • Web: www.lynn.edu
Support level: SP • Institution type: 4-year private

LEARNING DISABILITY PROGRAM AND SERVICES

Academic support services provide assistance to help students remain in college. The Academic Resource Center (ARC) is available to all students. The Advancement Program is designed for a limited number of students with LD who have the motivation and intellectual capacity for college-level work, yet whose skill and performance levels indicate that without support they would be at risk. In The Advancement Program (TAP), students enroll in regular college courses and, concurrently, in elective credit courses designed for this program. One three-credit specialized course is offered in the first semester. This course, Language and Learning, is diagnostic and offers an opportunity for students to explore their strengths, learning styles, and college skills. A research-based text, Frames of Mind, is required reading. Programs are scheduled for each individual with special consideration, usually resulting in a reduced academic course load. Tutorials, both individual and group, and study groups are facilitated by TAP personnel. Currently, 24 tutors holding MEds and PhDs provide support to students.

LD/ADHD ADMISSIONS INFORMATION

College entrance tests required: Yes
Nonstandardized tests accepted: Yes
Interview required: No
Essay required: No
Documentation required for LD: Psychoeducational evaluation
Documentation required for ADHD: Yes
Documentation submitted to: TAP
Special Ed. HS course work accepted: Yes

Specific course requirements for all applicants: Yes
Separate application required for services: No
# of LD applications submitted yearly: 500
# of LD applications accepted yearly: 300
Total # of students receiving LD/ADHD services: 268
Acceptance into program means acceptance into college: Students must be accepted into the University first and then are offered services through TAP.

ADMISSIONS

Students should submit the general application to Lynn University. Admissions criteria are dependent on the level of services required. Students needing the least restrictive services should have taken college-prep high school courses. Some students may be admitted provisionally after submitting official information. Other students may be admitted conditionally into the Frontiers Program. Typically, these students have an ACT of 18 or lower or an SAT of 850 or lower and 2.0 GPA. Students admitted conditionally take a reduced course load, no science for first semester, and 1 1/2 hours of scheduled tutoring. The Program Director and staff make a final recommendation on status to the Admission Committee regarding the admission of students to the Advancement Program. Interviews are strongly encouraged.

ADDITIONAL INFORMATION

All tests are monitored by TAP personnel, and advocacy work with faculty is provided by the director. TAP students may choose any major as they work toward degree completion in subsequent years. Students who continue to need support services after one year will continue in the program for specific tutoring, untimed tests, and program guidance as needed. Skills classes are offered for credit in Language and Learning Development. There is also one-to-one tutoring with professional tutors.

SUPPORT SERVICES CONTACT INFORMATION

Learning Disability Program/Services: The Advancement Program
Director: Gary Martin, LMCH
  E-mail: admission@lynn.edu
  Telephone: 561-237-7239
  Fax: 561-237-7094
Contact: Melanie Glines
  E-mail: admission@lynn.edu
  Telephone: 561-237-7900
  Fax: 561-237-7100

LEARNING DISABILITY SERVICES

Requests for the following services/accommodations will be evaluated individually based on appropriate and current documentation.

Allowed in Exams
  Calculator: Yes
  Dictionary: Yes
  Computer: Yes
  Spellchecker: Yes
Extended test time: Yes
Scribes: No
Proctors: Yes
Oral exams: Yes
Notetakers: Yes

Distraction-reduced environment: Yes
Tape recording in class: Yes
Books on tape from RFBD: No
Taping of books not from RFBD: No
Accommodations for students with ADHD: Yes
Reading machine: Yes
Other assistive technology: Yes
Priority registration: No

Added costs for services: $4,250 per semester
LD specialists: Yes
Professional tutors: 24
Peer tutors: No
Max. hours/wk. for services: Unlimited
How professors are notified of LD/ADHD: By student

GENERAL ADMISSIONS INFORMATION

Director of Admissions: Allen Mullen
Telephone: 800-888-LYNN

ENTRANCE REQUIREMENTS

20 total are recommended; 4 English recommended, 3 math recommended, 3 science recommended, 1 foreign language recommended, 2 social studies recommended, 2 history recommended, 5 elective recommended. High school diploma or GED required. Minimum TOEFL is 500. TOEFL required of all international applicants.

Application deadline: Rolling
Notification: Rolling
Average GPA: NR

Average SAT I Math: 482
Average SAT I Verbal: 471
Average ACT: 21

Graduated top 10% of class: NR
Graduated top 25% of class: NR
Graduated top 50% of class: NR

COLLEGE GRADUATION REQUIREMENTS

Course waivers allowed: No
Course substitutions allowed: Yes
In what subjects: Math and foreign language

ADDITIONAL INFORMATION

Environment: The University is located on 123 acres in a suburban area on Florida's Gold Coast.

Student Body
  Undergrad enrollment: 1,633
  Female: 54%
  Male: 46%
  Out-of-state: 61%

Cost Information
  Tuition: $17,300
  Room & board: $6,550
Housing Information
  University housing: Yes
  Percent living on campus: 55%

Greek System
  Fraternity: Yes
  Sorority: Yes
Athletics: NCAA Division II

UNIVERSITY OF FLORIDA

201 Criser Hall, Box 114000, Gainesville, FL 32611-4000
Phone: 352-392-1365 • Fax: 904-392-3987
E-mail: freshman@ufl.edu • Web: www.ufl.edu
Support level: CS • Institution type: 4-year public

LEARNING DISABILITY PROGRAM AND SERVICES

The University of Florida offers a full range of support services designed to assist students with learning disabilities. Support services are individually tailored to each student's needs and those supports may be modified to meet the specific demands and requirements of individual courses. Advisement and support services are available to students on an as-needed basis. Assistance can be provided regarding registration, learning strategies, classroom accommodations, and the University of Florida petition process.

LD/ADHD ADMISSIONS INFORMATION

College entrance tests required: Yes
Nonstandardized tests accepted: Yes
Interview required: NR
Essay required: No
Documentation required for LD: Psychoeducational evaluation
Documentation required for ADHD: Yes
Documentation submitted to: Office for Students with Disabilities
Special Ed. HS course work accepted: Yes

Specific course requirements for all applicants: Yes
Separate application required for services: No
# of LD applications submitted yearly: N/A
# of LD applications accepted yearly: N/A
Total # of students receiving LD/ADHD services: 100+
Acceptance into program means acceptance into college: Students must be admitted and enrolled at the University first (they can appeal a denial) and then may request services.

ADMISSIONS

The student with learning disabilities applies to the University under the same guidelines as all other students. However, students with learning disabilities may request a separate review. Students should check the box on the general application to request information and submit a personal statement describing how their learning disabilities may have had an impact or an effect on their grade point average or standardized test scores, if applicable. The required SAT or ACT varies according to the student's GPA. Students denied admission may petition for a review of their application. This review process petition should be directed to the Director of the Admissions.

ADDITIONAL INFORMATION

Skills workshops are offered in reading, note-taking, memory, and time management. The Dean of Students sponsors "Preview," an early registration and orientation program. Assistance can be provided regarding learning strategies, classroom accommodations, and petitions. Services are available to focus on strategic learning strategies and success strategies.

SUPPORT SERVICES CONTACT INFORMATION

Learning Disability Program/Services: Office for Students with Disabilities
Director: John Denny
  E-mail: jdenny@dso.ufl.edu
  Telephone: 352-392-1261
  Fax: 352-392-5566
Contact: Same

LEARNING DISABILITY SERVICES

Requests for the following services/accommodations will be evaluated individually based on appropriate and current documentation.

Allowed in Exams
  Calculator: Yes
  Dictionary: Yes
  Computer: Yes
  Spellchecker: Yes
Extended test time: Yes
Scribes: Yes
Proctors: Yes
Oral exams: Yes
Notetakers: Yes

Distraction-reduced environment: No
Tape recording in class: Yes
Books on tape from RFBD: Yes
Taping of books not from RFBD: Yes
Accommodations for students with ADHD: Yes
Reading machine: Yes
Other assistive technology: Yes
Priority registration: Yes

Added costs for services: No
LD specialists: Yes
Professional tutors: No
Peer tutors: No
Max. hours/wk. for services: As needed
How professors are notified of LD/ADHD: By student and program director

GENERAL ADMISSIONS INFORMATION

Director of Admissions: William Kolb
Telephone: 352-392-1365

ENTRANCE REQUIREMENTS

15 total are required; 4 English required, 3 math required, 3 science required, 2 science lab required, 2 foreign language required, 3 social studies required. High school diploma or GED required.

Application deadline: January 16
Notification: Within 3 weeks
Average GPA: 3.4

Average SAT I Math: 645
Average SAT I Verbal: 620
Average ACT: 28

Graduated top 10% of class: 66%
Graduated top 25% of class: 89%
Graduated top 50% of class: 99%

COLLEGE GRADUATION REQUIREMENTS

Course waivers allowed: No
Course substitutions allowed: Yes
In what subjects: Foreign language and math

ADDITIONAL INFORMATION

Environment: The University is located on 2,000 acres in a small city 115 miles north of Orlando, Florida, and 20 minutes from the Gainesville airport.

Student Body
  Undergrad enrollment: 32,680
  Female: 53%
  Male: 47%
  Out-of-state: 5%

Cost Information
  In-state tuition: $2,300
  Out-of-state tuition: $9,810
  Room & board: $5,440
Housing Information
  University housing: Yes
  Percent living on campus: 21%

Greek System
  Fraternity: Yes
  Sorority: Yes
Athletics: NCAA Division I

BRENAU UNIVERSITY

1 Centennial Circle, Gainesville, GA 30501
Phone: 770-534-6100 • Fax: 770-538-4306
E-mail: wcadmissions@lib.brenau.edu • Web: www.brenau.edu
Support level: CS • Institution type: 4-year private

LEARNING DISABILITY PROGRAM AND SERVICES

The Brenau Learning Center is a program for students with a diagnosed learning disability or attention deficit disorder. Students must also have average to above average academic aptitude with an adequate high school preparation for college studies. The program is designed to provide support services for students as they attend regular college courses. It also offers a more structured learning environment as well as the freedom associated with college living. Full-time students enroll in four or five courses per semester. Learning Center students receive academic advising from the College, as well as from the director of the program. Students have the opportunity to register early, which allows them to take required courses at the appropriate time in their college career. Many students become inactive in the program as they experience success and require less assistance. They may re-enter the program at any time. Brenau University attempts to offer a more personalized caring approach to college education. Faculty are very supportive of students who request extra help. So, in addition to receiving special services from the Learning Center, staff, and tutors, the student is being educated in an environment conducive to learning.

LD/ADHD ADMISSIONS INFORMATION

College entrance tests required: Yes
Nonstandardized tests accepted: Yes
Interview required: Yes
Essay required: No
Documentation required for LD: Psychological report
Documentation required for ADHD: Yes
Documentation submitted to: Admissions and Learning Center
Special Ed. HS course work accepted: Yes

Specific course requirements for all applicants: Yes
Separate application required for services: No
# of LD applications submitted yearly: 15–20
# of LD applications accepted yearly: 15
Total # of students receiving LD/ADHD services: 40–50
Acceptance into program means acceptance into college: Students can be reviewed by the LD Program Director, but must be admitted and enrolled at the University and then may request services.

Admissions

Regular admission criteria include an SAT of 900+ or ACT of 18+, and a GPA of 2.5+. Applicants with an LD not meeting regular admission criteria may be admitted through a "Learning Center Admission" and must participate in the LD program. These students should be "college-able," motivated, and have appropriate high school preparation. Students must have the intellectual potential and academic foundation to be successful. Applicants must provide documentation. Not all students with a diagnosed LD are eligible for the program; the learning differences must not be the primary result of emotional problems. Both the director of the LC and the Director of Admissions make a decision after reviewing SAT/ACT scores, academic performance and preparation, counselor's recommendation and other letters of reference, test results contained in the psychological evaluation, and a campus interview.

Additional Information

Learning Center students can register early and receive regular academic advising from the director of the program. Study-skills classes, including word processing, reading, and math-skills classes, are offered for credit. At all service levels students may take tests in an extended-time format where oral assistance is available. Learning Center students begin tutoring with professional tutors during the first week of the term and contract to regularly attend tutoring sessions throughout the semester. All LC students may receive one hour of educational support per week in addition to scheduled tutoring. Students may be tutored in one to four academic classes per semester. Skills classes in word processing, time management, study skills, and research may be taken for credit. LD services and accommodations are available for undergraduate and graduate students. Courses are offered in the summer and entering freshmen are encouraged to attend. Summer school allows students to get ahead with courses and take a reduced course load the first year.

SUPPORT SERVICES CONTACT INFORMATION

Learning Disability Program/Services: Learning Center (LC)
Director: Vincent Yamilkoski, EdD
  E-mail: vyamilkoski@lib.brenau.edu
  Telephone: 770-534-6134
  Fax: 770-534-6221
Contact: Sharon Underwood
  E-mail: sunderwood@ub.brenau.edu
  Telephone: 770-534-6133
  Fax: 770-534-6221

LEARNING DISABILITY SERVICES

Requests for the following services/accommodations will be evaluated individually based on appropriate and current documentation.

Allowed in Exams
  Calculator: Yes
  Dictionary: Yes
  Computer: Yes
  Spellchecker: Yes
Extended test time: Yes
Scribes: Yes
Proctors: Yes
Oral exams: Yes
Notetakers: Yes

Distraction-reduced environment: Yes
Tape recording in class: Yes
Books on tape from RFBD: Yes
Taping of books not from RFBD: No
Accommodations for students with ADHD: Yes
Reading machine: Yes
Other assistive technology: Yes
Priority registration: Yes

Added costs for services: $900 per course
LD specialists: Yes (2.5)
Professional tutors: 20
Peer tutors: No
Max. hours/wk. for services: 9
How professors are notified of LD/ADHD: By both student and director

GENERAL ADMISSIONS INFORMATION

Director of Admissions: Christina Cochran
Telephone: 770-534-6100

ENTRANCE REQUIREMENTS
4 English required, 3 math required, 2 science required, 2 science lab required, 2 social studies required, 7 elective required. High school diploma or GED required. Minimum TOEFL is 500. TOEFL required of all international applicants.

Application deadline: Rolling
Notification: Rolling
Average GPA: 3.2

Average SAT I Math: 502
Average SAT I Verbal: 528
Average ACT: NR

Graduated top 10% of class: NR
Graduated top 25% of class: NR
Graduated top 50% of class: NR

COLLEGE GRADUATION REQUIREMENTS

Course waivers allowed: No
Course substitutions allowed: No
In what subjects: All students take one beginning foreign language course (3 credits)

ADDITIONAL INFORMATION

Environment: Brenau University is in a small-city setting 50 miles northeast of Atlanta in the foothills of the Blue Ridge Mountains.

Student Body
  Undergrad enrollment: 613
  Female: 100%
  Male: 0%
  Out-of-state: 12%

Cost Information
  Tuition: $11,730
  Room & board: $6,876
Housing Information
  University housing: Yes
  Percent living on campus: 53%

Greek System
  Fraternity: No
  Sorority: Yes
Athletics: NAIA

EMORY UNIVERSITY

Boisfeuillet Jones Center, Atlanta, GA 30322
Phone: 404-727-6036 • Fax: 404-727-4303
E-mail: admiss@emory.edu • Web: www.emory.edu
Support level: CS • Institution type: 4-year private

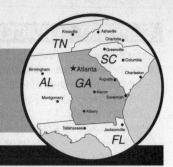

LEARNING DISABILITY PROGRAM AND SERVICES

Emory University ensures that all services/accommodations are accessible to students with disabilities. Accommodations are made on an individualized basis. Students are responsible for seeking available assistance and establishing their needs. The goals of Disability Services (DS) include: coordinating services to provide equal access to programs, services, and activities; reducing competitive disadvantage in academic work; providing individual counseling and referral; serving as an advocate for student needs; providing a variety of support services; and serving as a liaison between students and university officers or community agencies. Documentation for LD must include intelligence tests; specific cognitive processing; oral language assessment; social-emotional assessment; significant specific achievement deficits relative to potential; assessment instruments appropriate for adult population; and recommendations regarding accommodations for the student in an academic setting. ADHD documentation must include reported history of symptoms by age 7; self-report of three major behaviors from DSM-IV items; observations from two professionals; mandatory corroboration of behaviors by another adult (parent, relative, etc.); documentation on two rating scales of ADHD behaviors; recommendations regarding suggested accommodations.

LD/ADHD ADMISSIONS INFORMATION

College entrance tests required: Yes
Nonstandardized tests accepted: Yes
Interview required: No
Essay required: Yes
Documentation required for LD: Psychoeducational evaluation
Documentation required for ADHD: Yes
Documentation submitted to: Office of Disability Services
Special Ed. HS course work accepted: No

Specific course requirements for all applicants: Yes
Separate application required for services: Yes
# of LD applications submitted yearly: 100–150
# of LD applications accepted yearly: N/A
Total # of students receiving LD/ADHD services: 100–150
Acceptance into program means acceptance into college: Students must be admitted and enrolled at the University and then may request services.

ADMISSIONS

Students with learning disabilities are required to submit everything requested by the Office of Admission for regular admissions. Nonstandardized SAT/ACT may be submitted. Teacher and/or counselor recommendations may be weighted more heavily in the admissions process. A professional diagnosis of the learning disability with recommended accommodations is helpful. Essentially, each student with a disability is evaluated individually, and admitted based on potential for success in the Emory environment, taking into consideration the necessary accommodations requested. Documentation is required for services, not admissions. Once admitted, the Admissions Office sends a Self-Identification Form in the acceptance packet to each student who discloses a learning disability.

ADDITIONAL INFORMATION

The needs of students with LD are met through counseling and referral advocacy, and a variety of support services. Deans are notified by a report each semester of students who have self-identified as having LD. Tutoring is offered on a one-to-one basis or in small groups in most subjects. Students also are eligible for priority registration. Skills classes are offered, and the coordinator can monitor and track students to follow their progress. The coordinator meets with students to assess needs and develop an Individualized Service Plan. The coordinator is also an advocate for students and provides information to faculty to help with their understanding of providing accommodations to students with LD. DSS sends memos to professors to support student accommodation requests. DSS acknowledges they have sufficient verification to support the request and will provide the professor with the identified accommodations necessary. The Emory Students Enabling Association provides a support network for students with disabilities.

SUPPORT SERVICES CONTACT INFORMATION

Learning Disability Program/Services: Office of Disablility Services
Director: Gloria Weaver McCord
  E-mail: gmccoed@emory.edu
  Telephone: 404-727-6016
  Fax: 404-727-1126
Contact: Susan D. Cook-Prince
  E-mail: scook@emory.edu
  Telephone: 404-727-6016
  Fax: 404-727-1126

LEARNING DISABILITY SERVICES

Requests for the following services/accommodations will be evaluated individually based on appropriate and current documentation.

Allowed in Exams
  Calculator: Yes
  Dictionary: Yes
  Computer: Yes
  Spellchecker: Yes
Extended test time: Yes
Scribes: Yes
Proctors: Yes
Oral exams: Yes
Notetakers: Yes

Distraction-reduced environment: Yes
Tape recording in class: Yes
Books on tape from RFBD: Yes
Taping of books not from RFBD: Yes
Accommodations for students with ADHD: Yes
Reading machine: No
Other assistive technology: Yes
Priority registration: Yes

Added costs for services: No
LD specialists: Yes
Professional tutors: Yes
Peer tutors: Yes
Max. hours/wk. for services: 4 hours per course
How professors are notified of LD/ADHD: By the student and the program director

GENERAL ADMISSIONS INFORMATION

Director of Admissions: Jane Jordan
Telephone: 404-727-6036

ENTRANCE REQUIREMENTS
16 total are required; 4 English required, 3 math required, 2 science required, 2 science lab required, 2 foreign language required, 2 social studies required, 2 history required, 3 elective required. High school diploma is required and GED is not accepted. Minimum TOEFL is 600. TOEFL required of all international applicants.

Application deadline: January 15
Notification: April 1
Average GPA: 3.7

Average SAT I Math: 650
Average SAT I Verbal: 576
Average ACT: 28

Graduated top 10% of class: 88%
Graduated top 25% of class: 99%
Graduated top 50% of class: 100%

COLLEGE GRADUATION REQUIREMENTS

Course waivers allowed: No
Course substitutions allowed: Yes
In what subjects: Decisions made on a case-by-case basis

ADDITIONAL INFORMATION

Environment: The 631-acre campus is in a suburban section 5 miles northeast of Atlanta.

Student Body
  Undergrad enrollment: 6,316
  Female: 54%
  Male: 46%
  Out-of-state: 71%

Cost Information
  Tuition: $24,240
  Room & board: $7,868
Housing Information
  University housing: Yes
  Percent living on campus: 65%

Greek System
  Fraternity: Yes
  Sorority: Yes
  Athletics: NCAA Division III

GEORGIA SOUTHERN UNIVERSITY

PO Box 8024, Statesboro, GA 30460
Phone: 912-681-5391 • Fax: 912-681-5635
E-mail: admissions@gasou.edu • Web: www.gasou.edu
Support level: CS • Institution type: 4-year public

LEARNING DISABILITY PROGRAM AND SERVICES

Georgia Southern University wants all students to have a rewarding and pleasant college experience. The University offers a variety of services specifically tailored to afford students with learning disabilities an equal opportunity for success. These services are in addition to those provided to all students and to the access provided by campus facilities. Opportunities available through the Student Disability Resource Center program include Special Registration, which allows students to complete the course registration process without going through the standard procedure, and Academic/Personal Assistance for students who are having difficulty with passing a class and need help with time management, note-taking skills, study strategies, and self-confidence. The University has a support group designed to help students with disabilities deal with personal and academic problems related to their disability.

LD/ADHD ADMISSIONS INFORMATION

College entrance tests required: Yes
Nonstandardized tests accepted: Yes
Interview required: No
Essay required: No
Documentation required for LD: Psychoeducational evaluation
Documentation required for ADHD: Yes
Documentation submitted to: SDRC—after admission
Special Ed. HS course work accepted: Yes

Specific course requirements for all applicants: Yes
Separate application required for services: No
# of LD applications submitted yearly: N/A
# of LD applications accepted yearly: N/A
Total # of students receiving LD/ADHD services: 236
Acceptance into program means acceptance into college: Students must be admitted and enrolled at the University first and then be reviewed for services.

ADMISSIONS

There is no special admissions procedure for students with learning disabilities. The University system feels that all applicants must meet the same minimum requirements. Courses required for admission include: 4 years English, 3 years math, 3 years science, 2 years foreign language, and 3 years social studies.

ADDITIONAL INFORMATION

To ensure the provision of services, the Student Disability Resource Center office requests that any student with learning disabilities who will need accommodations and/or assistance identify him/herself as a student with a disability as soon as possible by either returning the Voluntary Declaration of Disability form found in the admissions acceptance packet or by contacting the SDRC office directly.

SUPPORT SERVICES CONTACT INFORMATION

Learning Disability Program/Services: Student Disability Resource Center
Director: Wayne Akins
  E-mail: cwatkins@gsix2.cc.gasou.edu
  Telephone: 912-871-1566
  Fax: 912-871-1419
Contact: Same

LEARNING DISABILITY SERVICES

Requests for the following services/accommodations will be evaluated individually based on appropriate and current documentation.

Allowed in Exams
  Calculator: Yes
  Dictionary: Yes
  Computer: Yes
  Spellchecker: Yes
Extended test time: Yes
Scribes: Yes
Proctors: Yes
Oral exams: Yes
Notetakers: Yes

Distraction-reduced environment: Yes
Tape recording in class: Yes
Books on tape from RFBD: Yes
Taping of books not from RFBD: Yes
Accommodations for students with ADHD: Yes
Reading machine: No
Other assistive technology: No
Priority registration: Yes

Added costs for services: No
LD specialists: Yes
Professional tutors: No
Peer tutors: Yes
Max. hours/wk. for services: Unlimited
How professors are notified of LD/ADHD: By student

GENERAL ADMISSIONS INFORMATION

Director of Admissions: Dr. Teresa Thompsen
Telephone: 912-681-5391

ENTRANCE REQUIREMENTS
15 total are required; 4 English required, 3 math required, 3 science required, 2 science lab required, 2 foreign language required, 3 social studies required. High school diploma is required and GED is not accepted.

Application deadline: July 1
Notification: Rolling
Average GPA: 2.9

Average SAT I Math: 492
Average SAT I Verbal: 496
Average ACT: 19

Graduated top 10% of class: NR
Graduated top 25% of class: NR
Graduated top 50% of class: NR

COLLEGE GRADUATION REQUIREMENTS

Course waivers allowed: No
Course substitutions allowed: Yes
In what subjects: Substitutions have only been granted in foreign language and a deficit area

ADDITIONAL INFORMATION

Environment: The campus is in a small town close to Savannah.

Student Body
  Undergrad enrollment: 12,909
  Female: 54%
  Male: 46%
  Out-of-state: 7%

Cost Information
  In-state tuition: $1,876
  Out-of-state tuition: $7,504
  Room & board: $4,154
Housing Information
  University housing: Yes
  Percent living on campus: 22%

Greek System
  Fraternity: Yes
  Sorority: Yes
Athletics: NCAA Division I

GEORGIA STATE UNIVERSITY

PO Box 4009, Atlanta, GA 30302-4009
Phone: 404-651-2365 • Fax: 404-651-4811
E-mail: admissions@gsu.edu • Web: www.gsu.edu
Support level: CS • Institution type: 4-year public

LEARNING DISABILITY PROGRAM AND SERVICES

Georgia State University is committed to helping each student, including those students with disabilities, realize his/her full potential. This commitment is fulfilled through the provision of reasonable accommodations to ensure equitable access to its programs and services for all qualified students with disabilities. In general, the University will provide accommodations for students with disabilities on an individualized and flexible basis. It is the student's responsibility to seek available assistance and to make his/her needs known. All students are encouraged to contact the Office of Disability Services and/or Student Support Services in the early stages of their college planning. The pre-admission services include information regarding admission requirements and academic support services. Students should register with both services before classes begin. This will assure that appropriate services are in place prior to the first day of classes. As a rule, the University does not waive academic requirements because of any disability. Therefore, the student should carefully evaluate degree requirements early in his/her studies. The only exception to this policy is if there is a documented learning disability that would hinder the learning of a foreign language, in which case a student may petition for a substitution in the foreign language requirement.

LD/ADHD ADMISSIONS INFORMATION

College entrance tests required: Yes
Nonstandardized tests accepted: Yes
Interview required: No
Essay required: No
Documentation required for LD: WAIS-III; Stanford-Binet; KBIT; WJ-R; WRAT-R: within 3 years
Documentation required for ADHD: Yes
Documentation submitted to: Disability Services—after enrollment
Special Ed. HS course work accepted: Yes

Specific course requirements for all applicants: Yes
Separate application required for services: N/A
# of LD applications submitted yearly: N/A
# of LD applications accepted yearly: N/A
Total # of students receiving LD/ADHD services: 149
Acceptance into program means acceptance into college: Students must be admitted and enrolled at the University first and then may request services or accommodations.

ADMISSIONS
Students with LD must meet the same admission criteria as all other applicants. The University uses a predicted GPA of 2.1 for admission to a degree program or a GPA of 1.8 for admission to Learning Support Systems. This is determined by the ACT/SAT I score and the high school GPA. The higher the GPA, the lower the ACT/SAT can be and vice versa. Course requirements include 4 years English, 3 years science, 3 years math, 3 years social science, and 2 years foreign language. (Substitutions are allowed for foreign language if the student has documentation that supports the substitution). Students may appeal an admission decision if they are denied, and could be offered a probationary admission. If a student contacts the Office of Disability Services and provides documentation of an LD, the office will write the Admissions Office and verify the existence of the LD.

ADDITIONAL INFORMATION
To receive LD services students must submit documentation that evaluates intelligence; academic achievement in reading, math, and written language; auditory/phonological processing; language; visual-perceptual-spatial-constructural capabilities; attention; memory; executive function; motor; and social emotional. Student Support Services provides individual and group counseling; tutoring; advocacy; taped texts; advising; readers; learning lab; computer training; and referral for diagnosis of LD. The University Counseling Center provides study-skills training; test-taking strategies; note-taking skills; textbook-reading skills; test anxiety and stress management; time management; organizational techniques; thesis and dissertation writing; and personal counseling. Passport is a special section of the Personal and Academic Development Seminar Class offered through the Learning Support Program, and is specifically designed for students with LD. The Office of Disability Services offers advisement, study lab, readers, and testing accommodations.

SUPPORT SERVICES CONTACT INFORMATION

Learning Disability Program/Services: Disability Services
Director: Caroline Gergely
  E-mail: disceg@langate.gsu.edu
  Telephone: 404-463-9044
  Fax: 404-463-9049
Contact: Louis Bedrossian

LEARNING DISABILITY SERVICES

Requests for the following services/accommodations will be evaluated individually based on appropriate and current documentation.

Allowed in Exams
  Calculator: Yes
  Dictionary: Yes
  Computer: Yes
  Spellchecker: Yes
Extended test time: Yes
Scribes: Yes
Proctors: Yes
Oral exams: Yes
Notetakers: Yes

Distraction-reduced environment: Yes
Tape recording in class: Yes
Books on tape from RFBD: Yes
Taping of books not from RFBD: Yes
Accommodations for students with ADHD: Yes
Reading machine: Yes
Other assistive technology: Yes
Priority registration: No

Added costs for services: No
LD specialists: Yes
Professional tutors: No
Peer tutors: Varies
Max. hours/wk. for services: Based on need and availability of space and staff
How professors are notified of LD/ADHD: By the student and by letter from ODS if requested

GENERAL ADMISSIONS INFORMATION

Director of Admissions: Diane Weber
Telephone: 404-651-2365

ENTRANCE REQUIREMENTS

15 total are required; 20 total are recommended; 4 English required, 4 English recommended, 3 math required, 4 math recommended, 3 science required, 3 science recommended, 2 science lab required, 3 science lab recommended, 2 foreign language required, 2 foreign language recommended, 1 social studies required, 1 social studies recommended, 2 history required, 2 history recommended, 4 elective recommended. High school diploma is required and GED is not accepted. Minimum TOEFL is 525. TOEFL required of all international applicants.

Application deadline: May 1
Notification: Rolling beginning 10/1
Average GPA: 3.2

Average SAT I Math: 521
Average SAT I Verbal: 525
Average ACT: 22

Graduated top 10% of class: NR
Graduated top 25% of class: NR
Graduated top 50% of class: NR

COLLEGE GRADUATION REQUIREMENTS

Course waivers No
Course substitutions allowed: Yes
In what subjects: Decided on a case-by-case basis with the recommendation of the student's major department

ADDITIONAL INFORMATION

Environment: The University's campus is in an urban area.

Student Body
  Undergrad enrollment: 16,309
  Female: 61%
  Male: 39%
  Out-of-state: 1%

Cost Information
  In-state tuition: $2,322
  Out-of-state tuition: $9,288
  Room & board: $7,948
Housing Information
  University housing: Yes
  Percent living on campus: 12%

Greek System
  Fraternity: Yes
  Sorority: Yes
Athletics: NCAA Division I

REINHARDT COLLEGE

7300 Reinhardt College Circle, Waleska, GA 30183
Phone: 770-720-5526 • Fax: 770-720-5602
E-mail: admissions@mail.reinhardt.edu • Web: www.reinhardt.edu
Support level: SP • Institution type: 4-year private

LEARNING DISABILITY PROGRAM AND SERVICES

The Academic Support Office (ASO) provides assistance to students with specific learning abilities or attention deficit disorders. Students are enrolled in regular college courses. The program focuses on compensatory skills and provides special services in academic advising and counseling, individual and group tutoring, assistance in writing assignments, note-taking, testing accommodations, and taped texts. The ASO was established in 1982 to provide assistance to students with learning disabilities who meet regular college entrance requirements, have a diagnosed LD, and may or may not have received any LD services in the past due to ineligibility for high school services, or a recent diagnosis.

LD/ADHD ADMISSIONS INFORMATION

College entrance tests required: Yes
Nonstandardized tests accepted: Yes
Interview required: Yes
Essay required: No
Documentation required for LD: WISC-R; WAIS-III; WJ or WRAT: within 3 years
Documentation required for ADHD: Yes
Documentation submitted to: Admissions and ASO
Special Ed. HS course work accepted: No

Specific course requirements for all applicants: Yes
Separate application required for services: Yes
# of LD applications submitted yearly: 70
# of LD applications accepted yearly: 30
Total # of students receiving LD/ADHD services: 60
Acceptance into program means acceptance into college: Students are admitted jointly by the College and ASO.

ADMISSIONS

Applicants with learning disabilities should request an ASO admission packet from Admissions; complete the regular application; check the ASO admission box; fill out the supplemental form from ASO; provide IEPs from as many years of high school as possible, psychological evaluations documenting the disability, and three references addressing aptitude, motivation, ability to set realistic goals, interpersonal skills, and readiness for college; and submit SAT/ACT scores. Students applying to the ASO program may be asked to interview with the ASO staff. Admission decisions are made by the Admissions Office with recommendations from the program director.

ADDITIONAL INFORMATION

The ASO is staffed by four full-time faculty members. Additional tuition is required for students enrolled in ASO tutorials. A generous financial aid program is available to all qualified students. Academic Support Services include faculty-led tutorials (for a fee); academic advisement and counseling; accommodative services for students with documented LD/ADHD such as individualized testing, note-takers, and the coordination of taped texts. All students admitted and enrolled in the ASO Program attend a regular student orientation program plus have an interview and orientation with the staff from the ASO Program.

SUPPORT SERVICES CONTACT INFORMATION

Learning Disability Program/Services: Academic Support Office (ASO)
Director: Sylvia Robertson
 E-mail: srr@reinhardt.edu
 Telephone: 770-720-5567
 Fax: 770-720-5602
Contact: Same

LEARNING DISABILITY SERVICES

Requests for the following services/accommodations will be evaluated individually based on appropriate and current documentation.

Allowed in Exams
 Calculator: Yes
 Dictionary: No
 Computer: Yes
 Spellchecker: Yes
Extended test time: Yes
Scribes: Yes
Proctors: Yes
Oral exams: Yes
Notetakers: Yes

Distraction-reduced environment: Yes
Tape recording in class: Yes
Books on tape from RFBD: Yes
Taping of books not from RFBD: No
Accommodations for students with
 ADHD: Yes
Reading machine: Yes
Other assistive technology: Yes
Priority registration: Yes

Added costs for services: $242 per
 credit hour
LD specialists: Yes (4)
Professional tutors: 4
Peer tutors: Yes
Max. hours/wk. for services:
 Unlimited
How professors are notified of
 LD/ADHD: By both student and
 director

GENERAL ADMISSIONS INFORMATION

Director of Admissions: Katherine Smith
Telephone: 770-479-1454

ENTRANCE REQUIREMENTS
13 total are required; 4 English required, 3 math required, 3 science required, 1 science lab recommended, 2 foreign language recommended, 3 social studies required, 2 history recommended, 2 elective recommended. High school diploma or GED required. Minimum TOEFL is 500. TOEFL required of all international applicants.

Application deadline: August 1
Notification: Rolling beginning 8/1
Average GPA: 2.9

Average SAT I Math: 470
Average SAT I Verbal: 485
Average ACT: 19

Graduated top 10% of class: NR
Graduated top 25% of class: NR
Graduated top 50% of class: NR

COLLEGE GRADUATION REQUIREMENTS

Course waivers allowed: No
Course substitutions allowed: N/A
In what subjects: N/A

ADDITIONAL INFORMATION

Environment: The College is located on a 600-acre campus in a small town 40 miles from Atlanta.

Student Body
 Undergrad enrollment: 1,190
 Female: 63%
 Male: 37%
 Out-of-state: 1%

Cost Information
 Tuition: $8,800
 Room & board: $4,716
Housing Information
 University housing: Yes
 Percent living on campus: 35%

Greek System
 Fraternity: Yes
 Sorority: Yes
Athletics: NAIA

UNIVERSITY OF GEORGIA

Terrell Hall, Athens, GA 30602
Phone: 706-542-8776 • Fax: 706-542-1466
E-mail: undergrad@admissions.uga.edu • Web: www.uga.edu
Support level: CS • Institution type: 4-year public

LEARNING DISABILITY PROGRAM AND SERVICES

The purpose of the Learning Disabilities Center (LDC) is to provide support and direct services to students who demonstrate a specific LD so that they may function as independently as possible while at the University. The objectives of the program are to: (1) assist students in understanding their disability; (2) coordinate information about other support services; (3) recommend modifications for the Regents Exam (required to graduate) and program of study where appropriate; and (4) consult with faculty. All UGA students whose LD has been confirmed by the LCD are eligible for support services. Students must meet the Learning Disability Criteria acceptable by the Georgia Board of Regents, including documentation within three years; average broad cognitive functioning; specific cognitive processing deficits; social-emotional assessment that doesn't suggest primary emotional basis for results; oral language assessment; significant specific achievement deficits relative to potential documented in the areas of written language, reading, and math; utilization of assessment instruments with appropriate age norms; and all standardized measures must be represented by standard score or percentile ranks based on published norms.

LD/ADHD ADMISSIONS INFORMATION

College entrance tests required: Yes
Nonstandardized tests accepted: Yes
Interview required: No
Essay required: No
Documentation required for LD: WAIS-III (or other IQ test); achievement assessment: within 3 years
Documentation required for ADHD: Yes
Documentation submitted to: Admissions and LDC
Special Ed. HS course work accepted: No

Specific course requirements for all applicants: Yes
Separate application required for services: No
# of LD applications submitted yearly: 30–61
# of LD applications accepted yearly: N/A
Total # of students receiving LD/ADHD services: 225–276
Acceptance into program means acceptance into college: Students must be admitted and enrolled at the University first and then may request services.

ADMISSIONS

Students with LD are encouraged to self-disclose on the general application form. This disclosure sets the process in motion, and the Admissions Office notifies the LDC. LDC contacts the applicant and offers to discuss services available, and then refers the student's name back to Admissions. LDC provides the Admissions Office with a diagnosis to assist with an admission decision. Students must submit documentation of their disability to be considered for special admissions. Admissions may be flexible with GPA and test scores, but students should take college-prep courses in high school. GPA is the most important criterion and the subscore on the verbal section of the ACT/SAT is weighted more heavily than math. Required SAT and GPA are adjusted in relation to general admission averages. The final decision is made by the Admissions Office.

ADDITIONAL INFORMATION

Specialists help with learning strategies for courses. Students meet with LD specialists to register quarterly and design a schedule that considers their LD along with curriculum requirements. Students are assisted in communicating their disabilities and learning needs with their instructors. Course substitutions for foreign language may be approved with appropriate documentation. Modifications for assignments and tests are designed to meet students' specific needs. Skills classes for college credit are offered to all students at UGA in study techniques, time management, problem-solving, research paper writing, and career selection. Students with ADHD are serviced by Disability Services.

SUPPORT SERVICES CONTACT INFORMATION

Learning Disability Program/Services: Learning Disabilities Center (LDC)
Director: Dr. Noel Gregg
  Telephone: 706-542-7034
  Fax: 706-583-0001
Contact: Same

LEARNING DISABILITY SERVICES

Requests for the following services/accommodations will be evaluated individually based on appropriate and current documentation.

Allowed in Exams
  Calculator: Yes
  Dictionary: Yes
  Computer: Yes
  Spellchecker: Yes
Extended test time: Yes
Scribes: Yes
Proctors: Yes
Oral exams: Yes
Notetakers: Yes

Distraction-reduced environment: Yes
Tape recording in class: Yes
Books on tape from RFBD: Yes
Taping of books not from RFBD: Yes
Accommodations for students with ADHD: Yes
Reading machine: Yes
Other assistive technology: Yes
Priority registration: Yes

Added costs for services: No
LD specialists: Yes (4)
Professional tutors: 5
Peer tutors: No
Max. hours/wk. for services: 2
How professors are notified of LD/ADHD: By both student and director

GENERAL ADMISSIONS INFORMATION

Director of Admissions: Nancy McBuss
Telephone: 706-542-8776

ENTRANCE REQUIREMENTS

20 total are required; 4 English required, 4 math required, 3 science required, 2 science lab required, 2 foreign language required, 3 social studies required, 4 elective required. High school diploma or GED required. Minimum TOEFL is 550. TOEFL required of all international applicants.

Application deadline: January 15
Notification: April 1
Average GPA: 3.6

Average SAT I Math: 602
Average SAT I Verbal: 599
Average ACT: 26

Graduated top 10% of class: 41%
Graduated top 25% of class: 78%
Graduated top 50% of class: 97%

COLLEGE GRADUATION REQUIREMENTS

Course waivers allowed: No
Course substitutions allowed: Yes
In what subjects: Foreign language

ADDITIONAL INFORMATION

Environment: The University is located on a large campus 80 miles from Atlanta.

Student Body
  Undergrad enrollment: 24,213
  Female: 56%
  Male: 44%
  Out-of-state: 10%

Cost Information
  In-state tuition: $2,506
  Out-of-state tuition: $10,024
  Room & board: $5,080
Housing Information
  University housing: Yes
  Percent living on campus: 18%

Greek System
  Fraternity: Yes
  Sorority: Yes
Athletics: NCAA Division I

UNIVERSITY OF IDAHO

UI Admissions Office, PO Box 444264, Moscow, ID 83844-4264
Phone: 208-885-6326 • Fax: 208-885-9119
E-mail: nss@uidaho.edu • Web: www.its/uidaho.edu/uihome
Support level: S • Institution type: 4-year public

LEARNING DISABILITY PROGRAM AND SERVICES

The University of Idaho has established services for students with disabilities in accordance with Section 504 of the Rehabilitation Act of 1973, as amended, and with the Americans with Disabilities Act (ADA) of 1990, as amended. Student Disability Services (SDS) provides disability support services to students with temporary or permanent disabilities (including learning disabilities and attention deficit disorder). Students requesting assistance must provide appropriate disability documentation to be kept on file in the SDS office and must provide adequate advance notice of such requests.

LD/ADHD ADMISSIONS INFORMATION

College entrance tests required: Yes
Nonstandardized tests accepted: Yes
Interview required: No
Essay required: No
Documentation required for LD: Psychoeducational evaluation
Documentation required for ADHD: Yes
Documentation submitted to: Student Disability Services
Special Ed. HS course work accepted: Case-by-case basis

Specific course requirements for all applicants: Yes
Separate application required for services: No
# of LD applications submitted yearly: N/A
# of LD applications accepted yearly: N/A
Total # of students receiving LD/ADHD services: 100
Acceptance into program means acceptance into college: Students must be admitted and enrolled at the University first and then may request LD services.

ADMISSIONS

Students must meet the general admission requirements. The following index is used for general admission: GPA 3.0 and no ACT/SAT required; GPA 2.6–2.99 and ACT 15+ or SAT 790+; GPA 2.5–2.59 and ACT 17+ or SAT 870+; GPA 2.4–2.49 and ACT 19+ or SAT 930+; GPA 2.30–2.39 and ACT 21+ or SAT 1000+; GPA 2.20–2.29 and ACT 23+ or SAT 1070+; plus 2.0 GPA in 4 years English, 3 years math, 1 year humanities or foreign language, 2.5 years social science, 3 years natural science plus electives. A freshman applicant who does not qualify for regular admission may be considered for provisional admission. A student seeking provisional admission must submit a written statement and three letters of recommendation. The student statement should include the student's goals, educational and/or professional objectives, an explanation of past academic performance, information and/or documentation regarding any extenuating circumstances, and anything else which may be pertinent to the applicant's request. The file is reviewed by the Admission Committee. Students' self-disclosure will have no effect on admission to the University. Students admitted specially or on probation must successfully complete 14 credits in four core areas over three semesters.

ADDITIONAL INFORMATION

Students with disabilities are asked to notify SDS as soon as possible to discuss specific disability-related concerns and needs. Students requiring academic assistance should also contact Student Support Services. This voluntary self-identification enables SDS to determine appropriate and reasonable accommodations to make classes, programs, services, and activities accessible to individuals with disabilities. Services from SDS include, but are not limited to, readers, note-takers, pre-registration assistance, new student orientation, proctor and test-taking arrangements, or help with any other disability needs. The Campus Guide for People with Disabilities describes some of these typical services.

SUPPORT SERVICES CONTACT INFORMATION

Learning Disability Program/Services: Student Disability Services
Director: Dianne Milhullin
  E-mail: sds@uidaho.du
  Telephone: 208-885-7716
  Fax: 208-885-9494
Contact: Lisa Birdsall
  E-mail: lisab@uidaho.edu
  Telephone: 208-885-7716
  Fax: 208-885-9494

LEARNING DISABILITY SERVICES

Requests for the following services/accommodations will be evaluated individually based on appropriate and current documentation.

Allowed in Exams
  Calculator: Yes
  Dictionary: Yes
  Computer: Yes
  Spellchecker: Yes
Extended test time: Yes
Scribes: Yes
Proctors: Yes
Oral exams: Yes
Notetakers: Yes

Distraction-reduced environment: Yes
Tape recording in class: Yes
Books on tape from RFBD: Yes
Taping of books not from RFBD: Yes
Accommodations for students with
  ADHD: Yes
Reading machine: No
Other assistive technology: Yes
Priority registration: Yes

Added costs for services: No
LD specialists: No
Professional tutors: Yes
Peer tutors: Yes
Max. hours/wk. for services: 5 hours
How professors are notified of
  LD/ADHD: By student

GENERAL ADMISSIONS INFORMATION

Director of Admissions: Dan Davenport
Telephone: 208-885-6326

ENTRANCE REQUIREMENTS
15 total are required; 4 English required, 3 math required, 3 science required, 1 science lab required, 1 foreign language required, 2 social studies required, 1 elective required. High school diploma or GED required. Minimum TOEFL is 525. TOEFL required of all international applicants.

Application deadline: August 1
Notification: Rolling beginning 2/15
Average GPA: 3.4

Average SAT I Math: 559
Average SAT I Verbal: 549
Average ACT: 23

Graduated top 10% of class: 19%
Graduated top 25% of class: 47%
Graduated top 50% of class: 77%

COLLEGE GRADUATION REQUIREMENTS

Course waivers allowed: No
Course substitutions allowed: Yes
In what subjects: Math and foreign language; students must request by petition

ADDITIONAL INFORMATION

Environment: The University is located on an 800-acre campus in a small town 90 miles south of Spokane, Washington.

Student Body
  Undergrad enrollment: 8,759
  Female: 46%
  Male: 54%
  Out-of-state: 24%

Cost Information
  In-state tuition: $2,348
  Out-of-state tuition: $8,348
  Room & board: $4,078
Housing Information
  University housing: Yes
  Percent living on campus: 45%

Greek System
  Fraternity: Yes
  Sorority: Yes
Athletics: NCAA Division I

University of Idaho

BARAT COLLEGE

700 East Westleigh Road, Lake Forest, IL 60045
Phone: 847-295-4260 • Fax: 847-604-6300
E-mail: admissions@barat.edu • Web: www.barat.edu
Support level: SP • Institution type: 4-year private

LEARNING DISABILITY PROGRAM AND SERVICES

The Learning Opportunities Program (LOP) is designed to meet the needs of college students with specific learning disabilities. The LOP began in 1980 and is approximately 7 percent of the Barat population. The LOP aims to help participants achieve academic success in college, function effectively in the classroom and in their personal lives, and prepare for a career or graduate school in their chosen disciplines. During the first year students met with their learning disabilities specialists twice a week for one-on-one tutoring sessions to aid in course work, remediate skills, develop effective study strategies, and/or learn compensatory skills. Specialists develop and implement individualized educational programs based on thorough diagnostic assessments administered to each student. The goal of LOP is for students to be phased out gradually as they become more independent academically and in other facets of college life. The program has three phases: Phase I students meet with LD specialist two hours per week; Phase II students meet one hour per week; and Phase III students meet half an hour per week or as needed. Usually students participate in LOP for at least two semesters.

LD/ADHD ADMISSIONS INFORMATION

College entrance tests required: Yes
Nonstandardized tests accepted: Yes
Interview required: Yes
Essay required: Yes
Documentation required for LD: Current WAIS-III or WISC-III (within three years), a learning disabilities diagnostic report
Documentation required for ADHD: Yes
Documentation submitted to: LOP
Special Ed. HS course work accepted: No

Specific course requirements for all applicants: Yes
Separate application required for services: No
# of LD applications submitted yearly: 60–80
# of LD applications accepted yearly: 15–21
Total # of students receiving LD/ADHD services: 45–55
Acceptance into program means acceptance into college: Students are admitted cooperatively by LOP and Admissions.

ADMISSIONS

The Barat College Learning Opportunities Program will consider for admission those students who have a history or current diagnosis of a specific learning disability. These students should have average or above-average ability, a strong desire to succeed in college, and a willingness to work hard. To apply, students submit a Barat application, two letters of recommendation, transcripts, SAT or ACT results, case history form, LD teacher report, school records (including case study evaluation report), outside evaluation results if available, and a release form. An interview is required for final candidates. The final decision is made by a committee comprised of the LOP Director, Director of Counseling and Director of the Special Education Department. Barat recommends students have 4 years English, 2 years math, 2 years science, 3 years social science, and 2 years foreign language (not required for admission).

ADDITIONAL INFORMATION

No credit is given for participation in the LOP. Students receive credit for course work the same as other students. Specialists work with students and have an understanding of each student's strengths and areas for improvement based on the initial diagnostic testing. Specialists plan and implement individually designed programs to aid students in their regular course work, remediate skills, and/or teach compensatory strategies. Tutorial sessions may also include instruction in time management, study skills, and self-advocacy. Specialists have ongoing communication with faculty, arrange and coordinate reasonable accommodations when appropriate, and help students access services such as textbooks on tape and assistive technology. Academic counseling and advisement are provided for program participants. When additional content-area tutoring is necessary, LOP will find and pay for one tutor per student each semester. Additional support is available to all students in the writing center, math lab, computer center, library, and career planning center. Additional content-area tutoring is provided on a limited as-needed basis.

SUPPORT SERVICES CONTACT INFORMATION

Learning Disability Program/Services: Learning Opportunities Program (LOP)
Director: Debbie Sheade, MA
  E-mail: dsheade@barat.edu
  Telephone: 847-604-6321
  Fax: 847-604-6377
Contact: Donna Witikka, Administrative Assistant
  E-mail: dwitikka@barat.edu
  Telephone: 847-604-6321
  Fax: 847-604-6377

LEARNING DISABILITY SERVICES

Requests for the following services/accommodations will be evaluated individually based on appropriate and current documentation.

Allowed in Exams
  Calculator: Yes
  Dictionary: Yes
  Computer: Yes
  Spellchecker: Yes
Extended test time: Yes
Scribes: Yes
Proctors: Yes
Oral exams: No
Notetakers: Yes

Distraction-reduced environment: Yes
Tape recording in class: Yes
Books on tape from RFBD: Yes
Taping of books not from RFBD: Yes
Accommodations for students with
  ADHD: Yes
Reading machine: No
Other assistive technology: No
Priority registration: Yes

Added costs for services:
  $675–$1,800 per semester
LD specialists: Yes (4)
Professional tutors: Yes
Peer tutors: Yes
Max. hours/wk. for services: 2
How professors are notified of
  LD/ADHD: By both student and
  director

GENERAL ADMISSIONS INFORMATION

Director of Admissions: Mary Kay Farrell
Telephone: 847-615-5678

ENTRANCE REQUIREMENTS
16 total are recommended; 4 English recommended, 2 math recommended, 2 science recommended, 2 foreign language recommended, 3 social studies recommended. High school diploma or GED required. Minimum TOEFL is 500. TOEFL required of all international applicants.

Application deadline: Rolling
Notification: Rolling
Average GPA: 3.2

Average SAT I Math: 490
Average SAT I Verbal: 500
Average ACT: 21

Graduated top 10% of class: 9%
Graduated top 25% of class: 25%
Graduated top 50% of class: 48%

COLLEGE GRADUATION REQUIREMENTS

Course waivers allowed: No
Course substitutions allowed: Yes
In what subjects: Determined on an individual basis

ADDITIONAL INFORMATION

Environment: The College is located on a 30-acre campus in the suburbs 25 miles north of Chicago.

Student Body
  Undergrad enrollment: 813
  Female: 74%
  Male: 26%
  Out-of-state: 18%

Cost Information
  Tuition: $13,590
  Room & board: $5,500
Housing Information
  University housing: Yes
  Percent living on campus: 36%

Greek System
  Fraternity: Yes
  Sorority: Yes
Athletics: NAIA

DePaul University

1 East Jackson Boulevard, Chicago, IL 60604-2287
Phone: 312-362-8300 • Fax: 312-362-5749
E-mail: admitdpu@wppost.depaul.edu • Web: www.depaul.edu
Support level: CS • Institution type: 4-year private

LEARNING DISABILITY PROGRAM AND SERVICES

Productive Learning Strategies (PLuS) is designed to service students with learning disabilities and/or attention deficit disorder who are motivated to succeed in college. The immediate goal is to provide learning strategies, based on students' strengths and weaknesses, to assist students in the completion of course work. The ultimate goal is to impart academic and study skills that will enable the students to function independently in the academic environment and competitive job market. PLuS provides intensive help on a one-to-one basis. It is designed to assist with regular college courses, improve learning deficits, and help the student learn compensatory skills. Students can choose to work with learning disability specialists whom they can meet for up to two hours per week.

LD/ADHD ADMISSIONS INFORMATION

College entrance tests required: Yes
Nonstandardized tests accepted: Yes
Interview required: Yes
Essay required: Yes
Documentation required for LD: WAIS-III academic achievement and information processing measures (could include Woodcock-Johnson psychoeducational battery)
Documentation required for ADHD: Yes
Documentation submitted to: PLuS Program
Special Ed. HS course work accepted: Yes, if they are developmental

Specific course requirements for all applicants: Yes
Separate application required for services: Yes
# of LD applications submitted yearly: 30
# of LD applications accepted yearly: 20-25
Total # of students receiving LD/ADHD services: 75
Acceptance into program means acceptance into college: Students must be admitted and enrolled at the University first and then may request services.

ADMISSIONS

There is no separate admission process for students with learning disabilities. Students with learning disabilities must be accepted to DePaul University before they can be accepted to PLuS. The diagnostic testing that is required, if done within the last three to five years, will be used in the evaluation. General admission criteria include a GPA of 2.5, top 40 percent of class, and ACT 21 or SAT 1000. Students should have 4 years of English, 3 years of math, 2 years of science, and 2 years of social studies (one history). Students with appropriate documentation may request substitutions in entrance requirements. Students may elect to self-disclose the disability during the admission process and submit their application to the attention of the PLuS Program. If the student does not have the required testing, PLuS will administer the appropriate assessments. Some students who are considered "high potential" but who have borderline admission criteria may qualify for admissions through the Bridge Program. This is an enhancement program for incoming freshmen. Bridge students may have an ACT of 18–20 or SAT of 850–880. (This program is not for students with learning disabilities although some students are learning disabled.) Bridge students must begin in a summer program prior to freshman year. Some students can be admitted on a probationary basis as Special Students. Adult students (over 24) can be admitted through the Adult Admissions Program.

ADDITIONAL INFORMATION

PLuS is housed in the Reading and Learning Lab and the program is only available to students with learning disabilities and/or attention deficit disorder. Some accommodations are offered through the Office for Students with Disabilties Students who do the best at DePaul and in the PLuS program are students who are highly motivated and who have received LD resource support in grade school and high school but were enrolled in mainstream classes. Accommodations include: extended time of exams, separate and distraction-free space to take exams, and books on tape. Services provided by PLuS include advocacy with professors two hours per week with a learning disabilities specialist to receive direct instruction in learning strategies, coping strategies, and mentoring. Students can choose to participate in this "fee-for-service" component of the program. Services and accommodations are available for undergraduate and graduate students.

SUPPORT SERVICES CONTACT INFORMATION

Learning Disability Program/Services: Productive Learning Strategies (PLuS) Program
Director: Stamatios Miras
  E-mail: kwold@wppost.depaul.edu
  Telephone: 773-325-4239
  Fax: 773-325-4673
Contact: Same

LEARNING DISABILITY SERVICES

Requests for the following services/accommodations will be evaluated individually based on appropriate and current documentation.

Allowed in Exams
  Calculator: Yes
  Dictionary: No
  Computer: Yes
  Spellchecker: Yes
Extended test time: Yes
Scribes: Yes
Proctors: Yes
Oral exams: Yes
Notetakers: Yes

Distraction-reduced environment: Yes
Tape recording in class: Yes
Books on tape from RFBD: Yes
Taping of books not from RFBD: Yes
Accommodations for students with ADHD: Yes
Reading machine: No
Other assistive technology: Yes
Priority registration: Yes

Added costs for services: $100 per semester
LD specialists: Yes (7)
Professional tutors: No
Peer tutors: No
Max. hours/wk. for services: 2
How professors are notified of LD/ADHD: By student

GENERAL ADMISSIONS INFORMATION

Director of Admissions: Paul Roberts (Interim)
Telephone: 312-362-8300

ENTRANCE REQUIREMENTS
16 total are required; 4 English required, 2 math required, 2 science required, 2 science lab required, 2 social studies required, 4 elective required. High school diploma or GED required. Minimum TOEFL is 550. TOEFL required of all international applicants.

Application deadline: August 15
Notification: Rolling beginning 10/15
Average GPA: 3.3
Average SAT I Math: 555
Average SAT I Verbal: 560
Average ACT: 24
Graduated top 10% of class: 18%
Graduated top 25% of class: 41%
Graduated top 50% of class: 68%

COLLEGE GRADUATION REQUIREMENTS

Course waivers allowed: No
Course substitutions allowed: Yes
In what subjects: This depends on the student's major course requirements. Foreign language and other courses that are not required for the major can be waived.

ADDITIONAL INFORMATION

Environment: DePaul has a 3-acre urban campus located in Chicago's Lincoln Park area, 3 miles north of the downtown area.

Student Body
  Undergrad enrollment: 12,436
  Female: 59%
  Male: 41%
  Out-of-state: 14%

Cost Information
  Tuition: $15,390
  Room & board: $6,675
Housing Information
  University housing: Yes
  Percent living on campus: 21%

Greek System
  Fraternity: Yes
  Sorority: Yes
Athletics: NCAA Division I

EASTERN ILLINOIS UNIVERSITY

600 Lincoln Avenue, Charleston, IL 61920
Phone: 217-581-2223 • Fax: 217-581-7060
E-mail: admissns@www.eiu.edu • Web: www.eiu.edu
Support level: S • Institution type: 4-year public

LEARNING DISABILITY PROGRAM AND SERVICES

EIU will provide services as deemed effective and reasonable to assist students with learning disabilities to obtain access to the University programs. Students applying to the University who are requesting support services and/or accommodations from the Office of Disability Services are required to submit documentation to verify eligibility under Section 504. The assessment and diagnosis of specific learning disabilities must be conducted by a qualified professional. The written diagnostic evaluation report should include the following information: diagnostic report clearly stating the learning disability and the rationale for the diagnosis; the tests administered and the specific scores including grade level scores, standard scores, and percentile scores; descriptive written text beyond that which is provided on a typical IEP and including qualitative information about the student's abilities; recommendations for accommodations that include specific suggestions based on the diagnostic evaluation results and supported by the diagnosis; and identifying information about the evaluator/diagnostician. The diagnostic tests should be current within the last three years; should be comprehensive and include a battery of more than one test and/or subtest; should include at least one instrument to measure aptitude or cognitive ability; and should include at least one measurement in reading, written language, and math.

LD/ADHD ADMISSIONS INFORMATION

College entrance tests required: Yes
Nonstandardized tests accepted: Yes
Interview required: No
Essay required: No
Documentation required for LD: Psychoeducational evaluation
Documentation required for ADHD: Yes
Documentation submitted to: Office of Disability Services—after admission
Special Ed. HS course work accepted: Yes, if college preparatory

Specific course requirements for all applicants: Yes
Separate application required for services: No
# of LD applications submitted yearly: N/A
# of LD applications accepted yearly: N/A
Total # of students receiving LD/ADHD services: 80–90
Acceptance into program means acceptance into college: Students must be admitted and enrolled at the University and then request services.

ADMISSIONS

All applicants must meet the same admission criteria. There is no special admission process for students with learning disabilities. General admission requires students to (1) rank in the top half of the class and have a minimum ACT of 18 or SAT of 860 or (2) rank in the top three-quarters of the class and have a minimum ACT of 22 or SAT of 1020. Additionally, all students must have 4 years of English, 3 years math, 3 years social science, 3 years laboratory science, and 2 years electives. Once admitted, students with learning disabilities or attention deficit disorder must provide appropriate documentation in order to access services and accommodations.

ADDITIONAL INFORMATION

Students should meet with the Office of Disability Services to discuss accommodations or make further arrangements as needed. Some services provided include priority registration, alternate format for classroom materials, note-takers, assistance locating tutors and liaison with tutors to develop effective study strategies, proctors, and liaison with instructors. Skills classes can be arranged in time management, note-taking, test-taking, and study strategies.

SUPPORT SERVICES CONTACT INFORMATION

Learning Disability Program/Services: Office of Disability Services
Director: Kathy Waggoner
E-mail: cfmpj@eiu.edu
Telephone: 217-581-6583
Fax: 217-581-7208
Contact: Same

LEARNING DISABILITY SERVICES

Requests for the following services/accommodations will be evaluated individually based on appropriate and current documentation.

Allowed in Exams
  Calculator: Yes
  Dictionary: Y/N
  Computer: Y/N
  Spellchecker: Yes
Extended test time: Yes
Scribes: Yes
Proctors: Yes
Oral exams: Yes
Notetakers: Yes

Distraction-reduced environment: Yes
Tape recording in class: Yes
Books on tape from RFBD: Yes
Taping of books not from RFBD: Yes
Accommodations for students with ADHD: Yes
Reading machine: Yes
Other assistive technology: Yes
Priority registration: Yes

Added costs for services: $5 per hour with Honors Tutorial
LD specialists: No
Professional tutors: No
Peer tutors: No
Max. hours/wk. for services: N/A
How professors are notified of LD/ADHD: By the student and Director

GENERAL ADMISSIONS INFORMATION

Director of Admissions: Dale Wolf
Telephone: 217-581-2223

ENTRANCE REQUIREMENTS
15 total are required; 4 English required, 3 math required, 3 science required, 3 science lab required, 3 social studies required, 2 elective required. High school diploma or GED required. Minimum TOEFL is 500. TOEFL required of all international applicants.

Application deadline: April 1
Notification: Rolling
Average GPA: NR

Average SAT I Math: NR
Average SAT I Verbal: NR
Average ACT: 22

Graduated top 10% of class: 11%
Graduated top 25% of class: 34%
Graduated top 50% of class: 77%

COLLEGE GRADUATION REQUIREMENTS

Course waivers allowed: No
Course substitutions allowed: Yes
In what subjects: Foreign language and math

ADDITIONAL INFORMATION

Environment: The University is in a small town 50 miles south of the University of Illinois.

Student Body
  Undergrad enrollment: 9,346
  Female: 58%
  Male: 42%
  Out-of-state: 2%

Cost Information
  In-state tuition: $2,391
  Out-of-state tuition: $7,174
  Room & board: $4,500
Housing Information
  University housing: Yes
  Percent living on campus: 50%

Greek System
  Fraternity: Yes
  Sorority: Yes
Athletics: NCAA Division I

ILLINOIS STATE UNIVERSITY

Admissions Office, Campus Box 2200, Normal, IL 61790-2200
Phone: 309-438-2181 • Fax: 309-438-3932
E-mail: ugradadm@ilstu.edu • Web: www.ilstu.edu
Support level: CS • Institution type: 4-year public

LEARNING DISABILITY PROGRAM AND SERVICES

The mission of the Disability Concerns office is to ensure the full and equal participation for persons with disabilities in the University community through empowering individuals, promoting equal access, encouraging self-advocacy, reducing attitudinal and communication barriers, and providing appropriate accommodation. The Disability Concerns program is designed to work with students who have learning disabilities on becoming academically and socially successful while attending Illinois State University. After a review of the appropriate documentation by the coordinator of the learning disability services and a consultation, accommodations can then be determined based on the needs of the individual. A psychoeducational evaluation consisting of the adult assessment scale is required. It should include test scores and the following: the diagnosis, including specific areas of the disability; the impact the disability has on the academic performance of the student; and the accommodations suggested in view of the impact of the disability on learning.

LD/ADHD ADMISSIONS INFORMATION

College entrance tests required: Yes
Nonstandardized tests accepted: Yes
Interview required: No
Essay required: No
Documentation required for LD: Psychoeducational evaluation
Documentation required for ADHD: Yes
Documentation submitted to: Disability Concerns
Special Ed. HS course work accepted: Yes

Specific course requirements for all applicants: Yes
Separate application required for services: No
# of LD applications submitted yearly: N/A
# of LD applications accepted yearly: N/A
Total # of students receiving LD/ADHD services: 130
Acceptance into program means acceptance into college: Students must be admitted and enrolled at the University first and then may request services.

ADMISSIONS

Admissions criteria for students with learning disabilities are the same as for other students at this time. Applicants with questions should contact the Disability Concerns office. In general, students are admissible if they are in the top three-fourths of their high school class and have an ACT of 23 or better. High school courses required include 4 years English, 3 years math, 2 years social science, 2 years science, 2 years electives. Students with learning disabilities who are borderline admits or who are denied admission may self-disclose and ask to be reviewed by Disability Concerns. The director will review the documentation and make a recommendation to Admissions.

ADDITIONAL INFORMATION

The following are options for accommodations based on appropriate documentation and needs: note-takers; peer tutors; readers; scribes; taped textbooks; computers; testing accommodations; conference with LD specialist; and quiet study rooms. LMS (Learning Through Mini Sessions) are designed to help students make college academics and college life a little less stressful. Sessions could include stress management, self-advocacy, test anxiety, communication skills, and organizational skills.

SUPPORT SERVICES CONTACT INFORMATION

Learning Disability Program/Services: Disability Concerns
Director: Ann M. Caldwell
  E-mail: ableisu@ilstu.edu
  Telephone: 309-438-5853
  Fax: 309-438-7713
Contact: Same

LEARNING DISABILITY SERVICES

Requests for the following services/accommodations will be evaluated individually based on appropriate and current documentation.

Allowed in Exams
  Calculator: Yes
  Dictionary: No
  Computer: Yes
  Spellchecker: Yes
Extended test time: Yes
Scribes: Yes
Proctors: Yes
Oral exams: Yes
Notetakers: Yes

Distraction-reduced environment: Yes
Tape recording in class: Yes
Books on tape from RFBD: Yes
Taping of books not from RFBD: Yes
**Accommodations for students with
  ADHD:** Yes
Reading machine: Yes
Other assistive technology: Yes
Priority registration: Y/N

Added costs for services: No
LD specialists: Yes (1)
Professional tutors: As needed
Peer tutors: As needed
Max. hours/wk. for services: Unlimited
**How professors are notified of
  LD/ADHD:** By both student and
  director

GENERAL ADMISSIONS INFORMATION

Director of Admissions: Steven Adams
Telephone: 309-438-2181

ENTRANCE REQUIREMENTS
15 total are required; 4 English required, 3 math required, 2 science required, 2 science lab required, 2 foreign language required, 2 social studies required, 2 elective required. High school diploma or GED required. Minimum TOEFL is 550. TOEFL required of all international applicants.

Application deadline: March 1
Notification: Rolling beginning 9/1
Average GPA: 3.21

Average SAT I Math: NR
Average SAT I Verbal: NR
Average ACT: 23

Graduated top 10% of class: 11%
Graduated top 25% of class: 38%
Graduated top 50% of class: 86%

COLLEGE GRADUATION REQUIREMENTS

Course waivers: No
Course substitutions allowed: Yes
In what subjects: Determined on a case-by-case basis

ADDITIONAL INFORMATION

Environment: The University is located on 850 acres in a small town 125 miles south of Chicago and 180 miles north of St. Louis.

Student Body
  Undergrad enrollment: 18,025
  Female: 58%
  Male: 42%
  Out-of-state: 1%

Cost Information
  In-state tuition: $3,332
  Out-of-state tuition: $7,275
  Room & board: $4,544
Housing Information
  University housing: Yes
  Percent living on campus: 37%

Greek System
  Fraternity: Yes
  Sorority: Yes
  Athletics: NCAA Division I

LINCOLN COLLEGE

300 Keokuk, Lincoln, IL 62656
Phone: 800-569-0556 • Fax: 217-732-7715
E-mail: rumler@lincolncollege.com • Web: www.lincolncollege.com
Support: S • Institution: 2-year private

LEARNING DISABILITY PROGRAM AND SERVICES

Lincoln College is committed to enhancing student achievement through supportive service community efforts in combination with parental involvement. The College offers personal attention and a number of supportive services to assist students. The Academic Enrichment Program meets every day to improve fundamental learning skills in writing, reading, mathematics, and oral communication. Study skills and study habits are also emphasized. Tutoring is assigned and each student's course schedule is strictly regulated. The Breakfast Club is for students who are failing two or more classes. These students meet with the College president and the academic dean to discuss ways to change direction and achieve academic success. Class attendance is monitored and faculty members inform the dean weekly if a student has missed class. Advisors help students to change counterproductive behaviors regarding attendance. C.A.S.P. (Concerned about Student Progress) warnings are sent the fifth week of each semester to provide an early indicator of below average performance, and allow students time to recover and change behaviors. The Connection Program targets incoming freshmen who may benefit from an established peer group. These groups of 8–10 meet with professors and foster awareness and build relationships.

LD/ADHD ADMISSIONS INFORMATION

College entrance tests required: No
Nonstandardized tests accepted: Yes
Interview required: Yes
Essay required: No
Documentation required for LD: Psychoeducational evaluation
Documentation required for ADHD: Yes
Submitted to: Supportive Educational Services
Special Ed. HS course work accepted: Yes

Specific course requirements for all applicants: Yes
Separate application required for services: No
# of LD applications submitted yearly: N/A
# of LD applications accepted yearly: N/A
Total # of students receiving LD/ADHD services: 180
Acceptance into program means acceptance into college: Students are admitted and enrolled at the College and then reviewed for supportive services.

ADMISSIONS

There is no special admissions process for students with learning disabilities. Students must submit the general application, a high school transcript, and counselor recommendation. Students with sub-17 ACT scores are required to attend the one-week Academic Development Seminar prior to the fall semester. Upon completing the Academic Development Seminar, a student's probationary status is removed. Students may be admitted and placed into a split semester, which means the student will take two courses per nine weeks if this is recommended by the Academic Development Seminar.

ADDITIONAL INFORMATION

Lincoln College offers the Academic Development Seminar for students the week before fall semester starts. Students learn writing and speaking skills, effective library skills, and science lab orientation. They develop effective student techniques; lab and field orientation; methods to evaluate social science graphs, charts, and maps; and concepts and values in the humanities. The Academic Writing Seminar is also offered one week in the summer to cover crucial college skills such as writing skill development; note-taking techniques; exam tips; speaking skills; writing to define and classify; college expectations; analytical thinking and writing; and writing to understand and evaluate.

SUPPORT SERVICES CONTACT INFORMATION

Learning Disability Program/Services: Supportive Educational Services
Director: Rod Rumler
　E-mail: rumler@lincolncollege.com
　Telephone: 800-569-0556 x250
　Fax: 207-732-7715
Contact: Same

LEARNING DISABILITY SERVICES

Requests for the following services/accommodations will be evaluated individually based on appropriate and current documentation.

Allowed in Exams
　Calculator: Yes
　Dictionary: Yes
　Computer: Yes
　Spellchecker: Yes
Extended test time: Yes
Scribes: No
Proctors: No
Oral exams: No
Notetakers: No

Distraction-reduced environment: Yes
Tape recording in class: Yes
Books on tape from RFBD: Yes
Taping of books not from RFBD: No
Accommodations for students with
　ADHD: Yes
Reading machine: No
Other assistive technology: No
Priority registration: Yes

Added costs for services: No
LD specialists: No
Professional tutors: 7
Peer tutors: 20–30
Max. hours/wk. for services: Unlimited
How professors are notified of
　LD/ADHD: By student

GENERAL ADMISSIONS INFORMATION

Director of Admissions: Rod Rumler
Telephone: 800-569-0556

ENTRANCE REQUIREMENTS

16 total are recommended; 4 English recommended, 3 math recommended, 3 science recommended, 2 foreign language recommended, 4 social studies recommended. Students with an ACT of 16 or better are admitted without restrictions. Those with an ACT below 16 may be admitted upon review. Conditional admits must complete an Academic Development Seminar.

Application deadline: Open
Notification: Rolling
Average GPA: 2.2–2.4

Average SAT I Math: NR
Average SAT I Verbal: NR
Average ACT: 18.5

Graduated top 10% of class: NR
Graduated top 25% of class: NR
Graduated top 50% of class: NR

COLLEGE GRADUATION REQUIREMENTS

Course waivers allowed: No
Course substitutions allowed: No
In what subjects: N/A

ADDITIONAL INFORMATION

Environment: The College has a suburban campus in Normal, Illinois, and a smal-town campus in Lincoln.

Student Body
　Undergrad enrollment: 725
　Female: 46%
　Male: 54%
　Out-of-state: 10%

Cost Information
　Tuition: $11,000
　Room & board: $4,700
Housing Information
　University housing: Yes
　Percent living on campus: 90%

Greek System
　Fraternity: Yes
　Sorority: Yes
Athletics: NJCAA

NATIONAL-LOUIS UNIVERSITY

2840 Sheridan Road, Evanston, IL 60201
Phone: 847-465-0575 • Fax: 847-465-0594
E-mail: nlnuinfo@wheeling1.nl.edu • Web: www.nl.edu
Support level: CS • Institution type: 4-year private

LEARNING DISABILITY PROGRAM AND SERVICES

The Center for Academic Development (CAD) is designed to assist students in their academic studies while they are pursuing degrees at NLU. The CAD offers academic support for all students admitted to the University and enrolled in regular and developmental college courses. The Center for Academic Development services is available to all students who might desire or be encouraged to partake in academic assistance such as subject area tutoring, study skills, etc. Emphasis is placed on individualized assistance. Special testing and academic services are available through the CAD for students with learning disabilities. The CAD provides tutoring and is the liaison between students and faculty for students who make reasonable progress toward a degree in one of the College programs.

LD/ADHD ADMISSIONS INFORMATION

College entrance tests required: Yes
Nonstandardized tests accepted: Yes
Interview required: No
Essay required: No
Documentation required for LD: At least WAIS-III; WJ
Documentation required for ADHD: Yes
Documentation submitted to: Center for Academic Development
Special Ed. HS course work accepted: No

Specific course requirements for all applicants: Yes
Separate application required for services: No
# of LD applications submitted yearly: N/A
# of LD applications accepted yearly: N/A
Total # of students receiving LD/ADHD services: 10
Acceptance into program means acceptance into college: Students must be accepted and enrolled at the University first and then may request services.

ADMISSIONS

Students must meet regular admission requirements of a 2.0 GPA in nondevelopmental academic courses. A learning specialist holds an informal assessment session with the enrolled student. Students should submit a statement from a diagnostician to Ms. Andreen A. Neukranz-Buter, MSW, (telephone: 847-465-5829, fax: 847-465-5610) who evaluates reports received and, along with the student, develops a letter of accommodations that the student will present to faculty. Alternative admission for all students is offered through Provisional Admission and/or Summer Admission.

ADDITIONAL INFORMATION

The Center for Academic Development is part of all National-Louis University Chicagoland campuses. Jady Piper is the coordinator at the Chicago Campus (312-261-3300), John Hopp is the coordinator at the Evanston Campus (847-256-5150, ext. 2548), and Sheila Stewart is the coordinator at the Wheaton and Wheeling Campuses (630-668-3838, ext. 4554). The Center for Academic Development is staffed by learning specialists and peer tutors. Some of services provided include the Summer Bridge Program, special advising, assistance in registration, individualized tutoring, organizational and student skill training, and an arrangement with faculty for modification of course presentation and examination. Support services and accommodations are offered to undergraduate and graduate students.

SUPPORT SERVICES CONTACT INFORMATION

Learning Disability Program/Services: Center for Academic Development
Director: Andreen Neukranz-Butler, Director of Diversity
  E-mail: aneukranz-butler@nl.edu
  Telephone: 847-465-5829
  Fax: 847-465-5610
Contact: Jady Piper
  Telephone: 312-261-3300

LEARNING DISABILITY SERVICES

Requests for the following services/accommodations will be evaluated individually based on appropriate and current documentation.

Allowed in Exams
  Calculator: Yes
  Dictionary: Yes
  Computer: Yes
  Spellchecker: Yes
Extended test time: Yes
Scribes: Yes
Proctors: Yes
Oral exams: No
Notetakers: Yes

Distraction-reduced environment: Yes
Tape recording in class: Yes
Books on tape from RFBD: Yes
Taping of books not from RFBD: No
Accommodations for students with ADHD: Yes
Reading machine: No
Other assistive technology: Yes
Priority registration: No

Added costs for services: No
LD specialists: Yes (1)
Professional tutors: 5
Peer tutors: 5
Max. hours/wk. for services: 2 hours per week per subject
How professors are notified of LD/ADHD: By student

GENERAL ADMISSIONS INFORMATION

Director of Admissions: Pat Patillo
Telephone: 847-465-0575, ext. 5612 or 312-621-9560, ext. 3450

ENTRANCE REQUIREMENTS
4 English recommended, 3 math recommended, 2 science recommended, 1 science lab recommended, 2 foreign language recommended, 3 social studies recommended.

Application deadline: Rolling
Notification: Rolling
Average GPA: NR

Average SAT I Math: NR
Average SAT I Verbal: NR
Average ACT: 18

Graduated top 10% of class: NR
Graduated top 25% of class: 19%
Graduated top 50% of class: 89%

COLLEGE GRADUATION REQUIREMENTS

Course waivers allowed: NR
Course substitutions allowed: Yes
In what subjects: Substitutions in various subjects may be allowed depending on specific college program.

ADDITIONAL INFORMATION

Environment: Formerly known as National College of Education, the University is located at 5 Chicagoland campuses: Chicago, Evanston, Wheaton, Wheeling, and Elgin, as well as in several other states.

Student Body
  Undergrad enrollment: 3,539
  Female: 76%
  Male: 24%
  Out-of-state: 1%

Cost Information
  Tuition: $13,095
  Room & board: $6,674 average
Housing Information
  University housing: Yes, at Evanston Campus
  Percent living on campus: 33% at Evanston Campus

Greek System
  Fraternity: Honorary
  Sorority: Honorary
Athletics: Intramural

NORTHERN ILLINOIS UNIVERSITY

Office of Admissions, Williston Hall 101, NIU, DeKalb, IL 60115-2854
Phone: 815-753-0446 • Fax: 815-753-1783
E-mail: admissions-info@niu.edu • Web: www.reg.niu.edu
Support level: CS • Institution type: 4-year public

LEARNING DISABILITY PROGRAM AND SERVICES

The main goal of the Center for Access Ability Resources (CAAR) is to create and maintain a supportive atmosphere to assist students with LD develop self-esteem, self-advocacy skills, and effective strategies for college success. CAAR is staffed by personnel who are supportive and sensitive to students. CAAR provides a comprehensive range of support services that are integrated within the University resources. Assistance must be requested by the student. The LD Coordinator assists students in identifying appropriate accommodations, compensatory and remediation strategies, and in the utilization of both on- and off-campus resources. Not all students are eligible for services. It is the responsibility of CAAR to see that qualified students who request services are provided appropriate accommodations. Instructors can also verify student accommodation requests through CAAR. The goal is to enhance student success through an individualized program of support services. To request and initiate services, students must submit to CAAR the necessary and appropriate official documentation verifying the disability.

LD/ADHD ADMISSIONS INFORMATION

College entrance tests required: Yes
Nonstandardized tests accepted: Yes
Interview required: Yes for CAAR
Essay required: No
Documentation required for LD: Psychoeducational evaluation within 3 years
Documentation required for ADHD: Yes
Documentation submitted to: Center for Access Ability Resources
Special Ed. HS course work accepted: No

Specific course requirements for all applicants: Yes
Separate application required for services: No
# of LD applications submitted yearly: N/A
# of LD applications accepted yearly: N/A
Total # of students receiving LD/ADHD services: 125–150
Acceptance into program means acceptance into college: Students admitted may request services. Students denied admission may appeal the decision and once admitted may request services.

ADMISSIONS

Regular admission requires: 50–99 percent class rank and 19 ACT or 34–49 percent class rank and 23 ACT. Course requirements include 4 years English, 2–3 years math, 2–3 years sciences, 3 years social studies, and 1–2 years of foreign language, art, or music. Substitutions may be allowed with appropriate documentation. Students with LD apply through regular admissions, but can disclose the LD and request special consideration if they feel that their entrance test scores or high school performance was adversely affected by special circumstances related to a documented disability. Special admission consideration for students with disabilities applies only to freshmen applicants who do not meet standard admission criteria and/or have already been denied admission. The special admission process involves (1) completing the standard NIU application and (2) attaching a "special consideration" letter asking that the application be given special consideration based on a diagnosed disability. It helps to describe the disability. This alerts Admissions to forward the application to CAAR. CAAR will need the following: (1) documentation of the disability with a personal statement explaining your interest in attending NIU, your academic and career goals, and any other information you would like to share, (2) three letters of recommendation from persons who have worked with you in an academic setting, and (3) any additional information about the disability that is pertinent. The admission process begins when all requested information has been received. Students may be contacted for an on-campus interview with a CAAR coordinator. CAAR staff make a recommendation to Admissions, who will notify students of the admission decision.

ADDITIONAL INFORMATION

Academic resources include priority registration; exam accommodations; limited tutoring; individualized study-skills and learning strategy advisement and instruction by LD specialists; reading and study techniques course taught by an LD specialist; foreign language course substitution with documentation; and taped texts. Other requests for course substitutions will be reviewed individually. Advocacy services include orientation, self-advocacy training, liaison with faculty, information on LD/ADHD-related events, and in-service training for faculty. Advisement resources include academic advising, referrals to University Counseling, and support and consultation by staff. Diagnostic evaluations for LD and ADHD are offered through referral to private diagnostician. Not all students are eligible for all services.

SUPPORT SERVICES CONTACT INFORMATION

Learning Disability Program/Services: Center for Access Ability Resources
Director: Nancy Kasinski
  E-mail: nancyk@niu.edu
  Telephone: 815-753-9734
  Fax: 815-753-9599
Contact: Garth Rubin
  E-mail: grubin@niu.edu
  Telephone: 815-753-9750
  Fax: 815-753-9599

LEARNING DISABILITY SERVICES

Requests for the following services/accommodations will be evaluated individually based on appropriate and current documentation.

Allowed in Exams
  Calculator: Yes
  Dictionary: Yes
  Computer: Yes
  Spellchecker: Yes
Extended test time: Yes
Scribes: Yes
Proctors: Yes
Oral exams: Yes
Notetakers: Yes

Distraction-reduced environment: Yes
Tape recording in class: Yes
Books on tape from RFBD: Yes
Taping of books not from RFBD: Yes
Accommodations for students with ADHD: Yes
Reading machine: Yes
Other assistive technology: Yes
Priority registration: Yes

Added costs for services: No
LD specialists: Yes (5)
Professional tutors: No
Peer tutors: No
Max. hours/wk. for services: Unlimited
How professors are notified of LD/ADHD: By student

GENERAL ADMISSIONS INFORMATION

Director of Admissions: Robert Burk
Telephone: 815-753-0446

ENTRANCE REQUIREMENTS

15 total are required; 4 English required, 2 math required, 4 math recommended, 2 science required, 4 science recommended, 1 science lab required, 2 science lab recommended, 1 foreign language required, 2 foreign language recommended, 2 social studies required, 3 social studies recommended, 1 history required. High school diploma or GED required. Minimum TOEFL is 525. TOEFL required of all international applicants.

Application deadline: August 1
Notification: Rolling
Average GPA: NR

Average SAT I Math: NR
Average SAT I Verbal: NR
Average ACT: 22

Graduated top 10% of class: 12%
Graduated top 25% of class: 36%
Graduated top 50% of class: 78%

COLLEGE GRADUATION REQUIREMENTS

Course waivers allowed: No
Course substitutions allowed: Yes
In what subjects: Primarily foreign language and math, but all requests are looked at individually

ADDITIONAL INFORMATION

Environment: The school is located on 460 acres in a small town 65 miles from Chicago.

Student Body
  Undergrad enrollment: 16,893
  Female: 54%
  Male: 46%
  Out-of-state: 4%

Cost Information
  In-state tuition: $4,347
  Out-of-state tuition: $7,415
  Room & board: $5,010
Housing Information
  University housing: Yes
  Percent living on campus: 33%

Greek System
  Fraternity: Yes
  Sorority: Yes
Athletics: NCAA Division I

NORTHWESTERN UNIVERSITY

PO Box 3060, 1801 Hinman Avenue, Evanston, IL 60204-3060
Phone: 847-491-7271 • Fax: 847-467-1317
E-mail: ug-admission@northwestern.edu • Web: www.northwestern.edu
Support level: CS • Institution type: 4-year private

LEARNING DISABILITY PROGRAM AND SERVICES

It is the policy at Northwestern University to ensure that no qualified student with a disability is denied the benefit of, excluded from participation in, or subjected to discrimination in any university program or activity.

LD/ADHD ADMISSIONS INFORMATION

College entrance tests required: Yes
Nonstandardized tests accepted: Yes
Interview required: N/A
Essay required: Yes
Documentation required for LD: WAIS-III
Documentation required for ADHD: Yes
Documentation submitted to: Services for Students with Disabilities—after admission
Special Ed. HS course work accepted: No

Specific course requirements for all applicants: Yes
Separate application required for services: No
# of LD applications submitted yearly: N/A
# of LD applications accepted yearly: N/A
Total # of students receiving LD/ADHD services: 120–175
Acceptance into program means acceptance into college: Students must be admitted and enrolled and then request services.

ADMISSIONS

There is no special admissions procedure for students with learning disabilities. All applicants must meet the general admission criteria. Most students have taken AP and Honors courses in high school and been very successful in these competitive college-prep courses. ACT/SAT tests are required and SAT II tests are recommended.

ADDITIONAL INFORMATION

Services are available for all students with disabilities and include Writing Center, comprehensive assistive technology, support groups, and individualized counseling. There are LD specialists on staff and all of the staff has knowledge in all disability categories. Students with learning disabilities must provide current psychoeducational evaluations normed on an adult population. Students with ADHD must provide a letter from an appropriate professional including a diagnosis, functional limitations, and recommendations. This documentation should be submitted to Services for Students with Disabilities.

SUPPORT SERVICES CONTACT INFORMATION

Learning Disability Program/Services: Services for Students with Disabilities
Director: Dannee Polomsky & Philip Romal
  E-mail: ssd@northwestern.edu
  Telephone: 847-467-5530
  Fax: 847-467-5531
Contact: Same

LEARNING DISABILITY SERVICES

Requests for the following services/accommodations will be evaluated individually based on appropriate and current documentation.

Allowed in Exams	**Distraction-reduced environment:** Yes	**Added costs for services:** No
Calculator: Yes	**Tape recording in class:** Yes	**LD specialists:** Yes
Dictionary: Yes	**Books on tape from RFBD:** Yes	**Professional tutors:** Yes
Computer: Yes	**Taping of books not from RFBD:** Yes	**Peer tutors:** No
Spellchecker: Yes	**Accommodations for students with**	**Max. hours/wk. for services:** Unlimited
Extended test time: Yes	**ADHD:** Yes	**How professors are notified of**
Scribes: Yes	**Reading machine:** Yes	**LD/ADHD:** By both student and
Proctors: Yes	**Other assistive technology:** Yes	director
Oral exams: Yes	**Priority registration:** Yes	
Notetakers: Yes		

GENERAL ADMISSIONS INFORMATION

Director of Admissions: Carol Lunkenheimer
Telephone: 847-491-7271

ENTRANCE REQUIREMENTS

16 total are recommended; 4 English recommended, 4 math recommended, 2 science recommended, 2 science lab recommended, 2 foreign language recommended, 4 social studies recommended, 3 elective recommended. High school diploma or equivalent is not required. Minimum TOEFL is 600. TOEFL required of all international applicants.

Application deadline: January 1	**Average SAT I Math:** 700	**Graduated top 10% of class:** 84%
Notification: April 15	**Average SAT I Verbal:** 680	**Graduated top 25% of class:** 96%
Average GPA: NR	**Average ACT:** 30	**Graduated top 50% of class:** 100%

COLLEGE GRADUATION REQUIREMENTS

Course waivers allowed: No
Course substitutions allowed: Yes
In what subjects: Foreign language when appropriate

ADDITIONAL INFORMATION

Environment: The University is located 10 miles from downtown Chicago.

Student Body	**Cost Information**	**Greek System**
Undergrad enrollment: 7,724	**Tuition:** $25,839	**Fraternity:** Yes
Female: 52%	**Room & board:** $7,776	**Sorority:** Yes
Male: 48%	**Housing Information**	**Athletics:** NCAA Division I
Out-of-state: 75%	**University housing:** Yes	
	Percent living on campus: 67%	

ROOSEVELT UNIVERSITY

430 South Michigan Avenue, Chicago, IL 60605
Phone: 312-341-3500 • Fax: 312-341-3655
E-mail: dessimm@admrs6k.roosevelt.edu • Web: www.roosevelt.edu
Support level: SP • Institution type: 4-year private

LEARNING DISABILITY PROGRAM AND SERVICES

The goal of the Learning and Support Services Program (LSSP) is to provide a highly individualized support system that will help students discover their learning style. The staff works with each student individually on reading comprehension, writing skills, note-taking, study skills, time management skills, and test-taking skills. Roosevelt's small classroom size provides an opportunity for students to get to know their professors, and the faculty has been very responsive to the needs of LSSP students. The program is for students who would otherwise experience difficulty with a regular college curriculum. Emphasis is placed on individual program planning, tutoring, arranged counseling, and modified test-taking. The program helps students to define their strengths so that they can overcome their weaknesses and become independent, successful college students.

LD/ADHD ADMISSIONS INFORMATION

College entrance tests required: Yes
Nonstandardized tests accepted: Yes
Interview required: No
Essay required: Yes
Documentation required for LD: Psychoeducational evaluation by licensed psychologist
Documentation required for ADHD: Yes
Documentation submitted to: DSS
Special Ed. HS course work accepted: No

Specific course requirements for all applicants: Yes
Separate application required for services: Yes
# of LD applications submitted yearly: 3–6
# of LD applications accepted yearly: 2–5
Total # of students receiving LD/ADHD services: 18–25
Acceptance into program means acceptance into college: Students are admitted directly into the University through LSSP.

ADMISSIONS

There is a special admissions process through LSSP. Students write a letter to the LSSP director to request services and state the purpose and reason for seeking help. After reviewing the letter, LSSP staff hold an informal interview assessment with the student. Applicants send reports to the LSSP with authorization for release of information. These reports should include the following: (1) most recent transcript and confidential records; (2) health and academic history; (3) test results and reports, including achievement, individual IQ or other measurements of academic performance; and (4) the latest IEP. The LSSP staff will evaluate the reports and an admission meeting will be held to determine eligibility and possible enrollment. Students may be admitted during the summer with probationary status.

ADDITIONAL INFORMATION

The Learning and Support Services Program is only available to students with learning disabilities. Assistance is available in course selection, required course readings, assignments, and more. A major department advisor is assigned to each student. Depending on individual needs, tutoring assistance may include course-related training, reading, writing, and spelling. Help is offered in specific problem areas such as note-taking, basic skills improvement, time management, and organization. Qualified counseling psychologists help students cope with personal concerns and advise them on career goals. Students are encouraged to use Roosevelt's Learning Resource Center and Writing Laboratory. Services and accommodations are available to undergraduate and graduate students. Students with learning disabilities are not required to take the Roosevelt University Assessment Test.

SUPPORT SERVICES CONTACT INFORMATION

Learning Disability Program/Services: Disabled Student Services (DSS)
Director: Nancy Litke
 E-mail: nlitke@roosevelt.edu
 Telephone: 312-341-3810
 Fax: 312-341-3735
Contact: Same

LEARNING DISABILITY SERVICES

Requests for the following services/accommodations will be evaluated individually based on appropriate and current documentation.

Allowed in Exams
 Calculator: Yes
 Dictionary: Yes
 Computer: Yes
 Spellchecker: Yes
Extended test time: Yes
Scribes: Yes
Proctors: Yes
Oral exams: Yes
Notetakers: Yes

Distraction-reduced environment: Yes
Tape recording in class: Yes
Books on tape from RFBD: Yes
Taping of books not from RFBD: Yes
**Accommodations for students with
 ADHD:** Yes
Reading machine: No
Other assistive technology: Yes
Priority registration: No

Added costs for services: $1,000 per
 semester
LD specialists: Yes (3)
Professional tutors: 3
Peer tutors: Yes
Max. hours/wk. for services: 2 hours
 per week plus unlimited time in
 writing lab
**How professors are notified of
 LD/ADHD:** By student

GENERAL ADMISSIONS INFORMATION

Director of Admissions: Brian Lynch
Telephone: 312-341-3515

ENTRANCE REQUIREMENTS

15 total are required; 16 total are recommended; 3 English required, 4 English recommended, 2 math required, 3 math recommended, 2 science required, 2 science recommended, 1 foreign language required, 2 foreign language recommended, 2 social studies required, 2 social studies recommended, 2 history required, 2 history recommended, 3 elective required, 1 elective recommended. Minimum TOEFL is 550.

Application deadline: Rolling
Notification: Rolling
Average GPA: 2.0 minimum

Average SAT I Math: NR
Average SAT I Verbal: NR
Average ACT: 19

Graduated top 10% of class: 15%
Graduated top 25% of class: 35%
Graduated top 50% of class: 65%

COLLEGE GRADUATION REQUIREMENTS

Course waivers allowed: Yes
Course substitutions allowed: Yes
In what subjects: Each request is considered individually and subject to department approval.

ADDITIONAL INFORMATION

Environment: Roosevelt University is located in an urban area in downtown Chicago.

Student Body
 Undergrad enrollment: 4,180
 Female: 61%
 Male: 39%
 Out-of-state: 2%

Cost Information
 Tuition: $10,930
 Room & board: N/A
Housing Information
 University housing: Yes
 Percent living on campus: 6%

Greek System
 Fraternity: Yes
 Sorority: Yes
Athletics: Intramural

SHIMER COLLEGE

PO Box 500, Waukegan, IL 60079-0500
Phone: 847-249-7175 • Fax: 847-249-8798
E-mail: admiss@shimer.edu • Web: www.shimer.edu
Support level: S • Institution type: 4-year private

LEARNING DISABILITY PROGRAM AND SERVICES

Shimer has no specific program for students with learning disabilities. Some students with relatively mild learning disabilities who have been unsuccessful in other settings have been successful at Shimer because of the unusual approach to education. Shimer offers an integrated curriculum where students read original sources and not textbooks. Students gather to discuss the books in small groups. Shimer has been able to meet the needs of students with learning disabilities who are motivated to seek this kind of education. Students are responsible for seeking the supportive help they want. The class size varies from 8 to 12 students, and a great deal of individual attention is available to all students.

LD/ADHD ADMISSIONS INFORMATION

College entrance tests required: Yes
Nonstandardized tests accepted: Yes
Interview required: No
Essay required: No
Documentation required for LD: Psychoeducational evaluation
Documentation required for ADHD: Yes
Documentation submitted to: Disability Services
Special Ed. HS course work accepted: Yes

Specific course requirements for all applicants: Yes
Separate application required for services: No
# of LD applications submitted yearly: N/A
# of LD applications accepted yearly: N/A
Total # of students receiving LD/ADHD services: NR
Acceptance into program means acceptance into college: Students must be admitted and enrolled in the College first and then may request services.

ADMISSIONS

The goal of Shimer is to select students who will benefit from and contribute to its intellectual community. Each applicant is considered on an individual basis. Motivation, intellectual curiosity, and commitment to a rigorous and integrative educational program are important qualifications. Shimer will consider the application of any individual who has the potential to perform well. Admissions standards are the same for all students. Admission is based on whether or not the College feels it can provide the services necessary for successful learning. Students are encouraged to have a personal interview (which can be conducted by telephone), write a personal essay, submit ACT/SAT scores, submit letters of recommendation, and have the psychoeducational reports sent to the admissions office. There are no minimum GPA or specific high school courses required. ACT/SAT scores are considered in the admission decision, but are not required. Writing samples and other personal contact will be used by the Admissions Committee to make an evaluation. A visit to campus is encouraged and an interview is highly recommended and, in some cases, required. The essay portion of the application asks the applicant to provide an analysis of academic experience and offers the opportunity to demonstrate creative talent. These essays are major criteria in determining candidacy for admission. Shimer will accept a limited number of students on a threshold basis. These students often lack specific evidence of academic achievement, but are able to convince the Admissions Committee of their commitment and potential. These students receive special guidance. Continuation after one semester is dependent upon academic achievement.

ADDITIONAL INFORMATION

Skills courses are offered to all students for credit in writing, reading, math, study strategies, and learning strategies. The skills developed in these courses do not depend upon earlier study in the core curriculum, so that most do not have prerequisites. Classes are never larger than 12 students. All courses are conducted through discussion and all course reading is from original sources. Extraordinary support is available to all students by faculty, staff, and other students.

SUPPORT SERVICES CONTACT INFORMATION

Learning Disability Program/Services: Disability Services
Director: George Krafcisin
Contact: David B. Buchanan
  Telephone: 847-249-7174
  Fax: 847-249-7171

LEARNING DISABILITY SERVICES

Requests for the following services/accommodations will be evaluated individually based on appropriate and current documentation.

Allowed in Exams
  Calculator: Yes
  Dictionary: Yes
  Computer: Yes
  Spellchecker: Yes
Extended test time: Yes
Scribes: No
Proctors: No
Oral exams: Yes
Notetakers: No

Distraction-reduced environment: Yes
Tape recording in class: No
Books on tape from RFBD: Yes
Taping of books not from RFBD: Yes
Accommodations for students with
  ADHD: Yes
Reading machine: No
Other assistive technology: No
Priority registration: No

Added costs for services: No
LD specialists: No
Professional tutors: Yes
Peer tutors: Yes
Max. hours/wk. for services: Unlimited
How professors are notified of
  LD/ADHD: By student

GENERAL ADMISSIONS INFORMATION

Director of Admissions: Bill Paterson
Telephone: 847-249-7175

ENTRANCE REQUIREMENTS
High school transcript or GED equivalent. One letter of recommendation required. Admission requirements are highly personalized. Interviews are required. ACT/SAT recommended but not required. Writing samples are used for admission.

Application deadline: Rolling
Notification: Rolling
Average GPA: NR

Average SAT I Math: Not required
Average SAT I Verbal: Not required
Average ACT: Not required

Graduated top 10% of class: NR
Graduated top 25% of class: NR
Graduated top 50% of class: NR

COLLEGE GRADUATION REQUIREMENTS

Course waivers allowed: No
Course substitutions allowed: No
In what subjects: N/A

ADDITIONAL INFORMATION

Environment: The school is located in a city setting, 40 miles north of Chicago and 40 miles south of Milwaukee.

Student Body
  Undergrad enrollment: 110
  Female: 61%
  Male: 39%
  Out-of-state: 60%

Cost Information
  Tuition: $14,370
  Room & board: $2,000
Housing Information
  University housing: Yes
  Percent living on campus: 70%

Greek System
  Fraternity: Yes
  Sorority: Yes
Athletics: Intramural

SOUTHERN ILLINOIS U.—CARBONDALE

Admissions & Records, Carbondale, IL 62901-4701
Phone: 618-453-4381 • Fax: 618-453-3250
E-mail: admrec@siu.edu • Web: www.siu.edu/oar/
Support level: SP • Institution type: 4-year public

LEARNING DISABILITY PROGRAM AND SERVICES

The Achieve Program is an academic support program for students with learning disabilities. The program provides comprehensive academic support services to meet the needs of students with previously diagnosed learning disabilities. Students interested in Achieve must make an application to the program and provide supporting documentation. All appropriate applicants must complete a two-day battery of diagnositc tests prior to entering the program. There are fees for application, diagnostic testing, and support services offered by Achieve. Students are accepted on a first-come, first-served basis providing they qualify for the program. Students are enrolled in regular college courses and are never restricted from any course offerings. Freshman-year students are enrolled as full-time students but are restricted to 12 semester hours. As students become more successful they may enroll in more semester hours.

LD/ADHD ADMISSIONS INFORMATION

College entrance tests required: Yes
Nonstandardized tests accepted: Yes
Interview required: Yes
Essay required: No
Documentation required for LD: Psychoeducational testing given by professional within 3 years
Documentation required for ADHD: Yes
Documentation submitted to: Project Achieve
Special Ed. HS course work accepted: Yes

Specific course requirements for all applicants: Yes
Separate application required for services: Yes
# of LD applications submitted yearly: 175
# of LD applications accepted yearly: 65
Total # of students receiving LD/ADHD services: 150
Acceptance into program means acceptance into college: Students are offered admission to the University and admission to Project Achieve.

ADMISSIONS

Application to the University and the program are separate. University application requires a general application form, ACT scores, and transcript. Students with an ACT of 20 and 4 years of English, 3 years of math, 3 years of science, and 3 years of social studies and electives are automatically admissible to the University. Applicants to Achieve Program are required to provide: Achieve application, $50 application fee, recent photo, and documentation of the LD. There is a fee of $1,000 for diagnostic testing (some fee waivers available), which is required before admission. The Achieve application can be submitted any time during high school (the earlier the better). Students who self-disclose on their applications will have them reviewed by the program, which provides a recommendation to Admissions. The required 20 ACT can be reviewed for Achieve Program applicants. For students not automatically admitted, Southern offers a selected admissions through the Center for Basic Skills. In addition, a two-year associate's program will consider admitting students not meeting minimum standards for regular admission.

ADDITIONAL INFORMATION

Students take tests in five subject areas and are assigned specific classes within those course areas. Peer tutors are assigned to assist students with understanding course material, studying and preparing for exams, homework assignments, projects, written work, and time management. Note-takers are hired to go into classes and take notes for students who demonstrate difficulty with visual-motor, auditory-memory-to-motor, and auditory comprehension tasks. Students must attend classes even if they are receiving note-taking support. Students may take exams and quizzes in the Achieve office, and may receive extended time, as well as a reader or writer if needed. Students may have textbooks and other written material taped. Some students will benefit from remediation of reading, spelling, math, and/or organizational deficits. Achieve students may take a developmental writing course before attempting the required English course. Graduate assistants work with students on a one-to-one basis so that the students have individual attention. Students have access to individualized tutoring, taped texts, test accommodations, remedial classes, developmental writing course, test proctoring, and advocacy service.

SUPPORT SERVICES CONTACT INFORMATION

Learning Disability Program/Services: Achieve Program
Director: Barbara Cordoni, EdD
  Telephone: 618-453-6120
  Fax: 618-453-3711
Contact: Sally DeDecker
  Telephone: 618-453-6131

LEARNING DISABILITY SERVICES

Requests for the following services/accommodations will be evaluated individually based on appropriate and current documentation.

Allowed in Exams
  Calculator: Yes
  Dictionary: Yes
  Computer: Yes
  Spellchecker: Yes
Extended test time: Yes
Scribes: Yes
Proctors: Yes
Oral exams: Yes
Notetakers: Yes

Distraction-reduced environment: Yes
Tape recording in class: Yes
Books on tape from RFBD: Yes
Taping of books not from RFBD: Yes
**Accommodations for students with
  ADHD:** Yes
Reading machine: Yes
Other assistive technology: Yes
Priority registration: Yes

Added costs for services: $2,200 per
  semester
LD specialists: Yes (17)
Professional tutors: Yes
Peer tutors: Yes
Max. hours/wk. for services:
  Unlimited
**How professors are notified of
  LD/ADHD:** By both student and
  director

GENERAL ADMISSIONS INFORMATION

Director of Admissions: Walker Allen
Telephone: 618-453-4381

ENTRANCE REQUIREMENTS
15 total are required; 4 English required, 3 math required, 3 science required, 3 social studies required, 2 elective required. High school diploma or GED required. Minimum TOEFL is 520. TOEFL required of all international applicants.

Application deadline: Rolling
Notification: Rolling
Average GPA: 2.2

Average SAT I Math: NR
Average SAT I Verbal: NR
Average ACT: 22

Graduated top 10% of class: 10%
Graduated top 25% of class: 30%
Graduated top 50% of class: 65%

COLLEGE GRADUATION REQUIREMENTS

Course waivers allowed: No
Course substitutions allowed: Yes
In what subjects: Foreign language and math

ADDITIONAL INFORMATION

Environment: The campus lies at the edge of the Shawnee National Forest, 6 hours south of Chicago.

Student Body
  Undergrad enrollment: 17,829
  Female: 43%
  Male: 57%
  Out-of-state: 17%

Cost Information
  In-state tuition: $3,011
  Out-of-state tuition: $6,021
  Room & board: $4,104
Housing Information
  University housing: Yes
  Percent living on campus: 24%

Greek System
  Fraternity: Yes
  Sorority: Yes
Athletics: NCAA Division I

SOUTHERN ILLINOIS U.—EDWARDSVILLE

Box 1047, Edwardsville, IL 62026-1080
Phone: 618-650-3705 • Fax: 618-650-2081
E-mail: admis@siue.edu • Web: www.siue.edu
Support level: CS • Institution type: 4-year public

LEARNING DISABILITY PROGRAM AND SERVICES

SIUE's philosophy is to assist students in becoming as independent as possible, and every effort has been made to eliminate barriers to learning. SIUE offers a full range of resources to support students with disabilities and help them attain their educational goals. Reaching goals starts with pre-admission planning and an assessment of the student's abilities and interests. The coordinator in the Office of Disabled Student Services (ODSS) will develop an understanding of the student's individual needs through counseling and academic advising. Early planning and testing will ensure that special needs are taken into consideration and that students can enjoy the full benefit of an educational experience at SIUE. Students are encouraged to contact ODSS as soon as they decide to enroll at the University in order to plan an individualized support program. SIUE does not have special classes for students with learning disabilities; however, the University does offer academic development classes for all students who need to develop their math, reading, and writing skills. New Horizons is an organization for students, faculty, and staff who are concerned with issues facing students with disabilities on campus. New Horizons' activities include advocacy, fund raising, guest speakers, and social activities.

LD/ADHD ADMISSIONS INFORMATION

College entrance tests required: Yes
Nonstandardized tests accepted: Yes
Interview required: No
Essay required: No
Documentation required for LD: Psychoeducational
   evaluation
Documentation required for ADHD: Yes
Documentation submitted to: Disability Support Services—
after admission
Special Ed. HS course work accepted: Y/N

Specific course requirements for all applicants: Yes
Separate application required for services: No
# of LD applications submitted yearly: N/A
# of LD applications accepted yearly: N/A
Total # of students receiving LD/ADHD services: 50
**Acceptance into program means acceptance into
   college:** Students must be accepted and enrolled at the
   University first and then may request LD services.

ADMISSIONS
Students with learning disabilities are required to submit the same general application form as all other students. Students should submit documentation of their learning disability in order to receive services once enrolled. This documentation should be sent to ODSS. Regular admissions criteria include 4 years English, 3 years math, 3 years science, 3 years social science, 2 years foreign language or electives (students with deficiencies need to check with the Office of Admission); a class rank in the top two-thirds, and an ACT minimum of 17 (average is 21) or SAT of 640–680. Students denied admission may appeal the decision.

ADDITIONAL INFORMATION
The advisers of ODSS will assist students with learning disabilities with pre-admission planning, including an assessment of abilities and interests. Counseling and academic advisement provides assistance in developing an understanding of individual needs. Skills classes are available in math, writing, and reading. Current resources include testing accommodations, assistance in writing/reading exams, assistance with library research, tutoring, and volunteer note-takers. In addition, the coordinator of ODSS acts as a liaison with faculty and staff regarding learning disabilities and accommodations needed by students. Services and accommodations are available for undergraduate and graduate students.

SUPPORT SERVICES CONTACT INFORMATION

Learning Disability Program/Services: Disability Support Services
Director: Jane Floyd-Hendey
  E-mail: jfloydh@siue.edu
  Telephone: 618-650-3782
  Fax: 618-650-5691
Contact: Same

LEARNING DISABILITY SERVICES

Requests for the following services/accommodations will be evaluated individually based on appropriate and current documentation.

Allowed in Exams
  Calculator: Yes
  Dictionary: Yes
  Computer: Yes
  Spellchecker: Yes
Extended test time: Yes
Scribes: Yes
Proctors: Yes
Oral exams: Yes
Notetakers: Yes

Distraction-reduced environment: Yes
Tape recording in class: Yes
Books on tape from RFBD: No
Taping of books not from RFBD: No
Accommodations for students with ADHD: Yes
Reading machine: Yes
Other assistive technology: Yes
Priority registration: Yes

Added costs for services: No
LD specialists: Yes (1)
Professional tutors: No
Peer tutors: Yes
Max. hours/wk. for services: Unlimited
How professors are notified of LD/ADHD: By student

GENERAL ADMISSIONS INFORMATION

Director of Admissions: Boyd Bradshaw
Telephone: 618-650-3705

ENTRANCE REQUIREMENTS

15 total are required; 4 English required, 3 math required, 3 science required, 3 science lab required, 2 foreign language recommended, 3 social studies required, 2 elective required. High school diploma or GED required. Minimum TOEFL is 550. TOEFL required of all international applicants.

Application deadline: July 31
Notification: Rolling
Average GPA: NR

Average SAT I Math: NR
Average SAT I Verbal: NR
Average ACT: 21

Graduated top 10% of class: 14%
Graduated top 25% of class: 39%
Graduated top 50% of class: 79%

COLLEGE GRADUATION REQUIREMENTS

Course waivers allowed: No
Course substitutions allowed: Yes
In what subjects: Math and foreign language

ADDITIONAL INFORMATION

Environment: The University is located on 2,664 acres 18 miles northeast of St. Louis.

Student Body
  Undergrad enrollment: 9,576
  Female: 58%
  Male: 42%
  Out-of-state: 13%

Cost Information
  In-state tuition: $2,574
  Out-of-state tuition: $5,148
  Room & board: $4,870
Housing Information
  University housing: Yes
  Percent living on campus: 24%

Greek System
  Fraternity: Yes
  Sorority: Yes
Athletics: NCAA Division II

Univ. of Illinois—Urbana-Champaign

901 West Illinois Street, Urbana, IL 61801
Phone: 217-333-0302 • Fax: 217-333-9758
E-mail: admissions@oar.uiuc.edu • Web: www.uiuc.edu
Support level: CS • Institution type: 4-year public

LEARNING DISABILITY PROGRAM AND SERVICES

The NCAA Division of Rehabilitation Education Services (DRES) assists qualified students with disabilities in the pursuit of their higher education objectives. DRES assists students with disabilities in gaining access to and benefiting from all the related experiences that are an integral part of a University of Illinois education. Professional staff are also available at DRES to assist university students in the following areas: planning and implementing academic accommodations, compensatory strategies, academic coaching, obtaining additional aids (e.g., interpreters, readers/writer), obtaining modified test accommodations, counseling, and priority registration/scheduling assistance. LD documentation should include: diagnostic interviews (developmental, medical, family histories); WAIS-III, Woodcock-Johnson test of cognitive ability, academic achievement battery, and a specific LD diagnosis by a qualified professional. ADHD documentation should include: evidence of early impairment, an extensive interview, developmental history, consideration of alternative causes, all appropriate neuropsych tests, extensive clinical summary, and specific DSM-IV diagnosis.

LD/ADHD ADMISSIONS INFORMATION

College entrance tests required: Yes
Nonstandardized tests accepted: Yes
Interview required: No
Essay required: No
Documentation required for LD: LD documentation should include: diagnostic interviews (developmental, medical, family histories); WAIS-III, Woodcock-Johnson tests of cognitive & academic achievement; and a specific LD diagnosis by a qualified professional
Documentation required for ADHD: Yes
Documentation submitted to: DRES
Special Ed. HS course work accepted: Yes

Specific course requirements for all applicants: Yes
Separate application required for services: Yes
# of LD applications submitted yearly: N/A
# of LD applications accepted yearly: N/A
Total # of students receiving LD/ADHD services: 125–150
Acceptance into program means acceptance into college: Students must be admitted and enrolled at the University first and then may request services.

Admissions

Applicants with LD are expected to meet the same admission criteria as all other applicants. Any tests for undergraduate and graduate admissions taken with accommodations are considered as competitive. Applicants whose qualifications are slightly below a college's admission guidelines are encouraged to use the "Background Statement" section on the application to provide additional information that could be useful in understanding the student's academic history. Students are encouraged to provide diagnostic evidence from a licensed clinical examiner. The University admits students to particular colleges on the basis of class rank, GPA, ACT/SAT scores, extracurricular activities, personal statements, achievements and challenge of curriculum. Prospective students should contact the appropriate college for complete course requirements. Required courses include 4 years English, 3 years math, 2 years foreign language, 2 years social science, and 2 years lab science.

Additional Information

Accommodations are individually student-centered. The student is expected to declare and document all concurrent disabilities for which services are expected. The design and implementation of accommodations depend on the student's perspective of his/her functional limitations relative to the academic requirements of each course. Timely communication to the learning disability specialist of any situations that are projected to need accommodations during the semester is essential. Individual inquiries and early contacts prior to campus residency strengthen the process of accommodation. Students with LD/ADHD can work with a specialist to develop compensatory strategies. Reading and Study Skills Workshops and Writer's Workshops are available for all students. Skills classes are offered in time management, test anxiety, stress management, and study strategies.

SUPPORT SERVICES CONTACT INFORMATION

Learning Disability Program/Services: Division of Rehabilitation Education Services (DRES)
Director: Karen Wold
  Telephone: 217-333-4600
  Fax: 217-333-0248
Contact: Kim Collins
  E-mail: kdcollin@uiuc.edu
  Telephone: 217-333-4603
  Fax: 217-333-0248

LEARNING DISABILITY SERVICES

Requests for the following services/accommodations will be evaluated individually based on appropriate and current documentation.

Allowed in Exams
  Calculator: Yes
  Dictionary: Yes
  Computer: Yes
  Spellchecker: Yes
Extended test time: Yes
Scribes: Yes
Proctors: Yes
Oral exams: Yes
Notetakers: Yes

Distraction-reduced environment: Yes
Tape recording in class: Yes
Books on tape from RFBD: Yes
Taping of books not from RFBD: Yes
Accommodations for students with ADHD: Yes
Reading machine: Yes
Other assistive technology: Yes
Priority registration: Yes

Added costs for services: No
LD specialists: Yes
Professional tutors: No
Peer tutors: No
Max. hours/wk. for services: Unlimited
How professors are notified of LD/ADHD: By student

GENERAL ADMISSIONS INFORMATION

Director of Admissions: Ruth Vedvik
Telephone: 217-333-0302

ENTRANCE REQUIREMENTS
4 English required, 3 math required, 2 science required, 2 science lab required, 2 foreign language required, 2 social studies required, 2 elective required. High school diploma or GED required. Minimum TOEFL is 550. TOEFL required of all international applicants.

Application deadline: January 1
Notification: Rolling
Average GPA: 3.5

Average SAT I Math: 652
Average SAT I Verbal: 608
Average ACT: 27

Graduated top 10% of class: 51%
Graduated top 25% of class: 85%
Graduated top 50% of class: 99%

COLLEGE GRADUATION REQUIREMENTS

Course waivers allowed: No
Course substitutions allowed: Yes
In what subjects: Substitutions only for foreign language and math

ADDITIONAL INFORMATION

Environment: The University has an urban campus 130 miles south of Chicago.

Student Body
  Undergrad enrollment: 27,908
  Female: 49%
  Male: 51%
  Out-of-state: 7%

Cost Information
  In-state tuition: $3,724
  Out-of-state tuition: $11,172
  Room & board: $5,844
Housing Information
  University housing: Yes
  Percent living on campus: 32%

Greek System
  Fraternity: Yes
  Sorority: Yes
Athletics: NCAA Division I

WESTERN ILLINOIS UNIVERSITY

1 University Circle, 115 Sherman Hall, Macomb, IL 61455-1390
Phone: 309-298-3157 • Fax: 309-298-3111
E-mail: wiuadm@wiu.edu • Web: www.wiu.edu
Support level: CS • Institution type: 4-year public

LEARNING DISABILITY PROGRAM AND SERVICES

Western Illinois University is committed to justice, equity, and diversity. Academically qualified students who have disabilities are an important part of our student body. Providing equal opportunities for students with disabilities is a campuswide responsibility and commitment. University personnel work with students to modify campus facilities and programs to meet individual needs. Disability Support Services is responsible for coordinating support services for Western Illinois University students who have disabilities. It is important to note that while services are available, there is no formal program for students with learning disabilities. WIU does not provide any remedial programs or offer any specialized curriculum. Students requesting accommodations must provide documentation verifying the specific learning disability. P.R.I.D.E. (Promoting the Rights of Individuals with Disabilities Everywhere) is an organization composed of students with and without disabilities. Members work together to remove attitudinal barriers within the University community. The group sponsors awareness-raising activities and serves as a resource for faculty, staff, and students who are interested in disability issues.

LD/ADHD ADMISSIONS INFORMATION

College entrance tests required: Yes
Nonstandardized tests accepted: Yes
Interview required: Y/N
Essay required: No
Documentation required for LD: Psychoeducational assessment: within 3 years
Documentation required for ADHD: Yes
Documentation submitted to: Disability Support Service
Special Ed. HS course work accepted: No

Specific course requirements for all applicants: Yes
Separate application required for services: No
# of LD applications submitted yearly: N/A
# of LD applications accepted yearly: N/A
Total # of students receiving LD/ADHD services: 105–135
Acceptance into program means acceptance into college: Students must be admitted and enrolled at the University and then can be reviewed for services.

ADMISSIONS

Students with learning disabilities must meet the same admission criteria as all applicants, which include 4 years English, 3 years social studies, 3 years math, 3 years science, and 2 years electives. Applicants must also have an ACT 22/SAT 1010 and a 2.2 GPA or ACT 18/SAT 850 and rank in the top 40 percent of their class, and have a 2.2 GPA. Students not meeting these standards may be considered for alternative admission. The application should be supported by a letter of recommendation from the counselor and a letter of appeal from the student. The Academic Services Program provides an opportunity for admission to a limited number of students yearly who do not meet the regular WIU admissions. Students considered for alternative admissions must have an ACT of 15 and a high school cumulative GPA of 2.2. Students admitted in the Academic Services Program are chosen on the basis of demonstrated academic potential for success. Several criteria are considered including, but not limited to high school academic GPA, grade patterns, references, and student letter expressing interest in the program.

ADDITIONAL INFORMATION

There are tutoring support services available to all WIU students through laboratories for writing and math, which are staffed by the English and mathematics departments. Students can receive one-to-one help with study skills including time management, note-taking skills, and exam preparation. There is tutoring available in some subjects, but there is no guarantee for tutoring in all subjects. Some tutors charge $4–$7 per hour, and some tutorials offered through the Office of Academic Services are free. Academic advisors in the Academic Services Program monitor student progress during each semester for students admitted in the program. These students are provided with tutorial support throughout freshman year. These students enroll in appropriate general education curriculum courses and introductory courses in their majors. The goal of the program is to promote the development of skills necessary for students to achieve academic success at WIU.

SUPPORT SERVICES CONTACT INFORMATION

Learning Disability Program/Services: Disability Support Services
Director: Joan Green
  E-mail: joan_green@ccmail.wiu.edu
  Telephone: 309-298-2512
  Fax: 309-298-2361
Contact: Myrna Galbraith
  E-mail: myrna_galbraith@ccmail.wiu.edu
  Telephone: 309-298-2512
  Fax: 309-298-2361

LEARNING DISABILITY SERVICES

Requests for the following services/accommodations will be evaluated individually based on appropriate and current documentation.

Allowed in Exams
  Calculator: Yes
  Dictionary: Yes
  Computer: Yes
  Spellchecker: Yes
Extended test time: Yes
Scribes: Yes
Proctors: Yes
Oral exams: Yes
Notetakers: Yes

Distraction-reduced environment: Yes
Tape recording in class: Yes
Books on tape from RFBD: Yes
Taping of books not from RFBD: Yes
Accommodations for students with ADHD: Yes
Reading machine: No
Other assistive technology: Yes
Priority registration: Yes

Added costs for services: No
LD specialists: Yes (1)
Professional tutors: No
Peer tutors: Yes
Max. hours/wk. for services: Unlimited
How professors are notified of LD/ADHD: By student

GENERAL ADMISSIONS INFORMATION

Director of Admissions: Karen Helmers
Telephone: 309-298-3157

ENTRANCE REQUIREMENTS
15 total are recommended; 4 English recommended, 3 math recommended, 3 science recommended, 3 social studies recommended. High school diploma or GED required. Minimum TOEFL is 550. TOEFL required of all international applicants.

Application deadline: July 31
Notification: August
Average GPA: NR

Average SAT I Math: NR
Average SAT I Verbal: NR
Average ACT: 21

Graduated top 10% of class: 7%
Graduated top 25% of class: 26%
Graduated top 50% of class: 64%

COLLEGE GRADUATION REQUIREMENTS

Course waivers allowed: Yes
Course substitutions allowed: Yes
In what subjects: Varies; students may submit a request for course substitution/waivers to the Council on Admissions, Graduation, and Academic Standards for review

ADDITIONAL INFORMATION

Environment: The University is located in a rural area 75 miles from Peoria.

Student Body
  Undergrad enrollment: 10,652
  Female: 51%
  Male: 49%
  Out-of-state: 3%

Cost Information
  In-state tuition: $2,982
  Out-of-state tuition: $5,964
  Room & board: $5,022
Housing Information
  University housing: Yes
  Percent living on campus: 52%

Greek System
  Fraternity: Yes
  Sorority: Yes
Athletics: NCAA Division I

ANDERSON UNIVERSITY

1100 East Fifth Street, Anderson, IN 46012
Phone: 765-641-4080 • Fax: 765-641-4091
E-mail: info@anderson.edu • Web: www.anderson.edu
Support level: CS • Institution type: 4-year private

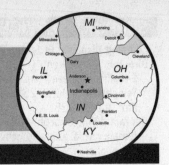

LEARNING DISABILITY PROGRAM AND SERVICES

It is the philosophy of Anderson University that those students who are qualified and have a sincere motivation to complete a college education should be given every opportunity to work toward that goal. Students with specific learning disabilities may be integrated into any of the many existing services at the Kissinger Learning Center or more individual programming may be designed. Students receive extensive personal contact through the program. The director of the program schedules time with each student to evaluate personal learning style in order to assist in planning for the most appropriate learning environment. One of the most successful programs is individual or small group tutorial assistance. Social and emotional support are also provided. The College strives to provide the maximum amount of services necessary to assist students with learning disabilities in their academic endeavors, while being careful not to create an over-dependency.

LD/ADHD ADMISSIONS INFORMATION

College entrance tests required: Yes
Nonstandardized tests accepted: Yes
Interview required: Yes
Essay required: No
Documentation required for LD: Psychoeducational evaluation
Documentation required for ADHD: Yes
Documentation submitted to: Disability Student Services
Special Ed. HS course work accepted: Y/N, will consult on individual basis

Specific course requirements for all applicants: Yes
Separate application required for services: No
# of LD applications submitted yearly: 25–31
# of LD applications accepted yearly: 20
Total # of students receiving LD/ADHD services: 78
Acceptance into program means acceptance into college: It is a joint decision between Admissions and the program.

ADMISSIONS

Students with specific learning disabilities who apply to Anderson do so through the regular admission channels. Documentation of a specific learning disability must be included with the application. Upon request for consideration for the program, prospective students are expected to make an on-campus visit, at which time a personal interview is arranged with the program director. All applicants are considered on an individual basis.

ADDITIONAL INFORMATION

Freshmen enrolled in the program are typically limited to 12–13 credit hours of course work during the first semester, including a two-hour study skills class. As students become more independent and demonstrate the ability to deal with increased hours, an additional course load may be considered. There are currently 42 students with LD and 41 students with ADHD receiving accommodations or services. Depending upon the specific needs of the student, all or a selected number of services may be provided including: assistance with advising, study skills instruction, time management, career counseling, alternative testing situations, and advocacy/liaison. The Kissinger Learning Center offers a variety of services, including a Writing Assistance Program directed by a faculty member of the English Department. Individuals needing further assistance receive a diagnostic evaluation, which enables staff to work more efficiently with school personnel in creating programs to fit the needs of students with learning disabilities. Students are fully integrated into the University and are expected to meet the same academic standards as all other students.

SUPPORT SERVICES CONTACT INFORMATION

Learning Disability Program/Services: Disabled Student Services
Director: Rinda Vogelgesang
  E-mail: rsvogel@anderson.edu
  Telephone: 765-641-4226
  Fax: 765-641-3851
Contact: Same

LEARNING DISABILITY SERVICES

Requests for the following services/accommodations will be evaluated individually based on appropriate and current documentation.

Allowed in Exams
  Calculator: Yes
  Dictionary: Yes
  Computer: Yes
  Spellchecker: Yes
Extended test time: Yes
Scribes: Yes
Proctors: Yes
Oral exams: Yes
Notetakers: Yes

Distraction-reduced environment: Yes
Tape recording in class: Yes
Books on tape from RFBD: Yes
Taping of books not from RFBD: No
Accommodations for students with
  ADHD: Yes
Reading machine: No
Other assistive technology: Yes
Priority registration: No

Added costs for services: No
LD specialists: Yes (2)
Professional tutors: 1
Peer tutors: 25
Max. hours/wk. for services:
  Unlimited
How professors are notified of
  LD/ADHD: By both student and
  director

GENERAL ADMISSIONS INFORMATION

Director of Admissions: Jim King
Telephone: 765-641-4080

ENTRANCE REQUIREMENTS

16 total are required; 20 total are recommended; 4 English required, 3 math required, 2 science required, 3 science recommended, 2 science lab required, 3 science lab recommended, 2 foreign language recommended, 2 social studies required, 3 social studies recommended, 2 history required, 5 elective recommended. TOEFL required of all international applicants.

Application deadline: August 1
Notification: Rolling beginning 7/1
Average GPA: 3.4

Average SAT I Math: 538
Average SAT I Verbal: 533
Average ACT: 24

Graduated top 10% of class: 23%
Graduated top 25% of class: 53%
Graduated top 50% of class: 85%

COLLEGE GRADUATION REQUIREMENTS

Course waivers allowed: No
Course substitutions allowed: Y/N
In what subjects: Not usually permitted, but will be considered on an individual basis.

ADDITIONAL INFORMATION

Environment: Anderson University is located on 100 acres 40 miles northeast of Indianapolis.

Student Body
  Undergrad enrollment: 1,977
  Female: 60%
  Male: 40%
  Out-of-state: 36%

Cost Information
  Tuition: $13,740
  Room & board: $4,540
Housing Information
  University housing: Yes
  Percent living on campus: 60%

Greek System
  Fraternity: Yes
  Sorority: Yes
Athletics: NCAA Division III

INDIANA UNIVERSITY—BLOOMINGTON

300 North Jordan Avenue, Bloomington, IN 47405-1106
Phone: 812-855-0661 • Fax: 812-855-5102
E-mail: iuadmit@indiana.edu • Web: www.indiana.edu
Support level: CS • Institution type: 4-year public

LEARNING DISABILITY PROGRAM AND SERVICES

The goal of the Office of Disabled Student Services is to provide services that enable students with disabilities to participate in, and benefit from all university programs and activities. There is no specific program for students with LD. However, there is a Learning Disabilities Coordinator who provides supportive services necessary to help students pursue their academic objectives. The Briscoe Academic Support Center offers free assistance to all IU students, night and day. Daily it is used for study groups, meetings, and advising. Evenings it provides free tutoring, advising, and academic support to assist with course assignments and studying. No appointments are necessary. Students with LD must provide current and appropriate psychoeducational evaluations that address aptitude; achievement; information processing; clear and specific evidence and identification of an LD; test scores/data must be included; evaluations must be done by a qualified professional; current IEPs are helpful. Students with ADHD must provide documentation that includes a clear statement of ADHD with a current diagnosis, including a description of supporting symptoms; current testing, preferably within three years; a summary of assessment procedures and evaluations used; a summary supporting diagnosis; medical history; suggestions of reasonable accommodations; and current IEP is helpful.

LD/ADHD ADMISSIONS INFORMATION

College entrance tests required: Yes
Nonstandardized tests accepted: Yes
Interview required: No
Essay required: No
Documentation required for LD: Psychoeducational
 evaluation
Documentation required for ADHD: Yes
Documentation submitted to: Disabled Student Services
Special Ed. HS course work accepted: No

Specific course requirements for all applicants: Yes
Separate application required for services: No
# of LD applications submitted yearly: N/A
# of LD applications accepted yearly: N/A
Total # of students receiving LD/ADHD services: 225
**Acceptance into program means acceptance into
 college:** Students must be admitted and enrolled at the
 University first and then may request services.

ADMISSIONS

There is no special admission process for students with learning disabilities. Each applicant is reviewed individually. IU is concerned with the strength of the College-prep program, including senior year, grade trends, and the student's class rank. Students falling below the minimum standards may receive serious consideration for admission if their grades have been steadily improving in a challenging college-prep program. Conversely, declining grades and/or a program of less demanding courses are often reasons to deny admission. The minimum admission standards include 4 years English, 3 years math, 1 year science, 2 years social science, plus additional courses in math, science, social science and/or foreign language to be competitive for admission. Indiana residents must complete Core 40 which includes a minimum of 28 semesters of college-prep courses. Nonresidents must complete a minimum of 32 semester college-prep classes. All students should be enrolled in at least three to four college-prep courses each semester. Students usually rank in the top one-third out-of-state and top half in-state. ACT/SAT are used primarily for advising.

ADDITIONAL INFORMATION

The LD specialist assists students with LD on an individual basis. Accommodations can be made to provide: test modifications; referrals to tutors; peer note-takers; books on tape; adaptive technology; and priority registration for students needing books on tape. Students must provide appropriate documentation. Students need to request a letter from DSS to give to their professors. Two years of foreign language are required for a degree from the College of Arts and Sciences. Students with a disability that impacts their ability to learn a foreign language must attempt taking one and the Dean will monitor the student's sincere effort to succeed. If the student is unsuccessful, there will be a discussion of alternatives. There are special math courses and one is a remedial course for credit. Currently, there are approximately 400 students with LD/ADHD receiving services.

SUPPORT SERVICES CONTACT INFORMATION

Learning Disability Program/Services: Disabled Student Services (DSS)
Director: Martha P. Jacques
  E-mail: dsscoord@indiana.edu
  Telephone: 812-855-7578
  Fax: 812-855-7650
Contact: Jody K. Ferguson, Learning Disabilities Coordinator
  Telephone: 812-855-3508
  Fax: 812-855-7650

LEARNING DISABILITY SERVICES

Requests for the following services/accommodations will be evaluated individually based on appropriate and current documentation.

Allowed in Exams
  Calculator: Yes
  Dictionary: Yes
  Computer: Yes
  Spellchecker: Yes
Extended test time: Yes
Scribes: Yes
Proctors: Yes
Oral exams: No
Notetakers: Yes

Distraction-reduced environment: Yes
Tape recording in class: Yes
Books on tape from RFBD: Yes
Taping of books not from RFBD: Yes
Accommodations for students with ADHD: Yes
Reading machine: Yes
Other assistive technology: Yes
Priority registration: Yes

Added costs for services: No
LD specialists: Yes (1)
Professional tutors: No
Peer tutors: Varies
Max. hours/wk. for services: Varies
How professors are notified of LD/ADHD: By student

GENERAL ADMISSIONS INFORMATION

Director of Admissions: Mary Ellen Anderson
Telephone: 812-855-0661

ENTRANCE REQUIREMENTS

14 total are required; 19 total are recommended; 4 English required, 4 English recommended, 3 math required, 4 math recommended, 1 science required, 3 science recommended, 1 science lab required, 3 foreign language recommended, 2 social studies required, 3 social studies recommended, 4 elective required, 2 elective recommended. High school diploma or GED required. Minimum TOEFL is 550. TOEFL required of all international applicants.

Application deadline: February 15
Notification: Rolling
Average GPA: NR

Average SAT I Math: 553
Average SAT I Verbal: 545
Average ACT: 24

Graduated top 10% of class: 21%
Graduated top 25% of class: 53%
Graduated top 50% of class: 91%

COLLEGE GRADUATION REQUIREMENTS

Course waivers allowed: No
Course substitutions allowed: Yes
In what subjects: Foreign language, depending on the documentation and the individual situation. There is an alternative track in Spanish for students with LD. There are also special tracks of math courses and one is a remedial math course for credit.

ADDITIONAL INFORMATION

Environment: The University is located in a small town 45 minutes from Indianapolis.

Student Body
  Undergrad enrollment: 29,383
  Female: 53%
  Male: 47%
  Out-of-state: 27%

Cost Information
  In-state tuition: $3,902
  Out-of-state tuition: $12,958
  Room & board: $5,608
Housing Information
  University housing: Yes
  Percent living on campus: 39%

Greek System
  Fraternity: Yes
  Sorority: Yes
Athletics: NCAA Division I

Indiana University—Bloomington

INDIANA WESLEYAN UNIVERSITY

4201 South Washington Street, Marion, IN 46953-4999
Phone: 800-332-6901 • Fax: 317-677-2333
E-mail: admissions@indwes.edu • Web: www.indwes.edu
Support level: S • Institution type: 4-year private

LEARNING DISABILITY PROGRAM AND SERVICES

The services offered at IWU are designed to assist students who have documented LD through advocacy and provision of appropriate accommodations. Student Support Services (SSS) provides tutoring, counseling, note-takers, and test accommodations. The Learning Center is available to all students who seek assistance with raising the quality of their academic work. Developmental educational courses are offered in reading improvement, fundamentals of communication, and skills for academic success.

LD/ADHD ADMISSIONS INFORMATION

College entrance tests required: No
Nonstandardized tests accepted: Yes
Interview required: No
Essay required: No
Documentation required for LD: Standardized intelligence or psychometric testing or other documentation related to disability
Documentation required for ADHD: Yes
Documentation submitted to: Student Support Services
Special Ed. HS course work accepted: No

Specific course requirements for all applicants: Yes
Separate application required for services: Yes
# of LD applications submitted yearly: 20–30
# of LD applications accepted yearly: 20–30
Total # of students receiving LD/ADHD services: 80
Acceptance into program means acceptance into college: Students are admitted to the University and to the program simultaneously.

ADMISSIONS

The Office of Admissions seeks students with at least a 2.0 GPA and an ACT of 18 or SAT I of 880. Students not meeting these requirements may be accepted on a conditional status and be required to enroll in a student success program designed to enhance their academic skills. Students with learning disabilities may self-disclose their LD or ADHD through a personal statement attached to the application for admission. There is a separate application for requesting services/accommodations for disabilities that is submitted after a student has been accepted and enrolled.

ADDITIONAL INFORMATION

All admitted students are given the Compass English Proficiency Test. If they score low, they are required to take developmental reading, writing, and study-skills classes. An SAT Verbal score below 350 or ACT English below 14 will also be indicators that the student should take developmental reading and fundamentals of communication classes. With appropriate documentation students with LD/ADHD may be eligible for some of the following services or accommodations: the use of a calculator, dictionary, computer or spellcheck in exams; extended time on tests; scribes; proctors; oral exams; note-takers; distraction-free environment; tape recorder in class; books on tape; assistive technology; priority registration; and workshops for all students in time management, test-taking skills, reading, and stress managment.

SUPPORT SERVICES CONTACT INFORMATION

Learning Disability Program/Services: Student Support Services (SSS)
Director: Jerry Harrell
  E-mail: jharrell@indwes.edu
  Telephone: 765-677-2257
  Fax: 765-677-2140
Contact: Same

LEARNING DISABILITY SERVICES

Requests for the following services/accommodations will be evaluated individually based on appropriate and current documentation.

Allowed in Exams
  Calculator: Yes
  Dictionary: Yes
  Computer: Yes
  Spellchecker: Yes
Extended test time: Yes
Scribes: Yes
Proctors: Yes
Oral exams: Yes
Notetakers: Yes

Distraction-reduced environment: Yes
Tape recording in class: Yes
Books on tape from RFBD: Yes
Taping of books not from RFBD: Yes
Accommodations for students with ADHD: Yes
Reading machine: Yes
Other assistive technology: Yes
Priority registration: Yes

Added costs for services: No
LD specialists: No
Professional tutors: No
Peer tutors: 40
Max. hours/wk. for services: Half-hour per week per course
How professors are notified of LD/ADHD: By student

GENERAL ADMISSIONS INFORMATION

Director of Admissions: Gaytha Holloway
Telephone: 800-332-6901

ENTRANCE REQUIREMENTS
High school diploma or GED required. The school seeks students with at least 2.0 GPA and 18 ACT or 880 SAT I. Conditional admits are offered.

Application deadline: August 15
Notification: Rolling
Average GPA: 2.0 minimum

Average SAT I Math: 440 minimum
Average SAT I Verbal: 440 minimum
Average ACT: 24

Graduated top 10% of class: 20%
Graduated top 25% of class: 48%
Graduated top 50% of class: 78%

COLLEGE GRADUATION REQUIREMENTS

Course waivers allowed: No
Course substitutions allowed: Yes
In what subjects: Varies based on course of study and specific disability; determined on a case-by-case basis

ADDITIONAL INFORMATION

Environment: The University is located on a 50-acre campus in a rural city 65 miles from Indianapolis and 50 miles south of Fort Wayne.

Student Body
  Undergrad enrollment: 2,000
  Female: 61%
  Male: 39%
  Out-of-state: 24%

Cost Information
  Tuition: $12,740
  Room & board: $4,940
Housing Information
  University housing: Yes
  Percent living on campus: 52%

Greek System
  Fraternity: No
  Sorority: No
Athletics: NAIA

MANCHESTER COLLEGE

604 College Avenue, N. Manchester, IN 46962
Phone: 219-982-5055 • Fax: 219-982-5043
E-mail: admitinfo@manchester.edu • Web: www.manchester.edu
Support level: CS • Institution type: 4-year private

LEARNING DISABILITY PROGRAM AND SERVICES

Manchester College does not have a specific program for students with learning disabilities. The College is, however, very sensitive to all students. The key word at Manchester College is "success," which means graduating in four years. The College wants all students to be able to complete their degree in four years. The College does provide support services to students identified as disabled to allow them to be successful. The goal is to assist students in their individual needs.

LD/ADHD ADMISSIONS INFORMATION

College entrance tests required: Yes
Nonstandardized tests accepted: Yes
Interview required: Yes
Essay required: No
Documentation required for LD: Psychoeducational evaluation
Documentation required for ADHD: Yes
Documentation submitted to: SSD
Special Ed. HS course work accepted: Yes

Specific course requirements for all applicants: Yes
Separate application required for services: No
# of LD applications submitted yearly: N/A
# of LD applications accepted yearly: N/A
Total # of students receiving LD/ADHD services: 40–50
Acceptance into program means acceptance into college: Students must be accepted and enrolled at the College first and then may request services.

ADMISSIONS

Students with learning disabilities submit the regular application form, and are required to meet the same admission criteria as all other applicants. Students are admitted to the College and use the support services as they choose. If special consideration for admission is requested, it is done individually, based on potential for graduation from the College. Manchester considers a wide range of information in making individual admission decisions. Students are encouraged to provide information beyond what is required on the application form if they believe it will strengthen their application or help the College to understand the students' performance or potential. Students who self-disclose the existence of a learning disability and are denied can ask to appeal the decision and have their application reviewed in a "different" way. The key question that will be asked is if the student can graduate in four years or, at the most, five years.

ADDITIONAL INFORMATION

College Study Skills, for one credit, is offered. A support group meets biweekly. No developmental or remedial courses are offered. A learning center provides tutoring for all students at the College. The College is in the process of developing a handbook that will describe services for students with disabilities. Services and accommodations are offered to undergraduate and graduate students.

SUPPORT SERVICES CONTACT INFORMATION

Learning Disability Program/Services: Services for Students with Disabilities
Director: Denise L.S. Howe
  E-mail: dshowe@manchester.edu
  Telephone: 219-982-5076
  Fax: 219-982-5043
Contact: Same

LEARNING DISABILITY SERVICES

Requests for the following services/accommodations will be evaluated individually based on appropriate and current documentation.

Allowed in Exams
  Calculator: No
  Dictionary: Yes
  Computer: Yes
  Spellchecker: Yes
Extended test time: Yes
Scribes: Yes
Proctors: Yes
Oral exams: Yes
Notetakers: Yes

Distraction-reduced environment: Yes
Tape recording in class: Yes
Books on tape from RFBD: No
Taping of books not from RFBD: No
Accommodations for students with ADHD: Yes
Reading machine: No
Other assistive technology: No
Priority registration: No

Added costs for services: No
LD specialists: Yes (1)
Professional tutors: No
Peer tutors: Yes
Max. hours/wk. for services: Unlimited
How professors are notified of LD/ADHD: By student and program director

GENERAL ADMISSIONS INFORMATION

Director of Admissions: JoLane Rohr
Telephone: 219-982-5055

ENTRANCE REQUIREMENTS

14 total are required; 17 total are recommended; 4 English required, 4 English recommended, 2 math required, 3 math recommended, 2 science required, 3 science recommended, 2 science lab required, 3 science lab recommended, 2 foreign language required, 2 foreign language recommended, 2 social studies required, 2 social studies recommended, 1 history required, 2 history recommended, 1 elective required, 2 elective recommended. High school diploma or GED required. Minimum TOEFL is 550. TOEFL required of all international applicants.

Application deadline: Rolling
Notification: Rolling beginning 9/1
Average GPA: NR

Average SAT I Math: 505
Average SAT I Verbal: 485
Average ACT: 22

Graduated top 10% of class: 20%
Graduated top 25% of class: 50%
Graduated top 50% of class: 81%

COLLEGE GRADUATION REQUIREMENTS

Course waivers allowed: No
Course substitutions allowed: No
In what subjects: Waivers/substitutions have never been requested

ADDITIONAL INFORMATION

Environment: The College is located in North Manchester, 35 miles west of Fort Wayne.

Student Body
  Undergrad enrollment: 1,091
  Female: 55%
  Male: 45%
  Out-of-state: 14%

Cost Information
  Tuition: $15,230
  Room & board: $5,610
Housing Information
  University housing: Yes
  Percent living on campus: 78%

Greek System
  Fraternity: Yes
  Sorority: Yes
Athletics: NAIA

UNIVERSITY OF INDIANAPOLIS

1400 East Hanna Avenue, Indianapolis, IN 46227
Phone: 317-788-3216 • Fax: 317-788-3300
E-mail: admissions@uindy.edu • Web: www.uindy.edu
Support level: SP • Institution type: 4-year private

LEARNING DISABILITY PROGRAM AND SERVICES

The University of Indianapolis offers a full support system for students with learning disabilities called B.U.I.L.D. (Baccalaureate for University of Indianapolis Learning Disabled). The goal of this program is to help students with learning disabilities reach their academic potential. Helen Keller expressed goal: "Although the world is full of suffering, it is also full of the overcoming of it." All students with LD at the University have reasonable modifications available to them at no extra charge. The B.U.I.L.D. program offers accommodations significantly more in depth than just minimal requirements. Services are extensive and the staff is very supportive and knowledgeable about learning disabilities.

LD/ADHD ADMISSIONS INFORMATION

College entrance tests required: Yes
Nonstandardized tests accepted: Yes
Interview required: No
Essay required: No
Documentation required for LD: IQ tests; reading and math tests: within 3 years
Documentation required for ADHD: Yes
Documentation submitted to: B.U.I.L.D.
Special Ed. HS course work accepted: Yes

Specific course requirements for all applicants: Yes
Separate application required for services: Yes
# of LD applications submitted yearly: 50–60
# of LD applications accepted yearly: 50–60
Total # of students receiving LD/ADHD services: 60
Acceptance into program means acceptance into college: Students must be admitted by the University and then admitted to B.U.I.L.D. If not accepted by Admissions, a committee confers.

ADMISSIONS

Admission to B.U.I.L.D. program occurs after a student has been accepted as a regular student, and students with LD must meet the University admissions requirements. However, flexibility is allowed to consider individual strengths. The student must submit the following: regular application for admission; B.U.I.L.D. application; high school transcript; current documentation regarding IQ scores, reading and math proficiency levels, primary learning style, and major learning difficulty; recommendations from an LD teacher discussing the applicant's main areas of strength and weakness; a recommendation from a mainstream teacher or guidance counselor; and an optional letter from an employer. After the directors of B.U.I.L.D. review the information, interviews will be arranged for those applicants being considered for final selection. Acceptance into the B.U.I.L.D. Program is determined by the program director.

ADDITIONAL INFORMATION

Tutorial coordinator assigns tutors to each student in B.U.I.L.D. All students must have at least two hours per week of individualized tutoring. Books on tape, test modifications, and group study are also provided. Course substitution is a possibility. B.U.I.L.D. offers three special courses to meet university requirements for English and math proficiency, all other classes are regular classes. Students are limited to 12 hours each semester until they can demonstrate academic success indicating they can handle the demands of a heavier course load. Other services include: specialized study skills course; specialized note-taking paper; test-taking arrangements; private study area; advice with course selection and career planning; possible course substitution; diagnostic testing referrals; and other aids such as books on tape, compresses-time tape recorders, and computers.

SUPPORT SERVICES CONTACT INFORMATION

Learning Disability Program/Services: Baccalaureate for University of Indianapolis Learning Disabled (B.U.I.L.D.)
Director: Deborah L. Spinney
  E-mail: dspinney@uindy.edu
  Telephone: 317-788-3536
  Fax: 317-788-3300
Contact: Same

LEARNING DISABILITY SERVICES

Requests for the following services/accommodations will be evaluated individually based on appropriate and current documentation.

Allowed in Exams
  Calculator: Yes
  Dictionary: Yes
  Computer: Yes
  Spellchecker: Yes
Extended test time: Yes
Scribes: Yes
Proctors: Yes
Oral exams: Yes
Notetakers: No

Distraction-reduced environment: Yes
Tape recording in class: Yes
Books on tape from RFBD: Yes
Taping of books not from RFBD: No
Accommodations for students with ADHD: Yes
Reading machine: Yes
Other assistive technology: Yes
Priority registration: Yes

Added costs for services: $3,700 per year
LD specialists: Yes (2)
Professional tutors: 15
Peer tutors: 35+
Max. hours/wk. for services: Unlimited
How professors are notified of LD/ADHD: By both student and director

GENERAL ADMISSIONS INFORMATION

Director of Admissions: Ron Wilks
Telephone: 217-788-3216

ENTRANCE REQUIREMENTS

15 total are recommended; 4 English recommended, 3 math recommended, 3 science recommended, 2 science lab recommended, 2 foreign language recommended, 3 social studies recommended. High school diploma or GED required. Minimum TOEFL is 500. TOEFL required of all international applicants.

Application deadline: September 15
Notification: Rolling beginning 8/1
Average GPA: 2.9

Average SAT I Math: 515
Average SAT I Verbal: 500
Average ACT: 22

Graduated top 10% of class: 23%
Graduated top 25% of class: 48%
Graduated top 50% of class: 80%

COLLEGE GRADUATION REQUIREMENTS

Course waivers allowed: No
Course substitutions allowed: Yes
In what subjects: Foreign language and math; substitution will be considered

ADDITIONAL INFORMATION

Environment: The 60-acre campus in a suburban neighborhood is located 10 miles south of downtown Indianapolis.

Student Body
  Undergrad enrollment: 2,856
  Female: 66%
  Male: 34%
  Out-of-state: 11%

Cost Information
  Tuition: $14,630
  Room & board: $5,225
Housing Information
  University housing: Yes
  Percent living on campus: 47%

Greek System
  Fraternity: Yes
  Sorority: Yes
Athletics: NCAA Division II

UNIVERSITY OF NOTRE DAME

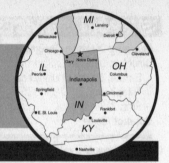

220 Main Building, Notre Dame, IN 46556
Phone: 219-631-7505 • Fax: 219-631-8865
E-mail: admissio.1@nd.edu • Web: www.nd.edu
Support level: S • Institution type: 4-year private

LEARNING DISABILITY PROGRAM AND SERVICES

It is the mission of the Office for Students with Disabilities (OSD) to ensure that Notre Dame students with disabilities have access to the programs and facilities of the University. OSD is committed to forming partnerships with students to share the responsibility of meeting individual needs. At the University of Notre Dame, students with disabilities may use a variety of services intended to reduce the effects that a disability may have on their educational experience. Services do not lower course standards or alter essential degree requirements, but instead give students an equal opportunity to demonstrate their academic abilities. Students can initiate a request for services by registering with the Office for Students with Disabilities and providing information that documents the disability. Individual assistance is provided in selecting the services that will provide access to the academic programs and facilities of the University.

LD/ADHD ADMISSIONS INFORMATION

College entrance tests required: Yes
Nonstandardized tests accepted: Yes
Interview required: No
Essay required: Yes
Documentation required for LD: Psychoeducational evaluation
Documentation required for ADHD: Yes
Documentation submitted to: Office for Students with Disabilities—after admission
Special Ed. HS course work accepted: No

Specific course requirements for all applicants: Yes
Separate application required for services: No
# of LD applications submitted yearly: N/A
# of LD applications accepted yearly: N/A
Total # of students receiving LD/ADHD services: 20
Acceptance into program means acceptance into college: Students must be accepted and enrolled at the University before they can access services.

ADMISSIONS

The University does not have a special admission process for students with learning disabilities. All students submit the same application and are expected to meet the same admission criteria. Admission to the University is highly competitive. The University seeks to enroll an exceptionally distinguished student body from among its broadly diverse and richly talented applicant pool. The admissions office prides itself on reviewing each application individually and with care. Students are expected to have 4 years English, 4 years math, 4 years science, 2 years foreign language, 2 years social studies, and 3 years of additional courses from these previous areas.

ADDITIONAL INFORMATION

Services for students with learning disabilities or attention deficit disorder include taped textbooks, note-takers, assistance with developing time management skills and learning strategies, and screening and referral for diagnostic testing. All students with disabilities are given assistance in developing a positive working relationship with faculty, facilitation of classroom accommodations, liaison with Vocational Rehabilitation and other state and local agencies, informal academic, personal and vocational counseling, and referral to other university resources. Currently 20 students with LD and 29 students with ADHD are receiving services/accommodations. Undergraduates and graduates with appropriate documentation are eligible to request services and accommodations.

SUPPORT SERVICES CONTACT INFORMATION

Learning Disability Program/Services: Office for Students with Disabilities
Director: Scott Howland
  E-mail: showland3@nd.edu
  Telephone: 219-631-7141
  Fax: 219-631-7939
Contact: Same

LEARNING DISABILITY SERVICES

Requests for the following services/accommodations will be evaluated individually based on appropriate and current documentation.

Allowed in Exams
  Calculator: Yes
  Dictionary: Yes
  Computer: Yes
  Spellchecker: Yes
Extended test time: Yes
Scribes: Yes
Proctors: Yes
Oral exams: Yes
Notetakers: Yes

Distraction-reduced environment: Yes
Tape recording in class: Yes
Books on tape from RFBD: Yes
Taping of books not from RFBD: Yes
Accommodations for students with ADHD: Yes
Reading machine: Yes
Other assistive technology: No
Priority registration: Yes

Added costs for services: No
LD specialists: No
Professional tutors: No
Peer tutors: No
Max. hours/wk. for services: Unlimited
How professors are notified of LD/ADHD: By student and director

GENERAL ADMISSIONS INFORMATION

Director of Admissions: Dan Saracino
Telephone: 219-631-7505

ENTRANCE REQUIREMENTS
16 total are required; 23 total are recommended; 4 English required, 4 English recommended, 3 math required, 4 math recommended, 2 science required, 4 science recommended, 2 foreign language required, 4 foreign language recommended, 2 history required, 4 history recommended, 3 elective required, 3 elective recommended. High school diploma is required and GED is not accepted. Minimum TOEFL is 550. TOEFL required of all international applicants.

Application deadline: January 9
Notification: April 1
Average GPA: NR

Average SAT I Math: 681
Average SAT I Verbal: 660
Average ACT: 31

Graduated top 10% of class: 84%
Graduated top 25% of class: 97%
Graduated top 50% of class: 99%

COLLEGE GRADUATION REQUIREMENTS

Course waivers allowed: No
Course substitutions allowed: No
In what subjects: N/A

ADDITIONAL INFORMATION

Environment: The University is located in a suburban area about an hour and a half from Chicago.

Student Body
  Undergrad enrollment: 8,038
  Female: 46%
  Male: 54%
  Out-of-state: 90%

Cost Information
  Tuition: $23,180
  Room & board: $5,920
Housing Information
  University housing: Yes
  Percent living on campus: 69%

Greek System
  Fraternity: Yes
  Sorority: Yes
Athletics: NCAA Division I

University of Notre Dame

UNIVERSITY OF SAINT FRANCIS

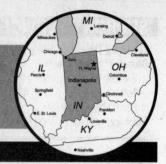

2701 Spring Street, Fort Wayne, IN 46808
Phone: 219-434-3279 • Fax: 219-434-3183
E-mail: admiss@sf.edu • Web: www.sfc.edu
Support level: CS • Institution type: 4-year private

LEARNING DISABILITY PROGRAM AND SERVICES

The Student Learning Center assists and acts as an advocate for students with disabilities. Students are encouraged to be self-advocates, as well as develop skills to become independent learners. The Learning Center strives to provide students with disabilities with special services and academic support needed to achieve success in the College environment. Students with disabilities are encouraged to meet with the Learning Center director prior to the start of the school year to discuss the types of accommodations necessary to provide the best opportunity for academic success.

LD/ADHD ADMISSIONS INFORMATION

College entrance tests required: Yes
Nonstandardized tests accepted: Yes
Interview required: No
Essay required: Yes
Documentation required for LD: The most recent psychological evaluation and the student's last individual education plan (within three years)
Documentation required for ADHD: Yes
Documentation submitted to: Student Learning Center—after admission
Special Ed. HS course work accepted: Yes

Specific course requirements for all applicants: Yes
Separate application required for services: No
# of LD applications submitted yearly: 15–30
# of LD applications accepted yearly: No limit
Total # of students receiving LD/ADHD services: 15–25
Acceptance into program means acceptance into college: Students must be admitted and enrolled at the College first and then may request services.

ADMISSIONS

There is no special admission process for students with learning disabilities. Entrance is based on an overall evaluation of the student's high school transcript, recommendations, and tests. The minimum ACT is 19 or SAT is 800. Automatic admission is given to students with a 920 SAT. College-prep course requirements include 4 years English, 3 years math, 2 years lab science, 2 years social studies, and 2 years foreign language. The minimum GPA is 2.2. Some students may be asked to come to campus for an interview and/or to write a personal statement or essay. Students may be admitted "on warning," on a 13-hour limit or a part-time basis.

ADDITIONAL INFORMATION

Incoming freshmen may be asked to take placement exams in reading, writing, and math to determine appropriate beginning level courses. Curriculum consideration is given to applicants whose test scores show that a limited number of credit hours would be helpful. Skills classes are offered in reading, writing, and math. The writing consultant helps students with all phases of the research paper or essay writing process including forming and refining ideas, planning a rough draft, revising, editing, and proofreading. Specialized services provided by the Student Learning Center are: accommodations on admission placement exams; alternative exam site; extended exam time; reading of exams or reading directions; carbonless paper for note-taking; assistance in ordering taped texts; altered exam procedures; large print; LD specialist for individuial assistance; peer tutors; academic progress monitoring with two reports per semester; letter to professors regarding accommodations; assistance with study and organizational skills; and assistance in facilitating a positive relationship with faculty and staff. Help is also available in the areas of time management, efficient study reading, memory techniques, concentration and motivation, test-taking strategies, and note-taking techniques.

SUPPORT SERVICES CONTACT INFORMATION

Learning Disability Program/Services: Student Learning Center
Director: Michelle Kruyer
  E-mail: mkruyer@sf.edu
  Telephone: 219-434-7597
Contact: Same

LEARNING DISABILITY SERVICES

Requests for the following services/accommodations will be evaluated individually based on appropriate and current documentation.

Allowed in Exams
  Calculator: Yes
  Dictionary: Yes
  Computer: Yes
  Spellchecker: Yes
Extended test time: No
Scribes: Yes
Proctors: Yes
Oral exams: Yes
Notetakers: Yes

Distraction-reduced environment: Yes
Tape recording in class: Yes
Books on tape from RFBD: Yes
Taping of books not from RFBD: Y/N
Accommodations for students with ADHD: Yes
Reading machine: Yes
Other assistive technology: Yes
Priority registration: No

Added costs for services: No
LD specialists: Yes (1)
Professional tutors: Varies
Peer tutors: Varies
Max. hours/wk. for services: Unlimited
How professors are notified of LD/ADHD: By both student and director

GENERAL ADMISSIONS INFORMATION

Director of Admissions: Dave McMahan
Telephone: 219-434-3279

ENTRANCE REQUIREMENTS
16 total are recommended; 4 English recommended, 3 math recommended, 2 science recommended, 2 science lab recommended, 2 foreign language recommended, 2 social studies recommended, 2 history recommended, 1 elective recommended. High school diploma or GED required. Minimum TOEFL is 500. TOEFL required of all international applicants.

Application deadline: Rolling
Notification: Rolling beginning 9/15
Average GPA: 2.9

Average SAT I Math: 473
Average SAT I Verbal: 480
Average ACT: 21

Graduated top 10% of class: 12%
Graduated top 25% of class: 32%
Graduated top 50% of class: 73%

COLLEGE GRADUATION REQUIREMENTS

Course waivers allowed: No
Course substitutions allowed: No
In what subjects: N/A

ADDITIONAL INFORMATION

Environment: The 70-acre campus is located west of Fort Wayne.

Student Body
  Undergrad enrollment: 794
  Female: 65%
  Male: 35%
  Out-of-state: 16%

Cost Information
  Tuition: $10,310
  Room & board: $4,270
Housing Information
  University housing: Yes
  Percent living on campus: 20%

Greek System
  Fraternity: Yes
  Sorority: Yes
  Athletics: NAIA

University of Saint Francis

UNIVERSITY OF SOUTHERN INDIANA

8600 University Boulevard, Evansville, IN 47712
Phone: 812-464-1765 • Fax: 812-465-7154
E-mail: enroll@usi.edu • Web: www.usi.edu
Support level: S • Institution type: 4-year public

LEARNING DISABILITY PROGRAM AND SERVICES

Staff provide support to assist students with disabilities so they can participate in educational programming. This mission is accomplished by offering student support and advocacy, being available for student and faculty consultation, coordinating accommodation services, and serving as a centralizing service for disability information for the University. Students must have a professionally diagnosed disabilty to qualify for disability support.

LD/ADHD ADMISSIONS INFORMATION

College entrance tests required: Yes
Nonstandardized tests accepted: Yes
Interview required: N/A
Essay required: No
Documentation required for LD: Complete diagnostic report including test scores, diagnosis, and recommendations for accommodations
Documentation required for ADHD: Yes
Documentation submitted to: Counseling Center—after admission
Special Ed. HS course work accepted: Yes

Specific course requirements for all applicants: Yes
Separate application required for services: No
# of LD applications submitted yearly: 25
# of LD applications accepted yearly: N/A
Total # of students receiving LD/ADHD services: 78
Acceptance into program means acceptance into college: Students must be admitted and enrolled at the University first and then may request services.

ADMISSIONS

Admissions criteria are the same for all students; however, the admissions office will always work with students on an individual basis if needed. In general, students with a 3.6 GPA or higher are admitted with honors. Students with a 2.0–3.5 GPA are admitted in good standing, and students with a GPA below a 2.0 are accepted conditionally. The conditional admissions procedure is for new freshmen who earned below a 2.0 in English, math, science, and social studies. The following are required for those admitted conditionally: freshman seminar; 2.0 GPA; registration through the University NCAA Division rather than a specific major; enrollment in no more than 12 credit hours. ACT/SAT scores are used for placement purposes.

ADDITIONAL INFORMATION

In order to receive support services, documentation of an LD must be provided by the student. Skills classes are offered in basic grammar, algebra review, reading, and study skills. Credit is given for the hours, but the grades are Pass/No Pass. There are no note-takers, but special supplies are provided to allow the students to get other students to carbon their notes in class. Other services include readers/taping services; test accommodations; tutor referral; advocacy and counseling; and career planning. Services and accommodations are available for undergraduate and graduate students.

SUPPORT SERVICES CONTACT INFORMATION

Learning Disability Program/Services: Counseling Center
Director: James Browning
 Telephone: 812-464-1867
 Fax: 812-464-1960
Contact: Leslie Smith
 E-mail: lmsmith@usi.edu

LEARNING DISABILITY SERVICES

Requests for the following services/accommodations will be evaluated individually based on appropriate and current documentation.

Allowed in Exams
 Calculator: Yes
 Dictionary: Yes
 Computer: Yes
 Spellchecker: Yes
Extended test time: Yes
Scribes: Yes
Proctors: Yes
Oral exams: Yes
Notetakers: Yes

Distraction-reduced environment: Yes
Tape recording in class: Yes
Books on tape from RFBD: Yes
Taping of books not from RFBD: Yes
Accommodations for students with ADHD: Yes
Reading machine: Yes
Other assistive technology: Yes
Priority registration: Yes

Added costs for services: No
LD specialists: No
Professional tutors: 40
Peer tutors: Yes
Max. hours/wk. for services: Unlimited
How professors are notified of LD/ADHD: By student

GENERAL ADMISSIONS INFORMATION

Director of Admissions: Eric Otto
Telephone: 812-464-1765

ENTRANCE REQUIREMENTS
18 total are recommended; 4 English recommended, 4 math recommended, 3 science recommended, 2 foreign language recommended, 2 social studies recommended, 2 history recommended, 2 elective recommended. High school diploma or GED required. Minimum TOEFL is 525. TOEFL required of all international applicants.

Application deadline: August 15
Notification: Rolling beginning 1/1
Average GPA: 2.8

Average SAT I Math: 478
Average SAT I Verbal: 478
Average ACT: 20

Graduated top 10% of class: 8%
Graduated top 25% of class: 26%
Graduated top 50% of class: 56%

COLLEGE GRADUATION REQUIREMENTS

Course waivers allowed: Not recommended
Course substitutions allowed: Yes
In what subjects: Math

ADDITIONAL INFORMATION

Environment: The University is located on 300 acres in a suburban area 150 miles south of Indianapolis.

Student Body
 Undergrad enrollment: 8,539
 Female: 60%
 Male: 40%
 Out-of-state: 9%

Cost Information
 In-state tuition: $2,918
 Out-of-state tuition: $7,148
 Room & board: $5,182
Housing Information
 University housing: Yes
 Percent living on campus: 30%

Greek System
 Fraternity: Yes
 Sorority: Yes
Athletics: NCAA Division II

VINCENNES UNIVERSITY

1002 N. First St., Vincennes, IN 47591
Phone: 812-888-4313 • Fax: 812-888-5707
E-mail: vuadmit@vunet.vinu.edu • Web: www.vinu.edu
Support: SP • Institution: 2-year public

LEARNING DISABILITY PROGRAM AND SERVICES

Students Transition into Education Program (STEP) is an LD support program for students in the mainstream. Students' strengths rather than deficits are the emphasis; compensatory techniques rather than remediation are the thrust. STEP is designed to give students the opportunity to develop their own unique abilities, achieve their highest academic potential, and develop a sense of self-worth and the skills needed to function and learn independently in college. STEP students take four semesters in Coping in College I–IV; the course teaches requisite social, study, and self-awareness skills and serves as a support group. The curriculum is practical and emphasizes active thinking, independent learning, student accountability, and the acquisition of specific strategies proven to improve academic performance. Coping in College I addresses self-advocacy, compensatory techniques, coping, adaptation, stress, and socialization; II emphasizes socialization and metacognitive skills; III further develops social skills and solidifies study skills; IV emphasizes career planning, job-search, and social skills, and includes the STEP retreat. Cope Student Support Services is a program designed to help students with all aspects of the College experience. This is a Trio Program requiring that the student meet one of three requirements: first generation college student, low income, or disabled.

LD/ADHD ADMISSIONS INFORMATION

College entrance tests required: No
Nonstandardized tests accepted: Yes
Interview required: N/A
Essay required: No
Documentation required for LD: Psychoeducational evaluation
Documentation required for ADHD: Yes
Submitted to: Admissions and STEP
Special Ed. HS course work accepted: Yes

Specific course requirements for all applicants: No
Separate application required for services: Yes
# of LD applications submitted yearly: 400
# of LD applications accepted yearly: 60
Total # of students receiving LD/ADHD services: 200
Acceptance into program means acceptance into college: Students must apply separately to the University and STEP or Cope. Students will be accepted to the University first and then to STEP or Cope.

ADMISSIONS

Students with learning disabilities must submit the general application form to Vincennes University. Vincennes offers open-door admissions to any student with a high school diploma or the GED. Students with learning disabilities must apply separately to STEP: send the STEP application; psychological evaluation; and letters of recommendation from LD specialists, counselors, or teachers. The transcript is of less importance and the recommendations are more important. Once accepted, students reserve a spot with a deposit of $110 to STEP. Deposits are refundable if students do not matriculate to Vincennes. Admission to the program is based on completion of the application process, determination of student eligibility, available funding, and space remaining. Space in the program is limited. Early application is important and the deadline date is February 1. Students applying to Cope should apply separately to the University prior to applying to STEP.

ADDITIONAL INFORMATION

STEP benefits include LD specialist for individualized tutoring/remediation; professional/peer tutoring; specialized remedial and/or support classes; weekly academic monitoring; coordinated referral to Counseling/Career Center; special classes; note-taking paper; reduced class load; audit class before taking it; test modifications; papers rather than tests; and alternative ways to demonstrate competency. STEP does not exempt students from classes, class requirements, or provide taped books and note-takers. Cope provides individual counselor to assist with needs; tutoring; progress reports; academic advising; appropriate accommodations; academic support groups; workshops on study skills, test anxiety, self-esteem, and interview skills. The Study Skills Center is open to all students and offers free tutoring; study skills classes in spelling, study skills, success strategies, and learning strategies; individualized materials to help improve performance in problem areas; assessment center; and study skills lab.

SUPPORT SERVICES CONTACT INFORMATION

Learning Disability Program/Services: Students Transition into Education Program (STEP)
Director: Jane Kavanaugh
  E-mail: jkavanaugh@vinu.edu
  Telephone: 812-888-4485
Contact: Susan Laue, Cope
  Telephone: 812-888-4212

LEARNING DISABILITY SERVICES

Requests for the following services/accommodations will be evaluated individually based on appropriate and current documentation.

Allowed in Exams
  Calculator: Yes
  Dictionary: Yes
  Computer: Yes
  Spellchecker: Yes
Extended test time: Yes
Scribes: No
Proctors: Yes
Oral exams: Yes
Notetakers: No

Distraction-reduced environment: Yes
Tape recording in class: No
Books on tape from RFBD: Yes
Taping of books not from RFBD: Yes
Accommodations for students with ADHD: Yes
Reading machine: Yes
Other assistive technology: Yes
Priority registration: Yes

Added costs for services: $300
LD specialists: Yes
Professional tutors: Yes
Peer tutors: Yes
Max. hours/wk. for services: Unlimited
How professors are notified of LD/ADHD: By student

GENERAL ADMISSIONS INFORMATION

Director of Admissions: Ann Skuce
Telephone: 812-888-4313

ENTRANCE REQUIREMENTS
"Open door" admissions. High school diploma or GED required. No ACT/SAT required.

Application deadline: Rolling
Notification: Rolling
Average GPA: NR

Average SAT I Math: NR
Average SAT I Verbal: NR
Average ACT: NR

Graduated top 10% of class: NR
Graduated top 25% of class: NR
Graduated top 50% of class: NR

COLLEGE GRADUATION REQUIREMENTS

Course waivers allowed: No
Course substitutions allowed: Yes
In what subjects: Handled individually

ADDITIONAL INFORMATION

Environment: The school is located on 95 acres 45 minutes south of Terre Haute.

Student Body
  Undergrad enrollment: 6,000
  Female: 43%
  Male: 57%
  Out-of-state: 9%

Cost Information
  On-state tuition: $1,800
  Out-of-state tuition: $3,200
  Room & board: $4,000
Housing Information
  University housing: Yes
  Percent living on campus: 48%

Greek System
  Fraternity: Yes
  Sorority: Yes
  Athletics: NJCAA

Vincennes University

DRAKE UNIVERSITY

2507 University, Des Moines, IA 50311
Phone: 515-271-3181 • Fax: 515-271-2831
E-mail: admitinfo@drake.edu • Web: www.drake.edu
Support level: S • Institution type: 4-year private

LEARNING DISABILITY PROGRAM AND SERVICES

Student Disability Services facilitates and enhances the opportunity for students with any type of disability to successfully complete their post-secondary education. The SDS is committed to enriching the academic experience of Drake students with disabilities through individualized assessment of accommodations and resource needs. To initiate a request for services, students should contact the SDS. An appointment will be made with a staff member to begin the registration process. Students are encouraged to meet with a SDS counselor each semester to identify accommodations that are needed. It is the students' responsibility to self-identify that they have a learning disability; to provide professional documentation of their disability; and to request the accommodations that they need The SDS office maintains a collection of information on disabilities, and there are many sources on the instruction and evaluation of students with disabilities. SDS encourages faculty, staff, and students to contact the office if they are interested in this type of information.

LD/ADHD ADMISSIONS INFORMATION

College entrance tests required: Yes
Nonstandardized tests accepted: Yes
Interview required: No
Essay required: No
Documentation required for LD: Psychoeducational evaluation
Documentation required for ADHD: Yes
Documentation submitted to: SDS—after admission
Special Ed. HS course work accepted: Yes

Specific course requirements for all applicants: Yes
Separate application required for services: No
# of LD applications submitted yearly: N/A
# of LD applications accepted yearly: N/A
Total # of students receiving LD/ADHD services: 35
Acceptance into program means acceptance into college: Students must be admitted and enrolled at the University first and then may request LD services.

ADMISSIONS

There is no special admission process for students with learning disabilities. All applicants are expected to meet the same admission criteria, including 16 academic college-prep courses with a minimum of 4 years English, 2 years math, 2 years science, 2 years social studies, 1 year history, and 2 years foreign language; 21 ACT or 970 SAT; and a minimum of a 2.0 GPA. Students must be admitted and enrolled in the University prior to seeking accommodations or services for a learning disability.

ADDITIONAL INFORMATION

The SDS, located in the American Republic Health Center, can offer students appointments at the pre-admission and pre-enrollment stages; review of Drake's policies and procedures regarding students with disabilities; identification and coordination of classroom accommodations; assessment of service needs; note-takers, scribes, and readers; referral to appropriate campus resources; advocacy and liaison with the University community; and training on the use of assistive technology. Services provided by the SDS do not lower any course standards or change any requirements of a particular degree. The services are intended to allow equal access and provide an opportunity for students with disabilities to demonstrate their abilities.

SUPPORT SERVICES CONTACT INFORMATION

Learning Disability Program/Services: Student Disability Services
Director: Interim
   Telephone: 1-800-44-DRAKE, ext. 3100
   Fax: 515-271-3016
Contact: Same

LEARNING DISABILITY SERVICES

Requests for the following services/accommodations will be evaluated individually based on appropriate and current documentation.

Allowed in Exams
  Calculator: Yes
  Dictionary: Yes
  Computer: Yes
  Spellchecker: Yes
Extended test time: Yes
Scribes: Yes
Proctors: Yes
Oral exams: Yes
Notetakers: Yes

Distraction-reduced environment: Yes
Tape recording in class: Yes
Books on tape from RFBD: Yes
Taping of books not from RFBD: Yes
Accommodations for students with
  ADHD: Yes
Reading machine: Yes
Other assistive technology: Yes
Priority registration: No

Added costs for services: No
LD specialists: No
Professional tutors: No
Peer tutors: Yes
Max. hours/wk. for services:
  Unlimited
How professors are notified of
  LD/ADHD: By student

GENERAL ADMISSIONS INFORMATION

Director of Admissions: Thomas Willoughlby
Telephone: 515-271-3181

ENTRANCE REQUIREMENTS
16 total are recommended; 4 English recommended, 3 math recommended, 2 science recommended, 2 foreign language recommended, 4 social studies recommended. High school diploma or GED required. Minimum TOEFL is 530. TOEFL required of all international applicants.

Application deadline: August 1
Notification: Rolling beginning 10/1
Average GPA: 3.5

Average SAT I Math: 581
Average SAT I Verbal: 566
Average ACT: 25

Graduated top 10% of class: 30%
Graduated top 25% of class: 62%
Graduated top 50% of class: 89%

COLLEGE GRADUATION REQUIREMENTS

Course waivers allowed: No
Course substitutions allowed: Yes
In what subjects: A special request can be made with appropriate documentation. Requests are evaluated individually.

ADDITIONAL INFORMATION

Environment: The campus is located in the suburbs of Des Moines.

Student Body
  Undergrad enrollment: 3,544
  Female: 61%
  Male: 39%
  Out-of-state: 60%

Cost Information
  Tuition: $17,580
  Room & board: $5,040
Housing Information
  University housing: Yes
  Percent living on campus: 64%

Greek System
  Fraternity: Yes
  Sorority: Yes
Athletics: NCAA Division I

Drake University

GRAND VIEW COLLEGE

1200 Grandview Avenue, Des Moines, IA 50316-1599
Phone: 515-263-2810 • Fax: 515-263-2974
E-mail: admiss@gvc.edu • Web: www.gvc.edu
Support level: CS • Institution type: 4-year private

LEARNING DISABILITY PROGRAM AND SERVICES

The Academic Success Program is available for all students on campus. The objective of the program is to provide a variety of learning environments and teaching techniques. Academic Success provides academic support programs, services, and courses designed to optimize student performance. Students who participate in the Center for Academic and Career Success Program make a smoother transition to Grand View, develop social and academic networks essential to their success, and benefit from informal student-faculty-staff interactions. Grand View is committed to enriching the academic experience of every qualified student with LD and endorses reasonable accommodations for participation in all programs and activities. Students are encouraged to make an appointment in the Academic Success Center to review college policies and procedures, request accommodations, develop an accommodation plan, or discuss personal advocacy issues.

LD/ADHD ADMISSIONS INFORMATION

College entrance tests required: Yes
Nonstandardized tests accepted: Yes
Interview required: No
Essay required: No
Documentation required for LD: Verification of learning disabilities by licensed psychologist required
Documentation required for ADHD: Yes
Documentation submitted to: Academic Success
Special Ed. HS course work accepted: Yes

Specific course requirements for all applicants: Yes
Separate application required for services: No
# of LD applications submitted yearly: N/A
# of LD applications accepted yearly: N/A
Total # of students receiving LD/ADHD services: 15
Acceptance into program means acceptance into college: Students must be admitted and enrolled and then may request services.

ADMISSIONS

There is no special admissions process for students with LD and ADHD. There is a probationary admit for students with an 18 ACT and a 2.0 high school GPA and below. This is offered to students who show that they are committed and have the potential for success at college.

ADDITIONAL INFORMATION

Academic Success Center provides resources which complement classroom instruction, enabling students to optimize their academic experience. Students can receive help with reading rate and reading comprehension, study skills, organizational skills, developing a personal management plan, test-taking strategies, writing skills, personalized instruction in math, and peer tutoring. The Career Center provides services, resources, and educational opportunities by assisting students in developing, evaluating, initiating, and implementing personal career and life plans. Faculty members serve as academic advisors. Core courses can have substitutions options. Other services or accommodations offered for students with appropriate documentation include the use of calculators, computers, or spellcheckers; extended testing time; scribes; proctors; oral exams; note-takers; distraction-free environment for taking tests; tape recording of lectures; and services for students with ADHD. There is one professional staff member who is certified in LD.

SUPPORT SERVICES CONTACT INFORMATION

Learning Disability Program/Services: Academic Success
Director: Carolyn Wassenaar
  E-mail: cwassenaar@gve.edu
  Telephone: 515-263-2971
  Fax: 515-263-2840
Contact: Same

LEARNING DISABILITY SERVICES

Requests for the following services/accommodations will be evaluated individually based on appropriate and current documentation.

Allowed in Exams
  Calculator: Yes
  Dictionary: Yes
  Computer: Yes
  Spellchecker: Yes
Extended test time: Yes
Scribes: Yes
Proctors: Yes
Oral exams: Yes
Notetakers: Yes

Distraction-reduced environment: Yes
Tape recording in class: Yes
Books on tape from RFBD: Yes
Taping of books not from RFBD: Yes
Accommodations for students with ADHD: Yes
Reading machine: No
Other assistive technology: No
Priority registration: Yes

Added costs for services: No
LD specialists: Yes (1)
Professional tutors: 1
Peer tutors: N/A
Max. hours/wk. for services: Unlimited
How professors are notified of LD/ADHD: By both student and director

GENERAL ADMISSIONS INFORMATION

Director of Admissions: Debbie Borger
Telephone: 515-263-2810

ENTRANCE REQUIREMENTS
17 total are required; 4 English required, 4 English recommended, 3 math required, 3 math recommended, 3 science required, 3 science recommended, 1 science lab required, 2 foreign language required, 2 foreign language recommended, 2 social studies required, 3 social studies recommended, 2 history required. High school diploma or GED required. Minimum TOEFL is 500. TOEFL required of all international applicants.

Application deadline: Rolling
Notification: Rolling
Average GPA: 2.9

Average SAT I Math: NR
Average SAT I Verbal: NR
Average ACT: 19

Graduated top 10% of class: 12%
Graduated top 25% of class: 38%
Graduated top 50% of class: 58%

COLLEGE GRADUATION REQUIREMENTS

Course waivers allowed: Not recommended
Course substitutions allowed: Yes
In what subjects: A special request can be made with appropriate documentation. Requests are evaluated individually.

ADDITIONAL INFORMATION

Environment: Located 200 miles from Kansas City and 250 miles from Minneapolis.

Student Body
  Undergrad enrollment: 1,419
  Female: 63%
  Male: 37%
  Out-of-state: 56%

Cost Information
  Tuition: $12,800
  Room & board: $3,985
Housing Information
  University housing: Yes
  Percent living on campus: 14%

Greek System
  Fraternity: No
  Sorority: No
  Athletics: NAIA

GRINNELL COLLEGE

PO Box 805, Grinnell, IA 50112
Phone: 641-269-3600 • Fax: 641-269-4800
E-mail: askgrin@grinnell.edu • Web: www.grinnell.edu
Support level: S • Institution type: 4-year private

LEARNING DISABILITY PROGRAM AND SERVICES

Grinnell College is dedicated to educating young people whose achievements show a high level of intellectual capacity, initiative, and maturity. Every year, this highly qualified group of students includes people with learning disabilities. Grinnell is committed to providing academic adjustments and reasonable accommodations for students with disabilities who are otherwise qualified for admission. Many of Grinnell's characteristics make it a positive educational environment for all students: an open curriculum, small classes, easy access to professors, and an openness to diversity. The Director of Academic Advising coordinates services for students with LD, arranges for academic accommodations, acts as a liaison to the faculty, and offers personal, individual assistance. Once students are admitted and they accept the offer of admission, Grinnell likes to plan with them for any reasonable accommodation they will need in order to enjoy a successful experience. Students have the responsibility to make their needs known. The most important factors for college success are seeking help early and learning to be self-advocates. Students are encouraged to notify the Director of Academic Advising about their needs before they arrive for the first semester. For planning purposes, sooner is always better.

LD/ADHD ADMISSIONS INFORMATION

College entrance tests required: Yes
Nonstandardized tests accepted: Yes
Interview required: No
Essay required: Yes
Documentation required for LD: Current written evaluation from a psychologist, LD specialist, or MD indicating results from testing; a specific diagnosis, a clinical summary, and recommendations for academic accommodation
Documentation required for ADHD: Yes
Documentation submitted to: Academic Advising
Special Ed. HS course work accepted: N/A

Specific course requirements for all applicants: Yes
Separate application required for services: No
# of LD applications submitted yearly: N/A
# of LD applications accepted yearly: N/A
Total # of students receiving LD/ADHD services: 13
Acceptance into program means acceptance into college: Students must be admitted and enrolled at the College first and then may request services.

ADMISSIONS

Grinnell welcomes applications from students with learning disabilities. While the same admissions standards apply to all students, the College does accept nonstandardized test scores. Students are advised to document their needs in the application for admission and explain how learning disabilities may have affected their secondary school performance. Interviews are encouraged. Grinnell is looking for a strong scholastic record from high school, recommendations, satisfactory results on the ACT/SAT, and specific units of high school course work, including 4 years English, 3 years math, 3 years social studies, 3 years science, 3 years foreign language. Applicants with appropriate documentation may substitute for some entrance requriements such as foreign language. The middle 50 percent range for the ACT is 28–31 and 1238–1433 for the SAT. Over 85 percent of the admitted students are from the top 20 percent of the class. The minimum GPA is a 2.5. Students are encouraged to have an interview either on or off campus.

ADDITIONAL INFORMATION

Students need to meet with professors and the Director of Academic Advising to plan for their individual needs. The Office of Academic Advising coordinates services for students and arranges for academic accommodations. The ADA Task Force ensures compliance with the Americans with Disabilities Act. The Reading Lab helps students improve reading speed, vocabulary, and reading comprehension. The Director of Academic Advising assists students with LD in identifying effective academic strategies. The Science and Math Learning Center provides instruction in math and science courses for students who want to strengthen their background in these areas. Student tutoring will help students make arrangements for tutoring at no charge. Additional resources include referral for LD testing, reduced course loads, untimed exams, personal counseling, and volunteers who are willing to read to students with learning disabilities. Skills classes for credit are offered in reading, writing, and math.

SUPPORT SERVICES CONTACT INFORMATION

Learning Disability Program/Services: Academic Advising Office
Director: Joyce M. Stern, Director of Academic Advising
  E-mail: sternjm@grinnell.edu
  Telephone: 641-269-3702
  Fax: 641-269-3710
Contact: Jo Calhoun

LEARNING DISABILITY SERVICES

Requests for the following services/accommodations will be evaluated individually based on appropriate and current documentation.

Allowed in Exams
  Calculator: Yes
  Dictionary: Yes
  Computer: Yes
  Spellchecker: Yes
Extended test time: Yes
Scribes: No
Proctors: No
Oral exams: Yes
Notetakers: Yes

Distraction-reduced environment: Yes
Tape recording in class: Yes
Books on tape from RFBD: No
Taping of books not from RFBD: No
Accommodations for students with
  ADHD: Yes
Reading machine: No
Other assistive technology: Yes
Priority registration: No

Added costs for services: No
LD specialists: No
Professional tutors: 7
Peer tutors: 50
Max. hours/wk. for services:
  Unlimited
How professors are notified of
  LD/ADHD: By both student and
  director

GENERAL ADMISSIONS INFORMATION

Director of Admissions: Jim Sumner
Telephone: 641-269-3600

ENTRANCE REQUIREMENTS
17 total are recommended; 4 English recommended, 4 math recommended, 3 science recommended, 3 science lab recommended, 3 foreign language recommended, 3 social studies recommended. High school diploma or GED required. Minimum TOEFL is 550. TOEFL required of all international applicants.

Application deadline: January 20
Notification: April 1
Average GPA: NR

Average SAT I Math: 658
Average SAT I Verbal: 673
Average ACT: 29

Graduated top 10% of class: 61%
Graduated top 25% of class: 90%
Graduated top 50% of class: 99%

COLLEGE GRADUATION REQUIREMENTS

Course waivers allowed: No
Course substitutions allowed: No
In what subjects: Not applicable because Grinnell has no general education requirements

ADDITIONAL INFORMATION

Environment: The College is located on 95 acres in a small town 55 miles east of Des Moines.

Student Body
  Undergrad enrollment: 1,344
  Female: 56%
  Male: 44%
  Out-of-state: 88%

Cost Information
  Tuition: $19,982
  Room & board: $5,820
Housing Information
  University housing: Yes
  Percent living on campus: 85%

Greek System
  Fraternity: Yes
  Sorority: Yes
Athletics: NCAA Division III

INDIAN HILLS COMMUNITY COLLEGE

525 Grandview Avenue, Ottumwa, IA 52501
Phone: 641-683-5111 • Fax: 641-683-5184
Web: www.ihec.cc.in.us
Support: CS • Institution: 2-year public

LEARNING DISABILITY PROGRAM AND SERVICES

The Success Center provides academic and physical accommodations and services for students with disabilities based on documented needs. Students with a documented learning disability or attention deficit disorder must provide current documentation that has been completed by a qualified professional. It is helpful to submit the most recent IEP.

LD/ADHD ADMISSIONS INFORMATION

College entrance tests required: No
Nonstandardized tests accepted: Yes
Interview required: Yes
Essay required: No
Documentation required for LD: WAIS-III; WJ
Documentation required for ADHD: Yes
Submitted to: Success Center
Special Ed. HS course work accepted: No

Specific course requirements for all applicants: No
Separate application required for services: No
# of LD applications submitted yearly: N/A
# of LD applications accepted yearly: N/A
Total # of students receiving LD/ADHD services: 400
Acceptance into program means acceptance into college: Students must be admitted and enrolled at the College prior to requesting services.

ADMISSIONS

Indian Hills Community College is an "open-door" institution. All students must present a high school diploma or GED or must earn one while enrolled in order to receive a college degree. ACT/SAT are not required, and there are no specific high school courses required for admission. Although an interview is not required, it is highly recommended. Students enroll with widely varying levels of achievement and differing goals, and some discover that they can move ahead more quickly. Applicants are required to submit a portfolio, which is reviewed by a selection committee. Many eventually enter one or more of the Indian Hills credit courses. A decision to move into college credit courses is made by staff members, parents, and the student involved.

ADDITIONAL INFORMATION

All students have access to skills classes in study skills and specialized vocabulary skills. These courses earn college credit. There are currently approximately 35 students with learning disabilities and 10 with attention deficit disorder receiving accommodations or services. There are academic support services for all students. Two staff members work full time as advocates for students to make sure all students receive their accommodations.

SUPPORT SERVICES CONTACT INFORMATION

Learning Disability Program/Services: Success Center
Director: Mary Stewart
  E-mail: mstewart@ihcc.cc.ia.us
  Telephone: 641-683-5155
  Fax: 641-683-5184
Contact: Same
  Telephone: 641-683-5128

LEARNING DISABILITY SERVICES

Requests for the following services/accommodations will be evaluated individually based on appropriate and current documentation.

Allowed in Exams
  Calculator: Y/N
  Dictionary: Yes
  Computer: Yes
  Spellchecker: Yes
Extended test time: Yes
Scribes: Yes
Proctors: Yes
Oral exams: Yes
Notetakers: Yes

Distraction-reduced environment: Yes
Tape recording in class: Yes
Books on tape from RFBD: Yes
Taping of books not from RFBD: Yes
Accommodations for students with ADHD: Yes
Reading machine: No
Other assistive technology: No
Priority registration: No

Added costs for services: No
LD specialists: Yes
Professional tutors: 9
Peer tutors: Yes
Max. hours/wk. for services: Unlimited
How professors are notified of LD/ADHD: Depends on wishes of student

GENERAL ADMISSIONS INFORMATION

Director of Admissions: Sally Harris
Telephone: 641-683-5155

ENTRANCE REQUIREMENTS
The College's "open door" admissions policy requires the student to have a high school or a GED equivalent. Students may complete these requirements while enrolled at the College. Some majors require specific math courses. ACT/SAT not required.

Application deadline: Rolling
Notification: Rolling
Average GPA: NR

Average SAT I Math: NR
Average SAT I Verbal: NR
Average ACT: NR

Graduated top 10% of class: NR
Graduated top 25% of class: NR
Graduated top 50% of class: NR

COLLEGE GRADUATION REQUIREMENTS

Course waivers allowed: No
Course substitutions allowed: No
In what subjects: N/A

ADDITIONAL INFORMATION

Environment: The College is located on 400 acres about 2 hours east of Iowa City or west of Des Moines.

Student Body
  Undergrad enrollment: 3,166
  Female: 50%
  Male: 50%
  Out-of-state: 7%

Cost Information
  In-state tuition: $1,860
  Out-of-state tuition: $2,760
  Room & board: $2,985
Housing Information
  University housing: Yes
  Percent living on campus: 15%

Greek System
  Fraternity: Yes
  Sorority: Yes
  Athletics: NJCAA

IOWA STATE UNIVERSITY

100 Alumni Hall, Ames, IA 50011-2011
Phone: 515-294-5836 • Fax: 515-294-2592
E-mail: admissions@iastate.edu • Web: www.iastate.edu
Support level: CS • Institution type: 4-year public

LEARNING DISABILITY PROGRAM AND SERVICES

ISU is committed to providing equal opportunities and facilitating the personal growth and development of all students. Several departments and organizations cooperate to accomplish these goals. The LD specialist assists students with issues relating to LD and helps them adjust to the University setting; provides a review of students' most current LD evaluation and documentation to determine the accommodations needed; offers assistance in articulating needs to faculty and staff; and may serve as a liaison in student/staff negotiations.

LD/ADHD ADMISSIONS INFORMATION

College entrance tests required: Yes
Nonstandardized tests accepted: Yes
Interview required: No
Essay required: No
Documentation required for LD: WAIS-III; or WISC-R (Part II) or WRAT-R: within 3 years
Documentation required for ADHD: Yes
Documentation submitted to: Disability Resources
Special Ed. HS course work accepted: Yes

Specific course requirements for all applicants: Yes
Separate application required for services: No
# of LD applications submitted yearly: N/A
# of LD applications accepted yearly: N/A
Total # of students receiving LD/ADHD services: 80
Acceptance into program means acceptance into college: Students must be admitted and enrolled at the University first and then may request services.

ADMISSIONS

Documentation should include demographic data about the student and examiner's qualifications; behavioral observation of the way students present themselves, manner of dress, verbal and nonverbal communication, interpersonal skills and behavior during testing; a narrative describing developmental and educational history; a description of the effect of the LD on academic learning; a report of the results of an assessment of intellectual functioning (including WAIS-R or WISC-R); a report of the results of academic testing including Woodcock-Johnson; testing for foreign language substitute; and specific recommendations concerning academic compensatory strategies and whether the student qualifies for specific academic accommodations. If a student is learning disabled and does not meet minimum requirements, the student can request a review. However, this is not a program for students with extreme deficits. Iowa State is looking for students who can succeed, have good verbal skills, and have an upward trend in grades. Students not meeting high school course requirements, but otherwise qualified, may be admitted after an individual review. The pattern on the ACT, not just the score, will be considered. General admission requirements include 4 years English, 3 years math, 3 years science, 2 years social studies (3 years for liberal arts and sciences plus 2 years foreign language); 3 years of high school foreign language satisfies the requirement to graduate from Iowa State; ACT 19 (SAT is accepted); requirements for students from out-of-state may be more difficult; there is an admission index indicating student rank and ACT scores. There is a Summer Trial Program for students not regularly admissible through test scores or class rank; students take 6 credits and get C or better; these students are often in the top 75 percent of their class but may not have a 25 ACT.

ADDITIONAL INFORMATION

The Academic Learning Lab is a "learning-how-to-learn" center designed to help all students; counselors work one-to-one to evaluate and identify problem study habits and devise strategies to improve them. The learning lab, tutoring, and Student Support Services are in one area called the Academic Success Center. ASC coordinates services including counseling, teaching reading, and study skills, and provides a list of tutors. The Writing Center, available for all students, helps students to write papers. The English department has a list of approved proofreaders. The LD specialist provides information about readers, note-takers, and scribes. SI is an academic assistance program attached to very difficult courses. Peer SI leaders attend classes and conduct biweekly sessions to help students learn and study the course material. Student Support Services is a federally funded program for students with LD and others qualified to receive academic support in the form of free tutoring and skill-building workshops.

SUPPORT SERVICES CONTACT INFORMATION

Learning Disability Program/Services: Disability Resources
Director: Gwen Woodward
  E-mail: gwenw@iastate.edu
  Telephone: 515-294-0644
  Fax: 515-294-5670
Contact: Same

LEARNING DISABILITY SERVICES

Requests for the following services/accommodations will be evaluated individually based on appropriate and current documentation.

Allowed in Exams
  Calculator: Yes
  Dictionary: Yes
  Computer: Yes
  Spellchecker: Yes
Extended test time: Yes
Scribes: Yes
Proctors: Yes
Oral exams: No
Notetakers: Yes

Distraction-reduced environment: Yes
Tape recording in class: Yes
Books on tape from RFBD: Yes
Taping of books not from RFBD: Yes
Accommodations for students with
  ADHD: Yes
Reading machine: Yes
Other assistive technology: Yes
Priority registration: No

Added costs for services: $3/hour for tutor
LD specialists: Yes (1)
Professional tutors: No
Peer tutors: Varies
Max. hours/wk. for services: .5
How professors are notified of LD/ADHD: By student

GENERAL ADMISSIONS INFORMATION

Director of Admissions: Marc Harding
Telephone: 515-294-5836

ENTRANCE REQUIREMENTS

4 English required, 3 math required, 3 science required, 2 science lab required, 2 foreign language recommended, 2 social studies required, 3 social studies recommended. High school diploma or GED required. Minimum TOEFL is 500. TOEFL required of all international applicants.

Application deadline: August 21
Notification: Rolling beginning 9/1
Average GPA: 3.5

Average SAT I Math: 610
Average SAT I Verbal: 590
Average ACT: 24

Graduated top 10% of class: 25%
Graduated top 25% of class: 56%
Graduated top 50% of class: 91%

COLLEGE GRADUATION REQUIREMENTS

Course waivers allowed: Yes
Course substitutions allowed: Yes
In what subjects: Foreign language

ADDITIONAL INFORMATION

Environment: Iowa State University is located on a 1,000-acre campus about 30 miles north of Des Moines.

Student Body
  Undergrad enrollment: 21,503
  Female: 45%
  Male: 55%
  Out-of-state: 17%

Cost Information
  In-state tuition: $2,906
  Out-of-state tuition: $9,748
  Room & board: $4,171
Housing Information
  University housing: Yes
  Percent living on campus: 35%

Greek System
  Fraternity: Yes
  Sorority: Yes
  Athletics: NCAA Division I

LORAS COLLEGE

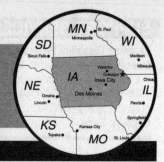

1450 Alta Vista, Dubuque, IA 52001
Phone: 800-245-6727 • Fax: 319-588-7119
E-mail: adms@loras.edu • Web: www.loras.edu
Support level: SP • Institution type: 4-year private

LEARNING DISABILITY PROGRAM AND SERVICES

Loras College provides a supportive, comprehensive program for the motivated individual with a learning disability. Students can be successful in Loras's competitive environment if they have had adequate preparation, are willing to work with program staff, and take responsibility for their own learning. The LD Program staff has two full-time specialists to serve as guides and advocates, encouraging and supporting students to become independent learners. Students with LD who are enrolled in college-preparatory courses in high school are the most appropriate candidates for the Loras program. Often high school students who previously were in LD programs, but are not currently receiving services, are appropriate candidates for the program if they have taken college-prep classes.

LD/ADHD ADMISSIONS INFORMATION

College entrance tests required: Yes
Nonstandardized tests accepted: Yes
Interview required: Yes
Essay required: Yes
Documentation required for LD: Psychoeducational evaluation
Documentation required for ADHD: Yes
Documentation submitted to: LD Program Director
Special Ed. HS course work accepted: Yes

Specific course requirements for all applicants: Yes
Separate application required for services: Yes
# of LD applications submitted yearly: 60
# of LD applications accepted yearly: 16
Total # of students receiving LD/ADHD services: 40
Acceptance into program means acceptance into college: Students are admitted into the LD Program and the College simultaneously. The decision is made by the LD Program director.

ADMISSIONS

Students may contact program staff in their junior year and request an early assessment of their chances for admission; the admission process will be explained and students will receive an application. Students should arrange for an evaluation documenting the learning disability if the evaluation is more than two years old, to include the WAIS-R, as well as achievement/diagnostic tests of reading, written expression, and math, and send the evaluation when completed. Transcript with 4 years English, 3 years math, 3 years social studies, 2–3 years science; ACT/SAT; and three letters of recommendation should be submitted by November 1 if students are applying for the Enhanced Program. Criteria for admission include strong average intelligence, class rank close to or above 50 percent, 2.0 GPA (minimum), 16+ ACT or 750 SAT. Students must be able to present their needs, strengths, and interests in a required interview with the LD Program director that is scheduled for those who are invited to visit after all materials have been received. An admission decision is made by the director of the LD Program.

ADDITIONAL INFORMATION

The Loras LD Program provides two levels of service: Enhanced and Mandated. The Enhanced Program for the first year students includes a two-credit class, Learning Strategies, both semesters of the first year; an individual meeting with program staff each week; and tutors, as needed. Upper-class, continuing students, and transfer students receive the same support with the exception of the class. The students in the Enhanced Program are also eligible to receive Mandated Services, which include note-takers, taped textbooks, and a place to take extended-time tests in a quiet room. Students in the Enhanced Program are charged a fee for services; those receiving only Mandated Services are not. Students who want Mandated Services are not required to self-disclose their need for services until after they are accepted to Loras. However, those who want the more comprehensive Enhanced Program should make their intention known on the application and submit all materials before the deadline of November 1 of senior year.

SUPPORT SERVICES CONTACT INFORMATION

Learning Disability Program/Services: Learning Disabilities Program
Director: Dianne Gibson
  E-mail: dgibson@loras.edu
  Telephone: 319-588-7134
  Fax: 319-557-4080
Contact: Rochelle Fury
  E-mail: rfury@loras.edu
  Telephone: 319-588-7134
  Fax: 319-557-4080

LEARNING DISABILITY SERVICES

Requests for the following services/accommodations will be evaluated individually based on appropriate and current documentation.

Allowed in Exams
  Calculator: Yes
  Dictionary: Yes
  Computer: Yes
  Spellchecker: Yes
Extended test time: Yes
Scribes: Yes
Proctors: Yes
Oral exams: Yes
Notetakers: Yes

Distraction-reduced environment: Yes
Tape recording in class: Yes
Books on tape from RFBD: Yes
Taping of books not from RFBD: Yes
Accommodations for students with ADHD: Yes
Reading machine: Yes
Other assistive technology: Yes
Priority registration: Yes

Added costs for services:
  $2,440–$3,020 for enhanced program
LD specialists: Yes (1)
Professional tutors: No
Peer tutors: 15
Max. hours/wk. for services:
  Unlimited
How professors are notified of LD/ADHD: By student

GENERAL ADMISSIONS INFORMATION

Director of Admissions: Tim Hauber
Telephone: 319-588-7236

ENTRANCE REQUIREMENTS
12 total are recommended; 4 English recommended, 3 math recommended, 3 science recommended, 2 foreign language recommended, 1 social studies recommended, 1 history recommended. High school diploma or GED required. Minimum TOEFL is 550. TOEFL required of all international applicants.

Application deadline: August 15
Notification: Rolling
Average GPA: 3.3

Average SAT I Math: 493
Average SAT I Verbal: 462
Average ACT: 22

Graduated top 10% of class: 18%
Graduated top 25% of class: 36%
Graduated top 50% of class: 67%

COLLEGE GRADUATION REQUIREMENTS

Course waivers allowed: Yes
Course substitutions allowed: No
In what subjects: Possible for math after attempting math course work; there is no foreign language requirement

ADDITIONAL INFORMATION

Environment: The College is located on 66 hilltop acres in northeast Iowa overlooking the Mississippi River.

Student Body
  Undergrad enrollment: 1,626
  Female: 53%
  Male: 47%
  Out-of-state: 42%

Cost Information
  Tuition: $15,190
  Room & board: $5,804
Housing Information
  University housing: Yes
  Percent living on campus: 69%

Greek System
  Fraternity: Yes
  Sorority: Yes
Athletics: NCAA Division III

SAINT AMBROSE UNIVERSITY

518 West Locust Street, Davenport, IA 52803-2898
Phone: 319-333-6300 • Fax: 319-333-6297
E-mail: mflahery@saunix.sau.edu • Web: www.sau.edu
Support level: CS • Institution type: 4-year private

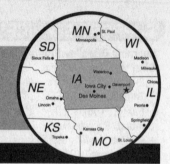

LEARNING DISABILITY PROGRAM AND SERVICES

St. Ambrose University's Services for Students with Disabilities is two dimensional. The first dimension is the education of the faculty to the specific needs of students. The second dimension is the development of services that allow programmatic access to students with disabilities. The key to both dimensions is the Coordinator of Services for Students with Disabilities. It is the responsibility of this individual to prepare seminars for the faculty and staff, to advise students, and to be the conscience of the St. Ambrose University community in regard to students with disabilities. Students with learning disabilities are provided with an individual program of services. Services do not lower academic standards, but rather help "level the playing field." The coordinator works with students to develop skills and select accommodations to compensate for their learning disabilities and become their own advocates.

LD/ADHD ADMISSIONS INFORMATION

College entrance tests required: Yes
Nonstandardized tests accepted: Yes
Interview required: No
Essay required: No
Documentation required for LD: Ability test (WAIS-III, Stanford-Binet-IV); achievement test (e.g. WJ, WIAT); information processing test
Documentation required for ADHD: Yes
Documentation submitted to: Admissions and Services for Students with Disabilities
Special Ed. HS course work accepted: Yes

Specific course requirements for all applicants: Yes
Separate application required for services: No
# of LD applications submitted yearly: N/A
# of LD applications accepted yearly: N/A
Total # of students receiving LD/ADHD services: 63
Acceptance into program means acceptance into college: Students must be admitted and enrolled at the University first and then may request services.

ADMISSIONS

Students meeting minimum admission requirements are not required to send additional information for admission purposes, but it is helpful in providing effective services. The general admission criteria include minimum ACT 20 or minimum 950 SAT; 2.5 GPA; and no specific courses are required. Students not meeting minimum requirements for admission may request special consideration by (1) submitting a regular application accompanied by a letter directed to the Dean of Admissions including a description of the LD, how the student has compensated for academic deficits, what resources were utilized in high school, and whether the student has independently requested accommodations; (2) submitting written assessment of learning problems (including all test scores) done by a certified professional, clearly stating that the student is LD and/or ADHD; (3) submitting recommendations from teachers who have first-hand knowledge of the student's academic abilities; and (4) scheduling a meeting with the coordinator of services. Students who have completed junior year may also attend the Summer Transition Program to assess their ability for regular admission. Students who do not meet the criteria are encouraged to contact the coordinator for additional consideration.

ADDITIONAL INFORMATION

Through the Office of Services for Students with Disabilities students may have access to the following services: academic advising; advocacy; alternate exam arrangements including extended time, large print, separate testing room, readers, scribes, or use of a computer; books on tape; assistive technology; equipment loans; LD specialist to provide one-to-one learning skills instruction; liaison with outside agencies; screening and referral for diagnosis of learning disabilities; and other accommodations to meet appropriate needs. A four-week Summer Transition Program is available for college-bound students with learning disabilities who have completed junior year in high school. Students do not have to be admitted to St. Ambrose to participate in this program, and completion of the program does not guarantee admission to the College. Students take "Intro to Psychology," tutoring, and study-skills sessions, where they receive instruction on study skills, note-taking, textbook reading, memorization strategies, and test preparation; LD Seminar, an informal discussion group on topics such as rights and responsibilities of LD, selecting accommodations, understanding LD, and self-advocacy; "Socializing in College," which relates to making new friends, dealing with stress, and communication skills. Tutors attend the psych class and assist students in applying learning skills to their course work.

SUPPORT SERVICES CONTACT INFORMATION

Learning Disability Program/Services: Services for Students with Disabilities
Director: Ann Austin
  E-mail: aaustin@saunix.sau.edu
  Telephone: 319-333-6161
  Fax: 319-333-6243
Contact: Same

LEARNING DISABILITY SERVICES

Requests for the following services/accommodations will be evaluated individually based on appropriate and current documentation.

Allowed in Exams
  Calculator: Yes
  Dictionary: Yes
  Computer: Yes
  Spellchecker: Yes
Extended test time: Yes
Scribes: Yes
Proctors: Yes
Oral exams: Yes
Notetakers: Yes

Distraction-reduced environment: Yes
Tape recording in class: Yes
Books on tape from RFBD: Yes
Taping of books not from RFBD: Yes
Accommodations for students with ADHD: Yes
Reading machine: Yes
Other assistive technology: Yes
Priority registration: No

Added costs for services: No
LD specialists: Yes (1)
Professional tutors: 2
Peer tutors: 36
Max. hours/wk. for services: Unlimited
How professors are notified of LD/ADHD: By student

GENERAL ADMISSIONS INFORMATION

Director of Admissions: Meg Flagherty
Telephone: 319-333-6300

ENTRANCE REQUIREMENTS

16 total are recommended; 4 English recommended, 2 math recommended, 2 science recommended, 1 foreign language recommended, 2 social studies recommended, 1 history recommended, 4 elective recommended. High school diploma or GED required. Minimum TOEFL is 500. TOEFL required of all international applicants.

Application deadline: Rolling
Notification: Rolling beginning 10/1
Average GPA: 3.1

Average SAT I Math: NR
Average SAT I Verbal: NR
Average ACT: 21

Graduated top 10% of class: 14%
Graduated top 25% of class: 33%
Graduated top 50% of class: 64%

COLLEGE GRADUATION REQUIREMENTS

Course waivers allowed: No
Course substitutions allowed: Yes
In what subjects: Foreign language, PE substitutions

ADDITIONAL INFORMATION

Environment: The campus is located in an urban area 180 miles west of Chicago.

Student Body
  Undergrad enrollment: 2,022
  Female: 60%
  Male: 40%
  Out-of-state: 36%

Cost Information
  Tuition: $13,890
  Room & board: $5,160
Housing Information
  University housing: Yes
  Percent living on campus: 45%

Greek System
  Fraternity: Yes
  Sorority: Yes
Athletics: NAIA

UNIVERSITY OF IOWA

107 Calvin Hall, Iowa City, IA 52242
Phone: 319-335-3847 • Fax: 319-333-1535
E-mail: admissions@uiowa.edu • Web: www.uiowa.edu
Support level: CS • Institution type: 4-year public

LEARNING DISABILITY PROGRAM AND SERVICES

The mission of LD/ADHD Services in the University of Iowa's Student Disability Services (SDS) is to facilitate individualized academic accommodations for eligible students. Each student has an assigned staff advisor who assists the student in identifying appropriate course accommodations, communicating classroom needs to faculty, and accessing other related services and resources. Students with LD/ADHD who believe they will need disability services in order to have an equal educational opportunity are encouraged to self-disclose their disability to SDS as soon as possible. Students who self-disclose when applying for admission will be contacted by SDS with information about LD/ADHD services at Iowa. They are encouraged to schedule an on-campus interview with the LD/ADHD coordinator in order to learn more about disability services for students with LD/ADHD and about the University.

LD/ADHD ADMISSIONS INFORMATION

College entrance tests required: Yes
Nonstandardized tests accepted: Yes
Interview required: No
Essay required: No
Documentation required for LD: Psycheducational evaluation
Documentation required for ADHD: Yes
Documentation submitted to: SDS and Admissions
Special Ed. HS course work accepted: No

Specific course requirements for all applicants: Yes
Separate application required for services: No
# of LD applications submitted yearly: 100+
# of LD applications accepted yearly: N/A
Total # of students receiving LD/ADHD services: 250–301
Acceptance into program means acceptance into college: Students must be admitted and enrolled in the University and then may request consideration for services. If denied admission, students may appeal the decision.

ADMISSIONS

General admission requires 4 years English, 3 years math, 3 years social studies, 3 years science, and 2 years foreign language. In-state residents must rank in top 50 percent of class or present an admission index score of 90. Nonresidents must rank in the top 30 percent or present an admission index of 100 (students with scores between 90-100 will be considered). The College of Engineering requires an ACT of 25 with a math score of 25+. There is a "special considerations" procedure for students not meeting general admission requirements who do not believe their academic record accurately reflects their ability to do college work. Students must submit a general application, transcript, and test scores; a letter disclosing the disability and requesting "special consideration," describing how the disability affected academic performance and what accommodations and compensation strategies are used to strengthen performance in deficit areas; a description of resources used and a statement explaining why the student may not have completed high school requirements, if applicable; letters from two people, not related, who can attest to the applicant's ability to be successful; and a diagnostic report verifying the disability and providing information about both the process and findings of the diagnostic assessment. The report should contain specific recommendations concerning the eligible academic accommodations, including whether the student qualifies for foreign language or math substitutions, and be signed by a licensed professional with the license number.

ADDITIONAL INFORMATION

Students requesting services and resources from Student Disability Services must self-disclose and provide satisfactory evidence of their disability-related eligibility for services. It is the responsibility of each student to determine whether or not to utilize services for which he or she is eligible. Services available through SDS for which students may be eligible on a case-by-case basis include pre-admission information, new student orientation, assistance in communicating with faculty and administrators, note-taking assistance, alternative examination services, obtaining audiotapes of required reading materials, referrals to other university resources for counseling, tutoring, study skills development, and time management training. SDS notes that due to the high demand for tutoring at the University, tutors are not always available for all courses.

SUPPORT SERVICES CONTACT INFORMATION

Learning Disability Program/Services: Student Disability Services (SDS)
Director: Mary Richard, Coordinator, LD/ADHD Services
  E-mail: mary-richard@uiowa.edu
  Telephone: 319-335-1462
  Fax: 319-335-3973
Contact: Same

LEARNING DISABILITY SERVICES

Requests for the following services/accommodations will be evaluated individually based on appropriate and current documentation.

Allowed in Exams
  Calculator: Yes
  Dictionary: Yes
  Computer: Yes
  Spellchecker: Yes
Extended test time: Yes
Scribes: Yes
Proctors: Yes
Oral exams: No
Notetakers: Yes

Distraction-reduced environment: Yes
Tape recording in class: Yes
Books on tape from RFBD: Yes
Taping of books not from RFBD: Yes
Accommodations for students with
  ADHD: Yes
Reading machine: Yes
Other assistive technology: Yes
Priority registration: Yes

Added costs for services: No
LD specialists: Yes (2)
Professional tutors: No
Peer tutors: Yes
Max. hours/wk. for services: 1
How professors are notified of
  LD/ADHD: By both student and
  director

GENERAL ADMISSIONS INFORMATION

Director of Admissions: Michael Barron
Telephone: 800-553-IOWA

ENTRANCE REQUIREMENTS
15 total are required; 4 English required, 3 math required, 3 science required, 2 foreign language required, 4 foreign language recommended, 3 social studies required. High school diploma or GED required. Minimum TOEFL is 530. TOEFL required of all international applicants.

Application deadline: May 15
Notification: Rolling beginning 9/15
Average GPA: 3.5

Average SAT I Math: 580
Average SAT I Verbal: 570
Average ACT: 24.5

Graduated top 10% of class: 20%
Graduated top 25% of class: 51%
Graduated top 50% of class: 90%

COLLEGE GRADUATION REQUIREMENTS

Course waivers allowed: No
Course substitutions allowed: Yes
In what subjects: High school math (algebra, algebra II, geometry)

ADDITIONAL INFORMATION

Environment: The University is on a 1,900-acre campus in a small city 180 miles east of Des Moines.

Student Body
  Undergrad enrollment: 19,284
  Female: 54%
  Male: 46%
  Out-of-state: 30%

Cost Information
  In-state tuition: $3,116
  Out-of-state tuition: $11,544
  Room & board: $4,870
Housing Information
  University housing: Yes
  Percent living on campus: 28%

Greek System
  Fraternity: Yes
  Sorority: Yes
  Athletics: NCAA Division I

UNIVERSITY OF NORTHERN IOWA

1222 West 27th Street, Cedar Falls, IA 50614-0018
Phone: 319-273-2281 • Fax: 319-273-2885
E-mail: admissions@uni.edu • Web: www.uni.edu
Support level: S • Institution type: 4-year public

LEARNING DISABILITY PROGRAM AND SERVICES

The Office of Disability Services is dedicated to serving the special needs of students at the University of Northern Iowa. The Office of Disability Services works with students to ensure that all persons with disabilities have access to university activities, programs, and services. Specialized services are provided to enhance the overall academic, career, and personal development of each person with a physical, psychological, or learning disability. Services are available to currently enrolled students, who must apply for services, and provide appropriate documentation to substantiate the claimed disability. RUN (Restrict Us Not) is a recognized student organization, sponsored by the Office of Disability Services.

LD/ADHD ADMISSIONS INFORMATION

College entrance tests required: Yes
Nonstandardized tests accepted: Yes
Interview required: NR
Essay required: No
Documentation required for LD: Psychoeducational evaluation
Documentation required for ADHD: Yes
Documentation submitted to: Office of Disability Services—after admission
Special Ed. HS course work accepted: Yes

Specific course requirements for all applicants: Yes
Separate application required for services: No
# of LD applications submitted yearly: N/A
# of LD applications accepted yearly: N/A
Total # of students receiving LD/ADHD services: 75
Acceptance into program means acceptance into college: Students must be admitted and enrolled at the University first and then may request services.

ADMISSIONS

There is no special admission process for students with learning disabilities. Students with disabilities are considered for admission on the same basis as all other applicants, and must meet the same academic standards. Students must have 4 years English, 3 years math, 3 years science, 3 years social studies, 2 years academic elective (can be foreign language). The University will accept college-preparatory courses taken through the special education department of the high school. Students must rank in the top half of their class, and submit either the ACT or the SAT.

ADDITIONAL INFORMATION

Services available include individualized pre-enrollment interview and orientation to disability services; preferred registration; list of students interested in serving as academic aides; alternative testing arrangements; auxiliary aides. The Center for Academic Achievement services all students at UNI who wish to receive additional academic support outside of the classroom. The center provides students with a variety of supportive services that will enhance academic achievement and success. Students may access help in writing assistance in any of their classes. Students may schedule a single appointment to work on a specific assignment or a regular appointment to work on a variety of assignments. Assistance with math skills is also available in the Math Lab. Services include one-to-one and small group instruction; individual instruction and practice through a variety of self-instructional modes; and review lessons to support the development and practice of concepts/skills taught in math courses. Drop-in hours are available.

SUPPORT SERVICES CONTACT INFORMATION

Learning Disability Program/Services: Disability Services
Director: David Towle, PhD
  E-mail: david.towle@uni.edu
  Telephone: 319-273-2676
  Fax: 319-273-6884
Contact: Jane Slykhuis, Coordinator
  E-mail: jane.slykhuis@uni.edu
  Telephone: 319-273-2676
  Fax: 319-273-6884

LEARNING DISABILITY SERVICES

Requests for the following services/accommodations will be evaluated individually based on appropriate and current documentation.

Allowed in Exams
  Calculator: Y/N
  Dictionary: No
  Computer: Yes
  Spellchecker: Yes
Extended test time: Yes
Scribes: Yes
Proctors: No
Oral exams: Yes
Notetakers: Yes

Distraction-reduced environment: Yes
Tape recording in class: Yes
Books on tape from RFBD: Yes
Taping of books not from RFBD: Yes
Accommodations for students with ADHD: Yes
Reading machine: No
Other assistive technology: No
Priority registration: Yes

Added costs for services: No
LD specialists: No
Professional tutors: No
Peer tutors: Yes
Max. hours/wk. for services: 1 hour per week per course
How professors are notified of LD/ADHD: By student and coordinator

GENERAL ADMISSIONS INFORMATION

Director of Admissions: Clark Elmer
Telephone: 319-273-2281

ENTRANCE REQUIREMENTS
15 total are required; 4 English required, 3 math required, 3 science required, 1 science lab recommended, 2 foreign language recommended, 3 social studies required, 2 elective required. High school diploma or GED required. Minimum TOEFL is 550. TOEFL required of all international applicants.

Application deadline: August 15
Notification: Rolling beginning 9/1
Average GPA: NR

Average SAT I Math: NR
Average SAT I Verbal: NR
Average ACT: 23

Graduated top 10% of class: 18%
Graduated top 25% of class: 50%
Graduated top 50% of class: 91%

COLLEGE GRADUATION REQUIREMENTS

Course waivers allowed: No
Course substitutions allowed: Yes
In what subjects: The University is in the process of establishing guidelines for waiver/substitutions in math and foreign language.

ADDITIONAL INFORMATION

Environment: The campus is in a small town about an hour and a half from Des Moines.

Student Body
  Undergrad enrollment: 12,100
  Female: 57%
  Male: 43%
  Out-of-state: 4%

Cost Information
  In-state tuition: $3,130
  Out-of-state tuition: $8,094
  Room & board: $4,160
Housing Information
  University housing: Yes
  Percent living on campus: 39%

Greek System
  Fraternity: Yes
  Sorority: Yes
Athletics: NCAA Division I

WALDORF COLLEGE

106 S. 6th Street, Forest City, IA 50436
Phone: 641-585-2450 • Fax: 515-582-8194
E-mail: admissions@waldorf.edu • Web: www.waldorf.edu
Support: CS • Institution: 2-year private

LEARNING DISABILITY PROGRAM AND SERVICES

The Learning Disabilities Program (LDP) fully integrates students with learning disabilities into mainstream courses. The program features a special orientation session, academic advising, tutoring, specialized services, and developmental courses. The LDP takes a holistic approach to address the social, emotional, and academic needs of the person with a learning disability. The LDP is learning-strategies-based. Students are accepted as individuals with the potential to succeed in college. The students have the opportunity to participate fully in college life and to experience academic success. Students benefit from a 12:1 student to instructor ratio, with each student having a laptop computer to use while a student. To be eligible for the Waldorf LDP, students must meet the following criteria: students must have psychological and achievement test results, preferably no more than two years old; students must have been involved with intervention on some level during high school; and students must exhibit a positive attitude and potential for good college success when appropriate learning strategies and coping skills are used.

LD/ADHD ADMISSIONS INFORMATION

College entrance tests required: Yes
Nonstandardized tests accepted: Yes
Interview required: Yes
Essay required: No
Documentation required for LD: Psychoeducational evaluation
Documentation required for ADHD: Yes
Submitted to: LDP
Special Ed. HS course work accepted: Yes

Specific course requirements for all applicants: Yes
Separate application required for services: No
# of LD applications submitted yearly: N/A
# of LD applications accepted yearly: 20
Total # of students receiving LD/ADHD services: 30
Acceptance into program means acceptance into college: Students are either admitted directly into the College and then request LDP or are reviewed by LDP and a joint decision is made.

ADMISSIONS

There is no special admissions process for students with learning disabilities. LDP students go through the regular admission procedures. General admission requirements include 4 years English, 2 years math, and science; ACT 18+ and a 2.0 GPA. There is a probationary admission for students not meeting the regular criteria. Students will be asked to participate in a special interview, either by phone or in person, in order to be considered for LDP. The number of spaces in LDP is limited. The stronger candidates are reviewed and admitted by the Office of Admission; the students with weaker records, who have a documented learning disability, are reviewed by the LDP director and the Office of Admission and they make a joint decision on admission.

ADDITIONAL INFORMATION

Services in the LDP include the following: specialized academic advising regarding schedules and academic classes; priority time and scheduling with the learning specialist; counseling services available upon referral or request; special orientation for LDP students at the beginning of the academic year, prior to the arrival of the other students; tutor time above and beyond the regular services available to all students; specialized materials and/or technology for LD students; priority assignment for developmental and study skills classes; as-needed academic and psychological testing with a learning-style emphasis; instructor notification of learning disability; and academic progress monitoring that will be shared with the student, and parents if permission is given. There are skills classes for credit in study skills, math/pre-algebra, reading, and writing. There is a one-day LD orientation prior to the beginning of the regular freshman orientation in the fall.

SUPPORT SERVICES CONTACT INFORMATION

Learning Disability Program/Services: Learning Disabilites Program (LDP)
Director: Rebecca Hill
  E-mail: hillb@waldorf.edu
  Telephone: 641-584-8207
  Fax: 641-584-8194
Contact: Same

LEARNING DISABILITY SERVICES

Requests for the following services/accommodations will be evaluated individually based on appropriate and current documentation.

Allowed in Exams
  Calculator: Yes
  Dictionary: Yes
  Computer: Yes
  Spellchecker: Yes
Extended test time: Yes
Scribes: No
Proctors: Yes
Oral exams: Yes
Notetakers: Yes

Distraction-reduced environment: Yes
Tape recording in class: Yes
Books on tape from RFBD: Yes
Taping of books not from RFBD: No
**Accommodations for students with
  ADHD:** Yes
Reading machine: No
Other assistive technology: No
Priority registration: Yes

Added costs for services: $400 per
  semester for freshmen, $300 per
  semester for sophomores
LD specialists: Yes
Professional tutors: 2
Peer tutors: 25
Max. hours/wk. for services:
  Unlimited
**How professors are notified of
  LD/ADHD:** By program director

GENERAL ADMISSIONS INFORMATION

Director of Admissions: Steve Lovick
Telephone: 641-585-8112

ENTRANCE REQUIREMENTS
Minimum GPA 2.0. One teacher/counselor recommendation is helpful. Interviews are required for some applicants. SAT/ACT required.

Application deadline: Rolling
Notification: Rolling
Average GPA: NR

Average SAT I Math: NR
Average SAT I Verbal: NR
Average ACT: 18+

Graduated top 10% of class: NR
Graduated top 25% of class: NR
Graduated top 50% of class: NR

COLLEGE GRADUATION REQUIREMENTS

Course waivers allowed: No
Course substitutions allowed: Yes
In what subjects: N/A

ADDITIONAL INFORMATION

Environment: The campus is in a small town.

Student Body
  Undergrad enrollment: 599
  Female: 47%
  Male: 53%
  Out-of-state: 25%

Cost Information
  Tuition: $13,522
  Room & board: $4,850
Housing Information
  University housing: Yes
  Percent living on campus: 71%

Greek System
  Fraternity: Yes
  Sorority: Yes
Athletics: NJCAA

BAKER UNIVERSITY

Eighth and Grove, Baldwin City, KS 66006
Phone: 785-594-8307 • Fax: 785-594-8372
E-mail: admission@george.bakeru.edu • Web: www.bakeru.edu
Support level: CS • Institution type: 4-year private

LEARNING DISABILITY PROGRAM AND SERVICES

Baker University feels that each student with an LD is unique and each LD is different. The University offers a program that is highly individualized. Students must self-identify to receive services, and the Coordinator of Academic Accommodations will work with students on an individual basis. Integration, self-advocacy, and individual responsibility are promoted and expected. The University acts only as a provider of academic accommodations by sending letters to faculty explaining the nature of the student's disability and suggested accommodations. Support services are designed to equalize opportunities for students with disabilities, not to lower academic standards or to alter the essential nature of the degree requirements. Students must provide appropriate documentation and request accommodations each semester in a timely manner. In addition, Baker University has a Learning Resource Center that is open to all students. Professional staff members and peer tutors are available to help. The LRC offers many resources that can aid in the students' educational endeavors.

LD/ADHD ADMISSIONS INFORMATION

College entrance tests required: Yes
Nonstandardized tests accepted: Yes
Interview required: No
Essay required: No
Documentation required for LD: IEP from high school or a psychological diagnostic report with accommodation suggestions within the last four years
Documentation required for ADHD: Yes
Documentation submitted to: Learning Resource Center
Special Ed. HS course work accepted: No

Specific course requirements for all applicants: Yes
Separate application required for services: No
# of LD applications submitted yearly: NA
# of LD applications accepted yearly: NA
Total # of students receiving LD/ADHD services: NR
Acceptance into program means acceptance into college: Students must be admitted and enrolled and then may request services.

ADMISSIONS

There is no special admission process for students with LD. The minimum ACT is 21 and the minimum GPA is 3.0. Students are required to have 4 years of English, 3 years of math, 3 years of natural science, 2–4 years of foreign language, 3 years of social studies, 1 year of fine arts, and 1 year of computer technology. Substitutions are not allowed. Students who do not meet the admission criteria may be admitted conditionally. Students not meeting admission criteria should provide a personal statement and self-disclose the LD to provide a better understanding of their academic challenges. Conditional applicants are reviewed by a special committee, which will make the admission decision. Students are encouraged to request an interview.

ADDITIONAL INFORMATION

Students with appropriate documentation could receive accommodations such as extended testing time, note-takers, readers, tutorial services in most subjects, distraction-free testing environment, reading machines, proctors, scribes, and sometimes oral exams. There is one LD specialist who is available for all students with disabilities. Occasionally, students may petition and receive a course substitution for a required course.

SUPPORT SERVICES CONTACT INFORMATION

Learning Disability Program/Services: Learning Resource Center
Director: Kathy Marian
  E-mail: marian@harvey.bakeru.edu
  Telephone: 785-594-8352
  Fax: 785-594-8367
Contact: Same

LEARNING DISABILITY SERVICES

Requests for the following services/accommodations will be evaluated individually based on appropriate and current documentation.

Allowed in Exams
  Calculator: Yes
  Dictionary: Yes
  Computer: Yes
  Spellchecker: Yes
Extended test time: Yes
Scribes: Yes
Proctors: Yes
Oral exams: NR
Notetakers: Yes

Distraction-reduced environment: Yes
Tape recording in class: Yes
Books on tape from RFBD: Yes
Taping of books not from RFBD: Yes
**Accommodations for students with
  ADHD:** Yes
Reading machine: Yes
Other assistive technology: Yes
Priority registration: No

Added costs for services: No
LD specialists: Yes (1)
Professional tutors: No
Peer tutors: 6
Max. hours/wk. for services:
  Unlimited
**How professors are notified of
  LD/ADHD:** By both student and
  director

GENERAL ADMISSIONS INFORMATION

Director of Admissions: Paige Illum
Telephone: 785-594-8307

ENTRANCE REQUIREMENTS

16 total are recommended; 4 English recommended, 3 math recommended, 3 science recommended, 2 foreign language recommended, 2 social studies recommended, 2 history recommended. High school diploma or GED required. Minimum TOEFL is 525. TOEFL required of all international applicants.

Application deadline: Rolling
Notification: Rolling
Average GPA: 3.4

Average SAT I Math: NR
Average SAT I Verbal: NR
Average ACT: 23

Graduated top 10% of class: 24%
Graduated top 25% of class: 47%
Graduated top 50% of class: 81%

COLLEGE GRADUATION REQUIREMENTS

Course waivers: No
Course substitutions allowed: No
In what subjects: In very special circumstances

ADDITIONAL INFORMATION

Environment: Located 35 miles from Kansas City.

Student Body
  Undergrad enrollment: 923
  Female: 58%
  Male: 42%
  Out-of-state: 35%

Cost Information
  Tuition: $12,900
  Room & board: $4,880
Housing Information
  University housing: Yes
  Percent living on campus: 95%

Greek System
  Fraternity: Yes
  Sorority: Yes
Athletics: NAIA

KANSAS STATE UNIVERSITY

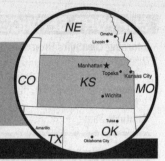

119 Anderson Hall, Manhattan, KS 66506
Phone: 785-532-6250 • Fax: 785-532-6393
E-mail: kstate@ksu.edu • Web: www.ksu.edu
Support level: CS • Institution type: 4-year public

LEARNING DISABILITY PROGRAM AND SERVICES

Kansas State provides a broad range of support services to students with learning disabilities through Disabled Student Services, as well as through numerous other university departments. Under DSS the Services for Learning Disabled Students serves as a liaison between students and instructors. The goals of the program are to recommend and provide accommodations and assistance tailored to the students' needs. Faculty and staff are sensitive to the special needs of the students and will work with them in their pursuit of educational goals. DSS works with students to plan accommodations that best aid the students to overcome areas of difficulty. DSS does not modify or reduce the content of courses. Rather, DSS helps to set up ways for students to demonstrate academic knowledge without interference from the disability. To qualify for services students must provide DSS with documentation of a learning disability that includes a complete record of all testing administered; a signed statement from a professional documenting LD; and information about strengths and weaknesses to help plan accommodations best suited to the student's needs. Many of the services provided take time to arrange. Consequently, students are encouraged to apply for services early in the process of planning for college.

LD/ADHD ADMISSIONS INFORMATION

College entrance tests required: Yes
Nonstandardized tests accepted: Yes
Interview required: No
Essay required: No
Documentation required for LD: WAIS-III; Woodcock-Johnson: within three years
Documentation required for ADHD: Yes
Documentation submitted to: DSS
Special Ed. HS course work accepted: Yes

Specific course requirements for all applicants: Yes
Separate application required for services: No
# of LD applications submitted yearly: 268
# of LD applications accepted yearly: All admitted to university with documentation
Total # of students receiving LD/ADHD services: 380–421
Acceptance into program means acceptance into college: Students must be admitted and enrolled at the University first and then may request services.

ADMISSIONS

There is no special admissions process for students with learning disabilities. Kansas State has open admissions for state residents. Out-of-state students must either meet the basic course requirements for general admissions to the University including 4 years English, 3 years math, 3 years science, 3 years social studies, and 1 semester of computer technology or be in the top one-thrid of their high school graduating class. High schools may recommend approval of course substitutions to the Regents. Special consideration may be given when requested. The Director of Support Services may be asked to consult with Admissions on individual applicants.

ADDITIONAL INFORMATION

To access support services students must provide DSS with verification of LD. A signed statement documenting LD qualifies students for services. Specific information about strengths and weaknesses helps DSS plan accommodations best suited to students' needs. Students contact Services for LD Students for services. Many services take time to arrange so early applications are encouraged. Students with LD are eligible for services such as test-taking accommodations; readers; assistance in obtaining taped texts; note-takers; taped lectures; and priority registration. Tutoring is offered in some freshman/sophomore classes. All students may attend an orientation meeting prior to registration freshman year. Special courses are offered in Enhanced University Experience to learn note-taking, textbook reading, and test-taking skills; math review for students experiencing difficulty with arithmetic computations; intermediate algebra; and college algebra. Services are available for undergrads and graduate students.

SUPPORT SERVICES CONTACT INFORMATION

Learning Disability Program/Services: Disability Support Services (DSS)
Director: Gretchen Holden
  E-mail: gretch@ksu.edu
  Telephone: 785-532-6441
  Fax: 785-532-6457
Contact: Andrea Blair
  E-mail: andreab@ksu.edu
  Telephone: 785-532-6441
  Fax: 785-532-6457

LEARNING DISABILITY SERVICES

Requests for the following services/accommodations will be evaluated individually based on appropriate and current documentation.

Allowed in Exams
  Calculator: Yes
  Dictionary: Yes
  Computer: Yes
  Spellchecker: Yes
Extended test time: Yes
Scribes: Yes
Proctors: Yes
Oral exams: Yes
Notetakers: Yes

Distraction-reduced environment: Yes
Tape recording in class: Yes
Books on tape from RFBD: Yes
Taping of books not from RFBD: Yes
Accommodations for students with ADHD: Yes
Reading machine: Yes
Other assistive technology: Yes
Priority registration: Yes

Added costs for services: No
LD specialists: Yes (1)
Professional tutors: No
Peer tutors: Yes
Max. hours/wk. for services: 3 hours
How professors are notified of LD/ADHD: By both student and director

GENERAL ADMISSIONS INFORMATION

Director of Admissions: Larry Moeder
Telephone: 785-532-6250

ENTRANCE REQUIREMENTS
14 total are required; 4 English required, 3 math required, 3 science required, 2 foreign language recommended, 2 social studies required, 1 history required. High school diploma or GED required. Minimum TOEFL is 550. TOEFL required of all international applicants.

Application deadline: August 1
Notification: Rolling beginning 9/1
Average GPA: 3.4

Average SAT I Math: NR
Average SAT I Verbal: NR
Average ACT: 23

Graduated top 10% of class: 24%
Graduated top 25% of class: 60%
Graduated top 50% of class: 89%

COLLEGE GRADUATION REQUIREMENTS

Course waivers: No
Course substitutions allowed: Yes
In what subjects: Math and foreign language

ADDITIONAL INFORMATION

Environment: The University is located on 664 acres in a suburban area 125 miles west of Kansas City.

Student Body
  Undergrad enrollment: 18,252
  Female: 47%
  Male: 53%
  Out-of-state: 7%

Cost Information
  In-state tuition: $2,333
  Out-of-state tuition: $9,260
  Room & board: $4,240
Housing Information
  University housing: Yes
  Percent living on campus: 30%

Greek System
  Fraternity: Yes
  Sorority: Yes
Athletics: NCAA Division I

PITTSBURG STATE UNIVERSITY

1701 South Broadway, Pittsburg, KS 66762-5880
Phone: 316-235-4251 • Fax: 316-235-6003
E-mail: psuadmit@pittstate.edu • Web: www.pittstate.edu
Support level: CS • Institution type: 4-year public

LEARNING DISABILITY PROGRAM AND SERVICES

The Learning Center at Pittsburg State University is committed to providing appropriate educational and related services to students with LD. PSU works hard to help meet the transition needs of new students with identified LD. The specific type of assistance is determined on an individual basis. Previous records and an interview determine the type and degree of assistance appropriate for the student. The main purpose of the LD Assistance Team is to assist students in understanding and preparing assignments and completing tests. The team provides a minimum amount of tutoring, but students should look to respective departments to provide these services. The key to their services is assistance. They do not provide content, information, or answers that do not reflect knowledge obtained by the student. Bright, highly motivated students with LD who are confident that they can succeed with hard work and supervision are welcomed to explore the educational possibilities at PSU.

LD/ADHD ADMISSIONS INFORMATION

College entrance tests required: Yes
Nonstandardized tests accepted: Yes
Interview required: No
Essay required: No
Documentation required for LD: A recent IEP or a current diagnosis
Documentation required for ADHD: Yes
Submitted to: Learning Center
Special Ed. HS course work accepted: Yes

Specific course requirements for all applicants: Yes
Separate application required for services: No
# of LD applications submitted yearly: 25
# of LD applications accepted yearly: 25
Total # of students receiving LD/ADHD services: 74
Acceptance into program means acceptance into college: Students must be admitted and enrolled and then request services.

ADMISSIONS

Students must meet the regular admissions criteria to the University. Upon acceptance, they should visit the campus in the spring, request to visit with a member of the Learning Disabilities Assistance Team, attend a summer orientation program on campus, and forward a copy of the most recent Individualized Education Plan or documentation from the high school or doctor stating the nature of the LD. Once on campus, students should contact the team for an appointment to plan a study schedule at the Learning Center.

ADDITIONAL INFORMATION

Specific assistance is determined on an individual basis based on documentation and an interview. Services provided by the Learning Disabilities Assistance Team include academic advising and planning; study skills strategies; testing modifications include extended time for tests, reading multiple choice and true-false tests verbatim, reading and defining words on a test (if the definition of that word does not give the student an unfair advantage in answering questions), reading and explaining what is being asked on short answer and essay tests; reading and helping the student understand the notes they took in class or the notes they took from their tape-recorded lectures; writing or typing a tape-recorded assignment prepared by the student; and reading and explaining the assignment to the student. The team will also monitor student's class attendance, study schedule, and free time schedule.

SUPPORT SERVICES CONTACT INFORMATION

Learning Disability Program/Services: Learning Center
Director: Dr. Nick A. Henry
  E-mail: nhenry@pittstate.edu
  Telephone: 316-235-4966
  Fax: 316-235-4520
Contact: Same

LEARNING DISABILITY SERVICES

Requests for the following services/accommodations will be evaluated individually based on appropriate and current documentation.

Allowed in Exams
  Calculator: Yes
  Dictionary: Yes
  Computer: Yes
  Spellchecker: Yes
Extended test time: Yes
Scribes: No
Proctors: Yes
Oral exams: Yes
Notetakers: No

Distraction-reduced environment: Yes
Tape recording in class: Yes
Books on tape from RFBD: No
Taping of books not from RFBD: No
**Accommodations for students with
  ADHD:** Yes
Reading machine: Yes
Other assistive technology: No
Priority registration: No

Added costs for services: No
LD specialists: Yes
Professional tutors: 5
Peer tutors: 2
Max. hours/wk. for services:
  Unlimited
**How professors are notified of
  LD/ADHD:** By student

GENERAL ADMISSIONS INFORMATION

Director of Admissions: Ange Peterson
Telephone: 316-235-4252

ENTRANCE REQUIREMENTS

Open admissions for in-state applicants; more competitive for out-of-state applicants, who must rank in the top 50 percent of their class and have a 2.0 GPA. TOEFL required of all international applicants. Minimum Toefl 520. High school diploma or GED required.

Application deadline: Rolling
Notification: Rolling
Average GPA: 2.0

Average SAT I Math: NR
Average SAT I Verbal: NR
Average ACT: 21

Graduated top 10% of class: NR
Graduated top 25% of class: 32%
Graduated top 50% of class: 63%

COLLEGE GRADUATION REQUIREMENTS

Course waivers allowed: No
Course substitutions allowed: Y/N
In what subjects: Usually not, but there is a petition process for this.

ADDITIONAL INFORMATION

Student Body
  Undergrad enrollment: 5,222
  Female: 48%
  Male: 52%
  Out-of-state: 13%

Cost Information
  In-state tuition: $2,172
  Out-of-state tuition: $6,982
  Room & board: $3,990
Housing Information
  University housing: Yes
  Percent living on campus: 20%

Greek System
  Fraternity: Yes
  Sorority: Yes
Athletics: NCAA Division II

Pittsburg State University

UNIVERSITY OF KANSAS

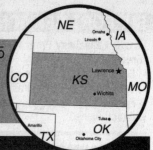

Office of Admissions and Scholarships, 1502 Iowa St., Lawrence, KS 66045
Phone: 785-864-3911 • Fax: 785-864-5006
E-mail: adm@ukans.edu • Web: www.ku.edu
Support level: S • Institution type: 4-year public

LEARNING DISABILITY PROGRAM AND SERVICES

The University accommodates the student with LD by understanding the student's ability and individualizing the services as much as possible. KU's philosophy is one of mainstreaming students with disabilities, including LD. Thus, there are no special classes, resource room, tutoring services, or other services specifically for the student with an LD. Course requirements and academic standards are not reduced. Rather, once the LD is adequately documented, the student receives classroom accommodations to meet specific individual needs. The Services for Students with Disabilities (SSD) also serves as a referral agent to other resources at the University and in the Lawrence community. Integration and mainstreaming, decentralized services with appropriate accommodations centrally coordinated, and student involvement and responsibility are critical aspects of the University's philosophy. Documentation is necessary and should include a recent diagnostic report of LD, and LD programs and progress will need to be identified. Students are encouraged to begin planning early so that programs are in place at the beginning of the semester to facilitate studies. The goal of SSD is to facilitate independence in preparation for needs after graduation.

LD/ADHD ADMISSIONS INFORMATION

College entrance tests required: Yes
Nonstandardized tests accepted: Yes
Interview required: No
Essay required: No
Documentation required for LD: WAIS-III; WJ
Documentation required for ADHD: Yes
Documentation submitted to: SSD
Special Ed. HS course work accepted: Yes, if college prep

Specific course requirements for all applicants: Yes
Separate application required for services: No
# of LD applications submitted yearly: N/A
# of LD applications accepted yearly: N/A
Total # of students receiving LD/ADHD services: 156
Acceptance into program means acceptance into college: Students must be admitted and enrolled at the University first (they can appeal a denial) and then may request services.

ADMISSIONS

All applicants are admitted using the same criteria. Students unable to meet admission criteria because of LD should submit a personal statement providing additional information, such as no foreign language taken in high school because of the LD. Applicants should contact SSD for information and an early assessment of needs. It is important to include recent documentation or diagnosis, samples of student's work, and parent and student statements regarding educational history. Regular admission requires (1) 2.5 GPA in Board of Regent courses including 4 years English, 3 years of college-prep math, 3 years natural science, 3 years social science, 2 years foreign language or (2) an ACT of 24 and a 2.0 GPA or (3) a 3.0 GPA and no cut-off on the ACT. The University is very concerned that a student with LD be competitive in this academic environment. If admission criteria are not met because of LD, the applicant should submit documentation and counselor recommendation, and the director of SSD will review and make a recommendation to Admissions to waive requirements.

ADDITIONAL INFORMATION

Skill workshops are available in study skills, time management, listening, note-taking, calculus, speed reading and reading comprehension, learning a foreign language, and preparing for exams. SSD also serves as an advocate or liaison for students. Tutoring services for students who meet qualifications are available through Supportive Educational Services at no cost. Private tutors can also be hired by the student for specific subjects. In neither instance is the tutor specifically trained regarding learning disabilities. SSD does not offer a reduced standard for academic performance, special classes, supplemental instruction, a learning center, special tutorial program, or exemption to graduation requirements. Services and accommodations are available for undergraduate and graduate students.

SUPPORT SERVICES CONTACT INFORMATION

Learning Disability Program/Services: Services for Students with Disabilities (SSD)
Director: Lorna Zimmer
  E-mail: lzimmer@ukans.edu
  Telephone: 785-864-2620
  Fax: 785-864-4050
Contact: Same

LEARNING DISABILITY SERVICES

Requests for the following services/accommodations will be evaluated individually based on appropriate and current documentation.

Allowed in Exams
  Calculator: Yes
  Dictionary: Yes
  Computer: Yes
  Spellchecker: Yes
Extended test time: Yes
Scribes: Yes
Proctors: No
Oral exams: Yes
Notetakers: Yes

Distraction-reduced environment: Yes
Tape recording in class: Yes
Books on tape from RFBD: Yes
Taping of books not from RFBD: Yes
Accommodations for students with ADHD: Yes
Reading machine: Yes
Other assistive technology: Yes
Priority registration: No

Added costs for services: No
LD specialists: No
Professional tutors: Yes
Peer tutors: Yes
Max. hours/wk. for services: Negotiated
How professors are notified of LD/ADHD: By student and coordinator of services

GENERAL ADMISSIONS INFORMATION

Director of Admissions: Alan Cerveny
Telephone: 785-864-3911

ENTRANCE REQUIREMENTS
14 total are required; 17 total are recommended; 4 English required, 4 English recommended, 3 math required, 4 math recommended, 3 science required, 3 science recommended, 1 science lab required, 1 science lab recommended, 2 foreign language recommended, 3 social studies required, 3 social studies recommended. High school diploma or GED required.

Application deadline: April 1
Notification: Rolling beginning 9/1
Average GPA: 2.0–2.9

Average SAT I Math: NR
Average SAT I Verbal: NR
Average ACT: 24

Graduated top 10% of class: 28%
Graduated top 25% of class: 58%
Graduated top 50% of class: 89%

COLLEGE GRADUATION REQUIREMENTS

Course waivers allowed: No
Course substitutions allowed: Yes
In what subjects: Generally in the areas of math, English, or foreign language

ADDITIONAL INFORMATION

Environment: The 1,000-acre campus is located in a small city 40 miles west of Kansas City.

Student Body
  Undergrad enrollment: 20,157
  Female: 53%
  Male: 47%
  Out-of-state: 24%

Cost Information
  In-state tuition: $2,333
  Out-of-state tuition: $9,260
  Room & board: $4,348
Housing Information
  University housing: Yes
  Percent living on campus: 51%

Greek System
  Fraternity: Yes
  Sorority: Yes
Athletics: NCAA Division I

EASTERN KENTUCKY UNIVERSITY

Coates Box 2A, Richmond, KY 40475
Phone: 859-622-2106 • Fax: 606-622-8024
E-mail: stephen.byrn@eku.edu • Web: www.eku.edu
Support level: CS • Institution type: 4-year public

LEARNING DISABILITY PROGRAM AND SERVICES

The mission of Project SUCCESS is to respond effectively and efficiently to the individual educational needs of eligible university students with learning disabilities through a cost-effective, flexible program of peer tutors, workshops, group support, and program referral. Upon admittance, Project SUCCESS develops an individualized program of services that serve to enhance the academic success of each student. The services a student utilizes will be determined in a conference between the student and the program director. All services are offered free of charge to the student. EKU also offers a summer transition program for students with learning disabilities. The program is designed to smooth the transition between high school and college. To apply for participation in Project SUCCESS, students are encouraged to visit both the campus and the Office of Services for Students with Disabilities. The student will be asked to fill out an application and provide appropriate, current documentation of the disability. The application for services through Project SUCCESS is in no way connected to admission to EKU.

LD/ADHD ADMISSIONS INFORMATION

College entrance tests required: Yes
Nonstandardized tests accepted: Yes
Interview required: Yes
Essay required: No
Documentation required for LD: Achievement; aptitude: within 3 years
Documentation required for ADHD: Yes
Documentation submitted to: Services for Students with Disabilities—after admission
Special Ed. HS course work accepted: Yes

Specific course requirements for all applicants: Yes
Separate application required for services: Yes
# of LD applications submitted yearly: 65
# of LD applications accepted yearly: 50
Total # of students receiving LD/ADHD services: 200
Acceptance into program means acceptance into college: Students must be admitted and enrolled at the University first and then may apply to Project SUCCESS.

ADMISSIONS

There are no special admissions criteria for students with learning disabilities. Students must be admitted and enrolled in the University in order to be eligible for entrance into Project SUCCESS. Full admission includes a 2.0 GPA and high school diploma, or GED or distance-learning degree; ACT 18 (with no score below 18 in English, Math, and Reading); completion of the Kentucky pre-college curriculum or its equivalent ACT scores of 21 in English, 20 in Math, 22 in Reading, and 21 in Science Reasoning. Students not meeting probationary admission (2.0 GPA, or GED or distance-learning diploma, etc.; ACT 15–17) may apply to attend EKU through a retention support program by applying for special admission. Collaborating retention support programs include Project SUCCESS.

ADDITIONAL INFORMATION

Project SUCCESS services provided include one-on-one tutoring, note-taking services, books on tape, test accommodations, advocacy, weekly seminars. Skills classes are offered in study skills, reading skills, weekly workshops in transition, time management, learning and study strategies, test-taking skills, developmental math, developmental reading, and developmental writing. A special summer program for pre-college freshmen with learning disabilities is offered. All services and accommodations are available for undergraduate and graduate students.

SUPPORT SERVICES CONTACT INFORMATION

Learning Disability Program/Services: Office of Services for Students with Disabilities
Director: Teresa Belluscio
E-mail: Disbellu@acs.eku.edu
Telephone: 859-622-1500
Fax: 859-622-6395
Contact: Same

LEARNING DISABILITY SERVICES

Requests for the following services/accommodations will be evaluated individually based on appropriate and current documentation.

Allowed in Exams
  Calculator: Yes
  Dictionary: Yes
  Computer: Yes
  Spellchecker: Yes
Extended test time: Yes
Scribes: Yes
Proctors: Yes
Oral exams: Yes
Notetakers: Yes

Distraction-reduced environment: Yes
Tape recording in class: Yes
Books on tape from RFBD: Yes
Taping of books not from RFBD: Yes
Accommodations for students with ADHD: Yes
Reading machine: Yes
Other assistive technology: Yes
Priority registration: Yes

Added costs for services: No
LD specialists: Yes (1)
Professional tutors: No
Peer tutors: 20
Max. hours/wk. for services: Unlimited
How professors are notified of LD/ADHD: By student

GENERAL ADMISSIONS INFORMATION

Director of Admissions: Stephen Byrn
Telephone: 859-622-2106

ENTRANCE REQUIREMENTS

13 total are required; 4 English required, 3 math required, 2 science required, 2 science lab required, 1 social studies required, 1 history required. High school diploma or GED required. Minimum TOEFL is 500. TOEFL required of all international applicants.

Application deadline: August 1
Notification: Rolling beginning 9/1
Average GPA: 3.1
Average SAT I Math: NR
Average SAT I Verbal: NR
Average ACT: 19
Graduated top 10% of class: NR
Graduated top 25% of class: 37%
Graduated top 50% of class: 77%

COLLEGE GRADUATION REQUIREMENTS

Course waivers allowed: Yes
Course substitutions allowed: Yes
In what subjects: Determined on a case-by-case basis

ADDITIONAL INFORMATION

Environment: The University is located on 350 acres in a small town 20 miles south of Lexington.

Student Body
  Undergrad enrollment: 12,676
  Female: 58%
  Male: 42%
  Out-of-state: 7%

Cost Information
  In-state tuition: $2,542
  Out-of-state tuition: $6,884
  Room & board: $3,796
Housing Information
  University housing: Yes
  Percent living on campus: 33%

Greek System
  Fraternity: Yes
  Sorority: Yes
Athletics: NCAA Division I

LEXINGTON COMMUNITY COLLEGE

203 Oswald Building, Lexington, KY 40506-0235
Phone: 859-257-4872
E-mail: lccinfo@lsu.uky.edu • Web: www.lcc.uky.edu
Support: S • Institution: 2-year public

LEARNING DISABILITY PROGRAM AND SERVICES

Lexington Community College has made a firm commitment to providing high quality post-secondary education to persons with disabilities. The Office of Services for Students with Disabilities seeks to ensure equal access and full participation for persons with disabilities in post-secondary education, and empower students to obtain the life skills necessary for a fulfilling productive lifestyle after leaving LCC. Students can request services by visiting Disability Support Services (DSS). Full participation in the DSS program is encouraged from the initial admission contact throughout the student's academic career. Positive peer contacts as well as guidance from the DSS coordinator and other faculty and staff also play a major role in encouraging participation in the DSS program.

LD/ADHD ADMISSIONS INFORMATION

College entrance tests required: Yes
Nonstandardized tests accepted: Yes
Interview required: No
Essay required: No
Documentation required for LD: Psychoeducational evaluation
Documentation required for ADHD: Yes
Submitted to: DSS
Special Ed. HS course work accepted: Yes, with appropriate documentation

Specific course requirements for all applicants: Yes
Separate application required for services: No
# of LD applications submitted yearly: N/A
# of LD applications accepted yearly: N/A
Total # of students receiving LD/ADHD services: 135+
Acceptance into program means acceptance into college: Students must be admitted and enrolled at LCC and then may request services.

ADMISSIONS

LCC offers an "open-door" admission to all applicants who meet the following requirements: proof of a high school diploma or the GED; ACT for placement not admission; 4 years English, algebra I & II, biology, chemistry or physics, U.S. history, and geometry; any areas of deficiency can be made up at LCC before enrolling in college courses; there is no required GPA or class rank. Students may live in the residence halls at the University of Kentucky and attend classes at LCC, which is located on the same campus as the University. There is an articulation agreement between LCC and the University of Kentucky. Students wishing to apply to Project Success must submit a separate application, call for an appointment, and bring supporting materials.

ADDITIONAL INFORMATION

DSS provides a full range of services, including academic advising, career counseling, supportive counseling, specialized computer software, recorded textbooks, note-taker, readers, writers/scribes, tutors, and testing accommodation. The DSS coordinator serves as student liaison with college faculty, staff and administrators, vocational rehabilitational counselors, and various other social service agencies. A case management approach is used to ensure continuity of services between agencies. LD assessments are available on campus for $175–$200. Study Strategies is offered for college credit. The Athena Club is a student organization created to assume an advocacy role on behalf of students with disabilities at LCC through education, recruiting, support groups, and social opportunities.

SUPPORT SERVICES CONTACT INFORMATION

Learning Disability Program/Services: Disability Support Services
Director: Veronica Miller
  E-mail: vimill@pop.uky.edu
  Telephone: 859-257-4872
Contact: Same

LEARNING DISABILITY SERVICES

Requests for the following services/accommodations will be evaluated individually based on appropriate and current documentation.

Allowed in Exams
  Calculator: Yes
  Dictionary: No
  Computer: Yes
  Spellchecker: Yes
Extended test time: Yes
Scribes: Yes
Proctors: Yes
Oral exams: Yes
Notetakers: Yes

Distraction-reduced environment: Yes
Tape recording in class: Yes
Books on tape from RFBD: Yes
Taping of books not from RFBD: Yes
Accommodations for students with ADHD: Yes
Reading machine: Yes
Other assistive technology: Yes
Priority registration: No

Added costs for services: No
LD specialists: No
Professional tutors: Yes
Peer tutors: Yes
Max. hours/wk. for services: 2 hours per week tutoring
How professors are notified of LD/ADHD: By student and program director

GENERAL ADMISSIONS INFORMATION

Director of Admissions: Shelbie Hugle
Telephone: 859-257-4872

ENTRANCE REQUIREMENTS
Open admissions except for health technology program. High school diploma or GED equivalent required. ACT/SAT required for applicants under 21 years old.

Application deadline: Rolling
Notification: Rolling
Average GPA: NR

Average SAT I Math: NR
Average SAT I Verbal: NR
Average ACT: NR

Graduated top 10% of class: NR
Graduated top 25% of class: NR
Graduated top 50% of class: NR

COLLEGE GRADUATION REQUIREMENTS

Course waivers allowed: No
Course substitutions allowed: Yes
In what subjects: Students may request substitutions for any course with the appropriate documentation.

ADDITIONAL INFORMATION

Environment: The College is located on the campus of the University of Kentucky.

Student Body
  Undergrad enrollment: 7,000
  Female: 58%
  Male: 42%
  Out-of-state: 4%

Cost Information
  In-state tuition: $1,950
  Out-of-state tuition: $4,860
  Room & board: $3,198
Housing Information
  University housing: Yes
  Percent living on campus: 1%

Greek System
  Fraternity: Yes
  Sorority: No
Athletics: Intramural

THOMAS MORE COLLEGE

333 Thomas More Parkway, Crestiew Hill, KY 41017
Phone: 859-344-3332 • Fax: 859-344-3444
E-mail: robert.mcdermott@thomasmore.edu • Web: www.thomasmore.edu
Support level: S • Institution type: 4-year private

LEARNING DISABILITY PROGRAM AND SERVICES

Thomas More College's Student Support Services program is committed to the individual academic, personal, cultural/social, and financial needs of the student. It is committed to promoting sensitivity and cultural awareness of the population served and to promoting varied on/off campus services and events that enhance the student's educational opportunities. A variety of support services are offered, including developmental courses, peer tutoring, and individual counseling. Students with deficits in speech/language, study skills, written expression, ongoing additional skills, perceptual skills, reading, speaking, math, fine motor, and ADHD/ADHD with or without LD are admissible. Students may need five years to graduate. The College offers small classes, excellent faculty, and solid preparation for the future.

LD/ADHD ADMISSIONS INFORMATION

College entrance tests required: Yes
Nonstandardized tests accepted: Yes
Interview required: No
Essay required: No
Documentation required for LD: Psychoeducational evaluation
Documentation required for ADHD: Yes
Documentation submitted to: Student Support Services—after admission
Special Ed. HS course work accepted: Yes

Specific course requirements for all applicants: Yes
Separate application required for services: No
# of LD applications submitted yearly: N/A
# of LD applications accepted yearly: N/A
Total # of students receiving LD/ADHD services: NR
Acceptance into program means acceptance into college: Students are admitted and enrolled at the College and then reviewed for services.

ADMISSIONS

There is no separate application required for an applicant with learning disabilities. All students must submit the general application for admission. A Student Support Services staff person is part of the Admissions Committee. Students with learning disabilities may be conditionally admitted so that they can receive extra support. General admission criteria include a recommendation for 4 years English, 2 years math, 2 years science, 2 years social studies, 2 years foreign language. Foreign language, and possibly math requirements, may be substituted for: ACT 19–23 or 950 SAT; rank in top half of class; and a B- average. The College can waive ACT/SAT scores after considering the student's LD status. A WAIS-R is not required, but diagnostic testing is encouraged before enrolling, as it is required to be on file before students can access services.

ADDITIONAL INFORMATION

Students with learning disabilities could be limited to 12–13 hours the first semester. Students' progress will be monitored. Some students may be required to take developmental courses based on the College's assessment of reading, writing, and math skills. Skills classes are paired with World History and there is college credit for skills classes in study skills, reading, and math. Some students are admitted on a conditional status and are given additional support through Student Support Services.

SUPPORT SERVICES CONTACT INFORMATION

Learning Disability Program/Services: Student Support Services
Director: Barbara S. Davis
  E-mail: barb.davis@thomasmore.edu
  Telephone: 859-344-3521
  Fax: 859-344-3342
Contact: Same

LEARNING DISABILITY SERVICES

Requests for the following services/accommodations will be evaluated individually based on appropriate and current documentation.

Allowed in Exams
  Calculator: No
  Dictionary: Y/N
  Computer: No
  Spellchecker: No
Extended test time: Yes
Scribes: Yes
Proctors: Yes
Oral exams: Yes
Notetakers: Yes

Distraction-reduced environment: Yes
Tape recording in class: Yes
Books on tape from RFBD: Yes
Taping of books not from RFBD: Yes
Accommodations for students with ADHD: Yes
Reading machine: No
Other assistive technology: No
Priority registration: No

Added costs for services: No
LD specialists: No
Professional tutors: 2
Peer tutors: 15
Max. hours/wk. for services: Unlimited
How professors are notified of LD/ADHD: Student and program director

GENERAL ADMISSIONS INFORMATION

Director of Admissions: Robert McDermott
Telephone: 859-344-3332

ENTRANCE REQUIREMENTS

12 total are required; 4 English required, 2 math required, 2 science required, 2 foreign language required, 2 social studies required. High school diploma or GED required. Minimum TOEFL is 515. TOEFL required of all international applicants.

Application deadline: August 15
Notification: Rolling
Average GPA: 3.1

Average SAT I Math: 480
Average SAT I Verbal: 528
Average ACT: 23

Graduated top 10% of class: 20%
Graduated top 25% of class: 21%
Graduated top 50% of class: 71%

COLLEGE GRADUATION REQUIREMENTS

Course waivers allowed: No
Course substitutions allowed: Yes
In what subjects: Foreign language and math

ADDITIONAL INFORMATION

Environment: The College is located on a 160-acre campus 8 miles from Cincinnati.

Student Body
  Undergrad enrollment: 1,273
  Female: 55%
  Male: 45%
  Out-of-state: 45%

Cost Information
  Tuition: $13,200
  Room & board: $2,400–$3,200
Housing Information
  University housing: Yes
  Percent living on campus: 18%

Greek System
  Fraternity: No
  Sorority: No
Athletics: NCAA Division III

WESTERN KENTUCKY UNIVERSITY

Potter Hall 117, 1 Big Red Way, Bowling Green, KY 42101-3576
Phone: 270-745-2551 • Fax: 270-745-6133
E-mail: admission@wku.edu • Web: www.wku.edu
Support level: S • Institution type: 4-year public

LEARNING DISABILITY PROGRAM AND SERVICES

The goal of the Equal Opportunity Program is to foster the full and self-directed participation of persons with disabilities attending the University. The service is established to facilitate the participation of students at Western Kentucky University by providing information on services, acting as liaison with faculty and staff for reasonable accommodation, and providing learning disability services. Office for Disability Services (ODS) coordinates support services so that students can be self-sufficient and can develop to their maximum academic potential. To be eligible for these services, documentation from a licensed professional must be provided. This documentation must be no more than three years old, state the nature of the disability, and clearly describe the kinds of accommodations recommended. Once accepted students should provide the documentation; discuss the disability and ways to accommodate special needs; arrange to take placement tests and register for classes early; contact instructors to learn what each instructor will require in terms of grading criteria, amount of weekly reading, and number and types of homework assignments and tests; order books on tape; and request alternative testing conditions, note-takers, and readers. Students needing specialized help beyond that offered by the University may need to seek financial assistance.

LD/ADHD ADMISSIONS INFORMATION

College entrance tests required: Yes
Nonstandardized tests accepted: Yes
Interview required: No
Essay required: No
Documentation required for LD: Psychoeducational evaluation
Documentation required for ADHD: Yes
Documentation submitted to: Equal Opportunity—after admission
Special Ed. HS course work accepted: No

Specific course requirements for all applicants: Yes
Separate application required for services: Yes
# of LD applications submitted yearly: 50
# of LD applications accepted yearly: 50
Total # of students receiving LD/ADHD services: 250
Acceptance into program means acceptance into college: Students must be admitted and enrolled at the University first and then may request services.

ADMISSIONS

There is no special admissions process for students with learning disabilities. All applicants must meet the same admission criteria and be a graduate of an accredited high school. High school courses required include 4 years English, 3 years math, 3 years social science, and 3 years science (one of which must be a lab). In-state residents must have a minimum 2.3 GPA or 18 ACT; out-of-state students must have a minimum 2.3 GPA and 18 ACT or 930 SAT. Factors considered for admission are ACT/SAT; high school performance; any post-secondary record; recommendations; personal qualifications and conduct; interview; and complete and accurate information listed on the application for admission. Students can be admitted by exception through the Director of Admissions. Admission to the Community College of Western Kentucky University is available to students with a high school diploma or equivalency certificate.

ADDITIONAL INFORMATION

The program for students with LD offers students adapted test administrations; taped textbooks; short-term loan of special equipment; reading referral services; faculty liaison; peer tutoring; academic, personal, and career counseling; and assistance with the Reading and Learning Labs. Academic advisors assist students in course selection. The University combines intensive academic advisement with special seminars to provide support during the freshman year. The University Counseling Services Center provides assistance in personal, social, emotional, and intellectual development. Skills classes are offered in math, reading, vocabulary, study skills, and English through the Community College. College credit is given for these classes. Services and accommodations are available for undergraduate and graduate students.

SUPPORT SERVICES CONTACT INFORMATION

Learning Disability Program/Services: Equal Opportunity/504/ADA Compliance
Director: Huda Melky
  E-mail: huda.melky@wku.edu
  Telephone: 270-745-5121
  Fax: 270-745-3199
Contact: Same

LEARNING DISABILITY SERVICES

Requests for the following services/accommodations will be evaluated individually based on appropriate and current documentation.

Allowed in Exams
  Calculator: Yes
  Dictionary: Yes
  Computer: Yes
  Spellchecker: Yes
Extended test time: Yes
Scribes: Yes
Proctors: Yes
Oral exams: Yes
Notetakers: Yes

Distraction-reduced environment: Yes
Tape recording in class: Yes
Books on tape from RFBD: Yes
Taping of books not from RFBD: No
Accommodations for students with ADHD: Yes
Reading machine: Yes
Other assistive technology: No
Priority registration: Yes

Added costs for services: No
LD specialists: No
Professional tutors: 15
Peer tutors: 20
Max. hours/wk. for services: Unlimited
How professors are notified of LD/ADHD: By student and program director

GENERAL ADMISSIONS INFORMATION

Director of Admissions: Sharon Dyrsen
Telephone: 270-745-2551

ENTRANCE REQUIREMENTS
4 English required, 3 math required, 3 science required (1 science lab required), 2 foreign language recommended, 3 social studies required. High school diploma or GED required. Minimum TOEFL is 525. TOEFL required of all international applicants.

Application deadline: August 1
Notification: Rolling
Average GPA: 3.08

Average SAT I Math: 500
Average SAT I Verbal: 500
Average ACT: 21

Graduated top 10% of class: 17.2%
Graduated top 25% of class: 40.4%
Graduated top 50% of class: 72%

COLLEGE GRADUATION REQUIREMENTS

Course waivers allowed: No
Course substitutions allowed: Yes
In what subjects: Handled on a case-by-case basis

ADDITIONAL INFORMATION

Environment: The University is located on 200 acres in a suburban area 65 miles north of Nashville.

Student Body
  Undergrad enrollment: 13,235
  Female: 58%
  Male: 42%
  Out-of-state: 15%

Cost Information
  In-state tuition: $2,150
  Out-of-state tuition: $6,450
  Room & board: $3,813
Housing Information
  University housing: Yes
  Percent living on campus: 32%

Greek System
  Fraternity: Yes
  Sorority: Yes
Athletics: NCAA Division I

LOUISIANA COLLEGE

1140 College Drive, Box 560, Pineville, LA 71359-0560
Phone: 318-487-7259 • Fax: 318-487-7550
E-mail: admissions@lacollege.edu • Web: www.lacollege.edu
Support level: SP • Institution type: 4-year private

LEARNING DISABILITY PROGRAM AND SERVICES

The goal of the Program to Assist Student Success (PASS) is to facilitate the academic success of students with disabilities and to serve as an advocate for the students. This highly individualized, limited enrollment program provides support services and personal attention to students who need special academic counseling, tutoring, or classroom assistance. Three levels of services are provided. Level I students are required to attend weekly individual counseling and tutoring sessions; the emphasis at this level is to provide individualized help to ensure the student's successful transition to college and to compensate for any identifiable disability. Level II students have, at a minimum, completed 24 hours of college credit at Louisiana College with at least a 2.5 grade point average; regularly scheduled individual counseling sessions continue to be provided; all other services continue to be available to the student as needed. Level III students have learned to compensate for their disability and are independently achieving college success; these students will have their progress monitored by the staff and tutoring will continue to be available. Any student not maintaining a 2.5 GPA must remain in or return to Level I.

LD/ADHD ADMISSIONS INFORMATION

College entrance tests required: No
Nonstandardized tests accepted: Yes
Interview required: No
Essay required: Yes
Documentation required for LD: Current professional
  evaluation
Documentation required for ADHD: Yes
Documentation submitted to: PASS
Special Ed. HS course work accepted: Yes

Specific course requirements for all applicants: Yes
Separate application required for services: Yes
# of LD applications submitted yearly: 15–20
# of LD applications accepted yearly: 8–13
Total # of students receiving LD/ADHD services: 25
**Acceptance into program means acceptance into
  college:** Students must be admitted and enrolled at the
  College first and then may request admission to PASS.

ADMISSIONS
All qualified applicants must submit the regular application, meet the general criteria for admission to Louisiana College, and have a diagnosed learning or physical disability. Successful applicants must have the intellectual potential (average to superior), the appropriate academic foundation (class standing and/or ACT/SAT scores), and the personal desire and motivation to succeed. The PASS director and staff make the final decision about admission to the program after reviewing the following: 20 or above on ACT or 930 or above on SAT; 4 years English, 3 years science, 3 years social studies, and 3 years math; 2.0 GPA; counselor's recommendation and other letters of reference; psychological or medical reports; and an essay outlining why the student feels he/she can succeed in college. At least one personal interview with student and parent(s) is required. Students are encouraged to apply early and will be advised of admission on or after May 31. There is an application evaluation fee of $25. Students may appeal to the Appeals Board if they are denied admission.

ADDITIONAL INFORMATION
Tutoring sessions are conducted in most subjects taken by Level I students. Additional tutorial help is available at the higher levels as needed. The PASS staff will carefully work with individual professors and the student's academic advisor to coordinate and accommodate the student's learning needs. Students admitted to PASS will remain in the program as long as they are at Louisiana College. Noncompliance with any component of the program may result in a student's dismissal from the program. Skills classes are offered in study techniques, test-taking strategies, and time management through orientation, and private tutoring from a PASS staff member. Incoming freshmen are encouraged to attend one summer session (five weeks) to become familiar with the campus and college life.

SUPPORT SERVICES CONTACT INFORMATION

Learning Disability Program/Services: Program to Assist Student Success (PASS)
Director: Betty P. Matthews
  E-mail: pass@lacollege.edu
  Telephone: 318-487-7629
  Fax: 318-487-7285
Contact: Same

LEARNING DISABILITY SERVICES

Requests for the following services/accommodations will be evaluated individually based on appropriate and current documentation.

Allowed in Exams
  Calculator: Yes
  Dictionary: Yes
  Computer: Yes
  Spellchecker: Yes
Extended test time: Yes
Scribes: Yes
Proctors: Yes
Oral exams: Yes
Notetakers: Yes

Distraction-reduced environment: Yes
Tape recording in class: Yes
Books on tape from RFBD: Yes
Taping of books not from RFBD: Yes
Accommodations for students with
  ADHD: Yes
Reading machine: No
Other assistive technology: No
Priority registration: No

Added costs for services: Per semester: Level I/$850; Level II/$450; Level III/$250
LD specialists: Yes (2)
Professional tutors: Yes
Peer tutors: Yes
Max. hours/wk. for services: 10
How professors are notified of LD/ADHD: By both student and director

GENERAL ADMISSIONS INFORMATION

Director of Admissions: Mandy Kinimer
Telephone: 318-487-7259

ENTRANCE REQUIREMENTS

17 total are required; 4 English required, 3 math required, 3 science required, 3 social studies required. High school diploma or GED required. Minimum TOEFL is 540. TOEFL required of all international applicants.

Application deadline: Rolling
Notification: August 15
Average GPA: 3.3

Average SAT I Math: NR
Average SAT I Verbal: NR
Average ACT: 23

Graduated top 10% of class: 35%
Graduated top 25% of class: 64%
Graduated top 50% of class: 90%

COLLEGE GRADUATION REQUIREMENTS

Course waivers allowed: No
Course substitutions allowed: Yes
In what subjects: Appeals for substitutions must be made to special committee. However, the director of PASS rarely makes such a recommendation.

ADDITIONAL INFORMATION

Environment: The College is located on 81 acres in a small town, 1 mile northeast of Alexandria.

Student Body
  Undergrad enrollment: 1,003
  Female: 59%
  Male: 41%
  Out-of-state: 5%

Cost Information
  Tuition: $6,210
  Room & board: $3,112
Housing Information
  University housing: Yes
  Percent living on campus: 45%

Greek System
  Fraternity: Yes
  Sorority: Yes
  Athletics: NAIA

LOUISIANA STATE U.—BATON ROUGE

110 Thomas Boyd Hall, Baton Rouge, LA 70803
Phone: 225-388-1175 • Fax: 225-388-4433
E-mail: lsuadmit@lsu.edu • Web: www.lsu.edu
Support level: CS • Institution type: 4-year public

LEARNING DISABILITY PROGRAM AND SERVICES

The Purpose of the Office of Disability Services (ODS) is to assist any student who finds his or her disability to be a barrier to achieving educational and/or personal goals. The Office provides support services to students with learning disabilities. ODS has a strong commitment to improving individual choices, personal control of essential resources, and integration into the University community. The consequences of the disability may include specialized requirements; therefore, the particular needs of each student are considered on an individual basis. ODS dedicates its efforts to meeting both the needs of students with disabilities and the interests of faculty, staff, and the University as a whole. It is the practice of the ODS that issues concerning accommodations of students with disabilities in academic and other programs and activities be resolved between the student requesting the accommodation and the University employee representing the department within which the academic program or service is located. After intervention, if the student does not find the provision of an accommodation satisfactory, the student may file a formal grievance.

LD/ADHD ADMISSIONS INFORMATION

College entrance tests required: Yes
Nonstandardized tests accepted: Yes
Interview required: No
Essay required: No
Documentation required for LD: WAIS-III; WJ
Documentation required for ADHD: Yes
Documentation submitted to: Office of Disability Service—after admission
Special Ed. HS course work accepted: No

Specific course requirements for all applicants: Yes
Separate application required for services: No
# of LD applications submitted yearly: N/A
# of LD applications accepted yearly: N/A
Total # of students receiving LD/ADHD services: 175
Acceptance into program means acceptance into college: Students must be accepted and enrolled at the University first and then may request services.

ADMISSIONS

There is no special admissions process for students with learning disabilities. All applicants must meet the general admission requirements, including 4 years English, 3 years math (including algebra I and II and an advanced math), biology, chemistry, physics, American and world history or social studies, foreign language, one-half year of computers, and 2 academic electives; ACT 20 or above or SAT 910 or above (exact scores are dependent on an individual student record); and a 2.3 GPA. If an applicant does not meet the general admission criteria but is borderline, the student can be admitted through the Access Program.

ADDITIONAL INFORMATION

Specialized support services are based on individual disability-based needs. Services available include disability management counseling; adaptive equipment loan; note-takers; referral for tutoring; assistance with enrollment and registration; liaison assistance and a referral to on-campus and off-campus resources; supplemental orientation to the campus; and advocacy on behalf of the students with campus faculty, staff, and students. The Learning Assistance Center is open to all students on campus. Computer labs, science tutoring, math lab, learning skills assistance, supplemental instruction, and skills classes in time management, test-taking strategies, note-taking skills, reading skills, and study skills are available. The decision to provide accommodations and services is made by the SSD after reviewing documentation. Currently there are 175 students with LD and 300 students with ADHD receiving services and accommodations.

SUPPORT SERVICES CONTACT INFORMATION

Learning Disability Program/Services: Office of Disability Services (ODS)
Director: Ben Cornwell
E-mail: bjcornw@lsu.edu
Telephone: 225-578-4401
Fax: 225-578-4560
Contact: Wendy Devall
Telephone: 225-578-4310
Fax: 225-578-4560

LEARNING DISABILITY SERVICES

Requests for the following services/accommodations will be evaluated individually based on appropriate and current documentation.

Allowed in Exams
  Calculator: Yes
  Dictionary: Yes
  Computer: Yes
  Spellchecker: Yes
Extended test time: Yes
Scribes: Yes
Proctors: Yes
Oral exams: Yes
Notetakers: Yes

Distraction-reduced environment: Yes
Tape recording in class: Yes
Books on tape from RFBD: Yes
Taping of books not from RFBD: Yes
Accommodations for students with
  ADHD: Yes
Reading machine: Yes
Other assistive technology: Yes
Priority registration: Yes

Added costs for services: No
LD specialists: Yes (1)
Professional tutors: Yes
Peer tutors: Yes
Max. hours/wk. for services:
  Unlimited
How professors are notified of
  LD/ADHD: By student

GENERAL ADMISSIONS INFORMATION

Director of Admissions: Natalie Rigsby
Telephone: 225-388-1175

ENTRANCE REQUIREMENTS

17 total are required; 4 English required, 3 math required, 3 science required, 2 foreign language required, 3 social studies required, 2 elective required. 2.3 GPA required. High school diploma or GED required. Minimum TOEFL is 500. TOEFL required of all international applicants.

Application deadline: June 1
Notification: Rolling beginning 9/1
Average GPA: 2.0–2.9

Average SAT I Math: NR
Average SAT I Verbal: NR
Average ACT: 20

Graduated top 10% of class: 25%
Graduated top 25% of class: 53%
Graduated top 50% of class: 84%

COLLEGE GRADUATION REQUIREMENTS

Course waivers allowed: No
Course substitutions allowed: No
In what subjects: N/A

ADDITIONAL INFORMATION

Environment: The University is located in an urban area in Baton Rouge.

Student Body
  Undergrad enrollment: 25,911
  Female: 53%
  Male: 47%
  Out-of-state: 8%

Cost Information
  In-state tuition: $2,301
  Out-of-state tuition: $6,501
  Room & board: $4,200
Housing Information
  University housing: Yes
  Percent living on campus: 23%

Greek System
  Fraternity: Yes
  Sorority: Yes
Athletics: NCAA Division I

NICHOLLS STATE UNIVERSITY

PO Box 2004, Thibodaux, LA 70310
Phone: 504-448-4507 • Fax: 504-448-4929
E-mail: nicholls@nicholls.edu • Web: www.nicholls.edu
Support level: S • Institution type: 4-year public

LEARNING DISABILITY PROGRAM AND SERVICES

The Center for the Study of Dyslexia offers assistance to serious, capable, students with learning disabilities at Nicholls State University who seek to earn an undergraduate degree. They believe that everyone has the right and the obligation to pursue the fulfillment of their learning potential. The center's programs are data driven, goal oriented, and committed to change. The center is committed to continually questioning and evaluating its own practices. It has its own research program and has close ties with leading scholars and researchers in dyslexia. The center is impressed with multisensory, linguistic, and direct instructional approaches, but to maintain its own integrity, it projects an orientation that is objective, open-minded, and directed toward the future. The goals of the center are focused on the need to increase the understanding of dyslexia and to upgrade and improve the accessibility and quality of the services that individuals with dyslexia depend upon to help them to become self-sufficient, well-adjusted, and contributing members of society.

LD/ADHD ADMISSIONS INFORMATION

College entrance tests required: No
Nonstandardized tests accepted: Yes
Interview required: Yes
Essay required: No
Documentation required for LD: Psychoeducational evaluation
Documentation required for ADHD: Yes
Documentation submitted to: Center for Study of Dyslexia—after admission
Special Ed. HS course work accepted: Yes

Specific course requirements for all applicants: Yes
Separate application required for services: Yes
# of LD applications submitted yearly: 60
# of LD applications accepted yearly: 50
Total # of students receiving LD/ADHD services: 100
Acceptance into program means acceptance into college: Students must be admitted and enrolled at the University first and then can request to be reviewed for services.

ADMISSIONS

There is no special admissions process for students with learning disabilities. The College has an "open admissions policy" for all graduates of high school or holders of a GED. The College recommends that students have 4 years English, 3 years math, 3 years science, 3 years social studies, and 2 years foreign language. ACT/SAT are not required for admission. The average high school GPA is 2.7 and the average ACT is 20. There are a limited number of openings in the center and students should apply early to assure space. The program seeks highly motivated students who have been diagnosed as having a learning disability. Admission decisions are made after careful review of all submitted documentation. The final decision is based upon selecting the option best suited to providing a successful experience at NSU for the student.

ADDITIONAL INFORMATION

The dyslexia center provides a support system; equipment; remediation; academic planning; resources; and assistance. With the student's permission, letters requesting appropriate classroom and testing accommodations are written to professors. Typical accommodations may include but are not limited to extended time; use of an electronic dictionary; oral reader; or use of a computer. Students meet weekly with an identified program coordinator and are enrolled in regular college classes. Other campus services for students with disabilities include the Office for Students with Disabilities; the Testing Center for special testing accommodations such as extended time or a quiet room; the Tutorial Learning Center for tutoring assistance; the University Counseling Center, which provides counseling directed at self-encouragement, self-esteem, assertiveness, stress management, and test anxiety; and the Computer Lab for assistance with written assignments. Assessment is available for a fee for students applying to the University.

SUPPORT SERVICES CONTACT INFORMATION

Learning Disability Program/Services: Center for the Study of Dyslexia
Director: Bill Borsky
  E-mail: dc-csr@mail.nich.edu
  Telephone: 504-448-4429
  Fax: 504-448-4423
Contact: Karen Chavrin
  E-mail: dc-klc@mail.nich.edu
  Telephone: 504-448-4214
  Fax: 504-448-4823

LEARNING DISABILITY SERVICES

Requests for the following services/accommodations will be evaluated individually based on appropriate and current documentation.

Allowed in Exams
  Calculator: Yes
  Dictionary: Yes
  Computer: Yes
  Spellchecker: Yes
Extended test time: Yes
Scribes: Yes
Proctors: Yes
Oral exams: Yes
Notetakers: No

Distraction-reduced environment: Yes
Tape recording in class: Yes
Books on tape from RFBD: Yes
Taping of books not from RFBD: No
Accommodations for students with ADHD: Yes
Reading machine: No
Other assistive technology: Yes
Priority registration: Yes

Added costs for services: $300 per semester
LD specialists: No
Professional tutors: 3
Peer tutors: No
Max. hours/wk. for services: 5
How professors are notified of LD/ADHD: By student

GENERAL ADMISSIONS INFORMATION

Director of Admissions: Becky Durocher
Telephone: 504-448-4507

ENTRANCE REQUIREMENTS
23 total are required; 4 English required, 3 math required, 3 science required, 2 foreign language recommended, 1 social studies required, 2 history required, 7 elective required. High school diploma or GED required. Minimum TOEFL is 500. TOEFL required of all international applicants.

Application deadline: August 15
Notification: Rolling
Average GPA: 2.9

Average SAT I Math: 480
Average SAT I Verbal: 460
Average ACT: 19

Graduated top 10% of class: 46%
Graduated top 25% of class: 56%
Graduated top 50% of class: 75%

COLLEGE GRADUATION REQUIREMENTS

Course waivers allowed: No
Course substitutions allowed: No
In what subjects: N/A

ADDITIONAL INFORMATION

Environment: The University is in a small town 1 hour from New Orleans.

Student Body
  Undergrad enrollment: 6,556
  Female: 62%
  Male: 38%
  Out-of-state: 2%

Cost Information
  In-state tuition: $2,368
  Out-of-state tuition: $7,504
  Room & board: $3,002
Housing Information
  University housing: Yes
  Percent living on campus: 15%

Greek System
  Fraternity: Yes
  Sorority: Yes
Athletics: NCAA Division I

UNIVERSITY OF NEW ORLEANS

Office of Admissions–AD 103, Lakefront, New Orleans, LA 70148
Phone: 504-280-6000 • Fax: 504-280-5522
E-mail: admissions@uno.edu • Web: www.uno.edu
Support level: S • Institution type: 4-year public

LEARNING DISABILITY PROGRAM AND SERVICES

The University of New Orleans is committed to providing all students with equal opportunities for academic and extracurricular success. The Office of Disability Services (ODS) office coordinates all services and programs. In addition to serving its primary function as a liaison between the student and the University, the office provides a limited number of direct services to students with all kinds of permanent and temporary disabilities. Services begin when a student registered with the University contacts the ODS office, provides documentation of the disability, and requests assistance. ODS encourages student independence, program accessibility, and a psychologically supportive environment, so students may achieve their educational objectives. ODS also seeks to educate the campus community about disability issues.

LD/ADHD ADMISSIONS INFORMATION

College entrance tests required: Yes
Nonstandardized tests accepted: Yes
Interview required: Yes
Essay required: No
Documentation required for LD: Psychoeducational
  evaluation
Documentation required for ADHD: Yes
Documentation submitted to: ODS—after admission
Special Ed. HS course work accepted: Yes, with
  appropriate documentation

Specific course requirements for all applicants: Yes
Separate application required for services: Yes
# of LD applications submitted yearly: N/A
# of LD applications accepted yearly: N/A
Total # of students receiving LD/ADHD services: 100+
**Acceptance into program means acceptance into
  college:** Students must be admitted and enrolled at the
  University first and then may request services.

ADMISSIONS

University of New Orleans does not have any special admissions process for students with learning disabilities. Students with learning disabilities should submit the general application form and are expected to meet the same admission standards as all other applicants. Any student who is denied admission may apply to the College Life Program, which is designed as an alternative admissions for "high risk" students (not only students with learning disabilities). This program is for students who need assistance in one or more academic areas. The students remain with this program until they are able to remediate their deficits and then transfer into the appropriate college.

ADDITIONAL INFORMATION

DSS provides regular support services to all UNO students. Drop-in tutoring for math and writing is available. Audiotapes are available in math and English courses. Tutors are available in the Learning Resource Center and Testing Centers in the library for test-taking, adaptive technology, and/or test administration. Developmental courses are offered in math and English, and skills classes are available for assistance in study techniques. PREP START is a special summer outreach program for recent high school graduates to gain admission to the University.

SUPPORT SERVICES CONTACT INFORMATION

Learning Disability Program/Services: Office of Disability Services (ODS)
Director: Janice G. Lyn, PhD
  E-mail: jlyn@uno.edu
  Telephone: 504-280-6222
  Fax: 504-280-3975
Contact: Amy King
  E-mail: aaking@uno.edu
  Telephone: 504-280-7284
  Fax: 504-280-7284

LEARNING DISABILITY SERVICES

Requests for the following services/accommodations will be evaluated individually based on appropriate and current documentation.

Allowed in Exams
  Calculator: Yes
  Dictionary: Yes
  Computer: Yes
  Spellchecker: Yes
Extended test time: Yes
Scribes: Yes
Proctors: Yes
Oral exams: Yes
Notetakers: Yes

Distraction-reduced environment: Yes
Tape recording in class: Yes
Books on tape from RFBD: Yes
Taping of books not from RFBD: Yes
Accommodations for students with ADHD: Yes
Reading machine: Yes
Other assistive technology: Yes
Priority registration: No

Added costs for services: No
LD specialists: No
Professional tutors: No
Peer tutors: No
Max. hours/wk. for services: Referred to Learning Resource Center
How professors are notified of LD/ADHD: By student and program director

GENERAL ADMISSIONS INFORMATION

Director of Admissions: Roslyn Shelley
Telephone: 504-280-7013

ENTRANCE REQUIREMENTS
4 English required, 3 math required, 3 science required, 2 science lab required, 2 foreign language required, 2 social studies required, 1 history required, 2 elective required. Minimum TOEFL is 500. TOEFL required of all international applicants.

Application deadline: August 18
Notification: Rolling
Average GPA: 2.83

Average SAT I Math: 523
Average SAT I Verbal: 534
Average ACT: 21

Graduated top 10% of class: 32%
Graduated top 25% of class: 73%
Graduated top 50% of class: 74%

COLLEGE GRADUATION REQUIREMENTS

Course waivers allowed: No
Course substitutions allowed: Yes
In what subjects: Foreign language and math with appropriate documentation

ADDITIONAL INFORMATION

Environment: The University is located on 345 acres in downtown New Orleans.

Student Body
  Undergrad enrollment: 11,872
  Female: 57%
  Male: 43%
  Out-of-state: 5%

Cost Information
  In-state tuition: $2,362
  Out-of-state tuition: $7,888
  Room & board: $3,150
Housing Information
  University housing: Yes
  Percent living on campus: 5%

Greek System
  Fraternity: Yes
  Sorority: Yes
Athletics: NCAA Division I

SOUTHERN MAINE TECHNICAL COLL.

Fort Road, South Portland, ME 04106
Phone: 207-767-9520 • Fax: 207-767-9671
E-mail: adms@smtc.edu • Web: www.smtc.net
Support: CS • Institution: 2-year public

LEARNING DISABILITY PROGRAM AND SERVICES

The Disability Services program is designed to offer academic support to students through various individualized services. Students can get professional faculty tutoring in their most difficult courses; learn about their specific learning style; improve concentration and memory; study more efficiently for tests; learn how to manage their time better; learn the basic skills that are the foundation of their specific technology; and use a computer toward processing, Internet research, and other computer applications. The NoveNET Learning Lab at SMTC uses a specially designed set of lessons and offers an alternative to adult education or other classes to complete high school level math, science, and English. The Learning Lab is a good place to become reacquainted with oneself as a learner; students can start using it anytime during the school year and work at their own pace; they can study only the lessons that they need; they can work at home on their own personal computer; there is an instructor available during regular lab hours; the instruction meets SMTC's prerequisite admissions requirements; it has day and evening hours; and it allows students to earn credit for work in math courses in the lab by Credit-by-Examination.

LD/ADHD ADMISSIONS INFORMATION

College entrance tests required: Yes, for some degrees
Nonstandardized tests accepted: Yes
Interview required: Recommended
Essay required: Yes
Documentation required for LD: Psychoeducational evaluation
Documentation required for ADHD: Yes
Submitted to: Disability Services
Special Ed. HS course work accepted: Yes

Specific course requirements for all applicants: Yes
Separate application required for services: No
# of LD applications submitted yearly: N/A
# of LD applications accepted yearly: N/A
Total # of students receiving LD/ADHD services: 60
Acceptance into program means acceptance into college: Students must be admitted and enrolled at the College first and then may request services.

ADMISSIONS

All students must meet the same admission criteria. There is no special admissions process for students with learning disabilities. All students have access to disability services, including those with a diagnosed learning disability. Applicants must submit a high school transcript, essay, and recommendation. Interviews are required. Students must have 2 years algebra, and 1 year biology, physics, or chemistry for most programs. SAT I is required for applicants to the associate's degree programs who have been out of high school two years or less. The ACT is not required. Students are expected to have a C average with at least a C in prerequisite courses. Assessment tests sometimes are required as well. Admission decisions are made by admissions and the program director. Conditional acceptance requires additional remedial courses, a C or better in all courses, and weekly contact with the Learning Assistance Center.

ADDITIONAL INFORMATION

Students with diagnosed LD, as well as any students with academic needs, are provided with tutoring by faculty and students; access to NoveNET; access to resources in study skills, in the form of personal advising/counseling, skill inventories, and study guides; and for LD, access to academic accommodations such as untimed exams, testing in a quiet area, and note-takers or readers. Other services are learning assessments; faculty consulting; curriculum development; preparation of materials to assist students in all courses; study skills counseling; academic advising; counseling and support for students with learning disabilities; access to multimedia self-teaching materials including computer-assisted instruction, videotapes, and audio cassettes; and microcomputers, and tape recorders. The College administers the ASSET test to any student who has not provided scores from the ACT or SAT.

SUPPORT SERVICES CONTACT INFORMATION

Learning Disability Program/Services: Disability Services
Director: Mark Krogman
  E-mail: mkrogman@smtc.net
  Telephone: 207-769-7368
  Fax: 207-767-6381
Contact: Gail Rowg
  Telephone: 207-767-9536

LEARNING DISABILITY SERVICES

Requests for the following services/accommodations will be evaluated individually based on appropriate and current documentation.

Allowed in Exams
  Calculator: Yes
  Dictionary: Yes
  Computer: Yes
  Spellchecker: Yes
Extended test time: Yes
Scribes: Yes
Proctors: Yes
Oral exams: Yes
Notetakers: Yes

Distraction-reduced environment: Yes
Tape recording in class: Yes
Books on tape from RFBD: Yes
Taping of books not from RFBD: Yes
Accommodations for students with ADHD: Yes
Reading machine: Yes
Other assistive technology: Yes
Priority registration: Yes

Added costs for services: No
LD specialists: Yes
Professional tutors: Yes
Peer tutors: Varies
Max. hours/wk. for services: As needed
How professors are notified of LD/ADHD: By student and disability service provider

GENERAL ADMISSIONS INFORMATION

Director of Admissions: Robert Welmont
Telephone: 207-767-9520

ENTRANCE REQUIREMENTS
Portfolio required for art program applicants. Auditions required for music program applicants. Additional admissions requirements vary by department.

Application deadline: Rolling
Notification: Rolling
Average GPA: 2.2 minimum

Average SAT I Math: NR
Average SAT I Verbal: NR
Average ACT: NR

Graduated top 10% of class: NR
Graduated top 25% of class: NR
Graduated top 50% of class: NR

COLLEGE GRADUATION REQUIREMENTS

Course waivers allowed: No
Course substitutions allowed: Yes
In what subjects: Limited

ADDITIONAL INFORMATION

Environment: The College, part of the Maine Technical College System, is located on a 50-acre campus.

Student Body
  Undergrad enrollment: 2,410
  Female: 38%
  Male: 62%
  Out-of-state: 9%

Cost Information
  In-state tuition: $2,150
  Out-of-state tuition: $4,230
  Room & board: $3,800
Housing Information
  University housing: Yes
  Percent living on campus: 7%

Greek System
  Fraternity: Yes
  Sorority: Yes
Athletics: NJCAA

UNITY COLLEGE

90 Quaker Hill Road, Unity, ME 04988-0532
Phone: 207-948-3131 • Fax: 207-948-6277
E-mail: admissions@unity.edu • Web: www.unity.edu
Support level: CS • Institution type: 4-year private

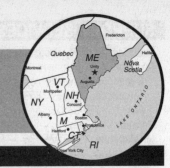

LEARNING DISABILITY PROGRAM AND SERVICES

Unity College offers services for students with learning disabilities and encourages them to begin their studies in the fall semester by enrolling in SAGE (Student Academic Growth Experience), which provides extensive academic and personal support to assist eligible students in making a successful transition to college. SAGE's central feature—the assignment of a faculty mentor to each student—assures individual attention through a structured learning partnership. While the program aims to improve students' skills and confidence to the point where they no longer need SAGE, some students may benefit from the program's support for an extended period, so may enroll in SAGE as needed on a semester-by-semester basis. The LRC (Learning Resource Center) provides a program for bright, highly motivated students. Students with learning disabilities follow a carefully coordinated program that combines regular course work, support services, and intensive individual work on contact. The LRC's staff includes faculty members, a learning disabilities specialist, a secretary, and peer tutors. The staff is available to help students develop effective learning strategies, with special emphasis placed on individual student needs. Most importantly, the LRC gives necessary attention to each student's academic and personal growth. With the support of the LRC, students gain confidence, knowledge, and skills to complete a high-quality education.

LD/ADHD ADMISSIONS INFORMATION

College entrance tests required: No
Nonstandardized tests accepted: Yes
Interview required: Yes
Essay required: Yes
Documentation required for LD: WAIS-III
Documentation required for ADHD: Yes
Documentation submitted to: Learning Resource Center
Special Ed. HS course work accepted: Yes

Specific course requirements for all applicants: Yes
Separate application required for services: No
# of LD applications submitted yearly: N/A
# of LD applications accepted yearly: N/A
Total # of students receiving LD/ADHD services: 60–75
Acceptance into program means acceptance into college: Students must be admitted and enrolled at the College prior to requesting services from the Learning Resource Center.

ADMISSIONS

To apply for admission, students with learning disabilities should submit the general college application and the results of recent diagnostic testing, including a WAIS-R. Students should submit other diagnostic materials that indicate their level of functioning. SAT and ACT scores are not required but should be submitted if available. Students also must send two letters of recommendation and their official high school transcript. The Office of Admissions may require an on-campus interview, on-campus testing, or submission of additional supporting materials. Students with learning disabilities may request an interview with the director of Student Support Services. Some students will be admitted with the stipulation that they enroll in SAGE. Other factors used in the admission decision include special talents, leadership, activities, and personality. Students not regularly admissible are reviewed by the LD specialist, who provides a recommendation to Admissions, and a joint decision is made.

ADDITIONAL INFORMATION

SAGE students negotiate a personalized learning plan with their faculty mentors in consultation with the instructor of the college strategies course, the LRC director and, if applicable, the LD specialist. SAGE students sign a contract of commitment to the plan and attend regular weekly planning sessions with their mentors. They also maintain regular contact with their classroom instructors, peer tutors, and, if appropriate, the LD specialist and/or the College counselor as specified in the learning plan. SAGE students also participate in a first-semester college strategies course that is linked to Perspectives on Nature, the first general education course in the Environmental Stewardship curriculum. Initially, faculty mentors help students interpret their placement results and set realistic goals. Over the course of the semester, they encourage their daily efforts, monitor their academic progress, and provide constructive feedback. Mentors guide students to accurately assess their own preparation for, and performance in, a variety of academic tasks. Working in concert with the instructors of the college strategies course, mentors also supervise students in constructing portfolios to document their developing competencies. The SAGE committee and the college strategies course instructors assess students' progress based on these portfolios.

SUPPORT SERVICES CONTACT INFORMATION

Learning Disability Program/Services: Learning Resource Center (LRC)
Director: James Reed
  E-mail: jreed@unity.edu
  Telephone: 207-948-3131, ext. 241
Contact: Ann Dailey
  Telephone: 207-948-3131, ext. 236

LEARNING DISABILITY SERVICES

Requests for the following services/accommodations will be evaluated individually based on appropriate and current documentation.

Allowed in Exams
  Calculator: Yes
  Dictionary: Yes
  Computer: Yes
  Spellchecker: Yes
Extended test time: Yes
Scribes: Yes
Proctors: Yes
Oral exams: Yes
Notetakers: Yes

Distraction-reduced environment: Y/N
Tape recording in class: Yes
Books on tape from RFBD: Yes
Taping of books not from RFBD: NR
Accommodations for students with ADHD: Yes
Reading machine: No
Other assistive technology: No
Priority registration: Yes

Added costs for services: No
LD specialists: Yes (1)
Professional tutors: Yes
Peer tutors: Yes
Max. hours/wk. for services: Unlimited
How professors are notified of LD/ADHD: By student and program director

GENERAL ADMISSIONS INFORMATION

Director of Admissions: John Craig
Telephone: 207-948-3131, ext. 231

ENTRANCE REQUIREMENTS
18 total are recommended; 4 English required, 4 math recommended, 2 science required, 2 foreign language recommended, 4 social studies recommended. High school diploma or GED required. Minimum TOEFL is 500. TOEFL required of all international applicants.

Application deadline: NR
Notification: Rolling beginning 12/1
Average GPA: 2.7

Average SAT I Math: 480
Average SAT I Verbal: 510
Average ACT: NR

Graduated top 10% of class: 3%
Graduated top 25% of class: 13%
Graduated top 50% of class: 48%

COLLEGE GRADUATION REQUIREMENTS

Course waivers allowed: Yes
Course substitutions allowed: Yes
In what subjects: Determined on a case-by-case basis

ADDITIONAL INFORMATION

Environment: The College is located on 185 acres in a rural community about 20 miles from Waterville.

Student Body
  Undergrad enrollment: 512
  Female: 31%
  Male: 69%
  Out-of-state: 64%

Cost Information
  Tuition: $12,795
  Room & board: $5,300
Housing Information
  University housing: Yes
  Percent living on campus: 80%

Greek System
  Fraternity: Yes
  Sorority: Yes
  Athletics: NAIA

UNIVERSITY OF MAINE—MACHIAS

Office of Admissions, 9 O'Brien Avenue, Machias, ME 04654
Phone: 207-255-1318 • Fax: 207-255-1363
E-mail: admissions@acad.umm.maine.edu • Web: www.umm.maine.edu
Support level: S • Institution type: 4-year public

LEARNING DISABILITY PROGRAM AND SERVICES

The University of Maine at Machias offers a personal approach to education. Students with documented disabilities may request modifications, accommodations, or auxiliary aids that will enable them to participate in and benefit from all post-secondary educational programs and activities. Students must provide current documentation completed within the last three years. This documentation should be submitted to the Student Resources Coordinator. The Student Resources Coordinator works one-on-one with any student who needs academic support. This support takes the form of working with methods specific to the LD. All accommodation requests must be processed through the Student Resources Coordinator.

LD/ADHD ADMISSIONS INFORMATION

College entrance tests required: Yes
Nonstandardized tests accepted: Yes
Interview required: No
Essay required: No
Documentation required for LD: WAIS-III; WJ
Documentation required for ADHD: Yes
Documentation submitted to: Admissions and Student Resources—after admissions
Special Ed. HS course work accepted: Yes

Specific course requirements for all applicants: Yes
Separate application required for services: No
# of LD applications submitted yearly: N/A
# of LD applications accepted yearly: N/A
Total # of students receiving LD/ADHD services: NR
Acceptance into program means acceptance into college: Students must be accepted and enrolled and then request services.

ADMISSIONS
There is no special admissions process for students with LD and ADHD. An interview is strongly suggested. Applicants in general have a 1000 on the SAT, rank in the top 50 percent of their senior class, and have a 3.0 GPA. Students seeking admission to an associate degree program should have a C average and rank in the top two-thirds of their senior class.

ADDITIONAL INFORMATION
One-on-one services are available upon request. One-on-one assistance is offered in the following areas: learning style and learning strategies, time management, organizing and writing papers, basic skills and study skills, anxiety management, major and career focus, assistance using the library, information and/or referral, advocacy, and peer tutoring. In order for a student to have a waiver or substitution of a course a Disabilities Committee meets to evaluate the documentation and make a recommendation to the vice president of academic affairs.

SUPPORT SERVICES CONTACT INFORMATION

Learning Disability Program/Services: Student Resources
Director: Jean Schild
  E-mail: jschild@acad.umm.maine.edu
  Telephone: 207-255-1228
  Fax: 208-255-4864
Contact: Same

LEARNING DISABILITY SERVICES

Requests for the following services/accommodations will be evaluated individually based on appropriate and current documentation.

Allowed in Exams
  Calculator: Yes
  Dictionary: Yes
  Computer: Yes
  Spellchecker: Yes
Extended test time: Yes
Scribes: Yes
Proctors: Yes
Oral exams: Yes
Notetakers: Yes

Distraction-reduced environment: Yes
Tape recording in class: Yes
Books on tape from RFBD: Yes
Taping of books not from RFBD: No
Accommodations for students with ADHD: Yes
Reading machine: No
Other assistive technology: Yes
Priority registration: Yes

Added costs for services: No
LD specialists: No
Professional tutors: No
Peer tutors: 14
Max. hours/wk. for services: Unlimited
How professors are notified of LD/ADHD: By director

GENERAL ADMISSIONS INFORMATION

Director of Admissions: David Baldwin
Telephone: 207-255-1218

ENTRANCE REQUIREMENTS

16 total are recommended; 4 English recommended, 3 math recommended, 2 science recommended, 2 science lab recommended, 2 foreign language recommended, 2 social studies recommended, 2 history recommended, 3 elective recommended. High school diploma or GED required. Minimum TOEFL is 500. TOEFL required of all international applicants.

Application deadline: Rolling
Notification: Rolling
Average GPA: 3.0

Average SAT I Math: 505
Average SAT I Verbal: 513
Average ACT: 23

Graduated top 10% of class: 17%
Graduated top 25% of class: 46%
Graduated top 50% of class: 89%

COLLEGE GRADUATION REQUIREMENTS

Course waivers allowed: Yes
Course substitutions allowed: Yes
In what subjects: Varies; disabilities committee makes recommendation to vice president of academic affairs for final determination

ADDITIONAL INFORMATION

Student Body
  Undergrad enrollment: 927
  Female: 67%
  Male: 33%
  Out-of-state: 22%

Cost Information
  In-state tuition: $3,150
  Out-of-state tuition: $7,860
  Room & board: $4,490
Housing Information
  University housing: Yes
  Percent living on campus: 36%

Greek System
  Fraternity: Yes
  Sorority: Yes
  Athletics: NAIA

UNIVERSITY OF NEW ENGLAND

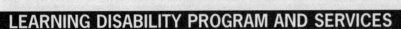

Hills Beach Road, Biddeford, ME 04005
Phone: 207-283-0171 • Fax: 207-294-5900
E-mail: jshea@mailbox.une.edu • Web: www.une.edu
Support level: S • Institution type: 4-year private

LEARNING DISABILITY PROGRAM AND SERVICES

The University of New England's Office for Students with Disabilities exists to ensure that the University fulfills the part of its mission that seeks to promote respect for individual differences and to ensure that no one person who meets the academic and technical standards requisite for admission to, and the continued enrollment at, the University is denied benefits or subjected to discrimination at UNE solely by reason of the disability. Toward this end, and in conjunction with federal and state laws, the University both accepts and provides reasonable accommodations for qualified students. Students with learning disabilities or attention deficit disorder must provide current documentation that identifies the specific disability. All documentation should be submitted to the Office of Students with Disabilities.

LD/ADHD ADMISSIONS INFORMATION

College entrance tests required: Yes
Nonstandardized tests accepted: Yes
Interview required: No
Essay required: No
Documentation required for LD: Psychoeducational evaluation
Documentation required for ADHD: Yes
Documentation submitted to: ILP
Special Ed. HS course work accepted: Yes

Specific course requirements for all applicants: Depends on major
Separate application required for services: No
# of LD applications submitted yearly: N/A
# of LD applications accepted yearly: N/A
Total # of students receiving LD/ADHD services: 25
Acceptance into program means acceptance into college: Students must be admitted and enrolled and then request services.

ADMISSIONS

All applicants must meet the same admission criteria. There is no separate process for students with LD/ADHD. General admission criteria include 4 years English, 2–4 years math, 2–4 years social studies, 2–4 years science, and 2–4 years foreign language. It is recommended that students submit an essay and have an interview. Interviews are especially helpful for borderline applicants. After being admitted, students may submit documentation to the Office for Students with Disabilities in order to request accommodations and services.

ADDITIONAL INFORMATION

Documentation requirements have been established by the Office for Students with Disabilities. Students with learning disabilities should submit psychoeducational assessment reports based on adult-normed tests of ability and achievement. Students with ADHD must also submit appropriate documentation from a qualified professional. Services could include priority registration, note-takers, scribes, proctors, and books on tape through the Recordings for the Blind and Dyslexic. Accommodations could include the use of a calculator, dictionary, computer, or spellchecker in exams; reduced-distraction site for exams; extended time on tests; oral exams; and assistive technology. All students have access to tutoring.

SUPPORT SERVICES CONTACT INFORMATION

Learning Disability Program/Services: Individual Learning Program (ILP)
Director: Susan Church, Coordinator
  E-mail: schurch@une.edu
  Telephone: 207-283-0171, ext. 2815
  Fax: 207-294-5927
Contact: Same

LEARNING DISABILITY SERVICES

Requests for the following services/accommodations will be evaluated individually based on appropriate and current documentation.

Allowed in Exams
  Calculator: Yes
  Dictionary: Yes
  Computer: Yes
  Spellchecker: Yes
Extended test time: Yes
Scribes: Yes
Proctors: Yes
Oral exams: Yes
Notetakers: No

Distraction-reduced environment: Yes
Tape recording in class: Yes
Books on tape from RFBD: Yes
Taping of books not from RFBD: Yes
Accommodations for students with
  ADHD: Yes
Reading machine: Yes
Other assistive technology: Yes
Priority registration: Yes

Added costs for services: No
LD specialists: No
Professional tutors: Yes
Peer tutors: Yes
Max. hours/wk. for services: Unlimited
How professors are notified of
  LD/ADHD: By student

GENERAL ADMISSIONS INFORMATION

Director of Admissions: Patricia T. Cribby
Telephone: 207-283-0171

ENTRANCE REQUIREMENTS

4 English required, 3 math required, 4 math recommended, 3 science required, 4 science recommended, 2 science lab required, 3 science lab recommended, 2 foreign language recommended, 2 social studies required, 4 social studies recommended, 2 history required, 4 history recommended, 4 elective recommended. High school diploma or GED required. Minimum TOEFL is 550. TOEFL required of all international applicants.

Application deadline: Rolling
Notification: Rolling beginning 2/15
Average GPA: 3.2

Average SAT I Math: 509
Average SAT I Verbal: 511
Average ACT: NR

Graduated top 10% of class: 17%
Graduated top 25% of class: 46%
Graduated top 50% of class: 80%

COLLEGE GRADUATION REQUIREMENTS

Course waivers allowed: Yes
Course substitutions allowed: Yes
In what subjects: Determined on an individual case-by-case basis

ADDITIONAL INFORMATION

Environment: The 121-acre campus is in a rural area 16 miles east of Portland.

Student Body
  Undergrad enrollment: 1,869
  Female: 81%
  Male: 19%
  Out-of-state: 50%

Cost Information
  Tuition: $16,350
  Room & board: $6,420
Housing Information
  University housing: Yes
  Percent living on campus: 45%

Greek System
  Fraternity: No
  Sorority: No
Athletics: NCAA Division III

University of New England

FROSTBURG STATE UNIVERSITY

FSU, 101 Braddock Road, Frostburg, MD 21532
Phone: 301-687-4201 • Fax: 301-687-7074
E-mail: fsuadmissions@frostburg.edu • Web: www.frostburg.edu
Support level: S • Institution type: 4-year public

LEARNING DISABILITY PROGRAM AND SERVICES

Frostburg State provides comprehensive support services for students with learning disabilities to assist them in achieving their potential. To be eligible for the Frostburg State University support services, admitted students must provide records of evaluation not more than three years old. Documentation should include a statement about the disability, functional limitations, supporting data and test results, and recommendations for accommodations. Services include advising and counseling by a qualified counselor familiar with each student's needs; assistance in course selection; guaranteed schedules; liaison with faculty; representation at Academic Standards Committee meetings; tutoring; and study-skills workshops. The goal of the programs is to provide appropriate support services to enhance learning, and to strive for student self-advocacy and understanding of and independence in learning style.

LD/ADHD ADMISSIONS INFORMATION

College entrance tests required: Yes
Nonstandardized tests accepted: Yes
Interview required: NR
Essay required: No
Documentation required for LD: Psychoeducational evaluation
Documentation required for ADHD: Yes
Documentation submitted to: Disability Support Services
Special Ed. HS course work accepted: Yes, case-by-case

Specific course requirements for all applicants: Yes
Separate application required for services: No
# of LD applications submitted yearly: N/A
# of LD applications accepted yearly: N/A
Total # of students receiving LD/ADHD services: 300
Acceptance into program means acceptance into college: Students must be admitted and enrolled and then may request services. There is an appeal procedure for students who are denied admission.

ADMISSIONS

There is no special admission procedure for students with learning disabilities. All students must complete the mainstream program in high school and meet all requirements for the University and the state. There is a Student Support Services/Disabled Student Services Information Form that must be completed by students to enroll in these programs. Admission to FSU is determined by the Admissions Office, which assesses an applicant's likelihood of success in a regular college program with Support Service assistance.

ADDITIONAL INFORMATION

Basic skills courses are available in time management, study techniques, organizational skills, and test-taking strategies. Other services include note-takers, dictation services, and readers. There is an orientation course to the University taught by an LD specialist. Students with LD or ADHD must provide current and appropriate documentation in order to receive services. Students who believe they may have a learning disability, but who have not been tested, may request testing and assessment for no fee.

SUPPORT SERVICES CONTACT INFORMATION

Learning Disability Program/Services: Disability Support Services
Director: Leroy Pullen
  E-mail: lpullen@frostburg.edu
  Telephone: 301-687-4483
  Fax: 301-687-4671
Contact: Same

LEARNING DISABILITY SERVICES

Requests for the following services/accommodations will be evaluated individually based on appropriate and current documentation.

Allowed in Exams
  Calculator: Y/N
  Dictionary: Y/N
  Computer: Yes
  Spellchecker: Y/N
Extended test time: Yes
Scribes: Yes
Proctors: Yes
Oral exams: Yes
Notetakers: Yes

Distraction-reduced environment: Yes
Tape recording in class: Yes
Books on tape from RFBD: Yes
Taping of books not from RFBD: Yes
Accommodations for students with ADHD: Yes
Reading machine: Yes
Other assistive technology: Yes
Priority registration: Yes

Added costs for services: No
LD specialists: No
Professional tutors: Yes (7)
Peer tutors: Yes
Max. hours/wk. for services: Varies
How professors are notified of LD/ADHD: Student presents accomodation letter

GENERAL ADMISSIONS INFORMATION

Director of Admissions: Dr. Stewart Tenent
Telephone: 301-687-4201

ENTRANCE REQUIREMENTS

15 total are required; 4 English required, 3 math required, 3 science required, 2 science lab required, 2 foreign language required, 3 social studies required. High school diploma or GED required. Minimum TOEFL is 560. TOEFL required of all international applicants.

Application deadline: Rolling
Notification: Rolling beginning 11/1
Average GPA: 3.0

Average SAT I Math: 490
Average SAT I Verbal: 490
Average ACT: NR

Graduated top 10% of class: NR
Graduated top 25% of class: NR
Graduated top 50% of class: NR

COLLEGE GRADUATION REQUIREMENTS

Course waivers allowed: No
Course substitutions allowed: Yes
In what subjects: Students may appeal for any course to be substituted. Appeals are determined on a case-by-case basis.

ADDITIONAL INFORMATION

Environment: The University in located on 260 acres in the Appalachian Highlands in a small town 150 miles northwest of Baltimore.

Student Body
  Undergrad enrollment: 4,313
  Female: 54%
  Male: 46%
  Out-of-state: 10%

Cost Information
  In-state tuition: $3,444
  Out-of-state tuition: $8,942
  Room & board: $5,266
Housing Information
  University housing: Yes
  Percent living on campus: 82%

Greek System
  Fraternity: Yes
  Sorority: Yes
Athletics: NCAA Division III

TOWSON UNIVERSITY

8000 York Road, Towson, MD 21252-0001
Phone: 410-704-2113 • Fax: 410-704-3030
E-mail: admissions@towson.edu • Web: www.towson.edu
Support level: CS • Institution type: 4-year public

LEARNING DISABILITY PROGRAM AND SERVICES

Towson University does not have a separate program for students with learning disabilities and/or attention deficit disorder. The University policy is to ask students what their needs are rather than to present them with a plan to which they must adapt. There is involvement in class selection. Professors are notified of students' disabilities, which eliminates the need for students to "explain" or "prove" their disability. Towson University also offers all students tutorial services, a Reading Center, and a Writing Lab. All students requesting services and/or accommodations must have an interview with the director of support services in order to establish what is necessary. Towson University's program for students with learning disabilities is individualistic, as the severity and compensating skills of the students are unique.

LD/ADHD ADMISSIONS INFORMATION

College entrance tests required: Yes
Nonstandardized tests accepted: Yes
Interview required: Yes
Essay required: No
Documentation required for LD: WAIS-III; WRAT-R; WJ: within 3 years
Documentation required for ADHD: Yes
Documentation submitted to: Disability Support Services
Special Ed. HS course work accepted: Yes

Specific course requirements for all applicants: Yes
Separate application required for services: Yes
# of LD applications submitted yearly: N/A
# of LD applications accepted yearly: N/A
Total # of students receiving LD/ADHD services: 375
Acceptance into program means acceptance into college: Students must be admitted and enrolled at the University first and then may request services.

ADMISSIONS

There is no question on the application that inquires about a learning disability. Students with learning disabilities who want special consideration and/or services should provide documentation and information about their learning disability. Exceptions to published entrance requirements are made by a committee for students with documented learning disabilities. Credentials are reviewed by a committee that has some flexibility in interpreting scores. Students submitting documentation should send copies to admissions and DSS. Interviews are recommended. The middle 50 percent SAT range for applicants is 1020–1180. Priority admission is granted to applicants with a GPA of 3.0 and 4 years English, 3 years social science, 3 years lab science, 3 years math, 2 years foreign language (waived with appropriate documentation) and an 1100 SAT. Courses taken in special education may be considered. Applicants with lower GPA and test scores will be considered after seventh semester grades on a space-available basis, with priority given to those with the highest GPA.

ADDITIONAL INFORMATION

Towson University provides students with learning disabilities the necessary accommodations based on recent psychoeducational evaluations. These accommodations are based on recommendations from the evaluation. The Learning Center provides reading and study skills development services. The Writing Lab provides assistance for students who need improvement in writing skills. A quiet study area is available. Additionally, the Disability Support Services provides note-takers; a resource room to be used for a quiet place to take a test; use of the services of a reader; extended testing time and other testing arrangements; student advocacy; interpretation of documentation; authorization of accommodations; assistance with implementation of reasonable accommodations; scribes and readers; short-term instructional support in time management, study and test-taking strategies, and reading and writing assistance; assistive technology; and referrals for other services. Students must be registered with RFB to get taped textbooks. Those textbooks not available through RFB may be requested from Disability Support Service.

SUPPORT SERVICES CONTACT INFORMATION

Learning Disability Program/Services: Disability Support Services
Contact: Ronni Uhland, Learning Disabilities Specialist
  E-mail: ruhland@towson.edu
  Telephone: 410-830-2638
  Fax: 410-830-4247
Contact: Susan Willemin, Learning Disabilities Specialist
  E-mail: swillemin@towson.edu
  Telephone: 410-830-3475
  Fax: 410-830-4247

LEARNING DISABILITY SERVICES

Requests for the following services/accommodations will be evaluated individually based on appropriate and current documentation.

Allowed in Exams
  Calculator: Yes
  Dictionary: Yes
  Computer: Yes
  Spellchecker: Yes
Extended test time: Yes
Scribes: Yes
Proctors: Yes
Oral exams: Yes
Notetakers: Yes

Distraction-reduced environment: Yes
Tape recording in class: Yes
Books on tape from RFBD: Yes
Taping of books not from RFBD: Yes
Accommodations for students with ADHD: Yes
Reading machine: Yes
Other assistive technology: Yes
Priority registration: Yes

Added costs for services: No
LD specialists: Yes (1)
Professional tutors: N/A
Peer tutors: Yes
Max. hours/wk. for services: Unlimited
How professors are notified of LD/ADHD: By student

GENERAL ADMISSIONS INFORMATION

Director of Admissions: Louise Shulack
Telephone: 410-704-2113

ENTRANCE REQUIREMENTS
24 total are required; 4 English required, 3 math required, 3 science required, 3 science lab required, 2 foreign language required, 3 social studies required, 6 elective required. High school diploma or GED required. Minimum TOEFL is 500. TOEFL required of all international applicants.

Application deadline: May 1
Notification: Rolling beginning 10/1
Average GPA: 3.3

Average SAT I Math: 551
Average SAT I Verbal: 544
Average ACT: 22

Graduated top 10% of class: 16%
Graduated top 25% of class: 49%
Graduated top 50% of class: 84%

COLLEGE GRADUATION REQUIREMENTS

Course waivers allowed: No
Course substitutions allowed: Yes
In what subjects: Varies based on individual need and current documentation

ADDITIONAL INFORMATION

Environment: The school is located on 306 landscaped and wooded acres minutes from downtown Baltimore.

Student Body
  Undergrad enrollment: 13,905
  Female: 60%
  Male: 40%
  Out-of-state: 18%

Cost Information
  In-state tuition: $3,605
  Out-of-state tuition: $10,491
  Room & board: $6,104
Housing Information
  University housing: Yes
  Percent living on campus: 33%

Greek System
  Fraternity: Yes
  Sorority: Yes
Athletics: NCAA Division I

U. OF MARYLAND—COLLEGE PARK

Mitchell Building, College Park, MD 20742-5235
Phone: 301-314-8385 • Fax: 301-314-9693
E-mail: um-admit@uga.umd.edu • Web: www.maryland.edu
Support level: CS • Institution type: 4-year public

LEARNING DISABILITY PROGRAM AND SERVICES

The goal of the Disability Support Services is to coordinate accommodations and services for students with learning disabilities and physical disabilities. Services are offered through the Learning Assistance Service as well, through accommodations as provided by the Disability Support Services. Students are expected to facilitate contact with instructors and negotiate any special accommodations. Students may request assistance from the Service Office in handling interactions with instructors. Commonly used services include testing assistance, note-takers, readers, and priority registration. Besides the standard accommodations, students receive support through special study skills course workshops, mentoring, and support groups.

LD/ADHD ADMISSIONS INFORMATION

College entrance tests required: Yes
Nonstandardized tests accepted: Yes
Interview required: No
Essay required: Yes
Documentation required for LD: Psychoeducational evaluation
Documentation required for ADHD: Yes
Documentation submitted to: Admissions and Disability Support Services
Special Ed. HS course work accepted: Yes

Specific course requirements for all applicants: Yes
Separate application required for services: No
# of LD applications submitted yearly: N/A
# of LD applications accepted yearly: N/A
Total # of students receiving LD/ADHD services: 400
Acceptance into program means acceptance into college: Students must be admitted and enrolled at the University first and then may request services.

ADMISSIONS

There is no special admissions or alternative admissions process for students with learning disabilities. Applicants with learning disabilities must meet general admissions criteria. The admission decision is based on courses taken in high school, which should include 4 years English, 3 years social studies, 2 years lab science, 3 years math, and 2 years foreign Language; GPA; SAT/ACT; class rank; personal statement; recommendations; and the psychoeducational evaluation. All freshmen applicants must submit a personal statement for admissions. The student may submit supporting documentation, which will be considered during the decision-making process. The Learning Disabilities Coordinator may review the documentation and make a recommendation to the admissions office. The final decision rests with the Office of Admissions.

ADDITIONAL INFORMATION

There is a math lab and writing center available for all students. There is no centralized tutoring service. However, limited free tutoring is available through departments. For most tutoring needs students need to hire their own tutors. There are approximately 500 students with either LD or ADHD currently receiving services or accommodations on campus. Notetakers are volunteers and could be students enrolled in the course. There is a mentoring program and support programs for students with disabilities. Priority registration is available. Services and accommodations are available to undergraduate and graduate students. There is a summer program for high school students. While it is not specifically for those with learning disabilities, these students could benefit from the program. The University is currently working on developing a special summer program for students with learning disabilities.

SUPPORT SERVICES CONTACT INFORMATION

Learning Disability Program/Services: Disability Support Services (DSS)
Director: Bill Scales, PhD
  E-mail: wrs@wam.umd.edu
  Telephone: 301-314-7682
  Fax: 301-405-0813
Contact: Peggy Hayeslip, LD Coordinator
  E-mail: mh185@umail.umd.edu
  Telephone: 301-314-9969
  Fax: 301-314-9011

LEARNING DISABILITY SERVICES

Requests for the following services/accommodations will be evaluated individually based on appropriate and current documentation.

Allowed in Exams
  Calculator: Yes
  Dictionary: No
  Computer: Yes
  Spellchecker: Yes
Extended test time: Yes
Scribes: Yes
Proctors: Yes
Oral exams: Yes
Notetakers: Yes

Distraction-reduced environment: Yes
Tape recording in class: Yes
Books on tape from RFBD: Yes
Taping of books not from RFBD: Yes
Accommodations for students with ADHD: Yes
Reading machine: Yes
Other assistive technology: Yes
Priority registration: Yes

Added costs for services: No
LD specialists: Yes
Professional tutors: No
Peer tutors: No
Max. hours/wk. for services: Unlimited
How professors are notified of LD/ADHD: By student

GENERAL ADMISSIONS INFORMATION

Director of Admissions: James Chistensen
Telephone: 800-422-5867

ENTRANCE REQUIREMENTS
16 total are required; 17 total are recommended; 4 English required, 3 math required, 4 math recommended, 2 science required, 2 science lab required, 3 foreign language required, 3 social studies required. High school diploma or GED required. Minimum TOEFL is 575. TOEFL required of all international applicants.

Application deadline: February 15
Notification: Rolling beginning 2/1
Average GPA: 3.7
Average SAT I Math: 610
Average SAT I Verbal: 590
Average ACT: NR
Graduated top 10% of class: 52%
Graduated top 25% of class: 87%
Graduated top 50% of class: 99%

COLLEGE GRADUATION REQUIREMENTS

Course waivers allowed: No
Course substitutions allowed: Yes
In what subjects: Math and foreign language

ADDITIONAL INFORMATION

Environment: The University is in a small town setting within proximity to Washington, D.C., and Baltimore.

Student Body
  Undergrad enrollment: 24,638
  Female: 49%
  Male: 51%
  Out-of-state: 26%

Cost Information
  In-state tuition: $4,334
  Out-of-state tuition: $12,406
  Room & board: $6,076
Housing Information
  University housing: Yes
  Percent living on campus: 38%

Greek System
  Fraternity: Yes
  Sorority: Yes
Athletics: NCAA Division I

U. OF MARYLAND—EASTERN SHORE

Office of Admissions, Backbone Road, Princess Anne, MD 21853
Phone: 410-651-6410 • Fax: 410-651-7922
E-mail: ccmills@mail.umes.edu • Web: www.umes.edu
Support level: CS • Institution type: 4-year public

LEARNING DISABILITY PROGRAM AND SERVICES

The Office of Services for Students with Disabilities assures the commitment of the University to provide access and equal opportunity to students with disabilities admitted to the University. Although there is no special curriculum for students with disabilities, services are designed to assist students in maximizing their academic potential. The focus is on supporting the positive development of students with disabilities.

LD/ADHD ADMISSIONS INFORMATION

College entrance tests required: Yes
Nonstandardized tests accepted: Yes
Interview required: No
Essay required: Yes
Documentation required for LD: Psychoeducational evaluation
Documentation required for ADHD: Yes
Documentation submitted to: Disability Office—after admission
Special Ed. HS course work accepted: Yes

Specific course requirements for all applicants: Yes
Separate application required for services: No
# of LD applications submitted yearly: 30+
# of LD applications accepted yearly: NR
Total # of students receiving LD/ADHD services: 25+
Acceptance into program means acceptance into college: Students must be admitted and enrolled at the University first and then may request services.

ADMISSIONS

There is no special admission. All applicants must meet the same criteria. General admission requirements include 4 years English, 3 years math, 2 years foreign language, 3 years social studies; minimum SAT of 750 and minimum GPA of 2.5 are recommended. In-state students who have a high school diploma and minimum C average may be admitted on the basis of the predictive index weighting SAT I scores and GPA.

ADDITIONAL INFORMATION

Tutoring is available in every subject for all students. There are skills courses offered in remedial math, reading, and writing.

SUPPORT SERVICES CONTACT INFORMATION

Learning Disability Program/Services: Office of Services for Students with Disabilities and Academic Support Services
Director: Dorling K. Joseph
  E-mail: djoseph@mail.umes.edu
  Telephone: 410-651-6461
  Fax: 410-651-6322
Contact: Same

LEARNING DISABILITY SERVICES

Requests for the following services/accommodations will be evaluated individually based on appropriate and current documentation.

Allowed in Exams
  Calculator: Yes
  Dictionary: Yes
  Computer: Yes
  Spellchecker: Yes
Extended test time: Yes
Scribes: Yes
Proctors: Yes
Oral exams: Yes
Notetakers: Yes

Distraction-reduced environment: Yes
Tape recording in class: Yes
Books on tape from RFBD: Yes
Taping of books not from RFBD: Yes
Accommodations for students with
  ADHD: Yes
Reading machine: No
Other assistive technology: No
Priority registration: No

Added costs for services: No
LD specialists: Yes (1)
Professional tutors: Yes
Peer tutors: Yes
Max. hours/wk. for services: Unlimited
How professors are notified of
  LD/ADHD: By student with letter

GENERAL ADMISSIONS INFORMATION

Director of Admissions: Cheryl Collier-Mills
Telephone: 410-651-6410

ENTRANCE REQUIREMENTS
20 total are required; 24 total are recommended; 4 English required, 3 math required, 2 science required, 2 science lab required, 2 foreign language required, 3 social studies required, 6 elective required. High school diploma or GED required. Minimum TOEFL is 500. TOEFL required of all international applicants.

Application deadline: July 15
Notification: Rolling
Average GPA: 2.7

Average SAT I Math: 410
Average SAT I Verbal: 430
Average ACT: NR

Graduated top 10% of class: NR
Graduated top 25% of class: NR
Graduated top 50% of class: NR

COLLEGE GRADUATION REQUIREMENTS

Course waivers allowed: No
Course substitutions allowed: Yes
In what subjects: All pending core course requirements

ADDITIONAL INFORMATION

Environment: The University is located on a 600-acre campus in a rural area 15 miles south of Salisbury.

Student Body
  Undergrad enrollment: 2,704
  Female: 57%
  Male: 43%
  Out-of-state: 26%

Cost Information
  In-state tuition: $3,994
  Out-of-state tuition: $8,497
  Room & board: $4,930
Housing Information
  University housing: Yes
  Percent living on campus: 56%

Greek System
  Fraternity: Yes
  Sorority: Yes
  Athletics: NCAA Division I

WESTERN MARYLAND COLLEGE

2 College Hill, Westminster, MD 21157
Phone: 410-857-2230 • Fax: 410-857-2757
E-mail: admissio@wmdc.edu • Web: www.wmdc.edu
Support level: CS • Institution type: 4-year private

LEARNING DISABILITY PROGRAM AND SERVICES

The goal of the College is to assist students with learning disabilities. More time is given to freshmen and transfer students to help with the transition into WMC. The Academic Skills Center provides three levels of services: Level I (no fee) students receive appropriate accommodations, tutoring, monthly support groups, and two hours a semester advising with ASC coordinator; Level II ($1,000 fee) provides Level I services and pre-scheduling of courses, consulting with ASC coordinator, Study Lab, five hours per week of study skills tutoring, and assignment to an ASC mentor; Level III ($1,500 fee) provides services from Level I and Level II and diagnostic testing, planning, developmental implementation, and evaluation of a yearly individualized academic program.

LD/ADHD ADMISSIONS INFORMATION

College entrance tests required: Yes
Nonstandardized tests accepted: Yes
Interview required: No
Essay required: Yes
Documentation required for LD: WAIS-III, psychoeducational testing: within three years
Documentation required for ADHD: Yes
Documentation submitted to: Academic Skills Center—after admission
Special Ed. HS course work accepted: No

Specific course requirements for all applicants: Yes
Separate application required for services: No
# of LD applications submitted yearly: 100
# of LD applications accepted yearly: 55
Total # of students receiving LD/ADHD services: 100
Acceptance into program means acceptance into college: Students must be admitted and enrolled at the College first and then may request services.

ADMISSIONS

The admission process is the same for all applicants. General admission criteria include a minimum 2.75 GPA in core academic courses including 4 years English, 3 years math, 3 years science, 3 years social studies, and 3 years foreign language (substitutions allowed in foreign language if appropriate). Any LD or ADHD documentation should be sent to ASC to be used after a student is admitted and enrolled.

ADDITIONAL INFORMATION

Enrolled new students must attend one Guidance Day during the summer prior to freshman year to select classes. Students with learning disabilities should attend an orientation meeting before college begins and schedule individual appointments with the ASC coordinator. All students must pass one math course. There is a basic math class and two math review courses for students needing more math foundation prior to taking the required course. One skills class is offered and students have access to unlimited tutoring.

SUPPORT SERVICES CONTACT INFORMATION

Learning Disability Program/Services: Academic Skills Center (ASC)
Director: Denise Marjarum
  E-mail: dmarjaru@wmdc.edu
  Telephone: 410-857-2504
  Fax: 410-386-4617
Contact: Same

LEARNING DISABILITY SERVICES

Requests for the following services/accommodations will be evaluated individually based on appropriate and current documentation.

Allowed in Exams
  Calculator: Yes
  Dictionary: Yes
  Computer: Yes
  Spellchecker: Yes
Extended test time: Yes
Scribes: Yes
Proctors: Yes
Oral exams: Yes
Notetakers: Yes

Distraction-reduced environment: Yes
Tape recording in class: Yes
Books on tape from RFBD: Yes
Taping of books not from RFBD: Yes
Accommodations for students with ADHD: Yes
Reading machine: No
Other assistive technology: Yes
Priority registration: Yes

Added costs for services: $1,250 per year
LD specialists: Yes (2)
Professional tutors: Yes
Peer tutors: 10
Max. hours/wk. for services: Unlimited
How professors are notified of LD/ADHD: By student

GENERAL ADMISSIONS INFORMATION

Director of Admissions: Marty O'Connell
Telephone: 410-857-2230

ENTRANCE REQUIREMENTS
18 total are required; 27 total are recommended; 4 English required, 3 math required, 4 math recommended, 3 science required, 4 science recommended, 2 science lab required, 3 science lab recommended, 3 foreign language required, 4 foreign language recommended, 3 social studies required, 4 social studies recommended, 2 history required, 3 history recommended, 4 elective recommended. High school diploma or GED required. Minimum TOEFL is 550. TOEFL required of all international applicants.

Application deadline: March 15
Notification: April 1
Average GPA: 3.4

Average SAT I Math: 567
Average SAT I Verbal: 564
Average ACT: 24

Graduated top 10% of class: 65%
Graduated top 25% of class: 73%
Graduated top 50% of class: 97%

COLLEGE GRADUATION REQUIREMENTS

Course waivers allowed: No
Course substitutions allowed: Yes
In what subjects: Foreign language

ADDITIONAL INFORMATION

Environment: The College is located on 160 acres in a small town 30 miles northwest of Baltimore.

Student Body
  Undergrad enrollment: 1,610
  Female: 56%
  Male: 44%
  Out-of-state: 31%

Cost Information
  Tuition: $20,550
  Room & board: $5,450
Housing Information
  University housing: Yes
  Percent living on campus: 74%

Greek System
  Fraternity: Yes
  Sorority: Yes
  Athletics: NCAA Division III

AMERICAN INTERNATIONAL COLLEGE

1000 State Street, Springfield, MA 01109-3184
Phone: 800-242-3142 • Fax: 413-737-2803
E-mail: inquiry@aic.edu • Web: www.aic.edu
Support level: SP • Institution type: 4-year private

LEARNING DISABILITY PROGRAM AND SERVICES

AIC believes that individuals who have learning disabilities can compensate for their difficulties and meet with success in the College environment. It is AIC's philosophy that the College is responsible for helping students with LD to become active participants in the learning process. AIC feels that the Supportive Learning Services Program has all the components necessary to allow for a successful college career for a student with learning disabilities. AIC models compensatory technique and teaches strategies to enable students to be effective in college and plan for their future. Students receiving Supportive Learning Services may elect to participate in the comprehensive services component in the Curtis Blake Center. Metacognitive strategies are taught in order to help students use their intellect more efficiently. The learning environment of the student is modified to promote learning. Students must have the intellectual ability necessary to meet the demands of a college curriculum, as well as motivation and commitment. Students are mainstreamed and may receive a minimum of two hours of tutoring/studying strategies weekly. Students create an Individual Educational Plan with their tutor freshman year and may take as few as four courses each semester. Students generally stay in the program for four years. In addition to comprehensive services, AIC also offers a limited services component which allows students with LD to reserve 5–10 hours of professional tutoring to be used over the semester. Additional hours can also be arranged for a fee.

LD/ADHD ADMISSIONS INFORMATION

College entrance tests required: No
Nonstandardized tests accepted: Yes
Interview required: Yes
Essay required: No
Documentation required for LD: Wechsler Adult Intelligence Scale and accompanying diagnosis; relevant diagnostic results of achievement testing
Documentation required for ADHD: Diagnosis of ADHD and psychoeducational assessment
Documentation submitted to: SLSP
Special Ed. HS course work accepted: Done on an individual basis

Specific course requirements for all applicants: Yes
Separate application required for services: No
# of LD applications submitted yearly: 250
# of LD applications accepted yearly: 35
Total # of students receiving LD/ADHD services: 60
Acceptance into program means acceptance into college: Simultaneous admission decisions are made by the program and Admissions.

ADMISSIONS

In addition to submitting an application to Admissions, students interested in applying for the support program must also contact the coordinator of SLSP. Applicants must schedule an on-campus interview with admissions and SLSP. Applicants must submit the results of the WAIS-R and accompanying report, relevant diagnostic material, and information about supportive assistance in the past. The College requires a high school transcript and ACT/SAT scores. There should be a strong indication of achievement and motivation in the fields of knowledge studied. The majority of applicants have a GPA of 2.0–3.0. Courses required include 16 academic units from English, math, science, and social studies. Foreign language is not required. The admission decision is made simultaneously between admissions and SLSP.

ADDITIONAL INFORMATION

At the heart of the services provided is a minimum of two hours of regularly scheduled direct, one-to-one assistance provided by a learning specialist. The specialist develops an individually tailored support program based on the student's needs. Priority is given to practical assistance to help students negotiate demands of the curriculum. Provisions can be made for more basic remediation of the student's learning difficulties. Specialists assist in course selection, organizing work and study schedules, and as a resource. Students have access to skills seminars in many areas. Classes in reading, spelling, math, study strategies, time management, written language, and handwriting are offered. The Supportive Learning Services Center is only open to students who are participating in the program. Services and accommodations are available to undergraduate and graduate students.

SUPPORT SERVICES CONTACT INFORMATION

Learning Disability Program/Services: Supportive Learning Services Program (SLSP)
Director: Dr. Mary Saltas
  E-mail: cbc2@alcstudent.com
  Telephone: 413-205-3426
  Fax: 413-205-3908
Contact: Ann Midura
  Telephone: 413-205-3426
  Fax: 413-205-3908

LEARNING DISABILITY SERVICES

Requests for the following services/accommodations will be evaluated individually based on appropriate and current documentation.

Allowed in Exams
  Calculator: Yes
  Dictionary: No
  Computer: Yes
  Spellchecker: Yes
Extended test time: Yes
Scribes: Yes
Proctors: Yes
Oral exams: Yes
Notetakers: No

Distraction-reduced environment: Yes
Tape recording in class: Yes
Books on tape from RFBD: Yes
Taping of books not from RFBD: Yes
Accommodations for students with ADHD: Yes
Reading machine: Yes
Other assistive technology: No
Priority registration: No

Added costs for services: $1,900 per semester
LD specialists: Yes (10)
Professional tutors: 9
Peer tutors: No
Max. hours/wk. for services: Unlimited
How professors are notified of LD/ADHD: By both student and director

GENERAL ADMISSIONS INFORMATION

Director of Admissions: Peter Miller
Telephone: 413-205-3201

ENTRANCE REQUIREMENTS

15 total are required; 4 English required, 2 math required, 2 science required, 2 foreign language recommended, 1 social studies required, 1 history required, 5 elective required. High school diploma or GED required. Minimum TOEFL is 500. TOEFL required of all international applicants.

Application deadline: Rolling
Notification: Rolling
Average GPA: 2.7

Average SAT I Math: 487
Average SAT I Verbal: 456
Average ACT: NR

Graduated top 10% of class: 9%
Graduated top 25% of class: 22%
Graduated top 50% of class: 67%

COLLEGE GRADUATION REQUIREMENTS

Course waivers allowed: No
Course substitutions allowed: No
In what subjects: Foreign language not required for graduation. May use Pass/Fail option for math.

ADDITIONAL INFORMATION

Environment: The school is located on 58 acres in Springfield, 75 miles west of Boston and 30 miles north of Hartford.

Student Body
  Undergrad enrollment: 1,426
  Female: 53%
  Male: 47%
  Out-of-state: 44%

Cost Information
  Tuition: $13,600
  Room & board: $7,112
Housing Information
  University housing: Yes
  Percent living on campus: 58%

Greek System
  Fraternity: Yes
  Sorority: Yes
  Athletics: NCAA Division II

BOSTON COLLEGE

140 Commonwealth Avenue, Devlin Hall 208, Chestnut Hill, MA 02467
Phone: 617-552-3100 • Fax: 617-552-0798
E-mail: ugadmis@bc.edu • Web: www.bc.edu
Support level: CS • Institution type: 4-year private

LEARNING DISABILITY PROGRAM AND SERVICES

There is no specific program at Boston College for students with LD. The Academic Development Center (ADC) offers instructional support to faculty and graduate students, special services to students with LD, and tutoring and skills workshops to all Boston College students. The ADC provides academic support to more that 250 BC students with LD. The ADC aims to help students with LD to become independent learners who understand their abilities and disabilities and can act effectively as self-advocates. The ADC also offers free tutoring to all students at BC. All tutors receive training and must be recommended or approved by the Chair of the Department for which the student will tutor. Students who are seeking support services are required to submit documentation to verify eligibility. Testing must be current, comprehensive, performed by a certified LD specialist or licensed psychologist, and there must be clear and specific evidence of an LD. Educational recommendations regarding the impact of the disability and accommodations recommended at the post-secondary level must be included. Documentation for ADHD must include an in-depth evaluation from the psychiatrist/psychologist/physician who made the diagnosis as well as specific educational recommendations.

LD/ADHD ADMISSIONS INFORMATION

College entrance tests required: Yes
Nonstandardized tests accepted: Yes
Interview required: No
Essay required: Yes
Documentation required for LD: Psychoeducational evaluation: within 3 years
Documentation required for ADHD: Yes
Documentation submitted to: Disability Services—after admission
Special Ed. HS course work accepted: No

Specific course requirements for all applicants: Yes
Separate application required for services: No
# of LD applications submitted yearly: N/A
# of LD applications accepted yearly: N/A
Total # of students receiving LD/ADHD services: 325
Acceptance into program means acceptance into college: Students must be admitted and enrolled and then request services

ADMISSIONS

Students with LD who self-disclose during the admission process may receive a second review by the Committee on Learning Disabilities. Some students may be given the option of a summer admit into a Transition Program the summer prior to freshman year. General admission requirements for BC are very competitive. The middle 50 percent for the SAT I is 1230–1370. SAT II: Subject Tests are required in writing, math and one additional subject. It is recommended that students have 4 years of English, 4 years of foreign language, 4 years of math, 3 years of science, and 3 years of social studies. All students must submit an essay and interviews are recommended. Students with LD who may be deficient in foreign language or math should provide documentation and request a substitution for these courses. Documentation of the LD should be sent to the Office of Admission. Students are encouraged to self-disclose during the admission process.

ADDITIONAL INFORMATION

Services offered by the Academic Development Center include a "Summer Transition Program" for entering freshmen students with LD; screening sessions for students who may have LD; individual consultations with a learning specialist; letters to faculty confirming and explaining the LD; reduced course load during the academic year combined with summer school; access to textbooks on tape; testing in a distraction-reduced room; workshops on study skills and time management; and small group seminars on learning strategies.

SUPPORT SERVICES CONTACT INFORMATION

Learning Disability Program/Services: Disability Services
Director: Dr. Kathleen Duggan
  E-mail: kathleen.duggan@bc.edu
  Telephone: 617-552-8055
  Fax: 617-552-6075
Contact: Same

LEARNING DISABILITY SERVICES

Requests for the following services/accommodations will be evaluated individually based on appropriate and current documentation.

Allowed in Exams
  Calculator: N/A
  Dictionary: N/A
  Computer: Yes
  Spellchecker: Yes
Extended test time: Yes
Scribes: N/A
Proctors: Yes
Oral exams: N/A
Notetakers: Yes

Distraction-reduced environment: Yes
Tape recording in class: Yes
Books on tape from RFBD: Yes
Taping of books not from RFBD: No
Accommodations for students with
  ADHD: Yes
Reading machine: Yes
Other assistive technology: No
Priority registration: Yes

Added costs for services: No
LD specialists: Yes (1)
Professional tutors: No
Peer tutors: 75
Max. hours/wk. for services: N/A
How professors are notified of
  LD/ADHD: By student

GENERAL ADMISSIONS INFORMATION

Director of Admissions: John Mahoney
Telephone: 617-552-3100

ENTRANCE REQUIREMENTS
20 total are recommended; 4 English recommended, 4 math recommended, 3 science recommended, 3 science lab recommended, 4 foreign language recommended, 2 social studies recommended. High school diploma or GED required. Minimum TOEFL is 550. TOEFL required of all international applicants.

Application deadline: January 15
Notification: April 15
Average GPA: NR

Average SAT I Math: 610–690
Average SAT I Verbal: 590–680
Average ACT: NR

Graduated top 10% of class: 62%
Graduated top 25% of class: 91%
Graduated top 50% of class: 100%

COLLEGE GRADUATION REQUIREMENTS

Course waivers allowed: Yes
Course substitutions allowed: Yes
In what subjects: Case-by-case basis

ADDITIONAL INFORMATION

Environment: Located six miles from Boston.

Student Body
  Undergrad enrollment: 9,190
  Female: 53%
  Male: 47%
  Out-of-state: 73%

Cost Information
  Tuition: $24,000
  Room & board: $8,500
Housing Information
  University housing: Yes
  Percent living on campus: 76%

Greek System
  Fraternity: No
  Sorority: No
Athletics: NCAA Division I

BOSTON UNIVERSITY

121 Bay State Road, Boston, MA 02215
Phone: 617-353-2300 • Fax: 617-353-9695
E-mail: admissions@bu.edu • Web: www.bu.edu
Support level: CS • Institution type: 4-year private

LEARNING DISABILITY PROGRAM AND SERVICES

Boston University recognizes that many students with a learning disability, attention disorder, or a mental disability can succeed in a university if they are provided with support services and appropriate accommodations. The Office of Disability Services, including its division of Learning Disability Support Services (LDSS), is committed to assisting individuals with disabilities in achieving fulfillment and success in all aspects of University life. As part of the Office of the Vice President and Dean of Students, the primary objective of LDSS is to foster academic excellence, personal responsibility, and leadership growth in students with disabilities through vigorous programming and the provision of reasonable accommodation services. LDSS seeks to further this commitment through the promotion of independence and self-advocacy in students with LD, ADHD, or other cognitive disabilities. The University does not waive program requirements or permit substitutions for required courses. Several degree programs have foreign language or mathematics requirements. The University considers these degree requirements essential to its programs.

LD/ADHD ADMISSIONS INFORMATION

College entrance tests required: Yes
Nonstandardized tests accepted: Yes
Interview required: No
Essay required: Yes
Documentation required for LD: Psychoeducational
   evaluation: within 3 years
Documentation required for ADHD: Yes
Documentation submitted to: LD Services—after admission
Special Ed. HS course work accepted: No

Specific course requirements for all applicants: Yes
Separate application required for services: No
# of LD applications submitted yearly: N/A
# of LD applications accepted yearly: N/A
Total # of students receiving LD/ADHD services: 550+
**Acceptance into program means acceptance into
   college:** Students must be admitted and enrolled at the
   University and then may request to be considered for
   services.

ADMISSIONS

All admissions decisions are made on an individualized basis by the Office of Undergraduate Admissions. Because requirements may vary substantially depending upon the College or program within the University, students are encouraged to contact BU for information regarding admissions requirements. BU expects that students with disabilities, including those with LD, will meet the same competitive admissions criteria as their peers without disabilities. Thus, there are no special admissions procedures for applicants with LD. The Office of Disability Services does not participate in any way in the application process or in admissions decisions.

ADDITIONAL INFORMATION

LDSS offers support services to students with LD/ ADHD including access to academic accommodations for which the student is eligible, counseling and support in self-advocacy, assistive technology, and LDSS skills workshops for academic and study strategies, note-taking, time management, and self-advocacy. Students are active in the accommodation process, and notify faculty about the implementation of approved accommodations. Students needing more extensive support may enroll in LDSS's Comprehensive Services, a fee-based program offering one-to-one strategy tutoring with a professional learning specialist. Tutoring covers writing development, critical reading, note-taking, study skills, testing strategies, time management, and organization. Tutoring is tailored to individual learning profile of strengths and weaknesses, academic program, other resources, and personal goals. Comprehensive Services strategy plan is designed in collaboration with the student, the learning specialist, and LDSS professional staff. Students must submit the results of a WAIS-R evaluation done within the past three years, including subtest scores and achievement battery. An on-campus interview is required. Applicants must also submit the regular Bradford application form; two recommendations, including one from a learning specialist with whom the student has worked closely; an original essay, a graded essay submitted as course work, including the teacher's comments; and standardized diagnostic reading results documenting the reading grade level and comprehension level. ACT/SAT scores are not required for students with learning disabilities. General admissions require a 2.0 GPA, 4 years English, 4 years math, 1 year lab science, and 1 year social studies.

SUPPORT SERVICES CONTACT INFORMATION

Learning Disability Program/Services: Learning Disability Services (LDS)
Director: Alan Mawrdy, Agency Director
  E-mail: ltg@bu.edu
  Telephone: 617-353-3658
  Fax: 617-353-9646
Contact: Leanne Goldman, LDS Coordinator
  E-mail: ltg@bu.edu
  Telephone: 617-353-3658
  Fax: 617-353-9446

LEARNING DISABILITY SERVICES

Requests for the following services/accommodations will be evaluated individually based on appropriate and current documentation.

Allowed in Exams	**Distraction-reduced environment:** Yes	**Added costs for services:** $1,660 per
Calculator: Yes	**Tape recording in class:** Yes	semester
Dictionary: No	**Books on tape from RFBD:** Yes	**LD specialists:** Yes (8)
Computer: Yes	**Taping of books not from RFBD:** Yes	**Professional tutors:** 8
Spellchecker: Yes	**Accommodations for students with**	**Peer tutors:** No
Extended test time: Yes	**ADHD:** Yes	**Max. hours/wk. for services:** 2
Scribes: Yes	**Reading machine:** Yes	**How professors are notified of**
Proctors: Yes	**Other assistive technology:** Yes	**LD/ADHD:** By student
Oral exams: Yes	**Priority registration:** No	
Notetakers: Yes		

GENERAL ADMISSIONS INFORMATION

Director of Admissions: Kelly Walter
Telephone: 617-353-2300

ENTRANCE REQUIREMENTS

15 total are required; 20 total are recommended; 4 English required, 4 English recommended, 3 math required, 4 math recommended, 3 science required, 4 science recommended, 3 science lab required, 4 science lab recommended, 2 foreign language required, 4 foreign language recommended. High school diploma or GED required. Minimum TOEFL is 215. TOEFL required of all international applicants.

Application deadline: January 1	**Average SAT I Math:** 640	**Graduated top 10% of class:** 57%
Notification: Mid-March thru mid-April	**Average SAT I Verbal:** 636	**Graduated top 25% of class:** 93%
Average GPA: 3.5	**Average ACT:** 28	**Graduated top 50% of class:** 99%

COLLEGE GRADUATION REQUIREMENTS

Course waivers allowed: No
Course substitutions allowed: No
In what subjects: N/A

ADDITIONAL INFORMATION

Environment: The University is located on a 131-acre campus in an urban area.

Student Body	**Cost Information**	**Greek System**
Undergrad enrollment: 17,819	Tuition: $25,872	Fraternity: Yes
Female: 59%	Room & board: $8,750	Sorority: Yes
Male: 41%	**Housing Information**	Athletics: NCAA Division I
Out-of-state: 75%	University housing: Yes	
	Percent living on campus: 66%	

CLARK UNIVERSITY

950 Main Street, Worcester, MA 01610
Phone: 508-793-7431 • Fax: 508-793-8821
E-mail: admissions@clarku.edu • Web: www.clarku.edu
Support level: CS • Institution type: 4-year private

LEARNING DISABILITY PROGRAM AND SERVICES

The learning disabilities services at Clark University, based within the Academic Advising Center, were developed to advocate and support the needs of the student with learning disabilities in a college environment. Strategies are developed to help the student with learning disabilities cope with the increased demands of the College curriculum. Resources are available to students who experience difficulties, and who may require some support or wish to learn more about their own learning styles. Support services in the AAC are coordinated with services offered by the University's Writing Center, Math Clinic, and Dean of Students. The most successful students are the ones who accept their disability, develop good self-advocacy skills, and are capable of good time management. The ultimate goal of Special Services is to help students improve their self-awareness and self-advocacy skills, and to assist them in being successful and independent in college.

LD/ADHD ADMISSIONS INFORMATION

College entrance tests required: Yes
Nonstandardized tests accepted: Yes
Interview required: NR
Essay required: No
Documentation required for LD: Psychoeducational evaluation
Documentation required for ADHD: Yes
Documentation submitted to: Academic Advising
Special Ed. HS course work accepted: Yes, individual basis

Specific course requirements for all applicants: Yes
Separate application required for services: Yes
# of LD applications submitted yearly: 150
# of LD applications accepted yearly: 70
Total # of students receiving LD/ADHD services: 150
Acceptance into program means acceptance into college: Students must be accepted and enrolled at the University first and then may request services.

ADMISSIONS

Special Services and the Office of Undergraduate Admissions work together in considering students for admission. Admission is based on ability, rather than disability. Applicants must meet standard admissions requirements. An interview with Clark's Special Services Office is highly recommended. If a student requires any classroom accommodations or support services, a diagnostic assessment completed within the last two years must be submitted, documenting the learning disability. This documentation is needed to evaluate the applicant's needs and determine what services the University can provide. The University looks at a student's upward trend in high school, as well as the challenge of the curriculum and the number of mainstream courses. Some special education courses in freshman year may be allowed if they have been followed by a college-prep curriculum during the rest of high school. The Director of Special Services makes a recommendation to Admissions about the applicant, but the final decision rests with the Office of Admission.

ADDITIONAL INFORMATION

An early orientation program two days prior to general orientation is designed to meet the needs of entering students with LD. This program is highly recommended as it provides intensive exposure to academic services on campus. Students take a reading comprehension and writing exam, and results are used to match students to the most appropriate academic program. Graduate students work with students on time management and organizational skills. Although note-takers are available, Special Services supplements with taping of lectures, and highly recommends that students use a cassette recorder with a count. It is also recommended that freshmen students take only three courses for the first semester. All students must complete one math course in basic algebra prior to graduating. The overall GPA of freshmen receiving services from Special Services is a 2.7. Clark offers space to an outside LD specialist who will provide tutoring and services for a fee. Services and accommodations are available to undergrads and graduates.

SUPPORT SERVICES CONTACT INFORMATION

Learning Disability Program/Services: Academic Advising
Director: Alan Bieri
  E-mail: abieri@clark.edu
  Telephone: 508-793-7468
  Fax: 508-421-3700
Contact: Maria Furtado
  E-mail: mfurtado@clarku.edu
  Telephone: 508-793-7431

LEARNING DISABILITY SERVICES

Requests for the following services/accommodations will be evaluated individually based on appropriate and current documentation.

Allowed in Exams
  Calculator: Yes
  Dictionary: Yes
  Computer: Yes
  Spellchecker: Yes
Extended test time: Yes
Scribes: Yes
Proctors: Yes
Oral exams: Yes
Notetakers: Y/N

Distraction-reduced environment: Yes
Tape recording in class: Yes
Books on tape from RFBD: Yes
Taping of books not from RFBD: Yes
Accommodations for students with
  ADHD: Yes
Reading machine: No
Other assistive technology: No
Priority registration: Yes

Added costs for services: No
LD specialists: Yes
Professional tutors: Yes
Peer tutors: Yes
Max. hours/wk. for services: Unlimited
How professors are notified of
  LD/ADHD: By student with letter

GENERAL ADMISSIONS INFORMATION

Director of Admissions: Maria Furtado
Telephone: 508-793-7431

ENTRANCE REQUIREMENTS
16 total are recommended; 4 English recommended, 3 math recommended, 3 science recommended, 2 science lab recommended, 2 foreign language recommended, 2 social studies recommended, 2 history recommended. High school diploma or GED required. Minimum TOEFL is 550. TOEFL required of all international applicants.

Application deadline: February 1
Notification: April 1
Average GPA: 3.3

Average SAT I Math: 584
Average SAT I Verbal: 590
Average ACT: 25

Graduated top 10% of class: 29%
Graduated top 25% of class: 63%
Graduated top 50% of class: 95%

COLLEGE GRADUATION REQUIREMENTS

Course waivers allowed: No
Course substitutions allowed: Yes
In what subjects: Foreign language with appropriate documentation

ADDITIONAL INFORMATION

Environment: The University is located on 45 acres in a small city 38 miles west of Boston.

Student Body
  Undergrad enrollment: 1,878
  Female: 60%
  Male: 40%
  Out-of-state: 60%

Cost Information
  Tuition: $24,400
  Room & board: $4,550
Housing Information
  University housing: Yes
  Percent living on campus: 71%

Greek System
  Fraternity: Yes
  Sorority: Yes
Athletics: NCAA Division III

CURRY COLLEGE

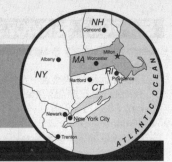

1071 Blue Hill Avenue, Milton, MA 02186
Phone: 617-333-2210 • Fax: 617-333-2114
E-mail: curryadm@curry.edu • Web: www.curry.edu
Support level: SP • Institution type: 4-year private

LEARNING DISABILITY PROGRAM AND SERVICES

The Program for Advancement of Learning (PAL) at Curry College is a comprehensive individualized program for students with specific learning disabilities. Students in PAL participate fully in Curry College course work and extracurricular activities. The goal of PAL is to facilitate students' understanding of their individual learning styles and to help them achieve independence as learners. Students' enpowerment is developed via intensive study of their own strengths, needs, and learning styles. PAL is a place where students are honored for the strengths and talents they bring to the learning process and are given the chance to demonstrate their abilities. PAL students are leaders on campus. PAL summer program is a three-week course that is strongly recommended for new students to ease the transition and provide excellent preparation.

LD/ADHD ADMISSIONS INFORMATION

College entrance tests required: Yes
Nonstandardized tests accepted: Yes
Interview required: Yes
Essay required: Yes
Documentation required for LD: Psychoeducational evaluation
Documentation required for ADHD: Yes
Documentation submitted to: PAL Program
Special Ed. HS course work accepted: Varies

Specific course requirements for all applicants: Yes
Separate application required for services: Yes
# of LD applications submitted yearly: 600
# of LD applications accepted yearly: 300
Total # of students receiving LD/ADHD services: 400
Acceptance into program means acceptance into college: The admission decision is made jointly by PAL and the Office of Admission.

ADMISSIONS

Applicants must submit the regular application, fee, official transcript, SAT or ACT (recommended), and counselor or teacher recommendation. For admission into the Program for Advancement in Learning the following needs to be submitted: diagnostic evaluations and other material which describe a specific learning disability; testing that includes the WAIS-III or WAIS-R accompanied by a narrative report, administered within two years of application; achievement testing indicating current levels in areas such as reading, written language, and math. An IEP (Individualized Educational Plan) or its equivalent is requested, if available. Interviews on campus are strongly recommended, and may be required of some applicants. Space is limited for the program.

ADDITIONAL INFORMATION

PAL students must commit to the program for at least one year, and have the option to continue with full or partial support beyond the first year. A three-week, three-credit summer PAL orientation session is strongly recommended. Students meet regularly with their own PAL instructor who is a learning specialist. The focus is on using strengths to improve skills in areas such as listening, speaking, reading, writing, organization and time management, note-taking, and test-taking skills. Students also receive help with readings, papers, and assignments for classes as the basis for learning about their unique learning style. The specialist reviews diagnostic testing to help the student understand the profile of strengths and needs. Students earn three credits toward graduation for the first year. Skills classes, for credit, are offered through the Essential Skills Center in developmental reading, writing, and math. Other special offerings include the following: diagnostic testing is available through the Educational Diagnostic Center at PAL.

SUPPORT SERVICES CONTACT INFORMATION

Learning Disability Program/Services: Program for Advancement of Learning (PAL)
Director: Dr. Lisa Ijiri
  Telephone: 617-333-2250
Contact: Susan Pratt, Coordinator
  E-mail: curryadm@curry.edu
  Telephone: 617-333-2250

LEARNING DISABILITY SERVICES

Requests for the following services/accommodations will be evaluated individually based on appropriate and current documentation.

Allowed in Exams
  Calculator: Y/N
  Dictionary: Y/N
  Computer: Y/N
  Spellchecker: Y/N
Extended test time: Yes
Scribes: No
Proctors: Yes
Oral exams: Y/N
Notetakers: Y/N

Distraction-reduced environment: Yes
Tape recording in class: Yes
Books on tape from RFBD: Yes
Taping of books not from RFBD: Yes
Accommodations for students with
  ADHD: Yes
Reading machine: Yes
Other assistive technology: Yes
Priority registration: No

Added costs for services: $2,000
  per year part time; $3,720 per
  year full time
LD specialists: Yes (28)
Professional tutors: Yes
Peer tutors: Yes
Max. hours/wk. for services: 2.5
  hours in PAL/Essential Skills
  Center is drop-in
How professors are notified of
  LD/ADHD: By the student

GENERAL ADMISSIONS INFORMATION

Director of Admissions: Micheal Poll
Telephone: 617-333-0500

ENTRANCE REQUIREMENTS
16 total are required; 4 English required, 3 math required, 2 science required, 2 science lab required, 1 social studies required, 1 history required, 5 elective required. High school diploma or GED required. Minimum TOEFL is 500. TOEFL required of all international applicants.

Application deadline: March 1
Notification: Rolling beginning 1/15
Average GPA: 2.3

Average SAT I Math: 420
Average SAT I Verbal: 440
Average ACT: NR

Graduated top 10% of class: 5%
Graduated top 25% of class: 22%
Graduated top 50% of class: 65%

COLLEGE GRADUATION REQUIREMENTS

Course waivers allowed: No
Course substitutions allowed: Yes
In what subjects: Varies

ADDITIONAL INFORMATION

Environment: Curry's 120-acre campus is minutes from metropolitan Boston.

Student Body
  Undergrad enrollment: 2,082
  Female: 53%
  Male: 47%
  Out-of-state: 40%

Cost Information
  Tuition: $17,160
  Room & board: $6,870
Housing Information
  University housing: Yes
  Percent living on campus: 60%

Greek System
  Fraternity: Yes
  Sorority: Yes
Athletics: NCAA Division III

DEAN COLLEGE

99 Main Street, Franklin, MA 02038
Phone: 508-541-8726 • Fax: 508-541-8726
E-mail: admissions@dean.edu • Web: www.dean.edu
Support: CS • Institution: 2-year private

LEARNING DISABILITY PROGRAM AND SERVICES

Dean College faculty and staff are committed to maintaining a caring and nurturing environment. While much of this support comes in the form of informal, face-to-face interactions, students will find that a number of programs have been developed specifically to provide students with structured guidance in both academics and student life. The Learning Center offers student academic support and assistance through the Berenson Writing Center, the Math Tutoring Program, Disability Support Services, and course-specific tutoring. Personalized Learning Services offers a comprehensive system of support for students with documented learning disabilities. Learning specialists work with students to develop customized programs that address both short-term and the skills and knowledge that create a foundation for success in future academic and professional settings. The goal of PLS is to assist students in becoming confident, successful, independent learners. This program is designed to help all students achieve their academic goals. The FACTS Advising Center (Financial, Academic, Career, Transfer, and Student life) provides comprehensive assistance and information to students. Students are assigned a personal advising team to guide them as they move through the academic year.

LD/ADHD ADMISSIONS INFORMATION

College entrance tests required: Yes	**Specific course requirements for all applicants:** No
Nonstandardized tests accepted: Yes	**Separate application required for services:** No
Interview required: Recommended	**# of LD applications submitted yearly:** N/A
Essay required: Yes	**# of LD applications accepted yearly:** N/A
Documentation required for LD: WAIS-III; WJ	**Total # of students receiving LD/ADHD services:** 70
Documentation required for ADHD: Yes	**Acceptance into program means acceptance into**
Submitted to: Disability Support Services	**college:** Students must be admitted and enrolled first
Special Ed. HS course work accepted: Yes	and then may request LD services.

ADMISSIONS

There is no special admission process for students with learning disabilities. All students submit the same general application. Every application is carefully reviewed by Admissions and students are selected based on their academic performance in high school, recommendations, and personal accomplishments. Students who self-disclose and submit documentation may have their materials reviewed by the LD specialist, who will make a recommendation to Admissions. There is no simple formula applied to an application. Dean strives to make the best match between what it offers as an institution and each student's skills, interests, and abilities. Interviews are highly recommeded. Students should have college-prep, including 4 years English and 3 years math. Interviews are not required but students must submit a counselor recommendation. SAT/ACT are required, but viewed as less important than school record. Students who do not meet the general admission requirements may be considered for conditional admission through successful completion of the Summer Bridge Program.

ADDITIONAL INFORMATION

Accommodations may include, but are not limited to, taped texts, access to computers, scribes and note-takers, alternative testing modes, and extended time for testing. The Learning Center provides free academic assistance and support services for all students through tutoring, workshops, and study groups. Professional and peer tutors are available throughout the day to assist students in developing writing, math, and study skills, and to provide course-specific tutoring. Personalized Learning Services offers tutorial support to students with documented LD, unique learning styles, or other diagnosed learning needs. Students meet weekly with LD specialist one-to-one or in small groups. Learning and study strategies taught by specialist include test-taking; test preparation; note-taking skills; time management; academic organization; reading comprehension; research and writing skills; and self-awareness and advocacy. The fee is $700–$3,500 per semester.

SUPPORT SERVICES CONTACT INFORMATION

Learning Disability Program/Services: Disability Support Services
Director: Paul Hastings
  E-mail: phastings@dean.edu
  Telephone: 508-541-1764
  Fax: 508-541-1918
Contact: Same

LEARNING DISABILITY SERVICES

Requests for the following services/accommodations will be evaluated individually based on appropriate and current documentation.

Allowed in Exams
  Calculator: Yes
  Dictionary: Yes
  Computer: Yes
  Spellchecker: Yes
Extended test time: Yes
Scribes: Yes
Proctors: Yes
Oral exams: Yes
Notetakers: Yes

Distraction-reduced environment: Yes
Tape recording in class: Yes
Books on tape from RFBD: Yes
Taping of books not from RFBD: Yes
**Accommodations for students with
  ADHD:** Yes
Reading machine: Yes
Other assistive technology: Yes
Priority registration: No

Added costs for services:
  $700–$3,500
LD specialists: 5
Professional tutors: 20
Peer tutors: 15
Max. hours/wk. for services: 5 hours
  per week
**How professors are notified of
  LD/ADHD:** By student

GENERAL ADMISSIONS INFORMATION

Director of Admissions: Kathleen Lynch, Dean
Telephone: 508-541-1547

ENTRANCE REQUIREMENTS
Essay required. Recommendations are helpful. Minimum 2.0 GPA required. Interview helpful. SAT/ACT required.

Application deadline: Rolling
Notification: Rolling
Average GPA: 2.0

Average SAT I Math: 450
Average SAT I Verbal: 450
Average ACT: NR

Graduated top 10% of class: NR
Graduated top 25% of class: NR
Graduated top 50% of class: NR

COLLEGE GRADUATION REQUIREMENTS

Course waivers allowed: No
Course substitutions allowed: No
In what subjects: N/A

ADDITIONAL INFORMATION

Environment: The campus is in a small town near Boston.

Student Body
  Undergrad enrollment: 850
  Female: 45%
  Male: 55%
  Out-of-state: 57%

Cost Information
  Tuition: $16,220
  Room & board: $7,920
Housing Information
  University housing: Yes
  Percent living on campus: 90%

Greek System
  Fraternity: No
  Sorority: No
Athletics: NJCAA

MOUNT IDA COLLEGE

777 Dedham Street, Newton, MA 02159
Phone: 617-928-4535 • Fax: 617-928-4507
E-mail: micadmsn@tiac.net • Web: www.mountida.edu
Support level: CS • Institution type: 4-year private

LEARNING DISABILITY PROGRAM AND SERVICES

Learning Opportunities Program (LOP) and Horizon Program provide additional academic support for students with LD. The programs focus on developing and strengthening individual learning styles that create successful, independent learning. Students are mainstreamed in a regular degree curriculum. Mount Ida goes the extra mile for all its students and the LOP is a natural extension of this philosophy. Students discover a supportive environment where a positive, successful experience is the goal. An important component of the LOP is the mentoring relationship with individual learning specialists. The Horizon program offers maximum academic support for a more gradual transition to college for students who have experienced academic challenges. It provides the support to help students transition from a structured high school environment to a more independent college experience. Students have all of the LOP services plus a half-hour of additional coaching, a reduced course load, supplemental support class, and appropriate accommodations.

LD/ADHD ADMISSIONS INFORMATION

College entrance tests required: Yes, for BA degree
Nonstandardized tests accepted: Yes
Interview required: As needed
Essay required: Optional
Documentation required for LD: WAIS-III
Documentation required for ADHD: Yes
Documentation submitted to: LOP
Special Ed. HS course work accepted: Yes

Specific course requirements for all applicants: No
Separate application required for services: Yes
# of LD applications submitted yearly: NR
# of LD applications accepted yearly: NR
Total # of students receiving LD/ADHD services: 100
Acceptance into program means acceptance into college: Students are admitted first to the College and then to the LOP/Horizon Program.

ADMISSIONS
There is no special admissions process for students with learning disabilities. ACT/SAT are required for admission to bachelor degree majors. An interview is strongly recommended. Students with disabilities should submit the WAIS-III, a test indicating appropriate reading grade level, and evaluative documentation of the learning disability.

ADDITIONAL INFORMATION
In the Learning Skills Laboratory students have an opportunity to work with Mount Ida faculty and students to improve study skills. Tutoring provided by professional tutors who are learning specialists is available two to three times per week. Each tutoring session is private and strategy based. These meetings focus on developing self-advocacy skills and independent learning skills. Other services include reduced course load, enrollment in Basic English, if needed, extended-time testing, notetaking, diagnostic testing, course substitutions, and counseling. Study skills courses in math and English are available. Additional support and content tutoring are offered in the Academic Success Center. The College also runs a Freshman Experience course that focuses on building the skills necessary to facilitate student success. Students work to identify and strengthen their individual learning styles.

SUPPORT SERVICES CONTACT INFORMATION

Learning Disability Program/Services: Learning Opportunities Program (LOP) and Horizon Program
Director: Jill Mehler
  Telephone: 617-928-4648
  Fax: 617-928-4507
Contact: Same

LEARNING DISABILITY SERVICES

Requests for the following services/accommodations will be evaluated individually based on appropriate and current documentation.

Allowed in Exams
  Calculator: Yes
  Dictionary: Yes
  Computer: No
  Spellchecker: Yes
Extended test time: Yes
Scribes: No
Proctors: No
Oral exams: Yes
Notetakers: Yes

Distraction-reduced environment: Yes
Tape recording in class: Yes
Books on tape from RFBD: Yes
Taping of books not from RFBD: Yes
Accommodations for students with ADHD: Yes
Reading machine: No
Other assistive technology: No
Priority registration: Yes

Added costs for services: $2,840 for LOP or Horizon
LD specialists: Yes (10)
Professional tutors: Yes
Peer tutors: Yes
Max. hours/wk. for services: 4
How professors are notified of LD/ADHD: By student and program director

GENERAL ADMISSIONS INFORMATION

Director of Admissions: Judy Kaufman, Dean of Admission
Telephone: 617-928-4535

ENTRANCE REQUIREMENTS
Minimum TOEFL is 425. TOEFL required of all international applicants.

Application deadline: Rolling beginning 10/1
Notification: Rolling beginning 3/1
Average GPA: 2.0–2.9

Average SAT I Math: NR
Average SAT I Verbal: NR
Average ACT: NR

Graduated top 10% of class: NR
Graduated top 25% of class: NR
Graduated top 50% of class: NR

COLLEGE GRADUATION REQUIREMENTS

Course waivers allowed: Yes
Course substitutions allowed: Yes
In what subjects: Varies based on the major and the learning-style issues

ADDITIONAL INFORMATION

Environment: Mount Ida's 85-acre campus is in a suburban neighborhood 8 miles west of Boston.

Student Body
  Undergrad enrollment: 1,200
  Female: 51%
  Male: 49%
  Out-of-state: 40%

Cost Information
  Tuition: $15,830
  Room & board: $8,950
Housing Information
  University housing: Yes
  Percent living on campus: 60%

Greek System
  Fraternity: No
  Sorority: No
Athletics: NCAA Division III

NORTHEASTERN UNIVERSITY

360 Huntington Avenue, 150 Richards Hall, Boston, MA 02115
Phone: 617-373-2200 • Fax: 617-373-8780
E-mail: admissions@neu.edu • Web: www.neu.edu
Support level: SP • Institution type: 4-year private

LEARNING DISABILITY PROGRAM AND SERVICES

The Disability Resource Center offers ongoing support and counseling services, academic advising, student advocacy, and help with course and exam modifications for students with LD. Students who apply must have the LD documented through a recent evaluation and the willingness to use the resources and services of the program. DRC serves students who have a wide range of learning problems, including specific reading or spelling disabilities, math disabilities, problems with organization, or difficulty maintaining attention. Students work on one-to-one basis and in small groups with a lerning disabilities specialist. There is no charge for basic support services. Persons with LD who need intensive support may be interested in the independent highly structured LD Program. Students meet with a psychologist and LD specialist who act as primary advisors to explore learning strengths and weaknesses and develop specific goals for each quarter. On the basis of individual need, each student receives 3–5 hours of one-on-one tutoring weekly. Program tutors maintain regular contact with instructors to monitor student progress. This privately sponsored program, only for students with LD, has an additional cost of $1,400 per quarter.

LD/ADHD ADMISSIONS INFORMATION

College entrance tests required: Yes
Nonstandardized tests accepted: Yes
Interview required: No
Essay required: Yes
Documentation required for LD: WAIS-III or WISC-R; psychoeducational evaluations: within 3 years
Documentation required for ADHD: Yes
Documentation submitted to: DRC
Special Ed. HS course work accepted: Decided by director of program

Specific course requirements for all applicants: Yes
Separate application required for services: N/A
# of LD applications submitted yearly: 50
# of LD applications accepted yearly: 12
Total # of students receiving LD/ADHD services: 300
Acceptance into program means acceptance into college: Students must be accepted and enrolled at the University first and then may request LD services from DRC or admission to the LD Program.

ADMISSIONS

There are two separate application processes involved in admission to Northeastern. Admission requirements to the University are the same for all students and any student may be eligible for help in the Disability Resource Center. General applicants have a 3.0 GPA and an average SAT of 1150. Depending on the program, courses, and diagnosis of the student's learning disability, courses may be substituted for admission. Students apply to the program after admission to the University. There is a separate application and interview needed for the Learning Disability Program, which is the independent program. Students must take a full 6–10 hour battery of tests for this program, and must also submit previous diagnostic tests. These students must have an interview. Notification of acceptance is sent from the Office of Admission.

ADDITIONAL INFORMATION

DRC services include note-taking services; readers and scribes; academic advice related to the disability; liaison and advocacy services; counseling and referral services; support groups; and Basic Skills courses taught by LD specialists in time management, learning strategies, study strategies, social skills, and perceptual skills. The LD program provides more intensive services including one-on-one tutoring 3–5 hours per week and close monitoring of the student's progress. There are currently 35 students enrolled in the program and there are always students waiting to be admitted (only a few new students are admitted yearly). The cost per term is $1,400. Documentation must address attention, perception, motor abilities, language, memory, processing speed, organization, emotional factors, and general intellectual and academic functioning. Services and accommodations are available for undergraduate and graduate students.

SUPPORT SERVICES CONTACT INFORMATION

Learning Disability Program/Services: Disability Resource Program (DRC)
Director: Dean Ruth Bork
   Telephone: 617-373-2675
   Fax: 617-373-7800
Contact: Debbie Auerbach
   Telephone: 617-373-2675
   Fax: 617-373-7800

LEARNING DISABILITY SERVICES

Requests for the following services/accommodations will be evaluated individually based on appropriate and current documentation.

Allowed in Exams
   Calculator: Yes
   Dictionary: Yes
   Computer: Yes
   Spellchecker: Yes
Extended test time: Yes
Scribes: Yes
Proctors: Yes
Oral exams: Yes
Notetakers: Yes

Distraction-reduced environment: Yes
Tape recording in class: Yes
Books on tape from RFBD: Yes
Taping of books not from RFBD: No
**Accommodations for students with
   ADHD:** Yes
Reading machine: Yes
Other assistive technology: Yes
Priority registration: No

Added costs for services: $1,400
   per quarter for the LD program
LD specialists: Yes (5)
Professional tutors: Yes
Peer tutors: Yes
Max. hours/wk. for services: Unlimited
**How professors are notified of
   LD/ADHD:** By student

GENERAL ADMISSIONS INFORMATION

Director of Admissions: Ronnie Patrick
Telephone: 617-373-2200

ENTRANCE REQUIREMENTS
17 total are recommended; 4 English recommended, 3 math recommended, 3 science recommended, 2 science lab recommended, 2 foreign language recommended, 3 social studies recommended, 2 history recommended. High school diploma or GED required. Minimum TOEFL is 550. TOEFL required of all international applicants.

Application deadline: March 1
Notification: Rolling
Average GPA: 3.1

Average SAT I Math: 572
Average SAT I Verbal: 553
Average ACT: 24

Graduated top 10% of class: 18%
Graduated top 25% of class: 51%
Graduated top 50% of class: 86%

COLLEGE GRADUATION REQUIREMENTS

Course waivers allowed: No
Course substitutions allowed: Yes
In what subjects: Foreign language and math

ADDITIONAL INFORMATION

Environment: The school is located on 55 acres in the city of Boston.

Student Body
   Undergrad enrollment: 12,300
   Female: 50%
   Male: 50%
   Out-of-state: 57%

Cost Information
   Tuition: $15,560
   Room & board: $9,135
Housing Information
   University housing: Yes
   Percent living on campus: 65%

Greek System
   Fraternity: Yes
   Sorority: Yes
Athletics: NCAA Division I

PINE MANOR COLLEGE

400 Heath Street, Chestnut Hill, MA 02467-2332
Phone: 617-731-7104 • Fax: 617-731-7199
E-mail: admission@pmc.edu • Web: www.pmc.edu
Support level: CS • Institution type: 2-year and 4-year private

LEARNING DISABILITY PROGRAM AND SERVICES

The Learning Resource Center is an expression of the College's strong commitment to the individual learning experience. The LRC supports and challenges students to realize their maximum academic potential in the way that best suits their individual learning styles. There are five professional tutors, writing tutors, math tutors, learning specialists, and the director, who provide tutoring that is individually tailored to the learning style and needs of the student. The tutoring is not content-oriented, but rather strategy-based and process-oriented. The LRC hopes that students with learning disabilities enter college with some compensatory techniques and study skills. The learning specialists furnish guidance and academic skills assistance to students whose learning disabilities create a gap between their true capacity and daily performance. The LRC serves the whole college population free of charge, whether or not a student has a documented learning disability.

LD/ADHD ADMISSIONS INFORMATION

College entrance tests required: Yes
Nonstandardized tests accepted: Yes
Interview required: No
Essay required: Yes
Documentation required for LD: WAIS-III or WISC-R with all subscores reported; achievement; and/or Woodcock-Johnson
Documentation required for ADHD: Yes
Documentation submitted to: LRC—after admission
Special Ed. HS course work accepted: Yes

Specific course requirements for all applicants: Yes
Separate application required for services: No
# of LD applications submitted yearly: N/A
# of LD applications accepted yearly: 40
Total # of students receiving LD/ADHD services: 20–36
Acceptance into program means acceptance into college: Students must be admitted and enrolled at the College prior to requesting services from the LRC.

ADMISSIONS

All applicants submit the same general application. Although not required, an interview is highly recommended. The average ACT is 19 or SAT 870. Courses required are 4 years English, 3 years math, 2 years science, 4 years social studies. Courses taken in special education are accepted. Admissions decisions are made by the Office of Admissions. However, the director of the LRC assists in interpreting testing and documentation and makes a recommendation to the Office of Admissions. Students are encouraged to self-disclose during the admission process. There is a special Optional Response Form that is used by the LRC after the student is accepted.

ADDITIONAL INFORMATION

LRC staff works with the students on a regular, once or twice a week basis or on a drop-in basis. Students also work closely with their academic advisors. LRC tutors offer diagnosis and remediation for students in academic difficulty; enrichment for successful students; and assistance to faculty and staff. The LRC can also obtain recorded textbooks and arrange for tutors and diagnostic testing. In addition, the following accommodations have proved useful: reduced course load each semester; additional time to complete exams, quizzes, or written assignments; and a separate room for examinations. Basic skills classes are offered in reading, math, learning strategies, written language, study strategies, and time management.

SUPPORT SERVICES CONTACT INFORMATION

Learning Disability Program/Services: Learning Resource Center (LRC)
Director: Mary Walsh
  E-mail: walshmar@pmc.edu
  Telephone: 617-731-7181
  Fax: 617-731-7199
Contact: Same

LEARNING DISABILITY SERVICES

Requests for the following services/accommodations will be evaluated individually based on appropriate and current documentation.

Allowed in Exams
  Calculator: Yes
  Dictionary: Yes
  Computer: Yes
  Spellchecker: Yes
Extended test time: Yes
Scribes: Yes
Proctors: Yes
Oral exams: Yes
Notetakers: Yes

Distraction-reduced environment: Yes
Tape recording in class: Yes
Books on tape from RFBD: Yes
Taping of books not from RFBD: No
Accommodations for students with
  ADHD: Yes
Reading machine: No
Other assistive technology: Yes
Priority registration: No

Added costs for services: $1,400
LD specialists: Yes (1)
Professional tutors: 5
Peer tutors: No
Max. hours/wk. for services:
  Unlimited
How professors are notified of
  LD/ADHD: By both student and
  director

GENERAL ADMISSIONS INFORMATION

Director of Admissions: Bill Nichols
Telephone: 617-731-7104

ENTRANCE REQUIREMENTS
4 English recommended, 3 math recommended, 3 science recommended, 2 foreign language recommended, 2 social studies recommended. High school diploma or GED required. Minimum TOEFL is 475. TOEFL required of all international applicants.

Application deadline: Rolling
Notification: Rolling
Average GPA: 2.5

Average SAT I Math: 420
Average SAT I Verbal: 440
Average ACT: 19

Graduated top 10% of class: 12%
Graduated top 25% of class: 32%
Graduated top 50% of class: 56%

COLLEGE GRADUATION REQUIREMENTS

Course waivers allowed: No
Course substitutions allowed: Yes
In what subjects: Mathematics

ADDITIONAL INFORMATION

Environment: Pine Manor is located on a 79-acre campus in Chestnut Hill, 5 miles west of Boston.

Student Body
  Undergrad enrollment: 306
  Female: 100%
  Male: 0%
  Out-of-state: 98%

Cost Information
  Tuition: $11,440
  Room & board: $7,245
Housing Information
  University housing: Yes
  Percent living on campus: 73%

Greek System
  Fraternity: Yes
  Sorority: Yes
Athletics: NCAA Division III

SMITH COLLEGE

7 College Lane, Northampton, MA 01063
Phone: 413-585-2500 • Fax: 413-585-2527
E-mail: admissions@smith.edu • Web: www.smith.edu
Support level: S • Institution type: 4-year private

LEARNING DISABILITY PROGRAM AND SERVICES

Smith College does not have a formal LD program. However, the College is both philosophically committed and legally required to enable students with documented disabilities to participate in college programs by providing reasonable accommodations for them. The Office of Disabilities Services (ODS) facilitates the provision of services and offers services aimed to eliminate barriers through modification of the program where necessary. A student may voluntarily register with ODS by completing a disability identification form and providing documentation of the disability, after which proper accommodations will be determined. Students with disabilities who need academic services are asked to make their needs known and to file timely request forms each semester with ODS for accommodations in course work. The College cannot make retroactive accommodations. Students are encouraged to tell professors about the accommodations needed. The College is responsible for providing that, within certain limits, students are not denied the opportunity to participate in college programs on the basis of a disability. The College will provide support services to students with appropriate evaluations and documentation. Students should contact the ODS for consultation and advice.

LD/ADHD ADMISSIONS INFORMATION

College entrance tests required: Yes
Nonstandardized tests accepted: Yes
Interview required: Yes
Essay required: Yes
Documentation required for LD: WAIS-III; WRAT; psychoeducational evaluation
Documentation required for ADHD: Yes
Documentation submitted to: ODS—after admission
Special Ed. HS course work accepted: No

Specific course requirements for all applicants: Yes
Separate application required for services: No
# of LD applications submitted yearly: N/A
# of LD applications accepted yearly: N/A
Total # of students receiving LD/ADHD services: Approximately 80
Acceptance into program means acceptance into college: Students must be accepted and enrolled at the College first and then may request services.

ADMISSIONS
There is no special admissions procedure for students with learning disabilities. Tests that evaluate cognitive ability, achievement, and information processing should be included with the regular application. It is also helpful to have a letter from a diagnostician documenting services that will be needed in college. SAT I and three SAT II: Subject Tests are required, or the ACT without SAT II: Subject Tests. Leniency may be granted in regard to a high school's waiving of foreign language requirements due to a learning disability. High school courses recommended are 4 years English composition and literature, 3 years foreign language (or 2 years in each of 2 languages), 3 years math, 2 years science, and 2 years history.

ADDITIONAL INFORMATION
Support services include readers, note-takers, scribes, assistive listening devices, typists, computing software and hardware, books on tape, writing counseling (more and/or longer appointments), peer tutoring, and time management/study skills training. The College will not provide services that create an undue burden for the College.

SUPPORT SERVICES CONTACT INFORMATION

Learning Disability Program/Services: Office of Disability Services (ODS)
Director: Laura Rauscher
 E-mail: lrausche@smith.edu
 Telephone: 413-585-2071
 Fax: 413-585-4498
Contact: Same

LEARNING DISABILITY SERVICES

Requests for the following services/accommodations will be evaluated individually based on appropriate and current documentation.

Allowed in Exams
 Calculator: Yes
 Dictionary: Yes
 Computer: Yes
 Spellchecker: Yes
Extended test time: Yes
Scribes: Yes
Proctors: No
Oral exams: Yes
Notetakers: Yes

Distraction-reduced environment: Yes
Tape recording in class: Yes
Books on tape from RFBD: Yes
Taping of books not from RFBD: Yes
Accommodations for students with
 ADHD: Yes
Reading machine: Yes
Other assistive technology: Yes
Priority registration: Yes

Added costs for services: No
LD specialists: No
Professional tutors: 2
Peer tutors: Yes
Max. hours/wk. for services: Unlimited
How professors are notified of
 LD/ADHD: By student with letter

GENERAL ADMISSIONS INFORMATION

Director of Admissions: Audrey Smith
Telephone: 413-585-2500

ENTRANCE REQUIREMENTS
15 total are recommended; 4 English recommended, 3 math recommended, 3 science recommended, 3 science lab recommended, 3 foreign language recommended, 2 history recommended. SAT I or ACT required; SAT II recommended. High school diploma or equivalent is not required. Minimum TOEFL is 600. TOEFL required of all international applicants.

Application deadline: January 15
Notification: April 1
Average GPA: 3.76

Average SAT I Math: 617
Average SAT I Verbal: 643
Average ACT: 27

Graduated top 10% of class: 59%
Graduated top 25% of class: 90%
Graduated top 50% of class: 99%

COLLEGE GRADUATION REQUIREMENTS

Course waivers allowed: No
Course substitutions allowed: No
In what subjects: Smith has no specific course requirements for graduation, though some majors have requirements.

ADDITIONAL INFORMATION

Environment: The 204-acre campus is located in a small city 85 miles west of Boston and 15 minutes from Amherst.

Student Body
 Undergrad enrollment: 2,630
 Female: 100%
 Male: 0%
 Out-of-state: 78%

Cost Information
 Tuition: $24,550
 Room & board: $8,560
Housing Information
 University housing: Yes
 Percent living on campus: 91%

Greek System
 Fraternity: No
 Sorority: Yes
Athletics: NCAA Division III

SPRINGFIELD COLLEGE

263 Alden Street, Springfield, MA 01109
Phone: 413-748-3136 • Fax: 413-748-3694
E-mail: admissions@spfldcol.edu • Web: www.spfldcol.edu
Support level: CS • Institution type: 4-year private

LEARNING DISABILITY PROGRAM AND SERVICES

Springfield College is committed to providing an equal educational opportunity and full participation in college activities for persons with disabilities. The Office of Student Support Services provides services that ensure that students with disabilities are given an equal educational opportunity and the opportunity for full participation in all college programs and activities. In addition to supporting students with disabilities, Student Support Services works with students who are having academic difficulty. Students can receive services by meeting with the director of Student Support Services to verify eligibility for services, identify student needs, and determine appropriate services and accommodations. To receive services students must provide documentation of their learning disability which is current and comprehensive with specific evidence and identification of a learning disability. Documentation should be no older than three years.

LD/ADHD ADMISSIONS INFORMATION

College entrance tests required: Yes
Nonstandardized tests accepted: Yes
Interview required: No
Essay required: Yes
Documentation required for LD: Any psychoeducational testing: within 3 years
Documentation required for ADHD: Yes
Documentation submitted to: Student Support Services—after admission
Special Ed. HS course work accepted: No

Specific course requirements for all applicants: Yes
Separate application required for services: No
# of LD applications submitted yearly: N/A
# of LD applications accepted yearly: N/A
Total # of students receiving LD/ADHD services: 150-160
Acceptance into program means acceptance into college: Students must be admitted and enrolled at the College and then can be reviewed for services.

ADMISSIONS

There is no special admissions process for students with learning disabilities. All applicants must submit the same general application and meet the same admission criteria. There is no minimum GPA required, although the average GPA is a 3.0. Courses required include 4 years English, 3 years math, 2 years history, and 2–3 years science. Admissions decisions are made by the Office of Admissions.

ADDITIONAL INFORMATION

Services provided through the Office of Student Support Services include taped textbooks; taped lectures; readers; alternative testing; note-takers; tutors; computers with spellcheck; Reading Edge; reduced course loads; study skills and time management; course accommodations; and course selection.

SUPPORT SERVICES CONTACT INFORMATION

Learning Disability Program/Services: Student Support Services
Director: Deb Dickens
  E-mail: ddickens@spfldcol.edu
  Telephone: 413-748-3768
  Fax: 413-748-3937
Contact: Same

LEARNING DISABILITY SERVICES

Requests for the following services/accommodations will be evaluated individually based on appropriate and current documentation.

Allowed in Exams
  Calculator: Yes
  Dictionary: Yes
  Computer: Yes
  Spellchecker: Yes
Extended test time: Yes
Scribes: Yes
Proctors: Yes
Oral exams: Yes
Notetakers: Yes

Distraction-reduced environment: Yes
Tape recording in class: Yes
Books on tape from RFBD: Yes
Taping of books not from RFBD: Yes
Accommodations for students with
  ADHD: Yes
Reading machine: No
Other assistive technology: Yes
Priority registration: No

Added costs for services: No
LD specialists: Yes (1)
Professional tutors: No
Peer tutors: Yes
Max. hours/wk. for services: Unlimited
How professors are notified of
  LD/ADHD: By both student and
  director

GENERAL ADMISSIONS INFORMATION

Director of Admissions: Mary DeAngelo
Telephone: 413-748-3136

ENTRANCE REQUIREMENTS
16 total are required; 4 English recommended, 2 math recommended, 2 science recommended, 2 foreign language recommended, 2 social studies recommended, 4 elective recommended. High school diploma or GED required. Minimum TOEFL is 525. TOEFL required of all international applicants.

Application deadline: April 11
Notification: Rolling
Average GPA: NR

Average SAT I Math: 510
Average SAT I Verbal: 500
Average ACT: NR

Graduated top 10% of class: 14%
Graduated top 25% of class: 35%
Graduated top 50% of class: 76%

COLLEGE GRADUATION REQUIREMENTS

Course waivers allowed: Yes
Course substitutions allowed: Yes
In what subjects: Foreign language

ADDITIONAL INFORMATION

Environment: The campus is in a suburban area about 30 minutes north of Hartford.

Student Body
  Undergrad enrollment: 2,046
  Female: 51%
  Male: 49%
  Out-of-state: 66%

Cost Information
  Tuition: $17,500
  Room & board: $6,050
Housing Information
  University housing: Yes
  Percent living on campus: 85%

Greek System
  Fraternity: Yes
  Sorority: Yes
Athletics: NCAA Division III

Springfield College

Univ. of Massachusetts—Amherst

Office of Undergraduate Admissions, 37 Mather Drive, Amherst, MA 01003
Phone: 413-545-0222 • Fax: 413-545-4312
E-mail: mail@admissions.umass.edu • Web: www.umass.edu
Support level: CS • Institution type: 4-year public

LEARNING DISABILITY PROGRAM AND SERVICES

Learning Disabilities Support Services (LDSS) is a support service for all students with documented LD. Students are eligible for services if they can document their LD with the appropriate diagnostic evidence. To be eligible, all students must provide one or more of the following types of documentation: an individualized educational plan indicating LD from elementary or secondary school; a report from a state-certified assessment center indicating LD; psychoeducational test results to be interpreted in the LDSS. Not all students with learning problems have learning disabilities. Only students with disabilities may be served by LDSS. Students whose predominate disability is a form of ADHD/ADHD are served by the Psychological Disability Services and not LDSS. Each student enrolled in LDSS is assigned a case manager who is a graduate student in education, counseling, or a related field. Case managers have prior relevant professional experience and are supervised by professional staff. Students work with the same case manager for the entire academic year on three objectives: understanding and obtaining accommodations needed; identifying and utilizing resources; and identifying and implementing learning strategies to compensate for the disability. The goal of LDSS is for students to become independent self-advocates by the time they graduate.

LD/ADHD ADMISSIONS INFORMATION

College entrance tests required: Yes
Nonstandardized tests accepted: Yes
Interview required: NR
Essay required: Yes
Documentation required for LD: Psychoeducational evaluation
Documentation required for ADHD: Yes
Documentation submitted to: LDSS—after admission
Special Ed. HS course work accepted: No

Specific course requirements for all applicants: Yes
Separate application required for services: No
# of LD applications submitted yearly: N/A
# of LD applications accepted yearly: N/A
Total # of students receiving LD/ADHD services: 400
Acceptance into program means acceptance into college: Students are admitted and enrolled to the University first and then reviewed for services.

ADMISSIONS

There are no special admissions criteria for students with learning disabilities. General admission requirements recommend that students be in the top 35 percent of their class with 3.0 GPA, SAT 1140, or ACT 24. Course requirements include 4 years English, 3 years math, 3 years social studies, 2 years science, and 2 years foreign language (this can be waived if it is part of the disability). Massachusetts students with learning disabilities do not need to submit ACT/SAT.

ADDITIONAL INFORMATION

Students and case managers prepare Learning Style Sheets for professors that request various accommodations, such as untimed exams, extended time on assignments, alternate form of tests, and note-taking. At mid-semester each professor who received an Accommodation Sheet receives a request from LDSS asking for the student's grades, attendance, and performance. There is individual tutoring weekly for most introductory level courses and math skills, study skills, language arts, written expression, time management, learning strategies, and organizational skills. Tutors are graduate students trained to work with LD. Students with LD can request to substitute foreign language with cultural courses. Disability Student Network is an organization designed to support the needs of students with disabilities.

SUPPORT SERVICES CONTACT INFORMATION

Learning Disability Program/Services: Learning Disabilities Support Services (LDSS)
Director: Diane Campbell
  E-mail: diane@acad.umass.edu
  Telephone: 413-545-4602
  Fax: 413-577-0691
Contact: Amanda Zygmont
  Telephone: 413-545-4602
  Fax: 413-577-0691

LEARNING DISABILITY SERVICES

Requests for the following services/accommodations will be evaluated individually based on appropriate and current documentation.

Allowed in Exams
  Calculator: Yes
  Dictionary: Yes
  Computer: Yes
  Spellchecker: Yes
Extended test time: Yes
Scribes: Yes
Proctors: Yes
Oral exams: Yes
Notetakers: Yes

Distraction-reduced environment: Yes
Tape recording in class: Yes
Books on tape from RFBD: Yes
Taping of books not from RFBD: Yes
Accommodations for students with ADHD: Yes, through Psychological Disabilities Services
Reading machine: Yes
Other assistive technology: Yes
Priority registration: Yes

Added costs for services: No
LD specialists: Yes (6)
Professional tutors: Yes
Peer tutors: Varies
Max. hours/wk. for services: 1 hour per week, more as available
How professors are notified of LD/ADHD: By student and service director

GENERAL ADMISSIONS INFORMATION

Director of Admissions: Kim Montague (interim director)
Telephone: 413-545-3712

ENTRANCE REQUIREMENTS
16 total are required; 4 English required, 3 math required, 3 science required, 2 science lab required, 2 foreign language required, 2 social studies required, 2 elective required. High school diploma or GED required. Minimum TOEFL is 550. TOEFL required of all international applicants.

Application deadline: February 1
Notification: Rolling beginning 12/15
Average GPA: 3.3

Average SAT I Math: 520–620 (mid-50% range)
Average SAT I Verbal: 510–620 (mid-50% range)
Average ACT: Accepted

Graduated top 10% of class: 19%
Graduated top 25% of class: 52%
Graduated top 50% of class: 91%

COLLEGE GRADUATION REQUIREMENTS

Course waivers allowed: No
Course substitutions allowed: Yes
In what subjects: College of Arts and Sciences students with a documented LD that prevents them from learning a foreign language may petition the foreign language department for a modification of the requirements. If granted, courses that fulfill culture intent and/or language are accepted.

ADDITIONAL INFORMATION

Environment: The University is located on 1,405 acres in a small town 90 miles west of Boston.

Student Body
  Undergrad enrollment: 19,061
  Female: 51%
  Male: 49%
  Out-of-state: 24%

Cost Information
  In-state tuition: $5,489
  Out-of-state tuition: $13,643
  Room & board: $4,986
Housing Information
  University housing: Yes
  Percent living on campus: 96%

Greek System
  Fraternity: Yes
  Sorority: Yes
Athletics: NCAA Division I

University of Massachusetts—Amherst

WHEATON COLLEGE

Office of Admission, Norton, MA 02766
Phone: 508-286-8251 • Fax: 508-286-8271
E-mail: admission@wheatoncollege.edu • Web: www.wheatoncollege.edu
Support level: S • Institution type: 4-year private

LEARNING DISABILITY PROGRAM AND SERVICES

Wheaton College encourages life-long learning by assisting students to become self-advocates and independent learners. The College does not have a special program for students with LD. The Assistant Dean for College Skills serves as the 504/ADA Coordinator. Students with LD can access services through the Dean. The Academic Advising Center houses the Dean of Academic Advising who holds drop-in office hours and assists students with petitions to the committee on Admissions and Academic Standing, Orientation, Probation, General Advising, and Incomplete Grade Resolution. The advising staff can assist with pressing advising questions. Students also have access to tutors, peer advisors, and preceptors who offer assistance with study strategies. All students have access to these services.

LD/ADHD ADMISSIONS INFORMATION

College entrance tests required: Yes
Nonstandardized tests accepted: Yes
Interview required: No
Essay required: Yes
Documentation required for LD: WAIS-III, WJ-R, Wechsler Memory Scales, aptitude, achievement, diagnostic interview, clinical summary, accomodations with rationale
Documentation required for ADHD: Yes
Documentation submitted to: Academic Support Services—after admission
Special Ed. HS course work accepted: Yes

Specific course requirements for all applicants: Yes
Separate application required for services: No
# of LD applications submitted yearly: N/A
# of LD applications accepted yearly: N/A
Total # of students receiving LD/ADHD services: N/A
Acceptance into program means acceptance into college: Students must be admitted and enrolled and then request services.

ADMISSIONS

All applicants must meet the same admission standards. Students with LD may choose to meet with the Assistant Dean for College Skills. Wheaton College does not require the ACT/SAT for admission. It is strongly suggested that students take 4 years of English, 3–4 years math, 3–4 years foreign language, 2 years social studies, 3–4 years science. Students are encouraged to take AP and honors courses and to also take courses in visual and performing arts. Wheaton will accept courses taken in the special education department. Students with LD are encouraged to self-disclose and provide current documentation. All LD testing information should be sent to both admissions and support services.

ADDITIONAL INFORMATION

Services for students with LD can include classroom accommodations, college skills workshops, course tutor program, general advising, and study strategy tutors as well as strategy workshops. Reasonable accommodations are available for students with appropriate documentation. There is a summer program available for students who wish to participate. Proctors are not offered because Wheaton has an Honor Code for exams.

SUPPORT SERVICES CONTACT INFORMATION

Learning Disability Program/Services: Academic Support Services
Director: Marty Bledsoe, Assistant Dean for College Skills
  E-mail: mbledsoe@wheatonma.edu
  Telephone: 508-286-8215
  Fax: 508-286-8276
Contact: Same

LEARNING DISABILITY SERVICES

Requests for the following services/accommodations will be evaluated individually based on appropriate and current documentation.

Allowed in Exams
  Calculator: Yes
  Dictionary: Yes
  Computer: Yes
  Spellchecker: Yes
Extended test time: Yes
Scribes: Yes
Proctors: No
Oral exams: Yes
Notetakers: Yes

Distraction-reduced environment: Yes
Tape recording in class: Yes
Books on tape from RFBD: Yes
Taping of books not from RFBD: Yes
Accommodations for students with
  ADHD: Yes
Reading machine: Yes
Other assistive technology: Yes
Priority registration: Yes

Added costs for services: N/A
LD specialists: No
Professional tutors: N/A
Peer tutors: N/A
Max. hours/wk. for services:
  Unlimited
How professors are notified of
  LD/ADHD: By both student and
  director

GENERAL ADMISSIONS INFORMATION

Director of Admissions: Gail Berson
Telephone: 508-286-3782

ENTRANCE REQUIREMENTS
16 total are recommended; 4 English recommended, 3 math recommended, 3 science recommended, 2 science lab recommended, 4 foreign language recommended, 2 social studies recommended. High school diploma or GED required. Minimum TOEFL is 550. TOEFL required of all international applicants.

Application deadline: February 1
Notification: April 1
Average GPA: 3.4

Average SAT I Math: 595
Average SAT I Verbal: 605
Average ACT: 25

Graduated top 10% of class: 27%
Graduated top 25% of class: 67%
Graduated top 50% of class: 92%

COLLEGE GRADUATION REQUIREMENTS

Course waivers allowed: Yes
Course substitutions allowed: Yes
In what subjects: Foreign language; by petition to committee

ADDITIONAL INFORMATION

Environment: Located 35 miles from Boston and Providence, Rhode Island.

Student Body
  Undergrad enrollment: 1,474
  Female: 64%
  Male: 36%
  Out-of-state: 64%

Cost Information
  Tuition: $24,225
  Room & board: $6,920
Housing Information
  University housing: Yes
  Percent living on campus: 99%

Greek System
  Fraternity: No
  Sorority: No
  Athletics: NCAA Division III

WHEELOCK COLLEGE

200 The Riverway, Boston, MA 02215
Phone: 617-879-2206 • Fax: 617-566-4453
E-mail: undergrad@wheelock.edu • Web: www.wheelock.edu
Support level: CS • Institution type: 4-year private

LEARNING DISABILITY PROGRAM AND SERVICES

The Disability Services Program in the Office of Academic Advising and Assistance (OAAA) at Wheelock College ensures that students with disabilities can actively participate in all facets of college life. They also provide and coordinate support services and programs that will enable students to maximize their educational potential. Students are encouraged to be independent individuals who know their strengths and develop compensatory skills for academic success. When working with students, the two major goals are to help with becoming independent and assisting in developing self-advocacy skills. Students with LD are encouraged to self-disclose to OAAA. Students are required to provide documentation from a qualified professional. Disability Services will assist in identifying appropriate accommodations based on the documentation provided.

LD/ADHD ADMISSIONS INFORMATION

College entrance tests required: Yes
Nonstandardized tests accepted: Yes
Interview required: N/A
Essay required: Yes
Documentation required for LD: Psychoeducational evaluation
Documentation required for ADHD: Yes
Documentation submitted to: Disability Services—after admission
Special Ed. HS course work accepted: Yes

Specific course requirements for all applicants: Yes
Separate application required for services: N/A
# of LD applications submitted yearly: N/A
# of LD applications accepted yearly: N/A
Total # of students receiving LD/ADHD services: 32
Acceptance into program means acceptance into college: Students must be admitted and enrolled and then may request services.

ADMISSIONS
There is no special admissions process for students with LD and ADHD. All applicants are expected to meet the general admission criteria. All students should have 4 years English, 1 year U.S. history and additional social studies, 3 years of college-prep math, and at least 1 lab science. Substitutions are not allowed for entrance requirements. Wheelock will accept courses in high school that were taken in the special education department. Students should feel free to self-disclose the disability in the application process.

ADDITIONAL INFORMATION
With appropriate documentation students may be eligible for the following services or accommodations: priority registration, letters informing the instructors of the disability and what reasonable accommodations the student will need, individual sessions with a learning specialist to help with time management, academic and organizational skills support. The Writing Center is available for all students interested in assistance with writing skills and peer tutors work one-on-one. Students may request referrals for peer tutors and study groups are available. In addition, workshops on the following topics are offered throughout the academic year: academic survival skills, reading skills, and Evaluation of Your Learning Style. Other academic supports include: academic advising, note-takers, textbooks on tape, testing modifications, readers, scribes, and referrals for diagnostic testing.

SUPPORT SERVICES CONTACT INFORMATION

Learning Disability Program/Services: Disability Services
Director: Denise Elliolt, Coordinator
  E-mail: delliolt@wheelock.edu
  Telephone: 617-879-2304
Contact: Same

LEARNING DISABILITY SERVICES

Requests for the following services/accommodations will be evaluated individually based on appropriate and current documentation.

Allowed in Exams
  Calculator: Yes
  Dictionary: Yes
  Computer: Yes
  Spellchecker: Yes
Extended test time: Yes
Scribes: Yes
Proctors: Yes
Oral exams: Yes
Notetakers: Yes

Distraction-reduced environment: Yes
Tape recording in class: Yes
Books on tape from RFBD: Yes
Taping of books not from RFBD: Yes
Accommodations for students with ADHD: Yes
Reading machine: No
Other assistive technology: Yes
Priority registration: Yes

Added costs for services: No
LD specialists: Yes (1)
Professional tutors: 1
Peer tutors: 25
Max. hours/wk. for services: Unlimited
How professors are notified of LD/ADHD: By both student and director

GENERAL ADMISSIONS INFORMATION

Director of Admissions: Joseph Chillo
Telephone: 617-879-2102

ENTRANCE REQUIREMENTS
16 total are required; 4 English required, 3 math required, 2 science required, 2 social studies required. High school diploma or GED required. Minimum TOEFL is 500. TOEFL required of all international applicants.

Application deadline: March 1
Notification: Rolling beginning 1/1
Average GPA: 2.9

Average SAT I Math: 470
Average SAT I Verbal: 491
Average ACT: NR

Graduated top 10% of class: 9%
Graduated top 25% of class: 21%
Graduated top 50% of class: 56%

COLLEGE GRADUATION REQUIREMENTS

Course waivers allowed: No
Course substitutions allowed: No
In what subjects: NA

ADDITIONAL INFORMATION

Environment: Located 2 miles from downtown Boston.

Student Body
  Undergrad enrollment: 632
  Female: 96%
  Male: 4%
  Out-of-state: 45%

Cost Information
  Tuition: $16,740
  Room & board: $6,615
Housing Information
  University housing: Yes
  Percent living on campus: 69%

Greek System
  Fraternity: No
  Sorority: No
Athletics: NCAA Division III

ADRIAN COLLEGE

110 South Madison Street, Adrian, MI 49221-2575
Phone: 800-877-2246 • Fax: 517-264-3331
E-mail: admission@adrian.edu • Web: www.adrian.edu
Support level: CS • Institution type: 4-year private

LEARNING DISABILITY PROGRAM AND SERVICES

Adrian College has extensive academic support services for all students with disabilities. The more the students are mainstreamed in high school, the greater their chances of success at Adrian in their mainstream program. There is no special or separate curriculum for students with learning disabilities. Project EXCEL is the umbrella program for all services at Adrian.

LD/ADHD ADMISSIONS INFORMATION

College entrance tests required: No
Nonstandardized tests accepted: Yes
Interview required: No
Essay required: No
Documentation required for LD: Current psychoeducational evaluation
Documentation required for ADHD: Yes
Documentation submitted to: Access—after admission
Special Ed. HS course work accepted: Yes

Specific course requirements for all applicants: Yes
Separate application required for services: Yes
# of LD applications submitted yearly: 10
# of LD applications accepted yearly: N/A
Total # of students receiving LD/ADHD services: 31
Acceptance into program means acceptance into college: Students must be accepted and enrolled at the College first and then may request services.

ADMISSIONS

Students with learning disabilities must meet regular admission criteria. Students should demonstrate the ability to do college-level work through an acceptable GPA in college-preparatory classes such as 4 years English, 2 years math, social studies, science, and foreign language, ACT (17+) or SAT, and a psychological report. Furthermore, by their senior year in high school, students should, for the most part, be mainstreamed. Courses taken in special education will be considered for admission. The applications of students who self-disclose are reviewed by Academic Services staff, not to determine admissions, but to start a documentation file. There is a special admissions program designed for students who demonstrate academic potential. This Special Admissions Support Program (SASP) requires students to sign a contract and maintain a certain GPA by the first semester each of the first two semesters.

ADDITIONAL INFORMATION

Course adaptations help to make courses more understandable. Skills classes are available in reading, math, study skills and research-paper writing, and students are granted credit toward their GPA. Support services and accommodations are available if appropriate in the following areas: extended time on tests; distraction-free testing environment; scribes; note-takers; proctors; use of calculators, dictionary, spellchecker, and computers in exams; taped textbooks; and reading machines. Tutorial assistance is available for all students and there are three-and-a-half LD specialists on staff.

SUPPORT SERVICES CONTACT INFORMATION

Learning Disability Program/Services: ACCESS, Academic Services
Director: Jane McCloskey
  E-mail: jmccloskey@adrian.edu
  Telephone: 517-265-5161
  Fax: 517-264-3181
Contact: Carol Tapp
  E-mail: ctapp@adrian.edu
  Telephone: 517-265-5161
  Fax: 517-264-3181

LEARNING DISABILITY SERVICES

Requests for the following services/accommodations will be evaluated individually based on appropriate and current documentation.

Allowed in Exams
  Calculator: Yes
  Dictionary: No
  Computer: Yes
  Spellchecker: Yes
Extended test time: Yes
Scribes: Yes
Proctors: Yes
Oral exams: Yes
Notetakers: Yes

Distraction-reduced environment: Yes
Tape recording in class: Yes
Books on tape from RFBD: Yes
Taping of books not from RFBD: Yes
Accommodations for students with ADHD: Yes
Reading machine: Yes
Other assistive technology: No
Priority registration: No

Added costs for services: No
LD specialists: Yes (3.5)
Professional tutors: No
Peer tutors: 30
Max. hours/wk. for services: Unlimited
How professors are notified of LD/ADHD: By both student and director

GENERAL ADMISSIONS INFORMATION

Director of Admissions: Janelle Sutkus
Telephone: 517-265-5161

ENTRANCE REQUIREMENTS
15 total are recommended; 4 English recommended, 2 math recommended, 2 science recommended, 2 foreign language recommended, 2 social studies recommended, 2 history recommended, 1 elective recommended. High school diploma or GED required. Minimum TOEFL is 475. TOEFL required of all international applicants.

Application deadline: August 15
Notification: Rolling
Average GPA: 3.1

Average SAT I Math: 500
Average SAT I Verbal: 590
Average ACT: 22

Graduated top 10% of class: 24%
Graduated top 25% of class: 42%
Graduated top 50% of class: 84%

COLLEGE GRADUATION REQUIREMENTS

Course waivers allowed: No
Course substitutions allowed: No
In what subjects: N/A

ADDITIONAL INFORMATION

Environment: The school is located on 100 acres in a residential section of Michigan, 35 miles northeast of Ann Arbor.

Student Body
  Undergrad enrollment: 1,049
  Female: 49%
  Male: 51%
  Out-of-state: 21%

Cost Information
  Tuition: $13,150
  Room & board: $4,320
Housing Information
  University housing: Yes
  Percent living on campus: 81%

Greek System
  Fraternity: Yes
  Sorority: Yes
Athletics: NCAA Division III

CALVIN COLLEGE

3201 Burton Street, S.E., Grand Rapids, MI 49546
Phone: 616-957-6106 • Fax: 616-957-8513
E-mail: admissions@calvin.edu • Web: www.calvin.edu
Support level: CS • Institution type: 4-year private

LEARNING DISABILITY PROGRAM AND SERVICES

The mission of Student Academic Services is to ensure that otherwise qualified students are able to benefit from a distinctly Christian education based on liberal arts. The Calvin community responds appropriately in a way that avoids handicapping the student with a disability. The coaching program is for students with learning disabilities, attention deficit disorders and other students who specifically need help with time management and study skills. The coaches give suggestions and feedback as well as encouragement on how to manage academics with other areas of life. First-year students are encouraged to apply for the Coaching Program at the beginning of the fall semester.

LD/ADHD ADMISSIONS INFORMATION

College entrance tests required: Yes
Nonstandardized tests accepted: Yes
Interview required: No
Essay required: Yes
Documentation required for LD: Psychoeducational evaluation
Documentation required for ADHD: Yes
Documentation submitted to: Student Academic Services—after admission
Special Ed. HS course work accepted: Decided on an individual basis

Specific course requirements for all applicants: Yes
Separate application required for services: No
# of LD applications submitted yearly: 25
# of LD applications accepted yearly: N/A
Total # of students receiving LD/ADHD services: 70
Acceptance into program means acceptance into college: Students must be admitted and enrolled at the College first and then may request services.

ADMISSIONS

There are no special admissions for students with learning disabilities. Applicants are expected to have an ACT of 20 (19 English and 20 Math) or SAT of 810 (390 Verbal and 420 Math). Courses required include 3 years English, 1 year algebra, 1 year geometry, and minimum of 2 years in any two of the following fields: social science, language, or natural science; 1 of the fields from math, foreign language, social science, and natural science must include at least 3 years of study. The Access Program is a conditional admission program for all students who do not meet admission requirements, but show promise of developing into successful college students.

ADDITIONAL INFORMATION

The Office of Student Academic Services is a learning center that is open to all students on campus. Skill classes are available in English, math, and study skills. These classes may be taken for college credit. The Coaching Program is an interactive relationship with another student who learns about the student's disability and learning style and then provides direction and strategies for the student. The program provides support in the areas of education and self-advocacy, time management, procrastination, note-taking, environment for studying, taking tests, and general organizational skills. Services and accommodations are offered to undergraduate and graduate students. Students who self-disclose and are admitted to the College are than reviewed for services.

SUPPORT SERVICES CONTACT INFORMATION

Learning Disability Program/Services: Student Academic Services
Director: James Mackenzie, PhD
   E-mail: jmackenz@calvin.edukbroeskst@calvin.edu
   Telephone: 616-957-6113
   Fax: 616-957-8551
Contact: Karen Broekstra
   E-mail: kbroeskst@calvin.edu
   Telephone: 616-957-6114
   Fax: 616-957-8551

LEARNING DISABILITY SERVICES

Requests for the following services/accommodations will be evaluated individually based on appropriate and current documentation.

Allowed in Exams
   Calculator: Y/N
   Dictionary: Y/N
   Computer: Y/N
   Spellchecker: Y/N
Extended test time: Yes
Scribes: Yes
Proctors: Yes
Oral exams: Y/N
Notetakers: Yes

Distraction-reduced environment: Y/N
Tape recording in class: Yes
Books on tape from RFBD: Yes
Taping of books not from RFBD: Yes
Accommodations for students with ADHD: Yes
Reading machine: No
Other assistive technology: No
Priority registration: Yes

Added costs for services: No
LD specialists: Yes
Professional tutors: 1
Peer tutors: 65
Max. hours/wk. for services: Unlimited for LD
How professors are notified of LD/ADHD: By the director

GENERAL ADMISSIONS INFORMATION

Director of Admissions: Dale Kuiper
Telephone: 616-957-6106

ENTRANCE REQUIREMENTS

12 total are required; 17 total are recommended; 3 English required, 4 English recommended, 3 math required, 3 math recommended, 2 science required, 2 science recommended, 1 science lab recommended, 2 foreign language recommended, 2 social studies required, 3 social studies recommended, 3 elective required, 3 elective recommended. High school diploma or GED required. Minimum TOEFL is 550. TOEFL required of all international applicants.

Application deadline: August 15
Notification: Rolling beginning 11/1
Average GPA: 3.5

Average SAT I Math: 597
Average SAT I Verbal: 594
Average ACT: 26

Graduated top 10% of class: 30%
Graduated top 25% of class: 56%
Graduated top 50% of class: 82%

COLLEGE GRADUATION REQUIREMENTS

Course waivers allowed: No
Course substitutions allowed: Yes
In what subjects: Foreign language with paper documentation

ADDITIONAL INFORMATION

Environment: The College is located on a 370-acre campus in a suburban area 7 miles southeast of Grand Rapids.

Student Body
   Undergrad enrollment: 4,263
   Female: 55%
   Male: 45%
   Out-of-state: 42%

Cost Information
   Tuition: $14,040
   Room & board: $4,890
Housing Information
   University housing: Yes
   Percent living on campus: 56%

Greek System
   Fraternity: Yes
   Sorority: Yes
Athletics: NCAA Division III

FERRIS STATE UNIVERSITY

420 Oak Street, Big Rapids, MI 49307
Phone: 231-591-2100 • Fax: 231-591-3944
E-mail: admissions@ferris.edu • Web: www.ferris.edu
Support level: CS • Institution type: 2-year and 4-year public

LEARNING DISABILITY PROGRAM AND SERVICES

Ferris State is committed to a policy of equal opportunity for qualified students. The mission of Disabilities Services is to serve and advocate for students with disabilities, empowering them for self-reliance and independence. Ferris State does not have a program for students with learning disabilities, but does provide a variety of support services and accommodations for students with documented learning disabilities that interfere with the learning process. Ferris State does not, however, attempt to rehabilitate learning disabilities. To obtain support services, students need to meet with the special needs counselor in the Academic Support Center. Students will complete a request for services application and a release form allowing the University to obtain a copy of the documentation of the disability. Documentation for LD/ADHD must be current and be submitted by a qualified professional. Professional development is offered to faculty and staff.

LD/ADHD ADMISSIONS INFORMATION

College entrance tests required: Yes
Nonstandardized tests accepted: Yes
Interview required: No
Essay required: No
Documentation required for LD: Psychoeducational report
Documentation required for ADHD: Yes
Documentation submitted to: Disability Services—after admission
Special Ed. HS course work accepted: Yes

Specific course requirements for all applicants: Yes
Separate application required for services: Yes
# of LD applications submitted yearly: 60–75
# of LD applications accepted yearly: 60–75
Total # of students receiving LD/ADHD services: 38
Acceptance into program means acceptance into college: Students must be admitted and enrolled at the University first and then may request services.

ADMISSIONS

Students with learning disabilities submit the general application form and should meet the same entrance criteria as all students. Qualified persons with disabilities may not be denied or subjected to discrimination in admission. There is no limit on the number of students admitted with disabilities. ACT scores are used for placement only and may not have an adverse effect on applicants with disabilities. No pre-admission inquiry regarding a possible disability can be made. Therefore, student with LD/ADHD are encouraged to self-disclose and provide information as to the extent of the disability. Sometimes a pre-admission interview is required if the GPA is questionable. In general students should have a 2.0 GPA, but some programs require a higher GPA and specific courses. Diverse curricula offerings and a flexible admissions policy allow for the admission of most high school graduates and transfer students. Some programs are selective in nature and require the completion of specific courses and/or a minimum GPA. The special needs counselor is involved in the admissions decision when there is a question about academic preparedness.

ADDITIONAL INFORMATION

Student Development Services offers tutoring for most courses. Flex tutoring is designed for in-depth clarification and review of subject material, and workshop tutoring is designed for short-term, walk-in assistance. The Collegiate Skills Program is designed to help academically underprepared students succeed in college by offering assistance in reading, writing, and study skills. Students also have an opportunity to develop skills in goal-setting, decision-making, and time management. The Academic Skills Center offers special instruction to assist students in improving their academic performance. Additionally, the following are offered: admission assistance; early registration; counseling/career awareness; academic assistance; campus advocacy; case conferences with referring agencies; and referrals to appropriate university and community agencies. There are currently 38 students with LD and 6 students with ADHD receiving services on campus.

SUPPORT SERVICES CONTACT INFORMATION

Learning Disability Program/Services: Disabilities Services
Director: Eunice Merwin
  E-mail: eunicemerwin@ferris.edu
  Telephone: 231-591-3772
  Fax: 231-591-3686
Contact: Ceytru Josephson
  E-mail: ceytrujosephson@ferris.edu
  Telephone: 231-591-5039

LEARNING DISABILITY SERVICES

Requests for the following services/accommodations will be evaluated individually based on appropriate and current documentation.

Allowed in Exams
  Calculator: Yes
  Dictionary: Yes
  Computer: Yes
  Spellchecker: Yes
Extended test time: Yes
Scribes: Yes
Proctors: Yes
Oral exams: Yes
Notetakers: Yes

Distraction-reduced environment: Yes
Tape recording in class: Yes
Books on tape from RFBD: Yes
Taping of books not from RFBD: Yes
Accommodations for students with ADHD: Yes
Reading machine: Yes
Other assistive technology: Yes
Priority registration: No

Added costs for services: No
LD specialists: Yes (1)
Professional tutors: 5
Peer tutors: 100
Max. hours/wk. for services: 2 subjects per week
How professors are notified of LD/ADHD: By director

GENERAL ADMISSIONS INFORMATION

Director of Admissions: Craig Westman
Telephone: 231-591-2100

ENTRANCE REQUIREMENTS
16 total are required; 19 total are recommended; 3 English required, 4 English recommended, 2 math required, 4 math recommended, 2 science required, 3 science recommended, 2 science lab required, 2 science lab recommended, 2 foreign language recommended, 2 social studies required, 2 social studies recommended, 2 history required, 2 history recommended, 2 elective required, 2 elective recommended. Minimum TOEFL is 500. TOEFL required of all international applicants.

Application deadline: Rolling
Notification: Rolling
Average GPA: 2.9

Average SAT I Math: NR
Average SAT I Verbal: NR
Average ACT: 19

Graduated top 10% of class: NR
Graduated top 25% of class: NR
Graduated top 50% of class: NR

COLLEGE GRADUATION REQUIREMENTS

Course waivers allowed: No
Course substitutions allowed: No
In what subjects: N/A

ADDITIONAL INFORMATION

Environment: The University is located on 600 acres 50 miles north of Grand Rapids.

Student Body
  Undergrad enrollment: 9,191
  Female: 44%
  Male: 56%
  Out-of-state: 5%

Cost Information
  In-state tuition: $4,238
  Out-of-state tuition: $8,851
  Room & board: $5,264
Housing Information
  University housing: Yes
  Percent living on campus: 41%

Greek System
  Fraternity: Yes
  Sorority: Yes
Athletics: NCAA Division II

Ferris State University

FINLANDIA UNIVERSITY

601 Quincy Street, Hancock, MI 49930
Phone: 906-482-5300 • Fax: 906-482-7383
Email: ben.larson@finlandia.edu • Web: www.finlandia.edu
Support: SP • Institution: 4-year private

LEARNING DISABILITY PROGRAM AND SERVICES

Through Finlandia's Learning Disabilities Program students will receive individual counseling, tutoring, academic advising, career counseling, and lots of support and encouragement. The LD Program is designed for students needing personalized attention and additional education before entering a liberal arts or career program. Careful academic planning is performed by the LD director to ensure that students carry a reasonable credit load that is sequential and well-balanced with attention to reading, written assignments, and other course requirements. The faculty is supportive and written and verbal communication between the LD director and faculty is frequent. Student performance is monitored and there are weekly scheduled meetings. The director is the advisor and support person overseeing and coordinating each individual's program. Self-advocacy and compensatory skills are goals, rather than remediation. There is a seven-day orientation prior to freshman year. Advisors work with students during the orientation to plan the best course of study, provide advice and assurance that the student will get what is needed in the program, provide encouragement, and may even be able to match the student with professors whose style of teaching best complements the student's style of learning.

LD/ADHD ADMISSIONS INFORMATION

College entrance tests required: No
Nonstandardized tests accepted: Yes
Interview required: Yes
Essay required: No
Documentation required for LD: WAIS-III; WJ
Documentation required for ADHD: Yes
Submitted to: Learning Disability Program
Special Ed. HS course work accepted: No

Specific course requirements for all applicants: Yes
Separate application required for services: No
# of LD applications submitted yearly: 15–25
# of LD applications accepted yearly: 15–20
Total # of students receiving LD/ADHD services: 30
Acceptance into program means acceptance into college: The students are reviewed jointly by the LD Program and the Office of Admission to reach an admission decision.

ADMISSIONS

General admission requirements must be met by all applicants. In addition, students with learning disabilities should submit an evaluation, made within the last three years, documenting the learning disability; an IEP; and a handwritten essay by the student describing the learning disability. Sometimes a telephone interview or visitation is requested to help determine eligibility for the program. An applicant must have the academic ability and background for work on a college level. Each applicant is evaluated individually by the director of the LD Program and the admissions staff. Depending on the high school information provided, some students will be given the dual designation of LD/Pre-College if the director of the program feels the student may be "at risk."

ADDITIONAL INFORMATION

The program director provides professors with a disability data sheet to request accommodations and also meets individually with faculty regarding student needs. Special services offered include alternative testing; individual counseling; career counseling; auxiliary aids and services; academic advising; computer-based instruction; group and individualized courses; support from the Teaching/Learning Center; and support from Student Support Services. The director of the program is certified to teach students with learning disabilities, and will help them set up a plan for growth and strength in areas that are challenging. Students will meet with their advisor once a week for as much or as little time as is needed. Students may take skills classes, for noncollege credit, in reading and study strategies. There is a one-week required summer orientation program for incoming freshmen.

SUPPORT SERVICES CONTACT INFORMATION

Learning Disability Program/Services: Learning Disabilities Program
Director: Barb Heuvers
  E-mail: admissions@finlandia.edu
  Telephone: 906-487-7276
  Fax: 906-482-7383
Contact: Same

LEARNING DISABILITY SERVICES

Requests for the following services/accommodations will be evaluated individually based on appropriate and current documentation.

Allowed in Exams
  Calculator: Yes
  Dictionary: Y/N
  Computer: Yes
  Spellchecker: Yes
Extended test time: Yes
Scribes: Yes
Proctors: Yes
Oral exams: Yes
Notetakers: Yes

Distraction-reduced environment: Yes
Tape recording in class: Yes
Books on tape from RFBD: Yes
Taping of books not from RFBD: No
Accommodations for students with ADHD: Yes
Reading machine: Yes
Other assistive technology: Yes
Priority registration: No

Added costs for services: No
LD specialists: Yes (1)
Professional tutors: 9
Peer tutors: 14
Max. hours/wk. for services: Unlimited
How professors are notified of LD/ADHD: By student and program director

GENERAL ADMISSIONS INFORMATION

Director of Admissions: Ben Larson
Telephone: 906-487-7310

ENTRANCE REQUIREMENTS
Applicants must have the academic ability and background for work on a college level. High school diploma or GED.

Application deadline: Rolling
Notification: Rolling
Average GPA: 2.5

Average SAT I Math: NR
Average SAT I Verbal: NR
Average ACT: 18

Graduated top 10% of class: 15%
Graduated top 25% of class: 33%
Graduated top 50% of class: 70%

COLLEGE GRADUATION REQUIREMENTS

Course waivers allowed: No
Course substitutions allowed: No
In what subjects: N/A

ADDITIONAL INFORMATION

Environment: The school is located in a beautiful and rugged area of the Upper Peninsula of Michigan.

Student Body
  Undergrad enrollment: 450
  Female: 69%
  Male: 31%
  Out-of-state: 24%

Cost Information
  Tuition: $9,500
  Room & board: $3,900
Housing Information
  University housing: Yes
  Percent living on campus: 45%

Greek System
  Fraternity: Yes
  Sorority: Yes
  Athletics: Intramural sports

GRAND VALLEY STATE UNIVERSITY

1 Campus Drive, Allendale, MI 49401
Phone: 616-899-6611 • Fax: 616-895-2000
E-mail: go2gvsu@gvsu.edu • Web: www.gvsu.edu
Support level: S • Institution type: 4-year public

LEARNING DISABILITY PROGRAM AND SERVICES

The Office of Academic Support at Grand Valley State University provides academic support services and accommodations that enhance the learning environment for students with disabilities and to help educate the University community on disability issues. In addition to the regular services, the University offers student skill assessment, academic and career advising, specialized tutoring, textbooks on tape, note-taking assistance, alternative test-taking assistance, peer mentoring, and counseling. OAS provides students with memoranda documenting their disability. The documentation will contain information on the nature of the disability and what academic accommodations the student may need.

LD/ADHD ADMISSIONS INFORMATION

College entrance tests required: Yes
Nonstandardized tests accepted: Yes
Interview required: No
Essay required: No
Documentation required for LD: Psychoeducational evaluation
Documentation required for ADHD: Yes
Documentation submitted to: Academic support—after admission
Special Ed. HS course work accepted: Yes

Specific course requirements for all applicants: Yes
Separate application required for services: Yes
# of LD applications submitted yearly: 20–55
# of LD applications accepted yearly: 11
Total # of students receiving LD/ADHD services: 198
Acceptance into program means acceptance into college: Students must be admitted and enrolled and then request services.

ADMISSIONS

Students are given the opportunity to provide documentation of their learning disability or attention deficit disorder. Information is reviewed by the Office of Academic Support and Admissions. Students interested in special accommodations need to submit both the regular admissions application and a separate application for the program. An evaluation report should include the summary of a comprehensive diagnostic interview. Standardized tests are required for admission. General admission requirements include 4 years English, 3 years math, 3 years social science, and 2 years science. The average ACT is a 23.1.

ADDITIONAL INFORMATION

Once admitted into the program students may request that an Instructor Progress Report be sent to each of their professors. The purpose of this report is to inform students of their current academic standing in a class. Academic Support staff provide the following services: work with students to help them improve their academic weaknesses and increase their areas of strength; academic and career advising; specialized tutoring in addition to the general tutoring available for all students; seminars on reading textbooks, note-taking, time management, test-taking strategies; tape recording of texts not available through RFBD; alternative test-taking; peer mentoring; counseling; and Organization for the Achievement of Disabled Students, which is a student organization to advance the educational and career goals of students with disabilities.

SUPPORT SERVICES CONTACT INFORMATION

Learning Disability Program/Services: Academic Support (OAS)
Director: Kathleen Vanderveen
  E-mail: vanderyk@gvsu.edu
  Telephone: 616-895-2490
  Fax: 616-895-3440
Contact: Sandy Sall
  E-mail: salls@gvsu.edu
  Telephone: 616-895-2490
  Fax: 616-895-3440

LEARNING DISABILITY SERVICES

Requests for the following services/accommodations will be evaluated individually based on appropriate and current documentation.

Allowed in Exams
  Calculator: Yes
  Dictionary: Yes
  Computer: Yes
  Spellchecker: Yes
Extended test time: Yes
Scribes: Yes
Proctors: Yes
Oral exams: Yes
Notetakers: Yes

Distraction-reduced environment: Yes
Tape recording in class: Yes
Books on tape from RFBD: Yes
Taping of books not from RFBD: Yes
Accommodations for students with ADHD: Yes
Reading machine: No
Other assistive technology: Yes
Priority registration: Yes

Added costs for services: No
LD specialists: No
Professional tutors: No
Peer tutors: 140
Max. hours/wk. for services: 4
How professors are notified of LD/ADHD: By student

GENERAL ADMISSIONS INFORMATION

Director of Admissions: Jodi Chychinski
Telephone: 616-895-2025

ENTRANCE REQUIREMENTS
20 total are required; 4 English required, 3 math required, 4 math recommended, 3 science required, 2 foreign language recommended, 3 social studies required, 7 elective required. High school diploma or GED required. Minimum TOEFL is 550. TOEFL required of all international applicants.

Application deadline: July 31
Notification: Rolling
Average GPA: 3.3
Average SAT I Math: NR
Average SAT I Verbal: NR
Average ACT: 23
Graduated top 10% of class: 16%
Graduated top 25% of class: 46%
Graduated top 50% of class: 82%

COLLEGE GRADUATION REQUIREMENTS

Course waivers allowed: No
Course substitutions allowed: No
In what subjects: N/A

ADDITIONAL INFORMATION

Environment: Located 12 miles from Grand Rapids.

Student Body
  Undergrad enrollment: 15,221
  Female: 60%
  Male: 40%
  Out-of-state: 3%

Cost Information
  In-state tuition: $4,272
  Out-of-state tuition: $9,244
  Room & board: $5,030
Housing Information
  University housing: Yes
  Percent living on campus: 25%

Greek System
  Fraternity: Yes
  Sorority: Yes
Athletics: NCAA Division II

MICHIGAN STATE UNIVERSITY

250 Administration Building, East Lansing, MI 48824-1046
Phone: 517-355-8332 • Fax: 517-353-1647
E-mail: admis@msu.edu • Web: www.msu.edu
Support level: CS • Institution type: 4-year public

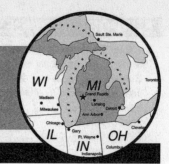

LEARNING DISABILITY PROGRAM AND SERVICES

MSU is serious in its commitment to helping students no matter what the disability. The OPHS/DRC (Office for Program for Handicapped Students/Disability Resource Center) mission is to be an advocate for the inclusion of students with disabilities into the total university experience. The OPHS purpose is to respond to the needs of students by providing resources that equalize their chances for success, support their full participation in all university programs, and act as a resource for the University community and the community at large. Students must provide recent documentation and history in the form of a school report, psychologist's assessment, or certification by other recognized authority and must contain a clearly stated diagnosis. Staff specialists focus on freshmen and transfer students during their transition and adjustment to the University environment. As students learn to utilize appropriate accommodations and strategies, a greater sense of independence is achieved, although classroom accommodations may still be necessary.

LD/ADHD ADMISSIONS INFORMATION

College entrance tests required: Yes
Nonstandardized tests accepted: Yes
Interview required: No
Essay required: No
Documentation required for LD: Psychoeducational evaluation
Documentation required for ADHD: Yes
Documentation submitted to: Resource Center for Disabilities—after admission
Special Ed. HS course work accepted: No

Specific course requirements for all applicants: Yes
Separate application required for services: No
# of LD applications submitted yearly: N/A
# of LD applications accepted yearly: N/A
Total # of students receiving LD/ADHD services: 140
Acceptance into program means acceptance into college: Students must be admitted and enrolled at the University first and then may request services.

ADMISSIONS

Admission for students with learning disabilities to the University is based on the same criteria used for all other students. College Achievement Admissions Program (CAAP) is an alternative admissions procedure for students who have academic potential but who would be unable to realize that potential without special support services due to their economic, cultural, or educational background. Students with learning disabilities should not send any documentation to the Office of Admissions. All documentation should be sent to OPHS/DRC.

ADDITIONAL INFORMATION

Specialists are available by appointment to provide information to students. Accommodations include taped texts; study strategy tutoring; voice output computers; and taping of lectures; extended time on tests, reader scribe, quiet room for tests, word processing and scribes; use of word processor; advocacy assistance from specialists and letters to professors; support groups through OPHS/DRC; and consultation with service providers. Various other resources on campus such as Learning Resource Center; Office of Supportive Services; MSU Counseling Center; and Undergraduate University Division of Academic Advising. The Learning Resource Center works with students with learning characteristics on an individual basis to help the student learn to utilize appropriate learning strategies and to mediate their learning environment.

SUPPORT SERVICES CONTACT INFORMATION

Learning Disability Program/Services: Resource Center for Persons with Disabilities
Director: Michael Hudson
  E-mail: mjh@msu.edu
  Telephone: 517-353-9642
  Fax: 517-438-3191
Contact: Elaine High
  E-mail: high@msu.edu
  Telephone: 517-432-4266
  Fax: 517-432-3191

LEARNING DISABILITY SERVICES

Requests for the following services/accommodations will be evaluated individually based on appropriate and current documentation.

Allowed in Exams
  Calculator: Yes
  Dictionary: Yes
  Computer: Yes
  Spellchecker: Yes
Extended test time: Yes
Scribes: Yes
Proctors: Yes
Oral exams: Yes
Notetakers: Yes

Distraction-reduced environment: Yes
Tape recording in class: Yes
Books on tape from RFBD: Yes
Taping of books not from RFBD: Yes
Accommodations for students with ADHD: Yes
Reading machine: Yes
Other assistive technology: Yes
Priority registration: Yes

Added costs for services: No
LD specialists: Yes (2)
Professional tutors: 1
Peer tutors: 10
Max. hours/wk. for services: Unlimited
How professors are notified of LD/ADHD: By student

GENERAL ADMISSIONS INFORMATION

Director of Admissions: Dr. Gordon Stanley
Telephone: 517-355-8332

ENTRANCE REQUIREMENTS
4 English required, 3 math required, 2 science required, 2 foreign language required, 3 social studies required. High school diploma or GED required. Minimum TOEFL is 550. TOEFL required of all international applicants.

Application deadline: July 30
Notification: Rolling
Average GPA: 3.5

Average SAT I Math: 572
Average SAT I Verbal: 551
Average ACT: 24

Graduated top 10% of class: 24%
Graduated top 25% of class: 60%
Graduated top 50% of class: 92%

COLLEGE GRADUATION REQUIREMENTS

Course waivers allowed: Y/N
Course substitutions allowed: Y/N
In what subjects: Decided on a case-by-case basis

ADDITIONAL INFORMATION

Environment: Michigan State is located 1 hour from Ann Arbor and 1.5 hours from Detroit.

Student Body
  Undergrad enrollment: 33,966
  Female: 53%
  Male: 47%
  Out-of-state: 9%

Cost Information
  In-state tuition: $5,093
  Out-of-state tuition: $12,675
  Room & board: $4,472
Housing Information
  University housing: Yes
  Percent living on campus: 44%

Greek System
  Fraternity: Yes
  Sorority: Yes
Athletics: NCAA Division I

NORTHERN MICHIGAN UNIVERSITY

1401 Presque Isle Avenue, 304 Cohodas, Marquette, MI 49855
Phone: 906-227-2650 • Fax: 906-227-1747
E-mail: admiss@nmu.edu • Web: www.nmu.edu
Support level: CS • Institution type: 4-year public

LEARNING DISABILITY PROGRAM AND SERVICES

Disability Services provides services and accommodations to all students with disabilities. The goals of Disability Services are to meet the individual needs of students. Student Support Services is a multifaceted educational support project designed to assist students in completing their academic programs at Northern Michigan University. The Student Support Services professional staff, peer tutors, mentors, and peer advisors provide program participants with the individualized attention needed to successfully complete a college degree. This program is funded through the U.S. Department of Education. Federal regulations require that all participants meet at least one of the following eligibility criteria: come from a low-income background; be a first generation college student; or have a physical or a learning disability.

LD/ADHD ADMISSIONS INFORMATION

College entrance tests required: Yes
Nonstandardized tests accepted: Yes
Interview required: No
Essay required: No
Documentation required for LD: WAIS-III; achievement
Documentation required for ADHD: Yes
Documentation submitted to: Disability Services—after admission
Special Ed. HS course work accepted: Yes

Specific course requirements for all applicants: Yes
Separate application required for services: Yes
# of LD applications submitted yearly: 80
# of LD applications accepted yearly: 80
Total # of students receiving LD/ADHD services: 80–170
Acceptance into program means acceptance into college: Students must be admitted and enrolled at the University first and then may request services.

ADMISSIONS

There are no special admissions for students with learning disabilities. All students submit the same general application, and are expected to have an ACT of 19 or higher and a high school GPA of at least 2.25. There are no specific high school courses required for admissions, although the University recommends 4 years English, 4 years math, 3 years history/social studies, 3 years science, 3 years foreign language, 2 years fine or performing arts, and 1 year computer instruction.

ADDITIONAL INFORMATION

The director of Disability Services works on a one-to-one basis with students as needed, and will also meet with students who do not have specific documentation if they request assistance. Skill classes are offered in reading, writing, math, study skills, sociocultural development, and interpersonal growth. No course waivers are granted for graduation requirements from NMU because the University views waivers as an institutional failure to educate its students with disabilities. Substitutions, however, are granted when appropriate. Services and accommodations are available for undergraduate and graduate students. Student Support Services provides each student with an individual program of educational support services including academic advising; basic skill building in reading, math, and writing; counseling; career advisement; developmental skill building; mentoring; support groups and study groups; tutoring from paraprofessionals; specialized tutors; group tutoring or supplemental instruction; and workshops on personal development and study skills improvement.

SUPPORT SERVICES CONTACT INFORMATION

Learning Disability Program/Services: Disability Services
Director: Lynn Walden, Coordinator
  E-mail: lwalden@nmu.edu
  Telephone: 906-227-1550
  Fax: 906-227-1510
Contact: Same

LEARNING DISABILITY SERVICES

Requests for the following services/accommodations will be evaluated individually based on appropriate and current documentation.

Allowed in Exams
  Calculator: Yes
  Dictionary: Yes
  Computer: Yes
  Spellchecker: Yes
Extended test time: Yes
Scribes: Yes
Proctors: Yes
Oral exams: Yes
Notetakers: Yes

Distraction-reduced environment: Yes
Tape recording in class: Yes
Books on tape from RFBD: Yes
Taping of books not from RFBD: Yes
Accommodations for students with ADHD: Yes
Reading machine: Yes
Other assistive technology: Yes
Priority registration: Yes

Added costs for services: No
LD specialists: Yes (1)
Professional tutors: No
Peer tutors: Yes
Max. hours/wk. for services: 2–4 hours per week per subject (more if needed)
How professors are notified of LD/ADHD: By program director

GENERAL ADMISSIONS INFORMATION

Director of Admissions: Gerri Daniels
Telephone: 906-227-2650

ENTRANCE REQUIREMENTS

12 total are required; 4 English required, 3 math required, 2 science required, 3 foreign language recommended, 3 social studies required, 3 history recommended. High school diploma or GED required. Minimum TOEFL is 500. TOEFL required of all international applicants.

Application deadline: Rolling
Notification: Rolling beginning 6/1
Average GPA: 2.5

Average SAT I Math: 525
Average SAT I Verbal: 530
Average ACT: 22

Graduated top 10% of class: NR
Graduated top 25% of class: NR
Graduated top 50% of class: NR

COLLEGE GRADUATION REQUIREMENTS

Course waivers allowed: No
Course substitutions allowed: Yes
In what subjects: Substitutions permitted to fulfill graduation requirement with appropriate documentation.

ADDITIONAL INFORMATION

Environment: The campus is located in an urban area about 300 miles north of Milwaukee, Wisconsin.

Student Body
  Undergrad enrollment: 8,366
  Female: 54%
  Male: 46%
  Out-of-state: 14%

Cost Information
  In-state tuition: $4,010
  Out-of-state tuition: $6,520
  Room & board: $4,780
Housing Information
  University housing: Yes
  Percent living on campus: 30%

Greek System
  Fraternity: Yes
  Sorority: Yes
Athletics: NCAA Division II

UNIV. OF MICHIGAN—ANN ARBOR

1220 Student Activities Building, Ann Arbor, MI 48109-1316
Phone: 734-764-7433 • Fax: 734-936-0740
E-mail: ugadmiss@umich.edu • Web: www.umich.edu
Support level: CS • Institution type: 4-year public

LEARNING DISABILITY PROGRAM AND SERVICES

The philosophy of Services for Students with Disabilities (SSD) is based on the legal actions described in Section 504 of the Rehabilitation Act of 1973. SSD services are dependent on self-advocacy of the students and are "nonintrusive," giving the students the responsibility to seek out assistance. SSD offers selected student services that are not provided by other University of Michigan offices or outside organizations. SSD assists students in negotiating disability-related barriers to the pursuit of their education; strives to improve access to university programs, activities, and facilities; and promotes increased awareness of disability issues on campus. SSD encourages inquiries for information and will confidentially discuss concerns relating to a potential or recognized disability and, if requested, provide appropriate referrals for further assistance.

LD/ADHD ADMISSIONS INFORMATION

College entrance tests required: Yes
Nonstandardized tests accepted: Yes
Interview required: NR
Essay required: Yes
Documentation required for LD: Psychoeducational evaluation
Documentation required for ADHD: Yes
Documentation submitted to: SSD
Special Ed. HS course work accepted: No

Specific course requirements for all applicants: Yes
Separate application required for services: No
# of LD applications submitted yearly: N/A
# of LD applications accepted yearly: N/A
Total # of students receiving LD/ADHD services: 250+
Acceptance into program means acceptance into college: Students must be admitted and enrolled at the University and then may be reviewed for services.

ADMISSIONS

Students with learning disabilities are expected to meet the same admission requirements as their peers. Courses required include 4 years English, 2 years foreign language (4 years recommended), 3 years math (4 years recommended including algebra, trigonometry, and geometry), 2 years biological and physical sciences (3 years recommended), 3 years history and the social sciences (2 years history recommended, including 1 year of U.S. history); 1 year hands-on computer study is strongly recommended, as is 1 year in the fine or performing arts, or equivalent preparation. Score range for the ACT is 25–29 and SAT 1170–1340. There is no set minimum GPA as it is contingent on several other factors. For students with learning disabilities, the Admissions Office will accept untimed test scores and letters of recommendation from LD specialists. When applying for admission to the University of Michigan, students with learning disabilities are encouraged to self-identify on the application form or by writing a cover letter.

ADDITIONAL INFORMATION

All accommodations are based on documented needs by the student. Services for students with learning disabilities include volunteer readers; volunteer tutors; referral for psychoeducational assessments; selected course book loans for taping; Franklin Spellers; free cassette tapes; APH 4-track recorders; advocacy and referral; advocacy letters to professors; limited scholarships; newsletters; volunteer note-takers; carbonized notepaper; free photocopying of class notes; free course notes service for some classes; many students eligible for assisted earlier registration; adaptive technology; and library reading rooms. SSD also provides appropriate services for students with "other health-related disabilities" such as ADHD. There is a special summer program at the University for high school students with learning disabilities. Services and accommodations are available for undergraduates and graduates.

SUPPORT SERVICES CONTACT INFORMATION

Learning Disability Program/Services: Services for Students with Disabilities (SSD)
Director: Stuart Segal, Coordinator
  E-mail: ssegal@umich.edu
  Telephone: 734-763-3000
  Fax: 734-936-3947
Contact: Same

LEARNING DISABILITY SERVICES

Requests for the following services/accommodations will be evaluated individually based on appropriate and current documentation.

Allowed in Exams
  Calculator: Yes
  Dictionary: Yes
  Computer: Yes
  Spellchecker: Yes
Extended test time: Yes
Scribes: Yes
Proctors: No
Oral exams: No
Notetakers: Yes

Distraction-reduced environment: Yes
Tape recording in class: Yes
Books on tape from RFBD: Yes
Taping of books not from RFBD: Yes
Accommodations for students with
  ADHD: Yes
Reading machine: Yes
Other assistive technology: Yes
Priority registration: Yes

Added costs for services: No
LD specialists: Yes (1)
Professional tutors: No
Peer tutors: No
Max. hours/wk. for services: Varies
How professors are notified of
  LD/ADHD: By student with letter

GENERAL ADMISSIONS INFORMATION

Director of Admissions: Theodore Spencer
Telephone: 734-764-7433

ENTRANCE REQUIREMENTS
15 total are required; 18 total are recommended; 4 English required, 4 English recommended, 3 math required, 4 math recommended, 2 science required, 3 science recommended, 1 science lab recommended, 2 foreign language required, 4 foreign language recommended, 3 social studies required, 3 social studies recommended, 2 history recommended. High school diploma or GED required. Minimum TOEFL is 560. TOEFL required of all international applicants.

Application deadline: February 1
Notification: Rolling beginning 9/1
Average GPA: 3.7

Average SAT I Math: 654
Average SAT I Verbal: 615
Average ACT: 27

Graduated top 10% of class: 63%
Graduated top 25% of class: 90%
Graduated top 50% of class: 99%

COLLEGE GRADUATION REQUIREMENTS

Course waivers allowed: No
Course substitutions allowed: Yes
In what subjects: Foreign language

ADDITIONAL INFORMATION

Environment: The campus is located in a suburban area about 30 minutes west of Detroit.

Student Body
  Undergrad enrollment: 24,412
  Female: 50%
  Male: 50%
  Out-of-state: 29%

Cost Information
  In-state tuition: $6,328
  Out-of-state tuition: $20,138
  Room & board: $5,780
Housing Information
  University housing: Yes
  Percent living on campus: 39%

Greek System
  Fraternity: Yes
  Sorority: Yes
Athletics: NCAA Division I

AUGSBURG COLLEGE

2211 Riverside Avenue South, Minneapolis, MN 55454
Phone: 612-330-1001 • Fax: 612-330-1590
E-mail: admissions@augsburg.edu • Web: www.augsburg.edu
Support level: SP • Institution type: 4-year private

LEARNING DISABILITY PROGRAM AND SERVICES

The Center for Learning and Adaptive Student Services (CLASS) program affirms Augsburg College's commitment to providing a high-quality liberal arts education for students by assisting students in developing self-confidence, independence, and self-advocacy skills in an academic setting. Augsburg has a commitment to recruit, retain, and graduate students with learning disabilities who demonstrate the willingness and ability to participate in college-level learning. Typically, the program provides a very intensive level of support to students during the early phases of their college career, while at the same time teaching them self-advocacy and independence skills. As students master these skills, they gradually assume an increasing degree of responsibility. It is expected that over time, CLASS students will develop an ability to advocate for themselves, gain working knowledge of the accommodations they need, and acquire the skills to access those accommodations independently.

LD/ADHD ADMISSIONS INFORMATION

College entrance tests required: Yes
Nonstandardized tests accepted: Yes
Interview required: Yes
Essay required: Yes
Documentation required for LD: Cognitive (e.g., WAIS-III); achievement (e.g., Woodcock-Johnson); measures of information processing and memory: within three years
Documentation required for ADHD: Yes
Documentation submitted to: CLASS
Special Ed. HS course work accepted: N/A

Specific course requirements for all applicants: Yes
Separate application required for services: Yes
# of LD applications submitted yearly: 140–161
# of LD applications accepted yearly: 70–91
Total # of students receiving LD/ADHD services: 120–160
Acceptance into program means acceptance into college: Students must be accepted and enrolled at the College first and then may request services.

ADMISSIONS

Applicants with learning disabilities must first complete the Augsburg application form. Students with a 2.5 GPA, rank in top half of class, or a 20 ACT are automatically admissible. Courses required include 4 years English, 3 years math, 3 years science, 2 years foreign language, and 3 years social studies (4 recommended). Students complete a brief application form and submit LD documentation directly to CLASS. The written diagnostic report must contain a definite statement that an LD is present. Specific recommendations about accommodations and academic strengths and weaknesses are valuable. A formal interview will be scheduled to allow the student to provide information and receive more details about accommodations at Augsburg. Students admitted on probation or as high-risk students must take a study skills class and earn a 2.0 GPA for the first year.

ADDITIONAL INFORMATION

Students admitted into CLASS are given individual assistance from application through graduation by learning specialists. Academic support includes assistance with registration and advising; guidance with course work; assistance with writing; instruction in learning strategies and compensatory techniques; help with improving basic skills; and advocacy. Accommodations include testing arrangements; access to computers and training; taped texts; the use of Kurzweil software; assistance in securing note-takers; assistance in obtaining tutors; and foreign language alternatives. There are also many community resources available. Currently there are 190 students with learning disabilities receiving services and accommodations. Undergraduates and graduates can access support services.

SUPPORT SERVICES CONTACT INFORMATION

Learning Disability Program/Services: Center for Learning and Adaptive Student Services (CLASS)
Director: Robert F. Doljanac
  E-mail: doljanac@augsburg.edu
  Telephone: 612-330-1648
  Fax: 612-330-1137
Contact: Same

LEARNING DISABILITY SERVICES

Requests for the following services/accommodations will be evaluated individually based on appropriate and current documentation.

Allowed in Exams
  Calculator: Yes
  Dictionary: Yes
  Computer: Yes
  Spellchecker: Yes
Extended test time: Yes
Scribes: Yes
Proctors: Yes
Oral exams: Yes
Notetakers: Yes

Distraction-reduced environment: Yes
Tape recording in class: Yes
Books on tape from RFBD: Yes
Taping of books not from RFBD: Yes
Accommodations for students with ADHD: Yes
Reading machine: No
Other assistive technology: Yes
Priority registration: No

Added costs for services: No
LD specialists: Yes (5)
Professional tutors: No
Peer tutors: 80
Max. hours/wk. for services: As needed
How professors are notified of LD/ADHD: By student

GENERAL ADMISSIONS INFORMATION

Director of Admissions: Sally Daniels
Telephone: 612-330-1581

ENTRANCE REQUIREMENTS

15 total are required; 6 total are recommended; 4 English required, 3 math required, 3 science required, 2 foreign language required, 3 social studies required, 4 social studies recommended, 2 history recommended. High school diploma or GED required. Minimum TOEFL is 520. TOEFL required of all international applicants.

Application deadline: August 15
Notification: Rolling
Average GPA: 3.2

Average SAT I Math: 574
Average SAT I Verbal: 545
Average ACT: 22

Graduated top 10% of class: 13%
Graduated top 25% of class: 38%
Graduated top 50% of class: 71%

COLLEGE GRADUATION REQUIREMENTS

Course waivers allowed: No
Course substitutions allowed: Yes
In what subjects: Foreign language

ADDITIONAL INFORMATION

Environment: The College is located on 25 acres near downtown Minneapolis.

Student Body
  Undergrad enrollment: 2,913
  Female: 60%
  Male: 40%
  Out-of-state: 13%

Cost Information
  Tuition: $17,070
  Room & board: $5,540
Housing Information
  University housing: Yes
  Percent living on campus: 54%

Greek System
  Fraternity: Yes
  Sorority: Yes
Athletics: NCAA Division III

COLLEGE OF ST. CATHERINE

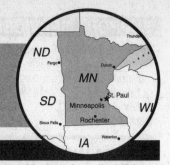

2004 Randolph Avenue, Saint Paul, MN 55105
Phone: 612-690-6505 • Fax: 612-690-8824
E-mail: admissions@stkate.edu • Web: www.stkate.edu
Support level: CS • Institution type: 4-year private

LEARNING DISABILITY PROGRAM AND SERVICES

The O'Neill Learning Center houses the special learning programs for students with learning disabilities. Accommodations are made on an individual basis. The Center's staff works with students and departments to provide reasonable and appropriate accommodations for access to and fair treatment in College programs and activities. Services are available to students who want to develop their academic potential and time management skills. The Learning Center and Counseling Center offer staff and services to accommodate students with learning disabilities. A reduced course load is strongly suggested for the student's first semester. Services include information sessions, faculty consultations, and early registration. While the College does not have all the resources that students with learning disabilities may need, it is committed to responding flexibly to individual needs.

LD/ADHD ADMISSIONS INFORMATION

College entrance tests required: Yes
Nonstandardized tests accepted: Yes
Interview required: No
Essay required: No
Documentation required for LD: Psychoeducational evaluation
Documentation required for ADHD: Yes
Documentation submitted to: O'Neill Center
Special Ed. HS course work accepted: Yes

Specific course requirements for all applicants: Yes
Separate application required for services: No
# of LD applications submitted yearly: NR
# of LD applications accepted yearly: NR
Total # of students receiving LD/ADHD services: 45
Acceptance into program means acceptance into college: Students must be admitted and enrolled at the College first and then may request services.

ADMISSIONS

There is no special admission procedure for students with learning disabilities, although the College tends to give special consideration if students self-disclose this information. The Director of Services for Students with Disabilities serves on the Admission Committee. The College of St. Catherine does not discriminate on the basis of disability in admission.

ADDITIONAL INFORMATION

Students with learning disabilities have access to support groups and practice in self-advocacy. In addition to the individual services offered by the O'Neill Center to all students, the following services are also available for students with documented disabilities: early registration; alternative testing, including time extensions and adaptive technology; note-taking; and one-to-one assistance from professional staff. Drop-in help is also available on a one-to-one basis from student assistants in writing, study skills, and time management.

SUPPORT SERVICES CONTACT INFORMATION

Learning Disability Program/Services: Resources for Disabilities/O'Neill Center
Director: Barbara Mandel
  E-mail: bjmandel@stkate.edu
  Telephone: 651-590-6706
  Fax: 651-690-6718
Contact: Same

LEARNING DISABILITY SERVICES

Requests for the following services/accommodations will be evaluated individually based on appropriate and current documentation.

Allowed in Exams
  Calculator: Yes
  Dictionary: Yes
  Computer: Yes
  Spellchecker: Yes
Extended test time: Yes
Scribes: Yes
Proctors: Yes
Oral exams: Yes
Notetakers: Yes

Distraction-reduced environment: Yes
Tape recording in class: Yes
Books on tape from RFBD: Yes
Taping of books not from RFBD: Yes
Accommodations for students with ADHD: Yes
Reading machine: Yes
Other assistive technology: Yes
Priority registration: Yes

Added costs for services: No
LD specialists: Yes (2)
Professional tutors: No
Peer tutors: Yes
Max. hours/wk. for services: Drop-in
How professors are notified of LD/ADHD: By student

GENERAL ADMISSIONS INFORMATION

Director of Admissions: Marleen Mohs
Telephone: 651-690-6000

ENTRANCE REQUIREMENTS
19 total are recommended; 4 English recommended, 3 math recommended, 2 science recommended, 4 foreign language recommended, 2 social studies recommended, 1 history recommended, 3 elective recommended. High school diploma or GED required. Minimum TOEFL is 500. TOEFL required of all international applicants.

Application deadline: Rolling
Notification: Rolling
Average GPA: 3.4

Average SAT I Math: 541
Average SAT I Verbal: 552
Average ACT: 22

Graduated top 10% of class: 19%
Graduated top 25% of class: 49%
Graduated top 50% of class: 79%

COLLEGE GRADUATION REQUIREMENTS

Course waivers allowed: No
Course substitutions allowed: Yes
In what subjects: Foreign language

ADDITIONAL INFORMATION

Environment: The College is located on 110 acres in an urban area in central St. Paul.

Student Body
  Undergrad enrollment: 2,545
  Female: 100%
  Male: 0%
  Out-of-state: 16%

Cost Information
  Tuition: $15,456
  Room & board: $4,550
Housing Information
  University housing: Yes
  Percent living on campus: 38%

Greek System
  Fraternity: No
  Sorority: No
Athletics: NCAA Division III

MOORHEAD STATE UNIVERSITY

Owens Hall, Moorhead, MN 56563
Phone: 218-236-2161 • Fax: 218-236-2168
E-mail: dragon@mnscu1.moorhead.msus.edu • Web: www.mnstate.edu
Support level: S • Institution type: 4-year public

LEARNING DISABILITY PROGRAM AND SERVICES

The University is committed to ensuring that all students have equal access to programs and services. The office of Services to Students with Disabilities addresses the needs of students who have disabilities. Any Moorhead State student with a documented learning disability is eligible for services.

LD/ADHD ADMISSIONS INFORMATION

College entrance tests required: Yes
Nonstandardized tests accepted: Yes
Interview required: No
Essay required: Yes
Documentation required for LD: Psychoeducational evaluation
Documentation required for ADHD: Yes
Documentation submitted to: Disability Services
Special Ed. HS course work accepted: Y/N

Specific course requirements for all applicants: Yes
Separate application required for services: No
# of LD applications submitted yearly: NA
# of LD applications accepted yearly: N/A
Total # of students receiving LD/ADHD services: 30–51
Acceptance into program means acceptance into college: Students must be accepted and enrolled at the University first and then may request services.

ADMISSIONS

There are no special admissions for students with learning disabilities. All students must meet the same criteria, including a rank in the top half of class or the following scores on standardized college admission tests: ACT 21+, PSAT 90+, or SAT 900+. They must also have 4 years English, 3 years math (2 algebra and 1 geometry), 3 years science (1 biological, 1 physical science, and at least 1 course must include significant laboratory experience), 3 years social studies (including American history and at least 1 course that includes significant emphasis on geography), 3 electives chosen from at least 2 of the following: world language, world culture, visual and performing arts. The New Center offers an alternative way to begin university studies to students who reside within the MSU service region.

ADDITIONAL INFORMATION

Skills courses are offered in study skills and test anxiety, and students may earn credits for these courses. Services and accommodations are available for undergraduate and graduate students.

SUPPORT SERVICES CONTACT INFORMATION

Learning Disability Program/Services: Disability Services
Director: Greg Toutges
  E-mail: toutges@mnstate.edu
  Telephone: 218-299-5859
  Fax: 212-287-5050
Contact: Same

LEARNING DISABILITY SERVICES

Requests for the following services/accommodations will be evaluated individually based on appropriate and current documentation.

Allowed in Exams
  Calculator: Yes
  Dictionary: Yes
  Computer: Yes
  Spellchecker: Yes
Extended test time: Yes
Scribes: Yes
Proctors: Yes
Oral exams: Yes
Note-takers: Yes

Distraction-reduced environment: Yes
Tape recording in class: Yes
Books on tape from RFBD: Yes
Taping of books not from RFBD: Yes
Accommodations for students with
  ADHD: Yes
Reading machine: Yes
Other assistive technology: Yes
Priority registration: Yes

Added costs for services: No
LD specialists: No
Professional tutors: No
Peer tutors: Yes
Max. hours/wk. for services: 1
How professors are notified of
  LD/ADHD: By director

GENERAL ADMISSIONS INFORMATION

Director of Admissions: Gina Munson
Telephone: 218-236-2161

ENTRANCE REQUIREMENTS
20 total are required; 4 English required, 3 math required, 2 science required, 2 foreign language recommended, 2 social studies required. High school diploma or GED required. Minimum TOEFL is 500. TOEFL required of all international applicants.

Application deadline: August 1
Notification: Rolling beginning 10/1
Average GPA: NR

Average SAT I Math: NR
Average SAT I Verbal: NR
Average ACT: 22

Graduated top 10% of class: 11%
Graduated top 25% of class: 39%
Graduated top 50% of class: 84%

COLLEGE GRADUATION REQUIREMENTS

Course waivers allowed: Not typically
Course waivers substitutions allowed: Yes
In what subjects: Varies based on disability and requirements of major

ADDITIONAL INFORMATION

Environment: The University has a suburban campus 240 miles northwest of Minneapolis.

Student Body
  Undergrad enrollment: 6,729
  Female: 63%
  Male: 37%
  Out-of-state: 39%

Cost Information
  In-state tuition: $2,728
  Out-of-state tuition: $6,118
  Room & board: $3,264
Housing Information
  University housing: Yes
  Percent living on campus: 26%

Greek System
  Fraternity: Yes
  Sorority: Yes
Athletics: NCAA Division II

ST. OLAF COLLEGE

1520 Street Olaf Avenue, Northfield, MN 55057-1098
Phone: 507-646-3025 • Fax: 507-646-3832
E-mail: admissions@stolaf.edu • Web: www.stolaf.edu
Support level: S • Institution type: 4-year private

LEARNING DISABILITY PROGRAM AND SERVICES

The goal of the services at St. Olaf is to provide equal access to a St. Olaf education for all students with disabilities. Because it is a small institution, they are able to work individually with students to reach this goal.

LD/ADHD ADMISSIONS INFORMATION

College entrance tests required: Yes
Nonstandardized tests accepted: Yes
Interview required: N/A
Essay required: Yes
Documentation required for LD: Statement (within three years) on letterhead of professional noting the history of the disability, testing done for diagnosis, effects of disability on academics, and possible recommendations
Documentation required for ADHD: Yes
Documentation submitted to: Academic Support Center
Special Ed. HS course work accepted: No

Specific course requirements for all applicants: Yes
Separate application required for services: No
# of LD applications submitted yearly: N/A
# of LD applications accepted yearly: N/A
Total # of students receiving LD/ADHD services: 16
Acceptance into program means acceptance into college: Students must be admitted and enrolled and then may request to be considered for services.

ADMISSIONS

All applicants must meet the same competitive admission criteria. There is no separate application process for students with learning disabilities or attention deficit disorder. Students are encouraged to self-disclose the disability in a personal statement. The middle 50 percent score range for the ACT is 25–30 and for the SAT 1170–1360. It's recommended that students have a strong academic curriculum with 4 years English, 3–4 years math, 3–4 years social studies, 3–4 years science, and 2–4 years foreign language. High school diploma is required and the GED is accepted. The TOEFL is required of all international applicants with a minimum score of 550. Once admitted, students with documented disabilities should have their current documentation sent to the Academic Support Center.

ADDITIONAL INFORMATION

All students have access to tutoring, math clinics, writing centers, study skills assistance, and weekly meetings, if necessary. Other accommodations and services are available with appropriate documentation including extended testing time; distraction-free testing environment; use of a calculator, dictionary, spellchecker or computer in exams; scribes; proctors; readers; note-takers; taped texts; and priority registration.

SUPPORT SERVICES CONTACT INFORMATION

Learning Disability Program/Services: Academic Support Center
Director: Peter Bolstad
  E-mail: bolstad@stolaf.edu
  Telephone: 507-646-3288
  Fax: 507-646-3750
Contact: Kathy Quade
  E-mail: quadek@stolaf.edu
  Telephone: 507-646-3288
  Fax: 507-646-3750

LEARNING DISABILITY SERVICES

Requests for the following services/accommodations will be evaluated individually based on appropriate and current documentation.

Allowed in Exams
  Calculator: Yes
  Dictionary: Yes
  Computer: Yes
  Spellchecker: Yes
Extended test time: Yes
Scribes: Yes
Proctors: Yes
Oral exams: Yes
Note-takers: Yes

Distraction-reduced environment: Yes
Tape recording in class: Yes
Books on tape from RFBD: Yes
Taping of books not from RFBD: Yes
Accommodations for students with ADHD: Yes
Reading machine: No
Other assistive technology: No
Priority registration: Yes

Added costs for services: No
LD specialists: No
Professional tutors: No
Peer tutors: 200
Max. hours/wk. for services: 3
How professors are notified of LD/ADHD: By student

GENERAL ADMISSIONS INFORMATION

Director of Admissions: Jana Kyle
Telephone: 507-646-3025

ENTRANCE REQUIREMENTS
15 total are recommended; 4 English recommended, 3 math recommended, 3 science recommended, 1 science lab recommended, 2 foreign language recommended. High school diploma or GED required. Minimum TOEFL is 550. TOEFL required of all international applicants.

Application deadline: Rolling
Notification: Rolling beginning 2/1
Average GPA: 3.7

Average SAT I Math: 626
Average SAT I Verbal: 626
Average ACT: 27

Graduated top 10% of class: 49%
Graduated top 25% of class: 79%
Graduated top 50% of class: 97%

COLLEGE GRADUATION REQUIREMENTS

Course waivers allowed: No
Course substitutions allowed: Yes
In what subjects: Foreign language; substitution is possible

ADDITIONAL INFORMATION

Environment: The College is located on 350 acres in a small town near Minneapolis.

Student Body
  Undergrad enrollment: 3,014
  Female: 57%
  Male: 43%
  Out-of-state: 45%

Cost Information
  Tuition: $19,400
  Room & board: $4,500
Housing Information
  University housing: Yes
  Percent living on campus: 96%

Greek System
  Fraternity: Yes
  Sorority: Yes
Athletics: NCAA Division III

UNIVERSITY OF MINNESOTA—DULUTH

23 Campus Center, Duluth, MN 55812
Phone: 218-726-7171 • Fax: 218-726-6394
E-mail: umdadmis@d.umn.edu • Web: www.d.umn.edu
Support level: CS • Institution type: 4-year public

LEARNING DISABILITY PROGRAM AND SERVICES

The Learning Disabilities Program strives to help students understand their disability, be able to clearly explain how it affects them academically, and be able to request the accommodations needed. The Learning Disabilities Program also provides guidance, advocacy, and assistance to students with documented learning disabilities, so that they can achieve to their fullest potential. Services and accommodations are provided on an individual and flexible basis. Once admitted, students needing special services have the responsibility of contacting the Access Center. Services include skills enhancement courses, assistance in arranging alternative testing and evaluation methods, priority registration, proofreading of written projects, advocacy with faculty, and support groups to meet expressed needs of students.

LD/ADHD ADMISSIONS INFORMATION

College entrance tests required: Yes
Nonstandardized tests accepted: Yes
Interview required: No
Essay required: No
Documentation required for LD: Psychoeducational
   evaluation: within 3 years
Documentation required for ADHD: Yes
Documentation submitted to: LD Program
Special Ed. HS course work accepted: No

Specific course requirements for all applicants: Yes
Separate application required for services: No
# of LD applications submitted yearly: N/A
# of LD applications accepted yearly: N/A
Total # of students receiving LD/ADHD services: 100
Acceptance into program means acceptance into
   college: Students must be admitted and enrolled at the University first and then may request services.

ADMISSIONS
All students must meet the regular university admission requirements. Admission criteria include an ACT of 19+ and rank in the top third of the high school class. Applicants who rank in the 40th to 65th percentile of their class (or below) are reviewed individually. Students with an identified learning disability may have their applications evaluated by a committee of admissions and disability services personnel. These students must provide documentation of a learning disability from high school, independent psychological testing clinic, or learning evaluation center. The admission decision is made jointly by the Program Director and the Director of Admission. Students who do not qualify for admission may take evening classes through University College. If they maintain a GPA of 2.0 or better they may be admitted to the regular college program.

ADDITIONAL INFORMATION
Any student admitted to the University with a verified learning disability is eligible for support services from the Access Center. Skills enhancement courses in writing, math, and study strategies are offered by the University. At the beginning of each quarter students needing special services must contact the Access Center and also notify instructors of special needs. Reading machines are available for all students in the library. Services and accommodations are available for undergraduate and graduate students.

SUPPORT SERVICES CONTACT INFORMATION

Learning Disability Program/Services: Learning Disabilities Program
Director: Penny Cragun
  Telephone: 218-726-8727
Contact: Judy Bromen, LD Coordinator
  Telephone: 218-726-7965

LEARNING DISABILITY SERVICES

Requests for the following services/accommodations will be evaluated individually based on appropriate and current documentation.

Allowed in Exams
  Calculator: Y/N
  Dictionary: Y/N
  Computer: Y/N
  Spellchecker: Y/N
Extended test time: Yes
Scribes: Yes
Proctors: Yes
Oral exams: Yes
Note-takers: Yes

Distraction-reduced environment: Yes
Tape recording in class: Yes
Books on tape from RFBD: Yes
Taping of books not from RFBD: Yes
Accommodations for students with
  ADHD: Yes
Reading machine: No
Other assistive technology: No
Priority registration: Yes

Added costs for services: No
LD specialists: Yes (2)
Professional tutors: No
Peer tutors: No
Max. hours/wk. for services: N/A
How professors are notified of
  LD/ADHD: By the student

GENERAL ADMISSIONS INFORMATION

Director of Admissions: Beth Esselstrom
Telephone: 218-726-7171

ENTRANCE REQUIREMENTS
14 total are required; 4 English required, 3 math required, 3 science required, 2 foreign language required, 2 social studies required. High school diploma or GED required. Minimum TOEFL is 550. TOEFL required of all international applicants.

Application deadline: August 1
Notification: Rolling beginning 9/1
Average GPA: 3.2

Average SAT I Math: NR
Average SAT I Verbal: NR
Average ACT: 23

Graduated top 10% of class: 17%
Graduated top 25% of class: 47%
Graduated top 50% of class: 86%

COLLEGE GRADUATION REQUIREMENTS

Course waivers allowed: By petition
Course substitutions allowed: By petition
In what subjects: Decisions are made on a case-by-case basis. Math and foreign language courses have been waived after the student has made an honest attempt at mastery.

ADDITIONAL INFORMATION

Environment: The University is located on a 250-acre campus in Duluth.

Student Body
  Undergrad enrollment: 8,605
  Female: 51%
  Male: 49%
  Out-of-state: 13%

Cost Information
  In-state tuition: $4,230
  Out-of-state tuition: $12,660
  Room & board: $4,338
Housing Information
  University housing: Yes
  Percent living on campus: 38%

Greek System
  Fraternity: Yes
  Sorority: Yes
Athletics: NAIA

UNIVERSITY OF SAINT THOMAS

2115 Summit Avenue, #32-F1, St. Paul, MN 55105-1096
Phone: 651-962-6150 • Fax: 651-962-6160
E-mail: admissions@stthomas.edu • Web: www.stthomas.edu
Support level: S • Institution type: 4-year private

LEARNING DISABILITY PROGRAM AND SERVICES

The mission of the Enhancement Program and Specialized Services is to ensure that all students with disabilities achieve their educational, career, and personal goals. Comprehensive support services and accommodations are offered that will allow the student equal access to all the University programs and facilities. Students qualify for services through the Enhancement Program upon self-disclosure and presentation of appropriate documentation of an LD/ADHD. Qualified students, along with the Enhancement Program staff, work to realize their potential for academic success. The staff acknowledges that individuals with documented disabilities have unique learning needs. Reasonable accommodations are arranged on an individual basis based on the disability and with the requirements of a particular course. To be eligible for these services, documentation from a licensed professional is required. The documentation should state the nature of the disability and the types of accommodations recommended by the licensed professional. The Enhancement Program represents an institutional commitment to individual guidance for students to develop the skills necessary to become independent lifelong learners.

LD/ADHD ADMISSIONS INFORMATION

College entrance tests required: Yes
Nonstandardized tests accepted: Yes
Interview required: No
Essay required: Yes
Documentation required for LD: A psychoeducational assessment completed within last three years, Woodcock-Johnson Test of Achievement, Wechsler Adult Intelligence Scale
Documentation required for ADHD: Yes
Documentation submitted to: Enhancement Program
Special Ed. HS course work accepted: Yes

Specific course requirements for all applicants: Yes
Separate application required for services: No
# of LD applications submitted yearly: 35–41
# of LD applications accepted yearly: All with documentation
Total # of students receiving LD/ADHD services: 180
Acceptance into program means acceptance into college: Students must be admitted and enrolled and then may request services.

ADMISSIONS

There are general requirements for admission; some exceptions are made on a case-by-case basis. The general requirements include an ACT score of 20/21, GPA of 3.0 or 35th to 40th percentile of a student's class, recommendations, and an essay. If it is known that a student has a disability, the Office of Admissions may ask the Director of the Enrichment Program to assess the documentation. The Office of Admission, has the final decision, but the Director of the Enhancement Program may be asked to provide information and recommendations. Students can be admitted on a probationary status. They will be required to develop an academic contract with a counselor and meet with that person regularly throughout the semester. Students cannot get an F in any of the classes. They must maintain this for two semesters, and if they do, they are then admitted regularly.

ADDITIONAL INFORMATION

Comprehensive services are available through a collaborative effort of the Enhancement Program counselors, the Accommodations Coordinator, and student employees. Academic and personal counseling is offered pertaining to the student's specific disability. Reasonable accommodations such as note-takers, readers, scribes, books on tape, alternate testing arrangements, and course/program modifications are offered if appropriate. The student's skills are assessed through a pre-screening interview to see if further testing is necessary, and the staff will collaborate with outside agencies for complete diagnostic services. The Enhancement Program offers a "testing, tutoring, and technology" center which houses adaptive technology. Additionally, they offer one-on-one tutoring that emphasizes strategies to improve course content and retention.

SUPPORT SERVICES CONTACT INFORMATION

Learning Disability Program/Services: Enhancement Program
Director: Kimberly Schumann (Associate)
  E-mail: kjschumann@stthomas.edu
  Telephone: 651-962-6315
  Fax: 651-962-6710
Contact: Same

LEARNING DISABILITY SERVICES

Requests for the following services/accommodations will be evaluated individually based on appropriate and current documentation.

Allowed in Exams
  Calculator: Yes
  Dictionary: Yes
  Computer: Yes
  Spellchecker: Yes
Extended test time: Yes
Scribes: Yes
Proctors: Yes
Oral exams: Yes
Note-takers: Yes

Distraction-reduced environment: Yes
Tape recording in class: Yes
Books on tape from RFBD: Yes
Taping of books not from RFBD: Yes
Accommodations for students with
  ADHD: Yes
Reading machine: Yes
Other assistive technology: Yes
Priority registration: Yes

Added costs for services: No
LD specialists: No
Professional tutors: No
Peer tutors: Yes
Max. hours/wk. for services:
  Unlimited
How professors are notified of
  LD/ADHD: By both student and
  director

GENERAL ADMISSIONS INFORMATION

Director of Admissions: Chris Getting
Telephone: 651-962-6150

ENTRANCE REQUIREMENTS

4 English recommended, 3 math required, 4 math recommended, 2 science recommended, 4 foreign language recommended. High school diploma or GED required. Minimum TOEFL is 550. TOEFL required of all international applicants.

Application deadline: N/A
Notification: Rolling beginning 10/1
Average GPA: 3.6

Average SAT I Math: 587
Average SAT I Verbal: 579
Average ACT: 25

Graduated top 10% of class: 32%
Graduated top 25% of class: 61%
Graduated top 50% of class: 93%

COLLEGE GRADUATION REQUIREMENTS

Course waivers allowed: Yes
Course substitutions allowed: Yes
In what subjects: Math and foreign language; with assistance, students petition the Committee on Studies

ADDITIONAL INFORMATION

Environment: Located 5 miles from downtown.

Student Body
  Undergrad enrollment: 5,469
  Female: 53%
  Male: 47%
  Out-of-state: 19%

Cost Information
  Tuition: $17,088
  Room & board: $5,407
Housing Information
  University housing: Yes
  Percent living on campus: 42%

Greek System
  Fraternity: Yes
  Sorority: Yes
Athletics: NCAA Division III

Univ. of Southern Mississippi

Box 5011, Hattiesburg, MS 39406
Phone: 601-266-5000 • Fax: 601-266-5148
E-mail: admissions@usm.edu • Web: www.usm.edu
Support level: S • Institution type: 4-year public

LEARNING DISABILITY PROGRAM AND SERVICES

The philosophy of USM is to provide services to students with learning disabilities to give them the maximum opportunity to complete a college education. The Office for Disability Accommodations (ODA) is USM's designated office to verify eligibility for accommodations under the American with Disabilities Act, and to develop and coordinate plans for the provision of such accommodations. After receiving documentation of the disability, ODA works with students to develop a plan for the provision of reasonable accommodations that are specific to their disabilities.

LD/ADHD ADMISSIONS INFORMATION

College entrance tests required: Yes
Nonstandardized tests accepted: Yes
Interview required: Yes
Essay required: No
Documentation required for LD: Full psychoeducational evaluation
Documentation required for ADHD: Yes
Documentation submitted to: Disability Accommodations
Special Ed. HS course work accepted: No

Specific course requirements for all applicants: Yes
Separate application required for services: No
# of LD applications submitted yearly: N/A
# of LD applications accepted yearly: N/A
Total # of students receiving LD/ADHD services: N/A
Acceptance into program means acceptance into college: Students must be admitted and enrolled in the University and then may request services.

ADMISSIONS

There is no special application for students with learning disabilities. Freshmen have specific curriculum, GPA and test score requirements. The mean ACT is 18, SAT 850, and the minimum GPA is 2.0. Course requirements include 4 years of English, 3 years of math, 3 years of social studies, 3 years of science and 2 electives. The admission decision for students with learning disabilities is made by the Director of OSSD. An interview is not required, but is preferred. The University offers a pre-admission summer program.

ADDITIONAL INFORMATION

In order to receive reasonable accommodations for a disability, students must file an application with OSS and provide current documentation of a disability. After an application is filed, students schedule an appointment with the OSS Coordinator, complete an Intake Form, and establish a plan for reasonable accommodations and services. The OSS helps students locate tutors, note-takers, and other ancillary aids for their classwork. The office works with Vocational Rehabilitation in order to pay for these services. The office staff works with students on a one-to-one basis in order to determine how they learn best. There are remedial programs in math, writing, and reading.

SUPPORT SERVICES CONTACT INFORMATION

Learning Disability Program/Services: Office for Disability Accommodations
Director: Suzy B. Hebert, Coordinator
 E-mail: suzanne.hebert@usm.edu
 Telephone: 601-266-5024
 Fax: 601-266-6035
Contact: Same

LEARNING DISABILITY SERVICES

Requests for the following services/accommodations will be evaluated individually based on appropriate and current documentation.

Allowed in Exams
 Calculator: Yes
 Dictionary: Yes
 Computer: Yes
 Spellchecker: Yes
Extended test time: Yes
Scribes: Yes
Proctors: Yes
Oral exams: Yes
Note-takers: Yes

Distraction-reduced environment: Yes
Tape recording in class: Yes
Books on tape from RFBD: Yes
Taping of books not from RFBD: Yes
Accommodations for students with ADHD: Yes
Reading machine: Yes
Other assistive technology: Yes
Priority registration: No

Added costs for services: No
LD specialists: No
Professional tutors: No
Peer tutors: Yes
Max. hours/wk. for services: Varies
How professors are notified of LD/ADHD: Letter from OSS

GENERAL ADMISSIONS INFORMATION

Director of Admissions: Dr. Homer Wesley
Telephone: 601-266-5000

ENTRANCE REQUIREMENTS

16 total are required; 4 English required, 3 math required, 3 science required, 2 science lab required, 2 foreign language required, 1 social studies required, 2 history required. High school diploma or GED required. Minimum TOEFL is 525. TOEFL required of all international applicants.

Application deadline: August 10
Notification: Rolling
Average GPA: 3.3

Average SAT I Math: NR
Average SAT I Verbal: NR
Average ACT: 22

Graduated top 10% of class: 37%
Graduated top 25% of class: 49%
Graduated top 50% of class: 81%

COLLEGE GRADUATION REQUIREMENTS

Course waivers allowed: No
Course substitutions allowed: Yes
In what subjects: Varies; substitutions only, with supporting documentation

ADDITIONAL INFORMATION

Environment: The University is located on 840 acres in a small city 90 miles southeast of Jackson.

Student Body
 Undergrad enrollment: 12,049
 Female: 60%
 Male: 40%
 Out-of-state: 14%

Cost Information
 In-state tuition: $2,970
 Out-of-state tuition: $6,898
 Room & board: $4,212
Housing Information
 University housing: Yes
 Percent living on campus: 33%

Greek System
 Fraternity: Yes
 Sorority: Yes
Athletics: NCAA Division I

EVANGEL UNIVERSITY

111 North Glenstone, Springfield, MO 65802
Phone: 417-865-2811 • Fax: 417-865-9599
E-mail: admissions@evangel.edu • Web: www.evangel.edu
Support level: CS • Institution type: 4-year private

LEARNING DISABILITY PROGRAM AND SERVICES

The Academic Support Center supports the needs of all students at Evangel University. The Center focuses on assisting students with improving academic skills so that they remain successful in college. The Center offers study skills assistance, tutorial services, and individual college planning. Group and individual support counseling is also available. Study skills are offered for credit. Checkpoint was established in response to the freshman progress reports and offers resources to at-risk students.

LD/ADHD ADMISSIONS INFORMATION

College entrance tests required: Yes
Nonstandardized tests accepted: Yes
Interview required: No
Essay required: Yes
Documentation required for LD: Psychoeducational evaluation
Documentation required for ADHD: Yes
Documentation submitted to: Academic Support Center
Special Ed. HS course work accepted: Yes, if it meets the current criteria

Specific course requirements for all applicants: Yes
Separate application required for services: No
# of LD applications submitted yearly: N/A
# of LD applications accepted yearly: N/A
Total # of students receiving LD/ADHD services: 27
Acceptance into program means acceptance into college: Students must be admitted and enrolled at the College first and then may request services.

ADMISSIONS

There is no special application for students with learning disabilities. All students must meet the same admission criteria. Evangel University looks at the completed application; ACT test is required, 2.0 GPA, pastor's recommendation, and high school recommendation. Course requirements include 3 years English, 2 years math, 2 years social science, and 1 year science. Students with documented LD can request a substitute for specific courses if their disability impacts their ability to learn that particular subject. Special admission to SOAR Program is offered to students with ACT scores between 14–17. These students will be enrolled in study-skills as well as other proficiency classes.

ADDITIONAL INFORMATION

Some study-skills classes are required for students who are admitted conditionally. The Academic Support Center offers tutoring, at no cost, in a variety of courses. The Center offers resources in such topics as personal growth; goal setting; self-concept enrichment; stress management; memory and concentration; test-taking; underlining; note-taking; outlining; reading a textbook; research; writing term papers; time scheduling; reading efficiency; and vocabulary. Additional resources include the design and implementation of individualized programs with an instructor; personal professional counseling at no charge; career counseling with the Director of Career Development Services; reading labs for increased reading speed; and tutoring in other classes at no charge. Checkpoint offers the following resources to students: performance assessments of text reading and note-taking; assessment of study and time management skills; personal interviews to help address academic difficulties; information about tutoring; and academic advising. SOAR is designed to assist selected provisionally admitted students during the first two semesters of college. SOAR courses focus on specific modules such as assessment and skills review in reading, math, and writing; study skills application; and career planning.

SUPPORT SERVICES CONTACT INFORMATION

Learning Disability Program/Services: Academic Support Center
Director: Dr. Laynah J. Rogers
 E-mail: rogersl@evangel.edu
 Telephone: 417-865-2811
 Fax: 417-865-1574
Contact: Same

LEARNING DISABILITY SERVICES

Requests for the following services/accommodations will be evaluated individually based on appropriate and current documentation.

Allowed in Exams
 Calculator: Yes
 Dictionary: Yes
 Computer: Yes
 Spellchecker: Yes
Extended test time: Yes
Scribes: Yes
Proctors: Yes
Oral exams: Yes
Note-takers: Yes

Distraction-reduced environment: Yes
Tape recording in class: Yes
Books on tape from RFBD: Yes
Taping of books not from RFBD: Yes
Accommodations for students with ADHD: Yes
Reading machine: Yes
Other assistive technology: Yes
Priority registration: No

Added costs for services: No
LD specialists: Yes (1)
Professional tutors: 1
Peer tutors: 8
Max. hours/wk. for services: Unlimited
How professors are notified of LD/ADHD: By both student and director

GENERAL ADMISSIONS INFORMATION

Director of Admissions: Andy Denton
Telephone: 417-865-2811

ENTRANCE REQUIREMENTS
14 total are recommended; 3 English recommended, 2 math recommended, 1 science recommended, 1 science lab recommended, 2 foreign language recommended, 2 social studies recommended, 3 elective recommended. Minimum TOEFL is 490. TOEFL required of all international applicants.

Application deadline: August 15
Notification: Rolling beginning 9/1
Average GPA: NR

Average SAT I Math: NR
Average SAT I Verbal: NR
Average ACT: 23

Graduated top 10% of class: NR
Graduated top 25% of class: NR
Graduated top 50% of class: NR

COLLEGE GRADUATION REQUIREMENTS

Course waivers allowed: No
Course substitutions allowed: Yes
In what subjects: Math

ADDITIONAL INFORMATION

Environment: The College is located on 80 acres in an urban area 225 miles west of St. Louis.

Student Body
 Undergrad enrollment: 1,616
 Female: 56%
 Male: 44%
 Out-of-state: 60%

Cost Information
 Tuition: $8,390
 Room & board: $3,440
Housing Information
 University housing: Yes
 Percent living on campus: 82%

Greek System
 Fraternity: Yes
 Sorority: Yes
Athletics: NCAA Division II

KANSAS CITY ART INSTITUTE

4415 Warwick Boulevard, Kansas City, MO 64111-1762
Phone: 816-474-5225 • Fax: 816-802-3309
E-mail: admiss@kcai.edu • Web: www.kcai.edu
Support level: S • Institution type: 4-year private

LEARNING DISABILITY PROGRAM AND SERVICES

The Academic Resource Center is committed to the educational development of students at Kansas City Art Institute. A recognition of the individual cognitive and creative styles of students of art and design is reflected in the comprehensive support service offered. The goal is to foster independent thinking and problem solving, resourcefulness, and personal responsibility. All KCAI students are invited to take advantage of the services provided by the ARC. Services are aimed at enhancing a student's experience throughout his/her academic career. The staff takes a holistic approach, and is committed to the educational, personal, and evolving professional development of all students. Students with formal documentation of a disability are encouraged to contact the ARC for assistance in arranging accommodations or developing self-advocacy strategies.

LD/ADHD ADMISSIONS INFORMATION

College entrance tests required: Yes
Nonstandardized tests accepted: Yes
Interview required: N/A
Essay required: Yes
Documentation required for LD: Any psychoeducational battery: within 3 years
Documentation required for ADHD: Yes
Documentation submitted to: Academic Resource Center
Special Ed. HS course work accepted: N/A

Specific course requirements for all applicants: Yes
Separate application required for services: No
# of LD applications submitted yearly: N/A
# of LD applications accepted yearly: N/A
Total # of students receiving LD/ADHD services: 15
Acceptance into program means acceptance into college: Students must be admitted and enrolled at the institute first and then may request services.

ADMISSIONS
Students with learning disabilities must demonstrate art ability through a portfolio review and meet a combination of academic criteria, like all applicants, but with a more specialized evaluation. Admitted students should have a minimum ACT of 20 or SAT of 950 and a 2.5 GPA. Students must have had at least 4 years of high school English. If the criteria are not met, applicants are considered in-depth via an admissions committee. An interview is recommended.

ADDITIONAL INFORMATION
Students are given assistance in the ARC on an individual basis. Students will consult with their academic advisor each semester about progress in their academic degree program. Advisors help assess progress toward a degree and provide guidance in course selection. Peer advisors are also available. The learning specialist helps students gain a more complete understanding of their individual learning styles, skills, strengths, and weaknesses to cope with the great demands of college courses. Assistance is available through study groups and one-on-one tutoring sessions to improve reading, writing, study, testing, and time management skills.

SUPPORT SERVICES CONTACT INFORMATION

Learning Disability Program/Services: Academic Resource Center (ARC)
Director: Mary Magers
 Telephone: 816-802-4852
 Fax: 816-802-3439
Contact: Same

LEARNING DISABILITY SERVICES

Requests for the following services/accommodations will be evaluated individually based on appropriate and current documentation.

Allowed in Exams
 Calculator: Yes
 Dictionary: Yes
 Computer: Yes
 Spellchecker: Yes
Extended test time: Yes
Scribes: No
Proctors: No
Oral exams: Yes
Note-takers: Yes

Distraction-reduced environment: Yes
Tape recording in class: Yes
Books on tape from RFBD: No
Taping of books not from RFBD: No
**Accommodations for students with
 ADHD:** Yes
Reading machine: No
Other assistive technology: No
Priority registration: No

Added costs for services: Student
 pays for note-taker
LD specialists: No
Professional tutors: 1
Peer tutors: 3
Max. hours/wk. for services:
 Unlimited
**How professors are notified of
 LD/ADHD:** By both student and
 director

GENERAL ADMISSIONS INFORMATION

Director of Admissions: Larry Stone
Telephone: 816-802-3300

ENTRANCE REQUIREMENTS

20 total are recommended; 4 English recommended, 3 math recommended, 3 science recommended, 3 social studies recommended, 3 elective recommended. High school diploma or GED required. Minimum TOEFL is 550. TOEFL required of all international applicants.

Application deadline: Rolling
Notification: Rolling
Average GPA: 3.3

Average SAT I Math: 541
Average SAT I Verbal: 563
Average ACT: 23

Graduated top 10% of class: 13%
Graduated top 25% of class: 33%
Graduated top 50% of class: 70%

COLLEGE GRADUATION REQUIREMENTS

Course waivers allowed: No
Course substitutions allowed: No
In what subjects: N/A

ADDITIONAL INFORMATION

Environment: The campus is located in an urban area in Kansas City.

Student Body
 Undergrad enrollment: 527
 Female: 51%
 Male: 49%
 Out-of-state: 84%

Cost Information
 Tuition: $17,974
 Room & board: $6,000
Housing Information
 University housing: Yes
 Percent living on campus: 20%

Greek System
 Fraternity: Yes
 Sorority: Yes
Athletics: None

SOUTHWEST MISSOURI STATE UNIV.

901 South National, Springfield, MO 65804
Phone: 417-836-5517 • Fax: 417-836-6334
E-mail: smsuinfo@mail.smsu.edu • Web: www.smsu.edu
Support level: CS • Institution type: 4-year public

LEARNING DISABILITY PROGRAM AND SERVICES

The Learning Diagnostic Clinic (LDC) is an academic support facility to assist students with psychological disabilities. The staff includes psychologists and learning specialists. LDC provides two levels of academic support to "qualified" individuals: One level of services includes those services that comprise basic accommodations guaranteed to the "qualified" students with disabilities under the law; these services are offered at no cost. The next level is called Project Success, an academic support program for college students with learning disabilities who desire more comprehensive services. This program provides academic and emotional support that will help to ease the transition to higher learning and the opportunity to function independently. Students applying to the Project Success program are required to have a psychoeducational evaluation by the LDC staff to ensure that the program is suitable for their needs and to provide appropriate accommodations. The fee for testing is $500. If background and documentation do not support a diagnosis of LD, alternatives and suggestions are discussed with the student. If the student wishes to appeal a decision not to provide services, he/she is referred to the ADA/504 Compliance Officer.

LD/ADHD ADMISSIONS INFORMATION

College entrance tests required: Yes
Nonstandardized tests accepted: Yes
Interview required: Yes
Essay required: No
Documentation required for LD: Psychoeducational
 evaluation
Documentation required for ADHD: Yes
Documentation submitted to: Disability Services
Special Ed. HS course work accepted: No

Specific course requirements for all applicants: Yes
Separate application required for services: No
# of LD applications submitted yearly: N/A
# of LD applications accepted yearly: N/A
Total # of students receiving LD/ADHD services: 160
Acceptance into program means acceptance into
 college: Students must be admitted and enrolled at the
 University first and then may request an application to
 LDC or Project Success.

ADMISSIONS

Students must be admitted to the University to be eligible for the services, and students with learning disabilities must meet the same requirements for admission to the University as all other applicants. There is a special application to be completed as well as a required evaluation fee for students requesting special services. Eligibility for admissions is based on a sliding scale determined by ACT scores and class rank. Application procedures to Progress Success are: gain acceptance to the University; self-identify and request application at LDC; submit application and requested information; and student is offered date for personal interview and testing or referred to other services; once interview and testing is completed the test data and information are evaluated by staff. The student is accepted or offered alternative suggestions.

ADDITIONAL INFORMATION

Students must self-identify as having a learning disability in order to request accommodations from LDC. Early referral permits the LDC more time to gather information and evaluate documentation. Appropriate accommodations are determined by the director and the student. The student is assigned to a graduate assistant who maintains contact, monitors progress, and assesses the effectiveness of accommodations. Project Success staff provides intensive remediation, focusing upon written language and mathematics strategies; caseworkers provide assistance/advocacy skills; tutors, trained by the LDC, are available to students enrolled in the Project Success program; the fee for this level of accommodations is $1,000 per semester. Basic services from LDC may include assistance in obtaining recorded textbooks, testing accommodations, counseling, advisement, and note-taking assistance; there is no fee for basic services.

SUPPORT SERVICES CONTACT INFORMATION

Learning Disability Program/Services: Learning Diagnostic Clinic (LDC)
Director: Stexe Capps, PhD
 E-mail: stevencapps@smsu.edu
 Telephone: 417-836-4787
 Fax: 417-836-5475
Contact: Terri Schrenk, MS

LEARNING DISABILITY SERVICES

Requests for the following services/accommodations will be evaluated individually based on appropriate and current documentation.

Allowed in Exams
 Calculator: Y/N
 Dictionary: Y/N
 Computer: Y/N
 Spellchecker: Y/N
Extended test time: Yes
Scribes: Yes
Proctors: Yes
Oral exams: Yes
Note-takers: Yes

Distraction-reduced environment: Yes
Tape recording in class: Yes
Books on tape from RFBD: Yes
Taping of books not from RFBD: Yes
Accommodations for students with ADHD: Yes
Reading machine: Yes
Other assistive technology: Yes
Priority registration: Yes

Added costs for services: No
LD specialists: Yes (3)
Professional tutors: No
Peer tutors: Yes
Max. hours/wk. for services: 1 hour per week per course
How professors are notified of LD/ADHD: By student and service coordinator

GENERAL ADMISSIONS INFORMATION

Director of Admissions: Don Simpson
Telephone: 417-836-5517

ENTRANCE REQUIREMENTS
16 total are required; 4 English required, 3 math required, 2 science required, 1 science lab required, 3 social studies required, 3 elective required. High school diploma or GED required. Minimum TOEFL is 500. TOEFL required of all international applicants.

Application deadline: August 1
Notification: Rolling beginning 8/1
Average GPA: 3.2

Average SAT I Math: NR
Average SAT I Verbal: NR
Average ACT: 23

Graduated top 10% of class: 21%
Graduated top 25% of class: 47%
Graduated top 50% of class: 82%

COLLEGE GRADUATION REQUIREMENTS

Course waivers allowed: No
Course substitutions allowed: Yes
In what subjects: In special circumstances

ADDITIONAL INFORMATION

Environment: The 200-acre rural campus is located 170 miles from Kansas City and 120 miles from St. Louis.

Student Body
 Undergrad enrollment: 14,515
 Female: 55%
 Male: 45%
 Out-of-state: 8%

Cost Information
 In-state tuition: $3,564
 Out-of-state tuition: $6,774
 Room & board: $3,846
Housing Information
 University housing: Yes
 Percent living on campus: 28%

Greek System
 Fraternity: Yes
 Sorority: Yes
 Athletics: NCAA Division I

UNIV. OF MISSOURI—COLUMBIA

230 Jesse Hall, Columbia, MO 65211
Phone: 573-882-7786 • Fax: 573-882-7887
E-mail: admissions@missouri.edu • Web: www.missouri.edu
Support level: CS • Institution type: 4-year public

LEARNING DISABILITY PROGRAM AND SERVICES

The mission of Disability Support Services is to encourage the educational development of students with a disability and to improve the understanding and support of the campus environment by: providing assistance to students with a documented disability and encouraging independence; serving as a liaison and advocate; working with students to ensure equal access to all programs and services. The Office for Disability Services (ODS) provides accommodations and support services within the resources of the University. The goal of the program is to promote independence and self-advocacy. In addition, ODS assists other college departments in providing access to services and programs in the most integrated setting possible. In order to access services or accommodations, students with LD must provide the most recent documentation indicating both ability, achievement, and IQ testing, performed by a qualified professional. Students with ADHD must have written documentation from a qualified professional stating client history, tests given, diagnosis, and accommodations recommended.

LD/ADHD ADMISSIONS INFORMATION

College entrance tests required: No
Nonstandardized tests accepted: Yes
Interview required: No
Essay required: No
Documentation required for LD: WAIS-III; WJ-R: within 3 years
Documentation required for ADHD: Yes
Documentation submitted to: Office of Disability Services
Special Ed. HS course work accepted: No

Specific course requirements for all applicants: Yes
Separate application required for services: No
# of LD applications submitted yearly: N/A
# of LD applications accepted yearly: N/A
Total # of students receiving LD/ADHD services: 100
Acceptance into program means acceptance into college: Students must be admitted and enrolled at the University and then may request services.

ADMISSIONS

There is no special admissions for students with learning disabilities. General admission is based on high school curriculum, ACT, and class rank. Applicants must have 4 years English, 4 years math, 3 years social studies, 3 years science, 2 years foreign language, and 1 unit of fine arts. Math, science, and foreign language requirements may be satisfied by completion of courses in middle school, junior high, or senior high. Any student with an ACT of 24 with the required courses is automatically admissible. Students with 23 ACT or 1050–1090 SAT need class rank of 48 percent; 22 ACT or 1010–1040 SAT need 54 percent; 21 ACT or 970–1000 SAT need 62 percent; 20 ACT or 930–960 SAT need 69 percent; 19 ACT or 890–920 SAT need 78 percent; 18 ACT or 840–880 SAT need 86 percent; 17 ACT or 800–830 SAT need 94 percent; ACT below 17 or SAT below 800 does not meet regular admission standards. Graduates of Missouri high schools who do not meet the standards for regular admission may be admitted on a conditional basis through summer session.

ADDITIONAL INFORMATION

Auxiliary aids and classroom accommodations include note-takers, lab assistants, readers, and specialized equipment. Testing accommodations include time extensions, quiet rooms, readers, scribes, or adaptive equipment. The learning disabilities specialist offers support and counseling in the areas of time management, study skills, learning styles and other academic and social issues. Group support is also available. Disabilities Services offers a mentoring program to provide first-year students the opportunity to meet with upperclassmen with disabilities. The Learning Center works cooperatively with DSO to provide individual tutoring free of charge. Other services include writing assistance, math assistance, test reviews, and help with reading comprehension and study skills.

SUPPORT SERVICES CONTACT INFORMATION

Learning Disability Program/Services: Office of Disability Services (ODS)
Director: Sarah Colby Weaver, PhD
  E-mail: weavers@missouri.edu
  Telephone: 573-882-4696
  Fax: 573-884-9272
Contact: Same

LEARNING DISABILITY SERVICES

Requests for the following services/accommodations will be evaluated individually based on appropriate and current documentation.

Allowed in Exams
  Calculator: Yes
  Dictionary: Yes
  Computer: Yes
  Spellchecker: Yes
Extended test time: Yes
Scribes: Yes
Proctors: Yes
Oral exams: Yes
Note-takers: Yes

Distraction-reduced environment: Yes
Tape recording in class: Yes
Books on tape from RFBD: Yes
Taping of books not from RFBD: Yes
Accommodations for students with ADHD: Yes
Reading machine: Yes
Other assistive technology: Yes
Priority registration: Yes

Added costs for services: No
LD specialists: Yes (1)
Professional tutors: 7
Peer tutors: 118
Max. hours/wk. for services: Unlimited
How professors are notified of LD/ADHD: By student

GENERAL ADMISSIONS INFORMATION

Director of Admissions: GeorgeAnn Porter
Telephone: 573-882-7786

ENTRANCE REQUIREMENTS
17 total are required; 4 English required, 4 math required, 3 science required, 1 science lab required, 2 foreign language required, 3 social studies required, 1 elective required. High school diploma or GED required. Minimum TOEFL is 500. TOEFL required of all international applicants.

Application deadline: Rolling
Notification: Rolling
Average GPA: NR

Average SAT I Math: NR
Average SAT I Verbal: NR
Average ACT: 25

Graduated top 10% of class: 34%
Graduated top 25% of class: 73%
Graduated top 50% of class: 91%

COLLEGE GRADUATION REQUIREMENTS

Course waivers allowed: Yes
Course substitutions allowed: Yes
In what subjects: Math and foreign language

ADDITIONAL INFORMATION

Environment: The University is located on 1,350 acres in a small town.

Student Body
  Undergrad enrollment: 17,346
  Female: 53%
  Male: 47%
  Out-of-state: 11%

Cost Information
  In-state tuition: $4,300
  Out-of-state tuition: $11,685
  Room & board: $4,700
Housing Information
  University housing: Yes
  Percent living on campus: 47%

Greek System
  Fraternity: Yes
  Sorority: Yes
Athletics: NCAA Division I

University of Missouri—Columbia

WASHINGTON UNIVERSITY IN ST. LOUIS

Campus Box 1089, One Brookings Drive, Saint Louis, MO 63130-4899
Phone: 314-935-6000 • Fax: 314-935-4290
E-mail: admissions@wustl.edu • Web: www.wustl.edu
Support level: CS • Institution type: 4-year private

LEARNING DISABILITY PROGRAM AND SERVICES

The Disability Resource Center recognizes that there are many types of disabilities that can hinder a student in showing his or her true academic ability. It is the goal of DSS to treat students with disabilities as individuals with specific needs and to provide services responsive to those needs. DSS provides a wide range of services and accommodations to help remove barriers posed by the students' disabilities. Students are encouraged to be their own advocates and have the major responsibility for securing services and accommodations. Reasonable accommodations will be made to assist students in meeting their individual needs. It is the goal of DSS to incorporate students with disabilities into the mainstream of the University community. Any student who has a permanent or temporary, psychological or physical disability is eligible for services. Students must self-identify and provide current documentation. The Director of DSS will work with the student to identify appropriate accommodations and services based upon documentation and previous experiences. Most accommodations resut from communication and agreements between the students and the classroom instructors.

LD/ADHD ADMISSIONS INFORMATION

College entrance tests required: Yes
Nonstandardized tests accepted: Yes
Interview required: Yes
Essay required: Yes
Documentation required for LD: Psychoeducational
  evaluation: within 3 years
Documentation required for ADHD: Yes
Documentation submitted to: Disability Resource Center
Special Ed. HS course work accepted: No

Specific course requirements for all applicants: Yes
Separate application required for services: No
# of LD applications submitted yearly: N/A
# of LD applications accepted yearly: N/A
Total # of students receiving LD/ADHD services: 73
**Acceptance into program means acceptance into
  college:** Students must be admitted and enrolled at the
  University first and then may request services.

ADMISSIONS

Washington University gives full consideration to all applicants for admission. There is no special admissions process for students with learning disabilities. Students may choose to voluntarily identify themselves as learning disabled in the admissions process. If they choose to self-identify, details of the history and treatment of the disability, how the individual has met different academic requirements in light of the disability, and the relationship between the disability and academic record help the University to understand more fully the applicant profile. This information can be helpful in the application process to explain, for example, lower grades in certain subjects. Washington University is a competitive school and looks for students with rigorous academic preparation, including 4 years English, 3–4 years math, 3–4 years science, 3–4 years social studies, and 2 years foreign language preferred but not required.

ADDITIONAL INFORMATION

The Learning Center services focus on reading, writing, vocabulary, time management, and study techniques. Skills classes are offered in time management, rapid reading, and self-advocacy, but they are not for credit. Common services and accommodations incude, but are not limited to: readers or scribes; note-takers; campus orientation; assistance in obtaining accommodations for professional exams; referral for disability evaluation; audiotaping class lectures; extra time to complete exams; alternative exam formats; and distraction-free exam sites. Services and accommodations are available for undergraduate and graduate students.

SUPPORT SERVICES CONTACT INFORMATION

Learning Disability Program/Services: Disability Resource Center (DRC)
Director: Fran Lang, PhD
  E-mail: drc@dosa.wustl.edu
  Telephone: 314-935-4062
  Fax: 314-935-8252
Contact: Donna Kepley
  E-mail: drc@dosa.wustl.edu
  Telephone: 314-935-4062
  Fax: 314-935-8272

LEARNING DISABILITY SERVICES

Requests for the following services/accommodations will be evaluated individually based on appropriate and current documentation.

Allowed in Exams
  Calculator: Yes
  Dictionary: Yes
  Computer: Yes
  Spellchecker: Yes
Extended test time: Yes
Scribes: Yes
Proctors: Yes
Oral exams: Yes
Note-takers: Yes

Distraction-reduced environment: Yes
Tape recording in class: Yes
Books on tape from RFBD: Yes
Taping of books not from RFBD: Yes
Accommodations for students with ADHD: Yes
Reading machine: Yes
Other assistive technology: Yes
Priority registration: No

Added costs for services: No
LD specialists: Yes (1)
Professional tutors: No
Peer tutors: Yes
Max. hours/wk. for services: Unlimited
How professors are notified of LD/ADHD: By both student and director

GENERAL ADMISSIONS INFORMATION

Director of Admissions: Nanette Tarbouni
Telephone: 800-638-0700

ENTRANCE REQUIREMENTS

18 total are recommended; 4 English recommended, 4 math recommended, 4 science recommended, 4 science lab recommended, 2 foreign language recommended, 4 social studies recommended, 4 history recommended. High school diploma or equivalent is not required. Minimum TOEFL is 550. TOEFL required of all international applicants.

Application deadline: January 15
Notification: April 1
Average GPA: NR

Average SAT I Math: 640–720
Average SAT I Verbal: 610–700
Average ACT: 28–31

Graduated top 10% of class: 85%
Graduated top 25% of class: 98%
Graduated top 50% of class: 100%

COLLEGE GRADUATION REQUIREMENTS

Course waivers allowed: No
Course substitutions allowed: No
In what subjects: N/A

ADDITIONAL INFORMATION

Environment: The Washington University campus is located 7 miles west of St. Louis on 169 acres.

Student Body
  Undergrad enrollment: 6,695
  Female: 51%
  Male: 49%
  Out-of-state: 88%

Cost Information
  Tuition: $25,700
  Room & board: $8,216
Housing Information
  University housing: Yes
  Percent living on campus: 77%

Greek System
  Fraternity: Yes
  Sorority: Yes
Athletics: NCAA Division III

WESTMINSTER COLLEGE

501 Westminster Avenue, Fulton, MO 65251-1299
Phone: 573-592-5251 • Fax: 573-592-5255
E-mail: admissions@jaynet.wcmo.edu • Web: www.westminster-mo.edu
Support level: SP • Institution type: 4-year private

LEARNING DISABILITY PROGRAM AND SERVICES

The goal of the Learning Disabilities Program is to give students with learning disabilities the special attention they need to succeed in basically the same academic program as that pursued by regularly admitted students. Westminster offers the students a supportive environment, small classes, and professors who are readily accessible. The LD staff offers intensive instruction in reading, writing, and study skills. Much of the instruction is conducted on a one-to-one basis, and is directed to the student's specific problem. Close supervision of the curriculum is essential in the freshman year, and the student's progress is monitored for any difficulties that may arise. The staff is LD certified and faculty members have the specific role of providing LD support.

LD/ADHD ADMISSIONS INFORMATION

College entrance tests required: Yes
Nonstandardized tests accepted: Yes
Interview required: Yes
Essay required: Yes
Documentation required for LD: WAIS-III; WISC III and written evaluation within two years; Woodcock-Johnson
Documentation required for ADHD: Yes
Documentation submitted to: Admissions and LD Program
Special Ed. HS course work accepted: No

Specific course requirements for all applicants: Yes
Separate application required for services: Yes
# of LD applications submitted yearly: 40–50
# of LD applications accepted yearly: 14–17
Total # of students receiving LD/ADHD services: 32
Acceptance into program means acceptance into college: Students are admitted jointly to the LD program and the College.

ADMISSIONS

There is a special application and admissions procedure for students with learning disabilities. Students submit a completed Westminster College application form and a separate application form for the LD Program; results of an eye and hearing exam; WAIS-R; WJ; achievement tests; SAT score of 900+ or ACT score of 19+ (untimed); two copies of the high school transcript; recent reports from school counselors, learning specialists, psychologists, or physicians who have diagnosed the applicant's disability; four recommendations from counselors or teachers familiar with the student's performance; and an evaluation from an educational specialist. An on-campus interview is required. Following the interview and a review of the file, the director and assistant director of the program confer and reach an admission decision usually within one week after the visit. Students are either admitted directly into the College and then reviewed for LD services or admitted into the LD Program, which results in an admission to the College.

ADDITIONAL INFORMATION

Students are mainstreamed and need a solid college-prep background in high school. There is a fee of $1,800 for the first year for the program and $900 thereafter. Students have access to unlimited tutoring. Learning resources include audiotapes of textbooks; self-instructional materials; special classes in study skills, reading and listening skills, test-taking strategies, time management, and English composition; and word processors to assist in writing instruction. The Student Development Center is a learning center that is open to all students.

SUPPORT SERVICES CONTACT INFORMATION

Learning Disability Program/Services: Learning Disabilities Program
Director: Hank F. Ottinger
  E-mail: ottingh@jaynet.wcmo.edu
  Telephone: 573-592-5304
  Fax: 573-592-5180
Contact: Same

LEARNING DISABILITY SERVICES

Requests for the following services/accommodations will be evaluated individually based on appropriate and current documentation.

Allowed in Exams
  Calculator: Yes
  Dictionary: No
  Computer: Yes
  Spellchecker: Yes
  Extended test time: Yes
  Scribes: Yes
  Proctors: Yes
  Oral exams: Yes
  Note-takers: Yes

Distraction-reduced environment: Yes
Tape recording in class: Yes
Books on tape from RFBD: Yes
Taping of books not from RFBD: Yes
Accommodations for students with ADHD: Yes
Reading machine: No
Other assistive technology: Yes
Priority registration: No

Added costs for services: $900 per semester
LD specialists: Yes (15)
Professional tutors: 2.5
Peer tutors: 20
Max. hours/wk. for services: Unlimited
How professors are notified of LD/ADHD: By director

GENERAL ADMISSIONS INFORMATION

Director of Admissions: Kelly Silvey
Telephone: 573-592-5195

ENTRANCE REQUIREMENTS

16 total are required; 4 English required, 3 math required, 3 science required, 2 science lab required, 3 foreign language recommended, 2 social studies required, 2 elective recommended. High school diploma or GED required. Minimum TOEFL is 550. TOEFL required of all international applicants.

Application deadline: Rolling
Notification: Rolling beginning 11/1
Average GPA: 3.4

Average SAT I Math: 546
Average SAT I Verbal: 563
Average ACT: 25

Graduated top 10% of class: 36%
Graduated top 25% of class: 53%
Graduated top 50% of class: 83%

COLLEGE GRADUATION REQUIREMENTS

Course waivers allowed: No
Course substitutions allowed: Y/N
In what subjects: Students can petition the faculty

ADDITIONAL INFORMATION

Environment: The 250-acre college campus is located in a small town 20 miles east of Columbia, Missouri.

Student Body
  Undergrad enrollment: 686
  Female: 43%
  Male: 57%
  Out-of-state: 28%

Cost Information
  Tuition: $14,060
  Room & board: $5,020
Housing Information
  University housing: Yes
  Percent living on campus: 75%

Greek System
  Fraternity: Yes
  Sorority: Yes
  Athletics: NCAA Division III

MONTANA STATE UNIV.—BILLINGS

1500 North 30th Street, Billings, MT 59101
Phone: 406-657-2158 • Fax: 406-657-2051
E-mail: keverett@msubillings.edu • Web: www.msubillings.edu
Support level: S • Institution type: 4-year public

LEARNING DISABILITY PROGRAM AND SERVICES

The mission of Disability Support Services is to encourage the educational development of students with disabilities and improve the understanding and support of the campus environment by providing assistance to students with disabilities, encouraging independence, and providing a supportive emotional atmosphere; serving as a liaison and advocate; and working with students to ensure equal access to all programs and services. MSU-Billings has a policy of providing reasonable accommodations to qualified students with a documented disability. Students requiring accommodations such as exam accessibility or reader services are encouraged to contact Disability Support Services at least four weeks before services are required. The guidelines utilized for providing services to students with LD are: (1) the student must meet the definition of LD set forth by the National Joint Committee on LD; (2) the student must have an LD diagnosed by a professional qualified to diagnose, and a statement of the disability and a summary of academic strengths and weaknesses must be included; (3) quantitative data acceptable for documentation must include standardized and informal measures including case histories, interviews, and previous records that confirm the learning problem; (4) DSS reserves the right to determine whether a student qualifies for services.

LD/ADHD ADMISSIONS INFORMATION

College entrance tests required: Yes
Nonstandardized tests accepted: Yes
Interview required: No
Essay required: No
Documentation required for LD: Must clearly state a learning disability or ADHD
Documentation required for ADHD: Yes
Documentation submitted to: DSS
Special Ed. HS course work accepted: Yes

Specific course requirements for all applicants: Yes
Separate application required for services: N/A
# of LD applications submitted yearly: N/A
# of LD applications accepted yearly: N/A
Total # of students receiving LD/ADHD services: 59
Acceptance into program means acceptance into college: Students must be admitted and enrolled at the University and then may request services.

ADMISSIONS

There is no special admission process for students with learning disabilities. All students must meet the same admission criteria. Freshmen applicants must meet one of the following conditions: (1) ACT of 22 or SAT 920; (2) 2.5 GPA; (3) rank in the top half of the class. Students must have 4 years English, 3 years math (students are encouraged to take math in senior year), 3 years social studies, 2 years laboratory science (1 year must be earth science, biology, chemistry, or physics), 2 years chosen from foreign language, computer science, visual and performing arts, vocational education that meet the Office of Public Instruction guidelines. Students not meeting the College-preparatory requirements have four options: (1) apply for an exemption by writing a letter and addressing special needs, talents, or other reasons; (2) enroll part-time in a summer session; (3) enroll as a part-time student with 7 or fewer credits the first semester; (4) attend a community college or other college and attempt at least 12 credits or make up any deficiency.

ADDITIONAL INFORMATION

Students must request services, provide documentation specifying a learning disability or ADHD, make an appointment for an intake with DSS, meet with professors at the beginning of each semester, and work closely with DSS. DSS must keep documentation and intake on file, make a determination of accommodations, issue identification cards to qualified students, and serve as a resource and a support. Services include course and testing accommodations; alternative testing; priority scheduling; technical assistance; liaison and referral services; taped textbooks; and career, academic, and counseling referrals. The use of computer, calculator, dictionary, or spellchecker is at the discretion of the individual professor, and based on the documented needs of the student. Services and accommodations are available for undergraduate and graduate students.

SUPPORT SERVICES CONTACT INFORMATION

Learning Disability Program/Services: Disability Support Services (DSS)
Director: Sharon Yazak
E-mail: syazak@msubillings.edu
Telephone: 406-657-2283
Fax: 406-657-2187
Contact: Same

LEARNING DISABILITY SERVICES

Requests for the following services/accommodations will be evaluated individually based on appropriate and current documentation.

Allowed in Exams
Calculator: Yes
Dictionary: No
Computer: Yes
Spellchecker: Yes
Extended test time: Yes
Scribes: Yes
Proctors: Yes
Oral exams: No
Note-takers: Yes

Distraction-reduced environment: Yes
Tape recording in class: Yes
Books on tape from RFBD: Yes
Taping of books not from RFBD: Yes
Accommodations for students with ADHD: Yes
Reading machine: Yes
Other assistive technology: Yes
Priority registration: Yes

Added costs for services: No
LD specialists: No
Professional tutors: 5
Peer tutors: 25
Max. hours/wk. for services: Varies
How professors are notified of LD/ADHD: By student

GENERAL ADMISSIONS INFORMATION

Director of Admissions: Karen Everet
Telephone: 406-657-2158

ENTRANCE REQUIREMENTS
14 total are required; 4 English required, 3 math required, 2 science required, 3 social studies required, 2 elective required. High school diploma or GED required. Minimum TOEFL is 525. TOEFL required of all international applicants.

Application deadline: July 1
Notification: Rolling
Average GPA: 2.9

Average SAT I Math: 483
Average SAT I Verbal: 503
Average ACT: 21

Graduated top 10% of class: 7%
Graduated top 25% of class: 22%
Graduated top 50% of class: 55%

COLLEGE GRADUATION REQUIREMENTS

Course waivers allowed: No
Course substitutions allowed: Yes
In what subjects: Foreign language and math under strict guidelines

ADDITIONAL INFORMATION

Environment: The campus is in an urban area.

Student Body
Undergrad enrollment: 3,826
Female: 64%
Male: 36%
Out-of-state: 7%

Cost Information
In-state tuition: $3,052
Out-of-state tuition: $8,227
Room & board: $4,500
Housing Information
University housing: Yes
Percent living on campus: 12%

Greek System
Fraternity: Yes
Sorority: Yes
Athletics: NCAA Division II

MONTANA TECH COLLEGE

1300 West Park Street, Butte, MT 59701
Phone: 406-496-4178 • Fax: 406-496-4710
E-mail: admissions@mtech.edu • Web: www.mtech.edu
Support level: CS • Institution type: 2-year

LEARNING DISABILITY PROGRAM AND SERVICES

All persons with disabilities have the right to participate fully and equally in the programs and services of Montana Tech. Tech is committed to making the appropriate accommodations. The primary contact and resource person for students with disabilities is the Dean of Students. The Dean serves as a general resource for all students who might need assistance. Availability of services from Disability Services is subject to a student's eligibility for these and any services. Students must provide appropriate and current documentation prior to requesting and receiving services or accommodations. All faculty and staff at the College are responsible for assuring access by providing reasonable accommodations. The Montana Tech Learning Center offers a variety of services to help students achieve their full academic potential. Tutors are available to help all students with course work in an assortment of subject areas. The TLC addresses the importance of developing basic college success skills.

LD/ADHD ADMISSIONS INFORMATION

College entrance tests required: Yes
Nonstandardized tests accepted: Yes
Interview required: No
Essay required: No
Documentation required for LD: Psychoeducational evaluation
Documentation required for ADHD: Yes
Documentation submitted to: Disability Services
Special Ed. HS course work accepted: No

Specific course requirements for all applicants: Yes
Separate application required for services: No
# of LD applications submitted yearly: N/A
# of LD applications accepted yearly: N/A
Total # of students receiving LD/ADHD services: N/A
Acceptance into program means acceptance into college: N/A

ADMISSIONS

There is no special admission process for students with LD or ADHD. Applicants must have a 22 ACT or 920 SAT I or be in the upper 50% of their high school class or have a 2.5 GPA. The GED is accepted. Students must have 14 academic high school credits including 4 years of English, 2 years of science, 3 years of math, 3 years of social studies, and 2 years from other academic areas, including foreign language, computer science, visual and performing arts, and vocational education. Interviews are not required and special education courses in high school are not accepted. Students who do not meet any of the general admission criteria may ask to be evaluated considering other factors. Students with LD/ADHD are encouraged to self-disclose in the admission process.

ADDITIONAL INFORMATION

The following types of services are offered to students with disabilities: responding to requests for accommodation; assistance in working with faculty members; text accommodation in concert with instructors; assistive technology; note-taking; disability evaluation and testing; and career services. Documentation to receive services should be sent directly to Disability Services. The Learning Center houses computer stations for students. In addition Montana Tech offers compensatory classes for students with LD in both math and English. Services and accommodations are available for undergraduate and graduate students.

SUPPORT SERVICES CONTACT INFORMATION

Learning Disability Program/Services: Disability Services
Director: Lee Barnett
  E-mail: lbarnett@mtech.edu
  Telephone: 406-496-3730
  Fax: 406-496-3710
Contact: Same

LEARNING DISABILITY SERVICES

Requests for the following services/accommodations will be evaluated individually based on appropriate and current documentation.

Allowed in Exams
  Calculator: No
  Dictionary: No
  Computer: Yes
  Spellchecker: No
Extended test time: Yes
Scribes: Yes
Proctors: Yes
Oral exams: Yes
Note-takers: Yes

Distraction-reduced environment: Yes
Tape recording in class: Yes
Books on tape from RFBD: Yes
Taping of books not from RFBD: Yes
Accommodations for students with
  ADHD: No
Reading machine: Yes
Other assistive technology: Yes
Priority registration: No

Added costs for services: No
LD specialists: 3
Professional tutors: 2
Peer tutors: 12
Max. hours/wk. for services:
  Unlimited
How professors are notified of
  LD/ADHD: By both student and
director

GENERAL ADMISSIONS INFORMATION

Director of Admissions: Ed Johnson
Telephone: 406-496-3732

ENTRANCE REQUIREMENTS
4 total are required; 4 English required, 4 English recommended, 3 math required, 4 math recommended, 1 science required, 2 science recommended, 1 science lab required, 2 science lab recommended, 2 foreign language required, 2 foreign language recommended, 3 social studies required, 3 history required. High school diploma or GED required. Minimum TOEFL is 525. TOEFL required of all international applicants.

Application deadline: Rolling
Notification: Rolling
Average GPA: 3.5

Average SAT I Math: 552
Average SAT I Verbal: 532
Average ACT: 22

Graduated top 10% of class: 20%
Graduated top 25% of class: 47%
Graduated top 50% of class: 78%

COLLEGE GRADUATION REQUIREMENTS

Course waivers allowed: N/A
Course substitutions allowed: N/A
In what subjects: N/A

ADDITIONAL INFORMATION

Environment: Located 65 miles from Helena.

Student Body
  Undergrad enrollment: 1,978
  Female: 45%
  Male: 55%
  Out-of-state: 12%

Cost Information
  In-state tuition: $3,006
  Out-of-state tuition: $8,530
  Room & board: $4,278
Housing Information
  University housing: Yes
  Percent living on campus: 15%

Greek System
  Fraternity: No
  Sorority: No
  Athletics: NAIA

ROCKY MOUNTAIN COLLEGE

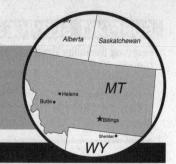

1511 Poly Drive, Billings, MT 59102-1796
Phone: 406-657-1026 • Fax: 406-259-9751
E-mail: admissions@rocky.edu • Web: www.rocky.edu
Support level: CS • Institution type: 4-year private

LEARNING DISABILITY PROGRAM AND SERVICES

Rocky Mountain College is committed to providing courses, programs, and services for students with disabilities. Services for Academic Success (SAS) provides a comprehensive support program for students with LD. To be eligible participants must meet one of the primary criteria: low-income family; first generation college student; or physical or learning disability. Participants must also be U.S. citizens and have an academic need for the program. Students are responsible for identifying themselves, providing appropriate documentation, and requesting reasonable accommodations. The program tailors services to meet the needs of the individuals. SAS welcomes applications from students who are committed to learning and who are excited about meeting the challenges of college with the support provided by the SAS staff. Research studies have shown that students who participate in student support services programs are more than twice as likely to remain in college and graduate as those students from similar backgrounds who do not participate in such programs. The SAS program is supported by a grant from the U.S. Department of Education and funds from Rocky Mountain College. The small size of the College, together with the caring attitude of the faculty and an excellent support program, make Rocky a "learning-disability-friendly" college.

LD/ADHD ADMISSIONS INFORMATION

College entrance tests required: Yes
Nonstandardized tests accepted: Yes
Interview required: No
Essay required: No
Documentation required for LD: Psychoeducational
  evaluation
Documentation required for ADHD: Yes
Documentation submitted to: SAS
Special Ed. HS course work accepted: No

Specific course requirements for all applicants: Yes
Separate application required for services: Yes
# of LD applications submitted yearly: 20
# of LD applications accepted yearly: 20
Total # of students receiving LD/ADHD services: 30–40
**Acceptance into program means acceptance into
  college:** Students must be admitted and enrolled at the
  College first and then reviewed for services.

ADMISSIONS

There is no special admissions application for students with learning disabilities. All applicants must meet the same criteria, which include an ACT of 21 or SAT of 1000, GPA of 2.5, and courses in English, math, science, and social studies. There is the opportunity to be considered for a conditional admission if scores or grades are below the cutoffs. However, to identify and provide necessary support services as soon as possible, students with disabilities are encouraged to complete a Services for Academic Success application form at the same time they apply for admission to Rocky Mountain College. Recommended courses for admissions include 4 years English, 3 years math, 3 years social science, 2 years lab science, and 2 years foreign language. Students who do not meet the normal admission requirements may be admitted conditionally.

ADDITIONAL INFORMATION

SAS provides a variety of services tailored to meet a student's individual needs. Services are free to participants and include developmental course work in reading, writing, and mathematics; study skills classes; tutoring in all subjects; academic, career, and personal counseling; graduate school counseling; accommodations for students with learning disabilities; alternative testing arrangements; taping of lectures or textbooks; cultural and academic enrichment opportunities; and advocacy. SAS staff meet with each student to talk about the supportive services the student needs, and then develop a semester plan. Skills classes for college credit are offered in math, English, and study skills.

SUPPORT SERVICES CONTACT INFORMATION

Learning Disability Program/Services: Services for Academic Success (SAS)
Director: Dr. Jane Van Dyk
  E-mail: vandykj@rocky.edu
  Telephone: 406-657-1128
  Fax: 406-259-9751
Contact: Same

LEARNING DISABILITY SERVICES

Requests for the following services/accommodations will be evaluated individually based on appropriate and current documentation.

Allowed in Exams
  Calculator: Yes
  Dictionary: Yes
  Computer: Yes
  Spellchecker: Yes
Extended test time: Yes
Scribes: Yes
Proctors: Yes
Oral exams: Yes
Note-takers: Yes

Distraction-reduced environment: Yes
Tape recording in class: Yes
Books on tape from RFBD: Yes
Taping of books not from RFBD: Yes
Accommodations for students with ADHD: Yes
Reading machine: No
Other assistive technology: Yes
Priority registration: Yes

Added costs for services: No
LD specialists: Yes (1)
Professional tutors: 2
Peer tutors: 30
Max. hours/wk. for services: Unlimited
How professors are notified of LD/ADHD: By both student and director

GENERAL ADMISSIONS INFORMATION

Director of Admissions: Craig Gould
Telephone: 406-657-1025

ENTRANCE REQUIREMENTS
4 English recommended, 3 math recommended, 2 science recommended, 2 science lab recommended, 2 foreign language recommended, 3 social studies recommended. High school diploma or GED required. Minimum TOEFL is 500. TOEFL required of all international applicants.

Application deadline: Rolling
Notification: Rolling beginning 10/1
Average GPA: 3.3

Average SAT I Math: 517
Average SAT I Verbal: 536
Average ACT: 22

Graduated top 10% of class: 12%
Graduated top 25% of class: 41%
Graduated top 50% of class: 70%

COLLEGE GRADUATION REQUIREMENTS

Course waivers allowed: Y/N
Course substitutions allowed: Y/N
In what subjects: Substitutions and waivers are provided on a limited basis

ADDITIONAL INFORMATION

Environment: The campus is located in a small town over 500 miles north of Denver, Colorado.

Student Body
  Undergrad enrollment: 801
  Female: 53%
  Male: 47%
  Out-of-state: 28%

Cost Information
  Tuition: $12,088
  Room & board: $4,147
Housing Information
  University housing: Yes
  Percent living on campus: 37%

Greek System
  Fraternity: Yes
  Sorority: Yes
  Athletics: NAIA

UNIV. OF MONTANA—MISSOULA

103 Lodge Building, Missoula, MT 59812
Phone: 406-243-6266 • Fax: 406-243-5711
E-mail: admiss@selway.umt.edu • Web: www.umt.edu
Support level: S • Institution type: 4-year public

LEARNING DISABILITY PROGRAM AND SERVICES

Disability Services for Students ensures equal access to the University by students with disabilities. DSS is a stand-alone student affairs office at the University. It is staffed by more than 10 full-time professionals. Students with learning disabilities have the same set of rights and responsibilities and the same set of services and accommodations offered other students with disabilities. Written documentation from a qualified diagnostician containing the diagnosis and functional limitation of the LD must be provided to DSS. It should be noted that DSS does not operate the same way many special education programs in secondary schools do. At the University, students have a right to access education; not a right to education. This means that DSS treats students as adults who succeed or fail on their own merits. Students should determine their needs, initiate requests for accommodations, and follow up with the delivery of those rights. DSS refrains from seeking out individuals for interventionist actions. Once a student makes the disability and needs known to DSS, DSS will provide the accommodations that will grant the student the right of equal access. Transitioning from high school to college is enhanced when students grasp and apply the principles of self-advocacy.

LD/ADHD ADMISSIONS INFORMATION

College entrance tests required: Yes
Nonstandardized tests accepted: Yes
Interview required: No
Essay required: No
Documentation required for LD: WAIS-III; one achievement battery unless ADHD is considered: within 3 years
Documentation required for ADHD: Yes
Documentation submitted to: Disability Services
Special Ed. HS course work accepted: N/A

Specific course requirements for all applicants: Yes
Separate application required for services: No
# of LD applications submitted yearly: N/A
# of LD applications accepted yearly: N/A
Total # of students receiving LD/ADHD services: NR
Acceptance into program means acceptance into college: Students must be admitted and enrolled at the University and then may be reviewed for services.

ADMISSIONS
Admissions criteria are the same for all applicants. However, consideration will be given to students who do not meet the general admissions criteria. General admission criteria include 22 ACT/1030 SAT; rank in the upper half of the class; 2.5 GPA. DSS will act as an advocate for students with learning disabilities during the admission process. Applicants not meeting admission criteria may request and receive a review of their eligibility by an admissions committee. Students should send documentation verifying the disability directly to the DSS office. Documentation should include a complete and current (within three to five years) psychological evaluation written by a qualified professional stating the diagnosis. Also in the report should be the list of standardized tests, relevant history, functional limitations, and recommended accommodations.

ADDITIONAL INFORMATION
Students with LD can expect reasonable accommodations to suit their individual needs. Accommodations may include a direct service or academic adjustment, but will not reduce the academic standards of the institution. Academic assistants at the University provide auxiliary aids such as reading textbooks and other instructional materials; scribing assignments or tests; assisting in library research; and proofreading materials. Services may include academic adjustments; admissions assistance; assistive technology; auxiliary aids; consultation with faculty; counseling; course waiver assistance; letter of verification; note-taking; orientation; priority registration; scribes; study-skills course; test accommodations services; and tutoring services. Academic adjustments may include extended testing time; substitute course requirements; or lecture notes from instructors.

SUPPORT SERVICES CONTACT INFORMATION

Learning Disability Program/Services: Disability Services for Students (DSS)
Director: James Marks
   E-mail: marks@selway.umt.edu
   Telephone: 406-243-2243
   Fax: 406-243-5330
Contact: Same

LEARNING DISABILITY SERVICES

Requests for the following services/accommodations will be evaluated individually based on appropriate and current documentation.

Allowed in Exams
   Calculator: Yes
   Dictionary: Yes
   Computer: Yes
   Spellchecker: Yes
Extended test time: Yes
Scribes: Yes
Proctors: Yes
Oral exams: Yes
Note-takers: Yes

Distraction-reduced environment: Yes
Tape recording in class: Yes
Books on tape from RFBD: Yes
Taping of books not from RFBD: Yes
Accommodations for students with
   ADHD: Yes
Reading machine: Yes
Other assistive technology: Yes
Priority registration: Yes

Added costs for services: 2
LD specialists: No
Professional tutors: No
Peer tutors: No
Max. hours/wk. for services:
   Unlimited
How professors are notified of
   LD/ADHD: By student

GENERAL ADMISSIONS INFORMATION

Director of Admissions: Frank Matoole
Telephone: 406-243-6266

ENTRANCE REQUIREMENTS
4 English required, 4 English recommended, 3 math required, 3 math recommended, 2 science required, 2 science lab required, 3 social studies required, 2 elective required. High school diploma or GED required. Minimum TOEFL is 500. TOEFL required of all international applicants.

Application deadline: Rolling
Notification: Rolling beginning 8/1
Average GPA: 3.2

Average SAT I Math: 540
Average SAT I Verbal: 550
Average ACT: 23

Graduated top 10% of class: 13%
Graduated top 25% of class: 35%
Graduated top 50% of class: 68%

COLLEGE GRADUATION REQUIREMENTS

Course waivers allowed: Yes
Course substitutions allowed: Yes
In what subjects: Any course that is not a core course, depending on the student's disability accommodations.

ADDITIONAL INFORMATION

Environment: The University's urban campus is 200 miles from Spokane.

Student Body
   Undergrad enrollment: 10,666
   Female: 53%
   Male: 47%
   Out-of-state: 26%

Cost Information
   In-state tuition: $3,064
   Out-of-state tuition: $8,311
   Room & board: $4,800
Housing Information
   University housing: Yes
   Percent living on campus: 21%

Greek System
   Fraternity: Yes
   Sorority: Yes
Athletics: NCAA Division I

WESTERN MONTANA COLLEGE

710 South Atlantic, Dillon, MT 59725
Phone: 406-683-7331 • Fax: 406-683-7493
E-mail: admissions@wmc.edu • Web: www.wmc.edu
Support level: S • Institution type: 4-year public

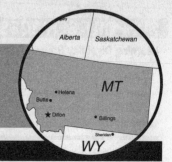

LEARNING DISABILITY PROGRAM AND SERVICES

Western Montana College strives to accommodate all students with special needs. These needs may be physical, social, and/or academic. Almost all services are free to the student. The Associate Dean of Students is in charge of making special accommodations available to students with learning disabilities. If an applicant has a documented learning disability and requests special accommodations for a class, he or she must contact the Associate Dean of Students so that arrangements can be made. The professor of the class, the Associate Dean, and the student will meet to set up an individualized educational plan for that class and documentation will be kept on file in the Student Life Office. Almost all services are free to the student.

LD/ADHD ADMISSIONS INFORMATION

College entrance tests required: Yes
Nonstandardized tests accepted: Yes
Interview required: No
Essay required: No
Documentation required for LD: Psychoeducational evaluation
Documentation required for ADHD: Yes
Documentation submitted to: Disability Services
Special Ed. HS course work accepted: Yes

Specific course requirements for all applicants: Yes
Separate application required for services: No
# of LD applications submitted yearly: N/A
# of LD applications accepted yearly: N/A
Total # of students receiving LD/ADHD services: 15
Acceptance into program means acceptance into college: Students must be admitted and enrolled at the College first and then may request services.

ADMISSIONS

The College has no special requirements other than those outlined by the state Board of Regents: a valid high school diploma or GED. Admission criteria for general admission include 4 years English, 3 years math, 3 years science, 3 years social studies, and 2 years from foreign language, computer science, visual or performing arts, or vocational education; 2.5 GPA (minimum 2.0 for students with learning disabilities); 20 ACT or 960 SAT I; top 50 percent of the class. Students with documented learning disabilities may request waivers or substitutions in courses affected by the disability. Because Western Montana is a small college, each individual can set up an admissions plan. There is a 15 percent "window" of exemption for some students who do not meet admission requirments. These students can be admitted provisionally if they provide satisfactory evidence that they are prepared to pursue successfully the special courses required.

ADDITIONAL INFORMATION

Students who present appropriate documentation may be eligible for some of the following services or accommodations: the use of calculators, dictionary, computer or spellchecker for tests; extended time on tests; distraction-free environment for tests; proctors; scribes; oral exams; note-takers; tape recorders in class; books on tape; and priority registration. The Learning Center offers skill-building classes in reading, writing, and math. These classes don't count toward a student's GPA, but do for athletic eligibility. Students whose ACT or entrance tests show that they would profit from such instruction will be placed in courses that will best meet their needs and ensure a successful college career. Free tutoring is available in most areas on a drop-in basis and/or at prescribed times. Services and accommodations are available for undergraduate and graduate students.

SUPPORT SERVICES CONTACT INFORMATION

Learning Disability Program/Services: Disability Services
Director: Chris Royer
  E-mail: c_royer@wmc.edu
  Telephone: 406-683-7723
  Fax: 406-683-7570
Contact: Same

LEARNING DISABILITY SERVICES

Requests for the following services/accommodations will be evaluated individually based on appropriate and current documentation.

Allowed in Exams
  Calculator: Yes
  Dictionary: Yes
  Computer: Yes
  Spellchecker: Yes
Extended test time: Yes
Scribes: Yes
Proctors: Yes
Oral exams: Yes
Note-takers: Yes

Distraction-reduced environment: Yes
Tape recording in class: Yes
Books on tape from RFBD: Yes
Taping of books not from RFBD: Yes
Accommodations for students with ADHD: Yes
Reading machine: No
Other assistive technology: No
Priority registration: Yes

Added costs for services: No
LD specialists: No
Professional tutors: 2
Peer tutors: 15
Max. hours/wk. for services: Unlimited
How professors are notified of LD/ADHD: By both student and director

GENERAL ADMISSIONS INFORMATION

Director of Admissions: Arlene Williams
Telephone: 406-683-7331

ENTRANCE REQUIREMENTS
16 total are required; 4 English required, 3 math required, 2 science required, 2 science lab required, 3 social studies required, 4 elective required. High school diploma or GED required. Minimum TOEFL is 500. TOEFL required of all international applicants.

Application deadline: July 1
Notification: Rolling beginning 9/1
Average GPA: 3.0

Average SAT I Math: 475
Average SAT I Verbal: 482
Average ACT: 20

Graduated top 10% of class: 6%
Graduated top 25% of class: 18%
Graduated top 50% of class: 55%

COLLEGE GRADUATION REQUIREMENTS

Course waivers allowed: Yes
Course substitutions allowed: Yes
In what subjects: General education courses

ADDITIONAL INFORMATION

Environment: The College is located on 20 acres in a small town about 60 miles south of Butte.

Student Body
  Undergrad enrollment: 1,160
  Female: 59%
  Male: 41%
  Out-of-state: 14%

Cost Information
  In-state tuition: $2,795
  Out-of-state tuition: $7,885
  Room & board: $3,800
Housing Information
  University housing: Yes
  Percent living on campus: 28%

Greek System
  Fraternity: Yes
  Sorority: Yes
Athletics: NAIA

UNION COLLEGE

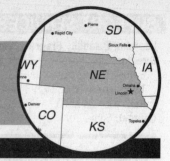

3800 South 48th Street, Lincoln, NE 68506-4300
Phone: 402-486-2504 • Fax: 402-486-2895
E-mail: ucenrol@ucollege.edu • Web: www.ucollege.edu
Support level: SP • Institution type: 4-year private

LEARNING DISABILITY PROGRAM AND SERVICES

The Teaching Learning Center is a specialized program serving the Union College student with learning disabilities/dyslexia and has now expanded to serve all students with disabilities. The Teaching Learning Center offers assistance to the serious, capable student with learning disabilities who seeks to earn an undergraduate degree in a Christian environment. In order to qualify for accommodations a student must have an IQ commensurate with college achievement; have a diagnosis based on current data, which will be reviewed by the Teaching Learning Center staff; complete admission procedures to Union College; take an untimed ACT; apply to the Teaching Learning Center and provide needed information; and arrange for a two-day visit to campus to complete diagnostic/prescriptive testing to determine needed accommodations and remediation. Students with LD in the program enroll in regular college classes, although a light load is initially recommended.

LD/ADHD ADMISSIONS INFORMATION

College entrance tests required: No
Nonstandardized tests accepted: Yes
Interview required: No (recommended)
Essay required: No
Documentation required for LD: Psychoeducational, preferably WAIS-III, Woodcock-Johnson
Documentation required for ADHD: Yes
Documentation submitted to: Teaching Learning Center
Special Ed. HS course work accepted: Yes

Specific course requirements for all applicants: Yes
Separate application required for services: Yes
# of LD applications submitted yearly: 60–70
# of LD applications accepted yearly: 58–69
Total # of students receiving LD/ADHD services: 80–90
Acceptance into program means acceptance into college: Students are admitted to the TLC program and the College jointly.

ADMISSIONS

There is no special admission process for students with learning disabilities. All applicants are expected to meet the same admission criteria, including 2.5 GPA; ACT of 16+; 3 years English, 2 years natural science, 2 years history, 2 years algebra, 3 years selected from English, math, natural science, social studies, religion, modern foreign language, or vocational courses. Students with course deficiencies can be admitted and make up the deficiencies in college. The staff from the Teaching Learning Center may review documentation from some applicants and provide a recommendation to the Office of Admissions regarding an admission decision. The final decision for admission into the program is made by TLC. Special Admission status is for students with no immediate plans to graduate. Temporary Admission status is valid on a semester-by-semester basis allowing students to secure official transcripts from high school or other colleges. This status is limited to three semesters. Conditional Admission status is for students who lack certain entrance requirements such as math, English, history, or science, which must be satisfied within the first year of attendance. A three-semester-hour course taken in college to remove an entrance deficiency is equivalent to one full year of a high school course.

ADDITIONAL INFORMATION

Reasonable accommodation is an individualized matter determined in consultation between the student, parents, project staff, and appropriate faculty members. Accommodations may include texts on tape; oral testing; individual testing; extended time/alternate assignments; note-takers; remediation; academic tutoring (additonal fee); counseling; instruction in word processing; and assistance with term papers. Skills classes for college credit are offered in reading, spelling, math, and writing. The Technology Resource Center for learning disabilities provides information on available technology such as four-track tape player (fits in your hand); Personal Voice Organizer; Language Master 600 (voice powered, hand-held dictionary, thesaurus, and word games); Calcu-Talk (scientific and financial talking calculator); plus laser printer, character recognition scanner and two personal computers with screen filters. Software includes Arkenstone (reads written page); Dragon Dictate (control computer by voice); Grammatik (analyzes and corrects grammar); Kurzweil (combines with scanner to convert written test to spoken word); Inspiration (allows the visual person to organize thoughts in outline and cluster form); and Telepathic II (word prediction engine).

SUPPORT SERVICES CONTACT INFORMATION

Learning Disability Program/Services: Teaching Learning Center (TLC)
Director: Jennifer Forbes
  E-mail: jeforbes@ucollege.edu
  Telephone: 402-486-2506
  Fax: 402-486-2895
Contact: Cindy Stanphill
  E-mail: tlc@ucollege.edu
  Telephone: 402-486-2506
  Fax: 402-486-2895

LEARNING DISABILITY SERVICES

Requests for the following services/accommodations will be evaluated individually based on appropriate and current documentation.

Allowed in Exams
  Calculator: Yes
  Dictionary: Yes
  Computer: Yes
  Spellchecker: Yes
Extended test time: Yes
Scribes: Yes
Proctors: Yes
Oral exams: Yes
Note-takers: Yes

Distraction-reduced environment: Yes
Tape recording in class: Yes
Books on tape from RFBD: Yes
Taping of books not from RFBD: Yes
Accommodations for students with ADHD: Yes
Reading machine: Yes
Other assistive technology: Yes
Priority registration: No

Added costs for services: $425 per semester, or by hour for tutors
LD specialists: 4
Professional tutors: 4
Peer tutors: 15–25
Max. hours/wk. for services: 2–5 hrs. per week; can apply for more
How professors are notified of LD/ADHD: By both student and director

GENERAL ADMISSIONS INFORMATION

Director of Admissions: Dan Londquist
Telephone: 518-388-6112

ENTRANCE REQUIREMENTS

Course requirements include 3 years English, 2 years science, 2 years history, 2 years math, and 3 years from core courses or vocational courses. Freshman applicants with a GPA below 2.5 or ACT below 20 percent will be admitted and enrolled in a freshman development program. Minimum TOEFL is 550. TOEFL required of all international applicants.

Application deadline: August 1
Notification: Rolling
Average GPA: NR

Average SAT I Math: NR
Average SAT I Verbal: NR
Average ACT: 18–25 (middle 50 percent range)

Graduated top 10% of class: 18%
Graduated top 25% of class: 18%
Graduated top 50% of class: 28%

COLLEGE GRADUATION REQUIREMENTS

Course waivers allowed: No
Course substitutions allowed: No
In what subjects: A request for a course waiver or substitution has never been made to the College.

ADDITIONAL INFORMATION

Environment: The College has a suburban campus near Lincoln.

Student Body
  Undergrad enrollment: 2,042
  Female: 54%
  Male: 46%
  Out-of-state: 75%

Cost Information
  Tuition: NR
  Room & board: $3,120
Housing Information
  University housing: Yes
  Percent living on campus: 66%

Greek System
  Fraternity: Yes
  Sorority: Yes
Athletics: NCAA Division III

WAYNE STATE COLLEGE

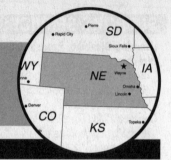

Office of Admissions, Wayne State College, Wayne, NE 68787
Phone: 402-375-7234 • Fax: 402-375-7204
E-mail: ssalmon@wscgate.wsc.edu • Web: www.wsc.edu
Support level: S • Institution type: 4-year public

LEARNING DISABILITY PROGRAM AND SERVICES

At Wayne State College students with Learning Disabilities and ADHD are provided an individualized, cooperatively planned program of accommodations and services that are structured yet integrated within existing college services and programs. Accommodations and services are matched to the individual student's needs and are provided free of charge. STRIDE (Student Taking Responsibility In Development and Education) is a program of student support services that includes individual attention, academic and personal support, and disability services. STRIDE services help new students adjust more quickly and fully to college life. Students with disabilities are one of the populations eligible for STRIDE. STRIDE expects students to place a high priority on academic performance, invest the time and effort needed for college-level learning, and take advantage of the services and programs available. Students with learning disabilities or attention deficit disorder must complete a special application for STRIDE and submit written information that verifies the disability diagnosis.

LD/ADHD ADMISSIONS INFORMATION

College entrance tests required: Yes
Nonstandardized tests accepted: Yes
Interview required: No
Essay required: No
Documentation required for LD: Psychoeducational evaluation
Documentation required for ADHD: Yes
Documentation submitted to: STRIDE
Special Ed. HS course work accepted: Yes

Specific course requirements for all applicants: Yes
Separate application required for services: No
# of LD applications submitted yearly: N/A
# of LD applications accepted yearly: N/A
Total # of students receiving LD/ADHD services: NR
Acceptance into program means acceptance into college: Students must be accepted and enrolled at the College first and then may request services.

ADMISSIONS
Admission to Wayne State College is open to all high school graduates or students with a GED equivalent. The College recommends that student take 4 years of English, 3 years of math, 3 years of social studies, and 2 years of science. Foreign language is not an entrance or graduation requirement. High school special education courses are accepted.

ADDITIONAL INFORMATION
Through the STRIDE program students have access to the following personal support services: a summer STRIDE pre-college experience; the STRIDE peer mentor program; academic, personal, and career counseling; and academic support services, including academic advising and course selection guidance, the Succeeding in College course, one-on-one peer tutoring, writing skills professional tutoring, individual study skills assistance in time management and organization, note-taking, and study techniques and test-taking strategies. STRIDE provides a cooperatively planned program of disability-related services and accommodations, tape recorded textbooks and materials, and alternative exam arrangements.

SUPPORT SERVICES CONTACT INFORMATION

Learning Disability Program/Services: STRIDE
Director: Dr. Jeff B. Carstens
  E-mail: jcarstens@wscgate.wsc.edu
  Telephone: 402-375-7500
  Fax: 402-375-7096
Contact: Same

LEARNING DISABILITY SERVICES

Requests for the following services/accommodations will be evaluated individually based on appropriate and current documentation.

Allowed in Exams
  Calculator: Yes
  Dictionary: Yes
  Computer: Yes
  Spellchecker: Yes
Extended test time: Yes
Scribes: Yes
Proctors: Yes
Oral exams: Yes
Notetakers: Yes

Distraction-reduced environment: Yes
Tape recording in class: Yes
Books on tape from RFBD: Yes
Taping of books not from RFBD: Yes
Accommodations for students with
  ADHD: Yes
Reading machine: Yes
Other assistive technology: No
Priority registration: Yes

Added costs for services: No
LD specialists: No
Professional tutors: 0
Peer tutors: 35
Max. hours/wk. for services: Unlimited
How professors are notified of
  LD/ADHD: By student

GENERAL ADMISSIONS INFORMATION

Director of Admissions: Susan Salmon
Telephone: 402-375-7236

ENTRANCE REQUIREMENTS
16 total are required; 4 English recommended; 3 math recommended; 3 science recommended; foreign language, fine and performing arts, and computer literacy recommended; 3 social studies recommended; 3 elective recommended. High school diploma or GED required. Minimum TOEFL is 550. TOEFL required of all international applicants.

Application deadline: August 1
Notification: Rolling
Average GPA: 2.5

Average SAT I Math: NR
Average SAT I Verbal: NR
Average ACT: 18–24

Graduated top 10% of class: 7%
Graduated top 25% of class: 24%
Graduated top 50% of class: NR

COLLEGE GRADUATION REQUIREMENTS

Course waivers allowed: NR
Course substitutions allowed: No
In what subjects: No foreign language required for graduation.

ADDITIONAL INFORMATION

Environment: The College is located in a rural area 45 miles southwest of Sioux City, Iowa.

Student Body
  Undergrad enrollment: 3,035
  Female: 57%
  Male: 43%
  Out-of-state: 20%

Cost Information
  In-state tuition: $2,100
  Out-of-state tuition: $3,900
  Room & board: $2,900
Housing Information
  University housing: Yes
  Percent living on campus: 53%

Greek System
  Fraternity: Yes
  Sorority: Yes
Athletics: NAIA

TRUCKEE MEADOWS COMM. COLL.

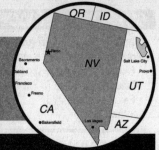

7000 Dandini Boulevard, Reno, NV 89512-3999
Phone: 775-784-6865 • Fax: 775-673-7028
Web: www.tmcc.edu
Support: CS • Institution: 2-year public

LEARNING DISABILITY PROGRAM AND SERVICES

The Learning Support Services Program provides a personalized, tailored program necessary for students with learning disabilities or nontraditional learning styles to succeed. TMCC is aware that there are many students with LD who are gifted and talented individuals. This program is designed for individuals with special learning abilities or nontraditional learning styles. Students are able to have the benefit of a small classroom setting but also have the opportunity to enroll concurrently in some classes at the University of Nevada—Reno. The program is also designed to allow the student to transfer all academic courses to UNR. Since there are only 20 freshman students in the program, there is much personal attention provided to each of them. These students can be successful in college.

LD/ADHD ADMISSIONS INFORMATION

College entrance tests required: No
Nonstandardized tests accepted: Yes
Interview required: Yes
Essay required: No
Documentation required for LD: WAIS-III and WJ
Documentation required for ADHD: Yes
Submitted to: Learning Support Services
Special Ed. HS course work accepted: Yes

Specific course requirements for all applicants: No
Separate application required for services: No
# of LD applications submitted yearly: 30–40
# of LD applications accepted yearly: 20
Total # of students receiving LD/ADHD services: 20–25
Acceptance into program means acceptance into college: Students must be admitted and enrolled at the College first and then may request admission to the Program or for services.

ADMISSIONS

The College is open admission for all students. ACT/SAT tests are not required for admission. Because of the extensive individualized support services provided, enrollment in the Learning Support Services Program is limited. Applicants are considered individually and selected on the basis of their intellectual ability, motivation, academic preparation, and potential for success in the program. For an individual to be considered for the program the following are necessary: secondary school transcript; medical or psychological statement of disability, special needs, strengths and weaknesses (diagnosis of the learning disability); test results of the WAIS-III; current achievement test results showing the level of proficiency in reading, spelling, written language and arithmetic; and a personal interview with the Learning Support Service Program counselor. Admission to the program is on a rolling basis. Students who have completed the full admission process will be notified immediately when a decision is reached by the LSS admissions committee.

ADDITIONAL INFORMATION

The Learning Support Service program is designed to meet the specific needs of each participating student. Individual services include an annual weekend orientation retreat, a Success Skills course, a minimum of three hours of tutoring per week, alternative testing methods (including the use of oral and extended time on tests), and extensive use of taped textbooks. In addition to the program, services and accommodations are available for other students with learning disabilities or attention deficit disorder. Currently, there are 75 students with LD and 15 students with ADHD receiving accommodations on campus.

SUPPORT SERVICES CONTACT INFORMATION

Learning Disability Program/Services: Learning Support Services Program
Director: Harry Heiser
  E-mail: heishc@aol.com
  Telephone: 530-832-4328
Contact: Same

LEARNING DISABILITY SERVICES

Requests for the following services/accommodations will be evaluated individually based on appropriate and current documentation.

Allowed in Exams
  Calculator: Yes
  Dictionary: Yes
  Computer: Yes
  Spellchecker: Yes
Extended test time: Yes
Scribes: Yes
Proctors: Yes
Oral exams: Yes
Notetakers: Yes

Distraction-reduced environment: Yes
Tape recording in class: Yes
Books on tape from RFBD: Yes
Taping of books not from RFBD: Yes
Accommodations for students with ADHD: Yes
Reading machine: No
Other assistive technology: Yes
Priority registration: Yes

Added costs for services: $3,800
LD specialists: Yes
Professional tutors: 5
Peer tutors: No
Max. hours/wk. for services: Unlimited
How professors are notified of LD/ADHD: By both student and director

GENERAL ADMISSIONS INFORMATION

Director of Admissions: Melissa Chorozsky
Telephone: 775-784-6865

ENTRANCE REQUIREMENTS
Open admissions. High school diploma or GED required. Specific courses are required for allied health programs.

Application deadline: Rolling
Notification: Rolling
Average GPA: NR

Average SAT I Math: NR
Average SAT I Verbal: NR
Average ACT: NR

Graduated top 10% of class: NR
Graduated top 25% of class: NR
Graduated top 50% of class: NR

COLLEGE GRADUATION REQUIREMENTS

Course waivers allowed: Yes
Course substitutions allowed: Yes
In what subjects: Foreign language

ADDITIONAL INFORMATION

Environment: The College is located on a suburban campus in a large city.

Student Body
  Undergrad enrollment: 9,142
  Female: 56%
  Male: 44%
  Out-of-state: 3%

Cost Information
  In-state: $1,250
  Out-of-state: $3,200
  Room & board: $6,024
Housing Information
  University housing: Yes (Reno)
  Percent living on campus: N/A

Greek System
  Fraternity: No
  Sorority: No
Athletics: NJCAA

UNIVERSITY OF NEVADA—LAS VEGAS

4505 Maryland Parkway, Box 451021, Las Vegas, NV 89154-1021
Phone: 702-895-3443 • Fax: 702-895-1118
E-mail: gounlv@ccmail.nevada.edu • Web: www.unlv.edu
Support level: S • Institution type: 4-year public

LEARNING DISABILITY PROGRAM AND SERVICES

The Disability Resource Center (DRC) provides academic accommodations for students with documented disabilities who are otherwise qualified for university programs. Compliance with Section 504 requires that reasonable academic accommodations be made for students with disabilities. These accommodations might include note-taking, testing accommodations, books on tape, readers, tutoring, priority registration, transition training, assistance with course registration and class monitoring, counseling, and information of the laws pertaining to disabilities. The center also serves as a resource area for all disability issues affecting students, faculty, and staff. To establish services, students will need to provide the DRC with appropriate documentation of their disability. Each semester a student wishes to receive assistance, a review of current documentation and assessment of the course needs will be made to determine the appropriate academic accommodations. On some occasions decisions are based on input from the students, faculty, and the designated DRC staff.

LD/ADHD ADMISSIONS INFORMATION

College entrance tests required: Yes
Nonstandardized tests accepted: Yes
Interview required: NR
Essay required: No
Documentation required for LD: Psychoeducational evaluation
Documentation required for ADHD: Yes
Documentation submitted to: DRC
Special Ed. HS course work accepted: Y/N

Specific course requirements for all applicants: Yes
Separate application required for services: No
# of LD applications submitted yearly: N/A
# of LD applications accepted yearly: N/A
Total # of students receiving LD/ADHD services: 454
Acceptance into program means acceptance into college: Students must be admitted and enrolled at the University first (appeal process is available) and then may request services.

ADMISSIONS

All applicants are expected to meet the same admission criteria, which include a 2.5 GPA and 13.5 college-prep courses or a 3.0 GPA and no specific high school courses. ACT/SAT are not required for admission, but are used for placement. Students are encouraged to self-disclose their learning disability and request information about services. DRC will assess the student's documentation and write a recommendation to the Office of Admission based on the director's opinion of the student's chance for success. Students denied admission may request assistance for an appeal through the director of the Disability Resource Center. This requires a special application with an explanation of the circumstances of previous academic performance. Students and not the parents should call DRC to inquire about initiating an appeal of the denial. Some of these students may be offered Admission By Alternative Criteria. If admitted on probation the students must maintain a 2.0 GPA for the first semester. Others can enter on Special Status as a part-time student, take 15 credits, and then transfer into the University.

ADDITIONAL INFORMATION

The Disabilities Resource Center offers help to all students on campus who have a diagnosed disability. Following the evaluation students meet with DRC director and staff to develop a plan for services. Students are encouraged to only enroll in 12 credit hours the first semester, including courses in abilities or skill development. Psychological services are available through the Counseling Office. Workshops are offered in time management, organization, test-taking strategies, and note-taking skills. DRC offers workshops to teach classroom success techniques and self-advocacy skills. Assistance is provided year-round to active students. Students remain active by signing a new contract for service before each semester. DRC hires enrolled students to be note-takers, readers, scribes, and proctors. Services are available to undergraduate and graduate students.

SUPPORT SERVICES CONTACT INFORMATION

Learning Disability Program/Services: Disability Resource Center (DRC)
Director: Anita Stockbauer
 E-mail: anitas@ccmail.nevada.edu
 Telephone: 702-895-0866
 Fax: 702-895-0651
Contact: Same

LEARNING DISABILITY SERVICES

Requests for the following services/accommodations will be evaluated individually based on appropriate and current documentation.

Allowed in Exams
 Calculator: Yes
 Dictionary: Yes
 Computer: Yes
 Spellchecker: Yes
Extended test time: Yes
Scribes: Yes
Proctors: Yes
Oral exams: Yes
Note-takers: Yes

Distraction-reduced environment: Yes
Tape recording in class: Yes
Books on tape from RFBD: Yes
Taping of books not from RFBD: Yes
Accommodations for students with ADHD: Yes
Reading machine: NR
Other assistive technology: Yes
Priority registration: Yes

Added costs for services: $20 per term, free for students who demonstrate financial need
LD specialists: No
Professional tutors: Yes
Peer tutors: Yes
Max. hours/wk. for services: 2 hours per week
How professors are notified of LD/ADHD: Bt students and program director

GENERAL ADMISSIONS INFORMATION

Director of Admissions: Susan Bozarth
Telephone: 702-895-3011

ENTRANCE REQUIREMENTS
14 total are required; 4 English required, 3 math required, 3 science required, 2 science lab required, 3 social studies required. High school diploma is required and GED is not accepted. Minimum TOEFL is 500. TOEFL required of all international applicants.

Application deadline: July 15
Notification: Rolling beginning 9/1
Average GPA: 3.2
Average SAT I Math: 513
Average SAT I Verbal: 495
Average ACT: 21
Graduated top 10% of class: 22%
Graduated top 25% of class: 50%
Graduated top 50% of class: 87%

COLLEGE GRADUATION REQUIREMENTS

Course waivers allowed: No
Course substitutions allowed: Yes
In what subjects: Foreign language only required for English majors. Substitutions are available. Math is required for graduation. All requests go to the Academic Standards Committee after initial approval.

ADDITIONAL INFORMATION

Environment: The University is located on 355 acres in an urban area minutes from downtown Las Vegas.

Student Body
 Undergrad enrollment: 17,327
 Female: 55%
 Male: 45%
 Out-of-state: 21%

Cost Information
 In-state tuition: $2,340
 Out-of-state tuition: $9,320
 Room & board: $5,800
Housing Information
 University housing: Yes
 Percent living on campus: 8%

Greek System
 Fraternity: Yes
 Sorority: Yes
 Athletics: NCAA Division I

UNIVERSITY OF NEVADA—RENO

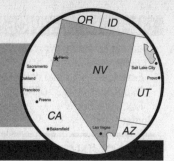

Admissions Office, Mailstop 120, Reno, NV 89557
Phone: 775-784-6865 • Fax: 775-784-4283
E-mail: unrug@unr.edu • Web: www.unr.edu
Support level: CS • Institution type: 4-year public

LEARNING DISABILITY PROGRAM AND SERVICES

The Disability Resource Center was created to meet the unique educational needs of students with disabilities. The purpose of the DRC is to ensure that students with disabilities have equal access to participate in, contribute to, and benefit from all university programs. The Center's goal is to act as a catalyst for elimination of barriers and to increase awareness of students with disabilities attending the University. The DRC staff is available to provide students with sensitive and individualized assistance at the student's request. Students who wish to request academic accommodations must provide the DRC with documentation of a verified disability. Appropriate services are determined and provided based upon the student's specific disability and the academic requirements of the appropriate department. Students need to request their desired accommodations at least four weeks prior to their actual need for accommodations. Students requesting accommodations must sign a Release of Information form giving DRC permission to discuss the student's educational situation with other professionals with a legitimate need to know. Students requesting accommodations will also be required to sign a Student Contract defining the student's responsibilities in receiving services.

LD/ADHD ADMISSIONS INFORMATION

College entrance tests required: No
Nonstandardized tests accepted: Yes
Interview required: Yes
Essay required: No
Documentation required for LD: Psychoeducational evaluation
Documentation required for ADHD: Yes
Documentation submitted to: Disability Resource Center
Special Ed. HS course work accepted: No

Specific course requirements for all applicants: Yes
Separate application required for services: Yes
# of LD applications submitted yearly: N/A
# of LD applications accepted yearly: 153
Total # of students receiving LD/ADHD services: 199
Acceptance into program means acceptance into college: Students must be admitted and enrolled and then may request services.

ADMISSIONS

There is no special admission process for students with LD or attention deficit disorders. However, students with LD/ADHD are encouraged to self-disclose if they do not meet general admission requirements and provide documentation. Admissions will consult with the DRC director during the admission process. General admission criteria include a 2.5 GPA; ACT of 20 in English and Math or SAT Verbal or Math of 500; 4 years of English, 3 years of math, 3 years of social studies, 3 years of natural science, and one-half year of computer literacy. Students may appeal to use a substitute course for one of the required courses for admission. Students who do not meet the general admission criteria may appeal. Some students may be admitted on appeal and brought in under a special admit.

ADDITIONAL INFORMATION

DRC provides accommodations and services tailored to the individual needs of each student. When appropriate, reasonable accommodations can include the following: reader services/books on tape; note-taking services; alternative testing accommodations/proctors/scribes; adaptive computer equipment access; accommodations counseling; registration assistance; faculty liaisons; learning strategies instruction; course substitutions; Math 019/119 (a two-semester course equivalent to Math 120); referrals to campus and community services; and other appropriate services as necessary. There is also a Writing Center, Tutorial Program, Math Lab, Counseling Center, and Women's Resource Center.

SUPPORT SERVICES CONTACT INFORMATION

Learning Disability Program/Services: Disability Resource Center
Director: Mary Zabel
  E-mail: mzabel@unr.edu
  Telephone: 775-784-6000
  Fax: 775-784-1353
Contact: Michelle Bruce
  E-mail: mbruce@unr.nevada.ed
  Telephone: 775-784-6000
  Fax: 775-784-1353

LEARNING DISABILITY SERVICES

Requests for the following services/accommodations will be evaluated individually based on appropriate and current documentation.

Allowed in Exams
  Calculator: Yes
  Dictionary: Yes
  Computer: Yes
  Spellchecker: Yes
Extended test time: Yes
Scribes: Yes
Proctors: Yes
Oral exams: Yes
Note-takers: Yes

Distraction-reduced environment: Yes
Tape recording in class: Yes
Books on tape from RFBD: Yes
Taping of books not from RFBD: Yes
Accommodations for students with ADHD: Yes
Reading machine: Yes
Other assistive technology: Yes
Priority registration: No

Added costs for services: No
LD specialists: Yes (1)
Professional tutors: No
Peer tutors: 50
Max. hours/wk. for services: 2 hrs per week per class
How professors are notified of LD/ADHD: By student

GENERAL ADMISSIONS INFORMATION

Director of Admissions: Melisa Choroszy
Telephone: 775-784-4700

ENTRANCE REQUIREMENTS
13 total are required; 4 English required, 3 math required, 3 science required, 2 science lab required, 3 social studies required and 1/2 computer literacy. High school diploma is required and GED is not accepted. Minimum TOEFL is 500.

Application deadline: Rolling
Notification: Rolling
Average GPA: 3.3

Average SAT I Math: 489
Average SAT I Verbal: 435
Average ACT: 22

Graduated top 10% of class: NR
Graduated top 25% of class: NR
Graduated top 50% of class: NR

COLLEGE GRADUATION REQUIREMENTS

Course waivers allowed: No
Course substitutions allowed: Yes
In what subjects: Foreign language as determined appropriate

ADDITIONAL INFORMATION

Environment: Located 400 miles from Las Vegas and 200 miles from San Francisco.

Student Body
  Undergrad enrollment: 9,402
  Female: 55%
  Male: 45%
  Out-of-state: 16%

Cost Information
  In-state tuition: $2,340
  Out-of-state tuition: $9,320
  Room & board: $5,295
Housing Information
  University housing: Yes
  Percent living on campus: 13%

Greek System
  Fraternity: Yes
  Sorority: Yes
Athletics: NCAA Division I

COLBY-SAWYER COLLEGE

100 Main Street, New London, NH 03257
Phone: 603-526-3700 • Fax: 603-526-3452
E-mail: csadmiss@colbysawyer.edu • Web: www.colby-sawyer.edu
Support level: CS • Institution type: 4-year private

LEARNING DISABILITY PROGRAM AND SERVICES

The goal of the Academic Development Center is to offer students with learning disabilities the same opportunities that the College extends to other students. This includes providing individualized, free-of-charge academic support services designed to enable Colby-Sawyer College students to realize their full academic potential. By way of implementation, the Academic Development Center staff members are trained to meet the academic needs of the entire student body by providing supplemental assistance to those who need help in specific courses and/or development of basic study skills, seek academic achievement beyond their already strong level, and/or have learning styles with diagnosed differences.

LD/ADHD ADMISSIONS INFORMATION

College entrance tests required: Yes
Nonstandardized tests accepted: Yes
Interview required: No
Essay required: Yes
Documentation required for LD: Psychoeducational
  evaluation—after admission
Documentation required for ADHD: Yes
Documentation submitted to: Academic Development Center
Special Ed. HS course work accepted: Yes

Specific course requirements for all applicants: Yes
Separate application required for services: No
# of LD applications submitted yearly: N/A
# of LD applications accepted yearly: N/A
Total # of students receiving LD/ADHD services: 75
**Acceptance into program means acceptance into
  college:** Students must be admitted and enrolled at the
  College first and then may request services.

ADMISSIONS

There is no special admissions process for students with learning disabilities. Students must submit one recommendation from their counselor and one from a teacher. An essay is also required. It is recommended that students have at least 15 units of college-preparatory courses. Students with documented learning disabilities may substitute courses for math or foreign language if those are the areas of deficit. GPA is evaluated in terms of factors that may have affected GPA, as well as a subjective assessment of students' chances of succeeding in college.

ADDITIONAL INFORMATION

Essential to the success of the Academic Development Center is the informal, individualized, nonjudgmental nature of the learning that occurs during tutoring sessions. Tutors must qualify for their jobs by presenting a GPA of 3.3 with no less than an A- in every course they designate as part of their area of expertise. Other services provided include: (1) Classroom modifications—students meet with a learning specialist to develop a "profile," which includes the student's learning style, learning strengths and weaknesses, and recommendations to professors for accommodations; (2) Special help—learning specialists assist students in improving study skills, and/or developing writing skills, and (3) Academic advising—each student has a faculty advisor, interested in student progress, who confers with students at regular intervals to set and achieve goals and select courses. There are currently 50 students with LD and 25 students with ADHD receiving services.

SUPPORT SERVICES CONTACT INFORMATION

Learning Disability Program/Services: Academic Development Center
Director: Mary Mar, PhD
  E-mail: mmar@colby-sawyer.edu
  Telephone: 603-526-3714
  Fax: 603-522-3452
Contact: Same

LEARNING DISABILITY SERVICES

Requests for the following services/accommodations will be evaluated individually based on appropriate and current documentation.

Allowed in Exams
  Calculator: Yes
  Dictionary: Yes
  Computer: Yes
  Spellchecker: Yes
Extended test time: Yes
Scribes: Yes
Proctors: Yes
Oral exams: Yes
Note-takers: Yes

Distraction-reduced environment: Yes
Tape recording in class: Yes
Books on tape from RFBD: Yes
Taping of books not from RFBD: No
Accommodations for students with ADHD: Yes
Reading machine: N/A
Other assistive technology: No
Priority registration: No

Added costs for services: No
LD specialists: Yes
Professional tutors: Yes (2)
Peer tutors: 22
Max. hours/wk. for services: Unlimited
How professors are notified of LD/ADHD: By student

GENERAL ADMISSIONS INFORMATION

Director of Admissions: Steve Cloniger
Telephone: 603-526-3700

ENTRANCE REQUIREMENTS
15 total are required; 4 English required, 3 math required, 2 science required, 2 science lab required, 2 foreign language required, 3 social studies required. High school diploma or GED required. TOEFL required of all international applicants.

Application deadline: Rolling
Notification: Rolling beginning 12/20
Average GPA: 2.8

Average SAT I Math: 497
Average SAT I Verbal: 504
Average ACT: 21

Graduated top 10% of class: NR
Graduated top 25% of class: NR
Graduated top 50% of class: NR

COLLEGE GRADUATION REQUIREMENTS

Course waivers allowed: No
Course substitutions allowed: Yes
In what subjects: Substitutions are usually unnecessary, but could be made under special circumstances

ADDITIONAL INFORMATION

Environment: The College has an 80-acre campus in a small town.

Student Body
  Undergrad enrollment: 808
  Female: 65%
  Male: 35%
  Out-of-state: 66%

Cost Information
  Tuition: $18,960
  Room & board: $7,240
Housing Information
  University housing: Yes
  Percent living on campus: 88%

Greek System
  Fraternity: Yes
  Sorority: Yes
Athletics: NCAA Division III

NEW ENGLAND COLLEGE

26 Bridge Street, Henniker, NH 03242
Phone: 603-428-2211 • Fax: 603-428-7230
E-mail: admission@nec.edu • Web: www.nec.edu
Support level: CS • Institution type: 4-year private

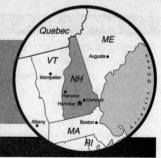

LEARNING DISABILITY PROGRAM AND SERVICES

The Academic Advising & Support Center provides services for all students in a welcoming and supportive environment. Students come to the Center with a variety of academic needs. Some want help writing term papers. Some feel they read too slowly or can't comprehend mathematics. Others are confused and anxious about their ability to perform as college students. Some students may have learning disabilities. The Center provides individual or small group tutoring, academic counseling, and referral services. Tutoring is available in most subject areas. The Center focuses primarily on helping students make a successful transition to New England College while supporting all students in their effort to become independent and successful learners. The support services meet the needs of students who do not require a formal, structured program, but who can find success when offered support by a trained and experienced staff in conjunction with small classes and personal attention by faculty. Typically these students have done well in "mainstream" programs in high school, when given assistance. Students with learning disabilities are encouraged to visit NEC and the Academic and Advising Support Center to determine whether the support services will adequately meet their academic needs.

LD/ADHD ADMISSIONS INFORMATION

College entrance tests required: No
Nonstandardized tests accepted: Yes
Interview required: Yes
Essay required: Yes
Documentation required for LD: WAIS-III, Woodcock-Johnson, reading, writing
Documentation required for ADHD: Yes
Documentation submitted to: Academic Advising and Support Center
Special Ed. HS course work accepted: Yes, case-by-case

Specific course requirements for all applicants: Yes
Separate application required for services: N/A
# of LD applications submitted yearly: N/A
# of LD applications accepted yearly: N/A
Total # of students receiving LD/ADHD services: 130
Acceptance into program means acceptance into college: Students must be admitted and enrolled at the College first and then may request services.

ADMISSIONS

Students with learning disabilities submit the general New England College application. Students should have a 2.0 GPA. SAT/ACT are optional. Course requirements include 4 years English, 2 years math, 2 years science, and 2 years social studies. Documentation of the learning disability should be submitted along with counselor and teacher recommendations. An interview is recommended. Successful applicants have typically done well in "mainstream" programs in high school when given tutorial and study skills assistance. The Academic Adventure Program is a four-week program open to all accepted students. Occasionally, NEC allows a handful of students to begin conditionally in the summer and tie admissions to performance in the summer program.

ADDITIONAL INFORMATION

Students may elect to use the Support Center services with regular appointments or only occasionally in response to particular or difficult assignments. The Center provides tutoring in content areas; computer facilities; study skills instruction; time management strategies; writing support in planning, editing, and proofreading; mathematics support; referrals to other college services; and one-on-one writing support for first-year students. Students are encouraged to use the word processors to generate writing assignments, and to use the tutors to help plan and revise papers. The writing faculty works closely with the center to provide coordinated and supportive learning for all students. Professional tutors work with students individually and in small groups. These services are provided in a secure and accepting atmosphere. Currently 20 percent of the student body has diagnosed LD.

SUPPORT SERVICES CONTACT INFORMATION

Learning Disability Program/Services: Academic Advising and Support Center
Director: Anna Carlson
 E-mail: acarslon@nec.edu
 Telephone: 603-428-2218
 Fax: 603-428-7230
Contact: Mary Lou Pashko
 Telephone: 603-428-2218
 Fax: 603-428-7230

LEARNING DISABILITY SERVICES

Requests for the following services/accommodations will be evaluated individually based on appropriate and current documentation.

Allowed in Exams
 Calculator: Yes
 Dictionary: No
 Computer: Yes
 Spellchecker: Yes
Extended test time: Yes
Scribes: Yes
Proctors: Yes
Oral exams: Yes
Note-takers: No

Distraction-reduced environment: Yes
Tape recording in class: Yes
Books on tape from RFBD: Yes
Taping of books not from RFBD: Yes
Accommodations for students with ADHD: Yes
Reading machine: No
Other assistive technology: No
Priority registration: No

Added costs for services: No
LD specialists: Yes (1)
Professional tutors: 6
Peer tutors: No
Max. hours/wk. for services: 5
How professors are notified of LD/ADHD: By student

GENERAL ADMISSIONS INFORMATION

Director of Admissions: Donald Parker
Telephone: 603-428-2223

ENTRANCE REQUIREMENTS

4 English required, 2 math required, 3 math recommended, 2 science required, 3 science recommended, 2 foreign language recommended, 3 social studies required, 1 history required. ACT/SAT are optional. High school diploma or GED required. Minimum TOEFL is 550. TOEFL required of all international applicants.

Application deadline: Rolling
Notification: Rolling beginning 12/18
Average GPA: 2.8

Average SAT I Math: NR
Average SAT I Verbal: NR
Average ACT: NR

Graduated top 10% of class: 21%
Graduated top 25% of class: 27%
Graduated top 50% of class: 43%

COLLEGE GRADUATION REQUIREMENTS

Course waivers allowed: No
Course substitutions allowed: No
In what subjects: It depends on the disability. Most frequent request is college-wide math requirement if not required for major.

ADDITIONAL INFORMATION

Environment: The College is located in the town of Henniker on 212 acres 17 miles west of Concord.

Student Body
 Undergrad enrollment: 724
 Female: 51%
 Male: 49%
 Out-of-state: 80%

Cost Information
 Tuition: $18,382
 Room & board: $6,538
Housing Information
 University housing: Yes
 Percent living on campus: 65%

Greek System
 Fraternity: Yes
 Sorority: Yes
 Athletics: NCAA Division III

New England College

NOTRE DAME COLLEGE

2321 Elm Street, Manchester, NH 03104-2299
Phone: 603-669-4298 • Fax: 603-644-8316
E-mail: admissions@notredame.edu • Web: www.notredame.edu
Support level: S • Institution type: 4-year private

LEARNING DISABILITY PROGRAM AND SERVICES

The learning disabilities support program at Notre Dame College is an accommodation, not a remediation program. All students are enrolled in regular classes. The Learning Enrichment Center is designed for the high school student who has the potential to earn a college degree, but needs support to compensate for a learning disability. Incoming students who wish to receive support should take the following steps: make an appointment with the Learning Enrichment Center Director to discuss concerns and necessary accommodations (the student should bring documentation of the learning disability to this meeting); take part in preparing a student profile with the Learning Enrichment Center Director; give copies of the completed student profile to each of the student's instructors; attend a weekly, pre-arranged meeting with the Learning Enrichment Center Director to monitor progress; seek tutoring as necessary or as recommended by the Learning Enrichment Center Director; and make a strong commitment to academics.

LD/ADHD ADMISSIONS INFORMATION

College entrance tests required: Yes
Nonstandardized tests accepted: Yes
Interview required: No
Essay required: No
Documentation required for LD: Psychoeducational evaluation
Documentation required for ADHD: Yes
Documentation submitted to: LEC
Special Ed. HS course work accepted: Yes

Specific course requirements for all applicants: Yes
Separate application required for services: No
# of LD applications submitted yearly: N/A
# of LD applications accepted yearly: N/A
Total # of students receiving LD/ADHD services: 28
Acceptance into program means acceptance into college: Students must be admitted and enrolled at the College and then may request services.

ADMISSIONS

Students with learning disabilities must submit a regular application for admission and be accepted under regular admission. The general admission requirements include 4 years English, 2 years foreign language, 2 years history, 2 years math, 2 years science, 2 years social studies; 880 SAT I; 2.0 GPA. Applicants desiring admission to the Learning Enrichment Center are encouraged to self-disclose and submit documentation to admissions of a diagnosed learning disability by a certified professional. There is some flexibility in SAT range. Self-disclosed LD documentation should include identification and description of the specific type of learning disability; description of the effects of the learning disability including strengths and weaknesses; learning style; and a recent Individualized Educational Plan. The admissions decision is made by both the Program Director and Admissions Director.

ADDITIONAL INFORMATION

The Learning Enrichment Center provides a quiet atmosphere to offer academic support and appropriate accommodations to all students, including students with documented learning disabilities. Services provided include assistance in writing college-level papers; help in studying for major tests and exams; guidance in study skills; tutoring in all subjects; workshops to review and relearn; and individualized support services and appropriate accommodations for students with learning disabilities. Study-skills classes for credit are offered in reading proficiency and basic English skills in writing.

SUPPORT SERVICES CONTACT INFORMATION

Learning Disability Program/Services: Learning Enrichment Center (LEC)
Director: Jane O'Neil
 E-mail: info@notredame.edu
 Telephone: 603-669-4294
Contact: Same

LEARNING DISABILITY SERVICES

Requests for the following services/accommodations will be evaluated individually based on appropriate and current documentation.

Allowed in Exams
 Calculator: Yes
 Dictionary: No
 Computer: Yes
 Spellchecker: No
 Extended test time: Yes
 Scribes: Yes
 Proctors: Yes
 Oral exams: Yes
 Note-takers: Yes

Distraction-reduced environment: Yes
Tape recording in class: Yes
Books on tape from RFBD: Yes
Taping of books not from RFBD: Yes
Accommodations for students with ADHD: Yes
Reading machine: Yes
Other assistive technology: No
Priority registration: No

Added costs for services: No
LD specialists: No
Professional tutors: Yes
Peer tutors: Yes
Max. hours/wk. for services: Unlimited
How professors are notified of LD/ADHD: By student and a profile completed by director

GENERAL ADMISSIONS INFORMATION

Director of Admissions: Patricia Doyle
Telephone: 603-669-4298

ENTRANCE REQUIREMENTS
16 total are required; 22 total are recommended; 4 English required, 2 math required, 4 math recommended, 2 science required, 3 science recommended, 1 science lab required, 2 foreign language recommended, 3 social studies required, 2 history required, 3 elective required. Minimum TOEFL is 500. TOEFL required of all international applicants.

Application deadline: Rolling
Notification: Rolling
Average GPA: 2.8

Average SAT I Math: 443
Average SAT I Verbal: 468
Average ACT: NR

Graduated top 10% of class: NR
Graduated top 25% of class: NR
Graduated top 50% of class: NR

COLLEGE GRADUATION REQUIREMENTS

Course waivers allowed: No
Course substitutions allowed: Yes
In what subjects: Case-by-case basis

ADDITIONAL INFORMATION

Environment: Notre Dame College is located on 7 acres in a suburban area north of Manchester.

Student Body
 Undergrad enrollment: 685
 Female: 76%
 Male: 24%
 Out-of-state: 31%

Cost Information
 Tuition: $15,367
 Room & board: $6,213
Housing Information
 University housing: Yes
 Percent living on campus: 19%

Greek System
 Fraternity: Yes
 Sorority: Yes
Athletics: NAIA

RIVIER COLLEGE

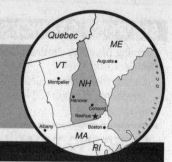

420 Main Street, Nashua, NH 03060
Phone: 603-897-8507 • Fax: 603-891-1799
E-mail: rivadmit@rivier.edu • Web: www.rivier.edu
Support level: S • Institution type: 4-year private

LEARNING DISABILITY PROGRAM AND SERVICES

Rivier College recognizes that learning styles differ from person to person. Physical, perceptual, or emotional challenges experienced by students may require additional supports and accommodations to equalize their opportunities for success. The College is committed to providing supports that allow all otherwise qualified individuals with disabilities an equal educational opportunity. Special Needs Services provides the opportunity for all individuals who meet academic requirements to be provided auxiliary services, facilitating their earning of a college education. To be eligible for support services students are required to provide appropriate documentation of their disabilities to the Coordinator of Special Needs Services. This documentation shall be provided from a professional in the field of psychoeducational testing or a physician and shall be current, within three to five years. This information will be confidential and is kept in the Coordinator's office for the purpose of planning appropriate support services. To access services students must contact the Coordinator of Special Needs Services before the start of each semester to schedule an appointment and provide documentation; together the Coordinator and the student will discuss and arrange for support services specifically related to the disability.

LD/ADHD ADMISSIONS INFORMATION

College entrance tests required: Yes
Nonstandardized tests accepted: Yes
Interview required: No
Essay required: Yes
Documentation required for LD: Psychoeducational evaluation: within 2 years
Documentation required for ADHD: Yes
Documentation submitted to: Special Needs Services
Special Ed. HS course work accepted: Yes

Specific course requirements for all applicants: Yes
Separate application required for services: No
# of LD applications submitted yearly: N/A
# of LD applications accepted yearly: N/A
Total # of students receiving LD/ADHD services: 25
Acceptance into program means acceptance into college: Students must be accepted and enrolled at the College first and then may request services.

ADMISSIONS

There is no special admissions process for students with learning disabilities. All applicants must meet the same criteria. Students should have a combined SAT of 820; GPA in the top 80 percent; and take college-prep courses in high school. Applicants not meeting the general admission requirements may inquire about alternative admissions. The College has a probational admit that requires students to maintain a minimum 2.0 GPA their first semester.

ADDITIONAL INFORMATION

Services available include academic, career, and personal counseling; preferential registration; classroom accommodations including tape recording of lectures, extended time for test completion, testing free from distractions, and note-takers; student advocacy; Writing Center for individualized instruction in writing and individualized accommodations as developed by the Coordinator of Special Needs Services with the student. Skills classes are offered in English and math and students may take these classes for college credit. Services and accommodations are available for undergraduate and graduate students.

SUPPORT SERVICES CONTACT INFORMATION

Learning Disability Program/Services: Special Needs Services
Director: Bess Arnold
  E-mail: barnold@rivier.edu
  Telephone: 603-897-8497
  Fax: 603-897-8887
Contact: Same

LEARNING DISABILITY SERVICES

Requests for the following services/accommodations will be evaluated individually based on appropriate and current documentation.

Allowed in Exams
  Calculator: Yes
  Dictionary: Yes
  Computer: Yes
  Spellchecker: Yes
Extended test time: Yes
Scribes: Yes
Proctors: Yes
Oral exams: Yes
Note-takers: Yes

Distraction-reduced environment: Yes
Tape recording in class: Yes
Books on tape from RFBD: Yes
Taping of books not from RFBD: No
Accommodations for students with ADHD: No
Reading machine: No
Other assistive technology: Yes
Priority registration: Yes

Added costs for services: No
LD specialists: No
Professional tutors: No
Peer tutors: No
Max. hours/wk. for services: N/A
How professors are notified of LD/ADHD: By both student and director

GENERAL ADMISSIONS INFORMATION

Director of Admissions: David Boisvert
Telephone: 603-897-8507

ENTRANCE REQUIREMENTS
16 total are recommended; 4 English recommended, 3 math recommended, 1 science recommended, 1 science lab recommended, 2 foreign language recommended, 2 social studies recommended, 1 history recommended, 3 elective recommended. High school diploma or GED required. Minimum TOEFL is 500. TOEFL required of all international applicants.

Application deadline: August 30
Notification: Rolling beginning 12/1
Average GPA: 3.0

Average SAT I Math: NR
Average SAT I Verbal: NR
Average ACT: NR

Graduated top 10% of class: 9%
Graduated top 25% of class: 24%
Graduated top 50% of class: 70%

COLLEGE GRADUATION REQUIREMENTS

Course waivers allowed: No
Course substitutions allowed: Yes
In what subjects: Each course substitution is looked at individually

ADDITIONAL INFORMATION

Environment: The College is located on 60 acres in a suburban area 40 miles north of Boston.

Student Body
  Undergrad enrollment: 1,546
  Female: 81%
  Male: 19%
  Out-of-state: 33%

Cost Information
  Tuition: $15,210
  Room & board: $6,100
Housing Information
  University housing: Yes
  Percent living on campus: 44%

Greek System
  Fraternity: No
  Sorority: No
  Athletics: NCAA Division III

SOUTHERN NEW HAMPSHIRE UNIV.

2500 North River Road, Manchester, NH 03108
Phone: 603-645-9611 • Fax: 603-645-9693
E-mail: admission@nhc.edu • Web: www.nhc.edu
Support level: CS • Institution type: 4-year private

LEARNING DISABILITY PROGRAM AND SERVICES

There is no formal learning disabilities program. The College does have a Learning Center that offers a wide range of academic support services. For the most part, successful students with learning disabilities will be those who are aware of their strengths and weaknesses and who actively seek help. The College does not offer an alternative curriculum.

LD/ADHD ADMISSIONS INFORMATION

College entrance tests required: No
Nonstandardized tests accepted: Yes
Interview required: Recommended
Essay required: Yes
Documentation required for LD: Psychoeducational evaluation
Documentation required for ADHD: Yes
Documentation submitted to: Disability Services
Special Ed. HS course work accepted: N/A

Specific course requirements for all applicants: Yes
Separate application required for services: No
# of LD applications submitted yearly: N/A
# of LD applications accepted yearly: N/A
Total # of students receiving LD/ADHD services: 115
Acceptance into program means acceptance into college: Students must be admitted and enrolled at the College first and then may request services.

ADMISSIONS

The College does not have a specific admissions process for students with learning disabilities. No pre-admission inquiry is made about applicants' disabilities, but self-disclosure can often be helpful in the admissions process. Through self-disclosure, an informed and fair decision can be made by the student and the College, regarding the suitability of this school in the pursuit of a college education. Students are encouraged to provide the following information: educational history including assessment measures and treatment of disability; accommodations needed; accommodations received in high school; coping skills that have been developed; and the relationship between the disability and the academic record.

ADDITIONAL INFORMATION

Tutoring is available on a one-to-one basis. Basic skills courses are offered in math, reading, and written language. College credit can be earned for reading and writing. Services and accommodations are available for undergraduate and graduate students. Some of the services or accommodations which may be available to students with appropriate documentation include the use of calculators, dictionary, computer or spellchecker on exams; extended time on tests; scribes; proctors; oral exams; note-takers; distraction-free testing environment; tape recorder in class; taped texts; and priority registration. There is a very strong advising system in the freshman year.

SUPPORT SERVICES CONTACT INFORMATION

Learning Disability Program/Services: Disability Services
Director: Hyla Jaffe, Coordinator
  E-mail: h.jaffe@snhu.edu
  Telephone: 603-668-2211
  Fax: 603-645-9648
Contact: Same

LEARNING DISABILITY SERVICES

Requests for the following services/accommodations will be evaluated individually based on appropriate and current documentation.

Allowed in Exams
  Calculator: Yes
  Dictionary: Yes
  Computer: Yes
  Spellchecker: Yes
  Extended test time: Yes
  Scribes: Yes
  Proctors: Yes
  Oral exams: Yes
  Note-takers: Yes

Distraction-reduced environment: Yes
Tape recording in class: Yes
Books on tape from RFBD: Yes
Taping of books not from RFBD: No
**Accommodations for students with
  ADHD:** Yes
Reading machine: Yes
Other assistive technology: Yes
Priority registration: Yes

Added costs for services: No
LD specialists: Yes (2)
Professional tutors: N/A
Peer tutors: N/A
Max. hours/wk. for services: N/A
**How professors are notified of
  LD/ADHD:** By student

GENERAL ADMISSIONS INFORMATION

Director of Admissions: Brad Pozhanski
Telephone: 603-645-9681

ENTRANCE REQUIREMENTS
16 total are required; 4 English required, 2 math required, 4 math recommended, 3 science recommended, 2 foreign language recommended, 2 social studies recommended. High school diploma or GED required. Minimum TOEFL is 500. TOEFL required of all international applicants.

Application deadline: Rolling
Notification: Rolling
Average GPA: 3.0

Average SAT I Math: 476
Average SAT I Verbal: 475
Average ACT: 20

Graduated top 10% of class: 3%
Graduated top 25% of class: 20%
Graduated top 50% of class: 44%

COLLEGE GRADUATION REQUIREMENTS

Course waivers allowed: No
Course substitutions allowed: No
In what subjects: N/A

ADDITIONAL INFORMATION

Environment: The College is located on 200 acres in a suburban area 55 miles north of Boston.

Student Body
  Undergrad enrollment: 4,058
  Female: 52%
  Male: 48%
  Out-of-state: 80%

Cost Information
  Tuition: $15,598
  Room & board: $6,790
Housing Information
  University housing: Yes
  Percent living on campus: 80%

Greek System
  Fraternity: Yes
  Sorority: Yes
  Athletics: NCAA Division II

UNIVERSITY OF NEW HAMPSHIRE

4 Garrison Avenue, Durham, NH 03824
Phone: 603-862-1360 • Fax: 603-862-0077
E-mail: admissions@unh.edu • Web: www.unh.edu
Support level: S • Institution type: 4-year public

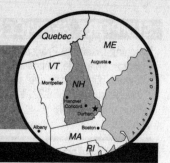

LEARNING DISABILITY PROGRAM AND SERVICES

UNH encourages students to self-disclose within the admissions procedure. There is no LD program. Rather services/accommodations are based on student self-disclosure and obtaining the proper guidelines for documentation of LD/ADHD. ACCESS Office: Support for Students with Disabilities is where students with documented disabilities can receive those accommodations and academic services which enable students to have equal access to the classroom. Additionally, students can learn and further develop their self-advocacy skills and increase their knowledge about communicating regarding their disability. Students need to be aware that "being tested for a learning disability," "having old documentation" (more than three years old), or being "previously coded in secondary education" in and of itself, does not necessarily mean that the student will be currently qualified with a disability under federal laws in college. UNH does not offer a program for subject area tutorial, nor are LD specialists on staff. Services and accommodations at UNH can be defined as those generic activities offered to ensure educational opportunity for any student with a documented disability. All students with LD/ADHD must provide current and appropriate documentation to qualify for services.

LD/ADHD ADMISSIONS INFORMATION

College entrance tests required: Yes
Nonstandardized tests accepted: Yes
Interview required: No
Essay required: Yes
Documentation required for LD: Psychoeducational evaluation
Documentation required for ADHD: Yes
Documentation submitted to: Access Office
Special Ed. HS course work accepted: Yes

Specific course requirements for all applicants: Yes
Separate application required for services: N/A
# of LD applications submitted yearly: N/A
# of LD applications accepted yearly: N/A
Total # of students receiving LD/ADHD services: 168
Acceptance into program means acceptance into college: Students must be admitted and enrolled at the University and then may be reviewed for services.

ADMISSIONS

Admissions criteria are the same for all applicants. Typically, students who are admitted to the University are in the top 30 percent of their class, have a B average in college-preparatory courses, and have taken 4 years of college-prep math, 3–4 years of a lab science, and 3–4 years of a foreign language; SAT I average range is 1050–1225 but there are no cutoffs (or equivalent ACT). There are no alternative options for admissions. Access has no involvement in any admissions decision. However, there is a member of the Admissions staff with a background in special education.

ADDITIONAL INFORMATION

Academic accommodations provided, based on documentation, include the following: individually scheduled meetings with ACCESS coordinator for guidance, advising, and referrals; mediation and advocacy; note-takers; scribes; proctors; readers; taped texts; extended exam time; distraction-free rooms for exams; alternative methods for exam administration; pre-registration priority scheduling; reduced course load; and faculty support letters. UNH does not provide a university-wide service or program for subject area tutoring; it is the student's responsibility to secure subject area tutoring. However, the Center for Academic Resources provides all students with drop-in tutoring in selected courses; referrals to free academic assistance opportunities and to private pay tutors; individualized study skills assistance; and peer support for academic and personal concerns. There is a federally funded grant that allows some students to receive free peer tutoring and reading/writing assistance with a specialist.

SUPPORT SERVICES CONTACT INFORMATION

Learning Disability Program/Services: ACCESS Office: Support for Students with Disabilities
Director: Margo W. Druschel
  E-mail: mwd@cisunix.unh.edu
  Telephone: 603-862-2607
  Fax: 603-862-4043
Contact: Same

LEARNING DISABILITY SERVICES

Requests for the following services/accommodations will be evaluated individually based on appropriate and current documentation.

Allowed in Exams
  Calculator: Yes
  Dictionary: Yes
  Computer: Yes
  Spellchecker: Yes
Extended test time: Yes
Scribes: Yes
Proctors: Yes
Oral exams: Yes
Note-takers: Yes

Distraction-reduced environment: Yes
Tape recording in class: Yes
Books on tape from RFBD: Yes
Taping of books not from RFBD: Yes
**Accommodations for students with
  ADHD:** Yes
Reading machine: No
Other assistive technology: Yes
Priority registration: Yes, limited

Added costs for services: No
LD specialists: No
Professional tutors: No
Peer tutors: Yes
Max. hours/wk. for services: Varies
**How professors are notified of
  LD/ADHD:** By the student and the
director after initial contact by the
student.

GENERAL ADMISSIONS INFORMATION

Director of Admissions: Mark Rubinstein (interim director)
Telephone: 603-862-1360

ENTRANCE REQUIREMENTS

18 total are recommended; 4 English recommended, 4 math recommended, 4 science recommended, 4 science lab recommended, 3 foreign language recommended, 3 social studies recommended. High school diploma or GED required. Minimum TOEFL is 550. TOEFL required of all international applicants.

Application deadline: February 1
Notification: April 15
Average GPA: 3.0

Average SAT I Math: 560
Average SAT I Verbal: 560
Average ACT: NR

Graduated top 10% of class: 19%
Graduated top 25% of class: 58%
Graduated top 50% of class: 94%

COLLEGE GRADUATION REQUIREMENTS

Course waivers allowed: No
Course substitutions allowed: Yes
In what subjects: Only in foreign language on a case-by-case basis by a petition process

ADDITIONAL INFORMATION

Environment: The University is located in a rural area about 1 hour north of Boston.

Student Body
  Undergrad enrollment: 10,927
  Female: 58%
  Male: 42%
  Out-of-state: 40%

Cost Information
  In-state tuition: $7,000
  Out-of-state tuition: $16,000
  Room & board: $4,800
Housing Information
  University housing: Yes
  Percent living on campus: 55%

Greek System
  Fraternity: Yes
  Sorority: Yes
Athletics: NCAA Division I

University of New Hampshire

CALDWELL COLLEGE

9 Ryerson Avenue, Caldwell, NJ 07006-9165
Phone: 973-618-3500 • Fax: 973-618-3600
E-mail: admissions@caldwell.edu • Web: www.caldwell.edu
Support level: CS • Institution type: 4-year private

LEARNING DISABILITY PROGRAM AND SERVICES

Caldwell College offers students with disabilities a support program through the Learning Center and the Office of Disability Services. Students with documentation of an LD are fully integrated into college degree programs of study, and, in addition, are offered support services. The Office of Disability Services functions as a service coordinator for students with disabilities, advocating with faculty for reasonable accommodations in accordance with the Americans with Disability Act.

LD/ADHD ADMISSIONS INFORMATION

College entrance tests required: Yes
Nonstandardized tests accepted: Yes
Interview required: No
Essay required: Yes
Documentation required for LD: WAIS-III and Woodcock-Johnson Psychoeducational Battery-Revised (WJPB-J)
Documentation required for ADHD: Yes
Documentation submitted to: Admissions and Office of Disability Services
Special Ed. HS course work accepted: Yes

Specific course requirements for all applicants: Yes
Separate application required for services: No
# of LD applications submitted yearly: N/A
# of LD applications accepted yearly: N/A
Total # of students receiving LD/ADHD services: N/A
Acceptance into program means acceptance into college: Students must be admitted and enrolled and then may request services.

ADMISSIONS

There is no special admissions process for students with LD and ADHD. There is a pre-freshman summer program for students considered at risk for success in the fall. The decision to advise a student for this program may be based on low SAT/ACT scores or a borderline (1.9) GPA. This conditional admission program is available to all applicants regardless of a disability. The middle50 percent SAT range for general admissions is 900. Additionally, students generally have a minimum GPA of 2.0, and have 16 high school academic units including 4 English, 2 years of foreign language, and 2 years of math, 2 years science and 1 year of history. With appropriate documentation applicants with LD may request to substitute some of the required courses with other high school courses.

ADDITIONAL INFORMATION

There is one LD specialist on staff and no fee charged for tutoring or other services. Individual tutoring sessions with a professional learning specialist are offered to help students improve organizational skills and promote self-advocacy. Meetings are also scheduled to facilitate advocacy in the form of accommodation letters to faculty and to coordinate peer tutoring. There is a Writing Center, Learning Center, supplemental instruction, and peer tutoring for all students. The library is equipped with various programs to assist students with disabilities.

SUPPORT SERVICES CONTACT INFORMATION

Learning Disability Program/Services: Office of Disability Services
Director: Joan Serpico, Coordinator
  E-mail: jserpico@caldwell.edu
  Telephone: 973-618-3645
  Fax: 973-618-3488
Contact: Same

LEARNING DISABILITY SERVICES

Requests for the following services/accommodations will be evaluated individually based on appropriate and current documentation.

Allowed in Exams
  Calculator: Yes
  Dictionary: Yes
  Computer: Yes
  Spellchecker: Yes
Extended test time: Yes
Scribes: Yes
Proctors: Yes
Oral exams: Yes
Note-takers: Yes

Distraction-reduced environment: Yes
Tape recording in class: Yes
Books on tape from RFBD: Yes
Taping of books not from RFBD: Yes
Accommodations for students with ADHD: Yes
Reading machine: Yes
Other assistive technology: Yes
Priority registration: No

Added costs for services: No
LD specialists: Yes (1)
Professional tutors: Varies
Peer tutors: Varies
Max. hours/wk. for services: Unlimited
How professors are notified of LD/ADHD: By both student and director

GENERAL ADMISSIONS INFORMATION

Director of Admissions: Ray Sheenan
Telephone: 973-618-3220

ENTRANCE REQUIREMENTS
16 total are required; 4 English required, 2 math required, 2 science required, 1 science lab required, 2 foreign language required, 1 history required, 5 elective required. High school diploma or GED required. Minimum TOEFL is 500. TOEFL required of all international applicants.

Application deadline: NR
Notification: Rolling beginning 12/15
Average GPA: 2.9

Average SAT I Math: 450
Average SAT I Verbal: 470
Average ACT: NR

Graduated top 10% of class: 5%
Graduated top 25% of class: 22%
Graduated top 50% of class: 48%

COLLEGE GRADUATION REQUIREMENTS

Course waivers allowed: NR
Course substitutions allowed: Yes
In what subjects: Foreign language; substitutions possible

ADDITIONAL INFORMATION

Environment: Located 10 miles from Newark, New Jersey, and 20 miles from New York City.

Student Body
  Undergrad enrollment: 1,844
  Female: 69%
  Male: 31%
  Out-of-state: 3%

Cost Information
  Tuition: $13,100
  Room & board: $6,250
Housing Information
  University housing: Yes
  Percent living on campus: 21%

Greek System
  Fraternity: No
  Sorority: No
Athletics: NAIA

FAIRLEIGH DICKINSON UNIVERSITY

1000 River Road, Teaneck, NJ 07666-1966
Phone: 800-338-8803 • Fax: 201-692-7319
E-mail: admissions@fdu.edu • Web: www.fdu.edu
Support level: SP • Institution type: 2-year and 4-year private

LEARNING DISABILITY PROGRAM AND SERVICES

The Regional Center for College Students with LD offers a structured plan of intensive advisement, academic support, and counseling services that is tailored to the unique needs of students with LD. The goal is to provide a framework within which college students with LD will develop the confidence to succeed in their studies and the independence to do their best. Planning, use of learning strategies, professional tutors, counseling, advisement, and accommodations are the cornerstones of the Regional Center. Staffed by professionals with support services at both the Teaneck and the Madison campus, the LD program and special services are free of charge. Assistance to students is intensive and the program is fully integrated into the course work. Students are in touch with faculty on a regular basis. The program encourages involvement in the community, particularly service-type activities relevant to the students with LD. Performance data are routinely reviewed to identify students in need of more intensive help. Upon admission students are invited to attend a summer orientation session. During this time, students meet with Center staff to develop an Individual Academic Plan in order to develop a class schedule with the right balance.

LD/ADHD ADMISSIONS INFORMATION

College entrance tests required: No
Nonstandardized tests accepted: Yes
Interview required: No
Essay required: No
Documentation required for LD: WAIS-III; WJ; PEB or
    equivalent: within 2 years
Documentation required for ADHD: Yes
Documentation submitted to: Regional Center
Special Ed. HS course work accepted: No

Specific course requirements for all applicants: Yes
Separate application required for services: Yes
# of LD applications submitted yearly: 225
# of LD applications accepted yearly: 40
Total # of students receiving LD/ADHD services: 120
Acceptance into program means acceptance into
    college: Students are accepted jointly by the Regional
    Center for College Students with Learning Disabilities
    and the Office of Admissions.

ADMISSIONS

Admissions decisions are made independently by FDA Admissions and the LD Program Admissions Director. Criteria include documentation of a primary diagnosis of learning disability made by licensed professionals and dated within 24 months of the application; evidence of adequate performance in mainstream college-prep high school courses; and evidence of motivation as reflected in recommendations. Students enrolled solely in special education high school classes are usually not admissible. Lower-level mainstream classes are acceptable from high schools offering different levels in the same subjects. ACT or SAT scores are required but are secondary to the above criteria. Previous school achievement and positive recommendations are viewed as the best predictors for success. Students with 2.5 GPA and 850 SAT can be accepted. General admissions require performance in the top two-fifths of the class or at least a B average and 850 SAT. If applicants are below a 2.5 GPA, they may be referred to the New College, a two-year college located on the Teaneck campus. Admission decisions are made after careful review.

ADDITIONAL INFORMATION

The New College offers a two-year liberal arts program on the Teaneck-Hackensack campus. Students with learning disabilities admitted to the New College can also receive specialized support services if admitted to the Regional Center. FDU students already enrolled in the University may request LD assessments on campus for no charge. Support sessions from trained professionals incorporate a variety of teaching techniques. There is a 15:1 ratio between students and LD specialists. Support sessions are small, individualized, and flexible. Students have priority registration. Students may also participate in math and writing workshops. Course advisement, priority registration, and counseling services are also provided. Services include recorded textbooks, extended testing time and other class support, technological support, and supervised study wherein students meet with specialists in study rooms.

SUPPORT SERVICES CONTACT INFORMATION

Learning Disability Program/Services: Regional Center for College Students with Learning Disabilities
Director: Dr. Mary Farrell
  E-mail: farrell@alpha.fdu.edu
  Telephone: 201-692-2087
  Fax: 201-692-2813
Contact: Same

LEARNING DISABILITY SERVICES

Requests for the following services/accommodations will be evaluated individually based on appropriate and current documentation.

Allowed in Exams
  Calculator: Yes
  Dictionary: No
  Computer: Yes
  Spellchecker: Yes
Extended test time: Yes
Scribes: No
Proctors: Yes
Oral exams: Yes
Note-takers: No

Distraction-reduced environment: Yes
Tape recording in class: Yes
Books on tape from RFBD: Yes
Taping of books not from RFBD: No
Accommodations for students with
  ADHD: Yes
Reading machine: No
Other assistive technology: No
Priority registration: Yes

Added costs for services: No
LD specialists: Yes (10)
Professional tutors: 10
Peer tutors: No
Max. hours/wk. for services: 8 hours
  for freshmen, 3 hours for sophomores,
  2 hours for juniors, 1 hour for seniors
How professors are notified of
  LD/ADHD: By director for freshmen
  and sophomores, then by student

GENERAL ADMISSIONS INFORMATION

Director of Admissions: Michael Hendricks
Telephone: 800-338-8803

ENTRANCE REQUIREMENTS
16 total are required; 16 total are recommended; 4 English required, 3 math required, 2 science required, 3 science recommended, 2 science lab required, 3 science lab recommended, 2 foreign language required, 2 history required, 3 elective required. High school diploma or GED required. Minimum TOEFL is 500.

Application deadline: Rolling
Notification: Rolling beginning 1/15
Average GPA: 3.0

Average SAT I Math: 460–570
Average SAT I Verbal: 460–570
Average ACT: NR

Graduated top 10% of class: 20%
Graduated top 25% of class: 38%
Graduated top 50% of class: 58%

COLLEGE GRADUATION REQUIREMENTS

Course waivers allowed: No
Course substitutions allowed: Yes
In what subjects: Math and foreign language substitutions may be granted if candidate qualifies for University policy.

ADDITIONAL INFORMATION

Environment: The Teaneck campus is located on the banks of the Hackensack River. It is within walking distance of The New College.

Student Body
  Undergrad enrollment: 2,100
  Female: 55%
  Male: 45%
  Out-of-state: 24%

Cost Information
  Tuition: $16,364
  Room & board: $5,000
Housing Information
  University housing: Yes
  Percent living on campus: 76%

Greek System
  Fraternity: Yes
  Sorority: Yes
Athletics: NCAA Division I

GEORGIAN COURT COLLEGE

900 Lakewood Avenue, Lakewood, NJ 08701-2697
Phone: 732-364-2200 • Fax: 732-364-4442
E-mail: admissions-ugrad@georgian.edu • Web: www.georgian.edu
Support level: CS • Institution type: 4-year private

LEARNING DISABILITY PROGRAM AND SERVICES

The Learning Center (TLC) is an assistance program designed to provide an environment for students with mild to moderate learning disabilities who desire a college education. The program is not one of remediation, but is an individualized support program to assist candidates in becoming successful college students. Emphasis is placed on developing self-help strategies and study techniques. To be eligible for the TLC program all applicants must submit the following: documentation for learning disability by a certified professional within a school system or state-certified agency; the documentation must be current within three years and must include identification and description of the learning disability including the student's level of academic performance and effect upon learning; a recent Individualized Education Plan; other evaluations or recommendations from professionals who have recently provided services to the student; and additional documentation upon request. All applicants must have a personal interview.

LD/ADHD ADMISSIONS INFORMATION

College entrance tests required: Yes
Nonstandardized tests accepted: Yes
Interview required: No
Essay required: Yes
Documentation required for LD: Psychoeducational evaluation
Documentation required for ADHD: Yes
Documentation submitted to: Learning Center
Special Ed. HS course work accepted: No

Specific course requirements for all applicants: Yes
Separate application required for services: No
# of LD applications submitted yearly: 120
# of LD applications accepted yearly: 12
Total # of students receiving LD/ADHD services: 23
Acceptance into program means acceptance into college: Students are admitted jointly into The Learning Center and Georgian Court College.

ADMISSIONS

Applicants must meet the following: 16 academic units that include four years English; 2 years foreign language; 2 years math; 1 year lab science; 1 year history; electives. The class rank and transcript should give evidence of the ability to succeed in college. Students must submit SAT scores. Conditional admission may be offered to some applicants. The Associate Director of Admissions is the liaison person between the admissions staff and the TLC.

ADDITIONAL INFORMATION

College graduation requirements are not waived for TLC students. Reduced course load is recommended for students with learning disabilities, and program completion may take longer than 4 years. A social worker and counselor are on the staff of the TLC to help students as well. TLC offers the following: an individualized support program; scheduled tutorial sessions with a learning disabilities specialist; faculty liaison; academic counseling; priority registration; organizational skills including time management, test-taking, note-taking, and outlining; study techniques; memory and concentration techniques; techniques for planning and writing research papers; and content tutoring if needed.

SUPPORT SERVICES CONTACT INFORMATION

Learning Disability Program/Services: The Learning Center (TLC)
Director: Patty Cohen
Telephone: 732-364-2200, ext. 659
Contact: Same

LEARNING DISABILITY SERVICES

Requests for the following services/accommodations will be evaluated individually based on appropriate and current documentation.

Allowed in Exams
  Calculator: Yes
  Dictionary: Yes
  Computer: Y/N
  Spellchecker: Y/N
Extended test time: Yes
Scribes: Yes
Proctors: Yes
Oral exams: Yes
Note-takers: Yes

Distraction-reduced environment: Yes
Tape recording in class: Yes
Books on tape from RFBD: Yes
Taping of books not from RFBD: No
Accommodations for students with ADHD: Yes
Reading machine: No
Other assistive technology: No
Priority registration: Yes

Added costs for services: $2,000 per year
LD specialists: Yes
Professional tutors: Yes
Peer tutors: Yes
Max. hours/wk. for services: Varies
How professors are notified of LD/ADHD: By student and program director

GENERAL ADMISSIONS INFORMATION

Director of Admissions: Marjorie Cook
Telephone: 732-364-2200

ENTRANCE REQUIREMENTS

16 total are required; 4 English required, 2 math required, 1 science required, 1 science lab required, 2 foreign language required, 1 social studies required, 6 elective required. High school diploma or GED required. Minimum TOEFL is 550. TOEFL required of all international applicants.

Application deadline: August 1
Notification: Rolling beginning 10/1
Average GPA: NR

Average SAT I Math: 455
Average SAT I Verbal: 482
Average ACT: NR

Graduated top 10% of class: 11%
Graduated top 25% of class: 47%
Graduated top 50% of class: 84%

COLLEGE GRADUATION REQUIREMENTS

Course waivers allowed: No
Course substitutions allowed: No
In what subjects: N/A

ADDITIONAL INFORMATION

Environment: Georgian Court College is a small private institution centrally located in New Jersey.

Student Body
  Undergrad enrollment: 1,355
  Female: 92%
  Male: 8%
  Out-of-state: 3%

Cost Information
  Tuition: $12,334
  Room & board: $4,000
Housing Information
  University housing: Yes
  Percent living on campus: 52%

Greek System
  Fraternity: Yes
  Sorority: Yes
Athletics: NAIA

KEAN UNIVERSITY

PO Box 411, Union, NJ 07083-0411
Phone: 908-527-2195 • Fax: 908-351-5187
E-mail: admitme@turbo.kean.edu • Web: www.kean.edu
Support level: CS • Institution type: 4-year public

LEARNING DISABILITY PROGRAM AND SERVICES

Kean University believes qualified students with difficulties processing oral and written material have the potential to earn a college degree if they are provided with certain individualized support services. These services are designed to help students develop skills to be independent, involved, responsible learners, and use their own assets to become successful learners. Students with LD attend the same classes and meet the same academic requirements as their peers. Once admitted to Kean University, students who choose to register with Project Excel may do so by providing complete documentation of a diagnosed disability. Students are asked to complete a Project Excel application after admission to Kean and answer questions such as: in what academic areas are you most and least successful; describe how the LD affects academic work; what support services are needed for success; describe any past special services received; identify high school mainstream courses; and when LD was diagnosed.

LD/ADHD ADMISSIONS INFORMATION

College entrance tests required: Yes
Nonstandardized tests accepted: Yes
Interview required: No
Essay required: No
Documentation required for LD: Psychoeducational battery within three years, test scores, diagnosis of LD, and professional summary
Documentation required for ADHD: Full written evaluation and diagnosis of ADHD performed by a qualified practitioner
Documentation submitted to: Project Excel
Special Ed. HS course work accepted: Yes

Specific course requirements for all applicants: Yes
Separate application required for services: No
# of LD applications submitted yearly: 15–20
# of LD applications accepted yearly: N/A
Total # of students receiving LD/ADHD services: 80–90
Acceptance into program means acceptance into college: Students must be admitted and enrolled at the College and then may request services through Project Excel.

ADMISSIONS

There is no special admissions process for students with LD. It is recommended that students self-disclose in the admission process. All applicants must meet the same admission criteria, which include 4 years English, 3 years math, 2 years social studies, 2 years science, and 5 elective credits. Courses taken in special education may be considered. SAT/ACT is required and the average SAT range is 950–1020. The minimum GPA is 2.8. The student must be highly motivated, able to do college work, be of at least average intelligence, have a documented learning disability, have areas of academic strength, and make a commitment to work responsibly and attend classes, tutoring, workshops, and counseling sessions. Students are encouraged to apply by early March.

ADDITIONAL INFORMATION

Project Excel does not provide remedial or developmental instruction. A number of services are available through Project Excel: diagnostic assessments; academic, career, and personal advisement/counseling; development of a College Education Plan (CEP) for the individual student; student advocacy with faculty; referral to other college services as appropriate, such as tutoring in basic skills and course materials. All information about the student's LD is held in strict confidence. Information shared on- or off-campus is only done with the student's signed consent. LD assessments are available for a fee of $250 for a professional assessment and $150 for an assessment from a student intern. All students in Project Excel select from the same schedule of classes and attend with all other students in the College.

SUPPORT SERVICES CONTACT INFORMATION

Learning Disability Program/Services: Project Excel
Director: Marie Segal, EdD
  E-mail: csi@turbo.kean.edu
  Telephone: 908-527-2380
  Fax: 908-527-2784
Contact: Same

LEARNING DISABILITY SERVICES

Requests for the following services/accommodations will be evaluated individually based on appropriate and current documentation.

Allowed in Exams
  Calculator: Yes
  Dictionary: Yes
  Computer: Yes
  Spellchecker: Yes
  Extended test time: Yes
  Scribes: No
  Proctors: Yes
  Oral exams: Yes
  Note-takers: No

Distraction-reduced environment: Yes
Tape recording in class: Yes
Books on tape from RFBD: Yes
Taping of books not from RFBD: No
Accommodations for students with ADHD: Yes
Reading machine: Yes
Other assistive technology: No
Priority registration: Yes

Added costs for services: No
LD specialists: Yes (3)
Professional tutors: N/A
Peer tutors: N/A
Max. hours/wk. for services: As needed
How professors are notified of LD/ADHD: By student

GENERAL ADMISSIONS INFORMATION

Director of Admissions: Audley Bridges
Telephone: 908-527-2195

ENTRANCE REQUIREMENTS
16 total are required; 4 English required, 3 math required, 2 science required, 2 foreign language recommended, 2 social studies required, 5 elective required. High school diploma or GED required.

Application deadline: June 15
Notification: Rolling
Average GPA: N/A

Average SAT I Math: 508
Average SAT I Verbal: 501
Average ACT: N/A

Graduated top 10% of class: 7%
Graduated top 25% of class: 32%
Graduated top 50% of class: 62%

COLLEGE GRADUATION REQUIREMENTS

Course waivers allowed: No
Course substitutions allowed: No
In what subjects: N/A

ADDITIONAL INFORMATION

Environment: The College is located on 151 acres in a suburban area 20 miles west of New York City.

Student Body
  Undergrad enrollment: 9,227
  Female: 65%
  Male: 35%
  Out-of-state: 5%

Cost Information
  In-state tuition: $3,373
  Out-of-state tuition: $5,070
  Room & board: $5,530
Housing Information
  University housing: Yes
  Percent living on campus: 11%

Greek System
  Fraternity: Yes
  Sorority: Yes
Athletics: NCAA Division III

MONMOUTH UNIVERSITY

Admiss., Monmouth U., 400 Cedar Ave., W. Long Branch, NJ 07764-1898
Phone: 732-571-3456 • Fax: 732-263-5166
E-mail: admission@monmouth.edu • Web: www.monmouth.edu
Support level: SP • Institution type: 4-year private

LEARNING DISABILITY PROGRAM AND SERVICES

Monmouth University recognizes the special needs of students with disabilities who are capable, with appropriate assistance, of excelling in a demanding college environment. Comprehensive support services and a nurturing environment contribute to their success. Monmouth's commitment is to provide a learning process and atmosphere that allows students to pursue their educational goals, realize their full potential, contribute actively to their community and society, and determine the direction of their lives. Students are enrolled in regular courses and are not isolated from the rest of the student body in any manner. Students with documented disabilities may request reasonable modifications, accommodations, or auxiliary aids. It is important that students disclose their disability and provide the required learning accommodations to DSS. Much of their success has to do with individual recognition of their specific learning needs combined with supportive faculty. Monmouth is very proud of the many important contributions of students with learning disabilities to life at the University.

LD/ADHD ADMISSIONS INFORMATION

College entrance tests required: Yes
Nonstandardized tests accepted: Yes
Interview required: Yes
Essay required: No
Documentation required for LD: Psychoeducational evaluation
Documentation required for ADHD: Yes
Documentation submitted to: Disability Services
Special Ed. HS course work accepted: Yes

Specific course requirements for all applicants: Yes
Separate application required for services: No
# of LD applications submitted yearly: 120–150
# of LD applications accepted yearly: 75
Total # of students receiving LD/ADHD services: 110
Acceptance into program means acceptance into college: Students are accepted jointly into the College and the learning disabilities program.

ADMISSIONS

There is no special admissions process for students with diagnosed learning disabilties. General admission requirements include 4 years of English, 3 years of math, 2 years of social science, 2 years of science and 5 electives from English, math, science, social studies and/or foreign language. Courses taken in the special education department may be accepted. The minimum GPA is 2.25. Students are encouraged to self-disclose if they believe that their high school performance needs an explanation.

ADDITIONAL INFORMATION

Students with documented disabilities may request reasonable modifications, accommodations, or auxiliary aids that will enable them to participate in and benefit from post-secondary educational programs and activities. These may include extended time, reader assistance, and note-takers. Monmouth University also offers a summer transition session during the University's freshman orientation, assistance with advocacy such as serving as liaison between the student and the professors.

SUPPORT SERVICES CONTACT INFORMATION

Learning Disability Program/Services: Department of Disability Services for Students
Director: Dr. David Nast
  E-mail: dnast@monmouth.edu
  Telephone: 732-571-3460
  Fax: 732-263-5126
Contact: Deanna Campbell
  E-mail: dcampbel@monmouth.edu
  Telephone: 732-571-3456
  Fax: 732-263-5166

LEARNING DISABILITY SERVICES

Requests for the following services/accommodations will be evaluated individually based on appropriate and current documentation.

Allowed in Exams	**Distraction-reduced environment:** Yes	**Added costs for services:** $7.50 per
Calculator: Yes	**Tape recording in class:** Yes	session for tutoring
Dictionary: Yes	**Books on tape from RFBD:** Yes	**LD specialists:** Yes (2)
Computer: Yes	**Taping of books not from RFBD:** Yes	**Professional tutors:** Yes
Spellchecker: Yes	**Accommodations for students with**	**Peer tutors:** 40–60
Extended test time: Yes	**ADHD:** Yes	**Max. hours/wk. for services:**
Scribes: Yes	**Reading machine:** Yes	Unlimited
Proctors: Yes	**Other assistive technology:** Yes	**How professors are notified of**
Oral exams: Yes	**Priority registration:** Yes	**LD/ADHD:** By both student and
Note-takers: Yes		director

GENERAL ADMISSIONS INFORMATION

Director of Admissions: Kelly McCrum
Telephone: 732-571-3456

ENTRANCE REQUIREMENTS
16 total are required; 4 English required, 3 math required, 2 science required, 1 science lab required, 2 foreign language recommended, 2 social studies recommended, 2 history required, 5 elective required. High school diploma or GED required. Minimum TOEFL is 525. TOEFL required of all international applicants.

Application deadline: March 1	**Average SAT I Math:** 523	**Graduated top 10% of class:** 10%
Notification: Rolling	**Average SAT I Verbal:** 526	**Graduated top 25% of class:** 26%
Average GPA: 3.0	**Average ACT:** 21	**Graduated top 50% of class:** 63%

COLLEGE GRADUATION REQUIREMENTS

Course waivers allowed: No
Course substitutions allowed: Yes
In what subjects: Determined on a case-by-case basis; most majors do not require foreign language

ADDITIONAL INFORMATION

Environment: The College is located on 125 acres in a suburb 60 miles south of New York City.

Student Body	**Cost Information**	**Greek System**
Undergrad enrollment: 4,193	**Tuition:** $15,758	**Fraternity:** Yes
Female: 57%	**Room & board:** $6,900	**Sorority:** Yes
Male: 43%	**Housing Information**	**Athletics:** NCAA Division I
Out-of-state: 6%	**University housing:** Yes	
	Percent living on campus: 35%	

NEW JERSEY CITY UNIVERSITY

2039 Kennedy Boulevard, Jersey City, NJ 07305-1597
Phone: 201-200-3234 • Fax: 201-200-2352
E-mail: admissions-@jcsl.jcstate.edu • Web: www.njcu.edu
Support level: SP • Institution type: 4-year public

LEARNING DISABILITY PROGRAM AND SERVICES

Project Mentor is a support program that "opens the door" to higher education for students with learning disabilities by providing them with a faculty mentor—a teacher, advisor, and facilitator—for their entire college career. A low-cost, four-week pre-college Summer Orientation Program prepares freshmen students for success in the academic setting. (Residential students pay for food and housing.) In addition to the traditional university admissions process there is an alternate admissions pathway through Project Mentor. Faculty mentors, advisement, priority registration, special tutorials, compensatory strategy development, counseling, and advocacy are among the many services that are available to student participants throughout the academic year.

LD/ADHD ADMISSIONS INFORMATION

College entrance tests required: Yes
Nonstandardized tests accepted: Yes
Interview required: Yes
Essay required: Yes
Documentation required for LD: Educational, psychological, and social evaluations (current within the past three years)
Documentation required for ADHD: Yes
Documentation submitted to: Project Mentor
Special Ed. HS course work accepted: No

Specific course requirements for all applicants: Yes
Separate application required for services: Yes
# of LD applications submitted yearly: 100
# of LD applications accepted yearly: 20–25
Total # of students receiving LD/ADHD services: 65–75
Acceptance into program means acceptance into college: Admission is given to the College and Project Mentor at the same time.

ADMISSIONS

Students with LD may gain admission through one of two procedures: (1) the traditional university admissions process: and (2) Project Mentor's alternate admissions process. These two procedures operate concurrently and their outcomes are independent of one another. A student who is admitted traditionally may receive all of the support and advocacy services available by providing LD documentation. To be considered for alternate admissions, students must submit recent documentation of the LD, evidence of motivation, and succesful academic performance. The Project Mentor Admissions Committee analyzes the documentation to gain a better understanding of the student's academic strengths and how the disability may impact academic performance. Members of the Project Mentor admissions committee will make their recommendations for admission to NJCU based on special criteria for candidates with LD who possess academic promise. Admitted students into Project Mentor must attend a summer program. All applicants to Project Mentor are requested to schedule an interview; submit recommendations or telephone calls from a high school counselor and/or teacher; and have a recent child study team evaluation. The admissions process involves a review of the psychoeducational report. Project Mentor is looking for students with the intellectual potential to achieve in a four-year college setting who were mostly in mainstream college-prep classes in high school. Although SAT scores are required, they are not used for admission purposes. All applications from students with learning disabilities are referred to Project Mentor. Project faculty review applications and make recommendations to the admissions office for acceptance, rejection, or trial status for a pre-college summer orientation program. The staff considers each candidate individually.

ADDITIONAL INFORMATION

Students meet once a week with mentors. Sessions might include instruction, counseling, and/or referral to services available to all students at the College. Exclusive tutorials for Project Mentor students are staffed by highly trained professionals. Mentors help the students to negotiate accommodations with their professors. Extending the limits on examinations, providing tutorial assistance, and permitting tape recording of lectures are among the types of accommodations provided. Professors try to provide for the special needs of students with learning differences/disabilities while maintaining appropriate academic standards.

SUPPORT SERVICES CONTACT INFORMATION

Learning Disability Program/Services: Project Mentor
Director: Beverly Barkon
  Telephone: 201-200-2091
  Fax: 201-200-3141
Contact: Same

LEARNING DISABILITY SERVICES

Requests for the following services/accommodations will be evaluated individually based on appropriate and current documentation.

Allowed in Exams
  Calculator: Yes
  Dictionary: Yes
  Computer: Yes
  Spellchecker: Yes
Extended test time: Yes
Scribes: Yes
Proctors: Yes
Oral exams: Yes
Note-takers: Yes

Distraction-reduced environment: Yes
Tape recording in class: Yes
Books on tape from RFBD: Yes
Taping of books not from RFBD: Yes
Accommodations for students with ADHD: Yes
Reading machine: No
Other assistive technology: Yes
Priority registration: Yes

Added costs for services: $400 per semester
LD specialists: Yes (2)
Professional tutors: 7
Peer tutors: No
Max. hours/wk. for services: As needed
How professors are notified of LD/ADHD: By student

GENERAL ADMISSIONS INFORMATION

Director of Admissions: Dee Blackman
Telephone: 201-200-3234

ENTRANCE REQUIREMENTS
High school diploma or GED required. Minimum TOEFL is 500. TOEFL required of all international applicants.

Application deadline: April 1
Notification: Rolling
Average GPA: 2.5

Average SAT I Math: 478
Average SAT I Verbal: 496
Average ACT: N/A

Graduated top 10% of class: 11%
Graduated top 25% of class: 32%
Graduated top 50% of class: NR

COLLEGE GRADUATION REQUIREMENTS

Course waivers allowed: No
Course substitutions allowed: Yes
In what subjects: Only in special cases

ADDITIONAL INFORMATION

Environment: The College is located on 150 acres in a suburban area 20 miles west of New York City.

Student Body
  Undergrad enrollment: 6,412
  Female: 61%
  Male: 39%
  Out-of-state: 1%

Cost Information
  In-state tuition: $2,880
  Out-of-state tuition: $4,898
  Room & board: $5,000
Housing Information
  University housing: Yes
  Percent living on campus: 5%

Greek System
  Fraternity: Yes
  Sorority: Yes
Athletics: NCAA Division III

RIDER UNIVERSITY

2083 Lawrenceville Road, Lawrenceville, NJ 08648
Phone: 609-896-5042 • Fax: 609-895-6645
E-mail: admissions@rider.edu • Web: www.rider.edu
Support level: CS • Institution type: 4-year private

LEARNING DISABILITY PROGRAM AND SERVICES

The Education Enhancement Program offers a range of services to help students with documented learning disabilities obtain appropriate accommodations. These services include screening and referral, supplementary assessment, and instructional services. The goal of the program is to assist students in becoming more independent and efficient learners. A learning disability specialist meets individually with students who have learning disabilities and/or attention deficit disorder. Students must initiate the request for this meeting and must supply documentation of the disability. These learning disability specialists conduct an intake interview and, based on the information resulting from this interview, refer students to appropriate support services. They also determine the appropriate academic adjustments.

LD/ADHD ADMISSIONS INFORMATION

College entrance tests required: Yes
Nonstandardized tests accepted: Yes
Interview required: If requested
Essay required: Yes
Documentation required for LD: Educational and psychological tests: within 3 years
Documentation required for ADHD: Yes
Documentation submitted to: Education Enhancement Program
Special Ed. HS course work accepted: No

Specific course requirements for all applicants: Yes
Separate application required for services: No
# of LD applications submitted yearly: N/A
# of LD applications accepted yearly: N/A
Total # of students receiving LD/ADHD services: 50
Acceptance into program means acceptance into college: Students must be admitted and enrolled at the University first and then may request services.

ADMISSIONS
There is no special admissions process for students with learning disabilities. All students must submit the general university application. Admissions criteria are based on the following: high school academic record and GPA of 2.0 or better; SAT or ACT test results; and a college writing sample (essay). Courses required include 16 acceptable units from a college-prep curriculum: 4 years English, 2 years math, sciences, foreign language, social science, and humanities. For students with a learning disability proper documentation recognizing the differing abilities of the student is requested. The Rider Achievement Program is for academically admissible students who are just below the admissions criteria for the regularly admitted student. The Educational Opportunity Fund Program is the state-funded program for academically disadvantaged or economically disadvantaged students.

ADDITIONAL INFORMATION
The Rider Learning Center provides individual and small group tutoring in writing, reading comprehension, and study strategies. The staff offers study strategy workshops and students have access to computers. The Mathematics Skill Lab provides a math course for students who do not meet the placement criteria for college-level math. The course is taught via individual tutoring, structured workshops, and computer-assisted instruction. The MSL staff offers weekly tutorial sessions for Finite Math, helps students prepare for the Algebra & Trig Qualifying Exam, and provides tutoring for other courses. Tutoring Services provide a peer tutoring program for students needing extra help. The Education Enhancement Program offers a course in College Reading and Introduction to Academic Reading.

SUPPORT SERVICES CONTACT INFORMATION

Learning Disability Program/Services: Education Enhancement Program
Director: Jacqueline Simon, PhD
 Telephone: 609-896-5244
Contact: Barbara Blandford, PhD
 E-mail: Blandfor@rider.edu
 Telephone: 609-896-5008

LEARNING DISABILITY SERVICES

Requests for the following services/accommodations will be evaluated individually based on appropriate and current documentation.

Allowed in Exams
 Calculator: Yes
 Dictionary: Yes
 Computer: Yes
 Spellchecker: Yes
Extended test time: Yes
Scribes: Yes
Proctors: Yes
Oral exams: Yes
Note-takers: Yes

Distraction-reduced environment: Yes
Tape recording in class: Yes
Books on tape from RFBD: Yes
Taping of books not from RFBD: Yes
Accommodations for students with
 ADHD: Yes
Reading machine: No
Other assistive technology: No
Priority registration: N/A

Added costs for services: No
LD specialists: Yes (2)
Professional tutors: 5
Peer tutors: 75
Max. hours/wk. for services: Usually
 not more than 3
How professors are notified of
 LD/ADHD: By the student and the
 program director

GENERAL ADMISSIONS INFORMATION

Director of Admissions: Susan Christian
Telephone: 609-896-5042

ENTRANCE REQUIREMENTS
16 total are required; 4 English required, 2 math required, 3 math recommended, 3 science recommended, 2 foreign language recommended, 2 social studies recommended, 2 history recommended. High school diploma or GED required. Minimum TOEFL is 550. TOEFL required of all international applicants.

Application deadline: Rolling
Notification: Rolling
Average GPA: 3.1

Average SAT I Math: 520
Average SAT I Verbal: 514
Average ACT: N/A

Graduated top 10% of class: 14%
Graduated top 25% of class: 20%
Graduated top 50% of class: 35%

COLLEGE GRADUATION REQUIREMENTS

Course waivers allowed: No
Course substitutions allowed: Yes
In what subjects: Substitutions are considered on a case-by-case basis through the Office of the Dean. The courses vary depending on students' individual disabilities and needs.

ADDITIONAL INFORMATION

Environment: The College is located on a 353-acre campus between Princeton and Trenton, New Jersey.

Student Body
 Undergrad enrollment: 4,205
 Female: 58%
 Male: 42%
 Out-of-state: 24%

Cost Information
 Tuition: $17,990
 Room & board: $7,380
Housing Information
 University housing: Yes
 Percent living on campus: 58%

Greek System
 Fraternity: Yes
 Sorority: Yes
Athletics: NCAA Division I

SETON HALL UNIVERSITY

Enrollment Services, 400 South Orange Avenue, South Orange, NJ 07079
Phone: 973-761-9332 • Fax: 973-275-2040
E-mail: thehall@shu.edu • Web: www.shu.edu
Support level: S • Institution type: 4-year private

LEARNING DISABILITY PROGRAM AND SERVICES

Student Support Services (SSS) is an academic program that addresses the needs of all eligible undergraduates. The program provides individual and group tutoring in many disciplines. Academic, career, and other counseling services are also available. The program provides individual and group tutoring in many disciplines. Special emphasis is placed on mathematics, laboratory sciences, and business. Student Support Services is especially attentive to the needs of students who can provide professional documentation of specific disabilities. Every effort is made to accommodate the special academic needs of these students by recommending extended test time and a distraction-free testing environment.

LD/ADHD ADMISSIONS INFORMATION

College entrance tests required: Yes
Nonstandardized tests accepted: Yes
Interview required: No
Essay required: No
Documentation required for LD: Psychoeducational evaluation
Documentation required for ADHD: Yes
Documentation submitted to: SSS
Special Ed. HS course work accepted: No

Specific course requirements for all applicants: Yes
Separate application required for services: No
# of LD applications submitted yearly: N/A
# of LD applications accepted yearly: N/A
Total # of students receiving LD/ADHD services: 30
Acceptance into program means acceptance into college: Students must be admitted and enrolled at the University first and then may request services.

ADMISSIONS

There is no special admissions process for students with learning disabilities, and all applicants must meet the same admission criteria. Courses required include 4 years English, 3 years math, 1 year lab science, 2 years foreign language, 2 years social studies, and 4 electives. The minimum SAT is 900. Students need to rank in the top two-fifths of their class and a minimum 2.5 GPA is recommended.

ADDITIONAL INFORMATION

In coordinating its activities with other departments of the University (such as Residence Life and Academic Services), Student Support Services works to assure that the University remains in compliance with all federal laws and regulations. Student Support Services also assists students in arranging for note-takers and obtaining adaptive equipment and textbooks or cassette tapes.

SUPPORT SERVICES CONTACT INFORMATION

Learning Disability Program/Services: Student Support Services
Director: Reverend Ray Frazier
  E-mail: fraziera@shu.edu
  Telephone: 973-761-9166
Contact: Same

LEARNING DISABILITY SERVICES

Requests for the following services/accommodations will be evaluated individually based on appropriate and current documentation.

Allowed in Exams
  Calculator: N/A
  Dictionary: N/A
  Computer: N/A
  Spellchecker: N/A
Extended test time: Yes
Scribes: No
Proctors: Yes
Oral exams: Yes
Note-takers: Yes

Distraction-reduced environment: Yes
Tape recording in class: Yes
Books on tape from RFBD: Yes
Taping of books not from RFBD: No
Accommodations for students with ADHD: Yes
Reading machine: Yes
Other assistive technology: Yes
Priority registration: No

Added costs for services: No
LD specialists: No
Professional tutors: Yes
Peer tutors: Yes
Max. hours/wk. for services: Based on need
How professors are notified of LD/ADHD: By student and program director

GENERAL ADMISSIONS INFORMATION

Director of Admissions: Alyssa McCloud
Telephone: 973-761-9332

ENTRANCE REQUIREMENTS
16 total are required; 4 English required, 3 math required, 1 science required, 1 science lab required, 2 foreign language required, 2 social studies required, 4 elective required. High school diploma or GED required. Minimum TOEFL is 550. TOEFL required of all international applicants.

Application deadline: March 1
Notification: Rolling beginning 12/1
Average GPA: NR

Average SAT I Math: 533
Average SAT I Verbal: 532
Average ACT: 23

Graduated top 10% of class: 15%
Graduated top 25% of class: 37%
Graduated top 50% of class: 67%

COLLEGE GRADUATION REQUIREMENTS

Course waivers allowed: No
Course substitutions allowed: No
In what subjects: N/A

ADDITIONAL INFORMATION

Environment: The University is located on 58 acres in a suburban area 14 miles west of New York City.

Student Body
  Undergrad enrollment: 5,465
  Female: 51%
  Male: 49%
  Out-of-state: 17%

Cost Information
  Tuition: $18,290
  Room & board: $7,722
Housing Information
  University housing: Yes
  Percent living on campus: 40%

Greek System
  Fraternity: Yes
  Sorority: Yes
Athletics: NCAA Division I

COLLEGE OF SANTA FE

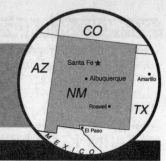

1600 St. Michaels Drive, Santa Fe, NM 87505-7634
Phone: 505-473-6133 • Fax: 505-473-6127
E-mail: admissions@csf.edu • Web: www.csf.edu
Support level: S • Institution type: 4-year private

LEARNING DISABILITY PROGRAM AND SERVICES

The Center for Academic Excellence is a federally funded Title IV Support Services Program designed to assist eligible students to graduate from CSF. There is no formal disabilities program at the College, but the students do have access to many services and accommodations. Students may receive services in basic skills instruction of reading, study strategies, writing, math, humanities, and science. Students work with the professional staff to set up a support program that meets their specific needs. The initial meeting is during registration. The classes at CSF are small and students have access to meetings with their professors. The instructors are very sensitive to the needs of students with learning disabilities. In order to be eligible for services students with learning disabilities must provide a current psychoeducational evaluation that identifies the learning disability. Once this documentation is on file with the Center for Academic Excellence, students may meet with staff to identify the necessary accommodations and services needed to be successful in college.

LD/ADHD ADMISSIONS INFORMATION

College entrance tests required: Yes
Nonstandardized tests accepted: Yes
Interview required: Yes
Essay required: Yes
Documentation required for LD: Psychoeducational
  evaluation: within 3 years
Documentation required for ADHD: NR
Documentation submitted to: Center for Academic Exchange
Special Ed. HS course work accepted: Yes

Specific course requirements for all applicants: Yes
Separate application required for services: No
# of LD applications submitted yearly: N/A
# of LD applications accepted yearly: N/A
Total # of students receiving LD/ADHD services: 50
**Acceptance into program means acceptance into
  college:** Students are admitted to the College and to
  the Center for Academic Excellence after applying for
  services.

ADMISSIONS

There is no separate admission process for students with learning disabilities/ADHD. Students with learning disabilities/ADHD are required to meet the general admission criteria. This includes course requirements of 3 years English, 2 years math, 2 years science, 2 years social science, and a recommendation of 2 years foreign language. All applicants are required to interview either in person or by telephone. Each applicant is evaluated individually. If admitted, students with a GPA inconsistent with their level of ability arrange for academic support from the Center for Academic Excellence. Copies of diagnostic examinations not more than three years old must document the student's learning disability or ADHD. The results of these tests are sent to the Center for Academic Excellence after the student is admitted.

ADDITIONAL INFORMATION

The following services are available: reading and study skills instructors to assist students in areas of comprehension and organization; mastery in time management, note-taking, textbook reading, and test-taking. Assistance is also available in dealing with math anxiety and integrating reading, writing, and study skills for specific courses. Staff is available to spend extra time with individual students who need additional assistance with various skills such as time management, organization, and studying techniques. There is a Reading and Study Skills Specialist who works one-on-one with students. Students are also assisted in developing self-advocacy skills.

SUPPORT SERVICES CONTACT INFORMATION

Learning Disability Program/Services: Center for Academic Excellence
Director: Tom Baumgartel
  Telephone: 505-473-6447
  Fax: 505-473-6124
Contact: David McCain
  Telephone: 505-473-6552

LEARNING DISABILITY SERVICES

Requests for the following services/accommodations will be evaluated individually based on appropriate and current documentation.

Allowed in Exams
  Calculator: Yes
  Dictionary: Yes
  Computer: Yes
  Spellchecker: Yes
Extended test time: Yes
Scribes: No
Proctors: Yes
Oral exams: Yes
Note-takers: Yes

Distraction-reduced environment: Yes
Tape recording in class: Yes
Books on tape from RFBD: Yes
Taping of books not from RFBD: Yes
Accommodations for students with ADHD: Yes
Reading machine: No
Other assistive technology: Yes
Priority registration: No

Added costs for services: No
LD specialists: No
Professional tutors: 4–5
Peer tutors: 10–15
Max. hours/wk. for services: 3
How professors are notified of LD/ADHD: By both student and director

GENERAL ADMISSIONS INFORMATION

Director of Admissions: Dale Reinhart
Telephone: 505-473-6133

ENTRANCE REQUIREMENTS
16 total are required; 20 total are recommended; 4 English required, 4 English recommended, 2 math required, 4 math recommended, 2 science required, 3 science recommended, 2 science lab required, 2 science lab recommended, 2 foreign language recommended, 2 social studies required, 2 social studies recommended, 2 history required, 2 history recommended, 4 elective required, 3 elective recommended. High school diploma or GED required. Minimum TOEFL is 550. TOEFL required of all international applicants.

Application deadline: Rolling
Notification: Rolling beginning 1/15
Average GPA: 3.2

Average SAT I Math: 524
Average SAT I Verbal: 579
Average ACT: 24

Graduated top 10% of class: 14%
Graduated top 25% of class: 37%
Graduated top 50% of class: 72%

COLLEGE GRADUATION REQUIREMENTS

Course waivers allowed: N/A
Course substitutions allowed: N/A
In what subjects: Foreign language is not required to graduate. All students must take the equivalent of Math 100 (pre-algebra). Students may waive out of the math requirement with a 20 on the math portion of ACT or 400 on SAT Math.

ADDITIONAL INFORMATION

Environment: The College is located on 118 acres in a suburban area of Santa Fe.

Student Body
  Undergrad enrollment: 1,316
  Female: 63%
  Male: 37%
  Out-of-state: 62%

Cost Information
  Tuition: $15,000
  Room & board: $4,892
Housing Information
  University housing: Yes
  Percent living on campus: 51%

Greek System
  Fraternity: No
  Sorority: No
  Athletics: Intramural

College of Santa Fe

NEW MEXICO INST. OF MINING & TECH.

Campus Station, 801 Leroy Place, Socorro, NM 87801
Phone: 505-835-5424 • Fax: 505-835-5989
E-mail: admission@admin.nmt.edu • Web: www.nmt.edu
Support level: S • Institution type: 4-year public

LEARNING DISABILITY PROGRAM AND SERVICES

New Mexico Tech does not have a specific program for students with LD. Services for students with disabilities are available in the Counseling and Student Health Center. Students must present recent documentation within the previous three years. The documentation should be sent to Services for Students with Disabilities. New Mexico Tech sends a letter to all admitted students asking those with disabilities to contact the Services for Students with Disabilities. There is a special application required after admission and enrollment in order to receive services or accommodations. The counseling staff works with students with disabilities on an individual basis to accommodate their special needs. Students may also use the counseling service to reduce their stress, think through problems or difficulties, clarify options, and express and explore feelings.

LD/ADHD ADMISSIONS INFORMATION

College entrance tests required: Yes
Nonstandardized tests accepted: Yes
Interview required: No
Essay required: No
Documentation required for LD: Psychoeducational evaluation
Documentation required for ADHD: Yes
Documentation submitted to: Services for Students with Disabilities
Special Ed. HS course work accepted: NR

Specific course requirements for all applicants: Yes
Separate application required for services: Yes
# of LD applications submitted yearly: N/A
# of LD applications accepted yearly: N/A
Total # of students receiving LD/ADHD services: 24
Acceptance into program means acceptance into college: Students must be admitted and enrolled and then may request services.

ADMISSIONS

There is no special admission process for students with LD. The minimum GPA is a 2.5; ACT composite score of 21 or higher or SAT I of 970 or higher. The College will accept the SAT but prefers the ACT. The GED is accepted with a score of 50 or higher. High school course requirements include 4 years of English; 2 years of science among biology, physics, chemistry and earth science; 3 years of math; and 3 years of social science, of which 1 must be history. Students are encouraged to self-disclose their disability during the admission process.

ADDITIONAL INFORMATION

Students will work with staff to determine appropriate accommodations or services. These services may include coordinating academic accommodations; extended time for tests; calculators in exams; skills classes in study strategies and time management. Tutorial services are available for all students on campus.

SUPPORT SERVICES CONTACT INFORMATION

Learning Disability Program/Services: Services for Students with Disabilities
Director: Dr. Judith Raymond
  E-mail: jraymond@admin.nmt.edu
  Telephone: 505-835-5094
  Fax: 505-835-5223
Contact: Same

LEARNING DISABILITY SERVICES

Requests for the following services/accommodations will be evaluated individually based on appropriate and current documentation.

Allowed in Exams
  Calculator: Yes
  Dictionary: No
  Computer: Yes
  Spellchecker: Yes
Extended test time: Yes
Scribes: Yes
Proctors: Yes
Oral exams: Yes
Note-takers: Yes

Distraction-reduced environment: Yes
Tape recording in class: Yes
Books on tape from RFBD: Yes
Taping of books not from RFBD: Yes
Accommodations for students with
  ADHD: Yes
Reading machine: No
Other assistive technology: Yes
Priority registration: Yes

Added costs for services: No
LD specialists: No
Professional tutors: No
Peer tutors: 50
Max. hours/wk. for services:
  Unlimited
How professors are notified of
  LD/ADHD: By student and director of
  services

GENERAL ADMISSIONS INFORMATION

Director of Admissions: Melissa Jaramillo-Fleming
Telephone: 505-835-5424

ENTRANCE REQUIREMENTS

15 total are required; 18 total are recommended; 4 English required, 4 English recommended, 3 math required, 4 math recommended, 2 science required, 4 science recommended, 2 science lab required, 3 science lab recommended, 2 foreign language recommended, 2 social studies required, 3 social studies recommended, 1 history required, 1 history recommended, 3 elective required. High school diploma or GED required. Minimum TOEFL is 540. TOEFL required of all international applicants.

Application deadline: August 1
Notification: Rolling
Average GPA: 3.6

Average SAT I Math: 620
Average SAT I Verbal: 587
Average ACT: 26

Graduated top 10% of class: 41%
Graduated top 25% of class: 74%
Graduated top 50% of class: 91%

COLLEGE GRADUATION REQUIREMENTS

Course waivers allowed: No
Course substitutions allowed: No
In what subjects: N/A

ADDITIONAL INFORMATION

Environment: Located 75 miles from Albuquerque.

Student Body
  Undergrad enrollment: 1,236
  Female: 36%
  Male: 64%
  Out-of-state: 19%

Cost Information
  In-state tuition: $1,704
  Out-of-state tuition: $7,030
  Room & board: $3,704
Housing Information
  University housing: Yes
  Percent living on campus: 42%

Greek System
  Fraternity: Yes
  Sorority: Yes
Athletics: NCAA Division I

NEW MEXICO STATE UNIVERSITY

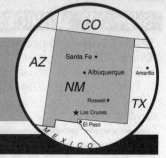

Box 30001, MSC 3A, Las Cruces, NM 88003-8001
Phone: 505-646-3121 • Fax: 505-646-6330
E-mail: admissions@nmsu.edu • Web: www.nmsu.edu
Support level: S • Institution type: 4-year public

LEARNING DISABILITY PROGRAM AND SERVICES

Services for Students with Disabilities is a component of the Office of Student Development. The staff is committed to providing information and services that assist students with disabilities in personal and academic adjustment to the University community. Services for Students with Disabilities provides assistance with procuring auxiliary aids, coordinating services and resources, and discussing special needs and accommodations, and serves as consultants regarding questions about various accommodations. They work with students to ensure that they have access to all programs and services that will effect their full participation in the campus community. Students are encouraged to contact Services for Students with Disabilities to discuss needs and to register for the program. Students should complete the Petition for Services for Students with disabilities and return it with the appropriate documentation for evaluation and review. A review committee will determine eligibility and the specific services and accommodations to be provided, and the student will be notified by the coordinator. This process takes time and students are encouraged to start the process as soon as possible.

LD/ADHD ADMISSIONS INFORMATION

College entrance tests required: Yes
Nonstandardized tests accepted: Yes
Interview required: No
Essay required: No
Documentation required for LD: Psychoeducational evaluation
Documentation required for ADHD: Yes
Documentation submitted to: SSD
Special Ed. HS course work accepted: Yes

Specific course requirements for all applicants: Yes
Separate application required for services: No
# of LD applications submitted yearly: N/A
# of LD applications accepted yearly: N/A
Total # of students receiving LD/ADHD services: 90
Acceptance into program means acceptance into college: Students must be admitted and enrolled at the University first and then may request services.

ADMISSIONS

Admission criteria are the same for all students. Admissions can be granted on a regular status or provisional status. Regular admission requires high school GPA of 2.5 and 21 ACT or 970 SAT. The SAT I is accepted; however, the ACT is preferred. Course requirements include 4 years English, 2 years science, 3 years math, and 3 years social studies (one must be history). Provisional status is possible for students who have a high school GPA of 2.1 and 18 ACT. Students admitted provisionally must take at least 6 but not more than 12 credits in a regular semester and at least 3, but not more than 6, in a summer session.

ADDITIONAL INFORMATION

The Center for Learning Assistance offers students the skills they need to excel in college. Students work with learning facilitators to develop or maximize the skills needed for college success. Assistance is offered in time management, concentration, memory, test preparation, test-taking, listening/note-taking, textbook-reading techniques, math/science study skills, reasoning skills, writing, spelling, and grammar. Student Support Services is a program of academic and personal support with the goal of improving the retention and graduation of undergraduate students with disabilities. A mentor is provided for all participants to help motivate them and tutors help with study skills in specific subjects. Students may have tutors in two subjects and can meet weekly. Other services available are early registration; note-taking services; readers; and test accommodations including extended time, a quiet location, scribes, readers, or other assistance with exams. All services are free.

SUPPORT SERVICES CONTACT INFORMATION

Learning Disability Program/Services: Services for Students with Disabilities (SSD)
Director: Jane Spinti
  E-mail: ssd@nmsu,edu
  Telephone: 505-646-6840
  Fax: 505-646-1975
Contact: Same

LEARNING DISABILITY SERVICES

Requests for the following services/accommodations will be evaluated individually based on appropriate and current documentation.

Allowed in Exams
  Calculator: Yes
  Dictionary: No
  Computer: Yes
  Spellchecker: Yes
Extended test time: Yes
Scribes: Yes
Proctors: Yes
Oral exams: Yes
Note-takers: Yes

Distraction-reduced environment: Yes
Tape recording in class: Yes
Books on tape from RFBD: Yes
Taping of books not from RFBD: Yes
Accommodations for students with ADHD: Yes
Reading machine: Yes
Other assistive technology: Yes
Priority registration: Yes

Added costs for services: No
LD specialists: No
Professional tutors: No
Peer tutors: 50
Max. hours/wk. for services: Unlimited
How professors are notified of LD/ADHD: Student and director of services

GENERAL ADMISSIONS INFORMATION

Director of Admissions: Angela Mora-Riley
Telephone: 505-646-3121

ENTRANCE REQUIREMENTS

10 total are required; 4 English required, 3 math required, 2 science required, 2 science lab required, 1 foreign language required. High school diploma or GED required. Minimum TOEFL is 500. TOEFL required of all international applicants.

Application deadline: NR
Notification: Rolling
Average GPA: 3.3

Average SAT I Math: NR
Average SAT I Verbal: NR
Average ACT: 21

Graduated top 10% of class: 20%
Graduated top 25% of class: 48%
Graduated top 50% of class: 79%

COLLEGE GRADUATION REQUIREMENTS

Course waivers allowed: Yes
Course substitutions allowed: Yes
In what subjects: Those the students negotiate with the College that handles their major field of study

ADDITIONAL INFORMATION

Environment: The University is located on 5,800 acres in a suburban area 40 miles north of El Paso, Texas.

Student Body
  Undergrad enrollment: 12,831
  Female: 53%
  Male: 47%
  Out-of-state: 25%

Cost Information
  In-state tuition: $2,502
  Out-of-state tuition: $8,166
  Room & board: $3,726
Housing Information
  University housing: Yes
  Percent living on campus: 25%

Greek System
  Fraternity: Yes
  Sorority: Yes
Athletics: NCAA Division I

ADELPHI UNIVERSITY

Levermore Hall 114, South Avenue, Garden City, NY 11530
Phone: 516-877-3050 • Fax: 516-877-3050
E-mail: admissions@adelphi.edu • Web: www.adelphi.edu
Support level: SP • Institution type: 4-year private

LEARNING DISABILITY PROGRAM AND SERVICES

The approach of the Learning Disabilities Program at Adelphi is to provide an atmosphere where students with LD/ADHD can realize their potential. The program is specially designed for students unable to process oral and written materials in conventional ways, but who excel in other ways. Each student is provided with the support of an interdisciplinary team of experienced professionals in tutoring and counseling. All instruction, counseling, and assessment is provided by more than 15 professionals with advanced degrees in special education and social work. Students meet individually with an educator and a counselor who work as a team. There is a mandatory five-week Summer Program prior to freshman year. Students must attend tutoring sessions two times a week, participate in all the program's services, and sign an agreement acknowledging their academic commitment. Students attend classes in their chosen major, and meet standard academic requirements. The goal is independence in the academic and the real world.

LD/ADHD ADMISSIONS INFORMATION

College entrance tests required: Yes
Nonstandardized tests accepted: Yes
Interview required: Yes
Essay required: Yes
Documentation required for LD: WAIS-III, WJ-R, specific LD diagnosis with psychoeducational evaluation
Documentation required for ADHD: Comprehensive evaluation with written interpretive report
Documentation submitted to: LD Program
Special Ed. HS course work accepted: No

Specific course requirements for all applicants: Yes
Separate application required for services: Yes
# of LD applications submitted yearly: 200
# of LD applications accepted yearly: 75–101
Total # of students receiving LD/ADHD services: 125
Acceptance into program means acceptance into college: Students must be admitted and enrolled at the University and then may request consideration for the program.

ADMISSIONS

The Admissions Committee reviews all submitted materials for a total picture of strengths and disabilities. Applicants with LD who show an ability to succeed academically are invited to interview. They must submit a high school transcript, documentation of LD, ACT/SAT scores and a recent testing. The director of the program is actively involved in the admissions decision, and conducts a highly individualized assessment of each applicant and the documentation. Motivation, college-prep courses, average or higher IQ (WAIS-III), interview, documentation, and a recommendation from an LD specialist are other factors that are used in making an admission decision. Prior to applying applicants should attend an information session conducted by the program. The program seeks highly motivated and socially mature individuals with average to superior intelligence who are capable of handling full academic schedules. Judgment of the professional staff will determine eligibilty for the program.

ADDITIONAL INFORMATION

Students receive intensive academic tutoring and individual counseling which begins in the summer program. Course content and requirements are never compromised for students with learning disabilities, but program procedures do help to ease the way in the classroom. For example, in individual tutorials professional special educators teach how to get the most of studies; instructors are privately notified in writing and by phone if program students are in their classes; students may tape record class lectures if note-taking is difficult; and individual counseling enables students to understand their behavior, reduce anxiety, and grow emotionally. Approximately 25 percent of these students make the Dean's List. There are currently 105 students with LD/ADHD receiving services.

SUPPORT SERVICES CONTACT INFORMATION

Learning Disability Program/Services: Learning Disabilities Program
Director: Susan Spencer
  E-mail: spencer@adelphi.edu
  Telephone: 516-877-4710
  Fax: 516-877-4711
Contact: Same

LEARNING DISABILITY SERVICES

Requests for the following services/accommodations will be evaluated individually based on appropriate and current documentation.

Allowed in Exams
  Calculator: Yes
  Dictionary: Yes
  Computer: Yes
  Spellchecker: Yes
Extended test time: Yes
Scribes: Yes
Proctors: Yes
Oral exams: No
Note-takers: Yes

Distraction-reduced environment: Yes
Tape recording in class: Yes
Books on tape from RFBD: Yes
Taping of books not from RFBD: Yes
Accommodations for students with ADHD: Yes
Reading machine: Yes
Other assistive technology: Yes
Priority registration: Yes

Added costs for services: $2,000 per semester
LD specialists: Yes (10)
Professional tutors: 10
Peer tutors: No
Max. hours/wk. for services: 3
How professors are notified of LD/ADHD: By both student and director

GENERAL ADMISSIONS INFORMATION

Director of Admissions: Esther Goodcuff
Telephone: 516-877-3050

ENTRANCE REQUIREMENTS
16 total are recommended; 4 English recommended, 3 math recommended, 3 science recommended, 2 foreign language recommended, 4 social studies recommended. High school diploma or GED required. Minimum TOEFL is 550. TOEFL required of all international applicants.

Application deadline: Rolling
Notification: Rolling beginning 10/1
Average GPA: 3.3

Average SAT I Math: 526
Average SAT I Verbal: 528
Average ACT: N/A

Graduated top 10% of class: 21%
Graduated top 25% of class: 52%
Graduated top 50% of class: 85%

COLLEGE GRADUATION REQUIREMENTS

Course waivers allowed: No
Course substitutions allowed: No
In what subjects: N/A

ADDITIONAL INFORMATION

Environment: The University is located on a 75-acre campus 20 miles from New York City.

Student Body
  Undergrad enrollment: 2,878
  Female: 70%
  Male: 30%
  Out-of-state: 10%

Cost Information
  Tuition: $14,750
  Room & board: $7,180
Housing Information
  University housing: Yes
  Percent living on campus: 25%

Greek System
  Fraternity: Yes
  Sorority: Yes
Athletics: NCAA Division II

BINGHAMTON UNIVERSITY

PO Box 6000, Binghamton, NY 13902-6001
Phone: 607-777-2171 • Fax: 607-777-4445
E-mail: admit@binghamton.edu • Web: www.binghamton.edu
Support level: CS • Institution type: 4-year public

LEARNING DISABILITY PROGRAM AND SERVICES

The Services for Students with Disabilities office provides assistance to students with physical or learning disabilities. They operate on the philosophy that the individuals they serve are students first and that their disabilities are secondary. Support services assist students in taking advantage of the opportunities at Binghamton and in making their own contributions to the University community.

LD/ADHD ADMISSIONS INFORMATION

College entrance tests required: Yes
Nonstandardized tests accepted: Yes
Interview required: N/A
Essay required: Yes
Documentation required for LD: Psychoeducational evaluation; completed no earlier than 11th or 12th grade
Documentation required for ADHD: Yes
Documentation submitted to: Services for Students with Disabilities
Special Ed. HS course work accepted: No

Specific course requirements for all applicants: Yes
Separate application required for services: No
# of LD applications submitted yearly: N/A
# of LD applications accepted yearly: N/A
Total # of students receiving LD/ADHD services: 63
Acceptance into program means acceptance into college: Students must be admitted to the University and then may request services and accommodations.

ADMISSIONS

Binghamton University welcomes applications from all qualified individuals. While there are no special admissions procedures or academic programs expressly for students with disabilities, the Services for Students with Disabilities office provides a wide range of support services to enrolled students. Diagnostic tests are not required for admissions, but students are encouraged to meet with the Director of Services for Students with Disabilities and to provide documentation in order to determine appropriate accommodations. Through nonmatriculated enrollment, students can take courses but are not enrolled in a degree program. If they do well, they may then apply for matriculation, using credits earned toward their degree. General admission criteria includes 4 years of English, 2.5 years of math, 2 years of social science, 2 years of science, 2 years of two foreign languages or 3 years of one foreign language in the same language. The middle 50 percent score range on the SAT is 1100–1330.

ADDITIONAL INFORMATION

Students with LD/ADHD may use all campuswide services plus receive accommodations and services through SSD. Accommodations which are available for students with appropriate documentation include extended testing time; low-distraction environments for tests; scribes; proctors; use of calculators, dictionary, spellchecker, and computers in exams; assistive technology including voice recognition software, screen readers software, print enlargment, assistive listening devices, and variable speed tape recorders on loan. Tutorial services are provided to undergraduate students at no charge for four hours per week. However, SSD can arrange for more than four hours per week at the student's expense. The University's Center for Academic Excellence provides peer tutoring to any student at no cost. The University has offered courses in College Study and Coping Skills and Applying Study Skills to Career Research. Availability of these courses each year is dependent on staffing. Students are provided memos of reasonable accommodation written by the SSD Director or Learning Disabilities Specialist, to be given to their professors. Services and accommodations are available for undergraduate and graduate students.

SUPPORT SERVICES CONTACT INFORMATION

Learning Disability Program/Services: Services for Students with Disabilities (SSD)
Director: B. Jean Fairbairn
  E-mail: bjfairba@binghamton.edu
  Telephone: 607-777-2686
  Fax: 607-777-6893
Contact: Diane Majewski
  E-mail: majewski@binghamton.edu
  Telephone: 607-777-2686
  Fax: 607-777-6893

LEARNING DISABILITY SERVICES

Requests for the following services/accommodations will be evaluated individually based on appropriate and current documentation.

Allowed in Exams
  Calculator: Yes
  Dictionary: Yes
  Computer: Yes
  Spellchecker: Yes
Extended test time: Yes
Scribes: Yes
Proctors: Yes
Oral exams: Yes
Note-takers: Yes

Distraction-reduced environment: Yes
Tape recording in class: Yes
Books on tape from RFBD: Yes
Taping of books not from RFBD: Yes
Accommodations for students with ADHD: Yes
Reading machine: Yes
Other assistive technology: Yes
Priority registration: Yes

Added costs for services: No
LD specialists: Yes (1)
Professional tutors: No
Peer tutors: 5
Max. hours/wk. for services: 4
How professors are notified of LD/ADHD: By student

GENERAL ADMISSIONS INFORMATION

Director of Admissions: Cheryl Brown
Telephone: 607-777-2171

ENTRANCE REQUIREMENTS

16 total are required; 4 English required, 3 math required, 4 math recommended, 2 science required, 4 science recommended, 3 foreign language required, 3 foreign language recommended, 2 social studies required, 3 history recommended. High school diploma or GED required. Minimum TOEFL is 550. TOEFL required of all international applicants.

Application deadline: February 15
Notification: Rolling beginning 1/15
Average GPA: 3.4

Average SAT I Math: 622
Average SAT I Verbal: 586
Average ACT: 26.5

Graduated top 10% of class: 53%
Graduated top 25% of class: 94%
Graduated top 50% of class: 100%

COLLEGE GRADUATION REQUIREMENTS

Course waivers allowed: No
Course substitutions allowed: Yes
In what subjects: Foreign language; substitutions are available when justified to the Academic Standards Committee of Harpur College, the only College at the University with a foreign language requirement

ADDITIONAL INFORMATION

Environment: The University has a suburban campus near Binghamton.

Student Body
  Undergrad enrollment: 9,858
  Female: 54%
  Male: 46%
  Out-of-state: 4%

Cost Information
  In-state tuition: $3,400
  Out-of-state tuition: $8,300
  Room & board: $5,772
Housing Information
  University housing: Yes
  Percent living on campus: 56%

Greek System
  Fraternity: Yes
  Sorority: Yes
  Athletics: NCAA Division I

COLGATE UNIVERSITY

13 Oak Drive, Hamilton, NY 13346
Phone: 315-228-7401 • Fax: 315-228-7544
E-mail: admission@mail.colgate.edu • Web: www.colgate.edu
Support level: CS • Institution type: 4-year private

LEARNING DISABILITY PROGRAM AND SERVICES

Colgate provides for a small student body a liberal arts education that will expand individual potential and ability to participate effectively in society's affairs. There are many resources available for all students. Colgate's goal is to offer resources and services within the campuswide support system that are responsive to the various talents, needs, and preferences of students with disabilities. In order for the University to understand and prepare for the accommodations that may be requested, students are asked to complete a confidential self-assessment questionnaire and provide appropriate documentation about their disability. The Director of Academic Support works with students and faculty to assure that the needs of students with disabilities are met; serves as clearinghouse for information about disabilities; provides training and individual consultation for all members of the Colgate community; and provides academic counseling and individualized instruction. Students should contact the Director of Academic Support to make the University aware of the existence of their learning disability. Seeking help early and learning to be a self-advocate are essential to college success.

LD/ADHD ADMISSIONS INFORMATION

College entrance tests required: Yes
Nonstandardized tests accepted: Yes
Interview required: N/A
Essay required: Yes
Documentation required for LD: Psychoeducational evaluation
Documentation required for ADHD: Yes
Documentation submitted to: Academic Program Support
Special Ed. HS course work accepted: No

Specific course requirements for all applicants: Yes
Separate application required for services: No
# of LD applications submitted yearly: N/A
# of LD applications accepted yearly: N/A
Total # of students receiving LD/ADHD services: 100
Acceptance into program means acceptance into college: Students must be admitted and enrolled at the University and then may be reviewed for services.

ADMISSIONS

There is no special admission process for students with learning disabilities. The Office of Admissions reviews the applications of all candidates for admission. The admissions staff looks for evidence of substantial achievement in a rigorous secondary school curriculum; one counselor recommendation; standardized testing; personalized essay; and extracurricular involvement. Also valued are qualities such as curiosity, originality, thoughtfulness, and persistence. Admission is very competitive. Criteria include 16 courses in a a college-preparatory program (20 recommended): 4 years English, 3–4 years math, 3–4 years science, 3–4 years social studies, and 3 years foreign language; ACT average is 29 or SAT I average 1348. Three SAT II tests are required including Writing and two others of student choice if the applicant submits the SAT II. However, SAT II tests are not required if the applicant submits the ACT.

ADDITIONAL INFORMATION

Students are encouraged to seek help early; meet with professors at the beginning of each semester to discuss approaches and accommodations that will meet their needs; and seek assistance from the Director of Academic Support and Disability Services, administrative advisor, and faculty advisor. Modifications in the curriculum are made on an individual basis. Colgate provides services in support of academic work on as-needed basis, such as assistance with note-takers; tape-recorded lectures; tutors; readers; and assistive technology. There is a Writing Center, Math Clinic and departmental tutoring and skills help are available in writing, reading, and study strategies. Services and accommodations are available for undergraduate and graduate students.

SUPPORT SERVICES CONTACT INFORMATION

Learning Disability Program/Services: Academic Program Support and Disability Services
Director: Lynn Waldman
  E-mail: lwaldman@mailcolgate.edu
  Telephone: 315-228-7225
  Fax: 315-228-7831
Contact: Same

LEARNING DISABILITY SERVICES

Requests for the following services/accommodations will be evaluated individually based on appropriate and current documentation.

Allowed in Exams
  Calculator: Yes
  Dictionary: Yes
  Computer: Yes
  Spellchecker: Yes
Extended test time: Yes
Scribes: Yes
Proctors: Yes
Oral exams: Yes
Note-takers: Yes

Distraction-reduced environment: Yes
Tape recording in class: Yes
Books on tape from RFBD: Yes
Taping of books not from RFBD: Yes
Accommodations for students with
  ADHD: Yes
Reading machine: Yes
Other assistive technology: Yes
Priority registration: Yes

Added costs for services: No
LD specialists: Yes (1)
Professional tutors: Yes
Peer tutors: Yes
Max. hours/wk. for services:
  Unlimited
How professors are notified of
  LD/ADHD: By student

GENERAL ADMISSIONS INFORMATION

Director of Admissions: Gary Ross
Telephone: 315-228-7401

ENTRANCE REQUIREMENTS
16 total are required; 20 total are recommended; 4 English required, 4 English recommended, 3 math required, 4 math recommended, 3 science required, 4 science recommended, 2 science lab required, 3 science lab recommended, 3 foreign language required, 4 foreign language recommended, 2 social studies required, 2 social studies recommended, 1 history required, 2 history recommended. High school diploma or GED required. Minimum TOEFL is 600. TOEFL required of all international applicants.

Application deadline: January 15
Notification: April 1
Average GPA: 3.4

Average SAT I Math: 670
Average SAT I Verbal: 650
Average ACT: 28

Graduated top 10% of class: 58%
Graduated top 25% of class: 86%
Graduated top 50% of class: 99%

COLLEGE GRADUATION REQUIREMENTS

Course waivers allowed: Y/N
Course substitutions allowed: Yes
In what subjects: All requests are considered on a case-by-case basis; foreign language is required for graduation from the University

ADDITIONAL INFORMATION

Environment: The University is located in a small town about 45 miles from Syracuse.

Student Body
  Undergrad enrollment: 2,773
  Female: 51%
  Male: 49%
  Out-of-state: 68%

Cost Information
  Tuition: $25,565
  Room & board: $6,330
Housing Information
  University housing: Yes
  Percent living on campus: 88%

Greek System
  Fraternity: Yes
  Sorority: Yes
Athletics: NCAA Division I

Colgate University

CONCORDIA COLLEGE

171 White Plains Road, Bronxville, NY 10708
Phone: 914-337-9300 • Fax: 914-395-4500
E-mail: admission@concordia-ny.edu • Web: www.concordia-ny.edu
Support level: SP • Institution type: 4-year private

LEARNING DISABILITY PROGRAM AND SERVICES

Concordia Connection is a program for students with LD who have demonstrated the potential to earn a college degree. Their commitment is to provide an intimate, supportive, and caring environment where students with special learning needs can experience college as a successful and rewarding endeavor. This is a mainstream program. Students are fully integrated into the College. During the fall and spring semesters students are registered for four or five classes. Additionally, students are registered for a one-credit independent study, which incorporates a weekly, one-hour group session with the director and staff that focuses on the development of individualized learning strategies. Progress is monitored and assessment of learning potential and academic levels is provided. The program's assistant director serves as the freshman advisor and coordinates support services. Enrollment is limited to 15 students. A three-day summer orientation and academic seminar is required for all new Concordia Connection students.

LD/ADHD ADMISSIONS INFORMATION

College entrance tests required: Yes
Nonstandardized tests accepted: Yes
Interview required: Recommended
Essay required: Yes
Documentation required for LD: WAIS-III; WJ: within 18 months
Documentation required for ADHD: Yes
Documentation submitted to: Concordia Connection
Special Ed. HS course work accepted: Depends on content

Specific course requirements for all applicants: Yes
Separate application required for services: No
# of LD applications submitted yearly: 40
# of LD applications accepted yearly: 9–12
Total # of students receiving LD/ADHD services: 20
Acceptance into program means acceptance into college: Students must be admitted to the College and then may request services. Some are reviewed by the LD program, which provides a recommendation to the admissions office.

ADMISSIONS

Students wishing to apply should submit the following documents to the Admissions Office: a Concordia Application; current transcript; SAT/ACT scores; documentation of LD, which must minimally include a WAIS-III profile with subtest scores within the past year and the most recent IEP; recommendations from LD specialist and guidance counselor; and an essay describing the nature of the LD and the effect on learning patterns and reason for pursuing college. Visits are encouraged. Applicants must be high school graduates, have a diagnosed LD, have college-prep courses, and be emotionally stable and committed to being successful. General admissions criteria include a B average; ACT/SAT, used to assess strengths and weaknesses rather than for acceptance or denial; college-preparatory courses in high school (foreign language is recommended but not required). Students with LD who self-disclose and provide documentation will be reviewed by the Admissions Office and the Director of Concordia Connection.

ADDITIONAL INFORMATION

The Concordia Connection provides services to all students. These include test-taking modifications, taped text books, computer access, and tutoring. Although there are no charges for students requesting peer tutoring, there is a $2,500 per semester charge for program services. Skills courses for credit are offered in time management, organizational skills, and study skills. The three-day summer orientation helps students get acquainted with support services; get exposure to academic expectations; review components and requirements of the freshman year; develop group cohesion; and explore individualized needs and strategies for seeking assistance.

SUPPORT SERVICES CONTACT INFORMATION

Learning Disability Program/Services: The Concordia Connection
Director: George Groth, PsyD, ext. 2361
  E-mail: ghg@concordia-ny.edu
  Telephone: 914-337-9300, ext. 2361
  Fax: 914-268-0399
Contact: Same

LEARNING DISABILITY SERVICES

Requests for the following services/accommodations will be evaluated individually based on appropriate and current documentation.

Allowed in Exams
  Calculator: Yes
  Dictionary: Yes
  Computer: Yes
  Spellchecker: Yes
Extended test time: Yes
Scribes: Yes
Proctors: Yes
Oral exams: Y/N
Note-takers: Yes

Distraction-reduced environment: Yes
Tape recording in class: Yes
Books on tape from RFBD: Yes
Taping of books not from RFBD: Yes
Accommodations for students with ADHD: Yes
Reading machine: No
Other assistive technology: No
Priority registration: Yes

Added costs for services: $2,500 per semester
LD specialists: 2
Professional tutors: 1
Peer tutors: 10
Max. hours/wk. for services: 6
How professors are notified of LD/ADHD: By student and program director

GENERAL ADMISSIONS INFORMATION

Director of Admissions: Rebecca Hendricks
Telephone: 914-337-9300, ext. 2149

ENTRANCE REQUIREMENTS
15 total are required; 4 English required, 3 math required, 2 science required, 2 foreign language recommended, 2 social studies required. High school diploma or GED required. Minimum TOEFL is 500. TOEFL required of all international applicants.

Application deadline: Rolling
Notification: Rolling beginning 11/15 early decision
Average GPA: 3.0

Average SAT I Math: 490
Average SAT I Verbal: 510
Average ACT: NR

Graduated top 10% of class: 16%
Graduated top 25% of class: 35%
Graduated top 50% of class: 66%

COLLEGE GRADUATION REQUIREMENTS

Course waivers allowed: Yes
Course substitutions allowed: Yes
In what subjects: Foreign language; American Sign Language may be substituted

ADDITIONAL INFORMATION

Environment: The College is in a suburban area approximately 15 miles north of New York City.

Student Body
  Undergrad enrollment: 599
  Female: 60%
  Male: 40%
  Out-of-state: 17%

Cost Information
  Tuition: $15,500
  Room & board: $6,900
Housing Information
  University housing: Yes
  Percent living on campus: 66%

Greek System
  Fraternity: Yes
  Sorority: Yes
  Athletics: NCAA Division II

Concordia College

CORNELL UNIVERSITY

Undergraduate Admissions, 410 Thurston Avenue, Ithaca, NY 14850
Phone: 607-255-5241 • Fax: 607-255-0659
E-mail: admissions@cornell.edu • Web: www.cornell.edu
Support level: CS • Institution type: 4-year public and private

LEARNING DISABILITY PROGRAM AND SERVICES

Cornell University is committed to ensuring that students with disabilities have equal access to all university programs and activities. Policy and procedures have been developed to provide students with as much independence as possible, to preserve confidentiality, and to provide students with disabilities the same exceptional opportunities available to all Cornell students. SDS, in concert with the Center for Learning and Teaching, provides a unique, integrated model to serve the needs of students with disabilities. A major goal of SDS is to develop self-advocacy skills for students with disabilities. This consists of: having a clear understanding of the disability; an understanding of how the disability affects functioning within the University community; and the ability to communicate this information.

LD/ADHD ADMISSIONS INFORMATION

College entrance tests required: Yes
Nonstandardized tests accepted: Yes
Interview required: N/A
Essay required: Yes
Documentation required for LD: Current comprehensive psychoeducational evaluation
Documentation required for ADHD: Yes
Documentation submitted to: Disability Services
Special Ed. HS course work accepted: No

Specific course requirements for all applicants: Yes
Separate application required for services: No
# of LD applications submitted yearly: N/A
# of LD applications accepted yearly: N/A
Total # of students receiving LD/ADHD services: 200
Acceptance into program means acceptance into college: Students must be admitted and enrolled at the University first and then may request services.

ADMISSIONS

Cornell does not have a special admissions process for students with learning disabilities. All students applying to Cornell are expected to meet the same admissions criteria. General admission requirements include 16 units of English, math, science, social studies, and foreign language. All of the seven colleges have their own specific requirements. Admission is very competitive and most of the admitted students rank, at least, in the top 20 percent of the class and have taken AP and Honors courses in high school. Students with learning disabilities who wish to self-disclose are encouraged to write a personal statement that will provide insight into the nature of the disability and how the student has compensated for the areas of deficit. All documentation should be sent directly to Disability Services.

ADDITIONAL INFORMATION

Students are encouraged to complete a Disability Self-Identification Form that is enclosed within acceptance materials. Disability Services welcomes a condensed version of the psychoeducational evaluation that could provide specific information regarding the disability and services/accommodations recommended. Once Disability Services has received a Learning Profile, it will help students find tutors, note-takers, readers, and recorded books, and work with professors to arrange for oral examinations and/or extended time on tests. Diagnostic testing, remedial courses, and tutors specifically trained to work with students with LD are not available at Cornell. The Learning Skills Center does provide general supportive services including classes and workshops in organizational skills, note-taking, and a peer support group that meets on a regular basis. The Learning Skills Center is open to all students. Skills classes are offered in reading comprehension, study skills, and note-taking. Services are available for undergraduate and graduate students.

SUPPORT SERVICES CONTACT INFORMATION

Learning Disability Program/Services: Disability Services, Office of Equal Opportunity (OEO)
Director: Matthew F. Tominey
  E-mail: clt_sds@cornell.edu
  Telephone: 607-255-4545
  Fax: 607-255-1562
Contact: Michele Fish
  E-mail: clt_sds@cornell.edu
  Telephone: 607-254-4545
  Fax: 607-255-1562

LEARNING DISABILITY SERVICES

Requests for the following services/accommodations will be evaluated individually based on appropriate and current documentation.

Allowed in Exams
  Calculator: Yes
  Dictionary: Yes
  Computer: Yes
  Spellchecker: Yes
Extended test time: Yes
Scribes: Yes
Proctors: Yes
Oral exams: No
Note-takers: Yes

Distraction-reduced environment: Yes
Tape recording in class: Yes
Books on tape from RFBD: Yes
Taping of books not from RFBD: Yes
Accommodations for students with ADHD: Yes
Reading machine: Yes
Other assistive technology: Yes
Priority registration: No

Added costs for services: No
LD specialists: Yes (2)
Professional tutors: No
Peer tutors: Yes
Max. hours/wk. for services: Unlimited
How professors are notified of LD/ADHD: By student

GENERAL ADMISSIONS INFORMATION

Director of Admissions: Wendy Sehaerer (interim director)
Telephone: 607-255-5241

ENTRANCE REQUIREMENTS
16 total are required; 4 English required, 4 English recommended, 3 math required, 3 math recommended, 3 science recommended, 3 science lab required, 3 science lab recommended, 3 foreign language recommended, 3 social studies recommended. High school diploma or equivalent is not required. Minimum TOEFL is 550. TOEFL required of all international applicants.

Application deadline: January 1
Notification: April 1
Average GPA: NR

Average SAT I Math: 700
Average SAT I Verbal: 660
Average ACT: 29

Graduated top 10% of class: 82%
Graduated top 25% of class: 94%
Graduated top 50% of class: 100%

COLLEGE GRADUATION REQUIREMENTS

Course waivers allowed: No
Course substitutions allowed: Yes
In what subjects: Foreign language in some majors

ADDITIONAL INFORMATION

Environment: Cornell is located 45 minutes from Syracuse on the southern end of Lake Cayuga in the Finger Lakes region.

Student Body
  Undergrad enrollment: 13,590
  Female: 47%
  Male: 53%
  Out-of-state: 55%

Cost Information
  Tuition: $24,760
  Room & board: $8,086
Housing Information
  University housing: Yes
  Percent living on campus: 62%

Greek System
  Fraternity: Yes
  Sorority: Yes
Athletics: NCAA Division I

DOWLING COLLEGE

Idle Hour Boulevard, Oakdale, NY 11769-1999
Phone: 800-369-5464 • Fax: 516-563-3827
E-mail: macdonar@dowling.edu • Web: www.dowling.edu
Support level: CS • Institution type: 4-year private

LEARNING DISABILITY PROGRAM AND SERVICES

Dowling College's Program for College Students with Learning Disabilities is a small, individualized program that provides for Cognitive Development. The College is looking for students who are committed to lifelong learning who have taken academically demanding courses in high school. They seek students who are eager and willing to persevere to achieve goals. Additionally, students need to be interested and involved in community and extracurricular activities. There is a fee of $1,500 per semester for services from the LD Program. Students must submit a recent psychoevaluation and IEP in order to be eligible to receive services or accommodations. Students are encouraged to make sure that their IEP includes all of the necessary accommodations. Students sign a contract promising to attend tutoring sessions and to attend all classes. Services are available all four years.

LD/ADHD ADMISSIONS INFORMATION

College entrance tests required: Yes
Nonstandardized tests accepted: Yes
Interview required: No
Essay required: No
Documentation required for LD: Psychological; IEP
Documentation required for ADHD: Yes
Documentation submitted to: Program for Students with LD
Special Ed. HS course work accepted: NR

Specific course requirements for all applicants: Yes
Separate application required for services: Yes
# of LD applications submitted yearly: 20
# of LD applications accepted yearly: 6–11
Total # of students receiving LD/ADHD services: 25
Acceptance into program means acceptance into college: Students must be admitted and enrolled and then may request services.

ADMISSIONS

Students must be admitted to Dowling College first and then may request an application to the Program for College Students with LD. Applicants to Dowling College are encouraged to submit either the ACT or SAT I. Students should have 16 academic courses in high school including 4 years of English. Students are encouraged to have an interview. Once a student with an LD has been admitted to the College, he or she may submit an application to the LD program. Both student and parent are required to complete an application. Students must submit their most recent IEP and psychoeducational evaluation. An interview is required, and the LD Program Director looks for students with tenacity and motivation. Approximately 25 students are admitted to the program each year.

ADDITIONAL INFORMATION

The Program for Students with Learning Disabilities offers support services in word processing and language development; a liaison between individual professors and students; weekly writing workshops; and a freshman college orientation for course requirements geared to the specific needs of students with LD. There is no learning resource center, but students have access to tutors who are available in the library. Tutors are trained to provide academic support. There is a Lab School at which students with learning disabilities may receive special tutoring two times a week in learning strategies. Students are eligible to receive all accommodations or services that are listed in their most recent IEP.

SUPPORT SERVICES CONTACT INFORMATION

Learning Disability Program/Services: Program for College Students with Learning Disabilities
Director: Dr. Dorothy Stracher
  Telephone: 631-244-3306
  Fax: 631-244-5036
Contact: Same

LEARNING DISABILITY SERVICES

Requests for the following services/accommodations will be evaluated individually based on appropriate and current documentation.

Allowed in Exams
  Calculator: Yes
  Dictionary: Yes
  Computer: Yes
  Spellchecker: Yes
Extended test time: Yes
Scribes: Yes
Proctors: Yes
Oral exams: Yes
Note-takers: Yes

Distraction-reduced environment: Yes
Tape recording in class: Yes
Books on tape from RFBD: Yes
Taping of books not from RFBD: Yes
Accommodations for students with ADHD: Yes
Reading machine: Yes
Other assistive technology: Yes
Priority registration: Yes

Added costs for services: $1,500 per semester
LD specialists: Yes (2)
Professional tutors: 25
Peer tutors: No
Max. hours/wk. for services: Unlimited
How professors are notified of LD/ADHD: By director

GENERAL ADMISSIONS INFORMATION

Director of Admissions: Nancy Brewer
Telephone: 800-369-5464

ENTRANCE REQUIREMENTS
16 total are recommended; 4 English recommended, 3 math recommended, 2 science recommended, 3 social studies recommended. High school diploma or GED required.

Application deadline: Rolling
Notification: Rolling
Average GPA: NR

Average SAT I Math: 430
Average SAT I Verbal: 438
Average ACT: 20.5

Graduated top 10% of class: 9%
Graduated top 25% of class: 33%
Graduated top 50% of class: 80%

COLLEGE GRADUATION REQUIREMENTS

Course waivers allowed: Yes
Course substitutions allowed: Yes
In what subjects: Foreign language

ADDITIONAL INFORMATION

Environment: Located 50 miles from New York City.

Student Body
  Undergrad enrollment: 2,922
  Female: 59%
  Male: 41%
  Out-of-state: 6%

Cost Information
  Tuition: $11,940
  Room & board: $2,650
Housing Information
  University housing: Yes
  Percent living on campus: 11%

Greek System
  Fraternity: No
  Sorority: No
Athletics: NCAA Division II

Dowling College

HOFSTRA UNIVERSITY

Admissions Center, Bernon Hall, Hempstead, NY 11549
Phone: 516-463-6700 • Fax: 516-463-5100
E-mail: hofstra@hofstra.edu • Web: www.hofstra.edu
Support level: SP • Institution type: 4-year private

LEARNING DISABILITY PROGRAM AND SERVICES

The Program for Academic Learning Skills (PALS) seeks candidates who have been diagnosed with learning disabilities and show above-average intellectual ability and emotional stability. The program concentrates on identifying qualified applicants for entrance to the University, and on enhancing the skills that will help students achieve academic success. This program is part of the Division of Special Studies. Normally, candidates will be accepted into PALS for a period of one academic year. In the first semester students enroll in courses offered through DSS, and in the second semester they enroll in regular Hofstra classes.

LD/ADHD ADMISSIONS INFORMATION

College entrance tests required: Yes
Nonstandardized tests accepted: Yes
Interview required: Yes
Essay required: No
Documentation required for LD: WAIS-III; IEP: within one year
Documentation required for ADHD: Yes
Documentation submitted to: Director of Admissions and PALS
Special Ed. HS course work accepted: Yes

Specific course requirements for all applicants: Yes
Separate application required for services: Yes
# of LD applications submitted yearly: 350
# of LD applications accepted yearly: 45–60
Total # of students receiving LD/ADHD services: 200
Acceptance into program means acceptance into college: Students who are admitted to PALS are automatically admitted to the University.

ADMISSIONS

Students with LD who are not admissible as regular students are invited to interview and may be offered admission to PALS. The Division of Special Studies, which administers PALS, has always conducted a highly individualized admissions process. Students with learning disabilities, who may be in the bottom 30 percent of their high school class and have an 800–850 SAT, may be eligible for the PALS program. The interview is very important and students may be asked to write an essay at this time. Only 18 of the 100 students accepted into the Division of Special Studies are learning disabled. PALS is looking for students who have the academic ability and potential to be successful in college; self-knowledge and understanding of strengths and weaknesses; and a willingness to work hard. There are no specific high school course requirements for PALS. In cooperation with the Admissions Office, candidates are encouraged to apply for admission for the fall semester. Admission decisions are made jointly by PALS and the Office of Admissions. Only in exceptional cases will applicants be admitted in midyear.

ADDITIONAL INFORMATION

There are course waivers available; however, the University prefers to substitute courses where possible. Once admitted the students meet with a specialist two times a week, and information regarding progress is shared with the family. Basic skills courses are offered in spelling, learning strategies, study strategies, time management, written language, and social skills.

SUPPORT SERVICES CONTACT INFORMATION

Learning Disability Program/Services: Program for Academic Learning Skills (PALS)
Director: I. H. Gotz, PhD
  E-mail: nucizg@hofstra.edu
  Telephone: 516-463-5841
  Fax: 516-463-4832
Contact: Same

LEARNING DISABILITY SERVICES

Requests for the following services/accommodations will be evaluated individually based on appropriate and current documentation.

Allowed in Exams
  Calculator: Yes
  Dictionary: Yes
  Computer: Yes
  Spellchecker: Yes
Extended test time: Yes
Scribes: Yes
Proctors: Yes
Oral exams: Yes
Note-takers: Yes

Distraction-reduced environment: Yes
Tape recording in class: Yes
Books on tape from RFBD: Yes
Accommodations for students with ADHD: Yes
Reading machine: Yes
Other assistive technology: Yes
Priority registration: No

Added costs for services: $5,000 for freshman year only
LD specialists: Yes (4.5)
Professional tutors: 5
Peer tutors: Yes
Max. hours/wk. for services: Unlimited
How professors are notified of LD/ADHD: By the student and the program director

GENERAL ADMISSIONS INFORMATION

Director of Admissions: Matthew Whelan
Telephone: 516-463-6700

ENTRANCE REQUIREMENTS
16 total are required; 20 total are recommended; 4 English required, 2 math required, 3 math recommended, 2 science required, 1 science lab required, 2 foreign language required, 3 social studies required, 3 history recommended, 4 elective required. High school diploma or GED required. Minimum TOEFL is 550. TOEFL required of all international applicants.

Application deadline: Rolling
Notification: Rolling
Average GPA: 2.8

Average SAT I Math: 555
Average SAT I Verbal: 548
Average ACT: 24

Graduated top 10% of class: 9%
Graduated top 25% of class: 49%
Graduated top 50% of class: 85%

COLLEGE GRADUATION REQUIREMENTS

Course waivers allowed: No
Course substitutions allowed: Yes
In what subjects: Foreign language

ADDITIONAL INFORMATION

Environment: Hempstead is a residential community on Long Island just outside New York City.

Student Body
  Undergrad enrollment: 9,346
  Female: 54%
  Male: 46%
  Out-of-state: 20%

Cost Information
  Tuition: $14,280
  Room & board: $7,240
Housing Information
  University housing: Yes
  Percent living on campus: 40%

Greek System
  Fraternity: Yes
  Sorority: Yes
Athletics: NCAA Division I

IONA COLLEGE

715 North Avenue, New Rochelle, NY 10801
Phone: 914-633-2502 • Fax: 914-633-2642
E-mail: icad@iona.edu • Web: www.iona.edu
Support level: SP • Institution type: 4-year private

LEARNING DISABILITY PROGRAM AND SERVICES

The College Assistance Program (CAP) offers comprehensive support and services for students with LD/ADHD. CAP is designed to encourage success by providing instruction tailored to individual strengths and needs. With success comes self-confidence and a greater ability to plan and achieve academic, personal, and career goals. Students take standard full-time course requirements to ensure the level of quality education expected of all degree candidates. Professional tutors teach individually appropriate strategies that cross disciplines. These skills are designed to facilitate the completion of assignments and to generate eventual academic independence. CAP staff encourages students to become active, involved members of the College community. All CAP freshmen must participate in a three-week summer orientation; the aim is to provide students with a solid foundation from which the College experience can begin with confidence. During the orientation, the staff instructs and guides students in intensive writing instruction and study, organizational, and time management skills; students are oriented to the College and services; individual learning styles are explored; opportunities are provided to practice self-advocacy; several workshops are offered in areas that meet the student's specific needs; and individual fall classes are developed. Semester services include supplementary advisement, counseling, regularly scheduled weekly skill-based tutoring with an LD professional, study groups, skills workshops, and provision of appropriate documented accommodations.

LD/ADHD ADMISSIONS INFORMATION

College entrance tests required: Yes
Nonstandardized tests accepted: Yes
Interview required: Yes
Essay required: Yes
Documentation required for LD: WAIS-III; IEP: within 2 years
Documentation required for ADHD: Yes
Documentation submitted to: CAP
Special Ed. HS course work accepted: No

Specific course requirements for all applicants: Yes
Separate application required for services: No
# of LD applications submitted yearly: 200+
# of LD applications accepted yearly: 20
Total # of students receiving LD/ADHD services: 65
Acceptance into program means acceptance into college: Students must be accepted and enrolled at the College first and then may request admission to CAP.

ADMISSIONS

All applicants must meet the same admission criteria, which include 4 years English, 1 year American history, 1 year social studies, 2 years foreign language (waivers granted), 1 year natural science, and 3 years math. Students should send the following to the CAP office: a complete psychological evaluation conducted within the past two years including the WAISS or WAIS-R subtest scores and a comprehensive report, a copy of the most recent Individualized Educational Plan; and two letters of recommendation (one from the learning disability instructor). A personal interview is required. CAP is designed for students with LD and ADHD who have been mainstreamed in their academic courses in high school. Students should be average or above average in intellectual ability, socially mature, emotionally stable, and motivated to work hard.

ADDITIONAL INFORMATION

CAP services include a freshman summer college transition program; supplementary academic advising and program planning based on each student's learning style; priority registration; two hours per week of scheduled skill-based individual tutoring with a professional learning specialist; additional tutoring sessions are possible; small group tutoring and workshops; testing accommodations; alternative testing procedures; special equipment; self-advocacy training; referrals to additional services on campus; and counseling services. The CAP director works with faculty to help them understand the problems faced by students with LD, and to explore creative ways to support the learning process. The Samuel Rudin Academic Resource Center (ARC) offers free services to all students who wish to improve their learning skills or who want academic support. ARC provides free reasonable services to all students with documented LD/ADHD.

SUPPORT SERVICES CONTACT INFORMATION

Learning Disability Program/Services: College Assistance Program (CAP)
Director: Madeline Packerman
  E-mail: mpackerman@iona.edu
  Telephone: 914-633-2582
  Fax: 914-633-2174
Contact: Same

LEARNING DISABILITY SERVICES

Requests for the following services/accommodations will be evaluated individually based on appropriate and current documentation.

Allowed in Exams
  Calculator: Yes
  Dictionary: Yes
  Computer: Yes
  Spellchecker: Yes
Extended test time: Yes
Scribes: Yes
Proctors: Yes
Oral exams: Yes
Note-takers: Yes

Distraction-reduced environment: Yes
Tape recording in class: Yes
Books on tape from RFBD: Yes
Taping of books not from RFBD: Yes
Accommodations for students with ADHD: Yes
Reading machine: Yes
Other assistive technology: Yes
Priority registration: Yes

Added costs for services: $1,000 per semester
LD specialists: Yes (10)
Professional tutors: 10
Peer tutors: No
Max. hours/wk. for services: No
How professors are notified of LD/ADHD: By student and program director

GENERAL ADMISSIONS INFORMATION

Director of Admissions: Tom Weeded
Telephone: 914-633-2502

ENTRANCE REQUIREMENTS
16 total are required; 17 total are recommended; 4 English required, 4 English recommended, 3 math required, 3 math recommended, 1 science required, 3 science recommended, 1 science lab required, 2 science lab recommended, 2 foreign language required, 2 foreign language recommended, 1 social studies required, 1 social studies recommended, 1 history required, 1 history recommended, 4 elective required, 3 elective recommended. High school diploma or GED required. Minimum TOEFL is 550. TOEFL required of all international applicants.

Application deadline: NR
Notification: Rolling beginning 1/1
Average GPA: 2.7

Average SAT I Math: 502
Average SAT I Verbal: 504
Average ACT: 20

Graduated top 10% of class: 14%
Graduated top 25% of class: 36%
Graduated top 50% of class: 76%

COLLEGE GRADUATION REQUIREMENTS

Course waivers allowed: No
Course substitutions allowed: Yes
In what subjects: Foreign language and math

ADDITIONAL INFORMATION

Environment: The College is located on 56 acres 20 miles northeast of New York City.

Student Body
  Undergrad enrollment: 3,422
  Female: 52%
  Male: 48%
  Out-of-state: 15%

Cost Information
  Tuition: $15,500
  Room & board: $8,835
Housing Information
  University housing: Yes
  Percent living on campus: 15%

Greek System
  Fraternity: Yes
  Sorority: Yes
Athletics: NCAA Division I

KEUKA COLLEGE

Office of Admissions, Keuka Park, NY 14478-0098
Phone: 315-279-5254 • Fax: 315-536-5386
E-mail: admissions@mail.keuka.edu • Web: www.keuka.edu
Support level: CS • Institution type: 4-year private

LEARNING DISABILITY PROGRAM AND SERVICES

The Academic Support Program will assist students in becoming competent, independent learners able to achieve their maximum potential in academic endeavors. Students with documented disabilities who are admitted and enrolled are encouraged to request services either in advance of the new semester or immediately at the beginning of the semester. Every effort is made to provide services and accommodations as quickly and appropriately as possible. It is the student's responsibility to contact the Academic Support Program office. The coordinator will meet with the student and review the documentation to create a plan of services and accommodations. The provision of services will be based on the specific diagnoses and recommendations of the professional performing the assessments. Students are encouraged to ensure that the diagnoses and all recommendations for accommodations are clearly stated within the report. Students who are eligible for testing accommodations will be required to make these arrangements with the professor prior to EVERY test of the semester, as well as signing up for each test with the Academic Support Program office.

LD/ADHD ADMISSIONS INFORMATION

College entrance tests required: Yes
Nonstandardized tests accepted: Yes
Interview required: No
Essay required: Yes
Documentation required for LD: Psychoeducational evaluation
Documentation required for ADHD: Yes
Documentation submitted to: Academic Support Program
Special Ed. HS course work accepted: NR

Specific course requirements for all applicants: Yes
Separate application required for services: No
# of LD applications submitted yearly: N/A
# of LD applications accepted yearly: N/A
Total # of students receiving LD/ADHD services: 45
Acceptance into program means acceptance into college: Students must be admitted and enrolled and then request services.

ADMISSIONS

There is no special admissions process available and all students are expected to meet the general admission criteria. Students are expected to rank in the top 50 percent of their high school class and have a minimum 2.8 GPA. Course requirements include 4 years of English, 3 years of history and 1 year of social studies, 2–3 years of math and science and 2 years of foreign language. An essay is required and a campus visit with an interview is recommended.

ADDITIONAL INFORMATION

The provision of support is based on the specific diagnosis and recommendations of the professional performing the assessments. Examples of some support services offered by the Academic Support Program are: testing accommodations, tutors (group and individual), individual appointments with professional staff members, career counseling, and books on tape. Workshops for all students are offered in note-taking strategies, testing strategies, time management and study skills. A Coaching Program for students with ADHD is also offered.

SUPPORT SERVICES CONTACT INFORMATION

Learning Disability Program/Services: Academic Support Program
Director: Nancy M. Bailey
  E-mail: nmbailey@mail.keuka.edu
  Telephone: 315-279-5636
  Fax: 315-279-5216
Contact: Beth Demay
  E-mail: belemay@mail.keuka.edu
  Telephone: 315-279-5636
  Fax: 315-279-5216

LEARNING DISABILITY SERVICES

Requests for the following services/accommodations will be evaluated individually based on appropriate and current documentation.

Allowed in Exams
  Calculator: Yes
  Dictionary: Yes
  Computer: Yes
  Spellchecker: Yes
Extended test time: Yes
Scribes: Yes
Proctors: Yes
Oral exams: Yes
Note-takers: Yes

Distraction-reduced environment: Yes
Tape recording in class: Yes
Books on tape from RFBD: Yes
Taping of books not from RFBD: Yes
Accommodations for students with
  ADHD: Yes
Reading machine: Yes
Other assistive technology: Yes
Priority registration: No

Added costs for services: No
LD specialists: Yes (2)
Professional tutors: 30–40
Peer tutors: No
Max. hours/wk. for services: No
How professors are notified of
  LD/ADHD: By student

GENERAL ADMISSIONS INFORMATION

Director of Admissions: Joel Wincowski
Telephone: 315-279-5254

ENTRANCE REQUIREMENTS
18 total are recommended; 4 English recommended, 3 math recommended, 3 science recommended, 2 science lab recommended, 3 foreign language recommended, 3 social studies recommended, 2 history recommended. High school diploma or GED required. Minimum TOEFL is 500. TOEFL required of all international applicants.

Application deadline: NR
Notification: Rolling beginning 9/1
Average GPA: 3.0

Average SAT I Math: 490
Average SAT I Verbal: 483
Average ACT: 21

Graduated top 10% of class: 7%
Graduated top 25% of class: 24%
Graduated top 50% of class: 60%

COLLEGE GRADUATION REQUIREMENTS

Course waivers allowed: Yes
Course substitutions allowed: Yes
In what subjects: Varies; must be appropriate and agreed upon by student, instructor, division chair, and registrar

ADDITIONAL INFORMATION

Environment: Located 50 miles from Rochester.

Student Body
  Undergrad enrollment: 952
  Female: 72%
  Male: 28%
  Out-of-state: 8%

Cost Information
  Tuition: $13,490
  Room & board: $6,750
Housing Information
  University housing: Yes
  Percent living on campus: 72%

Greek System
  Fraternity: No
  Sorority: No
Athletics: NCAA Division III

LONG ISLAND UNIV.—C.W. POST

720 Northern Boulevard, Brookville, NY 11548
Phone: 516-299-2900 • Fax: 516-299-2137
E-mail: enroll@cwpost.liu.edu • Web: www.liu.edu
Support level: SP • Institution type: 4-year private

LEARNING DISABILITY PROGRAM AND SERVICES

The Academic Resource Center (ARC) is a comprehensive support program designed for students with learning disabilities to help them achieve their academic potential in a university setting. The objective is to encourage students to become independent learners and self-advocates. Students participate in mainstream college courses and assume full responsibility for attendance in class and at the ARC. Students work with learning assistants on a one-to-one basis. Graduate assistants are students enrolled in the School of Education who are pursuing master's degrees. The graduate assistants help students make the transition from high school to college. They assist students in time management, organizational skills, note-taking techniques, study skills, and other learning strategies. Students are responsible for attendance and participation in meetings with the learning assistants. ARC staff communicates with professors, and students are tutored by learning assistants. Students learn time management, reading, study and test-taking strategies, organizational skills, and note-taking techniques. The ARC provides an environment that helps students demonstrate positive attitudes toward themselves and learning.

LD/ADHD ADMISSIONS INFORMATION

College entrance tests required: Yes
Nonstandardized tests accepted: Yes
Interview required: Yes
Essay required: Yes
Documentation required for LD: WAIS-III within last three years; IEP; any other testing should be sent (Woodcock-Johnson, etc.)
Documentation required for ADHD: Yes
Documentation submitted to: Academic Resource Center
Special Ed. HS course work accepted: Yes

Specific course requirements for all applicants: Yes
Separate application required for services: Yes
# of LD applications submitted yearly: 200
# of LD applications accepted yearly: 50–61
Total # of students receiving LD/ADHD services: 85–91
Acceptance into program means acceptance into college: Students must be accepted and enrolled at the University first and then may request services.

ADMISSIONS

The student must be admitted to the University first and then apply to the ARC. Acceptance into the University is separate and distinct from acceptance into the ARC. Students admitted to the University and who identify themselves as learning disabled are sent information and an application to apply to the ARC. Applications must include a Diagnostic Evaluation describing the specific LD; WAIS-R; and a handwritten essay indicating why the student is requesting admittance into the ARC. Once all of the information is on file the student will be invited to interview. This interview is an integral part of the admission process. Some students may be admitted through the General Studies Program if the GPA or tests are low. During an interview students must convince the Admissions Counselor that they have changed and are now willing to focus on studies. Motivation is very important. Students with an SAT below 800 or a Verbal below 450 are required to have either a B- average or 450 Verbal or 400 Math SAT. If students have a deficiency, the people responsible for testing must write letters stating what specifically in the test data indicates the students should be granted a waiver.

ADDITIONAL INFORMATION

Ancillary services include note-takers in individual course lectures; subject tutors; proctors; assistance securing books on tape; audio and video tapes to supplement learning; assistance with planning and scheduling classes; study and social skills workshops; and a mentor program. Other services include individualized learning strategies on a one-to-one basis two times a week; extended time and readers for exams; academic advisement and faculty liaison; and assistance in formulating an overall plan and structure when approaching an assignment. The program is a four-year program, but the majority of students opt to handle their own class work at the end of sophomore year. Freshmen are limited to 12 credits for their first semester, and all must enroll in a Freshman Seminar. There are no special or remedial classes.

SUPPORT SERVICES CONTACT INFORMATION

Learning Disability Program/Services: Academic Resource Center (ARC)
Director: Carol Rundlett
  Telephone: 516-299-2937
  Fax: 516-299-2126
Contact: Same

LEARNING DISABILITY SERVICES

Requests for the following services/accommodations will be evaluated individually based on appropriate and current documentation.

Allowed in Exams
  Calculator: Yes
  Dictionary: Yes
  Computer: Yes
  Spellchecker: Yes
Extended test time: Yes
Scribes: Yes
Proctors: Yes
Oral exams: Y/N
Note-takers: Yes

Distraction-reduced environment: Yes
Tape recording in class: Yes
Books on tape from RFBD: Yes
Taping of books not from RFBD: Yes
Accommodations for students with ADHD: Yes
Reading machine: Yes
Other assistive technology: Yes
Priority registration: No

Added costs for services: $1,600 per semester
LD specialists: Yes (1)
Professional tutors: 15–20
Peer tutors: No
Max. hours/wk. for services: Unlimited
How professors are notified of LD/ADHD: By both student and director

GENERAL ADMISSIONS INFORMATION

Director of Admissions: Susan Racanl
Telephone: 516-299-2900

ENTRANCE REQUIREMENTS

16 total are required; 24 total are recommended; 4 English required, 4 English recommended, 2 math required, 4 math recommended, 2 science required, 4 science recommended, 2 science lab required, 4 science lab recommended, 2 foreign language required, 4 foreign language recommended, 3 social studies required, 4 social studies recommended, 1 elective required. High school diploma or GED required. Minimum TOEFL is 500. TOEFL required of all international applicants.

Application deadline: Rolling
Notification: Rolling beginning 9/1
Average GPA: 3.0

Average SAT I Math: 518
Average SAT I Verbal: 517
Average ACT: NR

Graduated top 10% of class: 10%
Graduated top 25% of class: 26%
Graduated top 50% of class: 61%

COLLEGE GRADUATION REQUIREMENTS

Course waivers allowed: Yes
Course substitutions allowed: Yes
In what subjects: Math and foreign language core requirements only; a specific computer course for the core math requirement; English 7 & 8 (anthology courses) for foreign language

ADDITIONAL INFORMATION

Environment: The College is located on Long Island about 30 minutes from New York City.

Student Body
  Undergrad enrollment: 5,748
  Female: 57%
  Male: 43%
  Out-of-state: 6%

Cost Information
  Tuition: $16,100
  Room & board: $6,790
Housing Information
  University housing: Yes
  Percent living on campus: 37%

Greek System
  Fraternity: Yes
  Sorority: Yes
Athletics: NCAA Division II

MANHATTANVILLE COLLEGE

2900 Purchase Street, Admissions Office, Purchase, NY 10577
Phone: 914-323-5464 • Fax: 914-694-1732
E-mail: jflores@mville.edu • Web: www.mville.edu
Support level: CS • Institution type: 4-year private

LEARNING DISABILITY PROGRAM AND SERVICES

The Higher Education Learning Program (HELP) is designed to help motivated and committed students with learning disabilities successfully meet the academic challenge of the College experience. HELP offers a range of support services for students with learning disabilities throughout their years of college. HELP remains focused on instruction and applications of compensatory strategies to college content courses. The HELP Program offers a credit-bearing writing course, specifically designed for students with learning disabilities, which fulfills the College's writing requirement. Students in the HELP Program, as well as all students at the College, are entitled to reasonable accommodations and modifications. Students in the HELP Program are assisted by tutors in developing those advocacy skills needed to secure accommodations and modifications.

LD/ADHD ADMISSIONS INFORMATION

College entrance tests required: Yes
Nonstandardized tests accepted: Yes
Interview required: Yes
Essay required: No
Documentation required for LD: WAIS-III, achievement
Documentation required for ADHD: Yes
Documentation submitted to: HELP
Special Ed. HS course work accepted: Case-by-case basis

Specific course requirements for all applicants: Yes
Separate application required for services: No
# of LD applications submitted yearly: Varies
# of LD applications accepted yearly: N/A
Total # of students receiving LD/ADHD services: 46
Acceptance into program means acceptance into college: Joint decision but students are admitted to the College first then the program.

ADMISSIONS
Applicants must meet the requirements for general admission. These criteria include 3.0 GPA and 4 years English, 2 years math, 2 years science, 2 years foreign language, and 2 years history. The average ACT is 24 and SAT I is 1015. Applicants must also submit diagnostic testing identifying the learning disability.

ADDITIONAL INFORMATION
The core of the program is one-to-one tutoring in learning strategies directly applicable to course work. Services are individualized to accommodate the specific needs of each student and are coordinated and implemented by trained learning disabilities professionals.

SUPPORT SERVICES CONTACT INFORMATION

Learning Disability Program/Services: Higher Education Learning Program (HELP)
Director: Myra Gentiley
  E-mail: gentileym@mville.edu
  Telephone: 914-323-5124
  Fax: 914-323-5493
Contact: Same

LEARNING DISABILITY SERVICES

Requests for the following services/accommodations will be evaluated individually based on appropriate and current documentation.

Allowed in Exams
  Calculator: Y/N
  Dictionary: Y/N
  Computer: Y/N
  Spellchecker: Y/N
Extended test time: Yes
Scribes: Yes
Proctors: Yes
Oral exams: Yes
Note-takers: Yes

Distraction-reduced environment: Yes
Tape recording in class: Yes
Books on tape from RFBD: Yes
Taping of books not from RFBD: Yes
Accommodations for students with ADHD: Yes
Reading machine: Yes
Other assistive technology: Yes
Priority registration: No

Added costs for services: $3,000
LD specialists: Yes (10)
Professional tutors: Yes
Peer tutors: Yes
Max. hours/wk. for services: 3 hours per week
How professors are notified of LD/ADHD: By student and program director

GENERAL ADMISSIONS INFORMATION

Director of Admissions: Jose Flores
Telephone: 914-328-5124

ENTRANCE REQUIREMENTS

4 English required, 3 math required, 4 math recommended, 3 science required, 4 science recommended, 2 science lab required, 2 foreign language required, 3 social studies required, 4 social studies recommended, 3 history required. High school diploma or GED required. Minimum TOEFL is 550. TOEFL required of all international applicants.

Application deadline: March 1
Notification: Rolling beginning 1/5
Average GPA: 3.0

Average SAT I Math: 520
Average SAT I Verbal: 520
Average ACT: 23

Graduated top 10% of class: NR
Graduated top 25% of class: NR
Graduated top 50% of class: NR

COLLEGE GRADUATION REQUIREMENTS

Course waivers allowed: No
Course substitutions allowed: No
In what subjects: N/A

ADDITIONAL INFORMATION

Environment: The College is located on a 100-acre campus in a suburban area 25 miles north of New York City.

Student Body
  Undergrad enrollment: 1,581
  Female: 69%
  Male: 31%
  Out-of-state: 29%

Cost Information
  Tuition: $19,620
  Room & board: $8,320
Housing Information
  University housing: Yes
  Percent living on campus: 68%

Greek System
  Fraternity: Yes
  Sorority: Yes
Athletics: NCAA Division III

MARIST COLLEGE

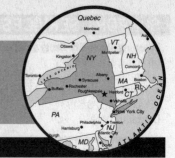

3399 North Road, Poughkeepsie, NY 12601-1387
Phone: 845-575-3226 • Fax: 845-575-3215
E-mail: admissions@marist.edu • Web: www.marist.edu
Support level: SP • Institution type: 4-year private

LEARNING DISABILITY PROGRAM AND SERVICES

Marist College believes that bright, motivated students with specific learning disabilities are more similar than different to other college students and can achieve a higher education. Marist offers a program of support for students with learning disabilities through the Learning Disabilities Program. Students receive a complement of academic services designed to meet individual needs. The program focuses on the development and use of strategies to promote independence and personal success. The philosophy of the program does not emphasize remediation, but rather the development of compensatory strategies. Each student is enrolled in credit-bearing courses and completes the same degree requirements as all students. Program staff work closely with faculty and administration and students are encouraged to discuss their learning disability with faculty. The goal is for each student to achieve the maximum level of independence possible and to become an effective self-advocate. Participation in the program is available on a continual basis for as long as the LD specialist and the student agree that is necessary.

LD/ADHD ADMISSIONS INFORMATION

College entrance tests required: Yes
Nonstandardized tests accepted: Yes
Interview required: NR
Essay required: Yes
Documentation required for LD: Psychoeducational evaluation
Documentation required for ADHD: Yes
Documentation submitted to: LD Program
Special Ed. HS course work accepted: No

Specific course requirements for all applicants: Yes
Separate application required for services: Yes
# of LD applications submitted yearly: 200–251
# of LD applications accepted yearly: 50+
Total # of students receiving LD/ADHD services: 75–80
Acceptance into program means acceptance into college: Students are admitted jointly into the College and the LD Program.

ADMISSIONS

Students with LD must submit an application for admission and all required materials to the Office of Admissions. A Supplementary Application for the LD Support Program must also be completed and sent directly to the OSS. Additionally, students must submit to the OSS the results of the WAIS-R, including subtest scores; calculated IQ and narrative; achievement testing with current levels of functioning in reading, mathematics, and written language; an unedited essay describing the impact of the LD on academic achievement; and a $20 fee. ACT/SAT scores are required of students with LD. After applications have been reviewed, those most qualified and suited to the program will be invited to interview. Students accepted into the program should have an acceptance and understanding of their LD; know their academic strengths and weaknesses; have college-prep courses; provide recommendations that communicate strengths, motivation to succeed, and willingness to accept and access supports; and have sound study skills and work habits. Admission to the program is competitive and students are encouraged to apply early. There is no early decision option.

ADDITIONAL INFORMATION

Upon enrollment students complete a comprehensive survey of abilities and attitudes toward academics. This survey is combined with diagnostic evaluations and the comprehensive record of students' performance to develop an Individual Support Service Plan. Students meet an LD specialist two times a week and typically concentrate on writing skills, note-taking, organizational skills, study skills, and testing strategies. Accommodations may include adaptive testing procedures; note-takers/tape recorders; scribes; taped textbooks/personal readers; use of adaptive equipment. A program fee is charged only for the services of the learning specialist. Students in the program also have access to content tutors and a counselor who can address academic, career, and personal issues. Services and accommodations are available for undergraduate and graduate students.

SUPPORT SERVICES CONTACT INFORMATION

Learning Disability Program/Services: Office of Special Services (OSS)/Learning Disabilities Program
Director: Linda Cooper
　Telephone: 845-575-3274
　Fax: 845-575-3011
Contact: Same

LEARNING DISABILITY SERVICES

Requests for the following services/accommodations will be evaluated individually based on appropriate and current documentation.

Allowed in Exams
　Calculator: Yes
　Dictionary: Yes
　Computer: Yes
　Spellchecker: Yes
Extended test time: Yes
Scribes: Yes
Proctors: Yes
Oral exams: Yes
Note-takers: Yes

Distraction-reduced environment: Yes
Tape recording in class: Yes
Books on tape from RFBD: Yes
Taping of books not from RFBD: Yes
Accommodations for students with ADHD: Yes
Reading machine: Yes
Other assistive technology: Yes
Priority registration: Yes

Added costs for services: $1,400 per semester
LD specialists: Yes
Professional tutors: 3
Peer tutors: 60
Max. hours/wk. for services: NR
How professors are notified of LD/ADHD: Student and program director

GENERAL ADMISSIONS INFORMATION

Director of Admissions: Jay Murray
Telephone: 845-575-3226

ENTRANCE REQUIREMENTS
16 total are required; 19 total are recommended; 4 English required, 4 English recommended, 3 math required, 4 math recommended, 3 science required, 4 science recommended, 2 science lab required, 3 science lab recommended, 3 foreign language recommended, 2 social studies required, 2 social studies recommended, 1 history required, 2 history recommended, 1 elective required. High school diploma or GED required. Minimum TOEFL is 550. TOEFL required of all international applicants.

Application deadline: February 15
Notification: March 15
Average GPA: 3.2

Average SAT I Math: 565
Average SAT I Verbal: 560
Average ACT: 24

Graduated top 10% of class: 18%
Graduated top 25% of class: 60%
Graduated top 50% of class: 98%

COLLEGE GRADUATION REQUIREMENTS

Course waivers allowed: Yes
Course substitutions allowed: Yes
In what subjects: Varies, mostly in math

ADDITIONAL INFORMATION

Environment: The College is located on 120 acres in upstate New York, 75 miles from New York City.

Student Body
　Undergrad enrollment: 4,713
　Female: 58%
　Male: 42%
　Out-of-state: 33%

Cost Information
　Tuition: $15,366
　Room & board: $7,828
Housing Information
　University housing: Yes
　Percent living on campus: 55%

Greek System
　Fraternity: Yes
　Sorority: Yes
Athletics: NCAA Division I

MARYMOUNT MANHATTAN COLLEGE

221 East 71st Street, New York, NY 10021 • Phone: 212-517-0430
Fax: 212-517-0465 • E-mail: admissions@mmm.edu
Web: www.marymount.mmm.edu/home.htm
Support level: SP • Institution type: 4-year

LEARNING DISABILITY PROGRAM AND SERVICES

Marymount Manhattan College's Program for Academic Access includes a full range of support services that center on academic and personal growth for students with learning disabilities. Students who have been admitted to the full-time program are required to demonstrate commitment to overcoming learning difficulties through regular attendance and tutoring. Academic advisement and counseling is provided to assist in developing a program plan suited to individual needs. The College is looking for highly motivated students with a commitment to compensate for their learning disabilities and to fully participate in the tutoring program. Once admitted into the program, students receive a program plan suited to their needs, based on a careful examination of the psycho-educational evaluations. Full time students sign a contract to regularly attend tutoring provided by professionals experienced within the field of LD. In addition to assisting students in the development of skills and strategies for their course work, LD specialists coach participants in the attitudes and behavior necessary for college success. Professors assist learning specialists in carefully monitoring students' progress throughout the academic year and arranging for accommodations. Students must submit a current and complete psychoeducational evaluation that meets the documentation guidelines by giving clear and specific evidence of the disability and its limitations on academic functioning in the diagnosis summary statement. Students with ADHD must have a licensed physician, psychiatrist or psychologist provide a complete and current documentation of the disorder.

LD/ADHD ADMISSIONS INFORMATION

College entrance tests required: Yes
Nonstandardized tests accepted: Yes
Interview required: Yes
Essay required: Yes
Documentation required for LD: Psychoeducational evaluation
Documentation required for ADHD: Yes
Documentation submitted to: Administration/Program for Academic Access
Special Ed. HS course work accepted: Yes

Specific course requirements for all applicants: Yes
Separate application required for services: No
# of LD applications submitted yearly: 40
# of LD applications accepted yearly: 25
Total # of students receiving LD/ADHD services: 25
Acceptance into program means acceptance into college: Students may be admitted to the College through the Program for Academic Access.

ADMISSIONS
Admission to Marymount Manhattan College's Program for Academic Access is based on a diagnosis of dyslexia, ADHD, or other primary learning disability; intellectual potential within the average to superior range; and a serious commitment in attitude and work habits to meeting the program and college academic requirements. Prospective students are required to submit the following: high school transcript or GED. Students are expected to have college prep courses in high school but foreign language is not required for admission; ACT or SAT are preferred but not required; results of a recent complete psychoeducational evaluation (within one year); letters of recommendation from teachers, tutors, or counselors; and a personal interview. Students may be admitted to the College through the Program for Academic Access. Students interested in being considered for admission through the program must self-disclose their LD/ADHD in a personal statement with the application. There is no fixed deadline for the application; however, there are a limited number of slots available.

ADDITIONAL INFORMATION
There are three LD professionals associated with the program. Students have access to two hours of tutoring per week plus drop-in tutoring. Skills classes are offered in study skills, reading, vocabulary development, and workshops in overcoming procrastination. The following services are offered to students with appropriate documentation: the use of calculators, computer and spellchecker in exams; extended time on tests; proctors; oral exams; distraction-free testing environment; tape recorder in class; books on tape; separate and alternative forms of testing; and priority registration. The program fee is $3,000 per academic year above tuition.

SUPPORT SERVICES CONTACT INFORMATION

Learning Disability Program/Services: Program for Academic Access
Director: Dr. Jacquelyn Bonomo (Acting)
 E-mail: jbonomo@mmm.edu
 Telephone: 212-774-0724
 Fax: 212-517-0541
Contact: Same

LEARNING DISABILITY SERVICES

Requests for the following services/accommodations will be evaluated individually based on appropriate and current documentation.

Allowed in Exams
 Calculator: Yes
 Dictionary: No
 Computer: Yes
 Spellchecker: Yes
Extended test time: Yes
Scribes: No
Proctors: Yes
Oral exams: Yes
Note-takers: No

Distraction-reduced environment: Yes
Tape recording in class: Yes
Books on tape from RFBD: Yes
Taping of books not from RFBD: No
Accommodations for students with ADHD: Yes
Reading machine: No
Other assistive technology: Yes
Priority registration: Yes

Added costs for services: $3,000 per year
LD specialists: Yes (3)
Professional tutors: 3
Peer tutors: No
Max. hours/wk. for services: 2
How professors are notified of LD/ADHD: By student

GENERAL ADMISSIONS INFORMATION

Director of Admissions: Thomas Friebel
Telephone: 212-517-0435

ENTRANCE REQUIREMENTS

16 total are required; 4 English required, 3 math required, 1 science required, 3 science recommended, 1 science lab required, 3 foreign language recommended, 3 social studies required, 4 elective required. High school diploma or GED required. Minimum TOEFL is 500. TOEFL required of all international applicants.

Application deadline: 3/5 Priority
Notification: Rolling
Average GPA: 3.4

Average SAT I Math: 510
Average SAT I Verbal: 540
Average ACT: 25

Graduated top 10% of class: 25%
Graduated top 25% of class: 75%
Graduated top 50% of class: 89%

COLLEGE GRADUATION REQUIREMENTS

Course waivers allowed: No
Course substitutions allowed: No
In what subjects: N/A

ADDITIONAL INFORMATION

Environment: Located on the upper east side of Manhattan.

Student Body
 Undergrad enrollment: 2,497
 Female: 79%
 Male: 21%
 Out-of-state: 35%

Cost Information
 Tuition: $13,050
 Room & board: $7,200
Housing Information
 University housing: Yes
 Percent living on campus: 23%

Greek System
 Fraternity: No
 Sorority: No
Athletics: Intercollegiate

NEW YORK UNIVERSITY

22 Washington Square North, New York, NY 10011
Phone: 212-998-4500 • Fax: 212-995-4902
E-mail: admissions@nyu.edu • Web: www.nyu.edu
Support level: CS • Institution type: 4-year private

LEARNING DISABILITY PROGRAM AND SERVICES

Success in college depends on such things as motivation, intelligence, talent, problem-solving abilities, and hard work. For students with learning disabilities these traits must be complemented by an understanding of their learning style and their ways of compensating for their disability. The Center for Students with Disabilities strives to help students capitalize on their strengths and minimize the impact of their learning disability. The goal of the Center is to assist students with learning disabilities to achieve the highest level of academic independence and progress possible. The Center provides support services and accommodations to all NYU students with learning disabilities. There is no fee. The Center can assist students in coping with their learning disability while working toward independence, competence, and a college degree. Students with LD requesting accommodations or services must provide appropriate documentation; must be clear and show a specific diagnosis of LD; evidence of a substantial limitation to academic functioning; must be recent and performed by a qualified professional. Students with ADHD must provide documentation showing a clear and specific diagnosis of ADHD; documentation must be comprehensive; specify the criteria for the diagnosis and an interpretive summary; and performed by a qualified professional.

LD/ADHD ADMISSIONS INFORMATION

College entrance tests required: Yes
Nonstandardized tests accepted: Yes
Interview required: No
Essay required: Yes
Documentation required for LD: Psychoeducational evaluation
Documentation required for ADHD: Yes
Documentation submitted to: The Center for Students with Disabilities
Special Ed. HS course work accepted: Yes

Specific course requirements for all applicants: Yes
Separate application required for services: Yes
# of LD applications submitted yearly: N/A
# of LD applications accepted yearly: N/A
Total # of students receiving LD/ADHD services: 225
Acceptance into program means acceptance into college: Students must be admitted and enrolled at the University first and then may request services.

ADMISSIONS
NYU is a competitive university that provides a challenging academic environment. Students who apply, including students with learning disabilities, must demonstrate the potential to do well. As part of the admission decision, a learning disability specialist may be consulted regarding recommendations for students who self-disclose their learning disability. Students with learning disabilities typically have to work hard and manage their time well, but also find that they learn and accomplish a great deal at NYU. General admission criteria include 4 years English, 3 years math, 3 years science, 2 years foreign language, and 3 years social studies; SAT/ACT and SAT II for the BA/MD program.

ADDITIONAL INFORMATION
Students can meet with a learning specialist to help develop compensatory skills, work on testing strategies, time management, reading efficiency, organization, effective writing, proofreading, note-taking, and study skills. Accomodations and services include test accommodations, which could include extended time, distraction-reduced test rooms, use of a computer or calculator, reader, scribe, and alternative formats for tests; assistance in arranging for taping of lectures and ordering books on tape; priority seating; and technology such as computers and readers. Not all students need all of these services. An accommodation plan is made with each student based on individual needs, keeping in mind the goal of encouraging independence. It is possible for a student with LD to petition for a waiver of certain course requirements. The decision to allow for a waiver is made on a case-by-case basis.

SUPPORT SERVICES CONTACT INFORMATION

Learning Disability Program/Services: Center for Students with Disabilities
Director: Michael Quagerelli
  E-mail: michael.quagerelli@nyu.edu
  Telephone: 212-998-4980
  Fax: 212-995-4114
Contact: Same

LEARNING DISABILITY SERVICES

Requests for the following services/accommodations will be evaluated individually based on appropriate and current documentation.

Allowed in Exams
  Calculator: Yes
  Dictionary: Yes
  Computer: Yes
  Spellchecker: Yes
Extended test time: Yes
Scribes: Yes
Proctors: Yes
Oral exams: Yes
Note-takers: Yes

Distraction-reduced environment: Yes
Tape recording in class: Yes
Books on tape from RFBD: Yes
Taping of books not from RFBD: Yes
Accommodations for students with
  ADHD: Yes
Reading machine: Yes
Other assistive technology: Yes
Priority registration: No

Added costs for services: No
LD specialists: Yes
Professional tutors: No
Peer tutors: Yes
Max. hours/wk. for services: 1–2
How professors are notified of
  LD/ADHD: By the student

GENERAL ADMISSIONS INFORMATION

Director of Admissions: Rich Avitabile
Telephone: 212-998-4500

ENTRANCE REQUIREMENTS
18 total are required; 4 English required, 3 math required, 4 math recommended, 3 science required, 2 science lab required, 2 foreign language required, 3 foreign language recommended, 4 history required. High school diploma or GED required. Minimum TOEFL is 600. TOEFL required of all international applicants.

Application deadline: January 15
Notification: April 1
Average GPA: 3.6

Average SAT I Math: 667
Average SAT I Verbal: 667
Average ACT: 29

Graduated top 10% of class: 70%
Graduated top 25% of class: 93%
Graduated top 50% of class: 100%

COLLEGE GRADUATION REQUIREMENTS

Course waivers allowed: Yes
Course substitutions allowed: Yes
In what subjects: Determined by an Academic Standards Committee on a case-by-case basis

ADDITIONAL INFORMATION

Environment: The University has an urban campus in New York City.

Student Body
  Undergrad enrollment: 18,628
  Female: 60%
  Male: 40%
  Out-of-state: 49%

Cost Information
  Tuition: $24,336
  Room & board: $9,226
Housing Information
  University housing: Yes
  Percent living on campus: 50%

Greek System
  Fraternity: Yes
  Sorority: Yes
Athletics: NCAA Division III

ROCHESTER INSTITUTE OF TECHNOLOGY

60 Lomb Memorial Drive, Rochester, NY 14623-5604
Phone: 716-475-6631 • Fax: 716-475-7424
E-mail: admissions@rit.edu • Web: www.rit.edu
Support level: SP • Institution type: 4-year private

LEARNING DISABILITY PROGRAM AND SERVICES

The Learning Development Center offers a variety of services for students. Disability Services reviews requests for disability accommodations and approves accommodations and coordinates services. The Learning Support Services provides regularly scheduled check-ins with a learning-support specialist who provides coaching in organizational skills, study strategies, and advocacy. This service is intended for any student who anticipates difficulty navigating the College environment. Lunch 'n' Learning Workshops are a series of one-hour workshops dealing with specific study topics or strategies such as procrastination, test preparation, time management, and study skills. The Office of Special Services offers peer tutoring two hours per week to all RIT students.

LD/ADHD ADMISSIONS INFORMATION

College entrance tests required: Yes
Nonstandardized tests accepted: Yes
Interview required: Yes (recommended)
Essay required: Yes
Documentation required for LD: Comprehensive psychological evaluation within three years
Documentation required for ADHD: Yes
Documentation submitted to: Learning Support Services
Special Ed. HS course work accepted: No

Specific course requirements for all applicants: Yes
Separate application required for services: N/A
# of LD applications submitted yearly: 70–86
# of LD applications accepted yearly: 150
Total # of students receiving LD/ADHD services: 388
Acceptance into program means acceptance into college: Students are admitted to the Institute and LSS simultaneously.

ADMISSIONS

There is no special admissions process for students with learning disabilities. However, students with learning disabilities may include a supporting essay. Although an interview is not required, it is recommended. The required scores on the SAT or ACT will depend on the College the student is applying to within RIT. It is also helpful to identify compensatory strategies used in high school and what will be needed for success in college. The admission decision is made jointly by the Program Chairperson and Director of Admission.

ADDITIONAL INFORMATION

RIT is currently serving over 600 students with disabilities of which 388 are currently students with learning disabilites or attention deficit disorder. LSS serves 70–85 students per year and all are either LD or ADHD. There are eight specialists on staff. Requests for accommodations and services are evaluated individually based on appropriate and current documentation. Services and accommodations that may be provided include calculator, dictionary, computer or spellchecker on exams; extended test time; scribes, proctors, note-takers, distraction-free environment; books on tape; assistive technology; and priority registration. Disability information is confidential. Students distribute copies of letters to professors which list approved accommodations only. Course substitutions are allowed depending on documentation. There are fees for Learning Support Services.

SUPPORT SERVICES CONTACT INFORMATION

Learning Disability Program/Services: Disability Services/Learning Support Services
Director: Pamela Lloyd, Coordinator
  E-mail: palldc@rit.edu
  Telephone: 716-475-7804
  Fax: 716-475-5832
Contact: Same

LEARNING DISABILITY SERVICES

Requests for the following services/accommodations will be evaluated individually based on appropriate and current documentation.

Allowed in Exams
  Calculator: Yes
  Dictionary: Yes
  Computer: Yes
  Spellchecker: Yes
Extended test time: Yes
Scribes: Yes
Proctors: Yes
Oral exams: Yes
Note-takers: Yes

Distraction-reduced environment: Yes
Tape recording in class: Yes
Books on tape from RFBD: Yes
Taping of books not from RFBD: Yes
Accommodations for students with ADHD: Yes
Reading machine: Yes
Other assistive technology: Yes
Priority registration: No

Added costs for services: For LSS only
LD specialists: Yes (8)
Professional tutors: Yes
Peer tutors: Yes
Max. hours/wk. for services: 12 hours weekly
How professors are notified of LD/ADHD: By student

GENERAL ADMISSIONS INFORMATION

Director of Admissions: Daniel Shelley
Telephone: 716-475-6631

ENTRANCE REQUIREMENTS

21 total are required; 21 total are recommended; 4 English required, 4 English recommended, 2 math required, 3 math recommended, 2 science required, 3 science recommended, 1 science lab required, 2 science lab recommended, 3 foreign language recommended, 4 social studies required, 4 social studies recommended, 9 elective required, 4 elective recommended. High school diploma or GED required. Minimum TOEFL is 525. TOEFL required of all international applicants.

Application deadline: March 15
Notification: Rolling beginning 3/1
Average GPA: 3.7

Average SAT I Math: 590
Average SAT I Verbal: 570
Average ACT: N/A

Graduated top 10% of class: 28%
Graduated top 25% of class: 60%
Graduated top 50% of class: 90%

COLLEGE GRADUATION REQUIREMENTS

Course waivers allowed: Yes
Course substitutions allowed: Yes
In what subjects: Varies based on the student's documentation

ADDITIONAL INFORMATION

Environment: RIT is located on a 1,300-acre campus 5 miles south of the city of Rochester, the third largest city in New York State.

Student Body
  Undergrad enrollment: 11,100
  Female: 33%
  Male: 67%
  Out-of-state: 40%

Cost Information
  Tuition: $18,633
  Room & board: $7,242
Housing Information
  University housing: Yes
  Percent living on campus: 60%

Greek System
  Fraternity: Yes
  Sorority: Yes
  Athletics: NCAA Division III

Rochester Institute of Technology

SAINT BONAVENTURE UNIVERSITY

PO Box D, St. Bonaventure, NY 14778
Phone: 716-375-2400 • Fax: 716-375-4005
E-mail: admissions@sbu.edu • Web: www.sbu.edu
Support level: CS • Institution type: 4-year private

LEARNING DISABILITY PROGRAM AND SERVICES

St. Bonaventure does not operate a specialized LD program but does provide services to students with identified disabilities. In the spirit of the federal mandates, reasonable accommodations are made for otherwise qualified students with disabilities. St. Bonaventure's Teaching and Learning Center is an intrinsic element of the University's goal of academic excellence. The credo is "to assist, not do." Once authentic, current documentation has been received, a careful review of the records will be conducted and an evaluation of appropriate accommodations will be made. Students who wait to identify themselves until after registration may find that some accommodations are not immediately available. Students with learning disabilities/attention deficit disorders who wish to request accommodations must meet with the Coordinator of Services for Students with Disabilities. It is the student's responsibility to deliver accommodation letters to professors after accommodations have been arranged. Accommodations are arranged each semester. Students are encouraged to discuss the disability with professors and arrange for specific accommodations for test taking and other course requirements. Students must contact the Coordinator of Services for Students with Disabilities to request a course substitution. The students need to accept responsibility for their own academic excellence and assistance will be provided.

LD/ADHD ADMISSIONS INFORMATION

College entrance tests required: Yes
Nonstandardized tests accepted: Yes
Interview required: No
Essay required: No
Documentation required for LD: WAIS-III; IEP; some memory and/or perceptual test: within three years
Documentation required for ADHD: Yes
Documentation submitted to: Services for Students with Disabilities
Special Ed. HS course work accepted: Yes

Specific course requirements for all applicants: Yes
Separate application required for services: No
# of LD applications submitted yearly: 15
# of LD applications accepted yearly: 15
Total # of students receiving LD/ADHD services: 51
Acceptance into program means acceptance into college: Students must be admitted and enrolled at the University first and then may request services.

ADMISSIONS
Students with learning disabilities must meet regular admission standards and complete the same admissions process as all applicants. The middle 50 percent ACT score range is 23–24 and SAT 1070–1110; the minimum GPA is a 3.0. Course requirements include 4 years English, 4 years social studies, 3 years math, 3 years science, 2 years foreign language (recommended). Special education courses may be considered. It is recommended that students self-disclose the disability in a personal statement. Once students are accepted and have enrolled they are encouraged to self-disclose their learning disability, if this has not already been done, and provide appropriate documentation to the Office of Services for Students with Disabilities. Documentation is reviewed and appropriate accommodations are arranged.

ADDITIONAL INFORMATION
Students with LD may obtain assistance with assessing learning strengths and weaknesses, and consult one-on-one or in groups to acquire a greater command of a subject, get help with a specific assignment, or discuss academic challenges. Services might include but are not limited to: alternative testing arrangements; taped texts and classes; word processor/spellcheck; note-takers; tutors; peer mentors; time management and study skills training; and weekly individual appointments. To order books on tape from RFBD, students should allow three months to secure these books in time. Assistance can be offered in requesting books on tape. Tutoring services are available to all students and are not intended to be a substitute for independent study or preparation.

SUPPORT SERVICES CONTACT INFORMATION

Learning Disability Program/Services: Services for Students with Disabilities
Director: Nancy A. Matthews
  E-mail: nmatthews@sbu.edu
  Telephone: 716-375-2065
  Fax: 716-375-2072
Contact: Same

LEARNING DISABILITY SERVICES

Requests for the following services/accommodations will be evaluated individually based on appropriate and current documentation.

Allowed in Exams		
Calculator: Yes	**Distraction-reduced environment:** Yes	**Added costs for services:** No
Dictionary: Yes	**Tape recording in class:** Yes	**LD specialists:** Yes (1)
Computer: Yes	**Books on tape from RFBD:** Yes	**Professional tutors:** 1
Spellchecker: Yes	**Taping of books not from RFBD:** Yes	**Peer tutors:** 60
Extended test time: Yes	**Accommodations for students with**	**Max. hours/wk. for services:** As
Scribes: Yes	**ADHD:** Yes	needed and as available
Proctors: Yes	**Reading machine:** No	**How professors are notified of**
Oral exams: Yes	**Other assistive technology:** No	**LD/ADHD:** By both student and
Note-takers: Yes	**Priority registration:** No	director

GENERAL ADMISSIONS INFORMATION

Director of Admissions: James Diriso
Telephone: 716-375-2400

ENTRANCE REQUIREMENTS

19 total are recommended; 4 English required, 4 English recommended, 3 math required, 3 math recommended, 3 science required, 3 science recommended, 3 science lab recommended, 2 foreign language required, 2 foreign language recommended, 4 social studies required, 4 social studies recommended. High school diploma or GED required. Minimum TOEFL is 550. TOEFL required of all international applicants.

Application deadline: April 1	**Average SAT I Math:** 541	**Graduated top 10% of class:** 14%
Notification: Rolling beginning 10/1	**Average SAT I Verbal:** 537	**Graduated top 25% of class:** 42%
Average GPA: 3.2	**Average ACT:** 22	**Graduated top 50% of class:** 76%

COLLEGE GRADUATION REQUIREMENTS

Course waivers allowed: No
Course substitutions allowed: Yes
In what subjects: Math and foreign language

ADDITIONAL INFORMATION

Environment: The University is located on 600 acres in a rural area 70 miles southeast of Buffalo.

Student Body	Cost Information	Greek System
Undergrad enrollment: 2,202	**Tuition:** $13,888	**Fraternity:** Yes
Female: 54%	**Room & board:** $5,800	**Sorority:** Yes
Male: 46%	**Housing Information**	**Athletics:** NCAA Division I
Out-of-state: 26%	**University housing:** Yes	
	Percent living on campus: 76%	

St. Lawrence University

Payson Hall, Canton, NY 13617
Phone: 315-229-5261 • Fax: 315-229-5818
E-mail: admissions@stlaw.edu • Web: www.stlawu.edu
Support level: S • Institution type: 4-year private

LEARNING DISABILITY PROGRAM AND SERVICES

The Office of Special Needs provides services to members of the University who either have identified themselves or believe they may have some type of learning disability. The office has several purposes: to serve students who are learning-challenged by documented disabilities; to help students get the academic help that they need; to put students in touch with other people on campus who can help; to advise and counsel students; to educate everyone on campus about special needs. The office works with students in developing Individual Educational Accommodations Plans for the purpose of receiving reasonable accommodations in their educational and residential life concerns. The service will also make referrals and advocate at several on-campus services, and if necessary, connect with state or regional support agencies. There is a Writing Center for help with writing assignments; peer tutors, for general assistance with academic work; and a Counseling Center and Health Center.

LD/ADHD ADMISSIONS INFORMATION

College entrance tests required: Yes
Nonstandardized tests accepted: Yes
Interview required: No
Essay required: Yes
Documentation required for LD: Psychoeducational evaluation
Documentation required for ADHD: Yes
Documentation submitted to: Office of Special Needs
Special Ed. HS course work accepted: Yes

Specific course requirements for all applicants: Yes
Separate application required for services: No
# of LD applications submitted yearly: N/A
# of LD applications accepted yearly: N/A
Total # of students receiving LD/ADHD services: 130–141
Acceptance into program means acceptance into college: Students must be accepted and enrolled at the University first and then may request services.

ADMISSIONS

There is no special admissions process for students with learning disabilities. All applicants must meet the same admission criteria, which include recommended courses of 4 years English, 3 years math, 3 years science, 3 years foreign language, 3 years social studies; SAT/ACT with the average SAT being 1130; an interview is recommended and can be done off campus with an alumni representative.

ADDITIONAL INFORMATION

Students need to be self-starters (to seek out the service early and follow through). They need to share as soon as possible the official documents that describe the learning disability so that the office can help develop the Individual Educational Accommodation Plan (IEAP). As soon as possible, students need to notify the professors and people in various offices about the learning disability. The Director of Services sends a memo to each professor that describes the student's IEAP, discloses that the student is a documented and endorsed learning-challenged student on file with the Office of Special Needs, and lists the accommodations necessary for the student to be successful in the course. Services and accommodations are available for undergraduate and graduate students.

SUPPORT SERVICES CONTACT INFORMATION

Learning Disability Program/Services: Office of Special Needs
Director: John Meagher, Director
  E-mail: jmeagher@stlawu.edu
  Telephone: 315-229-5104
  Fax: 315-229-7415
Contact: Same

LEARNING DISABILITY SERVICES

Requests for the following services/accommodations will be evaluated individually based on appropriate and current documentation.

Allowed in Exams
  Calculator: Yes
  Dictionary: Yes
  Computer: Yes
  Spellchecker: Yes
Extended test time: Yes
Scribes: Yes
Proctors: Yes
Oral exams: Yes
Note-takers: Yes

Distraction-reduced environment: Yes
Tape recording in class: Yes
Books on tape from RFBD: Yes
Taping of books not from RFBD: No
**Accommodations for students with
  ADHD:** Yes
Reading machine: Yes
Other assistive technology: Yes
Priority registration: Yes

Added costs for services: No
LD specialists: No
Professional tutors: No
Peer tutors: 75
Max. hours/wk. for services:
  Unlimited
**How professors are notified of
  LD/ADHD:** By both student and
  director

GENERAL ADMISSIONS INFORMATION

Director of Admissions: Terry Gouodrey
Telephone: 315-229-8261

ENTRANCE REQUIREMENTS

20 total are recommended; 4 English recommended, 4 math recommended, 4 science recommended, 4 foreign language recommended, 2 social studies recommended, 2 history recommended. High school diploma or GED required. Minimum TOEFL is 600. TOEFL required of all international applicants.

Application deadline: February 15
Notification: Rolling beginning 3/30
Average GPA: 3.3

Average SAT I Math: 570
Average SAT I Verbal: 570
Average ACT: 24

Graduated top 10% of class: 26%
Graduated top 25% of class: 60%
Graduated top 50% of class: 91%

COLLEGE GRADUATION REQUIREMENTS

Course waivers allowed: No
Course substitutions allowed: No
In what subjects: N/A

ADDITIONAL INFORMATION

Environment: The University is located on 1,000 acres in a rural area 80 miles south of Ottawa, Canada.

Student Body
  Undergrad enrollment: 1,969
  Female: 53%
  Male: 47%
  Out-of-state: 43%

Cost Information
  Tuition: $23,795
  Room & board: $7,475
Housing Information
  University housing: Yes
  Percent living on campus: 94%

Greek System
  Fraternity: Yes
  Sorority: Yes
Athletics: NCAA Division III

ST. THOMAS AQUINAS COLLEGE

125 Route 340, Sparkill, NY 10976
Phone: 914-398-4100 • Fax: 914-398-4224
E-mail: joestacenroll@rockland.net • Web: www.stac.edu
Support level: SP • Institution type: 4-year private

LEARNING DISABILITY PROGRAM AND SERVICES

Students need to be self-starters, seeking out the service early and following through. They need to share as soon as possible the official documents that describe the learning disability so that the office can help develop the Individual Educational Accommodation Plan (IEAP). As soon as possible, students need to notify the professors and people in various offices about the learning disability. The Director of Services sends a memo to each professor that describes the student's IEAP, discloses that the student is a documented and endorsed learning-challenged student on file with the Office of Special Needs, and lists the accommodations necessary for the student to be successful in the course. Services and accommodations are available for undergraduate and graduate students.

LD/ADHD ADMISSIONS INFORMATION

College entrance tests required: Yes
Nonstandardized tests accepted: Yes
Interview required: Yes
Essay required: Yes
Documentation required for LD: Psychological report, including adult intelligence test (WAIS-III) and social/emotional functioning; educational evaluation (complete); IEP, if available
Documentation required for ADHD: Yes
Documentation submitted to: The STAC Exchange
Special Ed. HS course work accepted: Yes

Specific course requirements for all applicants: Yes
Separate application required for services: Yes
# of LD applications submitted yearly: 90–120
# of LD applications accepted yearly: 20–25
Total # of students receiving LD/ADHD services: 65–70
Acceptance into program means acceptance into college: Students are admitted to the College and then to STAC.

ADMISSIONS

The STAC Exchange has a separate application and admissions process from the College itself. Admission to the program is limited to those students the program feels it can effectively serve, and is therefore extremely competitive. Students must be accepted by the College before their STAC Exchange application is evaluated. (SAT or ACT scores are required for regular college admission.) The following must be submitted to the STAC Exchange: a completed STAC application; high school transcripts (college transcripts for transfers); a letter of recommendation from a teacher; most recent IEP if available; and a comprehensive diagnostic assessment indicating an LD/ADHD completed within the last three years. This diagnostic assessment must include an adult intelligence test (WAIS-III), measures of achievement, evaluation of social/emotional functioning, and the specific effects of the LD/ADHD on the student's current academic performance. Reports are required; scores on an IEP are insufficient documentation. Students must also have a personal interview with STAC Exchange staff to be admitted into the program. Transfer applications are accepted.

ADDITIONAL INFORMATION

STAC has a director, assistant director, and trained staff of mentors. Mentors are professionals with post-college education and experience in some aspect of teaching. The director and assistant director are "hands-on" administrators who also provide mentoring. Mentoring differs from traditional tutoring in that students come to sessions having already attended classes and prepared initial course work. STAC Exchange students are required to attend regularly scheduled sessions with their own mentor and are encouraged to "drop-in" for additional help as needed. Workshops/seminars on organization and time management, note-taking, test-taking, interview skills, resume writing, and self-advocacy are provided based on needs and interests. Study groups in specific areas are offered dependent upon student need and staff expertise. STAC Exchange students are also provided with academic counseling, course advisement, and priority registration. The required summer program for incoming STAC freshmen is designed to learn the specific needs of each student, to begin preparing them for academic rigors of higher education, and to build a sense of trust and community within the group. This summer program also integrates the first half of a three-credit academic course whose topic may vary from year to year.

SUPPORT SERVICES CONTACT INFORMATION

Learning Disability Program/Services: The STAC Exchange
Director: Dr. Richard Heath
  E-mail: rheath@stac.edu
  Telephone: 845-398-4230
  Fax: 845-398-4229
Contact: Same

LEARNING DISABILITY SERVICES

Requests for the following services/accommodations will be evaluated individually based on appropriate and current documentation.

Allowed in Exams
  Calculator: Yes
  Dictionary: Yes
  Computer: Yes
  Spellchecker: Yes
Extended test time: Yes
Scribes: Yes
Proctors: Yes
Oral exams: Yes
Note-takers: Yes

Distraction-reduced environment: Yes
Tape recording in class: Yes
Books on tape from RFBD: Yes
Taping of books not from RFBD: No
Accommodations for students with ADHD: Yes
Reading machine: No
Other assistive technology: Yes
Priority registration: Yes

Added costs for services: $3,300 per year
LD specialists: Yes
Professional tutors: 8
Peer tutors: No
Max. hours/wk. for services: Unlimited
How professors are notified of LD/ADHD: By student

GENERAL ADMISSIONS INFORMATION

Director of Admissions: Tracey Howard
Telephone: 845-398-4100

ENTRANCE REQUIREMENTS

17 total are required; 4 English required, 2 math required, 2 science required, 1 foreign language required, 1 history required, 7 elective required. High school diploma or GED required. Minimum TOEFL is 500. TOEFL required of all international applicants.

Application deadline: Rolling
Notification: Rolling
Average GPA: 2.8

Average SAT I Math: 490
Average SAT I Verbal: 510
Average ACT: NR

Graduated top 10% of class: 15%
Graduated top 25% of class: 48%
Graduated top 50% of class: 88%

COLLEGE GRADUATION REQUIREMENTS

Course waivers allowed: No
Course substitutions allowed: Yes
In what subjects: Foreign language; students must have detailed documentation and must substitute courses in culture

ADDITIONAL INFORMATION

Environment: The school is located on 43 acres in a suburban area 15 miles from New York City.

Student Body
  Undergrad enrollment: 2,038
  Female: 58%
  Male: 42%
  Out-of-state: 35%

Cost Information
  Tuition: $11,100
  Room & board: $6,910
Housing Information
  University housing: Yes
  Percent living on campus: 35%

Greek System
  Fraternity: Yes
  Sorority: Yes
  Athletics: NAIA

SUNY AT ALBANY

1400 Washington Avenue, Albany, NY 12222
Phone: 518-442-5435 • Fax: 518-442-5383
E-mail: ugadmissions@albany.edu • Web: www.albany.edu
Support level: CS • Institution type: 4-year public

LEARNING DISABILITY PROGRAM AND SERVICES

The mission at the University is to provide a quality educational program to students with dyslexia/learning disabilities. Learning Disabilities Resource Program is a division of Student Affairs that seeks to empower students with LD to become successful decision makers and problem solvers. It also promotes increased sensitivity to and appreciation for the uniqueness of students with LD. The goal is to provide general support for students as they attempt to gain access to services and accommodations necessary to their success. The program provides a writing center staffed by faculty, advocacy, assistance with recommended courses, tutoring assistance, and a willingness to explore innovative ways of providing the most efficient assistance possible. The Mentor Program provides extra academic assistance and support for students with LD/ADHD. The mentor is a graduate student with a distinguished academic record who is paired with the mentee. They meet twice weekly and develop problem solving techniques. The mentor does not function as a content tutor, but does provide oversight and supervision for academic course work. The cost for the Mentor Program is $675 per semester.

LD/ADHD ADMISSIONS INFORMATION

College entrance tests required: Yes
Nonstandardized tests accepted: Yes
Interview required: No
Essay required: No
Documentation required for LD: IEP; WAIS-III
Documentation required for ADHD: Yes
Documentation submitted to: LDRP
Special Ed. HS course work accepted: Depends on course

Specific course requirements for all applicants: Yes
Separate application required for services: No
# of LD applications submitted yearly: N/A
# of LD applications accepted yearly: N/A
Total # of students receiving LD/ADHD services: 145
Acceptance into program means acceptance into college: Students must be accepted and enrolled at the University first and then may request services.

ADMISSIONS

There is no special application for applicants with LD. Applicants who self-disclose may have their application files reviewed by the Director of the LDRP and the Office of Admissions. Letters of recommendation, auxiliary testing, and a personal interview are helpful. Students must present 18 units from high school acceptable to the University, a 950 SAT score, a high school average of at least 85 percent, and class rank in the top one-third.

ADDITIONAL INFORMATION

Services include: pre-admission review of the applicant's file in conjunction with admissions and individual counseling and advisement to applicants and their families; counseling and support; auxiliary aids and services such as testing accommodations, assistance in locating note-takers and tutors, reading services, and loan of tape recorders; information and referral to campus resources; and consultation and advocacy. Students diagnosed with ADHD who have documented LD may receive support from the LDRP or, in some cases, from the Office of Disabled Student Services.

SUPPORT SERVICES CONTACT INFORMATION

Learning Disability Program/Services: Learning Disabilities Resource Program (LDRP)
Director: Carolyn Malloch
  E-mail: cmalloch@ua.mail.albany.edu
  Telephone: 518-442-5491
Contact: Same

LEARNING DISABILITY SERVICES

Requests for the following services/accommodations will be evaluated individually based on appropriate and current documentation.

Allowed in Exams
  Calculator: Yes
  Dictionary: No
  Computer: Yes
  Spellchecker: Yes
Extended test time: Yes
Scribes: Yes
Proctors: Yes
Oral exams: Yes
Note-takers: Yes

Distraction-reduced environment: Yes
Tape recording in class: Yes
Books on tape from RFBD: Yes
Taping of books not from RFBD: Yes
Accommodations for students with ADHD: Yes
Reading machine: Yes
Other assistive technology: Yes
Priority registration: Yes

Added costs for services: $6 per hours for tutors; $675 per semester for mentor program
LD specialists: Yes
Professional tutors: Yes
Peer tutors: Yes
Max. hours/wk. for services: Unlimited
How professors are notified of LD/ADHD: By student and program director

GENERAL ADMISSIONS INFORMATION

Director of Admissions: Harry W. Wood
Telephone: 518-442-5435

ENTRANCE REQUIREMENTS
18 total are required; 4 English required, 2 math required, 4 math recommended, 2 science required, 3 science recommended, 2 science lab recommended, 3 foreign language recommended, 3 social studies required, 5 elective required. High school diploma or GED required. Minimum TOEFL is 550. TOEFL required of all international applicants.

Application deadline: March 1
Notification: Rolling beginning 1/1
Average GPA: 3.5

Average SAT I Math: 550
Average SAT I Verbal: 558
Average ACT: NR

Graduated top 10% of class: 15%
Graduated top 25% of class: 49%
Graduated top 50% of class: 90%

COLLEGE GRADUATION REQUIREMENTS

Course waivers allowed: No
Course substitutions allowed: Yes
In what subjects: Case-by-case

ADDITIONAL INFORMATION

Environment: The University has an urban campus on 515 acres located on the fringe of the state capital.

Student Body
  Undergrad enrollment: 11,780
  Female: 49%
  Male: 51%
  Out-of-state: 4%

Cost Information
  In-state tuition: $4,338
  Out-of-state tuition: $9,238
  Room & board: $5,828
Housing Information
  University housing: Yes
  Percent living on campus: 58%

Greek System
  Fraternity: Yes
  Sorority: Yes
Athletics: NCAA Division I

SUNY AT FARMINGDALE

Admissions, Route 110, Farmingdale, NY 11735
Phone: 631-420-2200 • Fax: 631-420-2633
E-mail: admissions@farmingdale.edu • Web: www.farmingdale.edu
Support level: CS • Institution type: 4-year public

LEARNING DISABILITY PROGRAM AND SERVICES

There is no learning disabilities program at the College, but the Office for Students with Disabilities is dedicated to the principle that equal opportunity to realize one's full potential should be available to all students. In keeping with this philosophy, the staff offers individualized services to students with disabilities in accordance with their needs. Students may meet individually with a learning disability specialist or in group meetings. Services include academic remediation with emphasis on compensatory strategies; study skills strategies training; test accommodations; time management instruction; tutoring; and self-understanding of disability. The services offered strive to instill independence, self-confidence, and self-advocacy skills.

LD/ADHD ADMISSIONS INFORMATION

College entrance tests required: Recommended
Nonstandardized tests accepted: Yes
Interview required: No
Essay required: No
Documentation required for LD: WAIS-III; WJ
Documentation required for ADHD: Yes
Submitted to: Support Services for Students with Disabilities
Special Ed. HS course work accepted: Yes

Specific course requirements for all applicants: Yes
Separate application required for services: No
# of LD applications submitted yearly: N/A
# of LD applications accepted yearly: N/A
Total # of students receiving LD/ADHD services: 115–135
Acceptance into program means acceptance into college: Students must be admitted and enrolled at the University first (they can appeal a denial) and then may request services.

ADMISSIONS

There is no special admissions procedure for applicants with learning disabilities. Pre-college Pathways Program has more flexible entrance requirements. Elementary algebra is the minimum requirement in math. Students should self-identify on the application. Admission decisions are made by the Office of Admission. Students should submit psychoeducational reports and letters of recommendation and request a personal interview. Students are required to take the SAT/ACT. The University has "rolling admissions." Almost all of the programs accept students throughout the year.

ADDITIONAL INFORMATION

The University would like the high school Individualized Educational Plan (IEP) and the WAIS-R to help identify the services necessary to help the student to be successful. Services and accommodations available with appropriate documentation include extended testing time; distraction-free environment; calculator, computer, spellcheck, or dictionary in exams; note-takers; scribes; proctors; assistive technology; professional tutors; tape recording in class; and students are responsible for arranging for accommodations with professors.

SUPPORT SERVICES CONTACT INFORMATION

Learning Disability Program/Services: Support Services for Students with Disabilities
Director: Malka Edelman
  E-mail: edelmanp@farmingdale.edu
  Telephone: 631-420-2411
  Fax: 631-420-2163
Contact: Same

LEARNING DISABILITY SERVICES

Requests for the following services/accommodations will be evaluated individually based on appropriate and current documentation.

Allowed in Exams
  Calculator: Yes
  Dictionary: Yes
  Computer: Yes
  Spellchecker: Yes
Extended test time: Yes
Scribes: Yes
Proctors: Yes
Oral exams: Yes
Notetakers: Yes

Distraction-reduced environment: Yes
Tape recording in class: Yes
Books on tape from RFBD: No
Taping of books not from RFBD: No
Accommodations for students with ADHD: Yes
Reading machine: Yes
Other assistive technology: Yes
Priority registration: No

Added costs for services: No
LD specialists: 1
Professional tutors: Yes
Peer tutors: Yes
Max. hours/wk. for services: Unlimited
How professors are notified of LD/ADHD: By student

GENERAL ADMISSIONS INFORMATION

Director of Admissions: Kathreen Fitzwilliam
Telephone: 631-420-2411

ENTRANCE REQUIREMENTS
TOEFL required of all international applicants. Minimum TOEFL 500. Interviews for all applicants to advertising, art and design, or visual communications. High school diploma or GED required. ACT/SAT recommended.

Application deadline: Rolling
Notification: Rolling
Average GPA: NR

Average SAT I Math: 460
Average SAT I Verbal: 445
Average ACT: NR

Graduated top 10% of class: NR
Graduated top 25% of class: NR
Graduated top 50% of class: NR

COLLEGE GRADUATION REQUIREMENTS

Course waivers allowed:
Course substitutions allowed: Yes
In what subjects: Foreign language or math

ADDITIONAL INFORMATION

Environment: Farmingdale is a small town within easy access to New York City.

Student Body
  Undergrad enrollment: 5,800
  Female: 47%
  Male: 53%
  Out-of-state: 2%

Cost Information
  In-state tuition: $4,095
  Out-of-state tuition: $8,995
  Room & board: $6,114
Housing Information
  University housing: Yes
  Percent living on campus: 10%

Greek System
  Fraternity: Yes
  Sorority: Yes
Athletics: NCAA Division III

SUNY AT STONY BROOK

Office of Admissions, Stony Brook, NY 11794-1901
Phone: 631-632-6868 • Fax: 631-632-9898
E-mail: ugadmissions@notes.cc.sunysb.edu • Web: www.sunysb.edu
Support level: CS • Institution type: 4-year public

LEARNING DISABILITY PROGRAM AND SERVICES

Disability Support Services (DSS) coordinates advocacy and support services for students with disabilities. These services assist integrating students' needs with the resources available at the University to eliminate physical or programmatic barriers and to ensure an accessible academic environment. All information and documentation of student disabilities is confidential. Students are responsible for identifying and documenting their disabilities through the DSS office. Students receive assistance with special housing and transportation, recruitment of readers, interpreters, note-takers, test accommodations and counseling. A learning disabilities specialist is available for referral for diagnostic testing and educational programming, to meet accommodation needs, and to provide in-service training to the University community. A Supported Education Program offering individual counseling and group sessions is available for students with psychological disabilities. Students who anticipate requiring assistance should contact Disability Support Services as early as possible to allow time for implementing recommended services.

LD/ADHD ADMISSIONS INFORMATION

College entrance tests required: Yes
Nonstandardized tests accepted: Yes
Interview required: No
Essay required: No
Documentation required for LD: Psychoeducational evaluation: within 3 years
Documentation required for ADHD: Yes
Documentation submitted to: Disability Support Services
Special Ed. HS course work accepted: No

Specific course requirements for all applicants: Yes
Separate application required for services: No
# of LD applications submitted yearly: N/A
# of LD applications accepted yearly: N/A
Total # of students receiving LD/ADHD services: 125
Acceptance into program means acceptance into college: Students must be admitted and enrolled at the University first and then may request services.

ADMISSIONS

Admission decisions are based on grades, GPA and/or class rank and ACT/SAT. There is no separate or special admission because there are no developmental or remedial classes. However, each applicant who is identified as having a disability is given the special consideration of being reviewed by an Admissions counselor and a DSS staff member jointly. All special circumstances are taken into consideration. Students are encouraged to self-disclose the disability in the application process. The director of Disabilities Services will review documentation from students with learning disabilities and provide a recommendation to the Office of Admission.

ADDITIONAL INFORMATION

Types of services and accommodations available are: pre-registration advisement; liaison with faculty and staff; taped texts; learning strategies and time management training; assistance in locating tutors; assistance in arranging for note-takers and/or readers; tutorial computer programs; proctoring and/or modified administration of exams; support group; referral to appropriate campus resources; peer advising; and aid in vocational decision making. Services and accommodations are available to undergraduate and graduate students. No skills classes are offered.

SUPPORT SERVICES CONTACT INFORMATION

Learning Disability Program/Services: Disabilities Support Services
Director: Joanna Harris
  E-mail: j.jharris@notes.cc.sunysb.edu
  Telephone: 631-632-6748
  Fax: 631-632-6747
Contact: Same

LEARNING DISABILITY SERVICES

Requests for the following services/accommodations will be evaluated individually based on appropriate and current documentation.

Allowed in Exams
  Calculator: Yes
  Dictionary: Yes
  Computer: Yes
  Spellchecker: Yes
Extended test time: Yes
Scribes: Yes
Proctors: Yes
Oral exams: No
Note-takers: Yes

Distraction-reduced environment: Yes
Tape recording in class: Yes
Books on tape from RFBD: Yes
Taping of books not from RFBD: No
Accommodations for students with ADHD: Yes
Reading machine: Yes
Other assistive technology: Yes
Priority registration: Yes

Added costs for services: Tutoring fee
LD specialists: Yes (1)
Professional tutors: No
Peer tutors: 20
Max. hours/wk. for services: 2 hours per week
How professors are notified of LD/ADHD: By both student and director

GENERAL ADMISSIONS INFORMATION

Director of Admissions: Gigi Lemmens
Telephone: 631-689-6000

ENTRANCE REQUIREMENTS
14 total are required; 19 total are recommended; 4 English required, 4 English recommended, 3 math required, 4 math recommended, 3 science required, 4 science recommended, 3 foreign language recommended, 4 social studies required, 4 social studies recommended. High school diploma or GED required. Minimum TOEFL is 550. TOEFL required of all international applicants.

Application deadline: July 10
Notification: Rolling beginning 1/15
Average GPA: 3.2

Average SAT I Math: 588
Average SAT I Verbal: 545
Average ACT: 21

Graduated top 10% of class: 25%
Graduated top 25% of class: 63%
Graduated top 50% of class: 98%

COLLEGE GRADUATION REQUIREMENTS

Course waivers allowed: No
Course substitutions allowed: Yes
In what subjects: Math and foreign language

ADDITIONAL INFORMATION

Environment: The University is located on 1,100 acres in a suburban area on Long Island, 60 miles from New York City.

Student Body
  Undergrad enrollment: 13,257
  Female: 49%
  Male: 51%
  Out-of-state: 2%

Cost Information
  In-state tuition: $3,400
  Out-of-state tuition: $8,300
  Room & board: $6,524
Housing Information
  University housing: Yes
  Percent living on campus: 48%

Greek System
  Fraternity: Yes
  Sorority: Yes
  Athletics: NCAA Division I

SUNY COLLEGE AT POTSDAM

44 Pierrepont Avenue, Potsdam, NY 13676
Phone: 315-267-2180 • Fax: 315-267-2163
E-mail: admissions@potsdam.edu • Web: www.potsdam.edu
Support level: S • Institution type: 4-year public

LEARNING DISABILITY PROGRAM AND SERVICES

The State University of New York College at Potsdam is committed to the full inclusion of al individuals who can benefit from educational opportunities. Accommodative Services provides academic accommodations for all qualified students who have documented learning, emotional, and/or physical disabilities and need for accommodation. The ultimate goal is to promote individuals' independence within the academic atmosphere of the University. Students are assisted in this process by the support services and programs available to all Potsdam students. Students must submit (written) documentation of the disability and the need for accommodations. After forwarding documentation, students are encouraged to make an appointment to meet with the coordinator to discuss accommodations. All accommodations are determined on an individual basis. Accommodative Services makes every effort to ensure access to academic accommodations.

LD/ADHD ADMISSIONS INFORMATION

College entrance tests required: Yes
Nonstandardized tests accepted: Yes
Interview required: N/A
Essay required: No
Documentation required for LD: Comprehensive assessment by a licensed professional
Documentation required for ADHD: Yes
Documentation submitted to: Accommodative Services
Special Ed. HS course work accepted: No

Specific course requirements for all applicants: Yes
Separate application required for services: No
# of LD applications submitted yearly: N/A
# of LD applications accepted yearly: N/A
Total # of students receiving LD/ADHD services: 45–50
Acceptance into program means acceptance into college: Students must be admitted and enrolled at the University and then may request services.

ADMISSIONS

Students with learning disabilities must meet the same admission criteria as all applicants to the University. General admissions include an ACT of 20+ or SAT I of 960, 80 percent GPA, and 17 core courses including 3 years math, 2 years science, 4 years social studies, 4 years English, 3 years foreign language, and 1 year fine or performing arts. There is no conditional or probational admission plan. Students are encouraged to self-disclose the disability and provide appropriate documentation to Accommodative Services.

ADDITIONAL INFORMATION

Accommodations available through Accommodative Services include note-takers; test readers/books on tape; alternative testing such as extended time and/or distraction-reduced environment, exam readers/scribes, and word processor with spellcheck; loan of some equipment; additional services can include special registration and academic advising. Accommodative Services will assist students requesting nonacademic auxiliary aids or services in locating the appropriate campus resources to address the request. The College Counseling Center provides psychological services. The Early Warning System asks each instructor to indicate at midpoint in each semester if a student is making unsatisfactory academic progress. Results of this inquiry are sent to the student and advisor. Student Support Services provides academic support, peer mentoring, and counseling. Tutoring is available for all students on one-to-one or small group basis.

SUPPORT SERVICES CONTACT INFORMATION

Learning Disability Program/Services: Accommodative Services
Director: Sharon House
  E-mail: housese@potsdam.edu
  Telephone: 315-267-3267
  Fax: 315-267-3268
Contact: Same

LEARNING DISABILITY SERVICES

Requests for the following services/accommodations will be evaluated individually based on appropriate and current documentation.

Allowed in Exams
  Calculator: Yes
  Dictionary: Yes
  Computer: Yes
  Spellchecker: Yes
Extended test time: Yes
Scribes: Yes
Proctors: Yes
Oral exams: Yes
Note-takers: Yes

Distraction-reduced environment: Yes
Tape recording in class: Yes
Books on tape from RFBD: Yes
Taping of books not from RFBD: Yes
Accommodations for students with
  ADHD: Yes
Reading machine: Yes
Other assistive technology: Yes
Priority registration: Yes

Added costs for services: No
LD specialists: No
Professional tutors: No
Peer tutors: 180
Max. hours/wk. for services: 3
How professors are notified of
  LD/ADHD: By student

GENERAL ADMISSIONS INFORMATION

Director of Admissions: Thomas Nesbitt
Telephone: 315-267-2180

ENTRANCE REQUIREMENTS
18 total are required; 22 total are recommended; 4 English required, 4 English recommended, 3 math required, 4 math recommended, 2 science required, 3 science recommended, 1 science lab required, 2 science lab recommended, 3 foreign language required, 4 foreign language recommended, 4 social studies required, 4 social studies recommended. High school diploma or GED required. Minimum TOEFL is 520. TOEFL required of all international applicants.

Application deadline: Open
Notification: Rolling beginning 10/1
Average GPA: 3.2

Average SAT I Math: 531
Average SAT I Verbal: 537
Average ACT: 23

Graduated top 10% of class: 11%
Graduated top 25% of class: 33%
Graduated top 50% of class: 72%

COLLEGE GRADUATION REQUIREMENTS

Course waivers allowed: No
Course substitutions allowed: Yes
In what subjects: Substitution determined on a case-by-case basis

ADDITIONAL INFORMATION

Environment: The University is located on 240 acres in a rural area.

Student Body
  Undergrad enrollment: 3,580
  Female: 60%
  Male: 40%
  Out-of-state: 3%

Cost Information
  In-state tuition: $3,400
  Out-of-state tuition: $8,300
  Room & board: $6,100
Housing Information
  University housing: Yes
  Percent living on campus: 50%

Greek System
  Fraternity: No
  Sorority: No
  Athletics: NCAA Division III

SUNY COLLEGE OF TECH. AT ALFRED

Huntington Administration Bldg., Alfred, NY 14802
Phone: 800-425-3733 • Fax: 607-587-4299
E-mail: admissions@alfredstate.edu • Web: www.alfredstate.edu
Support level: S • Institution type: 2-year public

LEARNING DISABILITY PROGRAM AND SERVICES

The goal of the Office of Services for Students with Disabilities (SSD) is to ensure that students with disabilities, with appropriate documentation, have equal access to programs, activities, and services offered to other students. Once students present appropriate documentation, services are provided depending on individual needs. The Student Development Center has team of dedicated professionals committed to fostering personal and academic growth of all students. The centralized nature of the center allows for an important link among college supportive services dedicated to maximizing student growth and student success. The Alfred State Opportunity Program (ASOP) is a special admissions program designed to improve the student's opportunity to be academically successful. Reduced course loads and college-preparatory developmental courses assist students in meeting curricular prerequisites. Students should contact Learning Assistance and must provide adequate documentation before accommodations/services will be provided. The Services for Students with Disabilities counselor determines the extent of services provided.

LD/ADHD ADMISSIONS INFORMATION

College entrance tests required: No
Nonstandardized tests accepted: Yes
Interview required: No
Essay required: No
Documentation required for LD: Psychoeducational evaluation
Documentation required for ADHD: Yes
Documentation submitted to: SSD
Special Ed. HS course work accepted: Yes

Specific course requirements for all applicants: No
Separate application required for services: No
# of LD applications submitted yearly: N/A
# of LD applications accepted yearly: N/A
Total # of students receiving LD/ADHD services: 222
Acceptance into program means acceptance into college: Students must be admitted and enrolled at the College and then may request services.

ADMISSIONS

There is no special admission process for students with learning disabilities. All applicants must meet the same admission criteria. The minimum core courses that are preferred include 4 years English, 3 years math, 3 years science, 3 years social science, 2 years foreign language, and 1 year art. The minimum GPA is 74 percent. ASOP allows students to take three years to complete a two-year program.

ADDITIONAL INFORMATION

Services available through SSD include individual academic skills development; note-takers and scribes; readers; peer tutors; taped texts; testing accommodations; extended curricular programs; referral to other offices and agencies; specialized equipment loan; advocacy; and registration. ASOP provides counseling, extensive advising, and tutoring. Peer and professional tutors are available by appointment and provide course-specific assistance such as answers to questions, clarification of information, and drill and/or review for exams. Academic Skills Assistance for reading improvement, student success, and study skills can be provided through individual appointments, small group seminars, classroom instruction, or computer tutorials.

SUPPORT SERVICES CONTACT INFORMATION

Learning Disability Program/Services: Services for Students with Disabilities (SSD)
Director: Jeanne Mead
   Telephone: 607-587-3112
Contact: Same

LEARNING DISABILITY SERVICES

Requests for the following services/accommodations will be evaluated individually based on appropriate and current documentation.

Allowed in Exams
   Calculator: Yes
   Dictionary: Yes
   Computer: Yes
   Spellchecker: Yes
Extended test time: Yes
Scribes: Yes
Proctors: Yes
Oral exams: Yes
Note-takers: Yes

Distraction-reduced environment: Yes
Tape recording in class: Yes
Books on tape from RFBD: Yes
Taping of books not from RFBD: Yes
Accommodations for students with ADHD: Yes
Reading machine: Yes
Other assistive technology: Yes
Priority registration: Yes

Added costs for services: No
LD specialists: No
Professional tutors: Yes (1)
Peer tutors: 75
Max. hours/wk. for services: Unlimited
How professors are notified of LD/ADHD: SSD Counselors

GENERAL ADMISSIONS INFORMATION

Director of Admissions: Debra Goodrich
Telephone: 607-587-5111

ENTRANCE REQUIREMENTS
4 English recommended, 4 math recommended, 4 science recommended, 4 social studies recommended. Minimum TOEFL is 500. TOEFL required of all international applicants.

Application deadline: Rolling
Notification: Rolling beginning 11/1
Average GPA: 2.5

Average SAT I Math: 470
Average SAT I Verbal: 470
Average ACT: 19

Graduated top 10% of class: NR
Graduated top 25% of class: NR
Graduated top 50% of class: NR

COLLEGE GRADUATION REQUIREMENTS

Course waivers allowed: No
Course substitutions allowed: Yes
In what subjects: Math

ADDITIONAL INFORMATION

Environment: The University has a rural campus.

Student Body
   Undergrad enrollment: 2,733
   Female: 31%
   Male: 69%
   Out-of-state: 4%

Cost Information
   In-state tuition: $3,400
   Out-of-state tuition: $8,300
   Room & board: $5,668
Housing Information
   University housing: Yes
   Percent living on campus: 65%

Greek System
   Fraternity: Yes
   Sorority: Yes
Athletics: NCAA Division III

SUNY COLLEGE OF TECH. AT CANTON

French Hall, SUNY Canton, Canton, NY 13617
Phone: 315-386-7123 • Fax: 315-386-7929
E-mail: admissions@canton.edu • Web: www.canton.edu
Support level: S • Institution type: 2-year public

LEARNING DISABILITY PROGRAM AND SERVICES

At the State University of New York at Canton, College of Technology, the Accommodative Services Program is equipped to help students with learning disabilities make a smooth transition to college, and receive the necessary accommodations to ensure their academic success. The mission of the Office of Accommodative Services is to create a comprehensively accessible environment where individuals are viewed on the basis of ability, not disability. This supports the mission of SUNY Canton, a technical college offering two- and four-year degrees to a diverse student body. Prospective students are welcome to contact the Accommodative Services office with any questions. Although students with learning disabilities may register at the office at any time during their stay at SUNY Canton, they are encouraged to do so as early as possible. Students must register at the office in order to obtain the special resources and services. It is the students' responsibility to self-disclose, provide appropriate documentation, and request accommodations.

LD/ADHD ADMISSIONS INFORMATION

College entrance tests required: No
Nonstandardized tests accepted: Yes
Interview required: Preferred
Essay required: No
Documentation required for LD: A current (three years) IEP and a psychological evaluation
Documentation required for ADHD: Yes
Documentation submitted to: Accommodative Services
Special Ed. HS course work accepted: No

Specific course requirements for all applicants: Yes
Separate application required for services: No
# of LD applications submitted yearly: N/A
# of LD applications accepted yearly: N/A
Total # of students receiving LD/ADHD services: 77
Acceptance into program means acceptance into college: Students must be admitted and enrolled at the University first and then may request services.

ADMISSIONS

All students follow the same admissions procedure and are evaluated similarly for specific course placement. The Office of Accommodative Services is not directly involved in the admission process, but will usually meet with students (and families) during admission interviews. There are no specific course requirements as the requirements vary per curriculum, and foreign language is not required for admission. All students must have a high school diploma or the GED equivalent. No ACT/SAT tests are required for admission. Compass Tests are used for placement.

ADDITIONAL INFORMATION

A number of support services are offered on campus: Academic Advisement; Academic Computing Center; Canton Special Services Program; Counseling Center; Educational Opportunity Program; Learning Center; Math Lab; Writing Center; Tutoring; Science Learning Center. Services or accommodations could include testing accommodations; scribes, proctors; note-takers; books on tape; assistive technology; calculator, dictionary, computer or spellcheck in exams; distraction-free environment for tests; and priority registration. Acceptance into the University ensures that students will receive the services they request when they provide appropriate documentation.

SUPPORT SERVICES CONTACT INFORMATION

Learning Disability Program/Services: Accommodative Services (AS)
Director: Joel Bixby
　Telephone: 315-386-7392
　Fax: 315-379-3816
Contact: Veigh Mehan Lee
　E-mail: leev@canton.edu
　Telephone: 315-386-7392
　Fax: 315-379-3816

LEARNING DISABILITY SERVICES

Requests for the following services/accommodations will be evaluated individually based on appropriate and current documentation.

Allowed in Exams
　Calculator: Yes
　Dictionary: Yes
　Computer: Yes
　Spellchecker: Yes
Extended test time: Yes
Scribes: Yes
Proctors: Yes
Oral exams: Yes
Note-takers: Yes

Distraction-reduced environment: Yes
Tape recording in class: Yes
Books on tape from RFBD: Yes
Taping of books not from RFBD: Yes
Accommodations for students with ADHD: Yes
Reading machine: Yes
Other assistive technology: Yes
Priority registration: Yes

Added costs for services: No
LD specialists: No
Professional tutors: 12–25
Peer tutors: 12
Max. hours/wk. for services: As-needed basis
How professors are notified of LD/ADHD: By both student and director

GENERAL ADMISSIONS INFORMATION

Director of Admissions: David Gerlach
Telephone: 315-386-7123

ENTRANCE REQUIREMENTS
2 math recommended, 2 science recommended. High school diploma or GED required. Minimum TOEFL is 550. TOEFL required of all international applicants.

Application deadline: Rolling
Notification: Rolling beginning 12/1
Average GPA: N/A

Average SAT I Math: N/A
Average SAT I Verbal: N/A
Average ACT: N/A

Graduated top 10% of class: N/A
Graduated top 25% of class: N/A
Graduated top 50% of class: N/A

COLLEGE GRADUATION REQUIREMENTS

Course waivers allowed: No
Course substitutions allowed: Yes
In what subjects: Upon approval by dean's office; must satisfy graduation requirement

ADDITIONAL INFORMATION

Environment: The 550-acre campus is 135 miles northeast of Syracuse.

Student Body
　Undergrad enrollment: 2,260
　Female: 48%
　Male: 52%
　Out-of-state: 3%

Cost Information
　In-state tuition: $3,200
　Out-of-state tuition: $5,000
　Room & board: $5,510
　Housing Information
　　University housing: Yes
　　Percent living on campus: 43%

Greek System
　Fraternity: Yes
　Sorority: Yes
　Athletics: NAIA

SUNY College of Tech. at Delhi

Bush Hall, 2 Main St., Delhi, NY 13753
Phone: 607-746-4550 • Fax: 607-746-4104
E-mail: enroll@Delhi.edu • Web: www.delhi.edu
Support level: CS • Institution type: 2-year public

LEARNING DISABILITY PROGRAM AND SERVICES

SUNY-Delhi provides students with learning disabilities with academic support services and equipment, including professional tutors; exams in a distraction-free environment; submission of exams on tape or dictating exams to an attendant; remedial courses in reading, math, English, and study skills; and enlarged video display computer terminals. The coordinator of services often confers with students regarding their unique learning, study, and time management needs.

LD/ADHD ADMISSIONS INFORMATION

College entrance tests required: Yes
Nonstandardized tests accepted: Yes
Interview required: No
Essay required: No
Documentation required for LD: Psychoeducational evaluation within three years of admission and using adult standards (norms); IQ, achievement required
Documentation required for ADHD: Yes
Documentation submitted to: Center for Academic Services
Special Ed. HS course work accepted: Yes

Specific course requirements for all applicants: Yes
Separate application required for services: No
# of LD applications submitted yearly: N/A
# of LD applications accepted yearly: N/A
Total # of students receiving LD/ADHD services: No
Acceptance into program means acceptance into college: Students must be admitted and enrolled at the College and then may request services.

ADMISSIONS

The admission requirements are the same for all students. It is always helpful if students with learning disabilities present themselves as confident, independent, goal-oriented, and self-directed learners. The minimum GPA is 2.0 and course requirements depend on the major. Courses taken in special education may be considered. Students are encouraged to self-disclose the disability in a personal statement. Admission couselors will refer students to the coordinator if the student provides information about a disability. To be eligible for services students must disclose information about their learning disability/attention deficit disorder and meet with the coordinator of Services for Students with Disabilities. ASSET scores are used for placement within courses.

ADDITIONAL INFORMATION

The coordinator of services for students with learning disabilities is available to answer any questions regarding academic and nonacademic matters. The coordinator also serves as a campus referral service. There is a Writing Lab, Tutoring Lab, and Computer Lab available for all students. Skills classes are offered in test-taking strategies, time management, and study skills. Services and accommodations available with appropriate documentation include extended testing time for exams; distraction-free environments; calculator, dictionary, computer and spellcheck in exams; scibes; proctors; note-takers; books on tape; assistive technology; and course substituions for math or foreign language may be available in the Liberal Arts Program.

SUPPORT SERVICES CONTACT INFORMATION

Learning Disability Program/Services: The Center for Academic Services
Director: George E. Irwin, Coordinator
   E-mail: irwinge@delhi.edu
   Telephone: 607-746-4593
   Fax: 607-746-4368
Contact: Same

LEARNING DISABILITY SERVICES

Requests for the following services/accommodations will be evaluated individually based on appropriate and current documentation.

Allowed in Exams
   Calculator: Yes
   Dictionary: Yes
   Computer: Yes
   Spellchecker: Yes
Extended test time: Yes
Scribes: Yes
Proctors: Yes
Oral exams: Yes
Note-takers: Yes

Distraction-reduced environment: Yes
Tape recording in class: Yes
Books on tape from RFBD: Yes
Taping of books not from RFBD: No
**Accommodations for students with
   ADHD:** No
Reading machine: Yes
Other assistive technology: Yes
Priority registration: No

Added costs for services: No
LD specialists: Yes (1)
Professional tutors: 4
Peer tutors: 10
Max. hours/wk. for services: 2
**How professors are notified of
   LD/ADHD:** By student

GENERAL ADMISSIONS INFORMATION

Director of Admissions: Lawrence Barratt
Telephone: 607-746-4550

ENTRANCE REQUIREMENTS
4 English required, 1 math required, 2 math recommended, 1 science required, 2 science recommended, 1 science lab recommended, 3 social studies required, 1 history required. High school diploma or GED required.

Application deadline: Rolling
Notification: Rolling beginning 11/1
Average GPA: N/A

Average SAT I Math: N/A
Average SAT I Verbal: N/A
Average ACT: N/A

Graduated top 10% of class: N/A
Graduated top 25% of class: N/A
Graduated top 50% of class: N/A

COLLEGE GRADUATION REQUIREMENTS

Course waivers allowed: Yes
Course substitutions allowed: Yes
In what subjects: In liberal arts programs only

ADDITIONAL INFORMATION

Environment: The University is on 1,100 acres in a small town in upstate New York.

Student Body
   Undergrad enrollment: 1,893
   Female: 45%
   Male: 55%
   Out-of-state: 4%

Cost Information
   In-state tuition: $3,200
   Out-of-state tuition: $5,500
   Room & board: $5,320
Housing Information
   University housing: Yes
   Percent living on campus: 70%

Greek System
   Fraternity: Yes
   Sorority: Yes
Athletics: NCAA Division III

SYRACUSE UNIVERSITY

201 Tolley, Administration Building, Syracuse, NY 13244
Phone: 315-443-3611
E-mail: orange@syr.edu • Web: www.syracuse.edu
Support level: CS • Institution type: 4-year private

LEARNING DISABILITY PROGRAM AND SERVICES

The Office of Disability Services provides an integrated network of academic support, counseling, and advising services to meet the individual needs of students with diagnosed learning disabilities. Every student with learning disabilities who is accepted to the University is eligible for services, and must provide diagnostic information from which appropriate academic accommodations are determined. The staff is very supportive and sensitive to the needs of the students. Services are provided by a professional staff who sincerely care about the needs of every student. The program enables students to develop a sense of independence as they learn to advocate for themselves and become involved in their college education.

LD/ADHD ADMISSIONS INFORMATION

College entrance tests required: Yes
Nonstandardized tests accepted: Yes
Interview required: Yes
Essay required: Yes
Documentation required for LD: Psychoeducational
  evaluation
Documentation required for ADHD: Yes
Documentation submitted to: Office of Disability Services
Special Ed. HS course work accepted: No

Specific course requirements for all applicants: Yes
Separate application required for services: No
# of LD applications submitted yearly: N/A
# of LD applications accepted yearly: N/A
Total # of students receiving LD/ADHD services: 450
Acceptance into program means acceptance into
  college: Students must be admitted and enrolled at the
  University first and then may request services.

ADMISSIONS

All students must meet regular admission standards and submit the general application form. General admission criteria include 4 years English, 3–4 years math, 3–4 years science, 3–4 years social studies, 2 years foreign language; 25 ACT or 1100+ SAT I; B average or 80 percent or 3.0 GPA. Admissions does not factor disability issues into the admissions process. Students should not disclose information about a disability to Admissions, and no information or personal statement relating to the disability should be disclosed during the admission process. The Office of Disability Services should be contacted after a student is accepted to the University. Students' grades should show an upward trend. In the event that an applicant is denied admission to a specific course of study, an alternative offer may be suggested.

ADDITIONAL INFORMATION

Students with identified learning disabilities are provided with an integrated network of academic and counseling services to meet their individual needs. Services include note-takers, proofreaders, readers for exams and textbooks, and tutors. Accommodations include time extensions for exams, papers, or projects; alternative testing methods; and spelling waivers. The Office of Disability Services provides each student with an Accommodation letter to be used when the students meet with instructors to verify their LD status. To take advantage of these support services, diagnosed students must submit recent documentation of their learning disability. Summer Starts is a program lasting six weeks that is designed to enrich academic experience and ensure a smooth transition from high school to college with academic advising, orientation, tutoring, and career planning and counseling. Contact Joann May at 315-443-3867 or jamay@syr.edu. Services are offered to undergraduate and graduate students.

SUPPORT SERVICES CONTACT INFORMATION

Learning Disability Program/Services: Office of Disability Services
Director: Diana Darris
  E-mail: ddarris@syr.edu
  Telephone: 315-443-4498
  Fax: 315-443-1312
Contact: Same

LEARNING DISABILITY SERVICES

Requests for the following services/accommodations will be evaluated individually based on appropriate and current documentation.

Allowed in Exams
  Calculator: Yes
  Dictionary: Y/N
  Computer: Yes
  Spellchecker: Yes
Extended test time: Yes
Scribes: Yes
Proctors: Yes
Oral exams: Yes
Note-takers: Yes

Distraction-reduced environment: Yes
Tape recording in class: Yes
Books on tape from RFBD: Yes
Taping of books not from RFBD: Yes
Accommodations for students with ADHD: Yes
Reading machine: Yes
Other assistive technology: Yes
Priority registration: Yes

Added costs for services: 15–20 hours per semester are free, $8.60 per hour thereafter
LD specialists: Yes (1)
Professional tutors: Yes
Peer tutors: Yes
Max. hours/wk. for services: 20 hours per week for freshmen and sophomores; 18 hours per week for juniors and seniors
How professors are notified of LD/ADHD: By student

GENERAL ADMISSIONS INFORMATION

Director of Admissions: Susan Donovan
Telephone: 315-443-3611

ENTRANCE REQUIREMENTS
20 total are required; 21 total are recommended; 4 English required, 4 English recommended, 3 math required, 3 math recommended, 3 science required, 3 science recommended, 3 science lab required, 3 science lab recommended, 2 foreign language required, 3 foreign language recommended, 3 social studies required, 3 social studies recommended, 5 elective required, 5 elective recommended. High school diploma or GED required. Minimum TOEFL is 550. TOEFL required of all international applicants.

Application deadline: January 15
Notification: March
Average GPA: 3.5
Average SAT I Math: 610
Average SAT I Verbal: 590
Average ACT: NR
Graduated top 10% of class: 40%
Graduated top 25% of class: 77%
Graduated top 50% of class: 98%

COLLEGE GRADUATION REQUIREMENTS

Course waivers allowed: No
Course substitutions allowed: Yes
In what subjects: Students can petition for substitutions in math and foreign language. Substitutions must be approved by each College's academic committee. Documentation that recommends this as an accommodation must be on file in the Office of Disability Services.

ADDITIONAL INFORMATION

Environment: The school is located on 200 acres set on a hill overlooking the city of Syracuse.

Student Body
  Undergrad enrollment: 10,740
  Female: 54%
  Male: 46%
  Out-of-state: 53%

Cost Information
  Tuition: $21,500
  Room & board: $9,130
Housing Information
  University housing: Yes
  Percent living on campus: 72%

Greek System
  Fraternity: Yes
  Sorority: Yes
Athletics: NCAA Division I

UTICA COLLEGE OF SYRACUSE UNIV.

1600 Burrstone Road, Utica, NY 13502-4892
Phone: 315-792-3006 • Fax: 315-792-3003
E-mail: admiss@utica.ucsu.edu • Web: www.utica.edu
Support level: CS • Institution type: 4-year private

LEARNING DISABILITY PROGRAM AND SERVICES

Utica College is dedicated to ensuring reasonable access to programs and continuously seeks to augment and improve its services. The Academic Support Services Center provides counseling and academic support to an increasing number of students who identify themselves as LD. Accommodations are determined as a result of a diagnostic evaluation. Students are responsible for initiating a request for accommodations; for verification of a disability; and for contacting the support office as early as possible upon admission. The coordinator of student services determines eligibility for services based on documentation; consults with students about appropriate accommodations; assists students in self-monitoring the effectiveness of the accommodations; coordinates auxiliary services; reviews disability documentation and development of a needs assessment; provides information regarding legal rights and responsibilities of students; provides personal and educational counseling; and serves as an advocate.

LD/ADHD ADMISSIONS INFORMATION

College entrance tests required: Yes
Nonstandardized tests accepted: Yes
Interview required: No
Essay required: NR
Documentation required for LD: A written evaluation, including a discrepancy analysis, by licensed psychologist
Documentation required for ADHD: Yes
Documentation submitted to: Admissions and Learning Services
Special Ed. HS course work accepted: No

Specific course requirements for all applicants: Yes
Separate application required for services: No
# of LD applications submitted yearly: N/A
# of LD applications accepted yearly: N/A
Total # of students receiving LD/ADHD services: 85
Acceptance into program means acceptance into college: Students must be admitted and enrolled and then may request services.

ADMISSIONS

Utica College does not require standardized tests. Students are evaluated on an individual basis. Students should have 4 years of English, 3 years of social studies, 3 years of math, 3 years of science, and 2 years of foreign language. Special education courses are not accepted. Students with LD are encouraged to request an interview. Documentation of an LD should be sent to admissions and to support services. Students are encouraged to self-disclose the LD during the admission process.

ADDITIONAL INFORMATION

Student Services provides accommodations to students with LD based on appropriate and current documentation. Current documentation includes a written evaluation, including a discrepancy analysis, completed by a licensed psychologist or certified learning disability specialist, indicating the specific learning disability and the academic accommodations needed. Services could include priority registration, specific skill remediation, learning and study strategy development, referrals for diagnostic evaluation, time management strategies, individual peer tutoring; and other appropriate accommodations. Other accommodations could include such items as use of a tape recorder; time extensions for tests and/or alternative testing methods; note-takers; scribes; readers; tutors; and use of a proofreader to correct spelling on assignments outside of class. A disabilities form is provided stating what accommodations are appropriate in each individual case. It is the student's responsibility to notify instructors of the disability.

SUPPORT SERVICES CONTACT INFORMATION

Learning Disability Program/Services: Learning Services/Academic Support
Director: Stephen Pattarini
  E-mail: spattarini@utica.ucsu.edu
  Telephone: 315-792-3032
  Fax: 315-792-3292
Contact: Denise Williams
  E-mail: dwilliams@utica.ucsu.edu
  Telephone: 315-792-3032
  Fax: 315-792-3292

LEARNING DISABILITY SERVICES

Requests for the following services/accommodations will be evaluated individually based on appropriate and current documentation.

Allowed in Exams
  Calculator: Yes
  Dictionary: Yes
  Computer: Yes
  Spellchecker: Yes
Extended test time: Yes
Scribes: Yes
Proctors: Yes
Oral exams: Yes
Note-takers: Yes

Distraction-reduced environment: Yes
Tape recording in class: Yes
Books on tape from RFBD: Yes
Taping of books not from RFBD: Yes
Accommodations for students with ADHD: Yes
Reading machine: Yes
Other assistive technology: Yes
Priority registration: Yes

Added costs for services: No
LD specialists: Yes (1)
Professional tutors: 3
Peer tutors: 58
Max. hours/wk. for services: As available
How professors are notified of LD/ADHD: By student

GENERAL ADMISSIONS INFORMATION

Director of Admissions: Bob Croot
Telephone: 315-792-3006

ENTRANCE REQUIREMENTS
18 total are recommended; 4 English recommended, 3 math recommended, 3 science recommended, 2 science lab recommended, 3 social studies recommended. High school diploma or GED required. Minimum TOEFL is 500. TOEFL required of all international applicants.

Application deadline: Open
Notification: Rolling
Average GPA: 3.2

Average SAT I Math: 475
Average SAT I Verbal: 424
Average ACT: 21

Graduated top 10% of class: 12%
Graduated top 25% of class: 39%
Graduated top 50% of class: 73%

COLLEGE GRADUATION REQUIREMENTS

Course waivers allowed: No
Course substitutions allowed: Yes
In what subjects: Varies; substitutions can be made only if the course is not an essential component of the major

ADDITIONAL INFORMATION

Environment: The school has a suburban campus located 50 miles east of Syracuse.

Student Body
  Undergrad enrollment: 2,104
  Female: 62%
  Male: 38%
  Out-of-state: 8%

Cost Information
  Tuition: $16,844
  Room & board: $6,660
Housing Information
  University housing: Yes
  Percent living on campus: 45%

Greek System
  Fraternity: Yes
  Sorority: Yes
Athletics: NCAA Division III

APPALACHIAN STATE UNIVERSITY

Office of Admissions, PO Box 32004, Boone, NC 28608-2004
Phone: 828-262-2120 • Fax: 828-262-3296
E-mail: admissions@appstate.edu • Web: www.appstate.edu
Support level: CS • Institution type: 4-year public

LEARNING DISABILITY PROGRAM AND SERVICES

The University Learning Disability Program is part of a larger academic support service called the Learning Assistance Program. The LD Program is designed to provide academic services for students who self-identify on a voluntary basis and attend regular classes. Students with learning disabilities are totally integrated throughout the University community. Students are expected to communicate with their instructors regarding their specific needs. The Coordinator of Services works with students and faculty to implement needed services and accommodations. The needs of each student are considered and treated individually in consultation with the student and are based on current documentation of the learning disability.

LD/ADHD ADMISSIONS INFORMATION

College entrance tests required: Yes
Nonstandardized tests accepted: Yes
Interview required: No
Essay required: No
Documentation required for LD: Psychoeducational evaluation
Documentation required for ADHD: Yes
Documentation submitted to: LD Program
Special Ed. HS course work accepted: No

Specific course requirements for all applicants: Yes
Separate application required for services: No
# of LD applications submitted yearly: N/A
# of LD applications accepted yearly: N/A
Total # of students receiving LD/ADHD services: 200
Acceptance into program means acceptance into college: students must be accepted and enrolled at the University first and then must identify and provide documentation to be eligible for assistance.

ADMISSIONS

Students with learning disabilities are admitted to the University through the regular admission procedure. The minimum admissions requirements include 4 years English, 3 years math, 3 years science (1 in biology and 1 in a physical science), 2 years social science, and recommended 2 years foreign language, including 1 course in math and foreign language in senior year. Applicants may self-disclose on their applications. This information would support their application for admission. Personal statement, letters of recommendation, and school activities provide additional useful information. Once students have been accepted by the University, a form is provided in which the students can identify their disabilities. This identification process is necessary for the students to have access to the services of the LD Program. Students not regularly admissible may request a review of their application with additional or updated information.

ADDITIONAL INFORMATION

Tutoring is provided on a one-to-one basis for assistance with course content, as well as guidance in developing or improving learning skills. Tutors are trained in working with each student. Basic skills courses are available in memory skills, oral presentation, note-taking strategies, reading textbooks, written language, math, time management, and study strategies. Skills courses for no credit are offered in English and math. Services and accommodations are available for undergraduates and graduates.

SUPPORT SERVICES CONTACT INFORMATION

Learning Disability Program/Services: Learning Disability Program
Director: Suzanne T. Wehner
  E-mail: wehnerst@appstate.edu
  Telephone: 828-262-2291
  Fax: 828-262-6834
Contact: Same

LEARNING DISABILITY SERVICES

Requests for the following services/accommodations will be evaluated individually based on appropriate and current documentation.

Allowed in Exams
  Calculator: Y/N
  Dictionary: Y/N
  Computer: Y/N
  Spellchecker: Y/N
Extended test time: Yes
Scribes: Yes
Proctors: Yes
Oral exams: Yes
Note-takers: Yes

Distraction-reduced environment: Yes
Tape recording in class: Yes
Books on tape from RFBD: Yes
Taping of books not from RFBD: Yes
Accommodations for students with ADHD: Yes
Reading machine: Yes
Other assistive technology: Yes
Priority registration: Yes

Added costs for services: No
LD specialists: Yes (1)
Professional tutors: Yes
Peer tutors: Yes
Max. hours/wk. for services: Unlimited
How professors are notified of LD/ADHD: By both student and director

GENERAL ADMISSIONS INFORMATION

Director of Admissions: Joe Watts
Telephone: 828-262-2120

ENTRANCE REQUIREMENTS

20 total are required; 4 English required, 3 math required, 3 science required, 1 science lab required, 2 foreign language recommended, 1 social studies required, 1 history required. High school diploma or GED required. Minimum TOEFL is 500. TOEFL required of all international applicants.

Application deadline: October 15
Notification: Rolling beginning 11/16
Average GPA: 3.5

Average SAT I Math: 544
Average SAT I Verbal: 548
Average ACT: 24

Graduated top 10% of class: 12%
Graduated top 25% of class: 45%
Graduated top 50% of class: 85%

COLLEGE GRADUATION REQUIREMENTS

Course waivers allowed: No
Course substitutions allowed: Yes
In what subjects: Case-by-case basis via hearing procedure

ADDITIONAL INFORMATION

Environment: The University has a 255-acre campus in a small town 90 miles northwest of Winston-Salem.

Student Body
  Undergrad enrollment: 11,694
  Female: 50%
  Male: 50%
  Out-of-state: 11%

Cost Information
  In-state tuition: $962
  Out-of-state tuition: $8,232
  Room & board: $3,340
Housing Information
  University housing: Yes
  Percent living on campus: 48%

Greek System
  Fraternity: Yes
  Sorority: Yes
Athletics: NCAA Division I

DAVIDSON COLLEGE

PO Box 1737, Davidson, NC 28036-1719
Phone: 704-894-2230 • Fax: 704-894-2016
E-mail: admission@davidson.edu • Web: www.davidson.edu
Support level: CS • Institution type: 4-year private

LEARNING DISABILITY PROGRAM AND SERVICES

Students enroll in Davidson with a proven record of academic achievement and proven ability to utilize resources, perseverance and creativity to excel. The College provides services and accommodations to allow students an opportunity to continue to be successful. All students seeking accommodations on the basis of an LD must provide recent documentation. The evaluation should include recommendations for compensatory learning strategies used by the student and recommendations for accommodations and services to be provided by the College. The Dean of Students, with the student's permission, will notify professors of an individual student's need for adaptations. Accommodations are not universal in nature, but are designed to meet the specific need of the individual to offset a specific disability.

LD/ADHD ADMISSIONS INFORMATION

College entrance tests required: Yes
Nonstandardized tests accepted: Yes
Interview required: No
Essay required: No
Documentation required for LD: Psychoeducational evaluation—after matriculation
Documentation required for ADHD: Yes—after matriculation
Documentation submitted to: Associate Dean
Special Ed. HS course work accepted: No

Specific course requirements for all applicants: Yes
Separate application required for services: No
# of LD applications submitted yearly: N/A
# of LD applications accepted yearly: N/A
Total # of students receiving LD/ADHD services: 54
Acceptance into program means acceptance into college: Students must be admitted and enrolled and then may request services.

ADMISSIONS

There is no special admission process for students with LD, although the Admission Office may seek comments from support staff knowledgeable about LD. Students are encouraged to self-disclose the ADHD. The admission process is very competitive and the disclosure can help the Admission Office more fairly evaluate the transcript. This disclosure could address any specific academic issues related to the LD such as no foreign language in high school because of the specific LD or lower grades in math as a result of a math disability. The GPA is recalculated to reflect rigor with 97 percent of the accepted students having a recalculated GPA of 3.0. Students have completed at least 4 years of English, 3 years of math, 2 years of the same foreign language, 2 years of science, and 2 years of history/social studies. Courses taken in special education are not accepted. The middle 50 percent of students have an ACT between 28 and 31 or SAT I between 1240 and 1420. Interviews are not required but are recommended.

ADDITIONAL INFORMATION

Support services and accommodations available include, but are not limited to: referrals for appropriate diagnostic evaluation; individual coaching and instruction in compensatory strategies and study skills; consultation with faculty and staff; student support groups as requested; classroom accommodations such as extra test-taking time, taped texts, note-takers, use of tape recorders, use of computers with spellcheckers, individual space for study or test-taking; reduced course load; course substitutions or waivers (rarely). There is a math center, writing lab, peer tutoring, and skill class in time management for all students. There are 1.5 LD specialists on staff and peer tutoring for all students as needed.

SUPPORT SERVICES CONTACT INFORMATION

Learning Disability Program/Services: Associate Dean
Director: Associate Dean of Students Leslie Marsicano
  E-mail: lemarsic@davidson.edu
  Telephone: 704-894-2225
  Fax: 704-894-2849
Contact: Same

LEARNING DISABILITY SERVICES

Requests for the following services/accommodations will be evaluated individually based on appropriate and current documentation.

Allowed in Exams
  Calculator: Yes
  Dictionary: Yes
  Computer: Yes
  Spellchecker: Yes
Extended test time: Yes
Scribes: Yes
Proctors: Yes
Oral exams: No
Note-takers: Yes

Distraction-reduced environment: Yes
Tape recording in class: Yes
Books on tape from RFBD: Yes
Taping of books not from RFBD: NR
Accommodations for students with
  ADHD: Yes
Reading machine: No
Other assistive technology: No
Priority registration: No

Added costs for services: No
LD specialists: Yes (1)
Professional tutors: No
Peer tutors: 100
Max. hours/wk. for services:
  Unlimited
How professors are notified of
  LD/ADHD: By both student and
  director

GENERAL ADMISSIONS INFORMATION

Director of Admissions: Dr. Nancy Cable
Telephone: 704-894-2235

ENTRANCE REQUIREMENTS
16 total are required; 4 English required, 3 math required, 4 math recommended, 2 science required, 4 science recommended, 2 foreign language required, 4 foreign language recommended. High school diploma is required and GED is not accepted. Minimum TOEFL is 600. TOEFL required of all international applicants.

Application deadline: January 2
Notification: April 1
Average GPA: NR

Average SAT I Math: 663
Average SAT I Verbal: 659
Average ACT: 29

Graduated top 10% of class: 75%
Graduated top 25% of class: 95%
Graduated top 50% of class: 100%

COLLEGE GRADUATION REQUIREMENTS

Course waivers allowed: No
Course substitutions allowed: Yes
In what subjects: In any appropriate course

ADDITIONAL INFORMATION

Environment: Located 19 miles from Charlotte.

Student Body
  Undergrad enrollment: 1,679
  Female: 50%
  Male: 50%
  Out-of-state: 81%

Cost Information
  Tuition: $22,873
  Room & board: $6,572
Housing Information
  University housing: Yes
  Percent living on campus: 94%

Greek System
  Fraternity: Yes
  Sorority: No
Athletics: NCAA Division I

DUKE UNIVERSITY

2138 Campus Drive, Durham, NC 27708
Phone: 919-684-3214 • Fax: 919-681-8941
E-mail: undergrad-admissions@duke.edu • Web: www.duke.edu
Support level: CS • Institution type: 4-year private

LEARNING DISABILITY PROGRAM AND SERVICES

Duke University does not provide a formal, highly structured program for students with learning disabilities. The University does provide, however, significant academic support services for students through the Academic Resource Center (ARC). Students who submit appropriate documentation of their learning disability to the ARC Clinical Director are eligible for assistance in obtaining reasonable academic adjustments and auxiliary aids. In addition, the ASC Clinical Director and Instructors can provide individualized instruction in academic skills and learning strategies, academic support counseling, and referrals for other services. Students with learning disabilities voluntarily access and use the services of the ARC, just as they might access and use other campus resources. Student interactions with the ASC staff are confidential. The goals of the support services for students with learning disabilities are in keeping with the goals of all services provided through the ARC: to help students achieve their academic potential within the context of a competitive university setting; to promote a disciplined approach to study; and to foster active, independent learners.

LD/ADHD ADMISSIONS INFORMATION

College entrance tests required: Yes
Nonstandardized tests accepted: Yes
Interview required: Yes
Essay required: Yes
Documentation required for LD: Current psychoeducational testing: within 3 years
Documentation required for ADHD: Yes
Documentation submitted to: Services for Students with Disabilities
Special Ed. HS course work accepted: No

Specific course requirements for all applicants: Yes
Separate application required for services: No
# of LD applications submitted yearly: N/A
# of LD applications accepted yearly: N/A
Total # of students receiving LD/ADHD services: N/A
Acceptance into program means acceptance into college: Students must be admitted and enrolled at the University first and then may request services.

ADMISSIONS

There is no special admission process for students with learning disabilities. All applicants must meet the general Duke admissions criteria. Admission to Duke is highly competitive and most applicants are in the top 10% of their class. Most applicants have completed a demanding curriculum in high school including many Advanced Placement and Honors courses. Services and accommodations may be requested after enrollment in Duke.

ADDITIONAL INFORMATION

Assistance is available as needed from the student's Academic Dean and the Clinical Director of ARC. Students are encouraged to consult with their faculty advisor and the ARC, well in advance of registration, to determine the appropriate measures for particular courses. There is one staff member with special learning disability training, and three staff members who are writing/learning strategy instructors. Documentation and diagnostic tests are required for accommodations, not admissions. Students may also receive peer tutoring in introductory-level courses in several disciplines through the ARC Peer Tutoring Program. Up to 12 hours of tutoring in each course is offered at no additional charge. Students need to understand their learning disability, be able to self-advocate, and know what accommodations are necessary to assist them in being successful in college. Students are expected to work out reasonable accommodations with each of their professors. Outside testing referrals are made at the student's expense.

SUPPORT SERVICES CONTACT INFORMATION

Learning Disability Program/Services: Office of Services for Students with Disabilities
Director: Emma Swain
  E-mail: eswain@duke.edu
  Telephone: 919-684-5917
  Fax: 919-684-8934
Contact: Diane Alexander
  E-mail: dalex@pmac.duke.edu
  Telephone: 919-684-5917
  Fax: 919-684-8934

LEARNING DISABILITY SERVICES

Requests for the following services/accommodations will be evaluated individually based on appropriate and current documentation.

Allowed in Exams
  Calculator: Yes
  Dictionary: Yes
  Computer: Yes
  Spellchecker: Yes
Extended test time: Yes
Scribes: Yes
Proctors: Yes
Oral exams: No
Note-takers: Yes

Distraction-reduced environment: Yes
Tape recording in class: Yes
Books on tape from RFBD: NR
Taping of books not from RFBD: Yes
Accommodations for students with ADHD: Yes
Reading machine: Yes
Other assistive technology: Yes
Priority registration: No

Added costs for services: No
LD specialists: Yes (1)
Professional tutors: Yes
Peer tutors: 80
Max. hours/wk. for services: Unlimited
How professors are notified of LD/ADHD: By director

GENERAL ADMISSIONS INFORMATION

Director of Admissions: Christoph Guttentag
Telephone: 919-684-3214

ENTRANCE REQUIREMENTS

20 total are recommended; 4 English recommended, 3 math recommended, 3 science recommended, 3 foreign language recommended, 3 social studies recommended. High school diploma is required and GED is not accepted. TOEFL required of all international applicants.

Application deadline: January 2
Notification: April 15
Average GPA: N/A

Average SAT I Math: 700
Average SAT I Verbal: 685
Average ACT: 30

Graduated top 10% of class: 86%
Graduated top 25% of class: 98%
Graduated top 50% of class: 100%

COLLEGE GRADUATION REQUIREMENTS

Course waivers allowed: No
Course substitutions allowed: No
In what subjects: Students are only required to complete specific courses in 5 out of 6 subject areas, including foreign language, arts and literature, civilization, qualitative reasoning, social sciences, or natural sciences.

ADDITIONAL INFORMATION

Environment: The University is on 8,500 acres in a suburban area 285 miles southwest of Washington, D.C.

Student Body
  Undergrad enrollment: 6,325
  Female: 48%
  Male: 52%
  Out-of-state: 85%

Cost Information
  Tuition: $26,000
  Room & board: $7,628
Housing Information
  University housing: Yes
  Percent living on campus: 80%

Greek System
  Fraternity: Yes
  Sorority: Yes
Athletics: NCAA Division I

EAST CAROLINA UNIVERSITY

106 Whichard Building, Greenville, NC 27858
Phone: 252-328-6640 • Fax: 252-328-6945
E-mail: admis@mail.ecu.edu • Web: www.ecu.edu
Support level: CS • Institution type: 4-year public

LEARNING DISABILITY PROGRAM AND SERVICES

Through the Department for Disability Support Services, the University seeks to meet individual needs by coordinating and implementing internal policy regarding programs, services, and activities for individuals with disabilities. The department functions as a source of information and advice and as a communication link among individuals with disabilities, faculty and staff members, state rehab agencies, and the community at large. The overall purpose of the University's program for students with learning disabilities is to provide auxiliary support services, so they may derive equal benefits from all that East Carolina University has to offer. Individuals with learning disabilities and attention deficit disorders are required to provide the department with proper documentation of their disability. An acceptable psychoeducational evaluation administered within the past three years must be submitted to qualify for services. Students should schedule a meeting with the department well in advance of the beginning of their first semester to prevent delays in the planning of services. Students with LD or ADHD will receive a letter describing the services required to give to their instructors. With the exception of tutorial services for personal use, academic support services are provided at no cost.

LD/ADHD ADMISSIONS INFORMATION

College entrance tests required: Yes
Nonstandardized tests accepted: Yes
Interview required: No
Essay required: No
Documentation required for LD: Current psychoeducational battery
Documentation required for ADHD: Yes
Documentation submitted to: Disability Support Services
Special Ed. HS course work accepted: Yes, as long as it is an equivalent course

Specific course requirements for all applicants: Yes
Separate application required for services: No
# of LD applications submitted yearly: N/A
# of LD applications accepted yearly: N/A
Total # of students receiving LD/ADHD services: 100–150
Acceptance into program means acceptance into college: Students must be admitted and enrolled at the University first and then may request services.

ADMISSIONS

A student with a disability applies for admission and is considered for admission in the same manner as any other applicant. Neither the nature nor the severity of one's disability is used as a criterion for admission. Students with learning disabilities are admitted solely on academic qualifications. Out-of-state students must present slightly higher GPAs and test scores, but the minimum is 2.0 depending on the SAT. Test scores vary but the minimum out-of-state ACT is 19 and in-state is 17, and the average ACT is 21. The minimum SAT out-of-state is 1000 and in-state is 900, and the average SAT is 1030. Students must have taken 4 years English, 2 years social science, 3 years science (1 year biology, 1 year physical science), 3 years math; 2 years foreign language is recommended.

ADDITIONAL INFORMATION

Once admitted to the University, students must self-identify and register with the Department for Disability Support Services. Students must show official verification of their disability. Students will be assigned to academic advisors from the department. Once students enter their major fields of study, the department will still be available to provide advising assistance but never to the exclusion of the individual's assigned academic advisor. Alternative testing accommodations may include extended time, a noise-free environment, reader-assisted test taking, and other arrangements that satisfy the needs of the student. A maximum of double time can be allowed for student to complete a test or an exam. The University offers a modified language sequence for students enrolled in Spanish. There are several laboratories available, including the Writing Center, Reading Center, Mathematics Center, the Academic Support Center, and Computer Lab. Students pay for private tutoring. Skills classes for any student are available in time managment, test-taking/anxiety, study strategies, and academic motivation.

SUPPORT SERVICES CONTACT INFORMATION

Learning Disability Program/Services: Department for Disability Support Services
Director: C. C. Rowe
  Telephone: 252-328-6799
  Fax: 252-328-4883
Contact: Liz Johnston
  E-mail: johnstone@mail.ecu.edu
  Telephone: 252-328-0701
  Fax: 252-328-4883

LEARNING DISABILITY SERVICES

Requests for the following services/accommodations will be evaluated individually based on appropriate and current documentation.

Allowed in Exams
  Calculator: Yes
  Dictionary: Yes
  Computer: Yes
  Spellchecker: Yes
Extended test time: Yes
Scribes: Yes
Proctors: Yes
Oral exams: Yes
Note-takers: Yes

Distraction-reduced environment: Yes
Tape recording in class: Yes
Books on tape from RFBD: Yes
Taping of books not from RFBD: Yes
**Accommodations for students with
  ADHD:** Yes
Reading machine: Yes
Other assistive technology: No
Priority registration: Yes

Added costs for services: No
LD specialists: Yes
Professional tutors: No
Peer tutors: 10–15
Max. hours/wk. for services:
  Unlimited
**How professors are notified of
  LD/ADHD:** By student

GENERAL ADMISSIONS INFORMATION

Director of Admissions: Dr. Thomas E. Powell
Telephone: 252-328-6640

ENTRANCE REQUIREMENTS
20 total are required; 4 English required, 3 math required, 3 science required, 1 science lab required, 2 foreign language recommended, 2 social studies required, 1 history required. High school diploma or GED required. Minimum TOEFL is 550. TOEFL required of all international applicants.

Application deadline: March 15
Notification: Rolling beginning 10/1
Average GPA: 3.3

Average SAT I Math: 546
Average SAT I Verbal: 550
Average ACT: 20

Graduated top 10% of class: 13%
Graduated top 25% of class: 41%
Graduated top 50% of class: 83%

COLLEGE GRADUATION REQUIREMENTS

Course waivers allowed: No
Course substitutions allowed: Yes
In what subjects: Foreign language under special circumstances

ADDITIONAL INFORMATION

Environment: The school is located on over 370 acres within the city of Greenville, 85 miles from Raleigh.

Student Body
  Undergrad enrollment: 15,018
  Female: 58%
  Male: 42%
  Out-of-state: 15%

Cost Information
  In-state tuition: $1,195
  Out-of-state tuition: $9,058
  Room & board: $4,220
Housing Information
  University housing: Yes
  Percent living on campus: 31%

Greek System
  Fraternity: Yes
  Sorority: Yes
  Athletics: NCAA Division I

GUILFORD COLLEGE

5800 West Friendly Avenue, Greensboro, NC 27410
Phone: 336-316-2100 • Fax: 336-316-2954
E-mail: admission@guilford.edu • Web: www.guilford.edu
Support level: S • Institution type: 4-year private

LEARNING DISABILITY PROGRAM AND SERVICES

The Academic Skills Center serves the learning needs of a diverse campus by providing professional and peer tutoring, workshops, advocacy, and realistic encouragement. The focus is on self-advocacy and the articulation of both strengths and weaknesses. Faculty tutors work one-on-one with students in time management, study skills, test-taking, reading, math, science, and Spanish. A large Student Tutoring Service offers course-specific tutoring. The tutoring service also provides editors for students who need help checking final drafts. The center sponsors workshops and seminars on subjects pertaining to academic success. Faculty allow the usual accommodations requested by students: extra time, permission to use a computer for in-class work, testing in a less distracting environment, audiotaping classes, etc.

LD/ADHD ADMISSIONS INFORMATION

College entrance tests required: Yes
Nonstandardized tests accepted: Yes
Interview required: No
Essay required: Yes
Documentation required for LD: Full psychoeducational
  evaluation: within 5 years
Documentation required for ADHD: Yes
Documentation submitted to: Academic Skills Center
Special Ed. HS course work accepted: No

Specific course requirements for all applicants: Yes
Separate application required for services: No
# of LD applications submitted yearly: N/A
# of LD applications accepted yearly: N/A
Total # of students receiving LD/ADHD services: N/A
**Acceptance into program means acceptance into
  college:** Students must be accepted and enrolled into
  the College first and then may request services.

ADMISSIONS

Students with learning disabilities meet the same criteria as other students. The general admission criteria include the middle 50 percent range for the ACT 20–28 and the SAT 1030–1270 and GPA 2.8–3.4. Typically admitted students have 4 years English, 3 years math, 3–4 years natural science, 3 years social studies, 2 years foreign language. With appropriate documentation students with learning disabilities can substitute some high school courses in areas that impact their ability to learn. The ASC Director reviews files to make certain that the College can provide appropriate support services.

ADDITIONAL INFORMATION

Guilford is a writing-intensive place. The writing program is revision-driven and utilizes peer-editing and response groups. The Academic Skills Center (ASC) offers individualized professional tutoring in writing as well as work with trained student writing tutors. The ASC offers other services including faculty tutors to work one-on-one with students in time management, study skills, test-taking, reading, math, science, and Spanish. A large Student Tutoring Service offers course-specific tutoring. The center also sponsors workshops and seminars on subjects pertaining to academic success. Faculty allow the usual accommodations requested by students: extra time, permission to use a computer for in-class work, testing in a less distracting environment, and audiotaping classes. Students are encouraged to speak with professors early concerning particular needs. Guilford waives the foreign language requirement if students submit appropriate documentation and petition through ASC.

SUPPORT SERVICES CONTACT INFORMATION

Learning Disability Program/Services: Academic Skills Center
Director: Sue Keith
  E-mail: keith@rascal.guilford.edu
  Telephone: 336-316-2200
  Fax: 336-316-2930
Contact: Same

LEARNING DISABILITY SERVICES

Requests for the following services/accommodations will be evaluated individually based on appropriate and current documentation.

Allowed in Exams
  Calculator: Yes
  Dictionary: Yes
  Computer: Yes
  Spellchecker: Yes
  Extended test time: Yes
  Scribes: Yes
  Proctors: Yes
  Oral exams: Yes
  Note-takers: Yes

Distraction-reduced environment: Yes
Tape recording in class: Yes
Books on tape from RFBD: Yes
Taping of books not from RFBD: Yes
Accommodations for students with ADHD: Yes
Reading machine: Yes
Other assistive technology: Yes
Priority registration: Yes

Added costs for services: No
LD specialists: No
Professional tutors: 9
Peer tutors: 130
Max. hours/wk. for services: Unlimited
How professors are notified of LD/ADHD: By the student

GENERAL ADMISSIONS INFORMATION

Director of Admissions: Randy Doff
Telephone: 336-316-2100

ENTRANCE REQUIREMENTS
18 total are required; 4 English required, 3 math required, 4 math recommended, 2 science required, 2 science lab required, 2 foreign language required, 3 foreign language recommended, 2 social studies required, 3 social studies recommended, 1 history required, 2 elective required. High school diploma or GED required. Minimum TOEFL is 550. TOEFL required of all international applicants.

Application deadline: February 15
Notification: April 1
Average GPA: 3.1

Average SAT I Math: 557
Average SAT I Verbal: 579
Average ACT: 24

Graduated top 10% of class: 18%
Graduated top 25% of class: 42%
Graduated top 50% of class: 82%

COLLEGE GRADUATION REQUIREMENTS

Course waivers allowed: No
Course substitutions allowed: Yes
In what subjects: Foreign language and math

ADDITIONAL INFORMATION

Environment: The College is located on a suburban campus in a small city.

Student Body
  Undergrad enrollment: 1,246
  Female: 53%
  Male: 47%
  Out-of-state: 68%

Cost Information
  Tuition: $16,400
  Room & board: $5,610
Housing Information
  University housing: Yes
  Percent living on campus: 79%

Greek System
  Fraternity: Yes
  Sorority: Yes
  Athletics: NCAA Division III

LENOIR-RHYNE COLLEGE

Admissions Office, LRC Box 7227, Hickory, NC 28603
Phone: 828-328-7300 • Fax: 828-328-7378
E-mail: admission@lrc.edu • Web: www.lrc.edu
Support level: CS • Institution type: 4-year private

LEARNING DISABILITY PROGRAM AND SERVICES

The Lenoir-Rhyne College Disability Services Office strives to provide the highest quality service to each student with a disability through appropriate modification of college policies, practices, and procedures. It is the mission of the office to ensure that every student with a disability has an equal chance to benefit from college programs. Furthermore, the office emphasizes personal independence and responsibility, on the part of the student, in the provision of services. The office will also serve as a campus and community resource for information about people with disabilities and the issues that affect them.

LD/ADHD ADMISSIONS INFORMATION

College entrance tests required: Yes
Nonstandardized tests accepted: Yes
Interview required: No
Essay required: No
Documentation required for LD: Full psychoeducational evaluation with IQ scores listed
Documentation required for ADHD: Yes
Documentation submitted to: Admissions and Services for Students with LD
Special Ed. HS course work accepted: Yes

Specific course requirements for all applicants: Yes
Separate application required for services: No
# of LD applications submitted yearly: 25
# of LD applications accepted yearly: 20
Total # of students receiving LD/ADHD services: 25–30
Acceptance into program means acceptance into college: Students not admitted are reviewed by the LD program, which provides a recommendation to admissions. Once admitted they may request services.

ADMISSIONS

There is no special admissions process for students with learning disabilities. All students are reviewed on an individual case-by-case basis. Basic admissions criteria include 2.0 GPA, top 50 percent class rank, 850 SAT or 17 ACT, 4 years English, 3 years math, 1 year history, 2 years foreign language (substitution allowed).

ADDITIONAL INFORMATION

Advising and Academic Services Center offers a variety of services to help students achieve academic success through group peer tutoring, advising and assessment, and academic skills counseling. With appropriate documentation students with LD/ADHD may be eligible for some of the following services/accommodations: the use of calculators, dictionary, computer or spellcheck in exams; extended time on tests; distraction-free environment; scribe; proctor; oral exams; note-taker; tape recorder in class; books on tape; and substitution of the foreign language requirement. Students placed on academic probation by the College are monitored in the center. Also, the center provides access to supplementary computerized learning materials such as Learning Plus for prospective educators and computerized test preps for standardized tests such as the GMAT.

SUPPORT SERVICES CONTACT INFORMATION

Learning Disability Program/Services: Services for Students with Learning Disabilities
Director: Donavan Kirby
  E-mail: kirbydr@lrc.edu
  Telephone: 828-328-7296
  Fax: 828-328-7329
Contact: Same

LEARNING DISABILITY SERVICES

Requests for the following services/accommodations will be evaluated individually based on appropriate and current documentation.

Allowed in Exams
  Calculator: Yes
  Dictionary: Yes
  Computer: Yes
  Spellchecker: Yes
Extended test time: Yes
Scribes: Yes
Proctors: Yes
Oral exams: Yes
Note-takers: Yes

Distraction-reduced environment: Yes
Tape recording in class: Yes
Books on tape from RFBD: Yes
Taping of books not from RFBD: No
Accommodations for students with ADHD: Yes
Reading machine: No
Other assistive technology: No
Priority registration: No

Added costs for services: No
LD specialists: Yes (1)
Professional tutors: No
Peer tutors: 20–25
Max. hours/wk. for services: Unlimited
How professors are notified of LD/ADHD: By both student and director

GENERAL ADMISSIONS INFORMATION

Director of Admissions: Rachel Nichols
Telephone: 828-328-7300

ENTRANCE REQUIREMENTS
4 English required, 3 math required, 1 science required, 1 science lab required, 2 foreign language required, 1 social studies required, 1 history required. High school diploma or GED required. Minimum TOEFL is 500. TOEFL required of all international applicants.

Application deadline: Rolling
Notification: Rolling beginning 9/1
Average GPA: 3.5

Average SAT I Math: 519
Average SAT I Verbal: 517
Average ACT: 22

Graduated top 10% of class: 18%
Graduated top 25% of class: 50%
Graduated top 50% of class: 82%

COLLEGE GRADUATION REQUIREMENTS

Course waivers allowed: No
Course substitutions allowed: Yes
In what subjects: Foreign language substitution is available

ADDITIONAL INFORMATION

Environment: The College is located in a small town north of Charlotte.

Student Body
  Undergrad enrollment: 1,353
  Female: 64%
  Male: 36%
  Out-of-state: 29%

Cost Information
  Tuition: $12,870
  Room & board: $4,920
Housing Information
  University housing: Yes
  Percent living on campus: 60%

Greek System
  Fraternity: Yes
  Sorority: Yes
Athletics: NCAA Division II

NORTH CAROLINA STATE UNIVERSITY

Box 7103, Raleigh, NC 27695
Phone: 919-515-2434 • Fax: 919-515-5039
E-mail: undergrad_admissions@ncsu.edu • Web: www.ncsu.edu
Support level: CS • Institution type: 4-year public

LEARNING DISABILITY PROGRAM AND SERVICES

Services for students with learning disabilities are handled by the LD Coordinator through Disability Services for Students. The functions of the coordinator include identifying students with learning disabilities, helping to accommodate and interpret the needs of these students to the faculty, and providing services to students according to their individual needs. Support groups meet periodically to provide workshops, mutual support, and awareness of handicapped issues to the University community. The purpose of the services is to ensure that students with documented learning disabilities receive appropriate accommodations in order to equalize their opportunities while studying at NCSU.

LD/ADHD ADMISSIONS INFORMATION

College entrance tests required: Yes
Nonstandardized tests accepted: Yes
Interview required: N/A
Essay required: No
Documentation required for LD: WAIS-III: WJPEB-R, part II: within 3 years
Documentation required for ADHD: Yes
Documentation submitted to: DSS
Special Ed. HS course work accepted: Yes

Specific course requirements for all applicants: Yes
Separate application required for services: No
# of LD applications submitted yearly: N/A
# of LD applications accepted yearly: N/A
Total # of students receiving LD/ADHD services: 260–300
Acceptance into program means acceptance into college: Students must be admitted and enrolled at the University first and then may request services.

ADMISSIONS

Admission to the University for students with learning disabilities is determined on the basis of academic qualifications, and they are considered in the same manner as any other applicant. There is no pre-admission question regarding a learning disability. A cover letter from applicants, stating that a learning disability exists, alerts the admission staff to consider that there may be unusual circumstances. Self-disclosure of the learning disability could explain the high school record, such as late diagnosis and onset of LD accommodations or difficulty in particular subjects. General admission criteria include ACT 23–29 or SAT 1100–1300; over 75 percent of the students have a 3.5 GPA; course requirements include 4 years English, 3 years math, 3 years social studies, 3 years science, 2 years foreign language.

ADDITIONAL INFORMATION

All enrolled students may receive services and accommodations through the coordinator of learning disabilities of the DSS if they present appropriate documentation. The documentation should include a written report with a statement specifying areas of learning disabilities. Services and accommodations available with appropriate documentation include extended testing time for exams; distraction-free testing environments; calculator, dictionary, computer or spellcheck in exams; proctors; scribes; note-takers; books on tape; assistive technology; and priority registration. If new needs are identified, services are modified or developed to accommodate them.

SUPPORT SERVICES CONTACT INFORMATION

Learning Disability Program/Services: Disability Services for Students (DSS)
Director: Cheryl Branker, EdD
  E-mail: cheryl-branker@ncsu.edu
  Telephone: 919-515-7653
  Fax: 919-513-2840
Contact: Same

LEARNING DISABILITY SERVICES

Requests for the following services/accommodations will be evaluated individually based on appropriate and current documentation.

Allowed in Exams
  Calculator: Yes
  Dictionary: Yes
  Computer: Yes
  Spellchecker: Yes
Extended test time: Yes
Scribes: Yes
Proctors: Yes
Oral exams: Yes
Note-takers: Yes

Distraction-reduced environment: Yes
Tape recording in class: Yes
Books on tape from RFBD: Yes
Taping of books not from RFBD: Yes
Accommodations for students with ADHD: Yes
Reading machine: Yes
Other assistive technology: Yes
Priority registration: Yes

Added costs for services: No
LD specialists: Yes (2)
Professional tutors: 2
Peer tutors: 25
Max. hours/wk. for services: 3
How professors are notified of LD/ADHD: By both student and director

GENERAL ADMISSIONS INFORMATION

Director of Admissions: Dr. George Dickjson
Telephone: 919-515-2434

ENTRANCE REQUIREMENTS
15 total are required; 20 total are recommended; 4 English required, 3 math required, 4 math recommended, 3 science required, 1 science lab required, 2 foreign language required, 1 social studies required, 1 history required, 4 elective recommended. High school diploma is required and GED is not accepted. Minimum TOEFL is 550. TOEFL required of all international applicants.

Application deadline: February 1
Notification: Rolling beginning 10/15
Average GPA: 3.9

Average SAT I Math: 607
Average SAT I Verbal: 578
Average ACT: 25

Graduated top 10% of class: 37%
Graduated top 25% of class: 78%
Graduated top 50% of class: 98%

COLLEGE GRADUATION REQUIREMENTS

Course waivers allowed: No
Course substitutions allowed: Y/N
In what subjects: In some situations in foreign language

ADDITIONAL INFORMATION

Environment: The University sits on 623 acres in the central part of the state and has an adjacent 900-acre research campus.

Student Body
  Undergrad enrollment: 21,990
  Female: 42%
  Male: 58%
  Out-of-state: 8%

Cost Information
  In-state tuition: $1,860
  Out-of-state tuition: $11,026
  Room & board: $5,274
Housing Information
  University housing: Yes
  Percent living on campus: 33%

Greek System
  Fraternity: Yes
  Sorority: Yes
Athletics: NCAA Division I

North Carolina State University

St. Andrew's Presbyterian College

1700 Dogwood Mile, Laurinburg, NC 28352
Phone: 910-277-5555 • Fax: 910-277-5087
E-mail: admissions@sapc.edu • Web: www.sapc.edu
Support level: S • Institution type: 4-year private

LEARNING DISABILITY PROGRAM AND SERVICES

St. Andrews Presbyterian College acknowledges its responsibility, both legally and educationally, to serve students with learning disabilities by providing reasonable accommodations. These services do not guarantee success, but endeavor to assist students in pursuing a quality post-secondary education. Disability and Academic Support Services provides a full range of learning disability support services. The services are meant to help students devise strategies for meeting college demands and to foster independence, responsibility, and self-advocacy. Disability and Academic Support Services is committed to ensuring that all information regarding a student is maintained as confidential.

LD/ADHD ADMISSIONS INFORMATION

College entrance tests required: Yes
Nonstandardized tests accepted: Yes
Interview required: No
Essay required: Yes
Documentation required for LD: WAIS-III
Documentation required for ADHD: Yes
Documentation submitted to: Disability Services
Special Ed. HS course work accepted: Yes

Specific course requirements for all applicants: Yes
Separate application required for services: Yes
# of LD applications submitted yearly: N/A
# of LD applications accepted yearly: N/A
Total # of students receiving LD/ADHD services: 30
Acceptance into program means acceptance into college: Students must be admitted and enrolled at the College first and then may request services.

ADMISSIONS

Each application is reviewed on an individual basis. Factors considered are: SAT minimum of 700 or ACT minimum of 17; high school profile and courses attempted, as well as a minimum GPA of 2.0; essay and counselor and/or teacher recommendations are optional but strongly recommended. Courses recommended include 4 years English, 3 years science, 1 year social studies, 1 year history, and 2 years foreign language. Prospective students are strongly encouraged to visit the campus. Students with learning disabilities complete the regular admissions application. All students must meet the same admissions criteria. In order for the admissions committee to make the most informed decision, students are encouraged to self-disclose the existence of a learning disability in their personal statement. Any other personal information indicating the student's ability to succeed in college should also be included with the application. All documentation of a specific learning disability should be sent separately.

ADDITIONAL INFORMATION

All accommodations are based on the submitted, current documentation. Each case is reviewed individually. Disability Services reserves the right to determine eligibility for services based on the quality of the submitted documentation. The services and accommodations include note-taking, extended time on tests, alternative test formats, separate location for tests, books on tape through Recordings for the Blind and Dyslexic or from readers, and content tutoring through individual departments. Franklin Language Masters and audiocassette equipment are available for loan. All computers in computer labs are equipped with spellcheck. A Learning Resource Center is planned to open in the near future.

SUPPORT SERVICES CONTACT INFORMATION

Learning Disability Program/Services: Disability Services
Director: Interim
   Telephone: 910-277-5331
   Fax: 910-277-5020
Contact: Same

LEARNING DISABILITY SERVICES

Requests for the following services/accommodations will be evaluated individually based on appropriate and current documentation.

Allowed in Exams
   Calculator: Yes
   Dictionary: Yes
   Computer: Yes
   Spellchecker: Yes
Extended test time: Yes
Scribes: Yes
Proctors: Yes
Oral exams: Yes
Note-takers: Yes

Distraction-reduced environment: Yes
Tape recording in class: Yes
Books on tape from RFBD: Yes
Taping of books not from RFBD: Yes
Accommodations for students with ADHD: Yes
Reading machine: No
Other assistive technology: Yes
Priority registration: No

Added costs for services: No
LD specialists: No
Professional tutors: No
Peer tutors: 10–15
Max. hours/wk. for services: Unlimited
How professors are notified of LD/ADHD: By both student and director

GENERAL ADMISSIONS INFORMATION

Director of Admissions: Peg Crawford
Telephone: 910-277-5555

ENTRANCE REQUIREMENTS

11 total are required; 4 English recommended, 3 math recommended, 2 science recommended, 2 foreign language recommended, 2 history recommended. High school diploma or GED required. Minimum TOEFL is 500. TOEFL required of all international applicants.

Application deadline: Rolling
Notification: Rolling
Average GPA: 2.85

Average SAT I Math: 489
Average SAT I Verbal: 499
Average ACT: NR

Graduated top 10% of class: 34%
Graduated top 25% of class: 72%
Graduated top 50% of class: 97%

COLLEGE GRADUATION REQUIREMENTS

Course waivers allowed: No
Course substitutions allowed: Yes
In what subjects: Foreign language

ADDITIONAL INFORMATION

Environment: The College is located on 600 acres in a small town 40 miles southwest of Fayetteville.

Student Body
   Undergrad enrollment: 638
   Female: 60%
   Male: 40%
   Out-of-state: 50%

Cost Information
   Tuition: $13,515
   Room & board: $5,300
Housing Information
   University housing: Yes
   Percent living on campus: 85%

Greek System
   Fraternity: Yes
   Sorority: Yes
Athletics: NCAA Division II

UNIV. OF N. CAROLINA—CHAPEL HILL

Office of Undergraduate Admissions,
Jackson Hall 153A - Campus Box 2200, Chapel Hill, NC 27599
Phone: 919-966-3621 • Fax: 919-962-3045
E-mail: uadm@email.unc.edu • Web: www.unc.edu
Support level: CS • Institution type: 4-year public

LEARNING DISABILITY PROGRAM AND SERVICES

The Learning Disability Services (LDS) is one of seven units of Academic Support Services within the College of Arts and Sciences. The mission of LDS is to assist students in achieving their academic potential within the regular, academically competitive University curriculum. This is a comprehensive program with a team of LD/ADHD Specialists that meets both the letter and the spirit of the law. LDS works with students who are eligible for the services and is the service provider to students with documented LD/ADHD. LDS has developed innovative services for students with LD/ADHD in the College setting. A student's desire to learn new ways to learn becomes the foundation for direct services. LDS determines "reasonable" accommodations for students on a class-by-class basis each semester, based on each student's specific documented disability. Direct services focus on changes that students can make in how they learn. Students can meet as often as weekly in one-to-one sessions to learn more about their disability, develop self-advocacy skills, obtain referrals, and practice learning strategies. ADHD College Coaching services are available to assist ADHD students with the issues they experience in college.

LD/ADHD ADMISSIONS INFORMATION

College entrance tests required: Yes
Nonstandardized tests accepted: Yes
Interview required: No
Essay required: No
Documentation required for LD: Psychoeducational evaluation
Documentation required for ADHD: Yes
Documentation submitted to: LD Services
Special Ed. HS course work accepted: Yes

Specific course requirements for all applicants: Yes
Separate application required for services: No
# of LD applications submitted yearly: N/A
# of LD applications accepted yearly: N/A
Total # of students receiving LD/ADHD services: 350
Acceptance into program means acceptance into college: Students must be admitted and enrolled at the University and then may request consideration for LDS services.

ADMISSIONS

In terms of admission criteria for students with LD/ADHD, nonenrolled students can choose to voluntarily share documentation of their disability. If the student discloses a disability during admissions, his or her application is reviewed by Subcommittee "D" of the Admissions Committee. This subcommittee is made up of a number of campus professionals with expertise in disabilities, including the Director of the Learning Disabilities Services. Students with disabilities who apply for admissions have the right to refrain from disclosing. If, after being admitted, a student wishes to use LDS, that student would then submit documentation to be reviewed by the LD team.

ADDITIONAL INFORMATION

Accommodations provided include note-takers; taped textbooks; tutors in math or foreign language; extended time on tests; a distraction-free test environment; a reader during exams; a scribe to write dictated test answers; and a computer for writing test answers. Using the student's current course work, LDS can teach a range of strategies, including how to plan, draft, and edit papers; how to take lecture notes and reading notes; how to read critically and efficiently; how to manage time; and how to prepare for and take exams. Coaching services are available to help ADHD students deal with the serious time and task management problems that they frequently experience in college. ADHD students can choose to develop a partnership that assists them in developing and following specific short-term plans. Over time, ADHD College Coaching aims to help the student develop the awareness, thinking skills, patterns, and structures they need to compensate for how their ADHD affects their academic life. Group experiences are available to students each semester, based on their expressed interests. These can include support groups that promote understanding, acceptance, and pride; academic workshops that allow students to help each other learn specific skills; seminars that provide topical information from national experts; and panel discussions between students and university personnel.

SUPPORT SERVICES CONTACT INFORMATION

Learning Disability Program/Services: Learning Disabilities Services (LDS)
Director: Jane Byron
  E-mail: jsbyron@email.unc.edu
  Telephone: 919-962-7227
  Fax: 919-962-3674
Contact: Kim Allison

LEARNING DISABILITY SERVICES

Requests for the following services/accommodations will be evaluated individually based on appropriate and current documentation.

Allowed in Exams
  Calculator: Y/N
  Dictionary: Y/N
  Computer: Y/N
  Spellchecker: Y/N
Extended test time: Yes
Scribes: Yes
Proctors: Yes
Oral exams: Yes
Note-takers: Yes

Distraction-reduced environment: Yes
Tape recording in class: Yes
Books on tape from RFBD: Yes
Taping of books not from RFBD: Yes
Accommodations for students with ADHD: Yes, coaching
Reading machine: Yes
Other assistive technology: Yes
Priority registration: Yes

Added costs for services: No
LD specialists: Yes (4) LD, ADHD
Professional tutors: Yes
Peer tutors: Referrals
Max. hours/wk. for services: 2
How professors are notified of LD/ADHD: Faculty letter with student permission

GENERAL ADMISSIONS INFORMATION

Director of Admissions: Jerry Lucido
Telephone: 919-966-3621

ENTRANCE REQUIREMENTS

16 total are required; 4 English required, 3 math required, 3 science required, 4 science recommended, 1 science lab required, 2 foreign language required, 4 foreign language recommended, 1 social studies required, 1 history required, 1 history recommended, 1 elective required. High school diploma is required and GED is not accepted. Minimum TOEFL is 600. TOEFL required of all international applicants.

Application deadline: January 15
Notification: March
Average GPA: 4.0

Average SAT I Math: 629
Average SAT I Verbal: 622
Average ACT: 26

Graduated top 10% of class: 65%
Graduated top 25% of class: 92%
Graduated top 50% of class: 99%

COLLEGE GRADUATION REQUIREMENTS

Course waivers allowed: No
Course substitutions allowed: Yes
In what subjects: Foreign language and math

ADDITIONAL INFORMATION

Environment: The University is located in a suburban town near Raleigh.

Student Body
  Undergrad enrollment: 15,608
  Female: 61%
  Male: 39%
  Out-of-state: 18%

Cost Information
  In-state tuition: $2,365
  Out-of-state tuition: $11,531
  Room & board: $5,630
Housing Information
  University housing: Yes
  Percent living on campus: 43%

Greek System
  Fraternity: Yes
  Sorority: Yes
  Athletics: NCAA Division I

UNIV. OF N. CAROLINA—CHARLOTTE

9201 University City Boulevard, Charlotte, NC 28223-0001
Phone: 704-687-2213 • Fax: 704-687-6483
E-mail: unccadm@email.uncc.edu • Web: www.uncc.edu
Support level: S • Institution type: 4-year public

LEARNING DISABILITY PROGRAM AND SERVICES

The mission of Disability Services reflects the University's commitment to diversity by providing educational opportunities for persons with disabilities. This primary purpose is facilitated through ongoing research and development activities; development and presentation of educational seminars, workshops and training designed to increase knowledge of disability-related issues; and a case management system approach to service delivery. The professional staff in Disability Services assists students with learning disabilities to meet their individual needs. In all possible cases, UNC Charlotte will use existing resources for educational auxiliary aids. Services could include registration assistance, orientation to available services, individualized educational plan, special testing arrangements, counseling, and peer support services.

LD/ADHD ADMISSIONS INFORMATION

College entrance tests required: Yes
Nonstandardized tests accepted: Yes
Interview required: No
Essay required: No
Documentation required for LD: Psychoeducational evaluation
Documentation required for ADHD: Yes
Documentation submitted to: Disability Services
Special Ed. HS course work accepted: Yes

Specific course requirements for all applicants: Yes
Separate application required for services: No
# of LD applications submitted yearly: N/A
# of LD applications accepted yearly: N/A
Total # of students receiving LD/ADHD services: 127
Acceptance into program means acceptance into college: Students must be admitted and enrolled at the University first and then may request services.

ADMISSIONS

All applicants must meet the general admissions requirements and any special requirements for acceptance into a particular program of study. Students go through the regular application process. Applicants with learning disabilities are encouraged to provide information about their learning disability at the time of application for admission. The University reserves the right to withhold the admission of any applicant who fails to meet any of the requirements for admission. Students who are not otherwise qualified, and who provide documentation of a learning disability, may be reviewed by the Disability Services, which will give a recommendation to the Office of Admissions. Once students have been admitted and enrolled they may request the necessary services.

ADDITIONAL INFORMATION

Services offered include academic advisement/priority registration; assistive technology; taped textbooks; special test administration; note-takers; broad-based case management activities to include orientation and assessment for services; individual consultation/counseling 30 minutes weekly; workshops; referral for Tutorial Services and Learning. There is a tutoring center and a writing center. Currently there are 127 students with LD and 91 students with ADHD receiving services on campus. Students with ADHD must provide documentation that includes a diagnosis and a verification of the diagnosis.

SUPPORT SERVICES CONTACT INFORMATION

Learning Disability Program/Services: Disability Services
Director: Janet L. Filer
  E-mail: jfiler@email.uncc.edu
  Telephone: 704-547-4355
  Fax: 704-547-3226
Contact: Same

LEARNING DISABILITY SERVICES

Requests for the following services/accommodations will be evaluated individually based on appropriate and current documentation.

Allowed in Exams
  Calculator: Yes
  Dictionary: Yes
  Computer: Yes
  Spellchecker: Yes
Extended test time: Yes
Scribes: Yes
Proctors: Yes
Oral exams: Yes
Note-takers: Yes

Distraction-reduced environment: Yes
Tape recording in class: Yes
Books on tape from RFBD: Yes
Taping of books not from RFBD: Yes
Accommodations for students with
  ADHD: Yes
Reading machine: Yes
Other assistive technology: Yes
Priority registration: Yes

Added costs for services: No
LD specialists: No
Professional tutors: No
Peer tutors: Yes
Max. hours/wk. for services: 4
How professors are notified of
  LD/ADHD: By student and program director

GENERAL ADMISSIONS INFORMATION

Director of Admissions: Craig Fulton
Telephone: 704-547-3629

ENTRANCE REQUIREMENTS
16 total are required; 4 English required, 3 math required, 3 science required, 1 science lab required, 2 foreign language required, 2 social studies required, 1 history recommended, 2 elective required. High school diploma or GED required. Minimum TOEFL is 500. TOEFL required of all international applicants.

Application deadline: July 1
Notification: Rolling beginning 12/15
Average GPA: 3.5

Average SAT I Math: 529
Average SAT I Verbal: 514
Average ACT: 21

Graduated top 10% of class: 14%
Graduated top 25% of class: 52%
Graduated top 50% of class: 91%

COLLEGE GRADUATION REQUIREMENTS

Course waivers allowed: No
Course substitutions allowed: Yes
In what subjects: Substitutions in foreign language if supported by documentation; done only on a case-by-case basis

ADDITIONAL INFORMATION

Environment: The University is located on 1,000 acres 8 miles northeast of Charlotte.

Student Body
  Undergrad enrollment: 14,388
  Female: 54%
  Male: 46%
  Out-of-state: 12%

Cost Information
  In-state tuition: $1,920
  Out-of-state tuition: $9,190
  Room & board: $4,354
Housing Information
  University housing: Yes
  Percent living on campus: 27%

Greek System
  Fraternity: Yes
  Sorority: Yes
Athletics: NCAA Division I

University of North Carolina—Charlotte

Univ. of N. Carolina—Greensboro

123 Mossman Building, Greensboro, NC 27402-6170
Phone: 336-334-5243 • Fax: 336-334-4180
E-mail: undergrad_admissions@uncg.edu • Web: www.uncg.edu
Support level: CS • Institution type: 4-year public

LEARNING DISABILITY PROGRAM AND SERVICES

The University of North Carolina-Greensboro is committed to equality of educational opportunities for qualified students with disabilities. The goal of Disabled Student Services is to provide a full range of academic accommodations. Students who need tests offered in a nontraditional format may request this service. Modifications may include extended time, private room, reader, scribe, or use of word processor for essay examinations. Documentation must verify the use of special accommodations. The Disability Services office provides a handbook for students to use as a helpful guide in making their experience at UNCG a positive one.

LD/ADHD ADMISSIONS INFORMATION

College entrance tests required: Yes
Nonstandardized tests accepted: Yes
Interview required: No
Essay required: No
Documentation required for LD: Psychoeducational evaluation
Documentation required for ADHD: Yes
Documentation submitted to: Disability Services
Special Ed. HS course work accepted: No

Specific course requirements for all applicants: Yes
Separate application required for services: No
# of LD applications submitted yearly: N/A
# of LD applications accepted yearly: N/A
Total # of students receiving LD/ADHD services: 180
Acceptance into program means acceptance into college: Students must be admitted and enrolled at the University first and then may request services.

ADMISSIONS

There is no special admissions process for students with learning disabilities. Admissions is competitive and based on academic qualifications. Students with learning disabilities must submit the regular application and are considered for admission in the same manner as any other applicant. No pre-admission inquiry regarding the learning disability is made. However, it is helpful for the student to write a cover letter stating that a specific disability exists if support services will be necessary. This alerts the admissions staff to take this into consideration. It is highly recommended that the SAT or ACT be taken on an untimed basis if this gives a better estimate of the student's ability.

ADDITIONAL INFORMATION

DSS has several computers with word processors for registered students. Trained staff members are available for counseling to assist students with academic and/or personal problems. Voluntary note-takers are solicited through DSS, and photocopying is available. Students will meet with their faculty advisor to discuss courses that need to be taken, and DSS will "stamp" the students' registration cards to verify that they are registered with DSS and warrant priority registration. Assistance in securing taped textbooks through Recording for the Blind is provided, and a file of available readers is available for instances when materials are not available through RFB. Students are provided with information regarding campus tutorials and labs. Individual tutors are provided when it seems necessary. Students can receive help with study skills and time management techniques.

SUPPORT SERVICES CONTACT INFORMATION

Learning Disability Program/Services: Disability Services
Director: Patricia Bailey
  E-mail: plbailey@uncg.edu
  Telephone: 336-334-5440
  Fax: 336-334-4412
Contact: Same

LEARNING DISABILITY SERVICES

Requests for the following services/accommodations will be evaluated individually based on appropriate and current documentation.

Allowed in Exams
  Calculator: Yes
  Dictionary: Yes
  Computer: Yes
  Spellchecker: Yes
Extended test time: Yes
Scribes: Yes
Proctors: Yes
Oral exams: Yes
Note-takers: Yes

Distraction-reduced environment: Yes
Tape recording in class: Yes
Books on tape from RFBD: Yes
Taping of books not from RFBD: No
Accommodations for students with ADHD: Yes
Reading machine: Yes
Other assistive technology: Yes
Priority registration: Yes

Added costs for services: No
LD specialists: Yes
Professional tutors: No
Peer tutors: Yes
Max. hours/wk. for services: Depends on need
How professors are notified of LD/ADHD: By student

GENERAL ADMISSIONS INFORMATION

Director of Admissions: Jim Black (interim director)
Telephone: 336-334-5243

ENTRANCE REQUIREMENTS
15 total are required; 4 English required, 3 math required, 3 science required, 1 science lab required, 2 foreign language required, 2 social studies required, 1 history required, 1 elective required. High school diploma or GED required. Minimum TOEFL is 550. TOEFL required of all international applicants.

Application deadline: August 1
Notification: Rolling
Average GPA: 3.4

Average SAT I Math: 515
Average SAT I Verbal: 522
Average ACT: 20

Graduated top 10% of class: 14%
Graduated top 25% of class: 47%
Graduated top 50% of class: 86%

COLLEGE GRADUATION REQUIREMENTS

Course waivers allowed: No
Course substitutions allowed: Yes
In what subjects: Decided on a case-by-case basis in foreign language (they are the exception rather than the rule); all substitutions must be approved by a faculty committee

ADDITIONAL INFORMATION

Environment: The University is located on 178 acres in an urban area in Greensboro.

Student Body
  Undergrad enrollment: 10,021
  Female: 67%
  Male: 33%
  Out-of-state: 10%

Cost Information
  In-state tuition: $2,201
  Out-of-state tuition: $10,700
  Room & board: $4,742
Housing Information
  University housing: Yes
  Percent living on campus: 35%

Greek System
  Fraternity: Yes
  Sorority: Yes
Athletics: NCAA Division I

UNIV. OF N. CAROLINA—WILMINGTON

601 South College Road, Wilmington, NC 28403
Phone: 910-962-3243 • Fax: 910-962-3038
E-mail: admissions@uncwil.edu • Web: www.uncwil.edu
Support level: CS • Institution type: 4-year public

LEARNING DISABILITY PROGRAM AND SERVICES

The University's goal is to provide access to all of its academic programs, support services, and extracurricular activities, and to enrich academic and vocational experience while in college. The coordinator of Disability Services (DS) meets with the student in order to appraise special needs, make referrals, and arrange for special accommodations. The University has devoted much time and energy to meeting the requirements of Section 504 and ADA. This effort is exemplified by the accommodating services offered through DS for students with learning disabilities and by special cooperation of the faculty. As the number of students with learning disabilities attending UNCW increases, so does the University's commitment to make facilities and programs more accessible.

LD/ADHD ADMISSIONS INFORMATION

College entrance tests required: Yes
Nonstandardized tests accepted: Yes
Interview required: NR
Essay required: No
Documentation required for LD: WAIS-III; WJ
Documentation required for ADHD: Yes
Documentation submitted to: Disability Services
Special Ed. HS course work accepted: No

Specific course requirements for all applicants: Yes
Separate application required for services: Yes
# of LD applications submitted yearly: N/A
# of LD applications accepted yearly: N/A
Total # of students receiving LD/ADHD services: 200
Acceptance into program means acceptance into college: Students must be admitted and enrolled at the University first and then may request services.

ADMISSIONS

Students with learning disabilities must meet the same entrance requirements as all other applicants. Course requirements include 4 years English, 3 years math, 3 years science, 3 years social studies, 2 years foreign language.

ADDITIONAL INFORMATION

Services are provided based on individual need as assessed through recent diagnostic information and personal interview. As new needs are identified, services may be modified or developed to accommodate them. Newly accepted students interested in services should complete and sign the disclosure form that is included with the letter of acceptance. This information should then be forwarded to the Student Development Center. Current documentation must be sent to the coordinator of DS after acceptance to the University. Diagnostic testing must be conducted by a licensed professional, and an adequate report must include specific educational recommendations. Priority registration is available to all returning students registered with DSS. Services and accommodations are offered to undergraduate and graduate students.

SUPPORT SERVICES CONTACT INFORMATION

Learning Disability Program/Services: Disability Services (DS)
Director: Peggy Turner, PhD
  E-mail: turnerm@uncwill.edu
  Telephone: 910-962-3746
  Fax: 910-962-7124
Contact: Ginny Lundeen

LEARNING DISABILITY SERVICES

Requests for the following services/accommodations will be evaluated individually based on appropriate and current documentation.

Allowed in Exams
  Calculator: Y/N
  Dictionary: Y/N
  Computer: Y/N
  Spellchecker: Y/N
Extended test time: Yes
Scribes: Yes
Proctors: Yes
Oral exams: Yes
Note-takers: Yes

Distraction-reduced environment: Yes
Tape recording in class: Yes
Books on tape from RFBD: Yes
Taping of books not from RFBD: Yes
Accommodations for students with ADHD: Yes
Reading machine: Yes
Other assistive technology: Yes
Priority registration: Yes

Added costs for services: No
LD specialists: Yes (1)
Professional tutors: No
Peer tutors: Yes
Max. hours/wk. for services: Depends on need
How professors are notified of LD/ADHD: By student

GENERAL ADMISSIONS INFORMATION

Director of Admissions: Roxie Shabazz
Telephone: 910-962-3243

ENTRANCE REQUIREMENTS

4 English required, 3 math required, 3 science required, 1 science lab required, 2 foreign language required, 2 social studies required, 1 history required, 5 elective required. High school diploma or GED required. Minimum TOEFL is 580. TOEFL required of all international applicants.

Application deadline: February 15
Notification: May 1
Average GPA: 3.5

Average SAT I Math: 553
Average SAT I Verbal: 544
Average ACT: 23

Graduated top 10% of class: 18%
Graduated top 25% of class: 53%
Graduated top 50% of class: 94%

COLLEGE GRADUATION REQUIREMENTS

Course waivers allowed: No
Course substitutions allowed: Yes
In what subjects: Foreign language and math

ADDITIONAL INFORMATION

Environment: The University is located on a 650-acre urban campus.

Student Body
  Undergrad enrollment: 9,138
  Female: 60%
  Male: 40%
  Out-of-state: 13%

Cost Information
  In-state tuition: $1,102
  Out-of-state tuition: $8,452
  Room & board: $4,862
  Housing Information
    University housing: Yes
    Percent living on campus: 22%

Greek System
  Fraternity: Yes
  Sorority: Yes
Athletics: NCAA Division I

WAKE FOREST UNIVERSITY

Box 7305 Reynolda Station, Winston-Salem, NC 27109
Phone: 336-758-5201 • Fax: 336-758-4324
E-mail: admissions@wfu.edu • Web: www.wfu.edu
Support level: CS • Institution type: 4-year private

LEARNING DISABILITY PROGRAM AND SERVICES

The Learning Assistance Center (LAC) offers support for academic success. For students with documented disabilities, the program director will work with the student and members of the faculty to help implement any approved course accommodations. The students with learning disabilities have a series of conferences with staff members who specialize in academic skills and who help design an overall study plan to improve scholastic performance in those areas needing assistance. If special course accommodations are needed, the program director will serve as an advocate for the students with members of the faculty.

LD/ADHD ADMISSIONS INFORMATION

College entrance tests required: Yes
Nonstandardized tests accepted: Yes
Interview required: No
Essay required: Yes
Documentation required for LD: Psychoeducational
   evaluation: within 1 year
Documentation required for ADHD: Yes
Documentation submitted to: LAC
Special Ed. HS course work accepted: No

Specific course requirements for all applicants: Yes
Separate application required for services: No
# of LD applications submitted yearly: N/A
# of LD applications accepted yearly: N/A
Total # of students receiving LD/ADHD services: 18
Acceptance into program means acceptance into
   college: Students must be accepted and enrolled at the University first and then may request services.

ADMISSIONS

There are no special admissions. Students with learning disabilities submit the general Wake Forest University application and are expected to meet the same admission criteria as all applicants. Wake Forest does not accept the ACT. The middle 50 percent range for the SAT is 1240–1360. Course requirements include 4 years English, 3 years math, 1 year science, 2 years social studies, and 2 years foreign language. Students should self-disclose to the Learning Assistance Center after admission. Services are available to all enrolled students with documentation on file. Students are encouraged to provide a recent psychoeducational evaluation.

ADDITIONAL INFORMATION

The Learning Assistance Program staff will assist students with learning disabilities to learn new approaches to studying and methods for improving reading and comprehension, note-taking, time management, study organization, memory, motivation, and self-modification. The Learning Assistance Center offers peer tutoring services. In addition to one-on-one tutoring in most academic subjects, the LAC provides collaborative learning groups comprised of two to five students. The LAC also assists students who present special academic needs. Accommodations are determined based on appropriate documentation. Currently there are 30 students with LD and 23 with ADHD receiving accommodations or services on campus. Applications are accepted for course substitutions. All students with or without learning disabilities are eligible for group or individual tutoring in basic academic subjects. The tutors are advanced undergraduates or graduate students who have demonstrated mastery of specific subject areas and are supervised by the LAC staff for their tutoring activities. The LAC also offers all students individual academic counseling to help develop study, organization, and time-management strategies that are important for successful college-level learning.

SUPPORT SERVICES CONTACT INFORMATION

Learning Disability Program/Services: Learning Assistance Center (LAC)
Director: Van D. Westervelt, PhD
  Telephone: 336-759-5929
Contact: Same

LEARNING DISABILITY SERVICES

Requests for the following services/accommodations will be evaluated individually based on appropriate and current documentation.

Allowed in Exams
  Calculator: Yes
  Dictionary: Yes
  Computer: Yes
  Spellchecker: Yes
Extended test time: Yes
Scribes: No
Proctors: No
Oral exams: No
Note-takers: Yes

Distraction-reduced environment: Yes
Tape recording in class: Yes
Books on tape from RFBD: Yes
Taping of books not from RFBD: No
Accommodations for students with
  ADHD: Yes
Reading machine: No
Other assistive technology: No
Priority registration: No

Added costs for services: No
LD specialists: Yes (1)
Professional tutors: No
Peer tutors: 40
Max. hours/wk. for services:
  Unlimited
How professors are notified of
  LD/ADHD: By both student and
  director

GENERAL ADMISSIONS INFORMATION

Director of Admissions: William Starling
Telephone: 336-758-5201

ENTRANCE REQUIREMENTS
16 total are required; 20 total are recommended; 4 English required, 4 English recommended, 3 math required, 4 math recommended, 1 science required, 4 science recommended, 2 foreign language required, 4 foreign language recommended, 2 social studies required, 4 social studies recommended. High school diploma or GED required. Minimum TOEFL is 550. TOEFL required of all international applicants.

Application deadline: January 15
Notification: April 1
Average GPA: N/A

Average SAT I Math: 652
Average SAT I Verbal: 639
Average ACT: N/A

Graduated top 10% of class: 67%
Graduated top 25% of class: 98%
Graduated top 50% of class: 98%

COLLEGE GRADUATION REQUIREMENTS

Course waivers allowed: No
Course substitutions allowed: Yes
In what subjects: Foreign language

ADDITIONAL INFORMATION

Environment: The 550-acre campus is located in the Piedmont region of North Carolina.

Student Body
  Undergrad enrollment: 4,086
  Female: 52%
  Male: 48%
  Out-of-state: 71%

Cost Information
  Tuition: $22,410
  Room & board: $6,430
Housing Information
  University housing: Yes
  Percent living on campus: 78%

Greek System
  Fraternity: Yes
  Sorority: Yes
Athletics: NCAA Division I

WESTERN CAROLINA UNIVERSITY

242 HFR Administration, Cullowhee, NC 28723
Phone: 828-227-7317 • Fax: 828-227-7319
E-mail: cauley@wcu.edu • Web: www.wcu.edu
Support level: CS • Institution type: 4-year public

LEARNING DISABILITY PROGRAM AND SERVICES

The Disabled Student Services Program attempts to respond to the needs of students with learning disabilities by making services and equipment available as needed, and by making judicious use of reading and tutoring services. Each student in the program is assigned a counselor/advisor. The students must meet with this counselor at least twice a month to discuss topics such as academic progress, study skills, adjustment to college life, career decision-making, and personal concerns. In addition, students may take specially designed classes in English, reading, and study skills.

LD/ADHD ADMISSIONS INFORMATION

College entrance tests required: Yes
Nonstandardized tests accepted: Yes
Interview required: N/A
Essay required: No
Documentation required for LD: Psychoeducational evaluation: within three years
Documentation required for ADHD: Yes
Documentation submitted to: Student Support Services
Special Ed. HS course work accepted: No

Specific course requirements for all applicants: Yes
Separate application required for services: No
# of LD applications submitted yearly: N/A
# of LD applications accepted yearly: N/A
Total # of students receiving LD/ADHD services: 80–100
Acceptance into program means acceptance into college: Students must be admitted and enrolled at the University first and then may request services.

ADMISSIONS

Students with learning disabilities are admitted under the same standards as students who have no learning disability. Minimum GPA is 2.0 plus 4 years English, 3 years math, 3 years science, 3 years social studies, and 2 years foreign language (recommended). Nonstandardized ACT/SAT are acceptable. Students who are admitted are encouraged to take the Summer Term Enrichment Program (STEP) in order to "jump-start" their introduction to college. Students not admissible through the regular admission process may be offered a probationary admission and must begin in the summer prior to freshman year. The admission decision is made by the Admission Office.

ADDITIONAL INFORMATION

To qualify for services students must be enrolled at the University, be evaluated within the last three years, be willing to participate in additional evaluation to confirm the disability, and be willing to participate in planning support services. The following services or accommodations are available for students with appropriate documementation: the use of calculators, dictionary, computer or spellchecker in exams; extended time on tests; distraction-free environment; scribe; proctor; oral exams; note-taker; tape recorder in class; taped texts; and priority registration. All students have access to tutoring, writing and math center, technology assistance center, and counseling and psychological services. Admitted students should maintain good class attendance, strive for good grades, cooperate with counselors and advisors, set realistic career goals, and meet with the LD team. Services and accommodations are available for undergraduate and graduate students.

SUPPORT SERVICES CONTACT INFORMATION

Learning Disability Program/Services: Student Support Services
Director: Carol Mellen
  E-mail: mellen@wcu.edu
  Telephone: 828-227-7127
  Fax: 828-227-7078
Contact: Same

LEARNING DISABILITY SERVICES

Requests for the following services/accommodations will be evaluated individually based on appropriate and current documentation.

Allowed in Exams
  Calculator: Yes
  Dictionary: Yes
  Computer: Yes
  Spellchecker: Yes
  Extended test time: Yes
  Scribes: Yes
  Proctors: Yes
  Oral exams: Yes
  Note-takers: Yes

Distraction-reduced environment: Yes
Tape recording in class: Yes
Books on tape from RFBD: Yes
Taping of books not from RFBD: Yes
Accommodations for students with ADHD: Yes
Reading machine: Yes
Other assistive technology: Yes
Priority registration: Yes

Added costs for services: No
LD specialists: Yes (3)
Professional tutors: At times
Peer tutors: 20–50
Max. hours/wk. for services: NR
How professors are notified of LD/ADHD: By student through an educational support plan

GENERAL ADMISSIONS INFORMATION

Director of Admissions: Phil Cauley
Telephone: 828-227-7317

ENTRANCE REQUIREMENTS
20 total are required; 24 total are recommended; 4 English required, 3 math required, 3 science required, 3 science lab required, 2 foreign language recommended, 2 social studies required, 1 history required. Minimum GPA 2.0. High school diploma or GED required. Minimum TOEFL is 550. TOEFL required of all international applicants.

Application deadline: July 1
Notification: Rolling
Average GPA: 3.17

Average SAT I Math: 503
Average SAT I Verbal: 501
Average ACT: NR

Graduated top 10% of class: 8%
Graduated top 25% of class: 24%
Graduated top 50% of class: 56%

COLLEGE GRADUATION REQUIREMENTS

Course waivers allowed: Varies
Course substitutions allowed: Yes
In what subjects: Foreign language; other requirements will be received on an individual case-by-case basis

ADDITIONAL INFORMATION

Environment: The University is located on 400 acres in a rural area 50 miles southwest of Asheville.

Student Body
  Undergrad enrollment: 5,611
  Female: 52%
  Male: 48%
  Out-of-state: 7%

Cost Information
  In-state tuition: $1,022
  Out-of-state tuition: $8,292
  Room & board: $3,424
Housing Information
  University housing: Yes
  Percent living on campus: 44%

Greek System
  Fraternity: Yes
  Sorority: Yes
Athletics: NCAA Division I

WINGATE UNIVERSITY

Campus Box 3059, Wingate, NC 28174
Phone: 704-233-8200 • Fax: 704-233-8110
E-mail: admit@wingate.edu • Web: www.wingate.edu
Support level: CS • Institution type: 4-year private

LEARNING DISABILITY PROGRAM AND SERVICES

Wingate University provides a program designed to assist students with diagnosed specific learning disabilities/dyslexia. Wingate University is aware that the students with learning disabilities may be successful in the College environment, provided that their special needs are recognized and proper services are made available to them. The coordinator works closely with each student in an effort to maximize the opportunity for a successful college experience. While each student will have specific needs, there are some modes of assistance available to assist each student with the maximum support necessary. This assistance will include identifying strengths and weaknesses, balancing course selections, pre-registration, access to word processing, oral testing, extra testing time, taped texts, and tutoring. Success will be determined by the motivation and initiative of the individual student in seeking available assistance.

LD/ADHD ADMISSIONS INFORMATION

College entrance tests required: Yes
Nonstandardized tests accepted: Yes
Interview required: Yes
Essay required: Yes
Documentation required for LD: Psychoeducational
evaluation
Documentation required for ADHD: Yes
Documentation submitted to: Specific LD
Special Ed. HS course work accepted: Yes

Specific course requirements for all applicants: Yes
Separate application required for services: No
# of LD applications submitted yearly: N/A
# of LD applications accepted yearly: N/A
Total # of students receiving LD/ADHD services: 500–600
**Acceptance into program means acceptance into
college:** Students must be accepted and enrolled at the
University first and then may request services.

ADMISSIONS

All applicants must submit the general application and meet the same admission requirements. There is no special process for students with learning disabilities. Applicants must submit either SAT/ACT; two letters of recommendation; 2.7 GPA; and a short self-statement or essay; course requirements include 4 years English, 3 years math, 2 years history, 2 years science, 1 year social studies, and 2 years of foreign language are recommended. Once students are admitted and enrolled they should provide current documentation of specific learning disabilities in order to receive appropriate accommodations and services.

ADDITIONAL INFORMATION

Services for enrolled students include developing a plan for study, including choice of major, proper class load, liaison with faculty, informing faculty, and regular evaluation sessions; and additional guidance through the College's counseling program. With appropriate documentation students may have accommodations such as extended testing time; distraction-free environment for tests; calculator, dictionary, computer and spellcheck in exams; scribes; proctors; note-takers; tape recording in class; books on tape; peer tutoring; and priority registration. There are no waivers or substitutions for college graduation requirements.

SUPPORT SERVICES CONTACT INFORMATION

Learning Disability Program/Services: Specific Learning Disabilities
Director: Linda Stedje-Larson
   Telephone: 704-233-8269
Contact: Same

LEARNING DISABILITY SERVICES

Requests for the following services/accommodations will be evaluated individually based on appropriate and current documentation.

Allowed in Exams
   Calculator: Yes
   Dictionary: Yes
   Computer: Yes
   Spellchecker: Yes
Extended test time: Y/N
Scribes: Y/N
Proctors: Y/N
Oral exams: Y/N
Note-takers: Y/N

Distraction-reduced environment: Y/N
Tape recording in class: Y/N
Books on tape from RFBD: Yes
Taping of books not from RFBD: No
Accommodations for students with
   ADHD: Yes
Reading machine: No
Other assistive technology: No
Priority registration: Yes

Added costs for services: No
LD specialists: Yes (1)
Professional tutors: No
Peer tutors: Yes
Max. hours/wk. for services:
   Unlimited
How professors are notified of
   LD/ADHD: By student and coordinator

GENERAL ADMISSIONS INFORMATION

Director of Admissions: Walter Crutchfield
Telephone: 704-233-8200

ENTRANCE REQUIREMENTS

18 total are recommended; 4 English recommended, 3 math recommended, 2 science recommended, 1 science lab recommended, 2 foreign language recommended, 2 social studies recommended, 2 history recommended, 2 elective recommended. High school diploma or GED required. Minimum TOEFL is 550. TOEFL required of all international applicants.

Application deadline: August 1
Notification: Rolling beginning 10/1
Average GPA: 3.1

Average SAT I Math: 499
Average SAT I Verbal: 498
Average ACT: 22

Graduated top 10% of class: 18%
Graduated top 25% of class: 38%
Graduated top 50% of class: 70%

COLLEGE GRADUATION REQUIREMENTS

Course waivers allowed: No
Course substitutions allowed: No
In what subjects: N/A

ADDITIONAL INFORMATION

Environment: The University is located on 330 acres in a small town 25 miles east of Charlotte.

Student Body
   Undergrad enrollment: 1,115
   Female: 50%
   Male: 50%
   Out-of-state: 48%

Cost Information
   Tuition: $12,300
   Room & board: $5,200
Housing Information
   University housing: Yes
   Percent living on campus: 72%

Greek System
   Fraternity: Yes
   Sorority: Yes
   Athletics: NCAA Division II

MINOT STATE UNIVERSITY

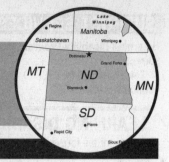

105 Simrall Blvd., Bottineau, ND 58318
Phone: 800-542-6866 • Fax: 701-288-5499
E-mail: groszk@misu.nodak.edu • Web: www.misu-b.nodak.edu
Support level: CS • Institution type: 2-year public

LEARNING DISABILITY PROGRAM AND SERVICES

The Learning Center provides a variety of academic support services to eligible students with LD. The Learning Center also provides individualized or small group instruction in English, algebra, biology, basic computer use, and other areas. Individuals are also provided with services that best meet their needs. In addition, study skills and reading improvement classes are offered for credit. An LD specialist/math instructor and an English/social studies instructor provide assistance in this program. Students planning to enroll at MSU-Bottineau should send documentation of the disability that is no more than three years old to the Learning Center. The documentation should include an intelligence assessment (preferably the WAIS-R); achievement testing such as the Woodcock-Johnson psychoeducational battery; and education recommendations such as accommodations provided in high school and a recent IEP. Students should visit the Learning Center as soon as they arrive on campus. Students will be asked to complete an application and the Learning Center instructor will review the class schedule and arrange for tutoring if needed.

LD/ADHD ADMISSIONS INFORMATION

College entrance tests required: No
Nonstandardized tests accepted: Yes
Interview required: No
Essay required: No
Documentation required for LD: Documentation is needed only if the student requests accommodation; psychological evaluation, recent IEP
Documentation required for ADHD: Yes
Documentation submitted to: Learning Center
Special Ed. HS course work accepted: Yes

Specific course requirements for all applicants: Yes
Separate application required for services: No
# of LD applications submitted yearly: N/A
# of LD applications accepted yearly: N/A
Total # of students receiving LD/ADHD services: 10–16
Acceptance into program means acceptance into college: Students must be admitted and enrolled and then may request services.

ADMISSIONS

Minot State University has an open admission policy. Applicants must present a high school diploma or equivalent such as a GED. Standardized tests are not required. Students are encouraged to self-disclose the disability during the application process so that the University may provide information about accessing support once enrolled. All students who enroll are asked to complete a questionnaire that asks them to identify academic support services that they feel they may need once on campus.

ADDITIONAL INFORMATION

The Learning Center offers free tutoring and is open to all students. Sessions are adapted to fit a student's schedule. Individual tutoring is available. Students may receive accommodations that include class scheduling, although priority registration is not offered. Skills courses are offered in note-taking strategies, test-taking tips, and memory aids. There is a one-credit reading improvement course that helps improve reading comprehension. Additional accommodations based on appropriate documentation could include extended testing time, note-takers, distraction-free testing environments, tape recorder in class, and auxiliary taping of books not available through RFBD. Partners Affiliated for Student Success is a consortium of educational institutions and businesses dedicated to assisting learners as they move from high school education to post-secondary education to work.

SUPPORT SERVICES CONTACT INFORMATION

Learning Disability Program/Services: Learning Center
Director: Jan Nahinurk
 E-mail: nahinurk@misu.nodak.edu
 Telephone: 701-228-5479
 Fax: 701-228-5468
Contact: Same

LEARNING DISABILITY SERVICES

Requests for the following services/accommodations will be evaluated individually based on appropriate and current documentation.

Allowed in Exams
 Calculator: Y/N
 Dictionary: Y/N
 Computer: Y/N
 Spellchecker: Y/N
Extended test time: Yes
Scribes: Y/N
Proctors: Y/N
Oral exams: Y/N
Note-takers: Yes

Distraction-reduced environment: Yes
Tape recording in class: Yes
Books on tape from RFBD: NR
Taping of books not from RFBD: Yes
Accommodations for students with
 ADHD: Yes
Reading machine: NR
Other assistive technology: NR
Priority registration: No

Added costs for services: No
LD specialists: Yes (1)
Professional tutors: 2
Peer tutors: Varies
Max. hours/wk. for services: Varies
How professors are notified of
 LD/ADHD: By both student and director

GENERAL ADMISSIONS INFORMATION

Director of Admissions: Ken Grosz
Telephone: 800-542-6866

ENTRANCE REQUIREMENTS

Core courses include 4 years English, 3 years math, 3 years social studies, and 3 years science. May apply online but need hard copy submitted also. ACT/SAT required.

Application deadline: Rolling
Notification: Rolling
Average GPA: 3.1

Average SAT I Math: NR
Average SAT I Verbal: NR
Average ACT: 21

Graduated top 10% of class: NR
Graduated top 25% of class: NR
Graduated top 50% of class: NR

COLLEGE GRADUATION REQUIREMENTS

Course waivers allowed: No
Course substitutions allowed: No
In what subjects: N/A

ADDITIONAL INFORMATION

Environment: Located in a small town 105 miles from Bismark.

Student Body
 Undergrad enrollment: 450
 Female: 52%
 Male: 48%
 Out-of-state: 14%

Cost Information
 In-state tuition: $1,632
 Out-of-state tuition: $4,357
 Room & board: $2,816
Housing Information
 University housing: Yes
 Percent living on campus: 51%

Greek System
 Fraternity: No
 Sorority: No
 Athletics: NAIA

NORTH DAKOTA STATE UNIVERSITY

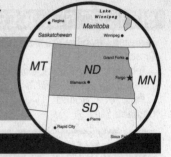

Box 5454, Fargo, ND 58105
Phone: 701-231-8643 • Fax: 701-231-8802
E-mail: NDSU_Admission@ndsu.nodak.edu • Web: www.ndsu.edu
Support level: CS • Institution type: 4-year public

LEARNING DISABILITY PROGRAM AND SERVICES

The mission of Disabilities Services is to assist students with disabilities in obtaining optimal access to educational programs, facilities, and employment at NDSU. Toward this end, the staff collaborates with other Counseling Center staff in providing consultation with students regarding accommodations that are therapeutic to their development as human beings and students. Disabilities Services works to provide equal access to academic programs, to promote self-awareness and advocacy, to educate the student body and faculty on disability-related issues, and to provide reasonable and appropriate accommodations. The staff educates faculty regarding the accommodation needs of students and works to ensure compliance with the Americans with Disabilities Act.

LD/ADHD ADMISSIONS INFORMATION

College entrance tests required: Yes
Nonstandardized tests accepted: Yes
Interview required: No
Essay required: No
Documentation required for LD: Psychoeducational evaluation
Documentation required for ADHD: Yes
Documentation submitted to: Disability Services
Special Ed. HS course work accepted: Yes

Specific course requirements for all applicants: Yes
Separate application required for services: No
# of LD applications submitted yearly: N/A
# of LD applications accepted yearly: N/A
Total # of students receiving LD/ADHD services: 80
Acceptance into program means acceptance into college: Students must be admitted and enrolled at the College first and then may request services.

ADMISSIONS
Students with learning disabilities submit the general application form and are expected to meet the same admission standards as all applicants. The ACT range is 20–22 and the minimum GPA is 2.5. Applicants are expected to have high school courses in math, including algebra and above, English, lab sciences, and social studies. Students with learning disabilities may include a self-disclosure or information explaining or documenting the disability. When necessary, an admission decision is made jointly by the Coordinator of the Program and the Admissions Office. In this case Disabilities Services would review the documentation and provide a recommendation to Admissions. Students can be admitted conditionally on probation and are required to take a study skills course.

ADDITIONAL INFORMATION
Skills courses are offered in study strategies, reading, computers, math, and science. A technology lab/resource room is available for student use. Assessment, counseling, and remedial support are coordinated through the Center for Student Counseling and Personal Growth. In addition, individual counseling, group support, career counseling, and personal/academic enrichment classes are offered. The NDSU Student Support Services Program provides tutoring and small group instruction. Students with appropriate documentation may request alternative testing accommodations. Skills classes are offered for credit for students with learning disabilities and ADHD. Additionally, Disabilities Services offers support groups for students with ADHD. Services and accommodations are available for undergraduate and graduate students.

SUPPORT SERVICES CONTACT INFORMATION

Learning Disability Program/Services: Disabilities Services
Director: Catherine Anderson
  E-mail: catherine_anderson@ndsu.nodak.edu
  Telephone: 701-231-7671
  Fax: 701-231-6318
Contact: Liz Gibb
  Telephone: 701-231-7714

LEARNING DISABILITY SERVICES

Requests for the following services/accommodations will be evaluated individually based on appropriate and current documentation.

Allowed in Exams
  Calculator: Y/N
  Dictionary: Y/N
  Computer: Yes
  Spellchecker: Y/N
Extended test time: Yes
Scribes: Yes
Proctors: Yes
Oral exams: Y/N
Note-takers: No

Distraction-reduced environment: Yes
Tape recording in class: Yes
Books on tape from RFBD: Yes
Taping of books not from RFBD: Yes
**Accommodations for students with
  ADHD:** Yes
Reading machine: Yes
Other assistive technology: Yes
Priority registration: Yes

Added costs for services: No
LD specialists: Yes (1)
Professional tutors: Yes
Peer tutors: No
Max. hours/wk. for services: 3 hours
  per class per week
**How professors are notified of
  LD/ADHD:** By student and program
  director

GENERAL ADMISSIONS INFORMATION

Director of Admissions: Dr. Kate Haugen
Telephone: 701-231-8643

ENTRANCE REQUIREMENTS
13 total are required; 4 English required, 3 math required, 3 science required, 3 science lab required, 3 social studies required. High school diploma or GED required. Minimum TOEFL is 525. TOEFL required of all international applicants.

Application deadline: August 15
Notification: Rolling beginning 8/1
Average GPA: 3.4

Average SAT I Math: NR
Average SAT I Verbal: NR
Average ACT: 23

Graduated top 10% of class: NR
Graduated top 25% of class: NR
Graduated top 50% of class: NR

COLLEGE GRADUATION REQUIREMENTS

Course waivers allowed: No
Course substitutions allowed: Yes
In what subjects: Yes, sometimes course substitutions are allowed

ADDITIONAL INFORMATION

Environment: The University is located in a small city 250 miles from Minneapolis, Sioux Falls, and Winnipeg, Canada.

Student Body
  Undergrad enrollment: 8,965
  Female: 43%
  Male: 57%
  Out-of-state: 45%

Cost Information
  In-state tuition: $2,886
  Out-of-state tuition: $7,028
  Room & board: $3,592
Housing Information
  University housing: Yes
  Percent living on campus: 34%

Greek System
  Fraternity: Yes
  Sorority: Yes
Athletics: NCAA Division II

BOWLING GREEN STATE UNIVERSITY

110 McFall Center, Bowling Green, OH 43403
Phone: 419-372-2086 • Fax: 419-372-6955
E-mail: admissions@bgnet.bgsu.edu • Web: www.bgsu.edu
Support level: S • Institution type: 4-year public

LEARNING DISABILITY PROGRAM AND SERVICES

The philosophy of the University is to level the playing field for students with LD and/or ADHD through the provision of appropriate accommodations and advocacy. The Office of Disability Services is evidence of BGSU's commitment to provide a support system that assists in conquering obstacles that persons with disabilities may encounter as they pursue their educational goals and activities. ODS hopes to recognize the diverse talents that persons with disabilities have to offer to the University and the community. ODS provides services on an as-needed basis. The Study Skills Lab is open to all BGSU students, and the extent of participation is determined by the student. No grades are given in the lab, participation is voluntary, and the program is individualized. The lab is not a tutorial service, but students will be shown efficient techniques for studying, reading textbooks, taking notes, time management, and strategies for effective test-taking and test preparation. Students are scheduled according to need and personal goals. They may attend workshops and/or request a standing weekly appointment.

LD/ADHD ADMISSIONS INFORMATION

College entrance tests required: Yes
Nonstandardized tests accepted: Yes
Interview required: No
Essay required: No
Documentation required for LD: Psychoeducational evaluation: within 3 years
Documentation required for ADHD: Yes
Documentation submitted to: Disability Service
Special Ed. HS course work accepted: Yes

Specific course requirements for all applicants: Yes
Separate application required for services: No
# of LD applications submitted yearly: N/A
# of LD applications accepted yearly: N/A
Total # of students receiving LD/ADHD services: 300–326
Acceptance into program means acceptance into college: Students must be accepted and enrolled at the University first and then may request services.

ADMISSIONS

There is no special application or special admissions process. Core courses preferred include 4 years English, 3 years math, 3 years science, 3 years social studies, 2 years foreign language, 1 year art. Students with LD may substitute foreign language with another core course. The minimum GPA is approximately 2.0. Students with LD submit the regular application and are encouraged to self-disclose their LD and arrange an interview with ODS to allow staff to discuss any documentation they may require and any concerns of the students. Additional information such as school or medical history that describes specific strengths and weaknesses is helpful in determining services necessary, once the student is admitted. Information documenting the LD should be sent to ODS. Students should submit the results of a psychoeducational evaluation or other testing and documentation that establishes the presence of a specific LD. Students should indicate accommodations that have worked successfully in high school. There is a Summer Freshman Program for freshmen applicants who do not meet the academic standards for fall admission.

ADDITIONAL INFORMATION

General services include priority registration; advising by sharing information on instructor's teaching and testing styles; Writing Lab for effective strategies; Study Skills Center for effective study skills, test-taking strategies, time management, and textbook reading skills; Math Lab, a walk-in lab for understanding basic and advanced concepts; computerized technology; note-takers, readers, and scribes; letters to professors explaining the disability and modifications needed; advocacy; and books on tape. To be eligible for test accommodations, students are required to provide documentation that provides a clear indication/recommendation for the need requested. Staffers work with the student to reach consensus on the type of accommodation. Test accommodations may include extended time, oral exams, take-home exams, open-book exams, readers, scribes, computers and spellcheck or grammar check, calculators, scratch paper with lines, speller's dictionaries, question clarification, modification of test response format, and quiet room.

SUPPORT SERVICES CONTACT INFORMATION

Learning Disability Program/Services: Disability Service for Students
Director: Rob Cunningham
  E-mail: rcunnin@bgnct.bgsu.edu
  Telephone: 419-372-8495
  Fax: 419-372-8496
Contact: Same

LEARNING DISABILITY SERVICES

Requests for the following services/accommodations will be evaluated individually based on appropriate and current documentation.

Allowed in Exams
  Calculator: Yes
  Dictionary: Yes
  Computer: Yes
  Spellchecker: Yes
Extended test time: Yes
Scribes: Yes
Proctors: Yes
Oral exams: Yes
Note-takers: Yes

Distraction-reduced environment: Yes
Tape recording in class: Yes
Books on tape from RFBD: Yes
Taping of books not from RFBD: Yes
Accommodations for students with ADHD: Yes
Reading machine: Yes
Other assistive technology: Yes
Priority registration: Yes

Added costs for services: No
LD specialists: No
Professional tutors: Yes
Peer tutors: Yes
Max. hours/wk. for services: Unlimited
How professors are notified of LD/ADHD: By student

GENERAL ADMISSIONS INFORMATION

Director of Admissions: Gary Swegan
Telephone: 419-372-7799

ENTRANCE REQUIREMENTS

16 total are required; 4 English required, 3 math required, 3 science required, 2 science lab required, 2 foreign language required, 3 social studies required. High school diploma or GED required. Minimum TOEFL is 500. TOEFL required of all international applicants.

Application deadline: July 15
Notification: Rolling beginning 10/1
Average GPA: 3.2

Average SAT I Math: 513
Average SAT I Verbal: 513
Average ACT: 22

Graduated top 10% of class: 12%
Graduated top 25% of class: 35%
Graduated top 50% of class: 73%

COLLEGE GRADUATION REQUIREMENTS

Course waivers allowed: Yes
Course substitutions allowed: Yes
In what subjects: Primarily foreign language; other requests will be considered

ADDITIONAL INFORMATION

Environment: The 1,250-acre campus is in a small town 25 miles south of Toledo.

Student Body
  Undergrad enrollment: 15,494
  Female: 57%
  Male: 43%
  Out-of-state: 6%

Cost Information
  In-state tuition: $4,330
  Out-of-state tuition: $10,228
  Room & board: $5,768
Housing Information
  University housing: Yes
  Percent living on campus: 44%

Greek System
  Fraternity: Yes
  Sorority: Yes
Athletics: NCAA Division I

CASE WESTERN RESERVE UNIVERSITY

103 Tomlinson Hall, 10900 Euclid Avenue, Cleveland, OH 44106-7055
Phone: 216-368-4450 • Fax: 216-368-5111
E-mail: admission@po.cwru.edu • Web: www.cwru.edu
Support level: S • Institution type: 4-year private

LEARNING DISABILITY PROGRAM AND SERVICES

The goals of Educational Support Services (ESS) are to provide reasonable accommodations and serve as an advocate for individuals with diagnosed learning disabilities. ESS ensures that students with disabilities have access to services and accommodations needed to make the College experience a positive and successful one. ESS provides academic support, special accommodations, and personal encouragement.

LD/ADHD ADMISSIONS INFORMATION

College entrance tests required: Yes
Nonstandardized tests accepted: Yes
Interview required: No
Essay required: Yes
Documentation required for LD: Psychoeducational evaluation
Documentation required for ADHD: Yes
Documentation submitted to: ESS
Special Ed. HS course work accepted: No

Specific course requirements for all applicants: Yes
Separate application required for services: No
# of LD applications submitted yearly: N/A
# of LD applications accepted yearly: N/A
Total # of students receiving LD/ADHD services: 25
Acceptance into program means acceptance into college: Students must be admitted and enrolled at the University first and then may request services.

ADMISSIONS

Students with learning disabilities are encouraged to apply to CWRU. Admission is highly competitive, but all applicants are evaluated on an individual basis. Students who feel additional information would be helpful to the Admission Committee are encouraged to provide diagnostic information about their individual situation. General admission criteria include 4 years English, 3 years math, 3 years social science, 1 year science, and 2–4 years foreign language. Students must also submit a writing sample and are encouraged to have an interview. Most admitted students rank in the top 20 percent of their class and have an SAT I of 1180–1380 or an ACT of 27–31.

ADDITIONAL INFORMATION

Skills courses are offered in study and learning strategies, time management, and reading. It is helpful for students to provide information regarding the nature of their disability so that services may be accommodated to their needs. High-performing students do well with the peer tutors available through ESS. These tutors are students who have successfully completed the appropriate course work and have been approved by faculty. Special arrangements are made by ESS for students to have alternative testing such as additional time and proctored examinations in alternative settings. Students with LD are eligible for books on tape through RFB. The ESS center has reading improvement software, word processing, and all network applications. A reading strategies tutorial program for one credit taught by a graduate student is also available for students with LD.

SUPPORT SERVICES CONTACT INFORMATION

Learning Disability Program/Services: Educational Support Services (ESS)
Director: Mayo Bulloch
  E-mail: mxb14@po.cwru.edu
  Telephone: 216-368-5230
Contact: Susan Sampson, Coordinator
  E-mail: sn617@po.cwru.edu

LEARNING DISABILITY SERVICES

Requests for the following services/accommodations will be evaluated individually based on appropriate and current documentation.

Allowed in Exams
  Calculator: Y/N
  Dictionary: Yes
  Computer: Y/N
  Spellchecker: Yes
Extended test time: Yes
Scribes: Yes
Proctors: Yes
Oral exams: Yes
Note-takers: Yes

Distraction-reduced environment: Yes
Tape recording in class: Yes
Books on tape from RFBD: Yes
Taping of books not from RFBD: Yes
Accommodations for students with ADHD: Yes
Reading machine: Yes
Other assistive technology: Yes
Priority registration: Yes

Added costs for services: No
LD specialists: No
Professional tutors: No
Peer tutors: Yes
Max. hours/wk. for services: Unlimited peer tutoring
How professors are notified of LD/ADHD: By student and program director

GENERAL ADMISSIONS INFORMATION

Director of Admissions: Elizebeth Woyczynski
Telephone: 216-368-4450

ENTRANCE REQUIREMENTS
16 total are required; 4 English required, 3 math required, 4 math recommended, 3 science required, 1 science lab required, 2 science lab recommended, 2 foreign language required, 3 foreign language recommended, 3 social studies required, 4 social studies recommended. High school diploma or GED required. Minimum TOEFL is 550. TOEFL required of all international applicants.

Application deadline: February 1
Notification: April 1
Average GPA: NR

Average SAT I Math: 680
Average SAT I Verbal: 650
Average ACT: 29

Graduated top 10% of class: 71%
Graduated top 25% of class: 91%
Graduated top 50% of class: 98%

COLLEGE GRADUATION REQUIREMENTS

Course waivers allowed: No
Course substitutions allowed: Yes
In what subjects: English composition

ADDITIONAL INFORMATION

Environment: The University is located on 128 acres 4 miles east of downtown Cleveland.

Student Body
  Undergrad enrollment: 3,434
  Female: 39%
  Male: 61%
  Out-of-state: 40%

Cost Information
  Tuition: $21,000
  Room & board: $6,250
Housing Information
  University housing: Yes
  Percent living on campus: 73%

Greek System
  Fraternity: Yes
  Sorority: Yes
Athletics: NCAA Division III

CENTRAL OHIO TECHNICAL COLLEGE

1179 University Drive, Newark, OH 43055
Phone: 740-366-9222 • Fax: 740-364-9531
Web: cotc.tee.oh.us
Support: CS • Institution: 2-year public

LEARNING DISABILITY PROGRAM AND SERVICES

The goals of Disability Services are to foster self-advocacy and independence. Disability Services provides diagnostic testing, counseling, and accommodations for students with learning disabilities. This is the only college in Ohio that provides free complete diagnostic testing. Placement tests are given after admissions. The Learning Assistance Center and Disability Services (LAC/DS) is the academic support unit. LAC/DS provides programs and services to any student desiring to strengthen academic skills. Students need to self-identify before scheduling classes. Early notice is needed for some services, such as alternate testing and recorded textbooks. The College advocates meeting the unique needs of students with disabilities, and accommodations provided allow for equal access to higher education.

LD/ADHD ADMISSIONS INFORMATION

College entrance tests required: No
Nonstandardized tests accepted: Yes
Interview required: No
Essay required: No
Documentation required for LD: WAIS-III; WJ
Documentation required for ADHD: Yes
Submitted to: Office for Disability Services
Special Ed. HS course work accepted: Yes

Specific course requirements for all applicants: Yes
Separate application required for services: No
# of LD applications submitted yearly: N/A
# of LD applications accepted yearly: N/A
Total # of students receiving LD/ADHD services: 70
Acceptance into program means acceptance into
   college: Students must be admitted and enrolled at the
   College first and then may request services.

ADMISSIONS

Admission is open to all applicants with a high school diploma or the GED, except in health programs. There are no specific course requirements. ACT/SAT tests are not required. To receive accommodations, the student's diagnostic test results and diagnosis must be within the past three years.

ADDITIONAL INFORMATION

The Learning Assistance Center is a learning center for students with learning disabilities and ADHD. Students who received learning disability services such as tutoring during their high school senior year are automatically eligible for services. The tutoring program includes peer tutoring in almost any course, scheduled at the student's convenience for two hours each week per course. The Academic Skills Lab has a Computer Lab; resources to improve reading, math, and language skills; word processing; and study aids for some courses and national tests. The Study Skills Workshop Series provides assistance in improving study skills and 50-minute workshops on time management, learning styles/memory, test preparation and test-taking, reading textbooks effectively, and note-taking. Students also have access to proctors, individualized instruction designed to meet special needs, advocacy assistance, diagnosis counseling, and assistance with accommodations.

SUPPORT SERVICES CONTACT INFORMATION

Learning Disability Program/Services: Office for Disability Services
Director: Phyllis E. Thompson, PhD
  E-mail: thompson.33@osu.edu
  Telephone: 740-366-9246
  Fax: 740-364-9641
Contact: Same

LEARNING DISABILITY SERVICES

Requests for the following services/accommodations will be evaluated individually based on appropriate and current documentation.

Allowed in Exams
  Calculator: Yes
  Dictionary: Yes
  Computer: Yes
  Spellchecker: Yes
Extended test time: Yes
Scribes: Yes
Proctors: Yes
Oral exams: Yes
Notetakers: Yes

Distraction-reduced environment: Yes
Tape recording in class: Yes
Books on tape from RFBD: Yes
Taping of books not from RFBD: Yes
Accommodations for students with ADHD: Yes
Reading machine: Yes
Other assistive technology: Yes
Priority registration: No

Added costs for services: No
LD specialists: Yes (1)
Professional tutors: No
Peer tutors: 70
Max. hours/wk. for services: Unlimited
How professors are notified of LD/ADHD: By student

GENERAL ADMISSIONS INFORMATION

Director of Admissions: John Merrin
Telephone: 740-366-9246

ENTRANCE REQUIREMENTS
Open admissions. High school diploma or GED required. Compass placement test accepted. Test may be waived with minimum SAT 500 or ACT 20.

Application deadline: Rolling
Notification: Rolling
Average GPA: NR

Average SAT I Math: NR
Average SAT I Verbal: NR
Average ACT: NR

Graduated top 10% of class: NR
Graduated top 25% of class: NR
Graduated top 50% of class: NR

COLLEGE GRADUATION REQUIREMENTS

Course waivers allowed: No
Course substitutions allowed: No
In what subjects: N/A

ADDITIONAL INFORMATION

Environment: The campus is located in a small town with easy access to Columbus.

Student Body
  Undergrad enrollment: 1,898
  Female: 70%
  Male: 30%
  Out-of-state: 1%

Cost Information
  In-state tuition: $2,538
  Out-of-state tuition: $4,698
  Room & board: N/A
Housing Information
  University housing: Yes
  Percent living on campus: 8%

Greek System
  Fraternity: No
  Sorority: No
Athletics: Intercollegiate

COLLEGE OF MOUNT SAINT JOSEPH

5701 Delhi Road, Cincinnati, OH 45233-1672
Phone: 513-244-4531 • Fax: 513-244-4629
E-mail: edward_eckel@mail.msj.edu • Web: www.msj.edu
Support level: SP • Institution type: 4-year private

LEARNING DISABILITY PROGRAM AND SERVICES

Project EXCEL is a comprehensive academic support program for students with learning disabilities enrolled in the College. The program's goals are to assist students in the transition from a secondary program to a college curriculum and to promote the development of learning strategies and compensatory skills that will enable students to achieve success in a regular academic program. The structure of the program and supportive environment at the Mount give Project EXCEL its singular quality. Project Excel offers students individualized attention and a variety of support services to meet specific needs, including supervised tutoring by professional tutors; monitoring of student progress; instruction in learning strategies, time management, and coping skills; and academic advising with attention to the students' specific learning needs. Students admitted to the program must maintain a 2.25 overall GPA, and their progress is evaluated on an ongoing basis.

LD/ADHD ADMISSIONS INFORMATION

College entrance tests required: Yes
Nonstandardized tests accepted: Yes
Interview required: Yes
Essay required: No
Documentation required for LD: Psychoeducational
evaluation: within 3 years
Documentation required for ADHD: Yes
Documentation submitted to: Project EXCEL
Special Ed. HS course work accepted: No

Specific course requirements for all applicants: Yes
Separate application required for services: Yes
# of LD applications submitted yearly: 50
# of LD applications accepted yearly: 30
Total # of students receiving LD/ADHD services: 90–101
**Acceptance into program means acceptance into
college:** Students are either admitted directly into EXCEL
and the College; or EXCEL reviews applicant and
recommends to Admissions; or they are admitted to the
College.

ADMISSIONS

Admission to Project EXCEL is multi-stepped, including an interview with the Program Director; completed general admission application; completed Project EXCEL forms (general information, applicant goal and self-assessment, and educational data completed by high school); psychoeducational evaluation; transcript; ACT minimum of 15 or SAT of 700–740; and a recommendation. The application is reviewed by the Project EXCEL Director and Project EXCEL Admission Committee. The diagnostic evaluation must indicate the presence of specific LD and provide reasonable evidence that the student can successfully meet college academic requirements. Academic performance problems that exist concomitantly with a diagnosed ADHD/ADHD will be considered in the review of the student's diagnostic profile. Students can be admitted to the College through Project EXCEL. Students not meeting all EXCEL admission requirements may be admitted part-time or on a probationary basis. Apply early. Other students not meeting admission requirements can take up to 6 hours per semester to a maximum of 13 hours. At that point, if they have a 2.0+ GPA they are admitted to the College.

ADDITIONAL INFORMATION

Project EXCEL students are assisted with course and major selection. Students are offered individualized attention and a variety of support services to meet specific needs, including supervised tutoring; monitoring of student progress; writing lab; note-takers; accommodated testing; instruction in learning strategies, time management, and coping skills; liaison with faculty; and academic advising with attention to specific learning needs. Students enroll in regular classes and must fulfill the same course requirements as all Mount students. The curriculum is closely supervised, and specialized instruction is offered in writing, reading, and study skills to fit the individual needs of the students. The program director serves as student advisor.

SUPPORT SERVICES CONTACT INFORMATION

Learning Disability Program/Services: Project EXCEL
Director: Jane Pohlman
  E-mail: jane_pohlman@mail.msj.edu
  Telephone: 513-244-4623
  Fax: 513-244-4222
Contact: Same

LEARNING DISABILITY SERVICES

Requests for the following services/accommodations will be evaluated individually based on appropriate and current documentation.

Allowed in Exams
  Calculator: Yes
  Dictionary: Yes
  Computer: Yes
  Spellchecker: Yes
Extended test time: Yes
Scribes: Yes
Proctors: Yes
Oral exams: Yes
Note-takers: Yes

Distraction-reduced environment: Yes
Tape recording in class: Yes
Books on tape from RFBD: Yes
Taping of books not from RFBD: Yes
Accommodations for students with ADHD: Yes
Reading machine: No
Other assistive technology: No
Priority registration: No

Added costs for services: $1,500 per semester
LD specialists: Yes (2)
Professional tutors: 15
Peer tutors: No
Max. hours/wk. for services: Unlimited
How professors are notified of LD/ADHD: By both student and director

GENERAL ADMISSIONS INFORMATION

Director of Admissions: Ed Eckel
Telephone: 513-244-4531

ENTRANCE REQUIREMENTS
13 total are required; 20 total are recommended; 4 English required, 4 English recommended, 2 math required, 4 math recommended, 2 science required, 4 science recommended, 1 science lab required, 2 science lab recommended, 2 foreign language required, 4 foreign language recommended, 1 social studies required, 2 social studies recommended, 1 history required, 4 history recommended, 1 elective required, 4 elective recommended. High school diploma or GED required.

Application deadline: August 15
Notification: Rolling beginning 10/1
Average GPA: 3.1

Average SAT I Math: 530
Average SAT I Verbal: 510
Average ACT: 22

Graduated top 10% of class: 21%
Graduated top 25% of class: 47%
Graduated top 50% of class: 79%

COLLEGE GRADUATION REQUIREMENTS

Course waivers allowed: No
Course substitutions allowed: Yes
In what subjects: Case-by-case basis

ADDITIONAL INFORMATION

Environment: The Mount is a Catholic, coeducational, liberal arts college located approximately 15 miles from downtown Cincinnati.

Student Body
  Undergrad enrollment: 2,061
  Female: 71%
  Male: 29%
  Out-of-state: 14%

Cost Information
  Tuition: $13,500
  Room & board: $5,100
Housing Information
  University housing: Yes
  Percent living on campus: 20%

Greek System
  Fraternity: Yes
  Sorority: Yes
Athletics: NCAA Division III

HOCKING COLLEGE

3301 Hocking Parkway, Nelsonville, OH 45764
Phone: 740-753-3591 • Fax: 740-753-1452
E-mail: hull.l@hocking.edu • Web: www.hocking.edu
Support: CS • Institution: 2-year public

LEARNING DISABILITY PROGRAM AND SERVICES

The Access Center Office of Disability Support Services (ACODS) is dedicated to serving the various needs of individuals with disabilities and to promoting their full participation in college life. The educational coordinator for students with disabilities helps any student with a learning disability successfully adjust to college life by finding the right fit between the instructional offerings of Hocking College and his/her own individualized learning and personal needs. This is accomplished in part by working with assessment and counseling professionals to assist students in identifying individualized programs of study and means for success by more closely aligning interest and abilities with instructor and program effectiveness. The accommodation process is one of collaboration between students and instructors with support from ACODS. Eligibility is determined on the basis of the presence of a disability and a need for services and accommodations to support an equal educational opportunity. Information from the disability documentation, the student's stated experience with services and accommodations that have been effective in the past, and ACODS professional judgment will be drawn upon in making the eligibility determination.

LD/ADHD ADMISSIONS INFORMATION

College entrance tests required: No
Nonstandardized tests accepted: Yes
Interview required: No
Essay required: No
Documentation required for LD: Psychoeducational evaluation preferred.
Documentation required for ADHD: Yes
Submitted to: Access Center
Special Ed. HS course work accepted: N/A

Specific course requirements for all applicants: No
Separate application required for services: Yes
# of LD applications submitted yearly: 50–75
# of LD applications accepted yearly: All who apply
Total # of students receiving LD/ADHD services: 200
Acceptance into program means acceptance into college: Students must be admitted and enrolled at the College first and then may request services.

ADMISSIONS

The College has open enrollment for any student with a high school diploma or equivalent. Students are not required to take any specific courses or have any specific test score on the ACT/SAT. Students requesting accommodations or services for learning disabilities must be admitted and enrolled, and then they may request services. Current documentation should be submitted.

ADDITIONAL INFORMATION

ACODS staff and the student work together to identify individual needs and then determine which of the support services and accommodations would enable the student to achieve academic potential. Strategies used to assist students with disabilities include assistance with instructional and supportive needs; aligning interest and abilities with instructor and program effectiveness; assurance that individual program implementation is consistent with the identified needs of the student; evaluation of problematic situations regarding modes of presentation that affect student performance and potential for success; assistance on course assignments, troubleshooting learning problems and assisting in solutions to situations that inhibit success; help in obtaining tutoring services; priority scheduling; liaison with community agencies; and advocacy. Quest for Success is a program designed especially for new students to help them prepare to start technical classes in the fall. Additional services include professional tutors in some mathematics and communications courses, Compu-Lenz to enlarge type on a computer screen and reduce glare, academic advising, and an educational coordinator to act as a liaison with college instructors and community agencies.

SUPPORT SERVICES CONTACT INFORMATION

Learning Disability Program/Services: Access Center
Director: Elaine Dabelko
  E-mail: dabelko_e@hocking.edu
  Telephone: 740-753-3591
  Fax: 740-753-4495
Contact: Kim Forbes Powell
  E-mail: forbes_k@hocking.edu
  Telephone: 740-753-3591
  Fax: 740-753-4097

LEARNING DISABILITY SERVICES

Requests for the following services/accommodations will be evaluated individually based on appropriate and current documentation.

Allowed in Exams
  Calculator: Yes
  Dictionary: No
  Computer: Yes
  Spellchecker: Yes
Extended test time: Yes
Scribes: Yes
Proctors: Yes
Oral exams: Yes
Notetakers: Yes

Distraction-reduced environment: Yes
Tape recording in class: Yes
Books on tape from RFBD: Yes
Taping of books not from RFBD: Yes
Accommodations for students with
  ADHD: Yes
Reading machine: Yes
Other assistive technology: Yes
Priority registration: No

Added costs for services: No
LD specialists: Yes
Professional tutors: 3
Peer tutors: Yes
Max. hours/wk. for services: Unlimited
How professors are notified of
  LD/ADHD: By student and program
  director

GENERAL ADMISSIONS INFORMATION

Director of Admissions: Dr. Candy Vanuko
Telephone: 740-753-3591, ext. 2803

ENTRANCE REQUIREMENTS
Open admissions. High school diploma or GED required. ACT/SAT scores are not required.

Application deadline: Rolling
Notification: Rolling
Average GPA: NR

Average SAT I Math: NR
Average SAT I Verbal: NR
Average ACT: NR

Graduated top 10% of class: NR
Graduated top 25% of class: NR
Graduated top 50% of class: NR

COLLEGE GRADUATION REQUIREMENTS

Course waivers allowed: No
Course substitutions allowed: Yes
In what subjects: N/A

ADDITIONAL INFORMATION

Environment: The College is located on 150 acres in a rural area with easy access to Columbus.

Student Body
  Undergrad enrollment: 5,070
  Female: 44%
  Male: 56%
  Out-of-state: 14%

Cost Information
  In-state tuition: $2,100
  Out-of-state tuition: $4,170
  Room & board: $2,535
Housing Information
  University housing: Yes
  Percent living on campus: 10%

Greek System
  Fraternity: Yes
  Sorority: Yes
Athletics: Intramural

KENT STATE UNIVERSITY

PO Box 5190, Kent, OH 44242-0001
Phone: 330-672-2444 • Fax: 330-672-2499
E-mail: kentadm@admissions.kent.edu • Web: www.kent.edu
Support level: CS • Institution type: 4-year public

LEARNING DISABILITY PROGRAM AND SERVICES

The goals and philosophy of the Student Disability Services (SDS) program are to promote student independence and self-advocacy at the College level. The University believes that the ability to do college work is highly correlated with grades in high school. Students with learning disabilities who receive accommodations in high school and who are academically successful are most likely to be successful at KSU. If an LD support system has been available, and the student has been diligent and still has a low GPA in high school, lack of skills or disabilities may be too severe for that student to be successful at KSU. Students should meet with an SDS staff member six months before enrollment to discuss needs and accommodations.

LD/ADHD ADMISSIONS INFORMATION

College entrance tests required: Yes
Nonstandardized tests accepted: Yes
Interview required: Yes
Essay required: No
Documentation required for LD: Psychoeducational evaluation
Documentation required for ADHD: Yes
Documentation submitted to: SDS
Special Ed. HS course work accepted: No

Specific course requirements for all applicants: Yes
Separate application required for services: No
# of LD applications submitted yearly: N/A
# of LD applications accepted yearly: N/A
Total # of students receiving LD/ADHD services: 250
Acceptance into program means acceptance into college: Students must be accepted and enrolled at the University first and then may request services or appeal a denial.

ADMISSIONS

Students with LD must meet the same admission criteria as all other applicants. There is no special admissions procedure for students with LD. However, the high school may adjust GPA if the student was not diagnosed until late in high school. Documentation of disability is required. In addition to having completed standard college-preparatory courses, applicants should be able to type or use a computer and a calculator and have skills in performing addition, subtraction, multiplication, and division using natural numbers, integers, fractions, and decimals. Students should also have highly developed study skills based on their specific strengths. The minimum GPA for admission is a 2.2 and 21 ACT or 870 SAT. Students who have been in the upper 60 percent of their high school class and have an ACT score of 19+ or SAT of 900+ do very well at KSU.

ADDITIONAL INFORMATION

It is recommended that all documentation be submitted prior to enrolling, as services include academic assistance in selecting courses. All students with documentation of a learning disability may utilize the academic and counseling services, such as: academic advising; developmental education courses for freshmen students with deficits in reading, writing and math; individual and small group tutoring; support groups; and individual and group study-skills help through the Academic Success Center. Services and accommodations are available for undergraduate and graduate students.

SUPPORT SERVICES CONTACT INFORMATION

Learning Disability Program/Services: Student Disability Services (SDS)
Director: Anne Jannarone
  E-mail: ajannaro@kent.edu
  Telephone: 330-672-3391
  Fax: 330-672-3763
Contact: Same

LEARNING DISABILITY SERVICES

Requests for the following services/accommodations will be evaluated individually based on appropriate and current documentation.

Allowed in Exams
  Calculator: Yes
  Dictionary: Yes
  Computer: Yes
  Spellchecker: Yes
  Extended test time: Yes
  Scribes: Yes
  Proctors: Yes
  Oral exams: No
  Note-takers: Yes

Distraction-reduced environment: Yes
Tape recording in class: Yes
Books on tape from RFBD: Yes
Taping of books not from RFBD: Yes
Accommodations for students with ADHD: Yes
Reading machine: No
Other assistive technology: Yes
Priority registration: Yes

Added costs for services: No
LD specialists: Yes
Professional tutors: 3
Peer tutors: 50
Max. hours/wk. for services: 4
How professors are notified of LD/ADHD: By student

GENERAL ADMISSIONS INFORMATION

Director of Admissions: Paul J. Deutsch
Telephone: 330-672-2444

ENTRANCE REQUIREMENTS
16 total are recommended; 4 English recommended, 3 math recommended, 3 science recommended, 2 science lab recommended, 2 foreign language recommended, 3 social studies recommended. High school diploma or GED required. Minimum TOEFL is 525. TOEFL required of all international applicants.

Application deadline: Rolling
Notification: Rolling beginning 10/1
Average GPA: 3.0

Average SAT I Math: 501
Average SAT I Verbal: 502
Average ACT: 21

Graduated top 10% of class: 10%
Graduated top 25% of class: 30%
Graduated top 50% of class: 64%

COLLEGE GRADUATION REQUIREMENTS

Course waivers allowed: No
Course substitutions allowed: Yes
In what subjects: Decisions are made by individual colleges, and they depend on the student's major.

ADDITIONAL INFORMATION

Environment: The University is a residential campus located on 1,200 acres 45 miles southeast of Cleveland.

Student Body
  Undergrad enrollment: 17,580
  Female: 60%
  Male: 40%
  Out-of-state: 6%

Cost Information
  In-state tuition: $4,234
  Out-of-state tuition: $9,410
  Room & board: $4,764
Housing Information
  University housing: Yes
  Percent living on campus: 34%

Greek System
  Fraternity: Yes
  Sorority: Yes
  Athletics: NCAA Division I

MIAMI UNIVERSITY

301 South Campus Avenue Building, Oxford, OH 45056
Phone: 513-529-2531 • Fax: 513-529-1550
E-mail: admission@muohio.edu • Web: www.muohio.edu
Support level: CS • Institution type: 4-year public

LEARNING DISABILITY PROGRAM AND SERVICES

The Learning Disabilities Program assists students in becoming independent and successful learners, preparing for meaningful careers, and achieving a positive college experience. The program staff coordinate university and community resources to meet the academic and personal needs of students with LD; assist faculty in understanding the characteristics and needs of these students; and provide services on an individual, confidential basis to students with appropriate documentation. All students with LD or ADHD are ultimately responsible for their own academic adjustment, including class attendance, assignments, and all other course requirements. It is the student's responsibility to ask for assistance. Appropriate services and accommodations are determined through a flexible, interactive process that involves the student and the Coordinator, and are arranged through dialogue with faculty and staff responsible for implementing many of these services or accommodations. Decisions about services and accommodations for students with LD are made on the basis of the disability documentation and the functional limitations caused by the disability, as well as the current needs of the student. Students with ADHD must meet with the LD Coordinator to initiate services after discussing disability-related needs and providing verification of the disability.

LD/ADHD ADMISSIONS INFORMATION

College entrance tests required: Yes
Nonstandardized tests accepted: Yes
Interview required: No
Essay required: Yes
Documentation required for LD: Psychoeducational evaluation
Documentation required for ADHD: Yes
Documentation submitted to: LDP
Special Ed. HS course work accepted: No

Specific course requirements for all applicants: Yes
Separate application required for services: No
# of LD applications submitted yearly: N/A
# of LD applications accepted yearly: N/A
Total # of students receiving LD/ADHD services: 475
Acceptance into program means acceptance into
   college: Students must be admitted and enrolled at the
   University first and then reviewed for services.

ADMISSIONS

Students with LD are admitted to Miami through the regular admission process; therefore, it is important to ensure that the information in the application accurately reflects a student's academic ability and potential. Students are expected to have 4 years English, 3 years math, 3 years science, 3 years social studies, 2 years foreign language, 1 year fine arts. Students with deficiencies may still be qualified for admission. Students may choose to indicate in their application the presence of an LD or ADHD, either through a personal essay or the "extenuating circumstances" statement. Also, students may voluntarily choose to submit other information that may help the Office of Admission to understand their unique learning strengths and needs. Applicants with LD are encouraged to meet with the LD Coordinator during the College search process to discuss the LD support program, the nature and extent of their disability, the types of accommodations that may be needed, and the program and course requirements in their field of study.

ADDITIONAL INFORMATION

Support services for students with learning disabilities include transition information; admission counseling; priority registration; classroom accommodations such as test modifications, extended exam time, etc.; academic assistance such as tutoring and study skills assistance; mentoring in learning strategies, time management and coping strategies; liaison with faculty; campus advocacy; and counseling and career awareness. The Orton Student Association is a student organization that provides a support system—academically, socially, emotionally, and personally—to students with LD. The group encourages and promotes student and faculty awareness of these conditions through outreach efforts. The Terry A. Gould LD Fund is an endowed account providing funds for instructional materials, program expenses, and conference opportunities for students with LD. The Office of Learning Assistance works with students encountering academic difficulties. The Tutorial Assistance Program provides peer tutors.

SUPPORT SERVICES CONTACT INFORMATION

Learning Disability Program/Services: Learning Disabilities Program
Director: Lois Philips
  E-mail: philplg@muohio,edu
  Telephone: 513-529-8741
  Fax: 513-529-8799
Contact: Doug Green
  Telephone: 513-529-8741

LEARNING DISABILITY SERVICES

Requests for the following services/accommodations will be evaluated individually based on appropriate and current documentation.

Allowed in Exams
  Calculator: Yes
  Dictionary: Yes
  Computer: Yes
  Spellchecker: Yes
Extended test time: Yes
Scribes: Yes
Proctors: Yes
Oral exams: Yes
Note-takers: Yes

Distraction-reduced environment: Yes
Tape recording in class: Yes
Books on tape from RFBD: Yes
Taping of books not from RFBD: Yes
Accommodations for students with ADHD: Yes
Reading machine: Yes
Other assistive technology: Yes
Priority registration: Yes

Added costs for services: No
LD specialists: Yes (2)
Professional tutors: No
Peer tutors: Yes (220)
Max. hours/wk. for services: Unlimited
How professors are notified of LD/ADHD: By student

GENERAL ADMISSIONS INFORMATION

Director of Admissions: Mike Mils
Telephone: 513-529-2531

ENTRANCE REQUIREMENTS

16 total are recommended; 4 English recommended, 3 math recommended, 3 science recommended, 2 foreign language recommended, 3 social studies recommended. High school diploma or GED required. Minimum TOEFL is 530. TOEFL required of all international applicants.

Application deadline: January 31
Notification: March 15
Average GPA: 3.63

Average SAT I Math: NR
Average SAT I Verbal: NR
Average ACT: 26

Graduated top 10% of class: 38%
Graduated top 25% of class: 79%
Graduated top 50% of class: 97%

COLLEGE GRADUATION REQUIREMENTS

Course waivers allowed: No
Course substitutions allowed: Yes
In what subjects: Foreign language and math, if not essential requirement for graduation in the student's major

ADDITIONAL INFORMATION

Environment: The University is in a small town northwest of Cincinnati.

Student Body
  Under grad enrollment: 14,914
  Female: 55%
  Male: 45%
  Out-of-state: 27%

Cost Information
  In-state tuition: $5,358
  Out-of-state tuition: $12,398
  Room & board: $5,830
Housing Information
  University housing: Yes
  Percent living on campus: 45%

Greek System
  Fraternity: Yes
  Sorority: Yes
  Athletics: NCAA Division I

MUSKINGUM COLLEGE

163 Stormont Drive, New Concord, OH 43762
Phone: 614-826-8137 • Fax: 614-826-8404
E-mail: adminfo@muskingum.edu • Web: www.muskingum.edu
Support level: SP • Institution type: 4-year private

LEARNING DISABILITY PROGRAM AND SERVICES

The PLUS Program provides students who have disabilities with the opportunity to reach their academic potential while at Muskingum College. A learning-strategies instructional model administered by a professional staff is the basis for PLUS support. Students may revise full program participation to maintenance (reduced fee) or independence (no fee) based on academic achievement. A full range of accommodations in addition to a structured tutorial are provided through the Center for Advancement of Learning, the framework for academic support at Muskingum College. Program participants must maintain a minimum of one hour of individual tutoring time per week for each class. The program offers no remedial or developmental instruction, encourages individual responsibility for learning, and acknowledges successful individual efforts. The program offers qualified students individual or small group content-based learning strategies, instruction, and content tutorial support. Parent contact is made each semester for students participating in the PLUS Program.

LD/ADHD ADMISSIONS INFORMATION

College entrance tests required: Yes
Nonstandardized tests accepted: Yes
Interview required: Yes
Essay required: No
Documentation required for LD: Aptitude test, achievement test, diagnostic statement of functional limitations
Documentation required for ADHD: Yes
Documentation submitted to: PLUS Program
Special Ed. HS course work accepted: No

Specific course requirements for all applicants: Yes
Separate application required for services: No
# of LD applications submitted yearly: 90–120
# of LD applications accepted yearly: 40–50
Total # of students receiving LD/ADHD services: 100–125
Acceptance into program means acceptance into college: Admission to the PLUS Program is an automatic admission to the College.

ADMISSIONS

Students may apply to the College and the PLUS Program after completing their junior year of high school. Admission for students with LD is based on a careful evaluation of all the materials that are submitted with the application. Students must submit: a completed application for admission (check the box for PLUS Program); ACT/SAT; current psycho-educational evaluation documenting disability and administered by a licensed psychologist, or medical diagnosis of ADHD; copy of current IEP and transition plan; and a detailed request for and description of auxiliary accommodations being requested. The student is evaluated for potential for academic success as a participant in the PLUS Program. Admission policies are flexible for students with LD, but a good distribution among college-prep courses is helpful. Students should submit recommendations from teachers or guidance counselor. Applicants are reviewed, and selected candidates are invited to interview. Space in the program is limited, and early application is encouraged. The admission decision is made jointly by the Program Director and Admissions Director.

ADDITIONAL INFORMATION

PLUS guides students toward increasing learning independence; assigns students to academic advisors and program advisors; and assists students in determining how to balance courses and create an appropriate course load each semester. Professionals provide tutorial services and coordinate appropriate testing and instructional accommodations. Students are provided with a combination of individual and small group tutorial support. Students participating in the full program must maintain a minimum of one contact hour of tutoring per week for each course. PLUS maintenance is recommended for upperclassmen as they progress successfully in college. High school juniors and seniors with LD can participate in a comprehensive, two-week summer experience, "First Step," to help them make the transition to college. The primary emphasis is on the application of learning strategies within the context of a college-level expository course. The program focuses on social and emotional changes associated with the transition to college.

SUPPORT SERVICES CONTACT INFORMATION

Learning Disability Program/Services: PLUS Program
Director: Jen E. Navicky
 E-mail: navicky@muskingum.edu
 Telephone: 740-826-8280
 Fax: 740-826-8285
Contact: Michelle Butler
 E-mail: butler@muskingum.edu
 Telephone: 740-826-8280
 Fax: 740-826-8285

LEARNING DISABILITY SERVICES

Requests for the following services/accommodations will be evaluated individually based on appropriate and current documentation.

Allowed in Exams
 Calculator: Yes
 Dictionary: Yes
 Computer: Yes
 Spellchecker: Yes
Extended test time: Yes
Scribes: Yes
Proctors: Yes
Oral exams: Yes
Note-takers: Yes

Distraction-reduced environment: Yes
Tape recording in class: Yes
Books on tape from RFBD: Yes
Taping of books not from RFBD: Yes
Accommodations for students with ADHD: Yes
Reading machine: Yes
Other assistive technology: Yes
Priority registration: Yes

Added costs for services: $1,050–2,100 pre semester for tutoring
LD specialists: Yes (17)
Professional tutors: 17
Peer tutors: 4
Max. hours/wk. for services: 6.5
How professors are notified of LD/ADHD: By both student and director

GENERAL ADMISSIONS INFORMATION

Director of Admissions: Beth Dalanzo
Telephone: 740-826-8041

ENTRANCE REQUIREMENTS
10 total are required; 15 total are recommended; 4 English required, 4 English recommended, 2 math required, 3 math recommended, 2 science required, 3 science recommended, 2 foreign language required, 2 foreign language recommended, 1 social studies required, 1 social studies recommended, 2 history required, 2 history recommended. High school diploma or GED required. Minimum TOEFL is 550. TOEFL required of all international applicants.

Application deadline: August 1
Notification: Rolling beginning 10/1
Average GPA: 3.2

Average SAT I Math: 539
Average SAT I Verbal: 539
Average ACT: 23

Graduated top 10% of class: 26%
Graduated top 25% of class: 53%
Graduated top 50% of class: 77%

COLLEGE GRADUATION REQUIREMENTS

Course waivers allowed: No
Course substitutions allowed: No
In what subjects: N/A

ADDITIONAL INFORMATION

Environment: The College is located on 215 acres in a rural area 70 miles east of Columbus.

Student Body
 Undergrad enrollment: 1,564
 Female: 52%
 Male: 48%
 Out-of-state: 15%

Cost Information
 Tuition: $12,250
 Room & board: $5,100
Housing Information
 University housing: Yes
 Percent living on campus: 75%

Greek System
 Fraternity: Yes
 Sorority: Yes
Athletics: NCAA Division III

OBERLIN COLLEGE

101 North Professor Street, Oberlin, OH 44074
Phone: 440-775-8411 • Fax: 440-775-6905
E-mail: college.admissions@oberlin.edu • Web: www.oberlin.edu
Support level: S • Institution type: 4-year private

LEARNING DISABILITY PROGRAM AND SERVICES

Personnel from the Office of Services for Students with Disabilities (OSSD) understand that challenge and provide services, as well as coordinate accommodations, to meet the needs of students who have disabilities. The goal is to maximize all the student's educational potential while helping him/her develop and maintain independence. The program philosophy is one that encourages self-advocacy. Students who are diagnosed by OSSD personnel as having an LD, as well as those who can provide documentation of a current diagnosis of an LD, are eligible for services. To verify a previously diagnosed LD, a student must provide a psychological assessment, educational test results, and a recent copy of an Individualized Education Program that specifies placement in a learning disabilities program. These documents will be reviewed by personnel from OSSD to determine eligibility. Students requesting services are interviewed by a learning disability counselor before a service plan is developed or initiated.

LD/ADHD ADMISSIONS INFORMATION

College entrance tests required: Yes
Nonstandardized tests accepted: Yes
Interview required: No
Essay required: No
Documentation required for LD: A recent psychological evaluation
Documentation required for ADHD: Yes
Documentation submitted to: OSSD
Special Ed. HS course work accepted: Yes

Specific course requirements for all applicants: Yes
Separate application required for services: No
# of LD applications submitted yearly: N/A
# of LD applications accepted yearly: N/A
Total # of students receiving LD/ADHD services: 90
Acceptance into program means acceptance into college: Students must be admitted and enrolled at the College first and then may request services.

ADMISSIONS

There is no special admissions procedure for students with LD. All applicants must meet the same admission requirements. Courses required include 4 years English and math and at least 3 years social science and science. GPA is typically a B average or better. ACT scores range between 25–30; SAT I scores range between 1100–1320 and SAT II scores range between 560–680 on each Reasoning Test. Students who self-disclose and provide documentation may have their files read by OSSD personnel, who will provide a recommendation to the Office of Admissions. Students who can provide valid and recent documentation of a psychoeducational diagnosis of an LD may receive services.

ADDITIONAL INFORMATION

A Learning Resource Center and an Adaptive Technology Center are available for all students. Skills classes are offered for college credit in reading, study skills, and writing. OSSD can arrange one or all of the following services for students with learning disabilities: quiet space for exams; extended examination time, up to twice the time typically allotted, based on diagnosis; oral exams; scribes; individual academic, personal, and vocational counseling; peer support groups for the development of academic strategies and psychosocial adjustments; computer resources for additional academic skill development and assistance; taped textbooks based on careful planning and lead time; priority academic scheduling; peer tutoring; diagnostic testing; new student orientation assistance; and faculty/staff consultation. In addition, OSSD can provide information about other support services sponsored by the College.

SUPPORT SERVICES CONTACT INFORMATION

Learning Disability Program/Services: Office of Services for Students with Disabilities (OSSD)
Director: Jane Boomer
  E-mail: jane.boomer@oberlin.edu
  Telephone: 440-775-8467
  Fax: 440-775-6724
Contact: Same

LEARNING DISABILITY SERVICES

Requests for the following services/accommodations will be evaluated individually based on appropriate and current documentation.

Allowed in Exams
  Calculator: Yes
  Dictionary: Yes
  Computer: Yes
  Spellchecker: Yes
Extended test time: Yes
Scribes: Yes
Proctors: Yes
Oral exams: Yes
Note-takers: Yes

Distraction-reduced environment: Yes
Tape recording in class: Yes
Books on tape from RFBD: Yes
Taping of books not from RFBD: Yes
Accommodations for students with ADHD: Yes
Reading machine: Yes
Other assistive technology: Yes
Priority registration: Yes

Added costs for services: No
LD specialists: No
Professional tutors: No
Peer tutors: 38
Max. hours/wk. for services: Unlimited
How professors are notified of LD/ADHD: By both student and director

GENERAL ADMISSIONS INFORMATION

Director of Admissions: Deborah Chermonte
Telephone: 440-775-8411

ENTRANCE REQUIREMENTS
4 English recommended, 4 math recommended, 3 science recommended, 3 science lab recommended, 3 foreign language recommended, 3 social studies recommended. High school diploma or GED required. Minimum TOEFL is 600. TOEFL required of all international applicants.

Application deadline: January 15
Notification: April 1
Average GPA: 3.6

Average SAT I Math: 644
Average SAT I Verbal: 685
Average ACT: 28

Graduated top 10% of class: 59%
Graduated top 25% of class: 87%
Graduated top 50% of class: 99%

COLLEGE GRADUATION REQUIREMENTS

Course waivers allowed: No
Course substitutions allowed: Yes
In what subjects: Case-by-case basis

ADDITIONAL INFORMATION

Environment: The College is located on 440 acres in a small town 35 miles southwest of Cleveland.

Student Body
  Undergrad enrollment: 2,951
  Female: 59%
  Male: 41%
  Out-of-state: 89%

Cost Information
  Tuition: $24,096
  Room & board: $6,178
Housing Information
  University housing: Yes
  Percent living on campus: 70%

Greek System
  Fraternity: Yes
  Sorority: Yes
  Athletics: NCAA Division III

OHIO STATE UNIVERSITY—COLUMBUS

Third Floor Lincoln Tower, 1800 Cannon Drive, Columbus, OH 43210
Phone: 614-292-3980 • Fax: 614-292-4818
E-mail: oafa@fa.adm.ohio-state.edu • Web: www.osu.edu
Support level: CS • Institution type: 4-year public

LEARNING DISABILITY PROGRAM AND SERVICES

The mission of the Office for Disability Services (ODS) is threefold: to seek to ensure that students can freely and actively participate in all facets of university life; to provide and coordinate support services and programs to maximize educational potential; and to increase the level of awareness among all members of the University community so that students with disabilities are able to perform at a level determined only by their abilities—not their disabilities. ODS helps students in their efforts to attain an excellent college education by promoting self-advocacy skills, self-understanding, and independence. Staff members are specialists in learning disabilities. Students are assigned to a counselor who understands their disability. Counselors assist and advise students about how to make the most of college life and, more importantly, will advise students on how to succeed academically. Disability Services matches services with students' needs. The staff recommends specific services, but students select the services that are suitable for them based upon recommendations.

LD/ADHD ADMISSIONS INFORMATION

College entrance tests required: Yes
Nonstandardized tests accepted: Yes
Interview required: No
Essay required: No
Documentation required for LD: Psychoeducational evaluation
Documentation required for ADHD: Yes
Documentation submitted to: ODS
Special Ed. HS course work accepted: Yes, with appropriate documentation

Specific course requirements for all applicants: Yes
Separate application required for services: No
# of LD applications submitted yearly: 200
# of LD applications accepted yearly: 100
Total # of students receiving LD/ADHD services: 800
Acceptance into program means acceptance into college: Students must be admitted and enrolled at the University and then may request services.

ADMISSIONS

Students with LD are admitted under the same criteria as regular applicants. However, consideration can be given to students with LD with support from ODS in instances where the student's rank, GPA, or lack of courses, such as foreign language, have affected their performance in high school. Applicants interested in services should submit a general application for admission to the Admissions Office; complete the section on the application form under Optional Personal Statement that gives students the opportunity to provide information if they feel that their high school performance was adversely affected by special circumstances; and submit documentation of the disability to ODS, including the latest IEP and the results of the last psychoeducational testing. ODS will review the application; look at course work and deficiencies; review services received in high school and determine if the student's needs can be met at OSU if the student is not normally admissible; look at when a diagnosis was made and at the IEP; and make a recommendation to Admissions. ODS will send a letter acknowledging receipt of the documentation. The letter will indicate whether services needed can be provided and if additional information is necessary.

ADDITIONAL INFORMATION

ODS is staffed by many specialists, including learning disability specialists and 10 counselors. The LD specialists will meet with students once a week. ODS can arrange for services including quiet studio space for exams; extended exam time; readers and/or scribes; computers for essay exams; access to class notes; taped textbooks through RFB; taping of textbooks not available through RFB; peer support groups to help develop academic strategies and psychosocial adjustment; peer tutoring for assistance in learning specific class material; diagnostic testing for learning disabilities; orientation assistance, including scheduling and training to assist in accessing services; Computer Learning Center and assistance in computer usage; priority academic scheduling; faculty-staff consultation; and family consultation. Noncredit workshops are offered on academic effectiveness from the Counseling Center and the Reading/Study Skills Program.

SUPPORT SERVICES CONTACT INFORMATION

Learning Disability Program/Services: Office for Disability Services (ODS)
Director: Ann Yurcisin
   E-mail: yurcisin.1@osu.edu
   Telephone: 614-292-3307
   Fax: 614-292-4190
Contact: Lois Burke
   E-mail: burke.4@osu.edu
   Telephone: 614-292-3307
   Fax: 614-292-4190

LEARNING DISABILITY SERVICES

Requests for the following services/accommodations will be evaluated individually based on appropriate and current documentation.

Allowed in Exams
   Calculator: Yes
   Dictionary: Yes
   Computer: Yes
   Spellchecker: Yes
Extended test time: Yes
Scribes: Yes
Proctors: Yes
Oral exams: Yes
Note-takers: Yes

Distraction-reduced environment: Yes
Tape recording in class: Yes
Books on tape from RFBD: Yes
Taping of books not from RFBD: Yes
Accommodations for students with
   ADHD: Yes
Reading machine: Yes
Other assistive technology: Yes
Priority registration: Yes

Added costs for services: No
LD specialists: Yes
Professional tutors: No
Peer tutors: Yes
Max. hours/wk. for services: Varies
How professors are notified of
   LD/ADHD: By student

GENERAL ADMISSIONS INFORMATION

Director of Admissions: Dr. Mable Freeman
Telephone: 614-292-3980

ENTRANCE REQUIREMENTS
4 English required, 4 English recommended, 3 math required, 4 math recommended, 2 science required, 3 science recommended, 2 science lab required, 2 foreign language required, 3 foreign language recommended, 2 social studies required, 3 social studies recommended, 1 elective required, 1 elective recommended. High school diploma or GED required. Minimum TOEFL is 500. TOEFL required of all international applicants.

Application deadline: February 15
Notification: Rolling beginning 10/1
Average GPA: NR

Average SAT I Math: 588
Average SAT I Verbal: 570
Average ACT: 25

Graduated top 10% of class: 32%
Graduated top 25% of class: 68%
Graduated top 50% of class: 95%

COLLEGE GRADUATION REQUIREMENTS

Course waivers allowed: No
Course substitutions allowed: Yes
In what subjects: Sometimes students can petition for a foreign language substitution after attempting foreign language in college

ADDITIONAL INFORMATION

Environment: The campus is in an urban area 4 miles from downtown Columbus.

Student Body
   Undergrad enrollment: 35,749
   Female: 49%
   Male: 51%
   Out-of-state: 13%

Cost Information
   In-state tuition: $4,383
   Out-of-state tuition: $12,732
   Room & board: $6,264
Housing Information
   University housing: Yes
   Percent living on campus: 85%

Greek System
   Fraternity: Yes
   Sorority: Yes
Athletics: NCAA Division I

OHIO UNIVERSITY—ATHENS

120 Chubb Hall, Athens, OH 45701
Phone: 740-593-4100 • Fax: 740-593-0560
E-mail: admissions.freshmen@ohiou.edu • Web: www.ohiou.edu
Support level: S • Institution type: 4-year public

LEARNING DISABILITY PROGRAM AND SERVICES

The Office for Institutional Equity helps students with disabilities coordinate the services needed to enjoy full participation in academic programs and campus life. Students are heard, advised, and assisted in achieving goals. Students are urged to have confidence in their abilities and to feel comfortable talking with their professors about their disability. Accommodations are a result of collaborative efforts between the student, faculty, and staff of the Office for Institutional Equity. The goal is to identify and strategize a plan to assist the student in achieving success in his/her educational pursuits. Students should provide the Office for Institutional Equity with a course schedule the first week of the quarter in order for professors to be notified of the student's status in the class. Students also need to communicate with professors in advance of requesting accommodations. Extra time to complete assignments and take tests can be arranged. Students should also take advantage of the tutoring sessions that can be arranged. It is very important that students understand that the accommodations requested may not be the ones considered reasonable by the University.

LD/ADHD ADMISSIONS INFORMATION

College entrance tests required: Yes
Nonstandardized tests accepted: Yes
Interview required: No
Essay required: No
Documentation required for LD: Psychoeducational evaluations
Documentation required for ADHD: Yes
Documentation submitted to: Disability Student Services
Special Ed. HS course work accepted: Yes

Specific course requirements for all applicants: Yes
Separate application required for services: N/A
# of LD applications submitted yearly: N/A
# of LD applications accepted yearly: N/A
Total # of students receiving LD/ADHD services: 278
Acceptance into program means acceptance into college: Students must be admitted and enrolled at the University first and then may request services.

ADMISSIONS

Applicants with learning disabilities are expected to meet the same admission criteria as all other applicants. General admission requires the applicant to be in the top 30 percent with 21 ACT or 990 SAT, or top 50 percent with 23 ACT or 1060 SAT. The middle 50 percent range for ACT is 22–26 and SAT 1030–1200. Course requirements include 4 years English, 3 years science, and 2 years of foreign language. Students can be admitted with deficiencies. Applicants with learning disabilities who meet the criteria should send documentation to special services after admission. Those students not meeting the admission criteria are encouraged to self-disclose by writing a narrative explaining the impact of the disability condition on the student's academic career as well as sending relevant documentation. This disclosure and accompanying documentation will be reviewed by Admissions. Students, in general, must demonstrate the ability to perform in a mainstream academic setting where support is available when needed. Counselor recommendation is very helpful for students who do not meet the traditional criteria.

ADDITIONAL INFORMATION

General services provided include advising referral and liaison, academic adjustments and classroom accommodations, priority scheduling, free tutoring through the Academic Advancement Center (four hours per course per week), and tutoring in writing and reading skills. Skills classes are offered in learning strategies, college reading skills, reading, speed, and vocabulary. Services are available to undergraduate and graduate students.

SUPPORT SERVICES CONTACT INFORMATION

Learning Disability Program/Services: Office for Institutional Equity/Disability Student Services
Director: Katherine Fahey
  Telephone: 740-593-2620
  Fax: 740-593-0790
  E-mail: fahey@oak.cats.ohiou.edu
Contact: Same

LEARNING DISABILITY SERVICES

Requests for the following services/accommodations will be evaluated individually based on appropriate and current documentation.

Allowed in Exams
  Calculator: Yes
  Dictionary: Yes
  Computer: Yes
  Spellchecker: Yes
Extended test time: Yes
Scribes: Yes
Proctors: No
Oral exams: Yes
Note-takers: No

Distraction-reduced environment: Yes
Tape recording in class: Yes
Books on tape from RFBD: Yes
Taping of books not from RFBD: No
Accommodations for students with
  ADHD: Yes
Reading machine: Yes
Other assistive technology: Scanner
  with computer
Priority registration: Yes

Added costs for services: No
LD specialists: No
Professional tutors: No
Peer tutors: 300
Max. hours/wk. for services: 4 hours
  per course per week through the
  Academic Advancement Center
How professors are notified of
  LD/ADHD: By both student and
  director

GENERAL ADMISSIONS INFORMATION

Director of Admissions: N. Kip Howard
Telephone: 740-593-4100

ENTRANCE REQUIREMENTS

19 total are recommended; 4 English recommended, 3 math recommended, 3 science recommended, 2 foreign language recommended, 3 social studies recommended, 2 history recommended, 2 elective recommended. High school diploma or GED required. Minimum TOEFL is 550. TOEFL required of all international applicants.

Application deadline: February 1
Notification: Rolling beginning 9/1
Average GPA: 3.4

Average SAT I Math: 550
Average SAT I Verbal: 550
Average ACT: 23

Graduated top 10% of class: 17%
Graduated top 25% of class: 46%
Graduated top 50% of class: 87%

COLLEGE GRADUATION REQUIREMENTS

Course waivers allowed: No
Course substitutions allowed: Y/N
In what subjects: Cas-by-case basis and not done as a general rule

ADDITIONAL INFORMATION

Environment: The University is in a small town south of Ohio State University.

Student Body
  Undergrad enrollment: 16,511
  Female: 55%
  Male: 45%
  Out-of-state: 10%

Cost Information
  In-state tuition: $5,085
  Out-of-state tuition: $10,704
  Room & board: $5,922
Housing Information
  University housing: Yes
  Percent living on campus: 42%

Greek System
  Fraternity: Yes
  Sorority: Yes
Athletics: NCAA Division I

UNIVERSITY OF CINCINNATI

PO Box 210091, Cincinnati, OH 45221-0091
Phone: 513-556-1100 • Fax: 513-556-1105
E-mail: admissions@uc.edu • Web: www.uc.edu
Support level: S • Institution type: 4-year public

LEARNING DISABILITY PROGRAM AND SERVICES

The University of Cincinnati does not have a specific structured learning disability program. However, students with learning disabilities who use academic accommodations and support services available through the Disability Services and other resources of the University find they can be successful in achieving their academic objectives. The goal of Disability Services is to provide the necessary accommodations to students in order for them to become successful and independent learners. Remedial developmental courses are available along with campuswide tutoring. To receive support services, students need to submit documentation from a licensed professional to the Disability Services Office. Service staff will work with students and faculty to arrange for special needs or accommodations.

LD/ADHD ADMISSIONS INFORMATION

College entrance tests required: Yes
Nonstandardized tests accepted: Yes
Interview required: No
Essay required: No
Documentation required for LD: Psychoeducational evaluation: within 3 years
Documentation required for ADHD: Yes
Documentation submitted to: Disability Services
Special Ed. HS course work accepted: According to the College

Specific course requirements for all applicants: Yes
Separate application required for services: No
# of LD applications submitted yearly: N/A
# of LD applications accepted yearly: N/A
Total # of students receiving LD/ADHD services: 250+
Acceptance into program means acceptance into college: Student must be admitted and enrolled at the University first and then may request services.

ADMISSIONS

There is no special admissions procedure for students with learning disabilities. The Admissions Office looks at each individual situation; there is no set rule for admissions and waivers. All students submit the general university application form. Course requirements and waivers depend upon the College within the University. General course requirements include 4 years English, 3 years math (4 for engineering), 2 years science, 2 years social studies, and 2 years foreign language (not required in business) or can substitute American Sign Language. University College is a two-year associate degree program that has an "open door" policy, no minimum GPA, no required tests, and no course requirements for entrance. Students may transfer to other majors after one year if they are doing well or may transfer into one of the four-year majors after receiving an associate degree. Students with learning disabilities are encouraged to request an interview with the Disability Services Office, which their parents may attend.

ADDITIONAL INFORMATION

Disabilities Services provides services and accommodations that are mandated under federal law. Support services include: note-taking, tutors, readers, taped textbooks, testing accommodations, scribes, loan of equipment, and library disability services. Peer tutoring is available as an accommodation at no cost. Students with appropriate documentation may request course substitutions in math or foreign language. Skills classes are offered for all students in time management, organizational skills, and study skills. University College offers developmental courses in effective reading, English, and mathematics as well as a college study course.

SUPPORT SERVICES CONTACT INFORMATION

Learning Disability Program/Services: Disability Services
Director: Debra Merchant
  E-mail: debra.merchant@uc.edu
  Telephone: 513-556-6823
  Fax: 513-556-1383
Contact: Same

LEARNING DISABILITY SERVICES

Requests for the following services/accommodations will be evaluated individually based on appropriate and current documentation.

Allowed in Exams
  Calculator: Yes
  Dictionary: Yes
  Computer: Yes
  Spellchecker: Yes
Extended test time: Yes
Scribes: Yes
Proctors: Yes
Oral exams: Yes
Note-takers: Yes

Distraction-reduced environment: Yes
Tape recording in class: Yes
Books on tape from RFBD: Yes
Taping of books not from RFBD: Yes
Accommodations for students with
  ADHD: Yes
Reading machine: No
Other assistive technology: Yes
Priority registration: Yes

Added costs for services: No
LD specialists: No
Professional tutors: Grad students
Peer tutors: Yes
Max. hours/wk. for services:
  Unlimited
How professors are notified of
  LD/ADHD: By both student and
  director

GENERAL ADMISSIONS INFORMATION

Director of Admissions: Terry Davis
Telephone: 513-556-1100

ENTRANCE REQUIREMENTS
16 total are required; 4 English required, 3 math required, 2 science required, 2 foreign language required, 2 social studies required, 2 elective required. High school diploma or GED required. Minimum TOEFL is 515. TOEFL required of all international applicants.

Application deadline: August 1
Notification: Rolling beginning 10/15
Average GPA: 3.2

Average SAT I Math: 556
Average SAT I Verbal: 548
Average ACT: 23

Graduated top 10% of class: 15%
Graduated top 25% of class: 36%
Graduated top 50% of class: 69%

COLLEGE GRADUATION REQUIREMENTS

Course waivers allowed: Yes
Course substitutions allowed: Yes
In what subjects: Foreign language and math

ADDITIONAL INFORMATION

Environment: The University is located on 392 acres in downtown Cincinnati.

Student Body
  Undergrad enrollment: 20,656
  Female: 48%
  Male: 52%
  Out-of-state: 11%

Cost Information
  In-state tuition: $4,467
  Out-of-state tuition: $12,744
  Room & board: $6,375
Housing Information
  University housing: Yes
  Percent living on campus: 41%

Greek System
  Fraternity: Yes
  Sorority: Yes
Athletics: NCAA Division I

UNIVERSITY OF TOLEDO

2801 West Bancroft, Toledo, OH 43606
Phone: 419-530-8888 • Fax: 419-530-4504
E-mail: enroll@utnet.utoledo.edu • Web: www.utoledo.edu
Support level: S • Institution type: 4-year public

LEARNING DISABILITY PROGRAM AND SERVICES

The University of Toledo sees its students as people first. To this end, the University strives to provide a nurturing environment to strengthen its students academically and socially. Specifically, the Office of Accessibility provides comprehensive support services to provide equal opportunity to students with disabilities as they pursue a post-secondary education. In order to engage services, students with learning disabilities and ADD/ADHD must provide the Office of Accessibility with a current psychoeducational evaluation that specifically identifies their disability and/or attention deficit disorder as adults. In order to understand the student's disability history better, students may also provide IEPs and/or documentation of services received in high school. The Office of Accessibility maintains the confidentiality of the psychoeducational evaluation and other supporting documentation. However, support service personnel, faculty directly involved with the student's classes, academic advisors, and administrative staff members exchange information with the Office of Accessibility regarding the nature of the student's disability, accommodations requested, and academic status. Students must sign a Confidentiality Agreement to indicate their understanding of the release of information to all involved in their academic success.

LD/ADHD ADMISSIONS INFORMATION

College entrance tests required: No
Nonstandardized tests accepted: Yes
Interview required: No
Essay required: No
Documentation required for LD: Psychoeducational evaluation
Documentation required for ADHD: Yes
Documentation submitted to: Office of Accessibility
Special Ed. HS course work accepted: Yes

Specific course requirements for all applicants: Yes
Separate application required for services: No
# of LD applications submitted yearly: N/A
# of LD applications accepted yearly: N/A
Total # of students receiving LD/ADHD services: 100
Acceptance into program means acceptance into college: Students are admitted and enrolled at the University and then, if eligible, receive accommodations.

ADMISSIONS
There is no separate admissions process for students with learning disabilities. All students must meet the same admission criteria. Admissions standards include GPA of at least 2.0 or the equivalent of a C GPA; 18 ACT or higher for Ohio residents and 21 ACT or 1000 SAT score for non-Ohio residents; 4 years English, 3 years math, 3 years science, 3 years social studies, and 2 years foreign language; and high school graduation requirements fulfilled or a successful passing score on the GED. Ohio residents not meeting these requirements are reviewed on an individual basis for admission consideration. Some programs, including engineering, nursing, physical therapy, pharmacy, pre-medical, pre-dentistry, and pre-veterinary, have higher requirements.

ADDITIONAL INFORMATION
Once students have been admitted to the University and have submitted documentation of their disability, they complete an intake process that delivers additional background information and sets up accommodations as dictated by the documentation. These services may include note-taking services, reader services for texts and tests, extended testing time, secondary academic advising, social/interpersonal counseling, disability verification to professors, disability advising, priority registration, and adaptive technology.

SUPPORT SERVICES CONTACT INFORMATION

Learning Disability Program/Services: Office of Accessibility
Director: Kendra Johnson
  E-mail: kjohnso3@utnet.utoledo.edu
  Telephone: 419-530-4981
  Fax: 419-530-6137
Contact: Same

LEARNING DISABILITY SERVICES

Requests for the following services/accommodations will be evaluated individually based on appropriate and current documentation.

Allowed in Exams
  Calculator: Yes
  Dictionary: Yes
  Computer: Yes
  Spellchecker: Yes
Extended test time: Yes
Scribes: Yes
Proctors: Yes
Oral exams: Yes
Note-takers: Yes

Distraction-reduced environment: Yes
Tape recording in class: Yes
Books on tape from RFBD: Yes
Taping of books not from RFBD: Yes
Accommodations for students with ADHD: Yes
Reading machine: No
Other assistive technology: No
Priority registration: Yes

Added costs for services: No
LD specialists: Yes
Professional tutors: No
Peer tutors: Yes (75+)
Max. hours/wk. for services: Unlimited
How professors are notified of LD/ADHD: By student and letter

GENERAL ADMISSIONS INFORMATION

Director of Admissions: Dick Eastop
Telephone: 419-530-8888

ENTRANCE REQUIREMENTS

3 English required, 4 English recommended, 3 math required, 3 math recommended, 3 science recommended, 1 science lab recommended, 2 foreign language recommended, 2 social studies required, 2 social studies recommended, 1 history recommended. High school diploma or GED required. Minimum TOEFL is 500. TOEFL required of all international applicants.

Application deadline: Rolling
Notification: Rolling beginning 10/1
Average GPA: 2.9

Average SAT I Math: 504
Average SAT I Verbal: 447
Average ACT: 20

Graduated top 10% of class: 14%
Graduated top 25% of class: 35%
Graduated top 50% of class: 62%

COLLEGE GRADUATION REQUIREMENTS

Course waivers allowed: No
Course substitutions allowed: Yes
In what subjects: Foreign language

ADDITIONAL INFORMATION

Environment: The University of Toledo is located on a 305-acre campus in Toledo, Ohio.

Student Body
  Undergrad enrollment: 16,729
  Female: 55%
  Male: 45%
  Out-of-state: 3%

Cost Information
  In-state tuition: $4,416
  Out-of-state tuition: $10,783
  Room & board: $5,096
Housing Information
  University housing: Yes
  Percent living on campus: 18%

Greek System
  Fraternity: Yes
  Sorority: Yes
Athletics: NCAA Division I

Ursuline College

2550 Lander Road, Pepper Pike, OH 44124-4398
Phone: 440-449-4203 • Fax: 440-684-6138
E-mail: admission@ursuline.edu • Web: www.ursuline.edu
Support level: CS • Institution type: 4-year private

LEARNING DISABILITY PROGRAM AND SERVICES

Ursuline College is a small Catholic college committed to helping students with learning disabilities succeed in their courses and become independent learners. The Program for Students with Learning Disabilities (PSLD) is a voluntary, comprehensive fee-paid program. PSLD's goals include providing a smooth transition to college life, helping students learn to apply the most appropriate learning strategies in college courses, and teaching self-advocacy skills. To be eligible for PSLD, a student must present documentation of an LD, which consists of a WAIS-R, the Woodcock-Johnson, and any other standardized measures of achievement. The psychoeducational evaluation must clearly indicate that the student has a specific learning disability and should have been conducted within the last three years. Students must have average to above-average intellectual ability and an appropriate academic foundation to succeed in a four-year liberal arts college.

LD/ADHD ADMISSIONS INFORMATION

College entrance tests required: Yes
Nonstandardized tests accepted: Yes
Interview required: Yes
Essay required: Yes
Documentation required for LD: WAIS-III/Woodcock-Johnson
Documentation required for ADHD: Yes
Documentation submitted to: PSLD
Special Ed. HS course work accepted: Yes

Specific course requirements for all applicants: Yes
Separate application required for services: Yes
# of LD applications submitted yearly: 6–11
# of LD applications accepted yearly: 9
Total # of students receiving LD/ADHD services: 25
Acceptance into program means acceptance into college: Students must be admitted and enrolled at the College first and then may request services.

ADMISSIONS

To participate in PSLD, students must first meet with the LD specialist to discuss whether the program is suitable for them. Students must then meet the requirements for clear or conditional admission to the College by applying to the admissions office and completing all regular admission procedures. Students with learning disabilities must meet the same requirements for admission to the College as all other students: 2.5 GPA and an ACT score of 17 or an SAT score of 850 for a "clear" admission. Courses recommended include 4 years English, 3 years social studies, 3 years math, 3 years science, 2 years foreign language. A student may receive a "conditional" admission if the GPA and ACT are lower. Course deficiencies must be removed prior to graduation from college. Students with conditional admission are limited to 12 credit hours per semester for the first year. The final admission decision is made by the Office of Admissions.

ADDITIONAL INFORMATION

PSLD is a program that features an orientation that provides a smooth transition to the College, acquaints students with mentors and other students in PSLD, and introduces students to high-tech equipment and computers in the LRC; individual bi-weekly one-hour sessions with an LD specialist to work on developing time-management and organizational skills, design learning strategies for success in college, and learn note-taking and test-taking skills; individual weekly one-hour sessions with a writing specialist who provides assistance with writing assignments in specific courses and who helps with developing skills in writing effective sentences, paragraphs, and essays; weekly academic-skills support groups with LD specialist to learn coping skills, develop self-advocacy skills, and receive support for dealing with classroom issues; and academic advising for guidance on choosing appropriate courses and scheduling appropriate number of credits each semester.

SUPPORT SERVICES CONTACT INFORMATION

Learning Disability Program/Services: Program for Students with LD (PSLD)
Director: Cynthia Russell
  E-mail: crussell@ursuline.edu
  Telephone: 440-646-8123
  Fax: 440-646-8318
Contact: Annette Gromada (LD Specialist)
  E-mail: agromada@ursuline.edu
  Telephone: 440-449-2046
  Fax: 440-646-8318

LEARNING DISABILITY SERVICES

Requests for the following services/accommodations will be evaluated individually based on appropriate and current documentation.

Allowed in Exams
  Calculator: Yes
  Dictionary: Yes
  Computer: Yes
  Spellchecker: Yes
Extended test time: Yes
Scribes: Yes
Proctors: Yes
Oral exams: Yes
Note-takers: Yes

Distraction-reduced environment: Yes
Tape recording in class: Yes
Books on tape from RFBD: Yes
Taping of books not from RFBD: Yes
Accommodations for students with ADHD: Yes
Reading machine: Yes
Other assistive technology: Yes
Priority registration: Yes

Added costs for services: $1,200 per semester
LD specialists: Yes (1)
Professional tutors: 3
Peer tutors: No
Max. hours/wk. for services: Unlimited
How professors are notified of LD/ADHD: By student

GENERAL ADMISSIONS INFORMATION

Director of Admissions: Jill Oakley-Jeppe
Telephone: 440-449-4203

ENTRANCE REQUIREMENTS

17 total are recommended; 4 English recommended, 3 math recommended, 3 science recommended, 2 science lab recommended, 2 foreign language recommended, 3 social studies recommended. Minimum TOEFL is 500. TOEFL required of all international applicants.

Application deadline: Rolling
Notification: Rolling
Average GPA: 3.1
Average SAT I Math: 445
Average SAT I Verbal: 451
Average ACT: 20
Graduated top 10% of class: 12%
Graduated top 25% of class: 41%
Graduated top 50% of class: 77%

COLLEGE GRADUATION REQUIREMENTS

Course waivers allowed: No
Course substitutions allowed: Yes
In what subjects: Substitutions are allowed with documentation of a disability in math and with approval of department chair of major. There is no foreign language requirement.

ADDITIONAL INFORMATION

Environment: The College is located in a suburban area about 20 miles from Cleveland.

Student Body
  Undergrad enrollment: 1,016
  Female: 93%
  Male: 7%
  Out-of-state: 1%

Cost Information
  Tuition: $13,500
  Room & board: $4,560
Housing Information
  University housing: Yes
  Percent living on campus: 10%

Greek System
  Fraternity: Yes
  Sorority: Yes
  Athletics: NAIA

WRIGHT STATE UNIVERSITY

3640 Colonel Glenn Highway, Dayton, OH 45435
Phone: 937-775-5700 • Fax: 937-775-5795
E-mail: admissions@wright.edu • Web: www.wright.edu
Support level: CS • Institution type: 4-year public

LEARNING DISABILITY PROGRAM AND SERVICES

The University is dedicated to the elimination of barriers that prevent intellectually qualified individuals with disabilities from attending colleges and universities across the country. Students with disabilities are encouraged to participate in all facets of university life according to their abilities and interests and to develop independence and responsibility to the fullest extent possible. The philosophy of the University is intended to stimulate students to pursue the career of study regardless of their learning disability. Through the Office of Disability Services, the University provides a comprehensive array of services on a campus with a long history of commitment to students with physical, visual, and/or learning disabilities. Students with learning disabilities may use a variety of services that will allow them to be equal and competitive in the classroom. A pre-service interview is required of all prospective students to discuss service needs. Eligibility for services is determined after documentation is received and the student has an individual interview.

LD/ADHD ADMISSIONS INFORMATION

College entrance tests required: Yes
Nonstandardized tests accepted: Yes
Interview required: Yes
Essay required: Yes
Documentation required for LD: WAIS-III; WRAT; WJ: within 3 years
Documentation required for ADHD: Yes
Documentation submitted to: Office of Disability Services
Special Ed. HS course work accepted: Yes

Specific course requirements for all applicants: Yes
Separate application required for services: Yes
# of LD applications submitted yearly: All who are eligible
# of LD applications accepted yearly: 300
Total # of students receiving LD/ADHD services: 200
Acceptance into program means acceptance into college: Students must be accepted and enrolled at the University first and then may request services.

ADMISSIONS

The University has an open admission policy for in-state students. ACT/SAT are used for placement, not admission. The middle 50 percent range for the ACT is 18–24 and SAT 990–1140. Students with LD must meet the identical criteria as all applicants and must be accepted prior to requesting service. However, out-of-state students are encouraged to self-disclose their learning disability and submit documentation to the Office of Disability Services prior to applying to the University if they would like to discuss eligibility for admission and services available on campus and determine if Wright State is a good fit for them. It is recommended that students self-disclose the LD if GPA or test scores are low and the student feels that LD disclosure is important in explaining academic or testing information. Course requirements include 4 years English, 3 years math, 3 years science and social science, 2 years foreign language, and 1 year fine arts. The Director of Disability Services encourages students and their families to visit and interview. Admissions would ask ODS to review documentation, transcripts, etc., and meet with the student to determine readiness for college. Students with a college-prep curriculum in high school have been more successful at Wright State than those who took a general curriculum. The final decision rests with Admissions.

ADDITIONAL INFORMATION

Conditional Admissions to the University is available to students who enter with a high school "deficiency." They must remove it before graduating from the University or complete developmental education courses. All new students attend summer orientation. A separate orientation is held prior to the start of fall quarter for students with learning disabilities. To determine eligibility for support services after admission, the following are required: results of psychological testing, a "Request for Support Services" form completed by the student, and a transcript of high school classes completed, as well as any post-secondary courses taken. Students must write a 100-word handwritten, uncorrected statement about why they are requesting support services through the Learning Disabilities Program. Application for services for ODS is separate and not connected to the application to the University. Interview and documentation are required.

SUPPORT SERVICES CONTACT INFORMATION

Learning Disability Program/Services: Office of Disability Services
Director: Jeff Vernooy
  E-mail: jeffrey.vernooy@wright.edu
  Telephone: 937-775-5680
  Fax: 937-775-5795
Contact: Judy Roberts
  E-mail: disability_services@wright.edu
  Telephone: 937-775-5680
  Fax: 937-775-5795

LEARNING DISABILITY SERVICES

Requests for the following services/accommodations will be evaluated individually based on appropriate and current documentation.

Allowed in Exams
  Calculator: Yes
  Dictionary: Yes
  Computer: Yes
  Spellchecker: Yes
Extended test time: Yes
Scribes: Yes
Proctors: Yes
Oral exams: Yes
Note-takers: Yes

Distraction-reduced environment: Yes
Tape recording in class: Yes
Books on tape from RFBD: Yes
Taping of books not from RFBD: Yes
Accommodations for students with ADHD: Yes
Reading machine: Yes
Other assistive technology: Yes
Priority registration: No

Added costs for services: No
LD specialists: Yes (1)
Professional tutors: No
Peer tutors: 35
Max. hours/wk. for services: 2 hours per class free, $5.50 per hour thereafter
How professors are notified of LD/ADHD: By student

GENERAL ADMISSIONS INFORMATION

Director of Admissions: Kathy Davis
Telephone: 937-775-5700

ENTRANCE REQUIREMENTS
12 total are required; 4 English required, 3 math required, 3 science required, 2 foreign language required. High school diploma or GED required. Minimum TOEFL is 500. TOEFL required of all international applicants.

Application deadline: Open
Notification: Rolling beginning 10/1
Average GPA: 3.0

Average SAT I Math: 500
Average SAT I Verbal: 501
Average ACT: 21

Graduated top 10% of class: 19%
Graduated top 25% of class: 37%
Graduated top 50% of class: 66%

COLLEGE GRADUATION REQUIREMENTS

Course waivers allowed: No
Course substitutions allowed: Yes
In what subjects: Foreign language and, in a few cases, math

ADDITIONAL INFORMATION

Environment: The University is located on 645 acres 8 miles northeast of Dayton.

Student Body
  Undergrad enrollment: 10,904
  Female: 56%
  Male: 44%
  Out-of-state: 3%

Cost Information
  In-state tuition: $4,128
  Out-of-state tuition: $8,256
  Room & board: $5,053
  Housing Information
    University housing: Yes
    Percent living on campus: 14%

Greek System
  Fraternity: Yes
  Sorority: Yes
Athletics: NCAA Division I

XAVIER UNIVERSITY

3800 Victory Parkway, Cincinnati, OH 45207-5311
Phone: 513-745-3301 • Fax: 513-745-4319
E-mail: xuadmit@xu.edu • Web: www.xu.edu
Support level: CS • Institution type: 4-year private

LEARNING DISABILITY PROGRAM AND SERVICES

The Learning Assistance Center's mission is threefold: to ensure that all students with disabilities can freely and actively participate in every aspect of college life; to provide academic support services so that students with disabilities have equal educational access; and to seek to educate the community at large.

LD/ADHD ADMISSIONS INFORMATION

College entrance tests required: Yes
Nonstandardized tests accepted: Yes
Interview required: NR
Essay required: Yes
Documentation required for LD: Psychoeducational evaluation
Documentation required for ADHD: Yes
Documentation submitted to: Learning Assistance Center
Special Ed. HS course work accepted: Yes

Specific course requirements for all applicants: Yes
Separate application required for services: No
# of LD applications submitted yearly: N/A
# of LD applications accepted yearly: N/A
Total # of students receiving LD/ADHD services: 163
Acceptance into program means acceptance into college: Students must be accepted and enrolled at the University first and then may request services.

ADMISSIONS

There is no special admissions process for students with learning disabilities. However, there is a "Freshman Success Program" for some admitted students who would benefit from a reduced course load and more guidance and mentoring.

ADDITIONAL INFORMATION

All students have access to the math lab, writing center, and tutoring center. Additionally, there are study skills classes offered in time management and test-taking strategies. Students with learning disabilities and/or ADHD also have access to support groups, special testing, and mentoring. Accommodations and services are available for undergraduates and graduates.

SUPPORT SERVICES CONTACT INFORMATION

Learning Disability Program/Services: Learning Assistance Center
Director: Sarah Kelly
  E-mail: kellys@admin.xu.edu
  Telephone: 513-745-3280
  Fax: 513-745-3387
Contact: Same

LEARNING DISABILITY SERVICES

Requests for the following services/accommodations will be evaluated individually based on appropriate and current documentation.

Allowed in Exams
  Calculator: Yes
  Dictionary: Yes
  Computer: Yes
  Spellchecker: Yes
Extended test time: Yes
Scribes: Yes
Proctors: Yes
Oral exams: Yes
Note-takers: Yes

Distraction-reduced environment: Yes
Tape recording in class: Yes
Books on tape from RFBD: Yes
Taping of books not from RFBD: Yes
Accommodations for students with
  ADHD: Yes
Reading machine: No
Other assistive technology: PM System
Priority registration: Yes

Added costs for services: No
LD specialists: Yes (1)
Professional tutors: No
Peer tutors: 35
Max. hours/wk. for services: Unlimited
How professors are notified of
  LD/ADHD: By program director

GENERAL ADMISSIONS INFORMATION

Director of Admissions: Marc Camille
Telephone: 513-745-3301

ENTRANCE REQUIREMENTS

15 total are recommended; 4 English recommended, 3 math recommended, 2 science recommended, 2 foreign language recommended, 2 social studies recommended, 2 elective recommended. High school diploma or GED required. Minimum TOEFL is 500. TOEFL required of all international applicants.

Application deadline: March 15
Notification: Rolling beginning 10/1
Average GPA: 3.5

Average SAT I Math: 570
Average SAT I Verbal: 572
Average ACT: 25

Graduated top 10% of class: 30%
Graduated top 25% of class: 57%
Graduated top 50% of class: 87%

COLLEGE GRADUATION REQUIREMENTS

Course waivers allowed: No
Course substitutions allowed: Yes
In what subjects: Substitutions only usually in math and foreign language

ADDITIONAL INFORMATION

Environment: Located 5 miles from downtown.

Student Body
  Undergrad enrollment: 4,019
  Female: 59%
  Male: 41%
  Out-of-state: 35%

Cost Information
  Tuition: $16,540
  Room & board: $6,960
Housing Information
  University housing: Yes
  Percent living on campus: 42%

Greek System
  Fraternity: No
  Sorority: No
Athletics: NCAA Division I

Xavier University

OKLAHOMA STATE UNIVERSITY

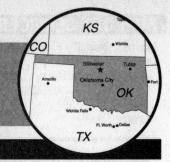

324 Student Union, Stillwater, OK 74078
Phone: 405-744-6858 • Fax: 405-744-5285
E-mail: admit@okstate.edu • Web: www.okstate.edu
Support level: S • Institution type: 4-year public

LEARNING DISABILITY PROGRAM AND SERVICES

Oklahoma State University does not have a formal learning disabilities program but uses a service-based model to assist the students in obtaining the necessary accommodations for specific learning disabilities. Students with learning disabilities may request priority enrollment and a campus orientation to assist in scheduling classes. Other services developed in coordination with the Special Education area work to minimize the students' difficulties in relation to course work. These services could include test accommodations, course substitutions, and independent study. The underlying philosophy of this program is to provide assistance to students to facilitate their academic progress. Student Disability Services (SDS) also acts as a resource for faculty and staff.

LD/ADHD ADMISSIONS INFORMATION

College entrance tests required: Yes
Nonstandardized tests accepted: Yes
Interview required: No
Essay required: No
Documentation required for LD: Adult-normed evaluations of ability and achievement, WAIS-III (ability), Woodcock-Johnson-R (achievement) and clear diagnostic statement
Documentation required for ADHD: Yes
Documentation submitted to: SDS
Special Ed. HS course work accepted: No

Specific course requirements for all applicants: Yes
Separate application required for services: No
# of LD applications submitted yearly: N/A
# of LD applications accepted yearly: N/A
Total # of students receiving LD/ADHD services: 120-131
Acceptance into program means acceptance into college: Students must be admitted and enrolled at the University first and then may request services.

ADMISSIONS

There is no special admissions policy for students with LD. However, if ability to meet admission criteria was impacted by a disability (such as late identification, no accommodations, or high school courses waived), students should include a personal statement with their application and contact Disability Services. General admission requirements include ACT of 22+ or SAT I of 1020+ or a 3.0 GPA and rank in the top third of the class. Course requirements include 4 years English, 3 years math, 2 years science, 2 years history, 1 year citizenship skills (economics, geography, government, or nonwestern culture), and 3 years from previous areas and/or computer science and/or foreign language. Students with appropriate documentation may be allowed to substitute courses for math or foreign language. Students not meeting admission requirements may qualify for admission through (1) Alternative Admission for students whose high school achievement is slightly below the standards and/or deficient in no more than one curricular unit (2) Summer Provision Program for students who meet all the curricular requirements and have a GPA of 2.5 or above, or ACT of 18 or above or SAT of 870 or above. These students may enter in the summer on probation and may be required to take placement tests prior to a final acceptance or (3) Adult admission for students over 21 or on active military duty with less than six college credits.

ADDITIONAL INFORMATION

There is a math lab and a writing center for all students. All students with LD/ADHD requesting accommodations or services must provide appropriate and current documentation. All diagnostic testing and documentation should be sent to Student Disability Services. There are currently 100 students with learning disabilities and 40 with ADHD receiving services on campus. The University also operates the Oklahoma City Technical Institute, which offers two-year, career-oriented programs.

SUPPORT SERVICES CONTACT INFORMATION

Learning Disability Program/Services: Student Disability Services (SDS)
Director: Michael Shuttic
  E-mail: shuttic@okstate.edu
  Telephone: 405-744-7116
  Fax: 405-744-8380
Contact: Same

LEARNING DISABILITY SERVICES

Requests for the following services/accommodations will be evaluated individually based on appropriate and current documentation.

Allowed in Exams
  Calculator: Yes
  Dictionary: Yes
  Computer: Yes
  Spellchecker: Yes
Extended test time: Yes
Scribes: Yes
Proctors: Yes
Oral exams: Yes
Note-takers: Yes

Distraction-reduced environment: Yes
Tape recording in class: Yes
Books on tape from RFBD: Yes
Taping of books not from RFBD: Yes
Accommodations for students with
  ADHD: Yes
Reading machine: Yes
Other assistive technology: Yes
Priority registration: Yes

Added costs for services: No
LD specialists: No
Professional tutors: No
Peer tutors: No
Max. hours/wk. for services:
  Unlimited
How professors are notified of
  LD/ADHD: By both student and
  director

GENERAL ADMISSIONS INFORMATION

Director of Admissions: Gordon Reese
Telephone: 405-744-7275

ENTRANCE REQUIREMENTS

15 total are required; 18 total are recommended; 4 English required, 4 English recommended, 3 math required, 3 math recommended, 2 science required, 2 science recommended, 2 science lab required, 2 science lab recommended, 2 foreign language recommended, 1 social studies required, 1 social studies recommended, 2 history required, 2 history recommended, 3 elective required, 3 elective recommended. High school diploma or GED required. Minimum TOEFL is 500. TOEFL required of all international applicants.

Application deadline: August 15
Notification: Rolling beginning 9/1
Average GPA: 3.5

Average SAT I Math: 559
Average SAT I Verbal: 552
Average ACT: 24

Graduated top 10% of class: 30%
Graduated top 25% of class: 59%
Graduated top 50% of class: 88%

COLLEGE GRADUATION REQUIREMENTS

Course waivers allowed: Yes
Course substitutions allowed: Yes
In what subjects: Varies based on degree requirements and major

ADDITIONAL INFORMATION

Environment: The 415-acre campus is located in a small city 65 miles north of Oklahoma City.

Student Body
  Undergrad enrollment: 16,203
  Female: 47%
  Male: 53%
  Out-of-state: 12%

Cost Information
  In-state tuition: $1,890
  Out-of-state tuition: $6,225
  Room & board: $4,716
Housing Information
  University housing: Yes
  Percent living on campus: 38%

Greek System
  Fraternity: Yes
  Sorority: Yes
  Athletics: NCAA Division I

UNIVERSITY OF OKLAHOMA

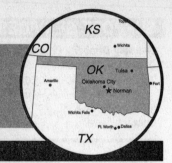

1000 Asp Avenue, Norman, OK 73019-4076
Phone: 405-325-2251 • Fax: 405-325-7124
E-mail: admrec@ouwww.ou.edu • Web: www.ou.edu
Support level: S • Institution type: 4-year public

LEARNING DISABILITY PROGRAM AND SERVICES

The Office of Disability Services provides support services and is committed to the goal of achieving equal educational opportunity and full participation for students with disabilities. In many cases, these services are developed in response to expressed student needs. There are no special LD or remedial classes. Students are encouraged to be self-advocates in making requests for reasonable academic accommodations. Assistance is to be used to support the accomplishment of educational goals. The coordinator of services sponsors the OU Association for Disabled Students, a student organization that provides a recognized forum for support, regular meetings, and social and recreational activities. Students must provide psychoeducational evaluations documenting learning disabilities in order to receive services. The evaluation should include full-scale, performance, and verbal IQ scores; scores from aptitude-achievement comparisons; and a summary and recommendations.

LD/ADHD ADMISSIONS INFORMATION

College entrance tests required: Yes
Nonstandardized tests accepted: Yes
Interview required: No
Essay required: No
Documentation required for LD: WAIS-III; WJ-R: within 3 years preferred
Documentation required for ADHD: Yes
Documentation submitted to: Office of Disability Services
Special Ed. HS course work accepted: Yes

Specific course requirements for all applicants: Yes
Separate application required for services: No
# of LD applications submitted yearly: N/A
# of LD applications accepted yearly: N/A
Total # of students receiving LD/ADHD services: 150
Acceptance into program means acceptance into college: Students must be admitted and enrolled at the University first and then may request services.

ADMISSIONS

Admission requirements for students with learning disabilities are the same as for all other students. Admission requirements include ACT 24 or SAT 1090 or rank in the top 30 percent of class or have a 3.0 GPA in the 15 core courses and have a minimum 22 ACT or 1010 SAT. Course requirements include 4 years English; 2 years science; 3 years math; 2 years social studies; 1 unit in economics, geography, government or nonwestern culture; and 3 additional subjects. Students who do not meet regular admission requirements will be considered for a number of alternative admission options. Decisions will be based on various criteria designed to identify applicants who have a reasonable chance for academic success. The Summer Provision Admission Program provides the opportunity to be admitted for the summer session and required to take one college-level English course and college algebra or equivalent. Students must complete each class with a C or better to continue at the University. The Alternative Admission Option is directed at students matriculating directly from high school who do not meet admission criteria. These students must submit a written statement concerning their background, educational goals, and why they feel they are prepared to be successful in college. Consideration will also be given to letters of recommendation attesting to motivation and potential for academic success. Admission in this category is limited and students are encouraged to submit application, test scores, and transcript as early as possible.

ADDITIONAL INFORMATION

After receiving academic advisement from the College, the student should make an appointment with Disabled Student Services. The office will also provide a personal campus orientation upon request. Services offered, based on individual needs, include alternative testing, readers, scribes, note-takers (who are volunteers), tutors, tape-recorded texts, and library assistance. Tutoring is provided on a one-to-one basis by peer tutors. Services are available for undergraduate and graduate students.

SUPPORT SERVICES CONTACT INFORMATION

Learning Disability Program/Services: Office of Disability Services
Director: Suzette Dyer
  E-mail: sdyer@ou.edu
  Telephone: 405-325-3852
  Fax: 405-325-4491
Contact: Same

LEARNING DISABILITY SERVICES

Requests for the following services/accommodations will be evaluated individually based on appropriate and current documentation.

Allowed in Exams
  Calculator: No
  Dictionary: No
  Computer: Yes
  Spellchecker: Yes
Extended test time: Yes
Scribes: Yes
Proctors: Yes
Oral exams: Yes
Note-takers: Yes

Distraction-reduced environment: Yes
Tape recording in class: Yes
Books on tape from RFBD: Yes
Taping of books not from RFBD: No
Accommodations for students with ADHD: Yes
Reading machine: Yes
Other assistive technology: Yes
Priority registration: Yes

Added costs for services: No
LD specialists: No
Professional tutors: No
Peer tutors: No
Max. hours/wk. for services: As needed
How professors are notified of LD/ADHD: By director

GENERAL ADMISSIONS INFORMATION

Director of Admissions: Pat Lynch (acting director)
Telephone: 405-325-2251

ENTRANCE REQUIREMENTS
15 total are required; 4 English required, 3 math required, 2 science required, 2 science lab required, 3 foreign language recommended, 1 social studies required, 2 history required, 3 elective required. High school diploma or GED required. Minimum TOEFL is 550. TOEFL required of all international applicants.

Application deadline: June 1
Notification: Rolling
Average GPA: 3.5

Average SAT I Math: NR
Average SAT I Verbal: NR
Average ACT: 25

Graduated top 10% of class: 31%
Graduated top 25% of class: 61%
Graduated top 50% of class: 89%

COLLEGE GRADUATION REQUIREMENTS

Course waivers allowed: No
Course substitutions allowed: Yes
In what subjects: Foreign language; students may petition for a substitution

ADDITIONAL INFORMATION

Environment: The 3,107-acre campus is located in a suburb 17 miles south of Oklahoma City.

Student Body
  Undergrad enrollment: 18,308
  Female: 50%
  Male: 50%
  Out-of-state: 17%

Cost Information
  In-state tuition: $1,890
  Out-of-state tuition: $6,225
  Room & board: $4,610
Housing Information
  University housing: Yes
  Percent living on campus: 20%

Greek System
  Fraternity: Yes
  Sorority: Yes
Athletics: NCAA Division I

UNIVERSITY OF TULSA

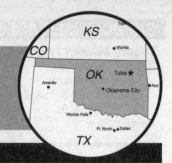

600 South College Ave., Tulsa, OK 74104
Phone: 918-631-2307 • Fax: 918-631-5003
E-mail: admission@utulsa.edu • Web: www.utulsa.edu
Support level: CS • Institution type: 4-year private

LEARNING DISABILITY PROGRAM AND SERVICES

The Center for Student Academic Support offers a comprehensive range of academic support services and accommodations to students with disabilities. The goal is to provide services which will, in combination with the resources and talents of the student, maximize the students' independence for full participation in the curriculum and provide an opportunity to achieve career goals. The policy of the University of Tulsa, in keeping with the Americans with Disabilities Act, is to provide reasonable accommodations for students with disabilities, including students with learning disabilities. Students who have specific disabilities that might impact their full access and participation in university programs are urged to provide the relevant documentation and make an appointment with the Coordinator of the Center for Student Academic Support.

LD/ADHD ADMISSIONS INFORMATION

College entrance tests required: Yes
Nonstandardized tests accepted: Yes
Interview required: No
Essay required: Yes
Documentation required for LD: Psychoeducational evaluation
Documentation required for ADHD: Yes
Documentation submitted to: Center for Academic Support
Special Ed. HS course work accepted: Yes

Specific course requirements for all applicants: Yes
Separate application required for services: Yes
# of LD applications submitted yearly: 80
# of LD applications accepted yearly: 74
Total # of students receiving LD/ADHD services: 15
Acceptance into program means acceptance into college: Students must be admitted and enrolled at the University and then may request services.

ADMISSIONS

All students must meet the general admissions requirements. Students with disabilities are not required to disclose information about the disability, but may voluntarily disclose or request information from CSAS. The University does not consider disabilities in the decision-making process, even if there is knowledge of the disability, without a request and disclosure by the applicant. Students may provide verification of the disability which should be submitted directly to CSAS. General admission requirements include 4 years English, 3 years math, 4 years science, and 2 years foreign language. No course substitutions are allowed. The average ACT is above 21 and for the SAT is 1080–1140. Students applying to the nursing or athletic training programs must submit a special application. Conditional admission is available for freshmen and probational admission is an option for transfer students. The student with learning disabilities also needs to complete the application form and intake sheet. Also required is documentation presented from a doctor stating diagnostic material and diagnosis of the disorder.

ADDITIONAL INFORMATION

Accommodations students might qualify for depending upon their documentation and needs include: extended time on tests, priority registration, testing in self-contained environment, use of spelling aids on written exams, texts on tape, note-takers, preferential seating, tests given orally, and enlarged print tests. Concerns regarding requests for a referral for evaluation of a learning disability should be directed to the Coordinator of the Center for Student Academic Support. Students with LD must provide documentation that includes tests of intellect and of achievement administered by a professional. Students with documented ADHD must provide behavior checklist (one completed by a doctor), a test of intellect, a test of attention, and a clinical interview that includes a history of the ADHD.

SUPPORT SERVICES CONTACT INFORMATION

Learning Disability Program/Services: Center for Student Academic Support
Director: Dr. Jane Corso
  E-mail: jane-corso@utulsa.edu
  Telephone: 918-631-2315
  Fax: 918-631-3459
Contact: Same

LEARNING DISABILITY SERVICES

Requests for the following services/accommodations will be evaluated individually based on appropriate and current documentation.

Allowed in Exams
  Calculator: Yes
  Dictionary: Yes
  Computer: Yes
  Spellchecker: Yes
Extended test time: Yes
Scribes: Yes
Proctors: Yes
Oral exams: No
Note-takers: Yes

Distraction-reduced environment: Yes
Tape recording in class: Yes
Books on tape from RFBD: Yes
Taping of books not from RFBD: Yes
Accommodations for students with ADHD: Yes
Reading machine: Yes
Other assistive technology: Yes
Priority registration: Yes

Added costs for services: NR
LD specialists: Yes
Professional tutors: 4
Peer tutors: 75
Max. hours/wk. for services: Unlimited
How professors are notified of LD/ADHD: By student and program director

GENERAL ADMISSIONS INFORMATION

Director of Admissions: John C. Corso
Telephone: 918-631-2307

ENTRANCE REQUIREMENTS
16 total are recommended; 4 English recommended, 3 math recommended, 3 science recommended, 2 science lab recommended, 2 foreign language recommended, 1 social studies recommended, 2 history recommended, 1 elective recommended. High school diploma or GED required. Minimum TOEFL is 500. TOEFL required of all international applicants.

Application deadline: Rolling
Notification: Rolling beginning 10/1
Average GPA: 3.7

Average SAT I Math: 610
Average SAT I Verbal: 610
Average ACT: 25

Graduated top 10% of class: 42%
Graduated top 25% of class: 74%
Graduated top 50% of class: 100%

COLLEGE GRADUATION REQUIREMENTS

Course waivers allowed: No
Course substitutions allowed: Yes
In what subjects: Foreign language and math based on documentation and whether the course is a fundamental part of major. Final decision is made by committee.

ADDITIONAL INFORMATION

Environment: The campus is in an urban area.

Student Body
  Undergrad enrollment: 2,874
  Female: 52%
  Male: 48%
  Out-of-state: 24%

Cost Information
  Tuition: $13,730
  Room & board: $4,810
Housing Information
  University housing: Yes
  Percent living on campus: 50%

Greek System
  Fraternity: Yes
  Sorority: Yes
Athletics: NCAA Division I

OREGON STATE UNIVERSITY

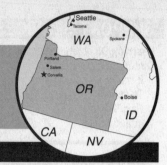

104 Kerr Administration, Corvallis, OR 97331-2106
Phone: 541-737-4411 • Fax: 541-737-2482
E-mail: osuadmit@orst.edu • Web: osu.orst.edu
Support level: S • Institution type: 4-year public

LEARNING DISABILITY PROGRAM AND SERVICES

OSU is committed to providing equal opportunity for higher education to academically qualified students without regard to disability. Services for Students with Disabilities (SSD) strives to be sensitive to the individual needs of students by offering a variety of services. Services rendered are dependent on the type of learning disability. Services are provided to ensure an equal opportunity to succeed but do not guarantee success. Self-advocacy and independence are promoted. SSD is available for all students who need extra services. The Educational Opportunities Program (EOP) offers students who are learning disabled, economically disadvantaged, or first-generation college-bound a variety of remedial courses for credit. EOP tries to provide tutoring for any undergraduate class if tutors are available. To be recognized as a person with a learning disability, students are required to submit documentation from a qualified educational evaluator. Preferred diagnostic testing would include at least one test in each of the following categories: cognitive, achievement, and processing. Other documentation specifying a learning disability without testing in the three categories mentioned must include an in-depth valid assessment of the disability by a qualified professional.

LD/ADHD ADMISSIONS INFORMATION

College entrance tests required: Yes
Nonstandardized tests accepted: Yes
Interview required: N/A
Essay required: Yes
Documentation required for LD: IQ; achievement tests; processing tests: within 3 years
Documentation required for ADHD: Yes
Documentation submitted to: SSD
Special Ed. HS course work accepted: No

Specific course requirements for all applicants: No
Separate application required for services: No
# of LD applications submitted yearly: 15
# of LD applications accepted yearly: 15
Total # of students receiving LD/ADHD services: 150
Acceptance into program means acceptance into college: Students must be admitted and enrolled at the University first and then may request services.

ADMISSIONS

All students must submit the general application for admission. If a student does not meet admissions requirements, admission will be denied. Enclosed with the notification, the student will receive information regarding petitioning for special admission. Students who want to petition their admission on the basis of a learning disability must submit all information required in the petition. Petitioning students must utilize the services of EOP. The director of SSD helps to make admission decisions and may recommend EOP for the student with LD. Regular admission requires a 3.0 GPA and special admit for students with 2.5. Students requesting services should self-identify; submit documentation of their LD, including educational history and diagnostic testing administered by professionals; and include information describing cognitive strengths and weaknesses, recommendations for accommodations or services, and any other additional information in the form of a family history. Students must also submit a handwritten one- to two-page statement outlining educational goals and explaining motivation to succeed at OSU. Students admitted through EOP must start in the summer and attend a required SSD orientation in the beginning of fall. EOP admission decision is made jointly between Admissions and EOP.

ADDITIONAL INFORMATION

Students with LD, whether admitted regularly or as special admits, are encouraged to apply for additional assistance from EOP, which can provide special counseling, tutoring, and intensive practice in study skills. Accommodations in instruction and related academic work may include alternative test methods such as extended testing time and use of resources such as calculators and dictionaries. Accommodations are negotiated with instructors, academic departments, and the College as appropriate. Personal counseling is available through the Counseling Center. The director acts as a liaison between students and faculty.

SUPPORT SERVICES CONTACT INFORMATION

Learning Disability Program/Services: Services for Students with Disabilities (SSD)
Director: Tracy Bentley-Townlin
E-mail: Tracey.Bentley@orst.edu
Telephone: 541-737-4098
Fax: 541-737-7354
Contact: Same

LEARNING DISABILITY SERVICES

Requests for the following services/accommodations will be evaluated individually based on appropriate and current documentation.

Allowed in Exams
  Calculator: Yes
  Dictionary: No
  Computer: Yes
  Spellchecker: Yes
Extended test time: Yes
Scribes: Yes
Proctors: Yes
Oral exams: Yes
Note-takers: Yes

Distraction-reduced environment: Yes
Tape recording in class: Yes
Books on tape from RFBD: Yes
Taping of books not from RFBD: Yes
Accommodations for students with
  ADHD: Yes
Reading machine: Yes
Other assistive technology: Yes
Priority registration: Yes

Added costs for services: No
LD specialists: No
Professional tutors: No
Peer tutors: Yes
Max. hours/wk. for services: Offered through EOP for all students, as available
How professors are notified of LD/ADHD: By student and SSD program director, depending on services

GENERAL ADMISSIONS INFORMATION

Director of Admissions: Robert Bontrager
Telephone: 541-737-4411

ENTRANCE REQUIREMENTS
4 English required, 3 math required, 2 science required, 1 science lab recommended, 2 foreign language required, 3 social studies required. High school diploma or GED required. Minimum TOEFL is 550. TOEFL required of all international applicants.

Application deadline: Rolling
Notification: Rolling beginning 8/1
Average GPA: 3.5

Average SAT I Math: 549
Average SAT I Verbal: 531
Average ACT: 23

Graduated top 10% of class: 21%
Graduated top 25% of class: 51%
Graduated top 50% of class: 85%

COLLEGE GRADUATION REQUIREMENTS

Course waivers allowed: No
Course substitutions allowed: Yes
In what subjects: On a case-by-case basis dependent on the major selected and documentation

ADDITIONAL INFORMATION

Environment: The University is located on 530 acres in a small town 85 miles south of Portland.

Student Body
  Undergrad enrollment: 13,776
  Female: 46%
  Male: 54%
  Out-of-state: 22%

Cost Information
  In-state tuition: $2,694
  Out-of-state tuition: $12,144
  Room & board: $5,508
Housing Information
  University housing: Yes
  Percent living on campus: 25%

Greek System
  Fraternity: Yes
  Sorority: Yes
Athletics: NCAA Division I

UNIVERSITY OF OREGON

1217 University of Oregon, Eugene, OR 97403-1217
Phone: 541-346-3201 • Fax: 541-346-5815
E-mail: uoadmit@oregon.uoregon.edu • Web: www.uoregon.edu
Support level: S • Institution type: 4-year public

LEARNING DISABILITY PROGRAM AND SERVICES

At the University of Oregon, Disability Services coordinates services and provides advocacy and support to students with documented learning disabilities. Eligibility for services must be supported by professional documentation of disability and need for services. Accommodations are determined on a case-by-case basis. Students who feel they are eligible for services should meet with a Disability Services Counselor. At this meeting students will be able to discuss the documentation process, services available, and their educational goals. Disability Services will work with students and faculty members to best accommodate needs. A general letter explaining the particular disability and suggested accommodations will be written, by request, to share with faculty at the students' discretion. This letter is reissued each academic term to designated instructors. Students with learning disabilities should be motivated, hard-working, and willing to take responsibility for meeting their educational goals.

LD/ADHD ADMISSIONS INFORMATION

College entrance tests required: Yes
Nonstandardized tests accepted: Yes
Interview required: No
Essay required: Yes
Documentation required for LD: Psychoeducational evaluation
Documentation required for ADHD: Yes
Documentation submitted to: Disability Services
Special Ed. HS course work accepted: Yes, evaluated case by case

Specific course requirements for all applicants: Yes
Separate application required for services: No
# of LD applications submitted yearly: N/A
# of LD applications accepted yearly: N/A
Total # of students receiving LD/ADHD services: 260
Acceptance into program means acceptance into college: Students must be admitted and enrolled at the University first and then may request services.

ADMISSIONS
Students with learning disabilities must meet the same admission criteria as all other applicants. Courses recommended for admission include 4 years English, 3 years math, 2 years science, 2 years foreign language, 3 years social studies, and 2 years electives. The average SAT is 1140 and the average GPA is 3.4. For students whose GPA falls below a 3.0, a chart shows required ACT/SAT scores. For example, students with a 2.99 GPA need an 830 SAT or 17 ACT, and students with a 2.0 GPA need a 1390 SAT or 32 ACT. Students not meeting the regular admission requirements who have extenuating circumstances due to a learning disability may request additional consideration of their application by a special committee. Students requesting a special review should forward the following to the admissions office: completed application form, a writing sample, two letters of recommendation, and documentation of the disability with information about how it has influenced the student's ability to meet minimum admission requirements. This information is required for special admission consideration based on a disability.

ADDITIONAL INFORMATION
Students are encouraged to take an active role in utilizing the services. Once admitted, students should meet with the counselor to discuss educational goals. Documentation will be put on file. Services available include note-takers; books on tape; modification of testing procedures, including additional testing time, audiotaped answers, having someone write dictated answers, large print, or taking the exam in a quiet location; Adaptive Technology Lab; and faculty liaison to assist in communicating needs to instructors and to help negotiate reasonable accommodations in courses and programs. The Office of Academic Advising provides counseling and assessment of progress toward graduation. The University requires two writing classes for graduation. In addition, the BS degree requires 1 year of college math, or 2 years of foreign language Writing and math are available.

SUPPORT SERVICES CONTACT INFORMATION

Learning Disability Program/Services: Disability Services
Director: Hilary Gerdes, PhD
  E-mail: disabsrv@darkwing.uoregon.edu
  Telephone: 541-346-3211
  Fax: 541-346-6048
Contact: Molly Sirois
  Telephone: 541-346-1155
  Fax: 541-346-6013

LEARNING DISABILITY SERVICES

Requests for the following services/accommodations will be evaluated individually based on appropriate and current documentation.

Allowed in Exams
  Calculator: Yes
  Dictionary: Yes
  Computer: Yes
  Spellchecker: Yes
Extended test time: Yes
Scribes: Yes
Proctors: Yes
Oral exams: Yes
Note-takers: Yes

Distraction-reduced environment: Yes
Tape recording in class: Yes
Books on tape from RFBD: Yes
Taping of books not from RFBD: Yes
Accommodations for students with
  ADHD: Yes
Reading machine: Yes
Other assistive technology: Yes
Priority registration: Yes

Added costs for services: $7–$10 per
  hour for tutoring
LD specialists: No
Professional tutors: Yes
Peer tutors: Yes
Max. hours/wk. for services: Varies
How professors are notified of
  LD/ADHD: By student and program
  director

GENERAL ADMISSIONS INFORMATION

Director of Admissions: Martha Pitts
Telephone: 541-346-3201

ENTRANCE REQUIREMENTS
14 total are required; 4 English required, 3 math required, 2 science required, 1 science lab recommended, 2 foreign language required, 3 social studies required. High school diploma or GED required. Minimum TOEFL is 500. TOEFL required of all international applicants.

Application deadline: February 1
Notification: Rolling beginning 11/2
Average GPA: 3.4

Average SAT I Math: 552
Average SAT I Verbal: 557
Average ACT: NR

Graduated top 10% of class: 20%
Graduated top 25% of class: 49%
Graduated top 50% of class: 83%

COLLEGE GRADUATION REQUIREMENTS

Course waivers allowed: No
Course substitutions allowed: Yes
In what subjects: In the extreme cases with appropriate documentation

ADDITIONAL INFORMATION

Environment: The University is located on 250 acres in an urban area of Eugene.

Student Body
  Undergrad enrollment: 14,076
  Female: 53%
  Male: 47%
  Out-of-state: 28%

Cost Information
  In-state tuition: $3,810
  Out-of-state tuition: $13,197
  Room & board: $5,690
Housing Information
  University housing: Yes
  Percent living on campus: 64%

Greek System
  Fraternity: Yes
  Sorority: Yes
Athletics: NCAA Division I

WESTERN OREGON UNIVERSITY

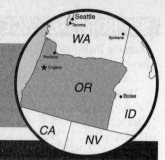

345 North Monmouth Avenue, Monmouth, OR 97361
Phone: 503-838-8211 • Fax: 503-838-8067
E-mail: wolfgram@wou.edu • Web: www.wou.edu
Support level: S • Institution type: 4-year public

LEARNING DISABILITY PROGRAM AND SERVICES

The mission of the Office of Disability Services is to remove barriers to learning for students with disabilities and to help ensure that these students access the tools and processes they need to create a successful experience at Western and beyond. These goals are realized by providing support services and information to help students develop skills such as self-advocacy, independence, identification and use of resources, appropriate use of problem-solving techniques, and accepting responsibility for one's actions. ODS strives to meet the individual needs of students with disabilities. The Student Enrichment Program (SEP) is designed to help students find success in college. The program's goals are to help SEP students develop writing, math, learning and critical thinking skills; maintain the necessary GPA to achieve individual goals; develop interpersonal communication skills; and achieve autonomy and maintain a sense of self-worth. Students who could benefit from SEP are those who enter the University without being completely prepared. SEP staff focus on working with individual needs. Eligibility is based on federal guidelines determined by (1) first-generation college-bound, (2) financial need, or (3) physical or learning disability; additionally, the student must have demonstrated academic need for the program.

LD/ADHD ADMISSIONS INFORMATION

College entrance tests required: Yes
Nonstandardized tests accepted: Yes
Interview required: No
Essay required: No
Documentation required for LD: Psychoeducational evaluation
Documentation required for ADHD: Yes
Documentation submitted to: Office of Disability Services
Special Ed. HS course work accepted: No

Specific course requirements for all applicants: Yes
Separate application required for services: Yes
# of LD applications submitted yearly: N/A
# of LD applications accepted yearly: N/A
Total # of students receiving LD/ADHD services: 60–70
Acceptance into program means acceptance into college: Students must be admitted and enrolled at the University first and then may request services.

ADMISSIONS

General admission requires a 2.75 GPA and ACT/SAT scores, which are used only as alternatives to the required GPA. Course requirements include 4 years English, 3 years math, 2 years science, 3 years social science, and 2 years of the same foreign language. Alternatives to course requirements require either a score of 470 or above on 3 SAT II: Subject Tests. The combined score must be 1410 or above. A limited number of students who do not meet the regular admission requirements, alternatives, or exceptions may be admitted through special action of an admissions committee. These students must submit by January 1 for first session and April 1 for the second session a personal letter of petition stating why they don't meet the admission requirements and what they are doing to make up deficiencies, and three letters of recommendation from school and community members.

ADDITIONAL INFORMATION

Skills classes are offered in academic survival strategies (no credit) and critical thinking (college credit). Other services include advocacy, computer stations, note-takers, readers and taping services, alternative testing, advisement, and assistance with registration. CEP offers counseling; basic math courses; advising; individualized instruction in reading, study skills, writing, and critical thinking; monitor programs; and workshops on study skills, research writing, math anxiety, rapid reading, note-taking, and time management. Services and accommodations are available for undergraduate and graduate students.

SUPPORT SERVICES CONTACT INFORMATION

Learning Disability Program/Services: Office of Disability Services
Director: Mary Crawford, JD
  E-mail: crawfom@wou.edu
  Telephone: 503-838-8250
  Fax: 503-838-8721
Contact: Same

LEARNING DISABILITY SERVICES

Requests for the following services/accommodations will be evaluated individually based on appropriate and current documentation.

Allowed in Exams
  Calculator: Yes
  Dictionary: Yes
  Computer: Yes
  Spellchecker: Yes
Extended test time: Yes
Scribes: Yes
Proctors: Yes
Oral exams: Yes
Note-takers: Yes

Distraction-reduced environment: Yes
Tape recording in class: Yes
Books on tape from RFBD: Yes
Taping of books not from RFBD: Yes
Accommodations for students with ADHD: Yes
Reading machine: Yes
Other assistive technology: Yes
Priority registration: No

Added costs for services: No
LD specialists: No
Professional tutors: No
Peer tutors: Yes
Max. hours/wk. for services: N/A
How professors are notified of LD/ADHD: By student and program director

GENERAL ADMISSIONS INFORMATION

Director of Admissions: Michael Cihak (interim director)
Telephone: 503-838-8211

ENTRANCE REQUIREMENTS
14 total are required; 4 English required, 3 math required, 2 science required, 1 science lab recommended, 2 foreign language required, 2 social studies required, 1 history required. High school diploma or GED required. Minimum TOEFL is 520. TOEFL required of all international applicants.

Application deadline: April
Notification: Rolling
Average GPA: 3.3

Average SAT I Math: 486
Average SAT I Verbal: 487
Average ACT: 21

Graduated top 10% of class: 9%
Graduated top 25% of class: 26%
Graduated top 50% of class: 47%

COLLEGE GRADUATION REQUIREMENTS

Course waivers allowed: No
Course substitutions allowed: Yes
In what subjects: Decisions are made on a case-by-case basis. There are no standard substitute classes.

ADDITIONAL INFORMATION

Environment: The University is located on 134 acres in a rural area 15 miles west of Salem.

Student Body
  Undergrad enrollment: 4,201
  Female: 60%
  Male: 40%
  Out-of-state: 8%

Cost Information
  In-state tuition: $2,520
  Out-of-state tuition: $10,038
  Room & board: $5,245
Housing Information
  University housing: Yes
  Percent living on campus: 24%

Greek System
  Fraternity: Yes
  Sorority: Yes
Athletics: Intramural

CLARION UNIVERSITY OF PENNSYLVANIA

Admissions Office, 840 Wood Street, Clarion, PA 16214
Phone: 814-393-2306 • Fax: 814-393-2030
E-mail: admissions@clarion.edu • Web: www.clarion.edu
Support level: CS • Institution type: 4-year public

LEARNING DISABILITY PROGRAM AND SERVICES

Clarion does not have a "special admissions" policy for students with learning disabilities nor does it offer a structured "LD Program." The Disability Support Services Program works to ensure educational parity for students with learning disabilities within a mainstream setting. Academic accommodations and support focuses on minimizing the effects of the disability. The Academic Support Services is the University's primary vehicle for providing a Tutoring Center and Academic Support Services, which is available to all students but are especially beneficial for students with learning disabilities. These services are free of charge and include extensive peer tutoring, study skills workshops, and individual "learning to learn" activities.

LD/ADHD ADMISSIONS INFORMATION

College entrance tests required: Yes
Nonstandardized tests accepted: Yes
Interview required: Yes
Essay required: No
Documentation required for LD: Psychoeducational evaluation
Documentation required for ADHD: Yes
Documentation submitted to: Student Support Services
Special Ed. HS course work accepted: Yes

Specific course requirements for all applicants: Yes
Separate application required for services: No
# of LD applications submitted yearly: N/A
# of LD applications accepted yearly: N/A
Total # of students receiving LD/ADHD services: 75
Acceptance into program means acceptance into college: Students must be accepted and enrolled at the University first and then may request services.

ADMISSIONS

Students with learning disabilities who wish to be admitted to the University must meet regular admission requirements. As part of the application process, students are encouraged to provide documentation of their learning disability in order to establish a clear need for individualized support services. Students should also include a copy of their Individualized Educational Plan from high school. Students not meeting the general admission criteria may be admitted by either the Academic Support Acceptance (these students are referred to Student Support Services) or Summer Start (probationary admittance).

ADDITIONAL INFORMATION

The staff in Student Support Services serve as liaisons between students and faculty to provide special considerations when appropriate. The program also provides academic advising, special topic seminars, reading/study skills workshops, and referral to other campus resources such as the Tutoring and Writing Centers. Services and accommodations are available to undergraduate and graduate students.

SUPPORT SERVICES CONTACT INFORMATION

Learning Disability Program/Services: Student Support Services Program
Director: Jennifer May
  E-mail: jmay@clarion.edu
  Telephone: 814-393-2095
  Fax: 814-393-2095
Contact: Same

LEARNING DISABILITY SERVICES

Requests for the following services/accommodations will be evaluated individually based on appropriate and current documentation.

Allowed in Exams
  Calculator: Y/N
  Dictionary: Y/N
  Computer: Y/N
  Spellchecker: Y/N
Extended test time: Yes
Scribes: Yes
Proctors: Yes
Oral exams: Yes
Note-takers: No

Distraction-reduced environment: Yes
Tape recording in class: Yes
Books on tape from RFBD: Yes
Taping of books not from RFBD: Yes
Accommodations for students with ADHD: Yes
Reading machine: Yes
Other assistive technology: Yes
Priority registration: Yes

Added costs for services: No
LD specialists: Yes (1)
Professional tutors: No
Peer tutors: 20
Max. hours/wk. for services: 1 hour per week per course
How professors are notified of LD/ADHD: By student and service coordinator

GENERAL ADMISSIONS INFORMATION

Director of Admissions: Sue McMillan (interim director)
Telephone: 814-393-2306

ENTRANCE REQUIREMENTS

4 English required, 2 math required, 4 math recommended, 3 science required, 4 science recommended, 2 foreign language recommended, 4 social studies required. High school diploma or GED required. Minimum TOEFL is 550. TOEFL required of all international applicants.

Application deadline: NR
Notification: Rolling beginning 10/1
Average GPA: 3.1

Average SAT I Math: 445
Average SAT I Verbal: 408
Average ACT: NR

Graduated top 10% of class: 6%
Graduated top 25% of class: 23%
Graduated top 50% of class: 58%

COLLEGE GRADUATION REQUIREMENTS

Course waivers allowed: Yes
Course substitutions allowed: Yes
In what subjects: Determined on a case-by-case basis

ADDITIONAL INFORMATION

Environment: The University is located on 100 acres in a small town 85 miles northeast of Pittsburgh.

Student Body
  Undergrad enrollment: 5,687
  Female: 61%
  Male: 39%
  Out-of-state: 2%

Cost Information
  In-state tuition: $4,713
  Out-of-state tuition: $6,523
  Room & board: $3,712
Housing Information
  University housing: Yes
  Percent living on campus: 35%

Greek System
  Fraternity: Yes
  Sorority: Yes
Athletics: NCAA Division II

COLLEGE MISERICORDIA

301 Lake Street, Dallas, PA 18612
Phone: 570-674-6460 • Fax: 570-675-2441
E-mail: admiss@miseri.edu • Web: www.miseri.edu
Support level: SP • Institution type: 4-year private

LEARNING DISABILITY PROGRAM AND SERVICES

All students who participate in the Alternate Learners Project (ALP) are enrolled in regular college classes. In most cases, they take a carefully selected, reduced credit load each semester. Students who participate in ALP are supported by an assortment of services delivered by a specially trained full-time staff. Services include "Learning Strategies," which are designed to make students more efficient, and accommodations designed to work around students' disabilities whenever possible. Upon entry each student develops an Individual Education Plan and signs a contract agreeing to weekly meetings with mentors. The ultimate goal of ALP is to help students with learning disabilities succeed in college.

LD/ADHD ADMISSIONS INFORMATION

College entrance tests required: Yes
Nonstandardized tests accepted: Yes
Interview required: Yes
Essay required: Yes
Documentation required for LD: Psychoeducational report
Documentation required for ADHD: Yes
Documentation submitted to: Admissions and ALP
Special Ed. HS course work accepted: No

Specific course requirements for all applicants: Yes
Separate application required for services: No
# of LD applications submitted yearly: 50
# of LD applications accepted yearly: 17
Total # of students receiving LD/ADHD services: 51
Acceptance into program means acceptance into college: There is a joint acceptance between ALP and the Office of Admissions.

ADMISSIONS

College Misericordia's experience with students with learning disabilities is that students who are highly motivated and socially mature have an excellent chance to be successful. Each applicant has to secure a standard admissions form, enclose a written cover letter summarizing the learning disability, and indicate a desire to participate in the ALP. Additionally, a copy of the psychological report should be submitted along with the high school transcript and three letters of recommendation (one must be written by a special education professional). Class rank is usually above the top 60 percent. ACT/SAT are required but not used in any way for LD admissions. Students and their parents will be invited to interviews. This interview is very important. The admission decision is made jointly by the Program Director and the Director of Admissions.

ADDITIONAL INFORMATION

All students served by ALP are asked to attend a summer program ($1,600) to learn strategies, understand needed accommodations, and learn about the College. The College, not ALP, offers several skills courses (noncredited) in basic areas such as reading, writing, and math. Services and accommodations are available for undergraduate and graduate students. College Misericordia offers a summer program for high school students with learning disabilities.

SUPPORT SERVICES CONTACT INFORMATION

Learning Disability Program/Services: Alternative Learners Project (ALP)
Director: Dr. Joseph Rogan
  E-mail: jrogan@miseri.edu
  Telephone: 570-674-6347
  Fax: 570-675-2441
Contact: Same

LEARNING DISABILITY SERVICES

Requests for the following services/accommodations will be evaluated individually based on appropriate and current documentation.

Allowed in Exams
  Calculator: Yes
  Dictionary: Yes
  Computer: Yes
  Spellchecker: Yes
Extended test time: Yes
Scribes: Yes
Proctors: Yes
Oral exams: Yes
Note-takers: Yes

Distraction-reduced environment: Yes
Tape recording in class: Yes
Books on tape from RFBD: Yes
Taping of books not from RFBD: No
Accommodations for students with ADHD: No
Reading machine: Yes
Other assistive technology: Yes
Priority registration: Yes

Added costs for services: No
LD specialists: Yes (4)
Professional tutors: No
Peer tutors: Yes
Max. hours/wk. for services: Unlimited
How professors are notified of LD/ADHD: By director

GENERAL ADMISSIONS INFORMATION

Director of Admissions: Jane Dassoye
Telephone: 717-675-4449

ENTRANCE REQUIREMENTS
16 total are required; 4 English required, 4 math required, 4 science required, 4 social studies required. High school diploma or GED required. Minimum TOEFL is 500. TOEFL required of all international applicants.

Application deadline: Rolling
Notification: Rolling beginning 9/1
Average GPA: 3.0

Average SAT I Math: 500
Average SAT I Verbal: 510
Average ACT: 23

Graduated top 10% of class: 27%
Graduated top 25% of class: 50%
Graduated top 50% of class: 75%

COLLEGE GRADUATION REQUIREMENTS

Course waivers allowed: Yes
Course substitutions allowed: Yes
In what subjects: Varies by curriculum/program

ADDITIONAL INFORMATION

Environment: The College is located on a 100-acre campus in a suburban small town 9 miles south of Wilkes-Barre.

Student Body
  Undergrad enrollment: 1,545
  Female: 74%
  Male: 26%
  Out-of-state: 24%

Cost Information
  Tuition: $15,800
  Room & board: $6,600
Housing Information
  University housing: Yes
  Percent living on campus: 55%

Greek System
  Fraternity: Yes
  Sorority: Yes
  Athletics: NCAA Division III

DICKINSON COLLEGE

PO Box 1773, Carlisle, PA 17013-2896
Phone: 717-245-1231 • Fax: 717-245-1442
E-mail: admit@dickinson.edu • Web: www.dickinson.edu
Support level: CS • Institution type: 4-year private

LEARNING DISABILITY PROGRAM AND SERVICES

Dickinson College is committed to providing reasonable accommodations to qualified individuals with disabilities. Students with disabilities will be integrated as completely as possible into the College community. Dickinson does not offer a specialized curriculum. Instead, a wide variety of ways to satisfy most requirements make it unnecessary for students to expect exemption from distribution requirements. Support is offered in designing an accommodations plan that identifies strengths, weaknesses and needs for reasonable accommodations. There are test accommodations, as appropriate, such as extended time, testing in a quiet location, readers, and tests in alternative formats. Also one-on-one assistance in developing study skills, time management, and compensatory learning strategies. In order to receive support services, students must submit documentation of the disability. Students with LD must send results of the most recent psychoeducational testing and IEP. Students with ADHD must send the most recent psychoeducational testing with appropriate behavioral rating scales and diagnosis of ADHD completed by a qualified physician.

LD/ADHD ADMISSIONS INFORMATION

College entrance tests required: Yes
Nonstandardized tests accepted: Yes
Interview required: No
Essay required: Yes
Documentation required for LD: Psychoeducational evaluation: within 3 years
Documentation required for ADHD: Yes
Documentation submitted to: Services for Students with Disabilities
Special Ed. HS course work accepted: No

Specific course requirements for all applicants: Yes
Separate application required for services: No
# of LD applications submitted yearly: N/A
# of LD applications accepted yearly: 26
Total # of students receiving LD/ADHD services: 40–60
Acceptance into program means acceptance into college: Students must be admitted and enrolled at the College and then may request services.

ADMISSIONS

There is no special admissions process for students with learning disabilities. Students should include a separate statement concerning their interest in disability services. ACT/SAT tests are not required. Students should have 4 years English, 3 years math, 3 years science, 2 years social studies, and 2 years foreign language. The minimum GPA is a 2.0.

ADDITIONAL INFORMATION

Skills classes are available in time management, note-taking, test-taking strategies, reading, and writing. Substitutions may be requested in foreign language, but only after attempting a language and demonstrating effort to pass the course. Support services could include extended testing time; distraction-free environment; scribes; proctors; note-takers; books on tape; peer tutors; and the use of calculator, dictionary, computer or spellchecker in exams.

SUPPORT SERVICES CONTACT INFORMATION

Learning Disability Program/Services: Services for Students with Disabilities
Director: Keith Jervis
  E-mail: jervis@dickinson.edu
  Telephone: 717-245-1485
  Fax: 717-245-1910
Contact: Same

LEARNING DISABILITY SERVICES

Requests for the following services/accommodations will be evaluated individually based on appropriate and current documentation.

Allowed in Exams
  Calculator: Yes
  Dictionary: Yes
  Computer: Yes
  Spellchecker: Yes
Extended test time: Yes
Scribes: Yes
Proctors: Yes
Oral exams: Yes
Note-takers: Yes

Distraction-reduced environment: Yes
Tape recording in class: Yes
Books on tape from RFBD: Yes
Taping of books not from RFBD: No
Accommodations for students with ADHD: Yes
Reading machine: Yes
Other assistive technology: No
Priority registration: No

Added costs for services: No
LD specialists: Yes (1)
Professional tutors: No
Peer tutors: 30
Max. hours/wk. for services: Unlimited
How professors are notified of LD/ADHD: By student

GENERAL ADMISSIONS INFORMATION

Director of Admissions: Christopher Seth Allen
Telephone: 717-245-1231

ENTRANCE REQUIREMENTS
16 total are required; 4 English required, 3 math required, 3 science required, 2 science lab required, 2 foreign language required, 3 foreign language recommended, 2 social studies required, 2 elective required. High school diploma or GED required. Minimum TOEFL is 550. TOEFL required of all international applicants.

Application deadline: February 1
Notification: March 31
Average GPA: NR

Average SAT I Math: 602
Average SAT I Verbal: 614
Average ACT: 26

Graduated top 10% of class: 50%
Graduated top 25% of class: 78%
Graduated top 50% of class: 97%

COLLEGE GRADUATION REQUIREMENTS

Course waivers allowed: No
Course substitutions allowed: Yes
In what subjects: Foreign language; students must attempt a language and demonstrate effort to pass the course

ADDITIONAL INFORMATION

Environment: The College is located on a 103-acre suburban campus.

Student Body
  Undergrad enrollment: 2,115
  Female: 61%
  Male: 39%
  Out-of-state: 57%

Cost Information
  Tuition: $25,250
  Room & board: $6,725
Housing Information
  University housing: Yes
  Percent living on campus: 92%

Greek System
  Fraternity: Yes
  Sorority: Yes
Athletics: NCAA Division III

DREXEL UNIVERSITY

3141 Chestnut Street, Philadelphia, PA 19104-2875
Phone: 215-895-2400 • Fax: 215-895-5939
E-mail: enroll@drexel.edu • Web: www.drexel.edu
Support level: S • Institution type: 4-year private

LEARNING DISABILITY PROGRAM AND SERVICES

Drexel University does not have a specific learning disability program, but services are provided through the Office of Disability Services. The professional staff works closely with the students who have special needs to ensure that they have the opportunity to participate fully in Drexel University's programs and activities. Drexel's Disability Services offers a two-hour "transition" program before each fall term for all entering freshmen with disabilities.

LD/ADHD ADMISSIONS INFORMATION

College entrance tests required: Yes
Nonstandardized tests accepted: Yes
Interview required: No
Essay required: No
Documentation required for LD: Psychoeducational evaluations and IEP
Documentation required for ADHD: Yes
Documentation submitted to: Office of Disability Services
Special Ed. HS course work accepted: No

Specific course requirements for all applicants: Yes
Separate application required for services: No
# of LD applications submitted yearly: N/A
# of LD applications accepted yearly: N/A
Total # of students receiving LD/ADHD services: 86
Acceptance into program means acceptance into college: Students must be admitted and enrolled at the University first and then may request services.

ADMISSIONS

The regular admission requirements are the same for all students, and there is no special process for students with learning disabilities. Students are encouraged to self-disclose and provide current documentation of their learning disabilities. General admission criteria include recommended courses of 4 years English, 3 years math, 1 year science, 1 year social studies, 7 years electives (chosen from English, math, science, social studies, foreign language, history, or mechanical drawing); interview recommended; average SAT is 1010, average GPA is 3.1, and 89 percent of the admitted students are in the top 60 percent of their high school graduating class.

ADDITIONAL INFORMATION

Services provided are tutors; readers; note-takers; proofreaders; LD specialists; personal academic and career counseling; liaison between student, faculty, and administration; priority scheduling; instructional modifications; augmented classes offered in math and English; and remedial services in study skills, writing, reading and math, time management, self-advocacy enhancement, and disability education for staff, faculty, and students. Currently there are 70 to 90 LD and 50 to 60 ADHD students receiving services or accommodations. The Office of Disability Services also provides assistance with academic accommodations and learning strategies, and follows through on all affirmative action and ADA requirements.

SUPPORT SERVICES CONTACT INFORMATION

Learning Disability Program/Services: Office of Disability Services (ODS)
Director: Robin Stokes
  E-mail: r528@drexel.edu
  Telephone: 215-895-2506
  Fax: 215-895-2500
Contact: Same

LEARNING DISABILITY SERVICES

Requests for the following services/accommodations will be evaluated individually based on appropriate and current documentation.

Allowed in Exams
  Calculator: Yes
  Dictionary: Yes
  Computer: Yes
  Spellchecker: Yes
Extended test time: Yes
Scribes: Yes
Proctors: Yes
Oral exams: Yes
Note-takers: Yes

Distraction-reduced environment: Yes
Tape recording in class: Yes
Books on tape from RFBD: Yes
Taping of books not from RFBD: Yes
Accommodations for students with ADHD: Yes
Reading machine: Yes
Other assistive technology: Yes
Priority registration: Yes

Added costs for services: No
LD specialists: No
Professional tutors: Yes
Peer tutors: Yes
Max. hours/wk. for services: 10 hours per week
How professors are notified of LD/ADHD: By student

GENERAL ADMISSIONS INFORMATION

Director of Admissions: David Eddy
Telephone: 215-895-2400

ENTRANCE REQUIREMENTS
3 math required, 1 science required, 1 science lab required, 1 foreign language recommended. High school diploma or GED required. Minimum TOEFL is 550. TOEFL required of all international applicants.

Application deadline: March 1
Notification: Rolling
Average GPA: 3.1

Average SAT I Math: 590
Average SAT I Verbal: 550
Average ACT: NR

Graduated top 10% of class: 22%
Graduated top 25% of class: 50%
Graduated top 50% of class: 85%

COLLEGE GRADUATION REQUIREMENTS

Course waivers allowed: No
Course substitutions allowed: Yes
In what subjects: Determined on a case-by-case basis. Depending on essential nature of course, degree, career field, and the limitations of the disability.

ADDITIONAL INFORMATION

Environment: The campus is located on 38 acres near the center of Philadelphia.

Student Body
  Undergrad enrollment: 10,582
  Female: 38%
  Male: 62%
  Out-of-state: 40%

Cost Information
  Tuition: $16,644
  Room & board: $8,705
Housing Information
  University housing: Yes
  Percent living on campus: 28%

Greek System
  Fraternity: Yes
  Sorority: Yes
Athletics: NCAA Division I

EAST STROUDSBURG U. OF PA

200 Prospect Street, E. Stroudsburg, PA 18301-2999
Phone: 570-422-3542 • Fax: 570-422-3933
E-mail: undergrads@po-box.esu.edu • Web: www.esu.edu
Support level: CS • Institution type: 4-year public

LEARNING DISABILITY PROGRAM AND SERVICES

There is no special program for students with learning disabilities at East Stroudsburg University. However, the University is committed to supporting otherwise qualified students with learning disabilities in their pursuit of an education. Disability Services offers students with LD academic and social support and acts as their advocate on campus. Students are encouraged to meet with the coordinator, once accepted, to schedule classes and to develop compensatory skills. Tutors are trained to be sensitive to individual learning styles.

LD/ADHD ADMISSIONS INFORMATION

College entrance tests required: Yes
Nonstandardized tests accepted: Yes
Interview required: No
Essay required: No
Documentation required for LD: Psychoeducational evaluation; IEP: most current
Documentation required for ADHD: Yes
Documentation submitted to: Disability Services
Special Ed. HS course work accepted: Yes

Specific course requirements for all applicants: Yes
Separate application required for services: Yes
# of LD applications submitted yearly: 143
# of LD applications accepted yearly: 60
Total # of students receiving LD/ADHD services: 25
Acceptance into program means acceptance into college: Students must be admitted and enrolled at the University first and then may request consideration for Disability Services.

ADMISSIONS

Students with learning disabilities file the general application form and are encouraged to complete the section titled "Disabilities Information" and forward documentation of their disability to Disability Services. Notification of a learning disability is used as a part of the admissions process only if the student is denied admission. At this time the admissions office waits for a recommendation from the learning disability specialist. The Office of Academic Support may request that the admissions office re-evaluate the student's application in light of information on the disability.

ADDITIONAL INFORMATION

There is a pre-admission summer program for Pennsylvania residents only called the "Summer Intensive Study Program." All entering freshmen and their parents are invited to participate in a two-day summer orientation. Drop-in labs are offered in math and writing, as are study-skills workshops. Students with learning disabilities may work individually with the Disability Services Coordinator. All students enrolled in the University have the opportunity to take skills classes in reading, composition, and math. Other services include workshops in time management and test-taking strategies as well as support groups. Services and accommodations are available for undergraduate and graduate students.

SUPPORT SERVICES CONTACT INFORMATION

Learning Disability Program/Services: Disability Services
Director: Edith F. Miller
　E-mail: emiller@po-box.esu.edu
　Telephone: 570-422-3954
　Fax: 717-422-3898
Contact: Same

LEARNING DISABILITY SERVICES

Requests for the following services/accommodations will be evaluated individually based on appropriate and current documentation.

Allowed in Exams
　Calculator: Yes
　Dictionary: Yes
　Computer: Yes
　Spellchecker: Yes
Extended test time: Yes
Scribes: Yes
Proctors: Yes
Oral exams: Yes
Note-takers: Yes

Distraction-reduced environment: Yes
Tape recording in class: Yes
Books on tape from RFBD: Yes
Taping of books not from RFBD: Yes
Accommodations for students with ADHD: Yes
Reading machine: Yes
Other assistive technology: Yes
Priority registration: Yes

Added costs for services: No
LD specialists: Yes
Professional tutors: 50
Peer tutors: 50
Max. hours/wk. for services: 2
How professors are notified of LD/ADHD: By the student and the program director

GENERAL ADMISSIONS INFORMATION

Director of Admissions: Alan Chesterton
Telephone: 570-422-3542

ENTRANCE REQUIREMENTS

18 total are recommended; 4 English recommended, 3 math recommended, 3 science recommended, 2 science lab recommended, 2 foreign language recommended, 4 social studies recommended. High school diploma or GED required. Minimum TOEFL is 500. TOEFL required of all international applicants.

Application deadline: March 1
Notification: Rolling beginning 11/1
Average GPA: N/A

Average SAT I Math: 475
Average SAT I Verbal: 480
Average ACT: N/A

Graduated top 10% of class: 4%
Graduated top 25% of class: 20%
Graduated top 50% of class: 64%

COLLEGE GRADUATION REQUIREMENTS

Course waivers allowed: No
Course substitutions allowed: Yes
In what subjects: Math and foreign language

ADDITIONAL INFORMATION

Environment: The 813-acre campus is set in the foothills of the Pocono Mountains.

Student Body
　Undergrad enrollment: 4,782
　Female: 58%
　Male: 42%
　Out-of-state: 17%

Cost Information
　In-state tuition: $3,618
　Out-of-state tuition: $9,046
　Room & board: $3,938
Housing Information
　University housing: Yes
　Percent living on campus: 44%

Greek System
　Fraternity: Yes
　Sorority: Yes
Athletics: NCAA Division II

EDINBORO UNIV. OF PENNSYLVANIA

Biggers House, Edinboro, PA 16444
Phone: 814-732-2761 • Fax: 814-732-2420
E-mail: eup_admissions@edinboro.edu • Web: www.edinboro.edu
Support level: CS • Institution type: 4-year public

LEARNING DISABILITY PROGRAM AND SERVICES

Edinboro is actively involved in providing services for students with learning disabilities. The Office for Students with Disabilities (OSD) provides services that are individually directed by the program staff according to expressed needs. There are different levels of services offered depending on the student's needs. Level A offers supervised study sessions with trained mentors two hours per day, with additional hours based on academic progress; writing specialists one to two hours weekly; computer lab; study lab; required appointment every two weeks with professional staff to review progress; and all services in Level D. To be eligible for Level B, students must maintain a 2.5 GPA and complete two or more semesters at Level A. Level B offers supervised study sessions with peer mentor one hour per day and two more hours based on progress; writing specialists one to two hours weekly; computer lab; study lab; a required appointment every two weeks with professional staff; and all services listed in Level D. Level C requires 2.5 GPA and one semester at Level B, and includes peer mentoring up to six hours weekly; writing specialists 1-2 hours weekly; computer lab; study lab; and all services in Level D. Level D provides assistance in arranging academic accommodations, including alternate test arrangements; priority scheduling; consultation with staff; and tape-recorded textbooks. Levels A, B, and C are fee-for-services levels.

LD/ADHD ADMISSIONS INFORMATION

College entrance tests required: Yes
Nonstandardized tests accepted: Yes
Interview required: Yes
Essay required: No
Documentation required for LD: WAIS-III and achievement testing: within 3 years
Documentation required for ADHD: Yes
Documentation submitted to: OSD
Special Ed. HS course work accepted: Yes

Specific course requirements for all applicants: Yes
Separate application required for services: No
# of LD applications submitted yearly: 40–100
# of LD applications accepted yearly: 40–60
Total # of students receiving LD/ADHD services: 285
Acceptance into program means acceptance into college: Students must be admitted and enrolled in the University and then may request services.

ADMISSIONS

Students with LD submit the general application form. Upon receipt of the application from the Admissions Office, it is suggested that students identify any special services that may be required and contact the OSD so that a personal interview may be scheduled. Occasionally, OSD staff are asked for remarks on certain files, but it is not part of the admission decision. Students must provide a multifactored educational assessment; grade-level scores in reading, vocabulary and comprehension, math, and spelling; an individual intelligence test administered by a psychologist, including a list of the tests given; and a list of recommended accommodations. Evaluations submitted must have been completed recently (within three years). Evaluations submitted must have been completed recently. The Trial Admissions Program (TAP) is a selective program for students whose academic credentials do not qualify them for direct admission. Students are reviewed for academic promise, motivation, and positive attitude.

ADDITIONAL INFORMATION

Students with LD are paired with peer mentors who help them with study skills, organizational skills, and time management skills. Students are recommended for different levels of services based on their needs. Students are not required to select a particular level, but OSD strongly recommends that students enroll for Level A if they have less than a 2.5 GPA. Specific academic scheduling needs may be complex, but students working through the OSD are given priority in academic scheduling. The Life Skills Center is a training area designed to enable students with disabilities to maximize their personal independence while completing their academic programs. Students enrolled in TAP must take a freshman orientation course, a developmental skill course, and nine semester hours in general education courses. Extensive tutoring is available for all students.

SUPPORT SERVICES CONTACT INFORMATION

Learning Disability Program/Services: Office for Students with Disabilities (OSD)
Director: Robert McConnell, PhD
  E-mail: mcconnell@edinboro.edu
  Telephone: 814-732-2462
  Fax: 814-732-2866
Contact: Kathleen Strosser
  E-mail: strosser@edinboro.edu
  Telephone: 814-732-2462
  Fax: 814-732-2866

LEARNING DISABILITY SERVICES

Requests for the following services/accommodations will be evaluated individually based on appropriate and current documentation.

Allowed in Exams
  Calculator: Yes
  Dictionary: Yes
  Computer: Yes
  Spellchecker: Yes
Extended test time: Yes
Scribes: Yes
Proctors: Yes
Oral exams: No
Note-takers: No

Distraction-reduced environment: Yes
Tape recording in class: Yes
Books on tape from RFBD: Yes
Taping of books not from RFBD: Yes
Accommodations for students with
  ADHD: Yes
Reading machine: Yes
Other assistive technology: Yes
Priority registration: Yes

Added costs for services: $306–
  $876; subject to change
LD specialists: Yes (2)
Professional tutors: 1
Peer tutors: 80
Max. hours/wk. for services: 12
How professors are notified of
  LD/ADHD: By student

GENERAL ADMISSIONS INFORMATION

Director of Admissions: Terrence Carlin
Telephone: 814-732-2761

ENTRANCE REQUIREMENTS
4 English recommended, 3 math recommended, 3 science recommended, 3 science lab recommended, 2 foreign language recommended, 3 social studies recommended, 4 history recommended, 4 elective recommended. High school diploma or GED required. Minimum TOEFL is 450. TOEFL required of all international applicants.

Application deadline: Rolling
Notification: Rolling
Average GPA: N/A

Average SAT I Math: 470
Average SAT I Verbal: 483
Average ACT: 19

Graduated top 10% of class: 5%
Graduated top 25% of class: 22%
Graduated top 50% of class: 56%

COLLEGE GRADUATION REQUIREMENTS

Course waivers allowed: No
Course substitutions allowed: Yes
In what subjects: Case-by-case basis

ADDITIONAL INFORMATION

Environment: Edinboro University is located on 600 acres in a small town 20 miles south of Erie.

Student Body
  Undergrad enrollment: 6,486
  Female: 57%
  Male: 43%
  Out-of-state: 8%

Cost Information
  In-state tuition: $3,792
  Out-of-state tuition: $5,688
  Room & board: $4,104
Housing Information
  University housing: Yes
  Percent living on campus: 32%

Greek System
  Fraternity: Yes
  Sorority: Yes
Athletics: NCAA Division II

GANNON UNIVERSITY

University Square, Erie, PA 16541
Phone: 814-871-7240 • Fax: 814-871-5803
E-mail: admissions@gannon.edu • Web: www.gannon.edu
Support level: SP • Institution type: 4-year private

LEARNING DISABILITY PROGRAM AND SERVICES

Gannon's Program for Students with Learning Disabilities (PSLD) provides special support services for students who have been diagnosed with either LD or ADHD yet who are highly motivated for academic achievement and have average-to-gifted intellectual potential. PSLD faculty are committed to excellence and strive to offer each student individually designed instruction. Students in the program may select any academic major offered by the University. Freshman-year support includes weekly individual sessions with instructor-tutors and a writing specialist, and small group meetings with a reading specialist. They also provide an advocacy seminar course which includes participation in small group counseling. Students declare a major at the beginning of the sophomore year and attend all regularly scheduled classes. There is limited space in PSLD, and students should check the appropriate box on the admissions application if this service applies. Gannon University provides a student-centered environment that helps to prepare undergraduate students for leadership roles within the University, in their chosen careers, and in the communities that they serve. Gannon assists students in achieving their intellectual, social, emotional, and spiritual potential.

LD/ADHD ADMISSIONS INFORMATION

College entrance tests required: Yes
Nonstandardized tests accepted: Yes
Interview required: Yes
Essay required: Yes
Documentation required for LD: Psychoeducational evaluation
Documentation required for ADHD: Yes
Documentation submitted to: Admissions and program for students with LD
Special Ed. HS course work accepted: Yes

Specific course requirements for all applicants: Yes
Separate application required for services: No
# of LD applications submitted yearly: 30
# of LD applications accepted yearly: 25
Total # of students receiving LD/ADHD services: 35–41
Acceptance into program means acceptance into college: The director of PSLD accepts students into the program and the University.

ADMISSIONS

Besides the regular application and interview there is a special admissions process for the student with learning disabilities. Students must check the box on the application indicating interest in the Learning Disabilities Program. Applicants must submit a psychoeducational evaluation, a high school transcript, two letters of recommendation, and a paragraph about why there is a need for support services. The program director and assistant director make an initial decision and advise Admissions on their decision. Students who are admitted conditionally must enter as undeclared majors until they can achieve a 2.0 GPA. Special education high school courses are accepted in certain situations.

ADDITIONAL INFORMATION

Specific features of the program include twice-weekly tutoring sessions with the program instructors to review course material, learn study skills relevant to material from courses, and focus on specific needs; and weekly sessions with the writing specialist for reviewing, editing, and brainstorming. A one-credit advocacy seminar course is part of the course load of first and second semester. This course covers self-advocacy, motivational techniques, college survival skills, the law and learning disabilities, and learning styles and strategies. Additional services available are computer access, taped textbooks, taping of classes, extended time on exams, scribes and/or dictation, and oral exams. There is a $600 fee for support services.

SUPPORT SERVICES CONTACT INFORMATION

Learning Disability Program/Services: Program for Students with Learning Disabilities
Director: Sister Joyce Lowery, SSJ, M.Ed.
  E-mail: lowrey@gannon.edu
  Telephone: 814-871-5326
  Fax: 814-871-5859
Contact: Jane Kanter
  E-mail: kanter@gannon.edu
  Telephone: 814-871-5360
  Fax: 814-871-5859

LEARNING DISABILITY SERVICES

Requests for the following services/accommodations will be evaluated individually based on appropriate and current documentation.

Allowed in Exams
  Calculator: Yes
  Dictionary: No
  Computer: Yes
  Spellchecker: Yes
Extended test time: Yes
Scribes: Yes
Proctors: Yes
Oral exams: Yes
Note-takers: No

Distraction-reduced environment: Yes
Tape recording in class: Yes
Books on tape from RFBD: Yes
Taping of books not from RFBD: Yes
Accommodations for students with
  ADHD: Yes
Reading machine: Yes
Other assistive technology: No
Priority registration: Y/N

Added costs for services: $300 per
  semester
LD specialists: Yes (1)
Professional tutors: 6
Peer tutors: No
Max. hours/wk. for services: 3
How professors are notified of
  LD/ADHD: By both student and
  director

GENERAL ADMISSIONS INFORMATION

Director of Admissions: Beth Nemenz
Telephone: 814-871-7240

ENTRANCE REQUIREMENTS
16 total are required; 4 English required, 4 math required, 2 science required. High school diploma or GED required. Minimum TOEFL is 500. TOEFL required of all international applicants.

Application deadline: Rolling
Notification: Rolling beginning 9/1
Average GPA: 3.2

Average SAT I Math: 519
Average SAT I Verbal: 524
Average ACT: 21

Graduated top 10% of class: 9%
Graduated top 25% of class: 35%
Graduated top 50% of class: 66%

COLLEGE GRADUATION REQUIREMENTS

Course waivers allowed: N/A
Course substitutions allowed: N/A
In what subjects: N/A

ADDITIONAL INFORMATION

Environment: The University is located on 13 acres in Erie, an urban area 135 miles north of Pittsburgh.

Student Body
  Undergrad enrollment: 2,470
  Female: 59%
  Male: 41%
  Out-of-state: 18%

Cost Information
  Tuition: $14,490
  Room & board: $5,850
Housing Information
  University housing: Yes
  Percent living on campus: 41%

Greek System
  Fraternity: Yes
  Sorority: Yes
Athletics: NCAA Division II

KUTZTOWN UNIV. OF PENNSYLVANIA

Admission Office, PO Box 730, Kutztown, PA 19530-0730
Phone: 610-683-4060 • Fax: 610-683-1375
E-mail: admission@kutztown.edu • Web: www.kutztown.edu
Support level: CS • Institution type: 4-year public

LEARNING DISABILITY PROGRAM AND SERVICES

The philosophy of the University is to provide equal opportunity to all individuals. Services for Students with Disabilities provides all necessary and reasonable services while fostering independence in the students. The services provided are in accordance with the needs of the students and the academic integrity of the institution. The office acts as an information and referral resource, provides direct services, coordinates services provided by other departments/agencies, and serves as a liaison between students with disabilities and university personnel working with students. Since information regarding a student's disability is not obtained through the admission process, it is the student's responsibility upon acceptance to the University to identify himself/herself to the program. Students are encouraged to do this as early as possible upon admission or even when contemplating application. This will provide an opportunity to assess the University's capability of responding to special needs and provide the students with opportunity to assess the services available at the University. The ADA/504 Coordinator works together with all university offices to help provide specific services as warranted by a diagnosis or clear need, as well as creative solutions to problems with which students with disabilities are confronted.

LD/ADHD ADMISSIONS INFORMATION

College entrance tests required: Yes
Nonstandardized tests accepted: Yes
Interview required: No
Essay required: No
Documentation required for LD: Psychoeducational evaluation
Documentation required for ADHD: Yes
Documentation submitted to: SSD
Special Ed. HS course work accepted: Yes

Specific course requirements for all applicants: Yes
Separate application required for services: No
# of LD applications submitted yearly: N/A
# of LD applications accepted yearly: N/A
Total # of students receiving LD/ADHD services: 278
Acceptance into program means acceptance into college: Students must be accepted and enrolled at the University first and then may request services.

ADMISSIONS

There is no special admissions process for students with learning disabilities. All applicants are expected to meet the same admission criteria, which include college-prep courses and SAT I of 900, with exceptions. Admission requirements are not so high that they impede access. An admissions exceptions committee considers applications that may warrant exceptions to the general admission standards. Students may enter through Extended Learning, and upon earning 21 credits, a student may be considered for regular matriculation. In-state residents who do not predict a 2.0 GPA may be considered for a five-week Summer Developmental Studies Session.

ADDITIONAL INFORMATION

The Coordinator of Human Diversity Programming is the initial resource person and record keeper who validates the existence of a disability and the need for any specific accommodations, and contacts faculty and other individuals who have reason to receive information. Academic assistance is provided through the Department of Developmental Studies. Students with LD are eligible to receive services and accommodations prescribed in the psychoeducational evaluation, extended time on exams, use of tape recorder, use of calculator, testing in a separate location, readers, spellcheck and grammar check on written assignments, scribes, 4-track cassette, tutorial assistance, early advisement and preregistration, computer assistive technology, and referrals. Individualized study skills assessments are made, and tutorial assistance is provided. Skills classes are offered in study skills, stress management, remedial math, English and reading, and ESL. Tutors are available to all students, and arrangements are made at no cost to the student.

SUPPORT SERVICES CONTACT INFORMATION

Learning Disability Program/Services: Services for Students with Disabilities
Director: Patricia Richter
  E-mail: richter@kutztown.edu
  Telephone: 610-683-4108
  Fax: 610-683-1520
Contact: Same

LEARNING DISABILITY SERVICES

Requests for the following services/accommodations will be evaluated individually based on appropriate and current documentation.

Allowed in Exams
  Calculator: Yes
  Dictionary: Yes
  Computer: Yes
  Spellchecker: Yes
Extended test time: Yes
Scribes: Yes
Proctors: Yes
Oral exams: Yes
Note-takers: Yes

Distraction-reduced environment: Yes
Tape recording in class: Yes
Books on tape from RFBD: Yes
Taping of books not from RFBD: Yes
Accommodations for students with
  ADHD: Yes
Reading machine: Yes
Other assistive technology: Yes
Priority registration: Yes

Added costs for services: No
LD specialists: Yes
Professional tutors: No
Peer tutors: Yes
Max. hours/wk. for services: As needed
How professors are notified of
  LD/ADHD: By student and program director

GENERAL ADMISSIONS INFORMATION

Director of Admissions: Robert McGowan
Telephone: 610-683-4060

ENTRANCE REQUIREMENTS

16 total are recommended; 3 math recommended, 3 science recommended, 2 foreign language recommended, 4 social studies recommended. High school diploma or GED required. Minimum TOEFL is 500. TOEFL required of all international applicants.

Application deadline: Rolling
Notification: Rolling beginning 9/1
Average GPA: NR

Average SAT I Math: 491
Average SAT I Verbal: 500
Average ACT: NR

Graduated top 10% of class: 4%
Graduated top 25% of class: 21%
Graduated top 50% of class: 60%

COLLEGE GRADUATION REQUIREMENTS

Course waivers allowed: No
Course substitutions allowed: Yes
In what subjects: Foreign language and math but only with strong diagnostic recommendations through the Undergraduate Exceptions Committee.

ADDITIONAL INFORMATION

Environment: The University is located on 325 acres in a rural area 90 miles north of Philadelphia.

Student Body
  Undergrad enrollment: 7,033
  Female: 60%
  Male: 40%
  Out-of-state: 13%

Cost Information
  In-state tuition: $4,448
  Out-of-state tuition: $10,236
  Room & board: $4,342
Housing Information
  University housing: Yes
  Percent living on campus: 35%

Greek System
  Fraternity: Yes
  Sorority: Yes
  Athletics: NCAA Division II

LEBANON VALLEY COLLEGE

101 North College Avenue, Annville, PA 17003-0501
Phone: 717-867-6181 • Fax: 717-867-6026
E-mail: admission@lvc.edu • Web: www.lvc.edu
Support level: S • Institution type: 4-year private

LEARNING DISABILITY PROGRAM AND SERVICES

The Office of Disability Services exists primarily to ensure full and equal opportunities to access the services, facilities and programs available at the College to all students with disabilities. Although the College does not offer a specialized curriculum for students with disabilities, it encourages students to utilize the ODS. Students requesting accommodations are required to submit documentation no more than three years old. Those students with ADHD must present historical information regarding behavioral patterns and academic performance. The assessment must also include observations from two professional, independent adults for verification. The Office of Disability Services will review the documentation and, in consultation with the student, develop a set of accommodations. Students will be provided with letters of verification that describe their accommodations, and are responsible for giving the letters to their instructors. Instructors may negotiate a modification of a particular accommodation with a student and/or the Office of Disability Services if there is a pedagogical reason for the change. Such a modification must be documented and signed by both the instructor and the student. If in any instance a student chooses not to make use of an accommodation, the student and the instructor must both sign a waiver form.

LD/ADHD ADMISSIONS INFORMATION

College entrance tests required: Yes
Nonstandardized tests accepted: Yes
Interview required: NR
Essay required: No
Documentation required for LD: Psychoeducational evaluation
Documentation required for ADHD: Yes
Documentation submitted to: Office of Disability Services
Special Ed. HS course work accepted: No

Specific course requirements for all applicants: Yes
Separate application required for services: No
# of LD applications submitted yearly: 50
# of LD applications accepted yearly: 10–16
Total # of students receiving LD/ADHD services: 40
Acceptance into program means acceptance into college: Students must be admitted and enrolled in college and then may request services.

ADMISSIONS

Disabilities are not considered in the admission decisions, and there is no special admissions process for students with LD and ADHD. General admission criteria include 4 years of English, 2 years of foreign language, 2 years of math, 1 year of science, and 1 year of social studies. With appropriate documentation, specific course requirements may be substituted with other college-prep courses. Once a student is admitted, he or she can be referred to the ODS for services and accommodations with appropriate documentation.

ADDITIONAL INFORMATION

Through consultation with the Coordinator of Disability Services, students can determine how to best meet the distribution of academic requirements and achieve their educational goals. ODS provides many support services including assistance in obtaining information to document a suspected disability; assistance in understanding the results of psychoeducational testing and their implications for the College academic environment; eight structured advising sessions during freshman year; academic advising; determination of course-specific accommodations each semester; one-on-one assistance in developing study skills, test-taking strategies, time management skills, and compensatory learning strategies; access to individualized assistance at the Writing Center; access to content-area tutors; advocacy with faculty and administration; assistance in developing self-advocacy skills; tape recorders; assistance in locating readers; and books on tape through RFBD.

SUPPORT SERVICES CONTACT INFORMATION

Learning Disability Program/Services: Office of Disability Services
Director: Ann H. Hohenwarter
 E-mail: hohenwar@ive.edu
 Telephone: 717-867-6158
 Fax: 717-867-6979
Contact: Same

LEARNING DISABILITY SERVICES

Requests for the following services/accommodations will be evaluated individually based on appropriate and current documentation.

Allowed in Exams
 Calculator: Yes
 Dictionary: Yes
 Computer: Yes
 Spellchecker: Yes
Extended test time: Yes
Scribes: Yes
Proctors: Yes
Oral exams: Yes
Note-takers: Yes

Distraction-reduced environment: Yes
Tape recording in class: Yes
Books on tape from RFBD: Yes
Taping of books not from RFBD: Yes
Accommodations for students with ADHD: Yes
Reading machine: Yes
Other assistive technology: No
Priority registration: Yes

Added costs for services: No
LD specialists: No
Professional tutors: No
Peer tutors: No
Max. hours/wk. for services: Unlimited
How professors are notified of LD/ADHD: By both student and director

GENERAL ADMISSIONS INFORMATION

Director of Admissions: Gillian J. Brown, Jr.
Telephone: 717-867-6181

ENTRANCE REQUIREMENTS
16 total are required; 4 English required, 2 math required, 3 math recommended, 1 science required, 3 science recommended, 1 science lab recommended, 2 foreign language required, 1 social studies required. High school diploma or GED required. Minimum TOEFL is 550. TOEFL required of all international applicants.

Application deadline: Open
Notification: Rolling beginning 10/20
Average GPA: NR

Average SAT I Math: 542
Average SAT I Verbal: 544
Average ACT: NR

Graduated top 10% of class: 35%
Graduated top 25% of class: 67%
Graduated top 50% of class: 91%

COLLEGE GRADUATION REQUIREMENTS

Course waivers allowed: No
Course substitutions allowed: Yes
In what subjects: Foreign language; substitution can be made if documentation supports it and it is not considered necessary to the major

ADDITIONAL INFORMATION

Environment: The campus is located in a rural area seven miles from Hershey.

Student Body
 Undergrad enrollment: 1,773
 Female: 59%
 Male: 41%
 Out-of-state: 21%

Cost Information
 Tuition: $17,870
 Room & board: $5,680
Housing Information
 University housing: Yes
 Percent living on campus: 75%

Greek System
 Fraternity: Yes
 Sorority: Yes
 Athletics: NCAA Division III

MERCYHURST COLLEGE

Admissions, 501 E. 38th Street, Erie, PA 16546
Phone: 800-825-1926 • Fax: 814-824-2071
E-mail: admug@mercyhurst.edu • Web: www.mercyhurst.edu
Support level: CS • Institution type: 4-year private

LEARNING DISABILITY PROGRAM AND SERVICES

The specialized program at Mercyhurst College is designed to assist students who have been identified as having LD. The emphasis is on students' individual strengths, abilities, and interests, as well as learning deficits. This program consists of a structured, individualized set of experiences designed to assist students with LD to get maximum value from their educational potential and earn a college degree. Students selecting the structured program for students with learning differences pay an additional fee for this service and must submit a recent psychological evaluation that includes the WAIS or WISC-R scores within two years; three letters of recommendation, one each from a math, English, and LD teacher or guidance counselor; SAT/ACT; and a written statement from a professional documenting the student's learning disability. Students choosing the structured program option must attend a summer session prior to entrance; classes may include Learning Strategies, Basic Writing, Communications, Career Planning, and Computer Competency. The program lasts five weeks and costs approximately $1,600 (includes room, board, and tuition). Students with learning differences who feel that they do not require a structured program may opt to receive support services through the Academic Support Center at no additional charge.

LD/ADHD ADMISSIONS INFORMATION

College entrance tests required: Yes
Nonstandardized tests accepted: Yes
Interview required: Yes
Essay required: No
Documentation required for LD: WISC or WAIS-III; complete psychological: within 2 years
Documentation required for ADHD: Yes
Documentation submitted to: Admissions and program for students with learning disabilities
Special Ed. HS course work accepted: No

Specific course requirements for all applicants: Yes
Separate application required for services: No
# of LD applications submitted yearly: 80
# of LD applications accepted yearly: 35
Total # of students receiving LD/ADHD services: 50
Acceptance into program means acceptance into college: Students must be admitted and enrolled at the College and then reviewed for services.

ADMISSIONS

To be eligible for any of the services at Mercyhurst, students with LD must adhere to the regular admission requirements and meet the regular admission criteria. General admission criteria include 2.5 GPA; ACT 19+ or SAT 900+; and 4 years English, 2 years social science, 3 years math, 2 years science, and 2 years foreign language (waivers and substitutions are determined on an individual basis). Students who do not meet the regular admissions standards are referred to Mercyhurst-McAuley and/or Mercyhurst-North East for consideration into the two-year division. Some students may be admitted on probation pending the completion of developmental course work. The College reserves the right to reject any student not meeting admission standards. The admission decisions are made jointly by the Director of Programs for Students with Learning Differences and the Office of Admission. Upon acceptance to the College, if the student wishes special services, she/he must identify herself/himself to the Admissions Office and, at that time, choose to receive services in one of two options available to students with documented learning differences. These programs are a structured program and a basic service program.

ADDITIONAL INFORMATION

The Structured Program for Students with Learning Differences provides special services, including Advisory Board, advocacy, alternative testing, books on tape though RFB, community skills, drop-in services, Kurzweil Personal Reader, midterm progress reports, note-takers, peer tutoring, professional advising/priority registration, special five-week Summer Orientation Program prior to freshman year, special section of Basic Writing, special section of Math Problem Solving, study hall (required of all freshman), and a support group.

SUPPORT SERVICES CONTACT INFORMATION

Learning Disability Program/Services: Program for Students with Learning Differences
Director: Dianne Rogers
  E-mail: drogers@mercyhurst.edu
  Telephone: 814-824-2450
  Fax: 814-824-2436
Contact: Same

LEARNING DISABILITY SERVICES

Requests for the following services/accommodations will be evaluated individually based on appropriate and current documentation.

Allowed in Exams
  Calculator: Yes
  Dictionary: Yes
  Computer: Yes
  Spellchecker: Yes
Extended test time: Yes
Scribes: Yes
Proctors: Yes
Oral exams: Yes
Note-takers: Yes

Distraction-reduced environment: Yes
Tape recording in class: Yes
Books on tape from RFBD: Yes
Taping of books not from RFBD: No
Accommodations for students with ADHD: Yes
Reading machine: Yes
Other assistive technology: Yes
Priority registration: Yes

Added costs for services: $1,200 per semester
LD specialists: Yes (1)
Professional tutors: No
Peer tutors: 30
Max. hours/wk. for services: Unlimited
How professors are notified of LD/ADHD: By both student and director

GENERAL ADMISSIONS INFORMATION

Director of Admissions: Robin Engel
Telephone: 814-824-2573

ENTRANCE REQUIREMENTS
16 total are recommended; 4 English recommended, 3 math recommended, 3 science recommended, 1 science lab recommended, 2 foreign language recommended, 1 social studies recommended, 2 history recommended. High school diploma or GED required. Minimum TOEFL is 550. TOEFL required of all international applicants.

Application deadline: Rolling
Notification: Rolling beginning 12/1
Average GPA: 3.2

Average SAT I Math: 532
Average SAT I Verbal: 549
Average ACT: 23

Graduated top 10% of class: 18%
Graduated top 25% of class: 45%
Graduated top 50% of class: 78%

COLLEGE GRADUATION REQUIREMENTS

Course waivers allowed: No
Course substitutions allowed: Yes
In what subjects: Foreign language

ADDITIONAL INFORMATION

Environment: The 80-acre campus of Mercyhurst overlooks Lake Erie.

Student Body
  Undergrad enrollment: 2,832
  Female: 57%
  Male: 43%
  Out-of-state: 43%

Cost Information
  Tuition: $13,190
  Room & board: $5,364
Housing Information
  University housing: Yes
  Percent living on campus: 70%

Greek System
  Fraternity: Yes
  Sorority: Yes
Athletics: NCAA Division II

Mercyhurst College

MESSIAH COLLEGE

One College Avenue, Grantham, PA 17027-0800
Phone: 717-691-6000 • Fax: 717-796-5374
E-mail: admiss@messiah.edu • Web: www.messiah.edu
Support level: S • Institution type: 4-year private

LEARNING DISABILITY PROGRAM AND SERVICES

Messiah College is committed to making reasonable accommodations for qualified students who present evidence of a disability. Documentation is reviewed, and, if adequate for determining eligibility, a plan of assistance is worked out with the student. The DS staff will assist the student in identifying accommodations needed in various classes and in communicating these needs to faculty. Students must make an appointment with DS to receive assistance in reviewing documentation and determining appropriate accommodations. DS may also require additional documentation or evaluations for determination of eligibility. Any costs incurred for evaluation are the responsibility of the student. Students who do not have documentation, but who think they may have a disability, may seek assistance from DS in locating screening services on campus. Students who are encouraged to pursue determination of eligibility or support services, but choose not to at the time, will be asked to sign a form indicating their preference in waiving their rights temporarily. Students may change their mind at a later date, as long as they are actively enrolled at Messiah College.

LD/ADHD ADMISSIONS INFORMATION

College entrance tests required: Yes
Nonstandardized tests accepted: Yes
Interview required: No
Essay required: Yes
Documentation required for LD: Psychoeducational report, IEP/504 service plan suggested to verify accommodations
Documentation required for ADHD: Yes
Documentation submitted to: Disability Services
Special Ed. HS course work accepted: Yes

Specific course requirements for all applicants: Yes
Separate application required for services: No
# of LD applications submitted yearly: NR
# of LD applications accepted yearly: NR
Total # of students receiving LD/ADHD services: 17
Acceptance into program means acceptance into college: Students must be admitted and enrolled and then may request services.

ADMISSIONS

All applicants must meet the same admission criteria. There is an extensive application process including letters of recommendation; ACT/SAT; high school transcript; essays; and a review by the Admissions officer/committee. Admission requirements include a minimum of a 3.0 GPA, 20 ACT or 1000 SAT, and 4 English, 2 math, 2 natural sciences, 2 social studies, and 6 electives (prefer that 2 of these be in foreign language). Foreign language is recommended but alternatives are considered with appropriate documentation. Some applicants who are borderline candidates may be reviewed and admitted through a program called START. These students are required to attend a two-week orientation prior to the beginning of freshman year. Messiah College makes all efforts to avoid any possible prejudice in the admission process. Students with disabilities are encouraged to self-disclose and request an interview with the DS Director. The Director can review the student's file and make a recommendation to the Office of Admission regarding a student's ability to succeed in college. Additionally, self-disclosure of a disability alerts the DS Office that the student has a potential disability that may make them eligible for accommodations.

ADDITIONAL INFORMATION

Commonly provided accommodations by the Disability Services include extended time for test-taking; proctored exams in an alternate location; assistance with getting notes; hard copies of transparencies; advocacy with instructors; taped textbooks for nonreaders; peer tutoring; referral source for other required services. Additionally, the Learning Center provides a range of tutorial services through trained peer tutors and the Writing Center provides peer tutors for written projects. Developmental Services offers assistance with time management, motivation, goal setting, reading skills, note-taking, learning theory, and taking exams.

SUPPORT SERVICES CONTACT INFORMATION

Learning Disability Program/Services: Disability Services
Director: Keith W. Drahn, PhD
 E-mail: kdrahn@messiah.edu
 Telephone: 717-766-2511
 Fax: 717-796-5217
Contact: Same

LEARNING DISABILITY SERVICES

Requests for the following services/accommodations will be evaluated individually based on appropriate and current documentation.

Allowed in Exams
 Calculator: Yes
 Dictionary: Yes
 Computer: Yes
 Spellchecker: Yes
Extended test time: Yes
Scribes: Yes
Proctors: Yes
Oral exams: Yes
Note-takers: Yes

Distraction-reduced environment: Yes
Tape recording in class: Yes
Books on tape from RFBD: Yes
Taping of books not from RFBD: Yes
Accommodations for students with
 ADHD: Yes
Reading machine: No
Other assistive technology: Yes
Priority registration: Yes

Added costs for services: No
LD specialists: No
Professional tutors: No
Peer tutors: 16
Max. hours/wk. for services: As available
How professors are notified of
 LD/ADHD: By director

GENERAL ADMISSIONS INFORMATION

Director of Admissions: William Strausbaugh
Telephone: 717-766-2511

ENTRANCE REQUIREMENTS

18 total are required; 23 total are recommended; 4 English required, 4 English recommended, 3 math required, 4 math recommended, 3 science required, 4 science recommended, 2 science lab required, 3 science lab recommended, 2 foreign language required, 3 foreign language recommended, 2 social studies required, 2 social studies recommended, 2 history required, 2 history recommended, 2 elective required, 4 elective recommended. High school diploma or GED required. Minimum TOEFL is 550. TOEFL required of all international applicants.

Application deadline: Rolling
Notification: Rolling
Average GPA: 3.7

Average SAT I Math: 581
Average SAT I Verbal: 586
Average ACT: 25

Graduated top 10% of class: 35%
Graduated top 25% of class: 64%
Graduated top 50% of class: 92%

COLLEGE GRADUATION REQUIREMENTS

Course waivers allowed: No
Course substitutions allowed: Yes
In what subjects: Foreign language; substitutions

ADDITIONAL INFORMATION

Environment: Small town 10 miles from Harrisburg.

Student Body
 Undergrad enrollment: 2,797
 Female: 61%
 Male: 39%
 Out-of-state: 51%

Cost Information
 Tuition: $15,830
 Room & board: $5,770
Housing Information
 University housing: Yes
 Percent living on campus: 89%

Greek System
 Fraternity: No
 Sorority: No
 Athletics: NCAA Division III

Messiah College

PENNSYLVANIA STATE U.—UNIV. PARK

201 Shields Building, University Park, PA 16802-3000
Phone: 814-865-5471 • Fax: 814-863-7590
E-mail: admissions@psu.edu • Web: www.psu.edu
Support level: CS • Institution type: 4-year public

LEARNING DISABILITY PROGRAM AND SERVICES

The goal of Penn State's academic support services for students with learning disabilities is to ensure that they receive appropriate accommodations so that they can function independently and meet the academic demands of a competitive university. Students with learning disabilities should be able to complete college-level courses with the help of support services and classroom accommodations. In order to receive any of the support services, students must submit documentation of their learning disability to the Learning Disability Specialist in the Office for Disability Services. Documentation should be a psychoeducational report from a certified or licensed psychologist done within the past three years for students with learning disabilities. The report should include measures of intellectual functioning (WAIS-III preferred) and measures of achievement which describe current levels of functioning in reading, mathematics, and written language. Students with ADHD/ADHD should have the professional who diagnosed them complete the ADHD Verification Form and submit it to the Office for Disability Services.

LD/ADHD ADMISSIONS INFORMATION

College entrance tests required: Yes
Nonstandardized tests accepted: Yes
Interview required: N/A
Essay required: No
Documentation required for LD: WAIS-III; WJ;
  neuropsychological if appropriate: within 3 years
Documentation required for ADHD: Yes
Documentation submitted to: Office for Disability Services
Special Ed. HS course work accepted: No

Specific course requirements for all applicants: Yes
Separate application required for services: No
# of LD applications submitted yearly: N/A
# of LD applications accepted yearly: N/A
Total # of students receiving LD/ADHD services: 234
Acceptance into program means acceptance into college: Students must be admitted and enrolled at the University and then may request services.

ADMISSIONS

There is no special application process for students with learning disabilities or attention deficit disorder, and these students are considered for admission on the same basis as other applicants. The minimum 50 percent of admitted students have a GPA between 3.47–3.85 and an ACT between 26–30 or SAT between 1160–1340. Course requirements include 4 years English, 3 years math, 3 years science, 2 years foreign language, and 3 years social studies. If the high school grades and the test scores are low, students may submit a letter explaining why their ability to succeed in college is higher than indicated by their academic records. The Admissions Office will consider this information as it is voluntarily provided. The acceptable ACT or SAT score will depend upon the high school grades and class rank of the student. Two-thirds of the evaluation is based on high school grades and one-third on test scores. Once admitted, students must submit documentation of their learning disability in order to receive support services. Students may seek admission as a provisional or nondegree student if they do not meet criteria required for admission as a degree candidate. Any student may enroll as a nondegree student.

ADDITIONAL INFORMATION

Students with LD are encouraged to participate in the Buddy Program; incoming students are matched with a "senior buddy" who is a current student with a disability and is available to share experiences with a junior buddy. Other services include audiotaped textbooks, arranging course substitutions with academic departments (when essential requirements are not involved), test accommodations, and individual counseling. Assistance with note-taking is offered through the ODS. Services are offered in a mainstream setting. The Learning Assistance Center operates a Math Center, Tutoring Center, Writing Center, and Computer Learning Center. Students may receive academic help either individually or in small groups for a number of different courses. One-to-one academic assistance is available through the Office of Disability Services. Graduate clinicians provide individual assistance with study skills, time management, and compensatory learning strategies. Currently 234 students with LD and 109 with ADHD are receiving services or accommodations.

SUPPORT SERVICES CONTACT INFORMATION

Learning Disability Program/Services: Office for Disability Services
Director: Bill Welsh
  E-mail: wjw9@psu.edu
  Telephone: 814-863-1807
  Fax: 814-863-3217
Contact: Same

LEARNING DISABILITY SERVICES

Requests for the following services/accommodations will be evaluated individually based on appropriate and current documentation.

Allowed in Exams
  Calculator: Yes
  Dictionary: Yes
  Computer: Yes
  Spellchecker: Yes
Extended test time: Yes
Scribes: Yes
Proctors: Yes
Oral exams: Yes
Note-takers: Yes

Distraction-reduced environment: Yes
Tape recording in class: Yes
Books on tape from RFBD: Yes
Taping of books not from RFBD: Yes
Accommodations for students with
  ADHD: Yes
Reading machine: Yes
Other assistive technology: Yes
Priority registration: Yes

Added costs for services: No
LD specialists: Yes (4)
Professional tutors: No
Peer tutors: No
Max. hours/wk. for services:
  Unlimited
How professors are notified of
  LD/ADHD: By student

GENERAL ADMISSIONS INFORMATION

Director of Admissions: Dr. Geoff Harford
Telephone: 814-865-5471

ENTRANCE REQUIREMENTS
4 English required, 3 math required, 3 science required, 2 foreign language required, 3 social studies required. High school diploma or GED required. Minimum TOEFL is 550. TOEFL required of all international applicants.

Application deadline: Rolling
Notification: Rolling beginning 11/30
Average GPA: 3.5

Average SAT I Math: 617
Average SAT I Verbal: 593
Average ACT: NR

Graduated top 10% of class: 44%
Graduated top 25% of class: 80%
Graduated top 50% of class: 96%

COLLEGE GRADUATION REQUIREMENTS

Course waivers allowed: No
Course substitutions allowed: Yes
In what subjects: Foreign language; student's documentation must support the need for it

ADDITIONAL INFORMATION

Environment: The school is located on over 5,000 acres in a small city 90 miles west of Harrisburg.

Student Body
  Undergrad enrollment: 34,406
  Female: 47%
  Male: 53%
  Out-of-state: 21%

Cost Information
  In-state tuition: $6,546
  Out-of-state tuition: $14,088
  Room & board: $4,910
Housing Information
  University housing: Yes
  Percent living on campus: 35%

Greek System
  Fraternity: Yes
  Sorority: Yes
Athletics: NCAA Division I

SETON HILL COLLEGE

Seton Hill Drive, Greensburg, PA 15601
Phone: 724-838-4255 • Fax: 724-830-1294
E-mail: admit@setonhill.edu • Web: www.setonhill.edu
Support level: S • Institution type: 4-year private

LEARNING DISABILITY PROGRAM AND SERVICES

Students who are eligible for, and are requesting, accommodations under the Americans with Disabilities Act are required to register with the coordinator of Disabled Student Services. Students work individually with the Disability Services coordinator to determine what learning or environmental supports are needed based on the documentation and recommendations for accommodations in the report. An individualized plan of accommodation will be developed with the student. It is the student's responsibility to implement the plan. The student should advise the coordinator of Disability Services if they experience any difficulties with their accommodation plan.

LD/ADHD ADMISSIONS INFORMATION

College entrance tests required: Yes
Nonstandardized tests accepted: Yes
Interview required: No
Essay required: No
Documentation required for LD: Psychoeducational evaluation
Documentation required for ADHD: Yes
Documentation submitted to: Office of Disability Services
Special Ed. HS course work accepted: NR

Specific course requirements for all applicants: Yes
Separate application required for services: No
# of LD applications submitted yearly: N/A
# of LD applications accepted yearly: N/A
Total # of students receiving LD/ADHD services: 20
Acceptance into program means acceptance into college: Students must be admitted to the College first and then may request services.

ADMISSIONS

The admissions process is the same for all students. Those with documentation supporting a disability are given the option of meeting with the Disability Services coordinator. There is a summer program, which targets math, English, and study skills. These are required programs for students with weak transcripts or low SAT/ACT scores who otherwise meet admissions standards. Students with documented learning disabilities may request course substitutions for deficiencies in entrance courses based on the LD. Pre-admission interviews are not required but are recommended.

ADDITIONAL INFORMATION

Accommodations may include but are not limited to priority registration, preferential seating, note-taking services, tape-recorded lectures, extended time for projects, extended time for quizzes and tests, testing in distraction-free environments, alternative testing formats, tutoring, counseling, course substitutions, use of assisted technologies such as spellcheck, computer-based programs, and scribe services. Students are responsible for notifying professors about their disability and requesting accommodations. Course substitution requests are reviewed and considered on an individual basis. Skills classes for college credit are offered in time management, note-taking strategies, test-taking strategies, and text reading.

SUPPORT SERVICES CONTACT INFORMATION

Learning Disability Program/Services: Disability Services
Director: Teresa A. Bassi
 E-mail: bassi@setonhill.edu
 Telephone: 724-838-4295
 Fax: 724-838-4233
Contact: Same

LEARNING DISABILITY SERVICES

Requests for the following services/accommodations will be evaluated individually based on appropriate and current documentation.

Allowed in Exams
 Calculator: Yes
 Dictionary: Yes
 Computer: Yes
 Spellchecker: Yes
Extended test time: Yes
Scribes: Yes
Proctors: Yes
Oral exams: Yes
Note-takers: Yes

Distraction-reduced environment: Yes
Tape recording in class: Yes
Books on tape from RFBD: Yes
Taping of books not from RFBD: Yes
Accommodations for students with
 ADHD: Yes
Reading machine: Yes
Other assistive technology: Yes
Priority registration: Yes

Added costs for services: No
LD specialists: No
Professional tutors: No
Peer tutors: Yes
Max. hours/wk. for services:
 Unlimited
How professors are notified of
 LD/ADHD: By student

GENERAL ADMISSIONS INFORMATION

Director of Admissions: Barbara Hinkle, VP of Enrollment Services
Telephone: 724-838-4255

ENTRANCE REQUIREMENTS
15 total are required; 15 total are recommended; 4 English required, 4 English recommended, 2 math required, 2 math recommended, 1 science required, 1 science recommended, 1 science lab required, 1 science lab recommended, 2 foreign language recommended, 2 social studies required, 2 social studies recommended, 4 elective required, 4 elective recommended. High school diploma or GED required. Minimum TOEFL is 500. TOEFL required of all international applicants.

Application deadline: Rolling
Notification: Rolling beginning 9/1
Average GPA: 3.3

Average SAT I Math: 500
Average SAT I Verbal: 540
Average ACT: NR

Graduated top 10% of class: 18%
Graduated top 25% of class: 45%
Graduated top 50% of class: 80%

COLLEGE GRADUATION REQUIREMENTS

Course waivers allowed: No
Course substitutions allowed: Yes
In what subjects: Varies; all appropriate substitutions are reviewed and considered

ADDITIONAL INFORMATION

Environment: The College is located in a small town 35 miles east of Pittsburgh.

Student Body
 Undergrad enrollment: 1,141
 Female: 83%
 Male: 17%
 Out-of-state: 17%

Cost Information
 Tuition: $15,225
 Room & board: $5,200
Housing Information
 University housing: Yes
 Percent living on campus: 54%

Greek System
 Fraternity: No
 Sorority: No
 Athletics: NAIA

TEMPLE UNIVERSITY

1801 North Broad Street, Philadelphia, PA 19122-6096
Phone: 215-204-7200 • Fax: 215-204-5694
E-mail: tuadm@mail.temple.edu • Web: www.temple.edu
Support level: CS • Institution type: 4-year public

LEARNING DISABILITY PROGRAM AND SERVICES

Disability Resources and Services is the primary department for disability-related information and services. DRS arranges academic adjustments and accommodations for students. Students must meet with their DRS advisor and review recommended academic adjustments. Documentation should contain the specific diagnosis and indicate the source used to make this determination. Students may take a copy of an accommodation letter prepared by DRS staff to their professors at the start of each semester. Faculty members cannot retroactively provide academic adjustments for course requirements for students who have not previously presented a letter supporting such requests. Faculty may not alter the essential function of a course. Discussions of disability-related needs and ways to adjust course requirements can be developed. As changes occur, updated information describing new requests must be provided.

LD/ADHD ADMISSIONS INFORMATION

College entrance tests required: Yes
Nonstandardized tests accepted: Yes
Interview required: No
Essay required: No
Documentation required for LD: Psychoeducational tests or IEP
Documentation required for ADHD: Yes
Documentation submitted to: Disability Resources
Special Ed. HS course work accepted: N/A

Specific course requirements for all applicants: Yes
Separate application required for services: N/A
# of LD applications submitted yearly: N/A
# of LD applications accepted yearly: N/A
Total # of students receiving LD/ADHD services: 290
Acceptance into program means acceptance into college: Students must be admitted and enrolled at the University and then may request services.

ADMISSIONS

DRS staff encourage students with LD/ADHD to use available accommodations/adjustments when taking standardized admissions examinations. In situations where standardized exams do not reflect academic potential because of a disability, applicants are encouraged to discuss anticipated strategies for success and explanations of past performance in a personal statement. General admission requirements include 4 years English, 3–4 years math, 2–3 years foreign language, 3 years social studies, 1 year science, 1 year arts, and 5 years other liberal arts/college-prep courses. Students may begin with a reduced load of courses. A six-week summer program is available for selected students (not specifically designed for students with LD).

ADDITIONAL INFORMATION

Making the Grade is a summer post-secondary transition program developed for high school graduates who have disabilities. Program goals include developing interpersonal skills; developing time management strategies; experience residential life; developing strategies for reading and writing; developing note-taking and organizational techniques; developing test-taking proficiencies; articulating an understanding of personal strengths and goals; and practicing self-advocacy approaches. There is a math lab, writing lab, tutoring, and study-skills program. Assistive technology available includes: Dragon Naturally Speaking, Jaws, LDDeluxe, and Alphasmart. Skills classes are offered in time management, test strategies, and reading strategies. Career recruitment, peer coaching, and support counseling are also available. Students experiencing difficulty in areas such as foreign language or math, that are not essential to a specific major, should meet with DRS staff to discuss alternatives and procedures.

SUPPORT SERVICES CONTACT INFORMATION

Learning Disability Program/Services: Disability Resources and Services
Director: Dorothy M. Cebula, PhD
  E-mail: hellodrs@astro.temple.edu
  Telephone: 215-204-1280
  Fax: 215-204-6794
Contact: Same

LEARNING DISABILITY SERVICES

Requests for the following services/accommodations will be evaluated individually based on appropriate and current documentation.

Allowed in Exams
  Calculator: Yes
  Dictionary: Yes
  Computer: Yes
  Spellchecker: Yes
Extended test time: Yes
Scribes: Yes
Proctors: Yes
Oral exams: Yes
Note-takers: Yes

Distraction-reduced environment: Yes
Tape recording in class: Yes
Books on tape from RFBD: Yes
Taping of books not from RFBD: Yes
**Accommodations for students with
  ADHD:** Yes
Reading machine: Yes
Other assistive technology: Yes
Priority registration: Yes

Added costs for services: No
LD specialists: Yes (1)
Professional tutors: No
Peer tutors: Varies
Max. hours/wk. for services: N/A
**How professors are notified of
  LD/ADHD:** By student

GENERAL ADMISSIONS INFORMATION

Director of Admissions: Timm Rinehart
Telephone: 215-204-7200

ENTRANCE REQUIREMENTS

16 total are required; 22 total are recommended; 4 English required, 4 English recommended, 3 math required, 4 math recommended, 2 science required, 3 science recommended, 1 science lab required, 2 science lab recommended, 2 foreign language required, 2 foreign language recommended, 2 social studies required, 2 social studies recommended, 1 history required, 2 history recommended, 2 elective required, 5 elective recommended. High school diploma or GED required. Minimum TOEFL is 525. TOEFL required of all international applicants.

Application deadline: April 1
Notification: Rolling beginning 12/1
Average GPA: 3.1

Average SAT I Math: 516
Average SAT I Verbal: 520
Average ACT: 20.5

Graduated top 10% of class: 17%
Graduated top 25% of class: 44%
Graduated top 50% of class: 81%

COLLEGE GRADUATION REQUIREMENTS

Course waivers allowed: No
Course substitutions allowed: Yes
In what subjects: Math and foreign language

ADDITIONAL INFORMATION

Environment: The University is located on a 76-acre urban campus.

Student Body
  Undergrad enrollment: 18,394
  Female: 58%
  Male: 42%
  Out-of-state: 22%

Cost Information
  In-state tuition: $6,322
  Out-of-state tuition: $11,450
  Room & board: $6,302
Housing Information
  University housing: Yes
  Percent living on campus: 22%

Greek System
  Fraternity: Yes
  Sorority: Yes
Athletics: NCAA Division I

Temple University

UNIVERSITY OF PITTSBURGH

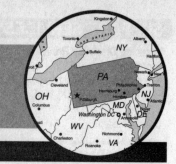

4227 Fifth Avenue, First Floor Masonic Temple, Pittsburgh, PA 15260
Phone: 412-624-7488 • Fax: 412-648-8815
E-mail: oafa+@pitt.edu • Web: www.pitt.edu
Support level: CS • Institution type: 4-year public

LEARNING DISABILITY PROGRAM AND SERVICES

To access services, students must refer themselves to Disability Resource Services and submit documentation of their learning disability. Once eligibility is established, students meet regularly with a DRS learning specialist who will assist the student in accessing resources and developing an individualized, comprehensive educational plan. The objective of DRS is to work closely with students to empower them to plan and implement a successful academic experience. The Transition Program is a program designed to assist students with LD in their transition into the University through the exploration and development of self-awareness and self-advocacy skills, and to educate students in the use of learning strategies designed to compensate for limitations imposed by the disability. The objective of this program is to positively impact the retention, matriculation, and academic performance of students with LD through the provision of transferable skills necessary for academic work, and to foster self-reliance and independence. Participants attend one group session weekly to discuss self-advocacy, rights and responsibilities, and general skills and strategies. Students also meet weekly with a DRS learning specialist to focus on individualized strategies and skills. There is no fee.

LD/ADHD ADMISSIONS INFORMATION

College entrance tests required: Yes
Nonstandardized tests accepted: Yes
Interview required: N/A
Essay required: No
Documentation required for LD: Full psychoeducational evaluation: within three years
Documentation required for ADHD: Yes
Documentation submitted to: Disability Resources
Special Ed. HS course work accepted: No

Specific course requirements for all applicants: Yes
Separate application required for services: No
# of LD applications submitted yearly: N/A
# of LD applications accepted yearly: N/A
Total # of students receiving LD/ADHD services: 343
Acceptance into program means acceptance into college: Students must be admitted and enrolled at the University and then may request services.

ADMISSIONS

Students with learning disabilities must meet the admission criteria established for all applicants. These criteria include ACT 22 or SAT 1000, class rank in top two-fifths, and college-prep courses. Students may be admitted on probation for one term, and having met the continuation policy at a minimum GPA of 2.0, will be permitted to continue. This applies only in the College of General Studies.

ADDITIONAL INFORMATION

DRS individually designs and recommends services to enhance the skills and personal development of the student. Services available may include exam accommodations; use of calculators, dictionary, computer or spellchecker in exams; scribes; proctors; distraction-free environments; taped textbooks; instructional strategy assistance; and adaptive computers. There are two LD specialists on staff.

SUPPORT SERVICES CONTACT INFORMATION

Learning Disability Program/Services: Disability Resources & Services
Director: Lynnett Van Slyke
  E-mail: vanslyket@pitt.edu
  Telephone: 412-648-7890
  Fax: 412-624-3346
Contact: Noreen Mazzocca
  E-mail: njm974@pitt.edu
  Telephone: 412-648-7890
  Fax: 412-624-3346

LEARNING DISABILITY SERVICES

Requests for the following services/accommodations will be evaluated individually based on appropriate and current documentation.

Allowed in Exams
  Calculator: Yes
  Dictionary: Yes
  Computer: Yes
  Spellchecker: Yes
Extended test time: Yes
Scribes: Yes
Proctors: Yes
Oral exams: Yes
Note-takers: No

Distraction-reduced environment: Yes
Tape recording in class: Yes
Books on tape from RFBD: Yes
Taping of books not from RFBD: Yes
Accommodations for students with ADHD: Yes
Reading machine: Yes
Other assistive technology: Yes
Priority registration: No

Added costs for services: No
LD specialists: Yes (2)
Professional tutors: No
Peer tutors: No
Max. hours/wk. for services: Unlimited
How professors are notified of LD/ADHD: By both student and director

GENERAL ADMISSIONS INFORMATION

Director of Admissions: Betsy Porter
Telephone: 412-624-7488

ENTRANCE REQUIREMENTS
15 total are required; 4 English required, 3 math required, 3 science required, 3 science lab required, 3 foreign language recommended, 1 social studies required, 4 elective required. High school diploma or GED required. Minimum TOEFL is 500. TOEFL required of all international applicants.

Application deadline: Rolling
Notification: Rolling
Average GPA: N/A

Average SAT I Math: 587
Average SAT I Verbal: 582
Average ACT: 25

Graduated top 10% of class: 30%
Graduated top 25% of class: 68%
Graduated top 50% of class: 96%

COLLEGE GRADUATION REQUIREMENTS

Course waivers allowed: No
Course substitutions allowed: Yes
In what subjects: Math, foreign language

ADDITIONAL INFORMATION

Environment: The University is located on a 132-acre urban campus.

Student Body
  Undergrad enrollment: 17,424
  Female: 53%
  Male: 47%
  Out-of-state: 14%

Cost Information
  In-state tuition: $6,422
  Out-of-state tuition: $14,104
  Room & board: $5,936
Housing Information
  University housing: Yes
  Percent living on campus: 35%

Greek System
  Fraternity: Yes
  Sorority: Yes
Athletics: NCAA Division I

University of Pittsburgh

WIDENER UNIVERSITY

One University Place, Chester, PA 19013
Phone: 610-499-4126 • Fax: 610-499-4676
E-mail: admissions.office@widener.edu • Web: www.widener.edu
Support level: CS • Institution type: 4-year private

LEARNING DISABILITY PROGRAM AND SERVICES

Enable is a structured mainstream support service designed to assist students enrolled in one of Widener's standard academic programs. Students wishing to use Enable services must submit a copy of the psychological testing, including intelligence and achievement testing that describes the nature of the learning disability. Each student in Enable is provided each week with two private counseling sessions with a learning specialist. Typically these sessions focus on time management, study skills, social and emotional adjustment, and academic planning. Enable serves as a campus advocate for the needs of students with LD by making sure that accommodations are provided when appropriate. Participation in Enable is included in the basic tuition charge. Thus, there is no extra fee for the services offered through Enable.

LD/ADHD ADMISSIONS INFORMATION

College entrance tests required: Yes
Nonstandardized tests accepted: Yes
Interview required: Yes
Essay required: Yes
Documentation required for LD: WAIS-III; achievement: within 3 years
Documentation required for ADHD: Yes
Documentation submitted to: Enable
Special Ed. HS course work accepted: Yes

Specific course requirements for all applicants: Yes
Separate application required for services: No
# of LD applications submitted yearly: N/A
# of LD applications accepted yearly: N/A
Total # of students receiving LD/ADHD services: N/A
Acceptance into program means acceptance into college: Students must be accepted and enrolled at the University first and then may request services.

ADMISSIONS

Students with learning disabilities submit the general application form. Admission decisions are made jointly by the Office of Admissions and the Director of Enable. Students should submit documentation, essay, and recommendations. ACT scores range between 17–27 and SAT scores range between 750–1300. There are no specific course requirements for admissions. High school GPA range is 2.0–4.0.

ADDITIONAL INFORMATION

Enable is a personalized academic advising and counseling service designed to help students with learning disabilities who meet university entrance requirements cope with the rigors of academic life. Students are assigned counselors who help them understand and accept their disabilities; provide academic advice; individualize learning strategies; teach self-advocacy; and link the students with the Reading and Academic Skills Center, Math Lab, Writing Center, and tutoring services. This office assures that professors understand which accommodations are needed. The Writing Center provides assistance with writing assignments and is staffed by professors. The Math Center offers individualized and group tutoring and is staffed by professors and experienced tutors. The Reading Skills Center assists in improving reading comprehension and study skills. Skills classes are available in college reading, math, and English; only three credits are accepted for college credit. The Academic Skills Program assists students who receive less than a 2.0 GPA in the fall semester.

SUPPORT SERVICES CONTACT INFORMATION

Learning Disability Program/Services: Enable
Director: LaVerne Ziegenfuss, PsyD
Telephone: 610-499-1270
Contact: Same

LEARNING DISABILITY SERVICES

Requests for the following services/accommodations will be evaluated individually based on appropriate and current documentation.

Allowed in Exams
Calculator: Yes
Dictionary: Yes
Computer: Yes
Spellchecker: Yes
Extended test time: Yes
Scribes: Yes
Proctors: Yes
Oral exams: Yes
Note-takers: Yes

Distraction-reduced environment: Yes
Tape recording in class: Yes
Books on tape from RFBD: Yes
Taping of books not from RFBD: No
Accommodations for students with ADHD: Yes
Reading machine: Yes
Other assistive technology: Yes
Priority registration: Yes

Added costs for services: No
LD specialists: 3
Professional tutors: 8
Peer tutors: 20
Max. hours/wk. for services: Unlimited
How professors are notified of LD/ADHD: By student

GENERAL ADMISSIONS INFORMATION

Director of Admissions: Dan Bowers
Telephone: 610-499-4126

ENTRANCE REQUIREMENTS
19 total are required; 23 total are recommended; 4 English required, 3 math required, 4 math recommended, 3 science required, 4 science recommended, 2 science lab required, 3 science lab recommended, 2 foreign language required, 4 foreign language recommended, 4 social studies required, 1 history required, 3 elective required. High school diploma or GED required. Minimum TOEFL is 500. TOEFL required of all international applicants.

Application deadline: Rolling
Notification: Rolling beginning 2/15
Average GPA: 3.2

Average SAT I Math: 500
Average SAT I Verbal: 495
Average ACT: N/A

Graduated top 10% of class: 26%
Graduated top 25% of class: 50%
Graduated top 50% of class: 95%

COLLEGE GRADUATION REQUIREMENTS

Course waivers allowed: No
Course substitutions allowed: No
In what subjects: N/A

ADDITIONAL INFORMATION

Environment: The University's 105-acre campus is located 15 miles south of Philadelphia.

Student Body
Undergrad enrollment: 2,235
Female: 45%
Male: 55%
Out-of-state: 35%

Cost Information
Tuition: $15,750
Room & board: $3,400
Housing Information
University housing: Yes
Percent living on campus: 62%

Greek System
Fraternity: Yes
Sorority: Yes
Athletics: NCAA Division III

BROWN UNIVERSITY

Box 1876, 45 Prospect Street, Providence, RI 02912
Phone: 401-863-2378 • Fax: 401-863-9300
E-mail: admission_undergraduate@brown.edu • Web: www.brown.edu
Support level: CS • Institution type: 4-year private

LEARNING DISABILITY PROGRAM AND SERVICES

The Students with Alternative Learning Styles is a mainstreaming program providing accommodations and services to enable students with LD to succeed at Brown. Counseling is available, as well as the Writing Center, Computer Center, and Student-to-Student (a peer counseling group). Testing accommodations are available. Students may petition to take a reduced course load.

LD/ADHD ADMISSIONS INFORMATION

College entrance tests required: Yes
Nonstandardized tests accepted: Yes
Interview required: No
Essay required: No
Documentation required for LD: One of following: WAIS-III, Woodcock-Johnson-R tests of cognitive ability, Kaufman Adolescent and Adult Intelligence Test
Documentation required for ADHD: Yes
Documentation submitted to: Disability Support Services
Special Ed. HS course work accepted: No

Specific course requirements for all applicants: Yes
Separate application required for services: No
# of LD applications submitted yearly: N/A
# of LD applications accepted yearly: N/A
Total # of students receiving LD/ADHD services: 200
Acceptance into program means acceptance into college: Students must be accepted and enrolled at the University first and then may request services.

ADMISSIONS

Admission is very competitive, and all students are required to submit the same application form and meet the same standards. Brown is a highly competitive university, and students have been enrolled in AP and honors courses in high school.

ADDITIONAL INFORMATION

Students requesting accommodations and/or support services must provide documentation of the existence of an LD. With appropriate documentation students may have access to the following services: extended testing time; note-takers; distraction-free testing environment; tape recorders; auxiliary taping of books; and other assistive technology. There is a writing center, an academic center, and professional tutors (for a fee) available for all students. There are no specific graduation requirements and students determine what group of courses to take. Services and accommodations are available for undergraduate and graduate students.

SUPPORT SERVICES CONTACT INFORMATION

Learning Disability Program/Services: Disability Support Services
Director: Elyse Chaplin, Director Disability Services
  Telephone: 401-863-9588
Contact: Admissions Office

LEARNING DISABILITY SERVICES

Requests for the following services/accommodations will be evaluated individually based on appropriate and current documentation.

Allowed in Exams
  Calculator: Yes
  Dictionary: Yes
  Computer: Yes
  Spellchecker: Yes
Extended test time: Yes
Scribes: No
Proctors: No
Oral exams: No
Note-takers: Yes

Distraction-reduced environment: Yes
Tape recording in class: Yes
Books on tape from RFBD: Yes
Taping of books not from RFBD: No
Accommodations for students with ADHD: Yes
Reading machine: Yes
Other assistive technology: Yes
Priority registration: No

Added costs for services: No
LD specialists: Yes (2)
Professional tutors: No
Peer tutors: Yes
Max. hours/wk. for services: As needed
How professors are notified of LD/ADHD: By both student and director

GENERAL ADMISSIONS INFORMATION

Director of Admissions: Michael Goldberger
Telephone: 401-863-2378

ENTRANCE REQUIREMENTS

16 total are required; 19 total are recommended; 4 English required, 4 English recommended, 3 math required, 4 math recommended, 3 science required, 4 science recommended, 2 science lab required, 3 science lab recommended, 3 foreign language required, 4 foreign language recommended, 2 history required, 2 history recommended, 1 elective required, 1 elective recommended. High school diploma is required and GED is not accepted. Minimum TOEFL is 600. TOEFL required of all international applicants.

Application deadline: January 1
Notification: April 1
Average GPA: N/A

Average SAT I Math: 690
Average SAT I Verbal: 690
Average ACT: 29

Graduated top 10% of class: 87%
Graduated top 25% of class: 97%
Graduated top 50% of class: 100%

COLLEGE GRADUATION REQUIREMENTS

Course waivers allowed: No
Course substitutions allowed: Yes
In what subjects: Varies

ADDITIONAL INFORMATION

Environment: The University is located on 146 acres in the urban area of Providence.

Student Body
  Undergrad enrollment: 6,029
  Female: 53%
  Male: 47%
  Out-of-state: 96%

Cost Information
  Tuition: $25,600
  Room & board: $7,346
Housing Information
  University housing: Yes
  Percent living on campus: 85%

Greek System
  Fraternity: Yes
  Sorority: Yes
Athletics: NCAA Division I

BRYANT COLLEGE

1150 Douglas Pike, Smithfield, RI 02917
Phone: 401-232-6100 • Fax: 401-232-6741
E-mail: admissions@bryant.edu • Web: www.bryant.edu
Support level: CS • Institution type: 4-year private

LEARNING DISABILITY PROGRAM AND SERVICES

The Academic Center for Excellence is dedicated to helping Bryant students achieve their goal of academic success. Basically, the center provides study skills training to help students become self-reliant, independent, and confident learners. This is achieved through this internationally accredited peer tutoring program and study skills instruction by professional staff. Group sessions as a mode of instruction are encouraged and the staff engages in a partnership with students to help them achieve their goals. The learning specialist provides support for students with LD. Consideration is given for reasonable modifications, accommodations, or auxiliary aids which will enable qualified students to have access to, participate in, and benefit from the full range of the educational programs and activities offered to all students. As a liaison among students, faculty, and administration, ACE encourages students with LD requiring special accommodations to schedule an appointment with a learning specialist as soon as they register for courses each semester.

LD/ADHD ADMISSIONS INFORMATION

College entrance tests required: Yes
Nonstandardized tests accepted: Yes
Interview required: No
Essay required: Yes
Documentation required for LD: Psychoeducational evaluation
Documentation required for ADHD: Yes
Documentation submitted to: Admissions and Academic Center for Excellence
Special Ed. HS course work accepted: No

Specific course requirements for all applicants: Yes
Separate application required for services: No
# of LD applications submitted yearly: N/A
# of LD applications accepted yearly: N/A
Total # of students receiving LD/ADHD services: 66
Acceptance into program means acceptance into college: Students must be admitted and enrolled and then may request services.

ADMISSIONS

If students self-disclose during the admission process, the Office of Admissions will forward documentation to the Academic Center for Excellence. If students do not self-disclose, they must schedule an appointment at ACE to do so. Students are encouraged to self-disclose and provide current documentation sent to admissions and to the ACE program. General admission criteria include an average GPA of 3.0 and 4 years of English, 2 years of social studies, at least 1 year of lab science, and 3 years of college-prep mathematics. Interviews are recommended. A probationary/conditional admission is available.

ADDITIONAL INFORMATION

Students with documented disabilities may receive accommodations and services based solely on the disability and appropriate services. Some of the accommodations could include extended testing time, readers, distraction-free environment, scribes, proctors, oral exams, note-takers, use of calculators, computers, spellcheckers, and books on tape through the RFBD. ACE provides learning specialists to assist students in college-level study-skill development. Learning specialists also help students find out what learning and study strategies work best for them. The College Reading and Learning Association certifies the Peer Tutoring Program and one-on-one tutoring is available in a variety of subjects. Students can drop in to work with a specialist or peer tutor in the Learning Labs. Study-skills workshops are offered covering topics such as time management, note-taking skills, test preparation, and combatting procrastination. The ACE course is a seven-week, voluntary enrollment study-strategies course designed to help students maintain superior GPAs. The Writing Center provides one-on-one conferencing in writing for all subjects. There are writing consultants, writing specialists, ESL writing specialists, and writing workshops.

SUPPORT SERVICES CONTACT INFORMATION

Learning Disability Program/Services: Academic Center for Excellence
Director: Laurie L. Hazard, EdD
  E-mail: lhazard@bryant.edu
  Telephone: 401-232-6746
  Fax: 401-232-6038
Contact: Selma (Sally) Riconscente
  E-mail: sriconsc@bryant.edu
  Telephone: 401-232-6532
  Fax: 401-232-6038

LEARNING DISABILITY SERVICES

Requests for the following services/accommodations will be evaluated individually based on appropriate and current documentation.

Allowed in Exams
  Calculator: Yes
  Dictionary: Yes
  Computer: Yes
  Spellchecker: Yes
Extended test time: Yes
Scribes: Yes
Proctors: Yes
Oral exams: Yes
Note-takers: Yes

Distraction-reduced environment: Yes
Tape recording in class: Yes
Books on tape from RFBD: Yes
Taping of books not from RFBD: No
Accommodations for students with ADHD: Yes
Reading machine: No
Other assistive technology: Yes
Priority registration: No

Added costs for services: No
LD specialists: Yes (1)
Professional tutors: 6
Peer tutors: 50
Max. hours/wk. for services: Unlimited
How professors are notified of LD/ADHD: By both student and director

GENERAL ADMISSIONS INFORMATION

Director of Admissions: Victoria LaFore
Telephone: 401-232-6346

ENTRANCE REQUIREMENTS
16 total are required; 4 English required, 3 math required, 4 math recommended, 1 science required, 3 science recommended, 1 science lab required, 2 foreign language recommended. High school diploma or GED required. Minimum TOEFL is 550. TOEFL required of all international applicants.

Application deadline: NR
Notification: Rolling beginning 11/1
Average GPA: 3.0

Average SAT I Math: 553
Average SAT I Verbal: 520
Average ACT: 22

Graduated top 10% of class: 16%
Graduated top 25% of class: 39%
Graduated top 50% of class: 79%

COLLEGE GRADUATION REQUIREMENTS

Course waivers allowed: No
Course substitutions allowed: No
In what subjects: Rarely provided

ADDITIONAL INFORMATION

Environment: The campus is located in a suburban area 12 miles from Providence.

Student Body
  Undergrad enrollment: 2,901
  Female: 41%
  Male: 59%
  Out-of-state: 76%

Cost Information
  Tuition: $18,480
  Room & board: $7,500
Housing Information
  University housing: Yes
  Percent living on campus: 73%

Greek System
  Fraternity: Yes
  Sorority: Yes
Athletics: NCAA Division II

JOHNSON & WALES U.—PROVIDENCE

8 Abbott Park Place, Providence, RI 02903-3703
Phone: 401-598-2310 • Fax: 401-598-2948
E-mail: admissions@jwu.edu • Web: www.jwu.edu
Support level: CS • Institution type: 4-year private

LEARNING DISABILITY PROGRAM AND SERVICES

Johnson & Wales University is dedicated to providing reasonable accommodations to allow students with learning disabilities to succeed in their academic pursuits. While maintaining the highest academic integrity, the University strives to balance scholarship with support services that will assist special needs students to function in the post-secondary learning process. It is important that these students identify themselves and present the appropriate neurological, medical, and/or psychoeducational documentation as soon as possible. Recommendations for specific accommodations will be based on the student's individual needs and learning style. The goal of the Student Success department is to support students in their efforts to develop their talents, empower them to direct their own learning, and lead them on the pathways of success.

LD/ADHD ADMISSIONS INFORMATION

College entrance tests required: Yes
Nonstandardized tests accepted: Yes
Interview required: No
Essay required: No
Documentation required for LD: Psychoeducational report
Documentation required for ADHD: Yes
Documentation submitted to: Admissions and Student Success
Special Ed. HS course work accepted: Yes

Specific course requirements for all applicants: Yes
Separate application required for services: No
# of LD applications submitted yearly: N/A
# of LD applications accepted yearly: N/A
Total # of students receiving LD/ADHD services: 550
Acceptance into program means acceptance into college: Students must be accepted and enrolled at the University first and then may request services.

ADMISSIONS

There is no special application process. Standardized tests are not required for admission, and foreign language is not required for admission. After the regular admissions process has been completed and the student is accepted, the student should self-identify and verify the learning disability with the appropriate neurological, medical, and/or psychoeducational documentation. This would include tests administered by the student's high school or private testing service within the past three years. Once admitted, a special needs advisor will meet with the student, and recommendations for specific accommodations will be based on the student's individual needs and learning styles. Any student admitted conditionally will be closely monitored by an academic counselor and must maintain a GPA of 2.0 (two terms below a 2.0 may result in dismissal).

ADDITIONAL INFORMATION

Academic counselors establish initial contact with probational, conditional, and special needs students. Counselors monitor and review grades and enforce academic policies. Accommodations could include decelerated course load, preferential scheduling, oral or extended time on exams, note-taker, use of tape recorder in class, LD support group, individualized tutoring, and a special needs advisor. Career counselors and personal counselors are also available. Program of Assisted Studies (PAS) provides a structured delivery of fundamental math, language, and major skills courses with a strong emphasis on learning-strategy instruction and professional advising and tutoring. The Learning Center offers group and/or one-to-one tutoring, writing skills, culinary skills, grammar fundamentals, study groups, and supplemental instruction groups. Freshman requirements include a course in study and social adjustment skills and a course to teach effective job-search techniques, including career planning, personal development, resume writing, and interview techniques. Services and accommodations are available for undergraduate and graduate students.

SUPPORT SERVICES CONTACT INFORMATION

Learning Disability Program/Services: Student Success/Special Needs
Director: Meryl Berstein
  E-mail: mberstein@jwu.edu
  Telephone: 401-598-4689
  Fax: 401-598-4657
Contact: Same

LEARNING DISABILITY SERVICES

Requests for the following services/accommodations will be evaluated individually based on appropriate and current documentation.

Allowed in Exams
  Calculator: Yes
  Dictionary: Yes
  Computer: Yes
  Spellchecker: Yes
Extended test time: Yes
Scribes: Yes
Proctors: Yes
Oral exams: Yes
Note-takers: Yes
	Distraction-reduced environment: Yes
	Tape recording in class: Yes
	Books on tape from RFBD: Yes
	Taping of books not from RFBD: Yes
	**Accommodations for students with
	  ADHD:** Yes
	Reading machine: No
	Other assistive technology: No
	Priority registration: Yes
		Added costs for services: No
		LD specialists: Yes (5)
		Professional tutors: 18
		Peer tutors: 15
		Max. hours/wk. for services:
		  Unlimited
		**How professors are notified of
		  LD/ADHD:** By both student and
		  director

GENERAL ADMISSIONS INFORMATION

Director of Admissions: Maureen Dumas
Telephone: 401-598-2310

ENTRANCE REQUIREMENTS

10 total are recommended; 4 English recommended, 3 math recommended, 1 science recommended, 2 social studies recommended. High school diploma or GED required. Minimum TOEFL is 550. TOEFL required of all international applicants.

Application deadline: Rolling **Notification:** Rolling beginning 10/1 **Average GPA:** 2.7	**Average SAT I Math:** N/A **Average SAT I Verbal:** N/A **Average ACT:** N/A	**Graduated top 10% of class:** 4% **Graduated top 25% of class:** 18% **Graduated top 50% of class:** 48%

COLLEGE GRADUATION REQUIREMENTS

Course waivers allowed: No
Course substitutions allowed: Yes
In what subjects: Foreign language

ADDITIONAL INFORMATION

Environment: The University is located on 100 acres with easy access to Boston.

Student Body
  Undergrad enrollment: 8,533
  Female: 48%
  Male: 52%
  Out-of-state: 70%
	Cost Information
	  Tuition: $13,740
	  Room & board: $6,150
	Housing Information
	  University housing: Yes
	  Percent living on campus: 47%
		Greek System
		  Fraternity: Yes
		  Sorority: Yes
		Athletics: NCAA Division III

PROVIDENCE COLLEGE

River Avenue and Eaton Street, Providence, RI 02918
Phone: 401-865-2535 • Fax: 401-865-2826
E-mail: pcadmiss@providence.edu • Web: www.providence.edu
Support level: CS • Institution type: 4-year private

LEARNING DISABILITY PROGRAM AND SERVICES

There is no formal program for students with LD. However, the Director of the Office of Academic Services and the faculty of the College are very supportive and are diligent about providing comprehensive services. The goal of the College is to be available to assist students whenever help is requested. After admission, the Disability Support Services Coordinator meets with the LD students during the summer, prior to entry, to help them select the appropriate courses for freshman year. Students are monitored for four years. The College makes every effort to provide "reasonable accommodations."

LD/ADHD ADMISSIONS INFORMATION

College entrance tests required: Yes
Nonstandardized tests accepted: Yes
Interview required: N/A
Essay required: Yes
Documentation required for LD: Psychoeducational evaluation after admission
Documentation required for ADHD: Yes
Documentation submitted to: Academic Services
Special Ed. HS course work accepted: No

Specific course requirements for all applicants: Yes
Separate application required for services: No
# of LD applications submitted yearly: N/A
# of LD applications accepted yearly: N/A
Total # of students receiving LD/ADHD services: 120
Acceptance into program means acceptance into college: Students must be accepted and enrolled at the College first and then may request services.

ADMISSIONS

There is no special admissions process for students with learning disabilities. However, an interview is highly recommended, during which individualized course work is examined. General course requirements include 4 years English, 3 years math, 3 years foreign language, 2 years lab science, 2 years social studies, and 2 years electives. Students with learning disabilities who have lower test scores but a fairly good academic record may be accepted. The Admissions Committee has the flexibility to overlook poor test scores for students with LD. Those who have higher test scores and reasonable grades in college-prep courses (C+/B) may also gain admission. Students should self-identify as learning disabled on their application.

ADDITIONAL INFORMATION

The following services and accommodatations are available for students presenting appropriate documentation: the use of calculators, dictionary, computer and spellchecker in exams; extended time on tests; distraction-free testing environment; scribes; proctors; oral exams; note-takers; tape recorders in class; assistive technology; and priority registration. Skills seminars, for no credit, are offered in study techniques and test-taking strategies. All students have access to the Tutorial Center and Writing Center. Services and accommodations are available for undergraduate and graduate students.

SUPPORT SERVICES CONTACT INFORMATION

Learning Disability Program/Services: Office of Academic Services
Director: Rose A. Boyle, Coordinator
   E-mail: rboyle@providence.edu
   Telephone: 401-865-2494
   Fax: 401-865-1219
Contact: Jennifer Rivera

LEARNING DISABILITY SERVICES

Requests for the following services/accommodations will be evaluated individually based on appropriate and current documentation.

Allowed in Exams
   Calculator: Yes
   Dictionary: Yes
   Computer: Yes
   Spellchecker: Yes
Extended test time: Yes
Scribes: Yes
Proctors: Yes
Oral exams: Yes
Note-takers: Yes

Distraction-reduced environment: Yes
Tape recording in class: Yes
Books on tape from RFBD: No
Taping of books not from RFBD: Yes
**Accommodations for students with
   ADHD:** Yes
Reading machine: Yes
Other assistive technology: Yes
Priority registration: Yes

Added costs for services: No
LD specialists: Yes
Professional tutors: No
Peer tutors: 30
Max. hours/wk. for services:
   Unlimited
**How professors are notified of
   LD/ADHD:** By student

GENERAL ADMISSIONS INFORMATION

Director of Admissions: Christopher Lydon
Telephone: 401-865-2535

ENTRANCE REQUIREMENTS
16 total are required; 18 total are recommended; 4 English required, 4 English recommended, 3 math required, 4 math recommended, 3 science required, 4 science recommended, 2 science lab required, 3 science lab recommended, 3 foreign language required, 3 foreign language recommended, 1 social studies required, 1 social studies recommended, 2 history required, 2 history recommended. High school diploma is required and GED is not accepted. Minimum TOEFL is 550. TOEFL required of all international applicants.

Application deadline: January 15
Notification: April 1
Average GPA: 3.4

Average SAT I Math: 595
Average SAT I Verbal: 585
Average ACT: 25

Graduated top 10% of class: 35%
Graduated top 25% of class: 71%
Graduated top 50% of class: 97%

COLLEGE GRADUATION REQUIREMENTS

Course waivers allowed: Yes
Course substitutions allowed: Yes
In what subjects: Those required by the student's disability

ADDITIONAL INFORMATION

Environment: Providence College has a 105-acre campus located in a small city 50 miles south of Boston.

Student Body
   Undergrad enrollment: 4,405
   Female: 58%
   Male: 42%
   Out-of-state: 76%

Cost Information
   Tuition: $18,440
   Room & board: $7,625
Housing Information
   University housing: Yes
   Percent living on campus: 66%

Greek System
   Fraternity: Yes
   Sorority: Yes
Athletics: NCAA Division I

RHODE ISLAND COLLEGE

Undergraduate Admissions, 600 Mt. Pleasant Ave., Providence, RI 02908
Phone: 401-456-8234 • Fax: 401-456-8817
E-mail: admissions@ric.edu • Web: www.ric.edu
Support level: CS • Institution type: 4-year private

LEARNING DISABILITY PROGRAM AND SERVICES

Rhode Island College strives to create and promote an environment that is conducive to learning for all students. Necessary accommodations require that administration, faculty, and staff be consistent and use flexibility in making adaptations, and that the students be flexible in adapting to and using alternative modes of learning and instruction. Students with disabilities may self-identify at any point, but are encouraged to do so at admission. A registration card is sent to all new students. Filling out this card and returning it to the Office of Student Life starts the process. Faculty are responsible for stating at the beginning of each semester verbally or in writing that the instructor is available to meet individually with students who require accommodations. The College wants students to feel comfortable requesting assistance, and faculty and fellow students are encouraged to be friendly and supportive. The College feels that the presence of students with individual ways of learning and coping serves as a learning experience for the professor, the student, and the class.

LD/ADHD ADMISSIONS INFORMATION

College entrance tests required: Yes
Nonstandardized tests accepted: Yes
Interview required: No
Essay required: No
Documentation required for LD: Psychoeducational evaluation
Documentation required for ADHD: Yes
Documentation submitted to: Admissions and Disability Services
Special Ed. HS course work accepted: No

Specific course requirements for all applicants: Yes
Separate application required for services: Yes
# of LD applications submitted yearly: N/A
# of LD applications accepted yearly: N/A
Total # of students receiving LD/ADHD services: 120
Acceptance into program means acceptance into college: Students must be admitted and enrolled and then may request services.

ADMISSIONS
Admission requirements are the same for all applicants. Students with LD/ADHD should submit the general application for admission. Students who do not meet admission requirements are considered as Conditional Admit regardless of a learning disability or attention deficit disorder. The majority of admitted students are ranked in the top 50 percent of their high school class.

ADDITIONAL INFORMATION
The Student Life Office provides the following services for students with appropriate documentation: one-to-one consultation; note-taking arrangements; use of a tape recorder in class; readers/recorders; registration assistance; disability discussion groups; and assistive technology. The Office of Academic Support and Information Services provides the following for all students: academic advisement; Academic Development Center; Math Learning Center; tutorial services; and the Writing Center. Students may request substitutions in courses not required by their major.

SUPPORT SERVICES CONTACT INFORMATION

Learning Disability Program/Services: Disability Services, Student Life Office
Director: Scott Kane, Associate Dean of Student Life
  E-mail: skane@ric.edu
  Telephone: 401-456-8061
  Fax: 401-456-8702
Contact: Sara W. Weiss, Peer Advisor for Students with Disabilities
  Telephone: 401-456-8061
  Fax: 401-456-8702

LEARNING DISABILITY SERVICES

Requests for the following services/accommodations will be evaluated individually based on appropriate and current documentation.

Allowed in Exams
  Calculator: Yes
  Dictionary: Yes
  Computer: Yes
  Spellchecker: Yes
Extended test time: Yes
Scribes: Yes
Proctors: No
Oral exams: Yes
Note-takers: Yes

Distraction-reduced environment: Yes
Tape recording in class: Yes
Books on tape from RFBD: Yes
Taping of books not from RFBD: Yes
Accommodations for students with ADHD: Yes
Reading machine: Yes
Other assistive technology: Yes
Priority registration: Yes

Added costs for services: No
LD specialists: Yes (2)
Professional tutors: No
Peer tutors: Yes (for all students)
Max. hours/wk. for services: As often as possible
How professors are notified of LD/ADHD: By both student and director

GENERAL ADMISSIONS INFORMATION

Director of Admissions: Holly Shadoin
Telephone: 401-456-8234

ENTRANCE REQUIREMENTS

4 English required, 3 math required, 2 science required, 2 science lab required, 2 foreign language required, 2 social studies required, 4 elective required. High school diploma or GED required. Minimum TOEFL is 550. TOEFL required of all international applicants.

Application deadline: May 1
Notification: Rolling beginning 12/15
Average GPA: NR

Average SAT I Math: 475
Average SAT I Verbal: 485
Average ACT: NR

Graduated top 10% of class: 8%
Graduated top 25% of class: 35%
Graduated top 50% of class: 80%

COLLEGE GRADUATION REQUIREMENTS

CCourse waivers allowed: No
Course substitutions allowed: Yes
In what subjects: English and others if not required by student's major

ADDITIONAL INFORMATION

Environment: Located a few miles from downtown Providence.

Student Body
  Undergrad enrollment: 6,917
  Female: 68%
  Male: 32%
  Out-of-state: 8%

Cost Information
  In-state tuition: $2,860
  Out-of-state tuition: $8,250
  Room & board: $5,946
Housing Information
  University housing: Yes
  Percent living on campus: 14%

Greek System
  Fraternity: Yes
  Sorority: Yes
Athletics: NCAA Division III

UNIVERSITY OF RHODE ISLAND

Undergraduate Admissions, 8 Ranger Road, Suite 1,
Kingston, RI 02881-2020 • Phone: 401-874-7000 • Fax: 401-874-5523
E-mail: uriadmit@uri.edu • Web: www.uri.edu
Support level: CS • Institution type: 4-year public

LEARNING DISABILITY PROGRAM AND SERVICES

Disability Services for Students will assist students in arranging accommodations, facilitate communication between students and professors, and help students to develop effective coping skills like time management, study skills, stress management, etc. Accommodations are provided to meet the specific needs of individual students. Students are encouraged to have an on-going relationship with DSS and the professional staff is able to meet with students as often as desired. Students with LD/ADHD who want to access services or accommodations must provide DSS with current documentation and communicate what needs are requested. Students are also expected to keep up with their requested accommodations (pick up, deliver, and return letters in timely manner) and be involved in the decision-making process when it comes to their needs. Students are encouraged to make accommodation requests as early as possible prior to the beginning of each semester.

LD/ADHD ADMISSIONS INFORMATION

College entrance tests required: Yes
Nonstandardized tests accepted: Yes
Interview required: No
Essay required: Yes
Documentation required for LD: Full psychoeducational testing including aptitude, achievement, and information processing
Documentation required for ADHD: Yes
Documentation submitted to: Admissions and Disability Services
Special Ed. HS course work accepted: N/A

Specific course requirements for all applicants: Yes
Separate application required for services: No
# of LD applications submitted yearly: N/A
# of LD applications accepted yearly: N/A
Total # of students receiving LD/ADHD services: 150
Acceptance into program means acceptance into college: Students must be admitted and enrolled and then request services.

ADMISSIONS

All applicants are expected to meet the general admission criteria. There is not a special process for students with LD/ADHD. General admission requirements expect students to rank in the upper 50 percent of their high school class and complete college-preparatory courses including English, math, social studies, science, and foreign language. If there is current documentation of a language-based LD there is a waiver for the foreign language admissions requirement, but students must self-disclose during the admission process.

ADDITIONAL INFORMATION

Students need to provide the Disability Services for Students office with current documentation of their disability that includes psychoeducational testing completed by a professional evaluator. DSS will assist students in arranging for accommodations, help to facilitate communication between students and professors, work with students to develop effective coping strategies, assist students with identifying appropriate resources and provide referrals, and offer support groups for students with ADHD and a group working toward enhanced awareness of disability issues. Accommodations are based solely on documented disabilities and eligible students have access to services such as priority registration, extended time on exams, permission to tape-record lectures, and access to a note-taker.

SUPPORT SERVICES CONTACT INFORMATION

Learning Disability Program/Services: Disability Services for Students
Director: Pamela A. Rohland
  E-mail: rohland@uri.edu
  Telephone: 401-874-2098
  Fax: 401-874-5574
Contact: Gail Faris Lepkowski, Coordinator
  E-mail: lepkowski@uri.edu
  Telephone: 401-874-2098
  Fax: 401-874-5574

LEARNING DISABILITY SERVICES

Requests for the following services/accommodations will be evaluated individually based on appropriate and current documentation.

Allowed in Exams
  Calculator: Yes
  Dictionary: Yes
  Computer: Yes
  Spellchecker: Yes
Extended test time: Yes
Scribes: Yes
Proctors: No
Oral exams: Yes
Note-takers: Yes

Distraction-reduced environment: Yes
Tape recording in class: Yes
Books on tape from RFBD: Yes
Taping of books not from RFBD: Yes
Accommodations for students with ADHD: Yes
Reading machine: Yes
Other assistive technology: Yes
Priority registration: Yes

Added costs for services: No
LD specialists: Yes (1)
Professional tutors: 20
Peer tutors: 100
Max. hours/wk. for services: Unlimited
How professors are notified of LD/ADHD: By both student and director

GENERAL ADMISSIONS INFORMATION

Director of Admissions: Dave Taggart
Telephone: 401-874-7100

ENTRANCE REQUIREMENTS
18 total are required; 18 total are recommended; 4 English required, 4 English recommended, 3 math required, 4 math recommended, 2 science required, 3 science recommended, 2 science lab required, 2 science lab recommended, 2 foreign language required, 3 foreign language recommended, 2 social studies required, 3 social studies recommended, 5 elective required, 5 elective recommended. High school diploma or GED required. Minimum TOEFL is 550. TOEFL required of all international applicants.

Application deadline: March 1
Notification: Rolling beginning 11/1
Average GPA: 3.4
Average SAT I Math: 546
Average SAT I Verbal: 544
Average ACT: 24
Graduated top 10% of class: 17%
Graduated top 25% of class: 53%
Graduated top 50% of class: 86%

COLLEGE GRADUATION REQUIREMENTS

Course waivers allowed: NR
Course substitutions allowed: Yes
In what subjects: Foreign language and more rarely math

ADDITIONAL INFORMATION

Environment: Located 30 miles from Providence.

Student Body
  Undergrad enrollment: 10,647
  Female: 56%
  Male: 44%
  Out-of-state: 38%

Cost Information
  In-state tuition: $3,464
  Out-of-state tuition: $11,906
  Room & board: $6,688
Housing Information
  University housing: Yes
  Percent living on campus: 37%

Greek System
  Fraternity: Yes
  Sorority: Yes
Athletics: NCAA Division I

CLEMSON UNIVERSITY

105 Sikes Hall, Box 345124, Clemson, SC 29634-5124
Phone: 864-656-2287 • Fax: 864-656-2464
E-mail: cuadmissions@clemson.edu • Web: www.clemson.edu
Support level: S • Institution type: 4-year private

LEARNING DISABILITY PROGRAM AND SERVICES

Student Disability Services coordinates the provision of reasonable accommodations for students with disabilities. All reasonable accommodations are individualized, flexible, and confidential based on the nature of the disability and the academic environment. Students requesting accommodations must provide current documentation of the disability from a physician or licensed professional. Reasonable accommodations will be made in the instructional process to ensure full educational opportunities. The objective is to provide appropriate services to accommodate the student's learning differences, not to lower scholastic requirements.

LD/ADHD ADMISSIONS INFORMATION

College entrance tests required: Yes
Nonstandardized tests accepted: Yes
Interview required: No
Essay required: No
Documentation required for LD: Psychoeducational
  evaluation: within 3 years
Documentation required for ADHD: Yes
Documentation submitted to: Student Disability Services
Special Ed. HS course work accepted: Yes

Specific course requirements for all applicants: Yes
Separate application required for services: No
# of LD applications submitted yearly: N/A
# of LD applications accepted yearly: N/A
Total # of students receiving LD/ADHD services: 230
**Acceptance into program means acceptance into
  college:** Students must be admitted and enrolled at the
  University and then may request services.

ADMISSIONS

All students must have the same admission criteria for the University. There is no separate application process for students with learning disabilities. General admission requirements include: ACT 22–27, SAT I 1080–1260, 4 years English, 3 years math, 3 years lab science, 3 years foreign language, and 3 years social studies. Students may request a waiver of the foreign language requirement by submitting a request to the Exceptions Committee. It is recommended that students self-disclose the learning disability if they need to explain the lack of a foreign language or other information which may help to understand their challenges.

ADDITIONAL INFORMATION

Appropriate accommodations are discussed with each student individually and confidentially. Some of the accommodations offered are assistive technology; note-takers, readers, and transcribers; course substitutions; exam modifications, computer, extended time, private and quiet room, readers and scribes; priority registration; and taped lectures. All students have access to peer tutoring, writing lab, and departmental tutoring. Assistive technology available includes screen readers, scanners, Dragon Dictate, and grammar check. Skills courses are offered in time management, test strategies, and study skills. Peer Academic Coaching is a collaborative process between students and a trained peer coach to improve academic and self-management skills through structure, support and compensatory strategies. Any student is eligible to participate in Peer Academic Coaching. There are currently 230 students with learning disabilities and 310 students with ADHD receiving services.

SUPPORT SERVICES CONTACT INFORMATION

Learning Disability Program/Services: Student Disability Services
Director: Bonnie Martin
  E-mail: bmartin@clemson.edu
  Telephone: 864-656-6848
  Fax: 864-656-6849
Contact: Same

LEARNING DISABILITY SERVICES

Requests for the following services/accommodations will be evaluated individually based on appropriate and current documentation.

Allowed in Exams
  Calculator: Yes
  Dictionary: Yes
  Computer: Yes
  Spellchecker: Yes
Extended test time: Yes
Scribes: Yes
Proctors: Yes
Oral exams: Yes
Note-takers: Yes

Distraction-reduced environment: Yes
Tape recording in class: Yes
Books on tape from RFBD: Yes
Taping of books not from RFBD: Yes
Accommodations for students with
  ADHD: Yes
Reading machine: Yes
Other assistive technology: Yes
Priority registration: Yes

Added costs for services: $3 per hour
  per tutor
LD specialists: No
Professional tutors: No
Peer tutors: 30
Max. hours/wk. for services:
  Unlimited
How professors are notified of
  LD/ADHD: By both student and
  director

GENERAL ADMISSIONS INFORMATION

Director of Admissions: Richard Barkley
Telephone: 864-656-2287

ENTRANCE REQUIREMENTS

19 total are required; 4 English required, 3 math required, 4 math recommended, 3 science required, 3 science lab required, 4 science lab recommended, 3 foreign language required, 3 social studies required, 1 history required, 2 elective required. High school diploma or GED required. Minimum TOEFL is 550. TOEFL required of all international applicants.

Application deadline: May 1
Notification: Rolling beginning 10/15
Average GPA: 3.6

Average SAT I Math: 597
Average SAT I Verbal: 575
Average ACT: 25

Graduated top 10% of class: 37%
Graduated top 25% of class: 70%
Graduated top 50% of class: 96%

COLLEGE GRADUATION REQUIREMENTS

Course waivers allowed: No
Course substitutions allowed: Yes
In what subjects: Math and foreign language, depending on the program of study

ADDITIONAL INFORMATION

Environment: The University is located on 1,400 acres in a small town.

Student Body
  Undergrad enrollment: 14,066
  Female: 45%
  Male: 55%
  Out-of-state: 30%

Cost Information
  In-state tuition: $3,280
  Out-of-state tuition: $9,266
  Room & board: $4,122
Housing Information
  University housing: Yes
  Percent living on campus: 47%

Greek System
  Fraternity: Yes
  Sorority: Yes
Athletics: NCAA Division I

LIMESTONE COLLEGE

1115 College Drive, Gaffey, SC 29340
Phone: 800-345-3792 • Fax: 864-487-8706
E-mail: admiss@saint.limestone.edu • Web: www.limestone.edu
Support level: CS • Institution type: 4-year private

LEARNING DISABILITY PROGRAM AND SERVICES

The Program for Alternative Learning Styles (PALS) was developed to service students with learning disabilities. Therefore, only students with documented learning disabilities are eligible to receive program services. For program purposes, LD refers to students with average to above average intelligence (above 90) who have a discrepancy between measured intelligence and achievement. PALS's biggest advantage is the follow-up system that is in place for the PALS students. Each student is very carefully monitored as to his/her progress in each course he or she takes. The students who are not successful are typically those students who do not take advantage of the system. With the follow-up system, the students in PALS are in no danger of "falling between the cracks." The tracking system is specifically designed to keep the professors, the director, and the students informed about their progress toward a degree from Limestone College.

LD/ADHD ADMISSIONS INFORMATION

College entrance tests required: No
Nonstandardized tests accepted: Yes
Interview required: Yes
Essay required: No
Documentation required for LD: WAIS-III and Woodcock-Johnson
Documentation required for ADHD: Yes
Documentation submitted to: PALS
Special Ed. HS course work accepted: Yes, with documentation

Specific course requirements for all applicants: Yes
Separate application required for services: Yes
# of LD applications submitted yearly: 15–20
# of LD applications accepted yearly: 13–19
Total # of students receiving LD/ADHD services: 19
Acceptance into program means acceptance into college: Students are admitted simultaneously into the College and to the PALS program.

ADMISSIONS

Students who self-disclose their LD and want the services of PALS must first be admitted to Limestone College either fully or conditionally. Students must submit a high school transcript with a diploma or GED certificate, SAT or ACT scores, and the general college application. The minimum GPA is a 2.0. To receive services through PALS, students must submit the most recent psychological report (within three years) documenting the existence of the LD. Only evaluations by certified school psychologists will be accepted. In addition, only intelligence test scores from the Stanford-Binet and/or Wechsler scales will be acceptable. All available information is carefully reviewed prior to acceptance. Students may be admitted provisionally provided they are enrolled in PALS. Students interested in PALS must arrange for an interview with the director of PALS in order to learn what will be expected of the student and what the program will and will not do for the student. After the interview is completed students will be notified of their eligibility for the PALS and be given the opportunity to sign a statement indicating their wish to participate or not to participate.

ADDITIONAL INFORMATION

During the regular academic year, students will receive special instruction in the area of study skills. The director of PALS is in constant communication with students concerning grades, tutors, professors, accommodations, time management, and study habits. Tutorial services are provided on an individual basis so that all students can reach their maximum potential. Skills classes are offered in math and reading. Other services include counseling, time management skills, and screening for the best ways to make accommodations. All freshmen or new students are required to pay the full fee for the first year of services ($3,000). After the first two semesters, that fee will be reduced by 50 percent for all students who meet the following GPA requirements: 2.0 GPA after two semesters; 2.3 GPA after four semesters; and 2.5 GPA after six semesters.

SUPPORT SERVICES CONTACT INFORMATION

Learning Disability Program/Services: Program for Alternative Learning Styles (PALS)
Director: Dr. Joe Pitts
  E-mail: jpitts@saint.limestone.edu
  Telephone: 864-488-4534
  Fax: 864-487-8706
Contact: Same

LEARNING DISABILITY SERVICES

Requests for the following services/accommodations will be evaluated individually based on appropriate and current documentation.

Allowed in Exams
  Calculator: Yes
  Dictionary: Yes
  Computer: Yes
  Spellchecker: Yes
Extended test time: Yes
Scribes: No
Proctors: No
Oral exams: Yes
Note-takers: No

Distraction-reduced environment: Yes
Tape recording in class: Yes
Books on tape from RFBD: Yes
Taping of books not from RFBD: No
Accommodations for students with ADHD: No
Reading machine: No
Other assistive technology: No
Priority registration: No

Added costs for services: $3,000 per year
LD specialists: No
Professional tutors: No
Peer tutors: 10
Max. hours/wk. for services: Unlimited
How professors are notified of LD/ADHD: By both student and director

GENERAL ADMISSIONS INFORMATION

Director of Admissions: Chris Phenicie
Telephone: 864-488-4553

ENTRANCE REQUIREMENTS
15 total are recommended; 4 English recommended, 3 math recommended, 3 science recommended, 2 science lab recommended, 3 foreign language recommended. Minimum TOEFL is 500. TOEFL required of all international applicants.

Application deadline: Rolling
Notification: Rolling
Average GPA: 2.9
Average SAT I Math: 446
Average SAT I Verbal: 480
Average ACT: 18
Graduated top 10% of class: 8%
Graduated top 25% of class: 15%
Graduated top 50% of class: 50%

COLLEGE GRADUATION REQUIREMENTS

Course waivers allowed: Yes
Course substitutions allowed: No
In what subjects: Foreign language

ADDITIONAL INFORMATION

Environment: The campus is located in an urban area 45 miles south of Charlotte.

Student Body
  Undergrad enrollment: 1,784
  Female: 58%
  Male: 42%
  Out-of-state: 20%

Cost Information
  Tuition: $10,000
  Room & board: $3,700
Housing Information
  University housing: Yes
  Percent living on campus: 44%

Greek System
  Fraternity: Yes
  Sorority: Yes
Athletics: NCAA Division II

SOUTHERN WESLEYAN UNIVERSITY

Wesleyan Drive, PO Box 1020, Central, SC 29630-1020
Phone: 864-644-5903 • Fax: 864-644-5032
E-mail: admissions@swu.edu • Web: www.swu.edu
Support level: CS • Institution type: 4-year private

LEARNING DISABILITY PROGRAM AND SERVICES

Southern Wesleyan University provides the environment for success. In accepting students with learning disabilities, the University is committed to providing special services and assistance to these students. Services are provided after an assessment of the students' particular needs. The objectives of the SWU program are to help students with learning disabilities make a smooth transition from high school to college, provide faculty with instructional methods, and help students know that they can graduate and be successful. Southern Wesleyan has a very friendly student body, and everyone works together like a family.

LD/ADHD ADMISSIONS INFORMATION

College entrance tests required: Yes
Nonstandardized tests accepted: Yes
Interview required: Yes
Essay required: No
Documentation required for LD: Psychoeducational evaluation
Documentation required for ADHD: Yes
Documentation submitted to: Student Support Services
Special Ed. HS course work accepted: Yes

Specific course requirements for all applicants: Yes
Separate application required for services: No
# of LD applications submitted yearly: N/A
# of LD applications accepted yearly: N/A
Total # of students receiving LD/ADHD services: 75
Acceptance into program means acceptance into college: Students are admitted directly into the University and to special services for exceptional students on campus with appropriate documentation.

ADMISSIONS

Applicants with learning disabilities are reviewed on the basis of high school transcript, SAT or ACT, personal interview, recommendations, and psychoeducational evaluation. Students may be conditionally admitted with less than a "C" average, an SAT lower than 740 or ACT lower than 19, or rank in the bottom 50 percent. High school courses should include 4 years English, 2 years math, 2 years science, 2 years social studies. Applicants not meeting these requirements may be admitted conditionally (on academic warning), on probation, or provisionally.

ADDITIONAL INFORMATION

There is a liaison person between faculty and students. Professors are available to students after class. Modifications can be made in test taking, which could include extended time and a quiet place to take exams. Additionally, students may receive assistance with note-taking. There are peer group study sessions for those students wishing this type of study experience.

SUPPORT SERVICES CONTACT INFORMATION

Learning Disability Program/Services: Student Support Services
Director: Randal Becker, PhD
  E-mail: rbecker@swu.edu
  Telephone: 864-639-2453
Contact: Same

LEARNING DISABILITY SERVICES

Requests for the following services/accommodations will be evaluated individually based on appropriate and current documentation.

Allowed in Exams
  Calculator: Y/N
  Dictionary: Yes
  Computer: N/A
  Spellchecker: N/A
Extended test time: Yes
Scribes: Yes
Proctors: Yes
Oral exams: Yes
Note-takers: Yes

Distraction-reduced environment: Yes
Tape recording in class: Yes
Books on tape from RFBD: Yes
Taping of books not from RFBD: Yes
Accommodations for students with
  ADHD: Yes
Reading machine: Yes
Other assistive technology: No
Priority registration: Yes

Added costs for services: No
LD specialists: Yes
Professional tutors: No
Peer tutors: Yes
Max. hours/wk. for services: 1 hour
  per week per course
How professors are notified of
  LD/ADHD: By student

GENERAL ADMISSIONS INFORMATION

Director of Admissions: Joy Bryant
Telephone: 864-644-5093

ENTRANCE REQUIREMENTS
12 total are required; 20 total are recommended; 4 English required, 4 English recommended, 2 math required, 3 math recommended, 2 science required, 4 science recommended, 2 foreign language recommended, 2 social studies required, 2 social studies recommended, 2 history recommended, 3 elective recommended. High school diploma or GED required. Minimum TOEFL is 500. TOEFL required of all international applicants.

Application deadline: Rolling
Notification: January 1
Average GPA: 3.2

Average SAT I Math: 473
Average SAT I Verbal: 490
Average ACT: 19

Graduated top 10% of class: 12%
Graduated top 25% of class: 39%
Graduated top 50% of class: 77%

COLLEGE GRADUATION REQUIREMENTS

Course waivers allowed: No
Course substitutions allowed: No
In what subjects: N/A

ADDITIONAL INFORMATION

Environment: The College is located midway between Charlotte, North Carolina, and Atlanta, Georgia, within sight of the Blue Ridge Mountains.

Student Body
  Undergrad enrollment: 1,472
  Female: 62%
  Male: 38%
  Out-of-state: 15%

Cost Information
  Tuition: $12,104
  Room & board: $4,290
Housing Information
  University housing: Yes
  Percent living on campus: 14%

Greek System
  Fraternity: Yes
  Sorority: Yes
  Athletics: NAIA

UNIV. OF SOUTH CAROLINA—COLUMBIA

Office of Admissions, Columbia, SC 29208
Phone: 803-777-7700 • Fax: 803-777-0101
E-mail: admissions-ugrad@sc.edu • Web: www.sc.edu
Support level: CS • Institution type: 4-year public

LEARNING DISABILITY PROGRAM AND SERVICES

The University's Office of Disability Services provides educational support and assistance to students with LD who have the potential for success in a competitive university setting. The Office of Disability Services is specifically designed to empower them with the confidence to become self-advocates and to take an active role in their education. The University works with each student on an individualized basis to match needs with appropriate services. The services are tailored to provide educational support and assistance to students based on their specific needs. The Office of Disability Services recommends and coordinates support services with faculty, administrators, advisors, and deans' offices. The nature and severity of LD may vary considerably. All requests are based on documented diagnostic information regarding each student's specific learning disability. The first step in accessing services from the Office of Disability Services is to self-disclose the disability and arrange an interview. During the interview, staff members will discuss the student's educational background and determine which services best fit his/her needs.

LD/ADHD ADMISSIONS INFORMATION

College entrance tests required: Yes
Nonstandardized tests accepted: Yes
Interview required: No
Essay required: No
Documentation required for LD: Psychoeducational evaluation
Documentation required for ADHD: Yes
Documentation submitted to: Disability Services
Special Ed. HS course work accepted: No

Specific course requirements for all applicants: Yes
Separate application required for services: No
# of LD applications submitted yearly: N/A
# of LD applications accepted yearly: N/A
Total # of students receiving LD/ADHD services: 200
Acceptance into program means acceptance into college: Students must be admitted and enrolled at the University first (they may appeal a denial) and then may request services.

ADMISSIONS

There is no special application or admission process for students with LD. Required scores on the SAT and ACT vary with class rank. Applicants must have a cumulative C+ average on defined college-preparatory courses, including 4 years English, 3 years math, 3 years science, 2 years of the same foreign language, 4 years elective, and 1 year physical education, as well as a 1200 SAT or 27 ACT. If they are denied admission or feel they do not meet the required standards, students may petition the Admissions Committee for an exception to the regular admissions requirements. Once admitted, students should contact the Educational Support Services Center to arrange an interview to determine which services are necessary to accommodate their needs.

ADDITIONAL INFORMATION

Services are individually tailored to provide educational support and assistance. All requests are based on documented diagnostic information. The program is designed to provide educational support and assistance, including analysis of learning needs to determine appropriate interventions, consulting with the faculty about special academic needs, monitoring of progress by a staff member, study skills training, and tutorial referrals. Special program accommodations may include a reduced course load of 9–12 hours, waivers/substitutions for some courses, and expanded pass/fail options. Special classroom accommodations may include tape recorders, note-takers, and extended time on tests.

SUPPORT SERVICES CONTACT INFORMATION

Learning Disability Program/Services: Office of Disability Services
Director: Karen Pettus
  E-mail: kpettus@gwm.sc.edu
  Telephone: 803-777-6742
  Fax: 803-777-6741
Contact: Graduate Assistant
  Telephone: 803-777-6472
  Fax: 803-777-6741

LEARNING DISABILITY SERVICES

Requests for the following services/accommodations will be evaluated individually based on appropriate and current documentation.

Allowed in Exams
  Calculator: Yes
  Dictionary: Yes
  Computer: Yes
  Spellchecker: Yes
Extended test time: Yes
Scribes: Yes
Proctors: Yes
Oral exams: Yes
Note-takers: Yes

Distraction-reduced environment: Yes
Tape recording in class: Yes
Books on tape from RFBD: Yes
Taping of books not from RFBD: Yes
Accommodations for students with ADHD: Yes
Reading machine: Yes
Other assistive technology: Yes
Priority registration: Yes

Added costs for services: No
LD specialists: Yes (1)
Professional tutors: No
Peer tutors: Yes
Max. hours/wk. for services: Unlimited
How professors are notified of LD/ADHD: By student

GENERAL ADMISSIONS INFORMATION

Director of Admissions: Terry Davis
Telephone: 800-868-5872

ENTRANCE REQUIREMENTS

19 total are required; 4 English required, 3 math required, 3 science required, 3 science lab required, 2 foreign language required, 2 social studies required, 1 history required, 4 elective required. High school diploma or GED required. Minimum TOEFL is 550. TOEFL required of all international applicants.

Application deadline: Rolling
Notification: Rolling beginning 10/1
Average GPA: 3.5

Average SAT I Math: 548
Average SAT I Verbal: 550
Average ACT: 24

Graduated top 10% of class: 30%
Graduated top 25% of class: 59%
Graduated top 50% of class: 90%

COLLEGE GRADUATION REQUIREMENTS

Course waivers allowed: Yes
Course substitutions allowed: Yes
In what subjects: Foreign language; students may petition their college for substitution if the requirement is not an integral part of the degree program

ADDITIONAL INFORMATION

Environment: The University is located on 242 acres in downtown Columbia.

Student Body
  Undergrad enrollment: 15,266
  Female: 55%
  Male: 45%
  Out-of-state: 12%

Cost Information
  In-state tuition: $3,768
  Out-of-state tuition: $10,054
  Room & board: $4,588
Housing Information
  University housing: Yes
  Percent living on campus: 40%

Greek System
  Fraternity: Yes
  Sorority: Yes
Athletics: NCAA Division I

BLACK HILLS STATE UNIVERSITY

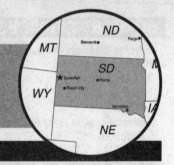

University Station, Box 9502, Spearfish, SD 57799-9502
Phone: 605-642-6259 • Fax: 605-642-6319
E-mail: admissions@mystic.bhsu.edu • Web: www.bhsu.edu
Support level: CS • Institution type: 2-year and 4-year public

LEARNING DISABILITY PROGRAM AND SERVICES

Student Support Services (SSS) ensures equal access and opportunities to educational programs for students with learning disabilities. Students requesting services must provide appropriate documentation. An individualized educational plan (IEP) is not sufficient documentation. Within the program, the Disabilities Services Coordinator arranges accommodations, counseling services, and campus awareness activities for students with disabilities. The algebra advisor, language/learning skills instructor, and academic and career advisor provide tutoring and advising services to encourage students with disabilities to achieve academic success. Students that participate in the SSS program can take advantage of a full range of services to assist in their academic pursuits.

LD/ADHD ADMISSIONS INFORMATION

College entrance tests required: Yes
Nonstandardized tests accepted: Yes
Interview required: No
Essay required: No
Documentation required for LD: Psychoeducational
  evaluation
Documentation required for ADHD: Yes
Documentation submitted to: SSS
Special Ed. HS course work accepted: No

Specific course requirements for all applicants: Yes
Separate application required for services: Yes
# of LD applications submitted yearly: All who apply
# of LD applications accepted yearly: All accepted
Total # of students receiving LD/ADHD services: 70
**Acceptance into program means acceptance into
  college:** Students must be accepted and enrolled at the
  University first and then may request services.

ADMISSIONS
General admission requirements include a C average, an ACT of 20, or rank in the upper two-thirds for residents or upper half for nonresidents. In addition, students must complete the following high school course work: 4 years English, 2 years lab science and 3 years math or 2 years math and 2 years lab science, 3 years social studies, .5 years of fine arts, and .5 years of computer science. Students who do not meet the admission requirements for general admissions will be admitted to the Junior College at Black Hills State. Course deficiencies must be satisfied within two years of admittance. There is complete open enrollment for summer courses also. Transfer students who do not meet admission requirements will be admitted on probationary status.

ADDITIONAL INFORMATION
During the first week of each fall semester students are required to attend a five-part advisory series to discuss academic plans, campus services, study skills, and career exploration. After the fifth session, students are formally admitted into the SSS Program. Accommodations include distraction-reduced exam site, extended testing time, note-takers, readers and scribes, and assistive technology. Services include advocacy training, coping strategies, study-skills strategies, time management skills, and tutors. The Student Assistance Center offers peer tutoring to all students in most subject areas. Basic skills instruction is available in English and math. A University Learning Skills course provides an introduction to college-level studies.

SUPPORT SERVICES CONTACT INFORMATION

Learning Disability Program/Services: Student Support Services
Director: Sharon Hemmingson
  E-mail: sharonhemmingson@bhsu.edu
  Telephone: 605-642-6259
  Fax: 605-642-6319
Contact: Same

LEARNING DISABILITY SERVICES

Requests for the following services/accommodations will be evaluated individually based on appropriate and current documentation.

Allowed in Exams
  Calculator: Yes
  Dictionary: Yes
  Computer: Yes
  Spellchecker: Yes
Extended test time: Yes
Scribes: Yes
Proctors: Yes
Oral exams: Yes
Note-takers: Yes

Distraction-reduced environment: Yes
Tape recording in class: Yes
Books on tape from RFBD: Yes
Taping of books not from RFBD: Yes
Accommodations for students with
  ADHD: Yes
Reading machine: Yes
Other assistive technology: No
Priority registration: No

Added costs for services: No
LD specialists: Yes
Professional tutors: Yes
Peer tutors: Yes
Max. hours/wk. for services: 40
How professors are notified of
  LD/ADHD: By student with letter

GENERAL ADMISSIONS INFORMATION

Director of Admissions: Steve Ochsner
Telephone: 605-642-6567

ENTRANCE REQUIREMENTS
14 total are required; 4 English required, 3 math required, 3 science required, 3 science lab required, 3 social studies required. High school diploma or GED required. Minimum TOEFL is 520. TOEFL required of all international applicants.

Application deadline: July 1
Notification: Rolling
Average GPA: 3.0

Average SAT I Math: NR
Average SAT I Verbal: NR
Average ACT: 21

Graduated top 10% of class: 4%
Graduated top 25% of class: 15%
Graduated top 50% of class: 46%

COLLEGE GRADUATION REQUIREMENTS

Course waivers allowed: No
Course substitutions allowed: No
In what subjects: Rarely

ADDITIONAL INFORMATION

Environment: The University is located on 123 acres in a small town 45 miles northwest of Rapid City.

Student Body
  Undergrad enrollment: 3,469
  Female: 60%
  Male: 40%
  Out-of-state: 26%

Cost Information
  In-state tuition: $3,153
  Out-of-state tuition: $6,973
  Room & board: $3,026
Housing Information
  University housing: Yes
  Percent living on campus: 25%

Greek System
  Fraternity: Yes
  Sorority: Yes
  Athletics: NAIA

SOUTH DAKOTA STATE UNIVERSITY

Box 2201, Brookings, SD 57007-0649
Phone: 605-688-4121 • Fax: 605-688-6384
E-mail: sdsu_admissions@sdstate.edu • Web: www.sdstate.edu
Support level: S • Institution type: 4-year public

LEARNING DISABILITY PROGRAM AND SERVICES

South Dakota State University is committed to providing equal opportunities for higher education to academically qualified students with LD who have a reasonable expectation of college success. The University does not offer a specialized curriculum, but it does share responsibility with students for modifying programs to meet individual needs. Students needing specialized tutoring service in reading and writing may have to seek assistance from Vocational Rehabilitation or personally pay for such help.

LD/ADHD ADMISSIONS INFORMATION

College entrance tests required: No
Nonstandardized tests accepted: Yes
Interview required: No
Essay required: No
Documentation required for LD: WAIS-III; WISC-R; WRAT
Documentation required for ADHD: Yes
Documentation submitted to: DSS
Special Ed. HS course work accepted: No

Specific course requirements for all applicants: Yes
Separate application required for services: Yes
# of LD applications submitted yearly: 60
# of LD applications accepted yearly: N/A
Total # of students receiving LD/ADHD services: 44
Acceptance into program means acceptance into college: Students must be admitted and enrolled at the University first and then may request services.

ADMISSIONS

Students with LD are required to submit the general application form. If they do not meet all of the course requirements, they may be admitted conditionally based on ACT scores or class rank. Courses required include 4 years English, 2–3 years math, .5 years computer science, 3 years social studies, 2–3 years science, and .5 years art or music. Students deficient in course requirements need an ACT of 22 (in-state or Minnesota) or 23 (out-of-state).

ADDITIONAL INFORMATION

A skills course is available entitled Mastering Lifelong Skills. Test proctoring for additional time, as well as reading or writing assistance with classroom exams, can be arranged. DSS will also assist students who are LD with finding readers or note-takers.

SUPPORT SERVICES CONTACT INFORMATION

Learning Disability Program/Services: Disabled Student Services (DSS)
Director: Nancy Schade, Coordinator
  E-mail: nancy_schade@sdstate.edu
  Telephone: 605-688-4496
  Fax: 605-688-5951
Contact: Same

LEARNING DISABILITY SERVICES

Requests for the following services/accommodations will be evaluated individually based on appropriate and current documentation.

Allowed in Exams
  Calculator: Yes
  Dictionary: No
  Computer: Yes
  Spellchecker: Yes
Extended test time: Yes
Scribes: Yes
Proctors: Yes
Oral exams: Yes
Note-takers: No

Distraction-reduced environment: Yes
Tape recording in class: Yes
Books on tape from RFBD: No
Taping of books not from RFBD: No
Accommodations for students with ADHD: No
Reading machine: No
Other assistive technology: Yes
Priority registration: Yes

Added costs for services: No
LD specialists: No
Professional tutors: No
Peer tutors: Yes
Max. hours/wk. for services: As needed
How professors are notified of LD/ADHD: By student and program director

GENERAL ADMISSIONS INFORMATION

Director of Admissions: Tracy Welsh
Telephone: 605-688-4121

ENTRANCE REQUIREMENTS
4 English required, 3 math required, 3 science required, 3 science lab required, 3 social studies required. High school diploma or GED required. Minimum TOEFL is 500. TOEFL required of all international applicants.

Application deadline: Rolling
Notification: Rolling
Average GPA: 3.3

Average SAT I Math: N/A
Average SAT I Verbal: N/A
Average ACT: 22

Graduated top 10% of class: 13%
Graduated top 25% of class: 35%
Graduated top 50% of class: 70%

COLLEGE GRADUATION REQUIREMENTS

Course waivers allowed: No
Course substitutions allowed: No
In what subjects: N/A

ADDITIONAL INFORMATION

Environment: The school is located on 220 acres in a rural area 50 miles north of Sioux Falls.

Student Body
  Undergrad enrollment: 7,382
  Female: 50%
  Male: 50%
  Out-of-state: 28%

Cost Information
  In-state tuition: $1,868
  Out-of-state tuition: $5,940
  Room & board: $2,864
Housing Information
  University housing: Yes
  Percent living on campus: 41%

Greek System
  Fraternity: Yes
  Sorority: Yes
Athletics: NCAA Division II

UNIVERSITY OF SOUTH DAKOTA

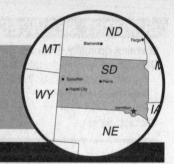

414 East Clark, Vermillion, SD 57069
Phone: 605-677-5434 • Fax: 605-677-6753
E-mail: admiss@usd.edu • Web: www.usd.edu
Support level: CS • Institution type: 4-year public

LEARNING DISABILITY PROGRAM AND SERVICES

The University of South Dakota Disability Services (USDDS) operates on the premise that students at the University are full participants in the process of obtaining appropriate accommodations for their disabilities. Students are encouraged to make their own decisions and become self-advocates for appropriate accommodations or services. The three main goals are to (1) help students become self-advocates, (2) provide better transition services into and out of college, and (3) to provide better instructional and support services. The University strives to ensure that all individuals with legally defined disabilities have access to the full range of the University's programs, services, and activities.

LD/ADHD ADMISSIONS INFORMATION

College entrance tests required: Yes
Nonstandardized tests accepted: Yes
Interview required: No
Essay required: No
Documentation required for LD: Psychoeducational evaluation
Documentation required for ADHD: Yes
Documentation submitted to: Disability Services
Special Ed. HS course work accepted: Limited

Specific course requirements for all applicants: Yes
Separate application required for services: Yes
# of LD applications submitted yearly: N/A
# of LD applications accepted yearly: N/A
Total # of students receiving LD/ADHD services: 115
Acceptance into program means acceptance into college: Students must be admitted and enrolled and then may request services.

ADMISSIONS

The general admission requirements include standing in the top 60 percent of the class, or an ACT score of 18 or above, or GPA of 2.6 with a C or higher in the required high school courses. Course requirements include 4 years of English or ACT English score of 17 or above or AP English score of 2 or above; 3 years of math or ACT math score of 17 or above or AP Calculus score of 2 or above; 3 years of lab science or ACT Science Reasoning score of 17 or above or AP Science of 2 or above; 3 years of social studies or ACT Reading score of 17 or above or AP Social Studies score of 2 or above; and one half-year of Fine Arts or AP Fine Arts score of 2 or above. Students are expected to be proficient in computer skills or they may be required to take specific computer skills courses at the University. Applicants to the associate degree program must meet the same criteria as general admissions or complete the General Equivalency Diploma with a combined score of at least 225 and a minimum score of 40 on each test. Applications submitted from students with deficiencies are reviewed on an individual basis. Nontraditional students (21 years or older) may be admitted at the University's discretion. There is an alternative option for the director of admissions to seek a recommendation from the director of Disability Services regarding admission questions for individuals with disabilities.

ADDITIONAL INFORMATION

Services are individualized for each student's learning needs. USDDS staff provide the following activities: planning, developing, delivering, and evaluating direct service programs; meeting individually with students for academic and related counseling and skill building; ensuring that students receive reasonable and appropriate accommodations that match their needs; consulting with faculty; and providing academic, career, and personal counseling referrals. Classroom accommodations include test modification, note-taking assistance, readers, books on tape, specialized computer facilities, and tutors.

SUPPORT SERVICES CONTACT INFORMATION

Learning Disability Program/Services: Disability Services
Director: Elaine Pearson
  E-mail: epearson@usd.edu
  Telephone: 605-677-6389
  Fax: 605-677-6752
Contact: Same

LEARNING DISABILITY SERVICES

Requests for the following services/accommodations will be evaluated individually based on appropriate and current documentation.

Allowed in Exams
  Calculator: Yes
  Dictionary: No
  Computer: Yes
  Spellchecker: Yes
Extended test time: Yes
Scribes: Yes
Proctors: Yes
Oral exams: Yes
Note-takers: Yes

Distraction-reduced environment: Yes
Tape recording in class: Yes
Books on tape from RFBD: Yes
Taping of books not from RFBD: Yes
Accommodations for students with ADHD: Yes
Reading machine: Yes
Other assistive technology: Yes
Priority registration: Yes

Added costs for services: No
LD specialists: Yes (1)
Professional tutors: No
Peer tutors: Yes
Max. hours/wk. for services: As available
How professors are notified of LD/ADHD: By student and program director

GENERAL ADMISSIONS INFORMATION

Director of Admissions: Paula Tacke
Telephone: 605-677-5434

ENTRANCE REQUIREMENTS

13 total are required; 4 English required, 3 math required, 3 science required, 3 social studies required. High school diploma or GED required. Minimum TOEFL is 550. TOEFL required of all international applicants.

Application deadline: Rolling
Notification: Rolling beginning 9/20
Average GPA: 3.2

Average SAT I Math: NR
Average SAT I Verbal: NR
Average ACT: 22

Graduated top 10% of class: 15%
Graduated top 25% of class: 37%
Graduated top 50% of class: 65%

COLLEGE GRADUATION REQUIREMENTS

Course waivers allowed: No
Course substitutions allowed: No
In what subjects: N/A

ADDITIONAL INFORMATION

Environment: Located 35 miles from Sioux City.

Student Body
  Undergrad enrollment: 5,147
  Female: 57%
  Male: 43%
  Out-of-state: 20%

Cost Information
  In-state tuition: $1,867
  Out-of-state tuition: $5,941
  Room & board: $2,946
Housing Information
  University housing: Yes
  Percent living on campus: 28%

Greek System
  Fraternity: Yes
  Sorority: Yes
Athletics: NCAA Division II

LEE UNIVERSITY

PO Box 3450, Cleveland, TN 37320-3450
Phone: 423-614-8500 • Fax: 423-614-8533
E-mail: admissions@leeuniversity.edu • Web: www.leeuniversity.edu
Support level: CS • Institution type: 4-year private

LEARNING DISABILITY PROGRAM AND SERVICES

Lee University provides an Academic Support Program for students. This service is free to students. It is the goal of the Lee University Academic Support Program to empower students to actualize all the academic potential that they can. The College offers a Peer Tutorial Program, which hires the best students on campus to share their time, experience, and insight in the course or courses that are most difficult for the students who need tutoring. In addition, the College provides direct assistance for any student to verify a learning disability. For these students, Lee University provides support teams, testing adjustments, classroom adjustments, tutoring, and personal monitoring. Students must initiate the request for special accommodations by applying at the Academic Support Program office. Lee University is committed to the provision of reasonable accommodations for students with disabilities.

LD/ADHD ADMISSIONS INFORMATION

College entrance tests required: Yes
Nonstandardized tests accepted: Yes
Interview required: Yes
Essay required: No
Documentation required for LD: Psychoeducational evaluation: within 3 years
Documentation required for ADHD: Yes
Documentation submitted to: Academic Support Program
Special Ed. HS course work accepted: Yes

Specific course requirements for all applicants: Yes
Separate application required for services: No
# of LD applications submitted yearly: 35
# of LD applications accepted yearly: 80%
Total # of students receiving LD/ADHD services: 150
Acceptance into program means acceptance into college: Students must be admitted and enrolled at the College first and then may request services.

ADMISSIONS

Each applicant is reviewed on a case-by-case basis. Each student must be able to perform successfully with limited support. ACT minimum is 17 or SAT 860. GPA required is 2.0. There are no specific course requirements. Students who do not meet the College policy for entrance are referred to a special committee for possible probational acceptance.

ADDITIONAL INFORMATION

The Academic Support Program is staffed by professional counselors, math and reading instructors, and a tutoring coordinator. The center has listening and study lab instructional materials, group study/discussion rooms, and tutoring services. The program provides readers and books on tape. Benefits included in the program are tutoring sessions with friendly and comfortable surroundings; two hours of tutoring per week per subject; tutoring in any subject, including biology, psychology, English, mathematics, religion, science, sociology, history, and foreign language. Freshmen are channeled into a gateway class, which provides study skills and time management skills.

SUPPORT SERVICES CONTACT INFORMATION

Learning Disability Program/Services: Academic Support Program
Director: Debrah Murray
 Telephone: 423-614-8181
 Fax: 423-614-8180
Contact: Gayle Gallaher, PhD
 Telephone: 423-614-8181
 Fax: 423-614-8179

LEARNING DISABILITY SERVICES

Requests for the following services/accommodations will be evaluated individually based on appropriate and current documentation.

Allowed in Exams
 Calculator: Y/N
 Dictionary: Y/N
 Computer: Y/N
 Spellchecker: Y/N
Extended test time: Yes
Scribes: Yes
Proctors: Yes
Oral exams: Yes
Note-takers: Yes

Distraction-reduced environment: Yes
Tape recording in class: Yes
Books on tape from RFBD: Yes
Taping of books not from RFBD: Yes
Accommodations for students with ADHD: Yes
Reading machine: No
Other assistive technology: No
Priority registration: No

Added costs for services: No
LD specialists: Yes (2)
Professional tutors: No
Peer tutors: 50
Max. hours/wk. for services: 2 hours per subject
How professors are notified of LD/ADHD: By student and program director

GENERAL ADMISSIONS INFORMATION

Director of Admissions: Phill Cook
Telephone: 423-614-8500

ENTRANCE REQUIREMENTS

4 English required, 4 English recommended, 3 math required, 3 math recommended, 2 science required, 2 science recommended, 1 foreign language required, 1 foreign language recommended, 2 social studies required, 2 social studies recommended, 1 history required, 1 history recommended. High school diploma or GED required. Minimum TOEFL is 450. TOEFL required of all international applicants.

Application deadline: September 1
Notification: Rolling beginning 9/1
Average GPA: 3.0

Average SAT I Math: NR
Average SAT I Verbal: NR
Average ACT: 22

Graduated top 10% of class: 20%
Graduated top 25% of class: 44%
Graduated top 50% of class: 72%

COLLEGE GRADUATION REQUIREMENTS

Course waivers allowed: No
Course substitutions allowed: No
In what subjects: N/A

ADDITIONAL INFORMATION

Environment: The College is located on 40 acres in a small town 25 miles from Chattanooga.

Student Body
 Undergrad enrollment: 3,155
 Female: 56%
 Male: 44%
 Out-of-state: 63%

Cost Information
 Tuition: $10,970
 Room & board: $4,020
Housing Information
 University housing: Yes
 Percent living on campus: 43%

Greek System
 Fraternity: Yes
 Sorority: Yes
Athletics: NAIA

MIDDLE TENNESSEE STATE UNIV.

Office of Admissions, Merfreesboro, TN 37132
Phone: 800-433-6878 • Fax: 615-898-5478
E-mail: admissions@mtsu.edu • Web: www.mtsu.edu
Support level: CS • Institution type: 4-year public

LEARNING DISABILITY PROGRAM AND SERVICES

The Learning Disabilities Program is a part of the Disabled Student Services office. The LD Program offers comprehensive support services for students diagnosed with LD and ADHD. Eligibility for the program requires admission to MTSU and documentation of the disability. The LD Program is designed to ensure students have an equal opportunity to pursue an education. Students with LD are held to the same academic standards as all students; however, accommodations are available to assist meeting these requirements. Accommodations are determined on an individual basis considering the student's strengths, course requirements, and documentation. To register with the LD Program, students schedule an appointment with the coordinator, complete the registration form, and provide the most current documentation of the disability.

LD/ADHD ADMISSIONS INFORMATION

College entrance tests required: No
Nonstandardized tests accepted: Yes
Interview required: No
Essay required: No
Documentation required for LD: Psychoeducational
  evaluation
Documentation required for ADHD: Yes
Documentation submitted to: Disabled Student Services
Special Ed. HS course work accepted: No

Specific course requirements for all applicants: Yes
Separate application required for services: No
# of LD applications submitted yearly: 40
# of LD applications accepted yearly: 80%
Total # of students receiving LD/ADHD services: 260
Acceptance into program means acceptance into
  college: Students must be admitted and enrolled and then
  may request services.

ADMISSIONS

There is no special admission process for students with LD. All students must meet the same general admission requirements. The minimum GPA is a 2.3. Students should have 4 years of English, 2 years of math, 2 years of science, 2 years of social studies, 2 years of foreign language, and visual/performing arts. Course substitutions are not allowed. The average ACT is 21 or 970 SAT. Students are encouraged to self-disclose a disability in a personal statement during the admission process, although this is not required.

ADDITIONAL INFORMATION

Students are encouraged to initiate contact with the LD Program coordinator early in the semester to determine the necessary accommodations. Once enrolled in courses students schedule regular meetings with the coordinator in order to monitor progress and/or determine the need for adjustments to the accommodations. Services/resources provided include orientation to the LD Program; orientation to the Adaptive Technology Center; assistance with the admission process; advising and strategic scheduling of classes; early registration of classes; tutorial services; test accommodations; note-takers, readers, scribes, books on tape; exploration of time management/note-taking strategies; career planning and employment strategies; and resume preparation. The Adaptive Technology Center provides training support for students, faculty and staff with disabilities in the use of adaptive/assistive technology application and devices. All disability documentation is conditional and is not released without the consent of the student.

SUPPORT SERVICES CONTACT INFORMATION

Learning Disability Program/Services: Disabled Student Services
Director: John Harris
  E-mail: jharris@mtsu.edu
  Telephone: 615-898-2783
  Fax: 615-898-4893
Contact: Melissa Smith
  E-mail: masmith@mtsu.edu
  Telephone: 615-904-8246
  Fax: 615-898-4893

LEARNING DISABILITY SERVICES

Requests for the following services/accommodations will be evaluated individually based on appropriate and current documentation.

Allowed in Exams
  Calculator: Yes
  Dictionary: Yes
  Computer: Yes
  Spellchecker: Yes
Extended test time: Yes
Scribes: Yes
Proctors: Yes
Oral exams: Yes
Note-takers: Yes

Distraction-reduced environment: Yes
Tape recording in class: Yes
Books on tape from RFBD: Yes
Taping of books not from RFBD: Yes
Accommodations for students with ADHD: Yes
Reading machine: Yes
Other assistive technology: Yes
Priority registration: Yes

Added costs for services: No
LD specialists: Yes (1)
Professional tutors: No
Peer tutors: Yes
Max. hours/wk. for services: Unlimited
How professors are notified of LD/ADHD: By student and director of services

GENERAL ADMISSIONS INFORMATION

Director of Admissions: Lynn Palmer
Telephone: 800-433-6878

ENTRANCE REQUIREMENTS
Minimum GPA is 2.3. Course requirements include 4 years English, 2 years math, 2 years science, 2 years social studies, 2 years foreign language, and visual or performing arts. Minimum TOEFL is 525. TOEFL required of all international applicants.

Application deadline: July 1
Notification: Rolling
Average GPA: 3.0

Average SAT I Math: 485
Average SAT I Verbal: 485
Average ACT: 22

Graduated top 10% of class: 17%
Graduated top 25% of class: 51%
Graduated top 50% of class: 64%

COLLEGE GRADUATION REQUIREMENTS

Course waivers allowed: Yes
Course substitutions allowed: Yes
In what subjects: On an individual basis.

ADDITIONAL INFORMATION

Environment: Located about 30 miles from Nashville.

Student Body
  Undergrad enrollment: 15,890
  Female: 53%
  Male: 47%
  Out-of-state: 5%

Cost Information
  In-state tuition: $1,906
  Out-of-state tuition: $6,732
  Room & board: $3,030
Housing Information
  University housing: Yes
  Percent living on campus: 25%

Greek System
  Fraternity: Yes
  Sorority: Yes
Athletics: NCAA Division I

Middle Tennessee State University

UNIVERSITY OF MEMPHIS

229 Administration Building, Memphis, TN 38152
Phone: 901-678-2111 • Fax: 901-678-3053
E-mail: recruitment@memphis.edu • Web: www.memphis.edu
Support level: CS • Institution type: 4-year public

LEARNING DISABILITY PROGRAM AND SERVICES

The University's LD/ADHD Program is designed to enhance academic strengths, provide support for areas of weakness, and build skills to help students with LD and ADHD compete in the College environment. The program encourages development of lifelong learning skills as well as personal responsibility for academic success. Training in college survival skills and regular meetings with the staff are emphasized during the first year to aid in the transition to college. Specific services are tailored to individual needs, considering one's strengths, weaknesses, course requirements, and learning styles. Students are integrated into regular classes and are held to the same academic standards as other students; however, academic accommodations are available to assist them in meeting requirements. The LD/ADHD program places responsibility on students to initiate services and follow through with services once they are arranged. Most students who use the appropriate services are successful in their academic pursuits.

LD/ADHD ADMISSIONS INFORMATION

College entrance tests required: No
Nonstandardized tests accepted: Yes
Interview required: No
Essay required: Yes
Documentation required for LD: WAIS-III; WJ
Documentation required for ADHD: Yes
Documentation submitted to: LD Program
Special Ed. HS course work accepted: Yes

Specific course requirements for all applicants: Yes
Separate application required for services: No
# of LD applications submitted yearly: N/A
# of LD applications accepted yearly: N/A
Total # of students receiving LD/ADHD services: 450
Acceptance into program means acceptance into college: Students must be accepted and enrolled at the University first and then may request services.

ADMISSIONS

If applicants with learning disabilities or ADHD choose to disclose their disability and provide professional medical documentation, exceptions to the regular admissions criteria may be made on an individual basis. Course requirements include 4 years English, 2 years science, 2 years foreign language, 2 years social studies, and 1 year visual or performing arts. It is recommended that students self-disclose their LD during the admission process if they do not meet regular admission requirements. Exceptions are made only for applicants who have at least a 17 ACT composite, 2.0 GPA, and no more than three high school curriculum deficiencies, only one of which can be math. Applicants who request admissions exceptions will be asked to provide two academic recommendations and a personal letter in addition to the documentation. Students requesting admissions exceptions based on learning disabilities or attention deficit disorders will have their documentation reviewed by the LD Coordinator to determine if the documentation is sufficient to meet qualifying criteria.

ADDITIONAL INFORMATION

Transitional studies courses are available in basic math, algebra, and composition for credit; however, they do not apply toward a degree. One-on-one instruction is available in note-taking, time management, and organization skills. The University also offers LD orientation (highly advised for incoming students), early registration, use of computers and adaptive software, preferential classroom seating, and two special sections of "Introduction to the University" geared to the needs of students with LD and ADHD. Services and accommodations are available for undergraduate and graduate students.

SUPPORT SERVICES CONTACT INFORMATION

Learning Disability Program/Services: Learning Disability Program
Director: Dona Sparger
  E-mail: dsparger@memphis.edu
  Telephone: 901-678-3304
  Fax: 901-678-3070
Contact: Same

LEARNING DISABILITY SERVICES

Requests for the following services/accommodations will be evaluated individually based on appropriate and current documentation.

Allowed in Exams
  Calculator: Yes
  Dictionary: Yes
  Computer: Yes
  Spellchecker: Yes
Extended test time: Yes
Scribes: Yes
Proctors: Yes
Oral exams: Yes
Note-takers: Yes

Distraction-reduced environment: Yes
Tape recording in class: Yes
Books on tape from RFBD: Yes
Taping of books not from RFBD: Yes
Accommodations for students with ADHD: Yes
Reading machine: Yes
Other assistive technology: Yes
Priority registration: Yes

Added costs for services: No
LD specialists: Yes (2)
Professional tutors: Yes
Peer tutors: Yes
Max. hours/wk. for services: Unlimited
How professors are notified of LD/ADHD: By both student and director

GENERAL ADMISSIONS INFORMATION

Director of Admissions: David Wallace
Telephone: 901-678-2111

ENTRANCE REQUIREMENTS
14 total are required; 16 total are recommended; 3 math required, 4 math recommended, 2 science required, 3 science recommended, 2 foreign language required, 2 social studies recommended. High school diploma or GED required. Minimum TOEFL is 500. TOEFL required of all international applicants.

Application deadline: August 1
Notification: Rolling
Average GPA: N/A

Average SAT I Math: N/A
Average SAT I Verbal: N/A
Average ACT: 22

Graduated top 10% of class: N/A
Graduated top 25% of class: N/A
Graduated top 50% of class: N/A

COLLEGE GRADUATION REQUIREMENTS

Course waivers allowed: No
Course substitutions allowed: Yes
In what subjects: Foreign language

ADDITIONAL INFORMATION

Environment: The University is located on 1,159 acres in an urban area.

Student Body
  Undergrad enrollment: 15,485
  Female: 57%
  Male: 43%
  Out-of-state: 12%

Cost Information
  In-state tuition: $3,000
  Out-of-state tuition: $8,100
  Room & board: $3,995
Housing Information
  University housing: Yes
  Percent living on campus: 14%

Greek System
  Fraternity: Yes
  Sorority: Yes
  Athletics: NCAA Division I

UNIV. OF TENNESSEE—CHATTANOOGA

615 McCallie Avenue, 131 Hooper Hall, Chattanooga, TN 37403
Phone: 423-755-4662 • Fax: 423-755-4157
E-mail: utcmocs@utc.edu • Web: www.utc.edu
Support level: CS • Institution type: 4-year public

LEARNING DISABILITY PROGRAM AND SERVICES

The College Access Program (CAP) at the University provides academic, social, and emotional support for students with learning disabilities. CAP provides academic advisement, tutoring in all course work, career planning, counseling, social skills development, survival skills, career advisement, word processing skills, extended time on tests, freshmen orientation, and psychological testing. "Start Smart" is a summer seminar for CAP students to prepare them for university course work and general adjustment to the University.

LD/ADHD ADMISSIONS INFORMATION

College entrance tests required: Yes
Nonstandardized tests accepted: Yes
Interview required: Yes
Essay required: No
Documentation required for LD: WJ; WAIS-III; achievement battery: within 3 years
Documentation required for ADHD: Yes
Documentation submitted to: CAP
Special Ed. HS course work accepted: Yes

Specific course requirements for all applicants: Yes
Separate application required for services: Yes
# of LD applications submitted yearly: 90
# of LD applications accepted yearly: 50
Total # of students receiving LD/ADHD services: 185
Acceptance into program means acceptance into college: Students must be admitted and enrolled at the University first in order to participate in CAP.

ADMISSIONS

Students with learning disabilities submit a general application to the Admissions Office and a special application to CAP. Applicants to CAP should also submit an LD evaluation, a transcript, and two letters of recommendation. Minimum admissions requirements are 2.0 GPA, 16 ACT or 760 SAT, and 4 years English, 3 years math, 2 years lab science, 1 year American history, 1 year European history or world history or world geography, 2 years foreign language, and 1 year fine arts. Students may be admitted conditionally if they fall below these guidelines and have only one unit deficiency. If the course deficiency is in the area of the LD, an appeals committee will sometimes allow a probationary admittance if CAP also accepts the student. Students admitted on condition must earn at least a 1.0 GPA their first semester or suspension will result. The Dean of Admissions or admission committee may recommend conditions for acceptance. Application to the Office for Students with Disabilities is a separate process and is not relevant to the admissions process.

ADDITIONAL INFORMATION

CAP does not, as a matter of policy, seek on a student's behalf a waiver of any course work. Students admitted conditionally may be required to carry a reduced course load, take specific courses, have a specific advisor, and take specific programs of developmental study. Upper-class and graduate student tutors, trained to work with students with learning disabilities, hold regularly scheduled, individualized tutoring sessions. The coordinator matches tutors with CAP students according to learning styles. Social skills development activities may involve video and role-playing situations in group form as well as during informal gatherings. There is a monthly publication, *The CAPsule*, for CAP students and parents. UTC offers developmental math and English courses for institutional credit. Services and accommodations are available for undergraduate and graduate students.

SUPPORT SERVICES CONTACT INFORMATION

Learning Disability Program/Services: Office for Students with Disabilities
Director: Debra Anderson
   E-mail: OSD-CAP@utc.edu
   Telephone: 423-755-4006
   Fax: 423-785-2288
Contact: Same

LEARNING DISABILITY SERVICES

Requests for the following services/accommodations will be evaluated individually based on appropriate and current documentation.

Allowed in Exams
   Calculator: Yes
   Dictionary: No
   Computer: Yes
   Spellchecker: Yes
Extended test time: Yes
Scribes: Yes
Proctors: Yes
Oral exams: Yes
Note-takers: Yes

Distraction-reduced environment: Yes
Tape recording in class: Yes
Books on tape from RFBD: Yes
Taping of books not from RFBD: Yes
Accommodations for students with ADHD: Yes
Reading machine: Yes
Other assistive technology: Yes
Priority registration: No

Added costs for services: $500 per semester
LD specialists: Yes (2)
Professional tutors: 18
Peer tutors: 12
Max. hours/wk. for services: Unlimited
How professors are notified of LD/ADHD: By student

GENERAL ADMISSIONS INFORMATION

Director of Admissions: Patsy Reynolds
Telephone: 423-755-4662

ENTRANCE REQUIREMENTS

14 total are required; 4 English required, 3 math required, 2 science required, 2 science lab required, 2 foreign language required, 1 social studies required, 1 history required. High school diploma or GED required. Minimum TOEFL is 500. TOEFL required of all international applicants.

Application deadline: August 1
Notification: Rolling beginning 10/1
Average GPA: 3.2

Average SAT I Math: N/A
Average SAT I Verbal: N/A
Average ACT: 22

Graduated top 10% of class: N/A
Graduated top 25% of class: 44%
Graduated top 50% of class: 84%

COLLEGE GRADUATION REQUIREMENTS

Course waivers allowed: No
Course substitutions allowed: No
In what subjects: N/A

ADDITIONAL INFORMATION

Environment: The University is located on 60 acres in an urban area in Chattanooga.

Student Body
   Undergrad enrollment: 6,993
   Female: 57%
   Male: 43%
   Out-of-state: 7%

Cost Information
   In-state tuition: $2,834
   Out-of-state tuition: $8,514
   Room & board: $4,548
Housing Information
   University housing: Yes
   Percent living on campus: 22%

Greek System
   Fraternity: Yes
   Sorority: Yes
Athletics: NCAA Division I

UNIVERSITY OF TENNESSEE—MARTIN

200 Hall-Moody, Administrative Building, Martin, TN 38238
Phone: 731-587-7020 • Fax: 731-587-7029
E-mail: jrayburn@utm.edu • Web: www.utm.edu
Support level: CS • Institution type: 4-year public

LEARNING DISABILITY PROGRAM AND SERVICES

The University believes students with learning disabilities can achieve success in college without academic compromise and can become productive, self-sufficient members of society. A preliminary interview will include a review of previous assessments of the disability and the collection of background information. If the results of the PACE evaluation show that the academic and social needs of the student can be met by PACE services, the student will work with a learning disabilities specialist to develop an individually designed program. University staff who work with PACE students receive training in understanding learning disabilities and teaching strategies that meet the individual student's needs. Graduate supervisors coordinate support services. PACE is designed to complement and supplement existing university support services available for all students.

LD/ADHD ADMISSIONS INFORMATION

College entrance tests required: Yes
Nonstandardized tests accepted: Yes
Interview required: Yes
Essay required: Yes
Documentation required for LD: WAIS-III; WJ: within 2 years
Documentation required for ADHD: Yes
Documentation submitted to: Director of PACE
Special Ed. HS course work accepted: Limited

Specific course requirements for all applicants: Yes
Separate application required for services: Yes
# of LD applications submitted yearly: 30–40
# of LD applications accepted yearly: N/A
Total # of students receiving LD/ADHD services: 75
Acceptance into program means acceptance into college: Admission to the University and PACE is simultaneous.

ADMISSIONS

Basically, applicants must meet regular admission criteria, including 16 ACT and 2.6 GPA or 19 ACT and 2.2 GPA. Some applicants are considered through Qualified Admission with a 14 ACT and 2.25 GPA. Course requirements include 4 years English, 3 years math, 2 years science, 2 years social studies, and 2 years foreign language. Each student is considered based on background, test scores, strengths/weaknesses, and motivation. Qualified students with learning disabilities should apply directly to both the PACE Center and the Office of Admissions. Students must complete all steps in both admission processes before an admission decision can be made. An interview is required for students applying to the PACE Program. Documentation should be sent to PACE. To be certain consideration is given to the learning disability, university decisions on acceptance are determined by both the PACE Center and the Admissions Office. Applicants are selected on the basis of intellectual potential (average to superior), motivation, academic preparation, and willingness to work hard.

ADDITIONAL INFORMATION

All freshmen students with LD selected to participate in PACE and admitted for fall semester must attend the second summer session program. Students take one selected university class in the mornings. In the afternoons, PACE staff teach learning strategies that can be applied to all future courses so that the students will have hands-on experience using the skills. The summer program will also address improvements in reading, spelling, written language, or math skills. Equally important are small group sessions to help students improve social skills. Students with ADHD must have comprehensive documentation in order to receive accommodations and services. There is a math lab and an English Writing Center. Students with appropriate documentation may be eligible to receive the following services: extended testing time; distraction-free testing environment; calculators, dictionary, computer and spellchecker in exams; proctors; oral exams; note-takers; tape recorders in class; books on tape; and tutoring. Services and accommodations are provided to undergraduate and graduate students.

SUPPORT SERVICES CONTACT INFORMATION

Learning Disability Program/Services: Program Access for College Enhancement (P.A.C.E.)
Director: Michelle Arant
  E-mail: marant@utm.edu
  Telephone: 901-587-7195
  Fax: 901-587-7956
Contact: Beth Vise
  E-mail: bavise@utm.edu
  Telephone: 901-587-7195
  Fax: 901-587-7956

LEARNING DISABILITY SERVICES

Requests for the following services/accommodations will be evaluated individually based on appropriate and current documentation.

Allowed in Exams
  Calculator: Yes
  Dictionary: Yes
  Computer: Yes
  Spellchecker: Yes
Extended test time: Yes
Scribes: Yes
Proctors: Yes
Oral exams: Yes
Note-takers: Yes

Distraction-reduced environment: Yes
Tape recording in class: Yes
Books on tape from RFBD: Yes
Taping of books not from RFBD: Yes
Accommodations for students with ADHD: Yes
Reading machine: Yes
Other assistive technology: No
Priority registration: No

Added costs for services: $500 per semester
LD specialists: Yes (2)
Professional tutors: 2
Peer tutors: 20
Max. hours/wk. for services: Unlimited
How professors are notified of LD/ADHD: By both student and director

GENERAL ADMISSIONS INFORMATION

Director of Admissions: Judy Rayburn
Telephone: 901-587-7032

ENTRANCE REQUIREMENTS
14 total are required; 4 English required, 3 math required, 2 science required, 1 science lab required, 2 foreign language required, 2 history required. High school diploma or GED required. Minimum TOEFL is 500. TOEFL required of all international applicants.

Application deadline: August 1
Notification: Rolling beginning 9/1
Average GPA: 3.3

Average SAT I Math: N/A
Average SAT I Verbal: N/A
Average ACT: 21

Graduated top 10% of class: 18%
Graduated top 25% of class: 40%
Graduated top 50% of class: 64%

COLLEGE GRADUATION REQUIREMENTS

Course waivers allowed: No
Course substitutions allowed: Yes
In what subjects: Math and foreign language

ADDITIONAL INFORMATION

Environment: The University is located on a 200-acre campus in a small town 100 miles north of Memphis.

Student Body
  Undergrad enrollment: 5,478
  Female: 43%
  Male: 57%
  Out-of-state: 6%

Cost Information
  In-state tuition: $2,172
  Out-of-state tuition: $7,432
  Room & board: $3,606
Housing Information
  University housing: Yes
  Percent living on campus: 40%

Greek System
  Fraternity: Yes
  Sorority: Yes
Athletics: NCAA Division I

University of Tennessee—Martin

ABILENE CHRISTIAN UNIVERSITY

Box 29000, Abilene, TX 79699
Phone: 915-674-2650 • Fax: 915-674-2130
E-mail: info@admissions.acu.edu • Web: www.acu.edu
Support level: CS • Institution type: 4-year private

LEARNING DISABILITY PROGRAM AND SERVICES

Alpha Academic Services is a Student Support Service program funded under Title IV legislation governing TRIO programs. The program strives to assist students in programs that move them toward independence in learning and living. The staff are specially trained instructors, peer tutors, counselors, and administrators who focus on the problems encountered by college students. Staff members help qualifying students find and apply solutions to their problems. Students qualify for services if they are first generation college students, economically disadvantaged, or students with disabilities. Alpha means one-on-one help with instruction and tutoring tailored to the students' unique needs. Students with learning disabilities may receive special accommodation services to assist them in achieving success in their university studies. Documentation of the disability is required in order to receive disability accommodations. Students must make an appointment to determine if they qualify to receive services.

LD/ADHD ADMISSIONS INFORMATION

College entrance tests required: Yes
Nonstandardized tests accepted: Yes
Interview required: Yes
Essay required: Yes
Documentation required for LD: Psychoeducational evaluation
Documentation required for ADHD: Yes
Documentation submitted to: Alpha Academic Services
Special Ed. HS course work accepted: Yes

Specific course requirements for all applicants: Yes
Separate application required for services: Yes
# of LD applications submitted yearly: 30–41
# of LD applications accepted yearly: 25–31
Total # of students receiving LD/ADHD services: 106
Acceptance into program means acceptance into college: Students must be admitted and enrolled at the University first and then may request services.

ADMISSIONS

All students must be admitted to the University and meet the same criteria for admission. Students with LD/ADHD who self-disclose may be admitted with lower SAT/ACT scores or class rank than required for general admission. Other relevant criteria are considered on an individual basis. Students with special needs must submit documentation to support a need for exception to normal admission requirements. Documentation is reviewed by an admissions panel which consists of the admissions counselor, an LD/ADHD specialist, and the Director of Admissions. An interview is required. Regular admissions criteria include 20 ACT (average is 24) or 960+ SAT I (average is 1075); college-preparatory courses including 3 years math, 3 years science, 4 years English, and 2 years foreign language (substitutions must be reasonable such as American Sign Language for foreign language); and rank in the top 50 percent of high school graduating class. Students with special needs may qualify for regular admission, probationary admission, or summer admission. Students admitted conditionally must take specified courses and demonstrate motivation and ability.

ADDITIONAL INFORMATION

Alpha Academic Services provides opportunities for individual instruction in basic skills areas such as writing, math, or study skills; assessment of learning preferences, strengths, and weaknesses; instruction and tutoring designed to fit the student's particular learning preferences and strengths and academic needs; classroom help such as readers, note-takers, alternative testing arrangements; personal, career, and academic counseling; and workshops on topics such as time management skills, resume writing, career placement, and study skills.

SUPPORT SERVICES CONTACT INFORMATION

Learning Disability Program/Services: Alpha Academic Services
Director: Gloria Bradshaw
  E-mail: bradshawg@acu.edu
  Telephone: 915-674-2750
  Fax: 915-674-6847
Contact: Ada Dodd or Jamie Jimenez
  Telephone: 915-674-2750
  Fax: 915-674-6847

LEARNING DISABILITY SERVICES

Requests for the following services/accommodations will be evaluated individually based on appropriate and current documentation.

Allowed in Exams
  Calculator: Yes
  Dictionary: Yes
  Computer: Yes
  Spellchecker: Yes
Extended test time: Yes
Scribes: Yes
Proctors: Yes
Oral exams: Yes
Note-takers: Yes

Distraction-reduced environment: Yes
Tape recording in class: Yes
Books on tape from RFBD: Yes
Taping of books not from RFBD: Yes
Accommodations for students with ADHD: Yes
Reading machine: Yes
Other assistive technology: Yes
Priority registration: No

Added costs for services: No
LD specialists: Yes (3)
Professional tutors: 4
Peer tutors: 20
Max. hours/wk. for services: Unlimited
How professors are notified of LD/ADHD: By both student and director

GENERAL ADMISSIONS INFORMATION

Director of Admissions: Tim Johnston
Telephone: 915-674-2650

ENTRANCE REQUIREMENTS

14 total are required; 14 total are recommended; 4 English required, 4 English recommended, 3 math required, 3 math recommended, 1 science required, 1 science recommended, 2 foreign language recommended, 2 social studies required, 2 social studies recommended, 2 history recommended. High school diploma or GED required. Minimum TOEFL is 525. TOEFL required of all international applicants.

Application deadline: August 1
Notification: Rolling
Average GPA: 3.4

Average SAT I Math: 555
Average SAT I Verbal: 555
Average ACT: 23

Graduated top 10% of class: 5%
Graduated top 25% of class: 21%
Graduated top 50% of class: 57%

COLLEGE GRADUATION REQUIREMENTS

Course waivers allowed: Yes
Course substitutions allowed: Yes
In what subjects: Math and foreign language

ADDITIONAL INFORMATION

Environment: The campus is in a suburban area 150 miles from Fort Worth.

Student Body
  Undergrad enrollment: 4,231
  Female: 55%
  Male: 45%
  Out-of-state: 33%

Cost Information
  Tuition: $10,410
  Room & board: $4,420
Housing Information
  University housing: Yes
  Percent living on campus: 88%

Greek System
  Fraternity: Yes
  Sorority: Yes
  Athletics: NCAA Division II

Abilene Christian University

LAMAR UNIVERSITY

PO Box 10009, Beaumont, TX 77710
Phone: 409-880-8888 • Fax: 409-880-8463
E-mail: admissions@hal.lamar.edu • Web: www.lamar.edu
Support level: S • Institution type: 4-year public

LEARNING DISABILITY PROGRAM AND SERVICES

Services are designed to help students become successful on the Lamar campus. Students with learning disabilities could qualify for registration assistance, tutoring, and other personalized services. Students are encouraged to notify the coordinator of services that specific disabilities exist, the modification needed, and preferably a conference prior to registration will allow the appropriate accommodations to be made. Prior to registration, students are requested to notify the coordinator of Services for Students with Disabilities regarding assistance and/or accommodation they anticipate will be needed during the course of instruction for which they plan to register.

LD/ADHD ADMISSIONS INFORMATION

College entrance tests required: No
Nonstandardized tests accepted: Yes
Interview required: Yes
Essay required: No
Documentation required for LD: Psychoeducational
  evaluation: within 3 years
Documentation required for ADHD: Yes
Documentation submitted to: SSWD
Special Ed. HS course work accepted: Yes

Specific course requirements for all applicants: Yes
Separate application required for services: No
# of LD applications submitted yearly: N/A
# of LD applications accepted yearly: N/A
Total # of students receiving LD/ADHD services: 24
**Acceptance into program means acceptance into
  college:** Students must be admitted and enrolled at the
  University and then may request services.

ADMISSIONS

Applicants with learning disabilities must meet the general admission requirements. Services will be offered to enrolled students who notify the coordinator of Services for Students with Disabilities. Students must be in top half of their class and complete 14 "solid" credits to be admitted unconditionally, including 4 years English, 3 years math (algebra I & II and geometry or higher), 2 years science (physical science, biology, chemistry, physics, or geology), 2.5 years social science, and 2.5 years electives (foreign language is recommended). A very limited number of applicants not meeting the prerequisites may be admitted on "individual approval." Those not in the top half must achieve a minimum composite score of 1000 SAT/21 ACT. Some students may be considered on an Individual Approval basis if they fail to meet Unconditional Admission. These students are subject to mandatory advisement; 6-credit limit in summer and 14 in fall term, and must successfully complete 9 hours with 2.0 GPA; students must meet these provisions or leave for one year.

ADDITIONAL INFORMATION

SSWD offers a variety of services designed to assist students in becoming full participating members of the University. Services or accommodations could include priority registration; alternative testing accommodations; copying of class notes; classroom accommodations; counseling for academic, personal, and vocational needs; note-takers; readers; textbooks on tape; and tutoring. Professional staff assist students with questions, problem solving, adjustment, decision making, goal planning, testing, and development of learning skills. Skills classes in study skills are offered, including developmental writing, reading, and math for credit. Students are referred to other offices and personnel in accordance with the needs and intents of the individual. Services and accommodations are available for undergraduate and graduate students.

SUPPORT SERVICES CONTACT INFORMATION

Learning Disability Program/Services: Services for Students with Disabilities (SSWD)
Director: Callie Trahan, Coordinator
  E-mail: trahancf@halilamar.edu
  Telephone: 409-880-8026
  Fax: 409-880-2225
Contact: Same

LEARNING DISABILITY SERVICES

Requests for the following services/accommodations will be evaluated individually based on appropriate and current documentation.

Allowed in Exams
  Calculator: Yes
  Dictionary: Yes
  Computer: Yes
  Spellchecker: Yes
Extended test time: Yes
Scribes: Yes
Proctors: Yes
Oral exams: Yes
Note-takers: Yes

Distraction-reduced environment: Yes
Tape recording in class: Yes
Books on tape from RFBD: Yes
Taping of books not from RFBD: Yes
Accommodations for students with
  ADHD: Yes
Reading machine: Yes
Other assistive technology: Yes
Priority registration: Yes

Added costs for services: No
LD specialists: No
Professional tutors: No
Peer tutors: 3
Max. hours/wk. for services: 15
How professors are notified of
  LD/ADHD: By student

GENERAL ADMISSIONS INFORMATION

Director of Admissions: James Rush
Telephone: 409-880-8888

ENTRANCE REQUIREMENTS

16 total are recommended; 4 English recommended, 3 math recommended, 2 science recommended, 2 social studies recommended, 2 elective recommended. High school diploma or GED required. Minimum TOEFL is 500. TOEFL required of all international applicants.

Application deadline: August 1
Notification: Rolling
Average GPA: N/A

Average SAT I Math: 459
Average SAT I Verbal: 413
Average ACT: 20

Graduated top 10% of class: 10%
Graduated top 25% of class: 27%
Graduated top 50% of class: 90%

COLLEGE GRADUATION REQUIREMENTS

Course waivers allowed: No
Course substitutions allowed: Yes
In what subjects: Must be determined to not be an essential element of the major.

ADDITIONAL INFORMATION

Environment: The University is located on 200 acres in an urban area 90 miles east of Houston.

Student Body
  Undergrad enrollment: 9,551
  Female: 55%
  Male: 45%
  Out-of-state: 1%

Cost Information
  In-state tuition: $864
  Out-of-state tuition: $5,976
  Room & board: $3,040
Housing Information
  University housing: Yes
  Percent living on campus: 11%

Greek System
  Fraternity: Yes
  Sorority: Yes
Athletics: NCAA Division I

MIDWESTERN STATE UNIVERSITY

3410 Taft Blvd., Wichita Falls, TX 76308
Phone: 940-397-4334 • Fax: 940-397-4672
E-mail: schoolrelations@nexus.mwsu.edu • Web: www.mwsu.edu
Support level: S • Institution type: 4-year public

LEARNING DISABILITY PROGRAM AND SERVICES

In accordance with Section 504 of the federal Rehabilitation Act of 1973 and the Americans with Disabilities Act of 1990, Midwestern State University endeavors to make reasonable adjustments in its policies, practices, services, and facilities to ensure equal opportunity for qualified persons with disabilities to participate in all educational programs and activities. Students requiring special accommodation or auxiliary aids must make application for such assistance through the Office of Disability Accommodations. The Office of Disability Accommodations focuses on helping students to negotiate all aspects of adapting to college life. These include academic, personal, career, and social concerns. To obtain services, students must be accepted for admission at MSU, complete an application form from the Office of Disability Accommodations, and supply verification of the disability.

LD/ADHD ADMISSIONS INFORMATION

College entrance tests required: Yes
Nonstandardized tests accepted: Yes
Interview required: No
Essay required: No
Documentation required for LD: WAIS-III, WJ
Documentation required for ADHD: Yes
Documentation submitted to: Disability Services
Special Ed. HS course work accepted: Yes

Specific course requirements for all applicants: Yes
Separate application required for services: No
# of LD applications submitted yearly: N/A
# of LD applications accepted yearly: N/A
Total # of students receiving LD/ADHD services: 20
Acceptance into program means acceptance into college: Students must be accepted and enrolled at the University first and then may request services.

ADMISSIONS
Unconditional acceptance by the University is available to the student who graduates from an accredited high school with 4 years of English, 3 years math, 2 years science, 60 percent high school rank, an ACT of 20 or more, or SAT of 840 or more. Admission by Review is an alternative admission with the same high school units as mentioned previously, but a high school rank between 40 and 60 percent, an ACT between 14 and 19, or an SAT of 560–839.

ADDITIONAL INFORMATION
The Office of Disability Accommodations arranges accommodations for the student with special needs. Help includes priority registration; testing arrangements; classroom accessibility; special equipment; and counseling for personal, academic, or vocational concerns. Skills courses for credit are offered in study skills and time management. Services and accommodations are available for undergraduate and graduate students.

SUPPORT SERVICES CONTACT INFORMATION

Learning Disability Program/Services: Office of Disability Services
Director: Debra J. Higginbotham
Telephone: 940-397-4618
Fax: 940-397-4814
Contact: Same

LEARNING DISABILITY SERVICES

Requests for the following services/accommodations will be evaluated individually based on appropriate and current documentation.

Allowed in Exams
  Calculator: Yes
  Dictionary: Yes
  Computer: Yes
  Spellchecker: Yes
Extended test time: Yes
Scribes: Yes
Proctors: Yes
Oral exams: Yes
Note-takers: Yes

Distraction-reduced environment: Yes
Tape recording in class: Yes
Books on tape from RFBD: Yes
Taping of books not from RFBD: No
Accommodations for students with ADHD: Yes
Reading machine: Yes
Other assistive technology: Yes
Priority registration: Yes

Added costs for services: No
LD specialists: No
Professional tutors: No
Peer tutors: Yes
Max. hours/wk. for services: Based on need
How professors are notified of LD/ADHD: By both student and director

GENERAL ADMISSIONS INFORMATION

Director of Admissions: Byllie Tims
Telephone: 940-397-4334

ENTRANCE REQUIREMENTS
4 English required, 3 math required, 2 science required, 6 elective required. High school diploma or GED required. Minimum TOEFL is 500. TOEFL required of all international applicants.

Application deadline: August 7
Notification: Rolling
Average GPA: N/A

Average SAT I Math: 479
Average SAT I Verbal: 471
Average ACT: 20

Graduated top 10% of class: 5%
Graduated top 25% of class: 27%
Graduated top 50% of class: 56%

COLLEGE GRADUATION REQUIREMENTS

Course waivers allowed: Yes
Course substitutions allowed: Yes
In what subjects: Varies; waivers and substitutions require an individual review by the Office of Disability Services, chair of the department, and vice president of academics

ADDITIONAL INFORMATION

Environment: The campus is located 135 miles northwest of Dallas.

Student Body
  Undergrad enrollment: 5,093
  Female: 57%
  Male: 43%
  Out-of-state: 7%

Cost Information
  In-state tuition: $2,500
  Out-of-state tuition: $6,804
  Room & board: $3,534
Housing Information
  University housing: Yes
  Percent living on campus: 12%

Greek System
  Fraternity: Yes
  Sorority: Yes
  Athletics: NAIA

SCHREINER COLLEGE

2100 Memorial Boulevard, Kerrville, TX 78028
Phone: 830-792-7217 • Fax: 830-792-7226
E-mail: tbrown@schreiner.edu • Web: www.schreiner.edu
Support level: SP • Institution type: 4-year private

LEARNING DISABILITY PROGRAM AND SERVICES

Extensive learning support is given to each student, and the ultimate goal is for students to be able to succeed without special help. The Learning Support Services (LSS) program is staffed by LD specialists and many tutors. Students with learning disabilities are enrolled in regular college courses and receive individual tutorial assistance in each subject. The goal of the service is to help students succeed in a rigorous academic environment.

LD/ADHD ADMISSIONS INFORMATION

College entrance tests required: Yes
Nonstandardized tests accepted: Yes
Interview required: NR
Essay required: Yes
Documentation required for LD: WAIS-III; achievement
Documentation required for ADHD: Yes
Documentation submitted to: LSS
Special Ed. HS course work accepted: No

Specific course requirements for all applicants: Yes
Separate application required for services: Yes
# of LD applications submitted yearly: 80
# of LD applications accepted yearly: 35
Total # of students receiving LD/ADHD services: 75
Acceptance into program means acceptance into college: Students admitted into the Learning Support Services program are automatically admitted into the College.

ADMISSIONS

Proof of high school diploma and all significant materials relevant to the specific learning disability must be submitted. Applicants should be enrolled in regular, mainstream English courses in high school. The Woodcock-Johnson Achievement Battery is preferred but other tests are accepted. An interview is required and is an important part of the admissions decision. Applicants are considered individually, and selected on the basis of their intellectual ability, motivation, academic preparation, and potential for success. LSS students are admitted contingent upon their participation in the program. Students admitted into LSS are automatically admitted into the College.

ADDITIONAL INFORMATION

Schreiner College offers both an associate's degree and a bachelor's degree. Individual skill development is available in study strategies, test taking, note-taking, reading, math, and written language. There is a professional counselor on staff.

SUPPORT SERVICES CONTACT INFORMATION

Learning Disability Program/Services: Learning Support Services (LSS)
Director: Jude Gallik
  Telephone: 830-729-7256
  Fax: 830-792-7448
Contact: Same

LEARNING DISABILITY SERVICES

Requests for the following services/accommodations will be evaluated individually based on appropriate and current documentation.

Allowed in Exams
  Calculator: No
  Dictionary: No
  Computer: Yes
  Spellchecker: Yes
Extended test time: Yes
Scribes: Yes
Proctors: Yes
Oral exams: Yes
Note-takers: Yes

Distraction-reduced environment: Yes
Tape recording in class: Yes
Books on tape from RFBD: Yes
Taping of books not from RFBD: Yes
Accommodations for students with ADHD: Yes
Reading machine: No
Other assistive technology: No
Priority registration: No

Added costs for services: $5,200
LD specialists: Yes (2)
Professional tutors: 18
Peer tutors: No
Max. hours/wk. for services: Unlimited
How professors are notified of LD/ADHD: By student and program director

GENERAL ADMISSIONS INFORMATION

Director of Admissions: Todd Brown
Telephone: 830-792-7217

ENTRANCE REQUIREMENTS
20 total are required; 4 English required, 4 math required, 2 science required, 2 science lab required, 2 foreign language required, 2 social studies required, 1 history required, 5 elective required. High school diploma or GED required. Minimum TOEFL is 550. TOEFL required of all international applicants.

Application deadline: August 1
Notification: Rolling beginning 9/1
Average GPA: 3.4

Average SAT I Math: 506
Average SAT I Verbal: 496
Average ACT: 21

Graduated top 10% of class: 22%
Graduated top 25% of class: 45%
Graduated top 50% of class: 75%

COLLEGE GRADUATION REQUIREMENTS

Course waivers allowed: No
Course substitutions allowed: Yes
In what subjects: Math and foreign language on a limited basis

ADDITIONAL INFORMATION

Environment: The College is located on 175 acres in a rural wooded area 60 miles northwest of San Antonio.

Student Body
  Undergrad enrollment: 762
  Female: 60%
  Male: 40%
  Out-of-state: 3%

Cost Information
  Tuition: $10,990
  Room & board: $6,480
Housing Information
  University housing: Yes
  Percent living on campus: 57%

Greek System
  Fraternity: Yes
  Sorority: Yes
Athletics: NAIA

SOUTHERN METHODIST UNIVERSITY

PO Box 750181, Dallas, TX 75275-0181
Phone: 214-768-2058 • Fax: 214-768-0103
E-mail: enrol_serv@mail.smu.edu • Web: www.smu.edu
Support level: CS • Institution type: 4-year private

LEARNING DISABILITY PROGRAM AND SERVICES

The goal of Services for Students with Disabilities is to provide students with disabilities services or reasonable accommodations in order to reduce the effects that a disability may have on their performance in a traditional academic setting. The coordinator of Services for Students with Disabilities provides individual attention and support for students needing assistance with any aspect of their campus experience, such as notifying professors, arranging accommodations, referrals, and accessibility. Students requesting LD assistance need to bring in their class schedules as soon as possible after receiving them to arrange accommodations in the desired classes. All students with LD who are requesting accommodations should have made their request with the coordinator of Services for Students with Disabilities within 30 days after the first day of classes. A student with ADHD must provide a report from either a physician or licensed psychologist that elaborates on how the student meets the diagnostic criteria for ADHD; limitations the student is likely to experience in an academic environment which are directly related to the disability (substantial limitation); and suggested accommodations with explanation of why the accommodations are needed to mitigate impact of ADHD on the student.

LD/ADHD ADMISSIONS INFORMATION

College entrance tests required: Yes
Nonstandardized tests accepted: Yes
Interview required: No
Essay required: Yes
Documentation required for LD: A full psychoeducational assessment conducted in the last three years
Documentation required for ADHD: Yes
Documentation submitted to: Services for Students with Disabilities
Special Ed. HS course work accepted: No

Specific course requirements for all applicants: Yes
Separate application required for services: No
# of LD applications submitted yearly: N/A
# of LD applications accepted yearly: N/A
Total # of students receiving LD/ADHD services: 143
Acceptance into program means acceptance into college: Students must be admitted and enrolled at the University and then may request services.

ADMISSIONS

There is no special admissions process for students with LD. If their standardized tests were administered under nonstandard conditions, this will not weigh unfavorably into the admission decision. Regular admission criteria include 4 years English, 3 years math, 3 years science, 3 years social studies, 2 years foreign language. Only foreign language may be waived with other appropriate and approved academic classes taken as substitutions. Candidates who exceed the minimum requirements are advantaged in the selection process.

ADDITIONAL INFORMATION

All students have access to tutoring, writing centers, study skills workshops, and classes to improve reading rate, comprehension, and vocabulary. Skills classes are offered in time management, test strategies, note-taking strategies, organizational skills, concentration, memory, and test anxiety. There are currently 170 students with learning disabilities and 146 students with ADHD receiving services.

SUPPORT SERVICES CONTACT INFORMATION

Learning Disability Program/Services: Services for Students with Disabilities
Director: Rebecca Marin, Coordinator
  E-mail: rmarin@mail.smu.edu
  Telephone: 214-768-4563
  Fax: 214-768-4572
Contact: Same

LEARNING DISABILITY SERVICES

Requests for the following services/accommodations will be evaluated individually based on appropriate and current documentation.

Allowed in Exams
  Calculator: Yes
  Dictionary: Yes
  Computer: Yes
  Spellchecker: Yes
Extended test time: Yes
Scribes: Yes
Proctors: No
Oral exams: Yes
Note-takers: Yes

Distraction-reduced environment: Yes
Tape recording in class: Yes
Books on tape from RFBD: Yes
Taping of books not from RFBD: Yes
Accommodations for students with
  ADHD: Yes
Reading machine: Yes
Other assistive technology: Yes
Priority registration: Yes

Added costs for services: No
LD specialists: Yes (1)
Professional tutors: No
Peer tutors: 50
Max. hours/wk. for services:
  Unlimited
How professors are notified of
  LD/ADHD: By both student and
  director

GENERAL ADMISSIONS INFORMATION

Director of Admissions: Ron Mass
Telephone: 214-768-2731

ENTRANCE REQUIREMENTS

15 total are required; 4 English required, 4 English recommended, 3 math required, 4 math recommended, 3 science required, 4 science recommended, 2 science lab required, 3 science lab recommended, 2 foreign language required, 3 foreign language recommended, 1 social studies required, 2 social studies recommended, 2 history required, 3 history recommended. High school diploma or GED required. Minimum TOEFL is 550. TOEFL required of all international applicants.

Application deadline: January 15
Notification: March 15
Average GPA: 3.2

Average SAT I Math: N/A
Average SAT I Verbal: N/A
Average ACT: N/A

Graduated top 10% of class: 31%
Graduated top 25% of class: 61%
Graduated top 50% of class: 88%

COLLEGE GRADUATION REQUIREMENTS

Course waivers allowed: No
Course substitutions allowed: Yes
In what subjects: Foreign language and math

ADDITIONAL INFORMATION

Environment: The University is located on a 163-acre suburban campus.

Student Body
  Undergrad enrollment: 5,662
  Female: 55%
  Male: 45%
  Out-of-state: 35%

Cost Information
  Tuition: $17,406
  Room & board: $7,177
Housing Information
  University housing: Yes
  Percent living on campus: 48%

Greek System
  Fraternity: Yes
  Sorority: Yes
Athletics: NCAA Division I

SOUTHWEST TEXAS STATE UNIVERSITY

601 University Drive, San Marcos, TX 78666
Phone: 512-245-2364 • Fax: 512-245-8088
E-mail: admissions@swt.edu • Web: www.swt.edu
Support level: CS • Institution type: 4-year public

LEARNING DISABILITY PROGRAM AND SERVICES

The mission of the Office of Disability Services (ODS) is to assist students with disabilities to independently achieve their educational goals and enhance their leadership development by ensuring equal access to all programs, activities, and services. This is accomplished through a decentralizing approach in providing education and awareness so that programs, activities, and services are conducted "in the most integrated setting appropriate." Students with learning disabilities are encouraged to self-identify and to submit documentation once admitted. By identifying and assessing student needs, ODS provides direct services and refers students to appropriate resources on and off campus. ODS also promotes awareness of the special needs and abilities of students with disabilities through educational events and outreach activities.

LD/ADHD ADMISSIONS INFORMATION

College entrance tests required: Yes
Nonstandardized tests accepted: Yes
Interview required: No
Essay required: No
Documentation required for LD: Psychoeducational evaluation
Documentation required for ADHD: Yes
Documentation submitted to: ODS
Special Ed. HS course work accepted: Yes

Specific course requirements for all applicants: Yes
Separate application required for services: No
# of LD applications submitted yearly: N/A
# of LD applications accepted yearly: N/A
Total # of students receiving LD/ADHD services: 350
Acceptance into program means acceptance into college: Students must be admitted and enrolled at the University first and then may request services.

ADMISSIONS

Students with LD must meet the same admission requirements as other applicants. A student whose educational and/or personal goals for success have been negatively impacted due to disability-related reasons may provide a supplemental essay with their application for admission. This information may be considered by the Admissions Office during the review process. General admission requirements include 4 years English, 3 years math, 2 years science, 3 years social studies, .5 years economics, and 2 years foreign language; 2.0 GPA or determined by class rank; 22 ACT is average and 850 SAT is middle 50 percent. Students who are not accepted are free to write letters of appeal to Admissions. All decisions are made by the Admissions Office. Probationary admission plans are available. Students not meeting the required rank in class may be admitted by review through Predicted Academic Success Option (PASO): students in top three-fourths may submit seventh semester transcript and a request that a PASO formula be attempted. (Students who rank in the fourth quarter are not eligible for PASO.) The formula used is an individual's high school rank in combination with ACT or SAT scores. If admitted, these students are placed on a one-semester contract set by the Director of Admissions.

ADDITIONAL INFORMATION

Specialized support services are based on the individual student needs. Services available could include advance registration; books on tape; special testing accommodations; readers; note-takers; liaison and advocacy between students, faculty and staff; assistance with tutoring; and an Academic Excellence seminar. Student Support Services provides one-on-one tutoring in limited subject areas. Remedial courses and an effective learning course are offered. An academic support group course covering various topics is offered for credit. Services and accommodations are available for undergraduate and graduate students. The following campus agencies provide students with special academic support services: ODS, Learning Resource Center, and Student Learning Assistance Center.

SUPPORT SERVICES CONTACT INFORMATION

Learning Disability Program/Services: Office of Disability Services (ODS)
Director: Tina Schultz
  E-mail: ts12@swt.edu
  Telephone: 512-245-3451
  Fax: 512-245-3452
Contact: Richard Poe (for LD/ADHD)
  E-mail: rp16@swt.edu
  Telephone: 512-245-3451
  Fax: 512-245-3452

LEARNING DISABILITY SERVICES

Requests for the following services/accommodations will be evaluated individually based on appropriate and current documentation.

Allowed in Exams
  Calculator: Yes
  Dictionary: Yes
  Computer: Yes
  Spellchecker: Yes
Extended test time: Yes
Scribes: Yes
Proctors: Yes
Oral exams: Yes
Note-takers: No

Distraction-reduced environment: Yes
Tape recording in class: Yes
Books on tape from RFBD: Yes
Taping of books not from RFBD: Yes
Accommodations for students with ADHD: Yes
Reading machine: Yes
Other assistive technology: Yes
Priority registration: Yes

Added costs for services: No
LD specialists: Yes (1)
Professional tutors: 1
Peer tutors: 15
Max. hours/wk. for services: Varies
How professors are notified of LD/ADHD: By student

GENERAL ADMISSIONS INFORMATION

Director of Admissions: Christy Shratichker
Telephone: 512-245-2364

ENTRANCE REQUIREMENTS

15 total are required; 21 total are recommended; 4 English required, 4 English recommended, 3 math required, 3 math recommended, 3 science required, 3 science recommended, 2 science lab required, 2 science lab recommended, 2 foreign language required, 3 foreign language recommended, 3 social studies required, 4 social studies recommended, 2 elective recommended. High school diploma or GED required. Minimum TOEFL is 550. TOEFL required of all international applicants.

Application deadline: July 1
Notification: Rolling beginning 10/1
Average GPA: 3.1

Average SAT I Math: 514
Average SAT I Verbal: 515
Average ACT: 21

Graduated top 10% of class: 15%
Graduated top 25% of class: 49%
Graduated top 50% of class: 93%

COLLEGE GRADUATION REQUIREMENTS

Course waivers allowed: No
Course substitutions allowed: Yes
In what subjects: Foreign language and math

ADDITIONAL INFORMATION

Environment: The 1,091-acre campus is located 30 miles south of Austin, and within easy access of San Antonio.

Student Body
  Undergrad enrollment: 18,856
  Female: 55%
  Male: 45%
  Out-of-state: 1%

Cost Information
  In-state tuition: $1,200
  Out-of-state tuition: $7,680
  Room & board: $4,349
Housing Information
  University housing: Yes
  Percent living on campus: 25%

Greek System
  Fraternity: Yes
  Sorority: Yes
Athletics: NCAA Division I

TEXAS A&M U.—COLLEGE STATION

Admissions Counseling, College Station, TX 77843-1265
Phone: 979-845-3741 • Fax: 979-847-8737
E-mail: admissions@tamu.edu • Web: www.tamu.edu
Support level: S • Institution type: 4-year public

LEARNING DISABILITY PROGRAM AND SERVICES

The Department of Student Life/Services with Disabilities (SSD) exists to provide an academic experience for all students that is fully inclusive and accessible. The philosophy of SSD is to empower students with the skills needed to act as their own advocates and succeed in the mainstream of the University environment. Services include testing, accommodations, note-takers, adaptive technology, interpreters, and registration assistance.

LD/ADHD ADMISSIONS INFORMATION

College entrance tests required: Yes
Nonstandardized tests accepted: Yes
Interview required: No
Essay required: No
Documentation required for LD: Comprehensive psychoeducational testing, intelligence and achievement scores, written report, WISC-III or WAIS-R with WJ
Documentation required for ADHD: Yes
Documentation submitted to: Services for Students with Disabilities
Special Ed. HS course work accepted: No

Specific course requirements for all applicants: Yes
Separate application required for services: Yes
# of LD applications submitted yearly: N/A
# of LD applications accepted yearly: N/A
Total # of students receiving LD/ADHD services: 160-181
Acceptance into program means acceptance into college: Students must be admitted and enrolled at the University first and then may request services.

ADMISSIONS

Applicants with learning disabilities submit the general application form and are considered under the same guidelines as all applicants. Students may have their application reviewed by requesting special consideration based on their disability and by providing letters of recommendation from their high school counselor stating what accommodations are needed in college to be successful. Admissions will be affected by the student's record indicating success with provided accommodations along with any activities and leadership skills. Students not meeting academic criteria for automatic admission may be offered admission to a Summer Provisional Program. These students must take 9–12 credits and receive a grade of C in each of the courses.

ADDITIONAL INFORMATION

Skill classes in math, reading, and writing are offered to the entire student body though the Center for Academic Enhancement. Some of these classes may be taken for college credit. Services and accommodations are available for undergraduate and graduate students. Services include a new Adaptive Technology Laboratory equipped with state-of-the-art technology for students with disabilities, including text-to-speech scanning for personal computer use.

SUPPORT SERVICES CONTACT INFORMATION

Learning Disability Program/Services: Services for Students with Disabilities
Director: Dr. Anne Reber
  E-mail: anne@studentlife.tamu.edu
  Telephone: 979-845-1637
  Fax: 979-458-1214
Contact: Same

LEARNING DISABILITY SERVICES

Requests for the following services/accommodations will be evaluated individually based on appropriate and current documentation.

Allowed in Exams
  Calculator: Yes
  Dictionary: Yes
  Computer: Yes
  Spellchecker: Yes
  Extended test time: Yes
  Scribes: Yes
  Proctors: Yes
  Oral exams: Yes
  Note-takers: Yes

Distraction-reduced environment: Yes
Tape recording in class: Yes
Books on tape from RFBD: Yes
Taping of books not from RFBD: Yes
Accommodations for students with ADHD: Yes
Reading machine: Yes
Other assistive technology: Yes
Priority registration: Yes

Added costs for services: No
LD specialists: No
Professional tutors: No
Peer tutors: No
Max. hours/wk. for services: Unlimited
How professors are notified of LD/ADHD: By student

GENERAL ADMISSIONS INFORMATION

Director of Admissions: Dr. Frank Ashley
Telephone: 979-845-3741

ENTRANCE REQUIREMENTS

4 English required, 4 English recommended, 3 math required, 3 math recommended, 2 science required, 3 science recommended, 2 science lab required, 2 science lab recommended, 2 foreign language required, 3 foreign language recommended, 2 social studies required, 2 social studies recommended, 1 history required, 1 history recommended. High school diploma is required and GED is not accepted. Minimum TOEFL is 550. TOEFL required of all international applicants.

Application deadline: February 15
Notification: Roling
Average GPA: N/A

Average SAT I Math: 603
Average SAT I Verbal: 577
Average ACT: 25

Graduated top 10% of class: 53%
Graduated top 25% of class: 87%
Graduated top 50% of class: 99%

COLLEGE GRADUATION REQUIREMENTS

Course waivers allowed: No
Course substitutions allowed: Yes
In what subjects: Math and foreign language have been the only ones requested

ADDITIONAL INFORMATION

Environment: The school is located on over 5,000 acres in a college town of 100,000 about 90 miles from Houston.

Student Body
  Undergrad enrollment: 36,229
  Female: 49%
  Male: 51%
  Out-of-state: 4%

Cost Information
  In-state tuition: $2,400
  Out-of-state tuition: $8,850
  Room & board: $5,164
Housing Information
  University housing: Yes
  Percent living on campus: 27%

Greek System
  Fraternity: Yes
  Sorority: Yes
Athletics: NCAA Division I

TEXAS A&M UNIV.—KINGSVILLE

Campus Box 105, Kingsville, TX 78363
Phone: 361-593-2315 • Fax: 361-593-2195
E-mail: lknippers@tamuk.edu • Web: www.tamuk.edu
Support: S • Institution: 4-year public

LEARNING DISABILITY PROGRAM AND SERVICES

The University is committed to providing an environment in which every student is encouraged to reach the highest level of personal and educational achievement. Students with disabilities may have special concerns and even special needs. Services vary according to the nature of the disability and are provided by the Center for Life Services and Wellness. Counseling services offer educational, vocational, and personal consultations, as well as tutoring, testing, and academic advising. Students with LD have access to note-takers, readers, writers, and other assistance that the University can provide. All students entering college as freshmen (or transfers with less than 30 hours) have the University's commitment to improve student achievement, retention, depth, and quality of instruction and services.

LD/ADHD ADMISSIONS INFORMATION

College entrance tests required: Yes
Nonstandardized tests accepted: Yes
Interview required: Yes
Essay required: No
Documentation required for LD: Psychoeducational evaluation
Documentation required for ADHD: Yes
Submitted to: Disabled Student Services
Special Ed. HS course work accepted: Yes

Specific course requirements for all applicants: No
Separate application required for services: No
# of LD applications submitted yearly: N/A
# of LD applications accepted yearly: N/A
Total # of students receiving LD/ADHD services: 190
Acceptance into program means acceptance into college: Students must be admitted and enrolled at the University first and then may request services.

ADMISSIONS

All applicants must meet the same general admission criteria. Admissions is very similar to "open-door" admissions and thus most applicants are admitted either conditionally or unconditionally, or on probation. ACT scores are 16+ or greater or SAT is 610 or greater. There are no specific courses required for entrance; however, it is recommended that students take 4 years English, 3 years math, 3 years science, 4 years social studies, 3 years foreign language, .5 year health, 1.5 years physical education, 1 year computer, 1 year art/speech, and 3 years electives. Students with LD are encouraged to self-disclose during the application process. There are two types of admission plans, conditional and unconditional. Unconditional admission is met by achieving 970 or above on the SAT. Conditional admission is achieved by scoring 810–960 on the SAT.

ADDITIONAL INFORMATION

Each freshman receives academic endorsement; developmental educational classes in writing, math, or reading (if necessary); tutoring or study groups; and academic rescue programs for students in academic jeopardy. Skills classes are offered for no credit in stress management and test anxiety. Letters are sent to faculty each semester, hand delivered by the student. DSS provides tutoring on a limited basis. Testing accommodations are available, but students are responsible for scheduling the tests. Accommodations include extended testing time, private rooms, scribes, and readers. DSS will also proctor the exam and return the test to the instructor. DSS relies on a volunteer program for note-takers. Services and accommodations are available to undergraduate and graduate students.

SUPPORT SERVICES CONTACT INFORMATION

Learning Disability Program/Services: Disabled Student Services
Director: Dr. Anne Reber, Coordinator of Student Life
  E-mail: anne@studentlife.tamu.edu
  Telephone: 512-593-3302
  Fax: 512-593-2006
Contact: Same

LEARNING DISABILITY SERVICES

Requests for the following services/accommodations will be evaluated individually based on appropriate and current documentation.

Allowed in Exams
  Calculator: Yes
  Dictionary: No
  Computer: Yes
  Spellchecker: Yes
Extended test time: Yes
Scribes: Yes
Proctors: Yes
Oral exams: Yes
Notetakers: Yes

Distraction-reduced environment: Yes
Tape recording in class: Yes
Books on tape from RFBD: Yes
Taping of books not from RFBD: No
Accommodations for students with ADHD: Yes
Reading machine: No
Other assistive technology: Yes
Priority registration: No

Added costs for services: No
LD specialists: No
Professional tutors: No
Peer tutors: Yes
Max. hours/wk. for services: Case-by-case decision
How professors are notified of LD/ADHD: By student and program director

GENERAL ADMISSIONS INFORMATION

Director of Admissions: Joe Estrada
Telephone: 361-593-2195

ENTRANCE REQUIREMENTS
2.0 GPA recommended. 4 English recommended, 3 math recommended, 4 social studies recommended, 3 science recommended, 3 foreign language recommended, 3 electives recommended, 1 fine art recommended, .5 health recommended, 1 computer recommended. SAT/ACT required. TOEFL required for international students.

Application deadline: NR
Notification: NR
Average GPA: NR
Average SAT I Math: NR
Average SAT I Verbal: NR
Average ACT: NR
Graduated top 10% of class: 12%
Graduated top 25% of class: 32%
Graduated top 50% of class: NR

COLLEGE GRADUATION REQUIREMENTS

Course waivers allowed: Yes
Course substitutions allowed: Yes
In what subjects: Case-by-case decision made by provost

ADDITIONAL INFORMATION

Environment: The 246-acre university campus is located 40 miles southwest of Corpus Christi.

Student Body
  Undergrad enrollment: 4,644
  Female: 47%
  Male: 53%
  Out-of-state: 1%

Cost Information
  In-state tuition: $2,607
  Out-of-state tuition: $9,057
  Room & board: $3,484
Housing Information
  University housing: Yes
  Percent living on campus: 35%

Greek System
  Fraternity: Yes
  Sorority: Yes
Athletics: NCAA Division I

TEXAS TECH UNIVERSITY

PO Box 45005, Lubbock, TX 79409-5005
Phone: 806-742-1480 • Fax: 806-742-0980
E-mail: nsr@ttu.edu • Web: www.texastech.edu
Support level: S • Institution type: 4-year public

LEARNING DISABILITY PROGRAM AND SERVICES

It is the philosophy of Texas Tech University to serve each student on a case-by-case basis. All services rendered are supported by adequate documentation. The University firmly believes that all students should be and will become effective self-advocates. Students with disabilities attending Texas Tech will find numerous programs designed to provide services and to promote access to all phases of university activity. Such programming is coordinated through the Dean of Students' office with the assistance of an advisory committee of both disabled and nondisabled students, faculty, and staff. Services to disabled students are offered through a decentralized network of university and nonuniversity resources. This means that many excellent services are available but that it is up to the student to initiate them. Each student is encouraged to act as his or her own advocate and take the major responsibility for securing services and accommodations. The Disabled Student Services team, Dean of Students' office, faculty, and staff are supportive in this effort.

LD/ADHD ADMISSIONS INFORMATION

College entrance tests required: Yes
Nonstandardized tests accepted: Yes
Interview required: No
Essay required: No
Documentation required for LD: Psychoeducational evaluation
Documentation required for ADHD: Yes
Documentation submitted to: Disabled Student Services
Special Ed. HS course work accepted: Yes

Specific course requirements for all applicants: Yes
Separate application required for services: No
# of LD applications submitted yearly: N/A
# of LD applications accepted yearly: N/A
Total # of students receiving LD/ADHD services: 450
Acceptance into program means acceptance into college: Students must be admitted and enrolled at the University first and then may request services.

ADMISSIONS

There is no special admissions process for students with LD, and all applicants must meet the same criteria. All students must have 4 years English, 3 years math, 2.5 years social studies, 2 years science, and 3.5 years electives. Any applicant who scores a 1200 on the SAT or a 29 on the ACT is automatically admitted regardless of class rank. Some students are admissible who do not meet the stated requirements, but they must have a 2.0 GPA for a provisional admission. After a student is admitted, Disabled Student Services requires documentation that provides a diagnosis, provides an indication of the severity of the disability, and offers recommendations for accommodations, in order for students to receive services.

ADDITIONAL INFORMATION

Support services through Disabled Student Services include Academic Support Services, which can help students develop habits enabling them to get a good education. Students may receive academic support services in the PASS (Programs for Academic Support Services) Center, which is open to all students on campus. Services offered free of charge include tutor referral services (paid by student); study skills group; hour-long workshops that target a variety of subjects from "Overcoming Math Anxiety" to "Preparing for Finals"; a self-help learning lab with videotapes; computer-assisted instruction; individual consultations assisting students with specific study problems; and setting study skills improvement goals. All students with LD are offered priority registration. Services and accommodations are available for undergraduate and graduate students.

SUPPORT SERVICES CONTACT INFORMATION

Learning Disability Program/Services: Disabled Student Services
Director: Frank Silvas, Director of Disabled Student Services
  E-mail: frank.silvas@ttu.edu
  Telephone: 806-742-2405
  Fax: 806-742-0138
Contact: Melissa Hays, Counseling Specialist
  E-mail: melissa.hays@ttu.edu

LEARNING DISABILITY SERVICES

Requests for the following services/accommodations will be evaluated individually based on appropriate and current documentation.

Allowed in Exams
  Calculator: Yes
  Dictionary: Y/N
  Computer: Yes
  Spellchecker: Yes
Extended test time: Yes
Scribes: Yes
Proctors: Yes
Oral exams: Yes
Note-takers: Yes

Distraction-reduced environment: Yes
Tape recording in class: Yes
Books on tape from RFBD: Yes
Taping of books not from RFBD: No
Accommodations for students with
  ADHD: Yes
Reading machine: Yes
Other assistive technology: Yes
Priority registration: Yes

Added costs for services: No
LD specialists: No
Professional tutors: Yes
Peer tutors: Yes
Max. hours/wk. for services: Unlimited
How professors are notified of
  LD/ADHD: By student

GENERAL ADMISSIONS INFORMATION

Director of Admissions: Marty Grassel
Telephone: 806-742-1480

ENTRANCE REQUIREMENTS

17 total are required; 4 English required, 3 math required, 2 science required, 2 science lab required, 2 foreign language required, 2 social studies required, 3 elective required. High school diploma is required and GED is not accepted. Minimum TOEFL is 550. TOEFL required of all international applicants.

Application deadline: August 1
Notification: Rolling
Average GPA: NR

Average SAT I Math: 554
Average SAT I Verbal: 537
Average ACT: 23

Graduated top 10% of class: 21%
Graduated top 25% of class: 49%
Graduated top 50% of class: 84%

COLLEGE GRADUATION REQUIREMENTS

Course waivers allowed: No
Course substitutions allowed: Yes
In what subjects: Possible in math and foreign language

ADDITIONAL INFORMATION

Environment: The University is located on 1,839 acres in an urban area in Lubbock.

Student Body
  Undergrad enrollment: 20,518
  Female: 46%
  Male: 54%
  Out-of-state: 4%

Cost Information
  In-state tuition: $1,797
  Out-of-state tuition: $8,277
  Room & board: $4,887
Housing Information
  University housing: Yes
  Percent living on campus: 26%

Greek System
  Fraternity: Yes
  Sorority: Yes
Athletics: NCAA Division I

UNIVERSITY OF HOUSTON

Office of Admissions, 4800 Calhoun, Houston, TX 77204-2161
Phone: 713-743-1010 • Fax: 713-743-9633
E-mail: admissions@uh.edu • Web: www.uh.edu
Support level: CS • Institution type: 4-year public

LEARNING DISABILITY PROGRAM AND SERVICES

The Center for Students with Disabilities provides a wide variety of academic support services to students with all types of disabilities. Its goal is to help ensure that these otherwise qualified students are able to successfully compete with nondisabled students by receiving equal educational opportunities in college as mandated by law. Through advocacy efforts and a deliberate, ongoing, public education program, the staff strives to heighten the awareness of needs, legal rights, and abilities of persons with handicapping conditions.

LD/ADHD ADMISSIONS INFORMATION

College entrance tests required: Yes
Nonstandardized tests accepted: Yes
Interview required: No
Essay required: No
Documentation required for LD: WAIS-III; WJ; or a neuropsychological evaluation: within 3 years
Documentation required for ADHD: Yes
Documentation submitted to: Center for Students with Disabilities
Special Ed. HS course work accepted: Yes

Specific course requirements for all applicants: Yes
Separate application required for services: No
# of LD applications submitted yearly: N/A
# of LD applications accepted yearly: N/A
Total # of students receiving LD/ADHD services: 185
Acceptance into program means acceptance into college: Students must be admitted and enrolled at the University first and then may request services.

ADMISSIONS

General admission requirements are: top 10 percent, no minimum on SAT or ACT; first quarter, 920 SAT I or 19 ACT; second quarter, 1010 SAT I or 21 ACT; third quarter, 1100 SAT I or 24 ACT; or fourth quarter, 1180 SAT I or 26 ACT. Courses required are 2 years English, 3 years math, 2 years science, and 3 years social studies. Applicants who do not qualify for admission may request a further review through the Individual Admission Process. The review will be based on an overall assessment of each applicant's circumstances in respect to potential for academic success. If an applicant to a program with different requirements does not meet the stated standards, but does meet the general admission requirements, then that applicant may be admitted to the University with an undeclared status.

ADDITIONAL INFORMATION

Students who come from an educationally and/or economically disadvantaged background may be eligible to participate in the UH "Challenger Program" which is designed to provide intense support to students who face obstacles in their efforts to successfully complete college. Services to all students include tutoring, counseling, financial aid advisement, and social enrichment. Remedial reading, writing, and study skills courses for three hours of noncollege credit are offered. There are also remedial courses for credit in English and college algebra. Other services include assistance with petitions for course substitutions, peer support groups, free carbonized paper for note-taking, textbooks and class handouts put on tape by office staff or volunteer readers, and advocacy for student's legal rights to "reasonable and necessary accommodations" in their course work. Extended tutoring is available at the Learning Support Services and Math Lab.

SUPPORT SERVICES CONTACT INFORMATION

Learning Disability Program/Services: Center for Students with Disabilities
Director: Cheryl Amoruso
    E-mail: camoruso@bayou.uh.edu
    Telephone: 713-743-5400
    Fax: 713-743-5396
Contact: Barbara H. Poursoltan, Asst. Director
    E-mail: bharmonp@bayou.uh.edu
    Telephone: 713-743-5400
    Fax: 713-743-5396

LEARNING DISABILITY SERVICES

Requests for the following services/accommodations will be evaluated individually based on appropriate and current documentation.

Allowed in Exams		
Calculator: Yes	**Distraction-reduced environment:** Yes	**Added costs for services:** No
Dictionary: Yes	**Tape recording in class:** Yes	**LD specialists:** Yes (1)
Computer: Yes	**Books on tape from RFBD:** Yes	**Professional tutors:** 1
Spellchecker: Yes	**Taping of books not from RFBD:** Yes	**Peer tutors:** Yes
Extended test time: Yes	**Accommodations for students with**	**Max. hours/wk. for services:** 2–4
Scribes: Yes	**ADHD:** Yes	**How professors are notified of**
Proctors: Yes	**Reading machine:** No	**LD/ADHD:** By student
Oral exams: Yes	**Other assistive technology:** Yes	
Note-takers: Yes	**Priority registration:** Yes	

GENERAL ADMISSIONS INFORMATION

Director of Admissions: Adrian Higgins
Telephone: 713-743-1010

ENTRANCE REQUIREMENTS
12 total are required; 4 English required, 3 math required, 2 science required, 2 science lab required, 2 foreign language recommended, 3 social studies required. High school diploma or GED required. Minimum TOEFL is 550. TOEFL required of all international applicants.

Application deadline: May 1	**Average SAT I Math:** 533	**Graduated top 10% of class:** 20%
Notification: Rolling beginning 1/16	**Average SAT I Verbal:** 515	**Graduated top 25% of class:** 48%
Average GPA: 3.0	**Average ACT:** 21	**Graduated top 50% of class:** 81%

COLLEGE GRADUATION REQUIREMENTS

Course waivers allowed: Yes
Course substitutions allowed: Yes
In what subjects: Foreign language course substitutions have been granted most recently

ADDITIONAL INFORMATION

Environment: The University is located on 540 acres in an urban area 3 miles from Houston.

Student Body	Cost Information	Greek System
Undergrad enrollment: 24,402	**In-state tuition:** $960	**Fraternity:** Yes
Female: 53%	**Out-of-state tuition:** $6,120	**Sorority:** Yes
Male: 47%	**Room & board:** $5,025	**Athletics:** NCAA Division I
Out-of-state: 2%	**Housing Information**	
	University housing: Yes	
	Percent living on campus: 9%	

University of Houston

UNIVERSITY OF NORTH TEXAS

PO Box 311277, Denton, TX 76203-1277
Phone: 800-868-8211 • Fax: 940-565-2408
E-mail: undergrad@unt.edu • Web: www.unt.edu
Support level: CS • Institution type: 4-year public

LEARNING DISABILITY PROGRAM AND SERVICES

The goal of the Office of Disability Accommodations is to ensure that qualified students with disabilities have access to reasonable and appropriate services and learning resources needed to facilitate matriculation and successful completion of academic programs at the University. The office serves as a liaison to ensure that assistance and/or accommodation/adjustments are available for students with disabilities to enable them full access to the educational facilities and services at the University. The office provides consultation and assistance to academic and general service offices in making adaptations and adjustments for students with disabilities. It also provides alternative testing sites and proctors when the academic department is unable to provide assistance.

LD/ADHD ADMISSIONS INFORMATION

College entrance tests required: Yes
Nonstandardized tests accepted: Yes
Interview required: NR
Essay required: No
Documentation required for LD: WAIS-III; WRAT-R; Nelson-Denny Reading test; Bender G
Documentation required for ADHD: Yes
Documentation submitted to: Office of Disability Services
Special Ed. HS course work accepted: No

Specific course requirements for all applicants: Yes
Separate application required for services: No
# of LD applications submitted yearly: N/A
# of LD applications accepted yearly: N/A
Total # of students receiving LD/ADHD services: 225+
Acceptance into program means acceptance into college: Students must be admitted and enrolled at the University first and then may request services. Students denied admission may appeal the decision.

ADMISSIONS

Students must apply directly to the Admissions Office and meet the current requirements. When a student makes a written request for waivers for admission requirements, the request is sent to an individual approval review committee for consideration. Students in the top 10 percent of their high school class must submit ACT/SAT scores but no specific score is required; students in the remainder of top quarter need minimum 920 SAT I or 19 ACT; the second quarter need a minimum 1010 SAT I or 21 ACT; the third quarter need a minimum 1100 SAT I or 24 ACT; and the fourth quarter need a minimum 1180 SAT I or 27 ACT. If a student is not accepted, there is an appeal process on the basis of the learning disability. These students may need letters of support, a statement of commitment from the student, and an evaluation of the documentation by the Disability Office. Admission decisions are made by the Office of Admissions and the Office of Disability Accommodations.

ADDITIONAL INFORMATION

The Center for Development Studies provides tutoring to build academic knowledge and skills in various subject areas; academic counseling to plan class schedules and to evaluate areas of strengths and weaknesses; personal counseling to develop greater self-understanding and to learn ways to cope with adjustments to college and the pressures of life; and study skills assessment for evaluating and improving academic performance. Skills courses for credit are offered in time management, career choice, and study skills. Students requesting a distraction-free environment for tests must provide the appropriate documentation. Calculators, dictionaries, computers, and spellcheckers are allowed with instructor's approval. Services and accommodations are available for undergraduate and graduate students.

SUPPORT SERVICES CONTACT INFORMATION

Learning Disability Program/Services: Office of Disability Accommodations
Director: Steve Pickett, MS, CRC
  E-mail: steve@dsa.admin.unt.edu
  Telephone: 940-565-4323
  Fax: 940-565-4376
Contact: Dee Wilson

LEARNING DISABILITY SERVICES

Requests for the following services/accommodations will be evaluated individually based on appropriate and current documentation.

Allowed in Exams
  Calculator: Y/N
  Dictionary: Y/N
  Computer: Y/N
  Spellchecker: Y/N
Extended test time: Yes
Scribes: Yes
Proctors: Yes
Oral exams: Yes
Note-takers: Yes

Distraction-reduced environment: Yes
Tape recording in class: Yes
Books on tape from RFBD: Yes
Taping of books not from RFBD: Yes
Accommodations for students with ADHD: Yes
Reading machine: Yes
Other assistive technology: Yes
Priority registration: Yes

Added costs for services: No
LD specialists: Yes (1)
Professional tutors: No
Peer tutors: Yes
Max. hours/wk. for services: Unlimited
How professors are notified of LD/ADHD: By student and program director

GENERAL ADMISSIONS INFORMATION

Director of Admissions: Marcilla Collinsworth
Telephone: 800-868-8211

ENTRANCE REQUIREMENTS

21 total are required; 4 English required, 4 math required, 3 science required, 3 foreign language required, 4 social studies required, 3 elective required. High school diploma or GED required. Minimum TOEFL is 550. TOEFL required of all international applicants.

Application deadline: August 22
Notification: Rolling beginning 6/15
Average GPA: NR

Average SAT I Math: 541
Average SAT I Verbal: 536
Average ACT: 22

Graduated top 10% of class: 11%
Graduated top 25% of class: 51%
Graduated top 50% of class: 84%

COLLEGE GRADUATION REQUIREMENTS

Course waivers allowed: No
Course substitutions allowed: Yes
In what subjects: Determined on a case-by-case basis by each department; approval is not automatic, it is dependent on the student's situation

ADDITIONAL INFORMATION

Environment: The University is located on 425 acres in an urban area 35 miles north of Dallas/Ft. Worth.

Student Body
  Undergrad enrollment: 20,449
  Female: 54%
  Male: 46%
  Out-of-state: 5%

Cost Information
  In-state tuition: $2,070
  Out-of-state tuition: $8,550
  Room & board: $8,192
Housing Information
  University housing: Yes
  Percent living on campus: 16%

Greek System
  Fraternity: Yes
  Sorority: Yes
  Athletics: NCAA Division I

UNIVERSITY OF TEXAS—EL PASO

500 W. University Ave., El Paso, TX 79968
Phone: 915-831-2811 • Fax: 915-831-2161
Web: www.utep.edu
Support level: S • Institution type: 4-year public

LEARNING DISABILITY PROGRAM AND SERVICES

The Disabled Student Services Office (DSSO) provides a program of support and advocacy for students with learning disabilities. Services offered include peer support group, assistance with learning strategies, note-takers for lectures, scribs/readers, extended time for in-class work, and altered format, such as oral exams. There is also a Tutoring and Learning Center with free services including study skill assistance, subject-area tutoring, life management skills, exam reviews, peer mentoring, and distance tutoring.

LD/ADHD ADMISSIONS INFORMATION

College entrance tests required: Yes
Nonstandardized tests accepted: Yes
Interview required: No
Essay required: No
Documentation required for LD: WAIS-III; WJ; Benton
   Visual Retention: recent
Documentation required for ADHD: Yes
Documentation submitted to: DSSO
Special Ed. HS course work accepted: Yes

Specific course requirements for all applicants: Yes
Separate application required for services: N/A
# of LD applications submitted yearly: N/A
# of LD applications accepted yearly: N/A
Total # of students receiving LD/ADHD services: 60
Acceptance into program means acceptance into
   college: Students must be accepted and enrolled at the
   University and then may request services.

ADMISSIONS

There is no special admissions process for students with learning disabilities. General admission criteria requires students to have a high school diploma and ACT/SAT; class rank or GPA are not considered. Course requirements include 4 years English, 3 years math, 3 years science, 4 years social studies, 3 years foreign language, .5 years health, 1 year fine arts, 1.5 years PE, and 1 year computer science. For students not otherwise eligible to enter due to grades or scores, a study skills class is required plus other courses from a course list.

ADDITIONAL INFORMATION

In order to receive services, students must meet with the Director of DSSO. Students need to provide current documentation from an appropriate licensed professional. Services offered to students, when appropriate, are diagnostic testing, peer support group, assistance with learning strategies, and priority registration. Classroom accommodations include note-takers, assistive technology, scribes, readers, extended testing time, and exam modifications. In the Tutoring and Learning Center, students can access study skills assistance, subject-area tutoring, life management skills, and a special needs room with state-of-the-art technology. Currently there are 60 students with LD and 17 with ADHD receiving services.

SUPPORT SERVICES CONTACT INFORMATION

Learning Disability Program/Services: Disabled Student Services Office
Director: Susan J. Lopez
E-mail: slopez@utep.edu
Telephone: 915-747-5148
Fax: 915-747-8712
Contact: Hector E. Flores
E-mail: hflores@utep.edu
Telephone: 915-747-5148
Fax: 915-747-8712

LEARNING DISABILITY SERVICES

Requests for the following services/accommodations will be evaluated individually based on appropriate and current documentation.

Allowed in Exams	**Distraction-reduced environment:** Yes	**Added costs for services:** No
Calculator: Yes	**Tape recording in class:** Yes	**LD specialists:** No
Dictionary: Yes	**Books on tape from RFBD:** Yes	**Professional tutors:** 63
Computer: Yes	**Taping of books not from RFBD:** Yes	**Peer tutors:** 12
Spellchecker: Yes	**Accommodations for students with**	**Max. hours/wk. for services:** 12
Extended test time: Yes	**ADHD:** Yes	**How professors are notified of**
Scribes: Yes	**Reading machine:** Yes	**LD/ADHD:** By student
Proctors: Yes	**Other assistive technology:** No	
Oral exams: Yes	**Priority registration:** Yes	
Note-takers: Yes		

GENERAL ADMISSIONS INFORMATION

Director of Admissions: Diana Guerrero
Telephone: 915-747-7345

ENTRANCE REQUIREMENTS
21 total are recommended; 4 English recommended, 4 math recommended, 3 science recommended, 3 foreign language recommended, 4 social studies recommended. High school diploma or GED required. Minimum TOEFL is 500.

Application deadline: July 31	**Average SAT I Math:** N/A	**Graduated top 10% of class:** 15%
Notification: N/A	**Average SAT I Verbal:** N/A	**Graduated top 25% of class:** 37%
Average GPA: 3.3	**Average ACT:** N/A	**Graduated top 50% of class:** 68%

COLLEGE GRADUATION REQUIREMENTS

Course waivers allowed: No
Course substitutions allowed: Yes
In what subjects: Math and foreign language

ADDITIONAL INFORMATION

Environment: The University is located on a 360-acre urban campus.

Student Body	**Cost Information**	**Greek System**
Undergrad enrollment: 12,955	In-state tuition: $1,776	Fraternity: Yes
Female: 54%	Out-of-state tuition: $7,152	Sorority: Yes
Male: 46%	Room & board: $5,165	Athletics: NCAA Division I
Out-of-state: 14%	**Housing Information**	
	University housing: Yes	
	Percent living on campus: 2%	

UNIV. OF TEXAS—PAN AMERICAN

1201 West University Drive, Edinburg, TX 78539
Phone: (956) 381-2206 • Fax: (956) 381-2212
E-mail: admissions@panam.edu • Web: www.panam.edu
Support level: S • Institution type: 4-year public

LEARNING DISABILITY PROGRAM AND SERVICES

The Office of Services for Persons with Disabilities (OSPD) is a component of the Division of Enrollment and Student Services at the University of Texas-Pan American. It is designed and committed to providing support services to meet the educational, career, and personal needs of persons with disabilities attending or planning to attend the University. Students requesting accommodations must put their requests in writing, must provide documentation from a professional who is qualified to diagnose and verify the particular disability; and the testing and documentation must be current within three years. OSPD will use the documentation to properly prepare an assistance plan for the student to use while enrolled at the University. It typically takes at least 30 days to process requests for services or accommodations.

LD/ADHD ADMISSIONS INFORMATION

College entrance tests required: Yes
Nonstandardized tests accepted: Yes
Interview required: Yes
Essay required: No
Documentation required for LD: Psychoeducational
  evaluation
Documentation required for ADHD: Yes
Documentation submitted to: OSPD
Special Ed. HS course work accepted: No

Specific course requirements for all applicants: Yes
Separate application required for services: No
# of LD applications submitted yearly: N/A
# of LD applications accepted yearly: N/A
Total # of students receiving LD/ADHD services: 34
Acceptance into program means acceptance into
  college: Students must be admitted and enrolled at the
  University first and then may request services.

ADMISSIONS

Students with learning disabilities must meet the same admission requirements as all other applicants. The criteria for entering freshmen are a high school diploma denoting graduation with "Honors" or "Advanced" or rank in the top 50 percent or 20+ ACT or 1200+ SAT; and 4 years English, 4 years math, 3 years science, 4 years social studies, 3 years foreign language, 1 year fine arts, 1.5 years PE, .5 years health, 0–1 year computers, and 2.5 years electives. Students not meeting these criteria may enroll through the Provisional Enrollment Program (PEP). PEP students must: attend orientation, be advised by counseling center, select classes prescribed, and participate in noncredit programs to develop study and academic skills. PEP students with a total of nine or more hours may fulfill criteria for regular admission by meeting specific requirements in GPA and completion of attempted hours. PEP students who do not have a 2.0 GPA after nine hours can take an additional semester if they have at least a 1.5 GPA and meet successful completion of attempted hours. Some students not eligible to continue may petition the Admissions Committee.

ADDITIONAL INFORMATION

OSPD provides the following services: assessment for special needs; note-takers; readers and writers; advisement, counseling, and guidance; assistance with admissions, orientation, registration; referral services to other university units; liaison between students, faculty, staff, and others; resolution of problems/concerns; computer hardware and software; reading machine. Skills classes for credit are offered in time management, test-taking strategies, note-taking skills, reading text, and stress management. OSPD assists students in preparing appeals and works with faculty/administrators to secure waivers. Services and accommodations are available for undergraduate and graduate students.

SUPPORT SERVICES CONTACT INFORMATION

Learning Disability Program/Services: Office of Services for Persons with Disabilities (OSPD)
Director: Rick Gray, RN, MBA
  E-mail: grayr@panam.edu
  Telephone: 956-316-7005
  Fax: 956-316-7034
Contact: Chris Iglesias, Coordinator
  E-mail: ospd@panam.edu
  Telephone: 956-316-7005
  Fax: 956-316-7034

LEARNING DISABILITY SERVICES

Requests for the following services/accommodations will be evaluated individually based on appropriate and current documentation.

Allowed in Exams
  Calculator: Yes
  Dictionary: Yes
  Computer: Yes
  Spellchecker: Yes
Extended test time: Yes
Scribes: Yes
Proctors: Yes
Oral exams: Yes
Note-takers: Yes

Distraction-reduced environment: Yes
Tape recording in class: Yes
Books on tape from RFBD: Yes
Taping of books not from RFBD: Yes
Accommodations for students with ADHD: Yes
Reading machine: Yes
Other assistive technology: Yes
Priority registration: Yes

Added costs for services: No
LD specialists: No
Professional tutors: 15
Peer tutors: 50
Max. hours/wk. for services: 40
How professors are notified of LD/ADHD: By both student and director

GENERAL ADMISSIONS INFORMATION

Director of Admissions: David Zuniga
Telephone: 956-381-2206

ENTRANCE REQUIREMENTS
24 total are required; 4 English required, 3 math required, 3 science required, 2 foreign language required, 3 social studies required, 3 elective required. Minimum TOEFL is 550. TOEFL required of all international applicants.

Application deadline: July 10
Notification: Rolling
Average GPA: N/A

Average SAT I Math: 455
Average SAT I Verbal: 445
Average ACT: 18

Graduated top 10% of class: 11%
Graduated top 25% of class: 35%
Graduated top 50% of class: 69%

COLLEGE GRADUATION REQUIREMENTS

Course waivers allowed: Yes
Course substitutions allowed: Yes
In what subjects: Varies based on the student's degree plan; requests can be made through the program advisors, department chairs, and the vice president for academic affairs; an appeal process is required

ADDITIONAL INFORMATION

Environment: The campus is in a small town near the Mexican border.

Student Body
  Undergrad enrollment: NR
  Female: 57%
  Male: 43%
  Out-of-state: 1%

Cost Information
  In-state tuition: $1,860
  Out-of-state tuition: $8,210
  Room & board: $5,531
Housing Information
  University housing: Yes
  Percent living on campus: 1%

Greek System
  Fraternity: Yes
  Sorority: Yes
  Athletics: NCAA Division I

BRIGHAM YOUNG UNIVERSITY

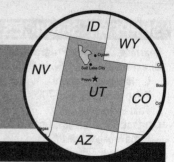

A-183 ASB, Provo, UT 84602-1110
Phone: 801-378-2507 • Fax: 801-378-4264
E-mail: admissions@byu.edu • Web: www.byu.edu
Support level: CS • Institution type: 4-year private

LEARNING DISABILITY PROGRAM AND SERVICES

The Services to Students with Learning Disabilities program works to provide individualized programs to meet the specific needs of each student, assisting in developing strengths to meet the challenges, and making arrangements for accommodations and special services as required. All accommodations are available on an individual case-by-case basis. Students with LD/ADHD must provide current documentation that demonstrates the presence of the disability. SDS can help students understand their disability, learn self-advocacy skills, and receive appropriate accommodations.

LD/ADHD ADMISSIONS INFORMATION

College entrance tests required: Yes
Nonstandardized tests accepted: Yes
Interview required: No
Essay required: Yes
Documentation required for LD: Psychoeducational evaluation
Documentation required for ADHD: Yes
Documentation submitted to: SSD
Special Ed. HS course work accepted: Yes

Specific course requirements for all applicants: Yes
Separate application required for services: Yes
# of LD applications submitted yearly: N/A
# of LD applications accepted yearly: N/A
Total # of students receiving LD/ADHD services: 101
Acceptance into program means acceptance into college: Students must be admitted and enrolled at the University first and then may request services.

ADMISSIONS

There is no special admission process for students with learning disabilities. The following factors are considered in the admission process: ecclesiastical evaluation, GPA, ACT, percentage of courses that are college preparatory, extracurricular activities, and an essay. Suggested courses include 4 years English, 3–4 years math, 2–3 years science, 2 years history or government, 2 years foreign language, and 2 years of literature or writing. Evaluations are made on an individualized basis with a system weighted for college-prep courses and core classes.

ADDITIONAL INFORMATION

Workshops are offered for noncredit. The following are some examples: math anxiety, memory, overcoming procrastination, self-appreciation, stress management, test taking, textbook comprehension, time management, and communication. Additional services include extended testing time, priority registration, distraction-free testing sites, reduced course loads, note-taking, alternative modes of evaluation, staggered exams, and counseling support and advising. Services and accommodations are available for undergraduate and graduate students.

SUPPORT SERVICES CONTACT INFORMATION

Learning Disability Program/Services: Services to Students with Learning Disabilities
Director: Paul Byrd
  Telephone: 801-378-2767
  Fax: 801-378-6667
Contact: Same

LEARNING DISABILITY SERVICES

Requests for the following services/accommodations will be evaluated individually based on appropriate and current documentation.

Allowed in Exams
  Calculator: Yes
  Dictionary: Yes
  Computer: Yes
  Spellchecker: Yes
Extended test time: Yes
Scribes: Yes
Proctors: Yes
Oral exams: Yes
Note-takers: Yes

Distraction-reduced environment: Yes
Tape recording in class: Yes
Books on tape from RFBD: Yes
Taping of books not from RFBD: Yes
Accommodations for students with ADHD: Yes
Reading machine: Yes
Other assistive technology: Yes
Priority registration: Yes

Added costs for services: No
LD specialists: Yes
Professional tutors: No
Peer tutors: Yes
Max. hours/wk. for services: Varies
How professors are notified of LD/ADHD: By student with letter

GENERAL ADMISSIONS INFORMATION

Director of Admissions: Jeff Tanner
Telephone: 801-378-1211

ENTRANCE REQUIREMENTS

4 English required, 4 English recommended, 3 math required, 4 math recommended, 2 science required, 3 science recommended, 2 science lab required, 3 science lab recommended, 2 foreign language required, 3 foreign language recommended, 2 history required, 2 history recommended. High school diploma or GED required. Minimum TOEFL is 500. TOEFL required of all international applicants.

Application deadline: February 15
Notification: Rolling
Average GPA: 3.7

Average SAT I Math: N/A
Average SAT I Verbal: N/A
Average ACT: 27

Graduated top 10% of class: 54%
Graduated top 25% of class: 88%
Graduated top 50% of class: 98%

COLLEGE GRADUATION REQUIREMENTS

Course waivers allowed: Yes
Course substitutions allowed: Yes
In what subjects: Foreign language and math

ADDITIONAL INFORMATION

Environment: The University is located in a suburban area 45 miles south of Salt Lake City.

Student Body
  Undergrad enrollment: 30,037
  Female: 53%
  Male: 47%
  Out-of-state: 71%

Cost Information
  Tuition: $2,830 ($4,330 for non-LDS members)
  Room & board: $4,454
Housing Information
  University housing: Yes
  Percent living on campus: 85%

Greek System
  Fraternity: Yes
  Sorority: Yes
Athletics: NCAA Division I

SOUTHERN UTAH UNIVERSITY

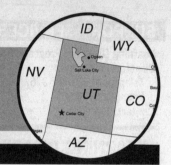

Admissions Office, 351 West Center, Cedar City, UT 84720
Phone: 435-586-7740 • Fax: 435-865-8223
E-mail: adminfo@suu.edu • Web: www.suu.edu
Support level: S • Institution type: 4-year public

LEARNING DISABILITY PROGRAM AND SERVICES

The philosophy of Student Support Services (SSS) is to promote self-sufficiency and achievement. SSS assists college students with developmental classes, skills courses, academic and tutorial support, and advisement. In particular, disabled students are encouraged and supported in advocating for themselves. The University provides a full variety of services and accommodations for all disabled students. The academic support coordinator assists students with enrollment in SSS and helps them identify academic areas where they feel a need to strengthen skills to assure college success.

LD/ADHD ADMISSIONS INFORMATION

College entrance tests required: Yes
Nonstandardized tests accepted: Yes
Interview required: No
Essay required: No
Documentation required for LD: Diagnostic test for LD, IEPs, recommendations
Documentation required for ADHD: Yes
Documentation submitted to: Students with Disabilities
Special Ed. HS course work accepted: No

Specific course requirements for all applicants: Yes
Separate application required for services: No
# of LD applications submitted yearly: N/A
# of LD applications accepted yearly: N/A
Total # of students receiving LD/ADHD services: 30
Acceptance into program means acceptance into college: Students must be admitted and enrolled at the University first and then may request services.

ADMISSIONS

Students with learning disabilities submit the general application form. Students must have at least a 2.0 GPA and show competency in English, math, science, and social studies. The University uses an admissions index derived from the combination of the high school GPA and results of either the ACT or SAT. If students are not admissible through the regular process, special consideration by a Committee Review can be gained through reference letters and a personal letter. The University is allowed to admit 5 percent in "flex" admission. These applications are reviewed by a committee consisting of the Director of Support Services and representatives from the Admissions Office. Students are encouraged to self-disclose their learning disability and submit documentation.

ADDITIONAL INFORMATION

Tutoring is available in small groups or one-to-one, free of charge. Basic skills classes, for credit, are offered in English, reading, math, math anxiety, language, and study skills. Students with LD/ADHD may enroll in Student Success Course, which is a course that focuses on developing effective habits. Students are supported as they practice these habits in a "Companion Class." This course also enhances time management skills and efficient information processing.

SUPPORT SERVICES CONTACT INFORMATION

Learning Disability Program/Services: Students with Disabilities
Director: Carmen R. Alldredge
  E-mail: alldredge@suu.edu
  Telephone: 435-865-8022
  Fax: 435-865-8235
Contact: Same

LEARNING DISABILITY SERVICES

Requests for the following services/accommodations will be evaluated individually based on appropriate and current documentation.

Allowed in Exams
  Calculator: Yes
  Dictionary: Yes
  Computer: Yes
  Spellchecker: Yes
Extended test time: Yes
Scribes: Yes
Proctors: Yes
Oral exams: Yes
Note-takers: Yes

Distraction-reduced environment: Yes
Tape recording in class: Yes
Books on tape from RFBD: Yes
Taping of books not from RFBD: Yes
Accommodations for students with
  ADHD: Yes
Reading machine: Yes
Other assistive technology: Yes
Priority registration: Yes

Added costs for services: No
LD specialists: No
Professional tutors: 4
Peer tutors: 6
Max. hours/wk. for services:
  Unlimited
How professors are notified of
  LD/ADHD: By both student and
  director

GENERAL ADMISSIONS INFORMATION

Director of Admissions: Dale Orton
Telephone: 435-586-7742

ENTRANCE REQUIREMENTS

11 total are recommended; 4 English recommended, 3 math recommended, 2 science recommended, 1 science lab recommended, 2 social studies recommended, 1 history recommended. High school diploma or GED required. Minimum TOEFL is 500. TOEFL required of all international applicants.

Application deadline: July 1
Notification: Rolling
Average GPA: 3.4

Average SAT I Math: 487
Average SAT I Verbal: 498
Average ACT: 22

Graduated top 10% of class: 16%
Graduated top 25% of class: 40%
Graduated top 50% of class: 75%

COLLEGE GRADUATION REQUIREMENTS

Course waivers allowed: Yes
Course substitutions allowed: Yes
In what subjects: Only on an individual basis after Southern Utah University policy process is completed.

ADDITIONAL INFORMATION

Environment: The University is in a small town 150 miles north of Las Vegas.

Student Body
  Undergrad enrollment: 4,166
  Female: 58%
  Male: 42%
  Out-of-state: 16%

Cost Information
  In-state tuition: $1,965
  Out-of-state tuition: $6,195
  Room & board: $3,300
Housing Information
  University housing: Yes
  Percent living on campus: 25%

Greek System
  Fraternity: Yes
  Sorority: Yes
Athletics: NCAA Division I

UTAH STATE UNIVERSITY

1600 Old Main Hill, Logan, UT 84322-1600
Phone: 435-797-1079 • Fax: 435-797-4077
E-mail: admit@admissions.usu.edu • Web: www.usu.edu
Support level: CS • Institution type: 4-year public

LEARNING DISABILITY PROGRAM AND SERVICES

The mission of the Disability Resource Center (DRC) is to provide support services to students with learning disabilities (and physical disabilities) in order to assist them in meeting their academic and personal goals. Staff members coordinate university support services, and help the students identify their needs, and overcome educational or attitudinal barriers that may prevent them from reaching their full educational potential. The DRC works to tailor services to students' individual needs. Many students use a combination of services to assist them academically, including campus orientation, registration referral, and academic advising to help them feel comfortable and to promote academic services.

LD/ADHD ADMISSIONS INFORMATION

College entrance tests required: Yes
Nonstandardized tests accepted: Yes
Interview required: No
Essay required: No
Documentation required for LD: Psychoeducational
  evaluation
Documentation required for ADHD: Yes
Documentation submitted to: DRC
Special Ed. HS course work accepted: Yes, if college-prep

Specific course requirements for all applicants: Yes
Separate application required for services: Yes
# of LD applications submitted yearly: N/A
# of LD applications accepted yearly: N/A
Total # of students receiving LD/ADHD services: 150
**Acceptance into program means acceptance into
  college:** Students must be admitted and enrolled at the
  University first and then may request services.

ADMISSIONS

All students submit the regular application. The minimum GPA is 2.0 plus 18 ACT. If the Admissions Committee does not admit the student with a learning disability, the Disability Resource Center will consult with Admissions on special admits. Students who know they have a learning disability should contact the DRC to find out the details. Each student is assessed individually for admission. Consideration is given to waiving certain entrance requirements, such as flexibility on the GPA, course requirements, and SAT or ACT scores (lower than 17 on the ACT).

ADDITIONAL INFORMATION

The Disability Resource Center provides the following services: registration assistance and priority registration; note-takers and readers trained to meet the needs of students with disabilities; taped textbooks; and accommodations for exams, including extended time and quiet testing rooms. Basic skills courses are offered in time management, learning strategies, reading, math, and study strategies. The DRC has developed an assistive technology lab with computers and adaptive equipment to promote independence in conducting research and completing class assignments.

SUPPORT SERVICES CONTACT INFORMATION

Learning Disability Program/Services: Disability Resource Center (DRC)
Director: Diane Craig Baum
  E-mail: dbaum @admissions.usu.edu
  Telephone: 435-797-2444
  Fax: 435-797-0130
Contact: Natalie Sterling
  Telephone: 435-797-3434

LEARNING DISABILITY SERVICES

Requests for the following services/accommodations will be evaluated individually based on appropriate and current documentation.

Allowed in Exams
  Calculator: Y/N
  Dictionary: Y/N
  Computer: Y/N
  Spellchecker: Y/N
Extended test time: Yes
Scribes: Yes
Proctors: Yes
Oral exams: Yes
Note-takers: Yes

Distraction-reduced environment: Yes
Tape recording in class: Yes
Books on tape from RFBD: Yes
Taping of books not from RFBD: Yes
Accommodations for students with ADHD: Yes
Reading machine: Yes
Other assistive technology: Yes
Priority registration: Yes

Added costs for services: No
LD specialists: Yes (1)
Professional tutors: No
Peer tutors: Yes
Max. hours/wk. for services: Varies
How professors are notified of LD/ADHD: By student

GENERAL ADMISSIONS INFORMATION

Director of Admissions: Lynn Poulsen
Telephone: 435-797-1079

ENTRANCE REQUIREMENTS
4 English required, 3 math required, 3 science required, 1 science lab required, 2 foreign language recommended, 1 history required, 4 elective required. High school diploma or GED required. Minimum TOEFL is 500. TOEFL required of all international applicants.

Application deadline: Rolling
Notification: Rolling
Average GPA: 3.4

Average SAT I Math: 536
Average SAT I Verbal: 533
Average ACT: 22

Graduated top 10% of class: 26%
Graduated top 25% of class: 53%
Graduated top 50% of class: NR

COLLEGE GRADUATION REQUIREMENTS

Course waivers allowed: No
Course substitutions allowed: Yes
In what subjects: Determined on a case-by-case basis

ADDITIONAL INFORMATION

Environment: The University is located on 332 acres 96 miles north of Salt Lake City.

Student Body
  Undergrad enrollment: 17,903
  Female: 52%
  Male: 48%
  Out-of-state: 27%

Cost Information
  In-state tuition: $2,314
  Out-of-state tuition: $7,003
  Room & board: $4,770
Housing Information
  University housing: Yes
  Percent living on campus: 14%

Greek System
  Fraternity: Yes
  Sorority: Yes
Athletics: NCAA Division I

CHAMPLAIN COLLEGE

163 South Willard Street, Box 670, Burlington, VT 05402-0670
Phone: 802-860-2727 • Fax: 802-860-2767
E-mail: admission@champlain.edu • Web: www.champlain.edu
Support level: S • Institution type: 4-year private

LEARNING DISABILITY PROGRAM AND SERVICES

Champlain College does not offer a special program for students with learning disabilities. Support services and academic accommodations are available when needed. Students with learning disabilities meet individually with a counselor at the start of the semester and are assisted in developing a plan of academic support. The counselor acts as liaison between the student and faculty. The Student Resource Center offers peer tutoring, writing assistance, accounting lab, math lab, and a study skill workshop series in note-taking; mastering a college text; writing, revising, and editing papers; and personal counseling. Students must provide documentation of the disability to Support Services for Students with Disabilities, which should include the most recent educational evaluation performed by a qualified individual, and a letter from any educational support service provider who has recently worked with the student would be most helpful. The letter should include information about the nature of the disability and the support services and/or program modifications provided.

LD/ADHD ADMISSIONS INFORMATION

College entrance tests required: Yes
Nonstandardized tests accepted: Yes
Interview required: N/A
Essay required: Yes
Documentation required for LD: The most recent psychoeducational evaluation, including WISC or WAIS-III and achievement testing
Documentation required for ADHD: Yes
Documentation submitted to: Admissions and Support Services for Students with Disabilities
Special Ed. HS course work accepted: Yes

Specific course requirements for all applicants: Yes
Separate application required for services: No
# of LD applications submitted yearly: N/A
# of LD applications accepted yearly: N/A
Total # of students receiving LD/ADHD services: 100–130
Acceptance into program means acceptance into college: Students must be admitted and enrolled at the College first and then may request services.

ADMISSIONS

There is no special admissions procedure for students with learning disabilities. Admissions are fairly flexible, although some requirements for certain majors are more difficult. Upward grade trend is very helpful and a good senior year is looked upon favorably. Recommendations are crucial. The College is very sensitive to students with learning disabilities and is most interested in determining if the students can succeed. Students may elect to self-disclose the learning disability during the admission process and the College will take this information into consideration when making admission decisions. Students may take a reduced load of 12 credits and still be considered full-time. The average ACT for applicants is a 20 and SAT 1100, and the minimum GPA is a 2.0.

ADDITIONAL INFORMATION

Students with LD who self-disclose receive a special needs form from the Coordinator of Support Services for Students with Disabilities, after they have enrolled in college courses. The coordinator meets with each student during the first week of school. The first appointment includes a discussion about the student's disability and the academic accommodations that will be needed. Accommodations could include but are not limited to tutoring, extended time for tests (in the Resource Center), readers for tests, use of computer, peer note-takers, tape recording lecture, and books on tape. With the student's permission, faculty members receive a letter describing the student's disability and discussing appropriate accommodations. The coordinator will continue to act as a liaison between students and faculty, consult with tutors, monitor students' academic progress, and consult with faculty as needed. Freshman Focus, a course designed to assist students in making a smooth transition to college, is available for students in certain majors.

SUPPORT SERVICES CONTACT INFORMATION

Learning Disability Program/Services: Support Services for Students with Disabilities
Director: Becky Peterson, Coordinator & Counselor
  E-mail: peterson@champlain.edu
  Telephone: 802-865-6425
  Fax: 802-860-2764
Contact: Same

LEARNING DISABILITY SERVICES

Requests for the following services/accommodations will be evaluated individually based on appropriate and current documentation.

Allowed in Exams
  Calculator: Yes
  Dictionary: Yes
  Computer: Yes
  Spellchecker: Yes
Extended test time: Yes
Scribes: Yes
Proctors: Yes
Oral exams: Yes
Note-takers: Yes

Distraction-reduced environment: Yes
Tape recording in class: Yes
Books on tape from RFBD: Yes
Taping of books not from RFBD: Yes
Accommodations for students with ADHD: Yes
Reading machine: Yes
Other assistive technology: Yes
Priority registration: No

Added costs for services: No
LD specialists: No
Professional tutors: No
Peer tutors: 30
Max. hours/wk. for services: 2
How professors are notified of LD/ADHD: By student

GENERAL ADMISSIONS INFORMATION

Director of Admissions: Josephine Churchill
Telephone: 802-860-2727

ENTRANCE REQUIREMENTS
7 total are required; 15 total are recommended; 4 English required, 3 math required, 1 math recommended, 3 science recommended, 2 science lab recommended, 2 foreign language recommended, 2 social studies recommended, 1 history recommended, 4 elective recommended. High school diploma or GED required. Minimum TOEFL is 450. TOEFL required of all international applicants.

Application deadline: Rolling
Notification: Rolling beginning 12/1
Average GPA: 3.0

Average SAT I Math: 500
Average SAT I Verbal: 490
Average ACT: 20

Graduated top 10% of class: 15%
Graduated top 25% of class: 35%
Graduated top 50% of class: 85%

COLLEGE GRADUATION REQUIREMENTS

Course waivers allowed: No
Course substitutions allowed: Y/N
In what subjects: Decided on a case-by-case basis

ADDITIONAL INFORMATION

Environment: The College is located on 16 acres in a small city surrounded by a rural area, mountains, and Lake Champlain.

Student Body
  Undergrad enrollment: 2,530
  Female: 55%
  Male: 45%
  Out-of-state: 50%

Cost Information
  Tuition: $10,905
  Room & board: $7,975
Housing Information
  University housing: Yes
  Percent living on campus: 26%

Greek System
  Fraternity: Yes
  Sorority: Yes
Athletics: NJCAA

GREEN MOUNTAIN COLLEGE

One College Circle, Poultney, VT 05764-1199
Phone: 802-287-8208 • Fax: 802-287-8099
E-mail: admiss@greenmtn.edu • Web: www.greenmtn.edu
Support level: CS • Institution type: 4-year private

LEARNING DISABILITY PROGRAM AND SERVICES

Green Mountain College provides accommodations for students with documented learning differences. The College believes that every student has the potential for academic success and strives to support students while teaching them independence and self-advocacy. The Learning Center (LC) functions as the primary source of information regarding academic issues relating to disabilities. Students seeking academic accommodations must self-identify and submit valid documentation of their learning needs. The LC staff determines which students are eligible for academic accommodations and works with the student and staff to develop and implement an accommodation plan that will allow the student an opportunity to succeed at college. Progress is monitored to ensure access to the necessary supports and to assist in fostering self-advocacy. The LC has six main functions: to provide academic support, primarily through one-on-one, small group, general content-area tutoring; to serve as the campus Writing Center; to support courses specifically designed for underprepared students; to provide support for foreign students; to be the campus center for academic issues relating to disabilities; and to provide workshops, seminars, and events with the goal of improving learning skills.

LD/ADHD ADMISSIONS INFORMATION

College entrance tests required: Yes
Nonstandardized tests accepted: Yes
Interview required: NR
Essay required: Yes
Documentation required for LD: Psychoeducational evaluation
Documentation required for ADHD: Yes
Documentation submitted to: LC
Special Ed. HS course work accepted: Yes

Specific course requirements for all applicants: Yes
Separate application required for services: No
# of LD applications submitted yearly: N/A
# of LD applications accepted yearly: N/A
Total # of students receiving LD/ADHD services: 50
Acceptance into program means acceptance into college: Students must be admitted and enrolled at the College and then reviewed for LC services.

ADMISSIONS

There is no special admissions process for students with learning disabilities. Students face the same admission criteria, which include ACT score of 19 or SAT score of 900; 2.0 GPA; 4 years English, 2–3 years history/social studies, 2 years science (with lab), 3 years math, and 2 years foreign language. All applications are carefully considered with the best interest of both the student and the College in mind. Green Mountain College has a probationary admission that limits the course load of the new student while requiring the student to make use of support services.

ADDITIONAL INFORMATION

The Learning Center provides support services to all students. The tutoring program uses a three-tiered approach: a drop-in clinic for immediate but temporary academic assistance; individually scheduled tutoring; or a more extensive schedule of one, two, or three tutoring sessions per week for tutorial help throughout a course. The Writing Center is open during drop-in hours. All new students take placement tests to assess their achievement in writing and mathematics. Students whose work is unsatisfactory are requested to rewrite assignments with the help of the Learning Center staff. Students underprepared in math are advised to take Basic Math or Beginning Algebra, and tutoring is available.

SUPPORT SERVICES CONTACT INFORMATION

Learning Disability Program/Services: The Learning Center (LC)
Director: Sue Zientara
  E-mail: zientaras@greenmtn.edu
  Telephone: 802-287-8288
  Fax: 802-287-8232
Contact: Same

LEARNING DISABILITY SERVICES

Requests for the following services/accommodations will be evaluated individually based on appropriate and current documentation.

Allowed in Exams
  Calculator: Yes
  Dictionary: Yes
  Computer: Yes
  Spellchecker: Yes
Extended test time: Yes
Scribes: Yes
Proctors: Yes
Oral exams: Yes
Note-takers: Yes

Distraction-reduced environment: Yes
Tape recording in class: Yes
Books on tape from RFBD: Yes
Taping of books not from RFBD: No
Accommodations for students with ADHD: Yes
Reading machine: No
Other assistive technology: No
Priority registration: Yes

Added costs for services: No
LD specialists: Yes (1)
Professional tutors: 4
Peer tutors: 10
Max. hours/wk. for services: Unlimited
How professors are notified of LD/ADHD: By student and program director

GENERAL ADMISSIONS INFORMATION

Director of Admissions: Merrilyn Tatarczuch-Koff
Telephone: 802-287-8208

ENTRANCE REQUIREMENTS
18 total are required; 2 total are recommended; 4 English required, 3 math required, 2 science required, 2 foreign language recommended, 1 social studies required, 2 history required, 6 elective required. High school diploma or GED required. Minimum TOEFL is 500. TOEFL required of all international applicants.

Application deadline: Rolling
Notification: Rolling beginning 9/1
Average GPA: 2.6

Average SAT I Math: 492
Average SAT I Verbal: 511
Average ACT: 20

Graduated top 10% of class: 8%
Graduated top 25% of class: 24%
Graduated top 50% of class: 55%

COLLEGE GRADUATION REQUIREMENTS

Course waivers allowed: No
Course substitutions allowed: No
In what subjects: N/A

ADDITIONAL INFORMATION

Environment: The campus is in a small town near Rutland.

Student Body
  Undergrad enrollment: 668
  Female: 49%
  Male: 51%
  Out-of-state: 91%

Cost Information
  Tuition: $17,000
  Room & board: $5,300
Housing Information
  University housing: Yes
  Percent living on campus: 89%

Greek System
  Fraternity: Yes
  Sorority: Yes
  Athletics: NAIA

JOHNSON STATE COLLEGE

337 College Hill, Johnson, VT 05656-9408
Phone: 802-635-1219 • Fax: 802-635-1230
E-mail: jcsapply@badger.jsc.vsc.edu • Web: www.jsc.vsc.edu
Support level: CS • Institution type: 4-year public

LEARNING DISABILITY PROGRAM AND SERVICES

Johnson State College provides services to students with learning disabilities through the Special Services Counselor. The fundamental purpose is to provide students with the appropriate services necessary to allow full participation in all Johnson State College academic programs. Students with learning disabilities are integrated fully into the College community. There is also a TRIO Program for 235 students meeting eligibility criteria, which include at least one of the following areas: be enrolled in one or more basic skills courses; SAT scores below 300 on either Verbal or Math sections; earned a GED; has below average high school grades; has not completed Algebra II or its equivalent in high school; or was conditionally accepted to the College. Students must also meet one of three criteria: (1) have a documented disability; (2) be a first generation college student; and (3) be economically disadvantaged. Eligible students receive intensive support services through the Academic Support Services program. The Learning Resource Center provides a friendly and supportive environment for any student who is academically struggling or underprepared to meet his or her educational goals. Services include group and peer tutoring, Math Lab, Writer's Workshop, and supplemental instruction.

LD/ADHD ADMISSIONS INFORMATION

College entrance tests required: Yes
Nonstandardized tests accepted: Yes
Interview required: N/A
Essay required: Yes
Documentation required for LD: Psychoeducational evaluation
Documentation required for ADHD: Yes
Documentation submitted to: Academic Support Services
Special Ed. HS course work accepted: N/A

Specific course requirements for all applicants: Yes
Separate application required for services: No
# of LD applications submitted yearly: N/A
# of LD applications accepted yearly: N/A
Total # of students receiving LD/ADHD services: 60
Acceptance into program means acceptance into college: Students must be admitted and enrolled at the College and then may request services.

ADMISSIONS

Upon consultation with the Academic Support Services office, all students with learning disabilities who demonstrate the academic ability to be successful are accepted. Modifications to entrance requirements are accommodated if a student is otherwise admissible. Course requirements include 4 years English, 2 years science, 2 years social science, and 3 years math. High school GPA minimum is a 2.0. The SAT score range is 700–940 for the middle 50 percent.

ADDITIONAL INFORMATION

Academic Support Services provides tutoring, academic advising, personal counseling, career exploration, college survival skills training workshops, and assistance with establishing appropriate and reasonable accommodations. Students should be self-advocates and are responsible for notifying instructors to arrange for accommodations. The Transition Year Experience (TYE) is available to all students who are conditionally accepted to JSC. It begins 1 week prior to freshman year and continues through 15 weeks of the fall semester. This innovative learning experience will help make the transition from high school to college a more positive and rewarding experience for students needing strong academic and individual support. Students earn a total of four college credits through the TYE designed to teach critical inquiry, study skills, general college survival skills, and self-advocacy.

SUPPORT SERVICES CONTACT INFORMATION

Learning Disability Program/Services: Academic Support Services
Director: Katherine Veilleux
  E-mail: veilleuk@badger.jsc.vsc.edu
  Telephone: 802-635-1259
  Fax: 802-635-1454
Contact: Dian Duranleau
  E-mail: duranled@badger.jsc.vsc.edu
  Telephone: 802-635-1259
  Fax: 802-635-1454

LEARNING DISABILITY SERVICES

Requests for the following services/accommodations will be evaluated individually based on appropriate and current documentation.

Allowed in Exams
  Calculator: Yes
  Dictionary: Yes
  Computer: Yes
  Spellchecker: Yes
Extended test time: Yes
Scribes: Yes
Proctors: Yes
Oral exams: No
Note-takers: Yes

Distraction-reduced environment: Yes
Tape recording in class: Yes
Books on tape from RFBD: Yes
Taping of books not from RFBD: Yes
Accommodations for students with ADHD: Yes
Reading machine: No
Other assistive technology: No
Priority registration: No

Added costs for services: No
LD specialists: Yes (1)
Professional tutors: 2
Peer tutors: 45
Max. hours/wk. for services: Unlimited
How professors are notified of LD/ADHD: By student

GENERAL ADMISSIONS INFORMATION

Director of Admissions: Kellie Rose
Telephone: 802-635-1219

ENTRANCE REQUIREMENTS
9 total are required; 15 total are recommended; 4 English required, 3 math required, 4 math recommended, 2 science required, 3 science recommended, 1 science lab required, 2 science lab recommended, 2 foreign language recommended, 2 social studies recommended, 2 history recommended. High school diploma or GED required. Minimum TOEFL is 500. TOEFL required of all international applicants.

Application deadline: Rolling
Notification: Rolling beginning 12/1
Average GPA: NR

Average SAT I Math: 490
Average SAT I Verbal: 500
Average ACT: N/A

Graduated top 10% of class: 6%
Graduated top 25% of class: 24%
Graduated top 50% of class: 52%

COLLEGE GRADUATION REQUIREMENTS

Course waivers allowed: Yes
Course substitutions allowed: Yes
In what subjects: Lower math may be substituted for one of the two math requirements if there is a math learning disability only.

ADDITIONAL INFORMATION

Environment: The College is located in a rural area 45 miles northeast of Burlington.

Student Body
  Undergrad enrollment: 1,361
  Female: 57%
  Male: 43%
  Out-of-state: 39%

Cost Information
  In-state tuition: $4,236
  Out-of-state tuition: $9,924
  Room & board: $5,346
Housing Information
  University housing: Yes
  Percent living on campus: 41%

Greek System
  Fraternity: Yes
  Sorority: Yes
Athletics: NCAA Division III

LANDMARK COLLEGE

River Road, South Putney, VT 05346
Phone: 802-387-6718 • Fax: 802-387-6868
E-mail: ljohnson@landmark.org • Web: www.landmarkcollege.org
Support: SP • Institution: 2-year private

LEARNING DISABILITY PROGRAM AND SERVICES

Landmark College is designed exclusively for high-potential students with dyslexia, specific learning disabilities, and/or ADHD. It is the only accredited college in the nation for students with LD/ADHD. More than 100 members of the faculty and professional staff devote their entire attention to providing the finest possible program for these students. The goal is to prepare students to enter or return to college. At Landmark, students do not bypass difficulties by using note-takers, taped books, or taking exams orally. Students must do their own work and Landmark teaches them how. Landmark's approach is unique and includes an individually designed tutorial program, very small classes, structured assignments, and an emphasis on constantly improving language and study skills.

LD/ADHD ADMISSIONS INFORMATION

College entrance tests required: No
Nonstandardized tests accepted: Yes
Interview required: Yes
Essay required: Yes
Documentation required for LD: Psychoeducational evaluation
Documentation required for ADHD: Yes
Submitted to: Landmark College
Special Ed. HS course work accepted: Yes

Specific course requirements for all applicants: N/A
Separate application required for services: No
# of LD applications submitted yearly: 700
# of LD applications accepted yearly: 300
Total # of students receiving LD/ADHD services: 320
Acceptance into program means acceptance into college: The program and the College are one and the same.

ADMISSIONS

Landmark College serves students whose academic skills have not been developed to a level equal to their intellectual capacity. Students must have average to superior intellectual potential, diagnosis of dyslexia, or another specific LD or ADHD, and high motivation. Applicants must have a willingness to undertake a rigorous academic program that does not provide bypass methods such as note-takers, books on tape, or oral exams. Focus instead is on individualized, intensive development and honing of academic skills. Qualified students must have a testing session and interview. An admission decision is made at this time. ACT/SAT are not required. There are no specific course requirements for admission, but students must take courses that lead to a high school diploma or the GED. Students may apply for admission for summer, fall, or spring semesters.

ADDITIONAL INFORMATION

Skills Development Summer Sessions ($7,300) help students develop the language and study skills needed for success in college. This program is open to students from other colleges or recent high school graduates, as well as those planning to attend Landmark. Students can get help with writing, reading, study skills, and understanding their own learning styles. Skills classes are offered to students on campus in study skills, math, written language, oral language, and content courses.

SUPPORT SERVICES CONTACT INFORMATION

Learning Disability Program/Services: Landmark College
Director: John Kipp
  Telephone: 802-387-4767
  Fax: 802-387-6868
Contact: Leatrice Johnson
  E-mail: ljohnson@landmarkcollege.org
  Telephone: 802-387-6718
  Fax: 802-387-6868

LEARNING DISABILITY SERVICES

Requests for the following services/accommodations will be evaluated individually based on appropriate and current documentation.

Allowed in Exams
  Calculator: Yes
  Dictionary: Yes
  Computer: Yes
  Spellchecker: Yes
Extended test time: Yes
Scribes: No
Proctors: No
Oral exams: Yes
Notetakers: No

Distraction-reduced environment: Yes
Tape recording in class: Yes
Books on tape from RFBD: Yes
Taping of books not from RFBD: No
Accommodations for students with ADHD: Yes
Reading machine: Yes
Other assistive technology: No
Priority registration: No

Added costs for services: No
LD specialists: Yes (100)
Professional tutors: 90
Peer tutors: No
Max. hours/wk. for services: Unlimited
How professors are notified of LD/ADHD: All students are LD/ADHD

GENERAL ADMISSIONS INFORMATION

Director of Admissions: Leatrice Johnson
Telephone: 802-387-6718

ENTRANCE REQUIREMENTS
Students must have a high school diploma or a GED equivalent. They must also have average to superior intellectual potential and have the willingness and ability to pursue a rigorous academic program. ACT/SAT not required. Interviews are required. Students must write a personal statement and submit three recommendations.

Application deadline: Rolling
Notification: Rolling
Average GPA: NR

Average SAT I Math: NR
Average SAT I Verbal: NR
Average ACT: NR

Graduated top 10% of class: NR
Graduated top 25% of class: NR
Graduated top 50% of class: NR

COLLEGE GRADUATION REQUIREMENTS

Course waivers allowed: No
Course Course substitutions allowed: No
In what subjects: N/A

ADDITIONAL INFORMATION

Environment: The College is located on 125 acres overlooking the Connecticut River Valley and the hills of Vermont and New Hampshire.

Student Body
  Undergrad enrollment: 320
  Female: 22%
  Male: 78%
  Out-of-state: 95%

Cost Information
  Tuition: $31,400
  Room & board: $6,000
Housing Information
  University housing: Yes
  Percent living on campus: 100%

Greek System
  Fraternity: Yes
  Sorority: Yes
Athletics: Intercollegiate and intramural

NEW ENGLAND CULINARY INSTITUTE

250 Main Street, Montpelier, VT 05602
Phone: 802-223-6324 • Fax: 802-223-0634
E-mail: ellenm@neculinary.com • Web: www.neculinary.com
Support level: CS • Institution type: 2-year private

LEARNING DISABILITY PROGRAM AND SERVICES

The New England Culinary Institute is in business to provide educational programs in the culinary arts, food and beverage management, basic cooking, and related areas that prepare students for employment and advancement in the hospitality industry. Students with LD/ADHD have found success at the institute, although sometimes it might take these students longer to finish a specific course or complete all of the graduation requirements. Some students with LD/ADHD may find the production kitchen learning environment, with its intensity, pressure, and long hours, a very demanding place. Almost all of the courses have a strong academic component, which requires comprehension and retention of a great deal of new information. Students with LD/ADHD often find the most success in the associate's segree of occupational studies program. Additionally, students are more successful if they have a strong work ethic and have had some experience in the food industry. The Learning Services Office provides services to all students and the coordinator is available five days a week to work with students one-on-one. The goal of Learning Services is to provide support to maximize culinary learning.

LD/ADHD ADMISSIONS INFORMATION

College entrance tests required: No
Nonstandardized tests accepted: Yes
Interview required: Recommended
Essay required: Yes
Documentation required for LD: Psychoeducational evaluation
Documentation required for ADHD: Yes
Submitted to: Learning Services
Special Ed. HS course work accepted: Yes

Specific course requirements for all applicants: No
Separate application required for services: No
# of LD applications submitted yearly: N/A
# of LD applications accepted yearly: N/A
Total # of students receiving LD/ADHD services: 47
Acceptance into program means acceptance into college: Students must be admitted and enrolled and then request services.

ADMISSIONS

There is no special admission process for students with LD or ADHD. Students who are applying for the AOS program must have a high school diploma or equivalency certificate, and must submit an essay and a minimum of one to three letters of recommendation. Interviews are recommended. Applicants may also be required to spend some time in the kitchen with one of the chefs. Students interested in the BA program must complete an associate's degree first. Applicants with LD/ADHD with appropriate documentation will be eligible to access accommodations once they are admitted and enrolled. Some students may wish to complete a Certificate in Basic Cooking first to determine their commitment and skills in the culinary arts.

ADDITIONAL INFORMATION

Students with LD/ADHD must provide appropriate documentation and meet with the Learning Center director in order to receive services. The director will verify the documentation, review the requests, and meet with the student to explain the learning services. Instructors are notified with student permission. Self-advocacy information is provided and a Learning Contract (if necessary) is written and signed by the student. Accommodations include oral and untimed tests, alternate test sites, use of dictionary during nonvocabulary tests, note-taking, individualized tutoring, use of calculators and computers, tape recording of lectures, and paper-writing assistance. Any student can access services through Learning Services. These services include one-on-one tutorials; small group workshops to refresh math skills; review sessions; opportunity to retake tests; computers; software to help with writing papers; reference books; and a quiet study/work space. This is a self-serve resource and they will try to work out all requests.

SUPPORT SERVICES CONTACT INFORMATION

Learning Disability Program/Services: Learning Services
Director: Jackie Burke
  E-mail: jackieb@neci.edu
  Telephone: 802-872-3409
  Fax: 802-872-3413
Contact: Same

LEARNING DISABILITY SERVICES

Requests for the following services/accommodations will be evaluated individually based on appropriate and current documentation.

Allowed in Exams
  Calculator: Yes
  Dictionary: Yes
  Computer: Yes
  Spellchecker: Yes
Extended test time: Yes
Scribes: Yes
Proctors: Yes
Oral exams: Yes
Notetakers: Yes

Distraction-reduced environment: Yes
Tape recording in class: Yes
Books on tape from RFBD: Yes
Taping of books not from RFBD: Yes
Accommodations for students with ADHD: Yes
Reading machine: No
Other assistive technology: Yes
Priority registration: No

Added costs for services: No
LD specialists: Yes
Professional tutors: 2
Peer tutors: 5
Max. hours/wk. for services: Unlimited
How professors are notified of LD/ADHD: By both student and director

GENERAL ADMISSIONS INFORMATION

Director of Admissions: Ellen McShane
Telephone: 802-872-3409

ENTRANCE REQUIREMENTS
High school diploma or GED required. Essay or personal statement and recommendations are important in the process.

Application deadline: Rolling
Notification: Rolling
Average GPA: NR

Average SAT I Math: NR
Average SAT I Verbal: NR
Average ACT: NR

Graduated top 10% of class: NR
Graduated top 25% of class: NR
Graduated top 50% of class: NR

COLLEGE GRADUATION REQUIREMENTS

Course waivers allowed: No
Course substitutions allowed: No
In what subjects: N/A

ADDITIONAL INFORMATION

Environment: The Institute is located in the city of Montpelier, 45 miles from Burlington.

Student Body
  Undergrad enrollment: 626
  Female: 25%
  Male: 75%
  Out-of-state: 70%

Cost Information
  Tuition: $18,205
  Room & board: $3,375
Housing Information
  University housing: Yes
  Percent living on campus: 80%

Greek System
  Fraternity: No
  Sorority: No
  Athletics: Intramural

New England Culinary Institute

NORWICH UNIVERSITY

Admissions Office, 65 South Main Street, Northfield, VT 05663
Phone: 800-468-6679 • Fax: 802-485-2032
E-mail: nuadm@norwich.edu • Web: www.norwich.edu
Support level: CS • Institution type: 4-year private

LEARNING DISABILITY PROGRAM AND SERVICES

The Learning Support Center (LSC) offers comprehensive support services in all areas of academic life. While Norwich does not have a formal program for students with learning disabilities, the University does offer support services on a voluntary basis. Students are instructed by the center staff in a wide range of study and college survival skills. The Center's staff work closely with advisors and faculty members, and are strong advocates for students with learning disabilities. The University stresses autonomy by providing a level of support that assists students with becoming responsible, thinking adults, and well-acquainted with their own needs and able to articulate them. Services are provided by a staff of professionals that includes LD specialists, study skills/writing specialists, and a basic math specialist. The professional staff is supplemented by a trained, well-supervised student tutorial staff.

LD/ADHD ADMISSIONS INFORMATION

College entrance tests required: Yes
Nonstandardized tests accepted: Yes
Interview required: No
Essay required: Highly recommended
Documentation required for LD: Comprehensive cognitive/ achievement with full report and diagnostic conclusion with recommendation: all within three years
Documentation required for ADHD: Yes
Documentation submitted to: Addmissions and LSC
Special Ed. HS course work accepted: No

Specific course requirements for all applicants: Yes
Separate application required for services: N/A
# of LD applications submitted yearly: N/A
# of LD applications accepted yearly: N/A
Total # of students receiving LD/ADHD services: 66
Acceptance into program means acceptance into college: Students must be admitted and enrolled at the University first and then may request services and accommodations.

ADMISSIONS

Students with learning disabilities submit a general application. Admission criteria include high school GPA of a C or better; SAT of 850 or equivalent ACT; participation in activities; and strong college recommendations from teachers, counselors, or coaches. There are no course waivers for admission. The University is flexible on ACT/SAT test scores. If grades and other indicators are problematic it is recommended that students provide detailed information to give a better understanding of the disability. A complete psychodiagnostic evaluation is required. A small number of students who do not meet the general admission requirements may be admitted if they show promise. An interview is highly recommended. In some cases the Director of Learning Support may review the admissions file and make a recommendation. There are limited "conditional" admission slots. Students are required to go to a college and take courses if their high school grades and/or SAT scores are below requirement.

ADDITIONAL INFORMATION

A telephone conversation or personal meeting with the LSC support personnel is encouraged prior to the start of college, so that work can begin immediately on preparing an individualized program. Students are responsible for meeting with each professor to discuss accommodations. Services begin with freshman placement testing designed to assess each individual's level of readiness for college-level reading, writing, and math. Other services include course advising with an assigned academic advisor, and advocacy for academic petitions. Services and accommodations are available for undergraduate and graduate students.

SUPPORT SERVICES CONTACT INFORMATION

Learning Disability Program/Services: Learning Support Center (LSC)
Director: Paula A. Gills
  E-mail: gills@norwich.edu
  Telephone: 802-485-2130
  Fax: 802-485-2580
Contact: Same

LEARNING DISABILITY SERVICES

Requests for the following services/accommodations will be evaluated individually based on appropriate and current documentation.

Allowed in Exams
  Calculator: Yes
  Dictionary: Yes
  Computer: Yes
  Spellchecker: Yes
  Extended test time: Yes
  Scribes: Yes
  Proctors: Yes
  Oral exams: Yes
  Note-takers: Yes

Distraction-reduced environment: Yes
Tape recording in class: Yes
Books on tape from RFBD: Yes
Taping of books not from RFBD: Yes
Accommodations for students with ADHD: Yes
Reading machine: No
Other assistive technology: No
Priority registration: Yes

Added costs for services: No
LD specialists: Yes (2)
Professional tutors: 9
Peer tutors: 5
Max. hours/wk. for services: Depends on staff availability
How professors are notified of LD/ADHD: By both student and director

GENERAL ADMISSIONS INFORMATION

Director of Admissions: Karen McGrath
Telephone: 800-468-6679

ENTRANCE REQUIREMENTS

4 English recommended, 3 math recommended, 3 science recommended, 2 foreign language recommended. High school diploma or GED required. Minimum TOEFL is 500. TOEFL required of all international applicants.

Application deadline: Rolling
Notification: Rolling beginning 10/1
Average GPA: 3.0

Average SAT I Math: N/A
Average SAT I Verbal: N/A
Average ACT: N/A

Graduated top 10% of class: 8%
Graduated top 25% of class: 21%
Graduated top 50% of class: 57%

COLLEGE GRADUATION REQUIREMENTS

Course waivers allowed: No
Course substitutions allowed: Yes
In what subjects: Foreign language; only with proof of inability to successfully function

ADDITIONAL INFORMATION

Environment: The University's two campuses, in Northfield (traditional) and Montpelier (low residency), are located 50 miles southeast of Burlington.

Student Body
  Undergrad enrollment: 2,214
  Female: 40%
  Male: 60%
  Out-of-state: 66%

Cost Information
  Tuition: $14,926
  Room & board: $5,718
Housing Information
  University housing: Yes
  Percent living on campus: 84%

Greek System
  Fraternity: Yes
  Sorority: Yes
Athletics: NCAA Division III

SOUTHERN VERMONT COLLEGE

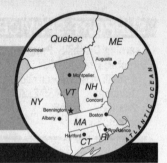

982 Mansion Drive, Bennington, VT 05201
Phone: 802-447-6304 • Fax: 802-447-4695
E-mail: admis@svc.edu • Web: www.svc.edu
Support level: SP • Institution type: 2-year and 4-year private

LEARNING DISABILITY PROGRAM AND SERVICES

The learning disability program at Southern Vermont College offers a highly supportive environment for students with special educational needs. Students who participate in the program are offered a wide range of support services tailored to their individual needs, and regularly scheduled tutorial sessions for academic support, study skills, and compensatory strategies. While support remains available throughout their college stay, students are strongly encouraged to seek support on a regularly scheduled, weekly basis at least during their freshman year. Varying levels of support are available throughout the academic years at Southern Vermont College. There is no additional fee for services. To be eligible to participate in the Disabilities Support Program, students must provide recent documentation specifying the nature of the learning disability or ADHD. An interview with the Disabilities Support Program staff is strongly recommended.

LD/ADHD ADMISSIONS INFORMATION

College entrance tests required: Yes
Nonstandardized tests accepted: Yes
Interview required: Yes
Essay required: Yes
Documentation required for LD: WAIS-III (within two years)
Documentation required for ADHD: Yes
Documentation submitted to: Disabilities Support Services
Special Ed. HS course work accepted: Yes

Specific course requirements for all applicants: Yes
Separate application required for services: No
# of LD applications submitted yearly: N/A
# of LD applications accepted yearly: N/A
Total # of students receiving LD/ADHD services: 70
Acceptance into program means acceptance into college: Students must be admitted and enrolled at the College first and then may request services.

ADMISSIONS

If a student with a documented learning disability does not meet regular admissions criteria, the LD Coordinator and review committee will further examine documentation and evaluation information. Each case is decided on an individual basis. Required documentation includes WAIS-R (within two years) with individual subscores indicating at least average ability in abstract reasoning; recent individualized achievement tests indicating grade equivalents in reading skills/comprehension, math, and written language skills. General admissions criteria include a minimum GPA of 2.0, 3 years English, 2 years math, and 2 years science (can substitute). No ACT/SAT is required or the student may take college placement tests in lieu of SAT/ACTs. Admissions decisions are made by the Office of Admissions.

ADDITIONAL INFORMATION

The Learning Cooperative Peer Tutorial Center is available to all students at the College. Peer tutors are provided for most courses offered at the College. There is walk-in tutoring with trained tutors. The Disabilities Support Program staff works with students and instructors to find learning strategies to help them succeed in college. Students may be placed in one of three classes: English composition and college math to master skills; literature course to improve general reading skills; and basic math, which is a self-paced course to strengthen math skills. Summer ACTion Program is available to all students accepted into the fall freshman class. This program provides an introduction to college life, dorm living, and the opportunity to earn college credits.

SUPPORT SERVICES CONTACT INFORMATION

Learning Disability Program/Services: Disabilities Support Program
Director: Todd Gerson
  E-mail: tgerson@svc.edu
  Telephone: 802-447-6360
  Fax: 802-447-4695
Contact: Same

LEARNING DISABILITY SERVICES

Requests for the following services/accommodations will be evaluated individually based on appropriate and current documentation.

Allowed in Exams
  Calculator: Yes
  Dictionary: No
  Computer: Yes
  Spellchecker: Yes
Extended test time: Yes
Scribes: Yes
Proctors: Yes
Oral exams: No
Note-takers: Yes

Distraction-reduced environment: Yes
Tape recording in class: Yes
Books on tape from RFBD: Yes
Taping of books not from RFBD: Yes
Accommodations for students with ADHD: Yes
Reading machine: Yes
Other assistive technology: Yes
Priority registration: Yes

Added costs for services: No
LD specialists: Yes (2)
Professional tutors: 2
Peer tutors: No
Max. hours/wk. for services: Unlimited
How professors are notified of LD/ADHD: By student

GENERAL ADMISSIONS INFORMATION

Director of Admissions: Elizabeth Gatti
Telephone: 802-447-6304

ENTRANCE REQUIREMENTS

16 total are recommended; 4 English required, 2 math required, 2 science recommended, 2 foreign language recommended, 3 social studies recommended, 2 history recommended. High school diploma or GED required. Minimum TOEFL is 500. TOEFL required of all international applicants.

Application deadline: Rolling
Notification: Rolling beginning 12/1
Average GPA: 2.8

Average SAT I Math: 474
Average SAT I Verbal: 473
Average ACT: 19.5

Graduated top 10% of class: 15%
Graduated top 25% of class: 41%
Graduated top 50% of class: 48%

COLLEGE GRADUATION REQUIREMENTS

Course waivers allowed: No
Course substitutions allowed: Yes
In what subjects: Math; course substitution considered only if, in spite of demonstrated efforts to master college math course material, the student has met with limited success

ADDITIONAL INFORMATION

Environment: The College is located in a town of 17,000, forty miles northeast of Albany, New York.

Student Body
  Undergrad enrollment: 515
  Female: 64%
  Male: 36%
  Out-of-state: 60%

Cost Information
  Tuition: $10,990
  Room & board: $5,450
Housing Information
  University housing: Yes
  Percent living on campus: 22%

Greek System
  Fraternity: Yes
  Sorority: Yes
Athletics: NCAA Division III

UNIVERSITY OF VERMONT

Office of Admissions, 194 South Prospect Street,
Burlington, VT 05401-3596 • Phone: 802-656-3370
Fax: 802-656-8611 • E-mail: admissions@uvm.edu • Web: www.uvm.edu
Support level: CS • Institution type: 4-year public

LEARNING DISABILITY PROGRAM AND SERVICES

The University provides a multidisciplinary program for students with LD. ACCESS works closely with students having learning problems to ensure that campuswide resources are used effectively. Initially, a comprehensive assessment is revised to identify students' strengths and weaknesses in learning. This information is used to carefully design classroom and study accommodations to compensate for learning problems. Through this process, students and program staff have identified a number of techniques and strategies to enable success at class and study tasks. The academic advising process for students with LD involves two offices: the academic advisor assigned by the College, and the professional staff of ACCESS who review tentative semester schedules to balance course format, teaching style, and workload with a student's learning strengths. The Learning Cooperative offers individual tutoring and assistance with reading, writing, study skills, and time management. The Writing Center assists with proofing and feedback on writing assignments. There is a developmental course called Conquering College. This is an individualized support service program designed to equalize educational opportunities for students with learning disabilities.

LD/ADHD ADMISSIONS INFORMATION

College entrance tests required: Yes
Nonstandardized tests accepted: Yes
Interview required: No
Essay required: Yes
Documentation required for LD: WAIS-III; or WJ I or II; achievement tests: within 3 years
Documentation required for ADHD: Yes
Documentation submitted to: ACCESS
Special Ed. HS course work accepted: Yes

Specific course requirements for all applicants: Yes
Separate application required for services: No
# of LD applications submitted yearly: N/A
# of LD applications accepted yearly: N/A
Total # of students receiving LD/ADHD services: 550
Acceptance into program means acceptance into college: Students must be admitted and then may request services. Some students are reviewed by the LD program, which provides consultation to Admissions.

ADMISSIONS

Students submit a regular UVM application to Admissions and all documentation of their disability to ACCESS. Students are encouraged to voluntarily provide documentation of their disability. ACCESS reviews documentation and consults with Admissions as to how the student's disability has affected their academic record. A clear understanding of the students' strengths and weaknesses in learning, and the influence of the disability on the current and past educational process, will enable a broader assessment of ability to meet academic qualifications, requirements, and rigors of UVM. Students with LD should submit a current educational evaluation that includes a measure of cognitive functioning and documentation of the learning problem(s). Students with ADHD are encouraged to provide documentation and information on how the ADHD had an impact on the educational setting. Course requirements include 4 years English, 3 years social science, 3 years math, 2 years physical sciences, and 2 years foreign language (math and foreign language can be waived with appropriate documentation.) Special education courses are acceptable if the student's high school gives high school credit for the courses. Self-disclosing in the application is a matter of personal choice. However, at UVM, disclosing a disability will absolutely not have a negative impact on a student's admissibility.

ADDITIONAL INFORMATION

UVM provides a multidisciplinary program for students with LD emphasizing development of academic accommodations; academic adjustments including note-taking, course substitution, course load reduction, extended test time, alternate test formats and computer/spellchecker; auxiliary services including taped tests, readers, tutoring, writing skill development, proofing services, reading skill development; academic advising and course selection; priority registration; learning strategies and study skills training; LD support group and counseling; faculty consultation and in-service training; and diagnostic screening and evaluation referral. Students with ADHD with appropriate documentation may receive help with class schedules, study activities to fit individual learning styles, support services, or accommodations in test conditions, course loads, and/or program requirements because of the severity of the disability.

SUPPORT SERVICES CONTACT INFORMATION

Learning Disability Program/Services: ACCESS
Director: Joe Pete Wilson
  E-mail: jwilson@zoo.uvm.edu
  Telephone: 802-656-7753
  Fax: 802-656-0739
Contact: Same

LEARNING DISABILITY SERVICES

Requests for the following services/accommodations will be evaluated individually based on appropriate and current documentation.

Allowed in Exams
  Calculator: Yes
  Dictionary: Yes
  Computer: Yes
  Spellchecker: Yes
Extended test time: Yes
Scribes: Yes
Proctors: Yes
Oral exams: Yes
Note-takers: Yes

Distraction-reduced environment: Yes
Tape recording in class: Yes
Books on tape from RFBD: Yes
Taping of books not from RFBD: Yes
Accommodations for students with
  ADHD: Yes
Reading machine: Yes
Other assistive technology: Yes
Priority registration: Yes

Added costs for services: $7 per hour
  for tutoring
LD specialists: Yes (4)
Professional tutors: 1
Peer tutors: 1
Max. hours/wk. for services: 1
How professors are notified of
  LD/ADHD: By both student and
  director

GENERAL ADMISSIONS INFORMATION

Director of Admissions: Don Honeman
Telephone: 802-656-3370

ENTRANCE REQUIREMENTS

16 total are required; 4 English required, 3 math required, 2 science required, 1 science lab required, 2 foreign language required, 3 social studies required. High school diploma or GED required. Minimum TOEFL is 550. TOEFL required of all international applicants.

Application deadline: January 15
Notification: March 31
Average GPA: NR

Average SAT I Math: 570
Average SAT I Verbal: 565
Average ACT: 24

Graduated top 10% of class: 18%
Graduated top 25% of class: 49%
Graduated top 50% of class: 87%

COLLEGE GRADUATION REQUIREMENTS

Course waivers allowed: Yes
Course substitutions allowed: Yes
In what subjects: Depends on departmental/college approval

ADDITIONAL INFORMATION

Environment: The University is located on 425 acres by Lake Champlain, 90 miles south of Montreal.

Student Body
  Undergrad enrollment: 8,618
  Female: 56%
  Male: 44%
  Out-of-state: 61%

Cost Information
  In-state tuition: $7,692
  Out-of-state tuition: $19,236
  Room & board: $5,806
Housing Information
  University housing: Yes
  Percent living on campus: 49%

Greek System
  Fraternity: Yes
  Sorority: Yes
Athletics: NCAA Division I

VERMONT TECHNICAL COLLEGE

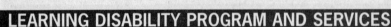

PO Box 500, Randolph Center, VT 05061
Phone: 802-728-1000
E-mail: rdistel@vtc.edu • Web: www.vtc.edu
Support: CS • Institution: 2-year public

LEARNING DISABILITY PROGRAM AND SERVICES

The goal of Services for Students with Disabilities is to ensure equal access to all VTC programs for all qualified students with disabilities; to help students develop the necessary skills to be effective at VTC and beyond; and to further students' understanding of how their disabilities affect them in school, work, and social settings.

LD/ADHD ADMISSIONS INFORMATION

College entrance tests required: Yes
Nonstandardized tests accepted: Yes
Interview required: Yes
Essay required: No
Documentation required for LD: WAIS-III; WJ
Documentation required for ADHD: Yes
Submitted to: Services of Students with Disabilities
Special Ed. HS course work accepted: Yes

Specific course requirements for all applicants: Yes
Separate application required for services: No
# of LD applications submitted yearly: N/A
# of LD applications accepted yearly: N/A
Total # of students receiving LD/ADHD services: 50
Acceptance into program means acceptance into college: Students must be admitted and enrolled at the College first and then may request services.

ADMISSIONS

There is no special admissions process for students with learning disabilities. In general, students have a GPA of 80% or higher. There is no cutoff score for the SAT. The program director can make recommendations to waive certain admission criteria if they discriminate against a student with a learning disability, and other evidence of a student's qualifications exist. General course requirements include algebra I and II, geometry, and physics or chemistry for engineering programs. Many students meet with the disabilities coordinator during the application process to discuss their needs. The Summer Bridge Program, an alternative admission plan, is a four-week math/physics and language arts program used as preparation for marginal freshmen who do not require the three-year program option. The three-year alternative admission option is for engineering students who need longer than two years to complete the program.

ADDITIONAL INFORMATION

The disabilities coordinator provides a variety of services, which include assessment of students' academic needs, coordination of tutoring to provide assistance with course material, and disabilities forum for students to share experiences and academic strategies that they have learned with other students. Individual tutoring is provided in writing and study skills, such as time management, effective textbook reading, learning strategies, and stress management. Also available are academic and career counseling and coordination of accommodations. There is a Learning Center open to all students on campus.

SUPPORT SERVICES CONTACT INFORMATION

Learning Disability Program/Services: Services for Students with Disabilities
Director: Barbara Bendix
  E-mail: bbendix@vtc.edu
  Telephone: 802-728-1278
  Fax: 802-728-1714
Contact: Same

LEARNING DISABILITY SERVICES

Requests for the following services/accommodations will be evaluated individually based on appropriate and current documentation.

Allowed in Exams
  Calculator: Y/N
  Dictionary: Y/N
  Computer: Y/N
  Spellchecker: Y/N
Extended test time: Yes
Scribes: Y/N
Proctors: Yes
Oral exams: Yes
Notetakers: Yes

Distraction-reduced environment: Yes
Tape recording in class: Yes
Books on tape from RFBD: Yes
Taping of books not from RFBD: No
Accommodations for students with ADHD: Yes
Reading machine: Yes
Other assistive technology: Yes
Priority registration: Yes

Added costs for services: No
LD specialists: Yes
Professional tutors: Yes
Peer tutors: Yes
Max. hours/wk. for services: Unlimited
How professors are notified of LD/ADHD: By student

GENERAL ADMISSIONS INFORMATION

Director of Admissions: Rosemary Distel
Telephone: 802-728-1243

ENTRANCE REQUIREMENTS

High school diploma or GED required. 3 math and 2 sciences required for engineering program. Other programs require 2 math and 2 science. ACT/SAT not required.

Application deadline: Rolling
Notification: Rolling
Average GPA: 2.0

Average SAT I Math: NR
Average SAT I Verbal: NR
Average ACT: NR

Graduated top 10% of class: NR
Graduated top 25% of class: NR
Graduated top 50% of class: NR

COLLEGE GRADUATION REQUIREMENTS

Course waivers allowed: No
Course substitutions allowed: No
In what subjects: N/A

ADDITIONAL INFORMATION

Environment: The College is located on 54 acres in a rural area.

Student Body
  Undergrad enrollment: 872
  Female: 25%
  Male: 75%
  Out-of-state: 30%

Cost Information
  Tuition: $4,380
  Room & board: $4,940
Housing Information
  University housing: Yes
  Percent living on campus: 79%

Greek System
  Fraternity: Yes
  Sorority: Yes
Athletics: Intramural and intercollegiate

COLLEGE OF WILLIAM AND MARY

PO Box 8795, Williamsburg, VA 23187-8795
Phone: 757-221-4223 • Fax: 757-221-1242
E-mail: admiss@facstaff.wm.edu • Web: www.wm.edu
Support level: CS • Institution type: 4-year public

LEARNING DISABILITY PROGRAM AND SERVICES

Disability Services at the College of William and Mary is available to all students with disabilities. Reasonable accommodations upon request are evaluated on an individual and flexible basis. Program goals include fostering independence, encouraging self-determination, emphasizing accommodations over limitations, and creating an accessible environment to ensure that individuals are viewed on the basis of ability and not disability. Individual accommodation needs are considered on a case-by-case basis in consultation with the student. The staff works with students and faculty to implement reasonable supports. Students anticipating the need for academic support must provide pertinent documentation in a timely manner in order to facilitate the provision of the service. Additional documentation may be requested and accommodation requests can be denied if they do not seem to be substantially supported. Documentation for LD/ADHD must include a comprehensive report of psychoeducational or neuropsychological assessment. The documentation must demonstrate the impact of the disability on major life activities and support all the recommended accommodations.

LD/ADHD ADMISSIONS INFORMATION

College entrance tests required: Yes
Nonstandardized tests accepted: Yes
Interview required: No
Essay required: Yes
Documentation required for LD: Psychoeducational evaluation
Documentation required for ADHD: Yes
Documentation submitted to: Disability Services
Special Ed. HS course work accepted: No

Specific course requirements for all applicants: Yes
Separate application required for services: No
# of LD applications submitted yearly: N/A
# of LD applications accepted yearly: N/A
Total # of students receiving LD/ADHD services: N/A
Acceptance into program means acceptance into college: Students must be admitted and enrolled and then may request services.

ADMISSIONS

Students go through a regular admissions process. Students must take either the SAT I or ACT and three SAT II: Subject Tests are recommended. Results of nonstandardized test administrations and documentation of disability may be submitted in support of any application, but are not essential for full consideration. Once admitted, students are fully mainstreamed and are expected to maintain the same academic standards as all other students.

ADDITIONAL INFORMATION

The staff of Disability Services works with the student and the faculty to implement reasonable accommodations such as peer note-takers, alternative test forms, textbook recording services, study skills training, and peer support groups. Disability-Related Program Access includes assistance with priority registration, liaison to the University, assistance with academic adjustments and curriculum alternatives, advocacy, in-service training for faculty and staff, and acquisition of adaptive equipment and/or software. The staff works closely with all college departments to identify appropriate options for accommodating students with disabilities.

SUPPORT SERVICES CONTACT INFORMATION

Learning Disability Program/Services: Disability Services
Director: Lisa Bickley
  E-mail: ljbick@wm.edu
  Telephone: 757-221-2510
  Fax: 757-221-2538
Contact: Same

LEARNING DISABILITY SERVICES

Requests for the following services/accommodations will be evaluated individually based on appropriate and current documentation.

Allowed in Exams
  Calculator: Y/N
  Dictionary: Y/N
  Computer: Yes
  Spellchecker: Y/N
Extended test time: Yes
Scribes: Yes
Proctors: Y/N
Oral exams: Y/N
Note-takers: Yes

Distraction-reduced environment: Yes
Tape recording in class: Y/N
Books on tape from RFBD: Yes
Taping of books not from RFBD: Y/N
Accommodations for students with ADHD: Yes
Reading machine: Yes
Other assistive technology: Yes
Priority registration: Yes

Added costs for services: No
LD specialists: Yes (1)
Professional tutors: No
Peer tutors: Yes
Max. hours/wk. for services: As needed
How professors are notified of LD/ADHD: Students must be admitted and enrolled and then may request services.

GENERAL ADMISSIONS INFORMATION

Director of Admissions: Karen Cotrell, Associate Provost (Interim)
Telephone: 757-221-3980

ENTRANCE REQUIREMENTS

4 English recommended, 4 math recommended, 4 science recommended, 3 science lab recommended, 4 foreign language recommended, 4 social studies recommended. High school diploma or equivalent is not required. Minimum TOEFL is 600. TOEFL required of all international applicants.

Application deadline: January 5
Notification: April 1
Average GPA: 4.0

Average SAT I Math: 654
Average SAT I Verbal: 663
Average ACT: 31

Graduated top 10% of class: 79%
Graduated top 25% of class: 97%
Graduated top 50% of class: 100%

COLLEGE GRADUATION REQUIREMENTS

Course waivers allowed: No
Course substitutions allowed: Rarely
In what subjects: Rarely provided in any subject

ADDITIONAL INFORMATION

Environment: Located 50 miles from Richmond.

Student Body
  Undergrad enrollment: 5,585
  Female: 57%
  Male: 43%
  Out-of-state: 36%

Cost Information
  In-state tuition: $4,800
  Out-of-state tuition: $17,000
  Room & board: $5,100
Housing Information
  University housing: Yes
  Percent living on campus: 77%

Greek System
  Fraternity: Yes
  Sorority: Yes
Athletics: NCAA Division I

FERRUM COLLEGE

PO Box 1000, Ferrum, VA 24088
Phone: 540-365-4290 • Fax: 540-365-4366
E-mail: admissions@ferrum.edu • Web: www.ferrum.edu
Support level: CS • Institution type: 4-year private

LEARNING DISABILITY PROGRAM AND SERVICES

Ferrum College does not have a program for students with learning disabilities, but does provide services to students with disabilities documentation. Ferrum also does not offer a comprehensive program or monitoring services. Students motivated to accept the assistance and academic accommodations offered frequently find Ferrum's services to be excellent.

LD/ADHD ADMISSIONS INFORMATION

College entrance tests required: Yes
Nonstandardized tests accepted: Yes
Interview required: No
Essay required: No
Documentation required for LD: Psychoeducational evaluation
Documentation required for ADHD: Yes
Documentation submitted to: Academic Resource Center
Special Ed. HS course work accepted: Yes, with documentation

Specific course requirements for all applicants: Yes
Separate application required for services: No
# of LD applications submitted yearly: N/A
# of LD applications accepted yearly: N/A
Total # of students receiving LD/ADHD services: NR
Acceptance into program means acceptance into college: Students must be admitted and enrolled at the College first and then may request services. There is an appeal process for students denied admission.

ADMISSIONS

Ferrum is proactive in terms of the admissions process for students with documentation of a disability. All students first go through the admissions process. If students are not admitted through the general admissions process, the committee can be requested to reconsider with the presentation of the documentation and a recommendation from the disability service provider. Those applicants who do not meet general admission criteria are encouraged to have an interview with the Office of Admissions. General admission criteria include 4 years English, 1 year math (3 recommended), 1 year science (3 recommended), 2 years foreign language, and 3 years social studies (recommended); SAT/ACT required (average ACT is 18 and average SAT I is 1040); the average GPA is 2.6.

ADDITIONAL INFORMATION

The Academic Resources Center is a learning center available for students with learning disabilities as well as all other students on campus. Some of the tutoring is provided by volunteer professors. Skills classes are offered for credit in study skills. Ferrum College offers a summer program for pre-college freshmen with learning disabilities.

SUPPORT SERVICES CONTACT INFORMATION

Learning Disability Program/Services: Academic Resources Center
Director: Nancy S. Beach
  E-mail: nbeach@ferrum.edu
  Telephone: 540-365-4270
  Fax: 540-365-4271
Contact: Same

LEARNING DISABILITY SERVICES

Requests for the following services/accommodations will be evaluated individually based on appropriate and current documentation.

Allowed in Exams
  Calculator: Yes
  Dictionary: Yes
  Computer: Yes
  Spellchecker: Yes
Extended test time: Yes
Scribes: Yes
Proctors: Yes
Oral exams: Yes
Note-takers: Yes

Distraction-reduced environment: Yes
Tape recording in class: Yes
Books on tape from RFBD: Yes
Taping of books not from RFBD: Yes
Accommodations for students with ADHD: Yes
Reading machine: Yes
Other assistive technology: Yes
Priority registration: Yes

Added costs for services: No
LD specialists: Yes (1)
Professional tutors: Yes
Peer tutors: Yes
Max. hours/wk. for services: Unlimited
How professors are notified of LD/ADHD: By student and program director

GENERAL ADMISSIONS INFORMATION

Director of Admissions: Gilda Woods
Telephone: 540-365-4290

ENTRANCE REQUIREMENTS
4 English recommended, 3 math recommended, 2 science recommended, 1 science lab recommended, 2 foreign language recommended, 3 social studies recommended, 2 elective recommended. High school diploma or GED required. Minimum TOEFL is 550. TOEFL required of all international applicants.

Application deadline: Rolling
Notification: Rolling
Average GPA: 2.6

Average SAT I Math: 447
Average SAT I Verbal: 452
Average ACT: NR

Graduated top 10% of class: 4%
Graduated top 25% of class: 16%
Graduated top 50% of class: 41%

COLLEGE GRADUATION REQUIREMENTS

Course waivers allowed: Y/N
Course substitutions allowed: Y/N
In what subjects: Discussed on a case-by-case basis

ADDITIONAL INFORMATION

Environment: The College is located in a rural area south of Roanoke.

Student Body
  Undergrad enrollment: 913
  Female: 41%
  Male: 59%
  Out-of-state: 16%

Cost Information
  Tuition: $11,900
  Room & board: $5,950
Housing Information
  University housing: Yes
  Percent living on campus: 77%

Greek System
  Fraternity: Yes
  Sorority: Yes
Athletics: NCAA Division III

GEORGE MASON UNIVERSITY

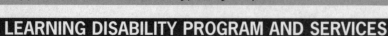

Undergrad. Admiss. Off., 4400 Univ. Dr. MSN 3A4, Fairfax, VA 22030-4444
Phone: 703-993-2400 • Fax: 703-993-2392
E-mail: admissions@gmu.edu • Web: www.gmu.edu
Support level: S • Institution type: 4-year public

LEARNING DISABILITY PROGRAM AND SERVICES

The University does not maintain a specific program for students with LD. George Mason is, however, committed to providing appropriate services and accommodations to allow identified students with disabilities to access programs. The Disability Resource Center is responsible for assuring that students receive the services to which they are entitled. Students must provide documentation and complete a Faculty Contact Sheet to receive documentation. DRC must confirm the students' requests for services.

LD/ADHD ADMISSIONS INFORMATION

College entrance tests required: Yes
Nonstandardized tests accepted: Yes
Interview required: Yes
Essay required: Yes
Documentation required for LD: Psychoeducational
   evaluation: within 3 years
Documentation required for ADHD: Yes
Documentation submitted to: DRC
Special Ed. HS course work accepted: Yes

Specific course requirements for all applicants: Yes
Separate application required for services: No
# of LD applications submitted yearly: N/A
# of LD applications accepted yearly: N/A
Total # of students receiving LD/ADHD services: 400
**Acceptance into program means acceptance into
   college:** Students must be admitted and enrolled at the
   University first and then may request services.

ADMISSIONS

Students with LD must submit the general George Mason University undergraduate application and meet the same requirements as all other applicants. Students are encouraged to self-disclose and provide documentation of their disability. Letters of recommendation are helpful for explaining weaknesses or problematic areas. Students who have deficiencies in required courses may request a waiver of the requirement. These requests are considered on an individual basis. General admission criteria include 4 years English, 3 years math (4 recommended), 1 year science (3 recommended), 3 years foreign language, 3 years social studies (4 recommended), and 3–4 year electives; ACT/SAT; and an interview is required.

ADDITIONAL INFORMATION

Students with LD may request extended testing time or alternative formats for exams, extended time for in-class writing assignments or short-term projects, note-takers, or use of a word processor for essay exams if documentation supports these modifications. Learning Services is a resource center for all students on campus. The center offers self-help skills classes in time management, organizational skills, and test-taking strategies. A Freshman Orientation class is offered for credit and some sections of this class are geared toward academic skills.

SUPPORT SERVICES CONTACT INFORMATION

Learning Disability Program/Services: Disability Resource Center
Director: Paul Bousel
   Telephone: 703-993-2474
   Fax: 703-993-2478
Contact: Deborah Wyne
   E-mail: dwyne@gmu.edu
   Telephone: 703-993-2478

LEARNING DISABILITY SERVICES

Requests for the following services/accommodations will be evaluated individually based on appropriate and current documentation.

Allowed in Exams	**Distraction-reduced environment:** Yes	**Added costs for services:** $7–$9 per
Calculator: Yes	**Tape recording in class:** Yes	hour for peer tutor
Dictionary: Yes	**Books on tape from RFBD:** Yes	**LD specialists:** No
Computer: Yes	**Taping of books not from RFBD:** Yes	**Professional tutors:** No
Spellchecker: Yes	**Accommodations for students with**	**Peer tutors:** Yes
Extended test time: Yes	**ADHD:** Yes	**Max. hours/wk. for services:** As
Scribes: Yes	**Reading machine:** Yes	needed
Proctors: Yes	**Other assistive technology:** Yes	**How professors are notified of**
Oral exams: Yes	**Priority registration:** Yes	**LD/ADHD:** By student and program
Note-takers: Yes		director

GENERAL ADMISSIONS INFORMATION

Director of Admissions: Eddie Tallent
Telephone: 703-993-2400

ENTRANCE REQUIREMENTS

18 total are required; 24 total are recommended; 4 English required, 4 English recommended, 3 math required, 4 math recommended, 3 science required, 4 science recommended, 3 science lab required, 4 science lab recommended, 2 foreign language required, 3 foreign language recommended, 3 social studies required, 4 social studies recommended, 3 elective required, 5 elective recommended. High school diploma or GED required. Minimum TOEFL is 570. TOEFL required of all international applicants.

Application deadline: February 1	**Average SAT I Math:** 532	**Graduated top 10% of class:** 17%
Notification: April 1	**Average SAT I Verbal:** 534	**Graduated top 25% of class:** 46%
Average GPA: 3.2	**Average ACT:** 21.5	**Graduated top 50% of class:** N/A

COLLEGE GRADUATION REQUIREMENTS

Course waivers allowed: No
Course substitutions allowed: Yes
In what subjects: Foreign language and, in some instances, analytical reasoning with specific documentation provided

ADDITIONAL INFORMATION

Environment: The University is located on 682 acres in a suburban area 18 miles southwest of Washington, D.C.

Student Body	**Cost Information**	**Greek System**
Undergrad enrollment: 15,185	**In-state tuition:** $2,376	**Fraternity:** Yes
Female: 56%	**Out-of-state tuition:** $11,220	**Sorority:** Yes
Male: 44%	**Room & board:** $5,400	**Athletics:** NCAA Division I
Out-of-state: 9%	**Housing Information**	
	University housing: Yes	
	Percent living on campus: 19%	

HAMPTON UNIVERSITY

Office of Admissions, Hampton University, Hampton, VA 23668
Phone: 757-727-5328 • Fax: 757-727-5095
E-mail: admit@hamptonu.edu • Web: www.hamptonu.edu
Support level: S • Institution type: 4-year private

LEARNING DISABILITY PROGRAM AND SERVICES

Hampton University is committed to assisting students with disabilities. The University seeks to help students achieve their academic potential within the academically competitive curriculum by providing a variety of accommodations. In the classroom, students may use a tape recorder and calculator, have a note-taker, selective seating, and ask for extended time for assignments. In an examination, they may have extended time, an alternate test form, a reader/scribe, an oral proctor, and a distraction-free environment. For services not available through Disability Services, referrals to other sources are made.

LD/ADHD ADMISSIONS INFORMATION

College entrance tests required: Yes
Nonstandardized tests accepted: Yes
Interview required: No
Essay required: Yes
Documentation required for LD: Psychoeducational
  evaluation: within 3 years
Documentation required for ADHD: Yes
Documentation submitted to: Testing Services
Special Ed. HS course work accepted: Yes

Specific course requirements for all applicants: Yes
Separate application required for services: No
# of LD applications submitted yearly: N/A
# of LD applications accepted yearly: N/A
Total # of students receiving LD/ADHD services: 25–30
**Acceptance into program means acceptance into
  college:** Students must be admitted and enrolled at the
  University first and then may request services.

ADMISSIONS
There is no special admission process for students with learning disabilities. All students are expected to meet the same admission criteria, which include 4 years English, 3 years math, 2 years science, 2 years history, and 6 electives; ACT/SAT with a minimum SAT of 800; rank in the top 50 percent of the class; and a minimum GPA of 2.0. Each applicant should present satisfactory credentials as to ability, character and health. Some students may be admitted through the summer Bridge Program if SAT scores are below 800 or the students are deficient in course requirements. These students take Placement Exams to determine the need for English, writing, reading, or science courses. Twenty percent of the class is admitted through Bridge.

ADDITIONAL INFORMATION
Accommodations in the classroom could include tape recorders or calculators; extended time for assignments; and note-takers. Accommodations in an examination could include distraction-free environment; extended time; alternate test formats; reader/scibe; printed copy of oral instructions; and oral proctor. Students who would like to receive disability services must contact the Section 504 Compliance Officer and provide documentation of the disability not older than three years. This Compliance Officer is responsible for qualifying students with disabilities for reasonable academic accommodations within the University. The Pre-college Program is open to all students. Freshmen on probation may take two nonrepeating courses in summer school. If they earn a C or better they may return for sophomore year.

SUPPORT SERVICES CONTACT INFORMATION

Learning Disability Program/Services: Testing Services/504 Compliance
Director: J. Halimah Rashada
  E-mail: janice.rashada@hamptonu.edu
  Telephone: 757-727-5493
  Fax: 757-727-5084
Contact: Same

LEARNING DISABILITY SERVICES

Requests for the following services/accommodations will be evaluated individually based on appropriate and current documentation.

Allowed in Exams
  Calculator: Yes
  Dictionary: Yes
  Computer: Yes
  Spellchecker: Yes
  Extended test time: Yes
  Scribes: Yes
  Proctors: Yes
  Oral exams: Yes
  Note-takers: Yes

Distraction-reduced environment: Yes
Tape recording in class: Yes
Books on tape from RFBD: Yes
Taping of books not from RFBD: No
Accommodations for students with ADHD: Yes
Reading machine: No
Other assistive technology: No
Priority registration: Yes

Added costs for services: No
LD specialists: No
Professional tutors: Yes
Peer tutors: 10
Max. hours/wk. for services: Unlimited
How professors are notified of LD/ADHD: By student

GENERAL ADMISSIONS INFORMATION

Director of Admissions: Leonard Jones, Jr.
Telephone: 757-727-5328

ENTRANCE REQUIREMENTS
17 total are required; 4 English required, 3 math required, 2 science required, 2 foreign language recommended, 2 history required, 6 elective required. High school diploma or GED required. Minimum TOEFL is 550. TOEFL required of all international applicants.

Application deadline: March 15
Notification: Rolling
Average GPA: 3.0

Average SAT I Math: 500
Average SAT I Verbal: 510
Average ACT: 19

Graduated top 10% of class: 24%
Graduated top 25% of class: 49%
Graduated top 50% of class: 99%

COLLEGE GRADUATION REQUIREMENTS

Course waivers allowed: No
Course substitutions allowed: Yes
In what subjects: Foreign language

ADDITIONAL INFORMATION

Environment: The University is located on 204 acres 15 miles west of Norfolk.

Student Body
  Undergrad enrollment: 4,891
  Female: 61%
  Male: 39%
  Out-of-state: 38%

Cost Information
  Tuition: $9,966
  Room & board: $5,090
Housing Information
  University housing: Yes
  Percent living on campus: 59%

Greek System
  Fraternity: Yes
  Sorority: Yes
Athletics: NCAA Division I

JAMES MADISON UNIVERSITY

Undergrad. Admission, Sonner Hall MSC 0101, Harrisonburg, VA 22807
Phone: 540-568-6147 • Fax: 540-568-3332
E-mail: gotojmu@jmu.edu • Web: www.jmu.edu
Support level: S • Institution type: 4-year public

LEARNING DISABILITY PROGRAM AND SERVICES

The Office of Disability Service (ODS) does not have a formal LD program, but students with learning disabilities are assisted individually and are eligible for appropriate accommodations. The mission of the ODS is to ensure that all students with disabilities can freely and actively participate in all facets of university life; to provide and coordinate support services and programs that enable students with disabilities to maximize their educational potential; and to assist students in the developmental process of transition to higher education, independence, and effective self-advocacy. The director functions as a liaison between students and the University community, and provides support in obtaining accommodations for equalizing academic success in the classroom. If the applicant is eligible for reevaluation through the school system, it is strongly advised to take advantage of the service before leaving high school. Current documentation with recommendations for post-secondary accommodations are crucial for providing appropriate services in college. Course substitution requests are dealt with on an individual basis. They may be appropriate for students for whom a particular subject has been a continuously documented obstacle to academic progress. Students should notify ODS upon enrollment if they want to seek a substitution for a course requirement. Substitutions are not guaranteed.

LD/ADHD ADMISSIONS INFORMATION

College entrance tests required: Yes
Nonstandardized tests accepted: Yes
Interview required: No
Essay required: Yes
Documentation required for LD: WAIS-III; achievement, information processing: within 4 years
Documentation required for ADHD: Yes
Documentation submitted to: ODS
Special Ed. HS course work accepted: No

Specific course requirements for all applicants: Yes
Separate application required for services: No
# of LD applications submitted yearly: N/A
# of LD applications accepted yearly: N/A
Total # of students receiving LD/ADHD services: 90
Acceptance into program means acceptance into college: Students must be admitted and enrolled at the University first and then may request services.

ADMISSIONS

The admissions team at JMU is highly sensitive and knowledgeable concerning students with learning disabilities and the admissions process. Admission decisions are made without regard to disabilities. All prospective students are expected to present academic credentials at or above the minimum standards for admission as established by the Admission Committee. After admission to JMU, documentation will be forwarded to ODS. Current recommendations for post-secondary accommodations are crucial for providing appropriate services in college. There are no specific courses required for admission into James Madison; however, students are expected to complete a solid college-prep curriculum. The middle 50 percent range for the ACT is 24–28, SAT 1110–1250 and GPA of 3.31–3.75. SAT II tests are required in writing and foreign language where applicable. The University uses class rank as one of the criteria reviewed, but does not use GPA.

ADDITIONAL INFORMATION

Some of the commonly used services are priority registration; the Support Lab, which houses equipment; academic advisors and academic services; and course scheduling information. Classroom accommodations include extended time for tests and written assignments, testing in a distraction-free environment, modification of exam format, volunteer note-takers, use of tape recorders in class, oral testing, scribes, use of computers for tests, and individual assistance as needed. Other university services include Reading and Writing Lab, Counseling and Student Development Center, and Academic Advising. Basic workshops for no credit are offered in study skills and self-advocacy. Services and accommodations are available for undergraduate and graduate students.

SUPPORT SERVICES CONTACT INFORMATION

Learning Disability Program/Services: Office of Disability Services (ODS)
Director: Louis Hedrick
 E-mail: hedriclj@jmu.edu
 Telephone: 540-568-6705
 Fax: 540-568-7099
Contact: Same
 E-mail: disability-svcs@jmu.edu

LEARNING DISABILITY SERVICES

Requests for the following services/accommodations will be evaluated individually based on appropriate and current documentation.

Allowed in Exams
 Calculator: Yes
 Dictionary: Yes
 Computer: Yes
 Spellchecker: Yes
Extended test time: Yes
Scribes: Yes
Proctors: Yes
Oral exams: Yes
Note-takers: Yes

Distraction-reduced environment: Yes
Tape recording in class: Yes
Books on tape from RFBD: Yes
Taping of books not from RFBD: Yes
Accommodations for students with ADHD: Yes
Reading machine: Yes
Other assistive technology: Yes
Priority registration: Yes

Added costs for services: No
LD specialists: No
Professional tutors: No
Peer tutors: No
Max. hours/wk. for services: Unlimited
How professors are notified of LD/ADHD: By the student and the program director

GENERAL ADMISSIONS INFORMATION

Director of Admissions: Michael Walsh
Telephone: 540-568-6147

ENTRANCE REQUIREMENTS

14 total are required; 22 total are recommended; 4 English required, 4 English recommended, 3 math required, 4 math recommended, 3 science required, 4 science recommended, 3 science lab recommended, 2 foreign language required, 3 foreign language recommended, 2 social studies recommended, 2 history required, 2 history recommended. High school diploma or GED required. Minimum TOEFL is 570. TOEFL required of all international applicants.

Application deadline: January 15
Notification: April 1
Average GPA: 3.4

Average SAT I Math: 588
Average SAT I Verbal: 582
Average ACT: N/A

Graduated top 10% of class: N/A
Graduated top 25% of class: N/A
Graduated top 50% of class: N/A

COLLEGE GRADUATION REQUIREMENTS

Course waivers allowed: No
Course substitutions allowed: Yes
In what subjects: Foreign language and math; typically substitutions are granted only when documentation is very recent, and specifically points to the need

ADDITIONAL INFORMATION

Environment: The University is located in the Shenandoah Valley surrounded by the Blue Ridge Mountains and the Alleghenies, 120 miles from Washington, D.C.

Student Body
 Undergrad enrollment: 14,156
 Female: 57%
 Male: 43%
 Out-of-state: 29%

Cost Information
 In-state tuition: $3,926
 Out-of-state tuition: $9,532
 Room & board: $5,182
Housing Information
 University housing: Yes
 Percent living on campus: 43%

Greek System
 Fraternity: Yes
 Sorority: Yes
 Athletics: NCAA Division I

James Madison University

LIBERTY UNIVERSITY

1971 University Blvd., Lynchburg, VA 24502
Phone: 504-582-2183 • Fax: 804-582-2421
E-mail: admissions@liberty.edu • Web: www.liberty.edu
Support level: CS • Institution type: 4-year private

LEARNING DISABILITY PROGRAM AND SERVICES

The primary purpose of the Bruckner Learning Center is to offer reading and study skills assistance to all students. The center provides individualized peer tutoring regularly or on a drop-in basis for English or math. There are three courses, each one semster hour long, provided for students wishing to develop reading and study skills: College Study Strategies, College Reading Improvement, and Individualized Laboratory in Reading and Study Strategies.

LD/ADHD ADMISSIONS INFORMATION

College entrance tests required: Yes
Nonstandardized tests accepted: Yes
Interview required: No
Essay required: Yes
Documentation required for LD: Latest IEP and/or psychological testing profile or other written information that describes the learning disability
Documentation required for ADHD: Yes
Documentation submitted to: Disability Academic Support
Special Ed. HS course work accepted: No

Specific course requirements for all applicants: Yes
Separate application required for services: No
# of LD applications submitted yearly: N/A
# of LD applications accepted yearly: N/A
Total # of students receiving LD/ADHD services: 60
Acceptance into program means acceptance into college: Students must be admitted and enrolled at the University first and then may request services.

ADMISSIONS

All applicants must submit an official transcript from an accredited high school and/or college, an official copy of a state high school equivalency diploma, or an official copy of the GED test results. The minimum acceptable unweighted GPA is 2.0. Applicants who fail to meet the minimum required GPA will be evaluated using other indicators of collegiate ability and may be admitted on Academic Warning. All applicants must submit ACT or SAT prior to admission. The minimum acceptable scores are SAT 800 or ACT 17.

ADDITIONAL INFORMATION

If a student's entrance test scores indicate a deficiency in English or math, then the student will enroll in a basic composition class or a fundamentals of math class. With the student's permission, instructors are provided with a written communication providing information about the student's specific disability and suggestions of appropriate accommodations. Students with a specific learning disability can be assigned to a faculty advisor who has had training in LD. This person advises students concerning academic loads and acts as a liaison between instructors and students regarding classroom accommodations. The Bruckner Learning Center provides individualized peer tutoring in most subjects on a weekly or drop-in basis.

SUPPORT SERVICES CONTACT INFORMATION

Learning Disability Program/Services: Office of Disability Academic Support
Director: Denny McHaney
E-mail: wdmchane@liberty.edu
Telephone: 804-582-2159
Fax: 804-582-2468
Contact: Same

LEARNING DISABILITY SERVICES

Requests for the following services/accommodations will be evaluated individually based on appropriate and current documentation.

Allowed in Exams
Calculator: No
Dictionary: No
Computer: No
Spellchecker: Yes
Extended test time: Yes
Scribes: Yes
Proctors: Yes
Oral exams: Yes
Note-takers: Yes

Distraction-reduced environment: Yes
Tape recording in class: Yes
Books on tape from RFBD: Yes
Taping of books not from RFBD: No
Accommodations for students with ADHD: Yes
Reading machine: No
Other assistive technology: No
Priority registration: Yes

Added costs for services: No
LD specialists: Yes (3)
Professional tutors: No
Peer tutors: 30
Max. hours/wk. for services: As needed
How professors are notified of LD/ADHD: By director

GENERAL ADMISSIONS INFORMATION

Director of Admissions: Ernie Rogers
Telephone: 804-582-2183

ENTRANCE REQUIREMENTS

17 total are recommended; 4 English recommended, 3 math recommended, 2 science recommended, 2 science lab recommended, 2 foreign language recommended, 2 social studies recommended, 2 elective recommended. High school diploma or GED required. Minimum TOEFL is 500. TOEFL required of all international applicants.

Application deadline: June 30
Notification: Rolling beginning 5/1
Average GPA: 3.1

Average SAT I Math: 504
Average SAT I Verbal: 486
Average ACT: 21

Graduated top 10% of class: NR
Graduated top 25% of class: NR
Graduated top 50% of class: NR

COLLEGE GRADUATION REQUIREMENTS

Course waivers allowed: No
Course substitutions allowed: No
In what subjects: N/A

ADDITIONAL INFORMATION

Environment: The 5,200-acre university is located in a suburban area 45 miles east of Roanoke.

Student Body
Undergrad enrollment: 5,942
Female: 49%
Male: 51%
Out-of-state: 62%

Cost Information
Tuition: $9,000
Room & board: $5,000
Housing Information
University housing: Yes
Percent living on campus: 67%

Greek System
Fraternity: Yes
Sorority: Yes
Athletics: NCAA Division I

OLD DOMINION UNIVERSITY

108 Rollins Hall, 5215 Hampton Boulevard, Norfolk, VA 23529-0050
Phone: 800-348-7926 • Fax: 757-683-3255
E-mail: admit@odu.edu • Web: www.odu.edu
Support level: CS • Institution type: 4-year public

LEARNING DISABILITY PROGRAM AND SERVICES

Student Support Services is a TRIO Program funded by the U.S. Department of Education providing academic support. The program is oriented to meet the needs of students according to their development level. Typically, students are newly diagnosed or recently transitioning to campus. The program assists students in achieving and maintaining the academic performance level required for satisfactory academic standing at the University, thereby increasing their chances of graduating. Services include on-site orientation programs, taped materials, tutorial services by peers, oral testing, untimed testing, and individual counseling. The students are respected as the primary source of knowledge of their needs.

LD/ADHD ADMISSIONS INFORMATION

College entrance tests required: Yes
Nonstandardized tests accepted: Yes
Interview required: No
Essay required: No
Documentation required for LD: WAIS-III; WISC-R; WJ: within 3 years
Documentation required for ADHD: Yes
Documentation submitted to: Director of Disability Services
Special Ed. HS course work accepted: Yes, if equivalent to high school course work

Specific course requirements for all applicants: Yes
Separate application required for services: Yes
# of LD applications submitted yearly: All
# of LD applications accepted yearly: All who provide adequate documentation
Total # of students receiving LD/ADHD services: 250
Acceptance into program means acceptance into college: Students must be admitted and enrolled at the University first and then may request services.

ADMISSIONS

There is no special admissions process for students with learning disabilities. Students are encouraged to include a cover letter identifying their learning disabilities and explaining weaknesses that may have affected their academic records. If students self-identify during the admissions process, the information may be used to support their application, but may not be used to their detriment. Clear and specific evidence and identification of a learning disability must be stated and the report must be conducted and written by a qualified professional. Students not meeting regular admission standards may be admitted through the Academic Opportunity Program. This is for 300 students with low test scores but high GPA. Others may be admitted through a Summer Transition Program or Individual Admission for nontraditional students. General admission criteria include 4 years English, 3 years math, 3 years science, 2 years foreign language, 3 years social studies, and 3 years history; ACT/SAT (with a minimum SAT of 850 and at least a 400 in the Verbal and the Math sections); rank in the top half of the class; and a minimum GPA of 2.0.

ADDITIONAL INFORMATION

Counseling and advising; study skills instruction; reading, writing, and math instruction; and tutorial assistance are available. Program staff design support services that focus on students' learning styles and special needs. There is a special section of Spanish for students with learning disabilities to meet the foreign language requirements as well as developmental math, reading, spelling, and writing.

SUPPORT SERVICES CONTACT INFORMATION

Learning Disability Program/Services: Disability Services
Director: Dr. Nancy Olthoff, PhD
  E-mail: disabilityservices@odu.edu
  Telephone: 757-683-4655
  Fax: 757-683-5356
Contact: LaCole Niles
  E-mail: Lniles@odu.edu
  Telephone: 757-683-6455
  Fax: 757-683-5356

LEARNING DISABILITY SERVICES

Requests for the following services/accommodations will be evaluated individually based on appropriate and current documentation.

Allowed in Exams
  Calculator: Yes
  Dictionary: Yes
  Computer: Yes
  Spellchecker: Yes
Extended test time: Yes
Scribes: Yes
Proctors: Yes
Oral exams: Yes
Note-takers: Yes

Distraction-reduced environment: Yes
Tape recording in class: Yes
Books on tape from RFBD: Yes
Taping of books not from RFBD: Yes
Accommodations for students with ADHD: Yes
Reading machine: Yes
Other assistive technology: Yes
Priority registration: Yes

Added costs for services: $8–$20 per hour
LD specialists: Yes (2)
Professional tutors: Yes
Peer tutors: Yes
Max. hours/wk. for services: Varies
How professors are notified of LD/ADHD: By both student and director

GENERAL ADMISSIONS INFORMATION

Director of Admissions: Alice McAdory
Telephone: 800-348-7926

ENTRANCE REQUIREMENTS
4 English recommended, 4 math recommended, 4 science recommended, 2 science lab recommended, 3 foreign language recommended, 4 history recommended. High school diploma or GED required. Minimum TOEFL is 550. TOEFL required of all international applicants.

Application deadline: February 15
Notification: March 15
Average GPA: 3.2

Average SAT I Math: 510
Average SAT I Verbal: 510
Average ACT: NR

Graduated top 10% of class: 19%
Graduated top 25% of class: 53%
Graduated top 50% of class: 90%

COLLEGE GRADUATION REQUIREMENTS

Course waivers allowed: No
Course substitutions allowed: Yes
In what subjects: Substitutions may be applied for in special cases

ADDITIONAL INFORMATION

Environment: The University is located on 46 acres in a suburban area of Norfolk.

Student Body
  Undergrad enrollment: 13,065
  Female: 56%
  Male: 44%
  Out-of-state: 9%

Cost Information
  In-state tuition: $2,184
  Out-of-state tuition: $9,774
  Room & board: $5,114
Housing Information
  University housing: Yes
  Percent living on campus: 23%

Greek System
  Fraternity: Yes
  Sorority: Yes
Athletics: NCAA Division I

UNIVERSITY OF VIRGINIA

Office of Admission, PO Box 400160, Charlottesville, VA 22904-4160
Phone: 804-982-3200 • Fax: 804-924-3587
E-mail: undergrad-admission@virginia.edu • Web: www.virginia.edu
Support level: CS • Institution type: 4-year public

LEARNING DISABILITY PROGRAM AND SERVICES

The University of Virginia is committed to providing equal access to educational and social opportunities for all disabled students. The Learning Needs and Evaluation Center (LNEC) is housed within the University's Center for Counseling and Psychological Services, and serves as the coordinating agency for services to all students with disabilities. The LNECs assists students with disabilities to become independent self-advocates, who are able to demonstrate their abilities both in the classroom and as members of the University community. The Center provides a number of services, including review of documentation supporting the disability, determination of appropriate academic accommodations, academic support services for students requiring assistance, and serves as a liaison with faculty and administrators. Information can be shared, with the student's permission, with university personnel who have an educational need to know. Once a learning disability is documented, the center assigns appropriate and reasonable accommodations and serves as a liaison with faculty and administrators. The center's primary purpose is to support the academic well-being of students with disabilities.

LD/ADHD ADMISSIONS INFORMATION

College entrance tests required: Yes
Nonstandardized tests accepted: Yes
Interview required: No
Essay required: Yes
Documentation required for LD: Psychoeducational evaluation
Documentation required for ADHD: Yes
Documentation submitted to: LNEC
Special Ed. HS course work accepted: Yes

Specific course requirements for all applicants: Yes
Separate application required for services: No
# of LD applications submitted yearly: N/A
# of LD applications accepted yearly: N/A
Total # of students receiving LD/ADHD services: 230
Acceptance into program means acceptance into college: Students must be admitted and enrolled at the University first and then may request services.

ADMISSIONS

The students with learning disabilities go through the same admissions procedure as all incoming applicants. After admission to the University, students must contact the LNEC in order to receive services. Students with learning disabilities admitted to the University have qualified for admission because of their ability. No criteria for admission are waived because of a disability. All applicants to UVA have outstanding grades, high rank in their high school class, excellent performance in Advanced Placement and Honor courses, superior performance on ACT/SAT I and SAT II, extracurricular success, special talents, and interests and goals. Letters of recommendation are required.

ADDITIONAL INFORMATION

Following acceptance of an offer of admission to the University, students with an LD or ADHD are advised to contact the LNEC in order to identify their need for services. All students seeking accommodations while at the University must provide acceptable documentation of their disability, including but not limited to a neuropsychological or psychoeducational evaluation report, completed by a licensed clinical psychologist or clinical neuropsychologist or clinical neuropsychologist that is current within three years of matriculation. The Learning Needs and Evaluation Center addresses such things as personal social skills, alternative speaking, reading, writing methods, and referral for tutors. Staff also consult with students about academic difficulties. Classes are offered in study skills and time management. Services and accommodations are available for undergraduate and graduate students.

SUPPORT SERVICES CONTACT INFORMATION

Learning Disability Program/Services: Learning Needs and Evaluation Center (LNEC)
Director: Jennifer Maedgen, PhD
  E-mail: jm3ef@virginia.edu
  Telephone: 804-243-5180
  Fax: 804-243-5188
Contact: Jill Napier
  E-mail: jjn@virginia.edu
  Telephone: 804-243-5180
  Fax: 804-243-5188

LEARNING DISABILITY SERVICES

Requests for the following services/accommodations will be evaluated individually based on appropriate and current documentation.

Allowed in Exams
  Calculator: Yes
  Dictionary: Yes
  Computer: Yes
  Spellchecker: Yes
  Extended test time: Yes
  Scribes: Yes
  Proctors: Yes
  Oral exams: Yes
  Note-takers: Yes

Distraction-reduced environment: Yes
Tape recording in class: Yes
Books on tape from RFBD: Yes
Taping of books not from RFBD: Yes
Accommodations for students with ADHD: Yes
Reading machine: Yes
Other assistive technology: Yes
Priority registration: Yes

Added costs for services: Some tutoring
LD specialists: Yes (3)
Professional tutors: Yes
Peer tutors: Yes
Max. hours/wk. for services: Individualized
How professors are notified of LD/ADHD: By student

GENERAL ADMISSIONS INFORMATION

Director of Admissions: John Blackburn
Telephone: 804-982-3200

ENTRANCE REQUIREMENTS
16 total are required; 4 English required, 4 math required, 5 math recommended, 2 science required, 4 science recommended, 2 foreign language required, 5 foreign language recommended, 1 social studies required, 3 social studies recommended. High school diploma or GED required. Minimum TOEFL is 550. TOEFL required of all international applicants.

Application deadline: January 2
Notification: April 1
Average GPA: 4.0

Average SAT I Math: 661
Average SAT I Verbal: 643
Average ACT: 28

Graduated top 10% of class: 83%
Graduated top 25% of class: 96%
Graduated top 50% of class: 99%

COLLEGE GRADUATION REQUIREMENTS

Course waivers allowed: Yes
Course substitutions allowed: Yes
In what subjects: Foreign language; waivers are allowed

ADDITIONAL INFORMATION

Environment: The 2,440-acre campus is located in a small city 70 miles northwest of Richmond.

Student Body
  Undergrad enrollment: 13,712
  Female: 54%
  Male: 46%
  Out-of-state: 30%

Cost Information
  In-state tuition: $3,046
  Out-of-state tuition: $16,295
  Room & board: $4,767
Housing Information
  University housing: Yes
  Percent living on campus: 48%

Greek System
  Fraternity: Yes
  Sorority: Yes
  Athletics: NCAA Division I

VIRGINIA INTERMONT COLLEGE

1013 Moore Street, Campus Box D-460, Bristol, VA 24201-4298
Phone: 540-466-7854 • Fax: 540-466-7855
E-mail: viadmit@vic.edu • Web: www.vic.edu
Support level: CS • Institution type: 4-year private

LEARNING DISABILITY PROGRAM AND SERVICES

Student Support Services provides free supportive services to students who participate in the program. There are extensive services offered to those with LD. The objective of the services is to help students stay in school and graduate. The department consists of a director/counselor, school psychologist/LD specialist, tutor coordinator, and an administrative assistant. Students work voluntarily with the staff as individuals or as a team to develop individual plans of support. Staff members act as advocates for students with faculty and administration and provide general faculty awareness and understanding of overall student needs without disclosure of confidentiality. Virginia Intermont staff and faculty have a commitment to the significance of the individual and to the value of personalizing education. The College provides quality education with extensive support services and accommodations, rather than altering admissions criteria or course requirements. Once admitted, students are encouraged to submit documentation of any special needs. This is usually in the form of psychoeducational test data and IEP from high school. All accommodations are provided at the request of students with documentation.

LD/ADHD ADMISSIONS INFORMATION

College entrance tests required: Yes
Nonstandardized tests accepted: Yes
Interview required: No
Essay required: No
Documentation required for LD: Psychoeducational
   assessment within: past three years
Documentation required for ADHD: Yes
Documentation submitted to: Student Support Services
   Special Ed. HS course work accepted: No

Specific course requirements for all applicants: Yes
Separate application required for services: No
# of LD applications submitted yearly: N/A
# of LD applications accepted yearly: N/A
Total # of students receiving LD/ADHD services: 30–40
**Acceptance into program means acceptance into
   college:** Students must be accepted and enrolled at the
   College first and then may request services.

ADMISSIONS

There is no special admissions procedure for the student with a learning disability. Documentation related to a learning disability may be submitted to the Office of Admissions with the general application or may be submitted separately to the Office of Student Support Services. Testing done by a high school psychologist is acceptable. General admission criteria: The average ACT is 21 or SAT 885; minimum 2.0 GPA is required; and a minimum of 15 units including 4 years English, 2 years math, 1 year lab science, 2 years social science, and 6 years electives. Virginia Intermont is more concerned with the student's quality of preparation than with the precise numerical distribution of requirements. Students not having the proper high school preparation or not meeting the normal admissions criteria may be required if admitted to take developmental courses as needed in math, English, reading, and/or study strategies. These courses would not count toward graduation, and the student would be limited to 14 hours in the first semester.

ADDITIONAL INFORMATION

Students with LD will be offered appropriate accommodations recommended by the learning specialist based on the documentation. Accommodations and/or services available to eligible students include individual personal and academic counseling, Freshman Placement Test accommodations, scribes, computer tests, extended time on tests, taped tests, peer and staff tutoring emphasizing unique techniques as needed, support groups, academic advising, diagnostic testing, liaison with faculty, tape recording of classes, assistance with course selection and registration, and optional reduced course load. A few accommodations require appointments, though generally there is an open door policy. Education 100 (one credit) taught by Student Support Services staff, is designed for students interested in improving academic skills. Topics covered in this course are individual learning styles, time-study management, note-taking, textbook reading, memory strategies, test-taking strategies, and test anxiety reduction.

SUPPORT SERVICES CONTACT INFORMATION

Learning Disability Program/Services: Student Support Services
Director: Talmage Dobbins
  E-mail: tdobbins@vic.edu
  Telephone: 540-466-7905
  Fax: 540-645-6493
Contact: Barbara Holbrook
  E-mail: bholbroo@vic.edu
  Telephone: 540-466-7905
  Fax: 540-645-6493

LEARNING DISABILITY SERVICES

Requests for the following services/accommodations will be evaluated individually based on appropriate and current documentation.

Allowed in Exams
  Calculator: Yes
  Dictionary: Yes
  Computer: Yes
  Spellchecker: Yes
Extended test time: Yes
Scribes: Yes
Proctors: Yes
Oral exams: Yes
Note-takers: Yes

Distraction-reduced environment: Yes
Tape recording in class: Yes
Books on tape from RFBD: Yes
Taping of books not from RFBD: Yes
Accommodations for students with
  ADHD: Yes
Reading machine: Yes
Other assistive technology: Yes
Priority registration: No

Added costs for services: No
LD specialists: Yes (1)
Professional tutors: No
Peer tutors: 30
Max. hours/wk. for services:
  Unlimited
How professors are notified of
  LD/ADHD: By both student and
  director

GENERAL ADMISSIONS INFORMATION

Director of Admissions: Robin Cozart
Telephone: 540-669-6101

ENTRANCE REQUIREMENTS
15 total are required; 4 English required, 2 math required, 1 science required, 1 science lab required, 2 social studies required, 6 elective required. High school diploma or GED required. Minimum TOEFL is 400. TOEFL required of all international applicants.

Application deadline: Rolling
Notification: Rolling
Average GPA: 3.0

Average SAT I Math: 460
Average SAT I Verbal: 485
Average ACT: 20

Graduated top 10% of class: 11%
Graduated top 25% of class: 29%
Graduated top 50% of class: 56%

COLLEGE GRADUATION REQUIREMENTS

Course waivers allowed: No
Course substitutions allowed: Y/N
In what subjects: Decided by committee on an individual basis

ADDITIONAL INFORMATION

Environment: The College is located on a 16-acre campus in the Blue Ridge Mountains.

Student Body
  Undergrad enrollment: 835
  Female: 75%
  Male: 25%
  Out-of-state: 34%

Cost Information
  Tuition: $11,890
  Room & board: $5,300
Housing Information
  University housing: Yes
  Percent living on campus: 56%

Greek System
  Fraternity: Yes
  Sorority: Yes
Athletics: NAIA

Virginia Intermont College

EASTERN WASHINGTON UNIVERSITY

526 Fifth Street, MS 148, Cheney, WA 99004
Phone: 509-359-2397 • Fax: 509-359-6692
E-mail: admissions@mail.ewu.edu • Web: www.ewu.edu
Support level: CS • Institution type: 4-year public

LEARNING DISABILITY PROGRAM AND SERVICES

Academically qualified students with disabilities are an integral part of the student population at EWU, and providing equal opportunities is a campuswide responsibility and commitment. Although the University does not offer a specialized curriculum, personnel work with students to modify programs to meet individual needs. Disability Support Services (DSS) is dedicated to the coordination of appropriate and reasonable accommodations for students with disabilities. These accommodations are based on individual needs so that each student may receive an equal opportunity to learn to participate in campus life; to grow emotionally and socially; and to successfully complete a program of study that will enable him or her to be self-supporting and remain as independent as possible. This is facilitated through support services, information sharing, advisement, and referral when requested. Students who wish services and support need to contact DSS so that the disability can be verified, needs determined, and timely accommodations made. In most cases, documentation by a professional service provider will be necessary. Information is kept strictly confidential. However, it is important to share information that will enable DSS staff to provide appropriate, reasonable, and timely services tailored to individual needs.

LD/ADHD ADMISSIONS INFORMATION

College entrance tests required: Yes
Nonstandardized tests accepted: Yes
Interview required: No
Essay required: No
Documentation required for LD: Psychoeducational
  evaluation: within 3 years
Documentation required for ADHD: Yes
Documentation submitted to: Disability Support Services
Special Ed. HS course work accepted: Yes

Specific course requirements for all applicants: Yes
Separate application required for services: No
# of LD applications submitted yearly: N/A
# of LD applications accepted yearly: N/A
Total # of students receiving LD/ADHD services: 70–80
**Acceptance into program means acceptance into
  college:** Students must be admitted and enrolled at the
  University first and then may request services.

ADMISSIONS

Individuals with disabilities are admitted via the standard admissions criteria that apply to all students. General admissibility is based on an index using GPA and test scores. The minimum GPA accepted is a 2.0. Required courses include 4 years English, 3 years math, 3 years social science, 2 years science (1 year lab), 2 years foreign language (American Sign Language accepted), and 1 year arts or academic elective. Special education courses are acceptable if they are courses that are regularly taught in the high school. However, all applicants must complete the required core courses. Students who do not meet the grade and test score admission scale may provide additional information to the Admission Office and request consideration through the Special Talent Admissions Process.

ADDITIONAL INFORMATION

Examples of services for students with specific learning disabilities include taped texts; equipment loan; alternative testing arrangements such as oral, extended time, relocation of testing site; note-takers; tutorial assistance (available to all students); referral to Learning Skills Center, Writers' Center, Mathematics Lab; accessible computer stations; and Kurzweil reading machine. Examples of services for students with ADHD are consultation regarding reasonable and effective accommodations with classroom professors; alternative testing; books on tape; note-takers; taped lectures; equipment loans; referrals to Learning Skills Center, Math Lab, Writers' Center, and Counseling and Psychological services; information on ADHD; and informal counseling. Skills classes for credit are offered in math, reading, time management, study skills, and writing skills. A Learning Skills Center and a Writing Center are open to all students. Services and accommodations are offered to undergraduate and graduate students.

SUPPORT SERVICES CONTACT INFORMATION

Learning Disability Program/Services: Disability Support Services
Director: Karen Raver
   E-mail: kraver@mail.ewu.edu
   Telephone: 509-359-6871
   Fax: 509-359-4673
Contact: Pam McDermott
   E-mail: pmcdermott@mail.ewu.edu
   Telephone: 509-359-6871
   Fax: 509-359-4673

LEARNING DISABILITY SERVICES

Requests for the following services/accommodations will be evaluated individually based on appropriate and current documentation.

Allowed in Exams
   Calculator: Yes
   Dictionary: Yes
   Computer: Yes
   Spellchecker: Yes
Extended test time: Yes
Scribes: Yes
Proctors: Yes
Oral exams: Yes
Note-takers: Yes

Distraction-reduced environment: Yes
Tape recording in class: Yes
Books on tape from RFBD: Yes
Taping of books not from RFBD: Yes
Accommodations for students with ADHD: Yes
Reading machine: Yes
Other assistive technology: Yes
Priority registration: Yes

Added costs for services: No
LD specialists: Yes
Professional tutors: 7
Peer tutors: 33
Max. hours/wk. for services: 19
How professors are notified of LD/ADHD: By both student and director

GENERAL ADMISSIONS INFORMATION

Director of Admissions: Michelle Whittingham
Telephone: 509-359-6582

ENTRANCE REQUIREMENTS

15 total are required; 4 English required, 3 math required, 4 math recommended, 2 science required, 1 science lab required, 2 foreign language required, 3 social studies required, 1 elective required. High school diploma or GED required. Minimum TOEFL is 525. TOEFL required of all international applicants.

Application deadline: Rolling
Notification: Rolling beginning 12/1
Average GPA: 3.3

Average SAT I Math: 502
Average SAT I Verbal: 502
Average ACT: 21

Graduated top 10% of class: 23%
Graduated top 25% of class: 48%
Graduated top 50% of class: 80%

COLLEGE GRADUATION REQUIREMENTS

Course waivers allowed: Yes
Course substitutions allowed: Yes
In what subjects: Only substitutions in math; possible waiver in foreign language

ADDITIONAL INFORMATION

Environment: The University is located on 35 acres in a small town 18 miles southwest of Spokane.

Student Body
   Undergrad enrollment: 7,149
   Female: 58%
   Male: 42%
   Out-of-state: 9%

Cost Information
   In-state tuition: $2,790
   Out-of-state tuition: $9,594
   Room & board: $4,558
Housing Information
   University housing: Yes
   Percent living on campus: 17%

Greek System
   Fraternity: Yes
   Sorority: Yes
Athletics: NCAA Division I

WASHINGTON STATE UNIVERSITY

342 French Administration Building, Pullman, WA 99164
Phone: 509-335-5586 • Fax: 509-335-4902
E-mail: admissions@wsu.edu • Web: www.wsu.edu
Support level: S • Institution type: 4-year public

LEARNING DISABILITY PROGRAM AND SERVICES

The Disability Resource Center (DRC) assists students who have a disability by providing academic services. The program may also refer students to other service programs that may assist them in achieving their academic goals. DRC will help students overcome potential obstacles so that they may be successful in their area of study. All academic adjustments are authorized on an individual basis. DRC coordinates services for students with LD. The program offers academic support in many different areas. To be eligible for assistance, students must be currently enrolled at Washington State University. They also must submit documentation of their disability. For a learning disability, the student must submit a written report that includes test scores and evaluation. It is the student's responsibility to request accommodations if desired. It is important to remember that even though two individuals may have the same disability, they may not necessarily need the same academic adjustments. DRC works with students and instructors to determine and implement appropriate academic adjustments. Many adjustments are simple creative alternatives for traditional ways of learning.

LD/ADHD ADMISSIONS INFORMATION

College entrance tests required: Yes
Nonstandardized tests accepted: Yes
Interview required: No
Essay required: No
Documentation required for LD: WAIS-III or WISC-R (within three years)
Documentation required for ADHD: Yes
Documentation submitted to: DRC
Special Ed. HS course work accepted: Yes

Specific course requirements for all applicants: Yes
Separate application required for services: No
# of LD applications submitted yearly: N/A
# of LD applications accepted yearly: N/A
Total # of students receiving LD/ADHD services: 283
Acceptance into program means acceptance into college: Students must be accepted and enrolled at the University first (they can appeal a denial) and then may request services.

ADMISSIONS
All students must meet the general admission requirements. The University looks at the combination of the scores on the ACT/SAT and the high school GPA. The standard admission criteria are based on an index score determined by 75 percent GPA and 25 percent SAT/ACT. Only 15 percent of new admissions may be offered under "special admission." Documentation of the learning disability and diagnostic tests should have been given less than three years before.

ADDITIONAL INFORMATION
General assistance to students with learning disabilities includes pre-admission counseling; information about disabilities; referral to appropriate community resources; academic, personal, and career counseling; information about accommodations; information about the laws pertaining to individuals with disabilities; and self-advocacy. Typical academic adjustments for students with learning disabilities may include note-takers and/or audiotape class sessions; and alternative testing arrangements; textbook taping or one-to-one readers; extended time for exams; essay exams taken on computer; and computers with voice output and spellcheckers. Services and accommodations are available for undergraduate and graduate students.

SUPPORT SERVICES CONTACT INFORMATION

Learning Disability Program/Services: Disability Resource Center (DRC)
Director: Susan Schaeffer, PhD
  Telephone: 509-335-1566
  Fax: 509-335-8511
Contact: Same

LEARNING DISABILITY SERVICES

Requests for the following services/accommodations will be evaluated individually based on appropriate and current documentation.

Allowed in Exams
  Calculator: No
  Dictionary: No
  Computer: Yes
  Spellchecker: Yes
  Extended test time: Yes
  Scribes: Yes
  Proctors: Yes
  Oral exams: Yes
  Note-takers: Yes

Distraction-reduced environment: Yes
Tape recording in class: Yes
Books on tape from RFBD: Yes
Taping of books not from RFBD: Yes
Accommodations for students with ADHD: Yes
Reading machine: No
Other assistive technology: No
Priority registration: Yes

Added costs for services: No
LD specialists: No
Professional tutors: No
Peer tutors: 50
Max. hours/wk. for services: Unlimited
How professors are notified of LD/ADHD: By student

GENERAL ADMISSIONS INFORMATION

Director of Admissions: Ken Vreeland (interim director)
Telephone: 509-335-5586

ENTRANCE REQUIREMENTS
15 total are required; 4 English required, 3 math required, 2 science required, 1 science lab required, 2 foreign language required, 2 social studies required, 1 history required, 1 elective required. High school diploma or GED required. Minimum TOEFL is 520. TOEFL required of all international applicants.

Application deadline: Rolling
Notification: Rolling
Average GPA: 3.4

Average SAT I Math: 527
Average SAT I Verbal: 531
Average ACT: N/A

Graduated top 10% of class: 40%
Graduated top 25% of class: 74%
Graduated top 50% of class: NR

COLLEGE GRADUATION REQUIREMENTS

Course waivers allowed: Yes
Course substitutions allowed: Yes
In what subjects: Foreign language

ADDITIONAL INFORMATION

Environment: The University is located on 600 acres in a small town 80 miles south of Spokane.

Student Body
  Undergrad enrollment: 16,839
  Female: 52%
  Male: 48%
  Out-of-state: 9%

Cost Information
  In-state tuition: $3,351
  Out-of-state tuition: $10,267
  Room & board: $4,826
Housing Information
  University housing: Yes
  Percent living on campus: 49%

Greek System
  Fraternity: Yes
  Sorority: Yes
Athletics: NCAA Division I

DAVIS & ELKINS COLLEGE

100 Campus Drive, Elkins, WV 26241
Phone: 304-637-1230 • Fax: 304-637-1800
E-mail: admiss@euclid.dne.wvnet.edu • Web: www.dne.edu
Support level: SP • Institution type: 4-year private

LEARNING DISABILITY PROGRAM AND SERVICES

Davis & Elkins offers a comprehensive support program for college students with learning disabilities. The goals blend with the College's commitment to diversity and providing a personalized education. The program goes well beyond accommodations or services by providing individualized instruction to meet each student's needs. The goal of the LD Program is to enable students diagnosed with LD/ADHD to function to the best of their ability. To meet this goal each student meets at least weekly for a regularly scheduled session with one of the three experienced learning disabilities specialists. The main focus of these meetings is to develop learning strategies and academic skills. Students may request extra assistance and use the lab as a study area. There is a $2,600 fee for first-year students. Applicants must submit complete and current documentation of the disability.

LD/ADHD ADMISSIONS INFORMATION

College entrance tests required: Yes
Nonstandardized tests accepted: Yes
Interview required: No
Essay required: Yes
Documentation required for LD: Complete psychological and academic battery; current within three years
Documentation required for ADHD: Yes
Documentation submitted to: LD Program
Special Ed. HS course work accepted: No

Specific course requirements for all applicants: Yes
Separate application required for services: Yes
# of LD applications submitted yearly: 50–80
# of LD applications accepted yearly: 10–31
Total # of students receiving LD/ADHD services: 50
Acceptance into program means acceptance into college: Students must be admitted and enrolled at the College first and then may request services.

ADMISSIONS

All applications are screened by the Learning Disabilties Program Director and the Director of Admissions. Students must be admitted to Davis and Elkins College prior to being considered for the program. The admissions counselors have been trained to recognize potentially successful students with learning disabilities. Students requesting admission to the program must meet admissions requirements; complete a separate application to the program; send complete and current documentation completed within the last three years; recommendation for participation in the program by a counselor or a learning specialist; copy of recent IEP, if available; a handwritten essay requesting services and indicating why services are being requested; and have a personal meeting to discuss needs and expectations.

ADDITIONAL INFORMATION

Services include individual sessions with certified LD specialists; individualized programs focusing on improved writing skills; test-taking techniques; note-taking and textbook usage; and time management strategies. Specialists help students develop a personalized program focusing on improving written work, identifying class expectations and preparing work to that level of expectation, test-taking skills, using textbooks and taking notes, and managing time effectively. Students also receive advising and registration assistance based on assessment information. Personnel in the LD program also assist the students with course selection and registration; orientation to college life; monitoring of classes throughout the year and help interpreting feedback from professors; coordination of tutoring, additional counseling, and career planning; and instructional program modification as needed.

SUPPORT SERVICES CONTACT INFORMATION

Learning Disability Program/Services: Learning Disabilities Program
Director: Judith Sabol McCauley
  E-mail: mccaulj@dne.edu
  Telephone: 304-637-1229
  Fax: 304-637-1413
Contact: Same

LEARNING DISABILITY SERVICES

Requests for the following services/accommodations will be evaluated individually based on appropriate and current documentation.

Allowed in Exams
  Calculator: Yes
  Dictionary: Yes
  Computer: Yes
  Spellchecker: Yes
Extended test time: Yes
Scribes: Yes
Proctors: Yes
Oral exams: Yes
Note-takers: Yes

Distraction-reduced environment: Yes
Tape recording in class: Yes
Books on tape from RFBD: Yes
Taping of books not from RFBD: Yes
**Accommodations for students with
  ADHD:** Yes
Reading machine: No
Other assistive technology: Yes
Priority registration: Yes

Added costs for services: $2,600 per year
LD specialists: Yes (3)
Professional tutors: Yes
Peer tutors: Yes
Max. hours/wk. for services: Unlimited
**How professors are notified of
  LD/ADHD:** By both student and director

GENERAL ADMISSIONS INFORMATION

Director of Admissions: Matt Shiflett
Telephone: 800-624-3157

ENTRANCE REQUIREMENTS
14 total are required; 4 English required, 3 math required, 3 science required, 1 science lab required, 1 foreign language required, 2 foreign language recommended, 3 social studies required. High school diploma or GED required. Minimum TOEFL is 500. TOEFL required of all international applicants.

Application deadline: Rolling
Notification: Rolling beginning 9/1
Average GPA: 3.1

Average SAT I Math: 473
Average SAT I Verbal: 490
Average ACT: 20

Graduated top 10% of class: 10%
Graduated top 25% of class: 25%
Graduated top 50% of class: 59%

COLLEGE GRADUATION REQUIREMENTS

Course waivers allowed: No
Course substitutions allowed: Yes
In what subjects: Varies; individual requests are reviewed by the dean

ADDITIONAL INFORMATION

Environment: The College is located in a community of 10,000 in the foothills of the Allegheny Mountains.

Student Body
  Undergrad enrollment: 658
  Female: 56%
  Male: 44%
  Out-of-state: 39%

Cost Information
  Tuition: $12,080
  Room & board: $5,330
Housing Information
  University housing: Yes
  Percent living on campus: 44%

Greek System
  Fraternity: Yes
  Sorority: Yes
Athletics: NCAA Division II

MARSHALL UNIVERSITY

400 Hal Greer Boulevard, Huntington, WV 25755
Phone: 304-696-3160 • Fax: 304-696-3135
E-mail: admissions@marshall.edu • Web: www.marshall.edu
Support level: SP • Institution type: 4-year public

LEARNING DISABILITY PROGRAM AND SERVICES

Higher Education for Learning Problems (HELP) encourages a feeling of camaraderie among the students enrolled in the program. HELP provides an individual tutoring program in course work, exceptions in testing, and a remedial program. Students work with LD specialists one-to-one, to improve reading, writing, and language skills. Counseling is provided on-site, and the large professional staff offers a variety of additional services. This program boasts a 95% success rate with students.

LD/ADHD ADMISSIONS INFORMATION

College entrance tests required: Yes
Nonstandardized tests accepted: Yes
Interview required: Yes
Essay required: Yes
Documentation required for LD: WAIS-III: within 3 years; achievement tests: within 1 year
Documentation required for ADHD: Yes
Documentation submitted to: HELP program
Special Ed. HS course work accepted: Yes

Specific course requirements for all applicants: Yes
Separate application required for services: Yes
# of LD applications submitted yearly: 300+
# of LD applications accepted yearly: 210
Total # of students receiving LD/ADHD services: 250
Acceptance into program means acceptance into college: Students must be accepted and enrolled at the University first and then may request admission to HELP.

ADMISSIONS

Students with learning disabilities must follow a special admissions procedure. These students must submit: an application; updated psychological and educational evaluation; one-page, handwritten statement by the student (no assistance) regarding why college is desirable; and two recommendations stating why the recommenders feel the student should attend college. Interviews are required; minimum GPA of 2.0, ACT 17+, or SAT 810+ (tests are unimportant for LD admit), plus 4 years English, 3 years social studies, and 2 years math. Students should schedule interview before January, and submit application to HELP no less than one year in advance of the proposed entry date to college. All applications must be received by December 31. Marshall University has a probationary admission if the reason for low GPA or test scores is convincing. There is a required five-week summer HELP Program for these incoming freshmen.

ADDITIONAL INFORMATION

The Summer Learning Disabilities Program is offered through HELP to incoming freshmen with learning disabilities. The program includes teachers with master's degrees in learning disabilities; a graduate assistant for each teacher who assists with tutoring course work (tutors are matched to students who have a learning style compatible to the teaching style of the tutor); no more than five students per group; note-taking skills and study skills; test-taking strategies; organization of time; improvement of basic skills in reading, spelling, written language, and mathematics; improvement of self-esteem and self-confidence. The cost is $1,000 for West Virginia residents, $1,300 for Metro area residents, and $2,000 for non–West Virginia residents. This does not include registration for classes students may take through the University. Students sign a release allowing HELP to talk to professors and parents. There is also a summer program for elementary and secondary students with learning disabilities.

SUPPORT SERVICES CONTACT INFORMATION

Learning Disability Program/Services: Higher Education for Learning Problems (H.E.L.P.)
Director: Dr. Barbara P. Guyer
  E-mail: guyerb@marshall.edu
  Telephone: 304-696-6317
  Fax: 304-696-3231
Contact: Lynne Weston
  E-mail: weston@marshall.edu
  Telephone: 304-696-6316
  Fax: 304-696-3231

LEARNING DISABILITY SERVICES

Requests for the following services/accommodations will be evaluated individually based on appropriate and current documentation.

Allowed in Exams
  Calculator: Yes
  Dictionary: Yes
  Computer: Yes
  Spellchecker: Yes
Extended test time: Yes
Scribes: Yes
Proctors: Yes
Oral exams: Yes
Note-takers: Yes

Distraction-reduced environment: Yes
Tape recording in class: Yes
Books on tape from RFBD: Yes
Taping of books not from RFBD: Yes
Accommodations for students with
  ADHD: Yes
Reading machine: Yes
Other assistive technology: Yes
Priority registration: Yes

Added costs for services: $250 per
  credit hour
LD specialists: Yes (15)
Professional tutors: 10
Peer tutors: No
Max. hours/wk. for services:
  Unlimited
How professors are notified of
  LD/ADHD: By student

GENERAL ADMISSIONS INFORMATION

Director of Admissions: James Harless
Telephone: 800-642-3463

ENTRANCE REQUIREMENTS
11 total are required; 2 total are recommended; 4 English required, 2 math required, 2 science required, 2 science lab required, 2 foreign language recommended, 3 social studies required. High school diploma or GED required. Minimum TOEFL is 500. TOEFL required of all international applicants.

Application deadline: Rolling
Notification: Rolling beginning 9/1
Average GPA: 3.3

Average SAT I Math: N/A
Average SAT I Verbal: N/A
Average ACT: 21

Graduated top 10% of class: N/A
Graduated top 25% of class: 52%
Graduated top 50% of class: 89%

COLLEGE GRADUATION REQUIREMENTS

Course waivers allowed: Yes
Course substitutions allowed: Yes
In what subjects: Foreign language and math

ADDITIONAL INFORMATION

Environment: Marshall University has a 55-acre urban campus located 140 miles east of Lexington, Kentucky.

Student Body
  Undergrad enrollment: 9,621
  Female: 55%
  Male: 45%
  Out-of-state: 16%

Cost Information
  In-state tuition: $2,160
  Out-of-state tuition: $6,364
  Room & board: $4,850
Housing Information
  University housing: Yes
  Percent living on campus: 20%

Greek System
  Fraternity: Yes
  Sorority: Yes
Athletics: NCAA Division I

WEST VIRGINIA UNIVERSITY

Admissions Office, PO Box 6009, Morgantown, WV 26506-6009
Phone: 304-293-2121 • Fax: 304-293-3080
E-mail: wvuadmissions@arc.wvu.edu • Web: www.wvu.edu
Support level: S • Institution type: 4-year

LEARNING DISABILITY PROGRAM AND SERVICES

The Office of Disability Services is available to all students on the campus of West Virginia University. Services are provided to better enable qualified students with disabilities to maximize their academic potential. It is the student's responsibility to provide documentation for the diagnosis prior to receiving accommodations based upon that disability. Each student's academic accommodations will be determined by the University on an individual basis. In order to meet the adult criteria of "disability" under federal laws, individuals must provide documentation of how the significant impairment "substantially limits" their academic functioning. A "significant impairment" means below average functioning. An IEP is not documentation of a disability for the purposes of providing accommodations at the College level.

LD/ADHD ADMISSIONS INFORMATION

College entrance tests required: Yes
Nonstandardized tests accepted: Yes
Interview required: No
Essay required: No
Documentation required for LD: Psychoeducational evaluation
Documentation required for ADHD: Yes
Documentation submitted to: WVU Learning Center
Special Ed. HS course work accepted: No

Specific course requirements for all applicants: Yes
Separate application required for services: No
# of LD applications submitted yearly: NA
# of LD applications accepted yearly: NA
Total # of students receiving LD/ADHD services: NA
Acceptance into program means acceptance into college: Students must be admitted and enrolled and then may request services.

ADMISSIONS

There is no special admissions process for students with LD and ADHD. In-state students must have a 2.0 GPA and out-of-state students must have a 2.25 GPA. Additionally, all applicants must have 4 years of English, 3 years of social studies, 3 years of math; 2 years of lab science and foreign language is recommended. Students are not encouraged to self-disclose a disability in a personal statement during the application process. Appropriate services/accommodations will be determined after the student is admitted.

ADDITIONAL INFORMATION

Requirements for the documentation of an LD include the following: a signed, dated comprehensive psychoeducational evaluation report indicating how the LD impacts academic performance and contributes to a "significant impairment" in academic functioning. The report should address aptitude, achievement, processing, and should include the WAIS and full Woodcock-Johnson Battery. A description of the functional limitations, which impact against the educational effort, must be included in the diagnostic report. Additionally, a documented history of previous accommodations received should be included. Documentation of ADHD must be in the form of a signed and dated report, by either a psychiatrist, neuropsychologist or licensed psychologist trained in the differential diagnosis. Additional information is required. There are no LD specialists on staff; however, counselors are available to provide services to all students. Some accommodations that are available with appropriate documentation include priority registration, course substitutions, extended testing time, note-takers, distraction-free environments, books on tape, and assistive technology.

SUPPORT SERVICES CONTACT INFORMATION

Learning Disability Program/Services: West Virginia University Learning Center
Director: T. Anne Hawkins
  E-mail: thawkins3@wvu.edu
  Telephone: 304-293-2316
  Fax: 304-293-3369
Contact: Same

LEARNING DISABILITY SERVICES

Requests for the following services/accommodations will be evaluated individually based on appropriate and current documentation.

Allowed in Exams
  Calculator: Yes
  Dictionary: Yes
  Computer: Yes
  Spellchecker: Yes
Extended test time: Yes
Scribes: Yes
Proctors: No
Oral exams: No
Note-takers: Yes

Distraction-reduced environment: Yes
Tape recording in class: Yes
Books on tape from RFBD: Yes
Taping of books not from RFBD: Yes
Accommodations for students with ADHD: Yes
Reading machine: Yes
Other assistive technology: Yes
Priority registration: Yes

Added costs for services: No
LD specialists: No
Professional tutors: No
Peer tutors: 65
Max. hours/wk. for services: Unlimited
How professors are notified of LD/ADHD: By both student and director

GENERAL ADMISSIONS INFORMATION

Director of Admissions: Cheng H. Khoo
Telephone: 304-293-2114

ENTRANCE REQUIREMENTS
12 total are required; 2 total are recommended; 4 English required, 3 math required, 2 science required, 2 science lab required, 2 foreign language recommended, 2 social studies required, 1 history required. High school diploma or GED required. Minimum TOEFL is 550. TOEFL required of all international applicants.

Application deadline: August 1
Notification: Rolling beginning 9/15
Average GPA: 3.2

Average SAT I Math: 521
Average SAT I Verbal: 514
Average ACT: 23

Graduated top 10% of class: 21%
Graduated top 25% of class: 45%
Graduated top 50% of class: 77%

COLLEGE GRADUATION REQUIREMENTS

Course waivers allowed: NR
Course substitutions allowed: Yes
In what subjects: Foreign language; substitutions possible

ADDITIONAL INFORMATION

Environment: Located 70 miles from Pittsburgh, Pennsylvania.

Student Body
  Undergrad enrollment: 15,463
  Female: 46%
  Male: 54%
  Out-of-state: 37%

Cost Information
  In-state tuition: $1,994
  Out-of-state tuition: $7,520
  Room & board: $5,152
Housing Information
  University housing: Yes
  Percent living on campus: 20%

Greek System
  Fraternity: Yes
  Sorority: Yes
Athletics: NCAA Division I

WEST VIRGINIA WESLEYAN COLLEGE

59 College Avenue, Buckhannon, WV 26201
Phone: 304-473-8510 • Fax: 304-473-8108
E-mail: admission@wvwc.edu • Web: www.wvwc.edu
Support level: SP • Institution type: 4-year private

LEARNING DISABILITY PROGRAM AND SERVICES

The College holds a strong commitment to providing excellent support to students with documented disabilities. An individually structured program has been designed to accommodate students with varying needs. Master's-level professionals in the fields of learning disabilities, reading, education, and counseling work to help each student design strategies for academic success. Accommodation plans are determined through a review of the documentation provided by the student and the recommendations of the student's Comprehensive Advisor, who works closely with each individual. Students who want to receive LD services must submit an educational assessment, completed within the last two to three years, to the Director of the Student Academic Support Services. Documentation must include the WAIS and the Woodcock-Johnson Standard Achievement Battery. Alternate achievement assessment will be considered with the approval of the Director. Both numeric scores and a narrative report, which interpret a perceived or diagnosed LD, are required. A copy of the IEP would be helpful. Documentation must be submitted in a timely manner in order to plan specialized advising, preferential registration, and the implementation of the appropriate accommodations.

LD/ADHD ADMISSIONS INFORMATION

College entrance tests required: Yes
Nonstandardized tests accepted: Yes
Interview required: No
Essay required: No
Documentation required for LD: WAIS-III (in the last two to three years) Woodcock-Johnson Achievement Battery
Documentation required for ADHD: Yes
Documentation submitted to: Student Academic Support Services
Special Ed. HS course work accepted: Yes

Specific course requirements for all applicants: Yes
Separate application required for services: No
# of LD applications submitted yearly: 150
# of LD applications accepted yearly: 90
Total # of students receiving LD/ADHD services: 103
Acceptance into program means acceptance into college: Students are admitted jointly into the College and SSSP.

ADMISSIONS

The Director of Student Academic Support Services reviews the application of students who self-disclose a learning disability or attention deficit disorder. Applicants are encouraged to submit a psychological evaluation if they believe it will help develop an accurate picture of student potential. Interviews are encouraged but not required unless it is determined that an interview could help the admissions team gain a better understanding of the applicant. The Academic Dean has the authority to offer special admission to some students not admitted through the regular application process. Application decisions are made jointly by the Director of Admission and the Director of Student Academic Support Services. General admission criteria include a GPA no lower than 2.0; 4 years English, 3 years math, 2 years science, 2 years social studies, 1 year history, and 3 years electives. No foreign language is required for admission. The middle 50 percent range for the ACT is 18–27 and SAT 800–1400. It is to the student's advantage to self-disclose a disability. If a student choses to self-disclose, the educational assessment is interpreted by the Director of Special Services, who may recommend admission based on the evaluation of the student's potentail for success in college.

ADDITIONAL INFORMATION

The Support for Students with Disabilities Office provides the following services when appropriate: individualized support from a Comprehensive Advisor who plans and coordinates accommodation of student needs and acts as a liaison with other departments; annual individualized accommodation plan with yearly updates of appropriate accommodations; preferential registration and specialized academic advising for the first three semesters; extended time and separate testing location for qualified students; limited noncredit practice as needed to support compostion courses; note-takers when necessary and appropriate; alternative textbook format; and individual peer tutoring. Some class offerings include: College Study Strategies; Developmental Math; Lindamood-Bell Learning Program (clinical instruction in phonemic awareness, comprehension skills, and application to course work); memory techniques; note-taking; techniques of reading; test-taking; time management; and visual thinking.

SUPPORT SERVICES CONTACT INFORMATION

Learning Disability Program/Services: Student Academic Support Services
Director: Mrs. Shawn Kuba
  E-mail: kuba_s@wvwc.edu
  Telephone: 304-473-8563
  Fax: 304-473-8497
Contact: Carolyn Baisden
  E-mail: baisden_c@wvwc.edu
  Telephone: 304-473-8563
  Fax: 304-473-8497

LEARNING DISABILITY SERVICES

Requests for the following services/accommodations will be evaluated individually based on appropriate and current documentation.

Allowed in Exams
  Calculator: Yes
  Dictionary: Yes
  Computer: Yes
  Spellchecker: Yes
Extended test time: Yes
Scribes: Yes
Proctors: Yes
Oral exams: Yes
Note-takers: Yes

Distraction-reduced environment: Yes
Tape recording in class: Yes
Books on tape from RFBD: Yes
Taping of books not from RFBD: Yes
Accommodations for students with ADHD: Yes
Reading machine: Yes
Other assistive technology: Yes
Priority registration: Yes

Added costs for services: Level I/$3,700; Level II/$2,000; Level III/$1,000; Level IV/$500
LD specialists: Yes (1)
Professional tutors: Yes
Peer tutors: 18
Max. hours/wk. for services: Unlimited
How professors are notified of LD/ADHD: By student

GENERAL ADMISSIONS INFORMATION

Director of Admissions: Robert Skinner
Telephone: 304-473-8510

ENTRANCE REQUIREMENTS

4 English required, 3 math required, 3 science required, 2 science lab required, 2 foreign language recommended, 2 social studies required, 3 social studies recommended, 2 history required, 2 history recommended, 3 elective required. High school diploma or GED required. TOEFL required of all international applicants.

Application deadline: August 1
Notification: Rolling beginning 11/15
Average GPA: 3.3

Average SAT I Math: 521
Average SAT I Verbal: 527
Average ACT: 23

Graduated top 10% of class: 23%
Graduated top 25% of class: 50%
Graduated top 50% of class: 80%

COLLEGE GRADUATION REQUIREMENTS

Course waivers allowed: Yes
Course substitutions allowed: Yes
In what subjects: Varies; any course where the request is appropriate; there is no foreign language requirement

ADDITIONAL INFORMATION

Environment: The College is located on 80 acres 135 miles from Pittsburgh in the Appalachian foothills.

Student Body
  Undergrad enrollment: 1,601
  Female: 57%
  Male: 43%
  Out-of-state: 48%

Cost Information
  Tuition: $16,800
  Room & board: $4,350
Housing Information
  University housing: Yes
  Percent living on campus: 85%

Greek System
  Fraternity: Yes
  Sorority: Yes
Athletics: NCAA Division II

ALVERNO COLLEGE

3400 South 43rd Street, PO Box 343922, Milwaukee, WI 53234-3922
Phone: 414-382-6100 • Fax: 414-382-6354
E-mail: admissions@alverno.edu • Web: www.alverno.edu
Support level: S • Institution type: 4-year private

LEARNING DISABILITY PROGRAM AND SERVICES

Alverno College is a small liberal arts college for women with approximately 2,000 students. The Instructional Services Center (ISC) provides academic support to Alverno students, and assists Alverno applicants in meeting admissions requirements. ISC offers courses in reading, writing, critical thinking, math, and algebra in order to develop academic skills as required on the basis of new student assessment results. ISC also offers tutorial support, course-based study groups, and workshops to provide an opportunity for small groups of students to study together under the direction of a peer tutor or an ISC teacher. There is also a Coordinator of Support Services for Students with Disabilities who assists the student to meet her academic potential through understanding of her learning needs, development of strategies and accommodations to maximize her strengths, and development of self-advocacy with faculty.

LD/ADHD ADMISSIONS INFORMATION

College entrance tests required: Yes
Nonstandardized tests accepted: Yes
Interview required: No
Essay required: Yes
Documentation required for LD: WAIS-III; WJ-R; WRAT-R: within 5–8 years
Documentation required for ADHD: Yes
Documentation submitted to: ISC
Special Ed. HS course work accepted: No

Specific course requirements for all applicants: Yes
Separate application required for services: No
# of LD applications submitted yearly: N/A
# of LD applications accepted yearly: N/A
Total # of students receiving LD/ADHD services: 60
Acceptance into program means acceptance into college: Students must be admitted and enrolled at the College first and then may request services.

ADMISSIONS

Admission criteria are the same for all students coming directly from high school. General admission requirements include 19+ ACT; 17 academic credits in college-prep courses with recommendations, including 4 years English, 2 years foreign language, 3 years math, 3 years science, 3 years social studies; and rank in the top half of graduating class. There is a college transition program for students who do not meet the admissions criteria but have academic potential.

ADDITIONAL INFORMATION

Classes are offered at a beginning level in reading and writing, math and algebra. Students may not substitute courses for math courses required to graduate, but intensive assistance is provided. Tutoring is provided through ISC, and an Academic Support Group for students with LD meets every two to three weeks to discuss topics such as self-advocacy, problem solving, writing letters, and communicating with professors. The College has a Math Resource Center and a Writing Resource Center available for all students.

SUPPORT SERVICES CONTACT INFORMATION

Learning Disability Program/Services: Instructional Services Center (ISC)
Director: Nancy Bornstein
 Telephone: 414-382-6353
Contact: Colleen Barnett, Coordinator
 Telephone: 414-382-6026

LEARNING DISABILITY SERVICES

Requests for the following services/accommodations will be evaluated individually based on appropriate and current documentation.

Allowed in Exams
  Calculator: Yes
  Dictionary: Yes
  Computer: Yes
  Spellchecker: Yes
Extended test time: Yes
Scribes: Yes
Proctors: Yes
Oral exams: Yes
Note-takers: Yes

Distraction-reduced environment: Yes
Tape recording in class: Yes
Books on tape from RFBD: Yes
Taping of books not from RFBD: No
**Accommodations for students with
  ADHD:** Yes
Reading machine: Yes
Other assistive technology: Yes
Priority registration: No

Added costs for services: No
LD specialists: No
Professional tutors: 10
Peer tutors: 25
Max. hours/wk. for services:
  Unlimited
**How professors are notified of
  LD/ADHD:** By the student and the
  program director

GENERAL ADMISSIONS INFORMATION

Director of Admissions: Owen Smith
Telephone: 414-382-6100

ENTRANCE REQUIREMENTS

17 total are required; 4 English recommended, 3 math recommended, 3 science recommended, 2 foreign language recommended, 3 social studies recommended. Minimum TOEFL is 500. TOEFL required of all international applicants.

Application deadline: August 1
Notification: Rolling
Average GPA: 3.0

Average SAT I Math: NR
Average SAT I Verbal: NR
Average ACT: 20

Graduated top 10% of class: 7%
Graduated top 25% of class: 29%
Graduated top 50% of class: NR

COLLEGE GRADUATION REQUIREMENTS

Course waivers allowed: No
Course substitutions allowed: No
In what subjects: Foreign language not required to graduate. Students must take a college algebra class to graduate.

ADDITIONAL INFORMATION

Environment: The campus is located in a suburban area on the southwest side of Milwaukee.

Student Body
  Undergrad enrollment: 1,982
  Female: 100%
  Male: 0%
  Out-of-state: 3%

Cost Information
  Tuition: $10,800
  Room & board: $4,250
Housing Information
  University housing: Yes
  Percent living on campus: 8%

Greek System
  Fraternity: No
  Sorority: Yes
Athletics: Intercollegiate

Alverno College

BELOIT COLLEGE

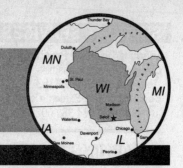

700 College Street, Beloit, WI 53511
Phone: 608-363-2500 • Fax: 608-363-2075
E-mail: admiss@beloit.edu • Web: www.beloit.edu
Support level: S • Institution type: 4-year private

LEARNING DISABILITY PROGRAM AND SERVICES

The goal of the Educational Development Program (EDP) is to provide support services and accommodations individually tailored to the needs of each student to enable the successful completion of the baccalaureate degree. EDP is a campus resource that provides opportunities for students to succeed. Beloit College students can qualify for EDP services based on any one of the following: (1) parents' educational attainment, (2) family income, (3) documented need for accommodations. EDP is funded through Beloit College in cooperation with the U.S. Department of Education. Participation is on a first-come, first-served basis for those who qualify and by the discretion of project staff.

LD/ADHD ADMISSIONS INFORMATION

College entrance tests required: Yes
Nonstandardized tests accepted: Yes
Interview required: No
Essay required: Yes
Documentation required for LD: Psychoeducational
    evaluation: within 3 years
Documentation required for ADHD: Yes
Documentation submitted to: EDP
Special Ed. HS course work accepted: Yes

Specific course requirements for all applicants: Yes
Separate application required for services: No
# of LD applications submitted yearly: N/A
# of LD applications accepted yearly: N/A
Total # of students receiving LD/ADHD services: 10–12
Acceptance into program means acceptance into
    college: Students must be admitted and enrolled at the
    College first and then may request services.

ADMISSIONS

There is no special admissions procedure for students with learning disabilities. Each student is reviewed individually and the final decision is made by the Office of Admission. The College is competitive in admissions, but there are no cutoffs for GPA or test scores.

ADDITIONAL INFORMATION

The Beloit Learning Resource Center offers additional services to the students in the areas of tutoring, study skills and time management, math and science tutoring and study groups, improvement of writing skills, advising, mentoring, reading speed and comprehension, and computer usage. Counseling services are offered in personal counseling, career guidance, and crisis intervention. Individual and self-help programs and small group workshops are available. Assessment tools are offered to help students determine individual strengths and weaknesses in reading rate, comprehension, and vocabulary, and there are a variety of handouts covering a wide range of academic skill areas such as studying, math, footnoting, and test taking.

SUPPORT SERVICES CONTACT INFORMATION

Learning Disability Program/Services: Educational Development Program (EDP)
Director: Gail Pizarro
  Telephone: 608-363-2031
  Fax: 608-363-2718
Contact: Same

LEARNING DISABILITY SERVICES

Requests for the following services/accommodations will be evaluated individually based on appropriate and current documentation.

Allowed in Exams
  Calculator: Yes
  Dictionary: Y/N
  Computer: Y/N
  Spellchecker: Y/N
Extended test time: Yes
Scribes: Yes
Proctors: Yes
Oral exams: Y/N
Note-takers: Yes

Distraction-reduced environment: Yes
Tape recording in class: Y/N
Books on tape from RFBD: No
Taping of books not from RFBD: No
Accommodations for students with
  ADHD: Yes
Reading machine: No
Other assistive technology: Yes
Priority registration: No

Added costs for services: No
LD specialists: No
Professional tutors: Yes
Peer tutors: Yes
Max. hours/wk. for services: No
How professors are notified of
  LD/ADHD: By the student and
  program director

GENERAL ADMISSIONS INFORMATION

Director of Admissions: Jim Zielinski
Telephone: 608-363-2500

ENTRANCE REQUIREMENTS
16 total are required; 4 English recommended, 3 math recommended, 3 science recommended, 3 science lab recommended, 2 foreign language recommended, 3 social studies recommended. High school diploma is required and GED is not accepted. Minimum TOEFL is 525. TOEFL required of all international applicants.

Application deadline: Rolling
Notification: Rolling beginning 2/1
Average GPA: 3.5

Average SAT I Math: 600
Average SAT I Verbal: 630
Average ACT: 27

Graduated top 10% of class: 30%
Graduated top 25% of class: 56%
Graduated top 50% of class: 91%

COLLEGE GRADUATION REQUIREMENTS

Course waivers allowed: No
Course substitutions allowed: No
In what subjects: N/A

ADDITIONAL INFORMATION

Environment: The College is located 50 miles south of Madison, 90 miles northwest of Chicago.

Student Body
  Undergrad enrollment: 1,254
  Female: 58%
  Male: 42%
  Out-of-state: 75%

Cost Information
  Tuition: $22,184
  Room & board: $5,078
Housing Information
  University housing: Yes
  Percent living on campus: 93%

Greek System
  Fraternity: Yes
  Sorority: Yes
  Athletics: NCAA Division III

MARIAN COLLEGE OF FOND DU LAC

45 South National Avenue, Fond du Lac, WI 54935
Phone: 920-923-7650 • Fax: 920-923-8755
E-mail: admissions@mariancollege.edu • Web: www.mariancollege.edu
Support level: CS • Institution type: 4-year private

LEARNING DISABILITY PROGRAM AND SERVICES

The Student Development Center offers services for students with LD. The ultimate goal of the Center is to provide the academic, social, and emotional support to students in order that they may maintain at least a 2.0 GPA and persevere to earn a college degree. The Student Development Center strives to provide a "neutral" area within which students can be accepted for who they are, and can begin moving toward meeting their own personal and academic goals.

LD/ADHD ADMISSIONS INFORMATION

College entrance tests required: Yes
Nonstandardized tests accepted: Yes
Interview required: No
Essay required: No
Documentation required for LD: Psychoeducational
   evaluation: within three years
Documentation required for ADHD: Yes
Documentation submitted to: Academic Support Services
Special Ed. HS course work accepted: Yes

Specific course requirements for all applicants: Yes
Separate application required for services: No
# of LD applications submitted yearly: 15–20
# of LD applications accepted yearly: 15–20
Total # of students receiving LD/ADHD services: 74
**Acceptance into program means acceptance into
   college:** Students must be admitted and enrolled at the
   College first and then may request services.

ADMISSIONS

There is no special application or admissions procedure for students with LD. Admission criteria include a 2.0 GPA, top 50 percent of class, and ACT of 18. All students, not just those with LD, are asked to meet two-thirds of these criteria. Students who do not meet two-thirds may be admitted on probation through a program called EXCEL. Students will be asked to submit three letters of recommendation supporting their ability to succeed in college-level course work. Students also may be asked to schedule a visit to Marian for a pre-admission interview during which their skills, attitudes, motivation, and self-understanding will be informally assessed. Students admitted provisionally may be admitted with limited credit status and may be required to take a freshman seminar course. Special education course work is accepted, but students are encouraged to be fully mainstreamed by senior year with minimal monitoring. Students who self-disclose their disability are given information on services available through the Student Development Center.

ADDITIONAL INFORMATION

The peer tutoring program helps students gain the confidence and skill necessary to successfully complete course work. To receive assistance students must disclose their disability. Skill classes are offered in English, math, and study skills, as well as computer-assisted instruction in math and basic skill areas. Other services include information on community, state, and national resources; assistance in writing and proofreading papers and assignments; tutors (individual and group); liaison service; assistance in working with instructors and course scheduling. Calculators are allowed in exams for students with a documented disability in math, and dictionaries are allowed in exams for students with a documented disability in written language. Assistance is determined for each individual based on assessment. All students have access to the tutoring program, the writing lab, and the computer lab. Services are available for undergraduate and graduate students.

SUPPORT SERVICES CONTACT INFORMATION

Learning Disability Program/Services: Student Development/Academic Support Services
Director: Cathy Mathweg
  E-mail: cmathweg@mariancollege.edu
  Telephone: 920-923-8117
  Fax: 920-923-8135
Contact: Same

LEARNING DISABILITY SERVICES

Requests for the following services/accommodations will be evaluated individually based on appropriate and current documentation.

Allowed in Exams
  Calculator: Yes
  Dictionary: Yes
  Computer: Yes
  Spellchecker: Yes
Extended test time: Yes
Scribes: Yes
Proctors: Yes
Oral exams: Yes
Note-takers: Yes

Distraction-reduced environment: Yes
Tape recording in class: Yes
Books on tape from RFBD: Yes
Taping of books not from RFBD: Yes
Accommodations for students with ADHD: Yes
Reading machine: Yes
Other assistive technology: Yes
Priority registration: No

Added costs for services: No
LD specialists: Yes
Professional tutors: 3
Peer tutors: 15
Max. hours/wk. for services: Unlimited
How professors are notified of LD/ADHD: By both student and director

GENERAL ADMISSIONS INFORMATION

Director of Admissions: Stacey Akey
Telephone: 920-923-7650

ENTRANCE REQUIREMENTS
17 total are required; 4 English required, 4 English recommended, 2 math required, 3 math recommended, 1 science required, 3 science recommended, 1 science lab required, 2 science lab recommended, 2 foreign language recommended, 1 social studies required, 2 social studies recommended, 2 history recommended. High school diploma or GED required. Minimum TOEFL is 525. TOEFL required of all international applicants.

Application deadline: Rolling
Notification: Rolling beginning 9/15
Average GPA: 2.9

Average SAT I Math: N/A
Average SAT I Verbal: N/A
Average ACT: 20

Graduated top 10% of class: 15%
Graduated top 25% of class: 30%
Graduated top 50% of class: 62%

COLLEGE GRADUATION REQUIREMENTS

Course waivers allowed: No
Course substitutions allowed: Yes
In what subjects: Not requested or needed; students have taken directed study-type classes to fulfill their math requirement; work one-to-one with tutor and weekly with instructor; have one year to complete a semester course; must attempt required course in traditional setting.

ADDITIONAL INFORMATION

Environment: Marian College is located on 50 acres in a suburb of Fond du Lac, 60 miles north of Milwaukee.

Student Body
  Undergrad enrollment: 1,571
  Female: 67%
  Male: 33%
  Out-of-state: 19%

Cost Information
  Tuition: $11,966
  Room & board: $4,364
Housing Information
  University housing: Yes
  Percent living on campus: 55%

Greek System
  Fraternity: Yes
  Sorority: Yes
  Athletics: NCAA Division III

Marian College of Fond du Lac

School Profiles • 701

MARQUETTE UNIVERSITY

PO Box 1881, Milwaukee, WI 53201-1881
Phone: 414-288-7302 • Fax: 414-288-3764
E-mail: Admissions@Marquette.edu • Web: www.Marquette.edu
Support level: S • Institution type: 4-year private

LEARNING DISABILITY PROGRAM AND SERVICES

The Office of Disability Services (ODS) is the designated office at Marquette University to coordinate accommodations for all students with identified and documented disabilities. Accommodations are determined on a case-by-case basis. In order to provide educational opportunities the student must seek assistance in a timely manner, preferably prior to the start of classes. Relevant documentation from an appropriate licensed professional that gives a diagnosis of the disability and how it impacts on participation in courses, programs, jobs, activities and facilities at Marquette is important. The student and a staff member from ODS will discuss the student's disability and how it will impact on the requirements of the student's courses. Based upon this evaluation the ODS Coordinator provides a range of individualized accommodations. For students who suspect they have a disability, a free informal screening for possible LD or ADHD can be provided from ODS. This screening process can determine if the student should have a formal testing battery done.

LD/ADHD ADMISSIONS INFORMATION

College entrance tests required: Yes
Nonstandardized tests accepted: Yes
Interview required: No
Essay required: Yes
Documentation required for LD: Psychoeducational
  evaluation
Documentation required for ADHD: Yes
Documentation submitted to: ODS
Special Ed. HS course work accepted: No

Specific course requirements for all applicants: Yes
Separate application required for services: No
# of LD applications submitted yearly: N/A
# of LD applications accepted yearly: N/A
Total # of students receiving LD/ADHD services: NR
Acceptance into program means acceptance into
  college: Students must be admitted and enrolled first and
  then may request services.

ADMISSIONS

There is no special admissions process for students with LD and ADHD. All applicants for admission must meet the same admission criteria. Marquette requires applicants to rank in the top 50 percent of their high school class (most rank in the top 25 percent) and have 4 years of English, 2–4 years of math and science, 2–3 years of social studies, 2 years of foreign language and other additional subjects.

ADDITIONAL INFORMATION

ODS provides a number of accommodations for students with LD and ADHD including taped texts and alternative testing arrangements. If a student's disability requires a backup note-taker, ODS assists students in locating or hiring note-takers and will provide noncarbon-required paper. Other methods of acquiring class material may include use of a tape recorder in class for later transcription, and photocopying class notes or copies of lecture notes. Advance notice of assignments, alternative ways of completing an assignment, computer technology, assistive listening devices, taped textbooks and course or program modifications are also available. To assist students with reading-related disabilities, the Kurzweil Omni 3000 Education System is available. Students also have access to the campus Writing Center, tutors, and general study skills assistance from the Office of Student Educational Services.

SUPPORT SERVICES CONTACT INFORMATION

Learning Disability Program/Services: Office of Disability Services
Director: Patricia L. Almon, Coordinator
E-mail: Patricia.Almon@marquette.edu
Telephone: 414-288-1645
Fax: 414-288-5799
Contact: Same

LEARNING DISABILITY SERVICES

Requests for the following services/accommodations will be evaluated individually based on appropriate and current documentation.

Allowed in Exams
  Calculator: Y/N
  Dictionary: Y/N
  Computer: Y/N
  Spellchecker: Y/N
Extended test time: Yes
Scribes: Y/N
Proctors: Y/N
Oral exams: Yes
Note-takers: Yes

Distraction-reduced environment: Yes
Tape recording in class: Yes
Books on tape from RFBD: Yes
Taping of books not from RFBD: Yes
Accommodations for students with ADHD: Yes
Reading machine: Yes
Other assistive technology: NR
Priority registration: Yes

Added costs for services: No
LD specialists: No
Professional tutors: No
Peer tutors: 35–40
Max. hours/wk. for services: 1 hour per week per course
How professors are notified of LD/ADHD: By student and director of services

GENERAL ADMISSIONS INFORMATION

Director of Admissions: Roby Blust
Telephone: 414-288-7302

ENTRANCE REQUIREMENTS
16 total are recommended; 4 English recommended, 3 math recommended, 3 science recommended, 2 foreign language recommended, 1 social studies recommended, 2 history recommended, 3 elective recommended. High school diploma or GED required. Minimum TOEFL is 525. TOEFL required of all international applicants.

Application deadline: Rolling
Notification: Rolling beginning 11/15
Average GPA: NR

Average SAT I Math: 584
Average SAT I Verbal: 576
Average ACT: 25

Graduated top 10% of class: 34%
Graduated top 25% of class: 66%
Graduated top 50% of class: 92%

COLLEGE GRADUATION REQUIREMENTS

Course waivers allowed: Yes
Course substitutions allowed: Yes
In what subjects: Foreign language

ADDITIONAL INFORMATION

Environment: Located in the city of Milwaukee, one hour from Madison.

Student Body
  Undergrad enrollment: 7,496
  Female: 55%
  Male: 45%
  Out-of-state: 52%

Cost Information
  Tuition: $18,180
  Room & board: $6,362
Housing Information
  University housing: Yes
  Percent living on campus: 34%

Greek System
  Fraternity: Yes
  Sorority: Yes
Athletics: NCAA Division I

RIPON COLLEGE

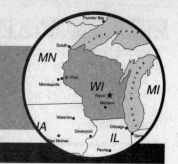

300 Seward Street, PO Box 248, Ripon, WI 54971
Phone: 800-947-4766 • Fax: 920-748-8335
E-mail: adminfo@ripon.edu • Web: www.ripon.edu
Support level: S • Institution type: 4-year private

LEARNING DISABILITY PROGRAM AND SERVICES

The Educational Development Program (EDP) provides a wide variety of services on the campus, including academic and personal counseling, study skills information, and tutoring. Although the focus of the program is on first generation students, students of higher need, and students who are learning disabled, other students who feel they might qualify are encouraged to contact the EDP office. EDP is a voluntary program that has been in existence at Ripon College since 1974. For the many students who have used its services, EDP has provided a network of support for academic, financial, and personal concerns. A group of peer contacts serves EDP by meeting regularly with students to facilitate communication between EDP participants and the office staff. For students who qualify, EDP offers free tutoring in specific subject areas. (All-campus tutoring is also available.) The tutors are upperclass students who have been recommended by their professors and trained by the EDP staff. These tutors serve as a supplement to faculty assistance. The aim of the tutoring program is to help students develop independent learning skills and improve their course grades. Although federal guidelines require a restriction on who "qualifies," the door to EDP remains open to all eligible students.

LD/ADHD ADMISSIONS INFORMATION

College entrance tests required: Yes
Nonstandardized tests accepted: Yes
Interview required: Yes
Essay required: No
Documentation required for LD: Psychoeducational evaluation
Documentation required for ADHD: Yes
Documentation submitted to: SSS
Special Ed. HS course work accepted: Yes

Specific course requirements for all applicants: Yes
Separate application required for services: No
# of LD applications submitted yearly: N/A
# of LD applications accepted yearly: N/A
Total # of students receiving LD/ADHD services: 10
Acceptance into program means acceptance into college: college: Students must be admitted and enrolled at the College and then may request services.

ADMISSIONS

Students with learning disabilities are screened by admissions and must meet the same admission criteria as all other applicants. There is no set GPA required; courses required include 4 years English, algebra and geometry, 2 years natural science, 2 years social studies, and 7 additional units. Students with learning disabilities who self-disclose are referred to Student Support Services when making prospective visits to the campus in order to ascertain specific needs and abilities of the student.

ADDITIONAL INFORMATION

EDP provides tutoring in subject areas; skills classes for no credit in time management, note-taking, test-taking strategies, reading college texts, writing papers, studying for and taking exams, and setting goals; and counseling/guidance. Student Support Services provides intensive study groups, LD support groups, and internships. EDP provides students with peer contacts who provide students with one-on-one support and is useful in helping students adjust to college life, to provide a contact for the student to go to with problems or issues, organize group tutoring, and to help students open their minds and see hope in their future.

SUPPORT SERVICES CONTACT INFORMATION

Learning Disability Program/Services: Student Support Services
Director: Dan Krhin
  E-mail: krhind@ripon.edu
  Telephone: 920-748-8107
  Fax: 920-748-8382
Contact: Same

LEARNING DISABILITY SERVICES

Requests for the following services/accommodations will be evaluated individually based on appropriate and current documentation.

Allowed in Exams
  Calculator: Yes
  Dictionary: No
  Computer: No
  Spellchecker: No
Extended test time: Yes
Scribes: Yes
Proctors: Yes
Oral exams: Yes
Note-takers: Yes

Distraction-reduced environment: Yes
Tape recording in class: Yes
Books on tape from RFBD: Yes
Taping of books not from RFBD: No
Accommodations for students with ADHD: Yes
Reading machine: Yes
Other assistive technology: No
Priority registration: No

Added costs for services: No
LD specialists: No
Professional tutors: Yes
Peer tutors: Yes
Max. hours/wk. for services: 3 hours per week per course
How professors are notified of LD/ADHD: By student and director

GENERAL ADMISSIONS INFORMATION

Director of Admissions: Scott Goplin
Telephone: 920-748-8107

ENTRANCE REQUIREMENTS
17 total are required; 4 English required, 2 math required, 4 math recommended, 2 science required, 4 science recommended, 2 foreign language recommended, 2 social studies required, 4 social studies recommended. High school diploma or GED required. Minimum TOEFL is 550. TOEFL required of all international applicants.

Application deadline: Rolling
Notification: Rolling beginning 9/1
Average GPA: 3.4

Average SAT I Math: 549
Average SAT I Verbal: 541
Average ACT: 24

Graduated top 10% of class: 24%
Graduated top 25% of class: 57%
Graduated top 50% of class: 86%

COLLEGE GRADUATION REQUIREMENTS

Course waivers allowed: Yes
Course substitutions allowed: Yes
In what subjects: Foreign language

ADDITIONAL INFORMATION

Environment: The College is located in a small town north of Milwaukee.

Student Body
  Undergrad enrollment: 862
  Female: 53%
  Male: 47%
  Out-of-state: 31%

Cost Information
  Tuition: $18,000
  Room & board: $4,400
Housing Information
  University housing: Yes
  Percent living on campus: 94%

Greek System
  Fraternity: Yes
  Sorority: Yes
Athletics: NCAA Division III

UNIV. OF WISCONSIN—EAU CLAIRE

105 Garfield Avenue, Eau Claire, WI 54701
Phone: 715-836-5415 • Fax: 715-836-2409
E-mail: ask-uwec@uwec.edu • Web: www.uwec.edu
Support level: CS • Institution type: 4-year public

LEARNING DISABILITY PROGRAM AND SERVICES

The University does not have a separate program for students with learning disabilities. However, many services provided would be beneficial. Documentation of a learning disability is required to receive services. Students should meet with staff in the Students with Disabilities Office two months before enrolling to ensure that needed services are in place. Academic adjustments or accommodations will be provided to meet the students' needs.

LD/ADHD ADMISSIONS INFORMATION

College entrance tests required: Yes
Nonstandardized tests accepted: Yes
Interview required: No
Essay required: No
Documentation required for LD: Psychoeducational
  evaluation: within 3 years
Documentation required for ADHD: Yes
Documentation submitted to: SSD
Special Ed. HS course work accepted: Y/N

Specific course requirements for all applicants: Yes
Separate application required for services: No
# of LD applications submitted yearly: N/A
# of LD applications accepted yearly: N/A
Total # of students receiving LD/ADHD services: 80
Acceptance into program means acceptance into
  college: Students must be admitted and enrolled at the
  University first and then may request services.

ADMISSIONS

Individuals with learning disabilities complete the standard university application form and must meet the regular university admission criteria. After a student is admitted, a copy of the diagnosis and assessment of the disability including educational recommendations should be submitted to Services for Students with Disabilities. Applicants for admission should rank in the top 50 percent of their class. Courses required include 4 years English, 3 years math, 3 years natural science, 3 years social science, 2 years foreign language, and 2 courses in any academic course or art, music, speech, and computer science. Students not admitted in the fall may find a January admission somewhat less competitive. Students must submit an ACT score and take placement tests in English, math, and other appropriate areas. Conditional student status is given during the summer and second semester of the academic year.

ADDITIONAL INFORMATION

Students must provide documentation prior to receiving appropriate accommodations. Some of the accommodations provided with appropriate documentation could include tutoring individually or in groups; readers; scribes; note-takers; taped textbooks; proofreaders; exam accommodations including extended time, readers and separate testing rooms. The Academic Skills Center offers individualized tutoring in math preparation and background, composition, reading, and study skills. Many departments on campus provide tutors to help students with course content. Students take a form completed by staff professors identifying appropriate accommodation requests. Students who are denied accommodations can appeal any denial by filing a complaint with the Affirmative Action Review Board. Services and accommodations are available to undergraduate and graduate students.

SUPPORT SERVICES CONTACT INFORMATION

Learning Disability Program/Services: Services for Students with Disabilities (SSD)
Director: Joseph C. Hisrich
  E-mail: hisrichjc@uwec.edu
  Telephone: 715-836-4542
  Fax: 715-836-3712
Contact: Beth Hicks
  E-mail: hicksea@uwec.edu
  Telephone: 715-836-4542
  Fax: 715-836-3712

LEARNING DISABILITY SERVICES

Requests for the following services/accommodations will be evaluated individually based on appropriate and current documentation.

Allowed in Exams
  Calculator: Yes
  Dictionary: Yes
  Computer: Yes
  Spellchecker: Yes
Extended test time: Yes
Scribes: Yes
Proctors: Yes
Oral exams: Yes
Note-takers: Yes

Distraction-reduced environment: Yes
Tape recording in class: Yes
Books on tape from RFBD: Yes
Taping of books not from RFBD: Yes
Accommodations for students with ADHD: Yes
Reading machine: Yes
Other assistive technology: Yes
Priority registration: Yes

Added costs for services: No
LD specialists: Yes (1)
Professional tutors: 6
Peer tutors: 40
Max. hours/wk. for services: Unlimited
How professors are notified of LD/ADHD: By student

GENERAL ADMISSIONS INFORMATION

Director of Admissions: Robert Lopez
Telephone: 715-836-5415

ENTRANCE REQUIREMENTS
17 total are required; 4 English required, 3 math required, 3 science required, 2 foreign language required, 3 social studies required, 2 elective required. High school diploma or GED required. Minimum TOEFL is 525. TOEFL required of all international applicants.

Application deadline: Rolling
Notification: Rolling beginning 12/1
Average GPA: NR

Average SAT I Math: 573
Average SAT I Verbal: 548
Average ACT: 23

Graduated top 10% of class: 21%
Graduated top 25% of class: 54%
Graduated top 50% of class: 93%

COLLEGE GRADUATION REQUIREMENTS

Course waivers allowed: No
Course substitutions allowed: Yes
In what subjects: Math and foreign language

ADDITIONAL INFORMATION

Environment: The 333-acre campus is in an urban setting 95 miles east of Minneapolis.

Student Body
  Undergrad enrollment: 10,101
  Female: 60%
  Male: 40%
  Out-of-state: 22%

Cost Information
  In-state tuition: $3,252
  Out-of-state tuition: $10,780
  Room & board: $3,435
Housing Information
  University housing: Yes
  Percent living on campus: 37%

Greek System
  Fraternity: Yes
  Sorority: Yes
Athletics: NCAA Division III

University of Wisconsin—Eau Claire

UNIV. OF WISCONSIN—LACROSSE

1725 State Street, LaCrosse, WI 54601-3742
Phone: 608-785-8939 • Fax: 608-785-6695
E-mail: admissions@uwlax.edu • Web: www.uwlax.edu
Support level: CS • Institution type: 4-year public

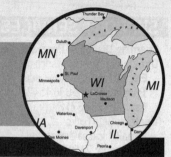

LEARNING DISABILITY PROGRAM AND SERVICES

The goal of the Disability Resource Services Office is to provide academic accommodations for students with learning disabilities in order for them to participate fully at the University. A number of academic and personal support services are available. Students must provide documentation (completed within the last three years) to verify the disability. The mission is to identify, reduce, or eliminate barriers in education for students with disabilities within the most integrated setting possible.

LD/ADHD ADMISSIONS INFORMATION

College entrance tests required: Yes
Nonstandardized tests accepted: Yes
Interview required: No
Essay required: No
Documentation required for LD: Psychoeducational evaluation: within three years
Documentation required for ADHD: Yes
Documentation submitted to: Diasability Resource Services
Special Ed. HS course work accepted: No

Specific course requirements for all applicants: Yes
Separate application required for services: Yes
# of LD applications submitted yearly: 40
# of LD applications accepted yearly: NR
Total # of students receiving LD/ADHD services: 140
Acceptance into program means acceptance into college: Students must be admitted and enrolled at the University first and then may request services.

ADMISSIONS

Admission criteria include an ACT of 23 and a class rank in the top 35 percent. There is limited admission for students with learning disabilities if they are close to the regular admission requirements. Students with learning disabilities are encouraged to self-disclose their disability. These applications are automatically referred to the program director who will then request a recent psychological report, three letters of recommendation, and a personal interview. The admissions office is sensitive to the director's opinions and will admit students recommended, who can succeed, even if these students do not meet standard admissions requirements.

ADDITIONAL INFORMATION

The program director writes a letter to all the student's professors explaining the student's learning disability and describing necessary modifications. The program director meets with freshmen every two weeks. A support group meets twice a month. Services include taped texts, testing accommodations, and note-takers. Students are encouraged to get tutoring through the academic departments. Tutorial assistance is offered through each department within the University. Skills classes are offered in reading, remedial English, and mathematics. Services and accommodations are available for undergraduate and graduate students.

SUPPORT SERVICES CONTACT INFORMATION

Learning Disability Program/Services: Disability Resource Services
Director: June Reinert, Coordinator
  Telephone: 608-785-6900
Contact: Same

LEARNING DISABILITY SERVICES

Requests for the following services/accommodations will be evaluated individually based on appropriate and current documentation.

Allowed in Exams
  Calculator: Yes
  Dictionary: Y/N
  Computer: Yes
  Spellchecker: Yes
Extended test time: Yes
Scribes: Yes
Proctors: Yes
Oral exams: Yes
Note-takers: Yes

Distraction-reduced environment: Yes
Tape recording in class: Yes
Books on tape from RFBD: Yes
Taping of books not from RFBD: Yes
**Accommodations for students with
  ADHD:** Yes
Reading machine: Yes
Other assistive technology: Yes
Priority registration: Yes

Added costs for services: No
LD specialists: Yes
Professional tutors: No
Peer tutors: Yes
Max. hours/wk. for services:
  Unlimited
**How professors are notified of
  LD/ADHD:** By student

GENERAL ADMISSIONS INFORMATION

Director of Admissions: Timothy R. Lewis
Telephone: 608-785-8067

ENTRANCE REQUIREMENTS
17 total are required; 23 total are recommended; 4 English required, 4 English recommended, 3 math required, 4 math recommended, 3 science required, 4 science recommended, 2 science lab required, 2 science lab recommended, 3 foreign language recommended, 3 social studies required, 4 social studies recommended, 4 elective required, 2 elective recommended. High school diploma or GED required. Minimum TOEFL is 550. TOEFL required of all international applicants.

Application deadline: January 15
Notification: Rolling beginning 9/15
Average GPA: 3.5

Average SAT I Math: NR
Average SAT I Verbal: NR
Average ACT: 24

Graduated top 10% of class: 26%
Graduated top 25% of class: 67%
Graduated top 50% of class: 98%

COLLEGE GRADUATION REQUIREMENTS

Course waivers allowed: Yes
Course substitutions allowed: Yes
In what subjects: Determined on a case-by-case basis

ADDITIONAL INFORMATION

Environment: The University is located on 119 acres, in a small city 140 miles west of Madison.

Student Body
  Undergrad enrollment: 8,487
  Female: 58%
  Male: 42%
  Out-of-state: 17%

Cost Information
  In-state tuition: $2,697
  Out-of-state tuition: $10,122
  Room & board: $3,450
Housing Information
  University housing: Yes
  Percent living on campus: 32%

Greek System
  Fraternity: Yes
  Sorority: Yes
Athletics: NCAA Division III

Univ. of Wisconsin—Madison

3rd Floor Armory and Gymnasium, 716 Langdon St., Madison, WI 53706
Phone: 608-262-3961 • Fax: 608-262-1429
E-mail: on.wisconsin@mail.admin.wisc.edu • Web: www.wisc.edu
Support level: CS • Institution type: 4-year public

LEARNING DISABILITY PROGRAM AND SERVICES

The McBurney Disability Resource Center LD Support Services seeks to provide students with equal access to the programs and activities of the University. LD staff work with students, staff, and faculty to promote students' independence and to ensure assessment of their abilities, not disabilities. LD staff work with students to determine disability-related accommodations and academic services that will maximize a student's opportunity for success. The LD staff consists of two part-time professionals. Over 450 undergraduate and graduate students with LD/ADHD are currently registered with the McBurney Center. Students with LD who tend to do well have graduated from competitive high school or college programs and are reasonably independent, proactive in seeking assistance, and use accommodations similar to those offered at the University.

LD/ADHD ADMISSIONS INFORMATION

College entrance tests required: Yes
Nonstandardized tests accepted: Yes
Interview required: No
Essay required: Yes
Documentation required for LD: Psychoeducational evaluation
Documentation required for ADHD: Yes
Documentation submitted to: McBurney Center
Special Ed. HS course work accepted: Possibly, depends on course description

Specific course requirements for all applicants: Yes
Separate application required for services: No
# of LD applications submitted yearly: N/A
# of LD applications accepted yearly: N/A
Total # of students receiving LD/ADHD services: 450
Acceptance into program means acceptance into college: Students must be accepted and enrolled at the University and then may request services.

ADMISSIONS

The admission process is the same for all applicants. Applicants not meeting regular admission criteria who self-disclose a disability can have their documentation reviewed by an Admissions Office liaison, and then sent to the McBurney Center. The disability could become a factor in admission when documentation is provided that clearly establishes the presence of a disability, shows its effect on education, and a record of academic achievement that meets guidelines suggesting potential success. Factors in the alternative admissions review process include disability information, grades, rank, test scores, course requirements completed, and potential for success. Examples of LD information include date of diagnosis or onset of disability and the ramifications of the disability on curricular requirements. If course requirements are directly impacted by the disability, resulting in low grades or the absence of courses, the GPA will be reviewed with and without those courses.

ADDITIONAL INFORMATION

The documentation must be completed by a professional qualified to diagnose an LD; must include results of a clinical interview and descriptions of the testing procedures, instruments used, test and subtest results reported in standard scores as well as percentile rank and grade scores where useful, and interpretation and recommendations based on data gathered. It must be comprehensive and include test results where applicable in intelligence, reading, math, spelling, written language, language processing, and cognitive processing skills. Testing should carefully examine areas of concern/weakness as well as areas of strengths; documentation should include a clear diagnostic statement based on the test results and personal history. Students may be eligible for advocacy/liaison with faculty and staff, alternative testing accommodations, curriculum modifications, disability management advising, learning skills training, liaison with Voc Rehab, McBurney Learning Resource Room card, note-taker, peer support groups, priority registration, taped texts, and course materials.

SUPPORT SERVICES CONTACT INFORMATION

Learning Disability Program/Services: McBurney Disability Resource Center
Director: J. Trey Duffy
  Telephone: 608-263-2741
  Fax: 608-265-2998
Contact: Cathy Trueba
  E-mail: cmtruerba@facstaff.wisc.edu
  Telephone: 608-263-2741
  Fax: 608-265-2998

LEARNING DISABILITY SERVICES

Requests for the following services/accommodations will be evaluated individually based on appropriate and current documentation.

Allowed in Exams
  Calculator: Y/N
  Dictionary: Y/N
  Computer: Y/N
  Spellchecker: Y/N
Extended test time: Yes
Scribes: Yes
Proctors: Yes
Oral exams: Yes
Note-takers: Yes

Distraction-reduced environment: Yes
Tape recording in class: Yes
Books on tape from RFBD: Yes
Taping of books not from RFBD: Yes
Accommodations for students with ADHD: Yes
Reading machine: Yes
Other assistive technology: Yes
Priority registration: Yes

Added costs for services: No
LD specialists: Yes (2)
Professional tutors: Yes
Peer tutors: Yes
Max. hours/wk. for services: 1 hour every 2 weeks on average
How professors are notified of LD/ADHD: By student

GENERAL ADMISSIONS INFORMATION

Director of Admissions: Rob Seltzer
Telephone: 608-262-39-61

ENTRANCE REQUIREMENTS
17 total are required; 20 total are recommended; 4 English required, 4 English recommended, 3 math required, 4 math recommended, 3 science required, 4 science recommended, 2 foreign language required, 2 foreign language recommended, 3 social studies required, 4 social studies recommended. High school diploma or GED required. Minimum TOEFL is 550. TOEFL required of all international applicants.

Application deadline: February 1
Notification: Rolling beginning 10/15
Average GPA: 3.6

Average SAT I Math: 638
Average SAT I Verbal: 611
Average ACT: 26

Graduated top 10% of class: 48%
Graduated top 25% of class: 90%
Graduated top 50% of class: 99%

COLLEGE GRADUATION REQUIREMENTS

Course waivers allowed: No
Course substitutions allowed: Yes
In what subjects: Foreign language

ADDITIONAL INFORMATION

Environment: The University is located in an urban area in the state capital.

Student Body
  Undergrad enrollment: 29,336
  Female: 53%
  Male: 47%
  Out-of-state: 40%

Cost Information
  In-state tuition: $3,650
  Out-of-state tuition: $12,400
  Room & board: $5,250
Housing Information
  University housing: Yes
  Percent living on campus: 50%

Greek System
  Fraternity: Yes
  Sorority: Yes
Athletics: NCAA Division I

University of Wisconsin—Madison

Univ. of Wisconsin—Milwaukee

PO Box 749, Milwaukee, WI 53201
Phone: 414-229-3800 • Fax: 414-229-6940
E-mail: webadmiss@des.uwm.edu • Web: www.uwm.edu
Support level: CS • Institution type: 4-year public

LEARNING DISABILITY PROGRAM AND SERVICES

The LD Program is a component of the Students Accessibility Center (SAC) at UWM, whose mission is to create an accessible community that provides equal access to all students. The Learning Disabilities Program offers a wide range of support services. The goal of the program is to provide an environment that encourages the development of the unique talents of each student. This program is well suited for those who can function independently with some academic support. Services provided include taped textbooks, tutorial services, special arrangements for test taking, note-takers, communication with professors, monitoring, and priority registration.

LD/ADHD ADMISSIONS INFORMATION

College entrance tests required: Yes
Nonstandardized tests accepted: Yes
Interview required: No
Essay required: No
Documentation required for LD: WAIS-III; WJ
Documentation required for ADHD: Yes
Documentation submitted to: LD Program
Special Ed. HS course work accepted: Yes

Specific course requirements for all applicants: Yes
Separate application required for services: No
# of LD applications submitted yearly: 25–50
# of LD applications accepted yearly: All accepted to UWM
Total # of students receiving LD/ADHD services: 125
Acceptance into program means acceptance into college: Students are admitted and enrolled at the University first and then may request services. Some students may apply directly through AOC.

ADMISSIONS

Admission into UWM is necessary for participation in the LD Program. Students apply directly to the Admissions Office. The LD Program does not make admission decisions. Students should send documentation to the LD Program and contact program when applying. The director of the LD Program can assist students with the admission process, and can make informal recommendations to the Admission Office on an individual basis. General admissions requires a 2.0 GPA. Students not regularly admissible, who are serious about continuing their education and show potential for university study, may apply through the Academic Opportunity Center (AOC). General admission requires a minimum 2.0 GPA. Students should submit a UWM application; send transcripts; take AOC placement tests; submit ACT/SAT; and schedule an interview. Approximately 60–75 students submit applications yearly through AOC. There is no limit to the number of students who can be admitted through the AOC each year.

ADDITIONAL INFORMATION

Students who may not be regularly admissible based on low GPA, ACT, SAT, or rank in class, or who lack academic units, or those who would benefit from intensive advising, may want to apply directly to AOC on their UWM application. Students will need to take the AOC test series, including math, English, and the Nelson Denny Reading Test. Students must also have an interview with an advisor in the AOC. The AOC will evaluate the student's potential in making an admission decision. AOC offers intensive advising, basic skills courses, and additional academic support. Students should contact the LD Program as they are applying to the University. An application must be made separately to the LD Program. Students will need to send current documentation to the LD Program and set up an Intake Interview.

SUPPORT SERVICES CONTACT INFORMATION

Learning Disability Program/Services: Learning Disabilities Program
Director: Laurie Peterson
  E-mail: lauriep@uwm.edu
  Telephone: 414-229-6239
  Fax: 414-229-2237
Contact: Same

LEARNING DISABILITY SERVICES

Requests for the following services/accommodations will be evaluated individually based on appropriate and current documentation.

Allowed in Exams
  Calculator: Yes
  Dictionary: Yes
  Computer: Yes
  Spellchecker: Y/N
Extended test time: Yes
Scribes: Yes
Proctors: Yes
Oral exams: Y/N
Note-takers: Yes

Distraction-reduced environment: Yes
Tape recording in class: Yes
Books on tape from RFBD: Yes
Taping of books not from RFBD: Yes
Accommodations for students with ADHD: Yes
Reading machine: Yes
Other assistive technology: Yes
Priority registration: Yes

Added costs for services: No
LD specialists: Yes (1)
Professional tutors: No
Peer tutors: Yes
Max. hours/wk. for services: 2–3
How professors are notified of LD/ADHD: By student and program director

GENERAL ADMISSIONS INFORMATION

Director of Admissions: Beth Weckmueller
Telephone: 414-229-6164

ENTRANCE REQUIREMENTS
17 total are required; 20 total are recommended; 4 English required, 4 English recommended, 3 math required, 4 math recommended, 3 science required, 4 science recommended, 1 science lab required, 2 science lab recommended, 2 foreign language recommended, 3 social studies required, 4 social studies recommended, 4 elective required. Minimum ACT of 21 and a rank in the top 50 percent of the high school class are required. High school diploma or GED required. Architecture and urban planning requires an ACT of 25 or SAT of 1140 and a rank in the top 25 percent of the class. Minimum TOEFL is 500. TOEFL required of all international applicants.

Application deadline: Rolling
Notification: Rolling beginning 9/30
Average GPA: NR

Average SAT I Math: 537.5
Average SAT I Verbal: 547.5
Average ACT: 22

Graduated top 10% of class: 7%
Graduated top 25% of class: 28%
Graduated top 50% of class: 67%

COLLEGE GRADUATION REQUIREMENTS

Course waivers allowed: Yes
Course substitutions allowed: Yes
In what subjects: Determined on a case-by-case basis

ADDITIONAL INFORMATION

Environment: The University is located on 90 acres in a residential area 90 miles north of Chicago.

Student Body
  Undergrad enrollment: 19,223
  Female: 54%
  Male: 46%
  Out-of-state: 6%

Cost Information
  In-state tuition: $3,764
  Out-of-state tuition: $13,212
  Room & board: $3,594
Housing Information
  University housing: Yes
  Percent living on campus: 13%

Greek System
  Fraternity: Yes
  Sorority: Yes
  Athletics: NCAA Division I

University of Wisconsin—Milwaukee

UNIV. OF WISCONSIN—OSHKOSH

Dempsey Hall 135, 800 Algoma Boulevard, Oshkosh, WI 54901
Phone: 920-424-0202 • Fax: 920-424-1098
E-mail: oshadmuw@uwosh.edu • Web: www.uwosh.edu
Support level: SP • Institution type: 4-year public

LEARNING DISABILITY PROGRAM AND SERVICES

Project Success is a language remediation project that is based on mastering the entire sound structure of the English language. These students are academically able and determined to succeed, in spite of a pronounced problem in a number of areas. Help is offered in the following ways: direct remediation of deficiencies through the Orton-Gillingham Technique; one-to-one tutoring assistance; math and writing labs; guidance and counseling with scheduling course work and interpersonal relations; untimed exams; and by providing an atmosphere that is supportive. The goal is for students to become language independent in and across all of these major educational areas: math, spelling, reading, writing, comprehension, and study skills. As full-time university students they will acquire language independence by mastering the entire phonetic structure of the American English language.

LD/ADHD ADMISSIONS INFORMATION

College entrance tests required: Yes
Nonstandardized tests accepted: Yes
Interview required: No
Essay required: No
Documentation required for LD: Full psychoeducational testing: within 3 years
Documentation required for ADHD: Yes
Documentation submitted to: Project Success
Special Ed. HS course work accepted: Yes

Specific course requirements for all applicants: Yes
Separate application required for services: No
# of LD applications submitted yearly: N/A
# of LD applications accepted yearly: N/A
Total # of students receiving LD/ADHD services: N/A
Acceptance into program means acceptance into college: Students are accepted jointly to Project Success and the University; however, they must submit separate applications for the program and the University.

ADMISSIONS
Students should apply to Project Success in their sophomore year of high school. Applicants apply by writing a letter, in their own handwriting, indicating interest in the program and why they are interested. Applications are processed on a first-come, first-served basis. Those interested should apply at least one to two years prior to desired entrance. Students and parents will be invited to interview. The interview is used to assess family dynamics in terms of support for the student, and reasons for wanting to attend college. The director is looking for motivation, stability, and the ability of the students to describe the disability. Acceptance into Project Success does not grant acceptance into the University. Admission to the University and acceptance into Project Success is a joint decision but a separate process is required for each. General admissions procedures must be followed before acceptance into the special program can be offered. ACT/SAT or GPA are not critical. Accepted students for Project Success are required to register for a summer term prior to freshman year.

ADDITIONAL INFORMATION
Incoming freshmen to Project Success must participate in an eight-week summer school program consisting of simultaneous multisensory instructional procedures (SMSIP). This procedure is used to teach study skills, reading, spelling, writing, and mathematical operations. Students are eligible for tutoring services and untimed testing opportunities. Services and accommodations are available for undergraduate and graduate students.

SUPPORT SERVICES CONTACT INFORMATION

Learning Disability Program/Services: Project Success
Director: William R. Kitz, PhD
  E-mail: kitz@uwosh.edu
  Telephone: 920-424-1033
Contact: Same

LEARNING DISABILITY SERVICES

Requests for the following services/accommodations will be evaluated individually based on appropriate and current documentation.

Allowed in Exams	**Distraction-reduced environment:** Yes	**Added costs for services:** No
Calculator: Yes	**Tape recording in class:** Yes	**LD specialists:** Yes (3)
Dictionary: Yes	**Books on tape from RFBD:** Yes	**Professional tutors:** Yes
Computer: Yes	**Taping of books not from RFBD:** Yes	**Peer tutors:** Yes
Spellchecker: No	**Accommodations for students with**	**Max. hours/wk. for services:** 5 hours
Extended test time: Yes	**ADHD:** Yes	for individual; unlimited group
Scribes: No	**Reading machine:** No	**How professors are notified of**
Proctors: Yes	**Other assistive technology:** Yes	**LD/ADHD:** By the student and the
Oral exams: No	**Priority registration:** Yes	director
Note-takers: No		

GENERAL ADMISSIONS INFORMATION

Director of Admissions: Jill Endries
Telephone: 920-424-0202

ENTRANCE REQUIREMENTS

17 total are required; 4 English required, 3 math required, 3 science required, 3 science lab required, 3 social studies required, 4 elective required. High school diploma or GED required. Minimum TOEFL is 525. TOEFL required of all international applicants.

Application deadline: August 1	**Average SAT I Math:** NR	**Graduated top 10% of class:** 12%
Notification: Rolling beginning 9/15	**Average SAT I Verbal:** NR	**Graduated top 25% of class:** 38%
Average GPA: NR	**Average ACT:** 22	**Graduated top 50% of class:** 86%

COLLEGE GRADUATION REQUIREMENTS

Course waivers allowed: Yes
Course substitutions allowed: Yes
In what subjects: Foreign language; special accommodations are in place relating to the foreign language requirement

ADDITIONAL INFORMATION

Environment: The campus is located 3 hours north of Chicago and 2 hours northeast of Madison.

Student Body	**Cost Information**	**Greek System**
Undergrad enrollment: 9,295	**In-state tuition:** $2,950	**Fraternity:** Yes
Female: 58%	**Out-of-state tuition:** $9,606	**Sorority:** Yes
Male: 42%	**Room & board:** $3,130	**Athletics:** NCAA Division III
Out-of-state: 4%	**Housing Information**	
	University housing: Yes	
	Percent living on campus: 34%	

University of Wisconsin—Oshkosh

UNIV. OF WISCONSIN—STEVENS POINT

Student Services Center, Stevens Point, WI 54481
Phone: 715-346-2441 • Fax: 715-346-3957
E-mail: admiss@uwsp.edu • Web: www.uwsp.edu
Support level: CS • Institution type: 4-year public

LEARNING DISABILITY PROGRAM AND SERVICES

The University does not have a formal program or a specialized curriculum for students with LD; rather it provides all of the services appropriate to ensure equal access to all programs. The University's philosophy is to provide what is mandated in order to enhance the student's academic success, and also to convey their concern for the student's total well-being. The director is a strong advocate for students. Students are encouraged to meet with the director prior to admissions for information about the services. A full range of accommodations are provided. The services provide a multisensory approach developing compensatory skills, not remediation, and utilize a developmental model for advising as well as psychosocial adjustment. Student success is contingent on many factors; some responsibilities belong to the student, others belong to the University, and others are shared by both. Students should make an appointment at the beginning of each semester; should not miss appointments; register with RFB for taped texts; make their needs known; and be a self-advocate. The Office of Disability Services (ODS) provides students with accommodations that are appropriate for the disability. Together, ODS and the student can work toward effective accommodations and utilization of support services and establish a working relationship based on trust and communication.

LD/ADHD ADMISSIONS INFORMATION

College entrance tests required: Yes
Nonstandardized tests accepted: Yes
Interview required: No
Essay required: No
Documentation required for LD: WAIS-III or WISC-R, WJ, as appropriate
Documentation required for ADHD: Yes
Documentation submitted to: N/A
Special Ed. HS course work accepted: No

Specific course requirements for all applicants: Yes
Separate application required for services: No
# of LD applications submitted yearly: N/A
# of LD applications accepted yearly: N/A
Total # of students receiving LD/ADHD services: 140
Acceptance into program means acceptance into college: Students must be admitted and enrolled at the University first and then may request services.

ADMISSIONS

There is no separate admission procedure for students with learning disabilities. However, students are encouraged to make a pre-admission inquiry and talk to the director of ODS. Students with learning disabilities who do not meet the combined class rank and ACT test score criteria of 64 should send a letter of recommendation from the high school LD specialist or counselor. Students should also meet with the Director of Disabled Student Services at Stevens Point if support is needed in the application process. The Director of Admission does have the flexibility to admit students with learning disabilities on a case-by-case basis.

ADDITIONAL INFORMATION

ODS provides accommodations that are appropriate to the disability, orientation assistance, taped textbooks, note-takers, proctors and scribes, adaptive testing, priority registration, assistance with life skills and advising, referral to tutoring and writing assistance, time management and study strategies training, notification to faculty/staff regarding necessary accommodations, assessment and referral services for those not yet diagnosed, and a commitment to keeping scheduled appointments and a corresponding commitment to being timely. The Tutoring-Learning Center schedules 30-minute tutoring sessions and small-group tutoring; tutoring is free for students wanting help with reading or writing assignments. Tutoring in subject areas is done in groups and there is a $10 enrollment fee; however, for most students, the fee is covered by various support programs.

SUPPORT SERVICES CONTACT INFORMATION

Learning Disability Program/Services: Office of Disability Services (ODS)
Director: John Timcak
  E-mail: jtimcak@uwsp.edu
  Telephone: 715-346-3365
  Fax: 715-346-2558
Contact: Same

LEARNING DISABILITY SERVICES

Requests for the following services/accommodations will be evaluated individually based on appropriate and current documentation.

Allowed in Exams
  Calculator: Yes
  Dictionary: Yes
  Computer: Yes
  Spellchecker: Yes
Extended test time: Yes
Scribes: Yes
Proctors: Yes
Oral exams: Yes
Note-takers: Yes

Distraction-reduced environment: Yes
Tape recording in class: Yes
Books on tape from RFBD: Yes
Taping of books not from RFBD: Yes
Accommodations for students with ADHD: Yes
Reading machine: Yes
Other assistive technology: Yes
Priority registration: Yes

Added costs for services: No
LD specialists: Yes (1)
Professional tutors: 3
Peer tutors: Yes
Max. hours/wk. for services: 2 hours per course
How professors are notified of LD/ADHD: By director

GENERAL ADMISSIONS INFORMATION

Director of Admissions: David Eckholm
Telephone: 715-346-2441

ENTRANCE REQUIREMENTS
17 total are required; 4 English required, 3 math required, 3 science required, 2 foreign language recommended, 3 social studies required, 4 elective required. High school diploma or GED required. Minimum TOEFL is 550. TOEFL required of all international applicants.

Application deadline: Rolling
Notification: Rolling
Average GPA: 3.4

Average SAT I Math: N/A
Average SAT I Verbal: N/A
Average ACT: 23

Graduated top 10% of class: 15%
Graduated top 25% of class: 50%
Graduated top 50% of class: 97%

COLLEGE GRADUATION REQUIREMENTS

Course waivers allowed: Yes
Course substitutions allowed: Yes
In what subjects: Math and foreign language

ADDITIONAL INFORMATION

Environment: The University of Wisconsin at Stevens Point is located on 335 acres 110 miles north of Madison.

Student Body
  Undergrad enrollment: 8,400
  Female: 56%
  Male: 44%
  Out-of-state: 7%

Cost Information
  In-state tuition: $3,165
  Out-of-state tuition: $10,693
  Room & board: $3,616
Housing Information
  University housing: Yes
  Percent living on campus: 36%

Greek System
  Fraternity: Yes
  Sorority: Yes
  Athletics: NCAA Division III

UNIV. OF WISCONSIN—WHITEWATER

800 West Main Street, Baker Hall, Whitewater, WI 53190
Phone: 262-472-1440 • Fax: 262-472-1515
E-mail: uwwadmit@uwwvax.uww.edu • Web: www.uww.edu
Support level: CS • Institution type: 4-year public

LEARNING DISABILITY PROGRAM AND SERVICES

The University of Wisconsin—Whitewater Project ASSIST offers support services for students with learning disabilities. The Project ASSIST Summer Transition Program is a four-week program in which students enroll in a three-credit study-skills class to enhance and develop learning strategies. Other instructional activities address comprehension concerns, study habits, time management, and self-advocacy skills. The philosophy of the Program is that students with LD can learn strategies to become independent learners.

LD/ADHD ADMISSIONS INFORMATION

College entrance tests required: Yes
Nonstandardized tests accepted: Yes
Interview required: Yes
Essay required: No
Documentation required for LD: WAIS-III; WJ
Documentation required for ADHD: Yes
Documentation submitted to: Project ASSIST
Special Ed. HS course work accepted: Yes, with documentation

Specific course requirements for all applicants: Yes
Separate application required for services: Yes
# of LD applications submitted yearly: 100
# of LD applications accepted yearly: 80
Total # of students receiving LD/ADHD services: 225
Acceptance into program means acceptance into college: Students must be admitted and enrolled at the University and then request services. Project ASSIST reviews some applications and makes recommendations to Admissions.

ADMISSIONS

All applicants must meet the same criteria for admission. Students should apply to both the University and Project ASSIST. General criteria include top 50 percent or combined class rank and ACT/SAT percentile equaling 100 or above. Those between 70 and 99 may be placed on the wait list. Course requirements include 4 English, 3 social studies, 3 sciences, and 4 electives. Students apply to the University Admissions first; after a decision is made to admit or deny, the director of Project ASSIST reviews the file to decide whether to make an exception for admission or whether the student may use services. If the director needs to make an exception for admissions, then the Summer Transition program is required and the students receive use of services for one year. Summer Transition Program is only offered to students with learning disabilities.

ADDITIONAL INFORMATION

Tutoring services are provided in a one-to-one setting where students work with tutors on strategies in the context of specific course work. Testing accommodations could include extra time, readers, scribes, computers and quiet rooms. Group sessions are held usually on a weekly basis, in which students either work on comprehension and application of specific course work, or learn a variety of skills and strategies such as test-taking and writing skills. Skills courses are offered for no credit in reading comprehension and writing.

SUPPORT SERVICES CONTACT INFORMATION

Learning Disability Program/Services: Project ASSIST
Director: Nancy Amacher
  E-mail: assist@mail.uww.edu
  Telephone: 262-472-4788
  Fax: 262-472-5210
Contact: Same

LEARNING DISABILITY SERVICES

Requests for the following services/accommodations will be evaluated individually based on appropriate and current documentation.

Allowed in Exams
  Calculator: Yes
  Dictionary: Yes
  Computer: Yes
  Spellchecker: Yes
  Extended test time: Yes
  Scribes: Yes
  Proctors: Yes
  Oral exams: Y/N
  Note-takers: Yes

Distraction-reduced environment: Yes
Tape recording in class: Yes
Books on tape from RFBD: Yes
Taping of books not from RFBD: Yes
Accommodations for students with ADHD: Yes
Reading machine: No
Other assistive technology: No
Priority registration: Yes

Added costs for services: Depends on one-to-one support
LD specialists: Yes
Professional tutors: 2
Peer tutors: 30
Max. hours/wk. for services: Unlimited
How professors are notified of LD/ADHD: By student

GENERAL ADMISSIONS INFORMATION

Director of Admissions: Dr. Tory McGuire
Telephone: 262-472-1440

ENTRANCE REQUIREMENTS
17 total are required; 4 English required, 3 math required, 3 science required, 2 science lab required, 3 social studies required, 4 elective required. High school diploma or GED required. Minimum TOEFL is 500. TOEFL required of all international applicants.

Application deadline: Rolling
Notification: Rolling beginning 8/15
Average GPA: NR

Average SAT I Math: NR
Average SAT I Verbal: NR
Average ACT: 22

Graduated top 10% of class: 9%
Graduated top 25% of class: 32%
Graduated top 50% of class: 77%

COLLEGE GRADUATION REQUIREMENTS

Course waivers allowed: No
Course substitutions allowed: No
In what subjects: N/A

ADDITIONAL INFORMATION

Environment: The University is located in a small town southwest of Milwaukee.

Student Body
  Undergrad enrollment: 9,339
  Female: 53%
  Male: 47%
  Out-of-state: 6%

Cost Information
  In-state tuition: $3,146
  Out-of-state tuition: $10,674
  Room & board: $3,284
Housing Information
  University housing: Yes
  Percent living on campus: 45%

Greek System
  Fraternity: Yes
  Sorority: Yes
  Athletics: NCAA Division III

University of Wisconsin—Whitewater

SHERIDAN COLLEGE

PO Box 1500, Sheridan, WY 82801
Phone: 307-674-6446 • Fax: 307-674-6446 x 6137
Web: www.sc.whecn.edu/general.html
Support level: S • Institution type: 2-year public

LEARNING DISABILITY PROGRAM AND SERVICES

Sheridan College has limited services available for students with learning disabilities. Students who have been enrolled in Special Education classes in high school may find that the college does not have the extensive services necessary for them to be successful. Students need to be self sufficient, because only a small percentage of the time of the two advisors/counselors are available to work with students with disabilities. Students requesting accommodations must provide psychoeducational evaluations and have these sent to the Counseling/Testing Offices. The college reserves the right to evaluate whether it can serve the needs of students.

LD/ADHD ADMISSIONS INFORMATION

College entrance tests required: No
Nonstandardized tests accepted: Yes
Interview required: No
Essay required: No
Documentation required for LD: Psychoeducational evaluation
Documentation required for ADHD: Yes
Submitted to: Admissions and Learning Center
Special Ed. HS course work accepted: Yes

Specific course requirements for all applicants: Yes
Separate application required for services: No
# of LD applications submitted yearly: N/A
# of LD applications accepted yearly: N/A
Total # of students receiving LD/ADHD services: N/A
Acceptance into program means acceptance into college: Students must be admitted and enrolled at the College and then may request services.

ADMISSIONS

There are no special admission procedures or criteria for students with learning disabilities. The college has open admissions and any student with a high school diploma or GED is eligible to attend. All students are treated the same and must submit the general college application for admission. Any information on learning disabilities provided is voluntarily given by the student. Students with learning disabilities must submit psychoeducational evaluations. The admission decision is made by the director of the program.

ADDITIONAL INFORMATION

The college offers tutoring, quiet places to take tests, readers, extended testing time, recorders, notetakers, and the availability of a few Franklin Spellers. Remediation courses are offered in arithmetic skills, spelling, vocabulary, reading, writing, and algebra. Other aids for students with learning disabilities include test-taking strategies, books on tape, tutoring one-on-one or in small groups in the Learning Center, and GED preparation and testing. Support services include career testing and evaluation, peer counseling, and personal and career development.

SUPPORT SERVICES CONTACT INFORMATION

Learning Disability Program/Services: Learning Center
Director: Elizabeth Stearns
  E-mail: estearns@sc.cc.wy.us
  Telephone: 307-674-6446
  Fax: 307-674-7205
Contact: Same

LEARNING DISABILITY SERVICES

Requests for the following services/accommodations will be evaluated individually based on appropriate and current documentation.

Allowed in Exams
  Calculator: Yes
  Dictionary: Yes
  Computer: Yes
  Spellchecker: Yes
Extended test time: Yes
Scribes: No
Proctors: Yes
Oral exams: Yes
Notetakers: No

Distraction-reduced environment: Yes
Tape recording in class: Yes
Books on tape from RFBD: Yes
Taping of books not from RFBD: Yes
Accommodations for students with ADHD: Yes
Reading machine: No
Other assistive technology: No
Priority registration: No

Added costs for services: No
LD specialists: No
Professional tutors: Yes
Peer tutors: Yes
Max. hours/wk. for services: As needed
How professors are notified of LD/ADHD: By student and program director

GENERAL ADMISSIONS INFORMATION

Director of Admissions: Zane Garstad
Telephone: 307-674-6446

ENTRANCE REQUIREMENTS
Open door admissions. High school diploma or GED required. Selective admission to nursing and dental hygiene programs

Application deadline: Rolling
Notification: Rolling
Average GPA: N/A

Average SAT I Math: NR
Average SAT I Verbal: NR
Average ACT: NR

Graduated top 10% of class: N/A
Graduated top 25% of class: N/A
Graduated top 50% of class: N/A

COLLEGE GRADUATION REQUIREMENTS

Course waivers allowed: No
Course substitutions allowed: No
In what subjects: N/A

ADDITIONAL INFORMATION

Environment: The College is located 30 miles southeast of Fresno.

Student Body
  Undergrad enrollment: 9,806
  Female: 59%
  Male: 41%
  Out-of-state: 6%

Cost Information
  In-state tuition: $690
  Out-of-state tuition: $1,872
  Room & board: $2,800
Housing Information
  University housing: Yes
  Percent living on campus: 5%

Greek System
  Fraternity: Yes
  Sorority: Yes
Athletics: NJCAA

Sheridan College

UNIVERSITY OF WYOMING

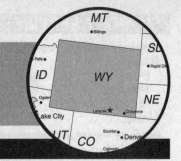

Admissions Office, PO Box 3435, Laramie, WY 82071
Phone: 307-766-5160 • Fax: 307-766-4042
E-mail: Why-Wyo@uyo.edu • Web: www.uwyo.edu
Support level: S • Institution type: 4-year public

LEARNING DISABILITY PROGRAM AND SERVICES

University Disability Support Services (UDSS) offers academic support services to students with physical, cognitive, or psychological disabilities. The goals are to promote the independence and self-sufficiency of students, and to encourage the provision of equal opportunities in education for students with disabilities. Any student enrolled at UW who has a documented disability is eligible for assistance. UDSS provides disability-related accommodations and services, technical assistance, consultations, and resource information. Recommended documentation includes a clear statement of the LD (documentation should be current, preferably within the last three years); a summary of assessment procedures and evaluation instruments used to make the diagnosis and a summary of the results, including standardized or percentile scores that support the diagnosis (LD testing must be comprehensive, including a measure of both aptitude and achievement in the areas of reading, mathematics, and written language); and a statement of strengths and needs that will impact the student's ability to meet the demands of college. Accommodations are collaboratively determined by the student and the assigned Disability Support Service Coordinator.

LD/ADHD ADMISSIONS INFORMATION

College entrance tests required: Yes
Nonstandardized tests accepted: Yes
Interview required: No
Essay required: No
Documentation required for LD: Psychoeducational evaluation
Documentation required for ADHD: Yes
Documentation submitted to: UDSS
Special Ed. HS course work accepted: Yes

Specific course requirements for all applicants: Yes
Separate application required for services: Yes
# of LD applications submitted yearly: 50
# of LD applications accepted yearly: No limit
Total # of students receiving LD/ADHD services: 90
Acceptance into program means acceptance into college: Students must be admitted and enrolled at the University first and then may apply for services.

ADMISSIONS

Students with learning disabilities must meet general admission requirements. If the students are borderline and have a documented learning disability, they are encouraged to self-identify to the director. Students who were diagnosed late in high school or began utilizing services late may be able to explain how this had an impact on academics. Students with learning disabilities who meet the general admission criteria request LD services after being admitted. Conditional admission is granted with GPA of 2.5 or GPA of 2.25 and 20 ACT or SAT of 960. Students with learning disabilities not meeting admission criteria and not qualifying for assured or conditional admission may request that their applications be reviewed again by the Office of Admission. The director may be asked to make a recommendation to the Office of Admission.

ADDITIONAL INFORMATION

Services include priority registration, readers, assistance with study skills, note-taking, test preparation, word processing orientation, equipment loan assistance, tutor referral, and advocacy for students via University Campus Access Committee. Auditory systems are also used to provide access to print mediums for persons with LD. Synthesized speech reinforces visual cues; grammar checking software is available to proof documents and to improve writing skills; writing skills may be improved through the use of word prediction software; and a voice recognition program may benefit those students who have learning disabilities that affect written expression.

SUPPORT SERVICES CONTACT INFORMATION

Learning Disability Program/Services: University Disability Support Services (UDSS)
Director: Chris Primus
  E-mail: cfprimus@uwyo.edu
  Telephone: 307-766-6189
  Fax: 307-766-4010
Contact: Same

LEARNING DISABILITY SERVICES

Requests for the following services/accommodations will be evaluated individually based on appropriate and current documentation.

Allowed in Exams
  Calculator: Yes
  Dictionary: Yes
  Computer: Yes
  Spellchecker: Yes
Extended test time: Yes
Scribes: Yes
Proctors: Yes
Oral exams: Yes
Note-takers: Yes

Distraction-reduced environment: Yes
Tape recording in class: Yes
Books on tape from RFBD: Yes
Taping of books not from RFBD: Yes
Accommodations for students with ADHD: Yes
Reading machine: Yes
Other assistive technology: Yes
Priority registration: Yes

Added costs for services: No
LD specialists: No
Professional tutors: Yes
Peer tutors: Yes
Max. hours/wk. for services: As available
How professors are notified of LD/ADHD: By the student and coordinator

GENERAL ADMISSIONS INFORMATION

Director of Admissions: Sara Alexson
Telephone: 307-766-5160

ENTRANCE REQUIREMENTS

13 total are required; 19 total are recommended; 4 English required, 4 English recommended, 3 math required, 3 math recommended, 3 science required, 3 science recommended, 3 science lab required, 3 science lab recommended. High school diploma or GED required. Minimum TOEFL is 525. TOEFL required of all international applicants.

Application deadline: August 10
Notification: Rolling
Average GPA: 3.4

Average SAT I Math: 555
Average SAT I Verbal: 540
Average ACT: 24

Graduated top 10% of class: 27%
Graduated top 25% of class: 49%
Graduated top 50% of class: 80%

COLLEGE GRADUATION REQUIREMENTS

Course waivers allowed: No
Course substitutions allowed: Yes
In what subjects: Substitutions are possible for foreign language and some math course requirements.

ADDITIONAL INFORMATION

Environment: The University is located on 785 acres in a small town 128 miles north of Denver.

Student Body
  Undergrad enrollment: 8,597
  Female: 52%
  Male: 48%
  Out-of-state: 26%

Cost Information
  In-state tuition: $2,817
  Out-of-state tuition: $8,279
  Room & board: $4,744
Housing Information
  University housing: Yes
  Percent living on campus: 26%

Greek System
  Fraternity: Yes
  Sorority: Yes
Athletics: NCAA Division I

QUICK CONTACT REFERENCE LIST

ALABAMA

Institution	City/State/Zip	Contact	Service	Phone
Auburn U.	Auburn U., AL 36849	Dr. Kelly Haynes	Students w/ Disabilities	334-844-2096
Auburn U.	Montgomery, AL 36124-4023	Tamara Massey	Special Services	334-244-3754
Gadsden St. C.C.	Gadsden, AL 35999	Dr. Judy Hill	Student Services	256-549-8271
Jacksonville St. U.	Jacksonville, AL 36265	Daniel Miller	Disability Support Services	205-782-5093
Samford U.	Birmingham, AL 35229	Marsha Hamby	Counseling Services	205-726-4078
U. of Alabama	Birmingham, AL 35294-1150	Tim Hunter	Disability Support Coordinator	205-934-4205
U. of Alabama	Huntsville, AL 35899	Delois H. Smith	Student Development Services	256-890-6203
U. of Alabama	Tuscaloosa, AL 35487	Jim Saski	The Office of Disabilities	205-348-7966
U. of Montevallo	Montevallo, AL 35115	Deborah S. McCune	Services for Students w/ Disabilities	205-665-6250
U. of South Alabama	Mobile, AL 36688-0002	Bernita Pulmas	Special Student Services	334-460-7212

ALASKA

Institution	City/State/Zip	Contact	Service	Phone
Sheldon Jackson C.	Sitka, AK 99835	Alice Smith	Learning Assistance Program	907-747-5235
U. of Alaska	Anchorage, AK 99508-8046	Lyn Stoller	Disability Support	907-786-4530
U. of Alaska	Fairbanks, AK 99775-7480	Jan Ohmsted	Disability Services	907-474-5655
U. of Alaska—Southeast	Juneau, AK 99801-8681	Robert Sewell	Counseling	907-465-6359

ARIZONA

Institution	City/State/Zip	Contact	Service	Phone
Arizona St. U.	Tempe, AZ 85287-3202	Tedde Scharf	Disability Resources for Students	480-965-1234
Coconino C.C.	Flagstaff, AZ 86004	Nancy Elliot	Disability Resources	520-527-1222
Embry—Riddle Aero. U. (AZ)	Prescott, AZ 86301-3720	Rosemary Carr	Student Success Program	520-708-3700
Gateway C.C.	Phoenix, AZ 85034	Emily Bluestine	Special Services	602-392-5049
Mesa C.C.	Mesa, AZ 85202	Judith Taussig	Disability Resources and Services	602-248-1826
Northern Arizona U.	Flagstaff, AZ 86011-4084	Dr. Marsha Fields	Disability Support Services	520-523-8773
Phoenix C.	Phoenix, AZ 85013	Ramona Shingler	Special Services	602-285-7477
Pima C.C.	Tucson, AZ 85702	Eric Morrison	Disabled Student Resources	520-206-6688
U. of Arizona	Tucson, AZ 85921	Dr. Sue Kroeger	SALT	520-621-7674

ARKANSAS

Institution	City/State/Zip	Contact	Service	Phone
Arkansas St. U.	State Univ., AR 72467	Dr. Jenifer Rice Mason	Disability Services	870-972-3964
Harding U.	Searcy, AR 72149	Dr. Linda Thompson	Student Support Services	501-279-4416
Henderson St. U.	Arkadelphia, AR 71999-0001	Vickie Muse	Disability Services	870-230-5451
NW Arkansas C.C.	Bentonville, AR 72712	Mike Kurk	Disability Service	501-619-4384
S. Arkansas U.	Magnolia, AR 71753-5000	Paula Washington-Wood	Student Disability Special Services	870-235-4145
U. of Arkansas	Fayetteville, AR 72701	Riqua Serebreni	Campus Access	501-575-3104

Institution	Contact	Address	Service	Phone
U. of Arkansas	Susan Queller	Little Rock, AR 72204	Disability Support Services	501-569-3143
U. of Arkansas	Micheal Washington	Pine Bluff, AR 71601-2799	Office of Veterans & Disability Services	870-543-8512
U. of Central Arkansas	Maurice Lee	Conway, AR 72035	Dean's Office	501-450-3167
U. of the Ozarks	Julia Frost	Clarksville, AR 72830	Jones Learning Center	501-979-1403

CALIFORNIA

Institution	Contact	Address	Service	Phone
Bakersfield C.	Tim Bohan	Bakersfield, CA 93305	Support Services Program	661-395-4334
Biola U.	Tim Engle	La Mirada, CA 90639	Services to the Disabled	562-944-0351
Butte C.C.	Richard Dunn	Oroville, CA 95965	Services for Students with Disabilities	530-895-2511
Cabrillo C.	Frank Lynch	Santa Cruz, CA 95060	Disabled Student Services	831-479-6379
Cabrillo C.	Deborah Shulman	Aptos, CA 95003	Learning Skills Program	831-479-6220
Calif Polytechnic St. U.	William Bailey	San Luis Obispo, CA 93407	Disability Resource Center	805-756-1395
Calif St. Polytechnic U.	Fred Henderson	Pomona, CA 91768	Disabled Student Services	909-869-3005
California St. U.	Lee Bettencourt	Turlock, CA 95832	Disabled Student Services	209-667-3159
California St. U.—Bakersfield	Janice Clalussen	Bakersfield, CA 93311	Services for Students with Disabilities	661-664-3360
California St. U.—Chico	Billie Jackson	Chico, CA 95929-0720	Disabilities Support Services	530-898-5959
California St. U.—Fullerton	Paul Miller	Fullerton, CA 92634	Disabled Student Services	714-278-2011
California St. U.—Hayward	Beth Darrow	Hayward, CA 94542	Learning Disabled Resources	510-885-3868
California St. U.—Long Beach	David Sanfilippo	Long Beach, CA 90840	Disabled Student Services	562-985-5401
California St. U.—Northridge	Lee Axelrod	Northridge, CA 91328-1286	Students with Disabilities Resource	818-677-2684
California St. U.—Sacramento	Patricia Sonntag	Sacramento, CA 95819	Services With Learning Disabilities	916-278-6955
Calif. St. U.—San Bernardino	Nicholas Erickson	San Bernardino, CA 92407	Learning Disability Program	909-880-5238
California St. U.—San Marcos	John Segoria	San Marcos, CA 92096-0001	Disabled Student Services	760-750-4905
Cerritos C.C.	Bob Hughlett	Norwalk, CA 90650	Disabled Students Programs & Services	562-860-2451
Chapman U.	Dr. Lynn Mayer	Orange, CA 92866	Center for Academic Success	714-997-6828
Citrus C.C.	Vince Mercurio	Glendora, CA 91741	Disabled Student Program	626-914-8677
City C. San Francisco	K. Kerr Schochet	Orinda, CA 94563	Disabled Student Services	415-239-3000
C. of Redwoods	Sandra Nightingale	Crescent City, CA 95531	Disabled Student Spec.	707-464-7457
Columbia C.C.	Suzanne Patterson	Sonora, CA 95370	Disabled Student Programs & Services	209-588-5133
Cuesta C.	Dr. Lynn Frady	San Luis Obispo, CA 93403	Learning Skills/Disability Services	805-546-3148
De Anza C.	Marilyn Rosenthal	Sunnyvale, CA 94087	Educational Diagnostic Center	408-864-8472
East Los Angeles C.	Therese Demir	Monterey Pk, CA 90025	DSPNS	323-265-8650
El Camino C.	Lucinda Aborn	Torrance, CA 90506	Special Resource Center	310-660-3296

Institution	City/Address	Contact	Service	Phone
Foothill C.	Los Altos, CA 94022	Diana Lydgate	STEP	650-949-7332
Grossmont C.	Ramona, CA 92065	Mary Paschke	LD Services	619-789-9706
Humboldt St. U.	Arcata, CA 95521-8299	Ralph Mc Farland	Disabled Student Services	707-826-4678
John F. Kennedy U.	Orinda, CA 94563	Terance Check	Student Disability Services	925-258-2317
Kings River C.	Reedley, CA 93654-2099	Sam Alvarado	Disabled Student Services	209-638-0332
Lake Tahoe C.C.	So. Lake Tahoe, CA 96150	Karen Macklin	Disability Resource Center	530-541-4660
Laney Colege	El Sobrante, CA 94803	Carol Dalissio	Disabled Student Program Services	510-464-3432
Long Beach City C.	Long Beach, CA 90808	Mark Matsui	Disabled Student Program Services	562-938-4111
Los Angeles City C.	Los Angeles, CA 90039	Susan Matranga	LD Services	323-953-4201
Loyola Marymount U.	Los Angeles, CA 90045	Patricia Robbins	Disability Support Services	310-338-4535
Master's C.	Newhall, CA 91322	Donna Hall	National Institute of Learning Disabilities	805-259-3082
Menlo C.	Atherton, CA 94027	Stan Wanat	Academic Success	650-688-3753
Occidental C.	Los Angeles, CA 90041	Diana Linden	Center for Teaching & Learning	323-259-2545
Oxnard C.	Oxnard, CA 93033	Ellen Young	Disabled Students Program & Services	805-986-5830
Pasadena City C.	Pasadena, CA 91106	Bianca Richards	Disabled Student Services	626-585-7127
Saddleback C.	Carlsbad, CA 92008	Randy Anderson	Special Services	949-582-4500
San Diego City C.	San Diego, CA 92101	Helen Elias	Disabled Student Program & Service	619-230-2513
San Diego St. U.	San Diego, CA 92182	Margo Bohr	Disabled Student Services	619-594-6473
San Francisco St. U.	San Francisco, CA 94132	Deidre De Freese	Disability Resource Center	415-338-6356
San Jose St. U.	San Jose, CA 95192	Martin Schulter	Disability Resource Center	408-924-6000
Santa Barbara City C.	Santa Barbara, CA 93109	Janet Shapiro	Disabled Student Services	805-965-0581
Santa Clara U.	Santa Clara, CA 95053	Ann Ravenscroft	Students with Disabilities Resources	408-554-4111
Santa Monica C.	Santa Monica, CA 90405	Ann Maddox	Learning Specialist Program	213-452-9265
Santa Rosa Junior C.	Santa Rosa, CA 95401	Pattie Wegman	Disability Resource Department	707-527-4906
Sierra C.	Rocklin, CA 95677	Dr. James Hirschinger	Learning Opportunities Center	916 781-0599
Sonoma St. U.	Rohnert Park, CA 94928	Linda Lipps	Disability Resourse Center	707-664-2677
Stanford U.	Stanford, CA 94305-3005	Joan Bisagno	Disability Resource Center	650-723-1066
Taft C.	Taft, CA 93268	Jeff Ross	Disabled Student Services	661-763-7700
U. of California—Berkeley	Berkeley, CA 94720-4250	Ed Rogers	Disabled Students' Program	510-642-0518
U. of California—Davis	Davis, CA 95616	Christine O'Dell	Learnining Disability Center	530-752-2971
U. of California—Irvine	Irvine, CA 92717	Ron Blosser	Office of Disability Services	949-824-6703
U. of California—Los Angeles	Los Angeles, CA 90095	Kathy Molini	Office for Students with Disabilities	310-825-1501
U. of California—Riverside	Riverside, CA 92521	Marcia Theise Schiffer	Services for Students w/ Disabilities	909-787-4538

Institution	Address	Contact	Service	Phone
U. of California—San Diego	La Jolla, CA 92093-0337	Roberta J Gimblett	Office for Students with Disabilities	858-534-4382
U. of California—Santa Barbara	Santa Barbara, CA 93106	Diane Glenn	Disabled Student Program	805-893-2182
U. of California—Santa Cruz	Santa Cruz, CA 95064	Sharyn Martin	Disability Resource Center	831-459-2089
U. of Redlands	Redlands, CA 92373-0999	Judy Bowman	Academic Support Services	909-335-4079
U. of San Diego	San Diego, CA 92110-2492	Betty Bacon	Disabilities Services	619-594-6473
U. of San Francisco	San Francisco, CA 94117	Tom Merrell	Services for Students w/ LD	415-422-6876
U. of Southern California	Los Angeles, CA 90089	Janet Eddy	Disability Services	213-740-0776
U. of the Pacific	Stockton, CA 95211	Howard Houck	Office of Disabilities Support	209-946-2458
Whittier C.	Whittier, CA 90608	Jamie Sheperd	Learning Support Services	562-907-4233

COLORADO

Institution	Address	Contact	Service	Phone
Colorado Mt. C.	Glenwood Springs, CO 81601	Shirley Bowen	Developmental Education	303-945-8691
Colorado School of Mines	Golden, CO 80401-1869	Ron Brummett	Student Development & Career Center	303-273-3297
Colorado St. U.	Fort Collins, CO 80523	Rosemary Kreston	Resources for Disabled Students	970-491-6385
Fort Lewis C.	Durango, CO 81301	Bob Lundquist	Learning Assistance Center	303-247-7383
Mesa St. C.	Grand Junctio, CO 81502-2647	Sandra J. Wymore	Education Access Service	970-248-1801
Northeastern Junior C.	Sterling, CO 80751	Nancy Mann	Study Skills Services	303-522-6600
Regis U.	Denver, CO 80221-1099	Dr. Koko Oyler	Disability Services	303-458-4941
U. of Colorado, Boulder	Boulder, CO 80309-0107	Cindy Donohue	Disability Services	303-492-8671
U. of Colorado, Col. Springs	Colorado Springs, CO 80933	Kaye Simonton	Disability Services	719-262-3065
U. of Colorado—Denver	Denver, CO 80217	Lisa McGill	Disability Support Department	303-556-8388
U. of Denver	Denver, CO 80208	Ted May	University Disability Services	303-871-2372
U. of Northern Colorado	Greeley, CO 80639	Nancy Kauffman	Disability Access Center	970-351-2289
U. of Southern Colorado	Pueblo, CO 81001	Pam Chambers	Disabilities Resources Office	719-549-2581
Western St. C. of Colorado	Gunnison, CO 81231	Layn Nelson	Student Support Services	970-943-2130

CONNECTICUT

Institution	Address	Contact	Service	Phone
Briarwood C.	Southington, CT 06489	Cynthia Clark	Services for Students with LD	860-628-4751
Central Connecticut St. U.	New Britain, CT 06050	Dr. George Tenney	Special Student Services	860-832-1957
Connecticut C.	New London, CT 06320	Susan Duques, PhD	Office of Disability Services	860-439-5428
Eastern Connecticut St. U.	Willimantic, CT 06226	Pamela Starr	Counseling for Students w/ Disabilities	860-465-5573
Fairfield U.	Fairfield, CT 06430-5195	Rev. W.L. O'Neil SJ	Student Support Services	203-254-4000
Housatonic C.	Bridgeport, CT 06608	Peter Anderheggen	Disability Support Services	203-332-5000
Mitchell C.	New London, CT 06320	Dr. Patricia Pezzullo	Learning Resource Center	860-701-5141

Institution	Location	Contact	Service	Phone
Quinnipiac C.	Hamden, CT 06518	John Jarvis	Learning Services	203-582-5390
Southern Connecticut St. U.	New Haven, CT 06515	Suzanne Tucker	Disability Resource Center	203-392-6828
U. of Connecticut	W. Hartford, CT 06117	J. Thierfeld-Brown	Disability Support Services	860-570-9188
U. of Connecticut	Storrs, CT 06269	Dr. Joseph Madaus	Students w/ Learning Disabilities	860-486-0178
U. of Hartford	West Hartford, CT 06117	Susan Fitzgerald	Learning Plus	860-768-5129
U. of New Haven	West Haven, CT 06516	Linda Copney Okeke	Disability Services	203-932-7331
Wesleyan U.	Middletown, CT 06459-0265	Vancenia Rutherford	Learning Disabilities Services	860-685-2600
Western Connecticut St. U.	Danbury, CT 06810	Helen Kreuger	Disability Services	203-837-9252
Yale U.	New Haven, CT 06520	Carolyn Barrett	Resource Office for Disabilities	203-432-2324

DELAWARE

Institution	Location	Contact	Service	Phone
Delaware Tech C.C.	Georgetown, DE 19947	Bonnie Hall	Student Support Services	302-856-5400
U. of Delaware	Newark, DE 19716-6210	David Johns	Special Services	302-831-1639

DISTRICT OF COLUMBIA

Institution	Location	Contact	Service	Phone
American U.	Washington, DC 20016	Helen Steinberg	Learning Services Program	202-885-3360
Catholic U. of America, The	Washington, DC 20064-0001	Bonnie McClellan	Disability Support Services	202-319-5618
Gallaudet U.	Washington, DC 20002	Patricia Tesar	Prog for Students w/ Other Disabilities	202-651-5256
George Washington U.	Washington, DC 20052	Christy Willis	Disability Support Services	202-994-8250
Georgetown U.	Washington, DC 20057	Marcia W. Fulk, M.Ed.	Learning Services	202-687-6985
Trinity C. (DC)	Washington, DC 20017-1094	Heather Robertson	Career Services	202-884-9643

FLORIDA

Institution	Location	Contact	Service	Phone
Barry U.	Miami Shores, FL 33161-6695	Dr. Jill Reed	Center for Advanced Learning	305-899-3485
Beacon C.	Leesburg, FL 34748	Dr. Deborah Brodbeck	Disability Service	352-787-7660
Broward C.C.	Ft. Lauderdale, FL 33301	Jean L. McCormick	Disability Services	954-761-7555
Edison C.C.	Fort Meyers, FL 33906	Kathy Doyle	Disability Services	941-489-9113
Embry-Riddle Aeronaut. U. (FL)	Daytona Beach, FL 32114	Maureen C. Bridger	Health Services	904-226-6036
Florida A&M U.	Tallahassee, FL 32307	Dr. Sharon Wooten	Learning Development & Evaluation Ctr.	850-599-8474
Florida Atlantic U.	Boca Raton, FL 33431	Nicole Rokos	Office for Students with Disabilities	561-297-3880
Florida International U.	Miami, FL 33199	Dianae Russell	Disability Services	305-348-3532
Florida St. U.	Tallahassee, FL 32306	Lauren Kennedy	Disabled Student Services	850-644-9566
Gulf Coast C.C.	Panama City, FL 32401	Linda Van Dalen	Disability Student Services	850-872-3834
Hillsborough C.C.	Tampa, FL 33631-3127	Joe Bentrovato	Disabled Services	813-253-7914
Indian River	Fort Pierce, FL 34981	Mary Sylvester	Disability Services	216-987-5106

Institution	Address	Contact	Service	Phone
Jacksonville U.	Jacksonville, FL 32211	Edward Alexander	Disabled Students Services	904-745-7070
Lynn U.	Boca Raton, FL 33431	Gary Martin	Advancement Program	561-237-7239
Pensacola Jr. C.	Pensacola, FL 32504	Linda Sheppard	Disabled Student Services	904-484-1637
Saint Thomas U.	Miami, FL 33054	Susan Angulo	Academic Enhancement	305-628-6713
Santa Fe C.C.	Gainsville, FL 32606	Doug Fols	Disability Resource Center	352-395-5948
Seminole C.C.	Sanford, FL 32773	Dorothy Paishon	Disabled Support Services	407-328-2109
St. Petersburg Jr. C.	St. Petersburg, FL 33733	Susan Blanchard	LD Support Program	813-791-3721
U. of Central Florida	Orlando, FL 32816	Dr. Philip Kalfin	Student Disability Services	407-823-2371
U. of Florida	Gainesville, FL 32611	John Denny	Students with Disabilities	352-392-1261
U. of Miami	Coral Gables, FL 33146	Judith Antinarella	Office for Students w/ LD	305-284-2374
U. of South Florida	Tampa, FL 33620	Dr. Server	Student Disability Services	813-974-4309
U. of Tampa	Tampa, FL 33606-1490	Robert Ruday	Dean's Office	813-253-2171

GEORGIA

Institution	Address	Contact	Service	Phone
Andrew C.	Cuthbert, GA 31740	Carol Trieble	Academic Support Services	912-732-6813
Armstrong St. C.	Savannah, GA 31419	Amelia Bunch	Disability Services	912-927-5271
Brenau U.	Gainesville, GA 30501	Dr. Vincent Yamilkoski	Learning Center	770-534-6134
Clark Atlanta U.	Atlanta, GA 30314	Ricky Robinson	Student Assistance	404-880-8771
Columbus C.	Columbus, GA 31907	Stacey Tuttle	Special Needs	706-568-2330
Darton C.	Albany, GA 31707	Louis Emond	Disabled Student Services	912-430-6729
DeKalb C.	Clarkston, GA 30021	Lisa Fowler	Ctr. for Disability Services	404-299-4118
Emory U.	Atlanta, GA 30322	Gloria McCord	Disability Services	404-727-6016
Gainesville C.	Gainesville, GA 30503	Diane Carpenter	Disability Services	770-718-3855
Georgia Institute of Tech.	Atlanta, GA 30332-0320	Caroline Gergely	Disabled Student Services	404-894-9191
Georgia Southern U.	Statesboro, GA 30460	Wayne Akins	Disabled Student Services	912-871-1566
Georgia St. U.	Atlanta, GA 30302-4009	Caroline Gergely	Disability Services	404-463-9044
Life C.	Marietta, GA 30060	Ann Drake	Academic Assistance Center	770-426-2725
Oglethorpe U.	Atlanta, GA 30319	Marsha Cooperman	Learning Disabilities Center	404-364-8869
Reinhardt C.	Waleska, GA 30183	Sylvia Robertson	Academic Support Office	770-720-5567
Southern Polytechnic St. U.	Marietta, GA 30060	Mary R. Stoy	Counseling & Disability Services	770-528-7226
Spelman C.	Atlanta, GA 30314	Coletta Hassel	Student Disability Services	404-681-3643
U. of Georgia	Athens, GA 30602	Dr. Noel Gregg	Learning Disabilities Center	706-542-7034
Valdosta St. U.	Valdosta, GA 31698	Kimberly Godden	Special Services Program	912-245-2498

HAWAII

Institution	City, State Zip	Contact	Program/Service	Phone
Chaminade U. of Honolulu	Honolulu, HI 96816	Dan Carmoney	Student Affairs	808-735-4852
Hawaii C.C.	Hilo, HI 96720	Karen Kane	Ha'awi Kokua Program	808-974-7741
U. of Hawaii—Hilo	Hilo, HI 96720-4091	Barbara Lee	Student Support Services	808-974-7619
U. of Hawaii—Manoa	Honolulu, HI 96822	Ann C. Ito	KOKUA Program	808-956-7511

IDAHO

Institution	City, State Zip	Contact	Program/Service	Phone
Boise St. U.	Boise, ID 83725	Blaine Eckles	Special Services	208-426-1583
Idaho St. U.	Pocatello, ID 83209-8270	Diane Jenkins	ADA Disabilities Center	208-282-3599
Lewis-Clark St. C.	Lewiston, ID 83501	Debbie Mundell	Counseling & Advising Dept	208-799-2211
U. of Idaho	Moscow, ID 83844-4140	Meredyth Goodwin	Student Disability Services	208-885-7716

ILLINOIS

Institution	City, State Zip	Contact	Program/Service	Phone
Aurora U.	Aurora, IL 60506	Jason Subblette	Student Services	630-844-5521
Barat C.	Lake Forest, IL 60045	Debbie Sheade	Learning Opportunities Program	847-604-6321
Benedictine U.	Lisle, IL 60532-0900	Donna DeSpain	Academic Resource Center	630-829-6000
Chicago St. U.	Chicago, IL 60628	Sandra Saunders	Abilities Office	773-995-4401
C. of Du Page	Glen Ellyn, IL 60137	Jacqueline Reuland	Special Student Services	630-942-2306
C. of Lake County	Grayslake, IL 60030	Bill Freitag	Special Needs	847-223-6601
Columbia C. (IL)	Chicago, IL 60605-1996	Laurie Ann Bender	Disability Support Services	312-663-1600
DePaul U.	Chicago, IL 60604	Stamatios Miras	Productive Learning	773-325-4239
Eastern Illinois U.	Charleston, IL 61920-3099	Kathy Waggoner	Disability Services	217-581-6583
Elgin C.C.	Elgin, IL 60123	Annabelle Rhoades	Disability Services	847-697-1000
Harper C.	Palatine, IL 60067	Tom Thompson	Center for Students with Disabilities	708-925-6266
Illinois Institute of Technology	Chicago, IL 60616	Charles Merbitz	Disability Resources	312-567-5744
Illinois St. U.	Normal, IL 61790	Ann Caldwell	Director of Office of Disability Concerns	309-438-5853
Ivy Tech St. C.	Evansville, IL 47710	Peg Ehlen	Special Needs	812-429-1386
John Wood C.C.	Quincy, IL 62301	Rose-Marie Akers	Support Services Center	217-224-6500
Joliet Junior C.	Joliet, IL 60436	Jewell Dennis	Special Needs Program	815-729-9020
Kankakee C.C.	Kankakee, IL 60901	Mary Jo Webers	Special Population & Instruc. Support.	815-933-0332
Lake Forest C.	Lake Forest, IL 60045	Elizabeth Fischer	Dean's Office	847-735-5200
Lakeland C.	Mattoon, IL 61938	Emily Hatke	Special Needs Resources	217-234-5259
Lincoln C.	Lincoln, IL 62656	Pat Burke	Supportive Educational Services	217-732-3155
Loyola U. of Chicago	Chicago, IL 60611	Pennie Marcus	Services for Students w/ Disabilities	773-508-2741

Institution	Location	Contact	Service	Phone
McHenry C.C.	Crystal Lake, IL 60012	Howard Foreman	Special Needs	815-455-8710
Morraine Valley C.C.	Palos Hills, IL 60465	Debbie Sievers	Center for Disability Services	708-974-5330
Morton C.	Cicero, IL 60650	Susan Pierce	Special Needs	708-656-8000
National-Louis U.	Evanston, IL 60201	Andreen Neukranz-Butler	Center for Academic Development	847-465-5829
North Central C.	Naperville, IL 60566	Deanne Wiedemann	Learning Disability Services	630-637-5264
Northeastern Illinois U.	Chicago, IL 60625	Victoria Amey-Flippin	HELP Program	773-583-4050
Northern Illinois U.	DeKalb, IL 60115	Nancy Kasinski	Ctr. for Access-Ability Resources	815-753-9734
Northwestern U.	Evanston, IL 60204	Dannee Polimski	Services for Students with Disabilities	847-467-5530
Oakton Community C.	Des Plaines, IL 60116	Linda McCann	ASSIST	847-635-1759
Parkland C.	Champaign, IL 61821	Norman Lambert	Disability Services	217-351-7632
Roosevelt U.	Chicago, IL 60605	Nancy Litke	Learning Support Services Program	312-341-3810
Saint Xavier U.	Chicago, IL 60655	Iraetta Lacey	Student Success/Learning Assist. Ctr.	773-298-3330
Schl. of Art Inst. of Chicago	Chicago, IL 60603	Judy Watson	Learning Center	312-345-3507
Shimer C.	Waukegan, IL 60079-0500	David Buchanan	Office of Admissions	847-249-7174
SIU—Carbondale	Carbondale, IL 62901-4710	Barbara Cordoni	Achieve Program	618-453-6120
SIU—Edwardsville	Edwardsville, IL 62026	Jane Floyd-Hendey	Disability Support Services	618-650-3726
U. of Chicago	Chicago, IL 60637	Aneesah Ali	Assistance for Disabled Students	773-702-5671
U. of Ill.—Urbana-Champaign	Urbana, IL 618-1	Karen Wold	Division Rehab-Education Services	217-333-4600
U. of Illinois—Chicago	Chicago, IL 60680	Richard Allegra	Disability Services	312-413-2183
Waubonsee C.C.	Sugar Grove, IL 60554	Iris Jorstad	Access Ctr. for Students w/ Disabilities	630-466-4811
Western Illinois U.	Macomb, IL 61455-1390	Joan Green	Disability Suport Services	309-298-2512
Will. Rainey Harper C.C.	Palatine, IL 60067	Tom Thompson	Access & Disabilities Services	847-925-6266

INDIANA

Institution	Location	Contact	Service	Phone
Anderson U.	Anderson, IN 46012	Rinda Vogelgesang	Disabled Student Services	765-641-4226
Ball St. U.	Muncie, IN 47306	Richard Harris	Office of Disabled Students	765-285-5293
Butler U.	Indianapolis, IN 46208	Michele Atterson	Student Disabilities Center	317-940-9308
DePauw U.	Greencastle, IN 46135	Dee Gardner	Academic Services	765-658-4027
Earlham C.	Richmond, IN 47374	Donna Keesling	Academic Support Services	765-983-1200
Goshen C.	Goshen, IN 46526-4794	Nancy Rhiner Nussbaum	Learning Resource Center	219-535-7576
Indiana St. U.	Terre Haute, IN 47809	Rita Worrall	Student Support Services	812-237-2300
Indiana U. SE	New Albany, IN 47150	Jodi Taylor	Students with Disabilities	812-941-2243
Indiana U. East	Richmond, IN 47374-1289	Sheryl Stafford	Student Support Services	765-973-8302

College	Location	Contact	Service	Phone
Indiana U.—Bloomington	Bloomington, IN 47405-7700	Jody Ferguson	Disabled Student Services	812-855-3508
Indiana U.—Purdue Univ.	Indianapolis, IN 46202-5143	Pamela King	Adaptive Educational Services	315-274-5555
Indiana U.—South Bend	South Bend, IN 46634-7111	Mark Dosch	Division of Disabled Student Services	219-237-4479
Indiana Wesleyan U.	Marion, IN 46953-4999	Jerry Harrell	Student Support Services	765-677-2257
IUPU—Ft. Wayne	Ft. Wayne, IN 46805	Susan Borrer	Disabled Student Services	219-481-6658
IVY Tech	Fort Wayne, IN 46805	Debra Clarke	Disability Services	219-480-4207
Manchester C.	N. Manchester, IN 46962	Denise Howe	Services for Students w/ Disabilities	219-982-5076
Marion C.	Indianapolis, IN 46222	Marge Batic	Learning Center	317-955-6150
Purdue U.—Calumet	Hammond, IN 46323-2094	Michelle Verduzco	Services for Students w/ Disabilities	219-988-2455
Purdue U.—West Lafayette	West Lafayette, IN 47907	Carol Danning	Adaptive Program	765-494-1247
St. Joseph's C.	Rensselaer, IN 47978	David Weed	Counseling Services	219-866-6116
Taylor U.	Upland, IN 46989	Edwin Welch	Academic Support Services	765-998-5523
Tri-St. U.	Angola, IN 46703	Marline Sweet	Special Students	219-665-4171
U. of Evansville	Evansville, IN 47722	Dr. Kim Ermi	Counselling & Testing Center	812-479-2663
U. of Indianapolis	Indianapolis, IN 46227	Deborah Spinney	BUILD Program	317-788-3536
U. of Notre Dame	Notre Dame, IN 46556	Scott Howland	Office for Students w/ Disabilities	219-631-7141
U. of Saint Francis	Fort Wayne, IN 46808	Michelle Kruger	Student Learning Center	219-434-7597
U. of Southern Indiana	Evansville, IN 47712	James Browning	Counseling Center	812-464-1867
Valparaiso U.	Valparaiso, IN 46383	John Ruff	Student Learning Center	219-464-5318
Vincennes U.	Vincennnes, IN 47591	J. Kavanaugh	STEP	812-888-4485
Wabash C.	Crawfordsville, IN 47933	Julia Rosenberg	Writing Center-Academic Support	765-361-6100

IOWA

College	Location	Contact	Service	Phone
Coe C.	Cedar Rapids, IA 52402	Lois Kabela-Coates	Academic Achievement Program	319-399-8547
Cornell C.	Mount Vernon, IA 52341	Michele Long	Dean's Office	319-895-4234
Des Moines Area C.C.	Ankney, IA 50021	Carol Grimm	Academic Achievement	515-964-6268
Drake U.	Des Moines, IA 50311	Interim	Disability Resource Center	515-271-1835
Graceland C.	Lamoni, IA 50140	Susan Knotts	Student Support Services	515-784-5226
Grand View C.	Des Moines, IA 50316-1599	Carolyn Wassenaar	Academic Success	515-263-2971
Grinnell C.	Grinnell, IA 50112	Joyce Stern	Academic Advising Office	641-269-3702
Hawkeye C.C.	Waterloo, IA 50704	Dianne Shoultz	Student Development	319-296-4014
Indian Hills C.C.	Ottumwa, IA 52501	Mary Stewart	Success Center	641-683-5128
Iowa Central C.C.	Ft. Dodge, IA 50501	S. Lumsden/C. Koeplin	Special Needs/VESS program	515-576-7201

Institution	Location	Contact	Service	Phone
Iowa St. U.	Ames, IA 50011-2011	Gwen Woodward	Disability Resources	515-294-0644
Iowa Wesleyan C.	Mount Pleasant, IA 52641	Kay Broywer	Learning Center	319-385-8021
Iowa Western C.C.	Council Bluffs, IA 51502	Chris Holst	Special Needs	712-325-3390
Loras C.	Dubuque, IA 52001	Dianne Gibson	Learning Disabilities Program	319-588-7134
Mount Saint Clare C.	Clinton, IA 52733-2967	Dean David Womack	Student Affairs	319-242-4023
Saint Ambrose U.	Davenport, IA 52803-2898	Ann Austin	Students with Disabilities	319-333-6161
Scott CC E. Iowa CC	Bettonderf, IA 52722	Jerri Crabtree	Student Support Services	319-441-4072
Southeastern C.C.	W. Burlington, IA 52655	Angela Orianodarnallo	Office for Students with Disabilities	319-752-8128
U. of Dubuque	Dubuque, IA 52001-5050	Jesse James	Admissions Office	319-589-3214
U. of Iowa	Iowa City, IA 52242	Mary Richard	Student Disability Services	319-335-1462
U. of Northern Iowa	Cedar Falls, IA 50614	David Towle, PhD	Disability Services	319-273-2676
Waldorf C.	Forest City, IA 50436	Rebecca Hill	LD Program	515-582-8207
Wartburg C.	Waverly, IA 50677	Lex Smith	Student Life	319-352-8260

KANSAS

Institution	Location	Contact	Service	Phone
Baker University	Baldwin City, KS 66006	Kathy Marian	Learning Resource Center	785-594-8352
Bethel C.	N. Newton, KS 67117	Sandra Zerger	Center for Academic Development	316-283-5359
Butler City C.C.	Eldorado, KS 67042	Lianne Fowler	Special Needs & Services	316-322-3166
Colby CC.	Colby, KS 67701	Monica Kane	Student Support Services	785-462-3984
Emporia St. U.	Emporia, KS 66801-5087	Trudi Benjamin	Project Challenge	316-341-5097
Hutchinson C.C.	Hutchison, KS 67502	Linda Dermyer	Disability Services	316-665-3554
Johnson City C.C.	Overland Park, KS 66210	Holly Dressler	Student Access Center	913-469-8500
Kansas City C.C.	Kansas City, KS 66112	Valerie Webb	Disability Support Services	913-596-9670
Kansas St. U.	Manhattan, KS 66506	Gretchen Holden	Disabled Student Services	785-532-6441
Pratt C.C.	Pratt, KS 67124	Registrar	Disability Services	316-672-5641
U. of Kansas	Lawrence, KS 66045	Lorna Zimmer	Services for Students with Disabilities	785-864-2620
Wichita St. U.	Wichita, KS 67260	Grady Landrum	Resource Center for Independence	316-978-6970

KENTUCKY

Institution	Location	Contact	Service	Phone
Bellarmine C.	Louisville, KY 40205	Dr. Ruth Garvey	Office of Student Affairs	502-452-8153
Brescia C.	Owensboro, KY 42301	Tersea Rilley	Student Support Services	800-264-1234
Eastern Kentucky U.	Richmond, KY 40475	Teresa Belluscio	Project Success	859-622-1500
Lexington C.C.	Lexington, KY 40506-0235	Veronica Miller	Disability Support Services	606-257-4872

School	Location	Contact	Service	Phone
Moorhead St.	Moorhead, KY 40351	Debra Reed	Disability Services	606-783-4204
Murray St. U.	Murray, KY 42071	Annazette Fields	Office of Equal Opportunity	270-762-3155
Northern Kentucky U.	Highland Heights, KY 41099	A. Dale Adams	Disability Services	606-572-5180
Southeast C.C.	Cumberland, KY 40823	Charles Sellars	Student Support Services	606-589-2145
Thomas More C.	Crestiew Hill, KY 41017	Barbara Davis	Student Support Services	606-344-3521
U. of Kentucky	Lexington, KY 40506	Jake Karnes	Disability Resource Office	859-257-2754
U. of Louisville	Louisville, KY 40292	Cathy Patus	Disability Resource Center	502-852-6938
Western Kentucky U.	Bowling Green, KY 42101	Huda Melkey	Office of Affirmative Action	270-745-5004

LOUISIANA

School	Location	Contact	Service	Phone
Louisiana C.	Pineville, LA 71359-0560	Betty Matthews	Pass Program	318-487-7629
LSU—Baton Rouge	Baton Rouge, LA 70803	Wendy Devall	Disability Services Office	225-388-4310
Loyola U. New Orleans	New Orleans, LA 70118	Sarah Smith	Acad. Enrichment and Disiblility Svcs.	504-865-2990
Nicholls St. U.	Thibodaux, LA 70310	Karen Chavrin	Center for the Study of Dyslexia	504-448-4214
Southeastern Louisiana U.	Hammond, LA 70402	Dr. June Williams	Student Life	504-549-2247
Southern U. of New Orleans	New Orleans, LA 70126	Dr. Zelma Frank	Student Support Services	504-286-5106
Tulane U.	New Orleans, LA 70118-5680	Dr. Peter Leviness	Disability Services	504-865-5113
U. of New Orleans	New Orleans, LA 70148	Dr. Janice G. Lyn	Disabled Student Services	504-280-6222
U. of Southwestern Louisiana	Lafayette, LA 70504	Page Salley	Services for Students w/ Disabilities	337-482-5252

MAINE

School	Location	Contact	Service	Phone
Bates C.	Lewiston, ME 04240-9917	Celeste Branham	Dean's Office	207-786-6222
Bowdoin C.	Brunswick, ME 04011-8441	Joanne Canning	Dean's Office	207-725-3866
Colby C.	Waterville, ME 04901-8840	Mark Serdjenian	Dean's Office	207-872-3106
Eastern Tech C.	Bangor, ME 04401	Dr. Rita Haunert	Disability Services	207-941-4655
Kennebec Valley Tech	Fairfield, ME 04937	Karen Normandin	Students With Disabilities	207-453-5019
N. Maine Tech C.	Presque Isle, ME 04769	Laura Flagg	Special Services	207-769-2461
S. Maine Tech C.	South Portland, ME 04106	Gail Rowe	Learning Assistance Center	207-767-9536
Unity C.	Unity, ME 04988-0532	Jim Reed	Learning Resource Center	207-948-3131
U. of Maine—Augusta	Bangor, ME 04401-4367	John Kapas	Cornerstone Program	207-621-3138
U. of Maine—Farmington	Farmington, ME 04938	Claire Nelson	Acad. Svcs. for Students w/ Disab.	207-778-7295
U. of Maine—Orono	Orono, ME 04469-5757	Ann Smith	Onward Program/Disabilities	207-581-2319
U. of Maine—Presque Isle	Presque Isle, ME 04769	Myrna Mc Gaffin	Student Support Services	207-768-9400
U. of Maine—Machias	Machias, ME 04654	Jean Schild	Student Resources	207-255-1228

Institution	Location	Contact	Service	Phone
U. of New England	Biddeford, ME 04005	Susan Church	Individual Learning Program	207-283-0171
U. of Southern Maine	Gorham, ME 4038	Joyce Branaman	Academic Support	207-780-4706
MARYLAND				
Allegheny C.	Cumberland, MD 21502	Carol Davis	Instructional Assistance Center	301-724-7700
Anne Arundel C.C.	Arnold, MD 21012	Lynn Williams	Disabled Student Services	410-541-2306
Baltimore City C.C.	Baltimore, MD 21215	Quismat Alim	Disabled Student Services	410-462-8585
Carroll C.C.	Westminster, MD 21157	Joyce Sebian	Student Support Services	410-386-8329
Catonsville C.C.	Catonsville, MD 21228	Jill Hodge	Special Student Population	410-455-4718
Cecil C.	North East, MD 20901	Mary Post	Academic Advising	410-287-6060
Charles Co. C.C.	La Plata, MD 20646	Penny Appel	Learning Assistance Center	301-934-2251
Essex C.C.	Baltimore, MD 21237	Beth Hunsinger	Office of Special Services	410-780-6741
Frostburg St. U.	Frostburg, MD 21532	Leroy Pullen	Disability Support Services	301-687-4483
Goucher C.	Baltimore, MD 21204-2794	Fronda Brown	Disability Specialist	410-337-6529
Hartford C.C.	Bel Air, MD 21015	Janet Medina	Learninng Support Services	410-836-4414
Hood C.	Fredrick, MD 21701	Lynn Schlossburg	Disability Services	301-696-3421
Howard C.C.	Columbia, MD 21044	Joan King	Learning Assistance Center	410-772-4619
Loyola C. (MD)	Baltimore, MD 21210	Katherine S. Milam	Academic Advising Department	410-617-2663
Montgomery C.	Rockville, MD 20850	Brenda Williams	Disability Support Services	301-294-9672
Morgan St. U.	Baltimore, MD 21251	Nina Dobson-Hopkins	Counseling Center	443-885-3130
Towson U.	Towson, MD 21252-0001	Ronni Uhland	Disability Support Services	410-830-2638
U. of Baltimore	Baltimore, MD 21201	Jacquelyn Truelore	Disability Support Services	410-837-4775
U. of Maryland—C. Park	College Park, MD 20742-5235	William Scales	Disability Support Services	301-314-7682
U. of Maryland—Eastern Shore	Princess Anne, MD 21853	Dorling Joseph	Student Development	410-651-6461
Western Maryland C.	Westminster, MD 21157	Denise Marjarum	Academic Skills Center	410-857-2504
MASSACHUSETTS				
American International C.	Springfield, MA 01109-3184	Prof. Mary M. Saltus	Supportive Learning Services	413-747-3426
Amherst C.	Amherst, MA 01002	Francis Tuleja	Services for Students with LD	413-542-2529
Anna Maria C.	Paxton, MA 01612	Livvy O.Tarleton	Learning Center	508-849-3356
Aquinas C.	Newton, MA 02458	Louis Silva	Academic Success Center	781-969-4400
Assumption C.	Worcester, MA 01615	Sister Ellen Guerin, RSN	Disabled Students Services	508-767-7487
Babson C.	Babson Park, MA 02157-0310	Alison Chase- Padulla	Disability Services/Office of Class Dean	617-239-4075

College	City/State	Contact	Department	Phone
Bentley C.	Waltham, MA 2452	Dr. Roger Danchise	Counseling & Student Development	781-891-2274
Berklee C. of Music	Boston, MA 02215	Micheline Beaudry	Learning Center	617-747-2667
Berkshire C.C.	Pittsfield, MA 01201	Pamela Farron	Services for Disabled Students	413-499-4660
Boston C.	Chestnut Hill, MA 02167	Kathleen Duggan	Disabled Student Services	617-552-8055
Boston U.	Boston, MA 02215	Alan Mawrdy	Learning Disability Support Services	617-353-3658
Brandeis U.	Waltham, MA 02254	Michele Rosenthal	Dean's Office-Academic Affairs	781-736-3470
Bridgewater St. C.	Bridgewater, MA 02325	Martha Jones	Office for Students with Disabilities	508-697-1200
Clark U.	Worcester, MA 01610-1477	Alan Bieri	Special Services	508-793-7468
C. of the Holy Cross	Worcester, MA 01610-2395	Dr. Matthew Toth	Disability Services	508-793-3363
Curry C.	Milton, MA 02186	Lisa Ijiri	Program for Advancement in Learning	617-333-2250
Dean C.	Franklin, MA 02038	Dr. Dave Richard	Personalized Learning Services	508-541-1508
Emerson C.	Boston, MA 02116-1511	Dr. Anthony Bashir	Learning Assistance Center	617-824-7874
Endicott C.	Beverly, MA 01915	Laura RossiLe	Student Support Program	978-232-2292
Fitchburg St. C.	Fitchburg, MA 01420-2697	Mary Wagner	Disability Services	978-665-3427
Framingham St. C.	Framingham, MA 01701	Maxine Keats	Academic Affairs Office	508-626-4905
Gordon C.	Wenham, MA 01984-1899	Ann Seavey	Academic Support	978-927-2306
Hampshire C.	Amherst, MA 01002	Kirsten Skorpen	Student Affairs Office	413-559-5849
Harvard and Radcliffe C.s	Cambridge, MA 02318	Louise Russell	Student Disability Resource Center	617-496-8707
Holyoke C.C.	Holyoke, MA 01040	Maureen Conroy	College Disability Services	413-552-2582
Lesley C.	Cambridge, MA 02138	Maureen Reilly	Disability Services	617-868-9600
Mass Bay C.C.	Wellesley Hills, MA 02181	Joe O'Neil	Disability Services	617-237-1100
Massasoit C.C.	Brockton, MA 02402	Nancy Sullivan	Disability Services	508-588-9100
Mt. Ida C.	Newton, MA 01259	Jill Mehler	Learning Opportunities Program	617-928-4648
Mt. Wachusett C.C.	Gardner, MA 01440	Juliette Loring	Students with Disabilities	978-632-6600
N. Adams St. C.	N. Adams, MA 01247	Linda Neville	Learning Center	413-664-6673
North Shore C.C.	Danvers, MA 01923	Helen Halloran	Student Disabilities Services	978-762-4000
Northeastern U.	Boston, MA 02115	Ruth K. Bork	Disability Resource Program	617-373-2675
Pine Manor C.	Chestnut Hill, MA 02167	Mary Walsh	Learning Resource Center	617-731-7181
Quinsigamond C.C.	Worcester, MA 01606	Marion Bergin	Disabilities Services	508-854-4471
Simmons C.	Boston, MA 02115	Diane Raymond	Academic Support	617-521-2212
Smith C.	Northampton, MA 01063	Laura Rauscher	Office of Disability Services	413-585-2071
Springfield C.	Springfield, MA 01109	Deborah Dickens	Student Support Service	413-748-3768
Springfield Tech C.C.	Springfield, MA 01105	Mary Moriarty	Disabled Student Services	413-781-7822

Institution	Location	Contact	Office/Service	Phone
St. C. at N. Adams	N. Adams, MA 01247	Terry Miller	Ctr. for Acad. Advancement Learning	413-662-5309
Stonehill C.	Easton, MA 02357-5610	Richard Grant	Academic Services	508-565-1306
Suffolk U.	Boston, MA 02114-4280	Dean Z. Tsige	Dean of Students Office	617-573-8239
Tufts U.	Medford, MA 02155	Medina Giulina	Academic Resource Center	617-627-3724
U. Mass.—Amherst	Amherst, MA 01003	Diane Campbell	Learning Disabilities Support Services	413-545-4602
U. Mass.—Boston	Boston, MA 02125-3393	Marty Bledsoe	Student Advising Office	617-287-5500
U. Mass.—Dartmouth	North Dartmouth, MA 02747	Carol Johnson	Disabled Student Services	508-999-8711
Wellesley C.	Wellesley, MA 02481	Stacey Bradlee	Learning & Teaching Center	781-283-2614
Western New England C.	Springfield, MA 01119	Bonnie Alpert	Student Disability Services	413-782-3111
Wheaton C. (MA)	Norton, MA 02766	Marty Bledsoe	Advising Center	508-285-8215
Wheelock C.	Boston, MA 02215	Denise Elliot	Disability Services	617-879-2102
Williams C.	Williamstown, MA 01267	Charles Toomajian	Assoc. Dean for Student Services	413-597-4037
Worcester Poly. Institute	Worcester, MA 01609	Ann Garvin	Office of Academic Advising	508-831-5381
Worcester St. C.	Worcester, MA 01602-2597	Dennis Lindblom	Disability Services Office	508-793-8000

MICHIGAN

Institution	Location	Contact	Office/Service	Phone
Adrian C.	Adrian, MI 49221-2575	Jane McCloskey	EXCEL	517-265-5161
Alma C.	Alma, MI 48801-1599	Dr. Robert Perkins	Center for Student Development	517-463-7225
Aquinas C.	Grand Rapids, MI 49506-1799	Jackie Sweeny	Academic Achievement Center	616-459-8281
Calvin C.	Grand Rapids, MI 49546	James MacKenzie	Student Academic Services	616-957-6113
Central Michigan U.	Mount Pleasant, MI 48859	Carol Wojcik	Academic Assistance	517-774-3018
Delta C.	Universal City, MI 48710	Dave Murley	Learning Disabilities Services	517-686-9573
Ferris St. U.	Big Rapids, MI 49307	Eunice Merwin	Disabilities Services	231-591-3772
Grand Rapids C.C.	Grand Rapids, MI 49503	Anne Sherman	Disability Support Services	616-234-4140
Grand Valley St. U.	Allendale, MI 49401	Katherine Vander Veen	Office of Academic Support	616-895-2490
Hope C.	Holland, MI 49422-9000	Jacqueline Heisler	Academic Support Center	616-395-7830
Itaska C.C.	Grand Rapids, MI 55744	Anne Vidovic	Support Services	218-327-4167
Kellogg C.C.	Battle Creek, MI 49017	Margaret Groner	Support Services	616-965-2633
Lansing C.C.	Lansing, MI 48901	Pamela Davis	Office Disability Services	517-483-1904
Madonna U.	Livonia, MI 48150-1173	Michael Meldrum	Educational Support Services	734-432-5641
Marygrove C.	Detroit, MI 48221	Donna Johnson	Support Services	313-927-1200
Michigan St. U.	East Lansing, MI 48824	Michael Hudson	Disability Resource Center	517-353-9642
Michigan Tech U.	Houghton, MI 49931	Dr. Gloria Melton	Handicapped Services	906-487-2212

College	Location	Contact	Service	Phone
North Central Michigan C.	Petoskey, MI 49770	Daniel Linnenberg	Special Populations	616-348-6687
Northern Michigan U.	Marquette, MI 49855	Lynn Walden	Disability Services	906-227-1550
Oakland C.C.	Auburn Hills, MI 48309	June Czopek	PASS Office	248-540-1532
Oakland U.	Rochester, MI 48309	Linda Sisson	Disability Support Services	248-370-2100
Saginaw Valley St. U.	University Ctr, MI 48152	Cynthia Woiderski	Disability Services	517-790-4168
Schoolcraft C.C.	Livonia, MI 48152	Pat Hurick	Special Needs	734-462-4436
Suomi C.	Hancock, MI 49930	Ben Larson	Learning Disabilities Program	906-487-7258
SW Michigan C.	Dowagiac, MI 49047	Linda Mangus	Special Needs	616-782-1312
U. of Michigan—Ann Arbor	Ann Arbor, MI 48109	Stuart Segal	Services for Students with Disabilities	734-763-3000
U. of Michigan—Flint	Flint, MI 48502	Trudie Hines	Student Development Center	810-762-3456
Wayne St. U.	Detroit, MI 48202	Donald Anderson	Education Access Service	313577-1851
Western Michigan U.	Kalamazoo, MI 49008	Beth Den Hartih	Disabled Student Resources	616-387-2116

MINNESOTA

College	Location	Contact	Service	Phone
Augsburg C.	Minneapolis, MN 55454	Robert Doljanac	CLASS Program	612-330-1648
Behel C.	St. Paul, MN 55112	Gretchen Wrobel	Disability Services	612-638-6403
Bimidji St. U.	Bimidji, MN 55601	Kathy Heagen	Educational Development Ctr.	218-755-3883
Carleton C.	Northfield, MN 55057	Hudlin Wagner	Support Services	507-646-4075
Century C.	White Bear Lake, MN 55110	Mary Bataglia	Disability Access	651-779-3354
C. of Saint Benedict	Saint Joseph, MN 56374	Michelle Sauer	Academic Advising	320-363-5011
C. of Saint Catherine, The	Saint Paul, MN 55105	Barbara Mandel	Resources for Disabilities	651-590-6706
C. of Saint Scholastica, The	Duluth, MN 55811-4199	Jay Newcomb	Academic Support Services	218-723-6552
Concordia C. (Saint Paul, MN)	Saint Paul, MN 55104-5494	Annette Carpenter	Students with Disabilities	612-641-8707
Fond du Lac C.C.	Cloquet, MN 55720	Bill Kallis	Office of Students with Disabilities	218-879-0815
Gustavus Adolphus C.	St. Peter, MN 56082	Julie Johnson	Academic Advising	507-933-8000
Hamline U.	Saint Paul, MN 55104	Barbara Simmons	Student Resource Center	651-523-2417
Hibbing C.C.	Hibbing, MN 55746	Bonnie Olson	Disability Services	218-262-7246
Inverhills C.C.	Invergr Hgts, MN 55076	Eve Nichols	Disabled Student Services	651-450-8628
Lake Superior C.	Duluth, MN 55811	Moly Johnson	Disability Services	218-733-7650
Lakewood C.C.	White Bear Lk, MN 55110	Ed Sapinski	Access Center	651-779-3354
Macalester C.	St. Paul, MN 55105	Micheal Dickel	Learning Center	651-696-6118
Mankato St. U.	Mankato, MN 56002	Gael Meicle	Learning Center	507-389-5902
Mesabi C.C.	Virginia, MN 55792	Robin Carr	Disability Services	218-749-7710

Institution	City, State ZIP	Contact	Office/Service	Phone
Minneapolis C.C.	Minneapolis, MN 55403	Jane Larson	Office for Students with Disabilities	612-341-7590
Moorhead St. U.	Moorhead, MN 56563	Greg Toutges	Disability Services	218-299-5859
N. Hennepin C.C.	Brooklyn Pk, MN 55445	Connie Sherman	Disability Access Services	612-493-0556
Normandale C.C.	Bloomington, MN 55431	Mary Jibben	Office for Students with Disabilities	612-832-6422
Riverland C.C.	Austin, MN 55912	Joe Davis	Student Success Center	507-433-0558
Rochester C.C.	Rochester, MN 55904	Travis Kromminga	Disabled Student Services	507-280-2968
Saint Cloud St. U.	Saint Cloud, MN 56303-1240	Bob Thienes	Learning Support Center	320-654-5959
Saint John's U.	Collegeville, MN 56321-7155	Susan Douma	Academic Advising	320-363-3246
Saint Mary's U.	Winona, MN 55987-1399	Joe Dulak	Study Skills Center	507-457-1414
Saint Olaf C.	Northfield, MN 55057-1098	Peter Bolstad	Academic Support Center	507-646-3288
Southwest St. U.	Marshall, MN 56258	Pam Ekstrom	Learning Resources	507-537-7285
U. of Minnesota	Crookston, MN 56716	Laurie Wilson	Office for Students w/ Disabilities	218-281-8587
U. of Minnesota—Duluth	Duluth, MN 55812-2496	Penny Cragun	Learning Disability Program	218-726-8727
U. of Minnesota—Minneapolis	Minneapolis, MN 55455	Margret Ottinger	Disability Services	612-626-8983
U. of Minnesota—Morris	Morris, MN 56267	Ferolyn Angell	Academic Assistance Office	320-589-6163
U. of St. Thomas	St. Paul, MN 55105-1096	Kimberly Schumann	Students with Disabilities	612-962-6315
Winona St. U.	Winona, MN 55987	Nancy Dumke	Disability Services	507-457-5600

MISSISSIPPI

Institution	City, State ZIP	Contact	Office/Service	Phone
Mississippi St. U.	Mississippi, MS 39762	Debbie Baker	Student Support Services	662-325-3335
U. of Mississippi	University, MS 38677	Ardessa Minor	Services for Students with Disabilities	662-232-7128
U. of Southern Mississippi	Hattiesburg, MS 39406	Suzy Hebert	Office of Svcs. for Stdnts w/ Disabilities	601-266-5024
William Carey C.	Hattiesburg, MS 39401-5499	Brenda Waldrip	Student Support Services	601-582-6209

MISSOURI

Institution	City, State ZIP	Contact	Office/Service	Phone
Blue River C.C.	Blue Springs, MO 64015-7242	Pat O'Neil	ACCESS Office	816-655-6077
Columbia C.	Columbia, MO 65216	Tonda March	Center for Academic Excellence	573-875-7611
Drury C.	Springfield, MO 65802-9977	Ann Nelms	Disabled Student Services	417-873-7419
Evangel U.	Springfield, MO 65802	Dr. Laynah Rogers	Academic Support Center	417-865-2811
Fontbonne C.	St. Louis, MO 63105	Jane Snyder	Academic Resource Center	314-889-4571
Kansas City Art Institute	Kansas City, MO 64111-1762	Mary Magers	Academic Resource Center	816-802-4852
Lindenwood C.	St. Charles, MO 63301-1695	Tonie Isenhour	Disability Services	636-949-2000
Longview Comm. C.	Lee Summit, MO 64081-2105	Connie Flick-Hruska	ACCESS Office	816-672-2254
Maple Woods C.C.	Kansas City, MO 64156	Barbara Schaefer	ACCESS Office	816-437-3192

College	Location	Contact	Service	Phone
Mineral Area C.	Park Hills, MO 63601	Margaret Scobee	Special Services	636-431-4593
Missouri Southern St. C.	Joplin, MO 64801-1595	Melissa Loger	Learning Center	417-625-9516
Missouri Valley C.	Marshall, MO 65340	Linda Kanagawa	Student Support Services	660-831-4210
Missouri Western St. C.	Saint Joseph, MO 64507	Ellen Smither	Non-Traditional Student Services	816-271-4280
NE Missouri St.	Kirksville, MO 63501	T.W. Sorrell	Services for Students with Disabilities	816-785-4478
Northwest Missouri St. U.	Maryville, MO 64468	Phil Kenkel	Director Student Support Services	660-562-1861
Penn Valley C.C.	Kansas City, MO 64110	Connie Spies	Access Office	816-759-4152
Saint Louis U.	Saint Louis, MO 63103	Charles Murphy	Student Disabilities Center	314-977-2930
Southwest Missouri St. U.	Springfield, MO 65804	Dr. Steve Capps	Learning Diagnostic Clinic	417-836-4787
St. Charles City C.C.	St. Peters, MO 63376	Pam Bova	Disabled Student Services	636-922-8247
St. Louis C.C.—Florissant Park	St. Louis, MO 63135	Suelaine Matthews	ACCESS Office	314-595-4549
St. Louis C.C.—Forest Park	St. Louis, MO 63110	Claudia Felsen	ACCESS Office	314-644-9243
St. Louis C.C.—Meramec	St. Louis, MO 63122	Linda Nissenbaum	ACCESS Office	314-984-7654
Three River C.C.	Poplar Bluff, MO 63901	Dr. Joseph Mick	Student Support Services	573-840-9650
Truman St. U.	Kirksville, MO 63501	T.W. Sorrell	Services for Students w/ Disabilities	660-785-4478
U. of Missouri—Columbia	Columbia, MO 65203	Sarah Colby Weaver	Disability Services	573-882-4696
U. of Missouri—Kansas City	Kansas City, MO 64110-2499	Scott Laurent	Disabled Students Center	816-235-5696
U. of Missouri—Rolla	Rolla, MO 65409	Denise Schlake	Chancellor for Student Affairs	573-341-4292
U. of Missouri—Saint Louis	Saint Louis, MO 63121	Marilyn Ditto	Director-Disability Access Services	314-516-5211
Washington U.	Saint Louis, MO 63130-4899	Dr. Fran Lang	Disabled Student Services	314-935-4062
Westminster C.	Fulton, MO 65251-1299	Hank Ottinger	Learning Disabilities Program	573-592-5304
William Jewell C.	Liberty, MO 64068	Dr. John Cain	Counseling and Testing	816-781-7700

MONTANA

College	Location	Contact	Service	Phone
Montana St. U.	Billings, MT 59101-0298	Sharon Yazak	Disability Support Services	406-657-2283
Montana St. U.	Bozeman, MT 59717	Mary Lukin	Learning Skills Advance by Choice	406-994-4541
Montana Tech. College	Butte, MT 59701	Lee Barnett	Disability Services	406-496-3730
Northern Montana C.	Harve, MT 59501	Susan Ransom	Student Support Services	406-265-4152
Rocky Mountain C.	Billings, MT 59102	Dr. Jane Van Dyk	Services for Academic Success	406-657-1128
U. of Montana	Missoula, MT 59812	Jim Marks	Disabiltiy Services for Students	406-243-2243
Western Montana C.	Dillon, MT 59725	Chris Royer	Disability Services	406-683-7723

NEBRASKA

College	Location	Contact	Service	Phone
Concordia C.	Seward, NE 68434	Grace-Ann Dolak	Academic Support	402-643-7250
Creighton U.	Omaha, NE 68178	Mr. Southerland	Educational Opportunity Program	402-280-2195

College	City, State ZIP	Contact	Service	Phone
Dana C.	Blair, NE 68008	Lori Nielsen	Academic Support Services	402-426-7334
Doane C.	Crete, NE 68333	Sheri Hanigan	Academic Support	402-826-8222
Metropolitan C.C.	Omaha, NE 68103	Norma Morehouse	Special Needs Program	402-289-1312
Southeast C.C.	Lincoln, NE 68520	Suzy Dunn	Disability Services	402-471-8532
Union C.	Lincoln, NE 68506-4300	Jennifer Forbes	Teaching Learning Center	402-486-2506
U. of Nebraska	Omaha, NE 68182	Janice Leuenbergere	Learning Center	402-554-2992
U. of Nebraska	Lincoln, NE 68588-0417	Marie Ward	Services for Students w/ Disabilities	402-472-3787
Wayne St. C.	Wayne, NE 68787	Jeff B. Carstens	Student Support Services	402-375-7096
West Nebraska C.C.	Scottsbluff, NE 69361-1899	Vanessa Pickett	Counseling Center	308-635-6090

NEVADA

College	City, State ZIP	Contact	Service	Phone
Truckee Meadows C.C.	Reno, NV 89512	Harry Heiser	Student Support Services	702-673-7286
U. of Nevada—Las Vegas	Las Vegas, NV 89154	Anita Stockbauer	Disability Resource Center	702-895-0866
U. of Nevada—Reno	Reno, NV 89557	Mary Zabel	Disabled Student Services	775-784-6000
West Nevada C.C.	Carson City, NV 89703	Lisa Wright	ADA Support Services	775-887-3059

NEW HAMPSHIRE

College	City, State ZIP	Contact	Service	Phone
Colby-Sawyer C.	New London, NH 03257	Dr. Mary Mar	Academic Development Center	603-526-3714
Dartmouth C.	Hanover, NH 03755	Nancy Pompian	Student Disabilities Center	603-646-2014
Franklin Pierce C.	Rindge, NH 03461-0060	Carol Siherly	Academic Services	603-899-4107
Keene St. C.	Keene, NH 03435	Alan Glotzer	Aspire Program	603-358-2353
New England C.	Henniker, NH 03242	Anna Carlson	Academic Advising and Support Center	603-428-2218
New Hampshire Tech	Manchester, NH 03102	Maxine Little	Support Services	603-669-4298
Notre Dame C.	Manchester, NH 03104-2299	Jane O'Neil	Learning Enrichment Center	603-669-4294
Rivier College	Nashua, NH 03060	Bess Arnold	Office of Special Needs Servcies	603-897-8497
Southern New Hampshire U.	Manchester, NH 03108	Hyla Jaffe		603-668-2211
U. of New Hampshire	Durham, NH 03824	Margo Druschel	The Access Office	603-862-2607

NEW JERSEY

College	City, State ZIP	Contact	Service	Phone
Bergen C.C.	Paramus, NJ 07652	Lynne Crawford	Student Support Services	201-447-9211
Brookdale C.C.	Lincroft, NJ 07738	Elizabeth Twohy	Disability and Adaptive Services	732-224-2730
Caldwell College	Caldwell, NJ 07006-9165	Joan Serpico	Office of Disability	973-618-3465
Camden County C.	Blackwood, NJ 08012	Anne-Marie Hoyle	PACS Program	609-227-7200
Centenary C.	Hackettstown, NJ 07840	Jeffrey Zimdahl	Disability Services	908-852-1400
C. of New Jersey, The	A. Degennaro, NJ 08650-4700	Carol Markayes	Office for Students w/ Differing Abilities	609-771-2571

College	Address	Contact	Program	Phone
County C. of Morris	Horizons Program, NJ 07869	Judy Kuperstein	Horizons Program	973-328-5284
Drew U.	Madison, NJ 07940	Edye Lawler	Academic Dean's Office	201-408-3514
Farleigh Dickinson U.	Teaneck, NJ 07666	Dr. Mary Farrell	Reg. Ctr. for College Students with LD	201-692-2087
Georgian Court C.	Lakewood, NJ 08701	Patty Cohen	The Learning Center	732-364-2200
Kean U.	Union, NJ 07083-0411	Dr. Marie Segal	Project Excel	908-527-2380
Middlesex C.C.	Edison, NJ 08818	Beth Lowe	Project Connections	732-906-2507
Monmouth U.	W. Long Branch, NJ 07764	Dr. David Nast	Support Services for Students with LD	732-571-3460
New Jersey City U.	Jersey City, NJ 07305	Beverly Bakron	Project Mentor	201-200-3023
Ocean County C.	Toms River, NJ 08754	Maureen Reustle	Disability Resource Center	732-255-0456
Princeton U.	Princeton, NJ 08544-0430	Sandra N. Silverman	Disability Services	609-258-3054
Ramapo C. of New Jersey	Mahwah, NJ 07430	Jean Balutanski	Office of Special Servcies	201-529-7514
Raritan Valley C.C.	Somerville, NJ 08876	Linda Baum	Special Education	908-526-1200
Rider U.	Lawrenceville, NJ 08648	Dr. Jacqueline Simon	Education Enrichment Program	609-896-5244
Rutgers U.	Piscataway, NJ 08854-8097	Cheryl Clarke	Concerns of Students with Disabilities	732-932-1711
Rutgers U.	Newark, NJ 07102-1896	James Credle	Dean's Office	973-353-5300
Salem C.C.	Carneys Point, NJ 08069	Richard Duffy	Special Population	609-299-3100
Seton Hall U.	South Orange, NJ 07079	Rev. Ray Frasier	Student Support Services	973-761-9166
Sussex C.C.	Newton, NJ 07860	Kathleen Okay	LD Program	973-300-2153

NEW MEXICO

College	Address	Contact	Program	Phone
C. of Santa Fe	Santa Fe, NM 84505	David McCain	Center for Academic Excellence	505-473-6447
Eastern New Mexico U.	Portales, NM 88130	Bernita Nutt	Services for Students with Disabilities	505-562-2280
New Mexico Junior C.	Hobbs, NM 88240	Marilyn Jackson	Special Needs Services	505-392-5411
N.M. Inst. of Mining & Tech.	Socorro, NM 87801	Dr. Judith Raymond	Services for Students with Disabilities	505-835-5094
New Mexico St. U.	Las Cruces, NM 88003	Jane Spinti	Services for Students with Disabilities	505-646-6840
Santa Fe C.C.	Santa Fe, NM 87502	Jill Douglas	Special Services	505-471-8200
U. of New Mexico	Albuquerque, NM 87131	Patty Useem	Special Services Program	505-277-8291

NEW YORK

College	Address	Contact	Program	Phone
Adelphi U.	Garden City, NY 11530	Susan Spenser	Program for Students with LD	516-877-4710
Barnard C.	New York, NY 10027	Susan Quinby	Disability Services	212-854-4634
Binghamton U.	Binghamton, NY 13902	Jean Fairbairn	Services for Student with Disabilities	607-777-2686
Bronx C.C.	Bronx, NY 10453	Marilyn Russell	Disabled Students	718-289-5151
Brooklyn C/CUNY	Brooklyn, NY 11210	Roberta Adleman	Services for Students with Disabilities	718-951-5363

College	Location	Contact	Service	Phone
Broome C.C.	Binghamton, NY 134902	Bruce Pomeroy	Student Support Services	607-778-5234
Buffalo St. C.	Buffalo, NY 14222	Rosell Park	Academic Skills Center	716-878-4041
C. of New Rochelle	New Rochelle, NY 10805-2339	Joan Bristol	Student Services	914-654-5364
C. of Staten Island C/CUNY	Staten Island, NY 10314	Dr. Audrey Glynn	Disability Services	718-982-2510
Canisius C.	Buffalo, NY 14208	Martha Veasey	Disabled Student Services	716-888-3748
Cayuga C.C.	Auburn, NY 13021	David Charland	Svcs. for Students with Special Needs	315-255-1743
Colgate U.	Hamilton, NY 13346	Lynn Waldman	Academic Program Support	315-228-7225
C. of Saint Rose, The	Albany, NY 12203	Mary Van Der Zee	Office of Students with LD	518-454-5299
Columbia Greene C.C.	Hudson, NY 12534	Bernadine Lamantia	Dean of Students	518-828-4181
Concordia C. (NY)	Bronxville, NY 10708	Dr. George Groth	The Concordia Connection	914-337-9300
Cornell U.	Ithaca, NY 14850	Matthew Tominey	Disability Svcs, Office of Eq. Opportunity	607-255-4545
Corning C.C.	Corning, NY 14830	Judy Northrop	Counseling for Students with Disabilities	607-962-9262
Culinary Institute of America	Hyde Park, NY 12538	in transition	Student Development	914-452-9600
Daemen C.	Amherst, NY 14226	Dr. Kathleen Boone	Disability Support Services	716-839-8301
Dowling C.	Oakdale, NY 11769-1999	Dr. Dorothy Stracher	College Students with LD	631-244-3306
D'Youville C.	Buffalo, NY 14201	Ms. Carolyn L. Boone	Disability Services	716-881-7728
Eastman School of Music	Rochester, NY 14627	Phyllis Wade	Office of the Dean of Students	716-274-1060
Finger Lakes C.C.	Canandaigua, NY 14424	Norah Nolin-Cramer	Services for Students with Disabilities	716-394-3500
Fordham U.	New York, NY 10458	Jeanne Pirozzi	Disabled Student Services	718-817-4362
Hamilton C.	Clinton, NY 13323	Louise Peckingham	Disabled Student Services	315-859-4305
Hofstra U.	Hempstead, NY 11549	Dr. Ignacio Gotz	PALS Program	516-463-5841
Houghton C.	Houghton, NY 14744	Arlene Lewis	Student Academic Services	716-567-9239
Hudson Valley C.C.	Troy, NY 12180	Pablo Negron	Disability Resource Center	518-270-7154
Hunter C. C/CUNY	New York, NY 10021	Sandra LaPorta	Office of Students with Disabilities	212-772-4857
Iona C.	New Rochelle, NY 10801	Madeline Packerman	College Assistance Program	914-633-2582
Jamestown C.C.	Jamestown, NY 14702	Nancy Callahan	Disability Support Services	716-665-5220
Jefferson C.C.	Watertown, NY 13601	Sheree Trainnam	Learning Skills Center	315-786-2377
Keuka College	Keuka Park, NY 14478-0098	Beth Demay	Academic Support Program	315-279-5636
Kingsborough C.C.	Brooklyn, NY 11235	Anthony Colarossi	Special Services	718-368-5175
LaGuardia C.C.	Long Island City, NY 11101	Matthew Joffre	Office for Students with Disabilities	718-482-5278
Le Moyne C.	Syracuse, NY 13214	in transition	Academic Support Center	315-445-4118
Lehman C/CUNY	Bronx, NY 10468	Marcos Gonzalez	Disability Issues	718-960-8700
Long Island U.—C.W. Post	Brookville, NY 11548-1300	Caroll Rundlett	Academic Resource Center	516-299-2937

College	Location	Contact	Service	Phone
Manhattan C.	Riverdale, NY 10471	Dr. Ross Pollack	Learning Disabilites Program	718-862-7101
Manhattanville C.	Purchase, NY 10577	Myra Gentiley	Higher Education Learning Program	914-323-5124
Marist C.	Poughkeepsie, NY 12601-1387	Linda Cooper	Office of Special Services	845-575-3274
Marymount C.	Tarrytown, NY 10591	Amanda Willoughby	Learning Services	914-332-8310
Marymount Manhattan C.	New York, NY 10021	Dr. Jacquelin Bonomo	Prog for Students w/ LD	212-774-0724
Mercy C.	Dobbs Ferry, NY 10522	Terry Rich	Support Services	914-693-4500
Mohawk Valley C.C.	Utica, NY 13501	Lynn Igoe	Services for Students with Disabilities	315-792-5413
Molloy C.	Rockville Centre, NY 11570	Sr. Burbana	STEEP Program	516-678-5000
Nassau C.C.	Garden City, NY 11530	Janice Schimsky	Center for Students with Disabilities	516-572-7241
NY Institute of Technology	Old Westbury, NY 11568-8000	Alice Heron Burke	Student Services	516-686-7683
New York U.	New York, NY 10011	Michael Quagerelli	Center for Students with Disabilities	212-998-4980
Niagara U.	Niagara University, NY 14109	Dianne Stoelting	Office of Academic Support	716-286-8076
NYU Para Educator Ctr	New York, NY 10003	Dr. Jane Herzog	Para Educator for Young Adults	212-998-5800
Onondaga C.C.	Syracuse, NY 13215	Roger Purdy	Svcs. for Students w/ Special Needs	315-469-2245
Paul Smith C.	Paul Smith's, NY 12970	Carol McKillip	Special Services	518-327-6425
Rensselaer Polytechnic Inst.	Troy, NY 12180	Debra Hamilton	Disabled Student Services	518-276-2746
Roberts Wesleyan C.	Rochester, NY 14624	Carol Ernsthausen	Learning Center	716-594-6270
Rochester Inst. of Technology	Rochester, NY 14623	Pamela Lloyd	Learning Support Services	716-475-7804
Rockland C.C.	Suffern, NY 10901	Ellen Spergel	Office of Disability Services	914-574-4312
Saint Bonaventure U.	St. Bonaventure, NY 14778	Nancy Mathews	Services for Students with Disabilities	716-375-2065
Saint John's U. (NY)	Jamaica, NY 11439	Jackie Lochrie	Student Services Coordinates Activities	718-990-6568
Saint Lawrence U.	Canton, NY 13617	John Meagher	Office of Special Needs	315-229-5104
Saint Thomas Aquinas C.	Sparkill, NY 10976	Richard Heath	THE STAC Exchange	845-398-4230
Schenectady C.C.	Schenectady, NY 12305	Tom Dotson	Disabled Student Services	518-381-1344
SUNY C. of Tech. at Alfred	Alfred, NY 14802	Jeanne Mead	Services for Students with Disabilities	607-587-3112
SUNY at Albany	Albany, NY 12222	Carolyn Malloch	Learning Disabilities Resource Program	518-442-5491
SUNY at Canton	Canton, NY 13617	Sharon House	Accommodative Services Department	315-386-7603
SUNY at Delhi	Delhi, NY 13753	George E. Irwin	Academic Success	607-746-4593
SUNY at Farmingdale	Farmingdale, NY 11735	Malka Edelman	Support Svcs. for Stdnts. w/ Disabilities	631-420-2411
SUNY at Stony Brook	Stony Brook, NY 11794	Joanna Harris	Disabled Services	631-632-6748
SUNY C. at Brockport	Brockport, NY 14420-2915	Vivian Vanderzell	Office for Students with Disabilities	716-395-5409
SUNY C. at Buffalo	Buffalo, NY 14222-1095	Marianne Savino	Special Services	716-878-4500
SUNY C. at Fredonia	Fredonia, NY 14063	Liza Smith	Disabled Student Support	716-673-3270

Institution	City/State	Contact	Service	Phone
SUNY C. at Geneseo	Geneseo, NY 14454-1471	Kelly Clark	Multicultural & Disability Services	716-245-5620
SUNY C. at New Paltz	New Paltz, NY 12561	Portia Lillo	Office of Disabled Student Services	914-257-3020
SUNY C. at Oneonta	Oneonta, NY 13820	Sandra Denicore	Learning Support Services	607-436-2137
SUNY C. at Oswego	Oswego, NY 13126	Bernardo Pelsawio	Office of Disabled Student Services	315-341-3358
SUNY C. at Plattsburgh	Plattsburgh, NY 12901-2681	Ms. Michele Carpentier	Student Support Services	518-564-2810
SUNY C. at Potsdam	Potsdam, NY 13676	Sharon House	Accommodative Services	315-267-3267
SUNY C. at Purchase	Purchase, NY 10577	Ronnie Mait	Special Services	914-251-6035
SUNY C. of Technology	Cobelskill, NY 12043	Anne Campbell	Counseling Center	518-234-5211
SUNY C. of Technology	Wellsville, NY 14895	Heather Meacham	Services for Students with Disabilities	607-587-3111
SUNY C. at Cortland	Cortland, NY 13045	Jody Siorini	Disabilities Services	607-753-2066
Syracuse U.	Syracuse, NY 13244	Diana Darris	Learning Disabilities Services	315-443-4498
Tompkins Cortland C.C.	Dryden, NY 13035	Tina Guason	Learning Assistance Services	607-844-8211
U. of Rochester	Rochester, NY 14627-0251	Vicki Roth	Learning Assistance Services	716-275-9049
Union C.	Schenectady, NY 12308	Kathleen J. Schurick	Student Affairs	518-388-6061
Utica C. of Syracuse U.	Utica, NY 13502-4892	Mr. Patterini	Academic Support	315-792-3032
Vassar C.	Poughkeepsie, NY 12604	Belinda Guthrie	Office of Disability Services	914-437-7584
Wagner C.	Staten Island, NY 10301	Christine Hagedorn	Academic Advisement Center	718-390-3340
Westchester C.C.	Valhalla, NY 10595	Marcia Kalkut	Disabled Students	914-785-6552

NORTH CAROLINA

Institution	City/State	Contact	Service	Phone
Appalachian St. U.	Boone, NC 28608	Suzanne T. Wehner	Learning Disability Program	828-262-2291
Ashville Buncombe C.	Ashville, NC 28801	Deborah Harmond	Special Needs	704-254-1921
Belmont Abbey C.	Belmont, NC 28012	Michelle Allen	Learning Disability Support Services	704-825-6820
Central Piedmont C.C.	Charlotte, NC 28235	Patricia Adams	Services for Students with Disabilities	704-330-6556
Davidson C.	Davidson, NC 28036	Leslie Marsicano	Dean of Students Office	704-894-2225
Duke U.	Durham, NC 27708	Emma Swain	Services for Students with Disabilities	919-684-5917
East Carolina U.	Greenville, NC 27858	C.C. Rowe	Disability Support Services	252-328-6799
Elon C.	Elon College, NC 27244	Priscilla Lipe	Svcs. for Stdnts. w/Spec. Learni. Needs	336-584-2212
Guilford C.	Greensboro, NC 27410	Sue Keith	Academic Skills Center	336-316-2200
Guilford Tech C.C.	Jamestown, NC 27282	Angela Leak	Academic Support Services	336-334-4822
Lenoir-Rhyne C.	Hickory, NC 28603	Donovan Kirby	Services for Students with LD	828-328-7296
Mars Hill C.	Mars Hill, NC 28754	Barbara Mc Kinney	Student Support Services	704-689-1464
Nash Community C.	Rocky Mount, NC 27804	Cynthia Hinnant	Compensatory Education Department	252-443-4011

College	Location	Contact	Service	Phone
North Carolina St. U.	Raleigh, NC 27695	Dr. Cheryl Branker	Disability Services for Students	919-515-7653
Richmond C.C.	Hamlet, NC 28345	Dr. John Wester	Student Development	910-582-7117
Rockingham C.C.	Wentworth, NC 27375	Jerry Melton	Student Development	910-582-7103
St. Andrews Presbyterian C.	Laurinburg, NC 28352	Interim	Disability Support Services	910-277-5331
Southwestern C.C.	Sylva, NC 28779	Cheryl Contino-Conner	Student Support Services	828-586-4091
U. of N. Carolina—Chapel Hill	Chapel Hill, NC 27599	Jane Byron	Learning Disabilities Services	919-962-7227
U. of N. Carolina—Charlotte	Charlotte, NC 28223-0001	Janet Filer	Disability Services	704-547-4355
U. of N. Carolina—Greensboro	Greensboro, NC 27402-6170	Patricia Bailey	Disability Services	336-334-5440
U. of N. Carolina—Wilmington	Wilmington, NC 28403	Dr. Peggy Turner	Disability Services	910-962-3746
Wake Forest U.	Winston-Salem, NC 27109	Van D. Westervelt	Learning Assistance Center	336-759-5929
Wake Tech C.C.	Raleigh, NC 27603	Janet Kilhen	Disability Support Services	919-662-3615
West Piedmont C.C.	Morgantown, NC 28655	Susan Andrea	Disabled Student Services	828-438-6050
Western Carolina U.	Cullowhee, NC 28723	Carol Mellon	Student Support Services	828-227-7127
Wingate U.	Wingate, NC 28174	Linda Stedje-Larson	Specific Learning Disabilities	704-233-8269
Winston-Salem St. U.	Winston-Salem, NC 27110	Myra Waddell	Academic Resource Center	336-750-2000

NORTH DAKOTA

College	Location	Contact	Service	Phone
Bismarck St. C.	Bismarck, ND 58506	Shirley Tioksin	Student Success Center	701-224-5426
Dickinson St. U.	Dickinson, ND 58601-4896	Susan Hupp	Student Support Services	701-483-2029
Minot St. U.	Minot, ND 58707	Jan Nahinurk	Disability Services	701-228-5479
North Dakota St. C.	Wahpeton, ND 58076-0002	Bonnie Johnson	Study Svcs. for Students w/ Disabilities	701-671-2335
North Dakota St. U.	Fargo, ND 58105-5226	Catherine Anderson	Disabilities Services	701-231-7671
United Tribes Tech C.	Bismarck, ND 58504	Royce Irwin	Student Support Services	701-255-3285
U. of North Dakota	Williston, ND 58801	Stephanie Turcotte	Disability Support Services	701-774-4220
U. of North Dakota	Grand Forks, ND 58202	Deb Glennen	Disabled Student Support Services	701-777-3426

OHIO

College	Location	Contact	Service	Phone
Antioch C.	Yellow Spring, OH 45387	England Kennedy	Academic Support Services	937-767-7331
Ashland U.	Ashland, OH 44805	Suzanne Salvo	Disability Services	419-289-4142
Baldwin-Wallace C.	Berea, OH 44017	Carol Templeman	Services for Students with Disabilities	440-826-2188
Bowling Green St. U.	Bowling Green, OH 43403	Robert D. Cunningham	Office of Disability Services	419-372-8495
Capital U.	Columbus, OH 43209	Richard Schalinske	Disability Concerns	614-236-6284
Case Western Reserve U.	Cleveland, OH 44106	Mayo Bulloch	Disability Support Services	216-368-5230
Central Ohio Tech C.	Newark, OH 43055	Dr. Phyllis Thompson	Disability Services	740-366-9246

Institution	City/State	Contact	Department/Service	Phone
Clark St. C.C.	Springfield, OH 45505	Mari Rae Kearney	Office of Student Services	937-328-6019
Cleveland St. U.	Cleveland, OH 44115	Mike Zuccaro	Disability Services	216-687-2015
C. of Mount Saint Joseph	Cincinnati, OH 45233-1630	Jane Pohlman	Project Excel	513-244-4623
C. of Wooster	Wooster, OH 44691	Pamela Rose	Learning Center	330-263-2595
Columbus St. C.C.	Columbus, OH 43216	Wayne Cocchi	Disability Services	614-227-2629
Cuyahoga C.C. Western	Parma, OH 44130	Mary Syarto	Access Office for Accommodation	216-987-2052
Denison U.	Granville, OH 43023	Jennifer Bestel	Office of Academic Support	740-587-6224
Franklin U.	Columbus, OH 43215-5399	Wayne Miller	Student Services	614-341-6256
Hiram C.	Hiram, OH 44234	Dr. Lynn B. Taylor	Counseling	330-569-5233
Hocking C.	Nelsonville, OH 45764	Elaine Dabelko	Access Center	740-753-3591
Kent St. U.	Kent, OH 44242-0001	Anne Jannarone	Student Disability Services	330-672-3391
Kenyon C.	Gambier, OH 43022	Jane Martindell	Academic Advising	740-427-5145
Lakeland C.C.	Kirtland, OH 44095	Alan Kirsh	Services for Students with Disabilities	440-953-7245
Lorain City C.C.	Elyria, OH 44035	Ruth Porter	Office for Special Needs Services	440-366-4058
Lourdes C.	Sylvania, OH 43560	Kim Grieve	Disability Services	419-885-3211
Marietta C.	Marietta, OH 45750	Dr. Marilyn Pasquerelli	Counseling Center	740-374-4784
Miami U.—Hamilton	Hamilton, OH 45011	Mary Vogel	Special Services	513-785-3211
Miami U.	Oxford, OH 45056	Lois Philips	Learning Disabilities Program	513-529-8741
Muskingum C.	New Concord, OH 43762	Jen E Navicky	PLUS Program	740-826-8280
North Central Tech C.	Mansfield, OH 44901	Sandra Lucky	Disability Services	419-755-4753
Oberlin C.	Oberlin, OH 44074	Jane Boomer	Off. of Serv. for Students w/ Disab.	440-775-8467
Ohio Dominican C.	Coumbus, OH 42319	Rose Ann Kalister	Academic Development	614-251-4511
Ohio Northern U.	Ada, OH 45810	Richanne Mankey	Student Affairs	419-772-2431
Ohio St. U.	Marion, OH 43302	Margaret Hazelett	Learning Disabilities Services	740-389-6247
Ohio St. U.—Columbus	Columbus, OH 43210-1200	Ann Yurcisin	Office for Disability Services	614-292-3307
Ohio St. U.—Newark	Newark, OH 43055	Dr. Phyllis Tompson	Learning Assistance Services	740-366-9246
Ohio U.—Athens	Athens, OH 45701	Katherine Fahey	Off. for Institutional Equity/Disab. Svcs.	740-593-2620
Ohio Wesleyan U.	Delaware, OH 43015	Dr. Blake Michael	Academic Advising	740-368-3275
Otterbein C.	Westerville, OH 43081	Ellen Kasulis	Learning Assistance Center	614-823-1362
Owens C.C.	Toledo, OH 43699	Beth Schefert	Disability Resource Services	419-661-7504
Raymond Walters C.	Cincinnati, OH 45236	John Kraimer	Disability Services	513-745-5670
Shawnee St. U.	Portsmouth, OH 45662	Royna Lattimore	Office of Special Needs Services	740-355-2276
Sinclair C.C.	Dayton, OH 45402	Robin Cooper	Disability Services	937-512-5113

Institution	Location	Contact	Office	Phone
Terra St. C.C.	Fremont, OH 43420	Richard Newman	Disability Services	419-334-8400
U. of Akron	Akron, OH 44325-2001	Grace E. Olmsted	Services for Students with Disabilities	216-972-7928
U. of Cincinnati	Cincinnati, OH 45221-0091	Debra Merchant	Disability Services	513-556-6823
U. of Dayton	Dayton, OH 45469-1611	Beatrice Bedard	Disabled Student Services	937-229-3684
U. of Findlay	Findlay, OH 45840	Branda Kane	Supporting Skills System	419-424-5532
U. of Toledo	Toledo, OH 43606-3390	Kendra Johnson	Office of Accessibility	419-530-4981
Ursuline C.	Pepper Pike, OH 44124-4398	Annette Gromada	Program for Students w/ LD	440-449-2046
Walsh U.	Canton, OH 44720	Ellen Kutz	Disability Services	330-499-8518
Washington St. C.C.	Marietta, OH 45750	Deborah Thomas	Student Development	740-374-8716
Wright St. U.	Dayton, OH 45435	Jeff Vernooy	Office of Disability Services	937-775-5680
Xavier U. (OH)	Cincinnati, OH 45207-2612	Sarah Kelly	Learning Assistance Center	513-745-3280

OKLAHOMA

Institution	Location	Contact	Office	Phone
Cameron U.	Lawton, OK 73505	Wayne Hatcher	Academic Dean's Office	580-581-2209
Oklahoma City C.C.	Oklahoma City, OK 73159	Pat Stone	Services to Students with Disabilities	405-682-1611
Oklahoma St. U.	Stillwater, OK 74078	Michael Shuttick	Student Disability Services	405-744-7116
Southeastern Oklahoma St. U.	Durant, OK 74701-0609	Jan Anderson	Students w/ Disabilities	580-924-0121
Tulsa Junior C.	Tulsa, OK 74119	Yolanda Williams	Disabled Student Resource Center	918-631-7115
U. of Oklahoma	Norman, OK 73019	Suzette Dyer	Office of Disability Services	405-325-3852
U. of Tulsa	Tulsa, OK 74104	Dr. Jane Corso	Center for Student Academic Support	918-631-2315

OREGON

Institution	Location	Contact	Office	Phone
Blue Mountain C.C.	Pendelton, OR 97801	Cynthia Hilden	Special Services Office	541-278-5796
Chemeketa C.C.	Salem, OR 97309	Michael Duggan	Office for Students with Disabilities	503-399-5192
Lane C.C.	Eugene, OR 97405	Leigh Alice Petty	Disabled Student Services	541-747-4501
Linn-Benton C.C.	Albany, OR 97321	Nancy Hart	Disabled Student Services	541-917-4999
Mt Hood C.C.	Gresham, OR 97030	Liz Johnson	Disability Services	503-491-7650
Oregon Institute of Technology	Klamath Falls, OR 97601	Ron McCutcheon	Campus Access and Equality	503-885-1031
Oregon St. U.	Corvallis, OR 97331-2133	Tracy Bentley-Townlin	Services for Students with Disabilities	541-737-4098
Portland St. U.	Portland, OR 97207	Lisa Wilson	Disability Services for Students	503-725-4005
Rogue C.C.	Grants Pass, OR 97527	Bonnie Reeg	Support Services	541-956-7500
Southern Oregon State U.	Ashland, OR 97520-5032	Patricia Sloan	Disabled Student Services	541-482-6411
Umpqua C.C.	Roseburg, OR 97470	Barbara Stoner	Disability Services	541-440-4600
U. of Oregon	Eugene, OR 97403-1217	Dr. Hilary Gerdes	Disability Services	541-346-3211
Western Baptist C.	Salem, OR 97301	Faythe Moore	Academic Services	503-375-7012

Institution	Location	Contact	Office	Phone
Western Oregon U.	Monmouth, OR 97361	Dr. Mary Crawford	Office of Disability Services	503-838-8250
Willamette U.	Salem, OR 97301	Robin Smithtro	Disability Services	503-370-6471
PENNSYLVANIA				
Albright C.	Reading, PA 19612	Tiffenia Archie	Learning Center	610-921-7662
Allentown C. of St. Fran.	Center Valley, PA 18034	Dr. Rosalyn Edman	Learning Center	610-282-1100
Bryn Mawr C.	Bryn Mawr, PA 19010-2899	Lois Mendez	Dean's Office	610-526-5372
Bucknell U.	Lewisburg, PA 17837-9988	Patti Flannery	Admissions Svcs. for Disabled Students	570-577-2000
Bucks County C.C.	Newton, PA 18940	M. Stevens Cooper	Program for Students with Disabilities	215-968-8463
Cabrini C.	Randor, PA 19087	Andrea Manovel	Learning Disabilities Services	610-902-8572
California U. of Pennsylvania	California, PA 15419	Cheryl Bilitski	CARE Dept	724-938-5781
Carlow C.	Pittsburgh, PA 15213	Andrea Beranek	College Learning Center	412-578-6136
Carnegie Mellon U.	Pittsburgh, PA 15213	Everett Tademy	Equal Opportunity Services	412-268-2012
Chatham C.	Pittsburgh, PA 15232	Janet James	College Learning Center	412-365-1611
Clarion U. of Pennsylvania	Clarion, PA 16214	Jennifer May	Student Support Services Program	814-393-2095
C. Misericordia	Dallas, PA 18612	Dr. Joseph Rogan	Alternative Learning Project	570-674-6347
C.C. of Allegheny County	Pittsburgh, PA 15212	Mary Beth Doyle	Support Svcs. for Stdnts. w/ Disabilities	412-237-4614
C.C. of Philadelphia	Philadelphia, PA 19130	Joan Monroe	Educational Support Services	215-751-8474
CCAC C. North	Pittsburgh, PA 15237	Kathleen White	Support Services	412-369-3686
Delaware Valley C.	Doylestown, PA 18901	Sharon Malka	Learning Support Services	215-489-2490
Dickinson C.	Carlisle, PA 17013-2896	Keith Jervis	Services for Students with Disabilities	717-245-1485
Drexel U.	Philadelphia, PA 19104	Robin Stokes	Office of Disability Services	215-895-2506
Duquesne U.	Pittsburgh, PA 15282	David Lachowski	Learning Skills Center	412-396-6035
East Stroudsburg U. of PA	East Stroudsb, PA 18301-2999	Dr. Edith Miller	Office of Disablitiy Services	570-422-3954
Edinboro U. of Pennsylvania	Edinboro, PA 16444	Dr. Robert McConnell	Office for Students with Disabilities	814-732-2462
Franklin & Marshall C.	Lancaster, PA 17604-3003	Kenneth John, PhD	Counseling Services	717-291-4083
Gannon U.	Erie, PA 16541	Sr. Joyce Lowrey, S.S.J.	Program for Students w/ LD	814-871-5326
Gettysburg C.	Gettysburg, PA 17325	Gailann Rickert	Academic Advising	717-337-6587
Harcum Jr C.	Bryn Mawr, PA 19010	Penny Caldwell	Talent Development	610-526-6034
Indiana U. of Penn	Indiana, PA 15705	Dr. Catherine Dugan	Advising and Testing Center	724-357-4079
Kutztown U. of Pennsylvania	Kutztown, PA 19530	Patricia Ritcher	Services for Students with Disabilities	610-683-4108
Lebanon Valley College	Annville, PA 17003-0501	Ann H. Hohenwarter	Office of Disability Services	717-867-6158
Lehigh U.	Bethlehem, PA 18015	Cheryl A. Ashcroft	Dean's Office	610-758-4152
Lock Haven U. of Pennsylvania	Lock Haven, PA 17745	Nate Hosley	Student Support Services	570-893-2324
Luzerne Cty. CC.	Naanticoke, PA 18634	Anna Mary McHugh	Learning Support Services	570-740-0771

College	Location	Contact	Service	Phone
Lycoming C.	Williamsport, PA 17701	Daniel Hertsock	Academic Resource Center	570-321-4294
Mercyhurst C.	Erie, PA 16546	Dianne Rogers	Program for Students with LDs	814-824-2450
Messiah C.	Grantham, PA 17027-0800	Dr. Keith Drahn	Disability Services	717-766-2511
Montgomery College CC.	Blue Bell, PA 19422	Saul Finkle	Services for Students with Disabilities	215-641-6574
Muhlenberg C.	Allentown, PA 18104-5596	Wendy Cole	Academic Support Services	610-821-3200
Northampton C.C.	Bethlehem, PA 18017	Laranie Demshock	Services for Disabled Students	610-861-5342
Penn St. U.—Delaware	Media, PA 19063-5596	Sharon Manco	Support Services	610-892-1461
Penn St. U.—Mont Alto	Mont Alto, PA 17237-9703	Nanette Hatzes	Learning Center	717-749-6045
Pennsylvania St. U.—U. Park	Univ. Park, PA 16802-3000	Bill Welsh	Learning Disabilities Support Services	814-863-1807
Robert Morris C.	Moon Township, PA 15108	Ms Marian Alverson	Student Enrollment	412-262-8349
Saint Joseph's U. (PA)	Philadelphia, PA 19131	Mr. Jim Scott	Services for Students with Disabilities	610-660-1774
Seton Hill College	Greensburg, PA 15601	Teresa A. Bassi	Disability Services	724-838-4295
Shippensburg U. of Penn.	Shippensburg, PA 17257-2299	Dr. Lois Waters	Office of Social Equity	717-477-1161
Slippery Rock U. of PA	Slippery Rock, PA 16057	Linda M. Smith	Office of Social Equity	724-738-2016
Temple U.	Philadelphia, PA 19122-6096	Dr. Dorothy Cebula	Disability Resources & Services	215-204-1280
U. of Pennsylvania	Philadelphia, PA 19104	Alice Nagle	Program for People with Disabilities	215-898-6993
U. of Pittsburgh—Johnstown	Johnstown, PA 15904	Diane VanBlerkom	Learning Resources Center	814-269-7109
U. of Pittsburgh—Pittsburgh	Pittsburgh, PA 15260	Noreen Mazzocca	Disability Resources & Services	412-648-7890
U. of Scranton	Scranton, PA 18510-4699	Judith Henning	Learning Resources Center	717-941-4038
Washington & Jefferson C.	Washington, PA 15301	Patricia Bright	Student Resource Center	724-223-5279
West Chester U. of PA	West Chester, PA 19383	Martin Patwell	Disability Services	610-436-3217
Widener U.	Chester, PA 19013-5792	Dr. L. Ziegenfuss	ENABLE	610-499-1270
Wilkes U.	Wilkes-Barre, PA 18766	Judith Fremont	Learning Center	570-831-4150

RHODE ISLAND

College	Location	Contact	Service	Phone
Brown U.	Providence, RI 02912	Dean Elyse Chaplin	Disability Services	401-863-9588
Bryant C.	Smithfield, RI 02917	Laurie Hazard	Academic Center for Excellence	401-232-6746
C.C. of Rhode Island	Warwick, RI 02856	Julie White	Access to Opportunity	401-825-2305
Johnson & Wales	Providence, RI 02903	Meryl Berstein	Student Success	401-598-4689
Providence C.	Providence, RI 02918	Rose Boyle	Office of Academic Services	401-865-2494
Rhode Island College	Providence, RI 02908	Scott Kane	Disability Services	401-456-8061
U. of Rhode Island	Kingston, RI 02881	Gail Lepkowski	Disability Services	401-874-2098

SOUTH CAROLINA

College	Location	Contact	Service	Phone
Citadel, The	Charleston, SC 29409	Dr. Barbara Zaremba	Academic Support Special Services	843-953-1820
Clemson U.	Clemson, SC 29634	Bonnie Martin	Student Disability Services	864-656-6848

C. of Charleston	Charleston, SC 29424	Bobbie D. Lindstrom	Special Needs Advising Plan Svcs.	843-953-1431
Francis Marion U.	Florence, SC 295001	Rebecca Lawson	Guidance and Placement	843-673-9407
Limestone C.	Gaffney, SC 29340	Dr. Joe Pitts	Program for Alternative Learning Styles	864-488-4534
Southern Wesleyan U.	Central, SC 29630-1020	Dr. Randel Becker	SNAPS	864-639-2453
USC—Lancaster	Lancaster, SC 29721	Dr. Eric Wolse	Academic Success Center	803-285-7471
USC—Aiken	Aiken, SC 29801	Kay Durden	Disability Services	803-641-3626
USC—Columbia	Columbia, SC 29208	Karen Pettus	Office of Disability Services	803-777-6742
USC—Spartanburg	Spartanburg, SC 29303	TBA	Disability Services	864-503-5123
York Tech C.	Clover, SC 29730	Nita Forrest	Student Support Services	803-327-8000

SOUTH DAKOTA

Augustana C. (SD)	Sioux Falls, SD 57197	Katrina Johnson	Svcs. for Students with Special Needs	605-336-0770
Black Hills St. U.	Spearfish, SD 57799	Sharon Hemmingson	Student Support Services	605-642-6259
Dakota St. U.	Madison, SD 57042	Nancy Moose	ADA Academic Services	605-256-5269
Dakota Wesleyan U.	Mitchell, SD 57301-4398	Sharlen Krause	Student Support Services	605-995-2902
National C.	Rapid City, SD 57709	Susan Watton	Learning Center	605-394-4821
Northern St. U.	Aberdeen, SD 57401	Karen Gerety	Learning Center	605-626-2371
South Dakota St. U.	Brookings, SD 57007-1198	Nancy Schade	Disabled Student Services	605-688-4496
U. of South Dakota	Vermillion, SD 57069	Elaine Pearson	Disability Services	605-677-6389

TENNESSEE

Chattanooga St. C.C.	Chattanooga, TN 37406	Cathy Lutes	Disability Services	423-697-4452
Clevland St. CC.	Cleveland, TN 37320	Amy Derrick	Disabilities Support Services	
East Tennessee St. U.	Johnson City, TN 37614-0731	Heidi Bimrose	Disability Services	423-439-8346
Lee U.	Cleveland, TN 37311	Debrah Murray	Serv. for Stud. with Except. Needs	423-614-8181
Middles Tennessee State U.	Murfreesboro, TN 37132	John Harris	Disabled Student Services	615-898-2783
Pellissippi St. Tech C.	Knoxville, TN 37933	Ron Emrich	Services for Students with Disabilities	865-694-6751
Rhodes C.	Memphis, TN 38112	Melissa Butler	Disability Services	901-843-3994
Tennessee St. U.	Nashville, TN 37209-1561	James D. Steely	Disability Services	615-963-7400
Tennessee Tech U.	Cookeville, TN 38505	Sammie Young	Disabled Services	931-372-6318
U. of Memphis	Memphis, TN 38152-6687	Dona Sparger	Learning Disability Program	901-678-3304
U. of Tenn. at Martin	Martin, TN 38238	Beth Vise	P.A.C.E.	901-587-7195
U. of Tenn.—Chattanooga	Chattanooga, TN 37403	Debra Anderson	Office for Students with Disabilities	423-755-4006
U. of Tenn.—Knoxville	Knoxville, TN 37996	Jan Howard	Disabled Student Services	865-974-6087
Vanderbilt U.	Nashville, TN 37203-1700	Sarah Ezell	Opportunity Development Center	615-322-4705

TEXAS

School	Contact	Address	Service	Phone
Abilene Christian U.	Gloria Bradshaw	Abilene, TX 79699	Alpha Academic Services	915-674-2750
Amarillo C.	Brenda Wilkes	Amarillo, TX 79178	Accessibility	806-371-5436
Austin C.C.	Judy Hubble	Cedar Park, TX 78613	Office for Students with Disabilities	512-223-2012
Central Texas C.	Jose Aponte	Killeen, TX 76540	Disability Support Services	254-526-1339
El Paso C.C.	Carol Jiodano	El Paso, TX 79998	Center for Students with Disabilities	915-831-2426
Lamar U.	Callie Trahan	Beaumont, TX 77710	Services for Students with Disabilities	409-880-8026
Lamar U.—Orange	Francis Ahearn	Orange, TX 77630	Disability Services	409-882-3379
Laredo C.C.	Sylvia Trevino	Laredo, TX 78040	Special Population	956-721-5137
Lee C.	Rosemary Coffmann	Baytown, TX 77522	Disabilities Services	281-425-6384
Midwestern St. U.	Debra Higginbotham	Wichita Falls, TX 76308-2099	Office of Disability Accommodations	940-397-4618
Saint Edward's U.	Lorrain Perea	Austin, TX 78704	Student Disability Office	512-448-8557
Schreiner C.	Jude Gallick	Kerrville, TX 78028-5697	Learning Support Services	830-792-7256
South Western Texas St. U.	Gina Schultz	San Marcos, TX 78666	Office of Disability Service	512-245-3451
Southern Methodist U.	Rebecca Marin	Dallas, TX 75275-0355	Services for Students w/ Disabilities	214-768-4563
Southwest Texas St. U.	Tina Schultz	San Marcos, TX 78666	Office of Disability Services	512-245-3451
Stephen F. Austin St. U.	Chuck Lopez	Nonacogdoches, TX 75962	Disability Services	936-468-3004
TCU	Jennifer Lowrance	Fort Worth, TX 76129	Student Disability Services	817-257-7486
Texas A&M U.	D. Brown Pearson	Kingsville, TX 78363	Services for Students with Disabilities	512-593-3302
Texas A&M U.—C. Station	Dr. Anne Reber	College Station, TX 77843	Services for Students with Disabilities	979-845-1637
Texas Tech U.	Frank Silvas	Lubbock, TX 79409-5005	Disabled Student Support	806-742-2405
Texas Woman's U.	Joanne Nunnelly	Denton, TX 76204-5679	Disability Support Services	817-898-3628
Tyler Jr. C.	Vickie Geisel	Tyler, TX 75711	Suport Services	903-510-2395
U. of Houston	Barbara Poursoltan	Houston, TX 77204	Center for Students with Disabilities	713-743-5400
U. of Houston—Downtown	Duraese Hall	Houston, TX 77002-1001	Disabled Student Services	713-221-8430
U. of North Texas	Steve Pickett	Denton, TX 76203-5358	Office of Disability Accommodations	940-565-4323
U. of Texas at Austin	Dr. Sherri Sanders	Austin, TX 78712	Academic Dean's Office	512-471-6259
U. of Texas—Dallas	Kerri Tate	Richardson, TX 75083-0688	Special Student Services	972-883-2111
U. of Texas—Edinburg	Caroline Rigly	Edinburg, TX 78539	Disability Services	210-381-2585
U. of Texas—El Paso	Hector Flores	El Paso, TX 79968	Disabled Student Service	915-747-5148
U. of Texas—Pan American	Chris Iglesias	Edinburg, TX 78539	Off. of Serv. for Persons with Disabilities	956-316-7005
U. of Texas—San Antonio	Lorraine Harrsion	San Antonio, TX 78249-0617	Disability Services	210-458-4157
Univesity of Texas at El Paso	Susan Lopez	El Paso, TX 79968	Disabled Student Services	915-747-5148
West St. Texas U.	Kay Kropff	Canyon, TX 79016	Special Populations Counseling Center	806-656-2392

UTAH

Institution	City	Contact	Office	Phone
Brigham Young U. (UT)	Provo, UT 84602-1110	Paul Byrd	Student Accomodations	801-378-2767
C. of East Utah	Price, UT 84501	Colleen Quigley	Disability Support Services	801-637-0489
Snow C.	Ephraim, UT 84627	Cyndi Crabb	Student Support Services	435-283-4021
Southern Utah U.	Cedar City, UT 84720	Carmen Alldredge	Student Support Services	435-865-8022
U. of Utah	Salt Lake City, UT 84112	Olga Nadeau	Center for Disability Services	801-581-5020
Utah St. U.	Logan, UT 84322	Diane Craig Hardman	Disability Resource Center	435-797-2444
Utah Valley C.C.	Orem, UT 84058	Michelle Lundell	Students with Disabilities	801-222-8000
Weber St. U.	Ogden, UT 84408-1103	Jeanne Pierce	Student Learning Center	801-626-7955

VERMONT

Institution	City	Contact	Office	Phone
Burlington C.	Burlington, VT 05401	Anne Lewis	Educational Resource Center (ERC)	802-862-9616
Castleton St. C.	Castleton, VT 05735	Maureen McMan	STEP Center	802-468-1392
Champlain C.	Burlington, VT 05402-0670	Becky Peterson	Support Svcs. for Stdnts. w/ Disabilities	802-865-6425
Green Mountain C.	Poultney, VT 05764-1199	Sue Zientara	Learning Center	802-287-8288
Johnson St. C.	Johnson, VT 05656	Katherine Veilleux	Academic Support Services	802-635-1259
Landmark C.	Putney, VT 05346	Maclean Gander	Landmark Pre-College	802-387-4767
Lyndon St. C.	Lyndonville, VT 05851	Peggy Hunter	Academic Support Services	802-626-6210
Marlboro C.	Marlboro, VT 05344	K.D. Maymard	Advising	802-257-4333
Middlebury C.	Middlebury, VT 05753-6002	Elizabeth Christensen	ADA Department	802-443-5851
Norwich U.	Northfield, VT 05663	Paula Gills	Learning Support Center	802-485-2130
Saint Michael's C.	Colchester, VT 05439	Edward Mahoney	Dean's Office	802-654-2000
Southern Vermont C.	Bennington, VT 05201	Todd Gerson	Disabilities Support Program	802-447-6360
Trinity C. of Vermont	Burlington, VT 05401	Patricia Amaerin	Learning Resourses Center	802-846-7060
U. of Vermont	Burlington, VT 05401	Nancy Oilker, EdD	Office of Specialized Student Services	802-656-7753
Vermont Technical C.	Randolph Center, VT 05061	Barbara Bendix	Services for Students with Disabilities	802-728-1278

VIRGINIA

Institution	City	Contact	Office	Phone
Blue Ridge C.C.	Weyers Cave, VA 24486	Suzanne Garritt	Disability Services	540-234-9261
Christopher Newport U.	Newport News, VA 23606	Debbie Whitt	Services to Students with Disabilities	757-594-8763
Clinch Valley C.	Wise, VA 24293	Julia Heise	Student Support Services	703-328-0176
C. of William and Mary	Williamsburg, VA 23187-8795	Lisa Bickley	Disability Services	757-221-2510
Eastern Mennonite U.	Harrisonburg, VA 22801	J. Coryell Hedrick	Learning Center	540-432-4233
Ferrum C.	Ferrum, VA 24088	Nancy Beach	Academic Resource Center	540-365-4270
George Mason U.	Fairfax, VA 22030-4444	Paul Bousel	Disability Resource Center	703-993-2474

Institution	Location	Contact	Service	Phone
Hampton U.	Hampton, VA 23668	Letizia Gambrell-Boone	Office of Section 504 Compliance	757-727-5493
Hollins C.	Roanoke, VA 24020	Rita Foster	Student Support Services	540-362-6404
James Madison U.	Harrisonburg, VA 22807	Louis Hedrick	Office of Disability Services	540-568-6705
Liberty U.	Lynchburg, VA 24502	Dr. Denny McHenry	Office of Disability Academic Support	804-582-2159
Longwood C.	Farmville, VA 23909	Scott Lissner	Academic Support Services	804-395-2392
Lynchburg C.	Lynchburg, VA 24501	Anne Smith	Disabled Student Services	804-544-8100
Mary Baldwin C.	Staunton, VA 24401	Beverly Askegaard	Learning Skills Center	540-887-7091
Mary Washington C.	Fredericksburg, VA 22401	Patricia Tracy	Office of Academic Services	540-654-4694
Marymount U.	Arlington, VA 22207	Dr. William Dinello	Disabled Student Services	703-284-1605
New River C.C.	Dublin, VA 24060	Jeananne Dixon	LEAP Center	540-674-3600
Old Dominion U.	Norfolk, VA 23529-0050	Nancy Olthoff, PhD	Disability Services	757-683-4655
Patrick Henry C.C.	Martinsville, VA 24115	Scott Guebert	Student Support Services	540-656-0257
Radford U.	Radford, VA 24142	Maureen Weyer	Disabled Student Services	540-831-5226
Randolph-Macon C.	Ashland, VA 23005	Sherry Schlenke	Learning Disabilities Support Services	804-752-7343
Roanoke C.	Salem, VA 24153-3794	Dr. Camille Miller	Student Support Services	703-375-2219
Saint Paul's C.	Lawrenceville, VA 23868	Dorothy Goodson	Disability Services	804-848-3111
Sweet Briar C.	Sweet Briar, VA 24595	Hope Walton	Academic Resource Center	804-289-8626
Thomas Nelson C.C.	Hampton, VA 23670	Thomas Kellen	Disabled Student Services	757-825-2827
Tidewater C.C.	Portsmouth, VA 23703	Sue Rice	LD Services	757-822-1225
U. of Richmond	Richmond, VA 23173	Hope Walton	Academic Skills Center	804-289-8626
U. of Virginia	Charlottesville, VA 22906	Jill Napier	Learning Needs & Evaluation Center	804-243-5180
Virginia Commonwealth U.	Richmond, VA 23284	Anna Ruiz	ADA Services	804-828-1347
Virginia Intermont College	Bristol, VA 24201-4298	Barbara Hollbrook	Student Support Services	540-466-7905
Virginia St. U.	Petersburg, VA 23806	Cassandra Thomas	Student Enrichment Center	804-524-5000
Virginia Tech	Blacksburg, VA 24061	Virginia Reilly	Special Services	540-231-3787
Virginia Western Comm. C.	Roanoke, VA 24038	Marsha Richardson	Student Support Services	540-857-7289

WASHINGTON

Institution	Location	Contact	Service	Phone
Bates Tech C.	Tacoma, WA 98405	Daniel Eberle	Special Needs	253-596-1698
Central Washington U.	Ellensburg, WA 98926-7463	Robert Cambell	Disability Support Services	509-963-2171
Eastern Washington U.	Cheney, WA 99004	Karen Raver	Disability Support Services	509-359-6871
Everett C.C.	Everette, WA 98201	Barbara Oswald	Disabled Student Services	425-388-9273
Evergreen St. C., The	Olympia, WA 98505	Linda Pickering	Student Access Services	360-866-6000
Gonzaga U.	Spokane, WA 99258	Susan Foster-Dow	Student Academic Services	509-328-4220

Institution	Contact	Address	Service	Phone
North Seattle C.C.	Rob Harden	Seattle, WA 98103	Disabled Students Services	206-527-7307
Pacific Lutheran U.	Wanda Wentworth	Tacoma, WA 98447-0003	Academic Assistance	253-535-7520
Pierce C.	Deborah Wynn	Tacoma, WA 98446	Special Needs	253-964-6527
Saint Martin's C.	Deborah DeBow	Lacey, WA 98503	Access Services	360-438-4580
Seattle Pacific U.	Richard Okamoto	Seattle, WA 98119	Disabled Student Services	206-281-2018
Seattle U.	Carol Schneider	Seattle, WA 98122	Student Learning Center	206-296-5740
Spokane Falls C.C.	Ben Webinger	Spokane, WA 99204	Disability & Support Services	509-533-3437
Tacoma C.C.	Kirsten Vallier	Tacoma, WA 98465	Disability Support Services	253-566-5838
U. of Puget Sound	Ivey West	Tacoma, WA 98416	Disability Services	253-875-3391
U. of Washington	Dyane Haynes	Seattle, WA 98195-5840	Disabled Student Services	206-543-8924
Washington St. U.	Susan Schaeffer	Pullman, WA 99164-4122	Disability Resources	509-335-1566
Western Washington U.	David Brunnemer	Bellingham, WA 98225	Disabled Student Services	360-650-3844
Whatcom C.C.	Bill Culwell	Bellingham, WA 98226	Disabled Student Services	360-676-2170
Yakima Valley	Bob Chavez	Yakima, WA 98907	Disability Services	509-574-4600

WEST VIRGINIA

Institution	Contact	Address	Service	Phone
Davis & Elkins C.	Judith Sabol McCauley	Elkins, WV 26241	Learning Disability Program	304-637-1229
Marshall U.	Dr. Barbara Guyer	Huntington, WV 25755	Student Help Program	304-696-6317
West Virginia St. C.	Jenny Fertig	Institute, WV 25112-1000	Collegiate Support Services	304-766-3000
West Virginia Tech	Kitty Polaski	Montgomery, WV 25136	Student Support Services	304-442-3188
West Virginia U.	T. Anne Hawkins	Morgantown, WV 26506-6009	Office of Disability Services	304-293-2316
West Virginia Wesleyan C.	Carolyn Baisden	Buckhannon, WV 26201	Special Support Services Program	304-473-8563

WISCONSIN

Institution	Contact	Address	Service	Phone
Alverno C.	Nancy Bornstein	Milwaukee, WI 53234-3922	Instructional Service Center	414-382-6353
Beloit C.	Gail Pizarro	Beloit, WI 53511	Educational Development Program	608-363-2031
Cardinal Stritch C.	Marcia Laskey	Milwaukee, WI 53217-3985	Academic Support	414-352-5400
Carroll C. (WI)	Amy Kallas	Waukesha, WI 53186	Disability Services	262-524-7333
Carthage C.	Laura Busch	Kenosha, WI 53140	Pace Center	262-551-8500
Concordia U. (WI)	Jean Timpel	Mequon, WI 53097	Tutoring Center	262-243-4216
Edgewood C.	Johanna O'Hatnich	Madison, WI 53711	Learning Resource Center	608-663-2247
Gateway Technical C.	Jo Bailey	Kenosha, WI 53144	Support Services	414-656-6960
Lawrence U.	M. Hemwall	Appleton, WI 54912-0599	Disability Services	414-832-6530
Marian C. of Fond Du Lac	Cathy Mathweg	Fond du Lac, WI 54935	Academic Support Services	920-923-8117

College	Location	Contact	Service	Phone
Marquette U.	Milwaukee, WI 53201-1881	Patricia Almon	Disability Services	414-288-1645
Milwaukee Inst. of Art & Des.	Milwaukee, WI 53202	Jennifer Crandall	Academic Support	414-276-7889
Milwaukee School of Eng.	Milwaukee, WI 53202-3109	Dr. Donald Ashby	Student Support Services	414-277-7281
Northland C.	Ashland, WI 54806	Melinda Merrill	Academic Skills Center	715-682-1803
Ripon C.	Ripon, WI 54971	Daniel J. Krhin	Student Support Services	920-748-8107
Saint Norbert C.	De Pere, WI 54115	K. Goode-Bartholomew	Academic Support Services	920-403-1326
U. of Wisconsin Oshkosh	Oshkosh, WI 54901	Dr. William Kitz	Project Success	920-424-1033
U. of Wisconsin—Eau Claire	Eau Claire, WI 54701	Joseph Hisrich	Services for Students with Disabilities	715-836-4542
U. of Wisconsin—Green Bay	Green Bay, WI 53411-7001	Elizabeth MacNeille	Educational Support	920-465-2671
U. of Wisconsin—LaCrosse	LaCrosse, WI 54601-3742	June Reinert	Disability Resource Services	608-785-6900
U. of Wisconsin—Madison	Madison, WI 53706	J. Trey Duffy	McBurney Disability Resource Center	608-263-2741
U. of Wisconsin—Milwaukee	Milwaukee, WI 53201	Laurie Peterson	Learning Disabilities Program	414-229-6239
U. of Wisconsin—Oshkosh	Oshkosh, WI 54901-8662	Bill Kitz	Project Success	920-424-1033
U. of Wisconsin—Parkside	Kenosha, WI 53141	Renee Sartin Kirby	Learning Disabilities Support Services	262-595-2610
U. of Wisconsin—Platteville	Platteville, WI 53818	Bernie Bernhardt	Special Services	608-342-1817
U. of Wisconsin—River Falls	River Falls, WI 54022	Carmen Croonquist	Challenge Program	715-425-3884
U. of Wisconsin—Stevens Pt.	Stevens Point, WI 54481	John Timcak	Disability Services	715-346-3365
U. of Wisconsin—Stout	Menomonie, WI 54751	Scott Bay	Student Support Services	715-232-2995
U. of Wisconsin—Superior	Superior, WI 54880	Karen Strewler	Special Services	715-394-8185
U. of Wisconsin—Whitewater	Whitewater, WI 53190	Nancy Amacher	Project Assist	262-472-4788
Viterbo C.	La Crosse, WI 54601	Jane Eady	Learning Center	608-796-3085
West Wisconsin Tech. C.	La Crosse, WI 54602	Kristina Puent	Svcs. for Students with Special Needs	608-789-9101
Wisconsin Indianhead Tech.	Shell Lake, WI 54871	in transition	Disability Services	715-468-2815

WYOMING

College	Location	Contact	Service	Phone
Laramie County C.C.	Cheyenne, WY 82007	Patty Pratz	Resource Center	307-778-1262
Sheridan C.	Sheridan, WY 82801	Elizabeth Stearns	Learning Center	307-674-6446
U. of Wyoming	Laramie, WY 82071	Chris Primus	Disability Support Services	307-766-6189

CANADA/ALBERTA

College	Location	Contact	Service	Phone
Grace MacEwan C.C.	Edmonton, AB T51 2P2	Abigail Parrish-Craig	Counseling & Special Services	780-497-5811
Lethbridge C.C.	Lethbridge, AB T1K 1L6	Julie Deimert	Support Services	403-320-3244
N. Alberta Inst. Tech.	Edmonton AB T5G 2R1	Shirley Kabachia	Services to Disabled Students	403-471-7551
S. Alberta Inst. Tech.	Calgary AB T2M 0L4	Judy Murphy	Students with Disabilites	403-284-7013
U. of Alberta	Edmonton AB T6G 2E8	Marion Vosahlo	Disabled Student Services	403-492-3381

CANADA/BRITISH COLUMBIA

Institution	Location	Contact	Service	Phone
Camosun C.	Victoria BC V8P 4X8	Susan McArthur	Adult Special Education	604-370-3325
Capilano C.	N. Vancouver BC V71 3H5	Jolene Bordewick	Disability Support Services	604-983-7527
C. of New Caledonia	Pr. George BC V2N 1P8	Fran Miller	ASE Division	604-562-2131
Kwantlen College	Surrey V3T BC 5H8	Susanne Dadson	Services for Stud. With Disabilities	604-599-2003
Langara C.	Vancover BC V5Y 2Z6	Wendy Keenlyside	Disabled Students	604-323-5635
Okanagan C.	Kelowna BC V1Y 4X8	Valerie Best	Disability Services	250-762-5445
Simon Fraser U.	Burnaaby BC V5A 1S6	Jeff Sugarman	Learning & Study	604-291-3877
U. of N. British Colum.	Prince Grge BC V2L 5P2	Jim Leonard	Student Services	250-960-6362
U. of British Columbia	Vancouver BC V6T 1Z1	Ruth Warick	Disabilities Resource Center	604-822-4677
U. of Victoria	Victoria BC V8W 3P2	David Clode	Student & Ancillary Services	250-721-8024

CANADA/MANITOBA

Institution	Location	Contact	Service	Phone
U. of Manitoba	Winnipeg MB R3T 2N2	Susan Ness	Disabilities Services	204-474-6213
U. of Winnipeg	Winnipeg MB R3B 2E9	Jess Urbuck	Services for Stud. With Special Needs	204-786-9771

CANADA/NEW BRUNSWICK

Institution	Location	Contact	Service	Phone
Mt. Allison U.	Sackville NB E0A 3C0	Jane Drover	Center for Learning Assistance	506-364-2527
U. of New Brunswick	Fredericton NB E3B 6E3	Sandra Latchford	Learning Center	506-453-3515

CANADA/NEWFOUNDLAND

Institution	Location	Contact	Service	Phone
Mem. U. Newfoundland	St. John's NF A1G 5S7	Donna Hardy	Student Development	709-737-7593

CANADA/NOVA SCOTIA

Institution	Location	Contact	Service	Phone
Dalhousie U.	Halifax NS B3H 4J2	Lynn Shokry	Services for Students w/ Disabilities	902-494-7077
St. Mary's U.	Halifax NS B3H 3C3	David Leitch	Support for Disabled Students	902-420-5449

CANADA/ONTARIO

Institution	Location	Contact	Service	Phone
Algoma U. C.	S. Ste. Marie ON P6A 2G4	Judy Syrette	Special Needs	705-949-2301
Cambrian C.	Sudbury ON P3A 3V8	S. Alcorn MacKay	Special Needs Center	705-566-8101
Canadore C.	N. Bay ON P1B 8K9	Dawson Pratt	Special Needs Services	705-474-7600
Carleton U.	Ottawa ON K1S 5B6	Larry McCloskey	Services for the Disabled	613-520-6608
Centennial C.	Scarborough ON M1K 5E9	Irene Volinets	Special Needs	416-694-3241
Durham C.	Oshawa ON L1H 7L7	Patricia Revell	Special Needs	416-576-0210
Fanshawe C.	London ON N5V 1W2	Grant Meadwell	Counseling & Student Life	519-452-4282
George Brown C.	Toronto ON M5T 2T9	Margueritge Wales	Special Needs	416-867-2620
Humber College	Rexdale ON M9W 5L7	Craig Barrett	Special Needs Office	416-675-6622

Institution	Address	Contact	Service	Phone
Lakehead U.	Thunder Bay ON P7B 5E1	Donna Grau	Learning Assistance	807-343-8086
Loyalist College	Belleville ON K8N 5B9	Catherine O'Rourke	Special Needs	613-962-0633
Mohawk College	Hamilton ON L8N 3T2	Rachel Mathews	Special Needs Office	416-575-2331
Nippissig U. College	N. Bay ON P1B 8L7	Bonie Houston	Special Needs Services	705-474-6431
Ontarion C. of Art	Toronto ON M5T 1W1	Cynthia Richardson	Special Needs	416-977-6000
Queen's U.	Kingston ON K7L 3N6	Allyson Harrison	Special Needs	613-545-6279
Seneca College	N. York ON M2J 2X5	Arthur Burke	Special Needs	416-491-5050
St. Clair C.	Windsor ON N9A 6S4	June Egan	Special Needs	519-966-1656
St. Lawrence C.	Brockville ON K6V 5X3	Gall Easton	Special Needs	613-345-0660
Sheridan C.	Oakville ON L6H 2L1	Linda DeJong	Special Needs	905-845-9430
Trent U.	Peterborough ON K9J 7B8	Eunice Lund-Lucas	Special Needs	705-748-1281
U. of W. Ontario	London ON N6A 3K7	Dr. Deb Stuart	Disabled Student Services	519-661-2147
U. of Waterloo	Waterloo ON N2L 3G1	Rose Padacz	Services for Disabled Persons	519-885-1211
U. of Windsor	Windsor ON N9B 3P4	Brooke White	Division of Student Develop. & Support	519-253-4232
York U.	N. York ON M3J 1P3	Marc Wilchesky	LD Programs	416-736-5297

CANADA/PRINCE EDWARD ISLAND

Institution	Address	Contact	Service	Phone
Holland U.	Charlottetn PE C1A 4Z1	Brian McMillan	Programs	902-566-9561

CANADA/QUEBEC

Institution	Address	Contact	Service	Phone
Concordia U.	Montreal PQ H4B 1R6	Leo Bissonnette	Services for Disabled Students	514-848-3518
Dawson C.	Montreal PQ H3Z 1A4	Alice Havel	Services for Students with Disabilities	514-931-8731
John Abbott C.	St. An. Belvue. PQ H9X 3L9	Gail Booth	Special Needs Learning Center	514-457-6610
McGill U.	Montreal PQ H3A 1X1	Joan Wolforth	Special Services	514-398-6009

CANADA/SASKATCHEWAN

Institution	Address	Contact	Service	Phone
SIAST-Kelsey	Saskatoon SK S7K 6B1	Tony Kessler	Dept. of Disabilities Services	306-933-6445
U. of Saskatchewan	Saskatoon SK S7N 0W0	Heather Kuttai	Disabled Student Services	306-966-5673

CANADA/YUKON

Institution	Address	Contact	Service	Phone
Yukon C.	Yukon YT Y1A 5K4	Catalina Colaci	Special Education	403-668-8785

ALPHABETICAL LIST OF COLLEGES BY LEVEL OF SUPPORT SERVICES

College/University	State	Support
Adelphi University	New York	SP
American International College	Massachusetts	SP
Augsburg College	Minnesota	SP
Barat College	Illinois	SP
Barry University	Florida	SP
Beacon College	Florida	SP
College Misericordia	Pennsylvania	SP
College of Mount Saint Joseph	Ohio	SP
Concordia College	New York	SP
Curry College	Massachusetts	SP
Davis & Elkins College	West Virginia	SP
Fairleigh Dickinson University	New Jersey	SP
Finlandia University	Michigan	SP
Gannon University	Pennsylvania	SP
Hofstra University	New York	SP
Iona College	New York	SP
Landmark College	Vermont	SP
Long Island University—C.W. Post	New York	SP
Loras College	Iowa	SP
Louisiana College	Louisiana	SP
Lynn University	Florida	SP
Marist College	New York	SP
Marymount Manhattan College	New York	SP
Marshall University	West Virginia	SP
Mitchell College	Connecticut	SP
Monmouth University	New Jersey	SP
Muskingum College	Ohio	SP
New Jersey City University	New Jersey	SP
Northeastern University	Massachusetts	SP
Regis University	Colorado	SP
Reinhardt College	Georgia	SP
Rochester Institute of Technology	New York	SP
Roosevelt University	Illinois	SP
Saint Thomas Aquinas College	New York	SP
Schreiner College	Texas	SP
Southern Illinois University—Carbondale	Illinois	SP
Southern Vermont College	Vermont	SP
Union College	Nebraska	SP
University of Arizona	Arizona	SP
University of Indianapolis	Indiana	SP
University of the Ozarks	Arizona	SP
University of Wisconsin—Oshkosh	Wisconsin	SP

College/ University	State	Support
Vincennes University	Indiana	SP
West Virginia Wesleyan College	West Virginia	SP
Westminster College	Missouri	SP

CS: COORDINATED SERVICES

College/ University	State	Support
Abilene Christian University	Texas	CS
Adrian College	Michigan	CS
American University	District of Columbia	CS
Anderson University	Indiana	CS
Appalachian State University	North Carolina	CS
Arizona State University	Arizona	CS
Baker University	Kansas	CS
Bakersfield College	California	CS
Binghamton University	New York	CS
Black Hills State University	South Dakota	CS
Boston College	Massachusetts	CS
Boston University	Massachusetts	CS
Brenau University	Georgia	CS
Brigham Young University	Utah	CS
Brown University	Rhode Island	CS
Bryant College	Rhode Island	CS
Cal Polytechnic State University—San Luis Obispo	California	CS
Caldwell College	New Jersey	CS
California State Polytechnic University—Pomona	California	CS
California State University—Chico	California	CS
California State University—Northridge	California	CS
California State University—San Bernardino	California	CS
Calvin College	Michigan	CS
The Catholic University of America	District of Columbia	CS
Central Ohio Technical College	Ohio	CS
Clarion University of Pennsylvania	Pennsylvania	CS
Clark University	Massachusetts	CS
Colby-Sawyer College	New Hampshire	CS
Colgate University	New York	CS
The College of Saint Catherine	Minnesota	CS
College of the Siskiyous	California	CS
College of William and Mary	Virginia	CS
Columbia Union College	Maryland	CS
Connecticut College	Connecticut	CS
Cornell University	New York	CS
Davidson College	North Carolina	CS
Dean College	Massachusetts	CS
DePaul University	Illinois	CS
Dickinson College	Pennsylvania	CS

Dowling College	New York	CS
Duke University	North Carolina	CS
East Carolina University	North Carolina	CS
East Stroudsburg Univ. of Pennsylvania	Pennsylvania	CS
Eastern Kentucky University	Kentucky	CS
Eastern Washington University	Washington	CS
Edinboro University of Pennsylvania	Pennsylvania	CS
Emory University	Georgia	CS
Evangel College	Missouri	CS
Fairfield University	Connecticut	CS
Ferris State University	Michigan	CS
Ferrum College	Virginia	CS
Florida A&M University	Florida	CS
Florida Atlantic University	Florida	CS
Florida State University	Florida	CS
George Washington University	District of Columbia	CS
Georgetown University	District of Columbia	CS
Georgia Southern University	Georgia	CS
Georgia State University	Georgia	CS
Georgian Court College	New Jersey	CS
Grand View College	Iowa	CS
Green Mountain College	Vermont	CS
Harding University	Arizona	CS
Hocking College	Ohio	CS
Illinois State University	Illinois	CS
Indian Hills Community College	Iowa	CS
Indiana University—Bloomington	Indiana	CS
Indian Hills Community College	Iowa	CS
Iowa State University	Iowa	CS
Jacksonville State University	Alabama	CS
Johnson and Wales University	Rhode Island	CS
Johnson State College	Vermont	CS
Kansas State University	Kansas	CS
Kean University	New Jersey	CS
Kent State University	Ohio	CS
Keuka College	New York	CS
Kutztown University of Pennsylvania	Pennsylvania	CS
Lee University	Tennessee	CS
Lenoir-Rhyne College	North Carolina	CS
Liberty University	Virginia	CS
Limestone College	South Carolina	CS
Louisiana State University—Baton Rouge	Louisiana	CS
Manchester College	Indiana	CS
Manhattan College	New York	CS
Manhattanville College	New York	CS

Marian College of Fond du Lac	Wisconsin	CS
Mercyhurst College	Pennsylvania	CS
Miami University	Ohio	CS
Michigan State University	Michigan	CS
Middle Tennessee State University	Tennessee	CS
Minot State University	North Dakota	CS
Montana Technical College	Montana	CS
Mount Ida College	Massachusetts	CS
National-Louis University	Illinois	CS
New England College	New Hampshire	CS
New England Culinary Institute	Vermont	CS
New York University	New York	CS
North Carolina State University	North Carolina	CS
North Dakota State University	North Dakota	CS
Northern Arizona University	Arizona	CS
Northern Illinois University	Illinois	CS
Northern Michigan University	Michigan	CS
Northwestern University	Illinois	CS
Norwich University	Vermont	CS
Ohio State University—Columbus	Ohio	CS
Old Dominion University	Virginia	CS
Pennsylvania State Univ.—University Park	Pennsylvania	CS
Pine Manor College	Massachusetts	CS
Pittsburgh State University	Kansas	CS
Providence College	Rhode Island	CS
Reedley College	California	CS
Rhode Island College	Rhode Island	CS
Rider University	New Jersey	CS
Rocky Mountain College	Montana	CS
Saint Ambrose University	Iowa	CS
Saint Bonaventure University	New York	CS
San Diego State University	California	CS
San Francisco State University	California	CS
San Jose State University	California	CS
Santa Clara University	California	CS
Santa Rosa Junior College	California	CS
Sheldon Jackson College	Alaska	CS
Sierra College	California	CS
Sonoma State University	California	CS
Southern Connecticut State University	Connecticut	CS
Southern Illinois University—Edwardsville	Illinois	CS
Southern Maine Technical College	Maine	CS
Southern Methodist University	Texas	CS
Southern New Hampshire University	New Hampshire	CS
Southern Wesleyan University	South Carolina	CS

Southwest Missouri State University	Missouri	CS
Southwest Texas State University	Texas	CS
Springfield College	Massachusetts	CS
SUNY at Albany	New York	CS
SUNY at Stony Brook	New York	CS
SUNY College of Technology at Farmingdale	New York	CS
SUNY College of Technology at Delhi	New York	CS
Syracuse University	New York	CS
Temple University	Pennsylvania	CS
Towson University	Maryland	CS
Truckee Meadows Community College	Nevada	CS
Unity College	Maine	CS
University of Alabama	Alabama	CS
University of California—Berkeley	California	CS
University of California—Los Angeles	California	CS
University of California—San Diego	California	CS
University of California—Santa Barbara	California	CS
University of Colorado—Boulder	Colorado	CS
University of Colorado—Colorado Springs	Colorado	CS
University of Connecticut	Connecticut	CS
University of Delaware	Delaware	CS
University of Denver	Colorado	CS
University of Florida	Florida	CS
University of Georgia	Georgia	CS
University of Hartford	Connecticut	CS
University of Houston	Texas	CS
University of Illinois—Urbana-Champaign	Illinois	CS
University of Iowa	Iowa	CS
University of Maryland—College Park	Maryland	CS
University of Maryland—Eastern Shore	Maryland	CS
University of Massachusetts—Amherst	Massachusetts	CS
University of Memphis	Tennessee	CS
University of Michigan—Ann Arbor	Michigan	CS
University of Minnesota—Duluth	Minnesota	CS
University of Missouri—Columbia	Missouri	CS
University of Nevada—Reno	Nevada	CS
University of North Carolina—Chapel Hill	North Carolina	CS
University of North Carolina—Greensboro	North Carolina	CS
University of North Carolina—Wilmington	North Carolina	CS
University of North Texas	Texas	CS
University of Pittsburgh	Pennsylvania	CS
University of Rhode Island	Rhode Island	CS
University of Saint Francis	Indiana	CS
University of San Francisco	California	CS
University of South Carolina—Columbia	South Carolina	CS

College/University	State	Support
University of South Dakota	South Dakota	CS
University of Southern California	California	CS
University of Tennessee at Chattanooga	Tennessee	CS
University of Tennessee at Martin	Tennessee	CS
University of the Pacific	California	CS
University of Tulsa	Oklahoma	CS
University of Vermont	Vermont	CS
University of Virginia	Virginia	CS
University of Wisconsin—Eau Claire	Wisconsin	CS
University of Wisconsin—LaCrosse	Wisconsin	CS
University of Wisconsin—Madison	Wisconsin	CS
University of Wisconsin—Milwaukee	Wisconsin	CS
University of Wisconsin—Stevens Point	Wisconsin	CS
University of Wisconsin—Whitewater	Wisconsin	CS
Ursuline College	Ohio	CS
Utah State University	Utah	CS
Utica College of Syracuse University	New York	CS
Vermont Technical College	Vermont	CS
Virginia Intermont College	Virginia	CS
Wake Forest University	North Carolina	CS
Waldorf College	Iowa	CS
Washington University in Saint Louis	Missouri	CS
Western Carolina University	North Carolina	CS
Western Connecticut State University	Connecticut	CS
Western Illinois University	Illinois	CS
Western Maryland College	Maryland	CS
Wheelock College	Massachusetts	CS
Widener University	Pennsylvania	CS
Wingate University	North Carolina	CS
Wright State University	Ohio	CS
Xavier University	Ohio	CS

S: SERVICES

College/ University	State	Support
Alverno College	Wisconsin	S
Aquinas College	Massachusetts	S
Beloit College	Wisconsin	S
Bowling Green State University	Ohio	S
Case Western Reserve University	Ohio	S
Champlain College	Vermont	S
Clemson University	South Carolina	S
College of Santa Fe	New Mexico	S
Drake University	Iowa	S
Drexel University	Pennsylvania	S
Eastern Illinois University	Illinois	S

Frostburg State University	Maryland	S
George Mason University	Virginia	S
Georgia State University	Georgia	S
Grand Valley State University	Michigan	S
Grinnell College	Iowa	S
Guilford College	North Carolina	S
Hampton University	Virginia	S
Indiana Wesleyan University	Indiana	S
James Madison University	Virginia	S
Kansas City Art Institute	Missouri	S
Lamar University	Texas	S
Lebanon Valley College	Pennsylvania	S
Lexington Community College	Kentucky	S
Lincoln College	Illinois	S
Loyola Marymount University	California	S
Marquette University	Wisconsin	S
Messiah College	Pennsylvania	S
Midwestern State University	Texas	S
Montana State University—Billings	Montana	S
Moorhead State University	Minnesota	S
New Mexico Institute of Mining and Technology	New Mexico	S
New Mexico State University	New Mexico	S
Nicholls State University	Louisiana	S
Notre Dame College	New Hampshire	S
Oberlin College	Ohio	S
Ohio University—Athens	Ohio	S
Oklahoma State University	Oklahoma	S
Oregon State University	Oregon	S
Ripon College	Wisconsin	S
Rivier College	New Hampshire	S
Saint Andrews Presbyterian College	North Carolina	S
Saint Lawrence University	New York	S
Seton Hall University	New Jersey	S
Seton Hill College	Pennsylvania	S
Sheridan College	Wyoming	S
Shimer College	Illinois	S
Smith College	Massachusetts	S
South Dakota State University	South Dakota	S
Southern Utah University	Utah	S
St. Olaf College	Minnesota	S
SUNY College at Potsdam	New York	S
SUNY College of Technology at Alfred	New York	S
SUNY College of Technology at Canton	New York	S
Texas A&M University—College Station	Texas	S
Texas Tech University	Texas	S

Thomas More College	Kentucky	S
University of Alabama—Huntsville	Alabama	S
University of Alaska—Anchorage	Alaska	S
University of Alaska—Fairbanks	Alaska	S
University of Cincinnati	Ohio	S
University of Idaho	Idaho	S
University of Kansas	Kansas	S
University of Maine—Machias	Maine	S
University of Montana—Missoula	Montana	S
University of Nevada—Las Vegas	Nevada	S
University of New England	Maine	S
University of New Hampshire	New Hampshire	S
University of New Haven	Connecticut	S
University of New Orleans	Louisiana	S
University of North Carolina—Charlotte	North Carolina	S
University of Northern Colorado	Colorado	S
University of Northern Iowa	Iowa	S
University of Notre Dame	Indiana	S
University of Oklahoma	Oklahoma	S
University of Oregon	Oregon	S
University of Redlands	California	S
University of Saint Thomas	Minnesota	S
University of Southern Colorado	Colorado	S
University of Southern Indiana	Indiana	S
University of Southern Mississippi	Mississippi	S
University of Texas—El Paso	Texas	S
University of Texas—Pan American	Texas	S
University of Toledo	Ohio	S
University of Wyoming	Wyoming	S
Washington State University	Washington	S
Wayne State College	Nebraska	S
Western Virginia University	Western Virginia	S
Western Kentucky University	Kentucky	S
Western Montana College	Montana	S
Western Oregon University	Oregon	S
Wheaton College	Massachusetts	S
Whittier College	California	S

INDEX

ABOUT THE AUTHORS

Marybeth Kravets has been a counselor and college consultant at Deerfield High School, a public high school in Deerfield, Illinois, for 22 years. She has also acted as an educational consultant to high schools, colleges, and families. She received her BA in education from the University of Michigan in Ann Arbor, Michigan, and her MA in counseling from Wayne State University in Detroit, Michigan. She is the President of the National Association for College Admission Counseling (NACAC) and previously served as the President of the Illinois Association for College Admission Counseling (IACAC) and Vice Chair for the Midwest Region of The College Board. In addition to co-authoring The K&W Guide, she also co-authored, with Dr. Michael Koehler, Counseling Secondary Students With Learning Disabilities: Ready To Use Guidelines, Techniques and Materials to Help Students Prepare for College and Work (The Center for Applied Research in Education, A Simon & Schuster Company) and has written articles for many professional journals. She has been a guest on NBC's Today show several times and has appeared on many other radio and television programs. She has presented at major conferences in the United States and Europe. She has been married to Alan Kravets since 1971, has four wonderful children, Wendy and husband Steve, Mark and wife Sara, Cathy and husband Cliff, and Dan and wife Andrea, and four delightful grandchildren, Allison, Connor, David, and Robert. For additional information or to contact Marybeth Kravets for consultation, write or call:

K&W
PO Box 187
Deerfield, IL 60015-0187
847-266-0457

Imy F. Wax, MS, is a certified licensed psychotherapist and educational consultant currently in private family practice. She has worked with adolescents and their families in high schools and social service settings. She received her BS from Mills College of Education in New York, New York, and her MS from Hunter College in New York, New York. Imy is a member of several professional and parental organizations. She has presented at both professional and parental conferences on such topics as "The Emotional Expectations of Parenting a Child with Learning Disabilities," and has written numerous articles in professional and parental journals. Imy conducts workshops for parents on raising children with learning disabilities and/or attention deficit/hyperactivity disorder. She has appeared as a guest on NBC's Today show as well as other television and radio shows. She is married to Howard Wax and has four children, two learning disabled and one who also has attention deficit/hyperactivity disorder. Her daughter, Debrah, was the inspiration for this book. For additional information or to contact Imy Wax for consultation or for presentations, write or call:

K&W
PO Box 187
Deerfield, IL 60015-0187
847-945-0913

NOTES

NOTES

NOTES

FIND US...

International

Hong Kong
4/F Sun Hung Kai Centre
30 Harbour Road, Wan Chai,
Hong Kong
Tel: (011)85-2-517-3016

Japan
Fuji Building 40, 15-14
Sakuragaokacho, Shibuya Ku,
Tokyo 150, Japan
Tel: (011)81-3-3463-1343

Korea
Tae Young Bldg, 944-24,
Daechi- Dong, Kangnam-Ku
The Princeton Review- ANC
Seoul, Korea 135-280,
South Korea
Tel: (011)82-2-554-7763

Mexico City
PR Mex S De RL De Cv
Guanajuato 228 Col. Roma
06700 Mexico D.F., Mexico
Tel: 525-564-9468

Montreal
666 Sherbrooke St.
West, Suite 202
Montreal, QC H3A 1E7 Canada
Tel: (514) 499-0870

Pakistan
1 Bawa Park - 90 Upper Mall
Lahore, Pakistan
Tel: (011)92-42-571-2315

Spain
Pza. Castilla, 3 - 5° A, 28046
Madrid, Spain
Tel: (011)341-323-4212

Taiwan
155 Chung Hsiao East Road
Section 4 - 4th Floor,
Taipei R.O.C., Taiwan
Tel: (011)886-2-751-1243

Thailand
Building One, 99 Wireless Road
Bangkok, Thailand 10330
Tel: (662) 256-7080

Toronto
1240 Bay Street, Suite 300
Toronto M5R 2A7 Canada
Tel: (800) 495-7737
Tel: (716) 839-4391

locations

National (U.S.)

We have over 60 offices around the United States and
run courses in over 400 sites. For courses and locations
within the U.S. call 1 (800) 2/Review and you will be
routed to the nearest office.

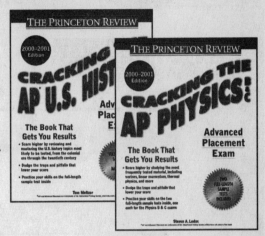
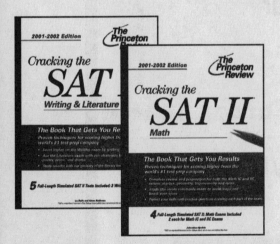

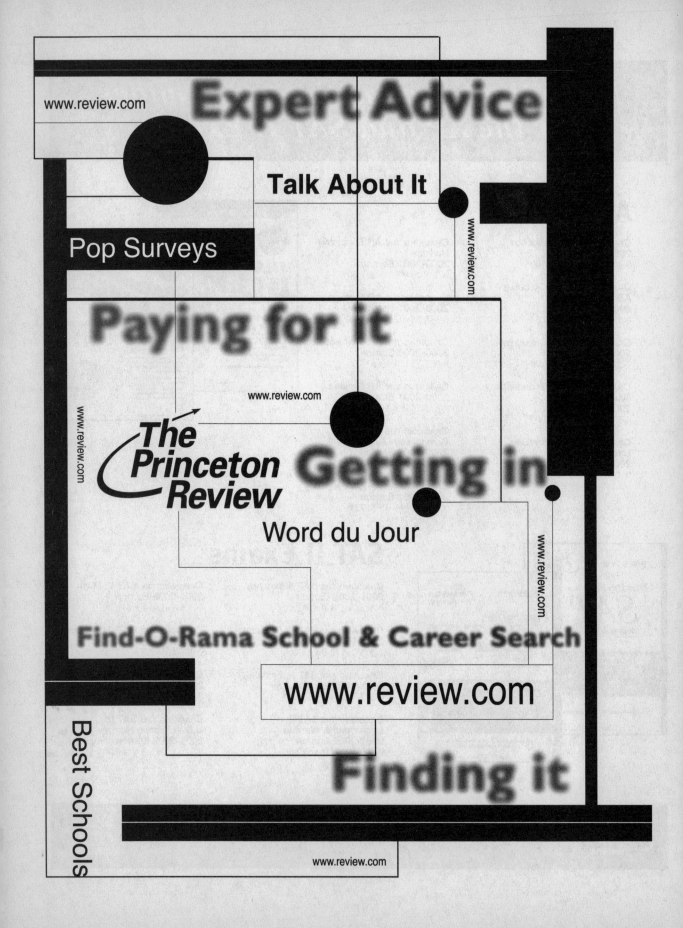